T0189807

Lecture Notes in Artificial Intelligence   11804

Subseries of Lecture Notes in Computer Science

More information about this series at http://www.springer.com/series/1244

Paulo Moura Oliveira · Paulo Novais ·
Luís Paulo Reis (Eds.)

Progress in Artificial Intelligence

19th EPIA Conference
on Artificial Intelligence, EPIA 2019
Vila Real, Portugal, September 3–6, 2019
Proceedings, Part I

 Springer

Editors
Paulo Moura Oliveira ⓘ
INESC-TEC
University of Trás-os-Montes
and Alto Douro
Vila Real, Portugal

Luís Paulo Reis ⓘ
LIACC/UP
University of Porto
Porto, Portugal

Paulo Novais ⓘ
University of Minho
Braga, Portugal

ISSN 0302-9743 ISSN 1611-3349 (electronic)
Lecture Notes in Artificial Intelligence
ISBN 978-3-030-30240-5 ISBN 978-3-030-30241-2 (eBook)
https://doi.org/10.1007/978-3-030-30241-2

LNCS Sublibrary: SL7 – Artificial Intelligence

This Springer imprint is published by the registered company Springer Nature Switzerland AG
The registered company address is: Gewerbestrasse 11, 6330 Cham, Switzerland

Preface

The EPIA Conference on Artificial Intelligence is a well-established European conference in the field of Artificial Intelligence (AI). In this 19th edition, EPIA 2019, took place in Vila Real at the University of Trás-os-Montes and Alto Douro (UTAD), during September 3–6, 2019 (https://epia2019.utad.pt/). Vila Real is a beautiful town in the heart of Douro Valley, a privileged wine region in Portugal. This is an elected place for the lovers of nature, food, and wine, whose people are well known for their hospitality.

Our society is undergoing a gradual process of transformation. We are moving at an accelerated pace towards an information and knowledge society where the introduction and use of AI and ITC technologies play a key role, which made EPIA 2019 even more challenging and exciting.

This conference is always organized under the auspices of the Portuguese Association for Artificial Intelligence (APPIA – http://www.appia.pt) and, as in previous editions, the program was based on a set of thematic tracks dedicated to specific themes of AI.

EPIA 2019 encompassed a record of 18 tracks devoted to different topics, plus a doctoral symposium and a panel session on "Societal AI." The selected tracks were: AIEd - Artificial Intelligence in Education, AI4G - Artificial Intelligence for Games, AIoTA - Artificial Intelligence and IoT in Agriculture, AIL - Artificial Intelligence and Law, AIM - Artificial Intelligence in Medicine, AICPDES - Artificial Intelligence in Cyber-Physical and Distributed Embedded Systems, AIPES - Artificial Intelligence in Power and Energy Systems, AITS - Artificial Intelligence in Transportation Systems, ALEA - Artificial Life and Evolutionary Algorithms, AmIA - Ambient Intelligence and Affective Environments, BAAI - Business Applications of Artificial Intelligence, GAI - General AI, IROBOT - Intelligent Robotics, KDBI - Knowledge Discovery and Business Intelligence, KRR - Knowledge Representation and Reasoning, MASTA - Multi-Agent Systems: Theory and Applications, SSM - Social Simulation and Modelling, and TeMA - Text Mining and Applications.

The conference program included three invited talks. Marco Dorigo (Université Libre de Bruxelles, Belgium) with a talk on "Swarm robotics: recent results and new research directions," Michael Wooldridge (University of Oxford, UK) with a talk on "Understanding Equilibrium Properties of Multi-Agent Systems," and Albert Bifet (Telecom ParisTech, France) with a talk on "Machine Learning for Data Streams."

For this edition, 252 paper submissions were received from 55 different countries to the thematic tracks. After a careful review process, 125 papers were selected to be presented in EPIA 2019. The papers acceptance rate was circa 49%. All of the papers were carefully revised by at least three reviewers of the corresponding track Program Committee. We thank the track organizing chairs, together with their respective Program Committee members, for their hard work of scientific reviewing.

Thanks are also due to all supporting organizations and conference sponsors, starting with SISCOG, our main sponsor to whom we sincerely address our thanks, but also Devscope. We would like to express our gratitude to all the Organizing Committee colleagues and track organizers. A special mention to Eduardo Solteiro Pires, José Boaventura Cunha, Teresa Paula Perdicoúlis, Tatiana Pinho, and Goreti Marreiros for their excellent work which was crucial for the successful realization of EPIA 2019.

Thank you all.

July 2019   Paulo Moura Oliveira
                                                                        Paulo Novais
                                                                     Luís Paulo Reis

EPIA-2019 Conference Organization

Event and Program Chairs

Paulo Moura Oliveira	INESC-TEC, University of Trás-os-Montes and Alto Douro, Portugal
Paulo Novais	ALGORITMI, University of Minho, Portugal
Luís Paulo Reis	LIACC, University of Porto, Portugal

International Steering Committee

Amedeo Cesta	CNR-ISTC, Italy
Ana Bazzan	Universidade Federal do Rio Grande do Sul, Brazil
Ana Paiva	Instituto Superior Técnico, Universidade de Lisboa, Portugal
Ernesto Costa	Universidade de Coimbra, Portugal
Eugénio Oliveira	Universidade do Porto, Portugal
François Pachet	Spotify, France
Helder Coelho	Universidade de Lisboa, Portugal
José Júlio Alferes	Universidade Nova de Lisboa, Portugal
Juan Pavón	Universidad Complutense Madrid, Spain
Luís Paulo Reis	Universidade do Porto, Portugal
Marco Dorigo	Université Libre de Bruxelles, Belgium
Paulo Novais	Universidade do Minho, Portugal
Pavel Brazdil	Universidade do Porto, Portugal
Peter McBurney	King's College London, UK
Ulrich Furbach	University of Koblenz, Germany

Organizing Chairs

Eduardo Solteiro Pires	INESC-TEC, UTAD, Portugal
José Boaventura Cunha	INESC-TEC, UTAD, Portugal
Paulo Jorge Matos	IPB, Portugal

Local Organizing Committee

César Analide	ALGORITMI, University of Minho, Portugal
Eduardo Solteiro Pires	INESC-TEC, Portugal
Goreti Marreiros	GECAD, IPP, Portugal
João Barroso	INESC-TEC, UTAD, Portugal
Lio Gonçalves	INESC-TEC, UTAD, Portugal
Paulo Martins	INESC-TEC, UTAD, Portugal
Ramiro Gonçalves	INESC-TEC, UTAD, Portugal

Raul Morais dos Santos	INESC-TEC, UTAD, Portugal
Tatiana Pinho	INESC-TEC, Portugal
Teresa Paula Perdicoúlis	ISR-Coimbra, UTAD, Portugal
Vítor Filipe	INESC-TEC, UTAD, Portugal

Proceedings Chairs

Eduardo Solteiro Pires	INESC-TEC, UTAD, Portugal
Tatiana Pinho	INESC-TEC, Portugal

Artificial Intelligence in Education (AIEd)

Organizing Committee

Vitor Santos	Nova University of Lisbon, Portugal
Leontios Hadjileontiadis	Aristotle University of Thessaloniki, Greece
João Barroso	INESC TEC, University of Trás-os-Montes and Alto Douro, Portugal
Dalila Durães	ESTG, Polytechnic Institute of Porto – Portugal

Program Committee

António Lopez Herrera	University of Granada, Spain
Bert Bredeweg	University of Amsterdam, The Netherlands
Goreti Marreiros	Polytechnic Institute of Porto, Portugal
Hélder Coelho	University of Lisbon, Portugal
Isabel Fernandez de Castro	University of the Basque Country, Spain
Jim Greer	University of Saskatchewan, Canada
Eduardo Solteiro Pires	INESC-TEC, University of Trás-os-Montes and Alto Douro, Portugal
Ernesto Costa	Coimbra University, Portugal
João Barroso	INESC-TEC, University of Trás-os-Montes and Alto Douro, Portugal
Leonardo Vanneschi	New University of Lisbon, Portugal
Leontios Hadjileontiadis	Khalifa University, UAE, and Aristotle University of Thessaloniki, Greece
Meni Tsitouridou	Aristotle University of Thessaloniki, Greece
Mauro Castelli	New University of Lisbon, Portugal
Monique Grandbastien	University of Nancy, France
Panagiotis Bamidis	Aristotle University of Thessaloniki, Greece
Paulo Novais	University of Minho, Portugal
Paulo Moura Oliveira	INESC-TEC, University of Trás-os-Montes and Alto Douro, Portugal
Peter Brusilovsky	University of Pittsburgh, USA
Peter Foltz	Pearson, USA
Pierre Dillenbourg	École Polytechnique Fédérale de Lausanne, Switzerland

Richard Cox	University of Sussex, UK
Sofia Dias	University of Lisbon, Portugal
Sofia Hadjileontiadou	Democritus University of Thrace, Greece
Tasos Mikropoulos	Aristotle University of Thessaloniki, Greece
Vitor Santos	New University of Lisbon, Portugal

Artificial Intelligence for Games (AI4G)

Organizing Committee

Alberto Simões	Polytechnic Institute of Cávado and Ave, Portugal
Antonios Liapis	University of Malta, Malta
Gustavo Reis	Polytechnic Institute of Leiria, Portugal

Program Committee

Carlos Martinho	IST, Universidade de Lisboa, Portugal
Christoph Salge	University of Hertfordshire, UK
David Carneiro	Universidade do Minho, Portugal
Daniele Gravina	University of Malta, Malta
Daniel Karavolos	University of Malta, Malta
David Melhart	University of Malta, Malta
Diego Perez Liebana	University of Essex, UK
Duarte Duque	Instituto Politécnico do Cávado e do Ave, Portugal
Éric Jacopin	ESM Saint-Cyr, France
Eva Hudlicka	Psychometrix Associates, USA
Fernando Silva	New York University, USA
Gabriella A. B. Barros	New York University, USA
João Dias	IST, Universidade de Lisboa, Portugal
José Valente de Oliveira	Universidade do Algarve, Portugal
Konstantinos Karpouzis	National University of Athens, Greece
Luís Paulo Reis	Universidade do Porto, Portugal
Marco Scirea	University of Southern Denmark, Denmark
Michael Green	New York University, USA
Nuno Rodrigues	Instituto Politécnico do Cávado e do Ave, Portugal
Pedro Moreira	Instituto Politécnico de Viana do Castelo, Portugal
Penousal Machado	Universidade de Coimbra, Portugal
Phil Lopes	GAIPS, Universidade de Lisboa, Portugal
Rui Prada	INESC-ID, IST, Universidade de Lisboa, Portugal

Artificial Intelligence and IoT in Agriculture (AIoTA)

Organizing Committee

José Boaventura Cunha	INESC-TEC, University of Trás-os-Montes and Alto Douro, Portugal
Josenalde Barbosa	Federal University of Rio Grande do Norte, Brazil

| Paulo Moura Oliveira | INESC-TEC, University of Trás-os-Montes and Alto Douro, Portugal |
| Raul Morais | INESC-TEC, University of Trás-os-Montes and Alto Douro, Portugal |

Program Committee

Andrés Muñoz Ortega	Universidad Católica de Múrcia, Spain
Aneesh Chauhan	Wageningen University and Research, The Netherlands
António Valente	INESC-TEC, University of Trás-os-Montes and Alto Douro, Portugal
Brett Whelan	University of Sydney, Australia
Bruno Tisseyre	Montpellier SupAgro, France
Carlos Eduardo Cugnasca	Escola Politécnica da Universidade de São Paulo, Brazil
Carlos Serôdio	CITAB, University of Trás-os-Montes and Alto Douro, Portugal
Eduardo Solteiro Pires	INESC-TEC, University of Trás-os-Montes and Alto Douro, Portugal
Emanuel Peres	INESC-TEC, University of Trás-os-Montes and Alto Douro, Portugal
Filipe Santos	INESC-TEC, Portugal
Francisco Rovira-Más	Polytechnic University of Valencia, Spain
Javier Sanchis Sáez	Universitat Politècnica de València, Spain
Javier Tardaguila	University of La Rioja, Spain
João Paulo Coelho	Instituto Politécnico de Bragança, Portugal
João Sousa	INESC-TEC, University of Trás-os-Montes and Alto Douro, Portugal
Jos Balendonck	Wageningen University and Research, The Netherlands
Jose Antonio Sanz	Universidad Pública de Navarra, Spain
Juan López Riquelme	Universidad Politécnica de Cartagena, Spain
K. P. Ferentinos	Hellenic Agricultural Organization, Greece
Kazuhisa Ito	Shibaura Institute of Technology, Japan
Laura Emmanuela Santana	Universidade Federal do Rio Grande do Norte, Brazil
Nieves Pávon-Pulido	Universidad Politécnica de Cartagena, Spain
Pedro Couto	CITAB, University of Trás-os-Montes and Alto Douro, Portugal
Pedro Melo-Pinto	CITAB, University of Trás-os-Montes and Alto Douro, Portugal
Tatiana Pinho	INESC-TEC, Portugal
Tomas Norton	KU Leven, Belgium
Sjaak Wolfert	Wageningen University and Research, The Netherlands
Veronica Saiz-Rubio	Polytechnic University of Valencia, Spain
Yuxin Miao	University of Minnesota, USA

Artificial Intelligence and Law (AIL)

Organizing Committee

Pedro Miguel Freitas	Universidade Católica Portuguesa, Portugal
Ugo Pagallo	University of Torino, Italy
Massimo Durante	University of Torino, Italy

Program Committee

Carlisle E. George	Middlesex University, UK
Giovanni Sartor	European University Institute, Italy
Isabel Ferreira	Universidade de Lisboa, Portugal
Luís Moniz Pereira	Universidade Nova de Lisboa, Portugal
Manuel David Masseno	Instituto Politécnico de Beja, Portugal
Migle Laukyte	University Carlos III of Madrid, Spain
Niva Elkin-Koren	University of Haifa, Israel, and Harvard University, USA
Paulo Novais	University of Minho, Portugal
Pompeu Casanovas	Universitat Autònoma de Barcelona, Spain, and Royal Melbourne Institute of Technology, Australia
Radboud Winkels	University of Amsterdam, The Netherlands
Thomas Gordon	University of Potsdam, Germany
Vicente Julián Inglada	Valencia University of Technology, Spain

Artificial Intelligence in Medicine (AIM)

Organizing Committee

Manuel Filipe Santos	University of Minho, Portugal
Carlos Filipe Portela	University of Minho, Portugal
Allan Tucker	Brunel University London, UK

Steering Committee

José Machado	University of Minho, Portugal
António Abelha	University of Minho, Portugal
Pedro Henriques Abreu	University of Coimbra, Portugal
Daniel Castro Silva	University of Porto, Portugal
Francesca Vitali	Pavia, Italy
Manuel Fernández Delgado	University of Santiago, Spain

Program Committee

Álvaro Silva	Abel Salazar Biomedical Sciences Institute, Portugal
Andreas Holzinger	Medical University Graz, Austria
António Abelha	University of Minho, Portugal

Antonio Manuel de Jesus Pereira   Polytechnic Institute of Leiria, Portugal
Barna Iantovics   Petru Maior University of Tîrgu-Mureş, Romania
Beatriz de la Iglesia   University of East Anglia, UK
Cinzia Pizzi   Università degli Studi di Padova, Italy
Filipe Pinto   Polytechnic Institute of Leiria, Portugal
Giorgio Leonardi   University of Piemonte Orientale, Italy
Göran Falkman   Universitet of Skövde, Sweden
Helder Coelho   University of Lisbon, Portugal
Helena Lindgren   Umeå University, Sweden
Hugo Peixoto   University of Minho, Portugal
Inna Skarga-Bandurova   East Ukrainian National University, Ukraine
José Machado   University of Minho, Portugal
José Maia Neves   University of Minho, Portugal
Júlio Duarte   University of Minho, Portugal
Luca Anselma   University of Turin, Italy
Michael Ignaz Schumacher   University of Applied Sciences Western Switzerland, Switzerland
Miguel Angel Mayer   Pompeu Fabra University, Spain
Miriam Santos   University of Coimbra, Portugal
Panagiotis Bamidis   Aristotelian University of Thessaloniki, Greece
Pedro Gago   Polytechnic Institute of Leiria, Portugal
Pedro Pereira Rodrigues   University of Porto, Portugal
Rainer Schmidt   Institute for Biometrics and Medical Informatics, Germany
Ricardo Martinho   Polytechnic Institute of Leiria, Portugal
Rui Camacho   University of Porto, Portugal
Salva Tortajada   Polytechnic University of Valencia, Spain
Teresa Guarda   State University Santa Elena Peninsula, Ecuador
Werner Ceusters   State University of New York at Buffalo, USA

Artificial Intelligence in Cyber-Physical and Distributed Embedded Systems (AICPDES)

Organizing Committee

Thiago RPM Rúbio   University of Porto, Portugal
Jean-Paul Jamont   Université Grenoble Alpes, France
Paulo Leitão   Polytechnic Institute of Bragança, Portugal

Program Committee

Adriano Pereira   Federal University of Minas Gerais, Brazil
Alberto Fernández   Universidad Rey Juan Carlos, Spain
Alois Zoitl   Fortiss GmbH, Germany
Benjamim Gateau   Luxembourg Institute of Science and Technology, Luxembourg

Christopher Frantz	University of Otago, New Zealand
Florentino Riverola	Universidad de Vigo, Spain
Gauthier Picard	ENS Mines Saint-Étienne, France
José Barbosa	Polythecnic Institute of Bragança, Portugal
Laurent Vercouter	LITIS, INSA de Rouen, France
Luis M. Camarinha-Matos	New University of Lisbon, Portugal
Marco Mendes	Schneider Electric Automation GmbH, Germany
Marie-Pierre Gleizes	IRIT, Université de Toulouse, France
Marin Lujak	École des Mines de Douai, France
Michael Mrissa	Université de Pau et des Pays de l'Adour, France
Michel Occello	Université Grenoble Alpes, France
Miguel Rebollo	Universitat Politècnica de València, Spain
Olivier Boissier	ENS Mines Saint-Étienne, France
Senén Barro	Universidad de Santiago de Compostela, Spain
Simon Mayer	University of St. Gallen and ETH Zurich, Switzerland
Stamatis Karnouskos	SAP, Germany
Tiberiu Seceleanu	ABB Corporate Research, Sweden
Zafeiris Kokkinogenis	University of Porto, Portugal

Artificial Intelligence in Power and Energy Systems (AIPES)

Organizing Committee

Zita Vale	Polytechnic of Porto, Portugal
Pedro Faria	Polytechnic of Porto, Portugal
Juan Manuel Corchado	University of Salamanca, Spain
Tiago Pinto	University of Salamanca, Spain

Program Committee

Ana Estanqueiro	LNEG−National Research Institute, Portugal
Bo Norregaard Jorgensen	University of Southern Denmark, Denmark
Carlos Ramos	Polytechnic Institute of Porto, Portugal
Chen-Ching Liu	Washington State University, USA
Dagmar Niebur	Drexel University, USA
Fernando Lopes	LNEG−National Research Institute, Portugal
Germano Lambert-Torres	Dinkart Systems, Brazil
Goreti Marreiros	Polytechnic Institute of Porto, Portugal
Gustavo Figueroa	Instituto de Investigaciones Eléctricas, Mexico
Hélder Coelho	University of Lisbon, Portugal
Isabel Praça	Polytechnic Institute of Porto, Portugal
Jan Segerstam	Empower IM Oy, Finland
João P. S. Catalão	University of Porto, Portugal
José L. Rueda	Delft University of Technology, The Netherlands
Kumar Venayagamoorthy	Clemson University, USA
Kwang Y. Lee	Baylor University, USA
Nikos Hatziargyriou	National Technical University of Athens, Greece

Nouredine Hadj-Said	Institut National Polytechnique de Grenoble, France
Olivier Boissier	École Nationale Supérieure des Mines de Saint-Étienne, France
Pablo Ibarguengoytia	Instituto de Investigaciones Eléctricas, Mexico
Peter Kadar	Budapest University of Technology and Economics, Hungary
Phuong Nguyen	Eindhoven University of Technology, The Netherlands
Pierluigi Siano	University of Salerno, Italy
Vladimiro Miranda	University of Porto, Portugal

Artificial Intelligence in Transportation Systems (AITS)

Organizing Committee

| Alberto Fernandez | Universidad Rey Juan Carlos, Spain |
| Rosaldo Rossetti | Universidade do Porto, Portugal |

Program Committee

Ana Bazzan	UFRGS, Brazil
Ana Paula Rocha	University of Porto, Portugal
Arnaud Doniec	IMT Lille Douai, France
Carlos A. Iglesias	Universidad Politécnica de Madrid, Spain
Carlos Lisboa Bento	University of Coimbra, Portugal
Eduardo Camponogara	UFSC, Brazil
Eftihia Nathanail	University of Thessaly, Greece
Eugénio Oliveira	University of Porto, Portugal
Franziska Klügl	Örebo University, Sweden
Gonçalo Correia	TU Delft, The Netherlands
Holger Billhardt	University Rey Juan Carlos, Spain
Javier Sanchez Medina	Universidad de Las Palmas de Gran Canaria, Spain
Jihed Khiari	NEC Laboratories Europe, Germany,
João Jacob	University of Porto, Portugal
João Mendes-Moreira	University of Porto, Portugal
Josep Salanova	Center for Research and Technology Hellas, Greece
Jürgen Dunkel	Hochschule Hannover, Germany
Luís Nunes	ISCTE-IUL, Portugal
Marcela Munizaga	University of Chile, Chile
Marin Lujak	IMT Lille Douai, France
Rui Gomes	University of Coimbra, Portugal
Soora Rasouli	Eindhoven University of Technology, The Netherlands
Sascha Ossowski	Rey Juan Carlos University, Spain
Tânia Fontes	University of Porto, Portugal

Artificial Life and Evolutionary Algorithms (ALEA)

Organizing Committee

Carlos Henggeler Antunes	INESC Coimbra, DEEC, University of Coimbra, Portugal
Leonardo Trujillo	Technical Institute of Tijuana, Mexico
Luca Manzoni	University of Milano-Bicocca, Italy
Ivo Gonçalves	INESC Coimbra, DEEC, University of Coimbra, Portugal

Program Committee

Antonios Liapis	Institute of Digital Games, University of Malta, Malta
Carlos M. Fonseca	Universidade de Coimbra, Portugal
Carlos Henggeler Antunes	INESC Coimbra, University of Coimbra, Portugal
Enrique Naredo Garcia	CentroGeo, Mexico
Eric Medvet	University of Trieste, Italy
Gabriela Ochoa	University of Stirling, UK
Gianluigi Folino	CNR-ICAR, Italy
Ivo Gonçalves	INESC Coimbra, University of Coimbra, Portugal
James Foster	University of Idaho, USA
Jin-Kao Hao	University of Angers, France
Julian Miller	University of York, UK
Leonardo Trujillo	Technical Institute of Tijuana, Mexico
Luca Manzoni	University of Milano-Bicocca, Italy
Luís Correia	University of Lisbon, Portugal
Luís Paquete	Universidade de Coimbra, Portugal
Marc Schoenauer	Inria, France
Mario Giacobini	University of Torino, Italy
Mauro Castelli	NOVA IMS, Portugal
Pablo Mesejo Santiago	University of Granada, Spain
Rui Mendes	Universidade do Minho, Portugal
Stefano Cagnoni	University of Parma, Italy

Ambient Intelligence and Affective Environments (AmIA)

Organizing Committee

Goreti Marreiros	Polytechnic Institute of Porto, Portugal
Paulo Novais	University of Minho, Portugal
Ana Almeida	Polytechnic Institute of Porto, Portugal
Sara Rodríguez	University of Salamanca, Spain
Peter Mikulecky	University of Hradec Kralove, Czech Republic

Program Committee

Amal Seghrouchni	Université Pierre et Marie Curie, France
Amilcar Cardoso	University of Coimbra, Portugal

Ana Almeida	Polytechnic Institute of Porto, Portugal
Ana Paiva	IST, Universidade de Lisboa, Portugal
Ângelo Costa	Universidade do Minho, Portugal
Antonio Caballero	University of Castilla-La Mancha, Spain
Antonio Camurri	University of Genoa, Italy
Boon Kiat-Quek	National University of Singapore, Singapore
Carlos Bento	University of Coimbra, Portugal
Carlos Iglesias	Universidad Politécnica de Madrid, Spain
Carlos Ramos	Polytechnic Institute of Porto, Portugal
César Analide	University of Minho, Portugal
Dante Tapia	University of Salamanca, Spain
Davide Carneiro	Polytechnic Institute of Porto, Portugal
Diego Gachet	European University of Madrid, Spain
Eva Hudlicka	Psychometrix Associates Blacksburg, USA
Fábio Silva	University of Minho, Portugal
Florentino Fdez-Riverola	University of Vigo, Spain
Goreti Marreiros	Polytechnic Institute of Porto, Portugal
Guillaume Lopez	Aoyama Gakuin University, Japan
Grzegorz Napela	AGH University of Science and Technology, Poland
Hoon Ko	Chosun University, South Korea
Ichiro Satoh	National Institute of Informatics, Japan
Javier Bajo	Polytechnic University of Madrid, Spain
Javier Jaen	Polytechnic University of Valencia, Spain
Jean Ilié	Université Pierre et Marie Curie, France
João Carneiro	Polytechnic Institute of Porto, Portugal
José Machado	University of Minho, Portugal
José Molina	University Carlos III of Madrid, Spain
José Neves	University of Minho, Portugal
Juan Corchado	University of Salamanca, Spain
Laurence Devillers	LIMS-CNRS, France
Lino Figueiredo	Polytechnic Institute of Porto, Portugal
Luís Macedo	University of Coimbra, Portugal
Paulo Novais	University of Minho, Portugal
Peter Mikulecky	University of Hradec Kralove, Czech Republic
Preuveneers	KU Leuven, Belgium
Ricardo Santos	Polytechnic Institute of Porto, Portugal
Rui José	University of Minho, Portugal
Sara González	University of Salamanca, Spain
Shin'Ichi Konomi	University of Tokyo, Japan
Tatsuo Nakajima	Waseda University, Japan
Tiago Oliveira	National Institute of Informatics, Japan
Vic Callaghan	Essex University, UK
Vicente Julián	Polytechnic University of Valencia, Spain

Business Applications of Artificial Intelligence (BAAI)

Organizing Committee

Célia Talma Gonçalves	CEOS - ISCAP P.PORTO, LIACC, Portugal
Carlos Soares	LIACC, INESC TEC, Universidade do Porto, Portugal
Eva Lorenzo Iglesias	UVIGO, Spain
Ana Paula Appel	IBM Research, Brazil
Eunika Mercier-Laurent	Global Innovation Strategies, Université Reims Champagne Ardenne, France
Eugénio Oliveira	LIACC, Universidade do Porto, Portugal

Program Committee

Adam Woznica	Expedia, Switzerland
Adrián Seara Veira	Universidad de Vigo, Spain
António Castro	LIACC-NIADR, University of Porto, Portugal
Carlos Rodrigues	Marionete, UK
Carmela Comito	ICAR-CNR, Italy
Dario Oliveira	IBM Research, Brazil
Efi Papatheocharous	Swedish Institute of Computer Science, Sweden
Elaine Ribeiro de Faria	Universidade Federal Uberlândia, Brazil
Francesca Spezzano	Boise State University, USA
Gustavo Batista	ICMC, USP, Brazil
Ida Mele	Università della Svizzera, Italy
Jean-Pierre Briot	Laboratoire d'Informatique de Paris 6 (Paris6-CNRS), France, and PUC-Rio, Brazil
Kaustubh Patil	MIT, USA
Lourdes Borrajo	Universidad de Vigo, Spain
Marisa Affonso Vasconcelos	IBM Research, Brazil
Miriam Seoane Santos	Universidade de Coimbra, Portugal
Paulo Cavalin	IBM Research, Brazil
Pedro Henriques Abreu	FCTUC-DEI, CISUC, Portugal
Peter Van der Putten	Pegasystems, Leiden University, The Netherlands
Rodrigo Mello	Universidade de São Paulo, Brazil
YongHong Peng	University of Sunderland, UK

General Artificial Intelligence (GAI)

Organizing Committee

Luís Paulo Reis	LIACC, University of Porto, Portugal
Paulo Moura Oliveira	INESC-TEC, UTAD, Portugal
Paulo Novais	ALGORITMI, University of Minho, Portugal

Program Committee

Amparo Alonso-Betanzos	University of A Coruña, Spain
Ana Paiva	INESC-ID, University of Lisbon, Portugal
Ana Paula Rocha	LIACC, University of Porto, Portugal
Andrea Omicini	Università di Bologna, Italy
Arlindo Oliveira	INESC-ID, IST, University of Lisbon, Portugal
Brígida Mónica Faria	Polytechnic Institute of Porto, Portugal
Carlos Bento	University of Coimbra, Portugal
Carlos M. Fonseca	University of Coimbra, Portugal
Carlos Ramos	Polytechnic Institute of Porto, Portugal
Cesar Analide	University of Minho, Portugal
Davide Carneiro	Polytechnic Institute of Porto, Portugal
Eric De La Clergerie	Inria, France
Ernesto Costa	University of Coimbra, Portugal
Francisco Pereira	Polytechnic Institute of Coimbra, Portugal
Gaël Dias	Normandy University, France
Goreti Marreiros	GECAD, Polytechnic Institute of Porto, Portugal
Henrique Lopes Cardoso	University of Porto, Portugal
João Balsa	BioISI-MAS, University of Lisbon, Portugal
João Gama	University of Porto, Portugal
João Leite	New University of Lisbon, Portugal
John-Jules Meyer	Utrecht University, The Netherlands
José Cascalho	University of Azores, Portugal
José Júlio Alferes	New University of Lisbon, Portugal
José Machado	University of Minho, Portugal
José Neves	University of Minho, Portugal
Juan Corchado	University of Salamanca, Spain
Juan Pavón	University Complutense de Madrid, Spain
Luís Antunes	University of Lisbon, Portugal
Luís Camarinha-Matos	New University of Lisbon, Portugal
Luís Cavique	University Aberta, Portugal
Luís Correia	University of Lisbon, Portugal
Luís Macedo	University of Coimbra, Portugal
Luís Seabra Lopes	University of Aveiro, Portugal
Mário J. Silva	University of Lisbon, Portugal
Miguel Calejo	Declarativa, Portugal
Mikhail Lavrentiev	Novosibirsk State University, Russia
Nuno Lau	University of Aveiro, Portugal
Paulo Cortez	University of Minho, Portugal
Paulo Quaresma	University of Évora, Portugal
Paulo Urbano	University of Lisbon, Portugal
Pedro Barahona	New University of Lisbon, Portugal
Pedro Rangel Henriques	University of Minho, Portugal
Penousal Machado	University of Coimbra, Portugal
Ricardo Santos	ESTG, Polytechnic Institute of Porto, Portugal

Rosaldo Rossetti	University of Porto, Portugal
Rui Prada	University of Lisbon, Portugal
Salvador Abreu	LISP, CRI, University of Évora, Portugal
Tatsu Naka	Waseda University, Japan
Vicente Julian	University of Politècnica de València, Spain
Victor Alves	University of Minho, Portugal

Intelligent Robotics (IROBOT)

Organizing Committee

Nuno Lau	Universidade de Aveiro, Portugal
João Alberto Fabro	Universidade Tecnológica Federal do Paraná, Portugal
Fei Chen	Istituto Italiano di Tecnologia, Italy
Luís Paulo Reis	LIACC, Faculdade de Engenharia da Universidade do Porto, Portugal

Program Committee

André Marcato	Universidade Federal de Juíz de Fora, Brazil
André Scolari Conceição	Universidade Federal da Bahia, Brazil
Anna Helena Costa	EPUSP, Brazil
António José Neves	Universidade de Aveiro, Portugal
António Paulo Moreira	Universidade do Porto, Portugal
Armando Pinho	Universidade de Aveiro, Portugal
Armando Sousa	Universidade do Porto, Portugal
Axel Hessler	TU Berlin, Germany
Brígida Mónica Faria	Instituto Politécnico do Porto, Portugal
Carlos Carreto	Instituto Politécnico da Guarda, Portugal
César Analide	Universidade do Minho, Portugal
Chengxu Zhou	Istituto Italiano di Tecnologia, Italy
Fanny Ficuciello	University of Naples Federico II, Italy
Fernando Osório	Universidade São Paulo, Brazil
Jorge Dias	ISR, Universidade de Coimbra, Portugal
Josemar Rodrigues de Souza	Brazil
Liming Chen	École Centrale de Lyon, France
Luís Correia	Universidade de Lisboa, Portugal
Luis Moreno Lorente	Universidad Carlos III Madrid, Spain
Luis Seabra Lopes	Universidade de Aveiro, Portugal
Marco Dorigo	Université Libre de Bruxelles, Belgium
Maxime Petit	École Centrale de Lyon, France
Mikhail Prokopenko	CSIRO ICT Centre, Australia
Nicolas Jouandeau	University of Paris 8, France
Nikolaos Tsagarakis	Istituto Italiano di Tecnologia, Italy
Paulo Urbano	Universidade de Lisboa, Portugal
Qinyuan Ren	Zhejiang University, China

Reinaldo Bianchi   IIIA-CSIC, Barcelona, Spain
Saeed Shiry Ghidary   Amirkabir University, Iran
Sanem Sariel Talay   Istanbul Technical University, Turkey
Yan Wu   Institute for Infocomm Research A*STAR, Singapore
Urbano Nunes   Universidade de Coimbra, Portugal

Knowledge Discovery and Business Intelligence (KDBI)

Organizing Committee

Paulo Cortez   University of Minho, Portugal
Alfred Bifet   Université Paris-Saclay, France
Luís Cavique   Universidade Aberta, Portugal
João Gama   INESC-TEC, University of Porto, Portugal
Nuno Marques   Universidade Nova de Lisboa, Portugal
Manuel Filipe Santos   University of Minho, Portugal

Program Committee

Alicia Troncoso   Pablo de Olavide University, Spain
Agnes Braud   University Robert Schuman, France
Alberto Bugarin   University of Santiago de Compostela, Spain
Alípio Jorge   University of Porto, Portugal
Amilcar Oliveira   Universidade Aberta, Portugal
André Carvalho   University of São Paulo, Brazil
Antonio Tallón-Ballesteros   University of Seville, Spain
Armando Mendes   University of Azores, Portugal
Bernardete Ribeiro   University of Coimbra, Portugal
Carlos Ferreira   Institute of Engineering of Porto, Portugal
Elaine Faria   Universidade Uberlândia, Brazil
Fátima Rodrigues   Institute of Engineering of Porto, Portugal
Fernando Bação   New University of Lisbon, Portugal
Filipe Pinto   Polytechnic Institute Leiria, Portugal
Karin Becker   UFRGS, Brazil
Leandro Krug Wives   UFRGS, Brazil
Manuel Fernandez Delgado   University of Santiago de Compostela, Spain
Marcos Domingues   University of São Paulo, Brazil
Margarida Cardoso   ISCTE, Portugal
Mark Embrechts   Rensselaer Polytechnic Institute, USA
Mohamed Gaber   University of Portsmouth, UK
Murate Testik   Hacettepe University, Turkey
Ning Chen   Institute of Engineering of Porto, Portugal
Phillipe Lenca   IMT Atlantique, France
Rita Ribeiro   Universidade do Porto, Portugal
Rui Camacho   University of Porto, Portugal
Sérgio Moro   ISCTE-IUL, Portugal
Ying Tan   Peking University, China

Knowledge Representation and Reasoning (KRR)

Organizing Committee

Eduardo Fermé	University of Madeira, Portugal
Ricardo Gonçalves	Universidade NOVA de Lisboa, Portugal
Matthias Knorr	Universidade NOVA de Lisboa, Portugal
Rafael Peñaloza	University of Milano-Bicocca, Italy
Jörg Pührer	TU Wien, Austria

Program Committee

Adila A. Krisnadhi	Universitas Indonesia, Indonesia
Alejandro Garcia	Universidad Nacional del Sur, Argentina
Amelia Harrison	University of Texas at Austin, USA
Bart Bogaerts	Vrije Universiteit Brussel, Belgium
Carlos Areces	Universidad Nacional de Córdoba, Argentina
Carmine Dodaro	University of Genova, Italy
Cristina Feier	University of Bremen, Germany
David Rajaratnam	University of New South Wales, Australia
Emmanuele Dietz Saldanha	Technische Universität Dresden, Germany
Fabrizio Maggi	University of Tartu, Estonia
Francesca Alessandra Lisi	Università degli Studi di Bari Aldo Moro, Italy
Gerhard Brewka	Leipzig University, Germany
Guohui Xiao	Free University of Bozen-Bolzano, Italy
Inês Lynce	University of Lisbon, Portugal
Ivan Varzinczak	Université d'Artois, France
João Leite	Universidade Nova de Lisboa, Portugal
João Marques-Silva	University of Lisbon, Portugal
José Júlio Alferes	Universidade Nova de Lisboa, Portugal
Jorge Fandinno	IRIT, France
Loizos Michael	Open University of Cyprus, Cyprus
Mantas Simkus	Vienna University of Technology, Austria
Maria Vanina Martinez	Universidad Nacional del Sur, Argentina
Marco Paulo Ferreirinha Garapa	University of Madeira, Portugal
Mario Alviano	University of Calabria, Italy
Matthias Thimm	Universität Koblenz-Landau, Germany
Marcelo Finger	University of São Paulo, Brazil
Maurício Duarte Luís Reis	University of Madeira, Portugal
Nicolas Troquard	Free University of Bozen-Bolzano, Italy
Orkunt Sabuncu	TED University Ankara, Turkey
Pedro Cabalar	Corunna University, Spain
Rafael Testa	University of Campinas, Brazil
Ramon Pino Perez	Yachay Tech University, Ecuador
Salvador Abreu	University of Évora, Portugal
Stefan Woltran	Vienna University of Technology, Austria

MultiAgent Systems: Theory and Applications (MASTA)

Organizing Committee

Henrique Lopes Cardoso	LIACC, Universidade do Porto, Portugal
Luís Antunes	BioISI-MAS, Universidade de Lisboa, Portugal
Viviane Torres da Silva	IBM Research, Brazil
Dave de Jonge	IIIA-CSIC, Spain

Steering Committee

Eugénio Oliveira	LIACC, Universidade do Porto, Portugal
Hélder Coelho	Universidade de Lisboa, Portugal
João Balsa	Universidade de Lisboa, Portugal
Luís Paulo Reis	LIACC, Universidade do Porto, Portugal

Program Committee

Adriana Giret	Universitat Politècnica de València, Spain
Alberto Fernandez	Universidad Rey Juan Carlos, Spain
Alejandro Guerra-Hernández	Universidad Veracruzana, Mexico
Ana Paula Rocha	Universidade do Porto, Portugal
Andrea Omicini	Università di Bologna, Italy
António Castro	TAP Air Portugal, LIACC, Portugal
Carlos Carracosa	Universitat Politècnica de València, Spain
Carlos Martinho	Instituto Superior Técnico, Portugal
Daniel Silva	University of Porto, Portugal
Diana Adamatti	Universidade Federal do Rio Grande, Brazil
F. Jordan Srour	American University of Beirut, Lebanon
Francisco Grimaldo	Universidad de Valencia, Spain
Jaime Sichman	Universidade de São Paulo, Brazil
Javier Carbó	Universidad Carlos III Madrid, Spain
João Leite	Universidade Nova de Lisboa, Portugal
John-Jules Meyer	Universiteit Utrecht, The Netherlands
Jordi Sabater-Mir	IIIA-CSIC, Spain
Jorge Gomez-Sanz	Universidad Complutense Madrid, Spain
Juan Antonio Rodriguez-Aguilar	IIIA-CSIC, Spain
Juan Burguillo	Universidad de Vigo, Spain
Juan Corchado	Universidad de Salamanca, Spain
Lars Braubach	Universität Hamburg, Germany
Laurent Vercouter	École Nationale Supérieure des Mines de Saint-Étienne, France
Luís Correia	Universidade de Lisboa, Portugal
Luís Macedo	Universidade de Coimbra, Portugal
Luís Nunes	ISCTE, Portugal

Michael Schumacher	University of Applied Sciences Western Switzerland, Switzerland
Marin Lujak	Institute Mines-Télécom, France
Neil Yorke-Smith	American University of Beirut, Lebanon
Olivier Boissier	École Nationale Supérieure des Mines de Saint-Étienne, France
Paolo Torroni	Università di Bologna, Italy
Paulo Novais	Universidade do Minho, Portugal
Rafael Bordini	Pontífica Universidade Católica do Rio Grande do Sul, Brazil
Ramón Hermoso	University of Zaragoza, Spain
Reyhan Aydogan	Özyeğin University, Turkey, and Delft University of Technology, The Netherlands
Wamberto Vasconcelos	University of Aberdeen, UK

Social Simulation and Modelling (SSM)

Organizing Committee

Luis Antunes	Universidade de Lisboa, Portugal
Pedro Campos	Universidade do Porto, Portugal
Shu-Heng Chen	National Chengchi University, Taiwan

Program Committee

Ana Bazzan	UFRGS, Brazil
Andrea Teglio	University Ca' Foscari of Venice, Italy
Annalisa Fabretti	University of Rome, Italy
Bruce Edmonds	Centre for Policy Modelling, UK
Claudio Cioffi-Revilla	George Mason University, USA
Cristiano Castelfranchi	ISTC-CNR, Italy
Frederic Amblard	Université Toulouse 1, France
Friederike Wall	Alpen-Adria-Universität Klagenfurt, Austria
Ghita Mezzour	International University of Rabat, Morocco
Hélder Coelho	Universidade de Lisboa, Portugal
João Balsa	Universidade Lisbon, Portugal
Luis R. Izquierdo	Universidad de Burgos, Spain
Nuno David	ISCTE-IUL, Portugal
Pedro Magalhães	ICS, Portugal
Pedro Santos	Instituto Superior Técnico, Portugal
Philippe Mathieu	Lille1 University, CRIStAL Lab, France
Pia Ramchandani	PwC and University of Pennsylvania, USA
Ramon Villa Cox	Carnegie Mellon, USA
Sérgio Bacelar	INE, Portugal
Tânya Araújo	ISEG, Portugal
Tim Verwaart	LEI Wageningen UR, The Netherlands

Text Mining and Applications (TeMA)

Organizing Committee

Joaquim Francisco Ferreira da Silva	Universidade Nova de Lisboa, Portugal
Altigran Soares da Silva	Universidade Federal do Amazonas, Brasil

Program Committee

Adeline Nazarenko	University of Paris 13, France
Alberto Diaz	Universidad Complutense de Madrid, Spain
Alberto Simões	Algoritmi Center, University of Minho, Portugal
Alexandre Rademaker	IBM Research Lab, Brazil
Antoine Doucet	University of Caen, France
António Branco	Universidade de Lisboa, Portugal
Béatrice Daille	University of Nantes, France
Belinda Maia	Universidade do Porto, Portugal
Bruno Martins	Instituto Superior Técnico, Universidade de Lisboa, Portugal
Eric de La Clergerie	Inria, France
Fernando Batista	Instituto Universitário de Lisboa, Portugal
Francisco Couto	Universidade de Lisboa, Portugal
Gaël Dias	University of Caen Normandy, France
Hugo Oliveira	Universidade de Coimbra, Portugal
Irene Rodrigues	Universidade de Évora, Portugal
Jesús Vilares	University of A Coruña, Spain
Katerzyna Wegrzyn-Wolska	ESIGETEL, France
Luciano Barbosa	Universidade Federal de Pernambuco, Brazil
Luisa Coheur	Universidade Técnica de Lisboa, Portugal
Manuel Vilares Ferro	University of Vigo, Spain
Mário Silva	Instituto Superior Técnico, Universidade de Lisboa, Portugal
Mohand Boughanem	University of Toulouse III, France
Nuno Marques	Universidade Nova de Lisboa
Pablo Gamallo	Santiago de Compustela, Spain
Paulo Quaresma	Universidade de Évora, Portugal
Pavel Brazdil	University of Porto, Portugal
Pável Calado	Instituto Superior Técnico, Universidade de Lisboa, Portugal
Sebastião Pais	Universidade da Beira Interior, Portugal
Sérgio Nunes	Faculdade de Engenharia, Universidade do Porto, Portugal
Vítor Jorge Rocio	Universidade Aberta, Portugal

Additional Reviewers

Abdelghany, Hazem
Abrishambaf, Omid
Adedoyin-Olowe, Mariam
Akermi, Imen
Alonso, Miguel A.
Bento, L. C.
Berger, Martin
Boufidis, Neofytos
Buisson, Jocelyn
Caled, Danielle
Canizes, Bruno
Casado-Vara, Roberto
Chamby-Diaz, Jorge C.
Darriba, Victor
de Melo Pinto Junior, Ubiratan
Doria, Nara
Doval Mosquera, Yerai
Fahed, Lina
Faia, Ricardo
Fernandes, Ramon
Ghomeshi, Hossein
González Briones, Alfonso
Jozi, Aria
Khorram, Mahsa
Krippahl, Ludwig

Lamurias, Andre
Lezama, Fernando
Mendes, Marco
Mitsakis, Evangelos
Morquecho, Edgar
Mu, Shenglin
Murphy, Aidan
Pandya, Kartik
Ribadas-Pena, Francisco J.
Sanchez Passos, Lúcio
Santana, Laura
Santos, Gabriel
Santos, Valéria
Shokri Gazafroudi, Amin
Silva, Cátia
Silva, Francisco
Simões, David
Soares, Joao
Sousa, Diana
Sutana, Ricardo
Teixeira, Brigida
Trigo, Luís
Tsaples, Georgios
Xin, Songyan

Contents – Part I

Artificial Intelligence and IoT in Agriculture

Artificial Intelligence and Law

Artificial Intelligence in Medicine

**Artificial Intelligence in Cyber-Physical and Distributed
Embedded Systems**

Artificial Intelligence in Power and Energy Systems

Artificial Life and Evolutionary Algorithms

Contents – Part II

General AI

Intelligent Robotics

Knowledge Discovery and Business Intelligence

Knowledge Representation and Reasoning

MultiAgent Systems: Theory and Applications

Social Simulation and Modelling

Text Mining and Applications

Artificial Intelligence in Education

Artificial Intelligence in Education

A Data Mining Approach Applied to the High School National Examination: Analysis of Aspects of Candidates to Brazilian Universities

Diego de Castro Rodrigues[1,2(✉)], Márcio Dias de Lima[2,3],
Marcos Dias da Conceição[1], Vilson Soares de Siqueira[1,2],
and Rommel M. Barbosa[2]

[1] Federal Institute of Tocantins, Dianópolis-TO and Colinas - TO, Tocantins, Brazil
diego.rodrigues@ifto.edu.br
[2] Federal University of Goiáis, Goiânia, Brazil
Rommel@inf.ufg.br
[3] Federal Institute of Goiâis, Goiânia, GO, Brazil
marcio.lima@ifg.edu.br
http://www.ifto.edu.br, http://www.inf.ufg.br, http://www.ifg.edu.br

Abstract. In many college courses in several countries are used exams in a national scale, such as Gaokao, in China, Scholastic Aptitude Test - SAT and the American College Testing - ACT in the United States of American, Yükseögretime Geçis Sinavi – YGS in Turkey, among others. This paper examines microdata from the High School National Examination (ENEM) database from Brazil. The database has 8,627,367 records, 166 attributes, and all experiments were performed based on the Spark architecture. The objective of this work is to examine microdata of the ENEM database applying data mining algorithms and creating an approach to handle big data and to predict the profile of those enrolled in ENEM. Through the standards found by the data mining algorithms with classification algorithms, it was possible to observe that family income, access to information, profession, and academic history of the parents were directly related to the performance of the candidates. And with a rules induction algorithm, it was possible to identify the patterns presented in each of the regions of Brazil, such as common characteristics when a candidate was approved and when not, essential factors as disciplines and particular characteristics of each region. This approach also enables the execution of large volumes of data in a simplified computational structure.

Keywords: Data mining · Artificial Intelligence · National Exam · Education

1 Introduction

The High School National Exam or ENEM (In Portuguese: *Exame Nacional do Ensino Médio*) was initially created in 1998 to evaluate students performance

© Springer Nature Switzerland AG 2019
P. Moura Oliveira et al. (Eds.): EPIA 2019, LNAI 11804, pp. 3–14, 2019.
https://doi.org/10.1007/978-3-030-30241-2_1

at the end of basic education and thus contribute to improvements to the education system by providing yearly indicators. The ENEM is a non-compulsory, standardized Brazilian national exam, managed and operated by the Ministry of Education National Institute for Educational Studies and Research (INEP). It tests the level of knowledge of the high school students in Brazil and is the second-biggest nationwide test in the world after the National Higher Education Entrance Examination, colloquially known as the "Gaokao" in China, which is taken by more than 9 million students [19]. In other countries, similar exams take place. In Turkey, for instance, the university entrance is solely determined by a national examination that happens in two phases: The exam is called The Transition to Higher Education Exam (Yüksekögretime Gecis Sinavi – YGS). Students whose YGS scores are higher than the minimum first stage score are allowed to take the Undergraduate Placement Examinations (Lisansa Yerlestirme Sinavlari – LYS) [8]. Japan has an exam offered by The National Center for University Admissions (Center Exam). All public universities, including the most prestigious universities, require the candidate to take another institution-specific secondary exam which takes place on the same day [7]. In the United States, students are required to do both, centralized exams like the Scholastic Aptitude Test (SAT), and also complete college-specific requirements, such as college admission essays. Students can apply to more than one college, but since the application process is costly, students typically send only a few applications. Another test is the American College Testing (ACT). Students who take the ACT receive a score report that shows their performance on each of the four subject tests (English, Mathematics, Social Studies, and Natural Sciences), as well as their composite score, which is the rounded average of four subtest scores. If a student scores above a certain threshold (determined by ACT) in a given subject, they are informed on the score report that they are college ready in that subject [5].

The ENEM exam comprises 180 multiple-choice questions and tests students in five main areas, namely human sciences and its technologies, mathematics and its technologies, natural sciences and its technologies, languages, and codes, as well as writing [9]. In many public and private post-secondary institutions in Brazil, the ENEM score is used as an admission exam for enrollment and also to obtain a high school degree certification. The University for All Program or ProUni (in Portuguese *Programa Universidade para Todos*) is a federal scholarship program, and it also uses the ENEM as a selection criterion to provide scholarships. Public universities have the autonomy to use the ENEM as a single stage of selection or to combine it with their selective processes. Through the Unified Selection System (Sisu), the vacancies for undergraduate courses are made available to the ENEM participants. The candidates are selected according to the grade obtained in the exam, within the number of places in each course, by the modality of competition. Recent researches have shown results of the effects of these entrances process. Kim et al. [11] investigated how a newly introduced school choice policy affected achievement gaps between private and public high schools in Seoul, South Korea. Anderson et al. [2] use regression discontinuity design to examine the effect of a system of public exam high schools, which admit students solely by pre-existing achievement, on student college entrance exam scores in Beijing, China. Pereira et al. [14] conducted a study applied to the context of Higher Education (HE) accreditation and evaluation in Brazil. He discussed recent reforms within the context of the Brazilian evaluation model. Almeida et al. [1] investigated how public school administrators react to government incentives based on past school performance. They used data from the Brazilian Student Evaluation Exam (*Prova Brasil – PB*) and the School Census to estimate the managerial effort function by quantile regression.

Viggiano et al. [17] investigated and compared the students' performance in ENEM 2010 in each Brazilian geographic region, considering different knowledge areas: Writing; Natural Sciences; Languages and Codes; Humanities and Mathematics. However, it was not found in the literature any work that used data mining in the Microdata ENEM. The Microdata ENEM database allows understood the socio-economic reality of the enrolled students, providing information on the profile of each participant of the exam. The classification of large amounts of data is becoming a necessary task in a significant number of real-world applications. Nevertheless, standard data mining techniques typically fail to tackle the high volume of data [12], like the one used in this work.

Yoo et al. [18] showed the results from correlation and regression analysis and identified significant variables in predicting student performance. In this study, SVM, J-48, and Naïve Bayes algorithms. The SVM performed better and was less sensitive to the change in the number of selected features. Janning et al. [10] applied SVM, decision trees (DCT) and k-Nearest-Neighbour (k-NN) approaches in a study recognizing the perceived task-difficulty of students interacting with an intelligent tutoring system. Beemer et al. [3] presented an ensemble learning approach for student study success analytics applications. Valdés et al. [16] used data mining in classification to analyze and then grade student models. This classification is intended to be used as a methodology to measure the portability of a student model and as a guide to find finding existing reusable models. Searching the literature was noticed that no work had used computational tools to handle large databases to study the socioeconomic profile of students that obtained the minimum required scored of 450 points in ENEM in order to have access to the scholarships offered by the Brazilian government. Likely due to the size of the ENEM database (2017), which contains more than 8 million the samples and requires more sophisticated computational tools to handle. In order to work on a dataset with such a large number of member registrations, it was necessary to combine different computational technologies, such as Spark [13], MySql [4], among others.

The Spark is an attractive platform for big data analysis widely used [6]. It also provides an interface to other established big data technologies. In this study, the ENEM microdata database was examined, applying data mining algorithms, and creating an approach to dealing with big data and predicting the profile of ENEM participants. The main contributions of the paper can be summarized as follows, investigation of the profiles of candidates enrolled in ENEM, new approach (methodology) for manipulation of extensive quantitative data, discovery of a relationship between candidate performance and socioeconomic conditions, use of the artificial intelligence algorithm to create the profiles of the enrolled students that have obtained a grade higher than 550 points minimum requirements to have access to Brazilian public universities.

2 Data Organization

The data used in this study is from Brazil's High School National Examination (ENEM) and is composed of one database termed ENEM microdata. It was obtained from the National Institute of Studies and Educational Research Anísio Teixeira (INEP) and referred to the year 2017. It was the most up-to-date database available mid of May 2018, when it was extracted to carry out the studies proposed in this work. The database has 8,627,367 records and 166 attributes. The attributes are composed of information related to the examination disciplines and social and economic information of each candidate from Brazil. Brazil has five regions (North has seven states, Northeast with nine states, Central-West has three states and Federal District, Southeast with four states, and South has three states).

3 Exam Organization

The National High School Examination (ENEM) consists of five areas of knowledge: Languages, Codes, and their Technologies, Mathematics and their Technologies, Natural Sciences and their Technologies, Human Sciences and their Technologies and writing assessment. Each area has a maximum score of one thousand points, and the arithmetic average demonstrates the candidate's overall performance.

The ENEM consists of 180 questions with five alternatives represented by A, B, C, D and E. The test is applied over two days, and the candidate must be present at all stages to complete the exam. It offers access to candidates for admission to public and private universities throughout Brazil and 34 universities in Portugal since 2014. For admission to public universities in Brazil, it is necessary to obtain an average score of 550 points or higher, and a grade above zero in the writing assessment. The minimum requirement for the candidate to apply for a scholarship or student financing, it is necessary to get a score above 450 points and grade above zero in the writing assessment. Additionally, to these basic and essential criteria, the candidate may be required to meet complementarity criteria that may vary according to the university and course.

4 Computational Experiments

The Fig. 1 presents the main steps performed to process the data, implement the data mining algorithm, and access the results of the experiment.

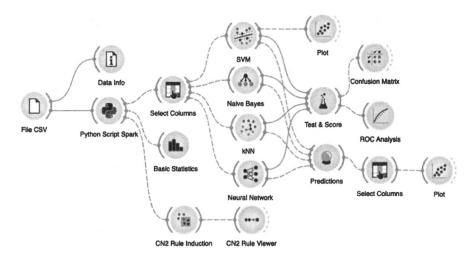

Fig. 1. Data mining process with ENEM data

All experiments were performed based on the Spark architecture where the data was loaded, cleaned and transformed. Was used the power of parallelism, to load the database into a Spark Data Frame (DF), transformed each attribute into its correct data type. The ENEM dataset has two types of data: integer and characters. Initially, the database has 8,627,367 records and 166 attributes. Following the execution of the data cleaning and transformations step, the dataset had 5,688,295 records and 48 attributes. Attributes with a better relationship with Q006 (What is your family's monthly income?). The result was a classification based on the information gain with the attributes Q025 (Does your residence have Internet access?), Q024 (Is there a computer in your residence?), Q001 (Until what grade did your father, or the man responsible for you, study?), Q003 (Which group contemplates the occupation closest to the occupation of your father or the man responsible for you.), Q004 (Which group contemplates the occupation closest to the occupation of your mother or the woman responsible for you.), Q002 (Until what grade did your mother, or the woman responsible for you, study?), Q037 (Reasons that led you to participate in ENEM: Get a scholarship).

Next, the dataset was transformed into the parquet data format and divided into eight parts, being each core of the computer processor responsible for one of the parts. Using Spark to perform this step, a gain in physical space of storage and processing was observed. The study dataset was uploaded in an average time of 30 s.

For the experiment the equipment used was a Mac Pro with 2.9 GHz Intel Core i7 processor with 4 physical processing cores and 4 virtual cores totaling 8 processing cores, dual-channel 16 GB 1600 MHz DDR3 RAM, Intel HD 4000 and 1536 MB graphics card and two 512 GB SSD with 6 GB per second write speed and data read. We used k-fold cross-validation (k = 20) to evaluate the algorithm's performance. K-Fold cross-validation is one way to improve over the holdout method. Was divided the data set into k subsets, and the holdout method is repeated k times. For each k, the subset k is the test set and the other k-1 subsets are put together to form a training set. Then, it calculates the average error in the k repetitions. The advantage of this method is that, independently of the data division, every data point gets to be in a test set exactly once, and gets to be in a training set k-1 times [15]. Each experiment was performed 50 times for statistical validation.

Also, in the Spark Environment, basic statistics were of fundamental importance to verify how the data behaved in the dataset, to execute classification algorithms and to initiate the prediction process of the selective results. A target attribute was needed in the step (Select Columns) shown in the scheme of experiments (see Fig. 2). After the selection of the target attribute, it started the execution process of the classification algorithms in the Spark environment. The result of the predictions of classifiers was compared to verify which had the best result to the stage in the step (Test & Score).

After compiling the results of the algorithms, it generated a dataset with the respective predictions. To showed the results was necessary to convert the data from the Spark environment to the Pandas data frame format, which is a non-parallel format. The Matplotlib tool was used in the visualization step to display the results of the classifiers graphically. Thus, facilitated the process of interpretation of the obtained results.

5   Results and Discussion

In order to better understand the results of the candidates' performance in the exam, it constructed intervals between 350 points and 800 points that determine the classification of the candidates by the algorithm based on the studies applied to the socioeconomic data. Another attribute that needs to be understood very well is Q006 (Family income), which is the candidate's family income with an interval starting from A to Q, where A is the lowest income (no income) and Q is the highest income, above 20 Brazilian minimum salaries (BRL 17,600 in 2019).

Figure 2(a-b) presents a relation of the level of education of the father and the mother where A is "low level of education" and H is "higher education". The family income has a range that goes from A lowest income to Q that is the highest income. The graphic shows the scoring range of candidates, the blue color is terrible grades, and yellow color are excellent grades. In Fig. 2(a-b) the highest concentration of bad grades is strongly related to the low income and the lower level of the parent's education. On the other hand, the candidates with the highest family income have the best grades. Some low-income candidates had good grades, but in these cases, the parents' level of schooling proved to be a differential for these candidates.

Figure 2(c-d) displays the relationship between the current occupation of father and mother, respectively, and the family income. Figure 2(c) shows a range from A to F, where A represents the worst jobs, and F represents the best jobs.

The highest concentration of low grades is in the A, B, C range, and higher grades concentrated between D and F. Figure 2(d) presented a similar behavior while maintaining the pattern seen in the previous figure. It also observed that, for both factors, the family income has a primary effect on the candidate's score.

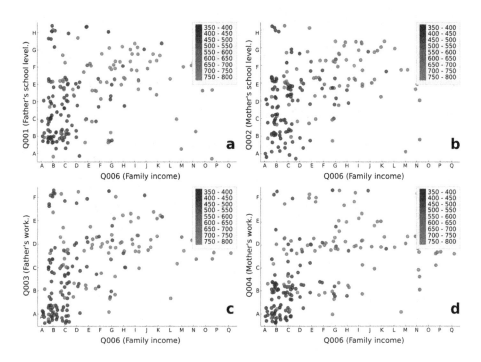

Fig. 2. The degree of parental study related to candidate performance

The relationship between access to information and family income (Q006), also considered the Fig. 3(a) identifies the number of computers in the applicant's house using ranges from A to E, where A represents no computer, B one computer, C two computers, D three computers, and E four or more computers. Figure 3(a) shows a concentration of higher grades between bands C and E for candidates who have low family income.

Figure 3(b) shows the relationship between internet access and family income, where A means that the candidate does not have the internet at home, and B means that the candidate has the internet at home. The highest concentration of good grades is associated with candidates who have access to the internet at home. Comparing Fig. 3(a) with Fig. 3(b), it is observed that access to information is a relevant factor in the overall performance of the candidates. Moreover, the family income was very relevant to identify the concentrations of candidates with good and bad scores.

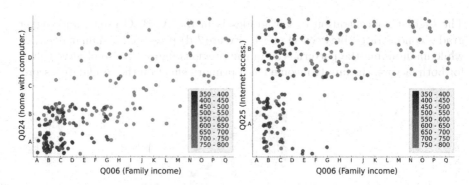

Fig. 3. Access to information

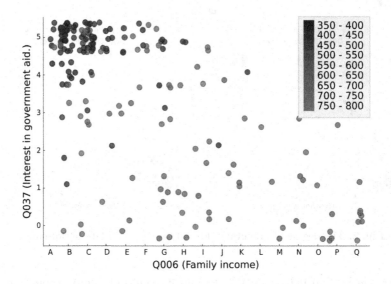

Fig. 4. Interest in aid or government financing

The family income and performance factors of the candidate presented in Fig. 4 shows the candidate's level of interest in taking the ENEM exam to receive government assistance for completing their studies. The Values in Fig. 4 range from 0 to 5, where 0 represents the candidates with the lowest interest in receiving government funding to finance their studies, and 5 are the candidates that have the most significant interest in being funded by the government. See that the higher concentration of low grades in the upper left corner is directly related to candidate's interest in obtaining government aid. University access policies may be the consequence of this behavior. For the candidate to apply for a scholarship or government aid, a minimum score of 450 points is required. However, to get admitted to a Brazilian public university, the candidate has to score, on average, at least 550 in ENEM. Another possible reason is that when analyzing the family income range of this group, we observe that the highest concentration of students highly interested in obtaining government aid is in the bands A, B, C and D which is a low family income for Brazilian standards.

Table 1 shows the performance achieved by the kNN, SVM, Neural Network, and Naïve Bayes models to describe the data using 20-fold cross-validation. The kNN model achieved the best accuracy rate of 99.00%, followed by Neural Network (85.90%), SVM (84.60%) and Naïve Bayes (82.20). The kNN, Naïve Bayes, Neural Network, and SVM model achieved the following precision rates: 99.00%, 88.40%, 85.30% and 83.90 respectively. The kNN model achieved the highest AUC-value (0.975), followed by Naïve Bayes (0.875), Neural Network (0.804) and SVM (0.791). Both accuracy and AUC-value can be used as evaluation criteria to determine which classification model is the best.

Table 1. Performance measure.

Method	ACC(%)	F1(%)	Precision(%)	Recall(%)	AUC
kNN	99.00	99.00	99.00	99.00	0.975
SVM	86.60	84.60	83.90	86.60	0.791
Neural Network	87.10	85.90	85.30	87.10	0.804
Naïve Bayes	79.40	82.20	88.40	79.40	0.875

Despite the excellent performance of the classifiers, the results provided by them present a confirmation of the behaviors already expected from the context of the data. To discover new rules and usage patterns among these stored data, we used another data mining method termed rules induction. Rules are one of the widely used techniques to present the obtained information. In order to discover unknown patterns, it applied the induction rules for each region of Brazil. Table 2 presents the best rules found for each of the regions.

In Table 2, rule 1 states that when the Languages and Codes' grade is below 427 points and the candidate studied some part of the elementary school in public school and the mother only has high school but did not complete the college, the candidate's performance in the test was below the average of 450 points. In rule 2, observed that in this region, there is a pattern of means above 450 points when the candidate presented test grades of Languages and Codes greater than 479. This test contemplates the disciplines of Portuguese language, literature, and foreign language, and human sciences.

In rule 3, when the candidates had a defined period of study or studied in the morning period or studied at night, despite presenting low grades in writing, they performed well in mathematics, and the average grade was over 450 points. In rule 4, it highlighted in this region that the candidates who did not show disapproval in high school obtained an average above 450 points.

Table 2. The main rules obtained by CN2 Rules induction algorithm.

Regions	Number	IF	THEN
North	Rule 1	NU_NOTA_LC <= 427.0 and Q002=E, Q042 != C	D_ AVERAGE =2
	Rule 2	NU_NOTA_LC >= 479.0	D_ AVERAGE =1
	Rule 3	NU_NOTA_MT >= 573.0 and Q049 != B	D_ AVERAGE =1
Northeast	Rule 4	Q049 ! = B and Q050 != B, Q050 != D	D_ AVERAGE =1
South	Rule 5	Q047=B and Q049=B, Q042 != C	D_ AVERAGE =1
Southeast	Rule 6	NU_NOTA_CH <= 410.0 and NU_NOTA_REDACAO <= 380.0, NU_NOTA_MT <= 426.0, Q050 != B	D_ AVERAGE =2
Central-West	Rule 7	Q003=E and Q045 != B, Q048=B	D_ AVERAGE =2

In rule 5, the candidates who studied high school in public school and part in private school independent of the study period, and with an elementary school in public school obtained an average higher than 450 points. Rule 6 states that those whose test scores for the natural sciences (NU_NOTA_CH) and writing were below average, and they did not drop out of high school, but disapproved at some point, had scored below the average of 450 points.

Rule 7, contemplates a legal guardian who has a right level education, such as medic, engineer, dentist, psychologist, economist, lawyer, judge, prosecutor, defender, delegate, lieutenant, captain, colonel, university professor, public or private entrepreneurs, politicians, entrepreneurs with more than 10 employees, the candidate failed a grade in elementary school, and has attended high school in different modalities, the average was below 450 points. With the application of induction rules, it was possible to identify the patterns presented in each of the regions of Brazil, identifying common characteristics of candidate who is approved and when one is not, identifying essential factors as disciplines and particular characteristics of each region.

We used an approach that allows the execution of large volumes of data in a simplified computational structure, defined by steps, to uploaded the dataset for Spark architecture and then transformed into the Parquet format, divided into multiple parts. Our approach evaluates each of these parts individually for the selection of algorithms, selection of variables, and generation of a new data set. Performing these steps in a single part of the dataset results in a faster evaluation of the efficiency of the algorithms for the dataset and facilitates the process of executing large amounts of data.

This process is performed for each of the parts to evaluate their performance and check for possible anomalies. After the execution of all the parts, the dataset is fully executed to evaluate the standards of the candidates. The partial results are compared to verify the behaviors of the parts of the dataset with the whole, using the strategy of small parts this facilitated the process of choosing the algorithms and selecting the variables of the study. A limitation is the more significant the dataset, the higher the size of the parts, so it is necessary to divide the maximum number of parts according to the maximum amount that the computer can perform with the Spark architecture, in most cases it is eight parts.

6 Conclusions and Future Work

In this study, we presented a data mining approach to handle large amounts of data with the help of Spark that enabled the investigation of ENEM candidates profiles. The approach taken allowed us to unravel the standards of the candidates who took the ENEM test and to further classify them through the test performance. Data mining algorithms were used to predict cases of excellent and poor performance. Through the standards found by the different classification algorithms kNN, SVM, Neural Network and Naïve Bayes, it was possible to observe that family income, access to information, occupation and academic history of the parents are directly related to the candidates' performance in the exam. Despite that, the excellent performance of the classifiers, the results provided by them present a confirmation of the behaviors already expected from the context of the data. So, with the application of induction rules, it was possible to identify the patterns presented in each of the regions of Brazil, identifying related points when the candidate is approved and when not, identifying essential factors as disciplines and particular characteristics of each region. Was used an approach that allows the execution of large volumes of data in a simplified computational structure, defined by steps, uploaded the dataset for Spark architecture, and then transformed into the Parquet format, divided into multiple parts. In future work, we plan to analyze data from all of ENEM's exams already conducted in Brazil and build models for patterns and forecasts to help public and private administrators make decisions about university access policies.

References

1. Almeida, A.T.C., Ramalho, H.M., Araujo Junior, I.T.: Managerial effort under asymmetric information: the case of public schools in Brazil. EconomiA **18**(3), 275–297 (2017)
2. Anderson, K., Gong, X., Hong, K., Zhang, X.: Do selective high schools improve student achievement? Effects of exam schools in China. China Econ. Rev. **40**, 121–134 (2016)
3. Beemer, J., Spoon, K., He, L., Fan, J., Levine, R.A.: Ensemble learning for estimating individualized treatment effects in student success studies. Int. J. Artif. Intell. Educ. **28**(3), 315–335 (2018)
4. DuBois, P., Hinz, S., Pedersen, C.: MySQL 5.0 Certification Study Guide (MySQL Press). MySQL Press (2005)
5. Foote, A., Schulkind, L., Shapiro, T.M.: Missed signals: the effect of ACT college-readiness measures on post-secondary decisions. Econ. Educ. Rev. **46**, 39–51 (2015)

6. Gounaris, A., Torres, J.: A methodology for spark parameter tuning. Big Data Res. **11**, 22–32 (2018)
7. Hafalir, I.E., Hakimov, R., Kübler, D., Kurino, M.: College admissions with entrance exams: centralized versus decentralized. J. Econ. Theor. **176**(15), 886–934 (2018)
8. Hatipoglu, Ç.: The impact of the university entrance exam on EFL education in Turkey: pre-service English language teachers' perspective. Procedia - Soc. Behav. Sci. **232**, 136–144 (2016)
9. INEP. Exame Nacional Do Ensino Médio - Enem (2018)
10. Janning, R., Schatten, C., Schmidt-Thieme, L.: Perceived task-difficulty recognition from log-file information for the use in adaptive intelligent tutoring systems. Int. J. Artif. Intell. Educ. **26**(3), 855–876 (2016)
11. Kim, Y.: The effects of school choice on achievement gaps between private and public high schools: evidence from the Seoul high school choice program. Int. J. Educ. Dev. **60**, 25–32 (2018)
12. Maillo, J., Triguero, I., Herrera, F.: A mapreduce-based k-nearest neighbor approach for big data classification. In: IEEE Trustcom/BigDataSE/ISPA, Helsinki, vol. 2, pp. 167–172 (2015)
13. Meng, X., et al.: MLlib: machine learning in apache spark. J. Mach. Learn. Res. **17**(1), 1235–1241 (2016)
14. Pereira, C.A., Araujo, J.F.F.E., de Lourdes Machado-Taylor, M.: The Brazilian higher education evaluation model: "SINAES" sui generis? Int. J. Educ. Dev. **61**, 5–15 (2018)
15. Polat, K., GÜneŞ, S.: Breast cancer diagnosis using least square support vector machine. Digit. Sig. Proc. **17**(4), 694–701 (2007)
16. Valdés Aguirre, B., Ramírez Uresti, J.A., du Boulay, B.: An analysis of student model portability. Int. J. Artif. Intell. Educ. **26**(3), 932–974 (2016)
17. Viggiano, E., Mattos, C.: O desempenho de estudantes no Enem 2010 em diferentes regiões brasileiras. Rev. Bras. de Estudos Pedagógicos **94**(237), 417–438 (2013)
18. Yoo, J., Kim, J.: Can online discussion participation predict group project performance? Investigating the roles of linguistic features and participation patterns. Int. J. Artif. Intell. Educ. **24**(1), 8–32 (2014)
19. Yue, C.: Expansion and equality in Chinese higher education. Int. J. Educ. Dev. **40**, 50–58 (2015)

Between Clones and Snow-Flakes: Personalization in Intelligent Tutoring Systems

Francisco Azeiteiro and Manuel Lopes[(✉)] [iD]

INESC-ID Instituto Superior Técnico, Lisbon, Portugal
manuel.lopes@tecnico.ulisboa.pt

Abstract. This work improves intelligent tutoring systems by combining the benefits of online personalization of contents with methods that have strong non-personalized long-term optimized policies.

Our hypothesis is that students are very diverse but they are not all completely different from each other. We will generalize previous algorithms by creating a new approach that (1) creates profiles of students based on historical data, (2) in real time is able to recognize the type of student that is being encountered, (3) personalizes their experience taking into account the information of similar students.

We perform several simulations to study the impact on teaching of the amount of data, the diversity of students, and errors in the estimation of parameters.

1 Introduction

In a perfect world students would have a learning experience perfectly personalized to their needs and interests. With so many student per class such personalization is very hard to achieve. With the help of Intelligent Tutoring Systems (ITS)[6] this might be possible as each student can have a set of exercises proposed and ordered according to their particular needs.

A great deal of work has considered how students learn [18] taking into account the human-factors, psychology, classroom dynamics, memory, among many other factors. A seminal work on this topic was the *Knowledge Tracing* framework [9] which builds a detailed cognitive model of the student, of its learning processes by considering a set of independent skills, the probability of learning them and the probability of correct or wrong answer in exercises that relies on those skills. Many recent extensions exist that try to improve the estimation of the student knowledge and also on how to learn the learning parameters of each student [1,4,5,10–12,17].

Researchers argue that if we know exactly how students learn then providing teaching materials and experiences would be trivial. Unfortunately requiring an accurate model of the students is too strong an assumption and might even be the wrong approach. Firstly, having an accurate model is very difficult. The amount of data required is too large, after acquiring the data of a particular student for

P. Moura Oliveira et al. (Eds.): EPIA 2019, LNAI 11804, pp. 15–26, 2019.
https://doi.org/10.1007/978-3-030-30241-2_2

a particular learning problem the ITS is no longer needed as the student finished the curriculum, and there are even computational problems in the identifiability of the parameters [2,3]. And, even if that was possible we would be assuming that all the students are similar and several recent results already showed that using the optimal policy for the average student is not good on average [7,13] and some degree of personalization is always needed.

Without personalized models, the main approach has been to consider an approximate model of a population of students and compute an optimal policy for that population [14,16]. This perspective assumes that students are clones of each other in that they share almost all the learning parameters. On the other side some researchers have considered that all students are different from each other [7,8]. This snow-flake perspective considers that each student has particular difficulties, learning parameters and initial knowledge. These methods have a potential of high personalization but without a model they cannot do long term planning and require too many interaction between the students and the ITS, which is not possible in many applications. Also, instead of relying on computational prohibitive methods such as POMDP [16] they rely on model-free efficient methods such as multi-armed bandits [8].

Hypothesis The hypothesis followed in that students have differences but they also share some similarities. If we can estimate in real time which type of students profile a particular student belongs, it is possible to personalize the learning experience. We are thus in between assuming that all students are similar and that all students are different. Challenges of this approach include accurately placing students on their correct group and making sure that the model parameters for each group of students are optimal.

2   Background

Formalization of a Learning Scenario. In a typical ITS we have a set of skills that we want to teach (sometimes also called knowledge components), a set of activities - that can include exercises, reading materials, videos or any other - that a teacher can choose from. For clarity we will use the following example during this article. We consider a list of exercises/activities A1 (Skill1); A2 (Skill1, Skill2); A3 (Skill1, Skill2, Skill3); B1 (Skill4); B2 (Skill4, Skill5); B3 (Skill4, Skill5, Skill6; C1 (Skill7); C2 (Skill7, Skill8) . Each of these exercises requires different skills in order for the student to succeed in solving them. Since there are typically too many activities to be explored it is expected to have a previously defined ZPD, which connects different activities via dependence relationships. Figure 1 shows the activity hierarchy used for the tests. An arrow indicates a prerequisite relationship - A2 is only added to the ZPD when the success rate in A1 passes the expansion threshold. Connections without arrows indicate activities without prerequisites between them which will be proposed when the leftmost activity gets a reward value lesser than or equal to zero - if the reward obtained for performing A3 is ever zero or less then the ZPD expands to include B2, but the opposite cannot happen.

There are some activities that are under a clear sequence of difficulty while others cannot be directly compared. A student might succeed in exercises of type A but not of type B while with another student the opposite may happen.

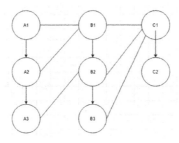

Fig. 1. Relationships between a series of different activities used for testing.

Knowledge Tracing (KT) [9] has been a popular approach to the student model. The original work uses a typical HMM [15] whose hidden states are whether or not the student has acquired a given skill. By solving exercises the students might acquire the associated skill. Whether or not the skill is acquired can be inferred by asking them to solve exercises and measuring the correctness of the answer. It is assumed that once a student learns a skill it cannot be forgotten.

A KT model for a given skill has four parameters: (i) $P(L_0)$ - the probability that the student possesses a particular skill prior to the first opportunity to apply it; (ii) $P(G)$ - the probability that the student will answer correctly to the question if the skill is in the unlearned state; (iii) $P(S)$ - the probability that the student will answer incorrectly if the skill is in the learned state; iv) $P(T)$ - the probability that the skill being learned transitions from the unlearned to the learned state after an opportunity to apply it.

Corbett and Anderson calculate how likely it is that a student understands a particular subject matter using the following formula:

$$P(L_n) = P(L_{n-1}|evd) + (1 - P(L_{n-1}|evd)) \times P(T) \qquad (1)$$

Where *evd* is the evidence consisting of the exercise proposed and if it was solved correctly or not.

The main application of KT has been to track if a student has acquired a given skill or not, while the problem of deciding what to present is always considered with other methods.

ZPDES. We will extend an approach based on multi-armed Bandits (MAB) due to its reduced computational cost and limited requirements in terms of student model. The ZPDES algorithm [8] is a tutoring model algorithm which requires little information from the student and cognitive models by attempting to estimate student competence online via a reward function. The subjects being taught are organized in skills, and the objective of this algorithm is to make sure that the students learn every skill. As in a typical MAB approach, the quality of each option (in this case each exercise) will increase if it gets a positive reward and reduce if it gets a negative reward. The reward is computed calculating the difference in amount of correct answers C_k of the last $d/2$ samples and the previous $d/2$ samples as follows: $r = \sum_{k=t-d/2}^{t} \frac{C_k}{d/2} - \sum_{k=t-d}^{t-d/2} \frac{C_k}{d-d/2}$

This allows to track if a given exercise is providing improvement in learning or not. An exercise that is always solved correctly does not provide a learning experience.

The following ZPDES parameters directly influence the number of time steps and probability of knowing every skill that the students have at the end of the ZPD: (i) β and η values, determining the confidence in a new reward value for $w_a \leftarrow \beta w_a + \eta r$ (ii) γ parameter, which determines the exploration rate when calculating the probability of selecting an activity to perform. (iii) The d parameter, which determines the number of most recent answers used to calculate the reward value from an activity, as well as the minimum amount of times that an activity needs to be proposed before the ZPD can expand from it. (iv) removal threshold - the success rate that an activity needs to have before it can leave the ZPD. (v) expansion threshold - the success rate that an activity needs to have before its dependent activities may join the ZPD.

Simulation of Student Populations. Different profiles of students will correspond to students that have different initial knowledge and different learning rates. We implement this through two attributes called baselearn (*bl*) and baseinit (*bi*), with *bl* influencing the probability that the student has of learning skills and *bi* influencing the probability of the student already knowing each skill before solving an exercise containing said skill.

Students are modeled with a KT formalism [9] as follows. Given a skill *sk* and a student *st*, the probability of the student learning that skill after each exercise, assuming that the student didn't know the skill before, is given $P(T_{st}) = b_1 bl_{st} + b_2 P(T_{sk})$, where bl_{st} is the student's baselearn attribute, $P(T_{sk})$ is the skill's transition probability, and b_1 and b_2 are two factors that influence the weight of $baselearn_{st}$ and $P(T_{sk})$, with $b_1 + b_2 = 1$. As a result from tests created with the objective of determining the b_1 and b_2 values to be used while making sure that both the student's learning speed and the skill's learning difficulty are taken into consideration, the used values are $b_1 = 0.55$ and $b_2 = 0.45$.

A similar equation was used to determine the student's probability of knowing the skill: $P(L_{0st}) = c_1 bi_{st} + c_2 P(L_{0sk})$ In this case the values used for c_1 and c_2 are 0.1 and 0.9 respectively, focusing on how well known the skill's domain is in general. Where $P(L_{0sk})$ is a skill specific probability of initially knowing the skill. The probability of student *st* learning a skill *sk* after performing an activity (or exercise) A which includes it is given by: $P(T) = (0.55 \times baselearn_{st} + 0.45 \times P(T_{sk})) \times w_{skA}$. Where w_{skA} is the weight that the skill has in the activity. This equation can be solved for *baselearn* as shown by $baselearn = \frac{P(T) - 0.45 P(T_{sk}) w_{skA}}{0.55 w_{skA}}$. Thanks to the Baum-Welch algorithm, it is possible to estimate the value of $P(T)$, which can then be used to recalculate the student's *baselearn* attribute.

3   The GOZPDES Algorithm

Our new approach contains several components: (i) a method to compare students and detect to which group a particular student belongs; (ii) a method to provide teaching examples for a particular group. A preliminary step requires information about previous students to create representative profiles of students and their respective optimized teaching experience. The algorithm is summarized in Algorithm 1.

Algorithm 1. GOZPDES

Offline Phase of Profile Creation from Historical Data;
begin
  Data: K skills to be learned
  Data: Graph of activities
  Data: N exercises from M students
  Result: Cluster of M students into P profiles
  Optimize Teaching parameters for each profile;
  Result: Optimized parameters for each profile
Online Phase with New Student;
begin
  new student;
  $\theta = \theta_{average}$;
  while *exercises in ZPD* **do**
    if *enough exercises to classify* **then**
      Estimate student parameters;
      Select most similar profile;
      $\theta = \theta_{profile}$
    activity ←ZPDES(θ);
    propose activity;
    observe answer and update ZPDES;

3.1   Measures of Similarity Between Students

Being the goal of this work to provide algorithms that personalize education as much as possible (all students are different) while simultaneously being able to use data from similar situations, (students are similar) we need to have some measures of similarity between students.

One constraint on this measure of similarity between students is that it needs to be data efficient. A trivial way would be to let the student go through the whole learning process and then compare the evolution and results, but then the knowledge learned about the student would not be needed anymore as the student already went through the learning process.

We have 3 main options for comparing students: perform a pre-test to identify the previous knowledge of the student; give an initial set of exercises and compare the success and errors; or give an initial set of exercises but compare based on learning parameters estimated from this initial and limited data. The first option requires a specific assessment period while the other two do not consider such different phase and can work while teaching. As we want to be data efficient we prefer methods that do not require pre-tests.

There are more fundamental differences between the three approaches, the first method compares previous knowledge, the second compares acquired knowledge, but the last one compares the learning process itself. In the second metric (based on success rates) we have a metric that compares students by measuring the distance between two vectors. Each vector contains the percentage of success in each type of exercise. The third metric (based on estimated parameters) uses the percentage of success in each type of exercise but applies an EM algorithm and then compares on the space of the estimated parameters. For our study we used a variant of the EM algorithm to estimate the baselearn (bl) and baseinit (bi) parameters.

The metric based on the parameters is expected to better compare the second but might require too many data points to be useful. To test this, We made several simulations to verify if similar students are classified as similar with each of the methods. With an increasing number of students we noticed that as the number of exercises increases comparing at the parameter level is able to do a better distinctions than comparing directly on the success rate of the exercises.

3.2   Creation of Student Profiles and Corresponding Teaching Policy

A profile of students is no more than a group of students that has very similar learning parameters that results in very similar teaching policies. If students are so similar that they will learn with the same sequence then they do not need to be individualized and can be considered clones of each other.

These profiles can be created automatically using clustering methods on the individual learning parameters. For each student in the dataset we can learn its learning parameters. Then a clustering method is done on the learned parameters. As the data is very sparse we do not learn all parameters in the typical BKT scenario but consider only the *baselearn* attribute that influences the learning rate.

Even in a small class of 30 students empirically we observe that there are between 5 to 10 different groups of students. The teaching policy could be optimized in different ways. To ensure further personalization and to make it consistent with the rest of the approach we will used ZPDES [8].

3.3   Teaching Policy Optimization

Each group of students will have a set of parameters that represent their learning behavior. For each student, or group of students sharing the same learning model, the optimal policy for teaching is different. This policy determines how the GOZPDES algorithm will function for each group. Within each group the parameters are chosen as the optimal values that minimize the average number of time steps for that group's student profile while maintaining the probability of learning all skills above a certain threshold. Since the parameters are optimal for the profile, then as long as the classification step is done correctly all students will have approximately optimal parameters.

3.4   Online Identification of Student Profile

With all the previous components we are now ready to accomplish the goal of our work. After a short number of exercises we will be able to identify to which profile each particular student belongs and provide each one with the best teaching strategy available.

Below are different conditions tested for deciding when to perform the *baselearn* estimation. Note that in some methods such estimation is not made.

1. Avg params - A set of average parameters obtained from previous tests are used from start to finish
2. A priori - A priori classification, performing a series of pre-tests and use observations obtained from there to estimate *baselearn* before placing the student into the ZPD. A time penalty is applied for this method to compensate for the time taken in pre-tests
3. A1 - Uses the observations obtained from activity A1 (as shown in Fig. 1) once the activity has been removed from the ZPD
4. A1/B1 - Uses the observations obtained from activities A1 and B1 once they have both been removed from the ZPD
5. 20 steps - Uses the observations obtained after 20 time steps (a time step is an attempt at solving an exercise, regardless of correctness)
6. 30 steps+ - Uses the observations obtained after 30 time steps, along with artificially increasing the estimated value slightly

4   Results

Creation of Student Profiles from Data. We performed several simulations to evaluate if we can create the student profiles from historical data. To do a systematic study, we generated 1100 students with *baselearn* parameters uniformly from 0.0 to 1.0. Then we let them go through the ITS until the termination condition and the results they have in each exercise will serve as database for the results.

Using a standard k-means for different numbers of classes we can see in Table 1 the obtained results. We can see that for any number of clusters the obtained means are very uniformly spread along the real distribution of data. Also, with the results we will see in the next section small differences in the estimation have little impact on the parameters of the policy, so in our case 3 to 5 student profiles would be ideal.

Table 1. Obtained clusters when running K-means for the estimated baselearn values with k = 3, 5, 7 or 9.

Num clusters	c1	c2	c3	c4	c5	c6	c7	c8	c9
3	0.2061	0.5296	0.8491	-	-	-	-	-	-
5	0.0942	0.3045	0.4913	0.6912	0.9425	-	-	-	-
7	0.0558	0.2031	0.3369	0.4721	0.6127	0.7571	0.9589	-	-
9	0.0545	0.1922	0.3081	0.3964	0.4787	0.5794	0.6878	0.8147	0.9773

GOZPDES Online Grouping and Teaching using ZPDES. This test measures the average number of time steps and probability of knowing all skills for all the conditions described. Depending on the condition, after a student is classified according to a given profile it will start using the optimal parameters for that profile, before that the average parameters are used. Detailed results are shown in Table 2 while results summarizing the main conclusions can be seen in Figs. 2 and 3.

Table 2. Average number of time steps and probability of knowing all skills, starting with default parameters and updating them dynamically at certain points through the model's execution. The conditions tested are performing the estimation after a certain number of time steps, a priori classification, after A1 has been removed from the ZPD, after both A1 and B1 are removed from the ZPD, using the average parameters throughout and the time taken if the classification had been perfect while ensuring a 97% probability of learning all skills.

Condition/Profile	$P_{0.1}$	$P_{0.2}$	$P_{0.3}$	$P_{0.4}$	$P_{0.5}$	$P_{0.6}$	$P_{0.7}$	$P_{0.8}$	$P_{0.9}$
20 steps time	283.9	210.1	177.4	150.6	137.7	123.0	116.4	107.7	102.5
20 steps %skills	98.5	98.2	97.1	96.2	95.8	93.3	91.1	90.5	86.5
A priori time	341.6	255.0	199.0	178.2	154.8	144.7	126.7	118.1	109.7
A priori %skills	99.3	97.5	92.5	97.3	90.6	86.6	98.4	93.8	91.6
A1 time	285.0	216.2	182.4	157.0	141.2	125.7	116.9	106.3	101.0
A1 %skills	98.5	98.1	96.8	96.0	94.5	92.9	88.4	88.5	86.1
A1/B1 time	285.0	223.4	181.0	162.4	143.7	130.4	120.3	114.5	107.0
A1/B1 %skills	99.0	98.0	96.9	95.1	92.5	89.2	86.5	85.0	81.7
Avg params time	284.2	211.8	181.2	157.5	140.6	129.6	120.2	114.3	108.7
Avg params %skills	98.0	97.9	96.8	95.9	91.4	89.2	84.2	81.8	77.1
30 steps+ time	282.5	208.6	173.9	147.4	130.9	117.2	109.0	101.9	95.3
30 steps+%skills	97.5	98.5	97.4	97.7	95.9	96.8	94.1	91.5	90.9
Optimal time	271.9	202.9	160.7	133.5	116.9	105.0	89.5	81.9	76.0

In order to obtain a better idea of how these methods behave on average, the mean and standard deviation for the average number of time steps and probability of learning all skills for each method was plotted using the values obtained for every student profile. Out of the conditions tested, the best one in terms of time and probability of learning is doing online classification after 30 time steps (the 30 steps+ condition).

The results, visible in Fig. 2, show that in terms of learning quality the "30+" condition has both a higher mean and lower standard deviation on average than every other method, as well as showing that the average parameters have the lowest mean and highest standard deviation value. This proves that treating all students equally leads to a suboptimal learning experience for most students. It is worth mentioning that every method ensured an average probability of knowing all skills of at least 90%, which is lower than the 97% threshold. This was expected since that threshold was defined for perfect classification of student profiles as opposed to this case's occasionally wrong classification of students which only use approximately optimal parameters as a natural approach of the grouping paradigm.

Analysis of the results shows that while the a priori classification does have the highest mean number of time steps, with the 30+ condition having the lowest one, the standard deviation is quite high for every method. This happens because there is a very large difference between the average number of time steps that a low *baselearn* student takes to go through the algorithm in comparison to a high *baselearn* student, ranging from approximately 280 to 100 in Table 2.

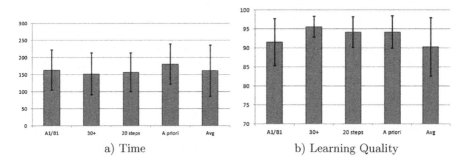

a) Time   b) Learning Quality

Fig. 2. Mean and standard deviation for the average number of time steps and probability of knowing all skills for each reestimation condition. The "30+" conditions yields the lowest mean number of time steps, along with the highest mean and lowest standard deviation in probability of learning all skills.

When grouping all students together, the time differences between the different methods are not statistically significant. For the learning quality the only difference that is statistically different is the condition 30+ being better than the avg condition (one-tailed t-test, p = 0.035). This proves that an online classification of student is not only possible but also provide gains in learning without

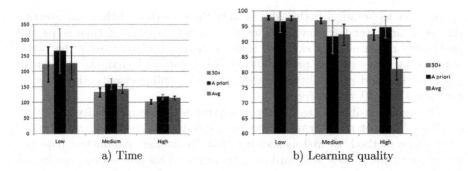

a) Time   b) Learning quality

Fig. 3. Comparison between the time and probability of knowing all skills in terms of mean and standard deviation for three conditions. Our method ("30+") guarantees a faster learning and more efficient for all student levels.

any cost in terms of learning time. Also, doing an a-priori classification does not seem to provide enough benefit for the extra cost paid.

Impact on each type of student. We do not want any potential gains for one type of student being dependent on leaving others behind. We summarize the results in Fig. 3 where we show the time it takes to learn all the skills and for a fixed time how much will they learn.

Although the probability of knowing all skills are all very similar for low *baselearn* students, our method "30+" clearly has the highest probability and lowest standard deviation for the students classified as "Medium". For the high *baselearn* group, however, the a priori method shows a higher average probability of knowing all skills. This happens due to the fact that faster learning students spend less time in the ZPD, meaning that the relative number of time steps that they are using the optimal parameters obtained by methods which require a certain number of time steps for their condition to trigger is greater than for slower students. This would also be the case for a system that treats all students differently, as it would require a much greater number of observations than those used by the online grouping estimation conditions which were attempted, meaning that it would not learn the optimal model parameters in time for them to be useful.

The improvement in terms of the average probability of knowing all skills by the end of the model's execution in comparison to using the average parameters from start to finish - the "Avg" values for this figure - are statistically significant for "High" *baselearn* for both the "30+" (one-tailed t-test, p = 0.004) and a priori (one-tailed t-test, p = 0.005) methods, along with for the "30+" online grouping estimation condition for "Medium" *baselearn* classifications (one-tailed t-test, p = 0.043).

In terms of the average number of time steps to go through the exercises, the results, also shown in Fig. 3, show that both the mean and standard deviation decrease for all methods as the average *baselearn* that the students were classified as having increases. The standard deviation for low *baselearn* students remains quite high, as even with this separation of students there is a large difference between the average number of time steps between students with *baselearn* values of, for example, 0.1 and 0.3 (approximately 280 to 180 time steps according to Table 2). No improvement in terms of mean was found to be statistically significant between methods on the same student type (for example, the 30+ method does not have a statistically significant improvement on the average number of time steps in comparison to the a priori method when comparing exclusively either the low, medium or high *baselearn* students). However, every method's transition to a better student type shows statistically significant improvements in comparison to the results on the previous students. The obtained p-values for the one-tailed t-tests were the following: 30+ low to medium: $p = 0.027$; 30+ medium to high: $p = 0.018$; A priori low to medium: $p = 0.034$; A priori medium to high: $p = 0.010$; Avg low to medium: $p = 0.0029$; Avg medium to high: $p = 0.016$.

5   Conclusions and Future Work

In this work we merge the advantages of approaches that provide optimal long-term teaching policies to students (but need to rely on considering all students as clones) with approaches that are fast to adapt to particular student characteristics (but cannot do long-term planning). We also wanted to see if the use of historical data of student could allows us to merge these approaches.

Our results showed that, given sufficient data, we can classify student in less than 30% of the time that they take to go through all the curriculum and then provide an optimal teaching experience after that. We also showed that teaching to the average model, or doing an a-priori test are worse strategies. Our results are stronger when we consider low, medium, and high learning rate students and see that the greater gains are obtained for the high learning rate students, but no group of student loses for being in this systems. For all student they either learn more and faster or are no worse than the standard approach of considering them all equal.

This work was made in simulation to ensure that we could control all the parameters of the process. Knowledge Tracing systems have been used very much in the research and in the real world to the point that we already trust that it is a good model for real students. Considering our results we expect that our system will provide greater gains when used in more heterogeneous classes but without any cost when the classes are homogeneous. Another important aspect is that this system is an extension of the ZPDES system that does not need prior information, but with our new system prior information can be used.

Acknowledgements. This work was partially by the Fundação para a Ciência e a Tecnologia with grants FCT: `UID/CEC/50021/2019` and `PTDC/CCI-COM/32378/2017`.

References

1. Baker, R.S.J., Corbett, A.T., Aleven, V.: More accurate student modeling through contextual estimation of slip and guess probabilities in bayesian knowledge tracing. In: Woolf, B.P., Aïmeur, E., Nkambou, R., Lajoie, S. (eds.) ITS 2008. LNCS, vol. 5091, pp. 406–415. Springer, Heidelberg (2008). https://doi.org/10.1007/978-3-540-69132-7_44
2. Beck, J.E., Chang, K.M.: Identifiability: a fundamental problem of student modeling. In: User Modeling 2007 (2007)
3. Beck, J.E., Xiong, X.: Limits to accuracy: how well can we do at student modeling? In: EDM (2013)
4. Cen, H., Koedinger, K., Junker, B.: Learning factors analysis-a general method for cognitive model evaluation and improvement. In: Intelligent Tutoring Systems (2006)
5. Chang, K., Beck, J., Mostow, J., Corbett, A.: A bayes net toolkit for student modeling in intelligent tutoring systems. In: Ikeda, M., Ashley, K.D., Chan, T.-W. (eds.) ITS 2006. LNCS, vol. 4053, pp. 104–113. Springer, Heidelberg (2006). https://doi.org/10.1007/11774303_11
6. Clancey, W.J.: Intelligent Tutoring Systems: A Tutorial Survey, p. 58 (1986)
7. Clement, B., Oudeyer, P.Y., Lopes, M.: A comparison of automatic teaching strategies for heterogeneous student populations. In: EDM (2016)
8. Clement, B., Roy, D., Oudeyer, P.Y., Lopes, M.: Multi-armed bandits for intelligent tutoring systems. J. Educ. Data Min. **7**(2), 20–48 (2015)
9. Corbett, A.T., Anderson, J.R.: Knowledge tracing: modeling the acquisition of procedural knowledge (1994). https://doi.org/10.1007/BF01099821
10. Dhanani, A., Lee, S.Y., Phothilimthana, P., Pardos, Z.: A comparison of error metrics for learning model parameters in bayesian knowledge tracing. In: International Conference on Educational Data Mining Workshops (2014)
11. González-Brenes, J.P., Mostow, J.: Dynamic cognitive tracing: towards unified discovery of student and cognitive models. In: EDM, pp. 49–56 (2012)
12. González-Brenes, J., Huang, Y., Brusilovsky, P.: General features in knowledge tracing: applications to multiple subskills, temporal item response theory, and expert knowledge. In: International Conference on Educational Data Mining (2014)
13. Lee, J.I., Brunskill, E.: The Impact on Individualizing Student Models on Necessary Practice Opportunities. In: Educational Data Mining, p. 8 (2012)
14. Psotka, J., Massey, L.D., Mutter, S.A.: Intelligent Tutoring Systems: Lessons Learned. Psychology Press, Hillsdale (1988)
15. Rabiner, L.R., Juang, B.H.: An introduction to hidden Markov models. IEEE Sign. Proc. Mag. **3**(1), 4–16 (1986)
16. Rafferty, A.N., Brunskill, E., Griffiths, T.L., Shafto, P.: Faster teaching via POMDP planning. Cogn. Sci. **40**(6), 1290–1332 (2016)
17. Villano, M.: Probabilistic student models: Bayesian belief networks and knowledge space theory. In: 1992 Intelligent Tutoring Systems (ITS) (1992)
18. Wang, M.C., Haertel, G.D., Walberg, H.J.: What Helps Students Learn? Spotlight on Student Success. Educational Leadership (1997)

Student Attention Evaluation System Using Machine Learning for Decision Making

Dalila Durães[1,2(✉)] [iD]

[1] CIICESI, ESTG, Polytechnic Institute of Porto, Felgueiras, Portugal
dad@estg.ipp.pt
[2] Algoritmi Research Centre/Department of Informatics, University of Minho,
Braga, Portugal

Abstract. The student attention evaluation is a very important feature that has a high influence on student results, so it's necessary to consider. This paper focuses on the evaluation of the student attention level using a machine learning categorization model using several machine learning techniques. The Support Vector Machine, Nearest Neighbor, Naive Bayes, Neural Networks and Random Forest algorithms are applied to model an intelligent system which will evaluate the attention level of the students. Thirteen important features such as alltime, percApp (time in the application), age, grade, behavior biometrics of keyboard (kdt - key down time, tbk – time between keys) and behavior biometrics of mouse (cd - click duration, mv – mouse velocity, ma – mouse acceleration, ddc – duration distance clicks, dplbc – distance point to line between clicks, dbc – distance between clicks, and tbc – time between clicks) are taken for training and testing. Above mentioned machine learning techniques are compared in terms of accuracy rate.

Keywords: Support Vector Machine · Nearest Neighbor ·
Naïve bayes algorithm · Neural Networks · Random Forest

1 Introduction

Nowadays, the main problem related to learning is the attention that the students dedicated to the execution of a task. Each person's level of attention is constantly affected using the Internet and social networks. These two factors have a high impact on the level of attention, as they offer a lot of information of public interest, adversely affecting the level of attention of the students. What will be presented in this work is the evaluation of the level of attention of the students since this determines the results they will get in learning. In this paper, we used machine learning techniques to build a model for decision making in terms of the student's level of attention. This model provides results that enable real-time decision making, in order to improve the level of attention. Specifically, we analyze the behavioural biometrics [1] and the dynamics of mouse and dynamic keyboard [2] to develop a non-intrusive method to assess the level of students' attention during the interaction with the computer.

Machine learning is a subdomain of artificial intelligence, which allows systems to learn by themselves. What is intended is that the machine learning architecture learns,

© Springer Nature Switzerland AG 2019
P. Moura Oliveira et al. (Eds.): EPIA 2019, LNAI 11804, pp. 27–34, 2019.
https://doi.org/10.1007/978-3-030-30241-2_3

develop and change dynamically when exposed to new data. In this work, we implement the concept of machine learning by introducing Support Vector Machine, Nearest Neighbor, Naives Bayes, Neural Network, and Random Forest methodologies to develop a model that allows decision making.

2   State of Art

Machining learning is a learning technique that finds patterns in data, patterns that provide knowledge and enable quick and accurate decision making. The output takes the form of predictions. The machining learning techniques seek structural descriptions that are learned descriptions that have become quite complex and are typically expressed as a set of rules. For any dataset, every instance used by machining learning algorithms is represented using the same set of features. These features can be binary, categorical or continuous. We call supervised learning if the instances are given with knowing label (which correspond to correct outputs). Unsupervised learning is where instances are unlabeled [3].The machining techniques allow the system to be trained and create a set of standards, enabling the creation of a prediction [4].

There are several algorithms that can be applied, namely Support Vector Machine (SVM), Nearest Neighbors, Naïve Bayes, Neural Networks and Random Forest. SVM is a supervised learning technique for data search, pattern acceptance and classification based on statistical learning theory [5]. The Nearest Neighbor algorithm is the simplest nonparametric decision procedure, which assigns the unclassified observation (input sample) the closest class/category/label of the sample (using metric) in the training set [6]. Naive Bayes offers a simple approach with clear semantics to represent the use and learning of probabilistic knowledge [4]. In recent years, neural networks were used to control design techniques and several solutions were presented for nonlinear systems [7, 8]. Random Forests are a combination of predictors of trees so that each tree depends on the values of a random vector sampled independently and with the same distribution for all trees in the forest [9].

3   Proposed Approach

Figure 1 presents a proposed approach of student attention evaluation system using machining learning for decision making. We can apply several learning models based in different type of exercises for improving student attention level like audio exercises, video exercises, text exercises and image exercises. However, to having decision making there are five steps as described in the following subsection.

- Behaviour Pattern Collection.
- Analysis of Collected Behaviour Pattern
- Classification Profile and Emotion Behaviour.
- Develop an Intelligent Model.
- Testing a Model

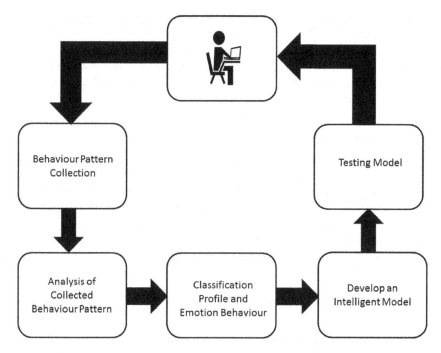

Fig. 1. Methodology of proposed approach.

3.1 Behaviour Pattern Collection

Since the study of behavioral features is mostly related to the individual's conduct habits, the calculation of attention level considers the individual's ID, actions of mouse and keyboard, and the application that the user used, which are monitored and acquired by the computation system [10, 11].

The process of feature extraction starts with the acquisition of interaction events, which is carried out by a specifically developed application that is installed in each computer or laptops. Logger applications that run in the background, collecting the necessary events and require no interaction by the user. It is thus non-intrusive [12, 13].

The devices that generate the raw data (e.g. soft sensors) describe the student's interaction with both mouse and keyboard. There are soft sensors that use information available from other measurements and process parameters to calculate an estimate of the quantity of raw data. The raw data generated is stored locally until it synchronizes with the web server in the cloud at regular intervals.

3.2 Analysis of Collected Behaviour Pattern

After pre-processing it, data are stored in database for future data mining. Through these techniques, it is possible to (1) study their behavioral patterns, so that we can obtain their behavioral pattern and their influence in the learning process; (2) study the relations between the affective reactions of the individual and their behavioral patterns in the cyberspace, so that we can make an evaluation of emotions and their influence in the learning process [14].

It is then necessary to process the information related to the events recorded and to transform this same information into the characteristics presented to study so that it can be withdrawn and analyzed the information coming from the record of events caused by the mouse and keyboard interaction [15].

3.3   Classification Profile and Emotion Behaviour

The individual logs created by the application for each user are processed to compile information that can characterize the user's behavior during their interaction with the computer. Through these features, it enables the development of a classification model capable of determining the task at hand executed by the user, given the influence of the user's biometric behaviors. For this study, keystroke dynamics, mouse dynamics, attention performance metrics, and type of learning style were selected to this end [16].

The emotions of the user's hand and by extension the movements of the computer mouse have a direct relation with the psychological – sentimental condition of the user. To be more specific, the way by which the mouse is moved (orbit, speed, intervals of immobility, direction) can demonstrate the user's condition [17, 18].

3.4   Develop an Intelligent Model

Based on the biometric characteristics obtained, the distribution of each characteristic (for example, mean, median, standard deviation, etc.) is presented at different scales. Hence the need to apply the scaling of resources (i.e., normalization techniques). Two methods were applied to max-min normalization and normalization of the Z score. The max-min normalization technique is a normalization strategy that linearly dimensions a characteristic value for the interval [0,1], based on the minimum and maximum of the set of observed values. That is, the minimum value of the resource value is mapped to 0, while the maximum value is mapped to 1. The Z-score technique is a substitute for the actual measurement and represents the distance from a value of the mean measured in standard deviation. This distribution technique is useful when relating different measurement distributions to each one, acting as a "common denominator".

Several classifiers were trained and tested in order to determine the most efficient method to categorize the student's level attention, where the most applied methods in the scientific literature were considered. The set of classification methods trained and tested were: Support Vector Machine, Nearest Neighbor, Naive Bayes, Neural Network and Random Forest [19, 20].

3.5   Testing Model

In this subsection, test data are given as input to the developed model and the outputs are compared with the actual output. Statistical comparison for classification done by each method is found using Percentage Accuracy.

4   Experimental Analysis and Discussion

In order to validate the proposed system, we have implemented it in a high school, which a group of volunteer students was selected. On different days, students had a class where they have access to an individual computer and two hours to complete a task. All involved participants presented computing proficiency and the rooms were equipped with similar computers, where each participant was randomly assigned to a computer. In addition to the biometrics features captured and each case study was labelled with the respective activity (i.e. video, image, text and audio editing).

Table 1 presents the set of results for the classifiers performance. With these results we can conclude that: (1) the Random Forest method presents the best performance overall, with a correct percentage of classifications of 87.5%, while the Support Vector Machine presents the worst performance according to the trained classification methods and tested; (2) the performance of the applied classifiers showed an improvement between [6.25%–25%], where the greatest improvement is verified in the neural network classifier; (3) the performance of the classifiers depends on the quality of the characteristics and the total number of case studies analyzed.

Table 1. Comparative analysis of machine learning categorization performance.

	Raw	Min-max normalization	Z-score
Support Vector Machine	37.5%	43.75%	37.5%
Nearest Neighbor	43.75%	62.5%	43.75%
Naives Bayes	68.75%	75%	68.75%
Neural Network	31.25%	56.25%	56.25%
Random Forest	81.25%	87.5%	87.5%

It was verified that the method Random Forest obtains better results and was selected to categorize the activity of the student. Moreover, this model was optimized through the application of hyper-parameter optimization. So, in order to optimize the Random Forest's classification performance, it was required to find the optimal number of leafs/features (i.e. between [1-11] leaf's/features) and number of trees (in this study it was modelled between [1-500] trees) that best suit the model and minimizes the validation error function.

The relevance of the characteristics of the model was also calculated and presented in Fig. 2. They are showing that the Activity Timer (alltime) is by far the most important to predict student activity, followed by percentage spend in the application (percentApp), and key down time (kdt).

The respective confusion matrix of the Random Forest's model is presented in Table 2 where only the Video activity presents a misclassification of 40% of total cases (i.e. 2/5 cases were misclassified as Audio editing activity).

32   D. Durães

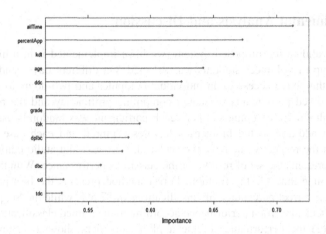

Fig. 2. Random forest: features relevance in activity classification.

Table 2. Random forest: confusion matrix.

	Audio	Image	Text	Video	Correct prediction (%)
Audio	2	0	0	0	100%
Image	0	6	0	0	100%
Text	0	0	3	0	100%
Video	2	0	0	3	60%

5 Conclusions

In this paper, an evaluation model is implemented using various machine learning techniques. A data set of 48 student records is performed for training and testing of SVM, Nearest Neighbor, Naive Bayes, Neural Network, and Random Forest algorithms. This work focused mainly on four different types of classes, such as audio, text, video and image, in order to evaluate student performance in a classroom using computers. These machine learning techniques ranked the results data obtained. This work is a non-invasive approach for a mentoring system based on the behaviour biometric analysis of the work during class.

As future work, the research will focus on: (1) increasing the number of available case studies to be analyzed; (2) increase the number of quality features that would allow a better monitoring of student's attention; (3) detailed analysis of the features that influence the performance of the student (e.g. through the correlation of students' final grade with biometric behaviours); and (4) definition of different student profile's to improve the adaptive learning mechanisms of the platform.

Acknowledge. This work has been supported by FCT – Fundação para a Ciência e Tecnologia within the Project Scope: UID/CEC/00319/2019.

References

1. Bhatnagar, M., Jain, R.K., Nilam, S.K.: A survey on behavioral biometric techniques: mouse vs. keyboard dynamics. In: IJCA Proceedings on International Conference on Recent Trends in Engineering and Technology, pp. 27–30 (2013)
2. Revett, K., Jahankhani, H., de Magalhães, S.T., Santos, H.M.D.: A survey of user authentication based on mouse dynamics. In: Jahankhani, H., Revett, K., Palmer-Brown, D. (eds.) ICGeS 2008. CCIS, vol. 12, pp. 210–219. Springer, Heidelberg (2008). https://doi.org/10.1007/978-3-540-69403-8_25
3. Maglogiannis, I.G. (Ed.).: Emerging Artificial Intelligence Applications in Computer Engineering: Real Word AI Systems with Applications in eHealth, HCI, Information Retrieval and Pervasive Technologies. IOS Press, Amsterdam, vol. 160, pp. 3–24 (2007)
4. Witten, I.H., Frank, E., Hall, M.A., Pal, C.J.: Data Mining: Practical Machine Learning Tools and Techniques. Morgan Kaufmann, Burlington (2016)
5. Suykens, J.A., Vandewalle, J.: Least squares support vector machine classifiers. Neural Process. Lett. 9(3), 293–300 (1999)
6. Cover, T.M., Hart, P.E.: Nearest neighbor pattern classification. IEEE Trans. Inf. Theor. 13(1), 21–27 (1967)
7. Durães, D., Carneiro, D., Jiménez, A., Novais, P.: Characterizing attentive behavior in intelligent environments. Neurocomputing 272, 46–54 (2018)
8. Pimenta, A., Carneiro, D., Neves, J., Novais, P.: A neural network to classify fatigue from human-computer interaction. Neurocomputing Elsevier 172, 413–426 (2016). https://doi.org/10.1016/j.neucom.2015.03.105. ISSN 0925-2312
9. Breiman, L.: Random forest. Mach. Learn. 45(1), 5–32 (2001)
10. Zhou, X., et al.: CyberPsychological computation on social community of ubiquitous learning. Comput. Intell. Neurosci. 2015, 12 (2015)
11. Carneiro, D., Novais, P., Pêgo, J.M., Sousa, N., Neves, J.: Using Mouse Dynamics to Assess Stress During Online Exams. In: Onieva, E., Santos, I., Osaba, E., Quintián, H., Corchado, E. (eds.) HAIS 2015. LNCS (LNAI), vol. 9121, pp. 345–356. Springer, Cham (2015). https://doi.org/10.1007/978-3-319-19644-2_29
12. Durães, D., Carneiro, D., Bajo, J., Novais, P.: Modelling a smart environment for nonintrusive analysis of attention in the workplace. J. Expert Syst. 35(5), e12275 (2018)
13. Pimenta, A., Carneiro, D., Novais, P., Neves, J.: Detection of Distraction and Fatigue in Groups through the Analysis of Interaction Patterns with Computers. In: Camacho, D., Braubach, L., Venticinque, S., Badica, C. (eds.) Intelligent Distributed Computing VIII. SCI, vol. 570, pp. 29–39. Springer, Cham (2015). https://doi.org/10.1007/978-3-319-10422-5_5
14. Dai, W., Duch, W., Abdullah, A., Xu, D., Chen, Y.-S.: Recent advances in learning theory. Comput. Intell. Neurosci. 4, 1–4 (2015)
15. Rodrigues M., Novais P., Santos M.: future challenges in intelligent tutoring systems – a famework. In: A. Méndez Villas, B. Gonzalez Pereira, J. Mesa González, J.A. Mesa González (Eds.) Publishers Formatex. Recent Research Developments in Learning Technologies: Proceedings of the 3rd International Conference on Multimedia and Information & Communication Technologies in Education (m-ICTE2005), pp. 929–934 (2005). ISBN 609-5994-5
16. Carneiro, D., Novais, P., Neves, J.: Conflict Resolution and its Context. LGTS, vol. 18. Springer, Cham (2014). https://doi.org/10.1007/978-3-319-06239-6
17. Carneiro, D., Novais, P.: Quantifying the effects of external factors on individual performance. Future Gener. Comput. Syst. 66, 171–186 (2017)

18. Durães, D., Bajo, J., Novais, P.: Analysis Learning Styles Though Attentiveness. In: Vittorini, P., Gennari, R., Di Mascio, T., Rodríguez, S., De la Prieta, F., Ramos, C., Azambuja Silveira, R. (eds.) MIS4TEL 2017. AISC, vol. 617, pp. 90–97. Springer, Cham (2017). https://doi.org/10.1007/978-3-319-60819-8_11
19. Borrajo, M., Baruque, B., Corchado, E., Bajo, J., Corchado, J.: Hybrid neural intelligent system to predict business failure in small-to-medium-size enterprises. Int. J. Neural Syst. **21** (04), 277–296 (2011)
20. Bajo, J., Paz, J., Rodríguez, S., González, A.: A new clustering algorithm applying a hierarchical method neural network. Logic J. IGPL **19**(2), 304–314 (2011)

Combining Sentiment Analysis Scores to Improve Accuracy of Polarity Classification in MOOC Posts

Herbert Laroca Pinto[1]([envelope]) [iD] and Vitor Rocio[1,2,3] [iD]

[1] Universidade Aberta de Portugal, Lisbon, Portugal
herbert.laroca@gmail.com, vitor.rocio@uab.pt
[2] INESC TEC, Porto, Portugal
[3] LE@D, Lisbon, Portugal

Abstract. Sentiment analysis is a set of techniques that deal with the verification of sentiment and emotions in written texts. This introductory work aims to explore the combination of scores and polarities of sentiments (positive, neutral and negative) provided by different sentiment analysis tools. The goal is to generate a final score and its respective polarity from the normalization and arithmetic average scores given by those tools that provide a minimum of reliability. The texts analyzed to test our hypotheses were obtained from forum posts from participants in a massive open online course (MOOC) offered by Universidade Aberta de Portugal, and were submitted to four online service APIs offering sentiment analysis: Amazon Comprehend, Google Natural Language, IBM Watson Natural Language Understanding, and Microsoft Text Analytics. The initial results are encouraging, suggesting that the average score is a valid way to increase the accuracy of the predictions from different sentiment analyzers.

Keywords: Sentiment analysis · Massive open online course · Polarity scores

1 Introduction

Individuals give opinions at every time. Unlike facts, which are objective and verifiable information, opinions are subjective information that expresses feelings, emotions, and personal assessments on the most varied subjects and interests, such as other individuals, entities, products or events. The sentiment analysis is the study of the analysis and application of the opinions, feelings, emotions and evaluations of individuals on the most varied themes, and can be done at the level of objects or events as well as the level of their properties or characteristics. The advance of information technology applications and the rise of applications such as social networks, discussion forums and distance learning environments has provided the creation of an additional environment for the widespread dissemination of opinion stored in digital devices in the form of textual data [11]. Thus emerges the MOOC – Massive Open Online Course, which is supported in a large-scale distance learning platform, and is popular with students and educators. The goal of the MOOC is to massify and popularize a new form of quality

© Springer Nature Switzerland AG 2019
P. Moura Oliveira et al. (Eds.): EPIA 2019, LNAI 11804, pp. 35–46, 2019.
https://doi.org/10.1007/978-3-030-30241-2_4

education offered by institutions of international renown, without restrictions both from the institution's viewpoint and from individual student participation, distributed across a wide variety of networks and domains of knowledge. Despite their great expansion and popularity, MOOC courses still have high dropout rates, pointing to a problem that still needs to be solved [1]. In this context, admitting that sentiments and emotions interfere positively or negatively in learning, researchers believe that educational environments would be more effective if they deal with the sentiments and emotions of the students, providing mechanisms of support, encouragement and retention of these same students [8].The goal of this paper is to improve on the results from individual sentiment analysis tools by combining their scores, using four available APIs on messages from MOOC forums of the Universidade Aberta de Portugal, namely AulAberta[1]. The four APIs chosen were: Amazon Comprehend, Google Natural Language, IBM Watson Natural Language Understanding, and Microsoft Text Analytics. These APIs were chosen because they are owned by big players in the industry [5]. This paper is divided into five parts. Part 1 presents the introduction and motivation of the work, as well as its initial concepts. Part 2 presents the related work. Part 3 shows the details of polarity classification of each API analyzed. Part 3 demonstrates the methodology used and all its steps, such as data collect, pre-processing, technologies and tools used. Part 4 shows the results obtained. Finally, part 5 concludes the paper, with the analysis of the results, limitations found and future work perspectives.

2   Related Work

Although MOOCs are relatively recent in the history of e-learning, there are already several works on the subject, both in the area of education and computer science. Most of the work that unifies MOOCs and the sentiment analysis aims to understand [9, 21] and help the prevention of drop-out [21] of students. Another part of the work provides tools for improve the students' learning process [18, 22] and help teachers' work [12, 20]. The data is obtained mainly from MOOCs platforms such as Coursera [14, 18] and edX [15]. Most of the work uses NLP tools and machine learning to perform the analysis [7, 20]. As a general rule, these works indicate the influence of sentiment and emotion in the learning processes of MOOCs, except in [9]. Some papers cite and analyze several success factors for learning in MOOCs, including the sentiment analysis [1, 14]. Polarity of messages can be estimated by available sentiment analysis tools, with more or less accuracy. Combining different classifiers has been explored as a way to improve accuracy of predictions [6]. Using ensemble methods, for instance, bootstrapping aggregation (or "bagging") [4], one can determine a final classification by a process of voting by the various tools, or an average score if the tools provide numerical values as their output. In this work we propose to use average scores to evaluate more accurately the polarity of sentiment in posts of a MOOC environment. The approach aims to increase reliability in the analysis of the polarity of sentiments, regardless of its purpose within the teaching and learning environment.

---

[1] https://aulaberta.uab.pt/.

3 Score and Polarity

The four APIs return the sentiment score at the analyzed document level. The Amazon Comprehend and IBM Watson Natural Language Understanding APIs provide the polarity label in addition to the score. The document is a message that represents the post of each student in the MOOC of AulAberta. Although all four APIs provide the score, there are some particularities that should be anticipated and addressed. The Amazon Comprehend API returns the scores as a percentage probability for each possible polarity in the text and the label is rated negative, neutral, positive or mixed, as shown in Fig. 1. In the example, there is a 95% chance of the sentiment of the document being positive. The mixed label is not implemented in the other APIs [2].

```
1  {
2  "SentimentScore": {
3    "Mixed": 0.030585512690246105,
4    "Positive": 0.94992071056365967,
5    "Neutral": 0.0141543131828308,
6    "Negative": 0.00893945890665054
7    },
8    "Sentiment": "POSITIVE",
9    "LanguageCode": "en"
10 }
```

Fig. 1. Return of amazon comprehend API in json format.

The Google Natural Language API returns as a score a number between −1 and 1, indicating the polarity of the sentiment as negative to −1 and positive to 1. This API does not return the label of sentiment polarity. Figure 2 illustrates the example of an API return. The Google Natural Language API also returns Magnitude, which is an indicator of the amount of negative or positive expressions in a text. The magnitude classification is not implemented in the other APIs [13].

```
1  {
2    "documentSentiment": {
3      "score": 0.2,
4      "magnitude": 3.6
5    },
6    "language": "en",
7  }
```

Fig. 2. Return of google natural language API in json format.

The IBM Watson Natural Language Understanding API returns the sentiment polarity label and a score that corresponds to a number between −1 and 1, indicating the polarity of the sentiment as negative to −1 and positive to 1. The returned labels are negative, neutral or positive [19] (Fig. 3).

```
1  "document": {
2    "score": 0.127034,
3    "label": "positive"
4  }
```

Fig. 3. Return of IBM watson natural language understanding API in json format.

The Microsoft Text Analytics API ranks text and generates the score with values between 0 and 1. The values closer to 1 indicate a positive sentiment polarity, while values closer to 0 indicate negative sentiment polarity. The API does not return the sentiment polarity label. The neutral values are classified with the score of 0.5 [16]

```
1 {'documents': [{'id': '1','score': 0.7673527002334595},
2                 {'id': '2','score': 0.1857409477233886},
3                 {'id': '3','score': 0.5}],
4 'errors': []}
```

Fig. 4. Return of microsoft text analytics API in json format.

To normalize the data generated by the APIs, we defined that the score will contain values between −1 and 1, with minus one (−1) being the most negative score, zero (0) is the neutral score and plus one (+1) the most positive score. Google and IBM already deliver their results in this format, but we need to pre-process the scores generated by the Amazon Comprehend and Microsoft Text Analytics APIs to enable standardization and further analysis.

4   Methodology

Basically, the methodology used followed the steps provided in [17], adding intermediate steps. Those steps are show in Fig. 5. In the data extraction stage the data is extracted from the source database from the MOOC platform and made available in text format for later collection. During the data collect step the data is collected and stored in a relational database. The pre-processing step makes modifications and adjustments to the data for later classification. The classification step makes the call of the APIs and stores the polarity of the sentiment in the relational database. Finally, the next step evaluates the classified data. Since the process of sentiment analysis was performed at the document level, it is not necessary to summarize the data because they are already at the desired level of granularity.

Fig. 5. Steps from the methodology used on the research.

4.1 Data Extraction

The data used in the research were extracted from the AulAberta relational database contained in the Moodle environment. At all, 990 posts were extracted. Of these 990 posts, 430 were classified as opinion information and 560 were classified as factual information [10]. This research considers only the posts that contain opinionated information, the rest being discarded. The data was extracted in text format, using the database's own database management platform extraction tools.

4.2 Data Collect and Pre-processing

After the extraction, student posts are collected and recorded in the research database, implemented using DBMS PostgreSQL[2]. The tool used for data collection and pre-processing was Knime[3]. During the collect it was necessary to perform two pre-processing routines of the posts. The first routine was the removal of HTML tags from the posts and the second routine was the deletion of posts with less than 30 characters (Fig. 6).

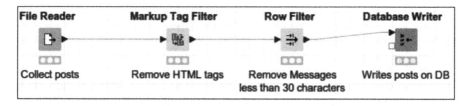

Fig. 6. Collect the posts of MOOCs from AulAberta.

After storing the data in the research database, the next step is to collect the score and label data from the sentiments of the posts, running the sentiment analysis process for each API. For this step, four programs were created in the Python programming language. Each program accesses its API, collects the score of each post and writes the information on the research database. The Google Natural Language and Microsoft Text Analytics APIs do not provide the sentiment label. In this case it was necessary to create a simple algorithm in the respective programs to generate the label. To normalize the Amazon Comprehend API score and to standardize the result, a simple expression SCORE * (−1) was used for the negative score (Fig. 7). In the example of Fig. 1,the positive score will be recorded as 0.94. If it were negative it would be recorded as −0.94.

---

[2] https://www.postgresql.org/.

[3] https://www.knime.com.

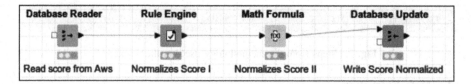

Fig. 7. Pre-processing amazon comprehend API scores.

The Microsoft Text Analytics API score should be normalized too to the standard score. In this case, the expression (SCORE − 0.5) * 2 was used for the positive score and (0.5 − SCORE) * (−2) was used for the negative score (Fig. 8). In the example of Fig. 4, the positive score 0.76 will be converted in 0.52 and recorded as the result of the expression (0.76 − 0.5) * 2. The score 0.18 will be converted in -0.64 and recorded as the result of the expression (0.5 − 0.18) * (−2).

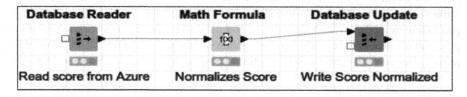

Fig. 8. Pre-processing microsoft text analytics API scores.

4.3   Classification

The normalized scores reflect the "votes" of the four tools, and to obtain a single value in order to classify the input, we can aggregate the individual scores, through a method of "bagging" (bootstrap aggregating) [4]. Bagging uses the results of classifiers on different training sets and determines a combined result by voting or averaging the individual results, thus reducing variance in the combined classifier. After the data collecting and pre-processing, the average of the scores generated by the analysis of each API (Fig. 9) is calculated. Hereafter the arithmetic average of the scores will be called the **average score** (1) and the polarity generated from this average score will be called the **average polarity**.

$$\textbf{AverageScore} = \sum \textbf{SCORES/n} \qquad (1)$$

The sentiment polarity is determined after calculating the average score (Fig. 10).

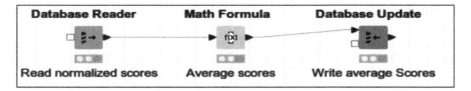

Fig. 9. Average score calculation.

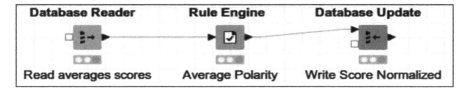

Fig. 10. Average polarity calculation.

4.4 Data Evaluation

Besides the manual classification of opinion or factual information, the posts were also classified by the polarity of sentiment. Data evaluation consists of comparing the manually defined polarities with the polarities generated by the APIs. The metrics used to evaluate the polarities were: recall, precision and F1-score (harmonic average between recall and precision) (Table 1).

Table 1. Elements for metric classification of posts [3]

		Prediction		
		Positive	Neutral	Negative
Correct	Positive	a	b	c
	Neutral	d	e	f
	Negative	g	h	i

The positive recall metric is defined as $R(pos) = a/(a + b + c)$, the positive precision metric is defined as $P(pos) = a/(a + d + g)$ and the positive harmonic average between P (pos) and R(pos) is defined as $F1(pos) = 2 \times (P \times R/P + R)$. Similarly, the neutral metric is defined as $R(neu) = e/(d + e + f)$, the neutral precision metric is defined as $P(neu) = e/(b + e + h)$ and the neutral harmonic average between P_0 and R_0 is defined as $F1(neu) = 2 \times (P \times R/P + R)$. Finally, the negative recall metric is defined as $R(neg) = i/(g + h + i)$, the negative precision metric is defined as $P(neg) = i/(c + f + i)$ and the negative harmonic average between P(neg) and R(neg) is defined as $F1(neg) = 2 \times (P \times R/P + R)$.

5 Results

The tables below demonstrate the values returned for each API and its respective measures. Table 2 shows the quantities of posts, classified as opinion and fact, as well as their total. Table 3 illustrates the number of posts classified by polarity for average score and each API. Table 4 shows the recall, precision and F1-score for average score and all APIs.

Table 2. Total of opinion and fact posts.

	Number of posts
Opinion	430
Fact	560
Total	990

Analyzing Table 3, the APIs and, consequently, the average score, tended towards positive polarity. Table 4 allows for some considerations: The Microsoft Text Analytics API did not classify the neutral sentiment for any opinion post. This fact is also shown in Table 3. Another consideration is that the average polarity did not identify neutral sentiments. This Fact is explained because the neutral polarity is valued by the score zero. Thus, for the average score to obtain the value zero, it is necessary that all scores have a value of zero, which did not occur in the data.

Table 3. Total of posts classified by polarity.

	Number of posts		
	Negative	Neutral	Positive
Human correct classified data	73	38	319
Amazon comprehend	11	203	216
Google natural language	26	66	338
Microsoft text analytics	57	0	373
IBM natural language understanding	21	21	388
Average score	23	0	407

In general, the average score obtained the best indicators, even with the zero values for the neutral polarities. Individually, the average score achieved the highest positive recall, the second highest negative recall, the lowest positive precision, the highest negative precision, the second highest positive F1-score, and the second highest negative F1-score. One reason that may explain the low positive precision is the fact that the average score has not classified any neutral polarity, all being classified as positive.

Table 4. Recall, precision and F1-score from average score and APIs.

	R+	R0	R-	P+	P0	P-	F1+	F10	F1-
Average score	**0,99**	**0,00**	**0,30**	**0,78**	**0,00**	**0,95**	**0,87**	**0,00**	**0,45**
IBM natural language	0,96	0,21	0,26	0,79	0,38	0,90	0,87	0,27	0,40
Microsoft text anal.	0,95	0,00	0,49	0,81	0,00	0,63	0,87	0,00	0,55
Google nat. language	0,88	0,31	0,24	0,83	0,18	0,69	0,85	0,23	0,36
Amazon comprehend	0,61	0,92	0,13	0,91	0,17	0,90	0,73	0,29	0,23

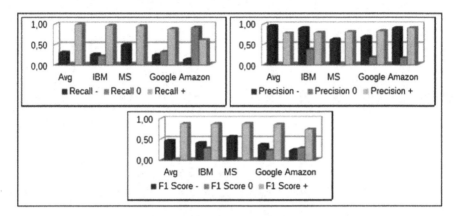

Fig. 11. Comparative chart of recall, precision and F1-score by average polarity and APIs.

The score determines the degree of reliability of the sentiment. If measurements are made with a reliability degree greater than 50% (scores with value greater than 0.50), for example, the results change, as showed in Tables 5 and 6. Figures 11 and 12 show comparative graphs of the metrics used in the average score and each API.

Table 5. Total of posts classified by polarity with scores above 50%.

	Number of posts		
	Negative	Neutral	Positive
Human correct classified data	8	1	177
Amazon comprehend	2	4	180
Google natural language	4	11	171
Microsoft text analytics	4	0	182
IBM natural language understanding	3	1	182
Average score	3	0	183

44   H. L. Pinto and V. Rocio

Table 6. Recall, precision and F1-score with scores above 50%.

	R+	R0	R-	P+	P0	P-	F1+	F10	F1-
Average score	**1,00**	**0,00**	**0,37**	**0,96**	**0,00**	**1,00**	**0,98**	**0,00**	**0,54**
IBM Natural Language	0,99	0,00	0,37	0,96	0,00	1,00	0,98	0,00	0,54
Microsoft text anal.	0,99	0,00	0,37	0,96	0,00	0,75	0,98	0,00	0,50
Google nat. language	0,98	0,00	0,25	0,96	0,00	1,00	0,97	0,00	0,40
Amazon comprehend	0,94	0,00	0,37	0,97	0,00	0,75	0,96	0,00	0,50

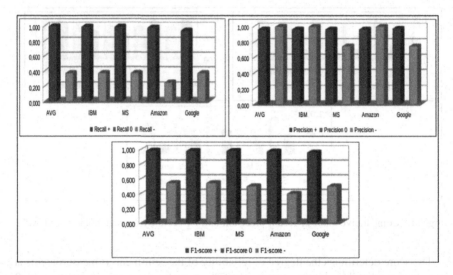

Fig. 12. Comparative chart of recall, precision and F1-score by average score and APIs with scores above 50%.

6 Conclusions and Future Works

The aim of this paper was to improve on the results of sentiment analysis by calculating the score obtained from the arithmetic average of four individual scores that are used to classify the sentiment polarity of a given text. As an example, we used the posts of participants in Universidade Aberta de Portugal's MOOC platform (AulAberta) and four sentiment analysis APIs: Amazon Comprehend, Google Natural Language, IBM Watson Natural Language Understanding and Microsoft Text Analytics. It is observed that in an academic environment such as AulAberta, facts have priority over opinion, in this case explained by the greater number of factual posts than opinionated ones. Another observation of interest is that all APIs generated more positive than negative values, a fact that can also be explained by the academic environment. The score indicates the percentage reliability of the sentiment analysis. It can be observed from the analyzed data that negative or positive sentiment with a score lower than .20 (20%)

do not have correct polarity prediction. Thus, if the average score method is applied to a set of scores with reliability greater than 50%, reliability and precision will be increased (Table 6). The advantage of using only the highest scores to compose the average is that the method's degree of reliability will be increased and only the best measurements of each API will be chosen. In this case, it is important to use more APIs to increase the score's measures. The introductory results show the potential of the method. The results showed that if scores with reliability greater than 50% were selected, the recall, precision and F1-score of the average score model exceeded the APIs individually. The average score (bagging) is expected to increase prediction accuracy, but further research is needed. For example, the average score should be adjusted to the neutral polarity rating within ranges of values close to zero, both positive and negative. The arithmetic average was obtained from four scores. If more scores are used the trend is that the reliability of the analysis will be increased. The low number of classified posts with negative or neutral sentiment reduces the significance of the results for these classifications. Finally, as this is an introductory work, it is intended in the future to apply the average score to other opinion bases, increase the amount of sentiment analysis APIs used or using other averages, such as the weighted arithmetic average, geometric average or the median.

References

1. Adamopoulos, P.: What makes a great MOOC? An interdisciplinary analysis of student retention in online courses. In: Proceedings of the 34th International Conference on Information Systems, ICIS, vol. 2013, Milan, Italy (2013)
2. Amazon Web Services, Inc. Amazon Comprehend - Developer Guide (2019). https://docs.aws.amazon.com/comprehend/latest/dg/comprehend-dg.pdf
3. Benevenuto, F., Ribeiro, F., Araújo, M.: Métodos para Análise de Sentimentos em mídias sociais. In: Brazilian Symposium on Multimedia and the Web. (Webmedia), Manaus, Brazil, p. 30 (2015). (in Portuguese)
4. Breiman, L.: Bagging predictors. Mach. Learn. **24**(2), 123–140 (1996)
5. Dale, R.: Text analytics APIs, Part 1: The bigger players. Nat. Lang. Eng. **24**(02), 317–324 (2018). https://doi.org/10.1017/S1351324918000013
6. Dietterich, T.G.: Ensemble methods in machine learning. In: Kittler, J., Roli, F. (eds.) MCS 2000. LNCS, vol. 1857, pp. 1–15. Springer, Heidelberg (2000). https://doi.org/10.1007/3-540-45014-9_1
7. Fei, H., Li, H.: The study of learners' emotional analysis based on MOOC. In: Xiao, J., Mao, Z.-H., Suzumura, T., Zhang, L.-J. (eds.) ICCC 2018. LNCS, vol. 10971, pp. 170–178. Springer, Cham (2018). https://doi.org/10.1007/978-3-319-94307-7_14
8. Jaques, P. A., Viccari, R. M.: Considering student's emotions in computer-mediated learning environments. In: Zongmin Ma. (Org.). Web-based Intelligent e-Learning Systems: Technologies and Applications. Information Science Publishing, Hershey 2006, pp. 122–138. IGI Global, Pennsylvania (2006). https://doi.org/10.4018/978-1-59140-729-4
9. Koutropoulos, A., et al.: Emotive vocabulary in MOOCs: context & participant retention. Eur. J. Open Distance E-Learn. (2012)
10. Liu, B.: Sentiment Analysis and Subjectivity. In: Handbook of Natural Language Processing 2nd(edn.) vol. 38 (2010)
11. Liu, B.: Sentiment analysis and opinion mining. Morgan & Claypool, San Rafael (2012)

12. Liu, Z., Zhang, W., Sun, J., Cheng, H. N. H., Peng, X., Liu, S.: Emotion and associated topic detection for course comments in a MOOC platform. In: 2016 International Conference on Educational Innovation through Technology (EITT), pp. 15–19. (2016). https://doi.org/10.1109/EITT.2016.11
13. Natural Language API Basics. https://cloud.google.com/natural-language/docs/basics
14. Pursel, B.K., Zhang, L., Jablokow, K.W., Choi, G.W., Velegol, D.: Understanding MOOC students: motivations and behaviours indicative of MOOC completion: MOOC student motivations and behaviors. J. Comput. Assist. Learn. 32(3), 202–217 (2016). https://doi.org/10.1111/jcal.12131
15. Robinson, C., Yeomans, M., Reich, J., Hulleman, C., Gehlbach, H.: Forecasting student achievement in MOOCs with natural language processing. In: Proceedings of the Sixth International Conference on Learning Analytics & Knowledge - LAK 2016, pp. 383–387. (2016). https://doi.org/10.1145/2883851.2883932
16. Sentiment analysis using the Text Analytics from Azure Cognitive Services - Microsoft Docs. https://docs.microsoft.com/en-us/azure/cognitive-services/text-analytics/how-tos/text-analytics-how-to-sentiment-analysis
17. Tsytsarau, M., Palpanas, T.: Survey on mining subjective data on the web. Data Min. Knowl. Disc. 24(3), 478–514 (2012). https://doi.org/10.1007/s10618-011-0238-6
18. Tucker, C., Pursel, B.K., Divinsky, A.: Mining student-generated textual data in MOOCs and quantifying their effects on student performance and learning outcomes. Comput. Educ. J. 5(4), 84–95 (2014)
19. Vergara, S., El-Khouly, M., Tantawi, M., Shireesh, M., Sri, L.: Building Cognitive Applications with IBM Watson Services: Volume 7 Natural Language Understanding. (2017)
20. Wang, L., Hu, G., Zhou, T.: Semantic analysis of learners' emotional tendencies on online MOOC education. Sustainability 10(6), 1921 (2018). https://doi.org/10.3390/su10061921
21. Wen, M., Yang, D., Rosé, C.P.: Sentiment analysis in MOOC discussion forums: what does it tell us. In: Proceedings of Educational Data Mining (2014)
22. Wong, J.-S., Pursel, B., Divinsky, A., Jansen, B.J.: An analysis of MOOC discussion forum interactions from the most active users. In: Agarwal, N., Xu, K., Osgood, N., (eds.) Social Computing, Behavioral-Cultural Modeling, and Prediction, vol. 9021, pp. 452–457 (2015) https://doi.org/10.1007/978-3-319-16268-3_58

Artificial Intelligence for Games

Artificial Intelligence for Games

Reinforcement Learning in Multi-agent Games: Open AI Gym Diplomacy Environment

Diogo Cruz[1], José Aleixo Cruz[1], and Henrique Lopes Cardoso[1,2(✉)]

[1] Faculdade de Engenharia, Universidade do Porto, Porto, Portugal
{up201105483,up201403526,hlc}@fe.up.pt
[2] Laboratório de Inteligência Artificial e Ciências dos Computadores (LIACC),
Porto, Portugal

Abstract. Reinforcement learning has been successfully applied to adversarial games, exhibiting its potential. However, most real-life scenarios also involve cooperation, in addition to competition. Using reinforcement learning in multi-agent cooperative games is, however, still mostly unexplored. In this paper, a reinforcement learning environment for the Diplomacy board game is presented, using the standard interface adopted by OpenAI Gym environments. Our main purpose is to enable straightforward comparison and reuse of existing reinforcement learning implementations when applied to cooperative games. As a proof-of-concept, we show preliminary results of reinforcement learning agents exploiting this environment.

Keywords: Reinforcement learning · Multi-agent games · Diplomacy · OpenAI Gym

1 Introduction

Artificial intelligence has grown to become one of the most notable fields of computer science during the past decade. The increase in computational power that current processors provide allows computers to process vast amounts of information and perform complex calculations quickly and cheaply, which in turn has renovated the interest of the scientific community in machine learning (ML). ML software can produce knowledge from data. Reinforcement learning (RL) [16] is an ML paradigm that studies algorithms that give a software agent the capability of learning and evolving by trial and error. The knowledge an RL agent acquires comes from interactions with the environment, from understanding what actions lead to what outcomes. While computers are getting better at overcoming obstacles using reinforcement learning, they still have great difficulty with acting in and adjusting to real-life scenarios.

Games have always been an essential test-bed for AI research. Researchers have focused mostly on adversarial games between two individual opponents, such as Chess [5]. Reinforcement learning, in particular, has been successfully applied in this type of games, with increasing efficiency over the past years.

© Springer Nature Switzerland AG 2019
P. Moura Oliveira et al. (Eds.): EPIA 2019, LNAI 11804, pp. 49–60, 2019.
https://doi.org/10.1007/978-3-030-30241-2_5

One of the first games for which RL techniques have been applied to develop software playing agents was backgammon [17], while recently more complex games like Go [15], Dota 2 [12] and a variety of Atari games [11] have been the main center of attention.

Games where negotiation and cooperation between players are encouraged but also allow changes in the relationships over time, have not been given the same amount of attention. Generally, these kinds of multi-agent games have a higher level of complexity: agents need not only to be concerned with winning the game, but they also need to coordinate their strategies with allies or opponents, either by competing or by cooperating, while considering the possibility of an opponent not fulfilling its part of the deal.

Experimenting with this type of games is important because they mimic the social interactions that occur in a society. Negotiating, reaching an agreement and deciding whether or not to break that agreement is all part of the daily life. Achieving cooperative solutions allows us to derive answers for real-life problems, for example, in the area of social science.

With this paper, we provide a tool that facilitates future research by making it easier and faster to build agents for this type of games. More specifically, we introduce an open-source OpenAI Gym environment which allows agents to play a board game called Diplomacy and evaluate the performance of state-of-the-art RL algorithms in that environment.

The rest of the paper is structured as follows. Section 2 introduces background information regarding Diplomacy, the BANDANA program (a game engine for Diplomacy) and the OpenAI Gym framework. Section 3 describes how the environment was developed and implemented. Section 4 contains experimental data from trials using the proposed environment. Section 5 contains the main conclusions of this work and considerations about future improvements.

2   Background

2.1   Diplomacy

Diplomacy [3] is a complex board game. This competitive game can be played with up to 7 players, each having the objective of capturing 18 *Supply Centers* that are placed over 75 possible *Provinces*, by moving the player's owned units across the board. Diplomacy is a game that involves adversarial as well as cooperative decisions. Players can communicate with each other to create deals. A deal can be an agreement or an alliance that the player uses in order to defend itself or attack a stronger opponent. Yet, the deals agents make are not binding and players may betray alliances. The social aspect of Diplomacy makes it a perfect test-bed for cooperation strategies in adversarial environments. Because the search-tree of Diplomacy is very large, the time and storage requirements of tabular methods are prohibitive. As such, approximate RL methods must be employed. Together with its social component, this makes Diplomacy a fit domain to explore using reinforcement learning techniques.

Several bots have been developed for Diplomacy. Up until recently, most approaches limited themselves to the no-press variant of the game (i.e., without negotiation). For a fairly recent list of works on both no-press and press variants, see Ferreira et al. [7]. De Jonge and Sierra [10] developed a bot called D-Brane, which encompasses both tactical and negotiation modules. D-Brane analyzes which agreements would result in a better tactical battle plan using Branch and Bound and is prepared to support an opponent, in the hopes of having the favor returned later in the game. D-Brane, however, was implemented in a variant of Diplomacy with binding agreements, explained in Sect. 2.2.

2.2 BANDANA

BANDANA [10] is a Java framework developed to facilitate the implementation of Diplomacy playing agents. It extends the DipGame [6] framework, providing an improved negotiation server that allows players to make agreements with each other. The Diplomacy league of the Automated Negotiating Agents Competition [9] asks for participants to conceive their submissions using the BANDANA framework.

Two types of Diplomacy players can be created using BANDANA – one can build a player that only makes tactical decisions or a player that also negotiates with its opponents. Tactical choices concern the orders to be given to each unit controlled by the player. Negotiations involve making agreements with other players about future tactical decisions. In the original Diplomacy game, these negotiations are non-binding, meaning that a player may not respect a deal it has reached. However, in BANDANA deals are binding: a player may not disobey an agreement it has established during the game. The removal of the trust issue that non-binding agreements bear simplifies the action space of mediation.

Tactics and negotiations in a BANDANA player are handled by two different modules. They may communicate with each other, but that is not mandatory. A complete BANDANA player consists of these two modules, that should obey to a defined interface.

To play a game of Diplomacy, BANDANA has a dedicated Java class which launches a game server and initializes each player. The game server is responsible for communicating the state of the game to the players and for receiving their respective actions. In the case of negotiation, BANDANA uses a separate server with a predefined message protocol that allows mediation. Players do not communicate directly with each other. The game continues until someone wins, or a draw is proposed and accepted by all surviving players.

Despite the fact that BANDANA facilitates the creation of a Diplomacy player, it is a Java-based platform, which makes it hard to connect with the most popular machine learning tools, often written in Python, such as Tensorflow [1] and PyTorch [13].

2.3 OpenAI Gym

OpenAI Gym [2] is a Python toolkit for executing reinforcement learning agents that operate on given environments. The great advantage that Gym carries is that it defines an interface to which all the agents and environments must obey.

Therefore, the implementation of an agent is independent of the environment and vice-versa. An agent does not need to be drastically changed in order to act on different environments, as the uniform interface will make sure the structure of the information the agent receives is almost the same for each environment. This consistency promotes performance comparison of one agent in different conditions, and of different agents in the same conditions. Two of the methods defined by the Gym interface are:

- `reset`: A function that resets the environment to a new initial *state* and returns its initial *observation*. It is used to initiate a new episode after the previous is done.
- `step`: A function that receives an *action* as an argument and returns the consequent *observation* (the state of the environment) and *reward* (the value of the state-action pair), whether the episode has ended (*done*) and additional information that the environment can provide (*info*).

Each environment must also define the following fields:

- `action space`: The object that sets the space used to generate an action.
- `observation space`: The object that sets the space used to generate the state of the environment.
- `reward range`: A tuple used to set the minimum and maximum possible rewards for a step.

This specification represents an abstraction that encompasses most reinforcement learning problems. Given that RL algorithms are very general and can be applied to a multitude of situations, being able to generate a model in different scenarios with good results is very beneficial, as it proves the algorithm usefulness. Also, as OpenAI Gym is built on Python, it is easier to connect Tensorflow and PyTorch with Gym agents and make use of the RL techniques that those frameworks provide. With this in mind, creating a Diplomacy environment for Gym would make it easier to implement RL agents that could play this game, and analyze their behavior. By taking the BANDANA framework and adapting it to the OpenAI Gym specification, a standard Diplomacy environment is created and can be explored by already developed agents, particularly RL agents. For instance, OpenAI maintains a repository containing the implementation of several RL methods [4] which are compatible with Gym environments. Employing these can lead to a better understanding of which methods perform better under the specific circumstances of Diplomacy and on other multi-agent cooperative scenarios. Also, if the model used to abstract Diplomacy is successful, it can be recycled to create environments for similar problems.

3   An OpenAI Gym Environment for Diplomacy

In this section we describe the proposed OpenAI Gym environment that enables Diplomacy agents to learn how to play the game. The main objective of the environment is to take advantage of the features that both OpenAI Gym and BANDANA offer. We also intend to allow different configurations of a Diplomacy board to be used in the environment, besides the standard one. We try to achieve this by making a bridge between both frameworks, permitting intercommunication. The OpenAI Gym environment created will be referred to as `gym-diplomacy` throughout the paper.

Because BANDANA offers the choice of creating a strategic or a negotiation agent, we built an environment for each case. The created environments are similar but with different scopes of action spaces and reward functions. The strategic environment allows the use of custom maps, however the negotiation environment does not.

The architecture of `gym-diplomacy`[1] is detailed in Sect. 3.1. The definition of the observation space and its set up will be described in Sect. 3.2. The *action space* for both strategic and negotiation scenarios are described in Sects. 3.3 and 3.4, respectively. The conversion of observation and action objects to a special OpenAI Gym class called `Spaces` is detailed in Sect. 3.5. The *reward function* that defines the reward that the agent will receive is described in Sect. 3.6.

3.1 `gym-diplomacy` Architecture

The design proposed is represented in Fig. 1. It consists of abstracting the Diplomacy game information provided by BANDANA to match the OpenAI Gym environment specification. We implement the methods required for a Gym environment, `reset` and `step`.

The BANDANA's features are inside the Gym environment. However, as a BANDANA player is written in Java and a Gym environment in Python, to exchange information we need to connect both using inter-process communication. For that, the server-client model was adopted using sockets as endpoints and Google's Protocol Buffers for data serialization.

When `reset` is called, the environment should return to its initial state, which means that it creates a new game. To do so, we make use of the BANDANA's `TournamentRunner` class to manage both the players and the game server. In the first reset call, the players and the game server are initialized, but in after calls the game server starts a new game without restarting the process. We then connect to our custom BANDANA player, retrieving the game's initial state iS. We created a Java class with the role of an adapter, which we attach to our BANDANA player, to convert the representation of the game state from the BANDANA format to OpenAI `Spaces` format so that the agent can interpret it, as explained in Sect. 3.5.

The OpenAI agent will analyze the received state and decide what its action A will be. When A is ready, the agent calls the `step` function, providing the action A it wants to execute as an argument. This action is also a `Spaces` object, so we need to convert it to a valid BANDANA action A'. We then pass the resulting action A' through our environment to the connected BANDANA player.

---

[1] Available at https://github.com/jazzchipc/gym-diplomacy.

The BANDANA player executes A', which generates a new game state nS. The reward R of the action A' is calculated by the adapter, using BANDANA functions. A binary value D, which informs if the current game has ended, is also determined. Then, nS is converted to a `Space` object nS' and the environment sends nS', R, and D back to the OpenAI agent, which makes use of the information in its learning module. An optional parameter I, corresponding to the optional debug information, may be passed to the agent.

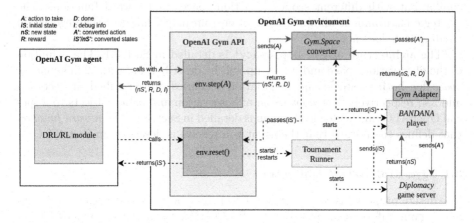

Fig. 1. Conceptual model of the Open AI Gym Diplomacy environment and agent. The solid and dashed arrows represent the interactions between the components when the agent calls the `step` and `reset` functions, respectively.

3.2 gym-diplomacy **Observation Space**

An observation of the Diplomacy game state should contain the most relevant information available to the player. In this case, the board gives that information. The information about all the *Provinces* is one possible representation of the current game state. Each *Province* may only be owned by player at a time, it may have a structure called *Supply Center* that players must capture to win the game, and it can only have at most one *Unit* placed in it. Therefore, for a standard board of Diplomacy, a list with the information of the 75 *Provinces* can be used to represent the board. Each element of this list is a tuple containing the *Province* owner, whether it has a *Supply Center*, and the owner of the unit if it has one.

3.3 gym-diplomacy **Strategy Action Space**

From the strategic point of view, for each turn, a player needs to give an order to each unit it has on the board. The number of units a player has corresponds to the number of *Supply Centers* it controls during a certain point of the game. There are 34 *Supply Centers* in a standard Diplomacy board. However, the maximum number of units a player can have at any given time is 17, because once a player holds 18 or more supply centers, it wins the game.

An order to an unit can be one of three possible actions: hold, move to, or support. The hold order directs the unit to defend its current position, while the move to order makes the unit attack the destination province; the support order tells the unit to support another order from the current turn.

For any player, Eq. 1 gives an upbound on the possible number of orders for each unit n_{orders}, where P is the number of *Provinces* in the board. If we consider only adjacent *Provinces*, the number of possible actions would be more precise, but this information is not part of the state representation. The BANDANA framework will examine invalid orders, such as moving a unit to a non-adjacent province, and will replace them with hold orders.

$$n_{orders} = 1 + 2P \tag{1}$$

3.4   gym-diplomacy Negotiation Action Space

From the negotiation point of view, in each turn a player needs to evaluate the current state of the board and decide if it is going to propose an agreement to its opponents. In the original version of Diplomacy, players talk freely, either privately or publicly. In BANDANA, however, to facilitate mediation between agents, there is an established negotiation protocol. According to it, a *Deal* is composed of two parts: a set of *Order Commitments* and a set of *Demilitarized Zones*. Any of these sets can be empty. An order commitment represents a promise that a power will submit a certain order o during a certain phase σ and a year y, represented by the tuple $oc = (y, \sigma, o)$. A demilitarized zone represents a promise that none of the specified Powers in the set A will invade or stay inside any of the specified provinces in set B during a given phase and year, represented by the tuple $dmz = (y, \sigma, A, B)$. Because a deal may contain any number of order commitments and demilitarized zones, and the year parameter can go up to infinity, the action space of negotiation is infinite as well. However, creating agreements several years in advance may not be advantageous, as the state of the board will certainly change with time. Therefore, a limit (y_{max}) can be considered for the number of years that should be planned ahead. Given the number of phases H, the number of units our player owns u_{own}, the number of units an opponent controls u_{op}, and the number of players L, the maximum number of deals becomes the value described in Eq. 4, where n_{oc} is the number of possible oc and n_{dmz} is the number of possible dmz.

$$n_{oc} = y_{max} * H * (u_{own} + u_{op}) * n_{orders} \tag{2}$$

$$n_{dmz} = y_{max} * H * L * 2^P \tag{3}$$

$$n_{deals} = 2^{(n_{oc} + n_{dmz})} \tag{4}$$

Because for each deal we may or may not select a possible oc and dmz, the number of possible arrangements, and therefore the negotiation action space grows exponentially with base 2 for each oc and dmz available. Equations 2 and 3 express the upper bound for the value of n_{oc} and n_{dmz}, respectively, where P is the number of provinces in the board. While we can shrink the action space by only allowing actions which are valid for a given state, the search tree is still extremely immense.

3.5 OpenAI Gym Spaces

In OpenAI Gym, the action and observation spaces are objects that belong to a subclass of the `Space` class. The one we found most appropriate to represent the Diplomacy action and observation space is the `MultiDiscrete` class. In a `MultiDiscrete` space, the range of elements is defined by one or more `Discrete` spaces that may have different dimensions. A simple `Discrete` space with dimension n is a set of integers $\{0, 1, \ldots, n-1\}$. To encode the observation space, we characterize each province i with a tuple of integers (o_i, sc_i, u_i), where o represents the player that owns province (0 if none), sc is 0 if the province does not have a supply center or 1 otherwise, and u represents the owner of the unit currently standing in the province (0 if none). We use a `MultiDiscrete` space with $3n_p$ `Discrete` spaces, where n_p is the number of provinces. An observation for 75 provinces then becomes:

$$\text{observation:} \ [(o_1, sc_1, u_1), (o_2, sc_2, u_2), \ldots, (o_{75}, sc_{75}, u_{75})]$$

For tactical actions, the translation to a `MultiDiscrete` space is done by associating an integer to each type of order and to each province. Let sp denote the order's starting province, o the type of order and dp the destination province. Then a tactic action is described by:

$$\text{tactic action:} \ (sp, o, dp)$$

When the action type is hold, the value of dp is disregarded.

Given the immense complexity of the negotiation action space, we reduced the scope of action of `gym-diplomacy`. Instead of deciding over the whole action space, we limit the possible actions to one oc per deal that consists of two `move to` orders: one for a player's own unit and the other for an opponent's unit. We currently represent the negotiation action space with a `MultiDiscrete` space with five `Discrete` spaces. Let sp_{own} and dp_{own} represent the starting and destination provinces, respectively, of the move order for the agent's own unit. Let op be the opponent we are proposing the deal to. Let sp_{op} and dp_{op} be the starting and destination provinces of the opponent's units. Then a negotiation action in our limited scope is given by:

$$\text{negotiation action:} \ (sp_{own}, dp_{own}, op, sp_{op}, dp_{op})$$

3.6 gym-diplomacy Reward Function

The objective of the agent is to win the game and, to achieve this, it is required to conquer a certain number of supply centers, that depends on the board configuration. A straightforward approach to defining a reward function is to give a positive reward for a win, a neutral reward for a draw, and a negative reward for a loss. While this approach is appropriate for a small board layout, for a standard board, this results in a sparse reward space, as the agent is only able to learn after the end of an episode. To foster the learning process, we also study a reward function that considers the supply centers that the agent conquers at each turn. Therefore, in the negotiation environment, the agent learns with each action, instead of each episode, while leading to the same global objective. The reward function $R_a(s, s')$ is described in Eq. 5, where r is a constant defining the reward for conquering one supply center and $SC(a)$ is the number of supply centers controlled in state a. It represents the reward of transitioning from state s to state s' after taking action a.

$$R_a(s, s') = r * (SC(s') - SC(s)) \tag{5}$$

4 Experimental Evaluation

Diplomacy presents an environment that is interesting to be used as a testbed for RL algorithms in a multi-agent perspective in two different approaches: strategic thinking and negotiation skills. In this section, we provide evidence that the strategic thinking needed for this game is still challenging for state-of-the-art RL algorithms. In the strategy experiment, we used an already implemented version of the Proximal Policy Optimization (PPO) [14] algorithm, from the stable-baselines repository [8]. In the negotiation experiment, we used an already implemented version of the Actor-Critic using Kronecker-Factored Trust Region (ACKTR) [18] algorithm, from the OpenAI baselines repository [4].

4.1 Strategic Environment Experiments

In order to test if the environment is viable to study RL algorithms, a simplified version of the game was created with fewer powers, provinces, and units. This is meant to reduce the observation space and the action space. This reduction will facilitate and accelerate the learning process which allows experimenting with different algorithms and developing a proper reward function.

In this version, named 'small', there are only 2 players and 19 provinces, of which 9 are supply centers. Both players start the game owning a single supply center. In this smaller board, a player must own 5 supply centers to win.

The PPO algorithm was used to train the agent. Figure 2 contains the result of an execution learning from scratch. The reward function is calculated at the end of each game. If the game does not end in a draw, the agent will receive a reward equal to its number of Supply Centers plus a bonus or penalty depending on the end game result. If it wins the game, the agent receives an extra positive reward of +5 (the total reward will be at least 10), while when losing it accumulates a penalty of −5 (the total reward will be within [−5, −1]).

A run of 10^4 steps was used to make a final evaluation of the trained agent. It has won 745 out of 796 games, which translates to 93.6% of victories (combination of solo victories and draws where the agent has more Supply Centers than the opponent). The mean reward was of 9.21, corresponding to 732 solo victories.

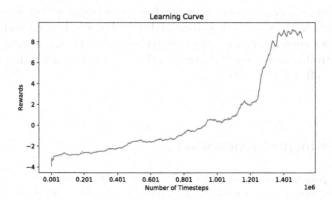

Fig. 2. Rewards per episode of a PPO agent in the 'small' board. A positive reward indicates that the agent was not eliminated from the game. A reward is higher than 10 when the agent has won the game.

4.2   Negotiation Environment Experiments

For negotiation scenarios, BANDANA does not allow a smaller map to be used. Therefore, we have used the standard 75 regions Diplomacy map for the negotiation experiments with all the 7 players. Because of the size of the action space, as mentioned in Sect. 3.4, we have started with a simple range of decision: the agent may only propose one deal per turn, to a single opponent, with only one order commitment. The order commitment is for the immediately following phase of the game and contains just two **move** orders.

Since negotiation does not directly affect the number of conquered supply centers, using the reward function in Eq. 5 could lead to inconsistent learning. For that reason, we use a different reward function to train the agent for negotiation. The agent receives a positive reward for each valid deal and a negative reward for each invalid deal it proposes. A deal is invalid if the player proposes to itself or if the orders inside the deal do not match the current state of the game. While this reward function does not directly lead to victory, it helps the agent to become better at negotiating. Because there is a time limit during the negotiation phase, it is important not to waste time by proposing invalid deals.

Figure 3 contains the average results of three different executions, all learning from scratch. Because each game may have a different number of turns, instead of showing the episode reward over the number of steps we show the average reward over the number of episodes.

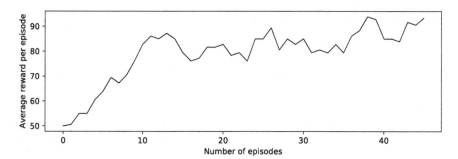

Fig. 3. Average rewards per episode (game) of an agent learning from scratch with ACKTR in the negotiation environment (3 executions over 46 episodes). The values have been smoothed using a window of size 3. Each game has a variable number of steps. A valid deal gets a positive reward +5, each invalid deal gets −5.

Because negotiation only takes place every two phases and is a rather long stage, running negotiation steps takes quite a bit of time, which limits the amount of training a player can have. However, the learning progress is evident, as the agent learns to propose more valid actions.

5   Conclusions

By combining the standardization of OpenAI Gym with the complexity of BANDANA, we have succeeded in facilitating the implementation of reinforcement learning agents for the Diplomacy game, both in the strategic and in the negotiation scenarios. We were able to create agents and to use already implemented algorithms, with little code adaptation. This achievement enables us to continue testing reinforcement learning techniques to improve Diplomacy players performance.

Some future enhancements include improving the representation of the action and observation space, as these are determinant in the performance of the techniques used. Diplomacy's environment execution is computationally heavy and determines the learning pace of our agents. Optimizing the environment execution is thus a relevant enhancement. Another improvement would be to let the developer define the reward function through a parameter of the environment.

References

1. Abadi, M., Agarwal, A., Barham, P., et al.: TensorFlow: large-scale machine learning on heterogeneous systems (2015). https://www.tensorflow.org/
2. Brockman, G., et al.: OpenAI gym. arXiv preprint. arXiv:1606.01540 (2016)
3. Calhamer, A.B.: The Rules of Diplomacy, 4th edn. Avalon Hill, Baltimore (2000)
4. Dhariwal, P., et al.: OpenAI baselines (2017)

5. Drogoul, A.: When ants play chess (or can strategies emerge from tactical behaviours?). In: Castelfranchi, C., Müller, J.-P. (eds.) MAAMAW 1993. LNCS, vol. 957, pp. 11–27. Springer, Heidelberg (1995). https://doi.org/10.1007/BFb0027053
6. Fabregues, A., Sierra, C.: DipGame: a challenging negotiation testbed. Eng. Appl. Artif. Intell. **24**(7), 1137–1146 (2011)
7. Ferreira, A., Lopes Cardoso, H., Reis, L.P.: Strategic negotiation and trust in diplomacy – the DipBlue approach. In: Nguyen, N.T., Kowalczyk, R., Duval, B., van den Herik, J., Loiseau, S., Filipe, J. (eds.) Transactions on Computational Collective Intelligence XX. LNCS, vol. 9420, pp. 179–200. Springer, Cham (2015). https://doi.org/10.1007/978-3-319-27543-7_9
8. Hill, A., et al.: Stable baselines (2018). https://github.com/hill-a/stable-baselines
9. de Jonge, D., Baarslag, T., Aydoğan, R., Jonker, C., Fujita, K., Ito, T.: The challenge of negotiation in the game of diplomacy. In: Lujak, M. (ed.) AT 2018. LNCS (LNAI), vol. 11327, pp. 100–114. Springer, Cham (2019). https://doi.org/10.1007/978-3-030-17294-7_8
10. de Jonge, D., Sierra, C.: D-Brane: a diplomacy playing agent for automated negotiations research. Appl. Intell. **47**(1), 158–177 (2017)
11. Mnih, V., et al.: Playing Atari with deep reinforcement learning. arXiv preprint. arXiv:1312.5602 (2013)
12. OpenAI: OpenAI five. https://blog.openai.com/openai-five/
13. Paszke, A., et al.: Automatic differentiation in PyTorch. In: NIPS-W (2017)
14. Schulman, J., Wolski, F., Dhariwal, P., Radford, A., Klimov, O.: Proximal policy optimization algorithms (2017)
15. Silver, D., et al.: Mastering the game of Go with deep neural networks and tree search. Nature **529**(7587), 484 (2016)
16. Sutton, R.S., Barto, A.G.: Reinforcement Learning: An Introduction, 2nd edn. The MIT Press, Cambridge (2018)
17. Tesauro, G.: TD-Gammon, a self-teaching backgammon program, achieves master-level play. Neural Comput. **6**(2), 215–219 (1994)
18. Wu, Y., Mansimov, E., Liao, S., Grosse, R.B., Ba, J.: Scalable trust-region method for deep reinforcement learning using kronecker-factored approximation. CoRR abs/1708.05144 (2017)

Voxel Based Pathfinding with Jumping for Games

Gabriel Silva[1], Gustavo Reis[1,2(✉)], and Carlos Grilo[1,2]

[1] School of Technology and Management,
Polytechnic Institute of Leiria, Leiria, Portugal
{gabriel.silva,gustavo.reis,carlos.grilo}@ipleiria.pt
[2] CIIC, Polytechnic Institute of Leiria, Leiria, Portugal

Abstract. Pathfinding plays a vital role in video games, whether in terms of gameplay mechanics or player immersion. Commonly used methods only allow the simplest types of movements like walking and running. Although seldom, other types of movement like swimming and flying are also considered. Even rarer are mechanisms that natively contemplate jumps, without the need of extra intervention of game developers. Most games overlook these movements on Non Player Characters, affecting player experience. This article discusses the limitations of Navigation Meshes when it comes to take jumps into consideration and proposes a new solution using grid-based any-angle pathfinding. Each cell of this navigation grid constitutes a voxel that delimits a small 3D space and is expressed in a shape of a cube. Voxels discretize the game world and are explored by a search algorithm to achieve pathfinding with jumps. Performance is critical and found paths should be optimal and efficient. Results show that the proposed solution can be successfully applied in game development.

Keywords: Pathfinding · Jumping AI · Path planning on grids · Voxel based worlds

1 Introduction

Nowadays, most video games employ at least some aspect of pathfinding and path following. These are responsible for the navigation of the agents in the game world, be they Player or Non Player Characters (NPCs), and can heavily influence gameplay features [1] as well as cinematic events. A lot of video games do not incorporate any jump behaviour for their agents because current methods do not offer an easy solution. These solutions require either manually marking every jump that an agent could potentially make or are very limited in the jump scenarios that can be recognized automatically. As a result, it is common to see games that do not allow jumping. These choices can severely impact the game experience by decreasing or increasing the game's difficulty or by affecting the sense of realism and immersion. For example, in a game where a NPC chases the player, it is easier to escape if the player can jump over walls but not the NPC. Besides, if nobody can jump, the game feels unrealistic since obstacles that the player perceives as easily crossed, like small rocks, have the same characteristics of an enormous wall.

© Springer Nature Switzerland AG 2019
P. Moura Oliveira et al. (Eds.): EPIA 2019, LNAI 11804, pp. 61–72, 2019.
https://doi.org/10.1007/978-3-030-30241-2_6

This article discusses the two most used pathfinding methods for continuous terrain contexts, Navigation Meshes and Grid Navigation, focusing on their advantages and limitations when supporting jumping behaviours. Navigation Meshes are the favoured method for pathfinding in recent 3D game developing and this is where jump integration would be most beneficial. However, assessing their limitations, the employed base pathfinding method for the proposed system was changed in favour of Navigation Grids. This discussion considers the NavMesh implementation present on Unreal Engine 4 (UE4), which employs the Recast algorithm [2].

2 Pathfinding Methods – Related Work

Pathfinding is the ability to find a path between a given start and end locations. This is a simple task for a player to do but, for an AI, the problem can be very complex. The AI must know where it can move, how to avoid obstacles and how to find the shortest path possible.

For an AI to navigate through a game world with a continuous terrain, first, it needs to employ a space discretization technique. This way, it can build a representation of the world with all valid and invalid positions that it can occupy. Once this is done, search algorithms can be applied to determine the best path for the agent to reach the goal. Most path finding algorithms use graph data structures to represent the world [3].

Space discretization can be an easy or difficult task depending on the game's requirements and features. In turn-based games, it is a common practice to divide the world space into small square or hexagonal sections that form a 2D grid. This way, each cell is either free or occupied by an obstacle and the AI can easily find the shortest sequence of valid movements from the start point to the goal. However, this solution only allows very simple movements for the agent: forward, back, right and left. Games that are looking for freer agent movements must employ other techniques [4].

Nowadays, NavMeshes are the go-to method when developing a 3D real-time game that requires pathfinding capabilities. The usage of navigation grids in conjunction with a search algorithm is also popular in some games [5], working particularly well in game worlds that can easily be divided in regular areas. These methods were chosen for further discussion because of their diffusion, simplicity and jumping integration capabilities; however, many other methods and discretization techniques still exist, some of which are described in [6].

2.1 Navigation Meshes

A navigation mesh is a graph data structure that contains the representation of the navigable areas in a game world. Using this, an AI agent knows where it can and cannot move. This is, essentially, a representation of a game map composed of polygons (polygon meshes), similar to the game floor mesh, but simpler and invisible. Adjacent polygons are connected to each other through nodes, which the agent can traverse.

With this representation, it is possible to move from point to point to cross an area or from node to node to move through different areas until a destination is reached. Untraversable areas do not have any nodes in them, being ignored by pathfinding operations.

To use this data structure, agents must project their real world locations to the correspondent ones on the NavMesh. If an agent is too far away from any point on the NavMesh, the projection fails, and the agent is not able to engage in any pathfinding operations.

The navigation mesh is usually constricted to walkable surfaces (see Fig. 1) and, therefore, agents will only consider areas of the map that are directly connected by ground to its location. This way, agents cannot climb walls to reach other areas, always requiring direct access through a stairs case or a ramp. Since no aerial locations are considered, it is impossible to include jumps, however, it is possible to let agents step over obstacles (see Sect. 3.2).

Fig. 1. NavMesh example on UE4. The ground area is not connected to the areas on top of the obstacles.

2.2   Regular Grids

Just like a chess board is divided in squares that form a grid, so can a game world be discretized into small cells. Agents can use this grid to know where they are and how can they reach a certain goal. Given a defined start and destination cell, one can calculate the shortest sequence of unblocked cells to reach the goal, effectively creating a path that the agent can follow.

Most games employ this method in a 2D context, where the agents can only move on two axes, however, this can also be used in a 3D context, in which cells are called *voxels*. These are usually expressed in a shape of a cube and it is possible to map a 3D space by arranging them in a 3D grid format. This way, each possible location on the grid is expressed by a voxel. This data structure can be easily integrated with many search algorithms and can quickly discretize the game world by overlapping and marking occupied cells as blocked (see Fig. 2). Pathfinding accuracy can be improved by increasing grid resolution, i.e. decreasing cell size [4].

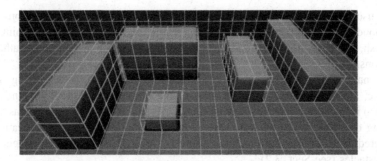

Fig. 2. Voxel grid example. Blocked voxels are represented by red cubes. For clarity, only voxels overlapping with obstacles are represented here. (Color figure online)

Voxels can be considered invalid if they are occupied by an obstacle or for other reasons. For example, if the agent body occupies multiple voxels, then a voxel is valid only if the other voxels next to it, needed by the agent, are unblocked. Once the grid is built and the voxels are tested for validity, it is possible to apply a search algorithm for pathfinding. This approach may have unrealistic restrictions when it comes to movement freedom, since the agent has to move through the centre of voxels, i.e. follow the grid connecting edges. The shortest path on the grid graph is probably not the shortest path in a continuous terrain [7]. However, these issues are not new and have been addressed by many solutions, some of which are described in [4, 5, 7].

Unlike NavMeshes, this approach maps all three-dimensional space, meaning that it accounts for different vertical positions of an agent. With NavMeshes, the location of an agent is always projected to the correspondent position on the NavMesh, ignoring the vertical coordinate. Mapping the vertical axis allows for other types of movement, like jumping, swimming and flying. For example, the game Drunk on Nectar uses a pathfinding system based on this approach for its flying creatures [8].

3 Integration of Jumping Behaviour on NavMeshes

NavMeshes represent the navigable areas of the environment. However, this data structure holds no information about areas in the air, meaning that if, for example, two surfaces are separated by a pit, it is the same as if they are separated by a wall. In these cases, no nodes will be present in these areas and, therefore, these will not be considered when calculating a path. Regarding jumping behaviours, this is the most disadvantageous aspect of NavMeshes and might be a reason for choosing another approach that does not suffer from this, like Regular Grids. However, even if difficult, it is still possible to build paths that use jumps with NavMeshes. This section focusses on the two most straightforward and efficient solutions, describing their principal limitations. More complex solutions have been developed by other authors, but these also tend to suffer from significant drawbacks, like the ones described in [9, 10], which only consider jumps when the agent reaches a dead end.

3.1 NavMesh Links

UE4 has implemented NavLinkProxys, objects that allow developers to manually connect a node from one area to a node of another on a NavMesh (see Fig. 3). The Unity game engine also employs NavMesh links to perform an equivalent functionality. Through these links, agents know that they can navigate directly between those points, for example, they might know that it is possible to fall down from a platform to land on another. These links only define that there is a valid path between the nodes, following it is entirely dependent on the path following process.

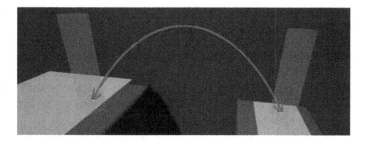

Fig. 3. Navigation link on UE4.

The usage of NavLinks does not increase the nodes of a NavMesh, it only connects two of them. This way, it is assumed that an agent can travel between them, just like any others. The two connected nodes can be far away from each other and the space between them will have no in-between nodes. However, when traversing through these segments, it is likely that the agent wrongly projects its location, potentially resulting in complications, like not knowing where it is on the NavMesh and failing ensuing pathfinding requests.

There are mechanisms that automatic detect jump scenarios and place NavLinks, e.g. [11]. However, these are very limited, leaving developers to manually place all or most links. This is a very repetitive task and may require a lot of manual work, just like creating a NavMesh manually, which makes this not a very good solution in the long run.

3.2 Manipulating the Agent Step Height

The *Agent Step Height* parameter of NavMeshes determines the maximum height differential between connected points on a terrain that the agent can traverse by walking. For example, it determines the maximum height of a stairs step that the agent can climb. This way, the pathfinding system assumes that an agent can step over obstacles if their height is smaller or equal to this value (see Fig. 4).

By increasing this value, the NavMesh covers a lot more areas of the environment and new paths can be found. The pathfinding process acts accordingly to these new areas and paths will feature areas where the agent could not walk on. However, when following these paths, the agent might get stuck at walls, because there is no

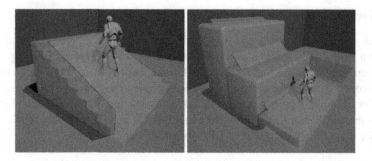

Fig. 4. Agent Step Height manipulation on UE4. Left: small Agent Step Height value; Right: big Agent Step Height value.

information on where to jump or land. It is possible to detect these situations and prompt a jump action, so it can continue with the path, but this has to be done separately from the NavMesh. For example, moving towards a wall triggers a jump. However, not every obstacle requires a jump to traverse it: the agent may be capable of walking over it or, sometimes, simply falling is sufficient.

Even if it is possible to support jump actions through NavMeshes, these are very limited. The agent will only jump from one platform to another if these are directly connected by the NavMesh. This only happens if the distance between them is not enough for the agent to fall through. The distance agents can jump down is always the same as they can jump up, severely reducing the usage cases that involve falling.

4   Voxel Pathfinding System Overview

The voxel pathfinding system must be able to navigate an agent in a game world. To do this, agents make pathfinding requests according to their characteristics. Requests are divided in three sequential phases: request preparation, path calculation and path following (see Fig. 5).

To handle pathfinding requests, the system must validate and prepare the input of each request. It is necessary to project the start and end locations, i.e. convert the real world location to the correspondent grid cell, and build an agent collision profile employed for later validations. Once these tasks are done, the search process may start.

The search is the most complicated and time-consuming operation of this system. This includes calculating the best path, while validating it according to the request collision profile, jump capabilities and imposed jump moment restrictions. To perform this, a variant of the A* algorithm is used to explore the solution space, calculate the shortest path possible and return it in the format of a list of locations on the grid.

During the Path Calculation phase, and after the voxel grid search, the resulting path is submitted to a smoothing process that seeks to shorten it, making it more appropriate for continuous spaces, i.e. allowing any-angle movements. To finalize, each location is marked with tags that mark where the agents must jump and land. At this stage, the final path is delivered to the path following process. This makes use of the locations and associated tags to correctly traverse the path while controlling the agent.

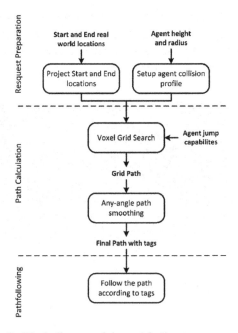

Fig. 5. Block diagram of the pathfinding request process.

Our system was implemented with the usage of a grid that discretizes the game world into cells/voxels. Built paths may include locations in the air, i.e. jumps, without the need of any kind of manual work.

5 Proposed Voxel Pathfinding Algorithm

The main goal of this research was to implement a navigation system as proof of concept that performs pathfinding operations supporting jump behaviours in an easy and transparent way that does not require any type of manual markings. For this purpose, the discretization technique chosen was a voxel grid, making it possible to map ground and air locations.

5.1 Constructing the Voxel Grid

Before handling requests, some voxel verifications must be performed. When placing the voxel grid, each voxel is verified if it is overlapping any map geometry. In this case, any obstruction in a voxel is sufficient to mark it as blocked. As a result, it is encouraged to align the grid with the map in the best possible way, i.e., in a manner that increases the number of unblocked cells. Considering that the voxel grid and map do not change, this process only needs to be done once.

Unblocked voxels that have a blocked voxel directly below them, are considered as ground (see Fig. 6), while all the remaining unblocked voxels are considered as air. This distinction is essential for the path validation process, which employs different validations methods for each type of voxel.

Fig. 6. Ground voxels identification. The underside/base of ground voxels is represented by the blue squares. (Color figure online)

5.2 Request Input Preparation

Before the search process, it is necessary to process the input of each request. The system must project the start and end locations, converting, if possible, a real world location in the correspondent voxel. Occasionally, valid positions in the real world correspond to invalid voxels. In these cases, it is necessary to find the best representative valid voxel, which is usually the closest valid voxel to the initial projection.

Each request is affiliated with an agent body size that can impact pathfinding, for example, a big agent is not capable of passing through a small gap. A voxel collision profile, i.e. a list of relative voxels positions that the agent occupies when positioned in the centre voxel, is constructed to be used in the search process to determine if the agent can stand on a given voxel without its body occupying any blocked voxels.

5.3 Search Algorithm

The search process is accomplished using the A* algorithm. This is a commonly used heuristic graph search algorithm that sorts nodes according to the value returned by the *evaluation function*

$$f(n) = g(n) + h(n),$$

where each node n represents a combination of a voxel and the movement state that lead there, $g(n)$ corresponds to the minimum cost between the start node and n and $h(n)$ corresponds to the estimated cost between n and the end node [12]. The algorithm selects to expand the next node with the smaller $f(n)$ value. Once a node is expanded, its neighbour nodes are added to the frontier list of nodes, sorted by the result of the evaluation function. As proven in [13], if the heuristic function *h* is admissible, then the result will always correspond to the shortest path on the grid. An admissible heuristic never overestimates the real shortest path cost to the goal.

To begin this process, the starting node is analysed. If this does not correspond to the end voxel, then it is expanded (i.e. nodes will be created for all adjacent voxels). Adjacent voxels are then validated and added to the frontier, only if these never were on it or if $g(n)$ is smaller than the previous cost of the same node. After adding nodes to the frontier, the first node is popped and analysed as already described. This cycle continues until either the frontier is empty or a node corresponding to the goal is reached.

In the interest of improving the length of the resulting paths, this system allows for voxels to be expanded in 26 directions, 6 straight and 20 diagonal directions from its centres. The cost $g(n)$ is exactly the shortest sum of distances between sequence of voxels that connect the start node to n. This way, nodes connected diagonally are picked over other ones, reducing the path's length.

The simplest and most used way to guarantee that the heuristic is admissible is by employing the Euclidean distance between nodes, which is always the shortest possible path cost between two points in a Euclidean world. However, the closer the heuristic value is to the real best possible cost, the less nodes are expanded and, therefore, the better the performance [12]. So, in this system, $h(n)$ is set to the minimum length of the path that complies with the allowed movements on the grid. This path uses primarily diagonal movements on the grid, only resorting to straight movement if required.

5.4   Node Identification and Validation

Nodes employed in the search process are composed of different properties according to their type, *ground* or *air*. Both have a correspondent voxel, but air nodes have two additional properties: voxel where the jump started and jump direction. As a result, ground nodes corresponding to the same voxel are always equal. However, air nodes with the same voxel can be different from each other. This is required due to air movement restrictions. Agents cannot change their velocity on the air and, therefore, cannot change the movement direction. The agent's jump capabilities also constrain its air movements, i.e. agents have a limit length they can jump up and forward.

This disparate behaviour causes air voxels to be expanded multiple times as there are many different nodes that could associate with them. The system exhausts every possible jump before moving away from the goal. This happens because the search algorithm is optimal. To avoid performance issues, mechanisms for controlling voxel expansion density (i.e. how many times a node with a certain voxel is added to the frontier) were implemented. These define an expansion threshold, ignoring new nodes if its voxel reached this limit. Even if no longer optimal, the performance increase is substantial and resulting paths are rarely affected.

Before adding nodes to the frontier, they must be first subjected to validations so that the resulting path is guaranteed to succeed when path following. There are two main types of validations: basic and jump. Basic validations include checking if the node's voxel and adjacent voxels defined by the agent collision profile are unblocked. Jump validations are more complex and are only applied to jump segments. These include checking if the agent's capabilities allow it to reach the voxel location, i.e., verify maximum height and length, and if its direction from the previous node is compatible with a linear jump that does not collide with any objects.

5.5 Smoothing Process and Final Output

The search process may not find the shortest path. Even in simple cases, where the best path is obviously a straight line from start to end, the produced path may contain multiple segments. This happens because the grid does not allow movement in any direction. This has already brought about the creation of variants of the A* that seek to improve this aspect, as seen in [5, 7]. However, these tend to encumber the search process, especially when many nodes are explored, which is common in a 3D context.

The proposed approach resolves around shortening the resulting paths of the search operation by verifying if it is possible to skip nodes (see Fig. 7). This process starts at the first node and tries to skip nodes to form the biggest linear segment possible. Once the segment is found, the system changes the start node to the one at the end of the segment and restarts the process until it reaches the end. This way, it allows for any-angle path planning even if it does not guarantee the absolute best results, in terms of length. This method is lighter than others that integrate similar operations on the search process because the result is already decided on and it only tries to shorten it. Jump segments are guaranteed to be linear, so all air nodes are always skipped.

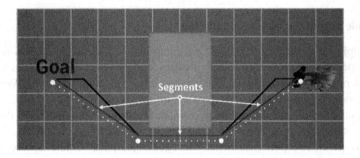

Fig. 7. Smoothing operation example. The black path was smoothed into the red path. (Color figure online)

6   Results and Discussion

The proposed system was implemented on UE4 and discussed results employ voxels with 1 m edges, the cost functions described in Sect. 5, a limit voxel density (maximum number of times nodes with a specific voxel can be expanded) of 5 and agents that can jump up to 2 m in altitude and 4 m in length. The experiments were executed on a computer with a core i7-7820HK processor and 16 GB of RAM and on single thread environment.

Pathfinding with jumps has the advantage of being able to find paths and reach locations that other commonly used methods cannot. For example, jumping between floating platforms. However, even in game worlds that are made so that agents can always reach the goal without jumping, supporting jumps in pathfinding still has benefits. When comparing the proposed pathfinding system with NavMeshes, it is possible to observe that paths can be improved, in terms of length, just by jumping over obstacles. This way, agents reach their destination much faster (see Fig. 8).

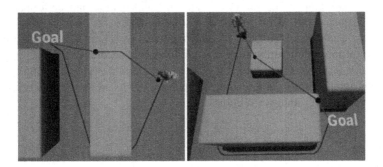

Fig. 8. Length advantage of pathfinding with jumps. Jump are represented by the black spheres.

In terms of performance, i.e. runtimes, results show that the number of jumps on a requested path significantly increases runtime. Detours also have this effect, since they force agents to move away from the goal to find a path (see Fig. 9) and, therefore, require more nodes to be explored in the search process.

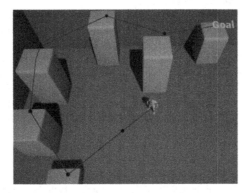

Fig. 9. Example of a complex path including jumps.

Pathfinding operations must be fast enough for the player not to notice any delay. This usually means 17 ms, which corresponds to the time in between frames on 60 fps game. Simple paths with two or less jumps and no detours take very little time to calculate, about, 0.1 ms. However, more complex paths, like the one at Fig. 9, take considerably more time, in this case 12.9 ms. If this path is representative of a complex pathfinding request path in a certain game, then it is possible to claim this system's suitability for that game.

7 Conclusion and Future Work

This article proposes a pathfinding mechanism with jumps that does not require extra manual work, using a voxel grid to discretize the game world space. Results show that the calculated paths can be significantly improved by considering jump actions. Execution times are supportable for video game implementation and performance constraints, which are critical in this context, can be improved through game specific adjustments. The natural advance of computational power increases over time the desirability of this solution, by improving runtimes and accuracy.

For future work, it would be interesting to include more complex jump scenarios considering momentum to adjust jump limitations and to employ parallelization and caching techniques to improve runtimes.

References

1. Sturtevant, Nathan R.: Moving path planning forward. In: Kallmann, M., Bekris, K. (eds.) MIG 2012. LNCS, vol. 7660, pp. 1–6. Springer, Heidelberg (2012). https://doi.org/10.1007/978-3-642-34710-8_1
2. Mononen, M.: Recast Navigation (2009). https://github.com/recastnavigation/recastnavigation. Accessed 16 July 2018
3. Madhav, S.: Game programming algorithms and techniques: a platform-agnostic approach. In: Pearson Education, pp. 180–192 (2014)
4. Daniel, K., Nash, A., Koenig, S., Felner, A.: Theta*: any-angle path planning on grids. J. Artif. Intell. Res. 39, 533–579 (2010)
5. Yap, P., Burch, N., Holte, R.C., Schaeffer, J.: Any-angle path planning for computer games. In: Proceedings of the Seventh AAAI Conference on Artificial Intelligence and Interactive Digital Entertainment (AIIDE-11), pp. 201–207 (2011)
6. Abd Algfoor, Z., Sunar, M.S., Kolivand, H.: A comprehensive study on pathfinding techniques for robotics and video games. Int. J. Comput. Games Technol. 2015, 11 (2015)
7. Nash, A., Koenig, S.: Any-angle path planning. AI Mag. 34(4), 85–107 (2013)
8. Sreedharan, V.: DoN AI Navigation–A free plugin for Unreal Engine 4, Drunk On Nectar - The Nature Simulator (2017). http://www.drunkonnectar.com/3d-pathfinding-ue4/. Accessed 16 Apr 2019
9. Andrade, E., Coelho, B., Reis, G., Grilo, C.: JumpingAI–autonomous jumping for unreal engine 4. In: Conference of Sciences and Arts of Video Games (Videogames 2017) (2017)
10. Rama, AI Navigation in C ++, Customize Path Following Every Tick. https://wiki.unreal-engine.com/AI_Navigation_in_C%2B%2B,_Customize_Path_Following_Every_Tick. Accessed 16 July 2018
11. Unity|Documentation : Building Off-Mesh Links Automatically. https://docs.unity3d.com/Manual/nav-BuildingOffMeshLinksAutomatically.html. Accessed 16 July 2019
12. Yao, J., Lin, C., Xie, X., Wang, A.J., Hung, C.-C.: Path planning for virtual human motion using improved A* star algorithm. In: 2010 Seventh International Conference on Information Technology: New Generations, pp. 1154–1158 (2010)
13. Hart, P.E., Nilsson, N.J., Raphael, B.: Formal basis for the heuristic determination of minimum cost paths. IEEE Trans. Syst. Sci. Cybern. 4(2), 100–107 (1968)

A Reliable Information Acquisition Model
for D&D Players

João Gabriel Gama Vila Nova$^{(\boxtimes)}$, Marcos Vinícius Carneiro Vital,
and Roberta Vilhena Vieira Lopes

Universidade Federal de Alagoas, Maceió, AL, Brazil
{jgg,rvvl}@ic.ufal.br, marcosvital@gmail.com

Abstract. This work has the objective to present a combat simulator model to
D&D players that considers the possibility of actions formalized in game rules
added with players' capability to acquire strategies that will guide them to
improve their performance during game simulations. The quality improvement
of the strategy adopted by the player with the proposed model, called Adaptive,
is evidenced through combat simulations between a team with and without the
ability to acquire information, or different levels of this ability, considering that
each player can have different levels of experience. It was noticed that the ability
to acquire trustworthy information can make the player's strategy improve
exponentially depending on the rate of information acquirement.

Keywords: Role-playing games · Strategy · Player behavior ·
Artificial intelligence

1 Introduction

Game Theory is a mathematical theory developed to describe situations that can be
observed when two or more players interact, and constitutes a language to describe
intentional and objective processes [1]. It contributes to amplify the ability to act
strategically, allowing to foresee the best results for players using the available
strategies. It has been applied to several areas of knowledge, such as in Economics,
Psychology, Sociology, Biology and Administration [2].

Regardless of the specific situation, players must make decisions that aim at
maximizing their gains, rather than cooperating as suggested by the Nash equilibrium
[1, 2]. Of course that, in some games - as in a role-playing games - gain can be many
things, such as building a captivating narrative. Yet, when game mechanics are analyzed in those games from a combat perspective, gain can be defined as players besting
their enemies with minor losses. But how to model the behavior of an inexperienced
player behavior? This can be done considering that sometimes an inexperienced player,
after some playthroughs, can win against an experienced player. The hypothesis to
explain this is the ability of an inexperienced player, besides learning from his own
errors and experiences, to seek reliable information during or between gaming matches.

Reliable information can be acquired throughout the evolution process of the
inexperienced player, and it can be obtained by various means: conversations with
other players, reading manuals, observing opponent's strategies, etc. To test the validity

© Springer Nature Switzerland AG 2019
P. Moura Oliveira et al. (Eds.): EPIA 2019, LNAI 11804, pp. 73–85, 2019.
https://doi.org/10.1007/978-3-030-30241-2_7

of the hypothesis presented, this article will show, in a combat simulation environment, the behavior of a team of players who knows the rules but are inexperienced when confronted by an experienced adversary team, considering that the inexperienced players can acquire reliable information between sessions.

1.1 Board Games and Tabletop Role-Playing Games

Board games have a long history in mankind, and can be traced back to 3 to 4 thousand years old, when Go was created in ancient China. Beyond just entertainment, board games have also been used as educational material in a wide range of situations including learning numerical-spatial relations in young children [3], medical training and health education [4], and computer science and programming skills [5].

A much more specific hobby, considered to be a very important evolution from board games and complex wargames, was born in 1974, when the first edition of Dungeons & Dragons (D&D) - considered to be the first "tabletop" Role-Playing Game (RPG) - was created. The first edition of D&D and the first RPG experiences that happened during the 70s were still very similar to the wargames they came from, but the development during the late 70s and early 80s expanded the gaming ideas to something closer to what we can see today [6].

Tabletop RPGs attempt to simulate imaginary situations set on real or fantasy settings, using game rules that usually relies on dice rolls and pre-set game statistics. In most games (as in D&D), each player creates a character following one or more rulebooks, describing their gaming statistics, the character history and personality. The game happens as one player, known as Dungeon Master (DM) in D&D games, describe a situation and the players describe and role-play their characters' actions.

Depending on the group play style and game system, this can escalate into complex collaborative storytelling and acting, and imagination plays an important role on a session. This led the development of research on areas as diverse as teaching, semiotics and psychology [7]. There is also evidence that tabletop RPGs players perform higher in creativity tests than digital RPGs players and non-players [8].

On the top of storytelling, acting and imagination, all RPGs relies on game rules to determine the performance and outcomes of a character's actions. In D&D this is usually resolved with a 20-sided dice roll, where the player must attain a target number that is calculated based on the result of the roll combined with the potential effects determined by the game rules (such as the character's abilities, the task difficulty, etc.) that can be added or subtracted. As D&D focus in heroic fantasy storytelling, combat against monsters and other enemies are commonplace on a gaming session, with conflict resolution requiring a vast set of rules and several dice rolls. As the game progress and the players' characters become more resourceful and obtain more abilities, preparing a session becomes a complex and challenging task for the DM, as the desired outcomes of combat situations becomes harder to foresee.

The tool that was used as a background for this work is being developed to tackle typical DM's challenges concerning combat balancing, as a successful D&D gaming session relies on presenting the players with combat and conflicts in a way that is challenging but not impossible to overcome. The SCURDD tool (in Portuguese, SCURDD stands for combat simulator using D&D rules) was created using the ruleset from D&D as presented on D&D Players' Handbook 3.5 edition, published by Wizards of the Coast in 2003, and its current stage simplifies the game ruleset and simulate straightforward combat situations that can be used by the DM to easily create and test encounters planned to be used on a session.

1.2 Related Work

The idea of combat simulations is not new to the D&D context, and other attempts were made to achieve a tool that can be used by the DM to create balanced encounters. A well-known tool is the D&D Encounter Simulator, that draw the rules from D&D 5th edition and simulates an encounter a thousand times, generating results statistics for the DM to evaluate [9]. This tool, however, uses a fixed set of playing strategies, and does not try to include the different levels of experience that can be held by players, nor the learning process that can be achieved between sessions. Those aspects are the main novelty brought by SCURDD when compared to similar systems.

The field of artificial intelligence have several applications related to games, including digital RPGs. AIs are used to simulate non player character behavior, to generate procedural content and many other tasks [10]. There is no academic record, however, of AI used to simulate behavior or learning in tabletop role-playing games.

2 The Simulation Tool: SCURDD

SCURDD is a system created with the objective of helping Dungeon Masters (DM) to balance their encounters in D&D v3.5. This game edition was chosen because, despite the existence of newer versions, it is still one of the most currently played versions of the system and, furthermore, has some peculiarities not shared with newer editions such as v4 and v5 do not have. In short, v3.5 has much more published content than v4 and v5, thus having more options for character customization, world building and game mechanics to challenge experienced players.

The tool aims to help balancing encounters by simulating combats with user inputted character sheets from a text file. Every character will be simulated in the system with an AI that fits better the user's gaming table. There are two main modules of AIs in SCURDD: A Skilled AI (SAI) and an Adaptive AI (AAI).

The SAI was created to simulate players with a good knowledge of D&D mechanics, who would know good strategies to control their characters, although not always the best ones. On the other hand, AAIs were made to represent beginner players, with little knowledge of the game, that could learn more after each session.

Since a real D&D game can potentially encompass an infinite set of possible player's decisions and character actions (as in most RPGs), SCURDD abstracts many rules and possibilities to a small set of character actions that are usually used during combat. Combat simulations starts as the game rules of D&D v3.5 states, by an Initiative Roll, that will determine the order of turns of characters actions from both teams. Following that, character actions at SCURDD current version are limited to: attacking, casting spells that does damage or heal (on a single or multiple targets) and moving at the battlefield. Character can act as their AI type commands or by following their team's messages. After doing its main turn action, such as an attack or casting a spell, a character may send a message to his team asking for healing or help to defeat his target. When a character can not get in range of an enemy in one movement action, it can spend its main action as an extra movement and then end its turn. When a character is reduced to 0 HP it is defeated and removed from that simulation, together with all messages concerning him.

The "help to defeat" message is sent when a character does damage to an enemy and makes the enemy get near death, while "need healing" is sent when the character is low on HP and ask for teammates to heal him. During combat simulations the user can follow what is happening in combat step-by-step with the output of SCURDD.

The team that wins a combat is the one with any number or characters alive after the defeat of all enemies. Character's statistics are recorded in logs with different complexities and information depending on their type of AI after each combat. At the end of all simulations, a log containing information about each character performance is generated in a text file so that the user can have further analysis of that simulation.

It this work, we will analyze the impact that a reliable information acquisition model can have into the strategies a player can use during a combat at a D&D game.

3   Skilled Artificial Intelligence

The Skilled Artificial Intelligence is one of the AI modules from SCURDD, it was created to represent a player with some knowledge about D&D rules and good strategies, but that is stagnant and can not evolve as the second AI model. In this way, it can also represent DM's NPCs and monsters, giving them good but fixed level of strategy. The SAI has two submodules, also known as Roles: Fighter and Spellcaster. Each one of these has a series of behaviors linked to their function.

Both SAI Fighters and Spellcasters have a straightforward vision for combat, following a basic strategy of fighting enemies using the best possible attack available from his list. This AI chooses his targets every turn based on a priority order (α) that focus: Proximity (β), Health Condition (δ) and Role (η) of opponent set X, as shown in the following equations:

$$\beta_X^R = \{i | \exists i \in X \left(\forall j \in X - \{i\} \left(\beta_i^R \leq \beta_j^R \right) \right)\} \tag{1}$$

$$\delta_X^R = \{i | \exists i \in X \left(\forall j \in X - \{i\} \left(\delta_i^R \geq \delta_j^R \right) \right)\} \tag{2}$$

$$\eta_X^R = \{i | \exists i \in X \left(\forall j \in X - \{i\} \left(\eta_i^R \geq \eta_j^R \right) \right)\} \tag{3}$$

Equation (1) reads as: there is an opponent i closer or equally distant as other opponents to the acting character of role R. Thus, β is the set of closest opponents to this character. Equation (2) reads as: there is an opponent i that is in worst or in equally bad health condition than other opponents of the acting character of role R. Thus, δ is the set of worst health conditioned opponents for this character. Equation (3) reads as:

there is an opponent i that has a more important or equally important role as the other opponents from the acting character of role R. Thus, η is the set of most important role opponents for that character.

The target's choice for a Fighter SAI is done first by searching for an opponent that is part of all three sets (β, δ and η). If that opponent does not exist, the AI will try to find one that fits in at least two other sets and, in the last case, the SAI will choose the closest enemy (β). This is demonstrated on Eq. (4):

$$
\alpha_O^{Fgt} = \begin{cases}
i \in \beta_O^{Fgt} \cap \delta_O^{Fgt} \cap \eta_O^{Fgt} & if \left(\beta_O^{Fgt} \cap \delta_O^{Fgt} \cap \eta_O^{Fgt} \right) \neq \emptyset \\
i \in \beta_O^{Fgt} \cap \delta_O^{Fgt} & if \left(\beta_O^{Fgt} \cap \delta_O^{Fgt} \right) \neq \emptyset \\
i \in \beta_O^{Fgt} \cap \eta_O^{Fgt} & if \left(\beta_O^{Fgt} \cap \eta_O^{Fgt} \right) \neq \emptyset \\
i \in \delta_O^{Fgt} \cap \eta_O^{Fgt} & if \left(\delta_O^{Fgt} \cap \eta_O^{Fgt} \right) \neq \emptyset \\
i \in \beta_O^{Fgt} & Otherwise
\end{cases}
\tag{4}
$$

When close to death, Fighters tend to get closer to Spellcasters allies that have healing spells, asking for their help. The target priority of Spellcasters is equal to Fighters, but before deciding to attack, they need to choose if they will heal himself or an ally with spells, if the character has this ability.

In this way, Spellcasters have, besides the previous sets of players, a set of allies A and the function ϕ that returns the health condition of allies, $i \in A$, that is used to construct the set of most wounded allies, defined in Eq. (5):

$$
\Phi_A^{Spc} = \{ i | \exists i \in A \left(\forall j \in A - i \left(\Phi_i^{Spc} \geq \Phi_j^{Spc} \right) \right) \}
\tag{5}
$$

The choice to heal an ally includes the own acting Spellcaster as the top priority if he is badly wounded. If it is not the case, the Spellcaster will try to heal the most wounded ally. If there is no ally badly wounded, the acting Spellcaster will choose to attack with magic or spells instead of healing. Spellcasters always choose their best available spell, since spells are a finite resource and eventually end. The choice of the target follows the same rules as the Fighter SAI as shown in Eq. (6):

$$
\alpha_A^{Spc} = \begin{cases}
Spellcaster & if \Phi_{Spc}^{Spc} \neq 0 \\
i \in \Phi_A^{Spc} & if \Phi_A^{Spc} \neq \emptyset \\
i \in \beta_A^{Spc} \cap \delta_A^{Spc} \cap \eta_A^{Spc} & if \left(\beta_A^{Spc} \cap \delta_A^{Spc} \cap \eta_A^{Spc} \right) \neq \emptyset \\
i \in \beta_A^{Spc} \cap \delta_A^{Spc} & if \left(\beta_A^{Spc} \cap \delta_A^{Spc} \right) \neq \emptyset \\
i \in \beta_A^{Spc} \cap \eta_A^{Spc} & if \left(\beta_A^{Spc} \cap \eta_A^{Spc} \right) \neq \emptyset \\
i \in \delta_A^{Spc} \cap \eta_A^{Spc} & if \left(\delta_A^{Spc} \cap \eta_A^{Spc} \right) \neq \emptyset \\
i \in \beta_A^{Spc} & Otherwise
\end{cases}
\tag{6}
$$

The SAI was developed based in production rules using author's vast knowledge about D&D after many years of playthrough, helped by researches and surveys with other players that share the hobby. It was created to represent not an expert and unbeatable player, but one with some skill in the game.

4 Adaptive Artificial Intelligence

The Adaptive Artificial Intelligence (AAI) was developed with the intent to simulate a player in the learning stages of the game, demonstrating the difficulties of learning how to use a character sheet without any experience in D&D. This AI consists of a series of behaviors that will represent the play style of a certain character under its control. These behaviors are separated in two types: Main Behaviors (MBs) and Sub Behaviors (SBs).

Main Behaviors are abstractions of combat behaviors that D&D characters usually have, and Sub Behaviors are inside details and specifications that some MBs need. The created MBs for the purpose of this simulator are:

- **Priority Attack Order (PAO):** Consists on the use priority of each attack in the character's attacks list over one another.
- **Priority Offensive Spell Order (POSO):** Equivalent to PAO, but for offensive spells, those that cause damage, from the character's spells list.
- **Priority Defensive Spell Order (PDSO):** Same from POSO, but for healing magic (magic that restore HP).
- **Priority Enemy Target (PET):** Priority for the purpose of deciding the enemy targets of character's attacks and spells. This MB has SBs that have priority among them, and the order of this priority is chosen during character's evolution. The SBs for PET are: *By Role*: Priority for targeting enemy characters of a determined role (e.g. Spellcasters > Fighters); *By Health*: Prioritize enemies with more or less HP; *By Proximity*: Prioritize enemies closer or farther away from the character.
- **Priority Allied Target (PAT):** It is the equivalent of PET but for allies, used for targeting characters when using healing spells or choosing allies for protection. This MB has the same SBs that of PET but are used for allies instead of enemies.
- **Movement Pattern (MP):** This MB specifies the way that a character moves in the battlefield. This way is specified by the SBs: *Closer to Enemy*: Characters tends to move in the direction of enemies during combat; *Closer to Ally*: Characters fight moving alongside allies or fight enemies close to them; *No Moving*: Characters tend to stay in place during combat, keeping their initial position in the simulation.
- **Message Reading (MR):** This behavior contemplates the attendance of a character about the messages from his team. This attendance is specified by the SBs: *Always Attend*: Character always attend to messages that he is capable of attending in the current turn; *50% to Attend*: Character has 50% to attend to a message that he is capable of; *Never Attends*: Character never attends to messages sent from his team, even if he is capable of doing it. Capability of attending a message is defined by the possibility to attend it in the current turn.
- **Play Style (PS):** The general play style of a character is defined in this MB, directing the method of attack and helping in prioritizing the actions and movement of a character during the simulation. This MB contain the SBs: *Aggressive*: This Play Style

comprehends stubborn and unilateral characters that focus all their effort in trying to cause the most damage possible. Aggressive characters only attack with their most prioritized attack from PAO or spell from POSO; *Balanced*: These characters try to cause damage and be somehow useful every turn, using not always their most prioritized attack or spell, varying it by the situation; *Defensive*: Defensive characters fight to eliminate enemies that are threatening their allies. Utilizing their PAT, they decide an ally to protect, heal and fight enemies that are current engaging this character in combat. It is possible for Defensive characters to have himself as his priority ally.

4.1   Scores and Statistics

After each combat simulation, logs containing statistics of each individual character are generated for that simulation. These statistics includes Physical Damage dealt (PD), Spell Damage (SD), Healing, Health Points left (HP) and Spell Uses (SU). Other values saved in logs are calculated based on these past statistics. These other values are the character Score and High-Performance Score (HPS).

The Score represents the punctuation a character reached in that simulation, and it is calculated summing Damage, Healing and HP statistics. Where Damage is the sum of PD and SD, Heal is equal to all Healing a character has done, if he is capable of using healing spells, and HP are the health points of this character at the end of combat, possibly 0 if he was defeated.

On the other hand, the HPS is a metric of possible performance for that character in that specific simulation. It is calculated as if the character could achieve 75% of his best performance in every action that he does (e.g. the character can do 10 damage at max per turn, his HPS would count as he has done at least 7.5 damage every turn in that simulation). The HPS calculate the possible performance for all character actions that influence his Score, including healing and damage capabilities in addition to health left at the end of combat.

In summary, the HPS is a possible reachable Score of 75% efficiency for that character in that simulation. We will be using all these statistics presented in this subsection to help the character to intuit a new set of MBs and SBs so that he can perform better. One important thing to notice is that the calculation of HPS is different based in the character' Role, because only Spellcasters can cast spells, and this ability changes the way we need to look at this HPS, affecting directly it's calculus.

4.2   AAI Evolution

After every simulation, characters bearing AAIs evolve using their logs from previous simulations. There are two main ways that the system can intuit changes on characters behaviors using their logs, and the first and simplest is to use only the last log to do it. The first way is used always until a character has at least two Best Scores, that are logs in which their Score reached at least half of the HPS for that simulation.

Using only their last log, the system calculates character's performance using those MBs and SBs, comparing it with the statistics contained in the log such as PD, SD, Healing, HP, and others depending on character's Role. Analyzing how well the character has done using those MBs and SBs, relating each one of them to a set of those statistics, the system applies probabilities of changes to this set of behaviors.

The parameterizations used in this method were made by simply dividing the odds of behavior changing equally between all related MBs, for example, the HP left at the end of a combat is related to the MBs PAT, MP and PS. This was a simple approach, but part of the future work is to analyze how can this parametrization impact in characters' performance. To demonstrate how the structure of probability attribution is working, the pseudocode presented in Algorithm 1 shows the logic behind the changes of behaviors related to the final HP of a Fighter character, being HPF the final HP in a simulation:

Algorithm 1: Probability Attribution related to HPF of Fighters

---

```
 1: procedure HPFBehavioralChanges(character, log)
 2:    float chances[]{PAT, MP, PS}
 3:    if character.Role = Fighter then
 4:       HPF = log.HP
 5:       HPMax = character.HPMax
 6:       if HPF < 0.5 * HPMax then
 7:          Chance of change for the PAT, MP and PS raise in 45%
 8:       if 0.5 * HPMax <= HPF and HPF < 0.75 * HPMax then
 9:          Chance of change for the PAT, MP and PS raise in 25%
10:       if 0.75 * HPMax <= HPF and HPF < HPMax then
11:          Chance of change for the PAT, MP and PS raise in 15%
12:       if HPF = HPMax then
13:          No extra chance is added to PAT, MP and PS
14:    if character.Role = Spellcaster then
15:       Similar comparisons are made
16:    return chances[]
```

The MBs presented in the algorithm are also affected by other analysis, like damage related ones, possibly reaching up to 95% chance of changing. The changing of an MB or SB is nothing more than the change to another random MB or SB different than the last. So, it is possible that an MB or SB is not changed if the random chance does not meet the probability of changing that behavior.

The other way to intuit changes on character's behaviors is using the list of Best Scores. When a character has at least two Scores that go over half of their respective HPS, the logs containing those Scores are added to a list of Best Score logs. The system will search for two of those logs in particular, first the one with the biggest numerical Score and second the log which has the smallest difference between its Score and it's HPS.

In that way, we call the first log the Best Score (BS) and second one the Smaller Difference from HPS (SDHPS). The choice of the SDHPS in detriment of searching for the second biggest numerical Score is done because the biggest numerical Score is not always the representation of a great performance. This happens because the longer a simulation is, the bigger will be Scores and HPSs for that simulation, and if the HPS is still much higher than the log Score, the character did not have a good performance.

Finally, have the system picked the BS and SDHPS among the Best Score logs, it will compare the set of MBs and SBs from both logs and assign the minimum changing chance for the MBs and SBs that are equal in both logs. This minimum changing chance is equal to 5%. The behaviors that are not equal in both logs are calculated as shown before, using comparisons with simulation metrics and assigning probabilities of change.

The only case when the chance of changing a behavior is 0% is when, apart from having equal behaviors among BS and SDHPS, this behavior is also listed in the Best Behaviors list for that character. This list and the subsystem of Insights and Learning Speed (LS) will be discussed in the next subsection.

Thus, using these two methods after every simulation character evolve each in a unique way, directing themselves to an "ideal" set of behaviors. The time that a character needs to reach this ideal set of behaviors depends mainly on his initial random set of MBs and SBs, his performance in combat and the Learning Speed chosen by the user.

4.3   Insights and Learning Speed

For the purpose of representing external knowledge acquirement such as, in the case of D&D, forum discussions, rule books and another player, we created the Insights and Learning Speed system. This system has also the function to help SCURDD give a reasonable output to the user in less than 1000 combat simulations.

The LS is a parameter chosen by the user after starting the simulations, when among the characters there is at least one with an AAI. This parameter varies from 1 to 5, the bigger the LS more chance to a character receive an Insight. Insights are like clues to ideal behaviors for a particular character, that are generated based on his character sheet and D&D knowledge from the authors and added to that character Best Behaviors list. This Best Behaviors list is a hardcoded list of best MBs and SBs combination for each type of character (Spellcaster and Fighter), created by analysis of many simulations done in the tool. As future work, we will develop a method to generate this list automatically with a more profound analysis of every character sheet, generating a unique list for every character.

After every simulation, apart from having the common evolution methods described in the last section, characters with AAI have a chance to receive an Insight based on their LS. This Insight will guide one of their MBs or SBs that still is not a Best Behavior to one. This makes that in future evolutions will be a greater chance of that behavior appearing among the Best Score logs, and in the BS or SDHPS.

5   Evaluation

To test the potential of both AIs a set of experiments were made, putting teams of SAIs and AAIs to battle against each other. Two teams (A and B) were generated with identical characters (3 Fighters and 1 Spellcaster each), them 1000 combat simulations were done between both teams in these three specific situations, where Team A is always composed of SAI characters and Team B of AAIs with different LSs: SAI vs AAI (LS = 1), SAI vs AAI (LS = 3) and finally, SAI vs AAI (LS = 5).

These simulations were made in both fixed and dynamic map environments, with a grid size of 8 × 10 squares. As both results turned to be very similar, we present here only the results from the fixed map tests.

The expertise from SAI over AAI can be noticed in Fig. 1, as Team A maintain a better win rate over Team B through all simulations, having a 54% win rate at the last 100 simulations. This happens because LS = 1 is the lowest rate of Insights receiving, so AAI characters will take longer to converge to their Best Behaviors making so that they lose more against a team that is already quite experienced.

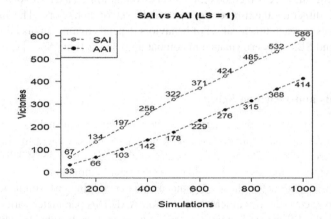

Fig. 1. Victories graph between a SAI team and an AAI team with LS = 1

The impact of LS is noticeable when we start using higher LSs. At LS = 3, the team composed of AAIs starts to overcome Team's A win count at around 300 simulations, as seen in Fig. 2. But still, the team with SAI put up a good competition, finishing 1000 simulations with only 10.6% less wins than the AAI Team, but with only 39% win rate in the last 100 simulations.

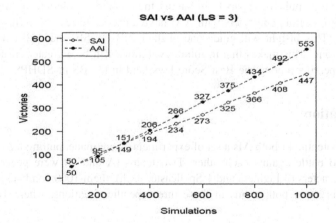

Fig. 2. Victories graph between a SAI team and an AAI team with LS = 3.

The impact of a higher LS from AAIs versus a fixed, but good, knowledge from SAIs can be totally perceived in Fig. 3, where LS = 5 is used. The team with AAIs bests their adversary even on the first 100 simulations, ending with over 35% more wins in comparison with Team A at 1000 simulations, that finish their last 100 simulations with only 25% win rate.

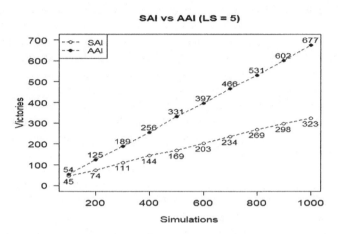

Fig. 3. Victories graph between an EAI team and an AAI team with LS = 5.

It is worth pointing out that with a sufficiently great number of simulations, an AAI Team always tend to overcome a SAI team using identical characters. Besides that, the exact victory count of each team can vary even in identical experiments since D&D is a game based in probabilities and dice rolls and SCURDD does represent it.

6   Discussion

Based on the experience gained with the work described in this paper, some insights can be taken about the AI modules presented and the hypothesis raised. First of all, using our described representations of an Skilled AI and an Adaptive AI for D&D v.3.5 players, we confirmed our hypothesis that a player with the ability to acquire reliable knowledge about the game could beat a more experienced player without this ability after a certain number of matches.

It was noticed that other than the rate of knowledge acquirement (Learning Speed), the overall complexity of a character's sheet and it's set of abilities directly impacts in the number of simulations needed to get to an ideal behavior set. This is noticeable in any field of work, since the effort to learn a subject is directly proportional to the complexity of this subject.

7 Conclusion and Future Work

In In this paper, we presented a model to represent a D&D player that is capable of learning not only through his experiences but through a reliable source of knowledge. This model, called AAI, was based in behaviors that abstracted the possible strategies of a player in battle. We then tested this model in our D&D combat simulation tool, SCURDD, against another group of characters controlled by a different type of AI.

Our idea was to test if a group of AAIs with no experience and a bad strategy set could learn through experience and external knowledge acquirement to beat a group of SAI characters that already have good experience but have no way to acquire knowledge. This way, our experiments demonstrated that, given a good rate of knowledge acquirement, the first group can prevail over the second, in a setting where both teams have identical characters and abilities.

However, the abstractions made in both AI models can have consequences in their performance. Further work is needed to investigate some of these issues, and testing the AI models performance versus groups of human players with different experiences level could be a good future experiment. Many abstractions were made to represent a D&D player within the constraints of our AAI and overall battle simulation, and there is still work to be done in order to improve the simulation tool, SCURDD, and our AI models to better represent real human players on a D&D combat environment. This future work includes optimization to implemented algorithms, usage of Neural Networks for training and evolution of player strategies and focus more on the role-playing aspect that influences player's choices in battle, such as his character's alignment or general way to deal with conflicts and certain situations.

References

1. Straffin, P.: Game Theory and Strategy, 5th edn. The Mathematical Association of America, United States of America (2004). https://doi.org/10.1137/1038146
2. Colman, A.: Game Theory & its Applications, 2nd edn. Routledge, London (2003). https://doi.org/10.4324/9780203761335
3. Laski, E.V., Siegler, R.S.: Learning from number board games: you learn what you encode. Dev. Psychol. **50**(3), 853–864 (2014)
4. Bochennek, K., Wittekindt, B., Zimmermann, S.Y., Klingebiel, T.: More than mere games: a review of card and board games for medical education. Med. Teach. **29**(9–10), 941–948 (2007). https://doi.org/10.1080/01421590701749813
5. Drake, P., Sung, K.: Teaching introductory programming with popular board games. In: Proceedings of the 42nd ACM Technical Symposium on Computer Science Education, pp. 619–624. ACM, USA (2011). https://doi.org/10.1145/1953163.1953338
6. Mason, P.: In search of the self: a survey of the first 25 years of anglo-american role-playing game theory. In: Montola, M., Stenros, J. (eds.) Beyond Role and Play: Tools, Toys and Theory for Harnessing the Imagination, pp. 1–15. Ropecon ry, Finland (2004)
7. Montola, M., Stenros, J.: Beyond Role and Play: Tools, Toys and Theory for Harnessing the Imagination, 1st edn. Ropecon ry, Finland (2004)

8. Chung, T.S.: Table-top role playing game and creativity. Thinking Skills Creativity **8**, 56–71 (2013). https://doi.org/10.1016/j.tsc.2012.06.002
9. DnD Encounter simulator GitHub page, https://github.com/matteoferla/DnD-battler. Accessed 29 Apr 2019
10. Yannakakis, G.N., Togelius, J.: A panorama of artificial and computational intelligence in games. IEEE Trans. Comput. Intell. AI Games **7**(4), 317–335 (2015). https://doi.org/10.1109/TCIAIG.2014.2339221

Solving Motion and Action Planning for a Cooperative Agent Problem Using Geometry Friends

Ana Salta[(✉)], Rui Prada, and Francisco Melo

Instituto Superior Técnico and INESC-ID, Av. Prof. Doutor Aníbal Cavaco Silva,
2744-016 Porto Salvo, Portugal
{anasalta,rui.prada}@tecnico.ulisboa.pt, fmelo@inesc-id.pt

Abstract. In this paper we discuss the development of agents for the Geometry Friends game, which poses simultaneously problems of planning and motion control in an physics-based puzzle and platform 2D world. The game is used in a competition, held yearly, that challenges participants to solve single player and cooperative levels. Our work addresses the two. The approach followed uses Rapidly-Exploring Random Trees with strategies to accelerate the search. When comparing with other agents on the competition, our results show that our agents can solve the single player challenges without overspecialization and are also promising for the cooperative levels with either agent-agent and human-agent players.

Keywords: Artificial agent · Rapidly-Exploring Random Trees ·
Motion planning · Motion control · Replanning ·
Human-agent cooperation

1 Introduction

Intelligent agents and Multi-Agent Systems (MAS) are becoming more popular as they simplify tasks from our daily activities to the industry world, scientific research and so forth. Planning and execution are subjects that have been explored with great interest for they can be applied to single agents and MAS in industries like robotics and video games. One of the most challenging problems for planning and execution is human-agent cooperation. If the agents are not able to perform their tasks well enough, even those that can be done by themselves, then they cannot aspire to cooperate with a human. Simple virtual problems are created, simulated and tested so their solution can be presented through their abstraction and easily adapted to similar real life problems. Many of these virtual problems are used in competition scenarios to appeal researchers to participate, like Geometry Friends [8], a cooperative physics-based puzzle and platform game with a problem of real time cooperation as well as motion planning and control. Solving problems like Geometry Friends which study cases of real time planning and fine motor coordination can help develop solutions for real life situations such as search and rescue, in which there is a necessity of

© Springer Nature Switzerland AG 2019
P. Moura Oliveira et al. (Eds.): EPIA 2019, LNAI 11804, pp. 86–97, 2019.
https://doi.org/10.1007/978-3-030-30241-2_8

highly efficient and effective responses from the involved agents, whether human or artificial. The main objective is to develop a pair of agents that can cooperate with another player, human or artificial. In this work, we select one of the most promising agents of the Geometry Friends competition, the RRT agents, which uses the Rapidly-Exploring Random Trees (RRT) algorithm, and study how to improve them by testing the combination of already proposed strategies, and by adding other strategies to help the search and control.

Our main contributions consist on a set of strategies to accelerate the RRT search, considering the context of the problem it might be used on, as well as a controller to follow the plan which acknowledges failed actions and attempts to recover from them. We then present a set of agents that perform well during the single player levels, without overspecialization, and are able to solve simple cooperation levels. This base work can be used to study further methods of cooperation and help open new doors to a generalized approach with applications in the real and virtual worlds.

In Sect. 2, we present the background to contextualize our work and the related work is referenced in Sect. 3. Sections 4 and 5 respectively describe the development of the agents for the single player and multiplayer levels. We then test and discuss the results in Sect. 6 with the final conclusions and future work discussion at Sect. 7.

2 Background

2.1 Geometry Friends

Geometry Friends [8] is a cooperative physics-based puzzle and platform game that has single and multiplayer modes. To succeed in the game, the player, or players, must catch all the diamonds present in each level by simply touching them. Some levels focus on puzzle-like problems and other levels focus on motion control. Figure 1 shows the actions each character can perform and an example of a cooperative level where the purple rhombus are the diamonds to catch and the black areas are platforms, obstacles the characters cannot get through.

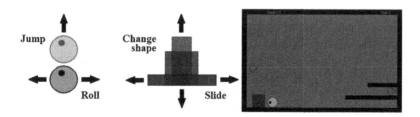

Fig. 1. Left: Characters possible actions. The circle can roll and jump while the rectangle can slide and change shape by morphing up or down. **Right:** Example of a cooperative level. To catch the diamond on the right, the rectangle must morph down and slide above the circle while next to the platform.

The main objective of this game is to study solutions for human-agent and agent-agent cooperation problems, from action planning to action coordination. To promote this, a competition is held each year where the proposed agents are tested with levels made public and others kept private.

2.2 Rapidly-Exploring Random Trees

The RRT algorithm was introduced by LaValle et al. [6] to solve the problems of other randomized approaches, like the non-uniform coverage of the state space and the planning not being suitable for nonholonomic or kinodynamic problems. A tree $\mathcal{T}$ is limited by K iterations representing the number of vertices of the tree. For each value of K, a random state x, outside $\mathcal{T}$, is selected for extension. The method of extension chooses the nearest state to the given state x, x_{near}, already in $\mathcal{T}$, with the help of a distance metric. With an action, u_{new}, that can be chosen randomly or by testing all possibilities, an attempt is made to move towards x, from x_{near}, by applying u_{new} to x_{near} for a period of time and verifying if the state x_{new} is generated. If x_{new} is the same as x, that state is considered reached, else it is considered as advanced. If the state x_{new} is not possible due to violations of some constraint, it is then considered as trapped. The goal of the algorithm is to search high-dimensional spaces with algebraic and differential constraints, by biasing the exploration to the unexplored state space and guide the search towards the randomly selected states [7].

3 Related Work

Some solutions have already been proposed for the single-player mode of Geometry Friends, including one that uses the RRT algorithm, the RRT agent [9]. The RRT agent shows promising results but is still not polished enough to solve some levels in a satisfactory way, mainly due to its controller, which fails to perform some actions of the plan, and the lack of replanning when the agent fails to do an action or the plan is invalidated by the other player.

Some strategies have already been suggested as an extension for the RRT algorithm. The Execution Extended RRT (ERRT) planner [2], for example, introduces replanning. The planner uses a waypoint cache of states from previous plans. When the RRT selects the next state, it is biased to choose a state from the cache instead of a random one from the free space, thus biasing the planner towards the previously successful plans. To avoid constant replanning in an environment that is constantly changing, the Variable Level-of-Detail (VLOD) strategy was proposed [13]. In these environments, it might be more efficient to execute the plan for a time interval and only then replan. When replanning, the search is focused on obtaining a path plan with short-term results while the future is seen in a more global way, but still giving a full start-goal path plan. To improve the efficiency of the RRT algorithm, strategies to bias the search towards the goal, like RRT-GoalBias, or towards an area around it, like RRT-GoalZoom, when selecting a state were also developed [7]. [12] suggested the use of tactics and skills, for the action selection, which introduces the Behavioral Kinodynamic Balanced Growth Trees (BK-BGT), that avoids the use of a distance metric, which can be hard to define, when choosing the next state in the tree, by choosing one already on the tree using the ratio between the average of the leaves depth and the average of the branching factor to decide if a random leaf or non-leaf state is selected.

We also want our solution to be a start towards a solution that can work on Geometry Friends cooperation levels, either agent-agent or human-agent players. For this we need to understand, in a simple way, what important factors the human cooperation has. The human interaction is based on aspects that are extremely complex to bring to the context of artificial agents. People actions are affected by social factors [1, 4, 11], culture, values, and even psychological states that might make the same person display different behavior towards similar situations [5]. Bradshaw et al. [1] mention that human coordination is done with the help of signals or other types of messages, meaning communication is essential to interaction. Human-agent communication is very limited in the game, turning this into a greater challenge. Teamwork and trust are also important forms of human interaction that is essential for the evolution of our societies. Van Wissen et al. [10] show that people do have different reactions and ways of playing when they believe that they are playing with humans or agents. When cooperating, an agent must be able to adapt to the human in order to achieve the common goals. For that, the agent needs to change its plan dynamically to follow the human's actions [4].

4   Single-Player Agents

Having a solid solution that can solve the single player levels is an important step during the cooperation levels since the agent should not be disturbed with planning and controlling difficulties that are not related to the cooperation itself. Both planning and control are presented as complex problems even for the single player levels due to the physics-based aspects of the game. Our agents first make a plan that can be either complete or partial. A plan contains a set of steps which indicate a position, velocity, the action that led to that position and velocity, and a number of diamonds, which correspond to a state the agent should arrive to. The controller then uses this information to guide the character, checking if the agent failed to reach a state at any time. When a partial plan is completed, or the agent fails to reach a state and recover from it, a new plan is made, repeating the process.

4.1   Planning

Geometry Friends is a game where planning has to be done in real time for it is not realistic to expect a human player will take more than a few seconds to start playing a level. Algorithm 1 shows the general idea of our version of RRT.

Algorithm 1. Adapted RRT

```
 1: function PLAN_UPDATE
 2:    if T == null then
 3:        BUILD_NEW_TREE();
 4:    end if
 5:    RUN_TREE(iterations);
 6:    if goal ! = null OR (TIME_LIMIT() AND best_state ! = null) then
 7:        return true;
 8:    else
 9:        return false;
10:    end if
11: end function
12: function BUILD_NEW_TREE
13:    T.INIT(x_init);
14:    state_matrix.INIT();
15: end function
16: function RUN_TREE(iterations)
17:    for k = 1 to iterations do
18:        x_rand ← SELECT_STATE();
19:        while x_rand == null do
20:            EXPAND_STATE_MATRIX();
21:            x_rand ← SELECT_STATE();
22:        end while
23:        EXTEND(T, x_rand);
24:    end for
25: end function
26: function EXTEND(x)
27:    u_new ← SELECT_ACTION();
28:    x_new ← APPLY_ACTION(x, u_new);
29:    if NEW_STATE(x_new) then
30:        T.ADD_STATE(x_new);
31:        if BEST_STATE(x_new) then
32:            best_STATE ← x_new
33:        end if
34:        if GOAL_REACHED(x_new) then
35:            goal ← x_new
36:        end if
37:    end if
38: end function
```

Since there can be various levels of complexity, it is hard to choose a good number of iterations for the RRT algorithm that is not too low to be possible to find a solution, nor too high to waste time searching for a better solution when a good one has already been found. To avoid this, we run the search several times with a lower number, X, of iterations, and at the end of each search, it is checked if a solution was found, running another X iterations on the same tree if that is not the case. The value of X can be 1 or a value high enough to significantly increase the changes of finding a better solution and be fast enough avoid having the agent staying still for more than a few seconds.

In an attempt to bias the search towards the goal we adapt the idea of LaValle et al. strategies of RRT-GoalBias and RRT-GoalZoom [7], during the algorithms state selection, along with Zickler et al. suggestion of the use of tactics and skills during the algorithms action selection [12]. For the tactics and skills, both agents have one tactic in a loop until all diamonds are caught, that can be divided in three stages: select diamond to collect; go to diamond platform; catch diamond. In a certain way, we divide the problem by assigning priorities when choosing a diamond to catch, since this will not compromise the solvability though, if not careful, might influence the solving time in a negative way. If there is a diamond in the same platform as the character, at a possible height for the character to catch, then this is the diamond to select. Otherwise the highest diamond on the highest platform is chosen since catching these first will not prevent to finish the level, in many cases.

We predict the application of an action on a state by using a simple forward model (predictor) for the circle and the game's own predictor for the rectangle. The predictors provided by the game are more accurate but too time expensive, hence the need to create our own. A simple model for the circle character was trivial to implement, though the same was not true for the rectangle hence keeping the original one. To avoid spending too much time searching around simple situations and too little on more complex ones, we use a dynamic time to predict the resulting state. The more complex a situation is, the shorter the time of the action simulation should be, so it can explore more states on the area around. We consider a complex situation, when an agent is on a short platform and rolling/sliding too much to the sides might make it fall when it should not. To choose how long the action simulation should be, we look at the platform width, and the shorter it is, less time is used for action simulation, meaning a bigger state exploration around the area. This strategy might be useful in any problem where it is possible to evaluate if a shorter time is needed, or if a longer time can be used. Another problem lies with the discretization of the state space. In our state space, a state is defined by the position of the agent, as well as its velocity, radius or height, depending if the agent is the circle or the rectangle, and a list of the uncaught collectibles. The state space of this problem is therefore theoretically infinite and so a discretization is needed for a fast search. To discretize we use a matrix of states, $Positions \times \#Diamonds$, to indicate whether or not a state has been reached. Though it is not the best representation, if the velocity and diamond ids are also considered, then the state space would still be big and the matrix consume too much memory. A state space that covers less of the real space can make the search faster but also impossible to solve. On the other hand, a big state space can slow down the search and disturb the level solving. Finding a balance that works for all kinds of levels is not trivial. To avoid this, we make the size of the search space dynamic by starting with a small matrix, dividing the width and height by a Y value, increasing it whenever the open list gets empty, and repopulating the new matrix with the previous states, re-opening those which actions did not previously generate a new state so there is no need for a new search.

In problems like these, where an incomplete plan might make it impossible to reach the main goal, partial plans should be avoided but, in some situations, taking too long to find a solution might be worse, which is the case where there is a time limit to solve a level. Sometimes a choice must be made between risking to solve part of the problem or none at all. For this, we give our agents some time to search for a solution, and when that time is up, the best plan so far is followed. When that plan is completed, an attempt is made to find the rest of the solution.

4.2   Control

A controller, that can easily guide the agent to the correct positions of the plan at the desired velocities, is necessary for this problem. The RRT agents [9] use such controller which, in part, uses information the agents get when simulating their actions, and a Proportional Integral-Derivative (PID) controller which we tested for our solution which did not work as expected for it would sometimes fail to guide the character to the right side, or to obtain the required velocity to jump/morph or fall. A PID controller has several parameters that must be well tuned, and that might have been where we failed to make it work properly. To solve this we then used a new approach loosely based on the PID. This version uses the idea of acceleration to compute the direction the agent must take. The acceleration of the agent is calculated between the updates. When computing if the agent should go left or right, the controller checks first if the agent is already going in the right direction. If so, and if its velocity is higher than the desired one, it returns the action that goes to the opposite of the point side. If slower, it first simulated if the agent can actually reach the desired position with the desired velocity from the position it is currently in or if the it needs to go on the opposite direction first. When the circle agent reaches a waypoint, it checks if it needs to jump, doing so if the case. The rectangle morphing is more complex. When the next action is morph and the agent is not falling, it is verified if the agent has achieved the desired height. If not, the agent morphs up or down accordingly. In case the next point is right below the agent and not on the same platform, the agent, most likely is between two platforms and needs to morph up to fall through them. When the agent is falling, the current action in the plan is performed so it can morph up or down if needed.

4.3   Plan Correction and Replanning

The described controller can still fail to execute an action at the right position, making the characters land on a different platform than the one in the next step of the plan. Other times, the controller has difficulty to reach the desired velocity or position, and keeps failing the same action, over and over. One of the reasons for this might be due to our action simulation during the search, that is prone to errors, as previously mentioned. It is crucial for the agents to know when such failed events happen, so they know they should stop following the current plan. To understand if a plan has failed, we give a time limit to reach the next step of the plan, as well as check if the agent is on the correct platform, meaning a platform from where it seems to be possible to reach the next step just by using the controller. If the time limit has been reached, or the agent is on a wrong platform then there is first an attempt to correct the plan. Sometimes, mainly when the agent falls into the wrong platform, that same platform might be on a step forward in the plan, which has the same number of caught diamonds. It also might happen to be in the same platform of a previous step, from which it might be useful to try again. If one of these steps is found, then the agent follows the plan from there. When no common step is found or the agent keeps failing to perform an action for n times, the agent then searches for a new plan.

5   Multiplayer Approach

The presented solution for single-player levels is enough to solve some cases where cooperative actions are needed. If there is a diamond where the other player needs only to position its character so the agent can use it as a platform, the agent is capable of finding a path if the other player positions the character at the right place. Even if the other player keeps its character still, the agent might find a way to push the other character to desired position to be possible to use as a platform, if possible. Though the problem does not involve the manipulation of objects, this solution is enough to be able to do so, in case these situations are added in.

Still, this is far from true cooperation and alterations are needed to create a version of the agents where they can solve more cooperative levels.

5.1   Planning

When searching for a solution, the agent now needs to simulate the actions of the partner besides their own, to know which changes the other character might do to the environment, as well as their possible positions. This means that, at each iteration of the RRT, the agent chooses a pair of actions, one of their own and one of their partner. This makes the state space of a multiplayer level exponentially bigger than of a single-player level, and the search time slower. The tactics and skills strategy can help reduce the number of times an action is uselessly selected and simulated and thus make the finding of a solution quicker. We keep the same tactic steps as in single-player mode: select diamond; go to diamond platform; catch diamond. While the main idea is the same, there is a difference in the last two steps. Going to a platform and catching a diamond has now skills that take into account cases where cooperation might be needed. Both agents, during the selection of an action, first call their skills to get their action, and with the resulting possible pair of actions which contain the selected one, call the skills of the other character to also get the action that might be more helpful in the current state. Currently, when following a plan, it is hard to understand if an action is needed for cooperation or not, so removing seemly useless actions from the plan might make the it not viable. By this reason, when cooperating, plan cleaning is not performed bringing new challenges for the controller when executing a plan.

5.2 Replanning

In cooperative levels, not only the plans are more complex, the other player can also get in the way of the agent plan during the execution, which make the use of replanning a greater necessity. Simply starting a new tree can be significantly inefficient due to the bigger search space. Strategies like ERRT [3] and VLOD [13] reduce the time of replanning. The ERRT strategy uses bins of old states from the previous trees to select randomly during state selection for extension. We availed the idea of using bins but we use a different approach by keeping them to understand if one was reached after applying a pair of actions. If so, this means the corresponding node of the tree, along with its descendants, can be connected to the selected node in the new tree and time spent in simulation can be avoided. As suggested by the VLOD strategy, we should avoid replanning until it is actually necessary. In this solution, only the next few steps of the plan are used when verifying if the other player has turned into an obstacle.

6 Results and Discussion

6.1 Single Player and Agent-Agent Cooperative Players

We test the discussed variants of the RRT to understand which got better performance. Table 1, shows the results of the search time of the circle agent with different techniques, while using our forward model for the action simulation of the circle search and the game's own forward model for the rectangle. We selected three easy, Fig. 2, medium, Fig. 3, and hard levels, Fig. 4, ran each 10 times and present the time average (in seconds). The Original+STP variant indicates that the state selection is done as in the original RRT but the action selection uses tactics and skills. The combination with better performance, in average, was the BGT-Bias+STP which uses BK-BGT with a Bias to a goal state for state selection and tactis and skills for action selection. To test our complete single-player

Fig. 2. Easy levels

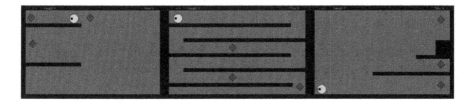

Fig. 3. Medium levels

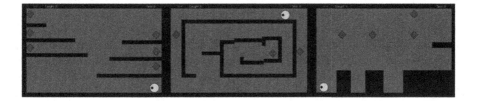

Fig. 4. Hard levels

and multiplayer solution, we compare our results to the contestants of the 2017 Geometry Friends Competition as well as some other available agents, as shown in Table 2.

Our agents rank in second place at the circle track and first at the rectangle and cooperative track, and though the latter is due to the lack of submitted agents for these tracks, it proves to overcome overspecialization. The cooperative track results are not good enough to conclude the agents can cooperate between themselves just with the solution as it is.

6.2 Human-Agent Cooperative Levels

To understand if our agents are currently capable of solving simple cooperative levels with human players, we prepared two sessions of tests. First we tested how human players worked as a team between themselves, to use as a base of comparison. We performed a set of tests with 8 two-player teams. The majority of the participants were casual players (61%), between 20 to 35 years old (92.3%), where almost half rarely or never play cooperative games (46.2%). Only two players had played Geometry Friends before this test. To simulate the lack of communication a human-agent team has, we asked our players to not communicate by

Table 1. Search time of the different RRT variants (average, in seconds)

Variant/Levels	Original	Bias	Zoom	BGT	BGT-Bias	Original+STP	BGT-Bias+STP
Easy	0.195	0.273	0.293	0.196	0.183	0.214	0.184
Medium	1.680	1.128	1.317	1.070	1.068	1.628	0.990
Hard	23.593	13.907	18.371	11.615	9.262	15.986	5.884

Table 2. Total scores of the agents on 2017 competition levels. C stands for Circle, R for Rectangle and Coop for Cooperative

Agent	Our Agents			KIT	RRT		Supervised	NRL	RL	Sub-Goal A*
Track	C	R	Coop	C	C	R	C	C	C	R
Points	3661	3139	2007	4203	1563	1234	1759	1925	2091	991

speaking or by using real world gestures, being possible to use the characters in an attempt to communicate. Then tests were executed with human-agent teams at a later stage. For this part, we first let the human players play with our agents without giving any information about them. After playing some levels, we asked their opinion about our agents through a questionnaire, and we then described their behavior, in a simple way, and asked to play again. This to understand if this new knowledge would change the opinion of the human players about our agents. Without communication, the human players showed to have difficulties to solve the levels as a team, as well as when they were playing with our agents. When asking for the players opinion about the agents level of intelligence, cooperation, and the players trust in the agent the answers were mainly positive, getting an average of 7 in a scale form 0 to 10 where we consider a negative response from 0 to 3, neutral from 4 to 6 and positive from 7 to 10. An interesting change happened after the players understood how the agents work. Though the players were more neutral regarding the rectangle (average of 6.5), many players changed their opinion about the circle agent for a more positive one (average of 7.8).

Even though our agents are not capable of differentiating a cooperative action from a simple waypoint in a plan, most human players believed the agents were cooperating with them. Having the agents rethink their plan, made the players believe the agents were adapting to them, even though they felt they add to adapt to the agents more times. Most players finished most levels under three minutes and, in most cases, the players felt their solving went well. We noticed that most players that had high expectations about the agents intelligence and capabilities do not work or study in any field of science.

7   Conclusions and Future Work

We address the problem of motion planning and execution in the Geometry Friends context which also challenges the agents to cooperate. Our proposed solution uses the algorithm RRT together with previously suggested strategies as well as new ones: use of dynamic discretization, dynamic prediction time for the action simulation, task priorities for biasing and partial planning. We also propose a controller that can follow said plan but can also understand when an action has failed and when it should try to recover using the same plan or re-plan from scratch. With this solution we are prepared to start to focus on the cooperation itself as future work.

Acknowledgements. This work was supported by national funds through Fundação para a Ciência e a Tecnologia (FCT-UID/CEC/50021/2019) and through the project AMIGOS (PTDC/EEISII/7174/2014).

References

1. Bradshaw, J., Feltovich, P., Matthew, J.: Human-agent interaction. In: Boy, G. (ed.) Handbook of Human-Machine Interaction, pp. 283–302. Ashgate Publishing Ltd., Farnham (2011)
2. Bruce, J., Veloso, M.: Real-time randomized path planning for robot navigation. In: IEEE/RSJ International Conference on Intelligent Robots and Systems (IROS), vol. 3, pp. 2383–2388 (2002). https://doi.org/10.1109/IRDS.2002.1041624
3. Bruce, J., Veloso, M.: Real-time randomized motion planning for multiple domains. In: Lakemeyer, G., Sklar, E., Sorrenti, D.G., Takahashi, T. (eds.) RoboCup 2006. LNCS (LNAI), vol. 4434, pp. 532–539. Springer, Heidelberg (2007). https://doi.org/10.1007/978-3-540-74024-7_55
4. Hoffman, G., Breazeal, C.: Collaboration in human-robot teams. In: Proceedings of the AIAA 1st Intelligent Systems Technical Conference, pp. 1–18 (2004). https://doi.org/10.2514/6.2004-6434
5. Kraus, S.: Human-agent decision-making: combining theory and practice. Electron. Proc. Theoret. Comput. Sci. **215**, 13–27 (2016). https://doi.org/10.4204/EPTCS.215.2
6. LaValle, S.M.: Rapidly-exploring random trees: a new tool for path planning. Technical report, TR 98-11 (1998). https://doi.org/10.1.1.35.1853
7. LaValle, S.M., Kuffner, J.J.: Rapidly-exploring random trees: progress and prospects, pp. 293–308 (2000) https://doi.org/10.1017/CBO9781107415324.004
8. Prada, R., Lopes, P., Catarino, J., Quiterio, J., Melo, F.S.: The geometry friends game AI competition. In: Proceedings of 2015 IEEE Conference on Computational Intelligence and Games, CIG 2015, pp. 431–438 (2015)
9. Soares, R., Leal, F., Prada, R., Melo, F.: Rapidly-exploring random tree approach for geometry friends. In: Proceedings of 1st International Joint Conference of DiGRA and FDG (2016)
10. Van Wissen, A., Gal, Y., Kamphorst, B.A., Dignum, M.V.: Human-agent teamwork in dynamic environments. Comput. Hum. Behav. **28**(1), 23–33 (2012). https://doi.org/10.1016/j.chb.2011.08.006
11. Weibel, D., Wissmath, B., Habegger, S., Steiner, Y., Groner, R.: Playing online games against computer- vs. human-controlled opponents effects on presence, flow, and enjoyment. Comput. Hum. Behav. **24**(5), 2274–2291 (2008). https://doi.org/10.1016/j.chb.2007.11.002
12. Zickler, S., Veloso, M.: Efficient physics-based planning: sampling search via non-deterministic tactics and skills. In: The 8th International Conference on Autonomous Agents and Multiagent Systems, pp. 27–34 (2009)
13. Zickler, S., Veloso, M.: Variable level-of-detail motion planning in environments with poorly predictable bodies. Frontiers Artif. Intell. Appl. **215**, 189–194 (2010). https://doi.org/10.3233/978-1-60750-606-5-189

Spatio-Temporal Attention Deep Recurrent Q-Network for POMDPs

Mariano Etchart[1(✉)], Pawel Ladosz[2], and David Mulvaney[1]

[1] Wolfson School of Mechanical, Electrical and Manufacturing Engineering,
Loughborough University, Loughborough, UK
`mariano.etchart@gmail.com`, `d.j.mulvaney@lboro.ac.uk`
[2] Department of Computer Science, Loughborough University, Loughborough, UK
`p.ladosz@lboro.ac.uk`

Abstract. One of the long-standing challenges for reinforcement learning agents is to deal with noisy environments. Although progress has been made in producing an agent capable of optimizing its environment in fully observable conditions, partial observability still remains a difficult task. In this paper, a novel model is proposed which inspired by human perception, utilizes two fundamental machine learning concepts, attention and memory, to better confront a noisy environment.

1 Introduction

Successful control policies may be obtained through reinforcement learning (RL), an agent's framework to learning by interacting in an environment. Traditionally, RL models are difficult to train and recent progress – made possible by a few tricks and the combination of deep learning [9] - has funnelled a large amount of attention to the field because of the ability to provide human-like performance [14]. Yet within the field, there exists several challenges that plague the RL communities. One of the prominent challenges is extending these control policies from relatively simple environments to more dynamic and noisy environments, owning to the nature of the real-world.

A large portion of research papers assume the RL problem to be fully observable, formalized as a Markov Decision Process (MDP) [3]. Although MDPs provide an adequate formalization of the reinforcement learning problem, when approaching real-world complexity, MDPs lack representing some of the features of how an agent sees an environment including partially observable states and redundant information. Having noted that performance drops and human-level performance has not yet been achieved in the games domain for partially observable environments, this paper proposes a model to operate under partially observable MDPs (POMDPs) by taking inspiration from human perception and proposes a combinational attention model (spatial and temporal) with memory to move towards a more robust agent who is better suited to handle nosier situations.

© Springer Nature Switzerland AG 2019
P. Moura Oliveira et al. (Eds.): EPIA 2019, LNAI 11804, pp. 98–105, 2019.
https://doi.org/10.1007/978-3-030-30241-2_9

Other approaches to POMDPs with deep reinforcement learning have managed to improve previous benchmarks in the Atari domain, although few have been specifically inspired by human cognition. To the knowledge of the authors, there have not been work on deep RL for POMDP with spatio-temporal attentional mechanisms. Variants of spatio-temporal attention have been used before for several applications including action recognition [19,20,24], caption generation and image classification [2], video recognition [5] and object tracking [25] and many more although have never been used for solving POMDPs before. Given the vast amount of research on the additive nature and synergic importance of spatial with temporal attention for human perception [4] in the cognitive neuroscience domain, one naturally wonders how this could be applied to an agent in Atari games in a noisy environment. This study hypothesizes that formulating an agent with a spatio-temporal attention mechanism for partially observable environments will perform more robustly and additively benefit from both mechanisms.

1.1 Partially Observable Markov Decision Processes

As an MDP represents the RL problem, POMDP represent a partially observable environment. Two variables are introduced to the MDP tuple, a set of observations Ω and the observation function O which connects the observations with the states. The probability of observing an observation $o \in \Omega$ in state s is O(s, o), and the POMDP can be summarized by the tuple {S,A,R,P, Ω,O}. In an POMDP, the environment only exhibits observations Ω and the states S are unknown. To create an POMDP for Atari games, one may simulate a POMDP by occulting a game screen with some probability. This technique was used in a study by Hausknecht et al. where a POMDP was created in the game of Pong with every game screen having 0.5 probability of being fully observable or completely occulted.

1.2 Related Works in POMDPs

POMDPs are known to be difficult problems to solve since an observation is not enough information to select an action and multiple observations are required to capture elements of the underlying state. In Hausknecht's study [6], a Deep Recurrent Q-Network (DRQN) is proposed and demonstrated to outperform DQN in partially observable MDPs. This is due to the correlations captured in the DRQN's recurrent neural network with long-short term memory cells and gives the agent an ability to integrate information through time to more robustly handle partial observability. Similarly the action-specific deep recurrent Q-network (ADRQN) [1] uses an RNN with an additional network, to keep track of the influence of certain observations over others. Both these recent models form part of approaches which utilize RNNs to encode the past in order to deal with noise and occulted observations.

On the other hand, Igl et al. argue that learning a policy in a partially observable environment with a Blackbox approach, such as in an RNN, can lead to a high reliance on these encodings of the past and that this implicit inference can lead to a less optimal solution for a complex environment [7]. Thus, it introduces a generative model of the environment and uses this to provide inference in the missing information. The approach uses the combination of encoding history in RNN like in DRQN or ADRQN, but also using belief inference with a variational auto-encoder with the argument that model-based and model free learning must be utilized together.

Other research into POMDPs assume transition probabilities, reward models and observation functions are known which is not the case when working towards real-world environments [16,17].

1.3 Deep Recurrent Q-Network

DQN's inability to deal with POMDPs was improved by the Deep Recurrent Q-Network (DRQN) from Hausknecht et al. [6] by adding an LSTM due to its ability to encode the history of past states and maintain longer term decencies between states. It implicitly maintains a history of previous state through its 3 gate structure (input, output and forget gate) determining which input features are more important than others. These additions to the network allow it to outperform DQN in partially observable environments, in the case of flickering Atari game screens. For this reason, the authors chose this as a starting point to deal with the problem of partial observability.

Model Architecture and Implementation. The DRQN architecture replaces the second-last fully connected layer in the DQN with a long-short term memory (LSTM) layer instead. This leads to an aspect of 'unrolling' the timesteps of the LSTM and backpropagation through time [22] must be used instead. Fundamentally, DQN and DRQN receive the input differently whereby DQN takes 4 frames at once and DRQN only a single frame. Although because of the aforementioned unrolling the DRQN maintains a history of the past 4 states (or for however long it is chosen to unroll). The DRQN and DQN trains by sampling experience tuples from a replay buffer [14] consisting of state, reward, action, and next state from one interaction with the environment. The entire DRQN is trained end-to-end including the LSTM layer, the loss function is the same as DQNs except for the added parameters of the LSTM layer:

$$L_i\left(\theta_i\right) = E_{(s_t, r_t, a_t, s_{t+1}) \sim D}[((r_t + \gamma \max_{a'} \hat{Q}\left(s_{t+1}, \; a_t' \middle| \theta_i\right) - Q\left(s_t, \; a_t \middle| \theta_i\right)) \;]$$

where θ is the weights and biases of the network, E is the set of experiences whereby D indicates the replay memory, $\hat{Q}$ is the Q-function of the target network and $(r_t + \gamma \max_{a'} \hat{Q}\left(s_{t+1}, \; a_t' \middle| \theta_i\right)$ represents the update target and $Q\left(s_t, \; a_t \middle| \theta_i\right)$ the current Q-value estimate. The optimizer tries to minimize this function in each iteration of training.

The DRQN was implemented by extending an already existing implementation of DQN. The RNN was unrolled for 4 timesteps. Refer to [6] for the entire network body.

1.4   Spatial Attention Model for POMDP

Visual attention [23] is a technique that allows an agent to focus on more relevant aspects of an input image and can therefore learn a policy associated with it more quickly because learning updates are more information efficient. This paper therefore introduces visual attention to the DRQN in order to exploit the fact that the entire spatial input is rarely needed to successfully learn policies, it is usually a very important subsection of the image that provides the information needed for learning. This is particularly true in some Atari games where the majority of the game screen is irrelevant or for aesthetics and only a small portion of the screen becomes essential to the decision making. Not only does this enable the agent to converge faster but increases the chances of learning correct policies.

Model Architecture and Implementation. The DRQN is augmented following an attention mechanism inspired by the Deep Attention Q-Network [21]. Soft attention uses the weighted sum of an attention matrix and the current input matrix in order to exemplify certain sections of the image more than others.

The attention network g is placed after the convolutional layers and before the LSTM. The input image is transformed into a set of vectors and then fed into the G network which consists of two linear layers and a SoftMax activation function. The output of the network may be summarized as such: $g\left(v_t^i, h_{t-1}\right) = softmax(linear(Tanh(Linear\left(v_t^i\right) + W h_{t-1})))$. Where Linear layers are affine transformations, v_t^i represents the input vectors of the image, h_{t-1} is the previous hidden state of the LSTM and W is a weight matrix with no bias. The output is then weighted and summed in order to find the context vector:

$$z_t = \sum_{i=1}^{L} g\left(v_t^i, h_{t-1}\right) * v_t^i$$

This simple addition allows the model to retain its differentiability and may still be trained end-to-end, therefore the loss function is the same as the one in DRQN with a larger θ to include additional parameters in the attention network.

1.5   Spatio-Temporal Model for POMDPs

Temporal attention performs the same selective approach as seen in spatial attention but in the time domain, choosing certain timesteps over others. Although there is a smaller body of research focusing on temporal attention in the machine learning community [12,18,25] , it is well-established in the neuroscientific community that the combination of spatial and temporal attention in human perception is a critical aspect of perceiving occulted and moving objects in time [4,11], two for the most prominent features of a flickering Atari game screen. The authors combine spatial and temporal attention in an attempt to recreate the additive effects [11] seen in human perception, in a deep RL agent.

Model Architecture and Implementation An attention network J is added in between the LSTM's timesteps to optimize for the most important states of the past history. In DRQN state are implicitly discriminated by the LSTM through its 3 gates, with the addition of the J network, states are being explicitly discriminated through the weights matrix of the attention network.

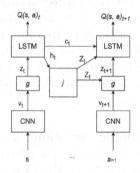

Fig. 1. Spatio-temporal attention DRQN netowork

The output of a LSTM is a hidden state which logically feeds into itself when unrolling the timesteps. During the unrolling, each hidden state is given an equal weight in a normal LSTM or in the DRQN, however in this case the hidden state is fed into the attention network before taking the weighted sum to find the context vector and then outputted to the LSTM for the next timestep as shown schematically in Fig. 1. The output of the J network is as follows: $j(h_{t-1}) = softmax(Tanh(Linear(h_{t-1}) + Wh_{t-1}))$. Where linear is an affine transformation with no bias, h_{t-1} represents the previous hidden state, and W is a weight matrix. The context vector is then thus calculated as the weighted sum:

$$z_t = \sum_{i=1}^{L} j(h_{t-1}) * h_{t-1}$$

The resulting model has spatial attention network G and temporal attention network J as shown in Fig. 1.

1.6 Training, Evaluation and Hyperparameters

On the ALE, policies were evaluated after 50k steps of training for 25k steps with an e-greedy policy of epsilon set to 0.05 and the average reward per episode was calculated. During training time polices took 50k exploration steps before beginning to train with an e-greedy policy of epsilon value of 1 annealed to 0.2 over 1 million steps. A discount factor of 0.99 was used and an asynchronous replay buffer size of 100k with batch size of 32. The optimizer used was Adam [8] with learning rate 0.0001. Target networks were updated every 1k steps, and

32 steps were sampled from the replay buffer to train the agent roughly every 4 steps taken in the environment. In all models 'smooth L1' loss was used which acts as a way to clip the error to improve stability in training.

In the flickering domain, almost all agents performed poorly as seen in previous studies. The spatial attention model and spatio-temporal attention model however performed marginally better than the DRQN, with the DRQN being unable to reach past a score of −15 ever and maintaining under −19 for the majority of epochs as seen in Fig. 2. Spatial attention showed more instability in the training than the other model with large oscillations. The spatio-temporal model managed to achieve the highest reward of the three in the same number of epochs.

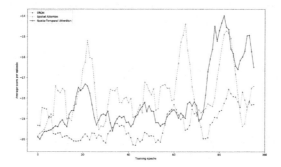

Fig. 2. Comparitive moving average of all models on Flickering Pong

The agents were evaluated in a fully observable environment to assess the generality of the models in both environments; fully and partially observable. In fully observable pong, the spatio-temporal attention agent performed worse than the DRQN in terms of rate of convergence and final score. The improvement in performance of spatial attention in partially observable environments simultaneously demonstrated poorer performance than DRQN in the fully observable case. It's rate of convergence does not match DRQN's as seen in Fig. 3.

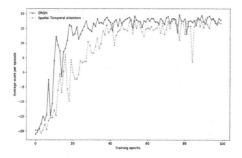

Fig. 3. DRQN and DRQN with spatial temporal attention in MDPs

2   Conclusions

In this paper, a novel model with attention and memory mechanisms was proposed. It was showed that the performance of the model was marginally better than the other model in a partially observable version of Pong, although did not show any improvements in the fully observable case. Since none of the algorithms manage to converge in the flickering domain for less than 5 million steps, more trials would have to be carried in order to ascertain that attention is key for partial observability. The authors are currently working towards the following directions (1) experimenting with extended tests covering 100 million steps or more, so that to ensure agents converge and the varying complexity of the environments is not a factor, (2) employing different environments such as those which are inherently partially observable since flickering a screen may not in fact adequately represent a noisy state since they are either fully observable or fully occulted, (3) Adopting other techniques such as neural episodic learning [15] where very valuable experience tuples are replayed multiple times. Other approaches with hard attention [13] or global approaches [10] may be taken.

References

1. On improving deep reinforcement learning for pomdps. CoRR abs/1804.06309 (2018), http://arxiv.org/abs/1804.06309, withdrawn
2. Ba, J., Grosse, R.B., Salakhutdinov, R.R., Frey, B.J.: Learning wake-sleep recurrent attention models. In: NIPS (2015)
3. Bellman, R.E.: A markovian decision process. In: MDP (1957)
4. Doherty, J.R., Rao, A., Mesulam, M.M., Nobre, A.C.: Synergistic effect of combined temporal and spatial expectations on visual attention. J. Neurosci.: Official J. Soc. Neurosci. **25**(36), 8259–8266 (2005)
5. Fu, Y., Wang, X., Wei, Y., Huang, T.S.: STA: Spatial-temporal attention for large-scale video-based person re-identification. CoRR abs/1811.04129 (2019)
6. Hausknecht, M.J., Stone, P.: Deep recurrent q-learning for partially observable MDPs. In: AAAI Fall Symposia (2015)
7. Igl, M., Zintgraf, L., Le, T.A., Wood, F., Whiteson, S.: Deep variational reinforcement learning for POMDPs. In: Dy, J., Krause, A. (eds.) Proceedings of the 35th International Conference on Machine Learning. Proceedings of Machine Learning Research, vol. 80, pp. 2117–2126. PMLR, Stockholmsmässan, Stockholm Sweden, 10–15 July 2018. http://proceedings.mlr.press/v80/igl18a.html
8. Kingma, D.P., Ba, J.: Adam: A method for stochastic optimization. CoRR abs/1412.6980 (2015)
9. LeCun, Y., Bengio, Y., Hinton, G.: Deep learning. Nature **521**(7553), 436 (2015)
10. Luong, T., Pham, H., Manning, C.D.: Effective approaches to attention-based neural machine translation. In: EMNLP (2015)
11. MacKay, A., Juola, J.F.: Are spatial and temporal attention independent? Percept. Psychophysics **69**(6), 972–979 (2007)
12. Meng, L., Zhao, B., Chang, B., Huang, G., Tung, F., Sigal, L.: Where and when to look? Spatio-temporal attention for action recognition in videos. CoRR abs/1810.04511 (2018)

13. Mnih, V., Heess, N., Graves, A., Kavukcuoglu, K.: Recurrent models of visual attention. In: Proceedings of the 27th International Conference on Neural Information Processing Systems - Volume 2, pp. 2204–2212. NIPS 2014, MIT Press, Cambridge, MA, USA (2014). http://dl.acm.org/citation.cfm?id=2969033.2969073

14. Mnih, V., et al.: Human-level control through deep reinforcement learning. Nature **518**, 529–533 (2015)

15. Pritzel, A., et al.: Neural episodic control. In: Precup, D., Teh, Y.W. (eds.) Proceedings of the 34th International Conference on Machine Learning. Proceedings of Machine Learning Research, vol. 70, pp. 2827–2836. PMLR, International Convention Centre, Sydney, Australia, 06–11 Aug 2017. http://proceedings.mlr.press/v70/pritzel17a.html

16. Roijers, D.M., Whiteson, S., Oliehoek, F.A.: Point-based planning for multi-objective POMDPs. In: Proceedings of the 24th International Conference on Artificial Intelligence, pp. 1666–1672. IJCAI 2015, AAAI Press (2015). http://dl.acm.org/citation.cfm?id=2832415.2832481

17. Ross, S., Pineau, J., Paquet, S., Chaib-draa, B.: Online planning algorithms for POMDPs. J. Artif. Int. Res. **32**(1), 663–704 (2008). http://dl.acm.org/citation.cfm?id=1622673.1622690

18. Song, J., Guo, Z., Gao, L., Liu, W., Zhang, D., Shen, H.T.: Hierarchical LSTM with adjusted temporal attention for video captioning. In: IJCAI (2017)

19. Song, S., Lan, C., Xing, J., Zeng, W., Liu, J.: Spatio-temporal attention-based lstm networks for 3D action recognition and detection. IEEE Trans. Image Proc. **27**(7), 3459–3471 (2018). https://doi.org/10.1109/TIP.2018.2818328

20. Song, S., Lan, C., Xing, J., Zeng, W., Liu, J.: An end-to-end spatio-temporal attention model for human action recognition from skeleton data (2017)

21. Sorokin, I., Seleznev, A., Pavlov, M., Fedorov, A., Ignateva, A.: Deep attention recurrent Q-network. CoRR abs/1512.01693 (2015)

22. Werbos, P.J.: Backpropagation through time: what it does and how to do it (1990)

23. Xu, K., et al.: Show, attend and tell: Neural image caption generation with visual attention. In: ICML (2015)

24. Yan, S., Smith, J., Lu, W., Zhang, B.: Hierarchical multi-scale attention networks for action recognition. Signal Processing Image Communication, vol. 61, August 2017. https://doi.org/10.1016/j.image.2017.11.005

25. Zhu, Z., Wu, W., Zou, W., Yan, J.: End-to-end flow correlation tracking with spatial-temporal attention. In: 2018 IEEE/CVF Conference on Computer Vision and Pattern Recognition, pp. 548–557 (2018)

Artificial Intelligence and IoT in Agriculture

Vineyard Segmentation from Satellite Imagery Using Machine Learning

Luís Santos[1,2(✉)], Filipe N. Santos[1], Vitor Filipe[1,2], and Pranjali Shinde[1]

[1] INESC TEC - INESC Technology and Science, Porto, Portugal
{luis.c.santos,fbnsantos,pranjali.shinde}@inesctec.pt
[2] UTAD - University of Trás-os-Montes e Alto Douro, Vila Real, Portugal
vfilipe@utad.pt

Abstract. Steep slope vineyards are a complex scenario for the development of ground robots due to the harsh terrain conditions and unstable localization systems. Automate vineyard tasks (like monitoring, pruning, spraying, and harvesting) requires advanced robotic path planning approaches. These approaches usually resort to Simultaneous Localization and Mapping (SLAM) techniques to acquire environment information, which requires previous navigation of the robot through the entire vineyard. The analysis of satellite or aerial images could represent an alternative to SLAM techniques, to build the first version of occupation grid map (needed by robots). The state of the art for aerial vineyard images analysis is limited to flat vineyards with straight vine's row. This work considers a machine learning based approach (SVM classifier with Local Binary Pattern (LBP) based descriptor) to perform the vineyard segmentation from public satellite imagery. In the experiments with a dataset of satellite images from vineyards of Douro region, the proposed method achieved accuracy over 90%.

Keywords: Vineyard · Satellite images · Machine learning · Agricultural robotics · Path planning

1 Introduction

The steep slope vineyards placed in the Douro Demarcated region (Portugal), UNESCO Heritage place, presents unique characteristics, which includes a number of robotic challenges. These challenges need to be overcomed so as to obtain a fully autonomous navigation system. Its unique characteristics present challenges in diverse robotic areas such as visual perception, localization, environmental modelling, control or decision making. An accurate map and localization system is crucial for safe autonomous navigation on the vineyard. However, Global Navigation Satellite Systems (GNSS) are not reliable, since the signal is constantly blocked by the hills. Dead reckoning sensors are also affected by harsh terrain conditions. Thus, VineSLAM algorithm [3] was proposed in the previous work. VineSLAM is a GNSS-freebase localization and mapping system for steep slope

© Springer Nature Switzerland AG 2019
P. Moura Oliveira et al. (Eds.): EPIA 2019, LNAI 11804, pp. 109–120, 2019.
https://doi.org/10.1007/978-3-030-30241-2_10

vineyard. This algorithm is based on the detection of natural features like trunks, performed with ViTruDe (Vineyard Trunks Detector), a tool to detect natural features in vineyards [4]. The mentioned approach for mapping, like any other SLAM approach, requires the robot to be physically available for navigation in the terrain. This represents an inconvenience for large dimension terrains like steep slope vineyards in Douro Region, for example, Sogrape wine production at "Quinta do Seixo" relies on 71 ha of vineyard [5]. The mapping process with a ground robot would result in a hugely time-consuming task which may be a market barrier for the robot. An alternative relies on detecting the rows of the vineyard from aerial/satellite imagery to construct a map ready for path planning of Autonomous Ground Robots (AGV).

This task requires two stages: segmentation of vineyards from satellite/aerial images; and processing of vineyards regions in order to detect paths between vegetation from which is built the occupation grid map. This article focuses on the first stage. This work considers a machine learning based approach (SVM classifier with Local Binary Pattern (LBP) based descriptor) to perform the vineyard segmentation from public satellite imagery. Besides, this approach is able to identify vineyards or to perform a more advanced classification considering other classes (such as roads or trees). In contrast to deep learning based approaches, which require large data-sets [6], our approach requires less training images and it is more time efficient during the training process.

Section 2 presents related work to path planning and agricultural image processing from aerial or satellite imagery. Section 3 describes the proposed machine learning approach for vineyard detection and Sect. 4 contains the results of the vineyard segmentation. The paper conclusions are presented in Sect. 5.

2   Related Work

Path planning consists in the task of finding the best possible path between two points, being that the definition of best path changes according to the required task. There are several path planning approaches such as potential field planners, RRT (Rapidly-exploring Random Tree), and grid map based search algorithms like Dijkstra or A*. [1, 2] Usually, path planning algorithms require a map with the environment characteristics (obstacles), and image analysis of aerial or satellite images could simplify the mapping process. The detection of vegetation characteristics resorting to aerial imagery is a recurrent topic with several works for diverse agricultural cultures. Works with Images obtained by Unmanned Aerial Vehicles (UAV) are predominant, but there are some approaches with very high-resolution satellite imagery. Mougel et al. [7] resorts to this type of images for tree crops monitoring performing tests with a regular vineyard and a peach groove to identify patterns. Karakizi et al. [8] also proposes a vineyard detection tool which extracts the vine canopy with very high-resolution satellite data. Torres et al. [9] presents a 3D monitoring tool with UAV technology. In the first stage, a digital surface model is created. This is followed by the Object-Based Image Analysis (OBIA) techniques used to extract several features from the vegetation such as canopy area, tree height and crop row position. OBIA is based on Otsu method. This is used to detect, classify, and perform automatic threshold in plantations of maize, wheat and sunflower with images captured from conventional and multispectral cameras placed in a UAV [11]. OBIA is also the chosen method for a cropland mapping tool with aircraft imagery. Different lands are identified with geographical object-based image analysis and random forest classification [10]. The Hough transform method is a technique for detecting patterns of points such as lines or parametric curves. This technique is widely used for crop rows detection either with aerial images or ground images [12] given that most of the plantations are disposed in straight lines. Ortiz *et al.* [13,14] proposes systems for weed mapping in crops using UAV imagery. In order to improve weed discrimination, the relative position of the weeds is given with respect to crop lines. Therefore, the authors present an accurate method to detect the crop in rows based on the Hough transform. Crop row detection is also a common case study for vineyards, resorting to different types of approaches. Smit *et al.* [15] developed a method to detect vine blocks, rows, and individual vines. The segmentation process is made with a combination of threshold and graph-based technique from multispectral images. Delenne *et al.* [16] provides a methodology for vineyard delineation using aerial images with a row extraction tool. This tool assumes that the rows are parallel and starts by filling the parcel with a high number of orientated lines, eliminating the false rows with a local minima identification. Further, to extract vine canopy vine rows, a study was performed comparing the following four methods: k-means cluster, artificial neural network, random forest and spectral indices, concluding that k-means method had the lowest performance while other methods had a satisfactory performance [17]. A skeletonization method with high resolution unmanned aerial systems (UAS) imagery was considered to reduce the complexity of agricultural scenes, simplifying the classification of features like vine rows [18]. Comba *et al.* [19] developed a work similar to the approach proposed in our work. With an image processing algorithm constituted by three steps (dynamic segmentation, Hough space clustering and total least squares), the authors are capable of segment vine rows in aerial images. The final result is an image liable to use as a map for path planning algorithms in AGVs. However, this is applied to a normal vineyard, without relevant slopes and total straight vine rows. In fact, all of the crop row detection state of the art address problems of straight line vegetation. Steep slope vineyards have the characteristics containing high slope terrains with curve vine rows. To the best of our knowledge, there are no approaches to segment steep slope vineyards which contain high sloppy terrains and inconstant vegetation curvatures.

3   Proposed Model for Vineyard Segmentation

The classification task was based on a Support Vector Machine (SVM) classifier running on ROS (Robot Operating System)[1]. A Region Descriptor is extracted

---

[1] ROS - http://www.ros.org/.

and used as input for the SVM classifier. Based on the training step, this tool is able to classify each image pixel according to the desired class objects. Figure 1 illustrates a diagram with information flow of the classification process. The descriptor is based in LBP (Local Binary Pattern) codes, a grey-level invariant texture primitive. The non-parametric LBP operator was introduced by Ojala *et al.* [20,21] for textured image description. The Original LBP works in a grid size of 3×3 for a given arbitrary pixel over an input grey-level image. The LBP code is computed by comparing the grey-level value of the centre pixel and its neighbours within the respective grid. The grey-value of the neighbouring pixels not covered by the grids are estimated by interpolation. The threshold stage is carried out with respect to the centre pixel, resulting in a binary number called LBP code. To describe the image texture, a LBP histogram (hLBP) is built from all binary patterns of each image pixel, as shown in Eq. (1), where K is the maximal LBP pattern value. Based on hLBP, two types of descriptors are constructed: *hLBP by colour* and *hLBP plus colour*, Fig. 2.

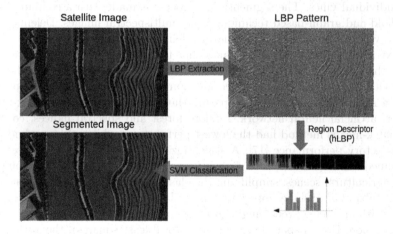

Fig. 1. Information flow of the classification process

$$
\begin{cases}
H(k) = \sum_{m=1}^{M} \sum_{n=1}^{N} f(LBP_{P,R}(m,n), \ k), & k \in [0, K] \\
f(x,y) = \begin{cases} 1, & x = y \\ 0, & otherwise \end{cases}
\end{cases}
\tag{1}
$$

The *hLBP by colour* contains one LBP histogram per colour, discretizing the colour ranges into n colours in RGB (Red, Green and Blue) space. The length of this descriptor is calculated with the multiplication between the number of LBP codes and the number of colour ranges. The LBP uniform variant is selected with 8 colour ranges. Considering $LBP_{8,2}^u$, the descriptor size has $59 \times 8 = 472$ bins. With this descriptor, the extractor in each pixel detects the related colour range and increments the histogram bin related to the LBP code extracted for

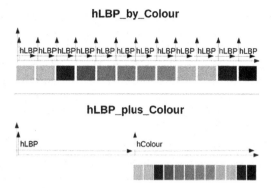

Fig. 2. Two descriptors selected: *hLBP by Colour* and *hLBP plus Colour* [4]

that pixel. *hLBP plus colour* is composed of two histograms, one for LBP codes and other for colour ranges. Its length is given by the number of LBP codes plus the number of colour ranges. Considering the $LBP_{8,2}$ with 8 colour ranges, the descriptor size is $256 + 8 = 264$ bins. With this descriptor, the extractor detects in each pixel the related colour range and increments the histogram bin related to that colour. Then, the pixel LBP code is extracted to increment the histogram bin related to that code [4].

These descriptors (*hLBP plus colour* and *hLBP by colour*) will feed a SVM classifier. SVM is a machine learning approach usually suited for two-group classification problems. The concept implements the following idea: input vector are non-linearly mapped to a high-dimension feature space. In this feature space, a linear decision surface is constructed [22]. Considering a problem of separating the set of training data $(x_1, y_1), ...(x_m, y_m)$ into two classes, where $x_i \in \mathbb{R}$ is a feature vector and $y_i \in \{-1, +1\}$ its class label. Assuming that the two classes can be separated by a hyperplane $w \cdot x + b = 0$ in some space $\mathbb{H}$, the optimal hyperplane is the one that maximizes the margin. A more detailed explanation about the SVM theory and libSVM (one of its variants implementation) is described by Chang *et al.* [23]. Although the SVM is originally designed for binary classification, there are extensions for multi-class scenarios. Typically the problem is decomposed into a series of two class problems, for which one-against-all is the earliest and one of the most widely used implementations [24].

4   Tests and Results

The *hLBP by colour* contains one LBP histogram per colour, discretizing the colour ranges into n colours in RGB (Red, Green and Blue) space. The length of this descriptor is calculated with the multiplication between the number of LBP codes and the number of colour ranges. The LBP uniform variant is selected with 8 colour ranges. Considering $LBP_{8,2}^{u}$, the descriptor size has $59 \times 8 = 472$ bins. With this descriptor, the extractor in each pixel detects the related colour range and increments the histogram bin related to the LBP code extracted for that pixel. *hLBP plus colour* is composed of just two histograms, one for LBP codes and other for colour ranges. Its length is given by the number of LBP codes plus the number of colour ranges. Considering the $LBP_{8,2}$ with 8 colour ranges, the descriptor size is $256 + 8 = 264$ bins. With this descriptor, the extractor detects in each pixel the related colour range and increments the histogram bin related to that colour. Then, the pixel LBP code is extracted to increment the histogram bin related to that code [4].

These descriptors (*hLBP plus colour* and *hLBP by colour*) will feed a SVM classifier. SVM is a machine learning approach usually suited for two-group classification problems. The concept implements the following idea: input vector are non-linearly mapped to a high-dimension feature space. In this feature space, a linear decision surface is constructed [22]. Considering a problem of separating the set of training data $(x_1, y_1), ... (x_m, y_m)$ into two classes, where $x_i \in \mathbb{R}$ is a feature vector and $y_i \in \{-1, +1\}$ its class label. Assuming that the two classes can be separated by a hyperplane $w \cdot x + b = 0$ in some space $\mathbb{H}$, the optimal hyperplane is the one that maximizes the margin. A more detailed explanation about the SVM theory and libSVM (one of its variants implementation) is described by Chang *et al.* [23]. Although the SVM is originally designed for binary classification, there are extensions for multi-class scenarios. Typically the problem is decomposed into a series of two class problems, for which one-against-all is the earliest and one of the most widely used implementations [24].

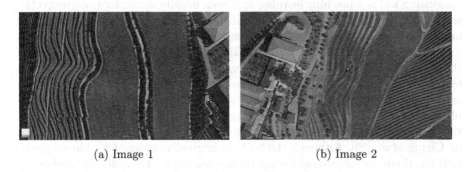

(a) Image 1   (b) Image 2

Fig. 3. Satellite Images considered for vineyard detection

4.1   Vineyard Detection with Two Classes

In this stage the SVM was trained to identify two classes from the satellite images: The "Vineyard" class contains different types of steep slope vineyard cultures such as traditional, one-line, two-line, terrace vineyards. The "Others" class contains roads, houses, river or other cultures. For this purpose, a data set was built with several sub-images belonging to the two classes, as specified in 1. In general, the number of images for the class "Vineyard" is larger due to the richness of wine cultures in the Douro Region. A bigger area was covered to obtain the images of the class "Others" in order to avoid a larger difference of images between the two classes. Some samples of these images are represented in Fig. 4. However, not all the images are used in the training process of the SVM. Some images are taken from the data set to test their accuracy after the training. The result of the algorithm accuracy test is shown in Table 1, where the tests of the SVM classifier are performed by running the detection with the test images of the data set.

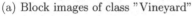

(a) Block images of class "Vineyard"   (b) Block images of class "Others"

Fig. 4. Samples of Image Blocks for SVM train and test

Table 1. Number of images available for the SVM train and test process

Classes	No of images	Train images	Test images	SVM classification test accuracy				
				hLBP_by_colour		Accuracy (%)	hLBP_plus_colour		Accuracy (%)
				Vineyard	Others		Vineyard	Others	
Vineyard	1310	1138	172	169	3	98	167	5	97
Others	1141	1028	113	4	109	96	5	108	95

Table 1 presents the training accuracy based on some images from the training dataset. In the classification of sub-images from the class "Vineyard", 5 images were classified as "Other", giving an accuracy of approximately 97%. However, this is based only in a small set of random sub-images selected to perform the test. To calculate the accuracy after running the detection, each image pixel will be compared to the same pixel in a ground truth image, revealing if that pixel was correctly identified. The results are expressed in Table 2, where TP and FP are True Positive and False Positive respectively. This table presents the accuracy and the metric F1 score common for binary classification problems. This metric combines, with a harmonic mean, Precision and Recall metrics. Recall is the number of items correctly identified as positive ("Vineyard") out of the total true positives ("Vineyard" and false "Others"). Precision is the number of items correctly identified as positive ("Vineyard") out of the total items identified as positive ("Vineyard" and false "Vineyard") [25]. So the maximum Recall minimizes false negative (false "Others") while maximum Precision minimizes false positives (false "Vineyard"). The segmentation results have an average accuracy of 90.05% with the descriptor *hLBP by Colour* and 86.9% with the descriptor *hLBP plus Colour*. The F1 score is also greater with the first descriptor, indicating that the number of false classifications is bigger with *hLBP by Colour*.

The images presented in Fig. 3 were considered to run the SVM classifier and the results are expressed in Fig. 5 using the descriptor *hLBP by Colour* and in Fig. 6 using the descriptor *hLBP plus Colour*. The colour map is related to the probability of each pixel to belong to the class "Vineyard" where blue represents the lowest probability and red the highest.

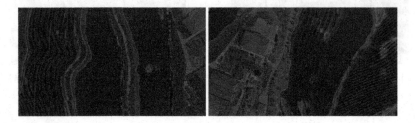

Fig. 5. Detection Results in colour map of class Vineyard using *hLBP by colour*: Blue: Low probability; Yellow: Medium probability; Red: High probability (Color figure online)

Table 2. Detection accuracy with ground truth image for two classes detection

	Classes	hLBP by colour		Accuracy (%)	F1 Score	hLBP plus colour		Accuracy (%)	F1 Score
		TP	FP			TP	FP		
Image 1	Vineyard	240857	16291	**92.4**	0.934	222690	25605	**89.6**	0.912
	Others	167320	17389			144096	17192		
Image 2	Vineyard	257025	7336	**87.7**	0.942	264691	11761	**84.2**	0.941
	Others	15667	24124			151251	21579		

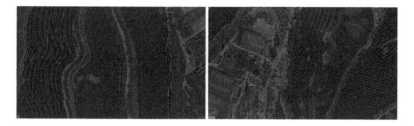

Fig. 6. Detection Results in colour map of class Vineyard using *hLBP plus colour*: Blue: Low probability; Yellow: Medium probability; Red: High probability (Color figure online)

4.2 Vineyard Detection with Four Classes

The extraction of more information from the satellite images, such as roads (for car traffic) or trees plantation, could be useful for other agricultural information systems. So, the SVM was trained considering four classes: Vineyard, Roads, Trees and Others. A new data set was created for the train and test process, with several images representing each class (Table 3). For this stage, only the descriptor *hLBP by colour* was considered, as the other descriptor has been shown to be less accurate in the preliminary experiments.

Table 3. Number of images available for the SVM train and test process and SVM test accuracy

Classes	No of images	Train images	Test images	SVM classification test				
				Vineyard	Trees	Road	Others	Accuracy (%)
Vineyard	1251	1091	160	153	4	1	2	96
Trees	433	393	40	2	38	0	0	95
Road	220	200	20	1	0	17	2	85
Others	294	242	52	2	2	0	48	92

The results are exposed in Fig. 7, where each class is represented by its corresponding colour. The accuracy details for each class are described in Table 4, where TP and FP represent True positive and False Positive respectively. The average accuracy for the classes "Vineyard" and "Others" is 87.6% while the detection in classes "Trees" and "Roads" have lower accuracy. One of the reasons for these results could be present in the resolution of the image, which might be too low to detect such details. The reduced number of images in the training data-set for the class "Road" also explains the poor classification results.

Fig. 7. Detection Results with 4 classes: Green - Vineyard; Blue - Trees; Yellow - Road; Red - Others (Color figure online)

Table 4. Detection accuracy with ground truth image for four classes detection

Classes	Image 1		Accuracy (%)	Image 2		Accuracy (%)
	TP	FP		TP	FP	
Vineyard	356779	22936	**94**	341577	56412	**85.8**
Trees	84939	62139	**57.8**	28906	39848	**42**
Road	7966	17277	**31.6**	16137	24173	**40**
Other	24129	7142	**77.2**	61666	4355	**93.4**

5   Conclusions

The proposed approach is capable to perform the segmentation of steep slope vineyard considering image satellite. The vineyard detection has an accuracy higher than 86% for all the performed tests, while for other classes the accuracy decreases. This happens because the training data set has more vineyard images than other images classes (roads, trees). The two proposed descriptors imply different results, where *hLBP by Colour* is more accurate than *hLBP plus Colour*. However, *hLBP plus Colour* has almost half of the size, decreasing the computational cost, not relevant for this kind of applications. Considering the simple case - single class classification - the detection accuracy reaches 92.4% with *hLBP by Colour*, and 89.6% with *hLBP plus Colour*.

Considering the approach using four classes, the classes "Vineyards" and "Others" accuracy was higher than 86% and 77%. The other two classes (Roads and trees) got a maximum accuracy of 58%. This happened due to the lower number of images available for the training data set.

As future work, this approach will be extended with the second stage - detection of paths between vegetation, that is, the free space between vine trees for robot's navigation. This will be useful for path planning tasks in autonomous ground robots. By detecting the vegetation and the free paths is possible to extract an occupation grid map for path planning algorithms, avoiding time-consuming for Robot setup of SLAM operations. To accomplish this, a more detailed classification will be performed in the segmented images of this article. The same SVM classifier will be tested using lower resolution images for the training step, and possibly a different region descriptor, i.e., HSV (hue, saturation and brightness) colour. Images with higher resolution or even different wave ranges (Normalised Difference Vegetation Index (NDVI)) will be tested.

Acknowledgements. This work is financed by the ERDF – European Regional Development Fund through the Operational Programme for Competitiveness and Internationalisation - COMPETE 2020 Programme within project POCI-01-0145-FEDER-006961, and by National Funds through the FCT – Fundação para a Ciência e a Tecnologia (Portuguese Foundation for Science and Technology) as part of project UID/EEA/50014/2013 and by through ANI - Agência Nacional de Inovação (Portuguese National Agency of Innovation) as part of project "ROMOVI: POCI-01-0247-FEDER-017945".

References

1. Coelho, F.O., Carvalho, J.P., Pinto, M.F., Marcato, A.L.: Direct-DRRT*: a RRT improvement proposal. In: 2018 13th APCA International Conference on Control and Soft Computing (CONTROLO), pp. 154–158. IEEE (2018)
2. Santos, L., et al.: Path planning aware of soil compaction for steep slope vineyards. In: 2018 IEEE International Conference on Autonomous Robot Systems and Competitions (ICARSC), pp. 250–255. IEEE (2018)
3. Santos, F.N., Sobreira, H., Campos, D., Morais, R., Moreira, A.P., Contente, O.: Towards a reliable robot for steep slope vineyards monitoring. J. Intell. Robotic Syst. **83**(3–4), 429–444 (2016)
4. Mendes, J., dos Santos, F.N., Ferraz, N., Couto, P., Morais, R.: Vine trunk detector for a reliable robot localization system. In: 2016 IEEE International Conference on Autonomous Robot Systems and Competitions (ICARSC), pp. 1–6. https://doi.org/10.1109/ICARSC.2016.68
5. Sogrape Wines. https://eng.sograpevinhos.com/regioes/Douro/locais/Quinta%20do%20Seixo. Accessed 18 June 2019
6. Kamilaris, A., Prenafeta, F.X.: Deep learning in agriculture: a survey. Comput. Electron. Agric. **147**, 70–90 (2018)
7. Mougel, B., Lelong, C., Nicolas, J.M.: Classification and information extraction in very high resolution satellite images for tree crops monitoring. In: Remote sensing for a changing Europe. Proceedings of the 28th Symposium of the European Association of Remote Sensing Laboratories, Istanbul, pp. 73–79 (2009)
8. Karakizi, C., Oikonomou, M., Karantzalos, K.: Vineyard detection and vine variety discrimination from very high resolution satellite data. Remote Sens. **8**(3), 235 (2016)
9. Sánchez, J., Granados, F., Serrano, N., Arquero, O., Peña, J.M.: High-throughput 3-D monitoring of agricultural-tree plantations with unmanned aerial vehicle (UAV) technology. PloS ONE **10**(6), e0130479 (2015)
10. Vogels, M.F.A., Jong, S.M., Sterk, G., Addink, E.A.: Agricultural cropland mapping using black-and-white aerial photography, object-based image analysis and random forests. Int. J. Appl. Earth Obs. Geoinf. **54**, 114–123 (2017)
11. Sánchez, J., Granados, F., Peña, J.M.: An automatic object-based method for optimal thresholding in UAV images: application for vegetation detection in herbaceous crops. Comput. Electron. Agric. **114**, 43–52 (2015)

12. Rovira, F., Zhang, Q., Reid, J.F., Will, J.D.: Hough-transform-based vision algorithm for crop row detection of an automated agricultural vehicle. Proc. Inst. Mech. Eng. Part D J. Automobile Eng. **219**(8), 999–1010 (2005)
13. Ortiz, M., Peña, J.M., Gutiérrez, P.A., Torres-Sánchez, J., Martínez, C., Granados, F.: A semi-supervised system for weed mapping in sunflower crops using unmanned aerial vehicles and a crop row detection method. Appl. Soft Comput. **37**, 533–544 (2015)
14. Ortiz, M., Gutierrez, P.A., Pena, J.M., Sanchez, J., Granados, F., Martinez, C.: Machine learning paradigms for weed mapping via unmanned aerial vehicles. In: 2016 IEEE Symposium Series on Computational Intelligence (SSCI), pp. 1–8. IEEE (2016)
15. Smit, J.L., Sithole, G., Strever, A.E.: Vine signal extraction-an application of remote sensing in precision viticulture. S. Afr. J. Enol. Viticulture **31**(2), 65–74 (2010)
16. Delenne, C., Durrieu, S., Rabatel, G., Deshayes, M.: From pixel to vine parcel: a complete methodology for vineyard delineation and characterization using remote-sensing data. Comput. Electron. Agric. **70**(1), 78–83 (2010)
17. Echeverría, C., Olmedo, G.F., Ingram, B., Bardeen, M.: Detection and segmentation of vine canopy in ultra-high spatial resolution RGB imagery obtained from unmanned aerial vehicle (UAV): a case study in a commercial vineyard. Remote Sens. **9**(3), 268 (2017)
18. Nolan, A.P., Park, S., Fuentes, S., Ryu, D., Chung, H.: Automated detection and segmentation of vine rows using high resolution UAS imagery in a commercial vineyard. In Proceedings of the 21st International Congress on Modelling and Simulation, Gold Coast, Australia, vol. 29, pp. 1406–1412, November 2015
19. Comba, L., Gay, P., Primicerio, J., Aimonino, D.R.: Vineyard detection from unmanned aerial systems images. Comput. Electron. Agric. **114**, 78–87 (2015)
20. Harwood, D., Ojala, T., Pietikäinen, M., Kelman, S., Davis, L.: Texture classification by center-symmetric auto-correlation, using Kullback discrimination of distributions. Pattern Recogn. Lett. **16**(1), 1–10 (1995)
21. Ojala, T., Pietikäinen, M., Harwood, D.: A comparative study of texture measures with classification based on featured distributions. Pattern Recogn. **29**(1), 51–59 (1996)
22. Cortes, C., Vapnik, V.: Support-vector networks. Mach. Learn. **20**(3), 273–297 (1995)
23. Chang, C.-C., Lin, C.-J.: LIBSVM : a library for support vector machines. ACM Trans. Intell. Syst. Technol. **2**, 27:1–27:27 (2011)
24. Liu, Y., Zheng, Y.F.: One-against-all multi-class SVM classification using reliability measures. In: Proceedings. 2005 IEEE International Joint Conference on Neural Networks, 2005, vol. 2, pp. 849–854. IEEE, July 2005
25. Espejo, B., Pellicer, F.J., Lacasta, J., Moreno, R.P., Soria, F.J.: End-to-end sequence labeling via deep learning for automatic extraction of agricultural regulations. Comput. Electron. Agric. **162**, 106–111 (2019)

Estimation of Vineyard Productivity Map Considering a Cost-Effective LIDAR-Based Sensor

Pedro Moura[1(✉)], Daniela Ribeiro[2], Filipe Neves dos Santos[1], Alberto Gomes[2], Ricardo Baptista[3], and Mario Cunha[1]

[1] INESC TEC - INESC Technology and Science, Porto, Portugal
pedro.h.moura@inesctec.pt
[2] FLUP - Faculty of Letters, University of Porto, Porto, Portugal
[3] FEUP - Faculty of Engineering, University of Porto, Porto, Portugal

Abstract. Viticulturists need to obtain the estimation of productivity map during the grape vine harvesting, to understand in detail the vineyard variability. An accurate productivity map will support the farmer to take more informed and accurate intervention in the vineyard in line with the precision viticulture concept. This work presents a novel solution to measure the productivity during vineyard harvesting operation realized by a grape harvesting machine. We propose 2D LIDAR sensor attached to low cost IoT module located inside the harvesting machine, to estimate the volume of grapes. Besides, it is proposed data methodology to process data collected and productivity map, considering GIS software, expecting to support the winemakers decisions. A PCD map is also used to validate the method developed by comparison.

Keywords: Agricultural IoT · Productivity maps · GIS

1 Introduction

The Portuguese vineyard regions are world renowned for its high quality patterns in wine production. This tradition has been extended for centuries and has been producing cultural landscapes that reflects the technical, social and economical evolution of the region.

Nowadays, the Portuguese vineyards are commonly characterized by their slopes and high stony soil shale that make of its cultivation authentic but difficult. Despite the techniques that have been adapted to the viticulture, the complexity that comes from these typical environmental conditions conducts to a low efficient of both labour and machinery and, consequently, to a low economic profitability. In order to improve the economic efficiency of vineyards, it should be considered an optimization to the management of the resources and the production data, based on recent knowledge and technology. The opportunity to support the winemakers decisions in rigorous and detailed productivity

© Springer Nature Switzerland AG 2019
P. Moura Oliveira et al. (Eds.): EPIA 2019, LNAI 11804, pp. 121–133, 2019.
https://doi.org/10.1007/978-3-030-30241-2_11

maps, can benefit the qualitative and quantitative levels of wine production [1]. In this context, solutions, as the implementation of load sensors combined with georeferencing techniques, have achieved some importance, during the last years, to evaluate the productivity of the vineyard.

This work aims to test a different solution to measure the productivity along each part of the vineyard, based on a LIDAR sensor located inside the harvest machine, We expected the solution can be able to measure the volume of production by detecting the height and shape of the grape load that is being accumulated. The data collected is processed and mapped, to allow the winemakers to understand and manage the variability of the productivity within the vineyard.

This paper is subdivided into six sections. Section 2 presents the related work, regarding methods to acquire the productivity map. Section 3 presents the proposed solution and hardware setup. Section 4 presents the algorithms to process data acquired by LIDAR sensor. Section 5 presents the results obtained. Finally, conclusions and future work to improve these results are referred into the last section.

2   Related Work

In the last decades, different techniques have been introduced to get an estimation of the vineyard productivity. Several measures, as bunches per vine, berries per bunch and weight of the berries have been used as output of different approaches. One of them is the manual counting of the productivity components, which is used in different regions of the world. Champagne and Cognac are example of that. Both are based in occasional sampling that limits its use for construction of productivity maps [3]. Focusing on another approach [2], the authors analyzed the variation of the tension of the vine bard wires and used it to extrapolate the production in time and space. However, this method still does not present sufficient results that reinforce its rigor in the quantitative analysis and its operability is difficult to achieve.

Recently, processing image approaches have been considered on the estimation process. Following this evolution, [6] proposed a set of procedures to measure the productivity by the direct analysis of the vine. A camera located in a side of a vehicle allowed to capture the images and map them along the vineyard trails. During this process, the grapes are detected with high detail, independently of its colour. Many other researchers have followed the processing image area, diversifying the sensors used [4,5]. Based on these studies, it is possible to verify that there are some limitations in the separation of grape bunches from the environment. Components as leafs and trunks can be in the origin of that challenge. Also the shape of the bunches and the lighting conditions can difficult the process. To solve this problems, the authors in [4] implemented technologies that allow to acquire night images. It was possible to overcome some obstacles, however as the image acquisition complexity increases, the difficulty of operation also increases.

The use of grape harvesting machines equipped with load sensors has also been growing up until the recent days. The information that comes from it when combined with georeferencing techniques allows the construction of productivity maps. A study done by the researchers in [1] followed this approach and, gathering a load sensor, a GPS antenna, a refractometer and a temperature sensor, it made possible to evaluate the machine performance and the vineyard productivity.

In order to synthesize the studies done until 2016, in [7] is made a review about the performance monitors that has been used in the harvesting machines. Solutions based in ultrasonic sensors and load sensors are analyzed. Focusing in the first one, the sensor was placed in the top of the container, allowing the measure of the grapes volume inside of it. If it is required collect the mass values of production, a conversion between volumetric and mass measurements has to be done, using the grape density coefficient. The need of that conversion is described as a disadvantage, as soon as the density coefficient varies with the berry size and grape moisture content. Errors will be introduced on the mass output if the coefficient remains constant. The load sensors, for its part, are strongly influenced by the displacement and vibrations of the machine as well as the slope of the vineyard. The measures are affected with some noise that can be reduced applying Kalman filters to the measures.

3   Hardware

The focus of this work is the vineyard production volume calculation, based on the container filling variations. A New Holland harvesting machine, shown in Fig. 1, was used for perform the tests.

Fig. 1. New Holland harvesting machine used for tests.

A LIDAR-Lite v1 sensor was placed inside the harvesting machine, on top of the container, connected to a servo-motor and to an AgIoT board, Fig. 2a,

(agiot.inesctec.pt). The first one can be described as a proximity and range sensor
that allows to measure the distance from the sensor to the object. Since it was
connected to a servo-motor, laser beams are fired with a wide range of about
115° and interleaved by three degrees, the reflections are caught and the measures
of distance between the sensor and the grapes are obtained. Considering that
distance and the height of the sensor from the base of the container, the height
and shape of the set of grapes are known, in the plan of the laser beam.

The AgIoT board combines the use of an ATMega32u4 microcontroller and
an Omega 2p microcomputer, aiming to control the servo-motor and collect the
data that comes from the sensor. The components were stored in the same box,
as shown in Fig. 2b.

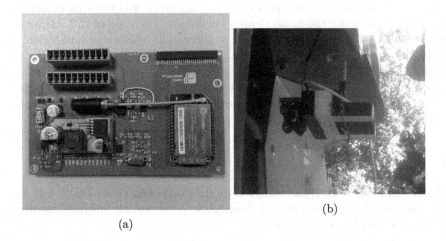

(a)   (b)

Fig. 2. (a) AgIoT board. (b) Integrated system between LIDAR, servo-motor and
AgIoT board.

4   Methodology

4.1   Production Volume Calculation

The hardware described in Sect. 3 and shown in Fig. 2b was implemented in the
harvesting machine and it was used for a sequence of tests during the grapes
collection season. Some logs were created to store the following data:

- Time stamp.
- Vineyard GPS position.
- Velocity of the harvester machine.
- Sensor orientation and correspondent distance measured.

Considering the sensor orientation, θ, and the distance, d, measured to the grape with a laser beam, the calculation of (x,y) coordinates became possible. Using the referential 1 presented in Fig. 3, the coordinates were calculated based on the formulas 1.

$$X_{1,G} = d * sin(\theta)$$
$$Y_{1,G} = d * cos(\theta) \tag{1}$$
$$-58° \leq \theta \leq 58°$$

Using each grape position measured with a zero reference located on the base, represented by X_2 axis, helps to make easier to calculate the production volume inside the container. Therefore, it was applied a linear transformation of the grape positions between referential 1 and referential 2, as shown in Fig. 3.

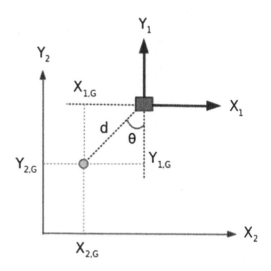

Fig. 3. Representation of (x,y) grape position in referential 1 and 2. Grey Rectangle represents the LIDAR. Green circle represents the grape. (Color figure online)

Once the (x,y) positions of the grapes have been determined in referential 2, the next step was the analysis of that values in order to know the possible outliers that comes from the measures collected. Followed that approach, it could be distinguished outliers outside and inside of the container. Focusing on the first ones, their presence can be observed in Fig. 6a, on Sect. 5, which represents the laser measures during the grape harvest. Note that the XY plan corresponds to a vertical plan of the container. In fact, comparing the shape created by the measures with the gray container of the machine, shown in Fig. 1, the filling happens as expected. However, the walls of the structure are represented as false grape points that would influence the production volume calculation. Therefore, all the points located outside of the limits defined by the container were discarded, as well as its own walls.

For its turn, inside the container, the outliers are related with the fall of the grapes. During the movement of the harvesting machine, if the LIDAR takes measures at the same time that the grape falls to the container, it can be detected before reaches the surface. For this reason, it is important to ensure that a variation in Y axis, between consecutive temporal samples, can't be higher than a defined threshold. On top of that, assuming that the grapes follow a Gaussian accumulation inside the container, the detection of outliers is also possible predicting the variations that can happen, in X and Y axis, between laser beams. Focusing in Fig. 4 and considering the laser beam orientations $\theta_a < \theta_b < \theta_c < \theta_d$, the assumptions described in Eq. 2 must be validated:

$$X_a < X_b < X_c < X_d$$
$$Y_a \leq Y_b \leq Y_c \tag{2}$$
$$Y_d \leq Y_c$$

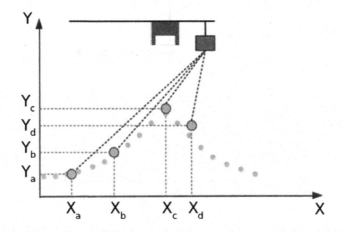

Fig. 4. Green circles represent grapes. Gray rectangle represents the LIDAR. Gray circles simulate a Gaussian distribution of the grapes. Blue dash lines represents the laser beams emitted by the LIDAR. Blue object represents the channel where the grapes fall to the container. (Color figure online)

After discard the outliers, the production volume was calculated with the remaining points of each sensor scanning. Since the points follow a Gaussian distribution, described in Eq. 3, the volume could be calculated using the integer of that as part of the equation. Each of the parameters was determined based on the points collected. The amplitude, A, was given by the difference between the higher and smaller Y value. The average of the distribution, u, was given by the X value that corresponds to the higher Y value. The offset, k, was given by the smaller Y value. The standard deviation, d, was determined applying the minimum squares method, which allows to find the best fit for a set of data, trying to minimize the sum of the squares of the differences between the estimated value and the observed data.

$$f(x) = A * \frac{1}{exp^{\frac{1}{2}*(\frac{x-u}{d})^2}} + k \tag{3}$$

Taking into account the profile area of the grapes distribution as well as the width of the harvesting machine, helps to calculate the production volume. Therefore, looking to Fig. 5, the profile area could be calculated as the sum of the Gaussian integer with the area below, given by the offset of the distribution. The resulting equations are formulated in 4 and 5 where A_P represents the profile area, V_M the volume, L_1 and L_2 define the limits of the machine in X axis, k the offset of the distribution and W_M the width of the machine.

$$A_P = \int_{L_1}^{L_2} f(x)\, dx + \int_{0}^{L_2} dxdy + \frac{L_1 * k}{2} \tag{4}$$

$$V_M = A_P * W_M \tag{5}$$

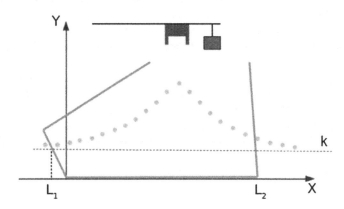

Fig. 5. The orange lines represent the walls of the container. The gray dashed curve represents the Gaussian distribution. The green dashed line represents the offset of the distribution. (Color figure online)

4.2   Geographic Information System

The analysis and manipulation of all the geographic data available were made with Geographical Information System tools. Therefore, combining the GPS position of each harvest point of the vineyard with the correspondent production volume, it was possible to design a productivity map with GIS software, firstly for each point and them for the entire harvested vineyard applying an interpolation method.

In a previous analysis of the harvesting points, there were negative values that could result from the failure of the sensor or discharges that the machine performed before starting a new grapes line, so these points were not counted in the volume points. Thus, 2343 (43.6%) of the 5373 initial registrations were eliminated. Even so, the harvesting points, on average, are spaced apart about 2–3 m.

Then, the volume values were multiplied by 1000, in order to have an integer value for the volume spatial representation per point and its spatial interpolation. The precise calculation of the volume collected at each point still lacks tuning and testing (in part due to the crushing of the bunch and reduction of the initial volume in the machine), so we chose to indicate a coefficient K that will give us in future the real volume collected for each point.

Considering that the measures of volume were obtained with a short distance between them, it was important to apply a spatial interpolation considering cells of 1 m by using Kriging interpolator, which use the points with known values to estimate the remaining ones, weighting them by local auto-correlation and general tendency of the collected data. The same process was performed for a raster dataset of Plant Cell Density values (obtained by UAV survey), in order to have a spatial comparison between these two variables. We compared the values by interpolation maps because it was not possible to compare both variables at the same points, due to the significant differences between the coordinates taken by the harvest machine and the high precision gathered with the UAV PCD survey.

The vineyard productivity maps were compared with maps NDVI (normalized difference vegetation index) maps and the PCD maps. This vegetation indexes (NDVI and PCD) were based on Sentinel-2 (S2) data (spatial resolution of 10m) from the Copernicus Open Access Hub. Both maps were used to test the connectivity between the data and it was expected to find some correlation with the volume of production.

5   Results

The methodology described in Sect. 4.1 was applied to some logs of data collected in the harvest season of 2018, applied in Celorico de Basto. Although multiple loads and unloads of the harvesting machine have been carried out, the following results will focus only in one process of that. Taking this into account, the first analysis of the filtration process was done in Fig. 6a and b. As can be seen, after remove the outliers, remained the points inside the container.

The results for one scan of the LIDAR are represented in Fig. 7a and b. When the filter was applied, the grapes that were falling and the points that were associated to the walls of the container disappear. Avoiding that outliers, the remaining points form a Gaussian curve as it was described in Sect. 4.1.

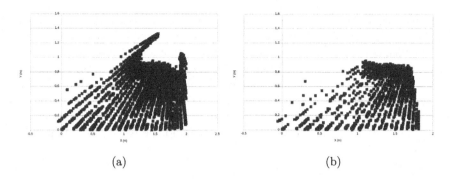

(a)   (b)

Fig. 6. Grape points, during one load process: (a) without filter (b) with filter

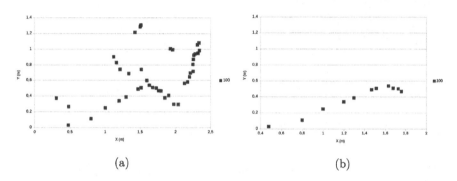

(a)   (b)

Fig. 7. Grape points, during one scan of the LIDAR: (a) without filter (b) with filter

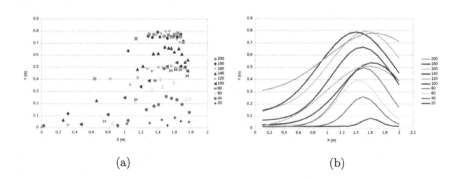

(a)   (b)

Fig. 8. (a) Grape points, during 10 scans of the LIDAR, each one represented by a different color (b) Gaussian distribution for the correspondent 10 scans.

Considering the use of the Gaussian curves to represent the grape points distribution, the results of 10 filtered scans are presented in Fig. 8a and b.

The final stage was to understand the impact that a implemented filter would have in the production volume along the grape harvest. In order to make it possible, in Fig. 9a and b, the cumulative volume, scan by scan, before and after the filtering, was represented. The filtered results suggest a smoothed growth of the production volume, when compared with the first ones. Some negative variations, that are not expected, were avoided and the results were improved.

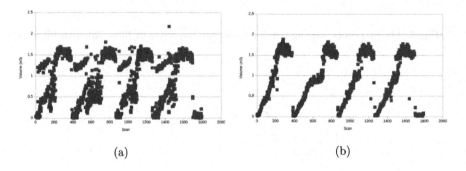

(a)   (b)

Fig. 9. Cumulative Volume calculated for each scan: (a) without filter (b) with filter.

Figure 10 presents the productivity map for the studied vineyard.

The analysis of the harvested points showed: (i) a large spatial variety in the harvest volume; (ii) the two classes with lower volume values are predominant; (iii) there are some points agglomerations with higher volume values, particularly in the NW sector of the vineyard.

This variability and the existence of well contrasted areas is evidenced in the interpolation map (Fig. 10) that presents the bards located in the northern sector of the vineyard as more productive when compared to the bards located to the south. The interpolation of Plant Cell Density values shows an alternation of bands with different values from south to north, evident in the AA' cross section (Fig. 10). The comparison between the interpolated volumes and the PCD, spatially, seems to demonstrate that at higher volume values and the values of PCD are associated, although this correspondence is tenuous.

Nevertheless, comparing it with the PCD map provided by Aveleda Company and shown in Fig. 10, it was possible to verify that the volume of production does not increase with the relative health of the vegetation. This fact is observed through the mismatch between both maps.

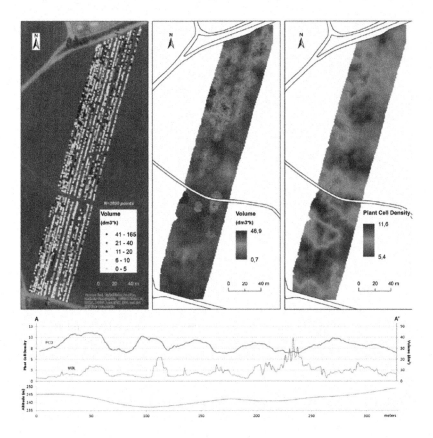

Fig. 10. Productivity maps of the Celorico de Basto vineyard: (a) harvest volume at each GPS point, spatial interpolation map of the harvest volume and spatial interpolation map of the Plant Cell Density; (b) AA' cross section along a bard showing the variation of harvest volume, Plant Cell Density and the bard altitude.

In terms of statistical correlation between of NDVI, PCD and harvest volume, the correlations are generally statistically no significant (Fig. 11). As expected, the highest correlation exists between NDVI values and plant density, although the vigour of the vines at harvest time is already weak, which may partly explain the low R^2 value.

Regarding the correlations between the NDVI, the harvest volume and the PCD, the correlations are very weak, which may be due to the way the volume data were collected during the harvesting process and that need adjustment in the future.

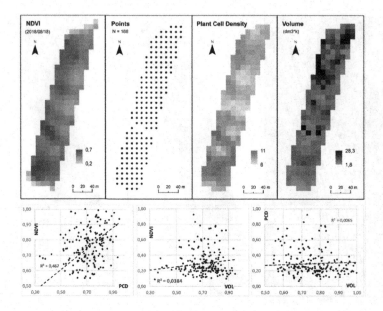

Fig. 11. Comparison of the vineyard productivity map with NDVI and PCD values: (a) Maps of NDVI values, Plant Cell Density and harvest volume interpolated to 188 vineyard points (pixel size of 10 m); (b) Correlations between the three variables.

6   Conclusions and Future Work

This work tests several techniques to estimate and map vineyard productivity, based on a LIDAR. Since the filtering is applied to the measures of the sensor, the grape points distribution in the container of the harvesting machine presents an expected Gaussian behaviour, suggesting a great potential of that. However, the small volume variations between scans coupled with the inability to take measurements away from the entire surface, introduced on this method some inaccuracies. Negative variations of the volume were calculated, affecting the construction of the productivity map. As the number of negative points increase, also the spatial interpolation increases, creating an higher error in the estimation. This may be the cause of the non-similarity between the productivity map and the PCD map.

The use of the LIDAR presents a great potential in the estimation of the grape positions inside the container. However, due to its one dimensional output, it is only possible to obtain a profile plan of the container filling. This fact limits the precision of the method since is necessary to approximate the grape distribution of the other profile plans to the one known. Therefore, in a future work would be interesting to use a two dimensional LIDAR that allows to create a three dimensional grape distribution during the filling of the container.

Acknowledgments. This work is funded by funds through the FCT - Fundação para a Ciência e a Tecnologia, I.P., within the framework of the project "Water-JPI/0012/2016". The authors would like to thank the EU and FCT for funding in the frame of the collaborative international consortium Water4Ever financed under the ERA-NET Water Works 2015 cofounded call. This ERA-NET is an integral part of the 2016 Joint Activities developed by the Water Challenge for a changing world joint programme initiation (Water JPI). The authors also thank to Aveleda S.A. for making available the harvest machinery for installation of AgIoT Lidar Sensor and allowing the collection of harvesting data.

References

1. Adamchuk, V.I., Hummel, J.W., Morgan, M.T., Upadhyaya, S.K.: On-the-go soil sensors for precision agriculture. Comput. Electron. Agric. **44**(1), 71–91 (2004). https://doi.org/10.1016/j.compag.2004.03.002
2. Blom, P.E., Tarara, J.M.: Trellis tension monitoring improves yield estimation in vineyards. HortScience **44**(3), 678–685 (2009)
3. Cunha, M., Ribeiro, H., Abreu, I.: Pollen-based predictive modelling of wine production: application to an arid region. Eur. J. Agron. **73**, 42–54 (2016). https://doi.org/10.1016/j.eja.2015.10.008
4. Font, D., Tresanchez, M., Martínez, D., Moreno, J., Clotet, E., Palacín, J.: Vineyard yield estimation based on the analysis of high resolution images obtained with artificial illumination at night. Sensors (Switzerland) **15**(4), 8284–8301 (2015). https://doi.org/10.3390/s150408284
5. Luo, L., Tang, Y., Lu, Q., Chen, X., Zhang, P., Zou, X.: A vision methodology for harvesting robot to detect cutting points on peduncles of double overlapping grape clusters in a vineyard. Comput. Ind. **99**, 130–139 (2018). https://doi.org/10.1016/j.compind.2018.03.017
6. Nuske, S., Wilshusen, K., Achar, S., Yoder, L., Narasimhan, S., Singh, S.: Automated Visual Yield Estimation in Vineyards, vol. 31, pp. 837–860 (2014). https://doi.org/10.1002/rob
7. Taylor, J.A., Sanchez, L., Sams, B., Haggerty, L., Jakubowski, R., Djafour, S., Bates, T.R.: Evaluation of a commercial grape yield monitor for use mid-season and at-harvest. J. Int. des Sciences de la Vigne et du Vin **50**(2), 57–63 (2016)

An Image-Based Deep Learning Model for Cannabis Diseases, Nutrient Deficiencies and Pests Identification

Konstantinos P. Ferentinos[1]([✉]) [iD], Myrto Barda[1] [iD],
and Dave Damer[2]

[1] Department of Agricultural Engineering Soil and Water Resources Institute,
Hellenic Agricultural Organization "Demeter", Athens, Greece
k.ferentinos@swri.gr
[2] Testfire Labs, Edmonton, Canada
dave@testfirelabs.com

Abstract. In this work, a deep learning system for cannabis plants disease, nutrient deficiencies and pests identification is developed, based on image data processed by convolutional neural network models. Training of the models was performed using image data available on the Internet, while database development included data cleansing by expert agronomists, basic image editing, and data augmentation techniques commonly used in deep learning applications in order to expand the rather limited amount of available data. Three fungi diseases, two pests and three nutrient deficiencies were included in the identification system, together with healthy plants identification. The final model reached a performance of 90.79% in successfully identifying cannabis diseases (or healthy plants) in previously "unseen" plant images. The most difficult cannabis problems to be identified were powdery mildew and potassium deficiency. Results showed that transfer learning from existing models specialized in similar tasks to the one under development, is more successful than using transfer learning from more general models. Finally, even though the amount of training images in some of the considered problems was significantly small, no correlation between model performance and the size of the training dataset for each category was found.

Keywords: Cannabis · Convolutional Neural Networks · Disease detection · Disease diagnosis

1 Introduction

Cannabis sativa L. is an important herbaceous species originating from Central Asia [1]. Based on ecological constraints, cannabis evolved somewhere in temperate latitudes of the northern hemisphere. Eurasia is favored as its primary region of origin [2]. Although cannabis has been practiced for centuries [3, 4], it has recently seen a resurgence of interest because of its multi-purpose applications, delivering fibers, seeds and pharmaceuticals. As the interest of cannabis cultivation is growing, hempseed production has risen from 35,321 tn in 1990 and 68,430 tn in 2011, to 102,416 tn in

© Springer Nature Switzerland AG 2019
P. Moura Oliveira et al. (Eds.): EPIA 2019, LNAI 11804, pp. 134–145, 2019.
https://doi.org/10.1007/978-3-030-30241-2_12

2017 [5]. Hemp has been used for its strong fiber since ancient times. Currently the fiber is used for light weight papers, insulation material and biocomposites. Moreover, cannabis outer and inner stem tissues can be used to make bioplastics and concrete-like material, respectively [1]. Hemp seeds can be consumed raw or pressed into hemp seed oil, which has an excellent fatty acid profile. Both seeds and oil are used for human food and animal feed. The non-psychotropic Cannabinoid CBD is an interesting pharmaceutical and food supplement which is also derived from industrial hemp. The legalized cultivation and distribution of cannabis for medicinal and even, in specific cases, recreational purposes is increasing, thus the increased cultivation is likely to cause an increase in pathogens that can negatively affect the production and quality of the crop [6].

On-site and real-time plant disease detection constitutes a challenge for cannabis producers, as today the plant is grown in open-field and greenhouse cultivations in a very wide geographical distribution, and is highly susceptible to infections, making early detection of signs and symptoms crucial to the quality and quantity of final production. Plant disease diagnosis through optical observation of the symptoms on plant leaves, incorporates a significantly high degree of complexity. Due to this complexity, even experienced agronomists and plant pathologists often fail to successfully diagnose specific diseases, pests or abiotic stresses, and are consequently led to mistaken treatments. Smart farming [7] is important for tackling the challenges of agricultural production in terms of sustainability, food security and environmental impact [8]. The existence of an automated computational system for the detection and diagnosis of plant pest and diseases symptoms, would offer a valuable assistance to the agronomist [9–11].

In recent years, Artificial Intelligence (A.I.) applications that use Machine Learning methodologies, have achieved exponential growth, leading to the development of novel methodologies and models, which now form a new A.I. field, that of Deep Learning [12]. Deep learning provides high accuracy, outperforming existing commonly used image processing techniques [13], since it exploits artificial neural network architectures that contain a quite large number of processing layers, as opposed to "swallower" architectures of more traditional neural network methodologies. Mainly because of the recent advances in the development of Graphics Processing Units (GPU) embedded processors, deep learning models are now computationally feasible, and have revolutionized sectors such as image recognition [14, 15], voice recognition [16], and other similarly complex processes that deal with the analysis of large volumes of data [17].

The introduction of these deep learning techniques into agriculture and in particular in the field of plant disease diagnosis [10], has only begun to take place in the last couple of years. The basic deep learning tool used in the majority of works is that of Convolutional Neural Networks (CNNs) [14]. CNNs have been widely applied for solving problems in the agricultural domain, including plant species classification [18, 19], weed detection [19, 20], pest image classification [21] and plant disease detection and diagnosis [11].

For plant diseases identification in particular, CNNs has achieved great success [22] and helped to overcome challenges in automatic plant disease recognition [23]. Mohanty et al. in [9] compared two well-known and established architectures of CNNs in the identification of 26 plant diseases, using an open database of leaves images of 14 different plants. Their results were very promising, with success rates in the automated identification up to 99.35%. However, a main drawback was that the entire photographic material included solely images in experimental (laboratory) setups, not in real conditions in the cultivation field. Sladojevic et al. in [24] developed a similar methodology for plant disease detection through leaves images using a similar amount of data available on the Internet, which included a smaller number of diseases (13) and different plants (5). Success rates of their models were between 91% and 98%, depending on the testing data. Pawara et al. in [25] compared the performance of some conventional pattern recognition techniques with that of CNN models, in plants identification, using three different databases of (a rather limited number of) images of either entire plants and fruits, or plant leaves, concluding that CNNs drastically outperform conventional methods. Ferentinos in [11] developed a CNN model for the detection of plant diseases among 58 different [plant, disease] combinations, which included 25 different plant species. The identification model was trained with images captured in both experimental and real-cultivation setups, and an overall performance reaching a 99.53% success rate. Even more recently, several other advanced CNN models have been developed for diseases identification in specific plant species [26–28].

In this work, a CNN model specialized on the identification of specific problems in cannabis plants is developed. The model is trained with a variety of images of healthy and infected cannabis leaves, and it covers the most common cannabis cultivation problems, including diseases, pests and nutrient deficiencies. Section 2 of the paper investigates these most common problems, especially for greenhouse cannabis cultivation, and defines the corresponding focus of this work. In addition, it describes the deep learning model design methodology that was followed, the data collection and manipulation processes for the development of the necessary image database, and the techniques used for data augmentation and creation of the training and testing datasets for model training and validation, respectively. Section 3 analyzes the performance of the developed models, leading to the selection of the final identification model. Finally, Sect. 4 concludes the paper with some relevant conclusions and plans for future work.

2   Materials and Methods

2.1   Common Problems of Cannabis Cultivation

Diseases of cannabis plants are caused by organisms (e.g., fungi) or abiotic sources (e.g., nutrient deficiencies). Environmentally stressed plants become predisposed to diseases. Stress includes drought, insufficient light, untoward temperatures, or growing plants in monoculture. Disease prevalence shifts between greenhouse crops and outdoor crops. Serious and most common flower and leaf cannabis diseases at an indoor cultivation are nutritional diseases, pink rot, gray mold, powdery mildew, brown blight, and virus diseases [29]. The most significant fungi attack in cannabis is gray mold, caused by *Botrytis cinerea* which thrives in temperate regions with high humidity and cold to moderate temperatures. The two most common leaf spot diseases are yellow leaf spot caused by two *Septoria* species [30], and brown leaf spot caused by about eight *Phoma* and *Ascochyta* species. These diseases rarely kill plants but sharply reduce crop yields [31]. In [6], powdery mildew infection on cannabis plants was caused by *Golovinomyces cichoracearum*, whereas powdery mildew on cannabis was previously reported to be caused by *Leveillula taurica* and *Sphaerotheca macularis* [32]. In [33], a high frequency of detection by PCR (84%) of *Golovinomyces* species in cannabis samples was reported, indicating that one of the most prevalent disease reported to affect cannabis is powdery mildew. The most common abiotic diseases on cannabis crop are nutrient deficiencies [34]. Generally, deficiencies of mobile nutrients (N, P, K, Mg, B, Mb) begin in large leaves at the bottom of the plants. Shortages of less mobile nutrients (Mn, Zn, Ca, S, Fe, Cu) usually begin in young leaves near the top. Cannabis grows best in a nutrient-rich, well-drained, well-structured, high organic matter, silty loam soil. Fiber crops require high soil N, high K, then in descending order: Ca, P, Mg, and micronutrients. Seed crops, compared to fiber crops, extract less K and more P from the soil [35].

The most common flower and leaf pests in closed cultivations of cannabis plants are spider mites (*Tetranychus urticae, Aculops cannabicola*), aphids (*Phorodon cannabis, Myzus persicae, Aphis fabae*), whiteflies (*Trialeurodes vaporariorum, Bemisia* spp.), thrips, and leafhoppers, whereas slugs, rodents, and birds are pests of seedlings and seeds [36], rarely found in greenhouse cultivations. The most important non-insect pests are spider mites which suck plant sap and are the most destructive pests of greenhouse-grown cannabis. Outdoor crops may also become infested by mites in warm climates. Two species are causing the biggest crop damage: the two spotted spider mite (*T. urticae*) and the carmine spider mite (*T. cinnabarinus*). The hemp russet mite (*A. cannabicola*) is equally destructive, but less commonly encountered.

Aphids also cause serious problems to cannabis. Some are specific feeders, such as the bhang aphid (*P. cannabis*) and hops aphid (*P. humuli*), while others are general feeders, such as the green peach aphid (*M. persicae*) and the black bean aphid (*A. fabae*). Aphids congregate on the underside of leaves and cause leaf wilting and yellowing, resulting sometimes in entire plant loss. Some aphids also infest flowering tops, which become hypertrophied or totally destroyed [36].

This work aims to detect and diagnose the most common diseases, pests and nutrient deficiencies of cannabis plants, focusing mainly on greenhouse cultivation. Thus, the problems shown in Table 1 were selected to be included in the initial deep learning model presented here.

2.2   Deep Learning Model Design

Artificial neural networks are mathematical models which are inspired by the network of neurons in the biological brain. Their main characteristic is the ability to be trained to perform a particular task using large amounts of data, through the process of supervised learning. During that process, neural networks "learn" to model some system with the use of specific data that contain matchings of inputs and outputs of the system to be modelled. CNNs [14] are an advanced form of traditional artificial neural networks, which have been evolved to focus mainly on applications with repeating patterns in different areas of the modeling space, as it happens, e.g., in image recognition applications. With the methodology used in their layering, CNNs manage to drastically

Table 1. Cannabis infections/problems identified by the proposed deep learning model.

Disease common name	Problem category	Involved organisms
Gray mold	Fungi	*Botrytis cinerea*
Powdery mildew	Fungi	*Golovinomyces* spp.
Yellow leaf spot	Fungi	*Septoria* spp.
Spider mites	Pests	*Tetranychus urticae, Aculops cannabicola*
Aphids	Pests	*P. cannabis, Myzus persicae, Aphis fabae*
Nitrogen deficiency	Nutrient deficiencies	N/A
Phosphorus deficiency	Nutrient deficiencies	N/A
Potassium deficiency	Nutrient deficiencies	N/A

reduce the required number of structural elements (number of artificial neurons) in comparison to traditional feedforward neural networks.

For image recognition in particular, several core architectures of CNNs have been developed [37–41]. Most specialized image recognition CNN models, usually use these core CNN architectures as a starting point for model development and training, rather than starting the model design and training from models with initially random weights. This is a process called transfer learning [42], which has proved to be extremely successful and resource-saving in a wide range of complicated tasks of visual imagery. Some specific applications may require special network architectures or large modifications of core architectures, but the majority of systems reach sufficient performance with the use of transfer learning from core CNN architectures.

Here, two transfer learning approaches were used and tested. In the first approach, CNN models were developed using transfer learning from three well known core CNN architectures that have been shown to work very well in the development of similar plant disease detection architectures [9, 11]: (a) AlexNet [37], (b) GoogLeNet [39], and (c) VGG16 [41]. These core models have been trained for object recognition in well-known, large image datasets, like Imagenet. In the second approach, a CNN model was developed using transfer learning from a very successful CNN model which is specialized in plant disease identification [11].

The plant disease identification model [11] that was used as a base model for the cannabis model developed in the second approach described before, was based on the VGG16 architecture [41]. An open database of 87,848 images was used for the development of that model, covering 25 different plants in a set of 58 distinct classes of [plant, disease] combinations, including healthy plants. The success rate of the model in identifying the correct [plant, disease] combination (or healthy plant) was 99.53%, making it probably one of the most powerful such models available, and surely the most widely applicable, as it not only included the largest variety of [plant, disease] combinations in the literature, but it also worked with images captured in both experimental and real cultivation setups. Thus, four different model design approaches were used in this work, resulting in four different CNN models, as presented in Table 2. Training was performed in MATLAB software package (by MathWorks®), using two NVIDIA® RTX2080 GPUs with the CUDA® parallel programming platform, in Linux environment (Ubuntu 18.04 LTS operating system).

Table 2. Basic features of the four CNN models developed for cannabis disease identification.

Model name	Base model for transfer learning	Base model reference
CANCNN1	AlexNet	[37]
CANCNN2	GoogLeNet	[39]
CANCNN3	VGG16	[41]
CANCNN4	58 [plant, disease] classes id. model	[11]

2.3   Data Collection and Manipulation

This work concerns the identification of 8 different problematic situations of cannabis plants, as well as healthy plants, comprising a set of 9 different classes. As mentioned in Sect. 2, five classes concerned corresponding plant diseases and infections, common for cannabis plants (gray mold, powdery mildew, yellow leaf spot, spider mites, and aphids), and three classes concerned nutrient deficiencies (nitrogen, phosphorus, and potassium). Images of healthy and diseased cannabis plants of various stages of the infections were collected from the Internet, using relevant keywords. The initially collected images were then filtered by expert agronomists to assure that they indeed belonged to their designated category. For training and testing of the developed CNN models, images of leaves of cannabis plants were used (single or multiple leaves). Thus, after data cleansing and some image manipulation involving extracting specific parts of entire images to form separate images of leaves, the number of images for each of the 9 classes (c0 – c8) were those shown in Table 3.

Table 3. Information and quantitative data of the collected cannabis leaves images.

Class	Problem name	No. of images	% of total images
c0	N/A (healthy plants)	102	20.4%
c1	Gray mold	57	11.4%
c2	Powdery mildew	69	13.8%
c3	Yellow leaf spot	19	3.8%
c4	Spider mites	59	11.8%
c5	Aphids	18	3.6%
c6	Nitrogen deficiency	72	14.4%
c7	Phosphorus deficiency	60	12.0%
c8	Potassium deficiency	44	8.8%
	TOTAL	500	100.0%

Figure 1 shows an example of each of the 9 classes. Images in the compiled database include photographs shot in both experimental conditions (e.g., on a table with uniform background) and real cultivation conditions. The database comprised of a total of 500 images, with the richest class (class c0 – healthy plants) containing 20.4% of them and the poorest class (class c5 – Aphids) containing 3.6% of them. It is obvious that there is a quite uneven distribution of images between the 9 classes (Table 3), which is something definitely not ideal for training a robust neural network model. However, the influence of dataset sizes in the performance of the final model is investigated and the corresponding results are presented in Sect. 3 below.

Fig. 1. Sample leaf images of the 9 classes in the database. c0: Healthy, c1: Gray mold, c2: Powdery mildew, c3: Yellow leaf spot, c4: Spider mites, c5: Aphids, c6: Nitrogen deficiency, c7: Phosphorus deficiency, c8: Potassium deficiency. (Color figure online)

No additional image editing was performed at the stage of developing the training/testing database. The alternative of using grayscale versions of the images for training was not considered, as previous works (e.g., [9]) have indicated that this approach does not improve the final classification performance of deep learning models in similar applications. The same holds for segmentation of the leaves from the background of the images, thus this additional step in the process was also not considered [11].

2.4   Training/Testing Datasets and Data Augmentation

The 500 images database was divided into two datasets, the training set, and the testing set, by randomly splitting the images so that 85% of them formed the training set, and 15% formed the testing set. Thus, 424 images were used for training the CNN models and the rest 76 images were kept for testing the performance of the models in classifying new, previously "unseen" images. In order to increase the rather limited size of the training data, several data augmentation techniques were also used and their influence in increasing the training performance of the models was investigated. These techniques included random rotations of images within ±10 to ±45°, and random image translations in both x and y dimensions. Finally, all images were resized to fit the necessary input dimensions of each tested architecture (227 × 227 pixels for AlexNet, and 224 × 224 for GoogLeNet, VVG16 and the [plant, disease] identification model of [11]).

3   Results

All four CNN models presented in Sect. 2.2 (Table 2) were trained using several different values for the training parameters concerning learning rate, batch size, momentum, etc. Also, all models were trained using either the original training data or the augmented training data, for comparison. Their performance on the testing dataset is shown in Table 4.

Table 4. Performance (correct classification rate) of different CNN models on the testing dataset.

Model	Trained on original data	Trained on augmented data
CANCNN1	81.58%	85.53%
CANCNN2	80.26%	86.84%
CANCNN3	82.89%	88.16%
CANCNN4	84.21%	90.79%

From the results presented in Table 4 it is clear that data augmentation played a crucial role in the development of models with high performance, and that CANCNN4 model, which was based on transfer learning from the plant/disease identification model presented in [11] outperformed the other three models which were based on more general network architectures. The performance of the final model achieved a 90.79% success rate on the testing dataset. Two versions of this specific model reached that success rate, with slightly different success rate distributions among the 9 classes under consideration. These distributions are presented in Table 5, and shown graphically in Fig. 2. The first version of the model (CANCNN4a) had a rather low performance in the case of class c8 (Potassium deficiency), thus the second version of the model (CANCNN4b) was selected as the final model of this work, which resulted in more uniform performance distribution among all 9 classes. Both versions had an overall performance rate of 90.79%, with their only difference being the batch size during training (64 for the first version and 32 for the second version). The results showed that the most difficult cannabis problems to be identified correctly were powdery mildew and potassium deficiency. Finally, these distribution results, when considered together with the number of available images for each category (Table 3), show that there is no actual correlation between model performance and the size of the training dataset for each category (Fig. 3).

Table 5. Success rates (%) for each class category (and overall performance) of the two versions of the best model architecture (CANCNN4).

Class	Category	CANCNN4a	CANCNN4b
c0	Healthy	100.00	100.00
c1	Gray mold	88.89	88.89
c2	Powdery mildew	80.00	70.00
c3	Yellow leaf spot	100.00	100.00
c4	Spider mites	100.00	100.00
c5	Aphids	100.00	100.00
c6	Nitrogen deficiency	100.00	100.00
c7	Phosphorus deficiency	88.89	88.89
c8	Potassium deficiency	57.14	71.43
	Overall	90.79	90.79

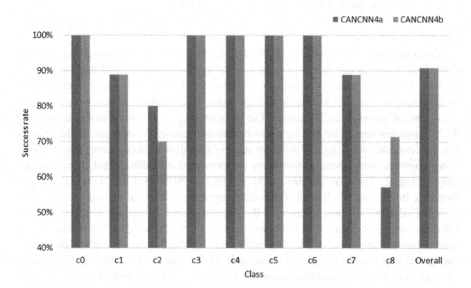

Fig. 2. Success rates distribution over each class category (and overall performance) of the two versions of the best model architecture (CANCNN4).

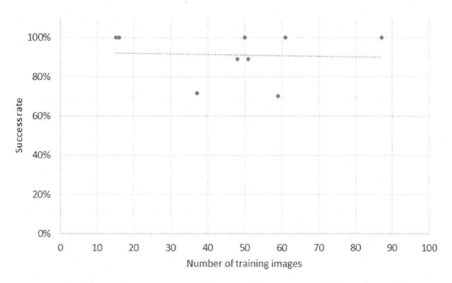

Fig. 3. Success rate per class of final model in relation to corresponding training data size of each class.

4 Conclusions

This work presents the development of specialized deep learning models, based on convolutional neural networks, for the identification of cannabis infections, concerning diseases, pests and nutrient deficiencies. Training of the models was performed using image data available on the Internet, while database development included data cleansing by expert agronomists, image editing to produce separate leaves images from photographs of multiple plants, and data augmentation techniques commonly used in deep learning applications in order to expand the rather limited amount of available data.

Four different CNN model approaches were investigated, concerning transfer learning from three well-known image classification CNN architectures and from one previously developed model for general plant disease identification, which included 28 different plant species (but no cannabis plants). The comparison results between the four approaches made clear that transfer learning from existing models specialized in similar tasks to the one under development, is more successful than using transfer learning from more general models. The performance of the final model, which reached a rate of 90.79% in correctly classifying testing images in either one of the 8 considered infections or as healthy, showed that the most difficult cannabis problems to be identified were powdery mildew and potassium deficiency. Even though the amount of training images in some of the considered problems was significantly small, no correlation between model performance and the size of the training dataset for each category was found, thus highlighting the power of CNNs and transfer learning in this specific task.

However, in order to develop a more robust disease identification system for cannabis, which would work in real cultivation conditions, much more training data need to be collected. As a future work, such data will be created in greenhouse cannabis cultivation conditions, and the model will be also further expanded to include more diseases and other common cannabis plants problems.

Acknowledgments. This research has been co-financed by the European Union and Greek national funds through the Operational Program Competitiveness, Entrepreneurship and Innovation, under the call RESEARCH – CREATE – INNOVATE (project code: T1EDK-02182).

References

1. Andre, C.M., Hausman, J.-F., Guerriero, G.: Cannabis sativa: the plant of the thousand and one molecules. Front. Plant Sci. **7**, 19 (2016)
2. Clarke, R.C., Merlin, M.D.: Cannabis: Evolution and Ethnobotany. University of California Press, Los Angeles and Berkeley (2013)
3. Clarke, R.C.: Marijuana Botany: An Advanced Study: The Propagation and Breeding of Distinctive Cannabis. Ronin Publishing, Oakland (1981)
4. Small, E.: Cannabis, a Complete Guide. CRC Press, Boca Raton (2017)
5. FAOSTAT. http://www.fao.org/faostat/en/#compare. Accessed 04 Apr 2019
6. Punja, Z.K.: Flower and foliage-infecting pathogens of marijuana (Cannabis sativa L.) plants. Can. J. Plant Pathol. **40**(4), 514–527 (2018)
7. Tyagi, A.C.: Towards a second green revolution. Irrig. Drainage **65**(4), 388–389 (2016)
8. Gebbers, R., Adamchuk, V.I.: Precision agriculture and food security. Science **327**, 828–831 (2010)
9. Mohanty, S.P., Hughes, D.P., Salathé, M.: Using deep learning for image-based plant disease detection. Front. Plant Sci. **7**, 1419 (2016)
10. Yang, X., Guo, T.: Machine learning in plant disease research. Eur. J. BioMed. Res. **3**(1), 6–9 (2017)
11. Ferentinos, K.P.: Deep learning models for plant disease detection and diagnosis. Comput. Electron. Agric. **145**, 311–318 (2018)
12. LeCun, Y., Bengio, Y., Hinton, G.: Deep learning. Nature **521**, 436–444 (2015)
13. Kamilaris, A., Prenafeta-Boldú, F.: Deep learning in agriculture: a survey. Comput. Electron. Agric. **147**, 70–90 (2018)
14. LeCun, Y., Bottou, L., Bengio, Y., Haffner, P.: Gradient-based learning applied to document recognition. Proc. IEEE **86**(11), 2278–2324 (1998)
15. Dan, C., Meier, U., Masci, J., Gambardella, L.M., Schmidhuber, J.: Flexible, high performance convolutional neural networks for image classification. In: Proceedings of the 22nd International Joint Conference on Artificial Intelligence, vol. 2, pp. 1237–1242 (2011)
16. Hinton, G., et al.: Deep neural networks for acoustic modeling in speech recognition: the shared views of four research groups. IEEE Sig. Process. Mag. **29**(6), 82–97 (2012)
17. LeCun, Y., Bengio, Y.: Convolutional networks for images, speech, and time series. In: The Handbook of Brain Theory and Neural Networks, vol. 3361(10). MIT Press (1995)
18. Grinblat, G.L., Uzal, L.C., Larese, M., Granitto, P.: Deep learning for plant identification using vein morphological patterns. Comput. Electron. Agric. **127**, 418–424 (2016)
19. Dyrmann, M., Jorgensen, R.N., Midtiby, H.S.: Detection of weed locations in leaf occluded cereal crops using a fully convolutional neural network. In: 11th European Conference on Precision Agriculture, pp. 842–847 (2017)
20. Dyrmann, M., Skovsen, S., Laursen, M.S., Jorgensen, R.N.: Using a fully convolutional neural network for detecting locations of weeds in images from cereal fields. In: 14th International Conference on Precision Agriculture, Montreal, Quebec, Canada (2018)

21. Cheng, X., Zhang, Y., Chen, Y., Wu, Y., Yue, Y.: Pest identification via deep residual learning in complex background. Comput. Electron. Agric. **141**, 351–356 (2017)
22. Toda Y., Okura F.: How convolutional neural networks diagnose plant disease. Plant Phenomics **2019**(9237136) (2019)
23. Barbedo, J.G.A.: Factors influencing the use of deep learning for plant disease recognition. Biosyst. Eng. **172**, 84–91 (2018)
24. Sladojevic, S., Arsenovic, M., Anderla, A., Culibrk, D., Stefanovic, D.: Deep neural networks based recognition of plant diseases by leaf image classification. Comput. Intell. Neurosci. **2016**, 11 (2016)
25. Pawara, P., Okafor, E., Surinta, O., Schomaker, L., Wiering, M.: Comparing local descriptors and bags of visual words to deep convolutional neural networks for plant recognition. In: 6th International Conference on Pattern Recognition Applications and Methods (2017)
26. Lin, K., Gong, L., Huang, Y., Liu, C., Pan, J.: Deep learning-based segmentation and quantification of cucumber powdery mildew using convolutional neural network. Front. Plant Sci. **10**, 155 (2019)
27. Barbedo, J.G.A.: Plant disease identification from individual lesions and spots using deep learning. Biosyst. Eng. **180**, 96–107 (2019)
28. An, J., Li, W., Li, M., Cui, S., Yue, H.: Identification and classification of maize drought stress using deep convolutional neural network. Symmetry **11**(2), 256 (2019)
29. McPartland, J.M.: A review of Cannabis diseases. J. Int. Hemp Assoc. **3**(1), 19–23 (1996)
30. McPartland, J.M.: Cannabis pathogens XI: Septoria spp. on Cannabis sativa, sensu strico. Sydowia **47**, 44–53 (1995)
31. McPartland, J.M.: Cannabis pathogens X: Phoma, Ascochyta and Didymella species. Mycologia **86**, 870–878 (1995)
32. McPartland, J.M.: Common names for diseases of Cannabis sativa L. Plant Dis. **75**, 226–227 (1991)
33. Thompson, G.R., et al.: A microbiome assessment of medical marijuana. Clin. Microbiol. Infect. **23**(4), 269–270 (2017)
34. Frank, M.: Marijuana Grower's Insider's Guide. Red Eye Press, Los Angeles (1988)
35. McPartland, J.M., Clarke, R.B., Watson, D.P.: Hemp Diseases and Pests Management and Biological Control. CABI Publishing, United Kingdom (2000)
36. McPartland, J.M.: Cannabis pests. J. Int. Hemp Assoc. **3**(2), 49–52 (1996)
37. Krizhevsky, A., Sutskever, I., Hinton, G.E.: Imagenet classification with deep convolutional neural networks. In: Pereira, F., Burges, C.J.C., Bottou, L., Weinberger, K.Q. (eds.) Advances in Neural Information Processing Systems, pp. 1097–1105 (2012)
38. Krizhevsky, A.: One weird trick for parallelizing convolutional neural networks arXiv:1404.5997 (2014)
39. Szegedy, C., Liu, W., Jia, Y., Sermanet, P., Reed, S., Anguelov, D., et al.: Going deeper with convolutions. In: Proceedings of the IEEE Conference on Computer Vision and Pattern Recognition (2015)
40. Sermanet, P., Eigen, D., Zhang, X., Mathieu, M., Fergus, R., LeCun, Y.: Overfeat: integrated recognition, localization and detection using convolutional networks arXiv:1312.6229 (2013)
41. Simonyan, K., Zisserman, A.: Very deep convolutional networks for large-scale image recognition arXiv:1409.1556 (2014)
42. Bengio, Y.: Learning deep architectures for AI. Found. Trends® Mach. Learn. **2**(1), 1–127 (2009)

Detection of Tomato Flowers from Greenhouse Images Using Colorspace Transformations

Manya Afonso[1]([✉]), Angelo Mencarelli[1], Gerrit Polder[1], Ron Wehrens[1],
Dick Lensink[2], and Nanne Faber[2]

[1] Wageningen University & Research, Wageningen, The Netherlands
{manya.afonso,angelo.mencarelli,gerrit.polder,ron.wehrens}@wur.nl
[2] Enza Zaden, Enkhuizen, The Netherlands
{d.lensink,n.faber}@enzazaden.nl

Abstract. In this paper we propose an image analysis method for detecting and counting tomato flowers from images taken in a greenhouse. Detecting and locating flowers is useful information for tomato growers and breeders, for phenotyping, yield prediction, and for automating procedures such as pollination and spraying. Since the tomato flowers are yellow, we first apply a set of grayscale transformations in which yellow regions stand out, and then threshold and combine them by a logical binary AND operation. Using more than one transform reduces the possibility of spurious detections due to non-flower regions of the image appearing yellow due to illumination conditions. Connected regions larger than a certain threshold are selected as instances belonging to the class flower. Experimental results over images acquired in a greenhouse using a Realsense camera show that this approach could detect flowers with a recall of 0.79 and precision of 0.77, which are comparable to the values reported in literature with higher resolution cameras closer to the flowers being imaged.

Keywords: Computer vision in agriculture · Phenotyping · Flower detection

1 Introduction

Accurate identification of fruits, flowers, stems, and other plant parts is an important step in precision agriculture problems such as automatic harvesting, phenotyping, and yield prediction. Image analysis and computer vision offer a quick and non-destructive way for these tasks as well as other related problems in agriculture such as plant identification, and pest and disease detection [7,16]. For horticultural crops, the number of flowers is important information in predicting the number of fruits harvested. The detection of flowers can be useful for automating procedures such as pollination [17] and spraying, pruning, and thinning to control the yield [3].

This research has been made possible by cofunding from Foundation TKI Horticulture & Propagation Materials.

ⓒ Springer Nature Switzerland AG 2019
P. Moura Oliveira et al. (Eds.): EPIA 2019, LNAI 11804, pp. 146–155, 2019.
https://doi.org/10.1007/978-3-030-30241-2_13

Our goal in this paper is to detect tomato flowers which are yellow, from images taken in a production greenhouse. Due to the small size of the flowers, variation in orientation, overlap and occlusions, and restrictions in camera placement and field of view, the detection of individual flower instances is a hard problem.

1.1 Related Work

A method for detecting tomato flowers from images taken by a drone flying through a greenhouse was proposed in [11]. This method used thresholding and morphological operations on the hue-saturation-value transform of the image followed by morphological operations to segment individual flowers. The drone could reach close enough to the flowers to be able to select a field of view that has the flowers in the foreground and reduces occlusions. The reported precision and recall were 0.80. Another work on tomato plant part detection [20] used a convolutional neural network with an architecture similar to VGG16 [14] and a region proposal network method similar to Fast-RCNN [6] and obtained a mean average precision of 0.84 for the flowers. This work used images with the flowers clearly visible in the foreground.

A general flower detection method proposed in [10] uses colorspace thresholding, shape modeling for the petals, and graph cuts to detect tulips, daffodils, and other commercially grown ornamental flowers. A method for detecting and counting grape flowers based on finding intensity peaks in the CieLAB color space and separating individual flowers based on quasi-spherical geometry was presented in [1,2]. A deep learning semantic segmentation method was used in [3,4] for detecting apple flowers.

Transfer learning for tomato flower detection from existing available datasets is difficult as there is no class called tomato flowers in large natural image processing datasets such as ImageNet [12]. The best known flower image datasets, the Oxford Visual Geometry Group flower dataset[1] [10] and the Kaggle flower classification challenge 2018 dataset[2] do not contain tomato flowers, and have the flowers appearing quite large in the images due to close camera placement.

1.2 Contribution

We develop a method for detecting individual tomato flower instances under our experimental setup which we describe in Sect. 2. Due to different cameras, imaging platforms, and proximity and fields of view of the cameras, the method from [11] is not directly applicable to our setup.

Suitable colorspaces in which tomato fruits or other plant parts such as stems have clearly different grayscale pixel values than the rest of the image, have been used to detect fruits [19] and stems [18]. We follow a similar approach and use colorspaces in which yellow flowers stand out. After thresholding these yellow

---

[1] http://www.robots.ox.ac.uk/~vgg/data/flowers/17/index.html.
[2] https://www.kaggle.com/c/fgvc2018-flower.

regions, morphological filling and connected component labeling are used to obtain individual flower instances. Since this method does not involve a training phase involving an annotated training ground truth dataset, we call the method an unsupervised object detector.

Experimental results show that our method achieves figures of merit which are close to those reported in previous work, under more difficult and restrictive experimental conditions. In particular, we use an Intel Realsense camera, which is an inexpensive sensor compared to the commercial digital and high definition cameras used in [11] and [20].

2   Materials and Methods

2.1   Images

The images were acquired with an Intel Realsense D435 camera, which is mounted on a moving platform that moves along the heating pipes of the greenhouse. The camera is at a height of 3 m from the ground, since the tomato flowers grow at the top of the plant stem. It is roughly at a distance of 0.5 m from the plants. The images were acquired during the morning on a cloudy day. The resolution of the color images is 1920×1080. As a result, the size of the flowers in the images can be as small as around 50 pixels, which is much smaller than the ones in [11] and [20] where the flowers are the foreground objects. Besides, it is not possible to adjust the field of view to zoom in on the flowers or to avoid occlusions since the imaging platform moves on a fixed track, unlike the drone used in [11].

For evaluating the flower detection method, a set of 44 images with a total of 132 flowers were annotated using the labelme tool[3] [13], which allows a polygon to be marked around the object of interest. Thus we obtain not just the bounding box, but also the pixels corresponding to each flower. Only the flowers which belong to the plant in the row being imaged, *i.e.*, the foreground, are annotated. Severely occluded and not fully open flowers are not annotated. For these cases, detection based on color alone is not feasible, so combining colorspace based detection along with other features like shape will be addressed in future work. An example image and the ground truth flower annotations overlaid on it are shown in Fig. 1, with the flowers zoomed in for better visibility.

2.2   Algorithm

The segmentation method was developed using the Halcon software from MVTec Software GmbH, Germany on a Linux Mint 18.2 system. The segmentation results were saved, and the evaluation with respect to the annotated ground truth was done in Matlab 2017 from The Mathworks, Natick MA, USA.

We know that the tomato flowers are yellow in color, and we assume that there are no other plant parts that are yellow. As in [19] and [11], we apply suitable colorspace transforms to the RGB (Red Green Blue) image in which objects

---

[3] https://github.com/wkentaro/labelme.

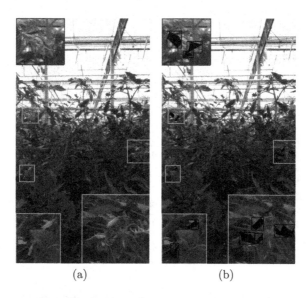

(a)   (b)

Fig. 1. (a) Example of an RGB image with the flowers zoomed in, (b) RGB image with annotated ground truth overlaid. (Color figure online)

of the color of interest stand out compared to the everything else in the image. Yellow regions were observed to stand out as brighter than the rest of the image in the B* color component of the CieLAB colorspace (L stands for luminance, and A* and B* are the color components), the in-phase (I) component of the YIQ (luminance, In-phase, Quadrature) colorspace [15], and in the difference of the red and green components. An example RGB image with these transforms is presented in Fig. 2.

Therefore we look for flowers by first segmenting the pixels in the image that are yellow, and then select connected regions as individual instances, through morphological operations. The sequence of steps is as follows:

1. **Image pre-processing:** We first discard red regions such as wires which can appear bright in the difference red $-$ green, which is one of the colorspace transformations that we use to detect yellow objects. This is done by applying the RGB to CieLAB transformation, and since the color red corresponds to a high value in the A* component, the red pixels are discarded by thresholding the A* component below the value 144, which was empirically found to be sufficient.

2. **Colorspace Transformation:** The colorspaces CieLAB and YIQ are obtained from the RGB image, and the difference between the red and green channels, $R - G$ is calculated.

3. **Thresholding:** Since yellow pixels are brighter than the rest in the above components, we apply a high threshold on each of them to select those pixels corresponding to the flowers. We define the threshold values on the CieLAB B*, YIQ I, and $R - G$ components as T_{B^*}, T_I, and T_{RG}, respectively.

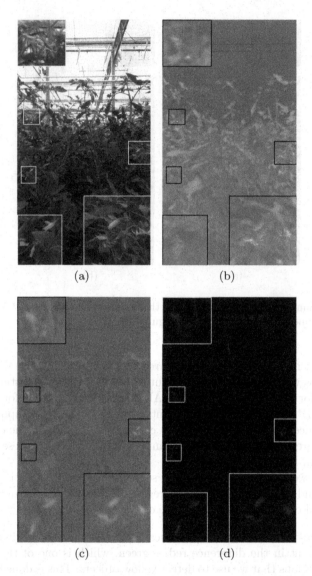

(a)   (b)

(c)   (d)

Fig. 2. Colorspace transformations in which yellow regions are visible: (a) RGB image, (b) Cielab B* component, (c) YIQ I component, (d) difference Red − Green. (Color figure online)

The yellow flower pixels are selected through a logical AND operation on the binary images resulting from the thresholding operations. This is expressed as,

$$\text{Yellow flower pixels} = (B^* > T_{B^*}) \cap (I > T_I) \cap (R - G > T_{RG}) \qquad (1)$$

4. **Instance detection:** A morphological operation to fill holes is applied on the binary image obtained above. Connected regions are determined using an 8-neighborhood. Regions whose areas are between 50 and 2000 pixels are selected as individual flowers. This range of values for the region area was chosen empirically.

2.3 Evaluation Procedure

We evaluate our flower detection method on the set of 44 annotated images. A detected instance is considered a true positive if it has a Jaccard Index similarity coefficient also known as intersection-over-union (IOU) [5] of 0.25 or more with a ground truth instance. The IOU is defined as the ratio of the number of pixels in the intersection to the number of pixels in the union. This value which is relatively low was chosen because the boundary regions of the flowers are not very sharp because of their relative small size in the images. A higher value can be expected to lower the precision and recall values, necessitating further processing to recover the boundary regions of the flower instances.

A detected flower which does not have sufficient overlap with any ground truth instance is considered a false positive. Those ground truth instances which did not overlap with any detected instance are considered false negatives. From these measures, the precision and recall were calculated,

$$\text{Precision} = \frac{TP}{TP + FP}, \tag{2}$$

$$\text{Recall} = \frac{TP}{TP + FN}, \tag{3}$$

where TP = the number of true positives, FP = the number of false positives, and FN = the number of false negatives.

For evaluating the segmentation at the pixel level, all instance masks in a given image detected by our method were combined into a single mask and compared to the pixel-wise ground truth. In this case, TP, FP, and FN refer to the number of pixels rather than the instances.

3 Results

The numbers of true positives, false positives, and false negatives along with the precision and recall for both, the instance level and pixel level segmentation of the flowers are presented in Table 1. The proposed method obtained a precision of 0.797 and a recall of 0.77 with the following parameter values: $T_{B^*} = 128$, $T_I = 160$, $T_{RG} = 20$. The value of the precision obtained by us although lower than the ones reported in [11] (0.80) and in [20] (0.84), was obtained on a more difficult experimental setup. The plot of the precision versus recall for different sets of these parameters, which are listed in Table 2, is presented in Fig. 5.

It can be seen from Table 1 that the pixel wise recall is significantly lower than the instance level recall, which implies that while our method is able to detect the central pixels of the flower instances, it loses the pixels closer to the edges.

Table 1. Figures of merit for segmentation of flowers using proposed method.

	True positives	False positives	False	Precision	Recall	IOU
Instance wise	100	26	32	0.797	0.773	–
Pixelwise	–	–	–	0.90	0.39	0.37

We present visual examples of the detection of flowers using the proposed method on two images, in Figs. 3(c) and 4(c). The ground truth flower instances along with the bounding boxes are shown in red, overlaid on the RGB images. The blue overlaid regions and bounding boxes correspond to detected flower instances. The flowers have been zoomed in, for better visual clarity.

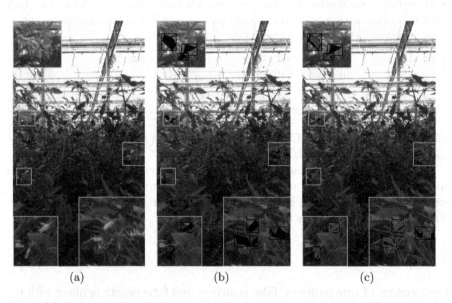

(a)　　　　　　　　　(b)　　　　　　　　　(c)

Fig. 3. (a) Example of an RGB image with the flowers zoomed in, (b) RGB image with annotated ground truth overlaid, (c) overlay with GT (red) and detections (blue). (Color figure online)

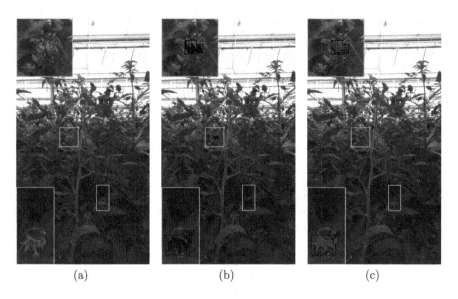

(a)   (b)   (c)

Fig. 4. (a) Example of an RGB image with the flowers zoomed in, (b) RGB image with annotated ground truth overlaid, (c) overlay with GT (red) and detections (blue). (Color figure online)

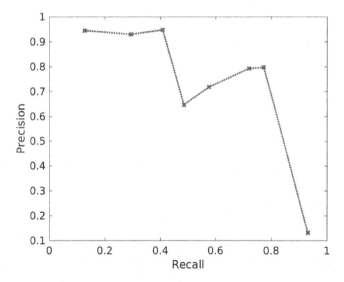

Fig. 5. Precision-Recall curve for different sets of parameters, from Table 2.

Table 2. Sets of values of the parameters of the proposed method, used in Fig. 5. Each column corresponds to a set of values, in increasing order of the recall values (left to right along the x axis).

T_{B^*}	128	128	128	170	128	160	128	128
T_I	160	160	160	160	160	160	160	150
T_{RG}	0	0	0	0	32	0	20	0
Min. area	500	300	200	50	50	50	50	50

4 Conclusions

We have presented an unsupervised method for detecting tomato flowers from images taken in a greenhouse with a Realsense camera, which was experimentally found to achieve a precision of 0.79 and recall of 0.77. These values are not far from those reported in previous work but with higher resolution and more expensive cameras and under relatively easier experimental setups. Thus, our method is able to come close to the level of state-of-the-art performance in flower detection, with a more difficult imaging setup and with a cheaper camera.

Current and future work include trying to improve the detection by using the depth channel from the Realsense camera to discard the background, and using the Maximally Stable Extremal Regions (MSER) method [9] to avoid having to empirically tune the parameters and to be able to deal with different measurement and ambient illumination conditions. The method proposed here can also be useful for preparing training data for deep learning object detectors such as the Mask Regional Convolutional Neural Network (MaskRCNN) algorithm [8]. An improvement in detection with occlusions and generalizability to different lighting conditions can be expected from deep learning. Transfer learning between images taken with other cameras such as plenoptic cameras will also be investigated.

References

1. Aquino, A., Millan, B., Gaston, D., Diago, M.P., Tardaguila, J.: vitisflower®: Development and testing of a novel android-smartphone application for assessing the number of grapevine flowers per inflorescence using artificial vision techniques. Sensors **15**(9), 21204–21218 (2015). https://doi.org/10.3390/s150921204. https://www.mdpi.com/1424-8220/15/9/21204
2. Aquino, A., Millan, B., Gutiérrez, S., Tardáguila, J.: Grapevine flower estimation by applying artificial vision techniques on images with uncontrolled scene and multi-model analysis. Comput. Electron. Agric. **119**, 92–104 (2015). https://doi.org/10.1016/j.compag.2015.10.009
3. Dias, P.A., Tabb, A., Medeiros, H.: Apple flower detection using deep convolutional networks. Comput. Ind. **99**, 17–28 (2018). https://doi.org/10.1016/j.compind.2018.03.010

4. Dias, P.A., Tabb, A., Medeiros, H.: Multispecies fruit flower detection using a refined semantic segmentation network. IEEE Robot. Autom. Lett. **3**(4), 3003–3010 (2018)
5. Csurka, G., Larlus, D., Perronnin, F.: What is a good evaluation measure for semantic segmentation? In: Proceedings of the British Machine Vision Conference. BMVA Press (2013)
6. Girshick, R.: Fast R-CNN. In: 2015 IEEE International Conference on Computer Vision (ICCV), pp. 1440–1448, December 2015. https://doi.org/10.1109/ICCV.2015.169
7. Gongal, A., Amatya, S., Karkee, M., Zhang, Q., Lewis, K.: Sensors and systems for fruit detection and localization: a review. Comput. Electron. Agric. **116**, 8–19 (2015). https://doi.org/10.1016/j.compag.2015.05.021. https://www.sciencedirect.com/science/article/pii/S0168169915001581
8. He, K., Gkioxari, G., Dollár, P., Girshick, R.: Mask R-CNN. In: 2017 IEEE International Conference on Computer Vision (ICCV), pp. 2980–2988. IEEE (2017)
9. Matas, J., Chum, O., Urban, M., Pajdla, T.: Robust wide-baseline stereo from maximally stable extremal regions. Image Vision Comput. **22**(10), 761–767 (2004)
10. Nilsback, M.E., Zisserman, A.: A visual vocabulary for flower classification. In: 2006 IEEE Computer Society Conference on Computer Vision and Pattern Recognition (CVPR 2006), vol. 2, pp. 1447–1454. IEEE (2006)
11. Oppenheim, D., Edan, Y., Shani, G.: Detecting tomato flowers in greenhouses using computer vision. World Acad. Sci. Eng. Technol. Int. J. Comput. Electr. Autom. Control Inform. Eng. **11**(1), 104–109 (2017)
12. Russakovsky, O., et al.: ImageNet large scale visual recognition challenge. Int. J. Comput. Vision (IJCV) **115**(3), 211–252 (2015). https://doi.org/10.1007/s11263-015-0816-y
13. Russell, B.C., Torralba, A., Murphy, K.P., Freeman, W.T.: LabelMe: a database and web-based tool for image annotation. Int. J. Comput. Vision **77**(1), 157–173 (2008). https://doi.org/10.1007/s11263-007-0090-8
14. Simonyan, K., Zisserman, A.: Very deep convolutional networks for large-scale image recognition. arXiv preprint. arXiv:1409.1556 (2014)
15. Szeliski, R.: Computer Vision: Algorithms and Applications. Springer, London (2010). https://doi.org/10.1007/978-1-84882-935-0
16. Wang, Z., Li, H., Zhu, Y., Xu, T.: Review of plant identification based on image processing. Arch. Comput. Methods Eng. **24**(3), 637–654 (2017). https://doi.org/10.1007/s11831-016-9181-4
17. Wood, R., Nagpal, R., Wei, G.Y.: Flight of the robobees. Sci. Am. **308**(3), 60–65 (2013)
18. Yamamoto, K., Guo, W., Ninomiya, S.: Node detection and internode length estimation of tomato seedlings based on image analysis and machine learning. Sensors **16**(7), 1044 (2016)
19. Zhao, Y., Gong, L., Huang, Y., Liu, C.: Robust tomato recognition for robotic harvesting using feature images fusion. Sensors **16**(2), 173 (2016)
20. Zhou, Y., Xu, T., Zheng, W., Deng, H.: Classification and recognition approaches of tomato main organs based on DCNN. Trans. Chin. Soc. Agric. Eng. **33**(15), 219–226 (2017)

Metbots: Metabolomics Robots
for Precision Viticulture

R. C. Martins[(✉)] [ID], S. Magalhães [ID], P. Jorge [ID], T. Barroso, and F. Santos [ID]

INESCTEC, Campus da FEUP, Rua Dr Roberto Frias, 4200-465 Porto, Portugal
rui.c.martins@inesctec.pt
http://www.inesctec.com/

Abstract. Metabolomics is paramount for precision agriculture. Knowing the metabolic state of the vine and its implication for grape quality is of outermost importance for viticulture and wine industry. The MetBots system is a metabolomics precision agriculture platform, for automated monitoring of vineyards, providing geo-referenced metabolic images that are correlated and interpreted by an artificial intelligence self-learning system for aiding precise viticultural practices. Results can further be used to analyze the plant metabolic response by genome-scale models. In this research, we introduce the system main components: (i) robotic platform; (ii) autonomous navigation; (iii) sampling arm manipulation; (iv) spectroscopy systems; and (v) non-invasive, real-time metabolic hyper-spectral imaging monitoring of vineyards. The full potential of the Metbots system is revealed when metabolic data and images are analyzed by big data AI and systems biology vine plant models, establishing a new age of molecular biology precision agriculture.

Keywords: Metabolism · Spectroscopy · Artificial intelligence ·
Autonomous systems · Non-invasive · 'In-vivo' monitoring

1 Introduction

Wine is a highly complex biotechnology product. It all begins at the vineyard, where the interaction of soil, climate and plant physiology, determines the desired characteristics. Producing high-quality wines on a constant basis is the major goal of precision viticulture.

Multi-spectral satellite, drone imaging and 'in-situ' sensors, when complemented with pattern recognition and artificial intelligence, are today the state-of-the-art of the 21st century viticulture [34]. Although aerial technologies are able to cover significant land masses [17,33,37], almost no information about the plant metabolism, grape quality and soil nutrients, is possible to be obtained from these methods. A characteristic example is the normalized difference vegetation index (NDVI). NDVI is poorly correlated to important metabolites, such

Supported by FCT project Metbots (POCI-01-0145-FEDER-031124).

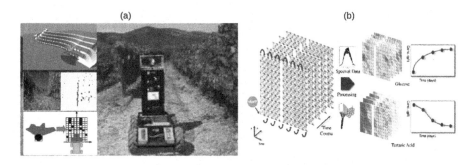

Fig. 1. Metbots metabolic imaging: (a) AgRob V16 robotic platform (navigation, positioning, sampling); (b) geo-referenced uv-vis-swnir hyperspectral metabolic imaging

as, the phenolic composition [17]. Only 'in-situ' technology is able to provide rich metabolic information.

'In-situ' technology is available to viticulture, such as: (i) computer vision: determining production yield [1,6]; (ii) soil composition (vis-swnir, x-ray fluorescence, LIBS) [31,32], and (iii) grape composition [23,36]. Uv-vis-swnir spectroscopy has shown to be a robust metabolomics tool in viticulture [8,23]. Parameters such as: degree Brix, total soluble solids [5,18], total acidity and reducing sugars and acids [9], and polyphenols [15]. Furthermore, results from 'in-situ' systems [12,36] have shown random sampling of grapes during traditional maturation control, and cannot describe the 'terroir' nor viticultural practices impact on grape quality. High-resolution geo-referenced metabolic imaging technology is able to characterize the impact of soil, climate and viticultural practices on grape quality, with emphasis on sugar/acids, anthocyanin, beta-carotene and lutein [23].

We developed a precision geo-referenced metabolic imaging using uv-vis-swnir spectroscopy [24]. The system accuracy was significantly increased by developing a big data self-learning AI methodology, for the accurate quantification and classification of spectral information, under complex variability and multi-scale interference. This new method has allowed to decrease most of quantification errors of previous technologies to low quantification errors [20].

Grape maturation was followed from May to September in experimental fields, using a geo-referenced sampling mesh (spectra and grape samples were collected at nodal points), mostly in Douro, Dão and Ribatejo, to grape varieties such as Tinta Roriz, Touriga Franca, Syrah, Touriga Nacional and Pinot Noir. The developed system performs geo-referenced metabolic images to: glucose, fructose, tartaric and malic acids, neoxanthins, zeoxanthins, anthocyanins, beta-carotene and lutein [13,21–23]. The user can visualize the metabolic evolution of grape maturation with a viewer software, and navigate along the field for obtaining the grape composition at the points of sampling an in-between, by the finite element method.

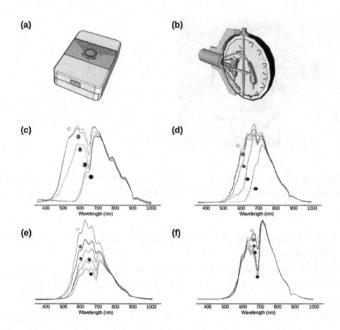

Fig. 2. Metbots IoT Spectroscopy System: (a) IoT Spectroscopy device; (b) Grape structures captured by light; and spectra along maturation from (c) grapes; (d) grape skins; (e) grape pulps and (f) grape seeds. The capacity of measuring these three structures is of most importance to wine quality, as different compounds are present in skin, pulp and seeds.

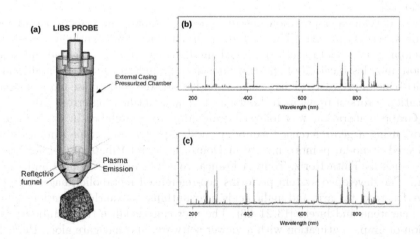

Fig. 3. Metbots LIBS system: (a) LIBS probe for agricultural applications; (b) leaf spectra without pesticide treatment; (c) leaf spectra with pesticide treatment.

Uv-vis-swnir is capable to show that: (i) the soil composition influences directly the grape maturation process; and (ii) irrigation regime influence on technical maturation (sugars/acids), anthocyanins and beta-carotenes [13,23].

The system is capable of monitoring chlorophyll-like compounds and carotenoids present in the grapes. These are important precursors of norisoprenoids, a key constituent of high-quality Port wine aromas. During Port wine ageing due to oxidation, beta-carotenes levels decrease, giving rise to TDN, vitispirane and TCH. In lutein supplemented wines, b-damascenone increases, and when supplemented with b-carotene, b-ionone and b-cyclocitral levels increase 2.5 times [13]. Carotenoids are known to depend on cultivar, climate conditions, viticultural region, irrigation, sunlight exposure and ripening stage [29].

Carotenoids are mostly present in the grape skin (65% of total berry carotenoids: lutein, xanthophyll and b-carotene), being easily detected by spectroscopy (Fig. 2). Carotenes are considered as light harvesters, as a protection to excessive light in unripe grapes. However, during maturation, grapes exposed to light have lower levels of carotene [8]. Oliveira et al. [29] also found that terrain elevation (lower temperatures and higher humidity) lead to the production of higher contents of carotenoids. Also, lower vegetative indexes correspond to lower carotenoid concentrations. Furthermore, soils with low water retention capacity always produce grapes with higher levels of carotenoids [29].

Figure 2 presents the current system under design and how it measures grape composition. It can work as portable miniature analyzer IoT device, that connects to a mobile phone or the AgRob V16 robot. The reflection probe in Fig. 2b uses a special designed fibre optics reflection probe, to provide spectral integration of the grape internal anatomy. With this configuration, the optics can obtain spectral information about the skin, pulp and seeds. Spectral integration is shown in Fig. 2c–f, where the grape spectra Fig. 2c is the integration of the skin (Fig. 2d), pulp (Fig. 2e) and seeds (Fig. 2e) spectra.

The miniaturized spectrometer can be used by a human to record the spectra (Fig. 2). It is not adequate for covering vast areas and difficult terrains, such as the Douro valley, and therefore this task is automated in Metbots. There is still very few available robots for agricultural applications. In fact, in the last two decades some robotic solutions were developed for specific tasks in agriculture, however, due to the characteristics of the terrain and the type of crops used, many of these solutions are not easily scalable and/or reproducible to other farms. The INESCTEC robotics lab has been developing steep slope robotic platforms [35] (AgRob V16 - agrob.inesctec.pt) and ROMOVI (P2020 project) [26] for operating in the Douro valley terrains, that overcame: GPS signal problems, harsh terrain conditions that limit instrumentation and slopes impose precise path planning.

The present generation of robots uses our developed VineSLAM system [35] takes into consideration the natural and artificial features of the vineyard to recognize the localization, compensating for poor GPS accuracy. Tests of AgRob V16 in a real steep slope vineyard show that this platform can overcome ditches,

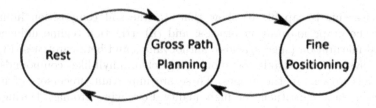

Fig. 4. Manipulation state machine

rocks and high slopes (30%). With a robust localization system, it can perform autonomously a crop monitoring task (crop yield, soil/air temperature/humidity and crop water stress index), being cost effective for the end-user.

The MetBots project main objective is to research and develop a robotic and AI system for metabolomics precision agriculture, using uv-vis-swnir and laser induced breakdown spectroscopy (LIBS), in conjunction with the AgRob V16 system (Fig. 1), to monitor the plant metabolism.

The project is divided into three main parts: (i) robotics and sensors - spectroscopy sensors are incorporated with the robotic platform for automatic monitoring; (ii) system infrastructure - where all the information is stored and processed by self-learning AI technology; and (iii) field tests - to validate the efficiency of automatic monitoring and diagnosis in real scenarios.

The research project is developed by Institute for Systems and Computer Engineering, Technology and Science (INESC TEC) and Duriense Viticultural Development Association Laboratories (ADVID), aiming to implement metabolic diagnosis in precision viticulture at the Portuguese Douro Valley wine region.

2   Manipulation

For a fully intelligent and autonomous system, it is required a robotic arm capable of handling the spectroscopy sensor, in order to copy the human behaviour on this task. However, autonomous sensing problem cannot be solved as some industrial problems, where static trajectories are predefined and the robot executes them repetitively. Instead, this case needs to accomplish active perception solutions [2] for grape recognition. So a complete manipulation solution has to accomplish the following steps: bunch of grapes and grapes detection and recognition [3,25], path planning [14,27], and trajectory control.

The Fig. 4 states the different stages of the manipulation sensing process. On rest state, a manipulator included sensor will continuously look to the vineyard searching for grapes bunches [3]. When a new bunch is detected, the system chooses if this bunch will be sampled. In a positive case, a gross planning is done to a near point of the bunch [14] and after a final path planning is made relative to the end-effector frame until the selected grape [25,27]. Finally, the manipulator returns to an initial standard position through a global path plan.

Table 1. Average quantification benchmark results for Tinta Roriz, Touriga Franca, Syrah and Cardinal cultivars

Parameter	Range	DL	R^2
Degree Brix	5.0–25.0	5.2	0.78
Glucose	1.3–160.0	7.3	0.77
Fructose	3.3–100.0	6.3	0.78
Malic Acid	1.0–10.0	0.37	0.82
Tartaric Acid	1.0–8.0	0.30	0.76

3 Spectroscopy Measurement Control

High-quality spectra, as shown in Fig. 2c, are necessary for accurate metabolite quantification. The spectral probe must contact the grape skin in order to avoid any reflections into the pin-hole receiver fiber (Fig. 2b). External fibers illuminate all regions of the grape, in order to obtain an integration of all grape structures (skin, pulp and seeds) (Fig. 2d to f).

Once the robotic arm positions the probe at 0.5 cm of the grape to be analyzed, the spectrometer data assumes positioning control. The spectra pattern is used to know if the probe is in the correct position, by the following procedure: (i) record spectra with the maximum power of the light source, while pushing forward the probe, until no surface reflection from the grape is detected; (ii) adjust the light source power and integration time for optimal spectra recording inside the linear region of quantification; and (iii) record the grape spectra.

The spectra pattern is analyzed by the projection into a principal components feature space, where a linear discriminant model, discriminates between the reflected light spectra and grape spectra.

4 Spectroscopy Processing

Vis-swnir spectrum were pre-processed to remove artifacts, such as, effects of baseline shifts, Mie and Rayleigh scattering and stray-light [7,10].

Correlation between spectra and grape composition was modelled by partial least squares regression (PLS) [11]. PLS is a linear multivariate model based on latent variables (eigenvectors/eigenvalues) that maximizes the co-variance matrix $(\mathbf{X}^t\mathbf{Y})$ between the spectrum matrix $(\mathbf{X})$ and the analytical chemistry data $(\mathbf{Y})$: $\mathbf{Y} = \mathbf{X}b + e$; where b translates the linear combination that projects the spectral information into the analytical chemistry data [30] (Fig. 5).

Grape variety may influence how we can relate the composition and spectral variation. Therefore, independent calibration predictive models were built for the different grape varieties: Touriga Nacional, Touriga Franca, Tinta Roriz, Syrah; and further table grapes of Cardinal variety. Representative samples across the different composition levels are paramount to build a globally stable PLS model.

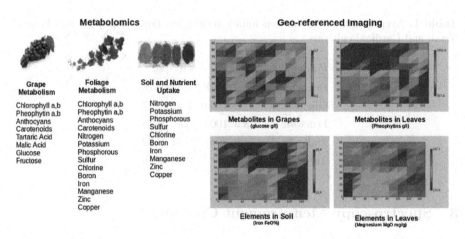

Fig. 5. Metbots metabolic geo-referenced uv-vis-swnir imaging in grapes, foliage and soil composition.

Therefore, each level of sugars and acids has the same level of representation in the global PLS model [4].

The PLS model describes a linear relationship between composition and spectral features. Such means that the correct number of latent variables (LV) is considered optimal, once it balances bias vs variance. In PLS modelling, the optimal number of LVs is considered the global minimum of the test set. This is the case in simple systems, where prediction errors increase due uncorrelated information present in the spectra. This does not happen when correlating grape spectra shown in Fig. 2 with composition, as the spectra is extremely rich in information about the grape composition. In this case, the PRESS continuously decreases, and no saddle point exits. Such means that we must ensure a new way of choosing the correct number of LVs that ensure model linearity, at the expense of higher variance, so that the PLS model can be used as a generalized linear model, capable of quantification along the range of variation.

To mitigate bias-variance and PLS linearity, we devised the following two step validation scheme:

i. global cross-validation: we used all data to develop the global model cross-validation PRESS curve and select solely the number of LVs that are with the steepest descent on PRESS optimization to the second step. The procedure is as follows: we devised the composition range into 50 intervals with n-k samples at each level. The remaining k samples were used to perform the model validation at each level. The cross-validation PRESS is computed for the k validation datasets, until all data is used to build validation datasets. The Kennard and Stone algorithm [16] was used to select representative samples at each level, so that all natural variability is all accounted for in the regression model, minimizing the risk of biased models. This scheme allows to set-up an uniform sampling bootstrapping and cross-validation [19].

ii. extrapolation cross-validation: using only the selected number of LVs in the previous step, we now must select the minimum number of LVs that allow to maintain a stable linear model, by minimizing biased predictions under extrapolation, so that:

$$Range(\%) = \frac{max(\mathbf{Y}) - min(\mathbf{Y})}{max(\mathbf{Y}^c) - min(\mathbf{Y}^c)} \tag{1}$$

where $\mathbf{Y}^c$ is the dataset used for the calibration, and $\mathbf{Y}$ the corresponding global calibration dataset. The objective of the 2nd step is to obtain the minimum number of LVs that hold a maximal range of prediction with minimal range of training set, so that a globally stable linear unbiased calibration is obtained. To further understand if the extracted PLS coefficients are statistically stable, 1000 boostrap samples with n-1 samples were used to determine the coefficients variation and significance assessed by the t-student test [19, 28].

This method allows to derive quantification for the major constituents of the grape, as presented in Table 1. PLS modeling allows to reasonably quantify 'in-situ' the degree Brix, glucose, fructose, malic and tartaric acids. The project aims to develop model calibrations also for: chlorophylls a and b, pheophytins a and b, anthocyanins and carotenoids, using uv-vis-swnir. The project will further explore the measurement of elements in soils and leaves (e.g. N, Fe, Cu, S, Cl, Mn, Zn, P, K) using LIBS spectroscopy, as well as, determine the amounts of applied agro-chemicals, as presented in Fig. 3, where trace levels of pesticide can be discriminated between control (Fig. 3b) and treated leaf (Fig. 3c).

5   Hyperspectral and Metabolic Imaging

Hyperspectral images are assembled from individual spectral measurements at nodal points from a pre-established geo-referenced mesh that minimizes sampling time (see Fig. 1). The robot is set into a pre-determined path to stop at specific vines, where it collects geo-referenced measurements. A part of this measurements is uv-vis-swnir and LIBS spectra. In uv-vis-swnir measurements, three grapes are measured at each vine. Each measurement takes approximately 1 min. Images are taken with 100 nodal points density per hectare, which can be done in approximately 2 h, depending on the 'terroir' topographic features. The metabolic image is reconstructed by inference of composition from spectral PLS regression models at each node. Metabolite gradients are interpolated using triangular finite elements, so that visualization is continuous across the vineyard mesh. Metabolic images can be validated by physical collection of samples at selected nodal points and performing corresponding laboratory chemical analysis.

The full potential of metabolic imaging using uv-vis-swnir and LIBS spectroscopy is presented in Fig. 4. Uv-vis-swnir and LIBS spectroscopy provides a comprehensive characterization of metabolites and nutrients, such as: chlorophylls a and b, pheophytins a and b, anthocyanins, carotenoids, tartaric and malic acids, degree Brix, glucose and fructose; as well as, major inorganic nutrients (nitrogen, potassium, phosphorous, sulfur, iron, magnesium, manganese, boron, zinc or copper). These parameters can be, for the first time, geo-referenced and compiled for grapes, leaves and soil; providing a significantly more complete set of information about the vine metabolism than previous technologies.

Metbots records information about plant metabolism. It is a new tool that opens precision viticulture to molecular biology viticultural management practices. Molecular information will allow to use data science/ artificial intelligence, to both analyze and predict the effects of agricultural practices, as well as, to make use of state of plant genome scale models, inferring the vine plant physiological response at the genetic, proteomic and metabolome levels. The Metbots project hopes to bring to the field, precision metabolomics and molecular biology, allowing producers and researchers to confront knowledge obtained under controlled laboratory or field test conditions, against what is observed in the open field by large scale sampling and integrative data from climate-soil-plant.

Acknowledgments. National Funds through FCT - Portuguese Foundation for Science and Technology, 'Metbots-Metabolomic Robots with Self-learning Artificial Intelligence for Precision Agriculture' Reference PTDC/EEI-ROB/31124/2017 and FEDER funds through the COMPETE 2020 Programme under the project number POCI-01-0145-FEDER-031124.

References

1. Arnó, J., Rosell, J.R., Blanco, R., Ramos, M.C., Martínez-Casasnova, J.A.: Spatial variability in grape yield and quality influenced by soil and crop nutrition characteristics. Precis. Agric. **13**(3), 393–410 (2012)
2. Bajcsy, R., Aloimonos, Y., Tsotsos, J.K.: Revisiting active perception. Auton. Robots **42**(2), 177–196 (2018). https://doi.org/10.1007/s10514-017-9615-3
3. Berenstein, R., Shahar, O.B., Shapiro, A., Edan, Y.: Grape clusters and foliage detection algorithms for autonomous selective vineyard sprayer. Intell. Serv. Robot. **3**(4), 233–243 (2010). https://doi.org/10.1007/s11370-010-0078-z
4. Bouveresse, E., Massart, D.: Improvement of the piecewise direct standardisation procedure for the transfer of NIR spectra for multivariate calibration. Chemometr. Intell. Lab. Syst. **32**(2), 201–213 (1996)
5. Dambergs, R., Cozzolino, D., Cynkar, W., Janik, L., Gishen, M.: The determination of red-grape quality parameters using the local algorithm. J. Near Infrared Spectrosc. **14**, 71–79 (2006)
6. Diago, M.P., Correa, C., Millan, B., Barreiro, P., Valero, C., Tardaguila, J.: Grapevine yield and leaf area estimation using supervised classification methodology on RGB images taken under field conditions. Sensors **12**(12), 16988–17006 (2012)
7. Feinholz, M., et al.: Stray light correction algorithm for multichannel hyperspectral spectrographs. Appl. Opt. **51**(16), 3631–3641 (2005)
8. Fernandes, A., et al.: Determination of anthocyanin concentration in whole grape skins using hyperspectral imaging and adaptive boosting neural networks. J. Food Eng. **105**(2), 216–226 (2011)

9. Fernández-Novales, J., López, M., Sánchez, M., Morales, J., González-Caballero, V.: Shortwave-near infrared spectroscopy for determination of reducing sugar content during grape ripening, winemaking, and aging of white and red wines. Food Res. Int. **42**(2), 285–291 (2009)
10. Gallagher, N., Blake, T., Gassman, P.: Application of extended inverse scatter correction to mid-infrared reflectance spectra of soil. J. Chemometr. **19**, 271–281 (2005)
11. Geladi, P., Kowalsky, B.: Partial least squares regression: a tutorial. Anal. Chem. Acta **185**, 1–17 (1986)
12. González-Caballero, V., Sánchez, M., Fernández-Novales, J., López, M., Pérez-Marín, D.: On-vine monitoring of grape ripening using near-infrared spectroscopy. Food Anal. Methods **5**(6), 1377–1385 (2012)
13. Guedes-Pinho, P., Martins, R., Vivier, M., Young, P., Oliveira, C., Silva-Ferreira, A.: Monitoring carotenoids and derived compounds in grapes and port wines: impact on quality, pp. 139–154 (2013)
14. Hwang, Y.K., Ahuja, N.: Gross motion planning—a survey. ACM Comput. Surv. **24**(3), 219–291 (1992). http://doi.acm.org/10.1145/136035.136037
15. Kemps, B., Leon, L., Best, S., Baerdemaeker, J., Ketelaere, B.: Assessment of the quality parameters in grapes using VIS/NIR spectroscopy. Biosyst. Eng. **105**(4), 507–513 (2010)
16. Kennard, R., Stone, L.: Computer aided design of experiments. Technometrics **11**, 137–148 (1969)
17. Lamb, D.W., Weedon, W.W., Bramley, R.G.V.: Using remote sensing to predict grape phenolics and colour at harvest in a cabernet sauvignon vineyard: timing observations against vine phenology and optimising image resolution. Aust. J. Grape Wine Res. **10**(1), 46–54 (2004)
18. Larrain, M., Guesalaga, A., Agosin, E.: Optimization of NIR spectral data management for quality control of grape bunches during on-vine ripening. IEEE Trans. Instrum. Meas. **57**(2), 294–302 (2008)
19. Manly, B.F.J.: Randomization, Bootstrap and Monte Carlo Methods in Biology, 2nd edn. (1998)
20. Martins, R.: Big data self-learning artificial intelligence methodology for the accurate quantification and classification of spectral information under complex variability and multi-scale interference (2018)
21. Martins, R., Silva-Ferreira, A.: Vinepat - facing the complexity of grape quality management and delivering a high-throughput device. In: XXXIV World Congress of Vine and Wine - The Wine Construction, Porto, Portugal, 20–27 June 2011 (2011)
22. Martins, R., Silva-Ferreira, A.: Vinepat - rapid, automated assessment and grading of fruit quality. In: Petrie, P.R. (ed.) ASVO Proceedings, Objective Measures of Wine and Grape Quality, Mildura, Australia, 25–26 July 2012 (2011)
23. Martins, R., Silva-Ferreira, A., Lopes, V.: Method and device for monitoring the production of grapes with UV-VIS-SWNIR (2013)
24. Martins, R., Sousa, N., Osorio, R.: Optical system for parameter charactreization of an element of body fluid or tissue (2014)
25. Mehta, S.S., Burks, T.F.: Vision-based control of robotic manipulator for citrus harvesting. Comput. Electron. Agric. **102**, 146–158 (2014). http://www.sciencedirect.com/science/article/pii/S0168169914000052
26. Mendes, J.M., dos Santos, F.N., Ferraz, N.A., et al.: Localization based on natural features detector for steep slope vineyards. J. Intell. Robot. Syst. (2019). https://doi.org/10.1007/s10846-017-0770-8

27. Mezouar, Y., Chaumette, F.: Path planning for robust image-based control. IEEE Trans. Robot. Autom. **18**(4), 534–549 (2002). https://doi.org/10.1109/TRA.2002. 802218

28. Neter, J., Kutner, M., Nachtsheine, C., Wasserman, W.: Applied Linear Statistical Models, 4th edn. IRWIN, Chicago (1996)

29. Oliveira, C., Silva-Ferreira, A., Mendes-Pinto, M., Hogg, T., Alves, F., Guedes-De-Pinho, P.: Carotenoid compounds in grapes and their relationship to plant water status. J. Agric. Food Chem. **51**(20), 5967–5971 (2003)

30. Phatak, A., Jong, S.: The geometry of partial least squares. J. Chemom. **11**, 311–338 (1997)

31. Ramirez-Lopez, L., Behrens, T., Schmidt, K., Stevens, A., Demattê, J., Scholten, T.: The spectrum-based learner: a new local approach for modelling soil VIS-NIR spectra of complex datasets. Geoderma **195–196**, 268–279 (2013)

32. Ramirez-Lopez, L., Behrens, T., Schmidt, K., Viscarra Rossel, R., Demattê, J., Scholten, T.: Distance and similarity-search metrics for use with soil VIS NIR spectra. Geoderma **199**, 43–53 (2013)

33. Raper, T.B., Varco, J.J.: Canopy-scale wavelength and vegetative index sensitivities to cotton growth parameters and nitrogen status. Precision Agric. **16**(1), 62–76 (2015)

34. Santesteban, L., Guillaume, S., Royo, J.B., Tisseyre, B.: Are precision agriculture tools and methods relevant at the whole-vineyard scale? Precision Agric. **14**(1), 2–17 (2013)

35. dos Santos, F.N., Sobreira, H., Campos, D., Morais, R., Moreira, A.P., Moreira, O.: Towards a reliable robot for steep slope vineyards monitoring (2016). https://doi.org/10.1007/s10846-016-0340-5

36. Sethuramasamyraja, B., Singh, H., Mazhuvancheriparambath, G.: Geospatial modeling of wine grape quality (anthocyanin) for optimum sampling strategy in mechanized on-the-go differential harvesting programs. Int. J. Eng. Sci. Technol. **2**(11), 6058–6073 (2010)

37. Zhang, C., Kovacs, J.M.: Canopy-scale wavelength and vegetative index sensitivities to cotton growth parameters and nitrogen status. Precision Agric. **13**(6), 693–712 (2012)

Nature Inspired Metaheuristics and Their Applications in Agriculture: A Short Review

Jorge Miguel Mendes[1,2](✉) (iD), Paulo Moura Oliveira[1,2] (iD),
Filipe Neves dos Santos[1] (iD), and Raul Morais dos Santos[1,2] (iD)

[1] INESC TEC – Institute for Systems and Computer Engineering,
Technology and Science, Pólo da UTAD, Vila Real, Portugal
{jorge.m.mendes,fbsantos}@inesctec.pt
[2] Engineering Department, UTAD – University of Trás-os-Montes e Alto Douro,
Quinta de Prados, Vila Real, Portugal
{oliveira,rmorais}@utad.pt

Abstract. Nature inspired metaheuristics algorithms have been the target of several studies in the most varied scientific areas due to their high efficiency in solving real world problems. This is also the case of agriculture. Among the most well-established nature inspired metaheuristics the ones selected to be addressed in this work are the following: genetic algorithms, differential evolution, simulated annealing, harmony search, particle swarm optimization, ant colony optimization, firefly algorithm and bat algorithm. For each of them, the mechanism that inspired it and a brief description of its operation is presented, followed by a review of their most relevant agricultural applications.

Keywords: Nature-inspired metaheuristics ·
Bio-inspired metaheuristics · Nabi in agroforestry applications ·
Precision agriculture

1 Introduction

Most engineering search and optimization problems are non-linear and with a high number of constraints. Consequently, finding optimal solutions to these problems requires efficient optimization algorithms [6]. Over the last decades, many algorithms have been studied and implemented with the aim of solving these problems with high degrees of complexity. These algorithms are called stochastic algorithms and, in general, they are of two types: heuristic and metaheuristic, with the term "meta" meaning "beyond" or "higher level" [77]. Given the high complexity of this type of problems it is hard to test all possible solutions/combinations. By using approximation algorithms it is possible to find, in a relatively short period of time, quality solutions to solve complex optimization problems. However there is no guarantee that optimal solutions are achieved. The two main components of any metaheuristic algorithm are: intensification

© Springer Nature Switzerland AG 2019
P. Moura Oliveira et al. (Eds.): EPIA 2019, LNAI 11804, pp. 167–179, 2019.
https://doi.org/10.1007/978-3-030-30241-2_15

and diversification (or exploitation and exploration) [7,70]. Diversification (or exploration) consists of looking for promising solutions in a wider search space, that still needs to be refined. This operation is equivalent to diversifying the search to avoid getting stuck in an local optimum (global search). These terms are usually used in general contexts. Intensification (or exploitation) consists of searching for a solution in a limited region of the search space in order to improve a promising solution already found. This operation is equivalent to refining the search in the proximity of the best solution found (local search). Usually these terms are used in population-based optimization techniques.

A large part of these metaheuristics are derived from the behavior of natural systems and are known as nature and bio-inspired (NABI) algorithms which, according to [45] can be organized into five categories: evolutionary algorithms; physical algorithms; swarm intelligence algorithms; bio-inspired algorithms; and other nature inspired algorithms. NABI metaheuristics have been subject to studies in a wide range of varied scientific areas [32]. This paper presents a literature review of the main nature and bio-inspired metaheuristics, with reference to their agricultural applications. It should be noted that this review is not an exhaustive review and was based in particular on results obtained through the Google Scholar, IEEE XPlore Digital Library and Science Direct platforms, using the following keywords: "heuristic"; "metaheuristic"; "metaheuristic in agriculture"; "natural-based metaheuristic"; "biological-based metaheuristic"; "genetic algorithms"; "genetic algorithms in agriculture"; and the same for all other metaheuristics discussed here. Some of the references were also obtained from other papers and not directly on the previously mentioned platforms.

The remaining of the paper is organized as follows: Sect. 2 presents a short review of some NABI algorithms found in the literature, with reference to the mechanism that inspired it, a description of its operation a web site where a MATLAB implementation of it can be downloaded and some of its agricultural applications. Section 3 concludes this review.

2   NABI Algorithms

Currently there is a huge number of NABI algorithms. Thus, in this study the following algorithms have been selected: (i) Genetic Algorithms (GA) [30]; (ii) Differential Evolution (DE) [62]; (iii) Simulated Annealing (SA) [36]; (iv) Harmony Search (HS) [25]; (v) Particle Swarm Optimization (PSO) [19]; (vi) Ant Colony Optimization (ACO) [15]; (vii) Firefly Algorithm (FA) [68]; (vii) Bat Algorithm (BA) [71]. The reason for selecting this algorithms are: (i) Most of these are considered well-established NABI metaheuristics with a wide range of successful applications including in agriculture. These are the cases for: GA, DE, SA, PSO and ACO; (ii) Some more recently NABI metaheuristics have also been applied to solve search and optimization problems in agriculture. In this section, the following methodology is used for each algorithm: (i) A brief overview is presented including their nature inspiration principles; (ii) Some agricultural applications are presented.

2.1 Genetic Algorithms

Initially developed by [30] in the 1960s, Genetic Algorithms (GA) are a meta-heuristic inspired by the process of natural selection that belongs to the class of evolutionary algorithms (EA) and are commonly used to generate quality solutions to problems of search and optimization. GA main operators are: selection, reproduction/crossover and mutation [44]. The evolutionary process begins with a set of chromosomes, called initial population. Each chromosome represents a solution to the problem to be solved, characterized by a set of parameters (variables) known as genes. In the original GA, the set of genes is represented using a binary string. A *fitness function* determines how suitable the chromosome is (the ability to compete with other chromosomes) and assigns it a fitness score representing the probability of being selected for reproduction. In the *selection*, the fittest chromosomes may be allowed to pass their genes to the next generation. Chromosomes with high fitness are more likely to be selected for reproduction. *Crossover* is the most significant GA operator, where a point of intersection within the genes is chosen randomly for each pair of parents to join. In certain offspring, some of their genes can be mutated, which implies that some bits may be inverted. The mutation occurs to maintain the population diversity and prevent premature convergence. The GA execution can end when the population stops converging (does not produce offspring which are significantly different from the previous generation), thus providing a set of solutions to a given problem [42]. Besides reproduction/crossover and mutation, it is possible to use other operators such as regrouping, colonization-extinction, or migration [3]. A MATLAB implementation of GA can be downloaded in [79].

In [47] a method is reported to create a suboptimal path of an agricultural mobile robot using a control technique combining a GA and a *Neural Network* (NN). [21] presents a multi-objective optimization methodology for adaptive wireless sensor network design and energy management. A precision agriculture sensor network application was used as an example. In [39], a GA and a *Support Vector Machine* (SVM) are proposed to forecast water consumption in agriculture. The predication of water consumption in agriculture is significant to set the planning of configuration optimization of water resources. [28] proposes a smart farming approach to perform weather forecasting using a GA and *Fast Fourier Transform* (FFT). The proposed model helps farmers to plan the agriculture activities.

In [48], the operation of water pumps in the irrigation systems, limited by the amount of available energy, was simulated and optimized in order to minimize energy consumption. [29] proposes an automated land partitioning using a GA, showing that it is possible to accelerate the process of partitioning. Land partitioning is one of the most significant problems within the land consolidation process being an important process to prevent land fragmentation and enhance agricultural productivity.

2.2   Differential Evolution

The first publication on Differential Evolution (DE) was reported by [62] in 1995. DE is similar to GA, since both are based on the principles of evolutionary biology, such as mutation, crossover and selection. The DE is an evolutionary based algorithm that natively support floating-point based solution representations [58]. According to [13], DE has a simple structure, easy to use, and with considerable speed and robustness, making it one of the best evolutionary type algorithms to solve real world optimization problems. DE is a search technique based on a vector population (*target vector* – contains the current solution; *mutant vector* – corresponds to the mutation of the target vector; *trial vector* – vector resulting after crossing operations between the target and mutant vectors). The basic idea behind DE is a new scheme for generating test parameter vectors. DE generates new parameter vectors by adding the weighted difference vector between two population members to a third member. If the resulting vector produces a lower objective function value than another population member, the newly generated vector replaces the vector with which it was compared. In addition, the best parameter vector is evaluated for each generation in order to track the progress made during the optimization process. Extracting the distance and the direction information from the population to generate random deviations result in an adaptive scheme with excellent convergence properties [54]. A MATLAB implementation of DE can be downloaded in [80].

Agricultural models are often associated with difficult-to-solve optimization problems. In [2] a multi-objective DE algorithm is presented using four strategies to solve a crop planning model with multiple constraints. The model objectives are to minimize irrigation water consumption and maximize total crop yield and total agricultural production. In [1] a DE algorithm is used to solve a crop planning problem. The three proposed objectives for the crop planning problem are maximization of total net benefit and total agricultural output while minimizing the total irrigation water used.

2.3   Simulated Annealing

The Simulated Annealing (SA) algorithm was proposed by [36] in 1983. It is a probabilistic technique inspired by heat treatment processes in the metallurgical area [9]. These metallurgical processes consist in heating and controlled cooling a material, thereby altering certain physical properties allowing, for example, to eliminate defects in the material [65]. The heating is done to a temperature above the recrystallization temperature of the metal, followed by slow and gradual cooling. SA accepts search moves to worse solutions (lesser quality) that allows some uphill steps so that it can escape from local minimums [34]. The acceptance of worse solutions is a fundamental property of metaheuristics because it allows for a wider search for the ideal solution. In SA, the slow cooling is interpreted as a slow decrease in the probability of accepting worse solutions as the solution search is explored. SA algorithm starts from an single initial solution. Then a neighboring solution is randomly selected and both solutions cost is evaluated.

If the new solution has a lower cost then the algorithm accepts it, otherwise it accepts it with a probability $e^{-\Delta/T}$ where Δ represents the difference between the solution costs and T is the temperature. Initially T assumes a predefined higher value and it is decreased progressively in each iteration. The termination criterion can be the temperature reaching zero [23]. A MATLAB implementation of SA can be downloaded in [84].

[52] proposes a new maximization methodology using SA techniques to recover energy, considering the feasibility of the pump working as a turbine installation within irrigation networks. SA techniques were used with different objective functions as well as different number of machines. The study presented in [40] attempted to characterize the spatial patterns of lead (Pb) in the soil of a rice field by comparing the sequential Gaussian simulation, SA techniques and *Kriging* methods. [5] addresses the potential of using area-based binocular stereo vision for three-dimensional (3D) analysis of single plants and estimation of geometric attributes such as height and total leaf area. To perform the stereo matching, a SA method was used to find the best candidates to match, taking neighboring pixels into consideration. [10] presents an innovative on-farm irrigation scheduling decision support method called the Canterbury Irrigation Scheduler (CIS) that is suitable when seasonal water availability is limited. The irrigation strategies are defined by a set of decision variables and optimized by using SA.

2.4 Harmony Search

Harmony Search (HS), presented by [25] in 2001, it is based on musical concepts and can be inserted in the class of physical-inspired metaheuristics. HS is a phenomenon-mimicking metaheuristic inspired by the improvisation process of jazz musicians [25]. An analogy is made between the improvisation process of a jazz band and an optimization process. Musicians try to find a satisfactory harmony that is determined by an aesthetic standard, in the same way that an optimization process looks for an optimal solution that is determined by an objective function [38]. In a simple way, each musician (decision variables) reproduces (generates) a note (a value) to find a better harmony (global optimum).

In the music process, the harmony quality is determined by the tone of each instrument, i.e. the value of the objective function is determined by the set of values assigned to each variable. The musician makes several attempts to find harmony, just as the HS algorithm performs several iterations until it finds the best solution. In short, it was found that both processes were intended to be optimal in their areas [57]. The HS is simple in concept, low in parameters, and easy in implementation [24], but very efficient. As described in [25], a set of solutions (Harmony memory) is generated randomly. Given this set of solutions, a new solution is generated and if it is better than the worst solution present in the Harmony memory, the worst solution is replaced by the new one. The process is repeated until a stopping criterion is satisfied. A MATLAB implementation of HS can be downloaded in [82].

In [64], an HS approach is proposed to optimize the coverage path planning (CPP) problem applied to aerial vehicles, intending to minimize the number of turns, to ensure that the mission time is likewise minimized. In [43], a system based on HS was developed allowing to predict the shoot length of a mustard plant. According to this study, measuring the plant growth with respect to shoot length is the most convenient method to estimate the plant production.

2.5   Particle Swarm Optimization

Particle Swarm Optimization (PSO) was developed by [19] in 1995, and it is a population-based stochastic optimization technique [35], inspired by the social behavior of swarms (e.g. bird flocks and fish shoals). In a simple way, the PSO optimizes a problem by trying to iteratively improve candidate solutions against a given quality measure. Potential solutions, called particles, "fly" through the search space according to some simple formulas [85], where the motion of each individual particle is influenced by its best known position, but also by other swarm particles best positions. This causes the swarm to move iteratively to the best solutions. A MATLAB implementation of PSO can be downloaded in [83].

In [33], a RBF neural network based on PSO is proposed to fuse the position information from multi-sensors to obtain more precise information in agriculture vehicle navigation. In [41], PSO and SVM are combined for agriculture water consumption forecasting that is important to optimize configuration of water resources. [60] presents a system based on PSO to solve sugarcane mechanical harvester route planning. A new particle encoding/decoding scheme has been devised for combining the path planning with the accessibility and split harvesting constraints. In [12], PSO is proposed as a new method to design an air temperature controller subject to restrictions. The controller outputs are computed to optimize the future behavior of greenhouse environment variables.

2.6   Ant Colony Optimization

Ant Colony Optimization (ACO) was initially proposed by [15] in 1992. The first algorithm aimed to look for an ideal path in a graph, based on the behavior of ants looking for the best path between their colonies and food sources. Later, in [17], the ACO metaheuristic was formalized as it is known today. It is known that when an ant of a certain specie finds a good (i.e., short) path from the colony to a food source, it creates a pheromone path. The path pheromone marking makes other ants more likely to follow it, and positive feedback eventually leads that all the ants follow a single path. However, over time, the pheromone path begins to evaporate, thus reducing its attracting force to new ants [14]. This evaporation has the advantage of avoiding convergence to a optimal local solution, because if there was no evaporation, the paths chosen by the first ants would tend to be overly attractive for the following ones and in that case the exploration of the solution space would be limited [18]. The ACO is therefore a probabilistic technique that exploits a similar mechanism through "virtual" ants [8] that walk around a graph representing the optimization problem to be solved [16]. A MATLAB implementation of ACO can be downloaded in [78].

In [46] a generic simulation-optimization framework for optimal irrigation and fertilizer scheduling is proposed. The problem is represented in the form of decision-tree graphs and ACO is used as the optimization mechanism. [4] proposes a task scheduling algorithm and a model to improve the farmers contracting process in small and medium-scale agriculture. In agriculture at this scale, it is usually not feasible for farmers to buy expensive equipment to perform the agricultural tasks, and thus it is common for farmers who own such equipment to work in neighboring farms.

2.7 Firefly Algorithm

The Firefly Algorithm (FA) was developed by [68] in 2008. It is an optimization algorithm based on the behavior of fireflies, also known as lightning bugs. This algorithm is inspired by light patterns and the behavior of fireflies, known to be bioluminescent organisms. It is based, therefore, on the ability of fireflies to vary the intensity of the luciferin emission which makes them appear to glow at different intensities. Currently it is known that this mechanism is associated with three main factors: prey attraction, defense against predators and mating. Fireflies of different species have different shades and patterns of light. Through these characteristics it is possible that a firefly recognizes other fireflies of the same species and chooses the best partner depending on the intensity of the light emitted by it. Light can also be used to attract prey, that is, if a firefly is hungry, the light will shine more intensely in order to make insect attraction more effective [37].

The FA begins with an initial population of fireflies. Then the quality of the current solution is evaluated, the population of fireflies is classified according to their physical values and the best individual of the population is selected. Lastly, all fireflies move toward the most attractive individual. The process is repeated until a stop condition is satisfied [22]. In [69] a new version of the FA for multimodal optimization applications was introduced. To simplify the description of the algorithm the following three rules were used: All fireflies are unisex and, in this way, a firefly can be attracted to any of the other fireflies, regardless of their sex; The attractiveness is proportional to the brightness of the fireflies, so it will always be the less brilliant firefly to move to the brightest. If there is not one firefly brighter than another, they will move randomly. However, the intensity (apparent brightness) decreases as their mutual distance increases; The brightness should be associated with the objective function and, for a maximization problem, it may be simply proportional to the value of that function. A MATLAB implementation of FA can be downloaded in [81].

In [31], a new method that uses an FA, with the objective of optimizing the operation of a reservoir of agricultural water supply is proposed. The used objective function was defined in a way to minimize the sum of the quadratic differences between the needs and the expenses of the reservoir divided by the maximum need during the operation. The performance of the used model was compared with the performance obtained using GA and PSO. In [66], the authors present an application of FA to estimate the water resources demand in Nanchang city of China. In this case, the use of these resources is divided in three main sectors: industry, consumption of the residents and agriculture.

2.8 Bat Algorithm

Bat Algorithm (BA) is a metaheuristic, developed by [71] in 2010, that showed a promising efficiency in solving global optimization problems [77]. This algorithm was inspired by the echolocation behaviour of microbats. This echolocation process can be summarized in the following 3 rules [75,76]: (i) All bats use echolocation to determine the distance to the obstacles in the surrounding environment, and they also have the ability to distinguish between food/prey and background barriers; (ii) To search for prey, bats ($i = 1, 2, ..., n$) randomly fly into a position (solution) x_i at a velocity v_i, with a fixed frequency f_{min} and loudness A_0. As they search for their prey, bats automatically adjust the wavelength (frequency) and the rate of pulse emission $r \in [0, 1]$, depending on the proximity of the target; (iii) Although the loudness can vary in many ways, it is supposed that the loudness varies from a large (positive) A_0 to a minimum constant value A_{min}.

BA essentially uses a frequency-tuning technique to control the dynamic behaviour of a swarm of bats and automatically balances exploration (long-range jumps around the global search space in order to avoid being trapped at a local maximum) with exploitation (look for more details around good solutions to find local maxima), by controlling loudness and pulse emission rates of simulated bats in the multi-dimensional search space [71]. A MATLAB implementation of BA can be downloaded in [72].

In [59], the authors propose a novel BA-based clustering approach for solving crop type classification problems using multispectral satellite images. According to the authors, all the information can be used in the overall improvement of the agricultural yield.

2.9 Other NABI Algorithms

There are some other NABI algorithms presented in the literature, such as Bacterial Foraging Optimization [51], Dendritic Cell Algorithm [27], Gravitational Search Algorithm [56], Bees Algorithm [53], Intelligent Water Drops Algorithm [61], Spiral Optimization Algorithm [63], Cuckoo Search Algorithm [74], Tabu Search Algorithm [26], River Formation Dynamics [55], Flower Pollination Algorithm [73] and Cuttlefish Optimization Algorithm [20]. Many others can be found in [11,45,50,67] and in [49] is presented a review of several Evolutionary and Bio-Inspired Algorithms in the context of environmental control of greenhouses, for single or multiple objectives, as well as current trends.

3 Conclusion

An introduction to nature and biologically inspired metaheuristics was presented followed by a review of a representative selected set and their most relevant agricultural applications. This set includes not only the most well-established NABI metaheuristics, but also some more recently introduced ones, with reported applications in agriculture. The number of applications found in the literature survey regarding the GA, DE, SA, HS, PSO, ACO, FA and BA algorithms, motivated their revision with more detail. From the reviewed applications it is possible to conclude that GA, DE, SA, PSO and ACO are the algorithms that present a greater number of applications in the agriculture scope, as expected, since they are some of the older and more well-established algorithms. However, newer algorithms such as HS, FA and BA also have some applications in this scope and it is expectable that the number of applications tends to increase in the nearby future due to the increasing adoption of precision agriculture techniques. Future work will involve a deeper critical analysis of the reviewed algorithms and works, as well as several other metaheuristics presented in Sect. 2.9.

Acknowledgements. This work was funded by FCT (Portuguese Foundation for Science and Technology), within the framework of the project "WaterJPI/0012/2016". The authors would like to thank the EU and FCT for funding in the frame of the collaborative international consortium Water4Ever financed under the ERA-NET Water Works 2015 cofounded call. This ERA-NET is an integral part of the 2016 Joint Activities developed by the Water Challenge for a changing world joint programme initiation (Water JPI). This work was developed under the Doctoral fellowship with the reference "SFRH/BD/129813/2017", from FCT.

References

1. Adeyemo, J., Bux, F., Otieno, F.: Differential evolution algorithm for crop planning: single and multi-objective optimization model. Int. J. Phys. Sci. **5**(10), 1592–1599 (2010)
2. Adeyemo, J., Otieno, F.: Differential evolution algorithm for solving multi-objective crop planning model. Agric. Water Manag. **97**(6), 848–856 (2010)
3. Akbari, R., Ziarati, K.: A multilevel evolutionary algorithm for optimizing numerical functions. Int. J. Industr. Eng. Comput. **2**(2), 419–430 (2011)
4. Alaiso, S., Backman, J., Visala, A.: Ant colony optimization for scheduling of agricultural contracting work. IFAC Proc. Vol. **46**(18), 133–137 (2013)
5. Andersen, H.J., Reng, L., Kirk, K.: Geometric plant properties by relaxed stereo vision using simulated annealing. Comput. Electron. Agric. **49**(2), 219–232 (2005)
6. Bäck, T., Fogel, D., Michalewicz, Z.: Handbook of evolutionary computation. Release **97**(1), B1 (1997)
7. Blum, C., Roli, A.: Metaheuristics in combinatorial optimization: overview and conceptual comparison. ACM Comput. Surv. (CSUR) **35**(3), 268–308 (2003)
8. Brezina Jr., I., Čičková, Z.: Solving the travelling salesman problem using the ant colony optimization. Manage. Inf. Syst. **16**(4), 010–014 (2011)
9. Brooks, S.P., Morgan, B.J.: Optimization using simulated annealing. Statistician **44**, 241–257 (1995)
10. Brown, P.D., Cochrane, T.A., Krom, T.D.: Optimal on-farm irrigation scheduling with a seasonal water limit using simulated annealing. Agric. Water Manage. **97**(6), 892–900 (2010)

11. Brownlee, J.: Clever Algorithms: Nature-Inspired Programming Recipes. Jason Brownlee, Melbourne (2011)
12. Coelho, J., de Moura Oliveira, P., Cunha, J.B.: Greenhouse air temperature predictive control using the particle swarm optimisation algorithm. Comput. Electron. Agric. **49**(3), 330–344 (2005)
13. Das, S., Suganthan, P.N.: Differential evolution: a survey of the state-of-the-art. IEEE Trans. Evol. Comput. **15**(1), 4–31 (2011)
14. Dias, J.A.C., Machado, P., Pereira, F.C.: Privacy-aware ant colony optimization algorithm for real time route planning. In: Proceedings of the World Conference on Transport Research, p. 9 (2013)
15. Dorigo, M.: Optimization, learning, and natural algorithms. Ph.D. thesis, Politecnico di Milano, Milano (1992)
16. Dorigo, M., Birattari, M.: Ant colony optimization. In: Sammut, C., Webb, G.I. (eds.) Encyclopedia of Machine Learning. Springer, Boston (2011). https://doi.org/10.1007/978-0-387-30164-8
17. Dorigo, M., Caro, G.D., Gambardella, L.M.: Ant algorithms for discrete optimization. Artif. Life **5**(2), 137–172 (1999)
18. Dorigo, M., Stültze, T.: Ant Colony Optimization. The MIT Press, Cambridge (2004)
19. Eberhart, R., Kennedy, J.: A new optimizer using particle swarm theory. In: Proceedings of the Sixth International Symposium on Micro Machine and Human Science, MHS 1995, pp. 39–43. IEEE (1995)
20. Eesa, A.S., Brifcani, A.M.A., Orman, Z.: Cuttlefish algorithm-a novel bio-inspired optimization algorithm. Int. J. Sci. Eng. Res. **4**(9), 1978–1986 (2013)
21. Ferentinos, K.P., Tsiligiridis, T.A.: Adaptive design optimization of wireless sensor networks using genetic algorithms. Comput. Netw. **51**(4), 1031–1051 (2007)
22. Fister, I., Fister Jr., I., Yang, X.S., Brest, J.: A comprehensive review of firefly algorithms. Swarm Evol. Comput. **13**, 34–46 (2013)
23. Fuchigami, H.Y.: Algoritmo simulated annealing para programação de flow shops paralelos proporcionais com tempo de setup (2011). www.din.uem.br/sbpo/sbpo2011/pdf/88031.pdf. Accessed 22 Mar 2019
24. Geem, Z.W.: Recent Advances in Harmony Search Algorithm. Studies in Computational Intelligence, vol. 270. Springer, Heidelberg (2010). https://doi.org/10.1007/978-3-642-04317-8
25. Geem, Z.W., Kim, J.H., Loganathan, G.V.: A new heuristic optimization algorithm: harmony search. Simulation **76**(2), 60–68 (2001)
26. Glover, F.: Tabu search–part i. ORSA J. Comput. **1**(3), 190–206 (1989)
27. Greensmith, J., Aickelin, U., Cayzer, S.: Introducing dendritic cells as a novel immune-inspired algorithm for anomaly detection. In: Jacob, C., Pilat, M.L., Bentley, P.J., Timmis, J.I. (eds.) ICARIS 2005. LNCS, vol. 3627, pp. 153–167. Springer, Heidelberg (2005). https://doi.org/10.1007/11536444_12
28. Gumaste, S.S., Kadam, A.J.: Future weather prediction using genetic algorithm and FFT for smart farming. In: 2016 International Conference on Computing Communication Control and automation (ICCUBEA), pp. 1–6. IEEE (2016)
29. Hakli, H., Harun, U.: A novel approach for automated land partitioning using genetic algorithm. Expert Syst. Appl. **82**, 10–18 (2017)
30. Holland, J.H.: Adaptation in Natural and Artificial Systems: An Introductory Analysis with Applications to Biology, Control, and Artificial Intelligence. MIT Press, Cambridge (1992)

31. Hosseini, M.S.M., Banihabib, M.E.: Optimizing operation of reservoir for agricultural water supply using firefly algorithm. J. Soil Water Resour. Conserv. **3**, 17 (2014)
32. Hussain, K., Salleh, M.N.M., Cheng, S., Shi, Y.: Metaheuristic research: a comprehensive survey. Artif. Intell. Rev., 1–43 (2018)
33. Ji, Y., Zhang, M., Liu, G., Liu, Z.: Positions research of agriculture vehicle navigation system based on radial basis function neural network and particle swarm optimization. In: 2010 Sixth International Conference on Natural Computation (ICNC), pp. 480–484. IEEE (2010)
34. Kendall, G.: AI methods - simulated annealing (2012). http://syllabus.cs.manchester.ac.uk/pgt/2017/COMP60342/lab3/Kendall-simulatedannealing.pdf. Accessed 19 Mar 2019
35. Kennedy, J.: The particle swarm: social adaptation of knowledge. In: IEEE International Conference on Evolutionary Computation, pp. 303–308. IEEE (1997)
36. Kirkpatrick, S., Gelatt, C.D., Vecchi, M.P.: Optimization by simulated annealing. Science **220**(4598), 671–680 (1983)
37. Krishnanand, K., Ghose, D.: Detection of multiple source locations using a glowworm metaphor with applications to collective robotics. In: Proceedings 2005 IEEE Swarm Intelligence Symposium, SIS 2005, pp. 84–91. IEEE (2005)
38. Lee, K.S., Geem, Z.W.: A new meta-heuristic algorithm for continuous engineering optimization: harmony search theory and practice. Comput. Methods Appl. Mech. Eng. **194**(36–38), 3902–3933 (2005)
39. Li, Y.z., Shan-shan, Y.: Application of SVM optimized by genetic algorithm in forecasting and management of water consumption used in agriculture. In: 2010 the 2nd International Conference on Computer and Automation Engineering (ICCAE). vol. 1, pp. 625–628. IEEE (2010)
40. Lin, Y.P., Chang, T.K., Teng, T.P.: Characterization of soil lead by comparing sequential gaussian simulation, simulated annealing simulation and kriging methods. Environ. Geol. **41**(1–2), 189–199 (2001)
41. Lu, S., Cai, Z.j., Zhang, X.b.: Forecasting agriculture water consumption based on PSO and SVM. In: 2009 2nd IEEE International Conference on Computer Science and Information Technology (ICCSIT), pp. 147–150. IEEE (2009)
42. Mallawaarachchi, V.: Introduction to genetic algorithms - including example code (2017). http://www.towardsdatascience.com/introduction-to-genetic-algorithms-including-example-code-e396e98d8bf3. Accessed 27 Mar 2019
43. Mandal, S.N., Ghosh, A., Choudhury, J.P., Chaudhuri, S.B.: Prediction of productivity of mustard plant at maturity using harmony search. In: 2012 1st International Conference on Recent Advances in Information Technology (RAIT), pp. 933–938. IEEE (2012)
44. Mitchell, M.: An Introduction to Genetic Algorithms. MIT Press, Cambridge (1998)
45. Nanda, S.J., Panda, G.: A survey on nature inspired metaheuristic algorithms for partitional clustering. Swarm Evol. Comput. **16**, 1–18 (2014)
46. Nguyen, D.C.H., Ascough II, J.C., Maier, H.R., Dandy, G.C., Andales, A.A.: Optimization of irrigation scheduling using ant colony algorithms and an advanced cropping system model. Environ. Model. Softw. **97**, 32–45 (2017)
47. Noguchi, N., Terao, H.: Path planning of an agricultural mobile robot by neural network and genetic algorithm. Comput. Electron. Agric. **18**(2–3), 187–204 (1997)

48. de Ocampo, A.L.P., Dadios, E.P.: Energy cost optimization in irrigation system of smart farm by using genetic algorithm. In: 2017 IEEE 9th International Conference on Humanoid, Nanotechnology, Information Technology, Communication and Control, Environment and Management (HNICEM), pp. 1–7 (2017)
49. Oliveira, P.M., Cunha, J., Pires, E.: Evolutionary and bio-inspired algorithms in greenhouse control: introduction, review and trends. In: Intelligent Environments (2017)
50. Orta, A.R., Fausto, F.A.: AISearch (2018). https://aisearch.github.io/. Accessed 16 Mar 2019
51. Passino, K.M.: Biomimicry of bacterial foraging for distributed optimization and control. IEEE Control Syst. 22(3), 52–67 (2002)
52. Pérez-Sánchez, M., Sánchez-Romero, F.J., López-Jiménez, P.A., Ramos, H.M.: Pats selection towards sustainability in irrigation networks: simulated annealing as a water management tool. Renew. Energy 116, 234–249 (2018)
53. Pham, D., Ghanbarzadeh, A., Koç, E., Otri, S., Rahim, S., Zaidi, M.: The bees algorithm technical note, pp. 1–57. Manufacturing Engineering Centre, Cardiff University, UK (2005)
54. Price, K., Storn, R.M., Lampinen, J.A.: Differential Evolution: A Practical Approach to Global Optimization. Natural Computing Series, 1st edn. Springer, Heidelberg (2005). https://doi.org/10.1007/3-540-31306-0
55. Rabanal, P., Rodríguez, I., Rubio, F.: Using river formation dynamics to design heuristic algorithms. In: Akl, S.G., Calude, C.S., Dinneen, M.J., Rozenberg, G., Wareham, H.T. (eds.) UC 2007. LNCS, vol. 4618, pp. 163–177. Springer, Heidelberg (2007). https://doi.org/10.1007/978-3-540-73554-0_16
56. Rashedi, E., Nezamabadi-Pour, H., Saryazdi, S.: GSA: a gravitational search algorithm. Inf. Sci. 179(13), 2232–2248 (2009)
57. Rodrigues, N.M.C.: Projeto de controladores PID com meta-heurísticas de inspiração natural e biológica. Master's thesis, University of Trás-os-Montes e Alto Douro (2017)
58. Rooy, N.A.: Differential evolution optimization from scratch with Python (2017). https://nathanrooy.github.io/posts/2017-08-27/simple-differential-evolution-with-python/. Accessed 19 Mar 2019
59. Senthilnath, J., Kulkarni, S., Benediktsson, J.A., Yang, X.S.: A novel approach for multispectral satellite image classification based on the bat algorithm. IEEE Geosci. Remote Sens. Lett. 13(4), 599–603 (2016)
60. Sethanan, K., Neungmatcha, W.: Multi-objective particle swarm optimization for mechanical harvester route planning of sugarcane field operations. Eur. J. Oper. Res. 252(3), 969–984 (2016)
61. Shah-Hosseini, H.: Intelligent water drops algorithm: a new optimization method for solving the multiple knapsack problem. Int. J. Intell. Comput. Cybern. 1(2), 193–212 (2008)
62. Storn, R., Price, K.: Differential evolution - a simple and efficient heuristic for global optimization over continuous spaces. Technical report TR-95-012, International Computer Science Institute (1995)
63. Tamura, K., Yasuda, K.: Primary study of spiral dynamics inspired optimization. IEEJ Trans. Electr. Electron. Eng. 6(S1), S98 (2011)
64. Valente, J., Del Cerro, J., Barrientos, A., Sanz, D.: Aerial coverage optimization in precision agriculture management: a musical harmony inspired approach. Comput. Electron. Agric. 99, 153–159 (2013)
65. Van Laarhoven, P.J., Aarts, E.H.: Simulated annealing. In: Simulated Annealing: Theory and Applications, vol. 37, pp. 7–15. Springer, Dordrecht (1987). https://doi.org/10.1007/978-94-015-7744-1_2

66. Wang, H., Wang, W., Cui, Z., Zhou, X., Zhao, J., Li, Y.: A new dynamic firefly algorithm for demand estimation of water resources. Inf. Sci. **438**, 95 (2018)
67. Xing, B., Gao, W.J.: Innovative Computational Intelligence: A Rough Guide to 134 Clever Algorithms. ISRL, vol. 62, 1st edn. Springer, Cham (2016). https://doi.org/10.1007/978-3-319-03404-1
68. Yang, X.S.: Nature-Inspired Metaheuristic and Algorithms, pp. 242–246. Luniver Press, Beckington (2008)
69. Yang, X.-S.: Firefly algorithms for multimodal optimization. In: Watanabe, O., Zeugmann, T. (eds.) SAGA 2009. LNCS, vol. 5792, pp. 169–178. Springer, Heidelberg (2009). https://doi.org/10.1007/978-3-642-04944-6_14
70. Yang, X.S.: Engineering Optimization: An Introduction with Metaheuristic Applications. Wiley, Hoboken (2010)
71. Yang, X.S.: A new metaheuristic bat-inspired algorithm. In: González, J.R., Pelta, D.A., Cruz, C., Terrazas, G., Krasnogor, N. (eds.) Nature Inspired Cooperative Strategies for Optimization (NICSO 2010), vol. 284, pp. 65–74. Springer, Heidelberg (2010). https://doi.org/10.1007/978-3-642-12538-6_6
72. Yang, X.S.: Bat algorithm (Demo), July 2012. https://www.mathworks.com/matlabcentral/fileexchange/37582-bat-algorithm-demo. Accessed 15 June 2019
73. Yang, X.-S.: Flower pollination algorithm for global optimization. In: Durand-Lose, J., Jonoska, N. (eds.) UCNC 2012. LNCS, vol. 7445, pp. 240–249. Springer, Heidelberg (2012). https://doi.org/10.1007/978-3-642-32894-7_27
74. Yang, X.S., Deb, S.: Cuckoo search via lévy flights. In: World Congress on Nature & Biologically Inspired Computing 2009, pp. 210–214. IEEE (2009)
75. Yang, X.S., Hossein Gandomi, A.: Bat algorithm: a novel approach for global engineering optimization. Eng. Comput. **29**(5), 464–483 (2012)
76. Yang, X.S., Papa, J.P.: Bio-inspired Computation and Applications in Image Processing. Academic Press, Amsterdam (2016)
77. Yang, X.S., Press, L.: Nature-Inspired Metaheuristic Algorithms, 2nd edn. Luniver Press, Frome (2010)
78. Yarpiz: Ant colony optimization (ACO), September 2015. https://www.mathworks.com/matlabcentral/fileexchange/52859-ant-colony-optimization-aco. Accessed 15 June 2019
79. Yarpiz: Binary and real-coded genetic algorithms, September 2015. https://www.mathworks.com/matlabcentral/fileexchange/52856-binary-and-real-coded-genetic-algorithms. Accessed 15 June 2019
80. Yarpiz: Differential evolution (DE), September 2015. https://www.mathworks.com/matlabcentral/fileexchange/52897-differential-evolution-de. Accessed 15 June 2019
81. Yarpiz: Firefly algorithm (FA), September 2015. https://www.mathworks.com/matlabcentral/fileexchange/52900-firefly-algorithm-fa. Accessed 15 June 2019
82. Yarpiz: Harmony Search (HS), September 2015. https://www.mathworks.com/matlabcentral/fileexchange/52864-harmony-search-hs. Accessed 15 June 2019
83. Yarpiz: Particle swarm optimization (PSO), September 2015. https://www.mathworks.com/matlabcentral/fileexchange/52857-particle-swarm-optimization-pso. Accessed 15 June 2019
84. Yarpiz: Simulated annealing (SA), September 2015. https://www.mathworks.com/matlabcentral/fileexchange/52896-simulated-annealing-sa. Accessed 15 June 2019
85. Zhang, Y., Wang, S., Ji, G.: A comprehensive survey on particle swarm optimization algorithm and its applications. Mathematical Problems in Engineering (2015)

On KNoT Meta-Platform for IoT-Based Control of Storage Grains

João Gabriel Quaresma de Almeida[1], Josenalde Oliveira[1(✉)],
and José Boaventura-Cunha[2,3]

[1] Federal University of Rio Grande do Norte, Macaíba 59280−000, Brazil
j.quaresmasantos_98@hotmail.com, josenalde@eaj.ufrn.br
[2] School of Science and Technology, University of Trás-os-Montes and Alto Douro,
Quinta de Prados, 5001−801 Vila Real, Portugal
jboavent@utad.pt
[3] INESC TEC Tehcnology and Science, Campus da FEUP, 4200−465 Porto, Portugal

Abstract. This work aims to develop an embedded system and mobile application within Internet of Things (IoT) context, which allow the evaluation of control techniques widely used in the industry, for both remote configuration and monitoring of environment inside storage silos in laboratory scale. The developed system contributes to the validation of the recent released KNoT meta platform and extends its application to agricultural area. Preliminary results for on-off and PID temperature control suggest its feasibility for remote transmission of setpoint data to local controllers and data acquisition for monitoring by a mobile application.

Keywords: Internet of Things · Grain storage · Smart farming · KNoT · IoT

1 Introduction

Grain storage is a key issue in agricultural industry [1]. Usually this storage is carried out in silos, where the grains are conserved, and which are subject to internal and external interference (biotic and abiotic factors) in the production cycle. Therefore, losses due to these factors have significant financial impact. Strict monitoring and control of ambience in silos is required, and thus, Internet of Things (IoT) is a promising and suitable solution related to the industry 4.0 concept [2], enabling remote management of such tasks. Although some previous works address issues such as storage, grain aeration, drying, temperature and humidity control [1,3,4] and consider some remote operation, they are not based on IoT techniques and concepts, such as cloud/fog computing, data platforms/dashboards, interchangeable data formats (JavaScript Object Notation JSON, Extensible Markup Language, XML), NoSQL databases, brokers and transmission protocols such as Message Queuing Telemetry Transport, MQTT. Among several IoT platforms already available, KNoT Network of Things (KNoT) is an open source, hardware and software meta platform for IoT [6]. As a meta platform it aims

P. Moura Oliveira et al. (Eds.): EPIA 2019, LNAI 11804, pp. 180–185, 2019.
https://doi.org/10.1007/978-3-030-30241-2_16

to connect several existing platforms ensuring interoperability of communication between the most diverse hardware (things), providing a set of development tools such as hardware nodes, protocol translation and software libraries. Since its release some academic works investigate benefits, drawbacks and limitations [7,8], extend software libraries [9] and integrates to FIWARE [10], but a few applications are available, as on work of [5], only for water consumption monitoring. This work extends KNoT application to agricultural processes and evaluates its feasibility to remote temperature setpoint transmission to a local controller and monitoring by a mobile application (Grain Control app). It is organized as follows: Sect. 2 describes KNoT architecture and components, while Sect. 3 details the materials and methods used to conduct the experiment. Section 4 presents some preliminary control results with remote setpoint profile and briefly discuss them. Section 5 suggests some final notes and further work.

2   KNoT

KNoT consists of a meta platform whose development is coordinated by the Center for Studies and Advanced Systems (CESAR, Pernambuco, Brazil), released in 2017, which implements the network architecture Hub-and-Spoke [8], that uses a central message broker. Figure 1 clearly shows the concept and main goal of the meta platform, which offers to the developer an interface of abstraction and homogeneity between low and high level layer heterogeneous devices and communication protocols. Therefore, it provides a single common access communication point.

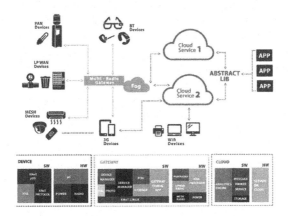

Fig. 1. KNoT architecture.   Source: slideshare.net/CESAR/knot-knot-network-of-things

The main components of KNoT are: KNoTCloud, an interface that is executed in the cloud, being responsible for managing users, applications and devices (things), as well as storing, retrieving and sharing the data of those devices;

KNoTThing is the hardware and software component that implements access to sensors and actuators physically connected to objects; Gateway, a component that acts as an intermediary between the layers of hardware and software responsible for directing messages between devices (KNoTThing) and the data storage cloud (KNoTCloud), abstracting protocols and physical means of communication together with connectivity to Internet.

3   Materials and Methods

In this work, an acrylic silo with laboratory scale (PP32, T & S Equipments, Brazil) is used to simulate storage grains, whose average temperature needs to be kept within previously defined setpoints, according to the specific grain type. The air flows vertically from a heater, crosses the grain mass (drawer) and exits the silo by an open hole on the top. The grain drawer has a design that allows a better dispersion of the airflow to reach the entire drying space. In order to get a more reliable internal temperature measurement, four NTC sensors were installed, besides the external NTC sensor. These four sensors are combined (homogeneous sensor fusion) and only the average temperature is transmitted through KNoT, and it is indeed the controlled variable. This solution reduces the need of KNoT things and has practical sense.

A manually flow adjustment (0–100 %) is provided by a potentiometer. An industrial PID controller (1100, Novus Automation, Brazil) drives a Solid State Relay (TSZC-40A, Metaltex, Brazil) connected to an electrical AC resistance. This particular controller model does not include a remote setpoint input, therefore a discrete PID algorithm was embedded into a Arduino UNO board (microcontroller ATmega328P), which acts as local controller and, simultaneously, as a KNoTThing, since the average temperature measurements are received from the silo, used as feedback signal for the PID, and also transmitted to the gateway (Raspberry 3 Model B+) through a radio module (NRF24L01, Nordic Semiconductor ASA, Norway) connect to both KNoTThing and gateway by Serial Peripheral Interface (SPI). All NTC sensors use Steinhart-Hart method. To keep track of KNoTThing measurements (remote setpoint and average temperature) the KNoT WebUI is a web interface running in the gateway, which holds a fog for local data, stored in a MongoDB database. Since Arduino UNO is the data acquisition device, a serial communication to a Python script reads and store data as a text file for further graphical analysis in Octave software.

3.1   App Development

As an intuitive machine-human interface, a mobile Android app was developed (beta-version, https://github.com/joaoGabriel55/GrainControl_app). It is possible to monitor the actual average temperature of the grain mass and also to inform a new setpoint to the KNoTThing, which acts also as the local controller. Both information are stored in a Firebase Real Time Database. It is one of several services provided by the Firebase platform, acquired by Google, considered a complete back-end solution for both mobile and web development. This service provides a non-relational database (NoSQL) used to store and synchronize data in real time, in JSON format. It follows that a Javascript code was developed to write and read data to/from Firebase.

4 Experimental Results and Discussion

Since setpoint values are provided by the mobile app, a feasibility study must consider possible delays and network bottlenecks, besides KNoT reliability to get/send data. For this particular case, since no critical timing is requested, an average time of two to three seconds was observed. To get parameters for the embedded PID, first the industrial PID ran with *autotune* mode turned on. This approach provided initial parameters: $K_P = \frac{1}{0.6}$, $K_I = \frac{K_P}{1.77}$, $K_D = 6 \times K_P$. Two well known control techniques were chosen: on-off and PID control, with three different air flow power/speeds (25%, 50% and 75%). Specifically for on-off control, hysteresis levels of 0.1, 0.5 and 1.0 were tested and considered acceptable for grain storage. Due to space limitations, only the flow at 75% case is shown for on-off strategy (Fig. 2), but in Table 1 results for other flow speeds can be compared and corroborates the expected result that better tracking ($ISE = \sum_{k=1}^{N} e^2(k)$) is achieved with minor $\Delta = 0.1$ at this flow speed, however with higher energy consumption. A similar conclusion can be observed for PID in Table 2, however, as expected its output is smoother (extends actuator lifetime) and keeps the process variable more stable after convergence, although with a slower response. The main purpose is not to compare on-off control to PID control, since are established methods, but to check the appropriate receive/send data to/from this very important control process in agriculture, based on the KNoT meta platform.

Table 1. On-off efficiency results

Hysteresis Region Δ	Blower power	$\sum_{k=1}^{N} e^2(k)$ *	$\sum_{k=1}^{N} u(k)$
1.0	25%	7.82 x 10^4	1563
	50%	9.59 x 10^4	1873
	75%	8.36 x 10^4	**2260**
0.5	25%	1.24 x 10^5	1549
	50%	8.47 x 10^4	1760
	75%	9.47 x 10^4	1673
1.0	25%	1.72 x 10^5	2106
	50%	1.41 x 10^5	2153
	75%	8.91 x 10^5	2151

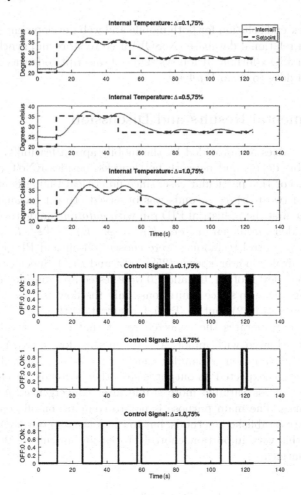

Fig. 2. Top plot: Average grain mass temperature using on-off control for power of 75% and $\Delta = 0.1, 0.5, 1.0$. Bottom plot: On-off control signal for power of 75% and $\Delta = 0.1, 0.5, 1.0$

Table 2. PID efficiency results

Blower power	$\sum_{k=1}^{N} e^2(k)$	$\sum_{k=1}^{N} u(k)$
25%	2.65 x 10^5	1.13 x 10^6
50%	1.94 x 10^5	1.31 x 10^6
75%	1.86 x 10^5	1.56 x 10^6

5   Final Notes

In this paper, the KNoT meta plaftorm is extended and evaluated for temperature control and monitoring within a storage silo. The results suggested that KNoT may be applied to agricultural problems without hard timing constraints, due to its dependency on the overall communication links. A set of software and hardware tools were combined to develop an embedded system with communication features, with a mobile application as machine-human interface. This app can be improved to other controlled variables as humidity, and, moreover, based on these measurements, prediction models could suggest suitable setpoints and vigor of the storage grain/seed.

References

1. Oliveira, J., Boaventura-Cunha, J., Oliveira, P.M.: Robust control of agroindustrial drying process of grains based on sliding modes and gravitational search algorithm. In: Garrido, P., Soares, F., Moreira, A.P. (eds.) CONTROLO 2016. LNEE, vol. 402, pp. 629–639. Springer, Cham (2017). https://doi.org/10.1007/978-3-319-43671-5_53
2. Alcácer, V., Cruz-machado, V.: Scanning the industry 4.0: a literature review on technologies for manufacturing systems. Eng. Sci. Technol. **22**(3), 899–919 (2019)
3. Visala, A., Oksanen, T., Oliveira, J.: Smooth adaptive robust temperature control of a seed drying system. Agricontrol **1**, 6–11 (2013)
4. Pereira Jr., M.: Application of supervisory fuzzy controller on a dryer in fertilizer industry. 82 f. Master thesis, Federal University of Ouro Preto (2018). (in Portuguese)
5. Dornelas, E., Oliveira, S.C.: Monitoring home water consumption using an IOT meta platform. Revista de Engenharia e Pesquisa Aplicada **2**(2) (2017). (in Portuguese)
6. KNOT. KNoT Network of things. CESAR, 2015. Source: https://www.knot.cesar.org.br/. 25 Apr 2019
7. Quaresma, J.G., Oliveira, J.: Machine-Human interface for control and instrumentation of grain storage silos within IoT context. Federal University of Rio Grande do Norte, Analysis and Systems Development (2018). (in Portuguese)
8. de Souza, D.A.M.: On gaps of KNoT IoT. Federal University of Pernambuco, Computer Center (2017). (in Portuguese)
9. Ribeiro, R.H.P.: KNoTPy: a library to device acquisition data connected to KNoT. Federal University of Pernambuco, Computer Center (2018). (in Portuguese)
10. Batista, C. P., Silva, P. V., Batista, T., Cavalcante, E.: Integrating platforms FIREWARE and KNoT for development of IoT applications. X SBCUP, pp. 1–6 (2018)

Grapevine Varieties Classification Using Machine Learning

Pedro Marques[1], Luís Pádua[1,2], Telmo Adão[1,2], Jonáš Hruška[1],
José Sousa[1], Emanuel Peres[1,2], Joaquim J. Sousa[1,2], Raul Morais[1,2],
and António Sousa[1,2(✉)]

[1] School of Science and Technology,
University of Trás-os-Montes e Alto Douro, Vila Real, Portugal
{pedro.marques, luispadua, telmoadao, jonash, jmsousa,
eperes, jjsousa, rmorais, amrs}@utad.pt
[2] Centre for Robotics in Industry and Intelligent Systems (CRIIS),
INESC Technology and Science (INESC-TEC), Porto, Portugal

Abstract. Viticulture has a major impact in the European economy and over the years the intensive grapevine production led to the proliferation of many varieties. Traditionally these varieties are manually catalogued in the field, which is a costly and slow process and being, in many cases, very challenging to classify even for an experienced ampelographer. This article presents a cost-effective and automatic method for grapevine varieties classification based on the analysis of the leaf's images, taken with an RGB sensor. The proposed method is divided into three steps: (1) color and shape features extraction; (2) training and; (3) classification using Linear Discriminant Analysis. This approach was applied in 240 leaf images of three different grapevine varieties acquired from the Douro Valley region in Portugal and it was able to correctly classify 87% of the grapevine leaves. The proposed method showed very promising classification capabilities considering the challenges presented by the leaves which had many shape irregularities and, in many cases, high color similarities for the different varieties. The obtained results compared with manual procedure suggest that it can be used as an effective alternative to the manual procedure for grapevine classification based on leaf features. Since the proposed method requires a simple and low-cost setup it can be easily integrated on a portable system with real-time processing to assist technicians in the field or other staff without any special skills and used offline for batch classification.

Keywords: Grapevine leaves · Classification · Precision viticulture ·
Digital image processing · Machine learning · Ampelography

1 Introduction

The common grapevine (*Vitis vinifera L.*) is spread mainly across the Mediterranean region and central Europe representing a major source of income to the local economy [1]. The lack of legislation and control of new plantations induced a widespread of this species along the years resulting in an increase of varieties [2]. This led to difficulties in their registration of designation of origin and their preservation. Currently just in the

Douro Demarcated Region (DDR), in Portugal, the number of recommended grapevine varieties is reaching about 120 according to *Instituto dos Vinhos do Douro e Porto* (IVDP). The uncontrolled proliferation and lack or no standard way of registration of new varieties that emerged in the meantime resulted in different designations attributed to similar varieties [2].

Traditionally, the classification process is manually conducted using ampelography [3]. This field is focused on the study, identification and classification of grapevine varieties based on the morphometric description of the characteristics of the plant mainly focused in the shape and color of the grapevine leaves, grape clusters and branches. Although, in Portugal, there are some specialized technicians in this field, they are almost retired, and the training of new technicians is costly and has a slow learning curve since it comes from experience and based on a manual process.

To cope with this problem, it is urgent to find new and automatic methods for grapevine varieties classification with acceptable results, at a faster rate, and with lower costs when compared with the manual procedure. A simple and low-cost setup is also required to allow an easy integration in a portable system suitable for field usage with real-time processing capabilities to assist the technicians or other staff without any special skills or offline for batch classification.

Different studies explore ways to make grapevine varieties classification using different approaches. Diago et al. [4] used a spectroscopy-based method for the identification and classification of grapevine varieties. It is based on local leaf hyper-spectral imaging and partial-least squares analysis. The classifier was created using 300 leaves, 100 images from three *Vitis vinifera L.* varieties (*Cv. Tempranillo, Grenache and Cabernet Sauvignon*). The authors report that the classifier performance for these three varieties exceeded 92% in all cases. Although the method presents fairly good results it relies on a hyperspectral sensor being not suitable for integration in a low-cost system. Furthermore, the leaves images were acquired in a controlled environment with constant illumination not compatible with field conditions where natural light is constantly changing.

Fuentes et al. [5] used machine learning algorithms based on morpho-colorimetric parameters and near-infrared (NIR) analysis separately were able to automatically classify leaves of 16 grapevine cultivars. The proposed method consists of an artificial neural network (ANN) model developed with morpho-colorimetric parameters as inputs, and 16 cultivars as targets, which obtained an accuracy of 94% to classify leaves for all studied cultivars. The ANN model obtained with the NIR spectra per leaf as inputs, and the real classification as targets, rendered 92% accuracy. The leaves features were extracted on laboratory using NIR spectrometry and a scanner to digitalize the leaves to perform the morpho-colorimetric analysis. The authors claim that the system can be used for in-field applications using equivalent portable equipment. However, the amount of equipment necessary to take to the field and the weather conditions (rain or dust) makes the system not practical to use in those situations.

A support vector machine (SVM) and ANNs are used by Gutiérrez et al. [6] for grapevine variety classification from in-field leaf spectroscopy. Spectral measurements were obtained on the NIR spectral range using a portable spectrophotometer. Authors used two datasets: (1) where spectra were collected from the adaxial side of 400 individual leaves of 20 grapevine varieties; (2) where two sets of spectra were collected, each one consisting on 48 measurements from individual leaves of six varieties. For the training of the models, SVMs and ANNs were employed using the pre-processed spectra as input and the varieties as the classes of the models. For the first dataset the best result from the classifiers was an 87.25% score. The second dataset reached a score of 77.08%.

In another study from the same research group, Gutiérrez et al. [7] proposed an approach for grapevine varieties classification using on-the-go hyperspectral imaging and machine learning algorithms. The imaging was performed using a hyperspectral camera and spectra were acquired over two different leaf phenological stages on the canopy of 30 different varieties. A total of 1,200 spectral samples were generated and SVM and ANNs were used. Authors report that the prediction performance this time was for individual varieties ranging from 83% to 99%. In both cases authors used a portable spectrophotometer to obtain the spectral measurements on the NIR part of the spectrum. Using this system implies the acquisition of expensive equipment which is not within reach of the common user searching for a simple and affordable system.

Karasik et al. [8] investigate the possibility of using a 3D tool for grape variety identification. Representative samples of grape pip populations were scanned followed by mathematical and statistical analysis. Using selected Fourier coefficients, the authors observed that a very clear separation was obtained between most of the varieties using their seeds, with only very few overlaps. The equipment used for data acquisition was a high-resolution 3D scanner with two cameras and a light projector. This equipment besides being expensive is not adaptable to a portable system. Also, the requirements for data acquisition are very strict once it needs a thorough cleaning of the seeds which is not compatible with in-field usage.

To overcome the major drawbacks associated with ampelography and the systems discussed above in related works concerning specifically their cost and lack of porta-bility a new method is proposed in this article. It consists in a fully automatic process which starts by extracting the features of a grapevine leaf from an RGB image given as input, and outputs the grapevine variety as the classification using Linear Discriminant Analysis machine learning algorithm. The results are similar to those obtained by the systems in related works with the advantage of being cost-effective setup and highly portable. The method was validated using data collected, in the field, during the grapevine vegetative growth cycle of 2017 season.

2   Materials and Methods

2.1   Data Acquisition

The data acquired for this study was obtained in vineyards from Quinta de Nossa Senhora de Lourdes which is located in Vila Real, Portugal within the campus of the University of Trás-os-Montes e Alto Douro (41°17'10.1"N, 7°44'12.8"W). Since these vineyards are mainly used for vineyard related research, it has several experimental plots, containing a wide range of grapevine varieties, which are already labelled with the respective classification. From the available varieties, three of the most common in Portugal were chosen, namely Touriga Nacional, Códega and Rabigato. For each of these varieties, 80 images of individual cut leaves were acquired in-field resulting in a total of 240 images. Imagery acquisition took place every week between 4th of May and 31st of July of 2017 using a Canon 600D camera with a 50 mm f1.4 lenses (Canon Inc., Tokyo, Japan). The RGB image of each leaf was acquired with a target in the background, this target was printed in white paper sheet and is composed by different colours that can be used for colour correction operations as well as scale bars. Imagery was acquired in a perpendicular angle relatively to the camera and with no artificial illumination, as illustrated in Fig. 1.

Fig. 1. Leaf image acquisition setup on the field.

2.2 Features Extraction

After a few meetings, and visit to vineyards, with specialized technicians in ampelography from IVDP, with a lifetime experience in the observation of grapevine varieties in the DDR, two main conclusions were drawn. Firstly, most features analyzed by these technicians are based on leaf observation, as it would be expected. Secondly, in some situations, the distinguishing features of the grapevine varieties are very subtle being needed to recur to other parts of plant characteristics e.g. smell, leaf texture, grapes and the vine sticks. In Table 1 is presented the early and late growth stages of the leaves analyzed in this study which illustrate also the small differences between some varieties and the high changes in varieties morphology in different growth stages.

Table 1. Selected grapevine varieties typical morphology in early and late growth stages

Growth stage	Touriga Nacional	Códega	Rabigato
Early			
Late			

This way, with these conclusions in mind, in this study it was intended to focus on grapevine feature extraction. Thus, 101 features were initially extracted from each leaf, which included 15 shape features (Appendix A) and 86 color features (Table 2, Appendix B).

Table 2. Extracted color features: (O) features removed after dimensionality reduction, and (●) features maintained in the final dataset.

Feature	Gray	RGBVI	Hue	Red	Green	Blue
Mean	●	O	●	●	●	●
Deviation	O	O	●	O	O	O
Softness	●	●	●	O	●	●
Contrast	●	O	●	●	●	●
Correlation	O	O	●	●	O	●
Energy	●	●	O	●	●	●
Homogeneity	O	●	O	O	O	O
MeanHist	O	●	O	●	●	●
VarianceHist	●	O	O	●	●	●
SkewnessHist	●	●	●	●	●	O
KurtosisHist	●	●	●	●	●	●
EnergyHist	O	●	●	●	●	O

For a correct shape features extraction, pixels correspondent to the grapevine leaf need to be isolated. To accomplish this, a mask was created binarizing the image using the Otsu method [9] to separate the leaf (foreground) from the other elements (background) (Fig. 2).

Fig. 2. Leaf binarized for shape features extraction.

To extract the color features (Table 2), the information of each image in RGB (Red, Green and Blue) was converted to grey scale, Red Green Blue Vegetation Index (RGBVI) [10] (Eq. 1) and hue, saturation, and value (HSV) color space.

$$RGBVI = \frac{G^2 - (R \times B)}{G^2 + (R \times B)} \qquad (1)$$

In Table 2 the rows represent the extracted features and the columns represent the color space or color band from where each feature was extracted in a total of 72 color features.

The remaining 14 color features were calculated by extracting, from the grey image and RGBVI image, 7 invariant moments as defined in [11]. After dimensionality reduction the 4th and 5th invariant moment calculated from the grey image was removed and the 2nd and 3rd invariant moment calculated from the RGBVI image were also removed.

2.3 Dataset

The dataset was created based on the extracted features and the cleaning of missing data. This step represented the removal of 22 samples from the dataset. The total number of samples after this operation is presented in Table 3.

Table 3. Dataset after the sample cleaning process.

Grapevine variety	Number of samples
Touriga Nacional	78
Códega	70
Rabigato	70

To reduce the dimensionality of the dataset a second step was applied, which consisted in the analysis of the feature's correlations (Fig. 3). This was accomplished by comparing each feature values with every other dataset feature value based on the Pearson Correlation Coefficient [12].

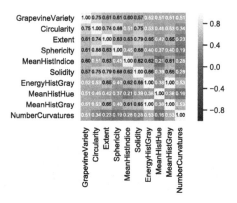

Fig. 3. Subset of features correlation matrix.

The individual features with highest correlation rate were recursively eliminated from the dataset. Usually the removal of highly correlated features does not affect the global performance of a classifier [13]. At the end of this stage the dimensionality of the dataset decreased from 101 features to 67 features.

2.4 Training

The dataset was divided into training set (80%) and test set (20%). The training data was used to test and compare 6 algorithms, among the most used in machine learning for multiclass classification problems present in python Scikit Learn library, to determine the most suitable for the proposed methodology (Table 4).

Table 4. Tested multiclass classification algorithms.

Acronym	Classification algorithm
LR	Logistic Regression [14]
LDA	Linear Discriminant Analysis [15]
KNN	K-Nearest Neighbours [16]
DT	Decision Tree [17]
GNB	Gaussian Naive Bayes [18]
SVM	C-Support Vector Classification [19]

The training data was split, to prevent overfitting, using 10-fold cross validation [20] (validation set) to evaluate the performance of the algorithms. In Fig. 4 each algorithm is represented by the mean and standard deviation of its performance in the validation set.

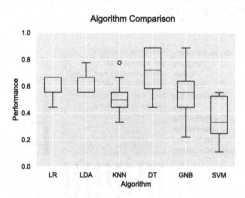

Fig. 4. Algorithm performance comparison.

Although Decision Tree (DT) presents the highest mean (72.2%) it is also the algorithm with one of the highest standard deviations (15.9%). Taking into account the highest mean and lowest standard deviation, the algorithm with the overall best performance was the Linear Discriminant Analysis (LDA) with a mean of 64.4% and a standard deviation of 8.3% over the validation set.

2.5   Classification

The test set (20%), remaining from the training step, was used, and the algorithm with better performance was chosen for classification (LDA). The LDA algorithm achieved an overall classification rate of 86.9% on the test data with the correct grapevine variety (Table 5).

Table 5. Grapevine varieties LDA classification performance.

Variety	Precision	Recall	F1-Score
Touriga Nacional	100%	60%	75%
Códega	75%	100%	86%
Rabigato	92%	92%	92%

The confusion matrix of the classification is presented in Fig. 5.

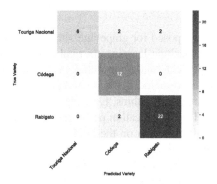

Fig. 5. Classification confusion matrix.

3   Results and Discussion

The number of images used in the experiments were enough to validate and prove the potential of the proposed methodology. Nevertheless, there is a need for acquisition of large amounts of images to fully explore the classification capabilities of the current method. The proposed method is fully ready to receive an increase in the number of grapevine varieties it can classify provided that the images for those varieties are available.

Although the number of features, extracted from the grapevine leaves, was initially large (101) it was possible to reduce the number of features (reduce dimensionality) without losing the proposed method classification capabilities. Even though 67 features were selected for the final dataset the dimensionality is still enough to support the introduction of new grapevine varieties for training and classification.

The initial dataset (240 samples) required a data cleaning which caused some loss of data (22 samples) which was negligible and evenly distributed among all grapevine varieties samples (10 maximum samples lost per variety).

The machine learning algorithms selected were among the most common ones used for multiclass classification problems. For the proposed methodology it was decided not to tune too much the algorithms since that could lead to overfitting. In the future, with larger datasets, the fine tuning can be done with more effectiveness.

The proposed method showed very promising classification capabilities (87% overall hit rate) considering the challenges presented by the leaves, even for an experienced technician, which had many shape irregularities and, in many cases, high color similarities for different varieties. Another factor that may have limited the overall performance of the proposed method is that the grape varieties can present great variabilities according to the age of the leaves. All these difficulties represented a big challenge in the extraction of shape and color information useful and meaningful enough to distinguish the 3 grapevine varieties.

4   Conclusions

An automatic method was proposed for grapevine varieties classification based on the plant leaves features using machine learning. In total 3 grapevine varieties were analyzed corresponding to 240 leaf images acquired in a vineyard. For each leaf 101 features were initially extracted including shape and color information. Based on this information 6 machine learning algorithms, typically used for multiclass classification problems, were evaluated. The classification performance of the proposed method was then validated using the collected data on the field.

In summary, the proposed methodology has shown very promising results compared with manual procedure observed on the field. It returns the grapevine classification at a much faster rate with an incomparable lower cost and without any special skills required for operation. The overall results suggest that the proposed method can be used as an effective alternative to the manual procedure for grapevine classification based on leaf features. Since the proposed method requires very simple and low-cost setup it can be easily integrated on a portable system with real time processing to assist the technicians on the field or offline for batch classification.

Acknowledgements. This work is financed by the ERDF – European Regional Development Fund through the Operational Programme for Competitiveness and Internationalisation - COMPETE 2020 Programme within project «POCI-01-0145-FEDER-006961», and by National Funds through the FCT – Fundação para a Ciência e a Tecnologia (Portuguese Foundation for Science and Technology) as part of project UID/EEA/50014/2013.

Appendix A

Feature	Description	Equation
Eccentricity [21–24]	Defined as the ratio of the length of main inertia axis of the ROI EA to the length of minor inertia axis of the ROI EB	$E = \frac{EA}{EB}$
Aspect Ratio [21–24]	Ratio between the maximum length Dmax and the minimum length D_{min} of the minimum bounding rectangle (MBR) of the leaf with holes	$AR = \frac{Dmax}{Dmin}$
Aspect Ratio 2	Same as Aspect Ratio but without considering the holes of the leaf	
Elongation [22–24]	From each point inside the ROI is calculated the minimal distance Dmin to the boundary contour ∂ ROI and its denoted by D_{me} its maximal value over the region	$D_{me} = \max_{x \in R} d(x, \partial ROI)$
	Then elongation is defined as:	$E = 1 - \frac{2D_{me}}{D_{ROI}}$
Solidity [21–24]	Describes the extent to which the shape is convex or concave	$S = \frac{A_{ROI}}{A_{CH}}$
Isoperimetric Factor [21–24]	If the closed contour ∂ ROI of length L(∂ROI) encloses a region ROI of area A (R), the isoperimetric factor is defined by	$IF = \frac{4\pi A(R)}{L(\partial ROI)^2}$
Maximal Indentation Depth [22, 23]	For each point on the contour of ROI is determined the distance to the convex hull, expressing this distance by a function. Then the Maximal Indentation Depth is the maximum of the function	
Rectangularity [21, 24]	Represents the ratio of A_{ROI} and the MBR (Mum Bounding Rectangle) area	$Rect = \frac{A_{ROI}}{D_{max} \times D_{min}}$
Convex Perimeter Ratio [25]	Represents the ratio of the P_{ROI} and the P_{CH}	$CPR = \frac{P_{ROI}}{P_{CH}}$
Circularity [21, 24]	Defined by all of the bounding points of the ROI $$C = \frac{\mu R}{\sigma R}$$ Where μR is the mean distance between the centre of the ROI and all of the bounding points, and σR is the quadratic mean deviation of the mean distance: $$\mu R = \frac{1}{N} \sum_{i=0}^{N-1} \|(x_i, y_i) - (\bar{x}, \bar{y})\|$$ $$\sigma R = \frac{1}{N} \sum_{i=0}^{N-1} \|((x_i, y_i) - (\bar{x}, \bar{y}) - \mu R)^2\|$$	

(continued)

(continued)

Feature	Description	Equation
Sphericity [25]	Represents the ratio between the R of incircle (in) of the ROI and the radius of the excircle (ex) of the ROI	$S = \frac{R_{in}}{R_{ex}}$
Entirety	Ratio between the difference between ACH and AROI, and the AROI	$Ent = \frac{A_{CH} - A_{ROI}}{A_{ROI}}$
Extent	Ratio between AROI and the product of BB width and height	$Ex = \frac{A_{ROI}}{BB_{Width} \times BB_{height}}$
Equiv Diameter	Calculates the D of a circle with the same area as the ROI	$ED = \sqrt{\frac{4 \times A_{ROI}}{\pi}}$
Number Curvatures [24, 26, 27]	Number of corners with 5×5 pixels neighbouring. In order to use K(n) for shape representation, it was quoted the function of curvature, K(n) as: $K(n) = \frac{\dot{x}(n)\ddot{y}(n) - \dot{y}(n)\ddot{x}(n)}{\left(\dot{x}(n)^2 + \dot{y}(n)^2\right)^{3/2}}$ Therefore, it is computed the curvature of a planar curve from its parametric representation. If n is the normalized arc-length parameter s, then: $K(s) = \dot{x}(s)\ddot{y}(s) - \dot{y}(n)\ddot{x}(n)$ However, the curvature function is computed only from parametric derivatives, and, therefore, it is invariant under rotations and translations. Though, the curvature measure is scale dependent, i.e., inversely proportional to the scale. A possible way to achieve scale independence is to normalize this measure by the mean absolute curvature, i.e., $K'(s) = \frac{K(s)}{\frac{1}{N}\sum_{s=1}^{N}|K(s)|}$ where N is the number of points on the normalized contour	

Appendix B

Feature	Description	Equation
Mean	Average of leaf pixel values	
Deviation	Standard deviation of leaf pixel values	
Softness	Calculate the smoothness of the image	$Sft = 1 - \frac{1}{1 + Deviation^2}$
Contrast	Returns the average of the measure of the intensity contrast between a pixel and its	$C = \sum_{i,j} |i - j|^2 p(i,j)$

(continued)

(continued)

Feature	Description	Equation
	neighbour over the whole image, also known as Variance	
Correlation	Returns the average of the measure of how correlated a pixel is to its neighbour over the whole image, where the range is between −1 and 1. Correlation is 1 or −1 for a perfectly positively or negatively correlated image. Correlation is NaN for a constant image	$Corr = \sum_{i,j} \frac{(i-\mu i)(j-\mu j)p(i,j)}{\sigma_i \sigma_j}$
Energy	Returns the average of the sum of squared elements in the GLCM, where the range is between 0 and 1. Energy is 1 for a constant image The property Energy is also known as uniformity, uniformity of energy, and angular second moment, and its calculated by:	$En = \sum_{i,j} p(i,j)^2$
Homogeneity	Returns the average of the value that measures the closeness of the distribution of elements in the GLCM to the GLCM diagonal, where the range is between 0 and 1. Homogeneity is 1 for a diagonal GLCM	$Homo = \sum_{i,j} \frac{p(i,j)}{1 + |i-j|}$
Mean Hist	Calculate the average of the approximate probability density of occurrence of the intensity in the histogram	
Variance Hist	Calculate the variance of the approximate probability density of occurrence of the intensity in the histogram	
Skewness Hist	Calculate the skewness of the approximate probability density of occurrence of the intensity in the histogram Skewness is a measure of the asymmetry of the data around the sample mean. If skewness is negative, the data are spread out more to the left of the mean than to the right. If skewness is positive, the data are spread out more to the right. The skewness of the normal distribution (or any perfectly symmetric distribution) is zero The skewness of a distribution is defined as: $Sk = \frac{E(x-\mu)^3}{\sigma^3}$ where μ is the mean of x, σ is the standard deviation of x, and E(t) represents the expected value of the quantity t	
Kurtosis Hist	Calculate the kurtosis of the approximate probability density of occurrence of the intensity in the histogram	

(continued)

(continued)

Feature	Description	Equation
	Kurtosis is a measure of how outlier-prone a distribution is. The kurtosis of the normal distribution is 3. Distributions that are more outlier-prone than the normal distribution have kurtosis greater than 3; distributions that are less outlier-prone have kurtosis less than 3 The kurtosis of a distribution is defined as $K = \frac{E(x-\mu)^4}{\sigma^4}$ where μ is the mean of x, σ is the standard deviation of x, and E(t) represents the expected value of the quantity t	
Energy Hist	Calculate the energy of the approximate probability density of occurrence of the intensity in the histogram	

References

1. Vivier, M.A., Pretorius, I.S.: Genetically tailored grapevines for the wine industry. Trends Biotechnol. **20**, 472–478 (2002)
2. This, P., Lacombe, T., Thomas, M.: Historical origins and genetic diversity of wine grapes. Trends Genet. **22**, 511–519 (2006)
3. Thomas, M.R., Cain, P., Scott, N.S.: DNA typing of grapevines: a universal methodology and database for describing cultivars and evaluating genetic relatedness. Plant Mol. Biol. **25**, 939–949 (1994)
4. Diago, M.P., Fernandes, A.M., Millan, B., Tardaguila, J., Melo-Pinto, P.: Identification of grapevine varieties using leaf spectroscopy and partial least squares. Comput. Electron. Agric. **99**, 7–13 (2013)
5. Fuentes, S., Hernández-Montes, E., Escalona, J.M., Bota, J., Gonzalez Viejo, C., Poblete-Echeverría, C., Tongson, E., Medrano, H.: Automated grapevine cultivar classification based on machine learning using leaf morpho-colorimetry, fractal dimension and near-infrared spectroscopy parameters. Comput. and Electr. in Agriculture **151**, 311–318 (2018)
6. Gutiérrez, S., Tardaguila, J., Fernández-Novales, J., Diago, M.P.: Support vector machine and artificial neural network models for the classification of grapevine varieties using a portable NIR spectrophotometer. PLoS ONE **10**, e0143197 (2015)
7. Gutiérrez, S., Fernández-Novales, J., Diago, M.P., Tardaguila, J.: On-The-Go hyperspectral imaging under field conditions and machine learning for the classification of grapevine varieties. Front. Plant Sci. **9**, 1102 (2018)
8. Karasik, A., Rahimi, O., David, M., Weiss, E., Drori, E.: Development of a 3D seed morphological tool for grapevine variety identification, and its comparison with SSR analysis. Sci. Rep. **8**, 6545 (2018)
9. Otsu, N.: A threshold selection method from gray-level histograms. IEEE Trans. Syst. Man Cybern. B Cybern. **9**, 62–66 (1979)

10. Bendig, J., et al.: Combining UAV-based plant height from crop surface models, visible, and near infrared vegetation indices for biomass monitoring in barley. Int. J. Appl. Earth Obs. Geoinf. **39**, 79–87 (2015)
11. Gonzalez, R.C., Woods, R.E.: Digital Image Processing, 4th edn. Pearson (2017)
12. Rodgers, J.L., Nicewander, W.A.: Thirteen ways to look at the correlation coefficient. Am. Stat. **42**, 59–66 (1988)
13. Guyon, I., Elisseeff, A.: An introduction to variable and feature selection. J. Mach. Learn. Res. **3**, 1157–1182 (2003)
14. Yu, H.-F., Huang, F.-L., Lin, C.-J.: Dual coordinate descent methods for logistic regression and maximum entropy models. Mach. Learn. **85**, 41–75 (2011)
15. Hastie, T., Tibshirani, R., Friedman, J.: The Elements of Statistical Learning: Data Mining, Inference, and Prediction. Springer Series in Statistics, 2nd edn. Springer, New York (2009). https://doi.org/10.1007/978-0-387-84858-7
16. Altman, N.S.: An introduction to kernel and nearest-neighbor nonparametric regression. Am. Stat. **46**, 175–185 (1992)
17. Breiman, L.: Classification and Regression Trees. Routledge, Boca Raton (2017)
18. Zhang, H.: The Optimality of Naive Bayes. In: FLAIRS2004 Conference (2004)
19. Guyon, I., Boser, B., Vapnik, V.: Automatic capacity tuning of very large VC-dimension classifiers. In: Proceedings Advances in Neural Information Processing Systems, vol. 5, pp. 147–155 (1992)
20. Kohavi, R.: A study of cross-validation and bootstrap for accuracy estimation and model selection, Montreal, vol. 14, pp. 1137–1145 (1995)
21. Du, J.-X., Wang, X.-F., Zhang, G.-J.: Leaf shape based plant species recognition. Appl. Math. Comput. **185**, 883–893 (2007)
22. Silva, P.F.B., Marçal, A.R.S., da Silva, R.M.A.: Evaluation of features for leaf discrimi-nation. In: Kamel, M., Campilho, A. (eds.) ICIAR 2013. LNCS, vol. 7950, pp. 197–204. Springer, Heidelberg (2013). https://doi.org/10.1007/978-3-642-39094-4_23
23. Pauwels, E.J., de Zeeuw, P.M., Ranguelova, E.B.: Computer-assisted tree taxonomy by automated image recognition. Eng. Appl. A.I. **22**, 26–31 (2009)
24. Yang, M., Kpalma, K., Ronsin, J.: A survey of shape feature extraction techniques. In: Yin, P.-Y. (ed.) Pattern Recognition, pp. 43–90. IN-TECH (2008)
25. Ghozlen, N.B., Cerovic, Z.G., Germain, C., Toutain, S., Latouche, G.: Non-destructive optical monitoring of grape maturation by proximal sensing. Sensors **2010**(10), 10040–10068 (2010)
26. Mokhtarian, F., Mackworth, A.K.: A theory of multiscale, curvature-based shape representation for planar curves. IEEE Trans. Pattern Anal. Mach. Intell. **14**, 789–805 (1992)
27. Jalba, A.C., Wilkinson, M.H.F., Roerdink, J.B.T.M.: Shape representation and recognition through morphological curvature scale spaces. IEEE Trans. Image Process. **2006**(15), 331–341 (2006)

Cyberphysical Network for Crop Monitoring and Fertigation Control

João Paulo Coelho[1,2(✉)] ⓘ, Higor Vendramini Rosse[1] ⓘ,
José Boaventura-Cunha[3,4] ⓘ, and Tatiana M. Pinho[4] ⓘ

[1] Instituto Politécnico de Bragança, Campus de Santa Apolónia,
5301-857 Bragança, Portugal
jpcoelho@ipb.pt
[2] Centro de Investigação em Digitalização e Robótica Inteligente (CeDRI),
Campus de Santa Apolónia, 5300-253 Bragança, Portugal
[3] Universidade de Trás-os-Montes e Alto Douro, Escola de Ciências e Tecnologia,
5000-801 Vila Real, Portugal
[4] INESC TEC Technology and Science, Campus da FEUP, 4200-465 Porto, Portugal

Abstract. The most current forecasts point to a decrease in the amount
of potable water available. This increase in water scarcity is a problem
with which sustainable agricultural production is facing. This has led
to an increasing search for technical solutions in order to improve the
efficiency of irrigation systems. In this context, this work describes the
architecture of an agent-based network and the cyberphysical elements
which will be deployed in a strawberry fertigation production plant. The
operation of this architecture relies on local information provided by
LoRA based wireless sensor network that is described in this paper.
Using the information provided by the array of measurement nodes,
cross-referenced with local meteorological data, grower experience and
the actual crop vegetative state, it will be possible to better define the
amount of required irrigation solution and then to optimise the water
usage.

Keywords: Cyberphysical system · Sensor network · LoRA WAN ·
Precision agriculture · Fertigation control

1 Introduction

The availability of water resources is a fundamental aspect to stabilise the human
activities and to maintain the equilibrium of the ecosystems. Besides the need
for drinkable water, societies depend on reliable supplies of water for distinct
activities such as agriculture and industry. However, it is anticipated that in
the near future the amount of available water *per capita* will decrease. There is
not a single, but several reasons that converge to this reduction tendency. The
two most cited ones are the climate changes felt all over the globe [6] and the
increasing population growth, specially in Africa and Asia [18]. A third reason,

© Springer Nature Switzerland AG 2019
P. Moura Oliveira et al. (Eds.): EPIA 2019, LNAI 11804, pp. 200–211, 2019.
https://doi.org/10.1007/978-3-030-30241-2_18

is the contamination of groundwater due to human activities such as sewers, landfills and over application of fertilisers in agriculture [3,19].

Agriculture is the basis of the modern societal structure and supports all the other sectors such as industry and services. As can be presumed, providing food for more than seven billion people world wide imposes a severe load on natural resources in general and in water in particular. Several strategies are currently being developed and applied in order to mitigate this phenomena. For example, the integration of rainwater harvesting systems, the use of fertigation plant growing systems, where both water and nutrients can be tightly controlled, and the integration of state-of-the-art information technologies in the production loop.

Fertigation is an advanced crop growing technique that provides precise injection of fertilisers and irrigation according to plant requirements, environmental conditions and substrate type. The use of fertigation systems has been increasingly popular as an alternative to more classical cultivation techniques. Worldwide, and at the present, more than 11 million hectares of area are associated to fertigation based production schemes. In the context of the Iberian peninsula, fertigation based crop growing systems are being increasingly used for intensive agriculture production [1,5]. Fertigation can be used both outdoor and indoor, with soil as the plant's support or using different substrates such as a mix made of coconut fibres. In this kind of process, soluble type nutrients, such as calcium nitrate and potassium nitrate, phosphoric acid are stored in tanks and injected into water. These solutions are then conduced down to the plant roots area through driplines. Figure 1 illustrates the overall architecture of a fertigation based system. Water is pumped from a reservoir down to the crop production lines. Along this process, venturi injectors apply a predefined amount of each type of nutrient which are stored in different tanks. Besides the nutrients, an additional tank containing an acid solution is also included in order to control the pH of the nutritive solution.

Instrumentation and measurement play a central role in fertigation systems. Besides pH, other variables such as electrical conductivity (EC) and nitrate levels are monitored for the quality of the nutritive solution. Moreover, plant tissue measurements, soil testing, and water analyses are fundamental to provide information about the current production state and to gather information regarding the overall health and productivity of the crop. Agriculture processes can be viewed as very complex time-varying systems since the plants absorb nutrients at different rates along their vegetative states. Failing to keep track on the above referred variables might significantly affect the yield and reduce the economic profit.

Commonly, the irrigation schedule is empirically defined from the farmer's experience or, in a semiautomatic way, based on indirect and imprecise information such as temperature, solar radiation or the water level present in the drainage channels. This form of control, however functional, does not take into consideration the real need for the vegetative development of the plant, the effective level of concentration of the fertigation solution and the difference of the

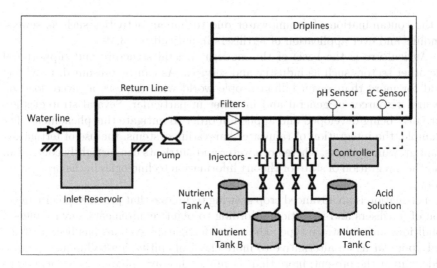

Fig. 1. Overall architecture of a fertigation based system.

environmental conditions, which can vary within the production area, and may cause saturation of nutritive compound or the opposite.

In this work, those problems are addressed by proposing a decentralised, agent-based control system for fertigation crop production. In particular, this strategy will be developed and field tested in a strawberry production plant. The devised control model strongly depends on local information gathered by an array of sensors scattered along the production area. The next section will provide an overview of the current scientific literature that documents the use of sensor networks in agriculture applications. Details regarding the proposed architecture and the experimental setup will be provided in Sect. 3.

2 Sensor Networks in Agriculture

The integration of electronic instrumentation and information technologies, within agricultural production loops, is not a recent subject but has been gaining momentum. Particularly, in the sensors network field, several papers have appeared in the literature during the last ten years.

For example, [21] has presented a method based on wireless sensor networks for potato farming that monitors and decode individual crops and requirements. Therefore, the farmers can potentially identify the various fertilisers, irrigation and other requirements. The authors propose an irrigation management model to estimate agricultural parameters using mathematical calculations and intelligent humidity sensors. In [15], the authors have proposed a smart wireless sensor network to collect data and make it available to end users. [20] present an IoT based systems which aims to provide smart farming systems to end users. Advantages of their approach regarding previous smart farms strategies were enumerated. In [4], they have proposed a method to promote smart agriculture by using automation and IoT technologies. In their paper, the authors have used a ZigBee network, cameras and actuators to implement real-time smart irrigation. More recently, [7] has put forward a sensor network targeting the measurement of soil moisture, air humidity and temperature. The focus of the aimed to support small producers where the owner of the property could access the information in real-time. In [10], a crop monitoring system has been developed aiming to regulate the water and fertiliser in a citrus fertigation production process. In their work, a ZigBee network was used to handle wireless communication. Finally, [16] has developed a wireless sensor network composed of several types of sensors where the acquired information was sent to a web page.

From this literature review, it is evident the use of ZigBee as the wireless communication technology that supports the sensor network information exchange. ZigBee is a technology based on the IEEE 802.15.4 international standard aiming short distances communication with a maximum throughput of 250 kbps. ZigBee has excellent features if a low bit rate local area network is to be implemented. However, it is not the only, or even the most suitable solution, if used within an IoT framework. Specially if large number of nodes are packed in a short area. In some applications, Bluetooth low energy (BLE), ANT, Z-Wave, NB-IoT, SigFox or LoRA can be better alternatives [2,11,12,17].

In this work, a LoRA based wide area network (WAN) is the solutions considered due to the following reasons: first the transceiver price, then the required bandwidth, the network configuration, the transmission range and its power consumption. The price is a fundamental criterion so that the solution can be attractive to the end user. It is important to underline that a large number of measurement nodes would need to be deployed as part of the supervising and control strategy described in this paper. A lower cost will allow a faster capital amortisation and will make it a more appealing solution. The remain reasons are of technical nature: the amount of data to be transmitted by each measurement node will not exceed a dozen of kB per day. The nodes will connect to gateways in a star topology and, in order to make the solution "plug & forget", power consumption is a fundamental issue and will be discussed in the following section.

3   Problem Statement

During this section, the problem addressed within this work will be detailed. First, it will be described the place and conditions where the experimental solution will be deployed. Then, in Subsect. 3.2, the measurement nodes will be described and how they communicate the data to a platform as a service (PaaS). In Subsect. 3.3, the overall agent-based control architecture will be presented. This approach will consider each crop growing stand as a cyberphysical system whose behaviour is monitored by an agent oriented platform.

3.1 Experimental Setup

The monitoring and control strategy described ahead, will be deployed and tested at the Hortiparsil installations. Hortiparsil is a Portuguese SME that produces strawberries using fertigation growing methods. Figure 2 shows a partial view of the growing stands layout.

Fig. 2. Growing stands at the Hortiparsil production greenhouse.

The Hortiparsil production scheme takes place indoor and is composed of several hundreds of growing platforms such as the ones depicted in Fig. 3. Each production row, with a length of around 40 m, is suspended from the greenhouse ceiling by steel cables and made from an iron based trellis, a plastic substrate support and the dripline.

The roots of each strawberry plant are buried in a support substrate made of coconut fibre. The dripline carries the fertigation solution and dispose it, drop by drop, near the plant roots. The irrigation solution not absorbed by the plant or the substrate is recovered at the end of the line and conduced, through hoses, back to the fertigation station inlet reservoir.

As referred during the introduction, the crop schedule irrigation plan is commonly established by the grower based on experience and intuition regarding the current crop nutritive needs. This irrigation scheme usually leads to a suboptimal use of water and nutrients. For this reason, this work proposes the use of an agent-based control framework where the production area will be divided into sectors and each sector, composed of a set of growing stands, will be upgraded to become a cyberphysical element. Sensor nodes will be placed along each section and will communicate data to a centralised data management and analytics platform. Details regarding this sensors network will be addressed in the next section.

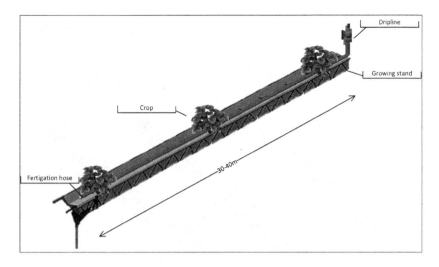

Fig. 3. Schematic diagram of the strawberries growing stands.

3.2   The Sensor Network

Each cyberphysical element will be composed by a set of neighbour growing platforms that share common environmental conditions. A set of measurement nodes (motes) will be distributed along the growing stands gathering information on substrate moisture, air temperature, solar radiation, pH, electrical conductivity, nitrites and nitrates. Artificial vision is also being considered in order to estimate the vegetative state of the crop. But at this point, the sensor network only involves data from environmental and substrate conditions.

The information sent by the motes will be filtered and organised by a software agent that will sent it trough TCP/IP to the PaaS. The communication between the agent and the motes is carried out through a Gateway connected to the motes by using a wireless point-to-multipoint LoRA based network architecture. Figure 4 presents an illustrative diagram of the structure of a generic cyberphysical element.

It is important to highlight that, the time constants involved in the irrigation process are high (generally from ten to sixty minutes depending on the weather conditions). For this reason, the amount of information sent by the transmitter resumes to less than 30 kB during a day time window. Hence, bandwidth is not a variable of concern. However, power consumption, range and number of nodes will steer the selection of the wireless data transmission technology.

With a bandwidth of 125 kHz, LoRA is the wireless digital data communication selected to the current sensors network. This technology supports several data rate modes that can range from 250 bps up to 5470 bps. This very low data rate is balanced by a transmission range that can reach 10 km. It is important to notice that to achieve such high distances it is very important to have a surrounding environment free of physical obstacles and with a high gain antenna.

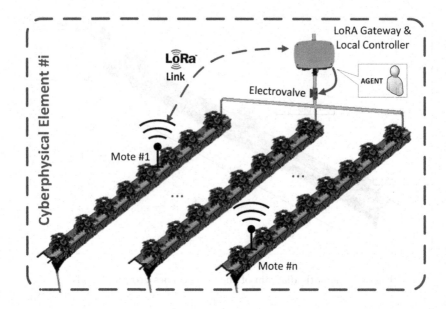

Fig. 4. Schematic diagram of a cyberphysical fertigation element.

From our experiments, 500 m is easily achieved with an isotropic antenna and through building type obstacles. Within the greenhouse, no such distances are required to be covered. However, the crop leafs will contribute to reduce the budget link between the motes and the gateway.

Even if other methods are being tested, at the moment the network operates with a master-slave topology where the measurement nodes are the slaves and the gateway behaves as the master. With a periodicity that could be define between 10 and 30 min, the master sends a request of information to the slaves and then enters into reception mode. The slaves, receiving this request, send the package containing the sensors information. It is worth to notice that all cyberphysical elements are autonomous in the sense that there is no synchronicity between gateways. However, due to high correlation between cyberphysical elements, the PaaS analytics will take this asynchronous incoming information to make a global decision regarding the irrigation schedule.

The number of motes in a sector will depend on the number of available growing stands. Some motes will be responsible to measure air temperature, substrate moisture and electrical conductivity and others will measure nitrites, nitrates and pH. The general architecture of each mote is represented in Fig. 5.

There are many challenges to be solved in the above architecture such as the choice of the sensors, the microcontroller and the power supply technology. Due to the large number of motes that will be installed in a typical cyberphysical element, one of the main concerns is the price. This condition is followed closely by the measurement node power consumption.

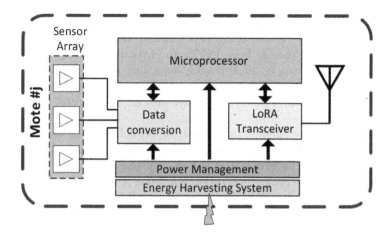

Fig. 5. Sensor nodes (motes) block diagram.

Regarding the sensors, at the present, the prototype is measuring the air temperature using a STLM20 analog temperature sensor. This device ranges from −40 °C to 85 °C with a quiescent power consumption of 15 μW and a shutdown power consumption lower than 70 nW. The substrate moisture is being acquired through an off-the-shelf capacitive type sensor. However, actually different types of sensors are being tested in order to find the one with lower power requirement.

The computation power of the mote is reduced to a simple low power 8 bit microcontroller. In this case, an ATMega328PB, running at 1 MHz with a supply voltage of 3.3 V. This device has a typical power consumption of around 1.5 mW dropping to 0.4 mW when in sleep mode.

The SX1272 LoRA modem is the element with higher power requirements. When in transmission mode, the consumption peaks to 300 mW lowering down to 60 mW when in receiving mode. In sleep mode, those values drop to a power near 0.25 mW. When it operates in the lowest transmission rate mode, the peak power required is only for a time window lower than 10 ms. For this reason, a power consumption average of around 1 mW must be supplied to the mote within a one day operation. That is, a total of 90 J of energy must be provided. A regular LiPo battery is able to pack 9000 J of energy which can lead to a 100 days of full operation until the battery is fully depleted. This solution is unacceptable and is not inline with the concept of "plug & forget" associated to IoT devices. For this reason, energy harvesting solutions are being considered to replace batteries. Nowadays, energy harvesting is considerably simple due to the fact that state-of-the-art DC-DC converters are able to accept input voltages as low as 20 mV and stepping it up to 3.3 V or even higher. For example, the LTC3108, from Analog Devices, is an integrated circuit designed to harvest the energy of thermometric sources. From the same company, the LTC3588 can be used for high impedance sources such as piezoelectric generators. Since the device will operate in a greenhouse, harvesting energy from the Sun is the obvious candidate for powering the device. In this context, we are currently evaluating the use of micro solar panels, from IXYX. In particular, the KXOB22-04X3L module with a total area of $40\,\text{mm}^2$ and, according to the manufacturer, an efficiency 20% higher than amorphous or polycristaline cells. This module is able to deliver a maximum power of 20 mW and an open circuit voltage near 2 V.

For the current mote, an integrates power supply solution is considered where energy will be harvested from the three above referred sources: the thermal difference between the substrate and the air will provide for a Seeback effect energy harvesters, the fertigation solution flow for a piezoelectric generator and the Sun for the micro solar panel. Energy storage will be handled by a capacitor instead of a battery. The main reason is due to the limited life expectancy of the battery when compared to capacitors. Even if batteries can pack a much higher energy value than capacitors, the life expectancy of a capacitor is much greater (theoretically infinite but, in practice, a difference of at least one figure is expected). Since the energy of a capacitor is given by:

$$E = \frac{1}{2}CV^2 \tag{1}$$

where C is its capacitance and V the voltage across its terminals, if the capacitor must be able to store the energy equivalent to two days of operation, $E = 200$ J which, for a 3.3 V output voltage, leads to a capacitor with a capacitance greater or equal to 37 F. For this capacitance value, a ultracapacitor must be considered. Indeed, the SAMXON 2.7 V, 60 F Ultracapacitor will be elected for the prototype. According to the above equation, it can store a total energy of 218 J which is aligned with the initial requirement.

The mote is only a small piece of the total integrated irrigation control system. The following section addresses the overall architecture where an agent-based decentralised model will be explained.

3.3   The Overall Agent-Based Architecture

The current work aims to develop an integrated solution to control the fertigation of a strawberry production process. As described in Subsect. 3.1, the crop is planted in suspended growing stands and the nutrition solution is carried to the plants through driplines. The current approach considers that this production scheme can be compared to a conventional industrial manufacturing line: the incoming raw material enters (in this case the fertigation broth, the solar radiation and remain environmental conditions) and the final product exits (the strawberries). Some of those variables can be controlled, for example the amount of each nutrient in the fertigation fluid but others are uncontrollable, such as the solar radiation, and must be viewed as disturbances. In this context, the fertigation based production line is even more complex than the common production lines found in typical industries due to the high influence that the uncontrollable disturbances have in the final production outcome. For this reason, it makes sense to migrate some of the Industry 4.0 paradigms into agriculture. In particular, the ones that lead to an increase in robustness, adaptability and waste reduction. Among other approaches, the use of decentralised control methods based on agents has proven to be an efficient solution in the management of complex industrial environments [8,9,13,14]. In agent-based systems, each agent can exchange information with the remain existing agents. Different types of agents are involved in the process: some of them have network management functions while others supervise the cyberphysical entities. In the current proposal, the cyberphysical elements are a collection of neighbour growing stands that share similar environmental conditions. For each cyberphysical element, the information of the current environmental and production conditions are delivered through an array of sensor nodes scattered along the growing stands of the sector. Details on those measurement devices have been provided in subsection 3.2. The overall agent-based fertigation control architecture is represented in Fig. 6.

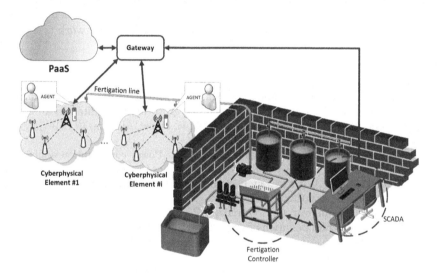

Fig. 6. Agent-based fertigation control architecture.

It is the responsibility of each agent to supervise the cyberphysical element state and to determine the fertigation level based on local information sent by the motes. They will also perform some important data analytics such as short-term environmental predictions. The motes information and the local predictions will be sent to a PaaS where this information will be crossed with data provided by meteorological servers in order to compute the irrigation requirements. This information will then be sent to the fertigation controller which, after approval by the grower, will execute the irrigation schedule.

It is expected that, with this architecture, the amount of water and nutrients used in the fertigation process will be reduced since the irrigation schedule will be defined based on the present plant needs, weather and actual substrate conditions forecast and not based on empirical rules.

4 Conclusion

The need of consciously use water resources has become a necessity due to the intensification of water scarcity. Intensive agriculture is one of the major players in water consumption and contamination due to the indiscriminate use of fertilisers and phytopharmaceuticals. This work addresses this problem by presenting a scalable, decentralised monitoring and predictive control system that will be field tested in a fertigation based strawberries growing production plant. The devised strategy relies on the information provided by a set of measurement nodes and using artificial intelligence techniques to compute the daily irrigation schedule. At the present time, we are engaged at developing the motes core hardware and testing the resiliency of the LoRA network in a point-multipoint network architecture. Trials are being conduced in order to define the energy harvesters operating bounds. Future work will address the implementation of the data analytics in the PaaS platform and the agent-based network.

References

1. Cameira, M., Pereira, A., Ahuja, L., Ma, L.: Sustainability and environmental assessment of fertigation in an intensive olive grove under mediterranean conditions. Agric. Water Manag. **146**, 346–360 (2014). https://doi.org/10.1016/j.agwat. 2014.09.007
2. Dementyev, A., Hodges, S., Taylor, S., Smith, J.: Power consumption analysis of bluetooth low energy, ZigBee and ANT sensor nodes in a cyclic sleep scenario. In: IEEE International Wireless Symposium (IWS). IEEE, April 2013. https://doi. org/10.1109/ieee-iws.2013.6616827
3. Egboka, B.C., Nwankwor, G.I., Orajaka, I.P., Ejiofor, A.O.: Principles and problems of environmental pollution of groundwater resources with case examples from developing countries. Environ. Health Perspect. **83**, 39–68 (1989). https://doi.org/ 10.1289/ehp.898339
4. Gondchawar, N., Kawitkar, P.D.R.S.: Smart agriculture using IoT and WSN based modern technologies. Int. J. Innovative Res. Comput. Commun. Eng. (2016)
5. Guzmán, M.: Protected crops in Spain: technology of fertigation control. In: Agri-Leadership Summit 2017 (2017)
6. Jimenez, B.E., et al.: Climate Change 2014: Impacts, Adaptation and Vulnerability. Contribution of Working Group II to the Fifth Assessment Report of the Intergovernmental Panel on Climate Change (2014)
7. Kiani, F., Seyyedabbasi, A.: Wireless sensor networks and Internet of Things in precision agriculture. Int. J. Adv. Comput. Sci. Appl. (2018)
8. Kong, L., Xiao, L.: A multi-layered control architecture of intelligent agent. In: IEEE International Conference on Control and Automation. IEEE, May 2007. https://doi.org/10.1109/icca.2007.4376602
9. Kouluri, M.K., Pandey, R.K.: Intelligent agent based micro grid control. In: 2nd International Conference on Intelligent Agent & Multi-Agent Systems. IEEE, September 2011. https://doi.org/10.1109/iama.2011.6049007

10. Kushal, M., Ghadge, H.K.G., Seeman, V.: Fertigation system to conserve water and fertilizers using wireless sensor network. Int. J. Eng. Res. Comput. Sci. Eng. (IJERCS) (2018)
11. Lauridsen, M., Vejlgaard, B., Kovacs, I.Z., Nguyen, H., Mogensen, P.: Interference measurements in the european 868 MHz ISM band with focus on LoRa and SigFox. In: IEEE Wireless Communications and Networking Conference (WCNC). IEEE, March 2017. https://doi.org/10.1109/wcnc.2017.7925650
12. Lee, J.S., Su, Y.W., Shen, C.C.: A comparative study of wireless protocols: bluetooth, UWB, ZigBee, and wi-fi. In: IECON 2007–33rd Annual Conference of the IEEE Industrial Electronics Society. IEEE (2007). https://doi.org/10.1109/iecon.2007.4460126
13. Leitao, P., Karnouskos, S., Ribeiro, L., Lee, J., Strasser, T., Colombo, A.W.: Smart agents in industrial cyber-physical systems. Proc. IEEE **104**(5), 1086–1101 (2016). https://doi.org/10.1109/jproc.2016.2521931
14. Luo, S., Hu, C., Zhang, Y., Ma, R., Meng, L.: Multi-agent systems using model predictive control for coordinative optimization control of microgrid. In: 20th International Conference on Electrical Machines and Systems (ICEMS). IEEE, August 2017. https://doi.org/10.1109/icems.2017.8056293
15. Mendez, G.R., Yunus, M.A.M., Mukhopadhyay, S.C.: A WiFi based smart wireless sensor network for monitoring an agricultural environment. In: IEEE International Instrumentation and Measurement Technology Conference Proceedings. IEEE, May 2012. https://doi.org/10.1109/i2mtc.2012.6229653
16. Moreno, C.D., Brox Jiménez, M., Alejandro Gersnoviez Milla, A., Márquez Moyano, M., Ortiz, M., Quiles Latorre, F.: Wireless sensor network for sustainable agriculture. Presented at Environment, Green Technology and Engineering International Conference (EGTEIC 2018), vol. 2, October 2018. https://doi.org/10.3390/proceedings2201302
17. Mroue, H., Nasser, A., Hamrioui, S., Parrein, B., Motta-Cruz, E., Rouyer, G.: MAC layer-based evaluation of IoT technologies: LoRa, SigFox and NB-IoT. In: IEEE Middle East and North Africa Communications Conference (MENACOMM). IEEE, April 2018. https://doi.org/10.1109/menacomm.2018.8371016
18. United Nations: World Population Prospects: The 2017 Revision. United Nations 2017 (2017)
19. Paralta, E., Fernandes, R., Carreira, P., Ribeiro, L.: Assessing the impacts of agriculture on groundwater quality using nitrogen isotopes. In: 2nd Workshop on Iberian Regional Working Group on Hardrock Hidrology (2005)
20. Ryu, M., Yun, J., Miao, T., Ahn, I.Y., Choi, S.C., Kim, J.: Design and implementation of a connected farm for smart farming system. In: IEEE SENSORS. IEEE, November 2015. https://doi.org/10.1109/icsens.2015.7370624
21. Shinighal, D.K., Srivastava, N.: Wireless sensor networks in agriculture: For potato farming. Int. J. Eng. Sci. Technol. (2010)

Soil Classification Based on Physical and Chemical Properties Using Random Forests

Didier Dias[1(✉)], Bruno Martins[2], João Pires[1], Luís M. de Sousa[3],
Jacinto Estima[4], and Carlos V. Damásio[1]

[1] NOVA LINCS and Faculdade de Ciências e Tecnologia,
Universidade Nova de Lisboa, Lisbon, Portugal
dn.dias@campus.fct.unl.pt
[2] INESC-ID and Instituto Superior Técnico, Universidade de Lisboa,
Lisbon, Portugal
[3] ISRIC - World Soil Information, Wageningen, The Netherlands
[4] INESC-ID and Instituto Politécnico de Setúbal, Lisbon, Portugal

Abstract. Soil classification is a method of encoding the most relevant information about a given soil, namely its composition and characteristics, in a single class, to be used in areas like agriculture and forestry. In this paper, we evaluate how confidently we can predict soil classes, following the World Reference Base classification system, based on the physical and chemical characteristics of its layers. The Random Forests classifier was used with data consisting of 6 760 soil profiles composed by 19 464 horizons, collected in Mexico. Four methods of modelling the data were tested (i.e., standard depths, n first layers, thickness, and area weighted thickness). We also fine-tuned the best parameters for the classifier and for a k-NN imputation algorithm, used for addressing problems of missing data. Under-represented classes showed significantly worse results, by being repeatedly predicted as one of the majority classes. The best method to model the data was found to be the n first layers approach, with missing values being imputed with k-NN ($k = 1$). The results present a Kappa value from 0.36 to 0.48 and were in line with the state of the art methods, which mostly use remote sensing data.

Keywords: Soil classification · Soil properties · Machine learning · Random Forests · Ensemble learning

1 Introduction

The soil corresponds to the most superficial layer of the planet, defined as starting from the surface and extending to the depth that plants roots reach. This value is usually limited to 200 cm for classification purposes [11,14]. To measure soil properties, it is usual to dig a vertical section of the land and extract the different layers of soil. These layers are easily distinguishable between them and

© Springer Nature Switzerland AG 2019
P. Moura Oliveira et al. (Eds.): EPIA 2019, LNAI 11804, pp. 212–223, 2019.
https://doi.org/10.1007/978-3-030-30241-2_19

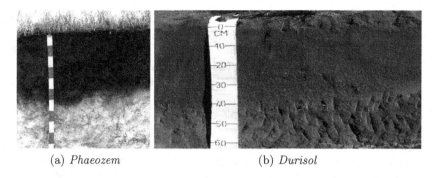

(a) *Phaeozem*   (b) *Durisol*

Fig. 1. Examples of soil profiles, taken from the ISRIC website and classified following WRB. On the left a soil identified as *Phaeozem* containing two horizons, a deep black mollic layer abruptly overlying a calcareous substrate, from a location in China. On the right, we have a dark red *Durisol* from South Africa. (Color figure online)

are referred to as horizons, while the whole vertical section containing all the layers is known as a profile, as seen in Fig. 1.

Many of the soil properties can be measured through laboratory testing, including the pH and electrical conductivity. To a non-expert, these variables are complex to understand. As such, soil classification systems were created to facilitate the understanding of this information. Most classification methods attribute a class to the profile, based on attributes from the layers like composition or colour. The most used systems are the World Reference Base (WRB) [11] and the USDA Soil Taxonomy [7]. The former, which we will be focusing on, is an international system with the intent of simplifying the communication between countries, while the latter was created in the USA, and was then adopted by many other countries. Other nations also have their own systems, which usually are not directly translatable to the two previous systems.

Studies in soil classification and mapping mainly do their predictions by resorting to remote sensing data, such as information on terrain slope or vegetation coverage [4,7,9,13]. This is due to the ease of access to satellite data that can provide information on some properties that are directly related to the soil classification. This method, however, requires actual soil measurements, and interpretations of these measurements made by domain experts, to be used not only as labels in the learning process but also as validation points. Another issue is that this data can usually only describe the surface of the land, while the classes are attributed based on measurements made at various depths.

In this paper we will take a different approach, using the properties of the various layers of a soil profile to infer its class. This is made with the purpose of finding relations between the observed properties and the classification, helping us classify other profiles that were analysed by experts but not classified, or that used different classification systems. This method may also help the expert classification where, with the measurements made on the soil, our algorithm may provide the most probable classes for the profile.

We used a database of around 48 000 soil profiles and their layers, made available by the International Soil Reference and Information Centre (ISRIC), in the World Soil Information System (WoSIS) [2]. About half of these profiles are classified following the World Reference Base (WRB) system, which we will be focusing on. To make our predictions we will be resorting to Random Forest classifiers while exploring different methods for modelling, cleaning, and imputing missing values in the available data.

The rest of this document is organised as follows: Sect. 2 covers related research. Section 3 provides an analysis of the data we will be using, also describing how it was treated. Section 4 presents the way that the data was modelled to be presented to the classifier. Section 5 presents the methods used for making predictions of the soil classes, while also covering the obtained results. Finally, Sect. 6 provides our conclusions and discusses possible future work.

2   Previous Related Work

Several previous studies have focused on comparisons between various machine learning algorithms for the soil classification problem. All of these previous efforts use remote sensing data as the main resource to inform the training of the models, while the actual soil measurements are used as ground truth.

The SoilGrids project [7] provides us with machine learning based predictions worldwide, with a resolution of 250 m, for soil properties like pH, organic carbon content and classification according to WRB and Soil Taxonomy. A total of 158 features were used in the different models, most generated from satellite data, and selected based on their representation of soil formation factors like vegetation and humidity. A model was trained for each predicted variable, and the algorithms used in the experiments were Random Forests, Gradient Boosting and Multinomial Logistic Regression. The results can be seen on the SoilGrids website[1]. This project used a previous iteration of the data set used in our paper but only resorted to its information for ground truth and validation purposes.

Meier et al. performed a comparison between 8 machine learning algorithms, applied to soil classification for a single tropical and mountainous region in Brazil [13]. As features to train the models, 73 covariates generated from satellite images were initially chosen but were then filtered using Random Feature Elimination (RFE) to a final total of 10 variables. As for ground truth for the classifiers, 140 soil profiles were measured and classified following the Brazilian National soil classification system. The algorithms that showed better results were Random Forests, AdaBoost and Gradient Tree Boosting, although, with the exception of Support Vector Machines (SVMs) using a polynomial kernel, all the procedures seemed to have a similar performance. All of the comparisons were performed using Cohen's Kappa to assess the quality of the results, generated from confusion matrices and with values from 0.42 to 0.48.

Brungard et al. performed a similar study, comparing 11 different algorithms for soil classification in three semi-arid regions of the USA [4]. Again, classified

---

[1] https://soilgrids.org.

profiles were used as validation points, 450 in this case, and only remote sensing data was used to train the models. Three different covariate groups were created, with the first consisting of variables chosen by soil experts. The second group was a union between the previous set and 113 additional features, and a final group was the result of filtering the second set using RFE. The results were substantially better when the third group of variables was used, through all algorithms. The authors found that the Random Forests classification algorithm provided the best results, followed by SVMs using a radial-basis kernel, when compared with the Kappa statistic, achieving values similar to those from the previous study from Meier et al. [13]. The imbalance and the number of classes was a decisive factor in the performance of the algorithms, which was observed when comparing the three studied regions.

Heung et al. focused on a single Canadian region and made a comparison of 10 classifiers using a set of 20 covariates, which were chosen from a larger set that was filtered using Principal Component Analysis [9]. The authors state that Random Forests proved to be the most accurate classifier and, while other classifiers had similar results, this method is substantially easier to parametrise and to train. The authors also mention that there is an accentuated imbalance in the data, where two of the 20 total classes account for more than 60% of the total size of the set. This is a recurring problem in the area, and the authors tested four sampling methods to decrease its impact: equal class, by-polygon, area weighted, and random oversampling applied to the weighted sampling [9]. The best results were achieved when using the area weighted sampling, seeing a significant increase compared to the remaining tests. This method relies on setting a number of samples equivalent to the proportion of the predominance in the area being studied. The use of random oversampling had negligibly better results, at the cost of a substantially larger processing time.

More recently, Hounkpatin et al. tried a different method for reducing the impact of the data imbalance in soil classification [10]. They applied a pruning approach to the majority class, removing a percentage of its values. This parameter was tested, and the best results were found when profiles contained by the lowest and highest 5%, of the cumulative percentage of the most important covariate, were removed. This was made to remove possible outliers and noisy data, while also resulting in more similar class sizes, providing an increase in the performance of the tested classifier, i.e. Random Forests. The use of random oversampling was tested after this first data treatment but only saw small improvements. The authors explain that repeating values in the classes with fewer data does not create new information, and can instead lead to overfitting.

3   The Data Set Used in Our Experiments

The soil classification is attributed to a profile, i.e. a vertical section containing a varied number of layers, named horizons [11,14]. Our tests regarding automated soil classification are based on data provided by ISRIC[2] through the WoSIS

---

[2] https://www.isric.org/.

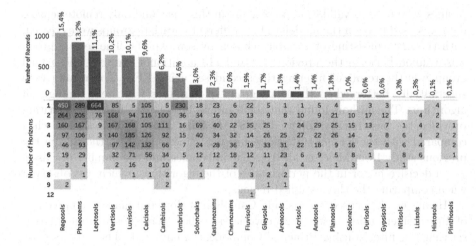

Fig. 2. Number of profiles per reference soil group, together with the number of horizons per profile, for the data subset covering Mexico.

database, containing 24 248 profiles labelled with WRB classes, totalling 94 895 horizons. In this section, we show the results from an analysis performed on the dataset and discuss the methods applied to treat missing values in the data.

3.1   Description and Analysis

WoSIS is a global database, with some exceptions in countries that use different classification systems, or empty regions where the soil is mostly homogeneous with a reduced number of uses for it [7]. Mexico has a large density of surveyed profiles, containing many different classes and consistent measurements, which led us to focus on this area for our preliminary study.

We used the broadest level of the WRB classification system, the Reference Soil Group (RSG), as a means to assess our results while reducing the number of possible classes. In Mexico, our data set contains 24 out of the total 32 RSG classes [11]. Analysing Fig. 2, we can see that we are dealing with a highly imbalanced dataset. While *Regosols* accounts for over 15% of the instances, there are 13 classes that have less than 2% of the total profiles recorded.

The number of horizons that constitute a profile can vary, although most classes tend to have 3 to 5 layers. Some classifications have a lower number of horizons, such as *Leptosols* in which most profiles have only a single layer, as seen in Fig. 2. Since the number of horizons seems to bring some information about the profiles' class, we added this feature to our data.

For each soil profile, we have the latitude and longitude of the location where the profile was sampled, and its classification. For the horizons we have data about the upper depth and the lower depth of the layer, meaning the depth where it starts and ends. The dataset also contains information on the average pH, electrical conductivity, organic carbon and calcium carbonate as well as the percentages for sand, silt and clay in the horizons.

3.2 Data Treatment and Dealing with Missing Values

One problem in our data is that there are many missing values, with some variables having such a low count of instances that the information that they can provide is negligible. As such, we decided to remove all the variables for which we have less than 1% of the total number of measurements (i.e., electrical conductivity). This was also made with the classes, removing those that appear in less than 0.25% of the total measurements, namely *Plinthosols* and *Histosols*. After this treatment, we ended up with only 11 features and 22 possible classes.

The remaining missing values in the soil properties were treated using an imputation method based on the k-Nearest Neighbours (k-NN) algorithm [6]. This procedure finds the k most similar samples by weighing them with the mean squared difference, based on the full set of variables for which the rows being compared have data. The resulting feature will be the average of the values observed in these neighbours, for that variable. The best value for k in this method was fine-tuned through experiments described further ahead in the paper. The data set was also normalised to have a mean of 0 and variance of 1.

4 Data Modelling

Our data is organised in layers, containing the properties of the soil at a given location, and a reference to the profile it belongs to. We have to model the data in such a way that we present a single instance per profile to our classifier so that it can correctly predict the classification for the whole profile, and not for each of the layers. An issue in this approach is that the number of layers that constitute a profile is variable, while the input of our classifier must be constant. In Fig. 3 we can see a profile with 6 layers, which we will use to exemplify our four developed methods of modelling the data, presented below.

N First Layers: The closer we are to the surface, the more information we can retrieve from the soil [7]. As such a simple method consists of using only the first N layers, a parameter which was varied in our experiments in order to find the best results. This not only reduces the impact of not using some information since the layers that may be skipped will always be the deepest, but it also provides us with flexibility regarding the number of layers. We may however not have enough data, e.g. in profiles for which we only have layers that go through 130 cm of depth. As an attempt to solve this last problem we repeat the deepest layer present in the instance.

Standard Depth: We also created a model based on the standard values that have been created for the depths of the layers: 0–5, 5–15, 15–30, 30–60, 60–100, and 100–200 cm [1]. To find the values for these layers we use the horizons, on

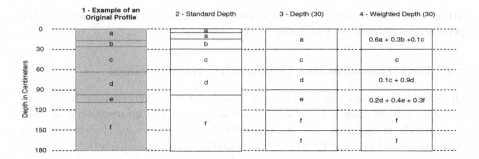

Fig. 3. Illustration for 3 of the different data modelling techniques that were used. The letters represent the value, for an arbitrary feature, in each layer.

our original data, that correspond to the middle point of the standard layers, e.g. 150 cm for the 100–200 cm layer. This may lead to some information not being used, as would be the case for layer e in Fig. 3. Again, we repeat the last layer if there are not enough horizons in the initial profile.

Thickness: In this approach, we focus on a predetermined thickness t for each measure, to a maximum depth m, until we have $\lfloor m/t \rfloor$ layers. Multiple values were tested for t, namely 10, 30 and 60 cm, while m was kept at 200 cm since it is the maximum depth allowed for classification purposes [11,14]. The deepest original horizon is repeated for missing layers and the values are extracted from the exact layer where the measurement will occur, independently of how much of the final layer is actually occupied by it. This may again lead to wasted information and, as an attempt to fix this issue, we developed a weighted approach.

Area Weighted Thickness: In this method, each horizon that is contained in the final layer contributes to the final value. This contribution is based on a weight, which is directly related to how much of the layer being analysed belongs to the final horizon, and where the sum of the weights must be equal to 1. An example for this can be seen in Fig. 3, more specifically by comparing the first layer of the thickness and weighted thickness approaches, where the first does not use any information from layer b. All of our features are numeric but, if that was not the case, this method would have to be modified since it does not work on categorical variables.

5 Experimental Validation

We developed and tested various ways to treat and model the data, prior to model training. This section first presents these tests and the methodology that they follow. A detailed analysis of the results is made afterwards.

5.1 Parameter Optimisation and Methodology

There are many variables that can be optimised, both in the classification method and in the data treatment procedures, in order to give us the best possible results. The following tests were made to optimise the parameters.

Model Training and Evaluation: The algorithm used in our experiments, i.e. the Random Forests classifier [3], was trained using cross-validation with 10 folds [13]. This was made with the intent of avoiding overfitting and to better estimate how our model would work on new instances.

To validate the results we used Cohen's Kappa [5]. This metric provides insights into the performance of a classifier while accounting for an agreement with the gold-standard due to chance, which is very important when the number of instances per class is imbalanced, as is the case in our data. The metric is computed from the confusion matrix, which we also analyse and present.

Classifier Parameters: The Random Forest classifier has various parameters to tune. In our research, the trees in the ensemble were grown according to the Gini impurity metric to split the nodes. In an initial filtering attempt, we used the RandomizedSearchCV algorithm, which tries random variations of the parameters. To further fine-tune the values found through this first phase, GridSearchCV was used. These methods, as well as the cross-validation and Random Forests procedures, are implemented in the *scikit-learn* package[3]. After the initial test, the values examined in more detail were:

- 1, 2, 3 for the minimum number of samples for a node to be a leaf.
- 2, 3, 6, 9, 12 for the minimum number of samples to split a node.
- 1000, 1100, 1200, 1300, 1400, 1500 for the number of trees to be used.

These values were tested only on the data that uses standard depth imputed with $k = 1$, to reduce the time to train models and evaluate results, since the best parameters should not differ much between the various modelling methods.

Data Treatment and Modelling: We used a k-NN imputation method, where the k is a parameter that can be tuned, changing the number of neighbours that are used for the imputation. With $k = 1$, we simply copy the value from the closest point, while with $k > 1$ the algorithm uses an average of the k neighbours' values. We tested this parameter with the values of 1, 2 and 3.

All of the different modelling techniques were tested, in conjunction with each value for k, to see which method performs better in our problem. The n first layers, thickness, and area weighted thickness variations also require parametrization. For the number of layers, we tested 1, 3, 5 and 7, while for thickness, the values used in our tests were 10, 30 and 60 cm.

---

[3] https://scikit-learn.org/.

5.2 Results and Discussion

We first tested different values for some of the many Random Forests hyper-parameters, using the standard depth modelling method and k-NN imputation with $k = 1$. The best parameters found for our problem were as follows:

- Minimum number of samples required for a node to be a leaf: 2 (default = 1)
- Minimum number of samples required to split a node: 6 (default = 2)
- Number of trees to be trained: 1300 (default = 100)

These parameters resulted in an overall improvement of about 4% in the Kappa score, over the default values in the *scikit-learn* library. After finding the best hyper-parameters for the classifier, we then proceeded to executing the remaining tests, which produced the results shown in Table 1.

Table 1. Results for the tests that were performed. The best results, using the Kappa measure and for each number of neighbours, are in bold. W = Weighted.

Neighbours (k) = 1			Neighbours (k) = 2			Neighbours (k) = 3		
Modelling	Kappa	Accuracy	Modelling	Kappa	Accuracy	Modelling	Kappa	Accuracy
Standard	0.443	0.502	Standard	0.456	0.514	Standard	0.446	0.504
Layers 1	0.438	0.500	Layers 1	0.440	0.501	Layers 1	0.436	0.497
Layers 3	0.469	0.527	**Layers 3**	**0.468**	**0.526**	**Layers 3**	**0.477**	**0.534**
Layers 5	**0.480**	**0.537**	Layers 5	0.465	0.522	Layers 5	0.471	0.528
Layers 7	0.466	0.524	Layers 7	0.464	0.521	Layers 7	0.471	0.529
Thickness 10	0.409	0.471	Thickness 10	0.420	0.482	Thickness 10	0.415	0.477
Thickness 30	0.418	0.480	Thickness 30	0.420	0.482	Thickness 30	0.419	0.481
Thickness 60	0.430	0.490	Thickness 60	0.427	0.487	Thickness 60	0.435	0.496
Thickness (W) 10	0.379	0.446	Thickness (W) 10	0.373	0.440	Thickness (W) 10	0.369	0.436
Thickness (W) 30	0.393	0.459	Thickness (W) 30	0.403	0.466	Thickness (W) 30	0.399	0.463
Thickness (W) 60	0.411	0.475	Thickness (W) 60	0.413	0.477	Thickness (W) 60	0.416	0.479

We can observe that our scores range from 0.36 to 0.48 in the Kappa index, and 0.43 to 0.53 in accuracy. These results are in line with the performances obtained in similar studies, which used only remote sensing data as well as smaller regions [4,12,13]. The tests that used $k = 2$ tend to have slightly worse results than the other variations. This may be explained by the case where the two nearest neighbours have very diverging values, resulting in a final property that is close to neither. The other values, $k = 1$ and $k = 3$, have very similar results since they minimise the problem discussed by either accepting a single value or by having a stronger smoothing effect on possible outliers.

The best modelling method used was the n first layers of the initial profile, with 3, 5 and 7 layers having very similar results in all the tests. The standard model provided slightly worse results, possibly explained by the loss of information when the layers in the initial profile do not correspond to the exact measurement depths, while the first method does prevent the loss of the first n horizons. This is preferable due to the lower layers containing less information.

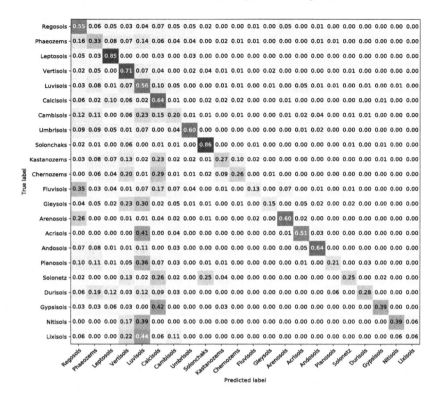

Fig. 4. Confusion matrix, ordered by the most representative classes, of the best model, i.e. using the first 5 layers and with data imputation based on $k = 1$

The thickness-based data modelling techniques proved to be the worst of the ones that were tested. With the decrease in the width of each layer, the results tend to worsen, possibly due to the increase in the horizons being repeated, and to overfitting. The weighted variant showed an overall worse performance between the two. While it uses all the information available in the original profile, we think that it may also have a smoothing effect, resulting in a less abrupt change of the properties between layers. This rapid change of the values might be necessary for classes where we have an overlap of contrasting layers.

A problem with our dataset, discussed in Sect. 3, is that the classes are very unbalanced. This is also shown in the confusion matrix, presented in Fig. 4, where the small classes tend to be predicted as the larger ones. Examples of this can be seen in *Regosols*, i.e. the class with the most instances in our data, where *Fluvisols* and *Arenosols* are predicted as belonging to the most frequent class, and in *Luvisols*, where classes such as *Nitisols* and *Lixisols* are regularly mistaken for the most representative class. This also informs us that these classes have very similar characteristics. To address these issues we could try to use sampling or pruning methods, as described in Sect. 2, or improve the data by adding new features and measures, helping our model distinguish these classes.

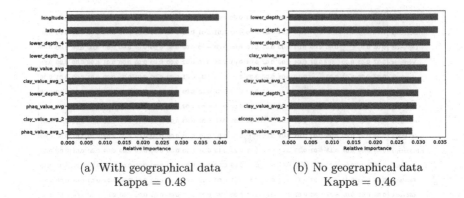

(a) With geographical data
Kappa = 0.48

(b) No geographical data
Kappa = 0.46

Fig. 5. The 10 most important features, as ranked by the Random Forest models with the best results: 5 First Layers with $k = 1$. lower_depth= lower depth, clay_value_avg = average clay percentage, phaq_value_avg = average pH measured in H2O, elcosp_value_avg = electrical conductivity in saturated paste. The numbers next to the variable names represent the layer from which the measure was taken where no number marks the first layer.

The Random Forests classifier provides us with the relative importance of the features used in its training, as presented in Fig. 5. One of the most important variables is the lower depth of the layers, showing a strong relationship with the RSG chosen by the predictor. The geographical position (i.e., latitude and longitude) of the profile is the most important feature. To test how much this impacted our classification we ran the same test while removing the latitude and longitude variables, resulting in a decrease of around 4% in the Kappa score. This shows that the location of the measure can greatly impact its classification, confirming the results of previous studies that also showed a high degree of spatial auto-correlation in soil properties, and thus also on classes [7].

6   Conclusions and Future Work

We evaluated the performance of Random Forest models for soil classification leveraging physical and chemical properties, obtaining results comparable to the state-of-the-art methods that use significantly different data, with the Kappa index ranging between 0.36 and 0.48. The method named n first layers was found to have the best performance, in terms of data preparation, while there are still problems when predicting the classes with less predominance in the data. For future work, other classifiers should be tested and compared with the results demonstrated in this paper, namely Gradient Tree Boosting and other tree ensemble methods designed specifically for geo-spatially referenced data [8]. On the data side, the region should be expanded, testing the classifiers on the whole dataset, using spatial interpolation on the available properties to support the creation of soil maps, and using pruning and sampling methods to reduce the imbalance in the class sizes. The introduction of new variables should also be addressed, mainly remote sensing data in complement to our variables, since these are the most used in the actual state of the art methods, and given that it would be interesting to see if the combined use of both types of data can improve the soil classification results.

Acknowledgments. This research was supported through Fundação para a Ciência e Tecnologia (FCT), through the project grant with reference PTDC/CCI-CIF/32607/2017 (MIMU), as well as through the INESC-ID (UID/CEC/50021/2019) and NOVA LINCS (UID/CEC/04516/2019) multi-annual funding.

References

1. Arrouays, D., McKenzie, N., de Forges, A.R., et al.: GlobalSoilMap: Basis of the Global Spatial Soil Information System. CRC Press, Leiden (2014)
2. Batjes, N.H., Ribeiro, E., Oostrum, A.v., et al.: Wosis: providing standardised soil profile data for the world. Earth Syst. Sci. Data **9**(1), 1–14 (2017)
3. Breiman, L.: Random forests. Mach. Learn. **45**(1), 5–32 (2001)
4. Brungard, C.W., Boettinger, J.L., Duniway, M.C., et al.: Machine learning for predicting soil classes in three semi-arid landscapes. Geoderma **239**, 68–83 (2015)
5. Congalton, R.G.: A review of assessing the accuracy of classifications of remotely sensed data. Remote Sens. Environ. **37**(1), 35–46 (1991)
6. Crookston, N.L., Finley, A.O.: yaimpute: an R package for KNN imputation. J. Stat. Softw. **23**(10), 16 (2008)
7. Hengl, T., de Jesus, J.M., Heuvelink, G.B., et al.: Soilgrids250m: global gridded soil information based on machine learning. PLoS ONE **12**(2), e0169748 (2017)
8. Hengl, T., Nussbaum, M., Wright, M.N., et al.: Random forest as a generic framework for predictive modeling of spatial and spatio-temporal variables. PeerJ **6**, e5518 (2018)
9. Heung, B., Ho, H.C., Zhang, J., et al.: An overview and comparison of machine-learning techniques for classification purposes in digital soil mapping. Geoderma **265**, 62–77 (2016)
10. Hounkpatin, K.O., Schmidt, K., Stumpf, F., et al.: Predicting reference soil groups using legacy data: a data pruning and random forest approach for tropical environment (Dano catchment, Burkina Faso). Sci. Rep. **8**(1), 9959 (2018)
11. IUSS Working Group WRB: World reference base for soil resources 2014, update 2015 international soil classification system for naming soils and creating legends for soil maps. World Soil Resources Reports No. 106, p. 192 (2015)
12. Jeune, W., Francelino, M.R., de Souza, E., et al.: Multinomial logistic regression and random forest classifiers in digital mapping of soil classes in Western Haiti. Rev. Bras. Cienc. Solo **42**, e0170133 (2018)
13. Meier, M., Souza, E.d., Francelino, M.R., et al.: Digital soil mapping using machine learning algorithms in a tropical mountainous area. Revista Brasileira de Ciência do Solo **42**, e0170421 (2018). http://dx.doi.org/10.1590/18069657rbcs20170421
14. Soil Survey Staff USA: Soil taxonomy: a basic system of soil classification for making and interpreting soil surveys. US Government Printing Office (1999)

Low-Cost IoT LoRa®Solutions
for Precision Agriculture
Monitoring Practices

Nuno Silva[1,5](✉) , Jorge Mendes[1,2] , Renato Silva[1] ,
Filipe Neves dos Santos[2] , Pedro Mestre[1,3,4] , Carlos Serôdio[1,3,4] ,
and Raul Morais[1,2,4]

[1] Departamento de Engenharias, Escola de Ciências e Tecnologia, UTAD – University
of Trás-os-Montes e Alto Douro, Quinta de prados, 5000-801 Vila Real, Portugal
nmsps@hotmail.com
[2] INESC TEC – Instituto de Engenharia de Sistemas e Computadores Tecnologia e
Ciência – Pólo da UTAD, 5000-801 Vila Real, Portugal
[3] Centro Algoritmi – Universidade do Minho,
Campus Azurém, 4800-058 Guimarães, Portugal
[4] CITAB – Centre for the Research and Technology of Agro-Environmental
and Biological Sciences, UTAD, Vila Real, Portugal
[5] IEETA – Institute of Electronics and Informatics Engineering of Aveiro,
Campus Universitário de Santiago, 3810-193 Aveiro, Portugal

Abstract. Emergent and established paradigms, such as the Internet
of Things (IoT), cloud and fog/edge computing, together with increasingly cheaper computing technologies – with very low power requirements, available to exchange data with increased efficiency – and intelligent systems, have evolved to a level where it is virtually possible
to create and deploy monitoring solutions, even in Precision Agriculture (PA) practices. In this work, LoRa®(Long Range) technology and
LoRaWAN™protocol, are tested in a Precision Viticulture (PV) scenario, using low-power data acquisition devices deployed in a vineyard
in the UTAD University Campus, distanced 400 m away from the nearest
gateway. The main goal of this work is to evaluate sensor data integration in the mySense environment, a framework aimed to systematize
data acquisition procedures to address common PA/PV issues, using
LoRa®technology. mySense builds over a 4-layer technological structure:
sensor and sensor nodes, crop field and sensor networks, cloud services
and front-end applications. It makes available a set of free tools based on
the Do-It-Yourself (DIY) concept and enables the use of low-cost platforms to quickly prototype a complete PA/PV monitoring application.

Keywords: LoRa · LoRaWAN · Data integration ·
Internet-of-Things · Precision Viticulture

© Springer Nature Switzerland AG 2019
P. Moura Oliveira et al. (Eds.): EPIA 2019, LNAI 11804, pp. 224–235, 2019.
https://doi.org/10.1007/978-3-030-30241-2_20

1   Introduction

The replacement of wired-based complex systems by wireless sensor networks (WSN), supported on efficient power management techniques, constitutes one of the greatest innovations of the last decade in infield monitoring. As such, Precision Agriculture/Precision Viticulture (PA/PV) monitoring systems, based on low-cost microcontrollers, can be spread out over wide areas without restrictions, according with each crops' needs. With wireless and standardized communications (e.g IEEE 802.15.4, IEEE 802.11, IEEE 802.15.1, LoRa, 3G/4G/5G, SigFox), this type of systems have dominated the publications spectrum in this field [4,5,11], being presented as easy-to-use solutions and boosters of data acquisition with an adjustable granularity, compatible with the desired spatial and temporal variability. From solutions that directly transmit sensor data to remote locations to those using infield base stations, large volumes of data are acquired and are readily available for further analysis and to support decision making in PA/PV management practices. Following this evolution, the recent paradigm of IoT began to be interesting in the field of agriculture. The availability of physical devices in the field – above or underground [13] – taking measurements and exchanging data with a cloud server, has enabled the design of simpler, cheaper and more energy efficient IoT devices, towards a real ubiquitous access (anywhere and anytime) to data and services.

Wireless data communication technologies like Bluetooth, IEEE 802.15.4/ZigBee, IEEE 802.11x, GSM/GPRS, among others, are traditionally used in IoT solutions for agriculture practices. Each technology is chosen depending on several factors such as the area to be covered, the location of the main/base/gateway data sink station, the availability of technology infrastructures and the available budget, among others. Bluetooth typically has a reduced range, ZigBee has a better range but it is also fairly constrained and GSM/GPRS is not available everywhere, particularly in rural areas. And, at some extent, all mentioned technologies consumes a fair share of energy, and some can be expensive.

Precision agriculture applications require monitoring solutions that can cover wide areas, in remote locations, and use very low-power devices, all in scenarios where data aggregation points may or may not exist. In addition, applications such as intelligent irrigation do not need high bandwidth but rather a large number of low cost sensors that collect data with sampling periods in the order of magnitude of the minute or even more.

This is precisely the concept where LPWAN (Low Power Wide Area Network) technologies fit, which stand out for the inherent long range and low power characteristics (long battery life to enable *"fit and forget"* or disposable end devices) and being the *"go-to"* technology for IoT applications where remote locations, easy deployment, thousands of connections per gateway and long battery life are required. Some examples of technologies that follows LPWAN concept are LoRa, Sigfox, RPMA (Random Phase Multiple Access), LTE-M or LTE-MTC (Long-Term Evolution Machine Type Communication), NB-IoT (Narrow Band IoT), EC-GSM-IoT (Extended Coverage GMS IoT).

LoRa as the lower physical layer, and LoRaWAN (Long Range Wide Area Network), acting mainly as a network layer protocol for managing communication between LPWAN gateways and end-node devices as a routing protocol, aims to become a global solution. According to [2], LoRa technology is the one with the best range, power and cost trade-off. LoRa uses a proprietary spread spectrum modulation technique derived from chirp spread spectrum (CSS) technology. LoRaWAN protocol defines three classes. Class A is the one with the lowest power budget since the end device is the one who starts the communication. After establishing a connection, a short window opens and bi-directional communications are allowed. All LoRa devices must at least comply with this class. Class B devices sync periodically where these syncs create listening windows allowing real bi-directional communications. For low-latency class C devices must be used where communication between end devices and gateways are always opened, increasing power budget significantly. Even though it is not absolutely necessary, a full fledged LoRa system needs gateways in its vicinity and that adds to the cost of the system. For maximum range, IoT nodes need to be in line of sight of the gateway.

In this work, the use of LoRa/LoRaWAN technologies is investigated in order to be effectively used in DIY devices in PA/PV applications. Besides presenting a small, low-cost device, the integration tools are also presented so that the mySense open environment (https://mysense.utad.pt), developed under a more structurant work, can accommodate the integration of data from LoRa devices using free of charge backend services such as The Things Network (https://www.thethingsnetwork.org) and WaveSys (https://iot.wavesys.pt).

The paper is organized as follows: after this introductory section, where the importance of LRWAN is justified in the context of PA/PV, Sect. 2 makes a survey on the use of LoRa technology applied to agriculture systems. Section 3 presents a small, unmanned low-cost data acquisition system that is being implemented to suffice some PA/PV needs in terms of field data gathering and communication using LoRa technologies. In addition, LoRaWAN integration with mySense environment is presented as part of the objective of promoting DIY solutions in PA/PV practices. Section 4 presents some results and Sect. 5 finishes the paper with some conclusions drawn from practical infield evaluation.

2   LoRa in IoT Agricultural Practices

A survey performed over the most recent published works on the use of LoRa technology applied to agricultural monitoring, revealed that this technology is not yet being widely used. However, works presented in [6,10] use LoRa technology and explore the main goals of using this technology. They need to cover a relatively large area with battery-operated devices and they do not have access to a GSM/GPRS network. In [6] the main goal is to collect vital signs and location of cows being the device placed on their collar. Using a SX1278 LoRa chip and an ultra-low power STM32L151 microcontroller they report a packet loss rate of 20% for a distance of about 2 Km between nodes and LoRa gateway. In

[10] the main goal is to monitor a starfruit plantation using pH and soil moisture sensors. Also using a (SX1276/SX1278) chip they opted for an Arduino board. Trees and other obstacles led to a packet loss rate of 20% for about 400 m of coverage. They developed an application that can be used with computers, tablets and smartphones.

An experimental performance evaluation of the LoRa technology was performed in a tree farm in [14]. Three end devices were positioned at 100, 150 and 200 m away from the gateway. Antennas heights where also varied from 0 m to 3 m from ground level. Data from several sensors were captured and transmitted. The goal was to verify how the physical layer parameters (PHY) of LoRa affected the transmissions. They concluded that the Spreading Factor (SF) and Coding Rate (CR) clearly affected transmissions, especially for greater distances. Bandwidth (BW) had the lowest impact. Reliability was affected by antenna height varying from 22% at 0 m height to 100% at 3 m height.

The work presented in [9] aims to monitor a forest where end nodes are scattered, using a drone, carrying a LoRa gateway, to collect end nodes data. Due to trees and some forest buildings the range is fairly affected leading authors to try this new approach. From time to time the drone makes a pass by the location of the end devices acting as a server of a network and the end devices as clients. The gateway is responsible to start the communication with the end devices, sending a broadcast signal, and once communication is established data can be streamed from, and to, the end devices. Data is sent to a cloud or is stored in an onboard memory depending if internet connection is available, or not.

Climate monitoring of a greenhouse in the production of mushrooms was accomplished in [8]. Temperature, relative humidity and Carbon Dioxide were measured with a low-cost and low power LoRa end device that transmitted data periodically to a LoRa gateway distanced by 100 m. Data is stored in an database server being accessed by using an application running in a smartphone, tablet or PC. Data is analysed locally in the LoRa gateway system also responsible to activate or deactivate control devices aiming to increase mushroom production. Heavier and thicker mushrooms were produced when compared to the traditional production scheme.

The system presented in [1] was tested with success in a vineyard for more than a year. It is composed by three services: data collection; data analytics; and control. There are two types of nodes: the collectors, responsible to collect data from sensors; and the executors, responsible for controlling any type of equipment such as sprinklers. The Things Network (TTN) services are used to store data and send control commands. Security is handed over the TTN security layers for the network and the application.

In [12] the purpose is the control of a drip irrigation system. In order to reduce costs, LoRa gateways and network servers were not considered. Instead, they use a master node that communicates with the other nodes using only the LoRa radio system. Because the master node is the one who initiates all communications there is no need to handle simultaneous multichannel receptions.

The master node creates an access point that can be accessed by any system (computer, tablet, smartphone, etc.) WiFi capable. Data can be requested from nodes or commands can be sent to them. To reduce the energy budget they limit commands, sent to each node, to 4 a day and designed the nodes with low power electronics. With four D-size batteries, each node may work for at least two years.

In [3] a data storage architecture dedicated to scientific research is presented where, in part, LoRa technology is used. The test bed is a system for bee health monitoring. Meteorologic data such as air temperature, relative humidity, barometric pressure and light, and bee hive data such as temperature, humidity, acceleration and air contaminants are sent to a cloud server using LoRa technology by means of a LoPy (PyCom, UK) microcontroller board and the TTN platform. The choice between SigFox and LoRa fell on the LoRa because the protocol limitation of 140 messages per day of Sigfox was not enough for system requirements. As future remarks, authors revealed the intention to implement the system based on the NB-IoT protocol discarding LoRa technology due to the need of deployment of technological network hardware, not needed with NB-IoT which depends on a cellular network.

3   Materials and Methods

In this section, an IoT device with LoRa/LoRaWAN data communication capability will be presented as well as the software tools developed for data integration in the mySense platform [7], an environment oriented to PA/PV applications. The goal is then for the mySense platform to accommodate LoRa devices that communicate with LoRaWAN gateways, which in turn enter the data collected using the REST API of the mySense platform. The objective is not to describe the mySense platform in its entirety but only what it is necessary for understanding how data from a LoRa device can be integrated.

In the case under study, a set of 2 devices send data periodically to the mySense environment each using different LoRaWAN gateways, where we investigated ways to integrate each one. As a result of this integration, the necessary steps have been described so that each user can use different LoRaWAN networks to get the data of their devices to the mySense environment.

3.1   The mySense Environment

mySense environment was conceived to act as a data warehouse where sensor data are stored and used in the most appropriate way depending on the particular application (e.g. smart irrigation, data analysis, alerts). It is built over a 4-layer technological structure, (Fig. 1): sensor and sensor nodes; crop field and sensor networks; cloud services; and front-end applications. It facilitates the use of low cost platforms such as Arduino and Raspberry Pi, making available a set of free tools and tutorials based on the DIY concept.

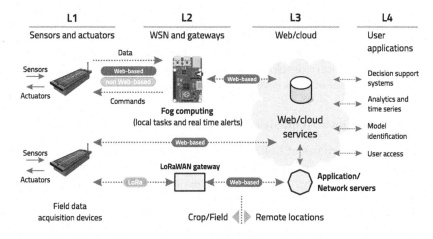

Fig. 1. 4-level management arrangements identified in the PA/PV data integration chain.

The main goals of mySense platform, whose environment is depicted in Fig. 2, are: to give support to the data collection stations (level 1) using common standardized data transfer technologies (IEEE 802.15.4/ZigBee, IEEE 802.11, GSM/GPRS, LoRa, etc); to give support for the installation of gateways (level 2), being possible to run local tasks following the fog or edge computing paradigms, and give support for storing data in the cloud (level 3); to promote high-level applications (level 4).

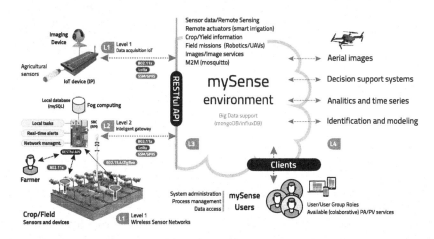

Fig. 2. Overview of the mySense environment.

In order to use the mySense platform an account must be created. Afterwards, user can deploy devices with data channels associated. API keys are automatically created for each device and channels, which are needed to send data to, or retrieve data from the object. From this point on, data can arrive from whatever device an user can imagine provided that it complies with the data formats allowed by the platform. The physical device, being it an Arduino, a Raspberry Pi and alike, proprietary development board, is not important, making mySense suitable for any kind of data gathering application.

3.2   The IoT Data Acquisition Device

One of the main purposes of LoRa technology is to allow that a device with low data rate needs can operate on batteries and have a relatively wide communication range. As a strategy to develop low-cost devices for PA/PV applications, an IoT node, the SPWAS'18 (Solar Powered Wireless Acquisition Station), presented in Fig. 3, was implemented so that it is possible to choose one from five possible communication technologies: Bluetooth, ZigBee, GSM/GPRS, LoRa or WiFi. SPWAS'18 is mainly powered by a 2000 mAh LiPo battery being recharged by a solar panel. The actual hardware, prepared for LoRa communication, can also be depicted in Fig. 3.

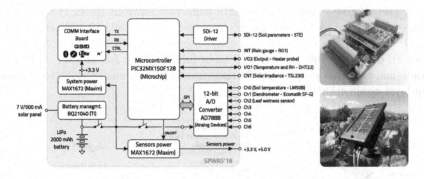

Fig. 3. Functional diagram of the SPWAS'18 device, an IoT node prepared for wireless communications such as Bluetooth, ZigBee, GSM/GPRS, LoRa or WiFi.

The SPWAS'18 device has the capability to connect up to 8 analog sensors and allows the connection of sensors with frequency output (such as solar radiation, TSL230, TAOS, USA), pluviometers and low-cost temperature and relative humidity combined sensor (such as DHT22, Aosong Electronics). An adapted RS485 driver enables the use of SDI-12 sensors. The processing unit is a low-cost 32-bit microcontroller (PIC32MX150F128, Microchip, USA) and the transceiver device is, in LoRa configuration, a RN2483 (Microchip, USA) transceiver module. It is a fully certified (LoRaWAN 1.0 specification) 433/868 MHz (Europe) module featuring LoRaWAN Class A protocol stack, enabling seamless connectivity to any LoRaWAN compliant network. It is ideal for low power, battery operated, applications.

3.3 Brokers and Gateways LoRaWAN

In typical IoT networks, a gateway is used to bridge devices to the Internet for a specific protocol. If the device supports the IP stack, the gateway, if used, needs only to relay data. In the case of the LoRaWAN protocol, routing and processing is needed before data coming from a device can be delivered to an application (end service). That is the function of a LoRaWAN network server or backend system such as the one provided by the TTN. These backend systems are positioned between the LoRa gateways and the application server taking care of the routing and processing of data.

A backend system is composed by several components that can be as simple as one component per function or several components per function allowing relations as one-to-many and many-to-many between components. Considering the simplest backend, it is composed by a Router, a Broker, a Network Server, an Handler and a Discovery Server. The LoRa gateways are connected to a Router that is responsible for managing gateways functionality. The Router is connected to one or more Brokers that are the central component of the backend system. Brokers are responsible to map a device to an application and to control uplink (device to application) or downlink (application to device) communications. The Network Server is specific for the LoRaWAN functionality. The Handler is the component that handles data of one or more applications.

A user sets up his own network, composed by one to several LoRa ready nodes, connecting them to a LoRa gateway. The gateway must be also LoRa capable and configured to work with a LoRaWAN backend system so that data can be routed to the application(s). An account must be created, by the user, in the backend system and device(s) must be configured and associated to applications. Once all this is done, data can flow from devices to applications and vice-versa.

3.4 Integration with mySense Platform

The UTAD university campus has around 140 ha of area, comprising a botanic garden, vineyards, educational buildings and other services. Two LoRaWAN gateways are installed for research purposes, one registered to the TTN backend system and the other to the Wavesys. The two will be tested under this work. Each one allows HTTP integration which means that posting data to other platforms using REST methods is possible. The API key and ObjectUID, obtained when a mySense account is created, are needed for the HTTP integration. Figure 4 shows an example of how to configure an HTTP integration to connect to a device registered in the mySense cloud.

The user must configure his nodes to send data in one of two formats. One of the formats is JSON (consult mySense platform for specific information), with two versions allowed, Fig. 5(a) and (b). A version 1, where only sensors data is sent. In this case, mySense takes the server time as the timestamp of the measurements (in order to reduce payload size). A version 2, where the timestamp of the measurements is also sent. Due to the LoRa protocol limit of

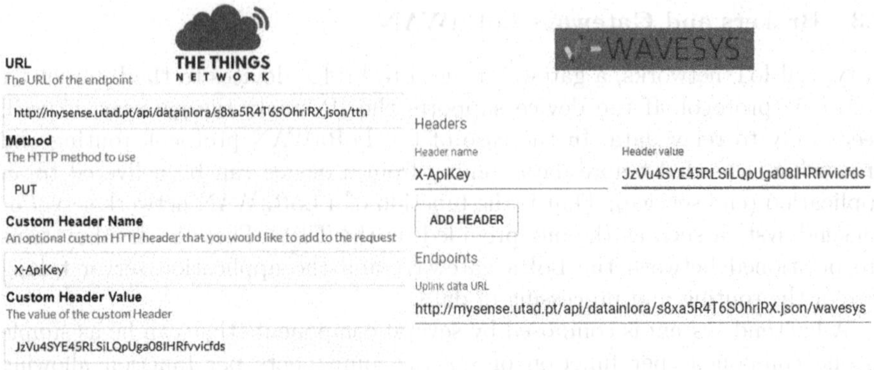

Fig. 4. HTTP integration using mySense access keys in the TTN and Wavesys servers.

242 bytes of data, the JSON formats allow a low number of sensor values (version 1) or only one value (version 2) to be sent. If the device has several sensors, then the format depicted in Fig. 5(c), may be considered. The exact number of values that can be sent depends on the format of the values, if double precision, if integer, etc. The simplified data format has a particularity in the part of the values. Suppose, for example, that a mySense object has three sensors. It is not required that all three values are sent for a particular timestamp. In this case two semicolons, one after the other, will indicate, for that position, that sensor has no value. For example, supposing that sensor 2 does not have a value, then data payload will be something like 2019021512300012.34;;65.21#.

```
{"formatver":"1.0",
 "dataarray":[
   {"ch":1, "value":14.41},
   {"ch":2, "value":60.25}
]}
```
a)

```
{"formatver": "2.0",
 "dataarray":[
   {"ts": "2019-04-09 16:44:00",
    "tsarray":[
      {"ch":1, "value":12.9}
    ]}
]}
```
b)

```
2019040916351514.41;60.25#

YYYYMMDDhhmmssv1;v2;v3;...;vi#
```

YYYY	= year	hh	= hours
MM	= month	mm	= minutes
DD	= day	ss	= seconds
vi	= value of sensor i	#	= frame end

c)

Fig. 5. The three data formats currently allowed by the mySense platform when using the LoRa parser: (a) JSON without timestamp; (b) JSON with timestamp; (c) Compact.

4   Results and Discussion

The board depicted in Fig. 3 was used to evaluate mySense data integration procedures using Wavesys and TTN backends. Data from temperature and relative humidity sensors was used. As previously mentioned, the data payload format 2, illustrated in Fig. 5(b) is the most complete because it allows defining sequences of data values for each timestamp. On the other hand, the format shown in Fig. 5(a) allows to send more samples without the need to send the timestamp, which allows some savings of the reduced space offered in a LoRa frame payload.

For applications that need to use this space more efficiently, the format shown in Fig. 5(c) may be the best option, but it is not, however, encoded in JSON. Figure 6 shows data retrieved from one SPWAS'18 IoT device data (mySense Data Port page).

⊞ **Data from** 2019-04-27 11:46:23 **to** 2019-04-30 11:46:23 [other time window]

Showing 25 ▾ records   Search:

Channels	1	2
Date and time ▾	Temperature	Humidity
2019-04-30 10:15:00	12.98	66.15
2019-04-30 10:00:00	13.92	67.41
2019-04-30 09:45:00	13.28	77.8
2019-04-30 09:30:00	13.12	60.11
2019-04-30 09:15:00	13.47	76.61
2019-04-30 09:00:00	12.83	60.33

Fig. 6. Example of a mySense data table regarding the SPWAS'18 IoT data.

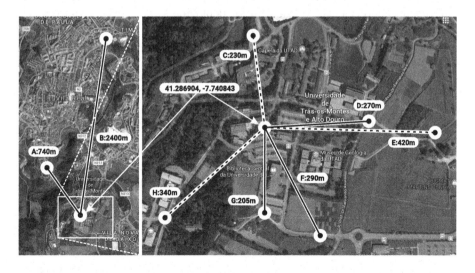

Fig. 7. Summary of range evaluation using a LoRa device.

During field evaluation, and between a particular SPWAS'18 device and a LoRaWAN gateway, it was verified that data communication success depends primarily on the alignment of device antennas. Regarding Fig. 7, no data loss was observed when devices were in line of sight (devices transmitting every minute during 20 min in each position). However, when some obstacles exist, transmission distance is greatly reduced. For instance, data-paths C, E and H were perturbed by trees and buildings and so even with a distance of 230 m, data loss was 100%. The fact that the two antennas were not in line of sight severely affected the communications range, leading to an obvious degradation, similar to that reported in the literature.

5   Conclusions and Future Remarks

The concept of LPWAN, where LoRa is included, came to address some issues related to the range of data communications, energy budget and device cost trade-off. LoRa solutions to be used in PA/PV monitoring practices are still few but tends to rise. The mySense environment, as a data integrator system for monitoring applications in PA/PV scenarios, now has, as a result of this work, the ability to offer LoRa solutions for this type of applications. The IoT device, with a total cost of less than 70 Euro, allows the development of DIY applications in these scenarios and can use free backends where any user can integrate with his mySense account.

There are still some implementation issues, but they are related to the size of the antennas and the range, the latter degrading significantly in the presence of obstacles. As expected, for applications with higher data rates or higher transmission rates, a LoRa system may not be enough to implement such a solution, but it is a very effective solution for deploying systems that require many low-cost devices with a low sensors count.

As future work, and in a line of research of free LoRa DIY solutions to offer within the scope of mySense open solutions, there is the intention to carry out more range and robustness tests of the process of transmitting data to the LoRaWAN gateways accessible in the vicinity.

Acknowledgements. The authors would like to acknowledge ERDF and North 2020 – North Regional Operational Program, as part of project "INNOVINE&WINE – Vineyard and Wine Innovation Platform" (NORTE-01-0145-FEDER-000038) for this research funding. This work was developed under the Doctoral fellowship with the reference SFRH/BD/137968/2018, from FCT (Portuguese Foundation for Science and Technology).

References

1. Davcev, D., Mitreski, K., Trajkovic, S., Nikolovski, V., Koteli, N.: IoT agriculture system based on LoRaWAN. In: 2018 14th IEEE International Workshop on Factory Communication Systems (WFCS), pp. 1–4, June 2018. https://doi.org/10.1109/WFCS.2018.8402368

2. de Carvalho Silva, J., Rodrigues, J.J.P.C., Alberti, A.M., Solic, P., Aquino, A.L.L.: LoRaWAN - a low power WAN protocol for Internet of Things: a review and opportunities. In: 2017 2nd International Multidisciplinary Conference on Computer and Energy Science (SpliTech), pp. 1–6, July 2017

3. Debauche, O., Moulat, M.E., Mahmoudi, S., Boukraa, S., Manneback, P., Lebeau, F.: Web monitoring of bee health for researchers and beekeepers based on the Internet of Things. Procedia Comput. Sci. **130**, 991–998 (2018). https://doi.org/10.1016/j.procs.2018.04.103

4. Hamouda, Y.E.M., Elhabil, B.H.Y.: Precision agriculture for greenhouses using a wireless sensor network. In: 2017 Palestinian International Conference on Information and Communication Technology (PICICT), pp. 78–83, May 2017. https://doi.org/10.1109/PICICT.2017.20

5. John, G.E.: A low cost wireless sensor network for precision agriculture. In: 2016 Sixth International Symposium on Embedded Computing and System Design (ISED), pp. 24–27, December 2016. https://doi.org/10.1109/ISED.2016.7977048

6. Li, Q., Liu, Z., Xiao, J.: A data collection collar for vital signs of cows on the grassland based on LoRa. In: 2018 IEEE 15th International Conference on e-Business Engineering (ICEBE), pp. 213–217, October 2018. https://doi.org/10.1109/ICEBE.2018.00041

7. Morais, R., et al.: mySense: a comprehensive data management environment to improve precision agriculture practices. Comput. Electron. Agric. **162**, 882–894 (2019). https://doi.org/10.1016/j.compag.2019.05.028

8. Nik Ibrahim, N.H., Ibrahim, A.R., Mat, I., Harun, A.N., Witjaksono, G.: LoRaWAN in climate monitoring in advance precision agriculture system. In: 2018 International Conference on Intelligent and Advanced System (ICIAS), pp. 1–6, August 2018. https://doi.org/10.1109/ICIAS.2018.854059

9. Park, S., Yun, S., Kim, H., Kwon, R., Ganser, J., Anthony, S.: Forestry monitoring system using LoRa and Drone. In: Proceedings of the 8th International Conference on Web Intelligence, Mining and Semantics, WIMS 2018, pp. 48:1–48:8. ACM, New York (2018). https://doi.org/10.1145/3227609.3227677. http://doi.acm.org/10.1145/3227609.3227677

10. Rachmani, A.F., Zulkifli, F.Y.: Design of IoT monitoring system based on LoRa technology for Starfruit plantation. In: TENCON 2018–2018 IEEE Region 10 Conference, pp. 1241–1245, October 2018. https://doi.org/10.1109/TENCON.2018.8650052

11. Sahitya, G., Balaji, N., Naidu, C.D., Abinaya, S.: Designing a wireless sensor network for precision agriculture using Zigbee. In: 2017 IEEE 7th International Advance Computing Conference (IACC), pp. 287–291, January 2017. https://doi.org/10.1109/IACC.2017.0069

12. Usmonov, M., Gregoretti, F.: Design and implementation of a LoRa based wireless control for drip irrigation systems. In: 2017 2nd International Conference on Robotics and Automation Engineering (ICRAE), pp. 248–253, December 2017. https://doi.org/10.1109/ICRAE.2017.8291389

13. Vuran, M.C., Salam, A., Wong, R., Irmak, S.: Internet of underground things in precision agriculture: architecture and technology aspects. Ad Hoc Netw. **81**, 160–173 (2018). https://doi.org/10.1016/j.adhoc.2018.07.017

14. Yim, D., et al.: An experimental LoRa performance evaluation in tree farm. In: 2018 IEEE Sensors Applications Symposium (SAS) (2018)

A Low-Cost System to Estimate Leaf Area Index Combining Stereo Images and Normalized Difference Vegetation Index

Jorge Miguel Mendes[1,2]([✉]) [iD], Vítor Manuel Filipe[1,2] [iD],
Filipe Neves dos Santos[1] [iD], and Raul Morais dos Santos[1,2] [iD]

[1] INESC TEC – Institute for Systems and Computer Engineering,
Technology and Science, Pólo da UTAD, Vila Real, Portugal
{jorge.m.mendes,fbsantos}@inesctec.pt
[2] Engineering Department, Quinta de Prados, UTAD – University of Trás-os-Montes
e Alto Douro, Vila Real, Portugal
{vfilipe,rmorais}@utad.pt

Abstract. In order to determine the physiological state of a plant it is necessary to monitor it throughout the developmental period. One of the main parameters to monitor is the Leaf Area Index (LAI). The objective of this work was the development of a non-destructive methodology for the LAI estimation in wine growing. This method is based on stereo images that allow to obtain a bard 3D representation, in order to facilitate the segmentation process, since to perform this process only based on color component becomes practically impossible due to the high complexity of the application environment. In addition, the Normalized Difference Vegetation Index will be used to distinguish the regions of the trunks and leaves. As an low-cost and non-evasive method, it becomes a promising solution for LAI estimation in order to monitor the productivity changes and the impacts of climatic conditions in the vines growth.

Keywords: Leaf Area Index ·
Normalized Difference Vegetation Index · Stereo images ·
Image segmentation · Vineyard monitoring · Remote sensing

1 Introduction

The estimation of a grapevine vigor can be considered a method to determine the grapes productivity and quality. There are many indices related to the characteristics of the vine foliage/canopy, however, the Leaf Area Index (LAI), an important vegetation biophysical parameter, is probably the most used in viticulture and aims to characterize the vigor and state of the vines development. The LAI is a dimensionless grandeur that is defined as the relationship between

© Springer Nature Switzerland AG 2019
P. Moura Oliveira et al. (Eds.): EPIA 2019, LNAI 11804, pp. 236–247, 2019.
https://doi.org/10.1007/978-3-030-30241-2_21

the leaf surface unilateral area and the soil unit surface area [1]. The leaf area distribution and its density, that is, the canopy shape, allows to gauge the solar radiation interception and distribution around the plant and, therefore, allows to determine its light, temperature and humidity microenvironments [20]. Leaf area produced by vines is associated with agronomic, biological, environmental and physiological processes and is a determining factor for their productivity, since the leaves are the main place where both photosynthesis and evapotranspiration processes are carried out [7].

LAI estimation is of great importance, particularly in the field of precision viticulture, since a high LAI is an indicator of high vigor, while a smaller LAI means loss of productive capacity. According to [8], leaves surface area influences the quantity and quality of the must produced by the grapes and there must be a balance between the leaf area and the productivity, in order to reach the desirable grapes ripeness and, thus, the quality of the wine. The LAI can also be used to adjust the dosage amount of plant protection products to avoid under dosing which would provide insufficient protection against pests or over dosage which has adverse environmental effects and increases costs. In [19] the importance of adapting the dosage following a LAI-based approach is highlighted.

LAI monitoring can make possible to understand, in the long-term, what are the productivity dynamic changes and the impacts of climatic conditions on the wine-growing ecosystem [23]. In addition, LAI can serve as an indicator of stress in vines and can be used to determine the relationship between environmental stress factors and the caused damages. LAI field measurement techniques can be complemented by emerging remote sensing techniques that have been shown to be an indispensable and necessary component for modeling and simulation of ecological variables and processes [9].

The methods used to estimate LAI can be divided into destructive or non-destructive methods and direct or indirect methods [11]. The destructive methods are those that involve the removal and analysis of parts of the plants, and non-destructive methods are those that do not involve the removal of parts of plants, thus preserving its integrity and allowing new LAI determinations to be carried out on the same plant. Direct methods consist of measurements made directly on plants, while indirect methods usually consist in the measurement of the total radiation that can penetrate through the canopy, in the use of empirical models or in the use of canopy images.

In this work we will present a low-cost system for the non-destructive LAI estimation based on stereo images and NDVI. This system will allow to monitor the canopy growth in order to predict the productivity changes and the impacts of climatic conditions in this growth.

This paper is organized as follows: after this introductory section, Sect. 2 provides a brief state of the art review with some indirect methods used to determine LAI. Section 3 presents the materials and methods of the developed system, where a description of the system architecture, the image acquisition mechanism, and the processing algorithms is made. Section 4 presents the results obtained, and finally, Sect. 5 concludes the paper with remarks for future work.

2 Related Work

Several methods have been developed for measuring LAI during the last few years [22]. Direct methods to determine LAI usually require measurement of the leaf area of leaves attached to the shoots, thus making them time-consuming and tedious. Thus, indirect methods have been the object of numerous studies [4,13, 15], since they allow to realize the LAI estimation in a fast, relatively precise and non-destructive way. In this section, some works developed in the wine-growing context that allow to determine the LAI using indirect methods are presented.

The LAI estimation on several grapevine crops, based on hyperspectral data, 2D RGB image mosaics and crop surface 3D models obtained from an unmanned aerial vehicle (UAV) was performed in [7]. The authors have presented promising experimental results that indicate that hyperspectral sensors, along with low-cost RGB cameras, can provide rich spectral information to accurately estimate the LAI of crops.

The viability of the use of LiDAR sensors in the LAI determination was evaluated in [1]. The LiDAR system was mounted on a tractor responsible for measuring the crop in a direction transverse to the bard, along the lines of the vines. Some geometric and structural parameters of the vines were calculated, namely height, cross-sectional area, canopy volume and plant area index. The relationship between the LAI and the canopy volume was evaluated through a linear regression that showed a good correlation between both. In [12] a LiDAR system was also used to map the LAI along a vineyard. Three LiDAR sensors were used and a study of the influence of the scanning method used (continuous or discontinuous systematic sampling) on the reliability of the resulting LAI maps was made. The proposed system allows to calculate the canopy surrounding vegetative area, which consists of the sum of the bard wall area in both sides of the line (excluding the gaps) and the upper part area. Nevertheless, a good relationship between crop volume values, measured using ultrasonic sensors, and LAI was obtained. In addition to the two papers presented above, there are several other LAI estimation systems based on LiDAR technology, from which stand out the systems proposed by [18,24] and [10].

An indirect method of estimating LAI based on a mobile application called PocketLAI was proposed in [2]. Captured images are automatically processed using a segmentation algorithm responsible for determining the opening fraction of the canopy, that is, the part of the canopy that allows the light passing. In [14] the performance of the PocketLAI mobile application and methods that use hemispheric photographs were evaluated in comparison to destructive methods for the LAI determination in vines. The authors recorded data from six trials in an experimental vineyard characterized by a high level of heterogeneity among the plants. It was also evaluated the possibility of combining remote sensing data and PocketLAI in situ estimations. [3] presented another mobile application called VitiCanopy, which allows to collect images of the vineyard in order to characterize several parameters of the canopy, among them the LAI. The application also allows to associate the value of the LAI to a location in the vineyard using the smartphone GPS (Global Positioning System) and GIS (Geographic Information System) techniques, allowing a fast and reliable evaluation of growth spatial and temporal dynamics of the canopy architecture. In addition to PocketLAI and VitiCanopy there are several applications that allows to calculate LAI, from which stand out Canopeo [16] and Easy Leaf Area [5].

The LAI mapping along two commercial vineyards using high resolution multispectral images collected by the IKONOS satellite in conjunction with soil measurements was performed in [6]. The satellite images were collected near the time of harvest, converted into radiance, georeferenced and transformed into NDVI. The conversion of NDVI maps to LAI was performed based on soil measurements at 24 calibration sites. According to studies found in the literature, the process of LAI estimation in vineyard using NDVI is usually accomplished through the use of aerial images obtained through drones or even satellites. These systems have the advantage of providing an estimate of the most embracing vineyard LAI, yet have associated higher costs. Our idea is to develop a low-cost system that any winemaker can put in his vineyard, and that allows to make a in loco LAI estimation.

3   Materials and Methods

In this section, we describe in detail the non-destructive LAI estimation system in vines proposed in this paper. The fundamental components of the developed system are defined, from the cameras used to acquire the images (input of the system), to the tools used to process them and to provide an output whose value represents the LAI of the studied vine.

3.1   System Architecture

The developed system architecture is divided into three main parts, Fig. 1: (i) power system; (ii) processing system; and (iii) stereo vision system. The power system consists of a 12 V lead battery, charged through a solar panel, and a 5 V DC-DC step-down voltage regulator. The processing system consists of two Single Board Computers (SBCs) Raspberry Pi (RPi), connected through an Ethernet connection. One works as a client and the other as a server. Its operation is explained in more detail in Sect. 3.3. The stereo vision system consists of two RPi NoIR camera boards, each one connected to a RPi. These cameras have no InfraRed (IR) filter, hence the name NoIR, and include a blue filter which, when used, allows to obtain conclusions about the health of the plants, by calculating several vegetation indices, namely the NDVI.

3.2   NDVI Calculation Using NoIR Camera

The NDVI value was calculated using an NGB (Near-infrared, Green, Blue) image obtained from one of the NoIR cameras with blue filter. An example of this image is shown in Fig. 2a. The NDVI value varies between −1 and +1 and,

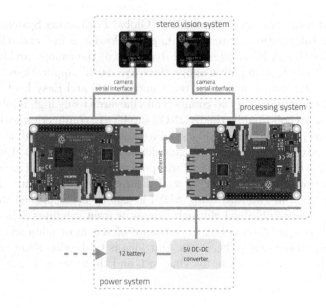

Fig. 1. System architecture proposed and developed in this work.

in this case, is given by the difference between the reflectances at the wavelength of the NIR (Near-InfraRed) and of the visible blue, divided by the sum of the reflectances at these two wavelengths, Eq. 1. The original NDVI formula uses red wavelength instead of blue, but we use blue because using the NoIR camera, red is replaced by NIR. According to [21], a NDVI value between −1 and 0 represents an inanimate or dead object, such as rocks dead plants, 0 to 0.33 represents an unhealthy plant or under stress, 0.33 to 0.66 represents a moderately healthy plant and 0.66 to 1 represents a very healthy plant.

$$NDVI = \frac{NIR - Blue}{NIR + Blue} \qquad (1)$$

After calculating the NDVI of the image shown in Fig. 2a, the image shown in Fig. 2b was obtained. In this particular case, as there is a lot of vegetation in the soil, it is the place where the NDVI value is highest. The trunks have an NDVI value close to 0, and the sky and masts have a negative value, according to the scale of Fig. 2c.

3.3   Image Acquisition

The server RPi is responsible for capturing an image (using the camera connected to it) and requesting another image from the client. The client, in turn, captures the image and returns it in response to the server for further processing. This image acquisition system was developed using sockets and the client-server model. It was possible to obtain a good synchronism between images, with an average lag of approximately 25 ms (as it is possible to observe in Fig. 3) which

(a) Image obtained using NoIR camera with blue filter.

(b) Resulting NDVI image.

(c) NDVI levels.

Fig. 2. Obtaining the NDVI image from the captured image using the NoIR camera with blue filter. (Color figure online)

is a perfectly acceptable value for this application. The images acquisition is performed according to the flowchart shown in Fig. 4.

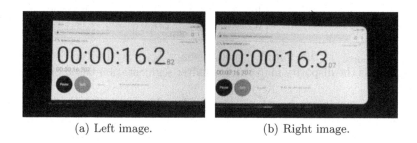

(a) Left image.

(b) Right image.

Fig. 3. Synchronism between stereo images.

3.4 Image Processing

The implemented image processing algorithm allows to obtain a LAI estimation through images acquired using the stereo vision system. The disparity between the acquired images is initially calculated. The position of a given object in one of the images is shifted in the other image by a number of pixels inversely proportional to the distance between the object and the camera [17]. This displacement is called disparity and when it is calculated, for each pixel of the image, allows to create a disparity map. This map was obtained using functions available in the OpenCV (Open Computer Vision) library, one of the most used in computer vision systems.

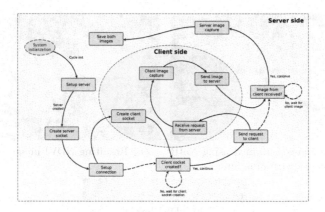

Fig. 4. Image acquisition system flowchart.

Next, a segmentation based on the NDVI value and on the depth obtained through the disparity map was performed. In segmentation based on NDVI, Eq. 2, are kept only the pixels where their value is higher than a certain minimum value ($ndvi_{min}$).

$$I_{disp\_seg\_ndvi}(i,j) = \begin{cases} I_{disp\_initial}(i,j), & \text{if } I_{ndvi}(i,j) \geq ndvi_{min} \\ 0 & \text{otherwise} \end{cases} \qquad (2)$$

where $I_{disp\_initial}$ is the initial disparity map, I_{ndvi} is the NDVI image and $I_{disp\_seg\_ndvi}$ is the disparity map obtained after segmentation based on the NDVI value.

In the segmentation based on depth value, Eq. 3, the regions that are at distance of the bard are selected, that is, between a minimum distance ($dist_{min}$) and a maximum distance ($dist_{max}$), discarding in this way all the regions that are in front of or behind it.

$$I_{disp\_final}(i,j) = \begin{cases} I_{disp\_seg\_ndvi}(i,j), & \text{if } dist_{min} \leq I_{disp\_seg\_ndvi}(i,j) \leq dist_{max} \\ 0 & \text{otherwise} \end{cases} \qquad (3)$$

where $I_{disp\_seg\_ndvi}$ is the disparity map obtained after segmentation based on the NDVI value, I_{disp_final} is the final disparity map obtained after segmentation based on depth value.

After the two previous segmentations have been made, the final disparity map, I_{disp_final}, is used to create a Point Cloud (PC) of the region of vine leaves.

The PC processing starts with the outliers removal in order to eliminate noise that may exist outside the zone of interest. This removal was performed using a *StatisticalOutlierRemoval* filter, which makes use of statistical analysis techniques to remove points that are isolated from the remaining ones.

After the outliers removal, a segmentation based on the PC points height, Eq. 4, is performed. In this segmentation all points that are below a certain minimum height (height$_{min}$) are removed. In this case, the points which are below the vine leaves region are removed, thus eliminating all points corresponding to the soil and trunk regions.

$$PC_{final}(x, y, z) = \begin{cases} PC_{initial}(x, y, z), & \text{if } z \geq \text{height}_{min} \\ 0 & \text{otherwise} \end{cases} \tag{4}$$

where PC$_{initial}$ is the initial PC and PC$_{final}$ is the final PC obtained after segmentation based on the PC points height.

Finally, using the `CloudCompare v2` software, the volume of the resulting region (canopy region), from which the LAI estimation is obtained, was calculated. The complete image processing flowchart is shown in Fig. 5.

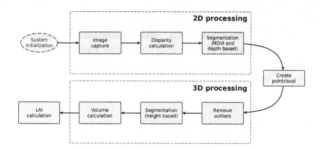

Fig. 5. Image processing flowchart.

3.5 LAI Estimation

Once the canopy volume was obtained, the LAI estimation was performed using a linear regression model proposed by [7]. This model was obtained by relating the measured LAI (ground truth) and the canopy volume of the vines, estimated from the crop 3D surface model. This linear regression is defined by Eq. 5 and according to the authors, the estimated volume of the canopy and the real LAI measurements have a coefficient of determination of 81.2%, a very acceptable value.

$$LAI = 0.09 \times \text{canopy}_{volume} + 0.1655 \tag{5}$$

4   Tests and Results

The tests of the developed system were carried out in a laboratory and then it was intended to verify its operation in a real environment in a vineyard located on the University of Tráis-os-Montes and Alto Douro campus, Vila Real, Portugal (41°17′13.1″N 7°44′08.5″W). It was not possible to preform tests using the images collected in the vineyard, since this work was developed during the period when the vines do not have leaves. In this way, the results presented in this section were obtained using images of trees located outside the laboratory where the tests were carried out and, as future work, we intend to repeat the tests using images collected in the vineyard.

The LAI determination process begins with the collection of stereo images, Fig. 6.

(a) Left image.   (b) Right image.

Fig. 6. Stereo image collected using two NoIR cameras.

Next, a disparity map is calculated, Fig. 7, where the lighter pixels correspond to regions closer to the camera and the darker pixels correspond to more distant regions. After the segmentation based on NDVI and depth, the PC was generated, having been obtained the result shown in Fig. 8.

Fig. 7. Disparity map obtained using stereo images.

Fig. 8. PC obtained using the disparity map.

The first step of PC processing consisted of outliers removal, and the result shown in Fig. 9 was obtained, where it can be verified that the points that were more dispersed were eliminated. The next step consisted of a segmentation based on PC points height, where it was supposed to remove part of the vines trunks, however, as in this case no images of the vines were used, the back tree has been manually removed in order to calculate the volume of a single tree. The result of this segmentation is shown in Fig. 10.

Then, the height of each PC point was determined and the volume of the tree was calculated, Fig. 11. In this case, the value of 4.46 m^3 was obtained.

Fig. 9. Obtained after outliers removal.

Fig. 10. PC of a single tree.

Finally, using the linear regression proposed by [7] (Eq. 5), an LAI of 0,57 was obtained.

(a) Front view.   (b) Top view.

Fig. 11. Height map of the PC.

5   Conclusion and Future Remarks

The grapevine vigor estimation can be considered a method to determine the produced grapes productivity and quality. There are many indices that allow to characterize the vigor and the state of development of the vines, but LAI and NDVI are the most used. The main objective of this work was the development of a system for the non-evasive LAI estimation in wine growing. The system is based on stereo images that allow to obtain a 3D representation of the bard, in order to facilitate the leaves region segmentation process, since to carry out this process only based on color information becomes practically impossible due to the high complexity of the application environment. The NDVI was used to distinguish the trunks from the leaves.

Most of the LAI determination indirect methods found in the literature are based on LiDAR technology, however this technology still has a much higher cost than normal image sensors, and thus, the proposed solution presents itself as a promising low-cost solution for the LAI estimation in order to monitor the productivity changes and the impacts of climatic conditions in the vines growth.

As future work, we intend to repeat the tests in real environment, once the vines development conditions allow it. It is also intended to make some changes in the system architecture, namely replacing the two NoIR cameras and the two RPis by two low-cost webcams (Logitech C270) and a single RPi. For such, it will be necessary to remove the webcams IR filter in order to allow to calculate NDVI. Further long-term perspectives are to perform a comparison of the proposed method versus other non-invasive methods published in the literature.

Acknowledgements. This work was funded by FCT (Portuguese Foundation for Science and Technology), within the framework of the project "WaterJPI/0012/2016". The authors would like to thank the EU and FCT for funding in the frame of the collaborative international consortium Water4Ever financed under the ERA-NET Water Works 2015 cofounded call. This ERA-NET is an integral part of the 2016 Joint Activities developed by the Water Challenge for a changing world joint programme initiation (Water JPI). This work was developed under the Doctoral fellowship with the reference "SFRH/BD/129813/2017", from FCT.

References

1. Arnó, J., et al.: Leaf area index estimation in vineyards using a ground-based lidar scanner. Precision Agric. **14**(3), 290–306 (2013)
2. Confalonieri, R., Francone, C., Foi, M.: The PocketLAI smartphone app: an alternative method for leaf area index estimation. In: Proceedings of the 7th International Congress on Environmental Modelling and Software, San Diego, CA, USA (2014)
3. De Bei, R., et al.: VitiCanopy: a free computer app to estimate canopy vigor and porosity for grapevine. Sensors **16**(4), 585 (2016)
4. Dobrowski, S., Ustin, S., Wolpert, J.: Remote estimation of vine canopy density in vertically shoot-positioned vineyards: determining optimal vegetation indices. Aust. J. Grape Wine Res. **8**(2), 117–125 (2002)
5. Easlon, H.M., Bloom, A.J.: Easy leaf area: automated digital image analysis for rapid and accurate measurement of leaf area. Appl. Plant Sci. **2**(7), 1400033 (2014)
6. Rituerto, A., Puig, L., Guerrero, J.J.: Comparison of omnidirectional and conventional monocular systems for visual SLAM. In: The 10th Workshop on Omnidirectional Vision, Camera Networks and Non-classical Cameras, OMNIVIS 2010. Zaragoza, Spain (2010)
7. Kalisperakis, I., Stentoumis, C., Grammatikopoulos, L., Karantzalos, K.: Leaf area index estimation in vineyards from uav hyperspectral data, 2D image mosaics and 3D canopy surface models. Int. Arch. Photogram. Remote Sensing Spatial Inf. Sci. **40**(1), 299 (2015)
8. Kliewer, W.M., Dokoozlian, N.K.: Leaf area/crop weight ratios of grapevines: influence on fruit composition and wine quality. Am. J. Enol. Viticulture **56**(2), 170–181 (2005)

9. Liu, J., Chen, J., Cihlar, J., Park, W.: A process-based boreal ecosystem productivity simulator using remote sensing inputs. Remote Sens. Environ. **62**(2), 158–175 (1997)
10. Llorens, J., Gil, E., Llop, J., et al.: Ultrasonic and lidar sensors for electronic canopy characterization in vineyards: advances to improve pesticide application methods. Sensors **11**(2), 2177–2194 (2011)
11. de Miguel, P.S., et al.: Estimation of vineyard leaf area by linear regression. Span. J. Agric. Res. **9**(1), 202–212 (2011)
12. del Moral-Martínez, I., et al.: Mapping vineyard leaf area using mobile terrestrial laser scanners: should rows be scanned on-the-go or discontinuously sampled? Sensors **16**, 119 (2016)
13. Oliveira, M., Santos, M.: A semi-empirical method to estimate canopy leaf area of vineyards. American journal of enology and viticulture **46**(3), 389–391 (1995)
14. Orlando, F., et al.: Estimating leaf area index (LAI) in vineyards using the PocketLAI smart-app. Sensors **16**(12), 2004 (2016)
15. Patakas, A., Noitsakis, B.: An indirect method of estimating leaf area index in cordon trained spur pruned grapevines. Scientia Horticulturae **80**, 299–305 (1999)
16. Patrignani, A., Ochsner, T.E.: Canopeo: a powerful new tool for measuring fractional green canopy cover. Agron. J. **107**(6), 2312–2320 (2015)
17. Raajan, N., Ramkumar, M., Monisha, B., Jaiseeli, C., et al.: Disparity estimation from stereo images. Procedia Eng. **38**, 462–472 (2012)
18. Sanz, R., et al.: Lidar and non-lidar-based canopy parameters to estimate the leaf area in fruit trees and vineyard. Agric. Forest Meteorol. **260**, 229–239 (2018)
19. Siegfried, W., Viret, O., Huber, B., Wohlhauser, R.: Dosage of plant protection products adapted to leaf area index in viticulture. Crop Prot. **26**(2), 73 (2007)
20. Smart, R.E.: Principles of grapevine canopy microclimate manipulation with implications for yield and quality: a review. Am. J. Enol. Viticulture **36**(3), 230–239 (1985)
21. Taipale, E.: NDVI and Your Farm: Understanding NDVI for Plant Health Insights. Sentera Precision Agriculture (2017). https://sentera.com/understanding-ndvi-plant-health/. Accessed March 2019
22. Welles, J.M.: Some indirect methods of estimating canopy structure. Remote Sensing Rev. **5**(1), 31–43 (1990)
23. Zheng, G., Moskal, L.M.: Retrieving leaf area index (LAI) using remote sensing: theories, methods and sensors. Sensors **9**(4), 2719–2745 (2009)
24. Zhu, X., et al.: Improving leaf area index (LAI) estimation by correcting for clumping and woody effects using terrestrial laser scanning. Agric. Forest Meteorol. **263**, 276–286 (2018)

Classification of an Agrosilvopastoral System Using RGB Imagery from an Unmanned Aerial Vehicle

Luís Pádua[1,2]([✉]) [iD], Nathalie Guimarães[1], Telmo Adão[1,2] [iD],
Pedro Marques[1] [iD], Emanuel Peres[1,2] [iD], António Sousa[1,2] [iD],
and Joaquim J. Sousa[1,2] [iD]

[1] School of Science and Technology,
University of Trás-os-Montes e Alto Douro, 5000-801 Vila Real, Portugal
{luispadua,nsguimaraes,telmoadao,pedro.marques,
eperes,amrs,jjsousa}@utad.pt
[2] Centre for Robotics in Industry and Intelligent Systems (CRIIS), INESC
Technology and Science (INESC-TEC), Porto 4200-465, Portugal

Abstract. This paper explores the usage of unmanned aerial vehicles (UAVs) to acquire remotely sensed very high-resolution imagery for classification of an agrosilvopastoral system in a rural region of Portugal. Aerial data was obtained using a low-cost UAV, equipped with an RGB sensor. Acquired imagery undergone a photogrammetric processing pipeline to obtain different data products: an orthophoto mosaic, a canopy height model (CHM) and vegetation indices (VIs). A superpixel algorithm was then applied to the orthophoto mosaic, dividing the images into different objects. From each object, different features were obtained based in its maximum, mean, minimum and standard deviation. These features were extracted from the different data products: CHM, VIs, and color bands. Classification process – using random forest algorithm – classified objects into five different classes: trees, low vegetation, shrubland, bare soil and infrastructures. Feature importance obtained from the training model showed that CHM-driven features have more importance when comparing to those obtained from VIs or color bands. An overall classification accuracy of 86.4% was obtained.

Keywords: Agrosilvopastoral systems · Unmanned aerial vehicles · Photogrammetric processing · Superpixels · Random forest

1 Introduction

Employing unmanned aerial vehicles (UAVs) in environmental monitoring activities is increasing, with a wide range of applications in forestry [1], agriculture [2], and grassland monitoring [3]. This remote sensing platform provides high flexibility by enabling superior temporal and spatial resolutions [4] with lower costs, in medium and small projects, when compared to traditional remote sensing platforms [5].

In the classification process of data, collected by UAVs, it is essential to select the best machine learning algorithm. There are three common algorithms being used in

© Springer Nature Switzerland AG 2019
P. Moura Oliveira et al. (Eds.): EPIA 2019, LNAI 11804, pp. 248–257, 2019.
https://doi.org/10.1007/978-3-030-30241-2_22

remote sensing: (1) random forest; (2) support vector machines; and (3) artificial neural networks. The selection of the most appropriate method is dependent on the type of problem being solved. In case of having multiple features but limited records, support vector machines might work better. In case of having a considerable number of records but less features, Neural Networks present better prediction/classification accuracy [6]. On the other hand, Random forest is a type of ensemble classifier that produces multiple decision trees by using a random subset of training samples and variables. It can handle high data dimensionality and multicollinearity swiftly and is insensitive to overfitting [7]. Indeed, random forest is widely used in remote sensing applications, being applied to urban vegetation mapping [8], land use and land cover mapping [9, 10], grassland classification [11] and tree species classification [12–14].

This study aims to classify an agrosilvopastoral system using a random forest algorithm and data driven from photogrammetric processing of UAV-based RGB imagery. Agrosilvopastoral systems can be defined as a collective name for land-use systems, which include the woody component (trees and/or shrubs), crops and cattle. Essentially, these systems are associated to a model of production and conservation centered on silvicultural practices and agricultural activities [15]. According to Nair [16] agrosilvopastoral systems "include the use of woody hedgerows for browse, mulch and green manure as well as for soil conservation".

This paper is structured as follows: the next section presents the study area, describes the UAV used and related imagery acquisition process. Methods used for imagery segmentation, features extracted, and the classification algorithm are also presented; Sect. 3 presents and discusses obtained results. The last section has some conclusions and describes steps towards future developments.

2   Materials and Methods

2.1   Study Area

The study area is located in north-eastern Portugal (41°22′43.8″N, 7°35′00.8″W) and is composed of trees (mainly *Pinus Pinaster* and *Castanea Sativa* Mill.), shrubland communities (*Cytisus striatus*), low-land vegetation and crops, such as grassland and potatoes, along with bare soil areas and some men-made infrastructures. An area overview is presented in Fig. 1. Pine trees are present in both the north and east sections of the study area, with some small trees located in the central section. Two chestnut plantations are also present: one located in the central section and a smaller plantation in the north section. Regarding shrubland communities, those are located throughout the study area, being prevalent around its boarders. Low-land vegetation is mainly located in the south section and is composed of grassland and a potato plantation. Bare soil areas are spread throughout the study area, some covered by dry vegetation – mostly in between pine trees and shrubs – and some granite stones near man-made infrastructures. As for the latter, they represent a smaller area in the south and southwest sections of the study area and are used mainly as livestock accommodations.

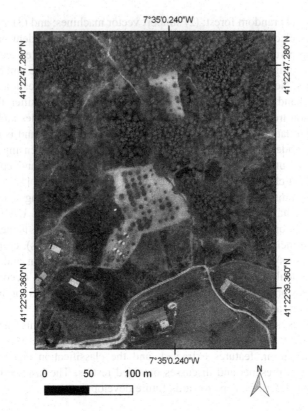

Fig. 1. General overview of the study area. Coordinates in WGS84 (EPSG:4326).

2.2   Data Acquisition

Aerial data acquisition was made using the DJI Phantom 4 (DJI, Shenzhen, China). It is cost-effective multi-rotor UAV equipped with a Global Navigation Satellite System (GNSS) receiver and a 12.4 MP RGB sensor mounted in a 3-axis electronic gimbal [17]. Its remote controller, which serves as ground station, enables the connection to a smartphone. Depending on the objective, there are different applications to perform image and video acquisition for this UAV model. In this study, it is intended to perform an autonomous flight to acquire aerial imagery for photogrammetric processing. As such, mission planning and data acquisition was done using Pix4Dcapture (Pix4D SA, Lausanne, Switzerland) in an Android smartphone: it enables the user to define an area to survey, setting different parameters, such as flight height, camera angle, UAV speed and images' overlap.

The UAV-based imagery acquisition was conducted in 21 May 2017 at 3 PM (GMT). A single-grid flight was performed at a flight height of 100 m from the take-off point, covering a 255 m × 150 m area. The RGB sensor was point towards a nadiral position, with a front overlap of 80% and a side overlap of 70%. These parameters were chosen based on previous studies [18]. A total of 102 images were acquired in four minutes, with a ground sample distance (GSD) of approximately 4 cm.

2.3   Photogrammetric Processing

The acquired UAV-based RGB high-resolution imagery was subjected to photogrammetric processing. This step was achieved using Pix4Dmapper Pro (Pix4D SA, Lausanne, Switzerland), which can transform a set of images into point cloud data using Structure from Motion (SfM) algorithms, by identifying common tie points. Moreover, it enables to compute different data products for geodetic analysis. The processing pipeline of Pix4Dmapper Pro is divided into three main steps: (i) initial processing, which is responsible for camera position, orientation optimization, computation of tie points, and for creating a sparse point cloud; (ii) point cloud and mesh, where the sparse point cloud is used, along with the imagery, to compute a dense point cloud; and (iii) DSM, orthophoto mosaic and index, which is mostly responsible for providing orthorectified raster outcomes by point cloud interpolation, such as digital surface models (DSMs), orthophoto mosaics, digital terrain models (DTMs) and vegetation indices (VIs) [17].

Within the scope of this study the initial processing was conducted using default parameters: a high point density was selected to generate the dense point cloud, and the latter was interpolated – by means of the inverse distances weighted (IDW) method with noise filtering and a sharp surface smoothing approach - to generate the raster outcomes. The photogrammetric processing generates: (i) a orthophoto mosaic; (ii) a RGB representation of the acquired imagery; (iii) a DSM that consists in a raster with altitude information of the above surface objects; (iv) a DTM in the shape of a raster with altitude information about points that corresponds to ground (some areas where ground was not directly visible were interpolated); and (v) the selected VIs.

Computed VIs are presented in Table 1. VIs are arithmetic operations using the different spectral bands. Depending on the sensor, bands other than RGB can be used (e.g. near infrared) with different narrowness levels [4]. Both RGBVI and GRVI shown to be good when discriminating vegetation from non-vegetation areas [19, 20]. GBVI, BRVI, BGVI were included in this study due to the usage of the blue band.

Table 1. Vegetation indices used in this study.

Vegetation index	Equation	Reference
Red Green Blue vegetation index (RGBVI)	$RGBVI = \dfrac{Green^2 - Blue \times Red}{Green^2 + Blue \times Red}$	Bendig et al. [21]
Green-Red vegetation index (GRVI)	$GRVI = \dfrac{Green - Red}{Green + Red}$	Tucker [22]
Green-Blue vegetation index (GRVI)	$GBVI = \dfrac{Green - Blue}{Green + Blue}$	
Blue/Red pigment index	$BRVI = \dfrac{Blue}{Red}$	Zarco-Tejada et al. [23]
Blue/Green pigment index	$BGVI = \dfrac{Blue}{Green}$	Zarco-Tejada et al. [23]

To have height information from the above ground objects, a CHM was calculated. This process was achieved by subtracting the DTM to the DSM [24], as presented in

(1). As such, altitude difference in both models is used as surface features height. QGIS raster calculator, a free and open source Geographic Information System (GIS) was used in this operation.

$$CHM = DSM - DTM \tag{1}$$

Moreover, the orthophoto mosaic was converted to a different color space – the hue saturation and value (HSV) color space [25].

2.4   Data Processing and Classification

The simple linear iterative clustering (SLIC) algorithm [26] was used to segment images into multiple superpixels. By applying superpixels oversegmentation to an image, compact and uniform groups of pixels that have similar characteristics are formed [27]. The orthophoto mosaic was used in this process.

Then, a dataset was created with properties obtained from the different available data products, divided into three categories: structural, spectral and color. As a structural product, the CHM was used. Spectral products were composed by the five computed VIs. Color products are composed of the red, green, blue and the hue (from HSV) bands. Therefore, only the pixels from each cluster were considered for data extraction. Then, four features were extracted from each product: the mean, maximum, minimum and standard deviation. To avoid potential outliers, minimum and maximum features were estimated using the 10% lower and higher values, respectively.

Considering the knowledge from the study area, each cluster was classified in five classes: (I) trees, encompassing forest trees and trees for agronomic purposes; (ii) low vegetation, composed of grassland and seasonal agriculture plantations; (iii) shrubland, which considers the shrub communities existing in the area and some shrubs located in forest canopy gaps; (iv) bare soil, encompassing areas with little to no ground vegetation and dry vegetation; (v) and infrastructures, composed of man-made buildings and stone walls. This process was achieved in QGIS by converting the super pixel objects to a polygon shapefile.

With the segmentation done, the features extracted, and data classified, a random forest model was trained for classification purposes. Data was divided into 75% for training and 25% for classification. Feature importance was also evaluated. For accuracy assessment, different metrics were evaluated, namely: producer accuracy, user accuracy, and the overall accuracy. Producer accuracy is obtained by the percentage of how many objects on the map are correctly labeled, including errors of omission and user accuracy is obtained by the percentage of all objects that were correctly identified, encompassing errors of commission.

3   Results and Discussion

Some of the digital products obtained through the photogrammetric processing – CHM, RGBVI, BGVI, BRVI, GBVI, and GRVI – are presented in Fig. 2. Differences between the computed VIs and the CHM height are clearly visible. The photogrammetric processing was done in about 1 h 30 m, using a workstation with two Intel® Xeon® CPU E5-2680 v4, 128 GB RAM, two Nvidia Quadro M4000 and 1 TB SSD.

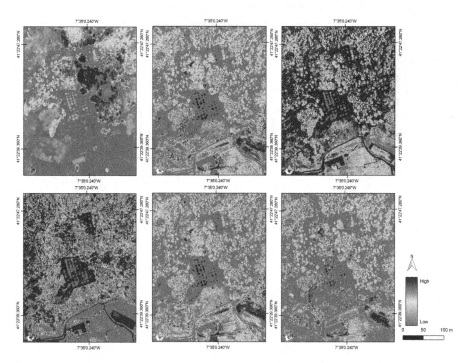

Fig. 2. Generated structural and spectral products in a color-coded representation. Top (left to right): CHM, RGBVI, and BGVI. Bottom (left to right): BRVI, GBVI, and GRVI. Coordinates in WGS84 (EPSG:4326).

The overall training accuracy, using random forest algorithm, was of 99.33%. Superpixels object size varied approximately from 5 m^2 to 90 m^2. As for features importance (Fig. 3), spectral features (VI-based) were the most relevant (35%), followed by color features (34%) and color features (31%). However, when individually analyzing each feature, the most relevant is CHM's mean value (10.8%), followed by CHM's maximum value (10.5%) and the blue band mean value (7.5%). By analyzing each digital outcome individually, CHM has the highest importance (32%). The VI with higher feature importance was the GRVI (12%). Considering color features, both blue and red bands had the higher importance (11% and 9%, respectively). When regarding feature parameter type (i.e. mean, maximum, minimum, and standard deviation) the mean value showed the higher percentage (34%), followed by the maximum (29%), minimum (23%) and, lastly, the standard deviation (14%).

A confusion matrix with the random forest classification results is provided in Table 2. The overall accuracy was 86.4%. Producer accuracy was higher for low vegetation class (91%), followed by tree class (90%), bare soil (86%), shrubland (79%) and infrastructure class (73%). User accuracy was higher for low vegetation (94%), followed by tree class (93%), infrastructure (89%), bare soil (84%), and shrubland (77%).

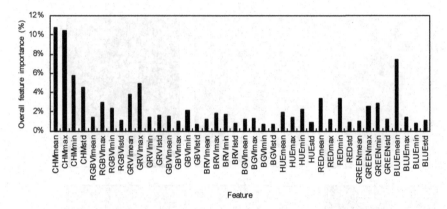

Fig. 3. Feature importance obtained from the random forest training process.

Table 2. Confusion matrix, with user accuracy, and producer accuracy for all classes, based on the number of detected superpixels.

	Trees	Low vegetation	Shrubland	Bare soil	Infrastructure	Producer (%)	User (%)
Trees	433	0	37	9	0	90.40	92.72
Low vegetation	0	94	5	4	0	91.26	94.00
Shrubland	26	3	255	36	1	79.44	77.04
Bare soil	8	2	33	269	0	86.22	84.33
Infrastructure	0	1	1	1	8	72.73	88.89

Feature importance measures shown a high value for the structural variables. Spectral VIs did not show greater importance, except for GRVI, being GBVI and BGVI the VIs with the lower importance. Among color features, blue and red bands shown the higher importance, with hue band from HSV color space not presenting a high importance. In the study of Melville et al. [11], a DSM was used, along with spectral bands driven from an hyperspectral sensor for grassland communities classification and similarly to this study, structural features had higher importance when compared with spectral features. As for feature parameter type, the mean and maximum were the most important: both presented more discrepancies between the different classes. As for minimum and standard deviation features, they shown lower importance. This can be related to the similarities of these features in all classes. For example, a superpixel object with a tree and a small portion of soil can present the same minimum value as an object from the soil class.

Regarding classification results (Table 2), some confusion between tree and shrubland classes was observed. This can be explained by the height similarity between some younger pine trees and shrubs, as well as the difficulty of photogrammetric techniques in penetrating the canopy [18], which results in wrong CHM estimates. As such, situations where shrublands are located in canopy gaps can be classified as being a tree. Furthermore, some soil objects were classified as shrub. These were related with objects located in shadowed areas. As for infrastructure results, these can be explained with the low number of objects representing this class (it was the less represented class), showing some imbalance in the dataset. The final classification image and its reference are presented in Fig. 4.

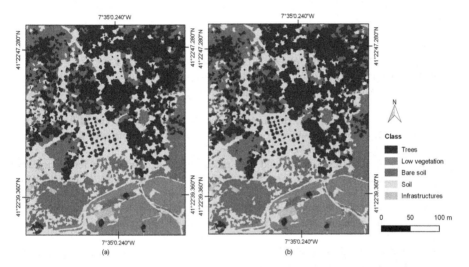

Fig. 4. Ground-truth classification (a) and random forest classification (b) of the study area. Coordinates in WGS84 (EPSG:4326).

4 Conclusions

This paper demonstrates the usefulness of random forest algorithm for classification of photogrammetric products obtained from UAV-based RGB imagery in an agrosilvopastoral system. Results indicated that UAV-based RGB imagery provides enough detail to classify different vegetation and non-vegetation objects. Moreover, encouraging accuracies were obtained in the random forest classification of the evaluated classes, being this a suitable approach for the characterization of agrosilvopastoral systems. The dataset used in this study shown to be effective for this purpose. Still, some concerns towards feature type selection must be considered in future studies.

Future developments should rely in exploring data acquisition in different flight heights, to obtain the best compromise towards data acquisition time and results accuracy. Other aspect is to explore other UAV-based imagery type, such as multispectral and thermal infrared imagery. Multispectral sensors can acquire data from other near infrared regions of the electromagnetic spectrum, which combined with temperature, may improve the classification results.

Acknowledgments. This work is financed by the ERDF – European Regional Development Fund through the Operational Programme for Competitiveness and Internationalisation - COMPETE 2020 Programme within project «POCI-01-0145-FEDER-006961» and by National Funds through the FCT – Fundação para a Ciência e a Tecnologia (Portuguese Foundation for Science and Technology) as part of project UID/EEA/50014/2013. The research activities of Luís Pádua were funded by the Portuguese Foundation for Science and Technology (SFRH/ BD/139702/2018).

References

1. Torresan, C., et al.: Forestry applications of UAVs in Europe: a review. Int. J. Remote Sens. **38**, 2427–2447 (2017). https://doi.org/10.1080/01431161.2016.1252477
2. Castaldi, F., Pelosi, F., Pascucci, S., Casa, R.: Assessing the potential of images from unmanned aerial vehicles (UAV) to support herbicide patch spraying in maize. Precision Agric. **18**, 76–94 (2017). https://doi.org/10.1007/s11119-016-9468-3
3. von Bueren, S.K., Burkart, A., Hueni, A., Rascher, U., Tuohy, M.P., Yule, I.J.: Deploying four optical UAV-based sensors over grassland: challenges and limitations. Biogeosciences **12**, 163–175 (2015). https://doi.org/10.5194/bg-12-163-2015
4. Pádua, L., et al.: UAS, sensors, and data processing in agroforestry: a review towards practical applications. Int. J. Remote Sens. **38**, 2349–2391 (2017). https://doi.org/10.1080/ 01431161.2017.1297548
5. Matese, A., et al.: Intercomparison of UAV, aircraft and satellite remote sensing platforms for precision viticulture. Remote Sens. **7**, 2971–2990 (2015). https://doi.org/10.3390/ rs70302971
6. Shakhatreh, H., et al.: Unmanned aerial vehicles: a survey on civil applications and key research challenges. arXiv:1805.00881 [cs] (2018)
7. Belgiu, M., Drăguţ, L.: Random forest in remote sensing: a review of applications and future directions. ISPRS J. Photogram. Remote Sens. **114**, 24–31 (2016). https://doi.org/10.1016/j. isprsjprs.2016.01.011
8. Feng, Q., Liu, J., Gong, J.: UAV remote sensing for urban vegetation mapping using random forest and texture analysis. Remote Sens. **7**, 1074–1094 (2015). https://doi.org/10.3390/ rs70101074
9. Akar, Ö.: The rotation forest algorithm and object-based classification method for land use mapping through UAV images. Geocarto Int. **33**(5). https://www.tandfonline.com/doi/abs/ 10.1080/10106049.2016.1277273
10. Ma, L., et al.: Evaluation of feature selection methods for object-based land cover mapping of unmanned aerial vehicle imagery using random forest and support vector machine classifiers. IJGI **6**, 51 (2017). https://doi.org/10.3390/ijgi6020051
11. Melville, B., Lucieer, A., Aryal, J.: Classification of lowland native grassland communities using hyperspectral unmanned aircraft system (UAS) imagery in the tasmanian midlands. Drones **3**, 5 (2019). https://doi.org/10.3390/drones3010005
12. Nevalainen, O., et al.: Individual tree detection and classification with UAV-based photogrammetric point clouds and hyperspectral imaging. Remote Sens. **9**, 185 (2017). https://doi.org/10.3390/rs9030185

13. Michez, A., Piégay, H., Lisein, J., Claessens, H., Lejeune, P.: Classification of riparian forest species and health condition using multi-temporal and hyperspatial imagery from unmanned aerial system. Environ. Monit. Assess. **188**, 146 (2016). https://doi.org/10.1007/s10661-015-4996-2

14. Goodbody, T.R.H., Coops, N.C., Hermosilla, T., Tompalski, P., Crawford, P.: Assessing the status of forest regeneration using digital aerial photogrammetry and unmanned aerial systems. Int. J. Remote Sens. **39**, 5246–5264 (2018). https://doi.org/10.1080/01431161.2017.1402387

15. Russo, R.O.: Agrosilvopastoral systems: a practical approach toward sustainable agriculture. J. Sustain. Agric. **7**, 5–16 (1996). https://doi.org/10.1300/J064v07n04_03

16. Nair, P.K.R.: Classification of agroforestry systems. Agroforest Syst. **3**, 97–128 (1985). https://doi.org/10.1007/BF00122638

17. Pádua, L., et al.: UAS-based imagery and photogrammetric processing for tree height and crown diameter extraction. In: Proceedings of the International Conference on Geoinformatics and Data Analysis, pp. 87–91. ACM, New York (2018). https://doi.org/10.1145/3220228.3220241

18. Dandois, J.P., Olano, M., Ellis, E.C.: Optimal altitude, overlap, and weather conditions for computer vision UAV estimates of forest structure. Remote Sens. **7**, 13895–13920 (2015). https://doi.org/10.3390/rs71013895

19. Motohka, T., Nasahara, K.N., Oguma, H., Tsuchida, S.: Applicability of green-red vegetation index for remote sensing of vegetation phenology. Remote Sens. **2**, 2369–2387 (2010). https://doi.org/10.3390/rs2102369

20. Marques, P., et al.: UAV-based automatic detection and monitoring of chestnut trees. Remote Sens. **11**, 855 (2019). https://doi.org/10.3390/rs11070855

21. Bendig, J., et al.: Combining UAV-based plant height from crop surface models, visible, and near infrared vegetation indices for biomass monitoring in barley. Int. J. Appl. Earth Obs. Geoinf. **39**, 79–87 (2015). https://doi.org/10.1016/j.jag.2015.02.012

22. Tucker, C.J.: Red and photographic infrared linear combinations for monitoring vegetation. Remote Sens. Environ. **8**, 127–150 (1979). https://doi.org/10.1016/0034-4257(79)90013-0

23. Zarco-Tejada, P.J., et al.: Assessing vineyard condition with hyperspectral indices: leaf and canopy reflectance simulation in a row-structured discontinuous canopy. Remote Sens. Environ. **99**, 271–287 (2005). https://doi.org/10.1016/j.rse.2005.09.002

24. Popescu, S.C.: Estimating biomass of individual pine trees using airborne lidar. Biomass Bioenerg. **31**, 646–655 (2007). https://doi.org/10.1016/j.biombioe.2007.06.022

25. Smith, A.R.: Color gamut transform pairs. In: Proceedings of the 5th Annual Conference on Computer Graphics and Interactive Techniques - SIGGRAPH 1978, pp. 12–19. ACM Press (1978). https://doi.org/10.1145/800248.807361

26. Achanta, R., Shaji, A., Smith, K., Lucchi, A., Fua, P., Süsstrunk, S.: SLIC superpixels compared to state-of-the-art superpixel methods. IEEE Trans. Pattern Anal. Mach. Intell. **34**, 2274–2282 (2012). https://doi.org/10.1109/TPAMI.2012.120

27. Crommelinck, S., Bennett, R., Gerke, M., Koeva, M.N., Yang, M.Y., Vosselman, G.: SLIC superpixels for object delineation from UAV data. ISPRS Ann. Photogramm. Remote Sens. Spatial Inf. Sci. **4**, 9–16 (2017). https://doi.org/10.5194/isprs-annals-IV-2-W3-9-2017

Digital Ampelographer: A CNN Based Preliminary Approach

Telmo Adão[1,2(✉)], Tatiana M. Pinho[1,2], António Ferreira[2],
António Sousa[1,2], Luís Pádua[2], José Sousa[2], Joaquim J. Sousa[1,2],
Emanuel Peres[1,2], and Raul Morais[1,2]

[1] INESC Technology and Science (INESC-TEC), 4200-465 Porto, Portugal
[2] University of Trás-os-Montes e Alto Douro, 5000-801 Vila Real, Portugal
telmoadao@utad.pt

Abstract. Authenticity, traceability and certification are key to assure both quality and confidence to wine consumers and an added commercial value to farmers and winemakers. Grapevine variety stands out as one of the most relevant factors to be considered in wine identification within the whole wine sector value chain. Ampelography is the science responsible for grapevine varieties identification based on (i) in-situ visual inspection of grapevine mature leaves and (ii) on the ampelographer experience. Laboratorial analysis is a costly and time-consuming alternative. Both the lack of experienced professionals and context-induced error can severely hinder official regulatory authorities' role and therefore bring about a significant impact in the value chain.

The purpose of this paper is to assess deep learning potential to classify grapevine varieties through the ampelometric analysis of leaves. Three convolutional neural networks architectures performance are evaluated using a dataset composed of six different grapevine varieties leaves. This preliminary approach identified Xception architecture as very promising to classify grapevine varieties and therefore support a future autonomous tool that assists the wine sector stakeholders, particularly the official regulatory authorities.

Keywords: CNN · Xception · ResNet · VGG · Precision viticulture ·
Ampelography · Grapevine identification · Wine Certification ·
Douro Demarcated Region

1 Introduction

The wine sector is one of the most relevant worldwide in the context of agro-food products, characterized by an interesting growth rate in recent years [1]. In fact, in 2018, the estimated world wine production was of 292.3 million hectoliters. Consumption follows this trend with an estimated volume of 246 million hectoliters. In terms of value, an increase of 1.2% was verified in the world wine market when compared to 2017, in a total of 31.3bn EUR [2]. The commercial value and authenticity of wine is usually related with its origin and certain regions are recognized for the production of high-quality wines [3]. As such, this sector is strategic, not only at economic, social and environmental levels, but also often represents a country's image

© Springer Nature Switzerland AG 2019
P. Moura Oliveira et al. (Eds.): EPIA 2019, LNAI 11804, pp. 258–271, 2019.
https://doi.org/10.1007/978-3-030-30241-2_23

in the world [4]. Through statistical analysis, it is possible to see that Europe has and will continue to have a world dominance in production, consumption and exports [5, 6]. In particular, Portugal has a long tradition in the production and export of wine [7], being Douro the first demarcated and regulated wine region in the world [8].

Due to increasingly demanding customers, wine producing countries have a continuously evolving interest in analytical characterization of wine to improve traceability, authentication and classification [9]. In addition, the implementation of stricter regulations is also a reality in this sector. Among them, certification of the protected designation of origin (PDO) can be highlighted as one of the most relevant implemented policies. In this context, the adoption of strategies that guarantee the control of the PDO and ensure the authenticity, and consequently the quality of the wine is essential [4, 7]. In Portugal, the Port and Douro Wines Institute, I. P. (IVDP, I.P.) has as its main task the control, certification, promotion and protection of the designations of origin "Porto" and "Douro" in the Douro Demarcated Region (DDR) [8]. Thus, it is important to analyze both the sources and factors that affect the wine production process, to improve its quality. Among them, grapevine variety, the geographical origin, harvest, among others [4] can be referred. Grapevine variety can be highlighted as one of the most important factors for the various stakeholders, from growers, to winemakers, regulatory authorities, consumers, etc., as it is essential to assure the correct identification of wines. Misidentification can lead to adulteration or fraud, which can have a significant impact in both financial costs and production volume to those involved in the value chain [3, 10].

There are several grapevine identification methods. Ampelography is one of the more traditional grapevine variety identification strategies, through visual inspection. Here, the mature leaf provides several essential descriptors to identify the grapevine variety [10]. However, ampelography is usually performed based on the user (ampelographer) experience. The current lack of ampelographic knowledge has raised some legal and commercial discussion [11]. In addition, variations in environmental, cultural and genetic conditions may also introduce uncertainty in the process [10]. Considering the mentioned issues, the use of reliable techniques that are not influenced by subjective interpretations or by the environment are essential tools for the correct identification of grape varieties [11], not only in the DDR context, but also regarding other realities worldwide.

Deep learning (DL) has been successfully applied as a modern and promising technique for image processing and data analysis in different agricultural application, such as leaf and crop type classification, plant disease detection, plant recognition, fruit counting, among others, as identified by Kamilaris et al. [12]. These authors also state that convolutional neural networks (CNNs) are used in more than half of the works that they addressed. Sequential, residual, pixel-wise and depth wise CNN architectures [13–17] are among those that can effectively be applied to address a particular classification problem, within a given context.

The purpose of this paper is to assess DL potential to classify grapevine varieties through the ampelometric analysis of leaves.

While differentiating similar *Vitis vinifera L.* subspecies may be challenging for humans [10], CNNs architectures are considered specialized in analysing data and extracting features that enable a problem's characterization, either from 1-D, 2-D or

N-D data structures (e.g. text files expressing characteristics and labelling, RGB images, hyperspectral data cubes). To assess CNNs' adequacy in supporting, complementing or autonomously performing grapevine varieties identification based on ampelographic analysis, 3 architectures – Visual Geometry Group (VGG)-16, ResNet and Xception – were both trained and tested. In this preliminary study, in which briefness was taken as a requirement, selection criteria considered important convolution strategies proposed in three distinct temporal moments: in-depth sequentiality, one of the earliest; residuality, a later one; and depth-wise separability, one of the most recent. The used dataset is composed of leaf images from 6 grapevine varieties – among the 115 recognized by the IVDP, I.P. [18] – commonly found in the DDR: Codega, Moscatel, Rabigato, Tinta Roriz, Tinto Cão and Touriga Nacional. Although, only visually discriminant phenological state imagery was considered. Moreover, 4 learning rate (LR) behaviour modelers – time-based decay, drop-based decay, exponential decay and Nadam – are also evaluated and discussed for each referred CNN architecture.

2 Related Work

DL is a modern and promising technique for image processing and data analysis, whose application domains include (but are not limited to) plant recognition, leaf and crop type classification and plant diseases detection [12]. Within plant recognition application domain, Grinblat et al. [19] used CNNs to identify plants through leaf veins morphology. With visualization-based models' technique, they were able to point out the most meaningful patterns. Similar research interests were pursued by Lee et al. [20], with 44 species of the Royal Botanic Gardens (Kew, England). Hall et al. [21] evaluated the robustness of traditional hand-crafted leaves features (e.g. length of contour, area convexity) and showed how CNNs, when combined with such features, can improve classification performance, while Reyes [22] proposed a fine-tuning strategy as a solution to transfer learned recognition capabilities from general domains to the specific challenge of plant identification task. In [23], remarkable results on image-based phenotyping classification have also been shown through the application of this class of computational learning, taking advantage of the discriminative power provided by the possibility of increasing the number of hidden layers within CNNs. Root and shoot features of plants were the focus of the learning/identification of that approach. Semantic segmentation using deep convolutions was authored by Mortensen et al. [24], resorting to close-up images of crops, data augmentation, manual annotation of 7 classes –among them barley, weed and soil- and a neural network. The potential of CNNs for segmenting plant species was emphasized.

In fact, the scientific community has been very active in developing DL-based solutions towards plant recognition [25, 26]. Requirements framed by land cover classification over remote sensing data can also be properly answered by DL, as shown by Kussul et al. [27], that compared random forests and neural networks relying on traditional fully connected multilayer perceptron with CNNs and concluded that the latter approach is more accurate in classifying summer crop types. Rußwurm and Körner [28] followed a similar research line, but considering multi-temporal classification over imagery lacking of radiometric and geometric pre-processing. Recurrent neural networks were adopted in this specific challenge involving a temporal sequence. Along with aforementioned DL applications, efforts to achieve computer-based recognition of plant diseases have been developed (e.g. [29–32]).

Regarding CNN architectures, Simonyan and Zisserman [13] proposed the VGG – named after authors' laboratory Visual Geometry Group –, which is a sequential network of simple implementation that relies on small convolution filters distributed among 16 or 19 weight layers. On the 2014 ImageNet Large Scale Visual Recognition Competition (ILSVRC) edition, VGG surpassed previous CNN architectures, including GoogLeNet – also known as Inception-V1 – [33] and Microsoft Research Asia (MSRA) proposal [34]. ResNet [14] is a deeper but also less complex architecture than VGG, that relies on layers' arrangement as learning residual functions. Variety regarding images' occupation by elements of interest, overfitting proneness related to deeper networks and careless convolution operations stacking leading to computational performance issues are aspects addressed in Inception-V1 [33], which performs based on wideness of instead of deepness, i.e., more filters operating at the same level. Improved versions include Inception-V2 and V3 [35], as well as V4 and Inception-ResNet (V1 and V2) [15]. The latter is a hybrid architecture that integrates the residual learning feature provided by ResNet. Crop-based experimental results from ImageNet dataset showed lower Top-1 and Top-5 error rates comparatively to both Inception-V3 and ResNet alone. Google's MobileNet [17] consists of a depth wise separable convolutions architecture that aims to setup lightweight deep neural networks – with fewer parameters to process and less complexity –, particularly useful for mobile and embedded vision applications. An improved version known as MobileNetV2 was recently released, relying in two main new features: linear bottlenecks between the layers and shortcut connections between the bottlenecks [36]. Xception [16] combines point-wise convolutions followed by depth-wise separable convolutions and residual connections (inspired by ResNet [14]). By exchanging the order of operations relatively to original depth-wise separable convolution – that starts by convoluting the channels and then the pixels – and, also, by removing intermediate rectified linear units (ReLU's) non-linearity, Xception reached state-of-the-art performances in tests with ImageNet dataset [37]. It also outperformed Inception-V3 training speed (steps/second) since it handles a more efficient number of parameters. To deal with vanishing-gradient issue, strengthen feature propagation, encourage feature reuse and reduce the number of parameters in problems requiring deeper convolutional networks, an architecture known as DenseNet [38] was proposed, pointing out and solving some of the weaker aspects of ResNet [14].

A relevant matter that has been studied by the machine/deep learning research community is the hyperparameters optimization. In this topic, grid search approach is often applied to select the best parameters among a finite universe defined by a user or programmer. Among these parameters, LR has a considerable weight in the success/failure of CNNs' convergence. While stochastic gradient descendant (SGD) strategy [39] uses LR, momentum, eventually, Nesterov accelerated gradient (NAG) [40] and schedulers capable of controlling LR progress and impulse – as addressed in [41], for example –, other adaptative approaches have been proposed, resulting from efforts to automatize and enhance CNNs' convergence (RMSProp [42], Adam [43], Nadam [44], etc.).

Following DL advances, many tools have been developed to facilitate the interface of programmers and users with the modelling of problems through convolutional neural networks, such as TensorFlow [45], Theano [46], Keras [47], Deep Learning Matlab Toolbox [48], Caffe [49], PyTorch [50] or even user-friendly studios such as Deep Cognition [51].

The next section describes a grapevine leaves dataset, as well as the training, evaluation and testing procedures of three CNNs architectures, involving LR schedulers and optimizers, as well as grid search, to assess DL capabilities in classification problems regarding grapevine varieties identification through leaves ampelometric analysis. Lastly, results are presented and discussed, and some conclusions are drawn.

3   Materials and Methods

This section presents the grapevine leaves dataset, data augmentation procedures followed, adopted CNN architectures, hyperparameters optimization and LR regulators employed.

3.1   Grapevine Leaves Dataset

A dataset consisting in a collection of grapevine leaves from 6 different varieties (2 plants per variety) – Touriga Nacional, Tinto Cão, Códega, Moscatel, Tinta Roriz and Rabigato – was prepared based on images acquired in the University of Trás-os-Montes e Alto Douro research farm vineyards (Nossa Senhora de Lourdes farm, Vila Real, Portugal: 41°17'11.5"N, 7°44'14.1"W). Whilst primarily used for research purposes, this farm, located within the DDR, possesses a diverse set of labelled and identified grapevine varieties. Weekly, during most of the 2017 season – specifically from May 4th to July 31st –, one leaf was picked from the same two previously selected plants of each grapevine variety (Fig. 1), put on top of a white sheet of paper and photographed (in the field), without any artificial lighting, using a Canon EOS 600D, equipped with a 50 mm f/1.4 objective lens (Canon, Ota, Tokyo, Japan). About 480 images were acquired: roughly 80 for each grapevine variety. Figure 2 presents specimens of the 6 grapevine varieties addressed in this work. Thereafter, images acquired under adverse lighting conditions, containing grapevine leaves wrongly framed and/or, somehow uncharacterized – due to, for example, disease, damage or early phenological state – were removed from the dataset to obtain a focused filtered subset, more suitable to be used as an unequivocal basis for the learning process. After clean-up, 52 images were conserved per grapevine variety group. Each image was then cropped using as criteria a minimal squared bounding box around leaves. Furthermore, images were also normalized to 300 × 300 pixels, keeping aspect ratio settings. Upon the resulting subset, a data augmentation process was carried out, replicating existing photos with transformations that included different rotations, contrasts/brightness, vertical/horizontal mirroring and scale variations. A successfully data augmentation was achieved to a total of 3120 images, 520 per grapevine variety, ensuring a balanced distribution. The process by which the final grapevine leaves dataset was attained is presented in Fig. 3.

Fig. 1. Location of the plants from which leaf images were acquired in Nossa Senhora de Lourdes farm (Vila Real, Portugal: 41°17'11.5"N, 7°44'14.1"W). For each of the 6 grapevine varieties, two apparently healthy plants were selected from the respective vine rows. An example image for the Rabigato variety is presented.

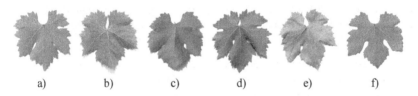

Fig. 2. Grapevine leaves acquired in the field, over a white background: (a) Touriga Nacional; (b) Tinto Cão; (c) Códega; (d) Moscatel; (e) Tinta Roriz; and (f) Rabigato.

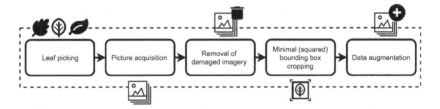

Fig. 3. Grapevine leaves' dataset development process: from in-field leaf-picking and image acquisition, to in-office removal of non-compliant imagery, cropping/resizing, and data augmentation operations.

3.2 Training, Evaluation and Testing Procedure

Three CNN architectures were tested – a simplified sequential VGG-16, ResNet, and Xception – to assess and compare their performance in learning/classifying grapevine

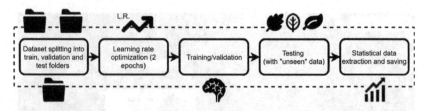

Fig. 4. Step-based process to train, evaluate and test CNN architectures: prepare the augmented dataset through splitting operations, optimize the learning process, train the CNNs and validate. Then, part of the augmented dataset is used to test the neural networks. Results are then analysed to assess performance.

varieties through proximity images acquired over a white background. Figure 4 presents the main steps regarding the training, evaluation and testing procedures.

The first step is to prepare the augmented dataset to be computed by CNN architectures, i.e. subsets for training, validation and testing were set up. While training data is used to handle features extraction for learning, validation data is used to monitor the learning process success and testing data is reserved for assessing accuracy rates, using unseen data. Respectively, 60%, 30% and 10% were the percentages chosen to randomly split the augmented dataset in all trials, without stratification.

Training/validation stage was carried out by 100 epochs, disregarding early stop controllers (for example, to deal with learning stagnation/recession). The following setup parameters were used as a transversal configuration:

- Batch size = 12 (maximum supported by graphic cards without memory leaks);
- Steps per epoch = Number of training images/Batch size;
- Validation steps = Number of validation images/Batch size;
- Target size for input layer = 300 (image width) × 300 (image height) × 3 (image channels);
- Class mode: categorical.

According to previous experience with CNNs, choosing an inappropriate initial LR might lead to an ineffective training, whose impact is observable through accuracy/loss indicators. In the worst-case scenario, these parameters cease to improve along the training, resulting in failure regarding the convergence of the models that, in turn, provide wrong predictions when confronted with unseen data. To tackle this issue, a preliminary step handling hyperparameter optimization is performed before the actual training, to find the most suitable initial LR among 0.1, 0.01 and 0.001, as depicted in Fig. 5.

In view of assessing typical behavioural modelers for LR, each CNN was tested with 3 different schedulers for stochastic gradient descendent (SGD), more specifically time-based, step-based and exponential decay, plus a relatively recent adaptive approach known as Nesterov Adam or Nadam optimizer, that automatically provides adjustments during the training, from epoch to epoch.

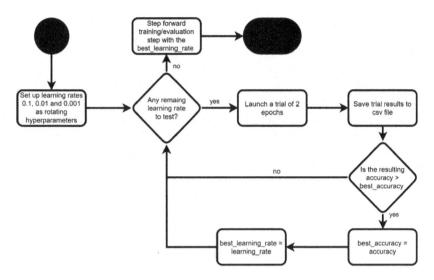

Fig. 5. Process to fine-tune LRs before the actual training/evaluation step.

Time-based, step-based and exponential decay are respectively modelled by Eqs. (1), (2) and (3), as presented in Eqs. (1), (2) and (3):

$$LR = LR \times 1/(1 + decay \times epoch) \tag{1}$$

$$LR = LRinit \times DropRate^{floor(epoch/epoch\_drop)} \tag{2}$$

$$LR = LRinit \times e^{-kt} \tag{3}$$

Due to initial LR variability deriving from the outcome possibilities implied in the preliminary step handling hyperparameter optimization, LR schedulers' profiles become susceptible of squeezing or expanding shape, which induces precocious or delayed plateauing, nearby zero. Thereby, dependent variables were isolated and modelled to ensure a decay coherency (proportionality) while dealing with such variability. For step-based scheduler, the *DropRate* variable was isolated and Eq. (4) was used to model decay.

$$DropRate = {}^{(epochs\_drop)}\!\!\sqrt{\left(LRinit^{flattern\_factor}\right)} \tag{4}$$

To model the exponential decay, variable k is presented as a function that adjusts the LR, while going throughout a specific number of epochs, as shown in Eq. (5).

$$k = \left(\log\left(LRinit^{flattern\_factor}\right) - \log(LRinit)\right)/(n\_epochs * \log(e)) \tag{5}$$

A *decay* of $1/n\_epochs$ was used to schedule the time-based decay. Variable *epochs_drop* was set to $n\_epochs/10$, to induce a decay at each 10 training epochs while using step-based scheduler. For both step-based and exponential decay schedulers, a *flatten_factor* of LRintial$^{2.25}$ was used to conduct a soft LR plateauing.

Implementation resorted to Keras supported by Tensorflow backend. Two graphical cards NVidea Quadro M4000 (Nvidia Corporation, Santa Clara, California, USA) – 1664 CUDA cores, 8 GB of GDDR5 memory and a maximum bandwidth of 192 GB/s – working in cooperation allowed to speed-up both training/validation and testing procedures. For each trial, several parameters were monitored to assess resulting models, such as processing time for both training and testing, accuracy indexes, trainable and non-trainable features number, as well as precision, accuracy, recall and F1-score – see Eqs. (6-9).

$$Accuracy = (TP + TN)/(TP + TN + FP + FN) \tag{6}$$

$$Recall = TP/(TP + FN) \tag{7}$$

$$Precision = TP/(TP + FP) \tag{8}$$

$$F1score = 2 \times (Precision \times Recall)/(Precision + Recall) \tag{9}$$

TP, TN, FP and FN correspond to true positive, true negative, false positive and false negative, respectively. The next section presents the results and a discussion, based on the aforementioned assessment parameters.

4 Results and Discussion

The results associated to the tests with the baseline implementations of VGG-16, ResNet and Xcpetion CNN architectures are presented in this section, wherein data regarding training/prediction time, as well as trainable parameters number are glimpsed. Furthermore, precision, recall, f1 and accuracy scores are also presented and discussed.

In what concerns processing time, Xception is the network architecture that took longer to train – approximately 5 h and 1 min – while both VGG and ResNet required roughly the same time, i.e., around 3 h and 15 min. To predict the 312 images reserved for testing purposes, computation time ranged between 12 and 17 s, wherein ResNet was slightly slower than Xception and VGG-16 was the fastest. On the other hand, the number of trainable parameters was much less efficient in VGG-16, in which more than the quadruple of features was highlighted, comparatively to ResNet and Xception. CNNs architectures predictive effectiveness results are summarized in Table 1.

Overall, the strategy combining point-wise and depth-wise convolutions and, also, residual connections adopted in Xception presented thorough accuracy/precision with a fewer number of trainable parameters, which corroborates with previous knowledge [16]. ResNet's residual connections alone reached 97% accuracy/precision, highlighting a quite acceptable classification effectiveness too. The very deep sequential nature of VGG-16 did not go further than 87.5% accuracy/precision, which seems to discourage the use of this kind of CNN architecture for class similarity problems within

Table 1. CNN architectures effectiveness evaluation. Metrics include F1, precision and recall scores per class, as well overall accuracy per CNN architecture. Only the best LR schedulers (LR sched. column) are shown for the sake of conciseness. Class numbers 0, 1, 2, 3, 4 and 5 correspond to Códega, Moscatel, Rabigato, Tinta Roriz, Tinto Cão and Touriga Nacional grapevine varieties, respectively.

	LR sched.	Class	F1	Precision	Recall	Accuracy
VGG	Exponential decay	0	0.874	0.882	0.865	0.875
		1	0.847	0.797	0.903	
		2	0.843	0.86	0.827	
		3	0.880	0.917	0.846	
		4	0.824	0.84	0.808	
		5	0.981	0.963	1.0	
		Avg	0.875	0.876	0.875	
Resnet	Step-based decay	0	0.954	0.912	1.0	0.971
		1	0.990	1.0	0.981	
		2	0.939	1.0	0.885	
		3	0.980	1.0	0.962	
		4	1.0	1.0	1.0	
		5	0.963	0.929	1.0	
		Avg	0.971	0.973	0.971	
Xception	Exponential and step-based decay	0	1.0	1.0	1.0	1.0
		1	1.0	1.0	1.0	
		2	1.0	1.0	1.0	
		3	1.0	1.0	1.0	
		4	1.0	1.0	1.0	
		5	1.0	1.0	1.0	
		Avg	1.0	1.0	1.0	

a given scope (e.g. grapevine varieties). Indeed, VGG's trainable parameters low-efficiency seem to negatively impact particularity-oriented discrimination processes.

Regarding LR schedulers, the ones based on SGD contributed more for the convergence of the selected CNNs architectures, specifically step-based and exponential decay. On the other hand, Nadam not only provided the worst precision/accuracy results, as it also failed in converging most of the tested CNN architectures. As such, the incorporation of ready-to-use adaptive methods like Nadam must be carefully considered, as they seem to be more prone to slow down or even preclude the training process than SGD-based schedulers.

As a final remark, one must consider that these results reflect the little number of used classes, phenological homogeneity, (white) background normalization and substantial data augmentation that should, however, and depending on the particular classification problem under analysis, be considered as a pertinent process to enhance CNN learning robustness.

5 Conclusions

Distinguishing species within vineyard cultivars is a decisive activity for the whole wine sector value chain. Currently, it is mainly carried out by human observers, trained to differentiate grapevine leaves specimens, sub-variants and/or other mutations arising from the effects of climate change and terroir characteristics, based on a visual insight. However, besides some uncertainty factors – e.g. human assessment subjectivity, inter/intra-species similarity – that can lead to classification errors, a worrying reduction of people holding this kind of ability/expertise has been witnessed, particularly in DDR. As such, this paper proposed a grapevine variety identification approach based on CNNs. More specifically, baseline implementations of VGG-16, ResNet and Xception architectures were assessed under 4 different LR schedulers each, against a vine leaf imagery dataset – constituted by 6 different grapevine varieties, common in the DDR – collected to establish an ampelometric knowledge base. Preliminary results point out Xception as a promising CNN architecture for grapevine variety identification, capable of achieving excellent (100%) recognition accuracy and precision, at least, while considering datasets purged of undesired conditions (phenological heterogeneity, natural background, etc.). Another noteworthy conclusion regards to LR schedulers, wherein SGD-based ones resulted in much more effective CNN convergences than using Nadam.

Future developments will address the following objectives: (i) to assess overfitting regarding different parameters such as variety, phenology and geographical location; (ii) to extend grapevine varieties dataset with a broader group of leaf images, encompassing more species and phenological states and taking advantage from a privileged interface with the DDR; (iii) to assess a wider set of acquisition conditions (light exposure, presence/absence of background, etc.), likely to influence CNNs action and, if possible, to address/overcome eventual poor effects; and (iv) to build a community CNN toolkit composed of an easy and intuitive interface for professionals/academics interested in training their own models for a given purpose and context, providing decision support powered by deep learning.

Acknowledgements. The authors would like to acknowledge project "CHIC – Cooperative Holistic View on Internet and Content" (N° 24498), financed the European Regional Development Fund (ERDF) through COMPETE2020 - the Operational Programme for Competitiveness and Internationalisation (OPCI) that partially supported this work, Port and Douro Wines Institute, I. P. (IVDP, I.P.) for their collaboration in this work.

Funding. This work is financed by the ERDF – European Regional Development Fund through the Operational Programme for Competitiveness and Internationalisation - COMPETE 2020 Programme within project «POCI-01-0145-FEDER-006961», and by National Funds through the FCT – Fundação para a Ciência e a Tecnologia (Portuguese Foundation for Science and Technology) as part of project UID/EEA/50014/2013.

References

1. Giacosa, E.: Wine consumption in a certain territory. Which factors may have impact on it? In: Grumezescu, A.M., Holban, A.M. (eds.) Production and Management of Beverages, pp. 361–380. Woodhead Publishing (2019). https://doi.org/10.1016/B978-0-12-815260-7.00012-2
2. OIV: State of the Vitiviniculture World Market: State of the sector in 2018. Organisation Internationale de la Vigne et du Vin (OIV) (2019)
3. Azcarate, S.M., et al.: Modeling excitation–emission fluorescence matrices with pattern recognition algorithms for classification of Argentine white wines according grape variety. Food Chem. **184**, 214–219 (2015). https://doi.org/10.1016/j.foodchem.2015.03.081
4. Moncayo, S., Rosales, J.D., Izquierdo-Hornillos, R., Anzano, J., Caceres, J.O.: Classification of red wine based on its protected designation of origin (PDO) using laser-induced breakdown spectroscopy (LIBS). Talanta **158**, 185–191 (2016). https://doi.org/10.1016/j.talanta.2016.05.059
5. Rinaldi, A.: Wine global trends. Traditional leaders and new markets. Rivista di Scienze del Turismo - Ambiente Cultura Diritto Economia **6**, 5–10 (2018). https://doi.org/10.7358/rst-2015-01-rina
6. Hogg, T., Rebelo, J.: Rumo Estratégico para o Setor dos Vinhos do Porto e Douro, Relatório Final - Estudos de base, Instituto dos Vinhos do Douro e do Porto, I.P. Universidade de Trás-os-Montes e Alto Douro, INNOVINE&WINE, Vila Real, Portugal (2014)
7. Panzone, L.A., Simões, O.M.: The importance of regional and local origin in the choice of wine: hedonic models of Portuguese wines in Portugal. J. Wine Res. **20**, 27–44 (2009). https://doi.org/10.1080/09571260902978527
8. Diário da República: Decreto Lei n° 173/2009 de 3 de Agosto (2009)
9. Gomez, F.J., Silva, M.F.: Microchip electrophoresis for wine analysis. Anal. Bioanal. Chem. **408**, 8643–8653 (2016). https://doi.org/10.1007/s00216-016-9841-0
10. Tassie, L.: Vine identification – knowing what you have (2010)
11. Garcia-Muñoz, S., Muñoz-Organero, G., Andrés, M.T. de, Cabello, F.: Ampelography - an old technique with future uses: the case of minor varieties of Vitis vinifera L. from the Balearic Islands. OENO One **45**, 125–137 (2011). https://doi.org/10.20870/oeno-one.2011.45.3.1497
12. Kamilaris, A., Prenafeta-Boldú, F.X.: Deep learning in agriculture: a survey. Comput. Electron. Agric. **147**, 70–90 (2018). https://doi.org/10.1016/j.compag.2018.02.016
13. Simonyan, K., Zisserman, A.: Very deep convolutional networks for large-scale image recognition. arXiv:1409.1556 [cs] (2014)
14. He, K., Zhang, X., Ren, S., Sun, J.: Deep residual learning for image recognition. arXiv: 1512.03385 [cs] (2015)
15. Szegedy, C., Ioffe, S., Vanhoucke, V., Alemi, A.: Inception-v4, Inception-ResNet and the impact of residual connections on learning. arXiv:1602.07261 [cs] (2016)
16. Chollet, F.: Xception: deep learning with depthwise separable convolutions. arXiv:1610.02357 [cs] (2016)
17. Howard, A.G., et al.: MobileNets: efficient convolutional neural networks for mobile vision applications. arXiv:1704.04861 [cs] (2017)
18. Diário da República: Portaria n.° 383/2017, de 20 de dezembro (2017)
19. Grinblat, G.L., Uzal, L.C., Larese, M.G., Granitto, P.M.: Deep learning for plant identification using vein morphological patterns. Comput. Electron. Agric. **127**, 418–424 (2016). https://doi.org/10.1016/j.compag.2016.07.003

20. Lee, S.H., Chan, C.S., Wilkin, P., Remagnino, P.: Deep-plant: plant identification with convolutional neural networks. In: 2015 IEEE International Conference on Image Processing (ICIP), pp. 452–456 (2015). https://doi.org/10.1109/ICIP.2015.7350839

21. Hall, D., McCool, C., Dayoub, F., Sunderhauf, N., Upcroft, B.: Evaluation of features for leaf classification in challenging conditions. In: 2015 IEEE Winter Conference on Applications of Computer Vision, pp. 797–804 (2015). https://doi.org/10.1109/WACV. 2015.111

22. Reyes, A.K., Caicedo, J.C., Camargo, J.E.: Fine-tuning deep convolutional networks for plant recognition. In: CLEF (Working Notes), vol. 1391, p. 9 (2015)

23. Pound, M.P., et al.: Deep machine learning provides state-of-the-art performance in image-based plant phenotyping. Gigascience **6**, 1–10 (2017). https://doi.org/10.1093/gigascience/ gix083

24. Mortensen, A.K., Dyrmann, M., Karstoft, H., Jørgensen, R.N., Gislum, R.: Semantic segmentation of mixed crops using deep convolutional neural network. In: CIGR-AgEng Conference, Aarhus, Denmark, 26–29 June 2016, Abstracts and Full papers, pp. 1–6 (2016)

25. Zhu, H., Liu, Q., Qi, Y., Huang, X., Jiang, F., Zhang, S.: Plant identification based on very deep convolutional neural networks. Multimed. Tools Appl. **77**, 29779–29797 (2018). https://doi.org/10.1007/s11042-017-5578-9

26. Lee, J.W., Yoon, Y.C.: Fine-grained plant identification using wide and deep learning model 1. In: 2019 International Conference on Platform Technology and Service (PlatCon), pp. 1–5 (2019). https://doi.org/10.1109/PlatCon.2019.8669407

27. Kussul, N., Lavreniuk, M., Skakun, S., Shelestov, A.: Deep learning classification of land cover and crop types using remote sensing data. IEEE Geosci. Remote Sens. Lett. **14**, 778–782 (2017). https://doi.org/10.1109/LGRS.2017.2681128

28. Rußwurm, M., Körner, M.: Multi-temporal land cover classification with sequential recurrent encoders. ISPRS Int. J. Geo-Inf. **7**, 129 (2018). https://doi.org/10.3390/ijgi7040129

29. Sladojevic, S., Arsenovic, M., Anderla, A., Culibrk, D., Stefanovic, D.: Deep neural networks based recognition of plant diseases by leaf image classification. https://www. hindawi.com/journals/cin/2016/3289801/. https://doi.org/10.1155/2016/3289801

30. Mohanty, S.P., Hughes, D.P., Salathé, M.: Using deep learning for image-based plant disease detection. Front Plant Sci. **7**, 1419 (2016). https://doi.org/10.3389/fpls.2016.01419

31. Amara, J., Bouaziz, B., Algergawy, A.: A deep learning-based approach for banana leaf diseases classification. In: BTW (2017)

32. Toda, Y., Okura, F.: How convolutional neural networks diagnose plant disease (2019). https://spj.sciencemag.org/plantphenomics/2019/9237136/.   https://doi.org/10.1155/2019/ 9237136

33. Szegedy, C., et al.: Going deeper with convolutions. arXiv:1409.4842 [cs] (2014)

34. He, K., Zhang, X., Ren, S., Sun, J.: Spatial pyramid pooling in deep convolutional networks for visual recognition. In: Fleet, D., Pajdla, T., Schiele, B., Tuytelaars, T. (eds.) ECCV 2014. LNCS, vol. 8691, pp. 346–361. Springer, Cham (2014). https://doi.org/10.1007/978-3-319-10578-9_23. arXiv:1406.4729 [cs]

35. Szegedy, C., Vanhoucke, V., Ioffe, S., Shlens, J., Wojna, Z.: Rethinking the inception architecture for computer vision. arXiv:1512.00567 [cs] (2015)

36. Sandler, M., Howard, A., Zhu, M., Zhmoginov, A., Chen, L.-C.: MobileNetV2: inverted residuals and linear bottlenecks. arXiv:1801.04381 [cs] (2018)

37. Russakovsky, O., et al.: ImageNet large scale visual recognition challenge. arXiv:1409.0575 [cs] (2014)

38. Huang, G., Liu, Z., van der Maaten, L., Weinberger, K.Q.: Densely Connected Convolutional Networks (2016)

39. Kiefer, J., Wolfowitz, J.: Stochastic estimation of the maximum of a regression function. Ann. Math. Statist. **23**, 462–466 (1952). https://doi.org/10.1214/aoms/1177729392
40. Nesterov, Y.E.: A method for solving the convex programming problem with convergence rate O(1/k^2). Dokl. Akad. Nauk SSSR **269**, 543–547 (1983)
41. Brownlee, J.: Deep learning with python: develop deep learning models on Theano and TensorFlow Using Keras, Melbourne, Australia
42. Tieleman, T., Hinton, G.: Lecture 6.5 - RMSProp: divide the gradient by a running average of its recent magnitude (2012)
43. Kingma, D.P., Ba, J.: Adam: a method for stochastic optimization. arXiv:1412.6980 [cs] (2014)
44. Dozat, T.: Incorporating Nesterov Momentum into Adam (2016)
45. TensorFlow. https://www.tensorflow.org/
46. Welcome — Theano 0.9.0 documentation. http://deeplearning.net/software/theano/
47. Keras Documentation. https://keras.io/
48. Deep Learning Toolbox. https://www.mathworks.com/products/deep-learning.html
49. Caffe|Deep L. Framework. https://caffe.berkeleyvision.org/
50. PyTorch. https://www.pytorch.org
51. Deep Cognition. https://deepcognition.ai/

Artificial Intelligence and Law

Artificial Intelligence and Law

Learning from Monkeys: Authorship Issues Arising from AI Technology

Jacopo Ciani[(⊠)]

Università degli Studi di Torino, 10100 Turin, Italy
jacopo.cianisciolla@unito.it

Abstract. Artificial intelligence is experiencing rapid growth, taking centre stage in R&D investments, policy-making forums and academic literature.

The protection of AI generated artwork under copyright law is only one of many policy questions across a range of issues within the intellectual property domain, considering AI as both object and subject of IP protection. However, it has already sparked debates all over the world for the re-examination of copyright legal framework. This Article wishes to contribute to this debate, addressing two research questions: (a) whether works independently created by artificial intelligence systems are eligible for copyright protection under the existing legal framework and (b) whether copyright is actually the best solution for protecting investments in robot-artists.

Keywords: Artificial intelligence · Machine-generated works of art · Copyright · Authorship · Autonomy

1 Introduction

Artificial intelligence (intelligence exhibited by machines [1], hereinafter only "AI") is experiencing rapid growth and taking centre stage in R&D investments [2], policy-making forums [3] and academic literature [4].

Policy documents as the U.S. Government's Report on Preparing for the future of Artificial Intelligence [5] and the draft report of the European Parliament to the Commission on Civil Law Rules on Robotics [6] surveyed its existing and potential applications, raised unanswered questions for society and public policy and made recommendations to governmental agencies and stakeholders for specific further actions.

Among them, the European Parliament called on the Commission to elaborate criteria for an "*own intellectual creation*" for copyrightable works produced through AI.

The G7 Countries as well, building on the debate initiated by the 2017 G7 ICT Ministerial in Torino, advocated the need for effective and adequate protection and enforcement of intellectual property rights among the principles, which should foster investments and trust in the Next Production Revolution and underpin growth in the global digital economy [7].

Intellectual property law [8] takes into consideration AI both as object or subject of protection. From the first point of view, the European Patent Office (EPO) released —

© Springer Nature Switzerland AG 2019
P. Moura Oliveira et al. (Eds.): EPIA 2019, LNAI 11804, pp. 275–286, 2019.
https://doi.org/10.1007/978-3-030-30241-2_24

for the first time—Guidelines on the patentability of AI and machine learning technologies [9]. Under the second aspect, instead, scholars explored the eligibility of AI-
generated works for different forms of IP protection, such as patent [10, 11], trade
secrecy law [12] and—of course—copyright [13–15].

This Article wishes to contribute to the latter point of debate, addressing two
research questions: (a) whether works independently created by artificial intelligence
systems are eligible for copyright protection under the existing legal framework (par.
Sect. 4) and (b) whether copyright is actually the best solution for protecting investments in robot-artists (par. Sect. 7).

2 The Automated Authorship Issue

Some scholars marked the computer authorship just as a "bad penny of a question"
[16]. They claimed that the underlying problems of assigning authorship of a work to
an "author", who is causally responsible for the work's existence, are more apparent
than real: "Old-fashioned pen-and-paper works raise all the same issues; there is
nothing new under the sun" [17].

On the contrary, it seems to me that the legal ownership over the results of any
inventive or creative activity should be a key issue to any regime based on exclusive
rights [18], therefore also to the copyright protection system [19]. Then, such a debate
very clearly fits within the wider discussion around the need of re-evaluation and
reform of the current copyright system.

Scholars addressing the topic in the past mostly focused either on whether copyright law permits the authorship of legal entities or on the challenges arising from
instances where multiple actors are involved in the creative process [20, 21]. Until
recently, instead, few studies have considered "non-human" authorship.

2.1 AI as a Human-Tool or as a Self-generating Source: A Matter
of Autonomy

When an AI system is employed as a tool for creating a work (so-called "computer-
aided works"), the individual using it will clearly be considered the author. Indeed,
machine-assistance does not disqualify the human agent from being deemed the author.
An example is the copyright treatment of photographs [22].

Yet, today we are in the throes of a technological revolution that may require us to
rethink the interaction between computers and the creative process. Indeed, we are
progressively dealing with agents, rather than simple tools [23]. More and more creative works are, in fact, the result of non-human creative processes, having been
entirely [24] left up to intelligent systems.

That said, to our purposes, it is of fundamental importance to understand the level
of autonomy of a machine, i.e., from the standpoint of the robotic engineer, the robot
ability "to operate in the real-world environment without any form of external control
for extended periods of time" [25]).

It may not be an easy task. Automated systems operate on several different degrees
of automation (i.e. interaction between the man and the machine), according to how

much control is yielded to the human operator. The terms "in the loop", "on the loop" or "out of the loop" are often used to distinguish between such different level of independence. It is even not unusual to find multiple degrees of autonomy depending on the kind of activity carried out by the machine. For instance, an art-creating robot can depend on a human operator for the acquisition of the previous art from which it can learn and be supervised during the manual working phase (for instance when keeping the brush in contact with the canvas). The selection of the right degree of autonomy (also referred to as dependability) may depend on several factors: (a) technological (like choosing the right balance between safety and performance), (b) social (e.g. social resistance by prospected users), (c) legal (inadequacy with respect to the legal system), or (d) ethical. On the latter point, guidance has been recently provided, among others [26], by the High-Level Expert Group on Artificial Intelligence established by the EU Commission, which recommended leaving little scope for AI's autonomy [27].

2.2 Examples of Artificially Intelligent Devices as the True "Authors" of Creative Works

Against this background, empirical evidence suggests that advanced forms of AI are able to generate new artworks, learning from inputs (pieces of art, musics, literary works etc.) provided by programmers and taking independent decisions, in a process akin to humans' reasoning. Racter, an artificial intelligence computer program is the author of randomly generated books based on grammar, syntactical rules and vocabulary provided by the creators of the program [28] (a more recent example is Brutus, developed by Selmer Bringsjord and his collaborators [29]). In other art-related fields, it should be mentioned Aaron, a program autonomously generating drawings and paintings, which was created in the 70s by an art professor and artist [30]. Another case in point is Sony's Flow Machines project, which has successfully created AI-written pop songs (see http://www.flow-machines.com). Other projects have seen AI programs writing poems and local news articles, editing photographs, and composing music [31].

Apparently, such artworks have also a significant financial value. The Portrait of Edmond de Belamy has been sold in auction at Christie's to an anonymous bidder for $435,000 (blowing the expected price of $7,000 out of the water) [32]. It has been created using a generative adversarial network (GAN), trained to seek patterns in a specific dataset and then create copies under the scrutiny of a "discriminator" network which spots the difference between the original and the sample and then checks if they are passable.

All these operations endow the algorithm with a novel sense of agency as it effectively acts in lieu of a human creator and behaves like one.

2.3 Oversimplifying the Way in Which Automated Systems Operate Would Be a Mistake

What is challenging here, before delving into any legal evaluation on computer authorship issues, is to fully perceive to what extent the human element (directly by human-in the-loop interventions or indirectly at the design stage) is present in the "intelligence" demonstrated by the algorithm [33].

In order to understand that and to localise informational control in the human or machine domain, it would be advisable to adopt a taxonomy of various degrees of automation. Such an effort has been already done in the domain of computer-assisted driving. Both the NHTSA or the Society of Automobile Engineers identified 5 levels of automation, between "No-Automation, Level 0", where the system automatically assists the driver to regain lost control of the vehicle and "Full Self-Driving Automation, Level 4", where the driver is not expected to become involved throughout the duration of the trip.

Lacking any indication in this regard, one runs the risk of oversimplifying the way in which automated systems operate, as well as providing unclear, unreliable and incomplete answers to the question of whether non-biologic entities may have autonomous standing under copyright law.

2.4   A Long-Standing Issue Offering Something New

Since traditional pillars of copyright law have been the humankind's central position in the creative universe [34] and the idea that technology represents no more than a tool in the hands of the author, such question brings to the surface serious challenges to the principles of the system.

Despite its recent appearance, the issue is not at all new. Already in 1978 the U.S. National Commission on New Technological Uses of Copyrighted Works (CONTU) addressed it. Its Final Report concluded that the development of an AI capable of independently creating works was *"too speculative to consider"* since *"there is no reasonable basis for considering that a computer in any way contributes authorship to a work produced through its use"* [35].

Today, it is easy to re-consider the situation with the benefit of hindsight and notice that CONTU's conclusions were mistaken [36].

3   The Monkey's Selfies Copyright Dispute

Few judicial rulings address what authorship means, or who is an author. Even fewer laws define authorship.

A valuable lesson in order to answer the proposed question may be given by *Naruto v David John Slater,* a popular dispute where the Northern District of California (no. 15-CV-04324) denied copyright protection to a monkey who authored self-portrait photographs [37].

This case arose out of allegations that Naruto, an Indonesian six-year-old crested macaque, took multiple selfies using Slater's camera. The complaint, filed by two animal-friendly associations, alleged that Slater published a book with the selfies, infringing on Naruto's copyright. The plaintiff alleged that Naruto authored the selfies by "independent, autonomous action" and was entitled to defendant's profit from the infringement of §106 and 501 of the U.S. Copyright Act of 1976. Indeed, the Act has "no definitional limitation" and "author", for the purpose of such legislation, may be anyone who creates an original work of authorship, including animals.

Judge W. H. Orrick, in a well supported and reasoned decision, dismissed the complaint on the grounds that Copyright Act "does not confer standing upon animals like Naruto". Indeed, if Congress and the President intended to extend the concept of authorship to animals, it could and should have said so plainly in the Copyright Act.

Arguments have been adduced in support from *Cetacean Cmty v. Bush* [386 F.3d 1169, 1175 (2004)], where the Ninth Circuit denied that the language of the statute under scrutiny evidenced congressional intent to confer standing on animals. Moreover, the Compendium of U.S. Copyright Offices Practices issued in December 2014 repeatedly refers to "persons" or "human beings" when analyzing authorship. As further detailed in § 313.2, titled "Works That Lack Human Authorship", "to qualify as a work of authorship a work must be created by a human being. Works that do not satisfy this requirement are not copyrightable".

On 20 March 2016, a notice of appeal was filed to the Ninth Circuit (no. 16-15469) Court of Appeals. Even if a settlement agreement between the parties was reached, the court found there were countervailing interests requiring it to fully adjudicate the matter. On April 23, 2018, the Ninth Circuit confirmed the previous ruling.

4   May a Non-human Be an Author?

This ruling, with copyright for animals out of the picture, might be easily applied, at least in the U.S., to artworks made by AI. Indeed, the U.S. Copyright Office Practices at § 313.2 (3d ed. 2014) clearly states that "*the Office will not register works produced by a machine or mere mechanical process that operates randomly or automatically without any creative input or intervention from a human author*".

Notwithstanding that copyright doctrine on authorship may reveal considerable variation in the comparison of common law and civil law systems, most national legal orders appear to agree that an author should be a human being. This is the result of the inquiry carried out by Ginsburg, exploring the concept of authorship in the US, the UK, Canada and Australia, as well as in the civil law countries of France, Belgium and the Netherlands [34].

A closer look at international conventions (par. Sect. 4.1), European Union directives (Sect. 4.2) and also at national copyright systems (Sect. 4.3) enables us to confirm this assumption.

4.1   International Conventions

Despite the number of international conventions in the field of copyright and neighbouring rights protection, the initial ownership of rights has not been subject to systematic international regulation so far.

The Berne Convention for the Protection of Literary and Artistic Works does not define authorship [38], nor provides guidance as to the meaning of the term "author". It just establishes that an author is whoever says he/she is, if his/her "name appears on the work in the usual manner", without clarifying if the person whose name appears must be a human being. Nonetheless, the leading authorities on the Berne Convention have agreed that this may be implicit [39, 40]. Indeed, both Article 6-bis and 7 of the Berne

Convention, making reference to the author's life and death (referring to the term of protection granted to the author), necessarily imply that the author can only be a physical person (similar provisions are contained in Article 23 and 25 of the Italian Copyright Act) [41, 42].

Likewise, both Article 27 of the Universal Declaration of Human Rights and Article 15 of the International Covenant on Economic, Social and Cultural Rights acknowledge to "everyone" "the right to the protection of the moral and material interests resulting from any scientific, literary or artistic production of which he is the author". As clarified by the preamble, "everyone" refers to "all members of the human family".

4.2 EU Directives

Also at European level, Directive 2001/29/EC on the harmonisation of certain aspects of copyright and related rights in the information society does not contain any definition of "author", nor of "copyright holder" and is silent on the legal capacity required in order to exercise the copyright holder's prerogatives. This silence should be interpreted in line with:

(a) Articles 1 to 21 of the Berne Convention: although the EU is not a party to it, it is nevertheless obliged, under Article 1(4) of the WIPO Copyright Treaty, to which it is a party and which Directive 2001/29 is intended to implement, to comply (see, to that effect, judgments of 9 February 2012, Luksan, C 277/10, EU:C:2012:65, paragraph 59 and the case-law cited);
(b) principles and rules already laid down in the previous Directives in force in this area (cf. Recital 20 of Dir. 2001/29/EC). In particular, Recital 13 of Directive 93/98/EEC harmonizing the term of protection of copyright and Article 4 Dir. 96/9/EC on the legal protection of databases both identify as authors respectively "one or more physical persons" or "the natural person or group of natural persons".

The adoption of the Directive 2019/790/EU of 17 April 2019 on copyright and related rights in the Digital Single Market, while includes relevant provision for the development and growth of AI in the European Union (as the mandatory copyright exception for Text and Data Mining under Articles 3 and 4), adds nothing new to this discussion.

Therefore, both international and EU legal framework, as they are currently configured, cannot vest copyright over a machine-generated work.

4.3   The "Intellectual" Link Between the "Work" and the "Author"

Italian Copyright Act has mainly followed the developments of relevant international and European Union law [20].

However, looking at it (as at many other national copyright systems, like the French one), may be interesting since it provides other relevant indications of the features that make one an "author".

Article 6 establishes that "Copyright shall be acquired on the creation of a work that constitutes the particular expression of an intellectual effort". This is usually understood (according to the settled case law of the Court of Justice of the European Union, particularly in its landmark *Infopaq* decision, C-5/08, ECLI:EU:C:2009:465) as meaning that a strong link should exist between authorship and originality assessment. An original work must "bear the imprint of the author's personality" (cf. Italian Supreme Court, 12 January 2018, no. 658).

From this perspective, the lack of the wilful intention to impress the stamp of its own personality on its artistic effort might be an argument for excluding the non-human creative activity from copyright protection. Indeed, there is large consensus that today's AI is "weak": it can act intelligently, but can not understand the true meaning of what it says or does [43].

4.4 AI's Lack of Legal Personhood

Nonetheless, AI's lack of wilful intention does not appear to be a decisive argument.

Most authors agree that the willingness of the creative act is not required for a proper attribution of authorship [41]. The awarding of the author's quality to minors and incapacitated persons may confirm this [44].

Echoing Teubner [45], nothing would prevent from creating legal actors (in this case copyright owners) by social attribution, without the need to possess any ontological human properties, such as reflexive capacities or empathy.

At this stage, however, AI and robots may be conceived as agents in contract and business law [46]. They may be also included in the class of morally accountable agents [47, 48], but they can in no way be treated as legal persons, in spite of the prevailing confusion on the legal notions of agency and personhood [46].

This certainly helps answering our first opening question. Awarding intelligent agents with copyright ownership is not and will not be a viable solution as long as the EU Parliament's heavy criticised proposal [6] for the introduction of a specific legal status for robots will remain just a proposal.

Therefore, the authorship issue can not be solved without a legislative intervention aimed at introducing an autonomous and specific legal standing for "e-persons" (issue tracing back in the legal literature to the 1980s [49, 50]). Prior to this development, any other subsequent question, like whether an AI generated artwork could fulfil the copyright legal requirements, appears to be premature.

5 Positive Legal Provisions Governing Computer-Generated Artworks

If and as long as AI remains without any legal standing, the only other question which makes sense at this stage is to determine who should be the author of a machine-generated artwork.

In the Naruto case, there is no trace of any answer to this issue: Judge Orrick never said whether Slater was entitled to copyright in the selfies, in its quality of owner of the camera.

Some guidance may be derived looking at a few common law jurisdictions.

U.K. Copyright, Designs and Patents Act, 1988 [§ 9(3)], Irish Copyright and Related Rights Act No. 28/2000 [§2(1)] and New Zealand's Copyright Act of 1994 (§ 2) vest copyright in works "generated by a computer in circumstances such that there is no human author" in "the person by whom the arrangements necessary for the creation of the work are undertaken". §12(3) of the UK 1988 Act also refers to the term of protection for the computer generated work as lasting for 70 years from the end of the year of creation.

However, there are serious doubts whether these provisions (occurred when today's advancements in automated creation were far from being foreseeable) could be interpreted as covering situations where the end work is created autonomously (indeed with humans not being active at all). Moreover, it is debated what "arrangements" actually means, who made them (the person who built the core AI system, or the person who trained it?), how proximate the person and their "arrangements" must be to the creation of the work and what does it happen if multiple contributors are involved in the development of the art-generating system. Much will depend on how a court would interpret this wording [22].

What we are sure of is that these provisions do not leave any room for the AI itself to be considered as an author for the purposes of copyright law. Conversely, they create a legal fiction of authorship by means of which copyright vests as a matter of law in a party who is not the author-in-fact.

6 Vesting Copyright in Persons Other Than Authors?

The common law system has no objections to the attribution of copyright to persons other than the author. For instance, it allows copyright law to protect the interest of professionals other than the author, such as in the case of phonograms producers or broadcasters [20, 44].

The latin-germanic copyright system struggles to cope with this tendency, since its fundamental structures rest heavily on the "intellectual" link. Thus, recognising authorship in favour of AI systems could mean disrupting the traditional notion of authorship [34, 38].

Many authors argue that this traditional "romantic" [51] view of copyright has been long abandoned [52]. At least since Dir. 2001/29, European copyright law shifted its attention towards protecting producers, investors and all those who contribute to the creation of the work in economic and financial terms rather than from the creative point of view [19, 53].

This change of perspective would be coherent with the information society's environment, characterised both by a growing dissociation between whoever engages in the creative effort and who else provides its economic funding and by the minor role played by the author's personality in the creative process.

The so-called "multiplayer model", describing the multiple stakeholders who are involved in the process through which artworks are created by AI systems (including software programmers, data and feedback suppliers, trainers, system owners and operators, employers, etc.), shows how the efforts of traditional copyright law to identify a single author today appears inadequate and anachronistic [54].

6.1 The Work Made for Hire Doctrine as a Fitting Legal Ground for Bypassing the Author-in-Fact

The legal fictions of granting exclusive rights to subjects other than the "author" already exist under copyright law. A well established example is the "work-for-hire" doctrine, where the employer (or other persons for whom the work was prepared) is "taken to be" the copyright holder over the economic exploitation of the work made for hire.

This doctrine already works for vesting rights of economic utilisation in the publishers of collective works and in the producers of cinematographic works, even if the authorship should belong to the editor or to the person who has organised the production.

Prima facie, it looks like a fitting framework within which to situate the problem of AI authorship. Indeed, it represents an existing mechanism for directly vesting copyright in a legal person who is not the author-in-fact [55]. To machine-generated works it would be applied for the same cultural reason behind its original introduction: holding out the prospect of economic reward as an incentive [56] to whom is directly concerned with investing in artistic works. Giving exclusive rights to AI programmers and owners would work as an incentive to the future development of the AI industry.

7 A Conclusion: A Neighbouring Right or a *Sui Generis* Right-Type of Protection for AI-Generated Artworks

This *rationale* does not coincide with that of copyright law. Indeed, the *rationale* for granting copyright is rewarding authorship. However, authorship is not a central element when dealing with AI-generated artworks. Instead, the right *rationale* for giving exclusive rights on them seems rather to be the protection of investments.

This shows that copyright actually is not the best suited legal framework where finding protection for AI-generated artworks.

Other legal tools, commons to the EU juridical tradition, may be more fit to the purpose. In particular, EU Member States should look at two past experiences: (a) the *sui generis* right on database protection and (b) the neighbouring rights in favour of producers and broadcasters [57].

Both regimes have been used to protect different kinds of investments. Therefore, the introduction of a neighbouring right-type of protection (or a *sui generis* one) in AI-created works would take better accounts of this kind of creativity, being more consistent with past policies and regulatory choices made by the Member States in this field, rather than adapting copyright features to the specific needs of AI [8].

This solution would be also coherent with Recital 5 Dir. 2001/29/EC, when Member States recognised that "no new concepts for the protection of intellectual property are needed, the current law on copyright and related rights should be adapted and supplemented to respond adequately to economic realities".

Such a new right should be shaped in full awareness of the existing and potential state of AI, after a careful comprehension of the various degrees of automation that may characterize the domain of computer-generated creativity (cf. par. Sect. 2.3).

References

1. Pagallo, U.: Intelligenza artificiale e diritto. Linee guida per un oculato intervento normativo. Sistemi Intelligenti **3**, 614 (2017)
2. WIPO, Technology Trends 2019: Artificial Intelligence, Geneva (2019)
3. WEF, World Economic Forum Annual Meeting 2017 System Initiatives Programme (2017). www3.weforum.org/docs/Media/AM17/AM17_System_Initiatives.pdf. Accessed 13 Apr 2019
4. Pagallo, U., Corrales, M., Fenwick, M., Forgò, N.: The rise of robotics & AI: technological advances & normative dilemmas. In: Corrales, M., Fenwick, M., Forgò, N. (eds.) Robotics, AI Future of Law. PLBI, pp. 1–13. Springer, Singapore (2018). https://doi.org/10.1007/978-981-13-2874-9_1
5. Executive Office of the President of the United States, Preparing for the future of artificial intelligence, Office of Science and Technology Policy (2016)
6. Nevejans, N.: European Civil Law Rules in Robotics, Study for the JURI Committee commissioned, supervised and published by the Policy Department for Citizens' Rights and Constitutional Affairs, PE 571.379 (2016), http://www.europarl.europa.eu/committees/fr/supporting-analyses-search.html. Accessed 13 Apr 2019
7. G7 ICT and Industry Ministers' Declaration, Making the next production revolution inclusive, open and secure, Torino, 25–26 September 2017, para 12j (2017)
8. Leroux, C., Labruto, R. (eds.): Suggestion for a Green Paper on Legal Issues in Robotics (2012). https://www.unipv-lawtech.eu/files/euRobotics-legal-issues-in-robotics-DRAFT_6j6ryjyp.pdf. Accessed 13 Aug 2019
9. EPO, Guidelines for Examination, Part G – Patentability, 3.3 Mathematical methods, 3.3.1 Artificial intelligence and machine learning. https://www.epo.org/law-practice/legal-texts/html/guidelines2018/e/g_ii_3_3_1.htm. Accessed 13 Apr 2019
10. Abbott, R.: I think, therefore I invent: creative computers and the future of patent law. Boston Coll. L. Rev. **57**, 1079–1080 (2016)
11. Samore, W.: Artificial intelligence and the patent system: can a new tool render a once patentable idea obvious? Syracuse Sci. Tech. L. Rep. **29**, 113 (2013)
12. Abbott, R.: Artificial intelligence, big data and intellectual property: protecting computer-generated works in the United Kingdom. In: Aplin, T. (ed.) Research Handbook on Intellectual Property and Digital Technologies. Edward Elgar (forthcoming)
13. Schafer, B., Komuves, D., Zatarain, J.M.N., Diver, L.: A fourth law of robotics? Copyright and the law and ethics of machine co-production. Artif. Intell. L. **23**(3), 217–240 (2015)
14. Clifford, R.D.: Intellectual property in the era of the creative computer program: will the true creator please stand up. Tul. L. Rev. **71**, 1675, 1685–1686, 1694–1695 (1996)
15. Farr, E.H.: Copyrightability of computer-created works. Rutgers Comput. Tech. L. J. **15**, 63–79 (1989)
16. Bridy, A.: Coding creativity: copyright and the artificially intelligent author. Stan. Tech. L. Rev. **5**(1), 52 (2012)
17. Grimmelmann, J.: There's no such thing as a computer-authored work—and it's a good thing, too. Colum. J. L. Arts **39**, 403 (2016)
18. Ubertazzi, L.C.: Profili soggettivi del brevetto, vol. 2. Giuffrè, Milano (1985)
19. Gioia, F.: I soggetti dei diritti, AIDA, vol. 80 (2002)
20. Ubertazzi, L.C.: I diritti d'autore e connessi. Scritti, II ed., Quaderni di AIDA, no. 5, pp. 21–34. Giuffrè, Milano (2003)
21. VerSteeg, R.: Defining "author" for purposes of copyright. Am. U. L. Rev. **45**, 1323 (1996)
22. Lambert, P.: Computer generated works and copyright: selfies, traps, robots, AI and machine learning. Eur. Intellect. Prop. Rev. **39**(1), 14 (2017)

23. Pagallo, U.: The Laws of Robot: Crimes, Contracts, and Torts. Law, Governance and Technology Series, vol. 10. Springer, Dordrecht (2013). https://doi.org/10.1007/978-94-007-6564-1

24. Pagallo, U.: Even angels need the rules: AI, roboethics, and the law. In ECAI 2016 22nd European Conference on Artificial Intelligence, The Hague, The Netherlands, 29 August–2 September 2016, Proceedings, p. 209. IOS Press (2016)

25. Lin, P., Abney, K., Bekey, G.: Robot ethics: mapping the issues for a mechanized world. Artif. Intell. **175**, 5–6 (2011)

26. Floridi, L., et al.: AI4People – an ethical framework for a good AI society: opportunities, risks, principles, and recommendations. Minds Mach. **28**(4), 689–707, 698 (2018). https://link.springer.com/article/10.1007%2Fs11023-018-9482-5. Accessed 13 Apr 2019

27. High-Level Expert Group on Artificial Intelligence, Ethics Guidelines for Trustworthy AI, 12 (2019). https://ec.europa.eu/digital-single-market/en/news/ethics-guidelines-trustworthy-ai. Accessed 13 Apr 2019

28. Butler, T.: Can a computer be an author? Copyright aspects of artificial intelligence. Comm/Ent L.S, **4**, 707–715 (1981)

29. Levy, D.: Robots Unlimited: Life in a Virtual Age, 160 et seq. Taylor & Francis (2005)

30. Boden, M.: The Creative Mind: Myths and Mechanisms, 159 et seq. Routledge, London (2004)

31. De Cock Buning, M.: Artificial Intelligence and the creative industry: new challenges for the EU paradigm for art and technology by autonomous creation. In: Barfield, W., Pagallo, U. (eds.) Research Handbook on the Law of Artificial Intelligence, p. 511, 515. Edward Elgar, Camberley (2018)

32. Jee, C.: A controversial artwork created by AI has hauled in $435,000 at auction, October 26 2018. MIT Technol. Rev. https://www.technologyreview.com/the-download/612348/a-controversial-artwork-created-by-ai-has-hauled-in-435000-at-auction/. Accessed 13 Apr 2019

33. Karanasiou, A.P., Pinotsis, D.A.: Towards a legal definition of machine intelligence: the argument for artificial personhood in the age of deep learning. In: Proceedings of ICAIL 2017, London, UK (2017)

34. Ginsburg, J.C.: The concept of authorship in comparative copyright law. DePaul L. Rev. **52**, 1063 (2003)

35. National Commission on New Technological Uses of Copyrighted Works (CONTU). Final report on the national commission on new technological uses of copyrighted works. Computer L. J. **3**, 53 (1981). http://repository.jmls.edu/jitpl/vol3/iss1/3. Accessed 20 June 2019

36. Miller, A.R.: Copyright protection for computer programs, databases, and computer-generated works: is anything new since CONTU? Harv. L. Rev. **977**, 1056–1072 (1993)

37. O'Connell, A.: Monkeys do not have standing under US Copyright Act. J. Intellect. Prop. L. Pract. **13**(8), 607–608 (2018)

38. Ricketson, S.: Reflections on authorship and the meaning of a "work" in Australian and Singapore copyright law. Sing. Acad. Law J. **24**, 792, 820 (2012)

39. Ricketson, S.: People or machines? The Berne Convention and the changing concept of authorship. Colum. VLA J. L. Arts **16**, 1 (1991)

40. Dietz, A.: The concept of authorship under the Berne Convention. RIDA **155**, 3 (1993)

41. De Sanctis, V.M.: I Soggetti del Diritto D'autore, vol. 19. Giuffrè, Milano (2000)

42. Kerever, A.: La determinazione dell'autore dell'opera, Dir. aut., 4 (1992)

43. Lim, A.: Robots aren't as smart as you think. MIT Technol. Rev. (2017). https://www.technologyreview.com/s/609223/robots-arent-as-smart-as-you-think/. Accessed 13 Apr 2019

44. Greco, P., Vercellone, P.: I diritti sulle opere dell'ingegno. In: Vassalli, F. (ed.) Trattato di Diritto Civile, vol. IX, no. 3, p. 213. UTET, Torino (1974)
45. Teubner, G.: Rights of non humans? Electronic agents and animals as new actors in politics and law. J. Law Soc. **33**(4), 497–521 (2006)
46. Pagallo, U.: Apples, oranges, robots: four misunderstandings in today's debate on the legal status of AI systems. Phil. Trans. R. Soc. **A376**, 20180168 (2018). http://dx.doi.org/10.1098/rsta.2018.0168. Accessed 20 June 2019
47. Durante, M.: Ethics, Law and the Politics of Information: A Guide to the Philosophy of Luciano Floridi. The International Library of Ethics, Law and Technology, vol. 18, p. 224. Springer, Amsterdam (2017). https://doi.org/10.1007/978-94-024-1150-8
48. Pagallo, U.: What robots want: autonomous machines, codes and new frontiers of legal responsibility. In: Hildebrandt, M., Gaakeer, J. (eds.) Human Law and Computer Law: Comparative Perspectives. IUSGENT, vol. 25, pp. 47–65. Springer, Dordrecht (2013). https://doi.org/10.1007/978-94-007-6314-2_3
49. Lehman-Wilzig, S.N.: Frankenstein unbound: towards a legal definition of artificial intelligence. Futures **13**(6), 442 (1981)
50. Solum, L.B.: Legal personhood for artificial intelligences. N. C. Law Rev. **70**, 1231 (1992)
51. Litman, J.: The public domain. Emory L. J. **39**, 965–1023 (1990)
52. Durham, A.L.: Copyright and information theory: toward an alternative model of authorship. BYU L. Rev. **69**, 99 (2004)
53. Benabou, V.-L.: Droit d'auteur, droits voisins et droit communautaire, Bruylant, Bruxelles, vol. 316 (1997)
54. Yanisky-Ravid, S., Liu, X.: When artificial intelligence systems produce inventions: the 3A era and an alternative model for patent law. Cardozo Law Rev. **39**, 2215 (2018)
55. Hristov, K.: Artificial intelligence and the copyright dilemma. IDEA **57**(3), 431 (2017)
56. Cubert, J.A., Bone, R.G.A.: The law of intellectual property created by artificial intelligence In: Barfield, W., Pagallo, U. (eds.) Research Handbook on the Law of Artificial Intelligence, vol. 411. Edward Elgar, Camberley (2018)
57. Ramalho, A.: Will robots rule the (artistic) world? A proposed model for the legal status of creations by artificial intelligence systems. J. Internet L. **21**(1), 1–25 (2017)

Legal Implications of Autonomous Vehicles: What We Know So Far and What's Left to Work On

Beatriz Assunção Ribeiro[1(✉)], Hélder Coelho[2],
Ana Elisabete Ferreira[3], and João Branquinho[4]

[1] Cognitive Science, University of Lisbon, Lisbon, Portugal
beatriz.smar@gmail.com
[2] Computation Department, University of Lisbon, Lisbon, Portugal
[3] Law, University of Coimbra, Coimbra, Portugal
[4] Philosophy Department, University of Lisbon, Lisbon, Portugal

Abstract. Autonomous Vehicles (AVs), from autonomy level 3 to 5 are expected to enter the EU market within a year and our infrastructures, as well as legal and social systems are hardly prepared to deal with this technology, which continues to advance rapidly right in front of us. The main purpose of this article is to critically analyse, from a cognitive science point of view, merging AI, philosophy and law, what has been done in this domain and what else requires immediate attention in order to allow AVs to perform a safe and uneventful entry in our society.

1 Introduction

AVs from autonomy level 3 to 5 (SAE International nomenclature) are expected to enter the EU market by 2020 (European Parliament News, 14, January, 2019), meaning that in less than a year this technology will assume, progressively, a fair share of the portion of the vehicles in the road. While some debate has been shed on the applicable legal system in the past few years, there's no doubt that determining a concrete legal regime is an urgent need (Fig. 1).

Though AVs are being tested intensively and extensively (by about 46 companies, which include Tesla, Alphabet, Amazon, Apple and Audi to name a few) there's still an undoubtedly large amount of work to be done. Until 2016, Google's AV test fleet had driven almost 2 million miles (Dwoskin and Fung 2016) which looks like a massive quantity of miles driven. But here's the trick: an AV might drive more than 3 million kilometres and still not be perfect while driving. On the other hand, humans grow up in the middle of other humans and have been confronted with behaviours that grow more familiar every day. Human's also deal with cars driving around the city, play with little toys that resemble cars, watch movies and sports related to vehicles throughout their life. Consequently, by the time a human being must take his driver's licence, though he's learning something new, a lot of those things seem quite natural, because driving simply joins two things which they know a lot about.

© Springer Nature Switzerland AG 2019
P. Moura Oliveira et al. (Eds.): EPIA 2019, LNAI 11804, pp. 287–298, 2019.
https://doi.org/10.1007/978-3-030-30241-2_25

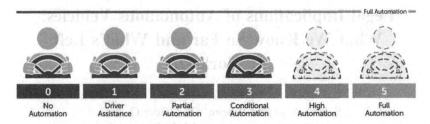

Fig. 1. Types of AVs and task distribution between human and AV (https://cleantechnica.com/2017/12/02/autonomous-driving-levels-0-5-implications/)

Humans are also able to learn from other people's mistakes, meaning they do not need to enrol other drivers to learn for that purpose, unlike AVs (Kalra 2017). Not only AVs need flawless technology, but also have no connection to the human context. In other words, while 2 million miles might look like a good number, it probably isn't.

In fact, a 2017 study using the CalTech Pedestrian Detection Benchmark data (video recorded from a vehicle's perspective) suggests a tenfold improvement in this technology is needed to replicate human performance (Zhang et al. 2018).

No discredit is meant at this point: this work has been done in a wide variety of everyday driving situations and is a truly significant and impressive achievement. However, making them work well enough to achieve acceptable safety levels will take another significant set of achievements. For example, if we consider the goal of making fully autonomous cars as safe as an aircraft, it would require a safety level of about 1 billion operating hours per catastrophic event (Koopman and Wagner 2017).

As a solution, Tesla created a *shadow mode*. In this mode, the system gathers sensor data and makes driving decisions just as if it was driving the vehicle, though no action is executed. The human driver maintains control of the vehicle and the simulated decisions of the shadow autonomous system are compared with the executed decisions of the driver in order to learn while the human is driving (Kalra 2017).

Facing the scenario where no legal rules exist to determine liability in the case of an accident with an AV, we will be forced to reach out for courts in every single event caused by an AV in order to know, casuistically, who should be accountable for the accident. This is not a viable solution. Not only the amount of legal cases would increase with the rising of AVs, but also because the intricacy of this technology would make it difficult to apply the known liability systems to each situation, especially considering the fact that currently every type of AV has a different computational architecture. Additionally, not every company shares their AVs architectures' structure as it may constitute a commercial advantage (Katrakazas 2015), which adds up to the complexity of the case. In the meantime, AVs brought us already serious situations when it comes to public security, namely the Tesla car that ran over a pedestrian in USA, last year in March, causing her death.

2 What We Know So Far

Regardless the absence of concrete legal rules in the domain, the EU has shown that is very much aware of the current issues. An example is the last report on the matter, *A Common EU Approach to Liability Rules* where the strong and weak points of each system are discussed and the elements that need further clarification are listed, including under the coverage of the Product Liability Directive (PDL).

It has been argued (Boulangé and Jaggie 2014) that, in the case of robots, the first step to define a legal system is to determine its *status*: define, exactly, what it is, and then confront this *status* with the available legal options. Pagallo (2013) did a great work on understanding the main traits of each type of robot that is planned in the near future, in his book *The Laws of Robots: Crimes, Contracts, and Torts.*

Globally, the author divides the possibilities into three categories: (1) legal person, (2) proper agent and (3) source of damage. Wandering down into each category, what it means, in practice, is that we must check whether a given robot shares enough attributes with human beings, therefore granting it something analogous to legal personality (1). If it has much more similarities, meaning more features in common, with the concept of thing, thus being considered a mere object, then the answer is to treat it as such (3). What can also happen is the robot not being completely alike to any of those categories and yet share some attributes with each one. We have, then, a proper agent (2), regardless of the legal terms we might want to apply to it.

Though never explaining why, the EU does not consider the option of guaranteeing legal personality to the AV, nor creating a distinct legal system, as the AV might represent a proper agent. This means the EU regards the AV as a mere object. In the light of this view (the AV as a source of damage), what is proposed in *A Common EU Approach to Liability Rules,* is an adaptation of the existent legal systems.

What adaptations does exactly the EU propose? First, a clarification of the concept of defective product used in the Product Liability Directive (PLD). The AVs are complex machines, and it is necessary to draw the line between what is a defective mechanism or software and what are conditions of the road or consequences of a bad weather. This one element that will help us to conclude if the failure is the manufacturer's responsibility, or the software developer or other party's fault.

What we also know is that the civil regime of subjective responsibility, used in some European Countries, which places the guilt on the driver, cannot be used because they won't, quite simply, make sense. This legal system assumes that the driver has, at the very least, some minimum degree of control over the driving process, something that, eventually, will no longer occur.

Finally, by far the most debated question is related with ethical programming. Though some authors argue that AVs won't need ethical rules, others and public in general seem to agree that there's a high probability that AVs will need it. Some of the reasons argued by Goodall (2014), include the unpredictability of human behaviour (a child that suddenly crossed the street to get his toy) and the unknown consequences that may arise from the commercialization of AVs in general.

Despite of the complications that arise from the direct application of the PLD, it will most likely be the chosen as the legal framework, not only because it does not require new legislation but instead a simple adaptation of an existent law, but also because it states rules that are already implanted in each state member. It's important to remember that implementation is a major difficulty when it comes to European law. In fact, The European Commission has been analysing the PLD and, as a follow-up, it will issue an interpretative guidance clarifying important concepts in the directive including in the light of technological developments which is indeed a big step in the field.

These clarifications by the EU are imminent and represent a massive effort to prepare our society for AVs. Nevertheless, we are still very much unprepared. The next part of the article sums up a few points that still need immediate attention in order for the AVs to perform a soft entry in our society.

3 What's Left to Work On

While reviewing the literature, we can summarise those things in three major categories: questions connected to public acceptance, questions related to safety (which include object detection, AV registration and titling, handover process and external conditions) and, finally, queries that concern regulatory gaps. Each of this categories will be reviewed from this point on.

3.1 Public Acceptance

When we have a new product but somewhat conventional, in the sense that it is not life changing, there's a clear method to be followed if that product is to be on the market. The entities involved in the production of this item (manufacturers or retailers) will carry out some market research so they can have an idea of the hypothetical disposition of the public to buy this new product.

Technology, on the other hand, follows a less uniformed path when it comes to implementation, since the technology which their complex structure depends on might evolve at different rates (Flynn 2007). For instance, AVs have been discussed publicly for more than ten years now, since the first Darpa Challenge in 2004, creating public debate and a wide spectrum of opinions.

While for some technologies, a simple market research might suffice to analyse public acceptance of a certain technology, others may require greater citizen consultation (Flynn 2007). This is, without a doubt, the case of AVs.

This is one of the biggest challenges the technology faces. While in 2016 the majority of European citizens (58%) would take a ride on an AV, this rate seems to have dropped since the latest accidents in the USA (European Commission 2018). We live in the world of social media, and if someone films an Uber's AV hitting trash cans on the road while delivering its order, because it simply did not detected them, the video rapidly goes viral, contributing to the opinion that AVs are still not good enough.

Most surveys that took place in 2018 show precisely this, namely the CARiD Survey, where 53% of respondents said they would feel somewhat or very unsafe riding in an AV (Casey 2018).

When it comes to regulators and developers, it seems that those same accidents have not gone under-appreciated by them. In fact, 81% of regulators said that continued efforts to develop and plan safety standards for experimental testing are necessary. The polls also concluded that executives from the tech and auto industries, as well as regulators, believe consumer perceptions are the top impediment to industry expansion (Perkins Coie's Survey 2019). This shows that, presently, only the highest safety and security standards will suffice, to gain societal acceptance (European Commission 2018).

Finally, in this regard, it's obvious that AVs will at least need to make sure that the occupants feel the vehicle's behaviour is safe (Koopman and Wagner 2017). This concerns quality and safety assurances, which is why safety is the second item on this article.

3.2 Safety

Object Detection. While it's appropriate to say that AVs can perform better than human drivers (Kalra 2017), because of better decision-making (e.g., more-accurate planning of driving manoeuvres), and execution (e.g., faster and more-precise control of steering), it's also true that humans still have a lot of tools that AVs lack.

The foundation of AV technology is effective detection. While no consensus has been achieved among manufacturers as to which of the many available classes of sensors perform best, many technologies and methods have been tested. The most common and effective combination is the utilisation of cameras (VLC), LiDAR and radar. Current state-of-the-art detection technologies vary widely in their potential to detect and avoid fatal collisions with pedestrians, from less than 30% (VLC alone) to over 90% (VLC+LiDAR+radar) of preventable fatalities (Combs et al. 2019). Needless to say, those rates correspond to testing in relatively controlled environment.

The combination of these technologies is essential since each one has weak points that need to be compensated by the others. For instance, VLC struggles to collect image data from dusk to dawn, and during adverse weather, showing considerate difficulties if confronted with a wet road. It's also ineffective to spot pedestrians on busy backgrounds and if travelling at high speeds (Jermakian and Zuby 2011; Zhang et al. 2017).

Although LiDAR may suppress the difficulties shown by the VLC during the night when roughly three quarters of pedestrian fatalities occur (LeVine 2017), it fails with non-grounded objects (Zhang et al. 2016) and it is unsuccessful during adverse weather, which leaves us solely with the radar in the event of rain. This latter is ineffective, for example, when pedestrians are stationary before impact (Zhang et al. 2017).

Additionally, there are a lot of *unknown unknowns* that might show, at any time. For example, a LiDAR-equipped AV prototype, by some reason, failed repeatedly to detect kangaroos on Australian roads. Though it might appear to be a detail, it leaves out the question of whether AVs are ready to recognise human beings if they do not behave in a convenient way, namely if a kid is hopping around (Deahl 2017).

In fact, pedestrians are, *per se*, an object hard to detect. Human beings can have a wide range of physical characteristics and appear in a variety of environments with different backgrounds, obstacles, and weather conditions, increasing the difficulty of being detected. Furthermore, human behaviour is as unpredictable as it can be, considering the unreasonable conduct many of us show in the street, such as crossing a red light, cross the road without looking or simply pranking (Koopman and Wagner 2017). Sensors can fail to identify pedestrians even in ideal conditions, especially when those pedestrians are small, too far or too close, or partially occluded by nearby objects (Dollar et al. 2012). Finally, cultural and regional (e.g. rural vs urban areas) differences in pedestrian and cyclists must be taken into consideration (Merat 2016).

AV Registration and Titling. Registration of AVs in an unquestionable safety measure. Level 3–5 AVs must be identified in the vehicle's title and registration, and this must include, specifically, the situations in which they are allowed to be operated without a driver and in which cases they are not. In this sense, strict procedures must be established to allow this registration and, above all, to guarantee it is always updated to the actual status of the AV. In other words, if the AV changed in some way, either because the software changed or simply because the AV went to the check-up, that must be included in this registration (Hedlung 2017).

There's also the question of knowing whether the AV occupant must have a licence to drive or not. Level 5 AVs won't probably require this licence, since they do not require human intervention in any case. Now, in the case of level 2–4 AVs, the occupant must have his licence, considering that he might be called to act in a specific situation (Hedlung 2017).

Unconstrained adaptation such as real time learning means that an AV can have different behaviour over time, including a different conduct than what was displayed during testing and certification (Rupp and King 2010). Considering the certification process as it is today it's nearly impossible to take into account all the behaviours the AV may have in the future. Therefore, we are merely certifying what is done in front of the certification entity but not this unknown future behaviour. With this said, this certification process needs to be reviewed (Koopman and Wagner 2017).

This is, however, the exact same process we use in order to get a licence. In fact, what one does in the driving exam does not prove that the person will be a safe driver (Kalra 2017). At the same time, we cannot compare AVs to a species with millions of years of evolution inserted in a community that designed and developed cars. We are intuitively prepared to act like a human being while an artificial species which has approximately 50 years of evolution knows nothing intuitively about the human world.

After the commercialisation and daily usage of AVs, each company will have certain statistical data and values associated to the car (Kalra and Paddock 2017), which makes everything easier, but this does not solve the problem of pre-market testing.

Handover. Regardless of what action we must perform, there's always some delay in human reaction. This delay gains specific relevance in the case of AVs, considering that some levels of autonomy, namely levels 3 and 4, imply changes of power in the driving process. So far, what studies have shown is that drivers experience a delay in regaining effective control following handover from the system (Morgan et al. 2016). More precisely, the VENTURER Trial 1 experiments (Axa, VENTURER Insurance and Legal Report 2017/18) found a time lag of three seconds between the warning and the effective takeover of the steering wheel, in a vehicle that was moving approximately at just 30 km/h. This delay may increase with speed, adverse weather or even by the simple fact that it is unexpected.

This is no surprise, in fact. Though autopilot did decrease the number of plane crashes, it also became one major cause for accidents, precisely because human beings were not made to simply sit, watch and wait for something to happen. Even the most observant human driver's attention will begin to wander off. When distracted, and then forced to act, because the system requires attention, human reaction time increases. In other words, when pilots have to regain power of the plane, they are less prepared to do so, since they were distracted before, with worse decision making than if they were simply focused on the task from the first moment (Gouraud 2017).

Therefore, handover in AVs must be implemented with caution. Not only because the responsibilities issues that arise from this mechanism (handover begs the question of knowing where human responsibility ends and insurance responsibility starts - Axa, VENTURER Insurance and Legal Report 2017/18), but also because someone might get injured in this time gap when no entity is actually in control of the wheel.

Despite requiring a very precise mechanism, one suggested approach in order to guarantee the absence of injured parties in the machine-human transition, is to provide an emergency or contingency plan that allows the human driver, that was distracted, to gain enough awareness of the context in order to be able to take over the wheel. This emergency plan could be, for instance, pull the AV to the side of the road (Koopman and Wagner 2017).

External Conditions. Even though object detection and prediction capacity of AVs might evolve to an optimum point, society will be forced to adapt the roads in order to make AVs' job easier. We must not only take into consideration the onboard technology but also the environment in which it is deployed (Oliver et al. 2018), since both factors will, eventually, create a synergetic influence, which will end up by bringing consequences to us.

In this sense, a more standardised environment and smart infrastructures are required (Oliver et al. 2018), namely higher roadway maintenance standards, such as clearer line painting and special traffic signals (Lawson 2018).

An also intriguing challenge is law compliance (Hedlung 2017). Human beings are provided with an intuitive system that allows them to break rules under some plausible justification. Day-to-day, on the road, this capacity allows traffic to flow normally. AVs, however, are designed to strictly follow the rules. This may not be a problem when the only type of cars in the street are AVs but until then this might pose an interesting conflict. For example, it is illegal to cross a double centre line, but if a vehicle on a two-lane road is parked in the travel lane and the road is clear ahead, common sense suggests that a car may cross the double line and pass the stopped vehicle (NHTSA 2016).

The key question, in this matter, is not only if and when will self-driving cars be ready for our roads, but rather if our roads will be ready for self-driving cars (Oliver et al. 2018).

3.3 Regulatory Gaps

Regulation is a sensitive matter in the sense that premature regulation might refrain technological development.

The classic example is the kind of regulation that requires AVs to be nearly perfect before they are allowed on the roads which could in turn prevent them from achieving required perfection. This would deny AVs the driving experience necessary to reach that level of performance (Kalra 2017). At the same time, safety is in jeopardy. Therefore, it is urgent to find balance in this process.

One previously mentioned regulatory gap is the handover process. In this sense, Axa Insurance and Legal Report describes a set of questions yet to be answered: (1) if the handover is unpredicted as a result of failures of system, should insurers seek rights of recovery against manufacturers? (2) If we face a situation where the driver is not able to take back control or didn't execute it properly, does the responsibility lie with the driver or with the manufacturer as a result of the failure of the system causing the unpredicted handover? (3) what is a 'reasonable' length of time for handover (Axa, VENTURER Insurance and Legal Report 2017/18)?

It is clear that well defined standards, justified by rigorous empirically-obtained data around how human drivers interact with automated driving systems for the purposes of passing control between an autonomous driving system and a human driver, are necessary. The justification for this assumption is the fact that the concept of negligence is usually outlined through the (hardly objective) notion of the reasonable driver (Axa, VENTURER Insurance and Legal Report 2017/18). In this sense what the medium driver would do in a specific context defines, *a contrario*, what negligence action is under that same circumstance. In other words, every action which does not constitute a reasonable action in terms of the medium driver, is a negligent conduct (unless we're under other kind of conditions that exclude guilt). Without those studies, it will be impossible to understand what the reasonable driver standard is, ultimately blocking the ascription of responsibility.

As previously mentioned, efforts are taking place in order to define whether software is a product, what exactly means a defective software and to what extent should we ascribe responsibilities to companies who develop their prototypes. In fact, with the adaptation of the PLD, we have one third of the problem solved. The other two thirds still correspond to open questions regarding the legal system that should be applied when the accident was not due to manufacturing defect but instead other conditions, such as driver distraction in handover.

The PLD, as it is today, determines that the burden of proof lies on the injured party. This is a major concern, since we're forcing the party that knows less about the technicalities of the product to prove that it didn't work as promised. The difficulties increase considerably if we think about all the errors or defects that have an unknown origin. Inversion of the burden of proof is, therefore, required. Regardless of how hard it might be to prove the existence or absence of the defect, it will always be easier and less expensive for the company who created the product.

Though expert assessment might be one way to solve this problem, it is still not clear the level of expertise required to be considered as such, given the different architectures in different cars. On the other hand, insurance companies or even the manufactures having an expert of their own, ready to go to court when necessary it's not exactly the most transparent or impartial measure.

Another suggestion to solve the proof in court has to do with data logs as the primary source of information. However, nobody is yet sure if the data from a vehicle that has malfunctioned can be trusted as accurate (Koopman and Wagner 2017).

The remaining question regards hacking and other cybernetic crimes. It is clear that failure to protect the AV against this kind of menaces will cause the developer to respond for it. Yet, we still don't know whom to ascribe responsibility when everything that could be done has been done and yet hacking still took place. And either way how can we prove that the developer failed to protect the AV? A possible solution might be to determine a minimum-security standard, though this standard must be updated regularly, given the fast evolution of this technology.

PDL aside, and apart from the undeniable necessity of insurance (yet to be created) for each AV on the road, we must not forget the relevance of defining a parallel system. Insurance must be mandatory in order to guarantee, through a simple process and no need to assess responsibilities to the detail, rapid compensation to the injured party. However, there may be the case when the injured party demands a higher compensation than what is covered by the insurance policy. Furthermore, if we are dealing with unknown situations, two systems working in parallel will grant a level of efficiency and flexibility that would be inconceivable with an isolated legal system.

Many options have been suggested for this second and parallel system, since adapting functional safety standards such as ISO 26262 to a simple adjustment of the several civil liability systems available in Europe, such as liability for the risk.

However, in the case of ISO 26262, the standards are intended for vehicles in which the human driver can ultimately correct for errors (Koopman and Wagner 2017; Kalra 2017), turning these norms obsolete towards fully autonomous vehicles that require no human intervention. ISO also requires the system to show detailed inputs and outputs, something highly unlikely in AVs, with large amounts of diverse, high-speed data coming from vehicle sensors (Koopman and Wagner 2017).

Liability for the risk - putting the weight on the owner - would make sense because the owner has an advantage in the utilisation of the AV. At the same time, as some might argue, it's extremely unfair to the user, since he has no control, in the slightest sense, of the driving process.

Resting the responsibility on the company who created the AV would make developers more conscious of safety. After all, the way they chose to program the vehicle is the first *sine qua non* condition for all that it is bound to happen with that AV. However, this doesn't seem quite right either. At a certain point, putting the weight on the company who created the AV would be similar to a father who still has to respond for his son actions, when his son is actually 35 years old. It will get to a point when companies can control the AV functioning as much as a parent can predict and control his child's behaviour.

Summarily, the main concern about the responsibility can be described as follows: we have an artificial entity (created by a company, a juridical person), with no legal personality whatsoever, that drives on its own through constant and complex decision making, while having its owner in its backseat (this last one being also a legal person), who has no influence on the driving process. If there's an accident, where's the responsibility core placed? In truth, there might not be one. This is the reason why some scholars have been defending a shared legal system for AVs.

In fact, this is a very reasonable suggestion, not only on behalf of what has been said regarding the absence of an authentic core of liability, but also because there are new risks that should be accountable, such as over reliance and misuse of the technology. Additionally, as far as we know, pedestrians can behave more recklessly towards AVs, trusting that the vehicle is effective enough to avoid any negative result (Kalra 2017). Finally, we are forced to consider the problem of occurrences that were inconceivable before the utilisation of the AV and yet happened (the famous *unknown unknowns*).

4 Conclusion

We live in the society of risk as described by Beck and in the era of mobility, when every city is now packed with rental bicycles and scooters nearly everywhere. AVs can and should be used to mitigate this risk. Whether AVs will be able to do this right from the first second they enter the market is still an open question. They do have the potential to do so, by eliminating many errors that human beings routinely make: they cannot be drunk, nor distracted or tired.

We cannot, however, sympathise with the idea of a commercialisation with no absolute guarantees of safety. A very clear standard of safety must be defined, and it should be, the very least, vision capacities and intelligent reactions at the human level. It makes no sense to replace one driver, under the justification that he is not good enough, for another that poses bigger risks.

Though we might accept a lower threshold of safety for early prototypes, while still demanding their demonstration and training in a controlled environment (for instance, places where crashes are less likely, easy to navigate and under good weather conditions), a higher threshold of safety would be warranted for widespread consumer use in uncontrolled environments (Kalra 2017).

At the same time, we need to find a way of increasing AVs experience, allowing them to improve their own safety, without jeopardising lives. In this regard, the creation of *special testing zones* (Santoni de Sio 2016), the *shadow mode* designed by Tesla and Data-sharing should also involve regular information about miles travelled, crashes, failures, and other information that can help provide early evidence of safety and safety concerns (Kalra 2017).

Regardless of the solutions to be found in this field, it is important to highlight the notion of responsible innovation, in the sense that an interdisciplinary and an anticipatory analysis of the issues at hand, based on pro-active ethics and values, is required (Santoni de Sio 2016).

References

Axa and Burges Salmon: Are we ready to "Handover" to Driveless Technology? VENTURER Insurance and Legal Report 2017/18

Boulangé, A., Jaggie, C.: Ethique, responsabilité et statut juridique du robot compagnon: revue et perspectives, Cognition, Affects et Interaction (2014). https://www.researchgate.net/publication/278625871_Cognition_Affects_et_Interaction

Casey, J.P.: CARiD survey suggests US public not ready for autonomous vehicles (2018). https://www.roadtraffic-technology.com/news/carid-survey-suggests-us-public-not-ready-autonomous-vehicles/. Accessed 5 Apr 2019

Combs, T.B., Sandt, L.S., Clamman, M.P., McDonal, N.C.: Automated vehicles and pedestrian safety: exploring the promise and limits of pedestrian detection. Am. J. Prev. Med. **56**(1), 1–7 (2019). https://doi.org/10.1016/j.amepre.2018.06.024

Communication from the Commission to the European Parliament, The Council, The European Economic and Social Committee and the Committee of the Regions, On the road to automated Mobility: an EU strategy for mobility of the Future (2018). https://eur-lex.europa.eu/LexUriServ/LexUriServ.do?uri=COM:2018:0283:FIN:EN:PDF

Deahl, D.: Volvo's self-driving cars are having trouble recognizing kangaroos. The Verge (2017). www.theverge.com/2017/7/3/15916076/volvo-self-driving-cars-trouble-recognizing-kangaroos

Dollar, P., Wojek, C., Schiele, B., Perona, P.: Pedestrian detection: an evaluation of the state of the art. IEEE Trans. Pattern Anal. Mach. Intell. **34**(4), 743–761 (2012). https://doi.org/10.1109/TPAMI.2011.155

Dwoskin, E., Fung, B.: For some safety experts, Uber's self-driving taxi test isn't something to hail. Washington Post (2016). https://www.washingtonpost.com/business/economy/for-some-safety-experts-ubers-self-driving-taxi-test-isntsomething-to-hail/2016/09/11/375f980a-769a-11e6-be4f-3f42f2e5a49e_story.html

European Parliament News (2019). http://www.europarl.europa.eu/news/en/headlines/economy/20190110STO23102/self-driving-cars-in-the-eu-from-science-fiction-to-reality. Accessed 9 Apr 2019

European Parliamentary Research Service, European Parliament, A Common EU Approach to Liability Rules, European Added Value Assessment Accompanying the European Parliament's legislative own-initiative report. Mady Delvaux, Rapporteur

Flynn, R.: Risk and the public acceptance of new technologies. In: Flynn, R., Bellaby, P. (eds.) Risk and the public acceptance of new technologies. Palgrave Macmillan, London (2007). https://doi.org/10.1057/9780230591288_1

Goodall, N.J.: Ethical decision making during automated vehicle crashes. Transp. Res. Rec. J. Transp. Res. Board (2014). https://doi.org/10.3141/2424-07

Gouraud, J., Delorme, A., Berberian, B.: Autopilot, mind wandering, and the out of the loop performance problem. Front. Neursci. (2017). https://doi.org/10.3389/fnins.2017.00541

Hedlung, J.: Autonomous vehicles meet human drivers: traffic safety issues for states. Prepared for Governors Highway Safety Association (2017). https://www.ghsa.org/sites/default/files/2017-01/AV%202017%20-%20FINAL.pdf

Jermakian, J.S., Zuby, D.S.: Primary pedestrian crash scenarios: factors relevant to the design of pedestrian detection systems. Insurance Institute for Highway Safety, Arlington, VA (2011). www.iihs.org/frontend/iihs/documents/masterfiledocs.ashx?id=1888

Kalra, N.: Challenges and approaches to realising AV safety. Testimony Presented to the House Energy and Commerce Committee, Subcommittee on Digital Commerce and Consumer

Protection. Published by the RAND Corporation, Santa Monica, California (2017). www.rand.org/content/dam/rand/pubs/testimonies/CT400/CT463/RAND_CT463.pdf

Kalra, N., Paddock, S.: Driving to Safety: How Many Miles of Driving Would It Take to Demonstrate Autonomous Vehicle Reliability? RAND Corporation, Santa Monica, California, RR-1478-RC, 2016 (2017). http://www.rand.org/pubs/research_reports/RR1478.html

Katrakazas, C., Quddus, M., Chen, W., Deka, L.: Real-time motion planning methods for autonomous on-road driving: State-of-the-art and future research directions. Transp. Res. Part C Emerg. Technol. 60, 416–442 (2015). https://doi.org/10.1016/j.trc.2015.09.011

Koopman, P., Wagner, M.: Autonomous vehicle safety: an interdisciplinary challenge. IEEE Intell. Transp. Syst. Mag. 9, 90–96 (2017). https://doi.org/10.1109/MITS.2016.2583491

Lawson, S.: Tackling the Transition to Automated Vehicles, Roads that Cars Can Read Report III, European Road Assessment Association (2018). https://bit.ly/2IrYTTQ

LeVine, S.: What it really costs to turn a car into a self-driving vehicle. Quartz (2017). https://qz.com/924212/what-it-really-costs-to-turn-a-car-into-a-self-driving-vehicle/

Merat, N.: House of Lords Science and Technology Committee inquiry into autonomous vehicles: supplementary written evidence (AUV0092). Institute for Transport Studies, University of Leeds (2016). http://data.parliament.uk/writtenevidence/committeeevidence.svc/evidencedocument/science-and-technology-committee-lords/autonomous-vehicles/written/43683.html

Morgan, P., Alford, C., Parkhurst, G.: Handover issues in autonomous driving: a literature review. Project Report. University of the West of England, Bristol, UK (2016). http://eprints.uwe.ac.uk/29167

National Highway Traffic Safety Administration: Automated Vehicles for Safety (2016). https://www.nhtsa.gov/technology-innovation/automated-vehicles-safety. Accessed 4 Apr 2019

Oliver, N., Potocnik, K., Calvard, T.: To make self-driving cars safe, we also need better roads and infrastructure. Harvard Bus. Rev. (2018). https://hbr.org/2018/08/to-make-self-driving-cars-safe-we-also-need-better-roads-and-infrastructure

Pagallo, U.: The Laws of Robots - Crimes, Contracts, and Torts. Springer, Dordrecht (2013). https://doi.org/10.1007/978-94-007-6564-1

Perkins Coie: Autonomous Vehicles Survey Report, January 2019. https://www.perkinscoie.com/images/content/2/1/v3/216738/2019-Autonomous-Vehicles-Survey-Report-v.3.pdf

Rupp, J.D., King, A.G.: Autonomous Driving – A Practical Roadmap. SAE International (2010). https://doi.org/10.4271/2010-01-2335

Santoni de Sio, F.: Ethics and Self-driving Cars: A White Paper on Responsible Innovation in Automated Driving Systems. Dutch Ministry of Infrastructure and Environment, Rijkswaterstaat (2016)

Zhang, S., Benenson, R., Omran, M., Hosang, J., Schiele, B.: Towards reaching human performance in pedestrian detection. IEEE Trans. Pattern Anal. Mach. Intell. 40(4), 973–986 (2018). https://doi.org/10.1109/tpami.2017.2700460. Caltech Pedestrian Detection Benchmark, Published 12 December 2016. www.vision.caltech.edu/Image_Datasets/CaltechPedestrians/

Zhang, L., Lin, L., Liang, X., He, K.: Is faster R-CNN doing well for pedestrian detection? In: Leibe, B., Matas, J., Sebe, N., Welling, M. (eds.) ECCV 2016. LNCS, vol. 9906, pp. 443–457. Springer, Cham (2016). https://doi.org/10.1007/978-3-319-46475-6_28

The Role of Artificial Intelligence in the European e-Justice Paradigm – Suiting Effective Judicial Protection Demands

Joana Covelo de Abreu$^{(\boxtimes)}$ (iD)

Law School, University of Minho, Campus de Gualtar, 4710-057 Braga, Portugal
jabreu@direito.uminho.pt

Abstract. Digital Single Market is the European Union (EU) political interest thought to adapt it to new ICT demands. Under this primary public interest, e-Justice paradigm was developed so new digital tools and technological systems could improve justice fields, especially on those cross-border litigations derived from fundamental freedoms' exercise. In the 2019–2023 e-Justice Action Plan, the Council focused the need to understand the full potential of artificial intelligence on justice fields. In the same way, also the European Parliament and the Commission acknowledged its vital role. The end of 2018 and the beginning of 2019 were fruitful periods on artificial intelligence domains, having the European Union established Working Parties and Expert Groups to apply these innovations on important economic and social sectors. Therefore, the Author tried to understand if these approaches are capable of fully overcoming the difficulties experienced in justice domains and, particularly, if these solutions are able to answer effective judicial demands in all its dimensions.

Keywords: Artificial intelligence · e-Justice · Effective judicial protection

1 European e-Justice and Digital Single Market – An Introduction

The EU established and is now developing a Digital Single Market as a general primary public interest which was embraced by both national and EU political agents [1] through its shared competences[1] under article 4 (2) (a) of the Treaty on the Functioning of the European Union (TFEU). In fact, for a long time, the EU trusted in its Member States' diligences of technological update, but it concluded it had to promote a tendential approach so all adopted digital solutions could be articulated and communicable between them. In fact, internet and digital technologies are changing the way the world works since they are integrated in all social and economic sectors, in an accelerated rhythm that demands a EU's coordinated action [2] since its Member States also

---

[1] The EU has shared competences with its Member States which means they have legislative power in those material domains. They will exercise that competence as follows: Member States will pursue their competence as long the European Union has not exercised its and will be able to exercise it again when the European Union has decided to exercise it – article 2 (2) of the TFEU.

P. Moura Oliveira et al. (Eds.): EPIA 2019, LNAI 11804, pp. 299–308, 2019.
https://doi.org/10.1007/978-3-030-30241-2_26

struggle with coincident issues but the national scale is too limited to allow them to take advantage of all opportunities and to face all transnational challenges. This led them to understand the EU level was the appropriated one to deal with those issues [2].

The European Commission (EC), on the topic "[a]n inclusive e-society", started to mention the need of "[...] interlinked and multi-lingual e-services, from e-government, e-justice [...]" [2], etc. Therefore, European e-Justice appeared as a political priority associated to the e-Government paramount through the e-Government Action Plan to the timeframe of 2016–2020. In this Action Plan it was mentioned the EC would make the needed efforts to digitally modernize also justice fields as already mentioned in the e-Justice Action Plan, namely through the e-Justice Portal (acting as a one-stop shop for justice information) but also referring to e-Codex, as "[...] go-live [...] tools for direct communications between citizens and courts in other Member States [...]" [3]. From this, it seemed that "[f]or politicians, electronic justice relates primarily to the creation of information systems for the organization of enormous amounts of legal questions and data" which could be "[...] considered a competitive advantage within the global economy" [4]. This association between e-Government and e-Justice paradigms – which was already clear since the early stages of the Digital Single Market's implementation, through the interoperability method's adoption (firstly thought to modernize administrative services) to electronic justice domains [5–8] – became clearly accepted in the Council's e-Justice Action Plan to 2019–2023. In fact, under the topic "[l]inks between e-Justice and eGovernment principles", the Council states that "[t]he work done in the field of e-Justice can benefit other fields" [9]: in fact, "[b]y allowing for easier access to information and justice, e-Justice should contribute to the development of the Digital Single Market which is one of the goals of eGovernment", leading to the idea that "[...] European e-Justice initiatives should strive for further consistency within the eGovernment Framework, having regard to the constitutional provisions concerning the judiciary in Member States (judicial independence and separation of powers)" [9].

European e-Justice has, nowadays, a double emblematic role: as a means to implement interoperable communication systems, so jurisdictional articulation can be facilitated, in an institutional level, and as a referral to effective judicial protection of those rights given to individuals by the EU legal order, through new approaches and updates. It is in this approach we must understand artificial intelligence's role and importance in the future of e-Justice in the EU.

2   2019–2023 European e-Justice – Council's Strategy and Action Plan

European e-Justice was firstly addressed, by the EU, in a coordinated way, in 2007, when the Council decided to establish a working party on the topic [10]. Since then, already three Multiannual Action Plans have been adopted by the Council: the one from 2009 to 2013; the one from 2014 to 2018; and, the most recent, from 2019 to 2023. But this paradigm was also pursued by the other European institutions: in 2008, the EC adopted a Communication under the theme "Towards a European e-Justice Strategy" [11]; and, in the same year, the European Parliament adopted a resolution on e-Justice, approved in plenary session [12]. Nowadays, "European e-Justice aims at improving access to justice in a pan-European context and is developing and integrating information and communication technologies into access to legal information and the workings of judicial systems" [9]. The Council also understood "[p]rocedures carried out in a digitised manner and electronic communication between those involved in judicial proceedings have become an essential component in the efficient functioning of the judiciary in the Member States" [9].

By evaluating the accomplishments of the previous period, the Council let know that the e-Justice Portal was improved through the inclusion of (i) more information (as those updates made on family law, on judicial professionals' formation in EU law, on victims' rights on criminal law proceedings and on the inclusion of consumers' protection legislation) [9]; (ii) search engines; (iii) interactive forms, as those related to small claims' procedure [13] and (iv) helping users to have a better experience [9]. Furthermore, in the previous period, digital tools were developed which "[...] now allow for digital judicial proceedings using secure electronic channels, secure communication between judicial authorities, easier information for citizens on legal provisions and access to certain national registers under the responsability of Member States or professional organisations" [9]. It also developed new search engines and included new data in the EUR-Lex website, allowing access to new normative acts (namely accessing Directives' national transposition measures) and jurisprudence. Institutionally, both the Council [14] and the EC [15] elaborated Progress Reports under the previous Action Plan.

In its Progress Report, the EC refers how the future Action Plan should be articulated, taking as referral the stakeholders' opinions on the matter. It mentions they have "[...] identified the following five domains that [...] should be focus of the next Action Plan" [15]: (1) artificial intelligence; (2) e-Codex; (3) interconnection of registers; (4) land registry interconnection; and (5) continuous development of e-Justice Portal [15].

Concerning the topic in hands, accordingly to the EC's report, "[...] 41% (19 out of 46 replies) indicated that AI should be used in the domain of justice or its possibilities should be explored" [15]. In fact, "[t]he current use of AI technologies is rather low" since, facing the question "Does your organisation currently use AI technologies in the justice domain?", "[a] total of 46 out of 56 (or 82%) stakeholders replied to this question, where 3 out of 46 respondents (or 7%) indicated that their organisation is using AI in the justice domain, while 37 out of 46 (or 80%) replied negatively" [15].

On its turn, the Council's strategy also considers artificial intelligence a vital path to be followed in this new period: under the topic "Evolutivity", the Council understands that "[l]egal tech domains such as Artificial Intelligence (AI), blockchain technology, e-Translation or virtual reality, for example, should be closely monitored, in order to identify and seize opportunities with a potential positive impact on e-Justice" [9]. However, the Council considers artificial intelligence can have a positive effect on e-Justice "[...] by increasing efficiency and trust" despite bearing in mind that "[a]ny future development and deployment of such technologies must take risks and challenges into account, in particular in relation to data protection and ethics" [9].

At the same time and following the same goals, the Council adopted the European e-Justice Action Plan, where it openly stated there were three objectives: "[...] access to information, e-Communication in the field of justice and interoperability" [16]. On what concerns artificial intelligence's impact on e-Justice, the Council understands its recent innovative impact, despite recognising "[i]ts implications in the field of e-Justice need to be further defined" [16]; for that, projects that have the ability to understand and "[d]efine the role which Artificial Intelligence might play in the field of justice" and to "[d]evelop an AI-tool for analysis of court decisions" are prioritized by the Council [16]. The Council also aims at establishing a "Chatbot for the e-Justice Portal" as it "[...] would assist the user and direct her/him to the information s/he is looking for" [16].

3 Artificial Intelligence and e-Justice Paradigm – Perceiving Their Synergetic Relationship Under Effective Judicial Protection Demands

In April 2018, the EC presented a Communication on Artificial Intelligence to analyse its impacts, advantages, strengths and threats and to realize how it can be put at the service of EU objectives and goals. For that purpose, the EC understood "[t]he EU must therefore ensure that AI is developed and applied in an appropriate framework which promotes innovation and respects the Union's values and fundamental rights as well as ethical principles such as accountability and transparency", especially because the EU is "[...] well placed to lead this debate on the global stage" [17]. Therefore, this Communication was aspiring, among other goals, at "[b]oost[ing] the EU's technological and industrial capacity and AI uptake across the economy, both by the private and public sectors" [17], especially those of e-Government and e-Justice acknowledged as secondary public interests and paramount in the 2017 Ministerial Declaration on e-Government [18] – as the EC understood, "AI can significantly improve public services [...]" since its mechanisms have the "[...] potential to analyse large amounts of data and help check how single market rules are applied" [17]. Artificial intelligence can also impact on "[...] public administrations (including justice)" [17] by making it "[...] available and accessible to all", by "[...] facilitat[ing] access of all potential users, especially small and medium-sized enterprises, companies from non-tech sectors and public administrations to the latest technologies and encourage[ing] them to test AI" [17].

In the timeframe of 2018–2020, the EC will invest around 1.5 billion euros in "[...] the uptake of AI across Europe, via a toolbox for potential users, with a focus on small and medium-sized enterprises, non-tech companies and public administrations: this will include an AI-on-demand platform giving support and easy access to the latest algorithms and expertise; a network of AI-focused Digital Innovation Hubs facilitating testing and experimentation; and a set-up of industrial data platforms offering high quality datasets" [17]. Notwithstanding, as another new reality, artificial intelligence "[...] can be used to positive but also to malicious ends" since, as it clearly creates new opportunities, "[...] also poses challenges and risks, for example in the areas of safety and liability, security (criminal use or attacks), bias, and discrimination" [17] – "[t]he emergence of AI, in particular the complex enabling ecosystem and the feature of autonomous decision-making, requires a reflection about the suitability of some established rules on safety and civil law questions on liability" [17].

Taking into consideration these developments and sensitivities, the EC established a High-level Expert Group on Artificial Intelligence; one of its deliverables was the publication, in April 2019, of an updated notion of artificial intelligence, in order to overcome some fears concerning its use and the role humans had on it. Insofar, the expert group proposed the updated notion, as follows:

"Artificial intelligence (AI) systems are software (and possibly hardware) systems designed by humans that, given a complex goal, act in the physical or digital dimension by perceiving their environment through data acquisition, interpreting the collected structured or unstructured data, reasoning on the knowledge, or processing the information, derived from this data and deciding the best action(s) to take to achieve the given goal. AI systems can either use symbolic rules or learn a numeric model, and they can also adapt their behaviour by analysing how the environment is affected by their previous actions" [19].

This notion came into light in the terms met, by the same Expert Group, in its draft of "Ethics guidelines for trustworthy AI", adopted on 18th December 2018.

Under it, the first "Key guidance for ensuring ethical purpose" was to assure an human centric AI: "[...] AI should be developed, deployed and used with an 'ethical purpose', grounded in, and reflective of, fundamental rights, societal values and the ethical principles of beneficence (do good), non-maleficence (do no harm), autonomy of humans, justice and explicability" [20], since artificial intelligence "[...] is one of the most transformative forces of our time, and is bound to alter the fabric of society" [20].

In fact, this approach gains particular new forms and relevance in legal domains and in justice fields where fundamental rights have to be met and enforced, despite the legal order that entails them; it seems it can meet effective judicial protection dimensions' fulfilment since artificial intelligence is being thought and implemented, not to substitute judicial operators, but to facilitate their tasks, namely those of repetitive nature (as of comparing settled case law, for instance).

That draft was not yet replaced by an effective Ethical Charter on the use of Artificial Intelligence in judicial systems. However, the Working Party on e-Law (e-Justice) has been meeting in Brussels, where they are addressing the topic "Innovative uses of technology – artificial intelligence", under which the European Ethical Charter on the use of artificial intelligence in judicial systems and their environment was presented by the Council of Europe (CoE) [21]. Furthermore, under article 6 (3) of the Treaty of the European Union (TEU), the protection of fundamental rights in the EU has to follow the minimum standard met in the European Convention of Human Rights (ECHR), under the CoE[2], being important to understand this European Ethical Charter, especially since all EU's Member States are also Parties of the ECHR. Therefore, this Ethical Charter will also influence the way EU is going to perceive artificial intelligence in justice fields.

---

[2] The Council of Europe is an international organization of human rights' protection of regional nature. It acts within the continent of Europe. The ECHR "constitutes the essential text in human rights and it represents the development and concretization, in the Council of Europe's scope, of the Universal Declaration on Human Rights" [22].

304 J. Covelo de Abreu

The Ethical Charter was adopted in order to sensitize "[...] public and private stakeholders responsible for the design and deployment of artificial intelligence tools and services that involve the processing of judicial decisions and data", but also "[...] public decision-makers in charge of the legislative or regulatory framework, of the development, audit or use of such tools and services" [23]. In fact, the use of those services in judicial systems aims at enhancing efficiency and quality but has to be carried in a way that fundamental rights are not undermined by that use. As acknowledged, "[j] udicial decision processing by artificial intelligence, according to their developers, is likely, in civil, commercial and administrative matters, to help improve the predictability of the application of the law and consistency of court decisions, subject to compliance with the principles set out below"; however, "[i]n criminal matters, their use must be considered with the greatest reservations in order to prevent discrimination based on sensitive data, in conformity with the guarantees of a fair trial" [23]. Therefore, despite the end for which the artificial intelligence software or hardware is due, "[...] it is essential that processing is carried out with transparency, impartiality and equity, certified by an external and independent expert assessment" [23].

The Ethical Charter presents five major principles to be met: (1) principle of respect for fundamental rights; (2) principle of non-discrimination; (3) principle of quality and security; (4) principle of transparency, impartiality and fairness; and (5) principle "under user control" [23].

On justice fields, effective judicial protection is both a general principle and a fundamental right, referring to the ability to enforce the rights attributed by a legal order before an impartial, independent and equidistant court. Insofar, effective judicial protection is based on several dimensions: right to action (the right to go to court to exercise those rights); rights of defence (the ability to question and contradict, before a court, the grounding presented by the other party in the litigation); the right to an impartial and independent court; the right to be represented by a lawyer; and the right to judicial support, especially when the plaintiff/ defendant are in financial distress.

With the principle of respect for fundamental rights, effective judicial protection receives the proper acknowledgment since, as stressed by the CoE, "[w]hen artificial intelligence tools are used to resolve a dispute or as a tool to assist in judicial decision-making or to give guidance to the public, it is essential to ensure that they do not undermine the guarantees of the right to access to the judge and the right to a fair trial (equality of arms and respect for the adversarial process)" [23], allowing to fully grasp and observe both right to action and defence rights. Furthermore, as "[t]hey should also be used with due respect for the principles of the rule of law and judges' independence in their decision-making process" [23], also the right to an impartial and independent court is duly observed and guaranteed.

The principle of non-discrimination aims at preventing the development/ intensification of any discrimination between individuals. In fact, artificial intelligence methods – as based on reproducing knowledge apprehended through data from different sources – have been struggling with the problem of reproducing existing discrimination "[...] through grouping or classifying data relating to individuals or groups of individuals", especially "[...] when the processing is directly or indirectly based on 'sensitive' data" [23]. In order to overcome those deficiencies, they are now aiming at enforcing "[…] corrective measures to limit or, if possible, neutralise these risks and as well as to awareness-raising among stakeholders" [23]. Recent approaches are now understanding these discriminations can be undermined by the use of machine learning and multidisciplinary scientific analysis; however, machine learning algorithms and their systematic technical workings are difficult to understand and to explain, particularly how that model arrived to that particular decision. In light of this, we believe their use must be encouraged but bearing in mind the particular challenge they posed and how their actions have to be monitored and regulated. By doing so, effective judicial protection will reach a higher standard since plaintiffs/defendants will understand algorithms are, in fact, correcting discrimination patterns that were detected, allowing justice being better met and served.

The principle of quality and security demands that "[d]ata based on judicial decisions that is entered into a software which implements a machine learning algorithm should come from certified sources and should not be modified until they have actually been used by the learning mechanism" [23]. By being as such, courts are able to rely on data already presented (as the case law already available through an algorithm), enhancing its independence and impartiality.

The principle of transparency, impartiality and fairness enhances the need to balance those dimensions with intellectual property rights over some processing methods. In order to do so, a "complete technical transparency" [23] must be the trend without forgetting trade secrets' protection. However, the best practice could be promoting a digital literacy of justice users and rising awareness of artificial intelligence's impact on justice fields ("[t]he system could also be explained in clear and familiar language by communicating […] the nature of the services offered, the tools that have been developed, performance and the risks of error" [23]).

Finally, the principle "under user control" demands that judicial operators become "[…] informed actors and in control of their choices" [23] by adopting guide books and wide and public debates on the matter: "[t]he user must be informed in clear and understandable language whether or not the solutions offered by the artificial intelligence tools are binding, of the different options available, and that s/he has the right to legal advice and the right to access a court" [23], being able to object and to be heard directly by a court.

As we were able to devise, all these principles also acknowledge and enforce all effective judicial protection dimensions. Both action and defence rights can benefit from artificial intelligence: if digital literacy is well provided and transparency methods are adopted, both plaintiff and defendant will gather "a certain amount of quantitative information (for example, the number of decisions processed to obtain the scale) and qualitative information (origin of decisions, representativeness of selected samples, distribution of decisions between different criteria such as the economic and social context) accessible to citizens and, above all, to the parties to a trial in order to understand how scales have been constructed, to measure their possible limits and to be able to debate them before a judge" [23]. Furthermore, parties cannot be found in an unbalanced position because of the use of technological means and all solutions must bear in mind both party types (with or without ICT familiarity), being important that "[…] no individuals are left alone in front of their screens", especially by being "[…] informed they can seek legal advice and [being] assisted where necessary" [23].

On judicial independence and impartiality, there is a need to provide software and hardware which do not put judges under any kind of external pressure, especially "[…] when decisions are taken and prompt their approval, or that the executive will monitor those who depart from the norm" [23].

Finally, on the right to be represented by a lawyer (and on having financial support on legal matters), artificial intelligence systems/mechanisms can have a positive impact since technological approaches on the matter will be less time consuming; however, in order to achieve it, "[p]rofessional practice should aim to minimise the risk that persons requiring legal advice may ultimately be deprived of it" [23]. In the same sense, new approaches to those that need legal aid because of financial distress have to be met in this new justice scenario where artificial intelligence might be a useful tool to overcome bureaucratic trends.

4   Conclusive Remarks

e-Justice paradigm was thought to overcome special barriers posed to cross-border litigations especially derived from fundamental freedoms' exercise. In fact, in an integrated EU, effective judicial protection was still difficult to achieve especially on those litigations where several Member States had a particular relation with the pleading object. Nowadays e-Justice Action Plan aims at strengthening digital approaches made under previous plans, but it also encloses the need to think, by inception, artificial intelligence in European justice fields.

As we were able to see, the end of 2018 and the beginning of 2019 were particularly keen on setting the tone on how artificial intelligence will reach EU's goals. Particularly on justice fields – and e-Justice matters – a Working Party, established under the Council of the EU, is making efforts to grasp the path to follow, taking as referral the Ethical Charter on artificial intelligence on justice fields of the CoE. Only time will tell us how the task, in the EU, will be carried out but, since the ECHR acts as a minimum referral of the Union's protection of fundamental rights, we are inclined to understand the path will be next to the one followed under the CoE. Furthermore, on justice matters, effective judicial protection acts as its grounding and teleology – insofar, the Ethical Charter seems to be fitted to this calling and is sufficiently scalable to answer its purposes. However, it is due better regulatory framework and details on how artificial intelligent systems will be applicable to justice fields, despite raising questions on how to promote this regulation because of judicial independence principle.

In a moment of transformation – and to grasp more integration – the EU has to reinvent itself, accompanying ICT innovation.

References

1. Abreu, J.C.: Digital Single Market under EU political and constitutional calling: European electronic agenda's impact on interoperability solutions. UNIO EU Law J. 3(1), 123–140 (2017)

2. European Commission: Communication from the Commission to the European Parliament, the Council, the European Economic and Social Committee and the Committee of the Regions – A Digital Single Market Strategy for Europe, Brussels, 6 May 2015, SWD (2015). 100 final. https://eur-lex.europa.eu/legal-content/EN/TXT/PDF/?uri=CELEX: 52015DC0192&from=EN. Accessed 12 Apr 2019

3. European Commission: Communication from the Commission to the European Parliament, the Council, the European Economic and Social Committee and the Committee of the Regions – EU eGovernment action Plan 2016–2020: "Accelerating the digital transformation of government", Brussels, 19 April 2016, COM (2016). 179 final. http://ec.europa.eu/ transparency/regdoc/rep/1/2016/EN/1-2016-179-EN-F1-1.PDF. Accessed 13 Apr 2019

4. Kengyel, M., Nemessányi, Z. (eds.): Electronic Technology and Civil Procedure. New Paths to Justice from Around the World. Springer, Dordrecht (2012). https://doi.org/10.1007/978-94-007-4072-3

5. Abreu, J.C.: A Justiça Eletrónica Europeia como paradigma de revisão do Regulamento n.º 1393/2007, relativo às citações/notificações de atos judiciais e extrajudiciais – sensibilidades preliminares à luz de uma integração judiciária. In: Calheiros, C., Monte, M.F., Pereira, M. A., Gonçalves, A. (Coords.) Direito na Lusofonia "Direito e Novas Tecnologias" – 5.º Congresso Internacional de Direito na Lusofonia, pp. 191–202. Escola de Direito da Universidade do Minho, Braga (2018)

6. Abreu, J.C.: Judicial interoperability in the e-Justice paradigm: perceiving e-CODEX as the proper answer? A synchronic melody for a judicial integration. PoLaR Portuguese Law J. 2 (1), 31–48 (2018)

7. Abreu, J.C.: A justiça eletrónica Europeia e a modernização do espaço de liberdade, segurança e justiça: a videoconferência no Regulamento n.º 1206/2001 ao serviço de uma integração judiciária. In: Carvalho, M.M., Messa, A.F., Nohara, I.P. (Coords.) Democracia Económica e Responsabilidade Social nas Sociedades Tecnológicas, pp. 93–116. Escola de Direito da Universidade do Minho, Braga (2019)

8. Silveira, A., Abreu, J.C.: Interoperability solutions under Digital Single Market: European e-Justice rethought under e-Government paradigm. Eur. J. Law Technol. 9(1) (2018). http:// ejlt.org/article/view/590/826

9. Council: 2019–2023 Strategy on e-Justice, 13 March 2019, 2019/C 96/04. https://eur-lex. europa.eu/legal-content/EN/TXT/PDF/?uri=CELEX:52019XG0313(01)&qid= 1555313597677&from=EN. Accessed 30 Mar 2019

10. Storskrubb, E.: E-Justice, innovation and the EU. In: Hess, B., Kramer, X.E. (eds.) From Common Rules to Best Practices in European Civil Procedure, pp. 271–302. Hart Publishing, Nomos, Max Planck Institute of Luxembourg for Procedural Law, Baden-Baden (2017)

11. European Commission: Communication from the Commission to the Council, the European Parliament and the European Economic and Social Committee – Towards a European e-Justice Strategy, Brussels, 30 May 2008, COM (2008). 329 final. https://eur-lex.europa.eu/ legal-content/EN/TXT/PDF/?uri=CELEX:52008DC0329&from=EN. Accessed 30 Mar 2019

12. European Parliament: European Parliament resolution with recommendations to the Commission on e-Justice, 18 December 2008, 2008/2125 (INI). http://www.europarl. europa.eu/sides/getDoc.do?pubRef=-//EP//TEXT+TA+P6-TA-2008-0637+0+DOC+XML +V0//EN&language=EN#BKMD-33. Accessed 30 Mar 2019

13. E-Justice Portal. https://e-justice.europa.eu/content_small_claims_forms-177-en.do. Accessed 30 Mar 2019

14. Council: Report on the progress of the 2014–2018 Action Plan on e-Justice, 10 October 2018, WK 598/2018 REV 2

15. European Commission: Evaluation study on the outcome of the e-Justice Action Plan 2014–2018 and the way forward – Final Report, DT4EU. https://publications.europa.eu/pt/publication-detail/-/publication/d72311d9-c070-11e8-9893-01aa75ed71a1/language-pt/format-PDF. Accessed 30 Mar 2019
16. Council: 2019–2023 Action Plan European e-Justice, 13 March 2019, 2019/C 96/05. https://eur-lex.europa.eu/legal-content/EN/TXT/PDF/?uri=CELEX:52019XG0313(02)&from=PT. Accessed 30 Mar 2019
17. European Commission: Communication from the Commission to the European Parliament, the European Council, the Council, the European Economic and Social Committee and the Committee of the Regions – Artificial Intelligence for Europe, Brussels, 25 April 2018, COM (2018). 237 final. https://eur-lex.europa.eu/legal-content/EN/TXT/PDF/?uri=CELEX:52018DC0237&from=EN. Accessed 15 Apr 2019
18. Tallinn Declaration on eGovernment at the ministerial meeting during Estonian Presidency of the Council of the EU, 6 October 2017. https://ec.europa.eu/digital-single-market/en/news/ministerial-declaration-egovernment-tallinn-declaration. Accessed 30 Mar 2019
19. European Commission – Independent High-level Expert Group on Artificial Intelligence: A definition of AI: main capabilities and disciplines, Brussels, 8 April 2019. https://ec.europa.eu/digital-single-market/en/news/definition-artificial-intelligence-main-capabilities-and-scientific-disciplines. Accessed 15 Apr 2019
20. European Commission – Independent High-level Expert Group on Artificial Intelligence, Draft Ethics guidelines for trustworthy AI – Executive Summary, Brussels, 18 December 2018. https://ec.europa.eu/digital-single-market/en/news/draft-ethics-guidelines-trustworthy-ai. Accessed 15 Apr 2019
21. Council of the European Union: ANP – EU Monitor: Working Party on e-Law (e-Justice). https://www.eumonitor.eu/9353000/1/j9vvik7m1c3gyxp/vkuv6fq8v8xv?ctx=vh1am07dxtwk&tab=1. Accessed 15 Apr 2019
22. Alvim, M.S.: Convenção Europeia dos Direitos do Homem (CEDH). In: Brandão, A.P, Coutinho, F.P., Camisão, I., Abreu, J.C. (Coords.) Enciclopédia da União Europeia, pp. 112–115. Petrony, Lisboa (2017)
23. Council of Europe – European Commission for the efficiency of justice: European Ethical Charter on the use of artificial intelligence in judicial systems and their environment, Strasbourg, 3–4 December 2018. https://rm.coe.int/ethical-charter-en-for-publication-4-december-2018/16808f699c. Accessed 15 Apr 2019

Artificial Intelligence in Medicine

Artificial Intelligence in Medicine

Heart Sounds Classification Using Images from Wavelet Transformation

Diogo Marcelo Nogueira[1(✉)], Mohammad Nozari Zarmehri[1,2],
Carlos Abreu Ferreira[1,3], Alípio M. Jorge[1,2], and Luís Antunes[1,2]

[1] INESC TEC, Porto, Portugal
diogo.m.nogueira@inesctec.pt
[2] Faculty of Science of University of Porto, Porto, Portugal
[3] Instituto Politécnico do Porto, Porto, Portugal

Abstract. Cardiovascular disease is the leading cause of death around the world and its early detection is a key to improving long-term health outcomes. To detect possible heart anomalies at an early stage, an automatic method enabling cardiac health low-cost screening for the general population would be highly valuable. By analyzing the phonocardiogram (PCG) signals, it is possible to perform cardiac diagnosis and find possible anomalies at an early-term. Accordingly, the development of intelligent and automated analysis tools of the PCG is very relevant.

In this work, the PCG signals are studied with the main objective of determining whether a PCG signal corresponds to a "normal" or "abnormal" physiological state. The main contribution of this work is the evidence provided that time domain features can be combined with features extracted from a wavelet transformation of PCG signals to improve automatic cardiac disease classification.

We empirically demonstrate that, from a pool of alternatives, the best classification results are achieved when both time and wavelet features are used by a Support Vector Machine with a linear kernel. Our approach has obtained better results than the ones reported by the challenge participants which use large amounts of data and high computational power.

Keywords: Phonocardiogram · Electrocardiogram · Wavelets · Time Features · Support Vector Machine

1 Introduction

Based on an estimation from the World Health Organization in 2012, Cardiovascular diseases are the main cause of death for approximately 17.5 million people around the world. Therefore, any contribution to help prevention of these diseases is highly valuable [11]. To help physician detecting any possible complication at an early stage, a dynamic method that enables low-cost cardiac health screening for the general population would be very useful. Furthermore, some cardiovascular conditions are well-reflected in the Heart Sound (HS) before their

P. Moura Oliveira et al. (Eds.): EPIA 2019, LNAI 11804, pp. 311–322, 2019.
https://doi.org/10.1007/978-3-030-30241-2_27

signatures appear in other signals such as ECG [6]. Thus, automated analysis and characterization of the PCG signal play a vital part in the diagnosis and monitoring of heart diseases.

Algorithms based on PCG signals to automatically classify normal and abnormal cardiac sounds have been proposed as tools for diagnostic support. These algorithms are composed of three main stages: A segmentation stage that helps to identify individual cardiac cycles; A feature extraction stage that provides the input for the last stage: feature classification. Despite there are already works, with good performances, there is still space to test new features in combination with well-performing classifiers in order to improve not only accuracy, but also specificity and sensitivity, which are very important for health applications.

The purpose of this study is to develop a new method for obtaining features for HS classification. In this work we transform a one-dimensional PCG signal into a two-dimensional wavelet transformation image, together with a group of time features (TF) of the signal.

In this direction, firstly, the PCG signal is divided into several segments using an ECG signal, which is recorded simultaneously, to identify the four HS sound states. Consequently, the features (wavelet image and time features) of each segment are collected. Lastly, several binary classifiers are used to classify the images into two classes: Normal and Abnormal. Our method is evaluated by using ECG and PCG signals that were made available in the 2016 PhysioNet Challenge [9].

The remainder of this paper is organized as follows. In Sect. 2, a brief description of ECG and PCG heart signals is presented. In Sect. 3, the current challenges in the study of heart signals and the related work are discussed, including different methods and approaches that can be used to extract features and classify HS. In Sect. 4, our methodology is described. In Sects. 5 and 6, results and discussion are presented, respectively. Finally, the paper is concluded in the last section.

2   Characteristics of ECG and PCG Heart Signals

One of the most important organs of a human body is the heart. The ECG and PCG signals are used in the diagnosis of possible abnormalities. The ECG signal consists of the recording of the variation of bioelectric potentials versus time of human heartbeats. The PCG is the recording of all the sounds made by the heart during a cardiac cycle. The PCG is very useful because it contains a great amount of physiological and pathological information regarding the human heart and vascular system [15].

In Fig. 1, we plot part of both ECG (the bottom of figure) and PCG signals (the top of the figure) to illustrate the relationship between them in the time domain. In addition to the four HS states (S1, Systole, S2, Diastole) a variety of other sounds, such as heart murmurs, may be present in the cardiac signal [4].

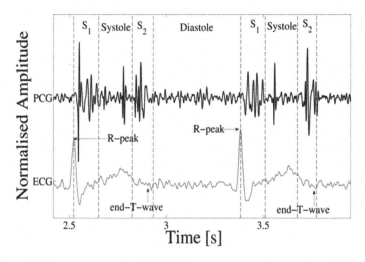

Fig. 1. Example of an ECG-labeled PCG, with the ECG and four states of the heart cycle (S1, Systole, S2, Diastole) shown. The R-peak and end-T-wave are labeled as reference for the approximate positions of S1 and S2, respectively [15].

3   State of the Art

3.1   Current Challenges

The development of appropriate algorithms that are able to detect heart diseases from heart sounds is an important challenge that has become the focus of work for many researchers. The ability to mathematically analyze and quantify the heart sounds represented on the PCG provides valuable information regarding the condition of the heart [13]. Some cardiovascular conditions are well-reflected in the HS before their signatures appear in other signals such as ECG [6]. Thus, automated analysis and characterization of the PCG signal play a vital part in the diagnosis and monitoring of heart diseases.

One important shortcoming of existing automatic HS classification techniques is the difficulty to distinguish some HS categories that correspond to different clinical conditions. This is in part due to the non-stationary characteristics of the PCG signals. The challenge currently faced by the scientific community is to find approaches with reasonable computational cost that can improve the performance in automatic diagnostic.

3.2   Related Work

The approaches for HS classification usually comprises three main stages: the first stage is focused on the detection of events such as S1 and S2 to identify individual cardiac cycles, and perform the segmentation of the PCG; The second stage corresponds to the feature extraction that provides the input for the last stage: feature classification.

The segmentation process of PCG signals is a very important task to perform diagnosis of cardiac pathologies with computer analysis. Thus, it is essential that different components of the heart cycle can be timed and separated. A large variety of algorithms that perform PCG segmentation have been presented in the literature. One of the most robust techniques to perform HS segmentation is using ECG gating. As was said above, there is a direct relationship between ECG and PCG main components. Correlation techniques have been used in [16], but this method shows limitations when the duration and the spectra of sound signal components show huge variations. It therefore requires user intervention. In [10], as the HS and ECG signals are time varying, the Instantaneous Energy is computed to characterize the temporal behavior of these signals and perform segmentation.

Regarding the second stage, the feature extraction, the features can be obtained using different analysis domains to ensure that the segments were described as thoroughly as possible. Since the analysis of HS is difficult to perform in the time domain due of noise interference and the overlapping of HS components, feature extraction is typically done over the frequency domain. Important feature extraction methods include the Fourier Transform [7], the Mel-frequency cepstral coefficients (MFCC) [12], the Discrete and Continuous Wavelet Transform coefficients [2]. Another type of features, which have already shown good results [5], are the features of the PCG signal, collected in the time domain.

In this work, we will perform a wavelet analysis of the PCG signals, and collect a group of time features from the signals. Wavelets-based approaches have been used in HS analysis because they are capable of providing both time and frequency information simultaneously in varying time and frequency resolutions (multiresolution analysis) [2].

After extracting the features, and regarding the modeling phase, most studies use Support Vector Machine (SVM) or Random Forest (RF). The SVM algorithm is known to generate highly accurate models. An approach for HS classification presented by Wu et al. reached an accuracy of 95%. This approach uses wavelet transform to extract the envelope of the PCG signals. The envelope is used to achieve the accurate position of S1 and S2. After that, they use as features, the area of PCG envelope and the wavelet energy, and their goal is determine if the heart sounds are "normal" or "abnormal" [17]. Although they achieved good results, the methodology was implemented in a dataset with only 35 PCG signals.

In [12], Nogueira et al. uses ECG and PCG collected simultaneously, with the aim of distinguishing if the PCG corresponds to a "normal" or "abnormal" physiological state. To do that, they segment the PCG signals into the fundamental HS using Springer's segmentation algorithm. After, they use time domain and MFCC features and to perform the classification. In the classification process, they evaluate three algorithms, and the best results (accuracy of 86.96%) are achieved with the SVM with radial basis function kernel. They use the dataset from the 2016 Physionet/Computing in Cardiology Challenge.

As can be seen from the list of works mentioned above, despite achieving good accuracy results so far, there is still space to test new features in combination with well-performing classifiers in order to improve not only accuracy, but also develop approaches with reasonable computational cost.

4   Methodology

In this work we propose a novel methodology to classify HS. The goal is to discriminate between "normal" and "abnormal" hearts conditions using PCG and ECG signals.

In our methodology, through the application of the wavelet analysis to the 1D PCG signal, we get as result a 2D image. Combining these image together with a set of TF, we get a group of features, that describes the segments, and can be used by several classifiers.

The methodology has five main steps:

- Segmentation of the PCG signal, identifying their four HS states;
- Perform a wavelet analysis for each PCG segment;
- Extract a group of eight time domain features for each PCG segment;
- Combine the two types of features collected (wavelets and TF) in one image, for each segment;
- Obtaining the classifier by training with a set of images generated from the normal and abnormal cases available.

Each component is described below in detail.

4.1   Heart Sound Database

In this work, the dataset from the 2016 Physionet/Computing in Cardiology Challenge [9] is used. The challenge database provides a large collection of HS recordings, obtained from different real-world clinical and nonclinical environments. We only use the training set A, which contains a total of 400 HS recordings and 400 ECG signals collected at the same time. We use the training set A, since it contains PCG and ECG signals collected simultaneously.

The HS recordings were divided into two types: normal and abnormal recordings. The abnormal recordings were collected from patients who suffered from a variety of illnesses. This fact will contribute to an abnormal class of signals, where we find signals that will generate very heterogeneous features. It is noteworthy that the number of normal recordings does not equal that of abnormal recordings, i.e., the dataset used is unbalanced. The distribution of the two classes in the dataset is approximately 70% of abnormal and 30% of normal recordings. More detailed information about the dataset can be found in [9].

4.2 Segmentation

First, each PCG signal is segmented into the fundamental heart sounds using Springer's segmentation algorithm [15]. This algorithm is based on a logistic regression hidden semi-Markov model to predict the most likely sequence of states. By applying this algorithm, we were able to identify exactly the beginning of each of the four fundamental heart sounds (S1, Systole, S2 and Diastole) in the PCG signals. Using this information, the original PCG signals are divided into short segments. The beginning of each heartbeat (S1) is selected as a starting point for the new segments. This was performed to ensure that the new segments, resulting from segmentation, were aligned during the feature extraction and the training of the classifier.

Starting from the S1 state, each segment is created with a length of three seconds. A total of 13375 segments of three seconds is produced from the original 400 PCG signals. Two examples of the produced segments are shown in the top of the Fig. 2. The figures show a segment of three seconds from the original one-dimensional PCG signal, with the identification of the HS states (red line).

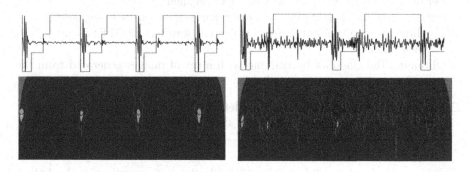

Fig. 2. Wavelet analysis of a normal PCG segment on the left, and an abnormal PCG segment on the right. (Color figure online)

4.3 Feature Extraction

After the segmentation step, two types of features from each segment of the PCG signals are collected: time domain features and wavelet transformation features. These features are described in the following subsections.

Time Features. For each segment, eight time-domain features were extracted, namely: average duration of states S1, Systole, S2, and Diastole; average duration of the intervals RR (the interval from the onset of one R-peak to the onset of the next one, one complete cardiac cycle); ratio between the duration of the Systole and the Diastole, in relation to the RR period of each heartbeat; and the ratio between the duration of the Systole and the Diastole of each heartbeat.

Wavelet Analysis. A wavelet transformation is used to convert a continuous time series (PCG signals) into wavelets. The Wavelet methodology is a reasonable choice to study periodic phenomena in time series, particularly in the presence of potential frequency changes across time. Wavelets-based approaches have the advantage of being able to provide both time and frequency information simultaneously in varying time and frequency resolutions (multi-resolution analysis) [1]. The Morlet wavelet transform of a time series (x_t) is defined as the convolution of the series with a set of "wavelet daughters" generated by the mother wavelet by translation in time (t) by τ and scaling by s:

$$Wave(\tau, s) = \sum_t x_t \frac{1}{\sqrt{s}} \psi^* \left(\frac{t - \tau}{s} \right) \tag{1}$$

Where * denotes the complex conjugate.

The position of the particular daughter wavelet in the time domain is determined by the localizing time parameter τ being shifted by a time increment of dt. The choice of the set of scales s determines the wavelet coverage of the series in the frequency domain. The local amplitude of any periodic component of the time series under investigation, and how it evolves with time, can then be retrieved from the modulus of its wavelet transform.

An image plot is a usual way to visualize the wavelet power spectrum. At the bottom of Fig. 2, there are two examples, resulting from the Wavelet analysis of the two PCG classes: the normal and abnormal, respectively. Looking at the wavelet analysis, the contour lines added to the wavelet power spectrum delineate areas of high significance. The color scale, which represents the wavelet power levels, was parameterized by taking into account the variation of its values. In the wavelet images, the black lines represent the periodicity of the PCG signal.

To perform the wavelet analysis of the signals, a set of adjustable parameters are used. These parameters and their values are shown in Table 1. The first five parameters are relative to the wavelet calculation, and the last two are relative to wavelet representation.

Table 1. A set of parameters used for wavelet analysis.

Parameter	Value of parameter
loess.span	0
dj	1/250
lowerPeriod	2
upperPeriod	175
n.sim	10
color.palette	rainbow(1000, 0, 0.74)
max.contour.segments	250000

The description of the parameters are as follow:

- *loess.span*: controls the degree of time series smoothing. With the value of zero, no smoothing is performed;
- *dj*: specifies the frequency resolution, i.e. sampling resolution on frequency domain;
- *lowerPeriod* and *upperPeriod*: define the lower and upper Fourier periods (in time units) for wavelet decomposition;
- *n.sim*: defines the number of simulations to perform the Wavelet analysis. By setting the "n.sim" parameter to ten, a compromise between the precision of the analysis and the computational time is established.

The values presented in Table 1, were chosen by a combination of initial manual exploration by the authors, followed by employing a random search through parameter space.

4.4 Data Preparation

In this stage, we had a total of 13375 segments of three seconds of PCG signal, resulting from the segmentation of the original 400 PCG signals. For each segment of three seconds of signal, we have a total of eight features from the time domain, and an image which is taken from the wavelet analysis of the segment. In order to use the wavelet images, as input parameter, in some classifiers (SVM and RF), the pixel values of the images are linearized by placing them sequentially in a single one-dimensional vector. In cases where we combine the time features with the wavelets, we simply concatenate the two vectors, corresponding the time features to the eight final elements of the vector.

Several experiments were carried out, using the collected features and several classifiers. Given the computational power available, we only use wavelet images with 64×64 and 90×90 dimensions, in order to reduce the dimensionality of the features, and try to obtain the best possible performance. We have also done some experiments, using the feature sets separately, to evaluate the impact that their joint use has on the results.

4.5 Classification of Heart Sound Images

We have tested different learning algorithms to the dataset obtained in the previous step to discriminate between normal and abnormal heart sounds. In our setup, these algorithms will first assign a class to each three seconds segment. In a second step, we group the predictions for the various segments of the same patient in order to classify each original PCG signal. Here, the classification is done by considering the percentage of segments classified as normal. If the percentage is above a pre-defined threshold then the patient's heart condition is classified as normal. Otherwise as abnormal. The value of the threshold was found empirically through exploration of the decision boundary on the posterior probability given by the classifiers. We have observed that the decision boundary on the posterior probability, which presents the best results overall, is around 30%, i.e., the original PCG signals which has at least 30% of the segments classified as Normal (minority class of the dataset) would be classified as Normal.

There is a wide variety of learning methods applied in the study of cardiac signals (ECG and PCG). In the proposed methodology, SVM, RF and the Convolutional Neural Network (CNN) are studied and evaluated. The SVM is used with a linear kernel and RF uses 400 trees and 200 variables randomly sampled at each split. With regard to the CNN, a LeNet-5 architecture [8] is trained and then applied to the test sets. CNN has two convolutional layers and two fully-connected layers and it uses a distributed representation to encode the categories at the output layer.

While the CNN allows the use of images directly as an input parameter, for the other classifiers, it is necessary to convert the images to a vector line (as explained in Sect. 4.4), so that it can be used as an input parameter.

4.6 Evaluation Metrics

In the classification process, the 13375 PCG segments generated were classified. Once the dataset used was unbalanced, consisting of approximately 70% abnormal segments and 30% normal segments, we performed a ten-fold stratified cross validation, ensuring that all the k test sets are disjoint. Additionally, it has been ensured that segments of the same patient are not placed in more than one fold.

Equations 2, 3 and 4 show the Sensitivity (Se), Specificity (Sp) and Overall metrics, respectively, which are used to evaluate the results. The overall was the evaluation metric used in the 2016 Physionet Challenge. It is also used in this paper in order to compare the results with those obtained in the challenge. The measures were defined using True Positive (TP), True Negative (TN), False Positive (FP) and False Negative (FN):

$$Se = \frac{TP}{TP + FN} \tag{2}$$

$$Sp = \frac{TN}{TN + FP} \tag{3}$$

$$Overall = \frac{Se + Sp}{2} \tag{4}$$

5   Experimental Results

In all the experimental setup, the square wavelet images with different dimensions are used. Due to the space limitation, only the most significant results (images with 64×64 and 90×90 dimensions with and without the TF) are shown.

In Table 2, the obtained results are also compared with a previous work [12]. In [12], a different methodology (using MFCC features together with TF) was

Table 2. Results obtained in the experiments. (*) A comparative result [12].

Features Type	Model	Sensitivity	Specificity	Overall
Wav(64)	SVM	0.8163	0.875	0.8456
Wav(64)	RF	0.8304	0.7089	0.7696
Wav(64)	CNN	0.773	0.2742	0.5236
Wav(64)+TF	SVM	0.8384	0.876	0.8572
Wav(64)+TF	RF	0.9929	0.6527	0.8228
Wav(64)+TF	CNN	0.795	0.4556	0.6253
Wav(90)	SVM	0.8865	0.8167	0.8516
Wav(90)	RF	0.9823	0.6196	0.8010
Wav(90)	CNN	0.7018	0.4126	0.5572
Wav(90)+TF	SVM	0.9045	0.8525	0.8785
Wav(90)+TF	RF	0.9929	0.6643	0.8286
Wav(90)+TF	CNN	0.7630	0.5592	0.6611
TF	SVM	0.835	0.6767	0.7559
5 MFCC+TF(*)	SVM	0.9187	0.8205	0.8696

applied to the same dataset. In that work, the best accuracy was 0.8696 which was obtained using SVM with the radial kernel.

The results show that the best experimental setup is images with 90 × 90 dimensions together with the TF features, achieving an accuracy of 0.8785. The best performance are obtained by using the SVM, with a linear kernel.

6   Discussion

The size of the images is used as a hyperparameter in the experimental setup to optimize the classification results. Due to the limitation of the computational resource, analyzing the images larger than 90 × 90 × 3 (three color layers - RGB) was not possible. The best results are obtained by using the SVM algorithm with a linear kernel followed by RF algorithm and CNN. Other classifiers are obtained lower results having low specificity values and in results low overall values. This is due to the high number of false positives which is the consequence of having unbalanced classes (30% and 70%) in the dataset. Using the wavelet images with the size of 90 × 90 together with the TF is obtained a sensitivity of 0.9045, a specificity of 0.8525 and an overall of 0.8785 which is the best experimental setup.

The CNN has the lowest accuracy which is related to the low amount of training data. The CNN performance is highly related to the amount of data used to train the network. Typically, the more data used for the training of the network, the better results will be obtained [14]. In this paper, only a small portion of the Physionet dataset is used for the training of the CNN due to the limitation in the computational power. Another important contribution is adding the TF to the wavelets features to improve the results. In all the experimental scenarios, a better classification accuracy is obtained when using the TF together with the wavelets features.

The overall scores for the top entries of the PhysioNet Challenge were very close to each other [3]. The difference in overall metric between the top place finisher (0.8602) and the 10th place (0.8263) was around 0.04%. Although the used dataset is smaller than the dataset used in the challenge, the class distribution is similar. The best result achieved is around 0.02 higher than the winner of the challenge. Furthermore, the best performance was achieved using a single SVM with a linear kernel, whereas other top place finishers of the challenge achieved high classification accuracies with an ensemble of classifiers [3]. Practically, a system that relies on only a single classifier, as opposed to a large ensemble, has the advantage of reducing the required computational resources.

7 Conclusion

In this work, we explore the dataset that was made available at Physionet databases. The goal is to discriminate between normal and abnormal hearts using PCG and ECG signals. Our approach included the segmentation of the heart signal, identifying the four states of the heart cycle, and creating three-second signal segments. From these segments, we extracted a set of time domain features and we perform the Wavelet analysis, in order to calculate the features of each segment of PCG signal, being these features used as input to our classifiers. We perform a binary classification that will assign a classification to all signal segments. Thereafter, it was necessary to group the predictions of the several segments to classify the original PCG signals.

The best performance was achieved using a SVM algorithm with a linear kernel which obtains an accuracy of 87.76%. The performance of the model was evaluated and compared to other classifiers. With the proposed approach we achieve a higher accuracy than the winner of the Physionet Challenge. The analysis of the results showed that the unbalanced dataset might be problematic for identifying the minority class, and the results could be improved by collecting more training data, and by balancing the dataset. One of the classifiers used was the CNN, which had worse results than the other classifiers. One possible cause for this is the small size of the dataset used, since this algorithm requires a large volume of data to converge.

As future work, we will investigate the usage of our methodology in larger datasets. Another future contribution will be the implementation of a dimension reduction process, in order to extract the most relevant information from the calculated features.

Acknowledgments. This work is financed by National Funds through the Portuguese funding agency, FCT - Fundação para a Ciência e a Tecnologia within project: UID/EEA/50014/2019.

References

1. Aguiar, L.F., Soares, M.J.: The continuous wavelet transform: a primer. NIPE Working Papers 16/2011, NIPE - Universidade do Minho, January 2011. https://ideas.repec.org/p/nip/nipewp/16-2011.html
2. Balili, C.C., Sobrepena, M.C.C., Naval, P.C.: Classification of heart sounds using discrete and continuous wavelet transform and random forests. In: 2015 3rd IAPR Asian Conference on Pattern Recognition (ACPR), pp. 655–659, November 2015
3. Clifford, G.D., et al.: Classification of normal/abnormal heart sound recordings: the PhysioNet/computing in cardiology challenge 2016. In: 2016 Computing in Cardiology Conference (CinC), pp. 609–612, September 2016
4. Ergen, B., Tatar, Y., Gulcur, H.O.: Time–frequency analysis of phonocardiogram signals using wavelet transform: a comparative study. Comput. Methods Biomech. Biomed. Eng. 15(4), 371–381 (2012)
5. Gomes, E., Bentley, P., Coimbra, M., Pereira, E., Deng, Y.: Classifying heart sounds: approaches to the PASCAL challenge. In: HEALTHINF 2013 - Proceedings of the International Conference on Health Informatics, pp. 337–340, January 2013
6. Huiying, L., Sakari, L., Iiro, H.: A heart sound segmentation algorithm using wavelet decomposition and reconstruction. In: Engineering in Medicine and Biology Society, vol. 4, pp. 1630–1633 (1997)
7. Kumar, D., Carvalho, P., Antunes, M., Paiva, R.P., Henriques, J.: Heart murmur classification with feature selection. In: 2010 Annual International Conference of the IEEE Engineering in Medicine and Biology, pp. 4566–4569, August 2010
8. LeCun, Y., et al.: Backpropagation applied to handwritten zip code recognition. Neural Comput. 1(4), 541–551 (1989)
9. Liu, C., Springer, D., Li, Q., et al.: An open access database for the evaluation of heart sound algorithms. Physiol. Meas. 37(12), 2181 (2016)
10. Malarvili, M.B., Kamarulafizam, I., Hussain, S., Helmi, D.: Heart sound segmentation algorithm based on instantaneous energy of electrocardiogram. In: Computers in Cardiology, pp. 327–330, September 2003
11. Mozaffarian, D., Benjamin, E.J., Go, A.S., et al.: Heart disease and stroke statistics—2016 update. Circulation (2015)
12. Nogueira, D.M., Ferreira, C.A., Jorge, A.M.: Classifying heart sounds using images of MFCC and temporal features. In: Oliveira, E., Gama, J., Vale, Z., Lopes Cardoso, H. (eds.) EPIA 2017. LNCS (LNAI), vol. 10423, pp. 186–203. Springer, Cham (2017). https://doi.org/10.1007/978-3-319-65340-2_16
13. Obaidat, M.S.: Phonocardiogram signal analysis: techniques and performance comparison. J. Med. Eng. Technol. 17(6), 221–227 (1993)
14. Shi, W., Gong, Y., Wang, J.: Improving CNN performance with min-max objective. In: Proceedings of the Twenty-Fifth International Joint Conference on Artificial Intelligence, IJCAI 2016, pp. 2004–2010 (2016)
15. Springer, D.B., Tarassenko, L., Clifford, G.D.: Logistic regression-HSMM-based heart sound segmentation. IEEE Trans. Biomed. Eng. 63(4), 822–832 (2016)
16. White, P.R., Collis, W.B., Salmon, A.P.: Time-frequency analysis of heart murmurs in children. In: IEE Colloquium on Time-Frequency Analysis of Biomedical Signals (Digest No. 1997/006), pp. 3/1–3/4 (1997)
17. Wu, J., Zhou, S., Wu, Z., Wu, X.m.: Research on the method of characteristic extraction and classification of phonocardiogram. In: 2012 International Conference on Systems and Informatics, pp. 1732–1735, May 2012

A Multi-modal Deep Learning Method for Classifying Chest Radiology Exams

Nelson Nunes[1]([envelope]), Bruno Martins[1], Nuno André da Silva[2], Francisca Leite[2], and Mário J. Silva[1]

[1] INESC-ID, Instituto Superior Técnico, Universidade de Lisboa, Lisbon, Portugal
{nelson.filipe,bruno.g.martins,mario.gaspar.silva}@tecnico.ulisboa.pt
[2] Hospital da Luz Learning Health, Luz Saude, Lisbon, Portugal
{nuno.asilva,francisca.leite}@hospitaldaluz.pt

Abstract. Non-invasive medical imaging techniques, such as radiography or computed tomography, are extensively used in hospitals and clinics for the diagnosis of diverse injuries or diseases. However, the interpretation of these images, which often results in a free-text radiology report and/or a classification, requires specialized medical professionals, leading to high labor costs and waiting lists. Automatic inference of thoracic diseases from the results of chest radiography exams, e.g. for the purpose of indexing these documents, is still a challenging task, even if combining images with the free-text reports. Deep neural architectures can contribute to a more efficient indexing of radiology exams (e.g., associating the data to diagnostic codes), providing interpretable classification results that can guide the domain experts. This work proposes a novel multi-modal approach, combining a dual path convolutional neural network for processing images with a bidirectional recurrent neural network for processing text, enhanced with attention mechanisms and leveraging pre-trained clinical word embeddings. The experimental results show interesting patterns, e.g. validating the high performance of the individual components, and showing promising results for the multi-modal processing of radiology examination data, particularly when pre-training the components of the model with large pre-existing datasets (i.e., a 10% increase in terms of the average value for the areas under the receiver operating characteristic curves).

Keywords: Classification of radiology exams ·
Machine learning in medicine · Learning from multi-modal data ·
Deep learning

1 Introduction

Chest radiography is globally the most common medical imaging examination. The interpretation of chest X-rays, involving specialized medical professionals, is critical for the screening, diagnosis, and management of many diseases.

© Springer Nature Switzerland AG 2019
P. Moura Oliveira et al. (Eds.): EPIA 2019, LNAI 11804, pp. 323–335, 2019.
https://doi.org/10.1007/978-3-030-30241-2_28

In recent years, leveraging the availability of large datasets [1,2], several authors have explored deep learning methods for the automated interpretation of chest radiography images, arguing that having automatic methods working at the level of practicing radiologists can provide substantial benefits in many medical settings, from improving workflow prioritization and assisting clinical coders, to supporting clinical decisions and large-scale screening initiatives. Many previous studies have, for instance, reported good results with methods based on Convolutional Neural Networks (CNNs) [3], in the task of coding chest radiography images according to classes conforming to the Fleischner Society's recommended glossary of terms for thoracic imaging [1,4].

Accurate models for data classification (e.g., for assigning images and/or text [5,6] to codes within standard clinical taxonomies) can significantly speed-up the coding process, decrease labor costs, increase coding consistency, and standardize the coding of legacy data. The picture archiving and communication systems (PACSs) and the radiology information systems (RISs) of many clinics/hospitals have large amounts of chest radiology images, stored together with free-text radiology reports summarizing their interpretation. Thus, we argue that the combination of state-of-the-art methods for image analysis [3] and natural language processing [7] can be particularly interesting in the context of coding legacy data, directly considering multi-modal contents (i.e., images together with existing text reports) as a way to improve the classification results.

In this paper, we introduce a novel multi-modal approach to classify chest radiology exams, combining convolutional and recurrent neural networks. For processing image data, we use a dual path convolutional neural network [8], combining ideas from both densely connected [9] and residual [10] networks. For processing text, we leverage pre-trained FastText [11] embeddings, together with Bidirectional Multiplicative Long Short-Term Memory (bi-mLSTM) units [12] for creating intermediate representations, which are finally combined through a multi-head attention mechanism [13]. Both parts of the model can be used in isolation, and they can be pre-trained using large existing datasets (i.e., the MIMIC-CXR [2] or CheXpert [1] datasets of chest radiology images, or the MIMIC-III [14] dataset of clinical texts). The complete model concatenates the representations from the convolutional and recurrent parts, and it can be trained end-to-end (or fine-tuned, in case we leverage pre-trained components) from data combining both modalities, e.g. using the standard back-propagation algorithm together with an optimization method such as Adam [15].

We report on experiments with four distinct datasets (i.e., frontal chest radiography images from the aforementioned MIMIC-CXR and CheXpert datasets, a subset of MIMIC-III corresponding to chest radiology free-text reports, and multi-modal instances from the OpenI dataset [16]), in all cases considering 14 labels for common diseases, and using stratified sampling [17–19] to split the data into training (75%) and testing (25%) sub-sets. Our tests contrasted single- versus multi-modal approaches, and they assessed the impact of model pre-training, evaluating results in terms of a variety of metrics (i.e., classification accuracy, coverage error, label ranking average precision, and micro- and macro-averaged values for precision, recall, F1, and Areas Under Receiver Operating Characteristic Curves (AUROCs)).

When using image contents alone, the convolutional model achieved 0.825 in micro-AUROC, a result that is in line with the current state-of-the-art (or even slightly better). On the OpenI dataset and leveraging pre-training, the complete model achieved 0.985 in micro-AUROC, 0.983 in accuracy, 1.547 in coverage error, and 0.966 in terms of label ranking average precision. These results confirm the usefulness of using multi-modal data. By leveraging existing datasets for model pre-training, very accurate results can be attained, opening the way to the development of tools for assisting clinical coders.

The next section describes related work, while Sect. 3 presents the proposed method. Section 4 details the evaluation methodology and the obtained results, also describing how visualizations based on pixel- and word-level attention can help to interpret the model predictions. Finally, Sect. 5 summarizes our conclusions and presents directions for future work.

2 Related Work

Large labeled datasets have recently driven deep learning methods to achieve expert-level performance on a variety of medical imaging interpretation tasks [1, 20–22]. Recent examples of publicly available datasets include MIMIC-CXR [2] and CheXpert [1] for the classification of chest X-ray images. Similarly, deep learning methods have also been used on tasks related to interpreting medical text, including the assignment of death certificates, discharge summaries, or other types of clinical text, to nodes in standardized taxonomies such as the International Classification of Diseases (ICD) [6,14]. Again, these studies have leveraged the availability of large labeled datasets, with a recent example being the MIMIC-III [14] database on patients admitted to critical care units, which includes free-text contents (e.g., radiology reports) associated with ICD codes.

A recent example for the use of deep learning on the task of coding medical text is the work reported by Duarte et al. [6], in which the authors evaluated the performance of a hierarchical attention network [23] on the task of classifying death certificates according to ICD-10, using the free-text descriptions in death certificates and associated autopsy reports. The proposed model combined recurrent units and attention mechanisms in a hierarchical arrangement (i.e., bi-directional Gated Recurrent Units (bi-GRUs) were used together with a neural attention layer to generate a representation for each sentence, and a separate combination of bi-GRUs with an attention layer was used to model the sequence of sentences associated with each certificate), generating meaningful intermediate representations for the textual contents. On a large dataset of death certificates collected from the mortality surveillance system of the Portuguese Ministry of Health, the authors obtained a high classification accuracy (e.g. 76.112%, 81.349%, and 89.320%, respectively for the classification of death certificates according to ICD full-codes, blocks, and chapters).

Karimi et al. [24] reported on the use of a Convolutional Neural Network (CNN), inspired on a previous method for general text classification [25], in the task of coding free-text radiology reports according to ICD codes. The authors used a grid-search procedure to optimize different parameters of the proposed model (e.g., type and dimensionality of word embeddings, activation functions on both the convolutional and fully-connected layers, and values for convolution filter size, depth, and stride), and also the training hyper-parameters (e.g., learning rate, batch size, number of epochs, and drop-out rates). The best configuration achieved an accuracy of 83.84%, with results suggesting that the use of pre-trained word embeddings over in-domain data can improve the overall classification accuracy.

On what concerns previous studies focusing on the analysis of medical images, specifically chest X-rays, Wang et al. introduced the ChestX-ray8 dataset of multi-labelled images with 8 disease labels [20]. Together with the dataset, the authors also reported on the classification results obtained with CNN model architectures (e.g., AlexNet, GoogLeNet, VGGNet-16 and ResNet-50), concluding that ResNet-50 significantly outperformed the other models (e.g., it achieved the highest AUROC in 7 of the 8 labels). The US National Institute of Health further expanded ChestX-ray8 into the ChestX-ray14 dataset, including more images and 6 additional disease labels. Using these data, Rajpurkar et al. [22] tested a 121-layer Dense Convolutional Network (DenseNet), achieving state-of-the-art results in all 14 pathologies, and detecting pneumonia from chest X-rays at a level exceeding practicing radiologists.

The previous work that is perhaps most similar to ours was reported by Wang et al. [21], addressing the combined use of text and image data. The authors presented a neural architecture for disease classification in chest X-ray exams, named text-image embedding network (TieNet). In brief, TieNet corresponds to an end-to-end architecture combing convolutional (ResNet-50) and recurrent (LSTM) layers, also enhancing the CNN-LSTM combination with attention-encoded text embeddings (AETE), a saliency weighted global average pooling (SW-GAP) layer, and a joint loss function.

TieNet explores the intuition that connecting CNN and LSTM networks can help the training of both. Specifically, image activations can be adjusted for the text embedding task, and the salient image features can be extracted by pooling based on high textual saliency. Concretely, the SW-GAP layer represents the global visual information, guided by both text and visual attention. In turn, the AETE layer uses attention to combine the most salient portions of the LSTM hidden states. The joint learning mechanism combines the results from the AETE and SW-GAP layers, concatenating both representations and feeding them to a final fully-connected layer, which outputs the multi-label classification results. The authors of TieNet discuss its application to classify chest X-rays exams using both image features and text embeddings extracted from the associated reports, and also as a complete reporting system (i.e., outputting disease classification and a preliminary report together). The classification results showed that TieNet achieves a high accuracy (e.g., 0.965 and 0.989 average in micro-AUROCs, respectively for the OpenI [16] and ChestX-ray14 datasets).

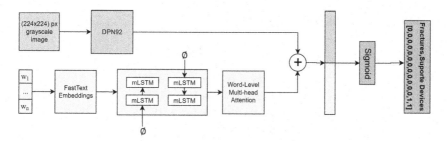

Fig. 1. Overview on the proposed neural architecture.

3   The Proposed Approach

The proposed network architecture has two separate branches that extract meaningful representations from the distinct information modalities, namely from X-ray images and associated radiology reports. Figure 1 provides an illustration.

The text classification branch has three main components: BioWordVec [26] pre-trained word embeddings, Bidirectional Multiplicative Long Short-Term Memory (bi-mLSTM) units [12], and a multi-head attention [13] mechanism. In turn, the image classification branch uses a modern CNN model called the Dual Path Network (DPN), more specifically the DPN-92 [8]. The complete network concatenates the representations from both branches, using the resulting features to inform a prediction layer. Although this fusion method is much simpler than the one used in the TieNet model [21], it allows us easily to pre-train the two branches of the network.

BioWordVec are FastText [11] word embeddings pre-trained over large biomedical corpora, specifically PubMed abstracts and clinical notes from MIMIC-III [26]. The FastText approach involves training embeddings for individual word tokens and character n-grams, allowing us to compute embeddings for out-of-vocabulary words, by averaging the embeddings for the corresponding n-grams. This aspect is particularly interesting for clinical text, where orthographic variations and typographical errors are often present.

Typical approaches for representing textual data involve Long Short-Term Memory (LSTM) units, i.e. neural networks that model sequential data by having a recurrent hidden state regulated by gates. A gate $f()$ decides which part of the memory cell will be forgotten, a gate $i()$ controls how much input information is added to the memory cell, and a gate $o()$ filters the cell memory, deciding how much to use for computing the output. The values for these gates are calculated based on linear combinations of the current input x_t and the previous state h_{t-1}, passed through an activation function (e.g., the logistic sigmoid $\sigma()$). LSTM units can be formally defined as follows, where $\odot$ corresponds to an element-wise multiplication, and y_t corresponds to the result from the LSTM unit (i.e., the hidden states) for each position t.

$$
\begin{aligned}
h_t &= \tanh\left(c_t\right) \odot o \\
c_t &= c_{t-1} \odot f + g \odot i \\
i &= \sigma\left(x_t \cdot W^{xi} + h_{t-1} \cdot W^{hi}\right) \\
f &= \sigma\left(x_t \cdot W^{xf} + h_{t-1} \cdot W^{hf}\right) \\
o &= \sigma\left(x_t \cdot W^{xo} + h_{t-1} \cdot W^{ho}\right) \\
g &= \tanh\left(x_t \cdot W^{xg} + h_{t-1} \cdot W^{hg}\right) \\
y_t &= h_t
\end{aligned}
\tag{1}
$$

Bi-directional LSTM units (bi-LSTMs) can be used to process a sequence of words both in a forward ($\overrightarrow{h_{it}}$), and in a backward direction ($\overleftarrow{h_{it}}$). By concatenating the states from two independent LSTM units (i.e., $h_{it} = [\overrightarrow{h_{it}}, \overleftarrow{h_{it}}]$), bi-LSTMs can provide a more wide-ranging summary of the information at each position i.

In our model, instead of standard bi-LSTMs, we used the recently proposed Multiplicative LSTM units (mLSTMs), also within a bi-directional arrangement. These units combine factorized hidden-to-hidden transitions (i.e. an idea taken from multiplicative recurrent neural networks) with the gating logic from LSTMs [12]. For a given input, mLSTMs can have different recurrent transition functions, and this approach can be formally defined as follows, where m_t represents an intermediate state.

$$
\begin{aligned}
h_t &= \tanh\left(c_t\right) \odot o \\
c_t &= c_{t-1} \odot f + g \odot i \\
m_t &= \left(x_t \cdot W^{xm}\right) \odot \left(h_{t-1} \cdot W^{ht}\right) \\
i &= \sigma\left(x_t \cdot W^{xi} + m_t \cdot W^{mi}\right) \\
f &= \sigma\left(x_t \cdot W^{xf} + m_t \cdot W^{mf}\right) \\
o &= \sigma\left(x_t \cdot W^{xo} + m_t \cdot W^{mo}\right) \\
g &= \tanh\left(x_t \cdot W^{xh} + m_t \cdot W^{mh}\right) \\
y_t &= h_t
\end{aligned}
\tag{2}
$$

Moreover, instead of the standard sigmoid activation function, we used the penalized hyperbolic tangent [27] as the activation function within the mLSTM units, penalizing negative inputs to create an additional non-linearity that facilitates model training, as shown in the next equation:

$$
f(x) = \begin{cases} \tanh(x) & \text{if } x > 0 \\ 0.25 \cdot \tanh(x) & \text{otherwise} \end{cases}
\tag{3}
$$

Previous experiments showed improved results when combining the penalized hyperbolic tangent with standard LSTM units, in a variety of NLP tasks [28].

The results from the bi-directional mLSTM units (i.e., the hidden states) can be combined through attention mechanisms, i.e. functions that map a context vector and a set of hidden state vectors into a single output vector [13,23]. The output vector is the result of a weighted sum of the hidden states, where the weights are computed by a score function that takes as input the context vector and each hidden state vector. A commonly used attention mechanism can be formally defined as follows:

$$s = \sum_t \left(\frac{\exp\left(\tanh(W \cdot y_t + b) \cdot u\right)}{\sum_{t'} \exp\left(\tanh(W \cdot y_{t'} + b) \cdot u\right)} \right) \times y_t \qquad (4)$$

In the previous equation, s corresponds to the text representation resulting from the attention weighting, while W, u and b are learned parameters, respectively a matrix of weights, the context vector, and a bias term. Multiplying the softmax outputs (i.e., the part in brackets) with each hidden state keeps the values of the words that are more significant for the task, and reduces the values for less important words. In our model, we used multiple attention mechanisms, thus considering multiple representations (i.e., different weights, learned independently in each attention head, associated with the different word positions). The output that is produced from the multi-head attention mechanism corresponds to the concatenation of the weighted value vectors of each head.

On what regards the branch from Fig. 1 that takes as input the image contents (i.e., a matrix of 224×224 values encoding pixel intensity in X-ray images), the Dual Path Network (DPN) combines ideas from the ResNet and DenseNet CNN architectures, through two distinct path topologies. The main idea is illustrated on Fig. 2, which contrasts DPNs against the standard ResNet and DenseNet architectures.

Residual Networks (ResNets) use skip connections to create paths propagating information from earlier to later layers, implicitly reusing features although lacking on the exploration of new features [10]. The skip connections in ResNet models are the result of adding the input features to the output features through a residual path. Dense Convolutional Networks (DenseNets), on the other hand, concatenate the input features with the outputs, exploring new features but suffering from higher redundancy [9]. Every DenseNet block receives the unmodified output of all previous blocks. Learning good representations benefits both from feature reuse and exploitation, thus motivating the combination of both aforementioned ideas.

Chen et al. [8] present DPNs in detail, including the parameters associated with the multiple modualized mirco-blocks that are stacked in the complete CNN architecture, while Krause et al. [12] describe mLSTMs, and Vaswani et al. [13] and Yang et al. [23] both present neural attention. The word embeddings and the output of each mLSTM layer have a dimensionality of 200, and the multi-head mechanism considers 4 heads of attention. We also used the DPN-92 version, with a total of 37.8×10^6 parameters. The complete model was implemented through the keras[1] deep learning library, and the source code supporting our experiments was also made available[2] on GitHub.

---

[1] http://keras.io/.

[2] http://github.com/nfrn/Multi-Modal-Classification-of-Radiology-Exams.

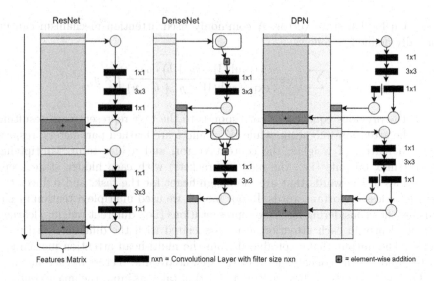

Fig. 2. ResNet, DenseNet, and DPN architectures as described by Chen et al. [8].

4   Experimental Evaluation

This section describes the experimental evaluation of the proposed network, first presenting the datasets and the experimental methodology, and then the obtained results.

4.1   Datasets and Experimental Methodology

Our experiments relied on four different datasets, including two datasets containing frontal chest X-ray images labeled according to 14 observation classes (i.e., CheXpert [1] and MIMIC-CXR [2]), one dataset of full-text radiology reports (i.e., a subset of the data from MIMIC-III [14] with the ICD labels converted to the same 14 observation classes), and the OpenI [16] multi-modal radiography dataset, collected from multiple institutes by Indiana University and containing frontal chest X-ray images together with full-text reports, also labeled according to the same 14 observation classes. Table 1 provides some general dataset characterization statistics.

MIMIC-CXR includes 371,920 chest X-rays, associated with 227,943 studies involving patients admitted to the Beth Israel Deaconess Medical Center, between 2011 and 2016. CheXpert consists of 224,316 chest X-rays from 65,240 patients, collected from Stanford Hospital between October 2002 and July 2017. In both cases, we considered only frontal view X-ray images (i.e., 250,044 instances from MIMIC-CXR, and 191,229 instances from CheXpert), merging both datasets for the experiments involving image data (i.e., when evaluating DPNs alone, or for pre-training the complete model in the case of multi-modal tests).

Table 1. Statistical characterization of the datasets used in the experiments.

Label	MIMIC-CXR	CheXpert	MIMIC-III	OpenI
No Finding	83,336	19,765	133,563	2,062
Enlarged Cardiomediastinum	18,240	19,578	608	0
Cardiomegaly	56,012	30,158	351	323
Lung/Airspace Opacity	60,196	98,759	62	417
Lung Lesion	8,315	8,149	9,741	1,291
Edema	43,812	61,535	4,635	67
Consolidation	16,614	37,396	43,006	28
Pneumonia	38,262	20,664	82,526	78
Atelectasis	61,108	59,658	287	349
Pneumothorax	12,953	20,408	16,241	25
Pleural Effusion	65,449	86,541	29,978	160
Pleural Other	3,009	4,318	896	37
Fracture	5,675	7,935	16,862	97
Support Devices	74,970	108,184	10,504	48
Total Number of Examples	250,044	191,229	261,091	3,689

MIMIC-III is a freely accessible critical care database containing, among other elements, radiology reports associated with ICD diagnostic codes (taken from patient discharge notes). We filtered the radiology reports according to the occurrence of key-phrases such as *chest*, *lungs* or *thorax*, and using the ICD codes that result from matching the 14 labels of the MIMIC-CXR dataset with the correspondent set of ICD codes. Finally, the complete OpenI dataset includes 3,851 radiology reports and the associated 7,784 chest X-ray images. We filtered the dataset to consider only 3,689 instances containing full-text reports and frontal X-ray images, labeled according to the 14 labels from MIMIC-CXR/CheXpert.

Taking into account the multi-label nature of the datasets, we considered stratification when dividing the data (i.e., the merging of MIMIC-CXR/CheXpert, and the subsets from MIMIC-III and OpenI) into training (75%) and testing (25%) splits. The stratification method balances the assignment of instances into splits, attending to the distribution of single classes and multi-class pairs [17,18].

Model training was made with batches of 64 instances, leveraging backpropagation together with the Adam optimization method [15]. The learning rate was initially set to 10^{-3}, and then refined through a criteria based on the loss over the training data, reducing it by a factor of 0.1 if the loss does not decrease during 5 consecutive epochs. The number of epochs was also defined through a criteria based on the training loss, stopping when the variation between consecutive epochs was less than 10^{-6}.

To assess the quality of the predictions, we used the following evaluation metrics: accuracy (i.e., average number of correct labels per instance), coverage

Table 2. Results for all the considered experimental settings.

Model	Accuracy	LRAP	CE	Precision		Recall		F1-score		AUROC	
				Micro	Macro	Micro	Macro	Micro	Macro	Micro	Macro
MIMIC-CXR/CheXpert	0.843	0.6531	5.085	0.499	0.235	0.485	0.244	0.492	0.197	0.825	0.656
MIMIC-III reports	0.938	0.8641	1.876	0.848	0.571	0.633	0.580	0.725	0.550	0.968	0.922
OpenI - Pre-trained image model	0.840	0.3565	5.796	0.423	0.142	0.282	0.040	0.338	0.052	0.621	0.500
OpenI - Pre-trained text model	0.900	0.6788	3.965	0.511	0.258	0.477	0.214	0.493	0.169	0.746	0.611
OpenI - Complete model	0.849	0.7508	2.601	0.741	0.202	0.358	0.072	0.483	0.102	0.882	0.608
OpenI - Pre-trained complete model	**0.983**	**0.9657**	**1.547**	**0.919**	**0.621**	**0.910**	**0.651**	**0.915**	**0.632**	**0.985**	**0.936**

error (CE) (i.e., how many labels, ranked according to prediction scores, need to be checked to cover all the true labels), label ranking average precision (LRAP), and micro- and macro-averaged scores for precision, recall, F1, and areas under ROC curves (AUROCs).

4.2   Experimental Results

Our tests considered three different settings: (i) use the DPN-92 model to classify X-ray images, leveraging the combined MIMIC-CXR/CheXpert data; (ii) use bi-directional mLSTMs, together with multi-head attention and BioWordVec embeddings, to classify chest radiology reports from MIMIC-III; and (iii) use the complete model to classify the multi-modal instances from the OpenI dataset, with and without model pre-training leveraging the remaining datasets. Table 2 presents the obtained results over the testing data splits. The first two rows correspond to Setting (i), the middle rows correspond to Setting (ii), and the last two rows to Setting (iii).

The complete model, leveraging both modalities with pre-trained weights and fine-tuned with the OpenI training split, achieved a very high performance in terms of the different metrics, outperforming methods using just a single modality, and/or methods without model pre-training. Pre-training, in particular, contributed significantly to the overall performance of the complete model (e.g., 15% improvement in accuracy, and 50% improvement in macro-AUROC).

In connection to the classification results, the proposed model also allows us to explore two distinct interpretability views. Using a gradient-weighted class activation map (Grad-CAM), it is possible to visualize which areas of the X-ray were more important to the classification decision [29]. Simultaneously, using the weights from the multi-head attention mechanism, it is possible to visualize which words in the full-text report were more important to the classification.

Figure 3 presents an example instance from the OpenI test split, correctly assigned to the classes *Support Devices* and *Lung Lesion*, together with the corresponding text report. The X-ray is overlayed with two Grad-CAM heatmaps, emphasizing the areas that were more important to support each classification decision (i.e., left and right X-ray images for *Support Devices* and *Lung Lesion*, respectively). The first heatmap clearly highlights the area corresponding to a medical device. The colored boxes over the text, on the right, denote word attention weights according to two of the attention heads (i.e., blue and green), also emphasizing words like *left upper lung* or *device*.

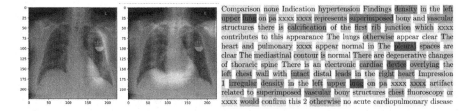

Fig. 3. Illustration for attention weights associated with an example instance from the OpenI test split, correctly labeled according to the class *Support Devices* and *Lung Lesion*. (Color figure in the online version)

5   Conclusions and Future Work

This paper presented a novel deep learning method for the multi-label classification of data from radiology exams according to 14 observation classes, combining both X-ray images and full-text reports. The complete model, with pre-trained weights leveraging large existing datasets and fine-tuned on instances from the OpenI dataset, achieved a high performance in terms of multiple evaluation metrics for multi-label classification. The obtained results confirm that the deep learning approach leveraging multi-modal data can indeed achieve a high accuracy in this domain, opening the way to the development of tools that can effectively assist medical professionals (e.g., clinical coders).

Despite the interesting results, there are also many ideas for future work. For instance, besides ResNet/DenseNet extensions, such as the Dual Path Network used in our study, other authors have instead proposed advanced models based on neural architecture search [30]. For future work, and particularly considering that we can easily have access to large datasets of chest X-ray images for supporting model (pre-)training, we plan to experiment with other types of CNN architectures for processing the image contents, e.g. similar to the recently proposed AmoebaNet [31]. Instead of the FastText embeddings used in our tests, we also plan to experiment with contextual word embeddings [32], which have achieved state-of-the-art results on several NLP benchmarks. Some recent studies have already advanced pre-trained contextual embeddings for clinical text [33].

Finally, the authors of the MIMIC-CXR [2] dataset plan to release an extended version, incorporating X-ray images together with the full-text reports. We also plan to evaluate the multi-modal approach on this larger dataset, once it becomes available.

Acknowledgements. Authors from INESC-ID were partially supported through Fundação para a Ciência e Tecnologia (FCT), specifically through the INESC-ID multi-annual funding from the PIDDAC programme (UID/CEC/50021/2019). We gratefully acknowledge the support of NVIDIA Corporation, with the donation of the Titan Xp GPU used in the experiments.

References

1. Irvin, J., et al.: CheXpert: a large chest radiograph dataset with uncertainty labels and expert comparison. In: Proceedings of the AAAI Conference on Artificial Intelligence (2019)
2. Johnson, A., et al.: MIMIC-CXR: a large publicly available database of labeled chest radiographs. arXiv preprint arXiv:1901.07042 (2019)
3. Khan, S., Rahmani, S., Shah, S.A., Bennamoun, M.: A guide to convolutional neural networks for computer vision. In: Synthesis Lectures on Computer Vision (2018)
4. Hansell, D.M., Bankier, A.A., MacMahon, H., McLoud, T.C., Muller, N.L., Remy, J.: Fleischner society: glossary of terms for thoracic imaging. Radiology **246**(3), 697–722 (2008)
5. Laserson, J., et al.: TextRay: mining clinical reports to gain a broad understanding of chest x-rays. In: Frangi, A.F., Schnabel, J.A., Davatzikos, C., Alberola-López, C., Fichtinger, G. (eds.) MICCAI 2018. LNCS, vol. 11071, pp. 553–561. Springer, Cham (2018). https://doi.org/10.1007/978-3-030-00934-2_62
6. Duarte, F., Martins, B., Pinto, C.S., Silva, M.J.: Deep neural models for ICD-10 coding of death certificates and autopsy reports in free-text. J. Biomed. Inform. **80**, 64–77 (2018)
7. Goldberg, Y.: Neural network methods for natural language processing. In: Synthesis Lectures on Human Language Technologies (2017)
8. Chen, Y., Li, J., Xiao, H., Jin, X., Yan, S., Feng, J.: Dual path networks. In: Proceedings of the Annual Conference on Neural Information Processing Systems (2017)
9. Huang, G., Liu, Z., van der Maaten, L., Weinberger, K.Q.: Densely connected convolutional networks. In: Proceedings of the IEEE Conference on Computer Vision and Pattern Recognition (2017)
10. He, K., Zhang, X., Ren, S., Sun, J.: Deep residual learning for image recognition. In: Proceedings of the IEEE Conference on Computer Vision and Pattern Recognition (2016)
11. Joulin, A., Grave, E., Bojanowski, P., Mikolov, T.: Bag of tricks for efficient text classification. In: Proceedings of the Conference of the North American Chapter of the Association for Computational Linguistics (2017)
12. Krause, B., Lu, L., Murray, I., Renals, S.: Multiplicative LSTM for sequence modelling. arXiv preprint arXiv:1609.07959 (2017)
13. Vaswani, A., et al.: Attention is all you need. In: Proceedings of the Annual Conference on Neural Information Processing Systems (2017)
14. Johnson, A.E.W., et al.: MIMIC-III, a freely accessible critical care database. Sci. Data **3**, 160035 (2016)
15. Kingma, D.P., Ba, J.: Adam: a method for stochastic optimization. arXiv preprint arXiv:1412.6980 (2015)
16. Demner-Fushman, D., et al.: Preparing a collection of radiology examinations for distribution and retrieval. J. Am. Med. Inform. Assoc. **23**(2), 304–310 (2016)

17. Szymański, P., Kajdanowicz, T.: A network perspective on stratification of multi-label data. In: Proceedings of the International Workshop on Learning with Imbalanced Domains: Theory and Applications (2017)
18. Sechidis, K., Tsoumakas, G., Vlahavas, I.: On the stratification of multi-label data. In: Gunopulos, D., Hofmann, T., Malerba, D., Vazirgiannis, M. (eds.) ECML PKDD 2011. LNCS (LNAI), vol. 6913, pp. 145–158. Springer, Heidelberg (2011). https://doi.org/10.1007/978-3-642-23808-6_10
19. Szymański, P., Kajdanowicz, T.: A scikit-based Python environment for performing multi-label classification. arXiv preprint arXiv:1702.01460 (2017)
20. Wang, X., Peng, Y., Lu, L., Lu, Z., Bagheri, M., Summers, R.M.: ChestX-ray8: hospital-scale chest X-ray database and benchmarks on weakly-supervised classification and localization of common thorax diseases. In: Proceedings of the IEEE Conference on Computer Vision and Pattern Recognition (2017)
21. Wang, X., Peng, Y., Lu, L., Lu, Z., Summers, R.M.: TieNet: text-image embedding network for common thorax disease classification and reporting in chest x-rays. In: Proceedings of the IEEE Conference on Computer Vision and Pattern Recognition (2018)
22. Rajpurkar, R.M., et al.: CheXNet: radiologist-level pneumonia detection on chest x-rays with deep learning. arXiv preprint arXiv:1711.05225 (2017)
23. Yang, Z., Yang, D., Dyer, C., He, X., Smola, A.J., Hovy, E.H.: Hierarchical attention networks for document classification. In: Proceedings of the Annual Conference of the North American Chapter of the Association for Computational Linguistics (2016)
24. Karimi, S., Dai, X., Hassanzadeh, H., Nguyen, A.: Automatic diagnosis coding of radiology reports: a comparison of deep learning and conventional classification methods. In: Proceedings of the Workshop on Biomedical Natural Language Processing (2017)
25. Kim, Y.: Convolutional neural networks for sentence classification. In: Proceedings of the Conference on Empirical Methods in Natural Language Processing (2014)
26. Chen, Q., Peng, Y., Lu, Z.: BioSentVec: creating sentence embeddings for biomedical texts. arXiv preprint arXiv:1810.09302 (2018)
27. Xu, B., Huang, R., Li, M.: Revise saturated activation functions. arXiv preprint arXiv:1602.05980 (2016)
28. Eger, S., Youssef, P., Gurevych, I.: Is it time to swish? Comparing deep learning activation functions across NLP tasks. In: Proceedings of the Conference on Empirical Methods in Natural Language Processing (2018)
29. Selvaraju, R., Cogswell, M., Das, A., Vedantam, R., Parikh, D., Batra, D.: Grad-CAM: visual explanations from deep networks via gradient-based localization. In: Proceedings of the IEEE International Conference on Computer Vision (2017)
30. Zoph, B., Vasudevan, V., Shlens, J., Le, Q.V.: Learning transferable architectures for scalable image recognition. In: 2018 IEEE/CVF Conference on Computer Vision and Pattern Recognition (2018)
31. Real, E., Aggarwal, A., Huang, Y., Le, Q.V.: Regularized evolution for image classifier architecture search. arXiv preprint arXiv:1802.01548 (2018)
32. Devlin, J., Chang, M.-W., Lee, K., Toutanova, K.: BERT: pre-training of deep bidirectional transformers for language understanding. arXiv preprint arXiv:1810.04805 (2018)
33. Alsentzer, E., et al.: Publicly available clinical BERT embeddings. arXiv preprint arXiv:1904.03323 (2019)

Named Entity Recognition in Portuguese Neurology Text Using CRF

Fábio Lopes[(✉)], César Teixeira[(✉)], and Hugo Gonçalo Oliveira[(✉)]

Center for Informatics and Systems, Department of Informatics Engineering,
University of Coimbra, Coimbra, Portugal
fadcl@student.dei.uc.pt, {cteixei,hroliv}@dei.uc.pt

Abstract. Automatic recognition of named entities from clinical text lightens the work of health professionals by helping in the interpretation and easing tasks such as the population of databases with patient health information. In this study, we evaluated the performance of Conditional Random Fields, a sequence labelling model, for extracting entities from neurology clinical texts written in Portuguese. More than achieving F1-scores of about 73% or 80%, respectively for a relaxed or strict evaluation, the more discriminant features in this task were also analyzed.

Keywords: Natural Language Processing ·
Named Entity Recognition · Portuguese clinical text ·
Machine learning · Conditional Random Fields

1 Introduction

The exponential growth of the computational resources allowed the increase of data production and storage. In the clinical field, there is much unstructured data, e.g., admission notes and diagnostic test reports, which contain information about the clinical status of the patients, e.g., their clinical evolution or the most frequent diseases during a time span [8]. Towards more efficient acquisition, it is fundamental to develop tools that can extract all this data and structure them in such a way that storage (e.g., in a relation database) and access are easier. Such tools are usually based on Natural Language Processing (NLP), a branch of Artificial Intelligence that deals with human language manipulation and understanding by machines.

In this work, we studied how to perform Information Extraction (IE), a subtask of NLP that aims to extract structured knowledge from text, in such a way that it becomes more easily interpretable. Specifically, we studied popular methods for Named Entity Recognition (NER) and their application to clinical text. NER is a subtask of IE that tackles the identification and classification of mentions of entities that are relevant for interpreting the text.

On the health domain, named entities (NE) may include the condition of the patient, the diagnostic tests and their results, and the treatments and how they were done.

© Springer Nature Switzerland AG 2019
P. Moura Oliveira et al. (Eds.): EPIA 2019, LNAI 11804, pp. 336–348, 2019.
https://doi.org/10.1007/978-3-030-30241-2_29

This study was triggered by our access to a collection of clinical documents in the Neurology service of the Coimbra University Hospital Centre (CHUC), in Coimbra, Portugal, and thus written in Portuguese. Additionally, although clinical text mining is not a new area, and there is much work in English written tests, Portuguese NLP studies are still scarce [3,10]. Given that languages are different, i.e., have different grammars, vocabulary, follow different writing styles, we aim to study whether it is possible to adopt state-of-the-art methods in NER from Portuguese clinical data, for its future application in CHUC. Therefore, instead of using exhaustive rule-based and dictionary-based models, we wanted to figure out how a machine learning model based on Conditional Random Fields (CRF) performs. Another goal of this study is to find out what are the most important features of Portuguese clinical texts.

In the next section we introduce state-of-art methods that have been used in NER. In Sect. 3 we show some statistics about our dataset, how were the texts labelled, and we explain the model that we are proposing. Section 4 reports on the obtained results – we achieved a micro average F1-score of about 73% and 80%, respectively for relaxed and strict evaluation. We conclude the paper with a brief discussion of the results.

2 Related Work

Several classes of named entities have been extracted from medical test reports, patient discharge letters and other hospital records. Those include medication information [5], or patient data, such as conditions, test results [9], therapeutics [3,9], or disorders [18,19].

NER has been tackled with unsupervised approaches, with rules based on regular expressions combined with the exploitation of medical vocabularies [5] or ontologies [3,18]. Mykowiecka et al. [9] handcrafted a set of rules and, despite achieving precision and recall above 80%, admitted that the rules are highly dependent on the quality of the reports. Skeppstedt et al. [18] assigned entity classes to tokens based on their presence in terminologies. If a token is assigned to more than one class, some classes are preferred over others (e.g., body structures are preferred over disorders and findings). Ferreira et al. [3] also exploits terminologies and reports results near 100% for most entity classes, but their model was only assessed on ten discharge letters.

Despite the high performances reported, the development of rule-based models is time-consuming due the exhaustive labour involved in the creation of rules and dictionaries, not to mention that these models are generally tuned for the target documents, thus making adaptation to other types of text difficult. Classification can also be quite slow, because it has to look up on dictionaries or compare with pre-designed templates for finding what class each token belongs. Furthermore, some words may appear in different entities (e.g., "tumor" can be labelled as a condition or a result of a diagnostic test; "lombar puncture" can be labelled as a diagnostic test or a therapy) which may not be distinguishable for models based on rules and dictionaries.

To make the development of NER models easier, it is fundamental to adopt machine learning algorithms, where the computer learns how to predict the class of an entity based on a set of annotated examples and extracted features. In this scope, NER is typically seen as a sequence-labelling task, and models for this purpose are often applied, e.g., Hidden Markov Models (HMM), Maximum Entropy Markov-Model (MEMM), Conditional Random Fields (CRF), Support Vector Machines (SVM) and Decision Trees. Yet, literature consistently suggests that the best results are obtained with CRFs [11,21].

CRF models have been trained on NER from clinical text [19] and outperformed rule-based systems in a similar scenario [18]. Relevant features for this purpose have been analysed [19] and included dictionary forms (lemmas) of the current and previous tokens; the Part-of-Speech (POS) tag of the current, following, and the two previous tokens; the terminology matching class for the current and the previous tokens; the compound splitting features for the current token; and the orthographic features for the current token.

Results of classic CRFs have also been improved by exploiting distributional semantic features[1], learned from large clinical corpora.

Prototypical representations of each NE class were learned by exploiting NE annotations and a distributional model based on random indexing [6]. Different types of neural word embeddings have also been learned for this purpose [22]: using word vectors of real numbers, discrete values, and based on a matrix with the prototypical words for each class based on normalized Pointwise Mutual Information (nPMI).

One of the issues behind the evaluation of this kind of data is that, in most languages, annotated datasets with clinical text are scarce, which makes it difficult to compare the results of different approaches. This happens not only due to the time-consuming human labour of annotating clinical text, which requires some degree of domain knowledge, but also because most collections of clinical data are not public, due to privacy legislation. This adds to the fact that there are different languages, with different specificities, which means that, results obtained for one language are often not directly replicable in other languages. On this aspect, most of the studies identified were for English, despite a minority for other languages, such as Polish [9], Swedish [19], and Portuguese [3]. Although the latter is our target language, their approach is mostly rule-based and does not apply machine learning.

3   Materials and Methods

This work tackles NER in Portuguese clinical text. For this purpose, a CRF classifier was adopted and its performance was analysed after training and test

---

[1] Distributional semantic models, or word embeddings, are typically learned from large collections of text and represent words by vectors of numbers, based on their distribution in text. This enables positioning words in a hyperplane and makes several processing tasks easier, such as computing semantic similarity with the cosine of the word vectors.

on a dataset of clinical cases, with labelled NEs. This section describes the dataset and its creation process. We further detail how the CRF works and how the best features were selected from the CRF weights.

3.1 Dataset

The dataset used has 281 textual documents reporting neurology clinical cases. They were collected from the numbers 1 and 2 of volume 17 of the clinical journal Sinapse[2], published by the Portuguese Society of Neurology [16,17].

Since all the texts were in a raw format, they first had to be preprocessed. This was made with NLPPort [13], a set of automatic tools for Portuguese NLP. More specifically, we used a tokenizer (TokPort) for splitting the text into tokens (e.g., words, punctuation); a POS-tagger (TagPort), for assigning a POS to each token (e.g., noun, verb); and LemPort, for normalizing the word into its lemma form. After preprocessing, the dataset was represented in the CoNLL format [20], with tokens in the first column, POS tags in the second, and lemmas in the third, as Table 1 illustrates. NE labels were to be added, manually, in the fourth column. For that, our starting point was the same guide used by Ferreira [4], written by physicians and linguists for the annotation of clinical text. Minor adaptations were made, namely: (i) the Location class was not considered because it does not represent clinical information; (ii) the classes

Table 1. Example of dataset annotation. Sentence: "...de 66 anos, com antecedentes de dislipidemia e síndrome depressiva, começou por..."

Token	POS tag	Lemma	IOB tag
de	prp	de	O
66	num	66	O
anos	n	ano	O
,	punc	,	O
com	prp	com	O
antecedentes	n	antecedente	B-DT
de	prp	de	O
dislipidemia	n	dislipidemia	B-C
e	conj-c	e	O
síndrome	n	síndrome	B-C
depressiva	adj	depressivo	I-C
,	punc	,	O
começou	v-fin	começar	O
por	prp	por	O

---

[2] http://www.sinapse.pt/archive.php.

Table 2. NE dataset description

NE	O	OR (%)	DO	DOR (%)
AS	2,488	15.59	1,412	16.14
C	3,887	24.35	2,203	25.18
CH	1,044	6.54	632	7.22
DT	1,519	9.52	883	10.09
EV	793	4.97	331	3.78
G	63	0.39	50	0.57
N	768	4.81	48	0.55
OBS	217	1.36	166	1.90
R	1,766	11.06	1,090	12.46
RA	71	0.45	14	0.16
T	2,041	12.79	1,012	11.57
THER	894	5.60	563	6.44
V	411	2.57	344	3.93
Total	15,962	100.00	8,748	100.00

CH: Characterization; T: Test; EV: Evolution;
G: Genetics; AS: Anatomical Site; N: Negation;
OBS: Additional Observations; C: Condition;
R: Results; DT: DateTime; THER: Therapeu-
tics; V: Value; RA: Route of Administration

Genetics and Additional Observations were added. The former identifies information about genes (e.g., "...variante do *gene CoQ2* em ..." (*...gene CoQ2 variant
in...*)), and the latter all the extra unlabelled information about the patient,
such as references to family diseases or patient opinions, among others (e.g.,
"...retomou Dasatinib (*decisão do doente* e *hematologista assistente*), desenvol-
vendo..."). This resulted in 13 NE classes, as illustrated in Table 2.

Entities are labelled with the Inside-Outside-Beginning (IOB) format, which
enables to identify whether the token is at the beginning (B) or inside (I) a NE,
or just not part of any NE (O).

Table 3 shows a quantitative analysis of the dataset with the number of tokens
for each IOB tag (NT), the number of distinct tokens (NDT), and respective
ratios in the dataset (NTR, NDTR). Table 2 has the number of NE occurrences (O), of distinct occurrences (DO), and their ratios (OR, DOR). The
dataset was labelled by one Biomedical Engineering student, but 30% of its
contents were later revised by two Biomedical Engineering students, two Data
Science PhD students, one Computer Science Professor working on NLP, and
one Physiotherapist. The agreement for the revised dataset was 95.8%, which is
a good compromise given that overlap between some classes is expected.

3.2   Feature Extraction

We considered a 5-token context window (current token, two previous and two following ones) for which the following *baseline* features were extracted:

- Orthographic and Morphological: token is a punctuation sign, total ASCII, all in lowercase, all in uppercase, numeric, alpha, alphanumeric; starts with uppercase character; ends in 'a', ends in 's'; plus token shape (sequence of lowercase and uppercase characters, numbers and punctuation), length, prefixes and suffixes. A 5-character window was used for both affixes.
- Linguistic: token, POS tag and lemma.

Table 3. Quantitative analysis of the dataset

IOB tags	NT	NTR (%)	NDT	NDTR (%)	Examples
B-AS	2,491	4.272	770	6.794	seio (B-AS)
I-AS	2,510	4.305	599	5.285	venoso (I-AS)
B-C	3,884	6.662	1,074	9.476	paramnésia (B-C)
I-C	3,634	6.233	1,269	11.196	reduplicativa (I-C)
B-CH	1,043	1.789	503	4.438	mais (B-CH)
I-CH	576	0.988	358	3.159	marcado (I-CH)
B-DT	1,516	2.600	280	2.470	18 (B-DT)
I-DT	2,495	4.279	378	3.335	semanas (I-DT)
B-EV	794	1.362	184	1.623	desenvolveu (B-EV)
I-EV	452	0.775	120	1.059	gradualmente (I-EV)
B-G	61	0.105	15	0.132	gene (B-G)
I-G	62	0.106	47	0.415	EGFR (I-G)
B-N	768	1.317	46	0.406	não (B-N)
I-N	2	0.003	2	0.018	impedindo (I-N)
B-OBS	217	0.372	153	1.350	restantes (B-OBS)
I-OBS	227	0.389	144	1.271	irmãos (I-OBS)
B-R	1,767	3.031	589	5.197	VS (B-R)
I-R	2,520	4.322	922	8.135	aumentada (I-R)
B-RA	71	0.122	14	0.124	intravenoso (B-RA)
I-RA	0	0.000	0	0.000	
B-T	2,041	3.501	490	4.323	estudo (B-T)
I-T	2,113	3.624	677	5.973	citogénico (I-T)
B-THER	894	1.533	384	3.388	correço (B-THER)
I-THER	709	1.216	332	2.929	de (I-THER)
B-V	410	0.703	276	2.435	0.8 (B-V)
I-V	584	1.002	112	0.988	células (I-V)
O	26,463	45.388	1,596	14.082	-
Total	58,304	100,000	11,334	100.000	-

Besides those features, we added features based on a FastText word embedding model [1], learned with the Gensim API [12] from 3,377 clinical texts, also from the Sinapse journal. Distributional features based on this model were: the most similar words and the IOB class, given by the nearest mean and median prototype vectors. The most similar words were those that maximized the cosine with the token word vector.

Prototype vectors were calculated using the word embeddings of the tokens of the dataset and their labels. First, normalized Pointwise Mutual Information (nPMI) [2] (Eq. 1) was computed to get the most important tokens for each IOB tag, because some tokens may appear in more than one IOB tag. Then, we got the vectors of each selected word and computed the mean and the median prototype vectors for each IOB tag. Finally, to get the features, we computed the cosine between the token word vector and each of the IOB tag prototype vectors, and selected the IOB tag of the nearest mean and median prototype vectors.

$$nPMI(label, word) = \ln \frac{p(label, word)}{p(label)p(word)} \times \frac{1}{-\ln p(label, word)} \tag{1}$$

3.3 Conditional Random Fields

CRF is a sequential supervised algorithm that enables automatic labeling of sequences based on undirected graphical models [7]. During training, the algorithm learns which feature functions increase the accuracy of the predictions and their weights. As shown in Eq. 2, these functions behave like rules and their weights represent whether the function promotes the predicted label or not. In our case, the weights are learned during the training phase, using a gradient descent using the limited-memory BFGS (L-BFGS) [15].

$$f_j(y_{i-1}, y_i, \mathbf{x}, i) = \begin{cases} 1 & \text{if word} = \text{"Epilepsia" and tag} = \text{"B-C"} \\ 0 & \text{else} \end{cases} \tag{2}$$

During the testing phase, the model maximizes the conditional probability of the output labels given the input features (Eq. 3). The naive method would be testing all the tag combinations, which is impossible for classifications with many different tags, because this approach has an exponential growth (a document with m tokens and k different tags would have k^m different labels). That is why dynamic programming is important during this phase. The Viberti algorithm [14] allows to find the most probable label without testing all the combinations. For training the classifier, we used the sklearn-crfsuite package[3].

$$P(y|\mathbf{x}) = \frac{\exp \sum_{i=1}^{n} \sum_j \lambda_j f_j(\mathbf{x}, i, y_{i-1}, y_i)}{\sum_{y' \in y} \exp \sum_{i=1}^{n} \sum_j \lambda_j f_j(\mathbf{x}, i, y'_{i-1}, y'_i)} \tag{3}$$

---

[3] https://sklearn-crfsuite.readthedocs.io/en/latest/index.html.

3.4 Feature Selection

As presented in Sect. 3.3, the CRF classifier gives one weight to each of the feature values during training. In other words, for the same feature there are different weights for different values (e.g. the word "Epilepsia" (*Epilepsy*) has a higher weight than "EEG" for the IOB tag "B-C"). We use those weights for finding which were the most relevant features. First, we convert each weight to their absolute value, because, depending on their meaning, weights could be positive or negative. Positive weights correspond to positive association between the feature and the proposed class while negative weights have the opposite meaning. We summed all those values for each feature and selected the feature with the maximum sum (max_{sum}). Then, we selected the features with a sum of weights above a certain threshold, computed by multiplying a certain percent with the max_{sum}. We present the grid search for the best percent threshold in Sect. 4.

4 Results and Discussion

To train CRF classifier, first we had to find the best parameters for L1 and L2 Regularization for the L-BFGS method. In order to find these two values, we made a Grid Search on the $[2^{-5}, 2^5]$ interval for both parameters. Figure 1 presents the macro F1-score for each pair of parameters, using relaxed evaluation. It shows that the best performances were achieved with the lower pair of values tested, 2^{-4} and 2^{-1} for L1 and L2 Regularization Coefficients, respectively since the classifier trained with this pair of parameters achieved the best performance. These values are consistent with the literature since low L1 and L2 Regularization Coefficients mean that the more important features take higher weights than the others, while with high regularization coefficients all the features take similar weights, in other words, none of them has discriminative power.

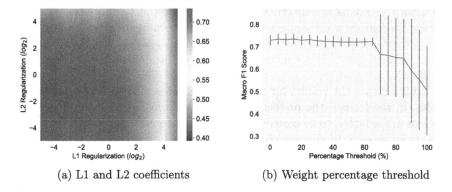

(a) L1 and L2 coefficients   (b) Weight percentage threshold

Fig. 1. Grid search of the classifier: L1 and L2 regularization coefficients and feature selection method

After finding the best parameters for the CRF, we searched for the best threshold for the feature selection method using a 10-fold cross validation. Figure 1b shows the macro F1-score using relaxed evaluation for each percentage threshold tested. It shows that the best performances were achieved for the thresholds between 0% and 25%, with 15% achieving the maximum macro F1-score. The abrupt fall at 70% is due to the result of removing features, such as POS tags, similar words and affixes from the surrounding tokens.

The best features for all the folds using a threshold of 15% were all the similar words, all the lemmas, only the nearest mean and median prototype vectors indexes of the current token, all the prefixes except the first character of the next token, all the suffixes except the last two, three, four and five characters for the current token, the POS tag of the current token, all tokens and all the token shapes except the token shape of the next token (112 features out of a total of 185 features).

The similar words are very useful for finding the real meaning of abbreviations, since their nearest words are their extended versions. For instance the most similar words for "EEG" are "Encefalografia" (*Encephalography*) and "Encefalograma" (*Encephalogram*). Not to mention that it is expected that nearest words belong to the same class. Tokens are useful because they are what is actually mentioned. Finally, lemmas are important as they allow to relate each IOB tag with the dictionary form of the word. This relation enables to classify with the same IOB tag even if the words are in different flexions. However, these last two features may lead to overfitting since they behave like a dictionary.

The features from the prototype vectors support the classification since each vector carries information of each IOB tag. It was already expected that the prefix and suffix features would be very important, because medical documents typically use many words with them. For example, the prefix "dis" means difficulty, "exo" means out, and "meta" alteration; the suffix "ase" means enzyme, "ismo" means disease and "oma" tumor. It was expected that all POS tags were important for each token classification, since they represent the grammatical function of each one and thus support sequential classification, i.e., some POS, such as nouns or adjectives, are prone to be the beginning of an entity. Finally, the feature word shape is very important because it carries almost all the morphological information for classifying entities as Value and DateTime. For instance, the token "18" is converted to "##" and the token "2/3" is converted to "#-#".

Table 4 shows the results for each NE class, presented in relaxed and strict modes. In the former, the predicted IOB tag is compared with the correct tag, whereas in the latter, to be correct, all the tokens of a NE must match the correct tags. Even though, in grid search and feature selection processes, we considered the results of non-NE (O tag), in the final results it was not considered since it does not represent any NE. We show the average results of a random 10-fold Cross Validation for each NE class as well as their micro, macro and weighted averages for all the folds.

Table 4. Relaxed and strict results

NE class	Recall (%)		Precision (%)		F1-Score (%)	
	Relax	Strict	Relax	Strict	Relax	Strict
AS	86.50 ± 1.93	74.56 ± 3.25	86.85 ± 2.52	76.47 ± 2.93	86.64 ± 1.17	75.47 ± 2.63
C	83.68 ± 2.52	75.18 ± 2.83	77.50 ± 1.67	72.13 ± 2.82	80.45 ± 1.59	73.61 ± 2.58
CH	41.13 ± 5.54	45.29 ± 4.80	53.60 ± 6.41	55.35 ± 4.68	46.34 ± 5.19	49.72 ± 4.31
DT	85.88 ± 2.19	72.25 ± 3.00	88.32 ± 3.75	78.30 ± 4.77	87.05 ± 2.51	75.14 ± 3.71
EV	82.30 ± 5.04	77.31 ± 6.51	87.86 ± 3.34	81.06 ± 5.93	84.89 ± 3.17	79.07 ± 5.69
G	74.36 ± 17.89	64.71 ± 19.49	97.50 ± 7.91	84.83 ± 18.70	82.77 ± 10.62	72.70 ± 18.15
N	92.94 ± 3.91	92.92 ± 3.91	98.06 ± 2.45	97.94 ± 2.37	95.36 ± 1.93	95.30 ± 1.88
OBS	20.41 ± 8.48	22.02 ± 8.17	54.64 ± 18.93	48.47 ± 14.64	28.67 ± 10.35	29.65 ± 9.59
R	73.87 ± 3.63	60.75 ± 5.10	71.28 ± 2.87	63.86 ± 3.68	72.47 ± 2.12	62.21 ± 4.04
RA	83.11 ± 20.83	83.11 ± 20.83	96.25 ± 8.44	96.25 ± 8.44	87.21 ± 13.53	87.21 ± 13.53
T	85.09 ± 3.12	78.77 ± 3.98	86.05 ± 3.82	79.72 ± 4.78	85.51 ± 2.58	79.19 ± 3.93
THER	75.38 ± 7.57	71.16 ± 5.98	83.53 ± 2.87	77.89 ± 5.25	79.12 ± 5.13	74.25 ± 4.79
V	85.50 ± 5.35	74.31 ± 8.54	91.91 ± 5.03	82.14 ± 8.57	88.48 ± 3.93	77.79 ± 7.07
mic Avg	79.85 ± 1.54	71.64 ± 1.83	81.14 ± 1.40	74.73 ± 1.81	80.49 ± 1.40	73.15 ± 1.80
mac Avg	74.63 ± 1.86	68.64 ± 2.24	82.57 ± 2.34	76.49 ± 1.58	77.30 ± 1.64	71.64 ± 1.76
Weighted Avg	79.85 ± 1.54	71.64 ± 1.83	80.96 ± 1.48	74.53 ± 1.88	80.10 ± 1.44	72.86 ± 1.82

The lowest performances were in Additional Observations and Characterization classes. The first was already expected because this class is too general and its labelling consists of tokens that do not belong to any other class (e.g., "restantes irmãos" (*remaining siblings*) and "abandono do acompanhamento médico" (*doctor abandonment*)). As for Characterization, its labelling depends on annotator reading, as some tokens can be Characterizations or Conditions (e.g., "suspeita" (*suspicion*) in "suspcita de Arterite de Takayasu" (*suspection of Takayasu's arteritis*) or "hipótese" (*hypothesis*) in "hipótese de AAC" (*hypothesis of AAC*)), which adds noise to the model. Anatomical Site, Condition, Genetics, Therapeutics and Value are classes presenting high classification performance. Anatomical Site has many equal different words repeated through the dataset that appear in similar contexts like "temporal" in "actividade paroxística temporal posterior" (*posterior temporal paroxysmal activity*) and in "córtex temporal superior" (*superior temporal cortex*). It has also different words that appear in similar contexts (e.g., "parietal" and "justa-ventricular" (*juxtaventricular*) in "lesão parietal" (*parietal injury*) and in "lesão justa-ventricular" (*juxtaventricular injury*)), a feature captured by the similar words feature. The same happens for Condition, and it further uses discriminatory affixes and usually appears in same contexts, near Anatomical Site, Test, Evolution or Therapeutics (e.g., "estenoses bilaterais" (*bilateral stenosys*), "Remissão dos sintomas" (*Remission of symptoms*), "terapêutica modificadora da doenãa" (*disease-modifying treatment*)). Genetics is mostly made of alphanumeric tokens and often contains "gene" in its beginning (e.g., "gene BRAF" or "LRRK2"). Therapeutics has discriminatory affixes as well since it covers active pharmaceutical ingredients ("azatioprina" or "dexametasona") or therapies to cure certain diseases ("imunoterapia" (*imunotherapy*), "corticoterapia" (*corticotherapy*) or "craniotomia descompressiva" (*decompressive craniectomy*). Value contains mostly numeric tokens and measurement units. Negation, Evolution and Route of Administration are classes with a large number of repeated tokens, generally near other classes like Conditions, Results, Therapeutics or Tests. Test has a low proportion of distinct tokens which makes it easier to identify. Result and Test classes are related because they usually appear next to each other (e.g., "biópsia muscular não revelou alterações" (*muscle biopsy revealed no changes*)), a feature captured by transition features developed by the CRF during the training phase. However, some occurrences of Result are classified as Conditions because there are cases when the class can be both (e.g., "hipodensidade" (*hypodensity*) or "malformação" (*malformation*)), which confuses the classifier. Finally, DateTime represents the chronology of actions or even their time duration, and is therefore found near Condition, Therapeutics or Test NEs. It is a class with a large number of repeated occurrences and has tokens that appear on similar contexts, for which similar word and cluster features are relevant. The high standard deviations in Genetics and Route of Administration are due to their low number of occurrences in the dataset, in other words each classification contributes with a high percentage value compared with NEs with several tokens. Route of Administration has the same values for both relaxed and strict evaluations because all its NEs have only one token.

5 Conclusion

This study assessed the performance of shallow machine learning algorithms, namely CRF, in NER from Portuguese clinical text. We report a micro average F1-score nearly 80% for relaxed evaluation and nearly 73% for strict evaluation. Although the grid search and feature selection results express little changes of performance over a considerable range of the tested parameters, it is important to say that the fact that we did not use a independent test set to check our model performance may introduce some bias on the final results. In order to get better results, more data needs to be annotated, for more efficient training of the classifier. Also, as the features from word embedding models rely on the training of this model, larger quantities of text will result in more suitable vector representations, towards more reliable associations.

Results of this study are useful for Hospital Neurology services, which may use this NLP tool for retrieving structured information from their raw reports. This will ease the population of databases, which will hopefully provide a more efficient way of analysing all the data, e.g., for finding relations between patient diseases and the therapeutics. As future work, we intend to compare these results with deep learning models such as state-of-art BiLSTM-CRF models in order to inspect their performance on Portuguese clinical texts. Also, we want to compare word embedding models trained with millions of general Portuguese texts with our word embedding models.

Acknowledgements. We acknowledge the financial support of Fundação para a Ciência e a Tecnologia through CISUC (UID/CEC/00326/2019).

References

1. Bojanowski, P., Grave, E., Joulin, A., Mikolov, T.: Enriching word vectors with subword information. Trans. Assoc. Comput. Linguist. **5**, 135–146 (2017)
2. Bouma, G.: Normalized (pointwise) mutual information in collocation extraction. In: Proceedings of GSCL, pp. 31–40 (2009)
3. Ferreira, L., Teixeira, A.J.S., Cunha, J.P.: Information extraction from Portuguese hospital discharge letters. In: VI Jornadas en Technologia del Habla and II Iberian SL Tech Workshop, pp. 39–42, January 2010
4. Ferreira, L.d.S.: Medical information extraction in European Portuguese. Ph.D. thesis, Universidade de Aveiro (2011)
5. Gold, S., Elhadad, N., Zhu, X., Cimino, J.J., Hripcsak, G.: Extracting structured medication event information from discharge summaries. In: AMIA Annual Symposium Proceedings, vol. 2008, pp. 237–241. American Medical Informatics Association (2008)
6. Henriksson, A., Dalianis, H., Kowalski, S.: Generating features for named entity recognition by learning prototypes in semantic space: the case of de-identifying health records. In: 2014 IEEE International Conference on Bioinformatics and Biomedicine (BIBM), pp. 450–457. IEEE (2014)
7. Klinger, R., Tomanek, K.: Classical probabilistic models and conditional random fields. Technical report TR07-2-013, Department of Computer Science, Dortmund University of Technology (2007). https://ls11-www.cs.uni-dortmund.de/_media/techreports/tr07-13.pdf
8. Lamy, M., Pereira, R., Ferreira, J.C., Vasconcelos, J.B., Melo, F., Velez, I.: Extracting clinical information from electronic medical records. In: Novais, P., et al. (eds.) ISAmI2018 2018. AISC, vol. 806, pp. 113–120. Springer, Cham (2019). https://doi.org/10.1007/978-3-030-01746-0_13
9. Mykowiecka, A., Marciniak, M., Kupść, A.: Rule-based information extraction from patients clinical data. J. Biomed. Inform. **42**(5), 923–936 (2009)
10. Névéol, A., Dalianis, H., Velupillai, S., Savova, G., Zweigenbaum, P.: Clinical natural language processing in languages other than English: opportunities and challenges. J. Biomed. Seman. **9**(1), 12 (2018)
11. Rais, M., Lachkar, A., Lachkar, A., Ouatik, S.E.A.: A comparative study of biomedical named entity recognition methods based machine learning approach. In: 2014 Third IEEE International Colloquium in Information Science and Technology (CIST), pp. 329–334. IEEE (2014)
12. Rehurek, R., Sojka, P.: Software framework for topic modelling with large corpora. In: Proceedings of the LREC 2010 Workshop on New Challenges for NLP Frameworks, pp. 45–50. ELRA, Valletta, Malta (2010)
13. Rodrigues, R., Oliveira, H.G., Gomes, P.: NLPPort: a pipeline for Portuguese NLP (Short paper). In: 7th Symposium on Languages, Applications and Technologies (SLATE 2018). OpenAccess Series in Informatics (OASIcs), vol. 62, pp. 18:1–18:9. Schloss Dagstuhl-Leibniz-Zentrum fuer Informatik, Dagstuhl, Germany (2018). https://doi.org/10.4230/OASIcs.SLATE.2018.18
14. Russell, S.J., Norvig, P.: Probabilistic reasoning over time. In: Limited, P.E. (ed.) Artificial Intelligence: A Modern Approach, Chap. 15, pp. 566–636, 3rd edn. Pearson, London (2010)

15. Sha, F., Pereira, F.: Shallow parsing with conditional random fields. In: Proceedings of the 2003 Conference of the North American Chapter of the Association for Computational Linguistics on Human Language Technology-Volume 1, pp. 134–141. Association for Computational Linguistics (2003)
16. Sinapse: Publicações da Sociedade Portuguesa de Neurologia, vol. 17:1. Sociedade Portuguesa de Neurologia, Lisbon (2017)
17. Sinapse: Publicações da Sociedade Portuguesa de Neurologia, vol. 17:2. Sociedade Portuguesa de Neurologia, Lisbon (2017)
18. Skeppstedt, M., Kvist, M., Dalianis, H.: Rule-based entity recognition and coverage of SNOMED CT in Swedish clinical text. In: LREC, pp. 1250–1257 (2012)
19. Skeppstedt, M., Kvist, M., Nilsson, G.H., Dalianis, H.: Automatic recognition of disorders, findings, pharmaceuticals and body structures from clinical text: an annotation and machine learning study. J. Biomed. Inform. **49**, 148–158 (2014)
20. Tjong Kim Sang, E.F., De Meulder, F.: Introduction to the CoNLL-2003 shared task: language-independent named entity recognition. In: Proceedings of the Seventh Conference on Natural Language Learning at HLT-NAACL 2003 - Volume 4, CONLL 2003, pp. 142–147. Association for Computational Linguistics, Stroudsburg (2003). https://doi.org/10.3115/1119176.1119195
21. Wang, Y., et al.: Supervised methods for symptom name recognition in free-text clinical records of traditional Chinese medicine: an empirical study. J. Biomed. Inform. **47**, 91–104 (2014)
22. Wu, Y., Xu, J., Jiang, M., Zhang, Y., Xu, H.: A study of neural word embeddings for named entity recognition in clinical text. In: AMIA Annual Symposium Proceedings, vol. 2015, pp. 1326–1333. American Medical Informatics Association (2015)

Intelligent Control of an Exoskeleton for Rehabilitation Purposes Using a ROS-Based Software Architecture

Nieves Pavón-Pulido[(✉)], Juan Antonio López-Riquelme, and Jorge J. Feliú-Batlle

Technical University of Cartagena, Cartagena 30620, Spain
nieves.pavon@upct.es

Abstract. This paper describes an open-source software architecture that allows an exoskeleton to be remotely used for rehabilitation purposes. The exoskeleton can be controlled through a Natural User Interface (NUI), which directly records the therapist's legs motion, from which, the input references that should be sent to the exoskeleton are calculated. The proposed architecture consists of a set of interconnected components, running independently, which use a middleware for transparently sharing information. In particular, a set of software components, executed as ROS nodes, solve the problems related to hardware issues and control strategies. An early prototype of the system has been tested and results are shown in this paper, together with a discussion about the advantages and disadvantages of the system.

Keywords: Exoskeleton · ROS · Machine learning · Mobile robots

1 Introduction

Population has remarkably aged in the last decades, and such aging actually goes on increasing [1, 2]. Medical advances, improvements in sanitation, feeding and taking certain preventive measures in the field of health are some of the reasons that motivate the growing of the elderly population. Although this can be considered as an excellent news, countless challenges are emerging on a great variety of contexts. Even more, when in many countries, the number of births is dramatically decreasing. This fact could generate a deep unbalance in society, since a reduced active population has to support an increasingly higher economic and social cost.

On the other hand, despite life expectancy has increased, quality of life for elderly people is not always as satisfactory as would be expected. Many diseases affect elderly population more virulently than in other age ranges. Specifically, disorders related to mobility are very common [3]. Such lack of mobility often worsens other illness, such as, cardiovascular problems, high blood pressure, diabetes, stroke risk or even those conditions related to mental and emotional health, among others.

In this context, it would be very interesting the application of rehabilitation techniques, particularly designed for elderly people with certain mobility problems [4], with the main purpose of enhancing, or even recovering, some damaged skills, thus allowing an indirect improvement of other physical and psychological conditions.

© Springer Nature Switzerland AG 2019
P. Moura Oliveira et al. (Eds.): EPIA 2019, LNAI 11804, pp. 349–360, 2019.
https://doi.org/10.1007/978-3-030-30241-2_30

In general, rehabilitation is defined as care that helps people to get back and keep abilities needed for daily day. Most rehabilitation procedures demand specialized staff and many of them requires assistive devices (that is, specific tools and equipment), to be used in a hospital environment. Therefore, due to the special characteristics of such procedures, its economic cost and the necessary labor are high. Furthermore, the assistance to this type of therapies often requires the displacement of patients to significantly specialized clinics, different from health centers that correspond to such patients.

On the other hand, the increase of patients together with the lack of medical staff frequently involve the saturation of waiting lists and, for elderly people, this situation could lead to an irreversible health state, for example, to the total loss of mobility, which would mean a huge loss of life quality, since it is not possible to lead an independent life in these conditions.

Obviously, the official governmental organisms are responsible to develop strategies to address all these issues for overcoming the problems of population aging, however, not always necessary measures are taken due to logistic difficulties or lack of budget.

In this context, technology could help health professionals to overcome or, at least, minimize the impact of such difficulties through research and development in the field of Cloud Computing, Internet of Things, Artificial Intelligence and Robotics, among others.

In literature, it is possible to find some interesting solutions, designed for improving elderly people quality life, as the result of many studies and research works carried out in the last decade. Many of these solutions integrate the concept of Ambient Assisted Living (AAL) [5] and Robotics, both at home [6, 7] and hospital environments. Telemedicine [8] is another way of enabling patients to be remotely attended, avoiding unnecessary and costly trips, and optimizing medical resources. However, in the field of rehabilitation, having specialized staff and equipment is usually essential, and remote attention could be difficult. In fact, there are not too many solutions focused on developing remotely controlled rehabilitation systems.

Despite the complexity involved in remotely applying rehabilitation procedures, some researchers are addressing this issue by using mobile robotic devices, in particular, the use of external exoskeletons [9] could be an excellent enabler for rehabilitation tasks. However, most of such solutions are experimental prototypes, not without problems that should be still tackled, some of which are closely related to the definition of a general software architecture that allows an optimal integration of firmware, low-level software and decoupled high-level software components that enable a transparent communication between modules.

Considering the aforementioned needs, an open-source system, which allows rehabilitation activities to be remotely carried out by using one of the exoskeletons developed as a result of the AAL European Project ExoLegs [10], is described in this paper. The software architecture uses ROS (Robotic Operating System) [11], as middleware to make communication between software components as easy and transparent as possible. Moreover, using ROS facilitates developers both the design and implementation of modules with new functionalities and the reuse of techniques and algorithms applied in Mobile Robotics, which could be meaningful in the context of exoskeleton control. In addition, the system is equipped with a RGB-D camera for acquiring visual information used as input of a Natural User Interface (NUI) [12] that helps expert therapists to design and remotely transfer the appropriate movements and/or exercises that the patient should perform.

The outline of the paper is as follows. Section 2 describes the system architecture, both hardware and software. It deepens in how a set of decoupled software components interact through ROS, with the aim of controlling the joints' position of the exoskeleton to generate trajectories useful for rehabilitation purposes. Furthermore, how the NUI allows therapists to use the system is also described. Section 3 shows the results of several experiments carried out in order to validate the proposed prototype. A discussion about the advantages and disadvantages of the system are also highlighted. Finally, Sect. 4 presents conclusions and future work.

2 System Architecture

The goal of the proposed system is helping therapists to remotely treat patients by means of rehabilitation exercises specifically designed for elderly people wearing an exoskeleton. This section explains how the software architecture allows hardware components to work together for meeting such objective.

2.1 Hardware Architecture

The main elements of the hardware architecture are an exoskeleton and a RGB-D camera (specifically the Kinect One V2 version) [13], in addition to the rest of devices needed to perform processing and communication tasks, such as two PCs (personal computers), one running Windows 10 and the other one running Ubuntu Linux 16.04.

Exoskeleton Description
The used exoskeleton is one of the designed and built as a result of the European project (AAL-010000-2012-15), EXO-LEGS (Exoskeleton Legs for Elderly Persons), included in the Ambient Assisted Living Joint Programme, which *"was aimed at developing lower body mobility exoskeletons for helping people move around to perform normal daily living tasks"*. In this work, the exoskeleton is not used for allowing people freely move at home or through other places, but it is considered as a wearable element that enables elderly patients, with a slight or moderate lack of mobility, to perform certain rehabilitation exercises.

The exoskeleton (see Fig. 1), consists of two legs with 3 motorized joints per leg, that is: hip, knee and ankle (see Fig. 1(a)). The motor model selected for all the joints, after studying the needs of effort and weight, is the Maxon brushless EC 60 flat motor of 400 W, 48 V of nominal voltage, with Hall sensors, and 470 g of weight. A Maxon planetary gearhead is matched to the motor, obtaining a reduction relation of 169:9. Moreover, the selected Maxon motor is equipped with a Maxon MILE inductive rotary encoder of 1024 PPR (pulse per revolution), whose operating principle provides several benefits in respect of that used in traditional encoders.

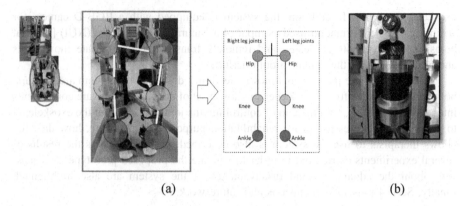

(a)   (b)

Fig. 1. One of the exoskeletons designed for the EXO-LEGS project. (a) Outline of the joints that shapes the exoskeleton. (b) Detail of one of the joints (specifically the left knee), moved by a Maxon EC60 flat motor.

Each motor (see Fig. 1(b)), is controlled by the small-sized and full digital Maxon EPOS2 50/5 [14] smart motion controller, capable of driving brushless EC motors with minimal torque ripple and low noise. It can be operated via any USB or RS232 interface or as a slave node in a CANopen network. Likewise, as an integrated position, velocity and current control functionality is available, this controller is an appropriate choice for sophisticated positioning applications.

Description of the RGB-D Camera for NUI

The Kinect One V2 RGB-D camera (see Fig. 2), has been selected, since the manufacturer offers a useful Software Development Kit (SDK), useful for performing tasks related to NUI, since it provides a set of software modules that help developers to design interfaces based on the human body motion by using skeleton tracking techniques.

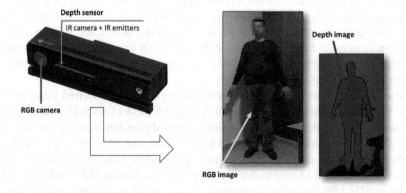

Fig. 2. Description of the Kinect One V2 camera and an example of RGB and depth images.

Kinect is a line of motion sensing input devices produced by Microsoft, initially developed as gaming accessory but currently focused on research and development. Specifically, the Kinect One was release in 2014 as an improvement of the first generation Kinect for Xbox 360, which was discontinued in 2015. This second generation camera uses a wide-angle TOF (Time-Of-Flight), camera and it is capable of processing 2 gigabits of data per second to read its environment. Moreover, the Kinect One is more accurate, since it gets three times the fidelity over its predecessor, its angle vision is 70° in horizontal and 60° in vertical, and it is possible to detect the position and orientation of 25 individual joints (including thumbs), by using certain specific modules of the available free SDK for skeleton tracking. In particular, it provides two corresponding images one for RGB information (with a maximum resolution of 1920 × 1080), and one for depth or distance to each RGB pixel (with a resolution of 512 × 424) in a range of 0.5–4.5 m, as Fig. 2 shows.

2.2 Software Architecture

The software architecture consists on a set of decoupled components (some of them running under ROS), executed in a distributed manner to meet the proposed goal of this work. That is, enabling the remote control of the exoskeleton, taking the angles of the leg joints of the therapist skeleton model (obtained from the images acquired with the Kinect sensor), as inputs, which will be sent to the corresponding ROS topics, where the commands for each joint of the exoskeleton are published.

An outline of the proposed global software architecture is shown in Fig. 3. All the modules that allows RGB-D images to be acquired and processed run in a PC under Windows 10. On the other hand, the exoskeleton is controlled by a PC running Ubuntu Linux 16.04; therefore, all the components related to the control of the exoskeleton joints have been written for being executed as ROS nodes, thus making communication easier, since a collection of ROS topics are available for publishing and subscription for all the software components.

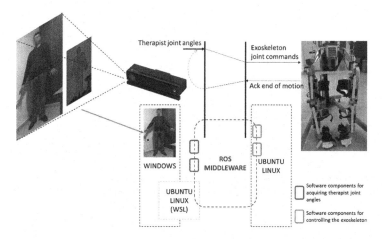

Fig. 3. General view of the global software architecture.

Description of the Software Components for Skeleton Tracking

As ROS is mainly designed for Linux, there is no an easy way of extending its functionality to a Windows-based system. However, Windows 10 currently includes the possibility of running a limited GNU/Linux environment through the Windows Subsystem for Linux (WSL). The WSL lets developers the execution of most command-line tools, utilities and applications, directly on Windows, without the overhead of a specific virtual machine; nevertheless, there exist some limitations, mainly related to hardware access. Consequently, it is not possible to directly access the Kinect sensor from Linux (via WSL). Apart from that, it is not feasible to use the Windows Kinect V2 SDK under Linux; then, skeleton tracking is only available under Windows.

With the aim of overcoming these difficulties, a software component has been written by using the IDE (Integrated Development Environment), Visual Studio and the appropriate functions included in the Kinect V2 SDK for tracking the skeleton of a user. Only the joints that belongs to the legs of such user are used for joint angles calculation. The collection of joint angles that define a motion through time are properly saved in a file, which can be read from another component written under Linux, running in the WSL. Given that ROS does run under the WSL Linux, a ROS node has been implemented to read the mentioned file, extract the set of joint angles and send the information to the exoskeleton throughout publishing the information in the suitable ROS topics. Furthermore, such node allows the subscription to those ROS topics that provides information about the exoskeleton state. Figure 4 summarizes the described pipeline.

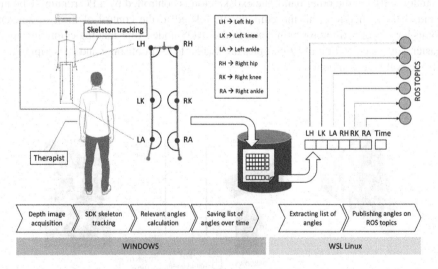

Fig. 4. Pipeline of the procedure that allows joint angles of the therapist to be recorded and sent through ROS by connecting software modules running on Windows and on WSL Linux.

Description of the Exoskeleton ROS Controller

As mentioned above, the exoskeleton consists on a list of 6 hardware modules, each of which includes a motor, a gearbox, an encoder and an EPOS2 50/5 controller.

From the software point of view, it is required a set of components, capable of interfacing with each EPOS2 controller, to be implemented by using the command library provided by the manufacturer, specifically, the Linux Shared Object Library `libEPOSCmd.so`. However, writing only the software that allows hardware devices to be accessed is not enough for developing the set of distributed software modules needed in this work. Likewise, the collection of components should be as decoupled as possible, run in real time and be easily extensible. Then, the ROS middleware has been selected as the base on which to design this part of the software architecture.

In fact, ROS is more than a simply middleware, which, at the low level, offers facilities for inter-process communication through publish/subscribe anonymous message passing, together with request/response remote procedure calls and a distributed parameter system. It could be also defined as *a flexible framework for writing robot software that comprises a set of tools, libraries and conventions aimed to simplify the complex task of creating robust robot behavior across many robotics platforms*. ROS encourages collaborative robotics software development; therefore, there exists a very active community that provides a wide variety of solutions to robotic problems distributed as ROS packages.

The exoskeleton control involves to implement a list of specific position controllers, one for each motor. As each motor has its own EPOS2 hardware controller, it is required to write software components capable of sending commands and reading the state of the motor through the EPOS2.

In the context of ROS, independent processes are launched as nodes. Nodes are combined into a graph and interact with one another using streaming topics (which are named buses, with an anonymous publish/subscribe semantics, for messages exchange), RPC (Remote Procedure Call) services and the Parameter Server (which is defined as a shared, multi-variate dictionary accessible via network, which enables nodes to store and retrieve parameters at runtime).

In this work, a node has been implemented for exposing the functionality of the exoskeleton through a set of parameters and topics. Once the node is being executed in the ROS environment, it is possible to send position commands to each joint through the corresponding topic. In addition, the state of each joint could be retrieved through another specific topic.

On the other hand, instead of using a ROS classical outline, where topics are created and managed in a custom way, the set of packages that comprise the `ros_-control` framework have been used [15]. Such packages are aimed to make controllers generic to all robots, by taking the joint state data from a robot's actuator's encoders and a set point as inputs to generate a specific behavior, by means of a generic control loop feedback, usually a PID controller that computes the output (position, velocity or effort), which should be sent to the actuator. Summarizing, as the authors of `ros_control` claims "*the ros_control framework provides the capability to implement (...), controllers with a focus on both real time performance and sharing of controllers in a robot-agnostic way*" [15].

One of the main advantages of using `ros_control` is that necessary robot interfaces and controllers needed in the system proposed in this paper are already implemented. Therefore, they can be directly used without the need of being rewritten them.

Although the use of `ros_control` offers many benefits, a deep analysis of the system that is expected to be developed is needed, before applying the principles of the mentioned framework. Once, the analysis stage is finished, it is possible to proceed to the implementation of the system. In particular, the steps followed are:

- It is necessary to define which robot interfaces are needed, according to the purpose of the robot, in this case, an exoskeleton capable of freely and independently moving each joint with certain limitations. In the proposed solution, 6 joints are available, and each one comprises values of position (`pos`), velocity (`vel`), effort (`eff`), defining the state, and a command (`cmd`), representing the set point that should be reached.
- Since only the position of each joint should be controlled, the hardware interfaces defined in `ros_control` that have been used are Joint State Interface and Position Joint Interface as Joint Command Interface. Therefore, it is possible to launch an existing controller, in particular, a Joint Position Controller to set the joint position, and a Joint State Controller for publishing the joint state for each exoskeleton joint.
- All the functionality of the exoskeleton mechanism has been implemented by a C++ class that inherits of the `hardware_interface::RobotHW` class, defined in the `hardware_interface` package.
- The code of the main program that is launched as a node (`mainnode`), for handling the exoskeleton, follows the typical outline defined by the `ros_control` framework, that is, a loop for reading the state, updating the controller and writing the actuation commands for each joint.
- A set of several configuration files are written for parameters and robot structure specification. In particular, an URDF (Unified Robot Description Format), file defines how the exoskeleton is assembled. This URDF file is also used for running Rviz and Gazebo simulations.
- A launch file has been written to run all the needed nodes: the `mainnode` that fully exposes the functionality of the exoskeleton and the `controller_manager` node. This last package provides a hard real time compatible loop to control the exoskeleton mechanism, since such mechanism is represented by a `hardware_interface::RobotHW` instance.

Figure 5 summarizes the performance of the designed ROS software architecture for handling and controlling the exoskeleton.

3 Results and Discussion

This section details how the system prototype has been validated. Furthermore, the advantages and drawbacks of the proposed solution are discussed, with the aim of enumerating which possible improvements should be carried out.

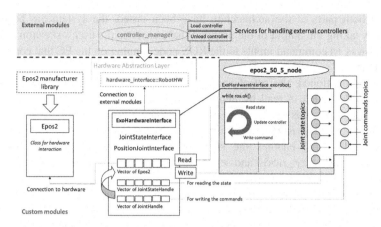

Fig. 5. Outline of the ROS software components that comprise the software architecture for controlling the exoskeleton. The node *epos2_50_5_node* is a program which executes a typical control loop, through the object *exorobot*, defined as an instance of *ExoHardwareInterface*, which implements the hardware interfaces used by any desired controller. Such class also allows the access to EPOS2 hardware devices by running functions of the manufacturer library. Joints' state and commands are properly exposes through topics.

Several tests have been applied to validate the performance of the software architecture, splitting such trials to those that prove how the skeleton of a human being is extracted by using the SDK provided by Microsoft, and those that allow the exoskeleton to be controlled by sending manual commands to the topics with the purpose of evaluating how it operates by means of certain tools, such as Rviz or Gazebo, see Fig. 6.

Sequence of motion done by a therapist user

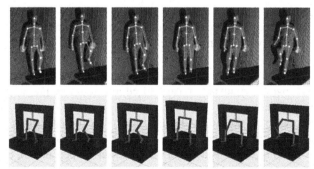

Sequence of motion done by a Rviz simulation of the exoskeleton according to recorded therapist's motions

Fig. 6. Example of test using Rviz for exoskeleton simulation according to the movements of the therapist.

Once both parts of the architecture have been tested, the system has been fully verified by taking the output of the program that generates the user's skeleton (running on Windows), as command inputs to the ROS node running on the PC that controls the exoskeleton.

As aforementioned, the set of angles corresponding to each joint are previously saved in a file which is read by another intermediary ROS node `wsl_intemerdiary_node` that runs on the same PC where the Kinect sensor is attached, through WSL Linux. Another ROS node `linux_intermediary_node`, running in the exoskeleton PC side enables the subscription to the ROS topics published by `wsl_intermediary_node` and sends the joint commands to the topics exposed by the `epos2_50_5_node` node.

Using two PCs that respectively executes Windows and Linux and shares information through the ROS middleware involves certain network requirements. In the experiments, both computers are located at the same subnetwork, and the ROS system has been deployed by taking into account several considerations: only one master is needed (in this case, the master runs on the PC that controls the exoskeleton), all the nodes are configure to use the same master, via the `ROS_MASTER_URI` environmental variable, bi-directional connectivity is ensured between the pair of machines on all ports and, finally, each machine advertises itself by a specific name that the rest of them can solve.

After properly validating the proposed system, the obtained results are good, since it has been demonstrated that it is possible to remotely control an exoskeleton, for rehabilitation purposes, just by using a NUI. The therapist can reproduce the movements that patients should do, simply recording such movements with a RGB-D camera, in this case, the Kinect One V2 sensor, manufactured by Microsoft. Furthermore, all the process could be carried out without the need of the patient is in the same room than the therapist. The main benefits of the proposed system are enumerated as follows:

- The exoskeleton is easy to wear, although certain trained staff would be needed, particularly, if it is applied on elderly people with reduced mobility.
- Therapists can easily use the system, because a NUI is highly usable and the training curve to learn how to drive the system is very low.
- Therapists can record motion exercises to be reproduced by the exoskeleton for different patients in different moments.
- Therapists could evaluate the results of the exercises, since the joints state of the exoskeleton (mainly parameters related to effort), could be properly saved during exercise execution.
- Patients can use the exoskeleton without the need of the presence of the therapist. Only it would be necessary the presence of a nurse or assistant that supervises the procedure. In fact, this could be done in any local (not necessarily specialized), clinic.

On the other hand, the system is still an early prototype that needs to be validated with elderly people and professionals related to rehabilitation tasks. Several drawbacks have been identified during validation process:

- Although the skeleton tracking technique developed by Microsoft has a good performance, in general, some poses are not properly recognized. As the library only offers the possibility of reading the skeleton joints but the algorithm to calculate them is not available as open source, it is not feasible to improve it.

- The Kinect One V2 sensor is clearly a very reliable and accurate RGB-D camera, but its availability is not ensured due to commercial reasons, since Microsoft has discontinued the manufacturing of all the Kinect sensor versions. Certainly, Microsoft continues to develop the platform for developers, with the most recent release Azure Kinect; however, it is not sure that this sensor is available in the future. Therefore, it would be recommendable to select other RGB-D model whose availability is guaranteed in the long term.

- If another RGB-D camera is used, the Microsoft SDK would be not compatible with it, and all the tracking skeleton designed software could not be reused. Consequently, it is important to develop a tracking skeleton technique independent of the camera model. In fact, authors of the work are currently working in a Deep Learning-based method to inference the position and orientation of each skeleton joint from raw depth data, in a sensor-agnostic way.

- Regarding the exclusive use of the ROS middleware for enabling sharing data and communication tasks, the main inconvenient is related to the network configuration, since ROS solutions for firewalls and other obstructions requires to create a virtual network to connect all the machines. Another more feasible approach to solve these problems could be the use of a Cloud-based solution, in such a way that all the processes that run on Windows could interact with the ROS middleware through a web ROS bridge.

Summarizing, although several drawbacks should be still overcome, the obtained results are promising, and all the aforementioned issues can be easily addressed to enhance the proposed system.

4 Conclusions and Future Work

In this work, a software architecture for allowing therapists to remotely control an exoskeleton for rehabilitation purposes has been presented. The system has been properly validated and advantages and disadvantages of the prototype have been highlighted. The main conclusion is that the design and study of this system prototype paves the path to get a better functional solution, ready to be tested in a real environment with elderly patients and therapists. This kind of system would clearly improve the methodology to apply rehabilitation exercises, by saving time, money and medical resources and overcoming logistic issues that often handicap the application of certain treatments, mainly when patients belongs to elderly population.

On the other hand, as mentioned in Sect. 3, authors are currently working in upgrading the system by rewriting the software components that control the RGB-D sensor for skeleton tracking by means of a Deep Learning-based technique. Furthermore, it is expected the Google Platform as a Service (PaaS) Google App Engine, to be used with the aim of linking the software components, when firewalls or other obstacles are present in the network.

Finally, validating the system in a real environment, with elderly users and therapists, and studying issues related to usability and acceptation of the system is expected to be tackled, in near future.

Acknowledgements. The engineer Jesús Damián Blasco deserves a special mention in this work for his support in several technical aspects. This article is the result of the activity carried out under the "Research Programme for Groups of Scientific Excellence at Region of Murcia" of the Seneca Foundation (Agency for Science and Technology of the Region of Murcia – 19895/GERM/15).

References

1. Lutz, W., Sanderson, W., Scherbov, S.: The coming acceleration of global population ageing. Nature Int. J. Sci. **451**(7179), 716–719 (2008)
2. United Nations: World Population Ageing. Report, New York (2017)
3. Tinetti, M.E.: Performance-oriented assessment of mobility problems in elderly patients. J. Am. Geriatr. Soc. **34**, 119–126 (1986)
4. Pitkala, K.H., Raivio, M.M., Laakkonen, M.-L., Tilvis, R.S., Kautiainen, H., Strandberg, T.E.: Exercise rehabilitation on home-dwelling patients with Alzheimer's disease - a randomized, controlled trial. Study protocol. Trials **11**(1), 92 (2010)
5. Memon, M., Wagner, S.R., Pedersen, C.F., Beevi, F., Hansen, F.O.: Ambient assisted living healthcare frameworks, platforms, standards, and quality attributes. Sensors **14**(3), 4312–4341 (2014)
6. Pavón-Pulido, N., López-Riquelme, J.A., Ferruz-Melero, J., Vega Rodríguez, M.A., Barrios-León, A.J.: A service robot for monitoring elderly people in the context of Ambient Assisted Living. J. Ambient Intell. Smart Environ. **6**(6), 595–621 (2014)
7. Pavón-Pulido, N., López-Riquelme, J.A., Pinuaga-Cascales, J.J., Morais, R.: Cybi: a smart companion robot for elderly people: improving teleoperation and telepresence skills by combining cloud computing technologies and fuzzy logic. In: Proceedings on IEEE International Conference on Autonomous Robot Systems and Competitions, Vila Real, pp. 198–203 (2015)
8. Bujnowska-Fedak, M.M., Grata-Borkowska, U.: Use of telemedicine-based care for the aging and elderly: promises and pitfalls. Smart Homecare Technol. TeleHealth **3**, 91–105 (2015)
9. Younbaek, L., et al.: Biomechanical design of a novel flexible exoskeleton for lower extremities. IEEE/ASME Trans. Mechatron. **22**(5), 2058–2069 (2017)
10. ExoLegs Homepage. http://www.aal-europe.eu/projects/exo-legs/. Accessed 29 Apr 2019
11. Quigley, M., et al.: ROS: an open-source Robot Operating System. In: ICRA Workshop on Open Source Software, vol. 3 (2009)
12. Pirker, J., Pojer, M., Holzinger, A., Gütl, C.: Gesture-based interactions in video games with the leap motion controller. In: Kurosu, M. (ed.) HCI 2017. LNCS, vol. 10271, pp. 620–633. Springer, Cham (2017). https://doi.org/10.1007/978-3-319-58071-5_47
13. Microsoft Kinect Homepage. https://developer.microsoft.com/es-es/windows/kinect. Accessed 21 Nov 2016
14. Maxon Motor Homepage. https://www.maxonmotor.com/maxon/view/product/control/Positionierung/347717. Accessed 21 Nov 2016
15. Chitta, S., et al.: ros_control: a generic and simple control framework for ROS. J. Open Source Softw. **2**(20), 456, 1–5 (2017)

Comparison of Conventional and Deep Learning Based Methods for Pulmonary Nodule Segmentation in CT Images

Joana Rocha[1,2(✉)], António Cunha[2,3], and Ana Maria Mendonça[1,2]

[1] Faculdade de Engenharia, Universidade do Porto,
FEUP Campus, Dr. Roberto Frias 4200-465, Porto, Portugal
joana866rocha@gmail.com
[2] INESC TEC – INESC Technology and Science,
FEUP Campus, Dr. Roberto Frias 4200-465, Porto, Portugal
[3] Universidade de Trás-os-Montes e Alto Douro,
Quinta de Prados, 5001-801 Vila Real, Portugal

Abstract. Lung cancer is among the deadliest diseases in the world. The detection and characterization of pulmonary nodules are crucial for an accurate diagnosis, which is of vital importance to increase the patients' survival rates. The segmentation process contributes to the mentioned characterization, but faces several challenges, due to the diversity in nodular shape, size, and texture, as well as the presence of adjacent structures. This paper proposes two methods for pulmonary nodule segmentation in Computed Tomography (CT) scans. First, a conventional approach which applies the Sliding Band Filter (SBF) to estimate the center of the nodule, and consequently the filter's support points, matching the initial border coordinates. This preliminary segmentation is then refined to include mainly the nodular area, and no other regions (e.g. vessels and pleural wall). The second approach is based on Deep Learning, using the U-Net to achieve the same goal. This work compares both performances, and consequently identifies which one is the most promising tool to promote early lung cancer screening and improve nodule characterization. Both methodologies used 2653 nodules from the LIDC database: the SBF based one achieved a Dice score of 0.663, while the U-Net achieved 0.830, yielding more similar results to the ground truth reference annotated by specialists, and thus being a more reliable approach.

Keywords: Computer-aided diagnosis · Conventional ·
Deep Learning · Lung · Nodule · Segmentation · Sliding Band Filter ·
U-Net

1 Introduction

Pulmonary nodules can be associated with several diseases, but a recurrent diagnosis is lung cancer, which is the main cause of cancer death in men and the second cause in women worldwide [10]. For this reason, providing an early detection and diagnosis to the patient is crucial, considering that any delay in cancer

© Springer Nature Switzerland AG 2019
P. Moura Oliveira et al. (Eds.): EPIA 2019, LNAI 11804, pp. 361–371, 2019.
https://doi.org/10.1007/978-3-030-30241-2_31

detection might result in lack of treatment efficacy. The advances of technology and imaging techniques such as computed tomography (CT) have improved nodule identification and monitoring. In a Computer-Aided Diagnosis (CAD) system, segmentation is the process of differentiating the nodule from other structures. However, this task is quite complex considering the heterogeneity of the size, texture, position, and shape of the nodules, and the fact that their intensity can vary within the borders. Data imbalance also poses a challenge, as in a CT scan less than 5% of the voxels belong to these lesions [11].

In biomedical image analysis, early methods (generally described as conventional) consisted of following a sequence of image processing steps (e.g. edge/line detectors, region growing) and mathematical models [4]. Among other conventional techniques, lesion detection and segmentation often imply the use of filters; e.g. the Sliding Band Filter can be used to develop an automated method for optic disc segmentation [2] and cell segmentation [6]. Such filter also proved to perform better than other local convergence index filters in pulmonary nodule detection [5].

Afterwards, the idea of extracting features and feeding them to a statistical classifier made supervised techniques become a trend. More recently, the trend is to use Deep Learning to develop models that are able to interpret what features better represent the data, but these require a large amount of annotated data, and have large computational cost. Medical imaging commonly relies on Convolutional Neural Networks (CNNs) [3]. For example, Fully Convolutional Networks are often applied for medical imaging segmentation [8], including encoder-decoder structures such as the SegNet, which are frequently used in semantic segmentation tasks [1]. The U-Net is a particular example of an encoder-decoder network for biomedical segmentation [7].

This work aims to precisely segment pulmonary nodules using a conventional approach, based on the Sliding Band Filter, and a Deep Learning based approach, more specifically the U-Net, and therefore evaluate and compare the performance of both methodologies.

2   Local Convergence Filters and the Sliding Band Filter

Local Convergence Filters (LCFs) estimate the convergence degree, C, of the gradient vectors within a support region R, toward a central pixel of interest $P(x, y)$, assuming that the studied object has a convex shape and limited size range. LCFs aim to maximize the convergence index at each image point, which is calculated minding the orientation angle $\theta_i(k, l)$ of the gradient vector at point (k, l) with respect to the line with radial direction i that connects (k, l) to P. The overall convergence is obtained by averaging the individual convergences at all M points in R, as written in Eq. 1, taken from [2].

$$C(x, y) = \frac{1}{M} \sum_{(k,l) \in R} \cos \theta_i(k, l)$$ (1)

LCFs perform better than other filters because they are not influenced by gradient magnitude, nor by the contrast with the surrounding structures. Being a member of the LCFs, the SBF also outputs a measure which estimates the degree of convergence of the gradient vectors. However, the position of the support region, which is a band of fixed width, is adapted according to the direction and the gradient orientation. The SBF studies the convergence along that band, ignoring the gradient's behaviour at the center of the object, which is considered irrelevant for shape estimation. Such feature makes this filter more versatile when it comes to detecting different shapes, even when they are not perfectly round, because the support region can be molded.

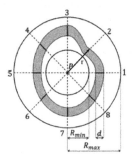

Fig. 1. Schematics of the Sliding Band filter with 8 support region lines (dashed lines, N = 8). Retrieved from [2].

The SBF searches each one of the N radial directions leading out of P for the position of the band of fixed width d that maximizes the convergence degree, as represented in Fig. 1. The search is done within a radial length that varies from a minimum ($Rmin$) to a maximum ($Rmax$) values, and so the filter's response is given by Eq. 2, where $\theta_{i,m}$ represents the angle of the gradient vector at the point m pixels away from P in direction i [2]. The coordinates of the band's support points $(X(\theta_i), Y(\theta_i))$ are obtained using Eq. 3, assuming that the center of the object is (x_c, y_c), and r_{shape} corresponds to the radius in direction i [9].

$$SBF(x,y) = \frac{1}{N} \sum_{i=0}^{N-1} \max_{Rmin \leq r \leq Rmax} \left[\frac{1}{d} \sum_{m=r-\frac{d}{2}}^{r+\frac{d}{2}} cos\theta_{i,m} \right] \tag{2}$$

$$\begin{cases} X(\theta_i) = x_c + r_{shape}(i) \times \cos(\theta_i) \\ Y(\theta_i) = y_c + r_{shape}(i) \times \sin(\theta_i) \\ r_{shape}(i) = \underset{Rmin \leq r \leq Rmax}{argmax} \left[\frac{1}{r} \sum_{m=r-\frac{d}{2}}^{r+\frac{d}{2}} cos\theta_{i,m} \right] \end{cases} \tag{3}$$

3   U-Net

The U-Net is a Fully Convolutional Network specially developed for biomedical image segmentation, thus requiring a smaller amount of parameters and computing time [7]. It resorts to data augmentation to simulate realistic elastic deformations, the most common variations in tissue, and so this network is able to work with less training data and still achieves a great performance.

The network, which is an example of an encoder-decoder architecture for semantic segmentation, includes a contracting path and an expansive path. The contracting path is also known as encoder, and can be seen as a common convolutional network with several convolutional layers, each followed by a ReLU and a max pooling layer. This path downsamples the input image into feature representations with different levels of abstraction. In other words, information about the features is gathered, while spatial information is shortened.

On the other hand, the expansive path takes advantage of a series of upconvolutions and concatenations, and thus the feature and spatial knowledge from the contracting path is associated with higher resolution layers. This causes the expansive path to be symmetrical to the contracting one, resulting in a U-shaped network. The precise segmentation is achieved with upsampling (resolution improvement) combined with high resolution features to localize the object.

4   Methodology

The following algorithms were applied on nodule candidates whose images are the output of a detection scheme. For each nodule, the 3D volume around its center was split into three anatomical planes (sagittal, axial, and coronal), resulting in three 80 × 80 pixel images per nodule. For clarity and brevity reasons, the method will be explained for a single plane (Fig. 2a for the conventional approach and Fig. 3a for the Deep Learning based one).

4.1   Conventional Approach

The SBF is first applied to get a better estimation of the nodule's center coordinates. Considering that most nodules have an overall uniform intensity, the nodules' images were processed by truncating any intensities much higher and lower than the nodule's. To do so, the nodule's average intensity was determined by calculating the mean of a matrix centered in the image. These steps result in a truncated mask, where there is already a very primitive segmentation (Fig. 2b) involving a low computational cost, which now needs substantial refinement.

The original nodule image, as well as the truncated nodule mask, are fed to the SBF and the filter's response in each pixel around the center of the image is calculated. The estimated nodule's center corresponds to the pixel which maximizes the response of the filter. With those coordinates, the SBF then evaluates the corresponding set of support points, returning the N border coordinates

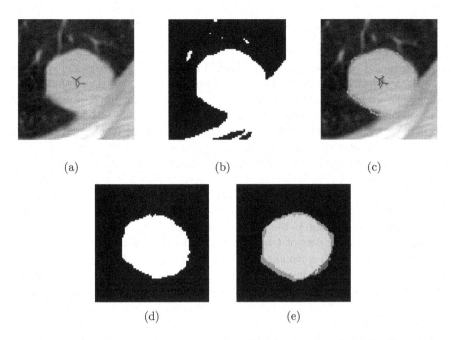

Fig. 2. Exemplification of the conventional methodology steps, where the blue mark is the center of the image, the green mark is the ground truth center of the nodule, and the red mark is the estimated center of the nodule. (Color figure online)

marked in Fig. 2c with yellow. To ensure the SBF is as precise as possible, a condition was added to force the cosine of the gradient vector's orientation angle to be null when the pixel which is being evaluated in a certain direction is null in the truncated mask. Ideally, this keeps the SBF from including in the segmentation non-nodular regions within the $Rmin$ and $Rmax$ limits. An outlier attenuation/removal step was implemented, minding the distance between consecutive border coordinates, and afterwards a binary mask with the initial SBF segmentation is created.

To further refine the segmentation and specifically select the nodular area, only the intersection of the SBF segmentation mask and the truncated nodule mask is considered, thus eliminating unwanted regions. Any cavities within the intersected binary masks are filled. By labeling all the different regions present in the intersected masks, which are identified by their connected components, it is possible to eliminate any region that has no connection to the nodule. This can be done by eliminating from the mask all regions that do not encompass the center of the image, as the nodule is always centered. After this step, the final segmentation mask is achieved, as exemplified in Fig. 2d.

4.2 Deep Learning Based Approach

The Deep Learning algorithm presented in this work was implemented using *Keras*, with a *TensorFlow* backend. The 2D images are imported and split into training, validation, and test sets. A condition was added to ensure that a nodule belongs exclusively to one of the sets, as it would not make sense to train and test the model using the same nodules. This way, the set of 2653 nodules was first split into training and test sets (80%–20%, respectively), and then 20% of the training set was used as validation set. Real-time data augmentation is applied to the training set, replicating tissue deformations through affine transformations (e.g. 0.2 degrees of shear and random rotation within a 90 degree range), and generating more training data with horizontal and vertical flips, as well as grayscale variations.

The architecture of the U-Net was kept as proposed in [7], where the contracting path includes four sets of two 3×3 unpadded convolutions, each followed by a ReLU with batch normalization, a 2×2 max pooling layer with stride equal to 2, and a dropout layer. The number of feature channels is doubled with each downsampling phase, which is repeated four times as mentioned above. Two 3×3 convolutions with ReLU, batch normalization, and dropout, are present at the end of this path, creating a bottleneck before the following path. The expansive path is comprised of four blocks which repeatedly have a deconvolution layer with stride equal to 2 (reducing the number of feature channels by half), a concatenation with the corresponding cropped feature map from the contracting path, and two 3×3 convolutions, each followed by ReLU with batch normalization. In order to achieve the segmentation result (pixel-wise classification task with two classes), the endmost layer includes a 1×1 convolution, using softmax activation. The pixel-wise probabilities face a 50% threshold to decide whether a pixel is nodular or not.

The network was trained with the Adam optimizer, to achieve faster a stable convergence. It was necessary to take into consideration the class imbalance within a sample (generally, there are more non-nodular pixels in an image than nodular ones), and so a Dice based loss function was selected. The training stage of the model is guided by two evaluation metrics: accuracy and Jaccard Index.

While training the model, callbacks were included. First, early stopping ensures the training ends when the validation loss stops improving. At the same time, the learning rate also reduces on plateau, meaning that it is reduced when the validation loss cannot reach a lower value. More specifically, the initial learning rate value is the default provided in the original paper for the Adam optimizer, and will be reduced by a factor of 0.1 (new learning rate = learning rate $\times$ 0.1), having a minimum accepted value of 0.00001.

The model is fit on batches with real-time data augmentation (using a batch size of 64 samples), allowing a maximum of 100 epochs. After analyzing the validation loss for every epoch, the training weights which maximize the evaluation metrics and minimize the loss are stored, to get the predictions of the test set. Figure 3b is the segmentation achieved by the U-Net for the nodule in Fig. 3a.

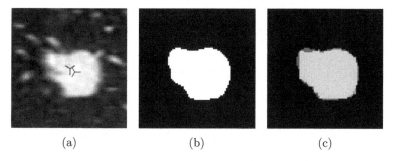

(a)   (b)   (c)

Fig. 3. Exemplification of the U-Net results, where the blue mark is the center of the image, the green mark is the ground truth center of the nodule. (Color figure online)

5   Results

The methods were evaluated on 2653 nodules, using as ground truth the segmentation masks from the LIDC database, which is publicly available and consists of lung cancer screening thoracic CT scans from 1010 patients. The results for the conventional approach, exhibited in Table 1, were obtained with the SBF parameter values N = 64, d = 7, Rmin = 1 and Rmax = 25, which were established empirically to maximize the algorithm's performance. This method achieved a Dice score of 0.663, while having Precision and Recall values of 0.710 and 0.732, respectively. On the other hand, the U-Net test set predictions achieved a loss value of 0.172, accuracy of 0.992, and Dice score of 0.830, while having Precision and Recall values of 0.792 and 0.898. The U-Net model exhibited fast convergence (after 14 epochs), and did not overfit to the training data, considering the validation loss is similar to the training loss (Fig. 4). The SBF needed approximately 5 hours to run, while the U-Net had a reasonable training time of roughly 8 hours on a NVidia GeForce GTX 1080 GPU (8 GB).

Table 1. Evaluation metrics achieved by the conventional and Deep Learning based methods.

	Dice coefficient	Precision	Recall
SBF	0.663	0.710	0.732
U-Net	0.830	0.792	0.898

To illustrate the performance of the methods presented in this work, a comparison plot was created (Figs. 2e and 3c), in which the green pixels belong exclusively to the ground truth mask, the red pixels belong exclusively to the achieved result using the proposed method, and the yellow pixels belong to both - meaning that the yellow pixels mark the correct predictions made by the algorithm. Figure 5 compares the performance of each algorithm, using these plots.

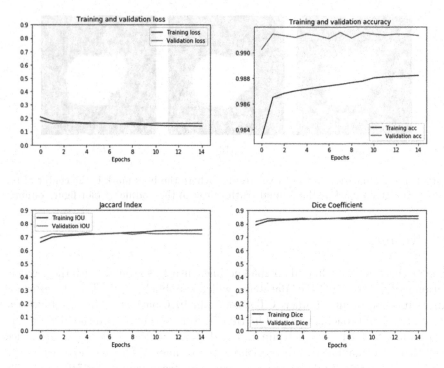

Fig. 4. Training and validation results of the U-Net model.

Considering that the SBF was evaluated on a set of 2653 nodules, and the U-Net was evaluated on 531 nodules (20% of the database), the following analysis is done minding the performance of both methodologies for the same set of 531 nodules, randomly selected in the U-Net algorithm. The proposed conventional approach exhibits a highly satisfactory performance when dealing with well-circumscribed solid nodules. The nodules that have a pleural tail generally have the thin structure ignored by the algorithm, which does not include it in the segmentation mask, while the specialists consider the tail as part of the nodule. In spite of vascularized nodules entailing an inherent difficulty when it comes to distinguishing the nodule from the attached vessels, the SBF based approach is frequently able to separate them and create a mask which does not include the non-nodular structures. The algorithm's performance is also satisfying when dealing with nodules whose intensities vary within their border (e.g. calcific and cavitary nodules), as it is able to ignore the cavities/calcific regions during the segmentation process. The main flaws of the algorithm appear when dealing with juxtapleural nodules, since it often does not know where the nodule ends and the pleura begins, thus only being able to estimate the boundary to some extent. Overall, the less satisfying results are mainly due to the unexpected shape of the nodule, or because the nodule does not have a clear margin (e.g. non-solid nodules/ground glass opacities).

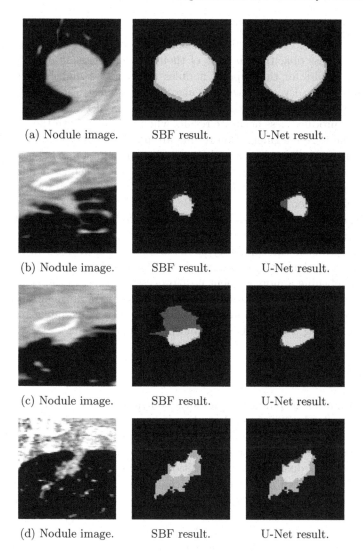

(a) Nodule image.   SBF result.   U-Net result.

(b) Nodule image.   SBF result.   U-Net result.

(c) Nodule image.   SBF result.   U-Net result.

(d) Nodule image.   SBF result.   U-Net result.

Fig. 5. Comparison between methodologies: in nodule (a) both methodologies are successful, in nodule (b) the SBF outperforms the U-Net, in nodule (c) the U-Net outperforms the SBF, and finally in nodule (d) none of the methodologies have a satisfying result.

Similarly to the SBF based approach, the U-Net is able to clearly segment well-circumscribed solid nodules, as well as cavitary, calcific, and vascularized nodules. This network also agrees with the previous approach when it comes to nodules with pleural tail, in the sense that it does not encompass the tail in the segmentation mask, unlike suggested by the specialists. However, the U-Net certainly outperforms the conventional approach, as it is able to deal nearly perfectly with juxtapleural nodules, achieving very accurate segmentation results in such cases. It also achieves better results when presented with non-solid nodules/ground glass opacities, in spite of their inherent segmentation complexity, and so the results for this type of nodules may also be slightly different from the ground truth. Even though the algorithm demonstrates a certain degree of dexterity when dealing with irregular shaped nodules in comparison to the SBF, it still produces less accurate results when presented with these situations. However, the U-Net segmentation results are in general very similar to the ones given by the specialists, hence its great performance in comparison to the SBF based approach. In some cases, the U-Net is even able to achieve a more uniform detailed segmentation in comparison to the specialists', which may be justified by its pixel-wise perspicacity.

Additional efforts can be done in future work to improve the algorithms' performance, namely develop a more adequate pre-processing for the input images, in order to promote the capability of the segmentation process. In the conventional approach, the border coordinates may be refined for the juxtapleural nodules by establishing a more efficient post-processing stage. In the Deep Learning approach, the most straightforward way to enhance its performance in non-solid or irregular shaped lesions would be to add more of these examples to the training set, promoting a more advanced and perceptive learning.

6   Conclusion

The segmentation of pulmonary nodules contributes to their characterization, which makes it a key to assess the patient's health state. This way, a segmentation step implemented within a CAD system can help the physician to establish a more accurate diagnosis. However, the automation of such task is hampered by the diversity of nodule shape, size, position, lighting, texture, etc. The proposed conventional approach deals with these challenges by implementing the Sliding Band Filter to find the coordinates of the borders, and achieves a Dice score of 0.663 when tested with the LIDC database. On the other hand, the Deep Learning based approach achieves a Dice score of 0.830, using the U-Net. Both performances are impaired by irregular shaped/non-solid nodules, and in the case of the convencional approach by juxtapleural nodules as well, and so future work includes the refinement of the methods to deal with these particular challenges. However, they are promising segmentation tools for well-circumscribed, solid, cavitary, calcific, and vascularized nodules. This way, the comparison of the conventional and Deep Learning based approaches explored the advantages and disadvantages of each technique, establishing the U-Net as the most efficient method in this case - particularly efficient for obvious lesions, and able to overcome to a certain extent the high variability of nodular structures. Consequently, the satisfactory segmentation results achieved by the U-Net in this work lead to further insights on nodule characterization, contributing to the development of a decision support system, which may be able to assist the physicians to establish a reliable diagnosis based on the analysis of such characteristics.

Acknowledgements. This work is financed by National Funds through the Portuguese funding agency, FCT – Fundação para a Ciência e a Tecnologia within project: UID/EEA/50014/2019.

References

1. Badrinarayanan, V., Kendall, A., Cipolla, R.: SegNet: a deepconvolutional encoder-decoder architecture for imagesegmentation, November 2015. arXiv:1511.00561 [cs]. http://arxiv.org/abs/1511.00561
2. Dashtbozorg, B., Mendonça, A.M., Campilho, A.: Optic disc segmentation using the sliding band filter. Comput. Biol. Med. **56**, 1–12 (2015). https://doi.org/10.1016/j.compbiomed.2014.10.009. https://linkinghub.elsevier.com/retrieve/pii/S0010482514002832
3. Jiang, F., et al.: Medical image semantic segmentation based on deep learning. Neural Comput. Appl. **29**(5), 1257–1265 (2018). https://doi.org/10.1007/s00521-017-3158-6. https://link.springer.com/10.1007/s00521-017-3158-6
4. Litjens, G., et al.: A survey on deep learning in medical image analysis. Med. Image Anal. **42**, 60–88 (2017). https://doi.org/10.1016/j.media.2017.07.005. https://linkinghub.elsevier.com/retrieve/pii/S1361841517301135
5. Pereira, C.S., Mendonça, A.M., Campilho, A.: Evaluation of contrast enhancement filters for lung nodule detection. In: Kamel, M., Campilho, A. (eds.) ICIAR 2007. LNCS, vol. 4633, pp. 878–888. Springer, Heidelberg (2007). https://doi.org/10.1007/978-3-540-74260-9_78
6. Quelhas, P., Marcuzzo, M., Mendonca, A.M., Campilho, A.: Cell nuclei and cytoplasm joint segmentation using the sliding band filter. IEEE Trans. Med. Imaging **29**(8), 1463–1473 (2010). https://doi.org/10.1109/TMI.2010.2048253. https://ieeexplore.ieee.org/document/5477157/
7. Ronneberger, O., Fischer, P., Brox, T.: U-Net: convolutional networks for biomedical image segmentation. In: Navab, N., Hornegger, J., Wells, W.M., Frangi, A.F. (eds.) MICCAI 2015. LNCS, vol. 9351, pp. 234–241. Springer, Cham (2015). https://doi.org/10.1007/978-3-319-24574-4_28
8. Roth, H.R., et al.: Deep learning and its application to medical image segmentation, March 2018. arXiv:1803.08691 [cs]. https://doi.org/10.11409/mit.36.63. http://arxiv.org/abs/1803.08691
9. Shakibapour, E., Cunha, A., Aresta, G., Mendonça, A.M., Campilho, A.: An unsupervised metaheuristic search approach for segmentation and volume measurement of pulmonary nodules in lung CT scans. Exp. Syst. Appl. **119**, 415–428 (2019)
10. Torre, L.A., Siegel, R.L., Jemal, A.: Lung cancer statistics. In: Ahmad, A., Gadgeel, S. (eds.) Lung Cancer and Personalized Medicine. AEMB, vol. 893, pp. 1–19. Springer, Cham (2016). https://doi.org/10.1007/978-3-319-24223-1_1
11. Wang, S., et al.: Central focused convolutional neural networks: developing a data-driven model for lung nodule segmentation. Med. Image Anal. **40**, 172–183 (2017). https://doi.org/10.1016/j.media.2017.06.014. https://linkinghub.elsevier.com/retrieve/pii/S1361841517301019

Intelligent Virtual Assistant for Promoting Behaviour Change in Older People with T2D

João Balsa[1]([✉])(ID), Pedro Neves[1], Isa Félix[2](ID), Mara Pereira Guerreiro[2,3](ID), Pedro Alves[1], Maria Beatriz Carmo[1](ID), Diogo Marques[1], António Dias[1], Adriana Henriques[2](ID), and Ana Paula Cláudio[1](ID)

[1] Biosystems & Integrative Sciences Institute (BioISI), Faculdade de Ciências da Universidade de Lisboa, Lisbon, Portugal
{jbalsa,mbcarmo,apclaudio}@ciencias.ulisboa.pt,
{fc51688,fc51686,fc47847,fc47811}@alunos.fc.ul.pt
[2] Unidade de Investigação e Desenvolvimento em Enfermagem (ui&de), Escola Superior de Enfermagem de Lisboa, Lisbon, Portugal
{isafelix,mara.guerreiro,ahenriques}@esel.pt
[3] CiiEM, Instituto Universitário Egas Moniz, Monte de Caparica, Portugal

Abstract. We present a version of an application prototype developed in the context of the *VASelfCare* project. This application works as an intelligent anthropomorphic virtual relational agent that has the role of assisting older people with Type 2 Diabetes Mellitus (T2D) in medication adherence and lifestyle changes.

In this paper, we focus on the development of the dialogue component of the system and in what we consider one of the main original contributions: the incorporation, in the way the dialogue flows, of Behaviour Change Techniques (*BCTs*), identified in the context of the Behaviour Change Wheel framework.

We also describe the general architecture of the system, including the graphical component. Tests on the prototype pre-requisites were conducted with health professionals and older adults with T2D within five primary care units of the Portuguese National Health Service. Overall, these tests yielded encouraging data and endorsed our approach.

Keywords: Intelligent virtual assistants · Relational agents · Behaviour change · *mHealth* applications · Diabetes

1 Introduction

With the advances in mobile computing, numerous applications have been developed with the goal of responding to people's diverse needs in the health domain. Those are generally referred to as *mHealth applications*. Highlighting the components related to artificial intelligence, we present in this paper an application prototype that, as far as we know, goes beyond what is currently available.

The drive for our work lies in three dimensions: *medical*—how to help older people with T2D cope with the disease, *behavioural*—how to promote behaviour

© Springer Nature Switzerland AG 2019
P. Moura Oliveira et al. (Eds.): EPIA 2019, LNAI 11804, pp. 372–383, 2019.
https://doi.org/10.1007/978-3-030-30241-2_32

change, when needed, and *computer science* (artificial intelligence and computer graphics)—how to develop a virtual assistant, as an intelligent relational agent, to achieve a specific goal. These aspects are central to the *VASelfCare* project, from which the application we describe emerged.

The importance of T2D in modern societies has been extensively established in the literature. T2D affects approximately 425 million adults (20–79 years) [14]. Around one-quarter of people over the age of 65 years have diabetes and one-half of older adults have pre-diabetes [10]. The prevalence of T2D continues to increase steadily as more people live longer [27]. In 2016, an estimated 1.6 million deaths were directly caused by diabetes. Almost half of all deaths attributable to high blood glucose occur before the age of 70 years [27], however there are many people with T2D, older than 70 years that can be expected to live more than a decade of healthy life expectancy [23]. A vital aspect of diabetes care is diabetes self-management education and support; the latter is recommended to assist older people with implementing and sustaining skills and behavioural changes and may be delivered using technology-based programs [1]. It is important to empower older people for self-care and help them to perform self-management behaviours, including *medication* management, eating a *healthy diet* and being *physically active.*

The management of long-term conditions, such as diabetes, places a substantial burden on health care systems, particularly in the context of an ageing society. The use of electronic health (eHealth) systems, accessible through mobile phones, tablets or computers, offers new opportunities to manage these conditions in a convenient, affordable and scalable fashion, by supporting self-care and/or health care professionals' monitoring and communication. The effect of mobile health interventions on glycemic control in T2D patients has been demonstrated by recent systematic reviews [12,13]. For example, Cui et al. [12] estimated a significant effect of mobile applications in HbA1c (*Glycated hemoglobin*). These effects can be important if achieved by patients on their own, without the additional cost of involving healthcare professionals. Pal et al. [24] pointed out that, in the interventions analysed, the theoretical basis and the behaviour change techniques (BCTs), which are the active ingredients of interventions, were not always described. This impairs the generation of evidence on the most effective BCTs to achieve the desired impact and curtails replication.

We address these issues by carefully designing a theory-driven and evidence-based intervention, resorting to an anthropomorphic virtual assistant (VA) that supports medication adherence and lifestyle change (healthy diet and physical activity). The VA was developed as an intelligent relational agent; the use of these agents has shown effectiveness and acceptability for older people, including those with limited health literacy [4,5], and may promote engagement over time.

At the current stage, the main challenge is to have a virtual assistant that performs a daily dialogue with the patient over the course of several weeks, to promote and sustain desirable behaviours. Unlike traditional VAs, that perform a single interaction, the VA in our project should be able to establish a relation with the patient over a series of interactions. In this context, it is crucial that the

VA exhibits human-like intelligent behaviour in two dimensions: in the way each daily dialogue flows, and ensuring coherence across daily interventions towards desirable behaviours. To achieve this, we used a rule-based engine to model the dialogue flow in two levels: a bottom-level with the definition of specific portions of the interaction; and a meta-level, which enables a general characterisation of the dialogue flow, in order to incorporate context specific knowledge.

The remainder of our paper is organised as follows. In Sect. 2, we analyse the most relevant related work. In Sect. 3, we present the core of our contribution, describing the way the interaction was designed. In Sect. 4, we give an overall perspective of the application prototype. In Sect. 5, we present some evaluation results. Finally, in Sect. 6, we present some conclusions.

2   Related Work

Detailing the active ingredients and intervention features of behavioural T2D interventions is crucial to deliver effective replicable strategies with impact in clinical outcomes. Overall, there is a paucity of evidence on the effects of the active ingredients of multi-component interventions and their impact on changes in HbA1c, in particular concerning *mHealth* solutions using virtual assistants.

Several models and taxonomies have been developed to guide intervention content and streamline reporting the effects of behavioural interventions. The *Behaviour Change Wheel* (BCW) framework [19] offers a systematic and structured method of intervention development. It organises content and components of behavioural interventions into nine *intervention functions* (IFs): restrictions, environmental restructuring, modelling, enablement, training, coercion, incentivization, persuasion and education. IFs represent how an intervention might change the target behaviour. To translate the general IFs into specific replicable techniques, Michie and colleagues [20] recommend the Behaviour Change Techniques Taxonomy (BCTTv1), which reports the active ingredients of an intervention—behaviour change techniques (BCTs).

The BCTTv1 has been validated and is used to design and retrospectively evaluate and aggregate effect sizes of health interventions [21]. Developing an understanding of the theoretical basis of effective interventions can inform future development. A scoping review [15], on the contents of the eHealth interventions targeting persons with poorly controlled T2D identified 31 BCTs most frequently used based on the BCTTv1, such as "instruction on how to perform a behaviour", "adding objects to the environment", "self-monitoring on outcomes of behaviour", "social support (practical)", "feedback on outcomes of behaviour" and "prompts/cues". These findings are corroborated by previous literature [24,26]. Pal et al. [24] demonstrated that the most common BCTs with significant impact on HbA1c in computer-based interventions were: "prompt self-monitoring of behavioural outcomes" and "provide feedback on performance".

The importance of *mHealth apps* (mobile Health applications, typically for iOS or Android devices), has been accompanying the development of mobile technologies. Bhuyan et al. [3] developed a study in which they concluded that among the adults that use mHealth apps, 60% considered them as useful in achieving health behaviour goals. In another study, Morrissey et al. [22] surveyed 166 apps aimed at promoting medical adherence in order to find if they incorporate any established BCT. This study concluded that, from the 93 possible techniques [20], only a total of 12 were found in the evaluated apps. This result clearly shows that there is still a lot of work to be done in incorporating BCT research results in available applications.

Regarding the use of relational agents (virtual humans, designed to build long-term socio-emotional relationships with users), Bickmore et al. (for instance [4–6]) have been the most active group, researching interventions in several areas.

Rule-based approaches to dialogue management have been explored, namely in the context of spoken dialogue systems. As mentioned by [9], systems like the one of [7, 25] and [18] (this using also probabilities), use *handcrafted* rule-base systems to manage the *action-selection* process of a dialogue, that is, to determine *what to say next*.

Unlike most of these systems, in our prototype the user input is generally limited to a set of options. There are two main reasons underlying this choice: the nature of target users (older people, possibly with low literacy) and potential unintended consequences of free dialogues, as pointed out in a recent review of conversational agents in healthcare [17].

3 Intelligent Relational Interaction

We now describe our approach. We will first explain how the intervention was designed, and then how it was modelled using a rule-based approach.

3.1 Intervention Design

The intervention has two distinct phases: (1) *evaluation* and (2) *follow-up*. The main purpose of the evaluation phase is to collect data on the user's characteristics pertaining to the three components: *diet, physical activity* and *medication*, for future tailoring of the intervention. In the subsequent *follow-up* phase, the main goal is to promote the desired behaviour or to maintain it. In this paper we focus on this *follow-up* phase, since it is the most interesting from an artificial intelligence perspective.

Each daily interaction with the virtual assistant is structured according to the literature on relational agents [5], that recommends the dialogue should follow some general sequential steps. These steps are: (1) *opening*; (2) *social talk*; (3) *review tasks*; (4) *assess*; (5) *counselling*; (6) *assign tasks*; (7) *pre-closing*; and (8) *closing*. A detailed description of each of these steps can be found in [8].

The dialogue structure is common for the three intervention components. The design of the software prototype intervention and the dialogue creation was guided by the BCW [19]. This approach enhanced the development process based on an evidence-based selection of the intervention components (BCTs), ensuring that the intervention targets the underlying determinants of behaviour.

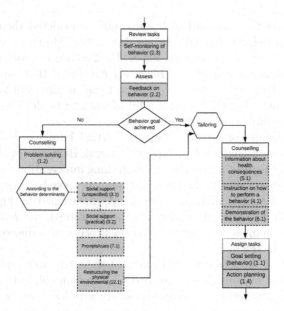

Fig. 1. BCTs distribution according to standard dialogue steps in an interaction. *Dotted lines indicate BCTs that are operationalised depending on the context (tailoring or behaviour targeting). Numbers represent the BCT code according to BCTTv1.*

Suitable and potential effective BCTs were incorporated in different steps of the interaction. The selected BCTs are exclusive of a particular dialogue step in all intervention components. In our view, the operationalisation in the first two and of the last two dialogue steps does not represent a behaviour change technique, according to the above mentioned BCTTv1 taxonomy [20]. Specific BCTs are operationalised according to tailoring principles, including constructs such as lack of knowledge, or by a previously defined behaviour target. Figure 1 represents the BCTs distribution according to the standard dialogue steps in the follow-up phase.

3.2 Rule-Based Component

In order to incorporate the desired BCTs in the dialogue flow, the interaction is controlled by a rule engine. Rules define the flow of the dialogue in two ways. At a lower level, they have the role of representing a handcrafted portion of the dialogue, that might, for instance, materialise the local application of a specific BCT. At a higher level, they are responsible for managing the overall interaction flow, for instance, the realisation that the dialogue should go to next step, or that a different component should be addressed.

The way this works is illustrated in Fig. 2. This figure represents the flow of the dialog for one day of interaction. There is an organisation in modules.

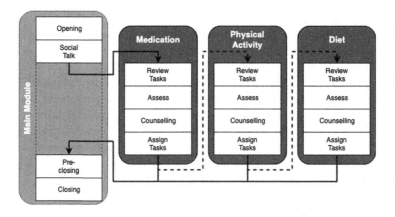

Fig. 2. Module interaction in the rule-based system.

The main module includes the four steps—*Opening, Social Talk, Pre-Closing* and *Closing*—that are always executed; the first two at the beginning and the other two at the end. Then, the modules that incorporate some BCT are started according to the defined protocol (first, *medication*, then *physical activity*, and finally *diet*). The duration of the evaluation phase varies between one and three days, depending on the component. For each component, the follow-up phase depends on patient adherence to the target behaviour and can be delivered ranging from eight days to several weeks. In Fig. 2 the dotted lines represent the possibility, inferred or not by the rule engine, of including more than one component in a single interaction. Multi-behaviour interactions do not go through all the dialogue steps for each component on a daily basis.

4   The *VASelfCare* application

The central element of the *VASelfCare* application is an anthropomorphic female character (called Vitória) which plays the role of an intelligent virtual assistant and is capable of speaking (articulates speech while the corresponding subtitles appear on the screen) and express emotions through facial and body animations. The overall development of the app's interface was guided by usability principles for older people with T2D [2]. For example, redundancy of both audio and written information may help reduce any communication shortcomings, such as lower eyesight accuracy and hearing deficits.

The user communicates with the VA using buttons to choose the answers or alternatives that determine the course of the dialogue. Besides, the user can also insert specific values in the interface of the app, such as the daily number of steps or the glycaemia level. Such values are used to produce graphics that ease the process of obtaining a general idea about the overall evolution over time of the diabetic patient that is using the app.

The app can be used in two modes by the patient: (i) daily interaction with the VA, fed by past records and information inputted during the interaction; and (ii) ad-hoc access to update records or to consult its own evolution over time in terms of T2D self-management.

The app runs in tablets (OS – Android 7.0; CPU – Snapdragon 435; RAM: 3 GB; ROM: 32 Gb) and does not depend on the existence of an active Internet connection. The app in each tablet will be used by one patient only at a time. All records concerning this patient are kept on a local database in the tablet. Periodically the information is copied to a server for a posterior analysis.

The virtual assistant chosen for this first prototype is a female 3D model, obtained from Daz3[1].

4.1   Application Architecture

The core of *VASelfCare* technological solution is implemented in *Unity*[2]. Although best known as a game engine, it suits adequately the requirements of our application, with the possibility of defining multiple views, each with their own purpose, as well as the transitions between them.

The architecture comprises 3 main components: the *Core*, the *Dialogue Creator* and the *Speech Generator* (Fig. 3). The *Core* controls the interface and the flow of the execution. The *Dialogue Creator* is the component used to define the speech of the VA and the choices presented to the user while the interaction with the user is taking place. Finally, the *Speech Generator* creates the audio and viseme files to support the VA's articulated speech.

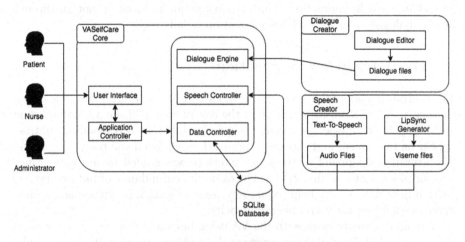

Fig. 3. *VASelfCare* application architecture.

---

[1] https://www.daz3d.com.
[2] https://unity.com/.

The *User Interface* module provides several views for the patient: (i) to log-in; (ii) to interact with the virtual assistant; (iii) to register personal data, such as daily number of steps walked, blood glucose levels or weight; (iv) to access personal information, such as, prescribed anti-diabetic medication or charts with the registered data over time; (v) to view the assigned self-care plans; and (vi) to access advice information about the diet, physical activity and medication.

The *Application Controller* manages the flow of the execution being responsible for the logical sequence of the application and for communicating with the other components of the VASelfCare Core. The *Dialogue Engine* corresponds to what was described in the previous section.

The *Dialogue Creator* component corresponds to the definition of the hand-crafted portion of the dialogues (the lower-level mentioned earlier).

To convert the written dialogues into audio files a Text-To-Speech software is used, *Speech2Go*[3]. The speech rate has been slowed down, taking in consideration the target population. The *LipSync Generator*, developed in the context of a previous project [11] is used to convert text to viseme files. Audio and viseme files are read simultaneously to provide Vitória's articulated speech.

4.2 Implementation

As mentioned above, the core of the solution is implemented in *Unity*. For the rule engine, the choice was CLIPS[4]. It is a rule-based programming language that uses a forward-chaining inference engine (based on the RETE algorithm). Originally developed by NASA in 1985, and presented as an expert system tool, it has been subject to continuous improvements and extensions, and has been used in diverse artificial intelligence applications. Our work uses version 6.4, launched in 2018.

Implementation raised some technology integration challenges that need to be solved by the team. For instance, being C# the primary development language used with *Unity*, we had to wrap CLIPS in a plugin that provided the necessary functions to interact with the rule engine. This allows the CLIPS engine to be started from within the application code, the reception of the question and possible answers that are present in the rule currently being executed by the CLIPS engine, and the selection of a specific answer (given by the user in the application), thus making CLIPS infer the next rule to fire.

Besides the two main components just described, some other auxiliary tools were used or developed in the context of this work: *YARN*, a dialogue editor used to create the dialog structure; and a *YARN→CLIPS translator*, a tool developed in the project, used to translate from the YARN language to CLIPS language.

5   Evaluation

Although the feasibility trial will start only in a couple of months, the project protocol comprises iterative tests with older people with T2D and health

---

[3] https://harposoftware.com.

[4] http://clipsrules.sourceforge.net/.

professionals during the software development phase (with ethics approval by ARSLVT[5]. In this paper we report on the evaluation of pre-requisites, which was conducted through interactions with the first prototype.

5.1 Participants and Procedure

Nurses, physicians and older people with T2D were purposively sampled within five primary care units of the Portuguese National Health Service. A sample size of five to ten individuals in each group was envisaged. Nineteen healthcare professionals (12 nurses and 6 physicians; mean 46.22, min 25 max 63) plus nine adults with T2D accepted to participate. Older people's age ranged between 66 and 89 years (mean 71).

The data collection instrument was a previously piloted self-administered questionnaire; it was comprised by three parts: social-demographic questions, closed and open-ended questions about the prototype. Most questions were common for both groups, but healthcare professionals had two additional open-questions and there were differences in three closed-questions. Participants responded to closed-questions on a 5-point Likert scale, with anchor points from (1) strongly disagree to strongly agree (5).

Questionnaires were completed following an explanation of the study by a research team member and signing informed consent. Data were collected in individual face-to-face session, which lasted between 40 to 50 min. Participants were asked to use the prototype independently, guided by a script that covered a full interaction with the virtual assistant (medication adherence component; evaluation phase) and other prototype features.

5.2 Results and Discussion

Overall, the most frequent score was 4 (46,9%). Patients' opinions tended to be more positive than healthcare professionals, but differences only reached statistical significance in what concerned the virtual assistant facial expression (mean value for professionals 3.37 vs older adults 4.33, $t = 3.00$, $p = 0.006$). Therefore, the remaining data were analysed together.

In general, the least encouraging opinions were related to the VA's appearance and facial expressions. This also emerged in textual data as a negative aspect under the theme technology; for example, one professional said "Facial expressions are weird" (6_IDP1)[6]. Respondents' opinions on other aspects of the interface were also generally positive. The statements that characters on the screen could be read well received only positive answers (mean 4.57; min 4; max 5).

Both groups agreed that the application was easy to use (mean 4.11, min 3 max 5; mean 4.56, min 4 max 5 for professionals and patients respectively). This was corroborated by findings under the category intuitiveness: "Easy to handle and understand" (4_IDP1). The statement "I would like to try the application

---

[5] Regional Health Administration of Lisbon and Tagus Valley.
[6] We include participants' ids to guarantee traceability.

for a few weeks" received positive answers from patients (mean 4,56, min 4 max 5). However, textual data indicates that both groups envisaged difficulties, as illustrated by the accounts of four patients under the technology theme "(People) are not used to use technology" (5_ID1). Results highlight the need for training older people with T2D in using a potentially new technology. This was already planned in the project protocol and mirrors the procedures adopted in similar studies [16].

Patients were satisfied with Vitória's final feedback on their answers to questions posed in the evaluation phase (mean 4.56, min 4 max 5). In summary, answers to closed-questions indicate, overall, a positive opinion about the prototype. Textual data from both professionals and patients yielded numerous suggestions to inform pre-requisites, coded in four categories: "monitoring", "medication", "physical activity" and "diet".

Data on negative aspects in several themes can also point out opportunities for improvement (e.g. background colours of the prototype were considered gloomy). These data has been addressed in the iterative software development process. Interestingly, results from these tests with patients and health professionals are overall consistent with the ones obtained from academic nurses with expertise in primary care, which we have previously reported [8]. Such consistence across distinct groups (academics, care providers and patients) is encouraging and endorses the approach we developed based on previous research and clinical literature for the Portuguese context. Future tests, entailing a longer contact with the prototype and its components, will provide additional data in this respect.

6   Conclusions

We presented the most relevant aspects of an application designed for an intervention with older people with T2D. The Intelligent Virtual Assistant that we developed, incorporates a solid behaviour change theory in the dialogue flow, making the VA a relational agent with unique and original features regarding the model that supports the way it interacts with the user. Besides, it has a human appearance, that subtly evolves according to the emotions it intends to express.

Initial evaluation results are positive, endorsing the first developments and indicating that the prototype was well-received by patients and health professionals.

Acknowledgements. The authors are indebted to other *VASelfCare* team members for their contribution to the software development (http://vaselfcare.rd.ciencias.ulisboa.pt/). This work was supported by FCT and Compete 2020 (grant number LISBOA-01-0145-FEDER-024250). It is also supported by UID/MULTI /04046/2019 Research Unit grant from FCT, Portugal (to BioISI).

References

1. American Diabetes Association: 5. Lifestyle Management: Standards of Medical Care in Diabetes - 2019. Diabetes Care **42**(Suppl. 1), S46 (2019)
2. Arnhold, M., Quade, M., Kirch, W.: Mobile applications for diabetics: a systematic review and expert-based usability evaluation considering the special requirements of diabetes patients age 50 years or older. J. Med. Internet Res. **16**(4), 1–18 (2014)
3. Bhuyan, S.S., et al.: Use of mobile health applications for health-seeking behavior among US adults. J. Med. Syst. **40**(6), 153 (2016)
4. Bickmore, T.W., et al.: A randomized controlled trial of an automated exercise coach for older adults. J. Am. Geriatr. Soc. **61**(10), 1676–1683 (2013)
5. Bickmore, T.W., Caruso, L., Clough-Gorr, K., Heeren, T.: 'It's just like you talk to a friend' relational agents for older adults. Interact. Comput. **17**(6), 711–735 (2005)
6. Bickmore, T.W., Puskar, K., Schlenk, E.A., Pfeifer, L.M., Sereika, S.M.: Maintaining reality: relational agents for antipsychotic medication adherence. Interact. Comput. **22**, 276–288 (2010)
7. Boye, J.: Dialogue management for automatic troubleshooting and other problem-solving applications. In: Proceedings of the 8th SIGDial Workshop on Discourse and Dialogue, pp. 247–255 (2007)
8. Buinhas, S., et al.: Virtual assistant to improve self-care of older people with type 2 diabetes: first prototype. In: García-Alonso, J., Fonseca, C. (eds.) IWoG 2018. CCIS, vol. 1016, pp. 236–248. Springer, Cham (2019). https://doi.org/10.1007/978-3-030-16028-9_21
9. Burgan, D.: Dialogue Systems & Dialogue Management. Tech. rep., National Security & ISR Division Defence Science and Technology Group (2017)
10. Centers for Disease Control and Prevention: National Diabetes Statistics Report: Estimates of Diabetes and Its Burden in the United States. Atlanta, GA: Centers for Disease Control and Prevention (2017)
11. Cláudio, A.P., Carmo, M.B., Pinto, V., Cavaco, A., Guerreiro, M.P.: Virtual humans for training and assessment of self-medication consultation skills in pharmacy students. In: 10th International Conference on Computer Science and Education (ICCSE), pp. 175–180 (2015)
12. Cui, M., Wu, X., Mao, J., Wang, X., Nie, M.: T2DM self-management via smartphone applications: a systematic review and meta-analysis. PLoS ONE **11**(11), 1–15 (2016)
13. Hou, C., Carter, B., Hewitt, J., Francisa, T., Mayor, S.: Do mobile phone applications improve glycemic control (HbA1c) in the self-management of diabetes? A systematic review, meta-analysis, and GRADE of 14 randomized trials. Diabetes Care **39**(11), 2089–2095 (2016)
14. Karuranga, S., da Rocha Fernandes, J., Huang, Y., Malanda, B. (eds.): IDF Diabetes Atlas, 8th edn. International Diabetes Federation, Brussels (2017)
15. Kebede, M.M., Liedtke, T.P., Möllers, T., Pischke, C.R.: Characterizing active ingredients of eHealth interventions targeting persons with poorly controlled type 2 diabetes mellitus using the behavior change techniques taxonomy: scoping review. J. Med. Internet Res. **19**(10) (2017)
16. King, A.C., et al.: Testing the comparative effects of physical activity advice by humans vs. computers in underserved populations: The COMPASS trial design, methods, and baseline characteristics. Contemp. Clin. Trials **61**, 115–125 (2017)

17. Laranjo, L., et al.: Conversational agents in healthcare: a systematic review. J. Am. Med. Inform. Assoc. **25**(9), 1248–1258 (2018)
18. Lison, P.: A hybrid approach to dialogue management based on probabilistic rules. Comput. Speech Lang. **34**(1), 232–255 (2015)
19. Michie, S., Atkins, L., West, R.: The Behaviour Change Wheel : A Guide to Designing Interventions. Silverback Publishing, London (2014)
20. Michie, S., et al.: The behavior change technique taxonomy (v1) of 93 hierarchically clustered techniques: building an international consensus for the reporting of behavior change interventions. Ann. Behav. Med. **46**, 81–95 (2013)
21. Michie, S., Wood, C.E., Johnston, M., Abraham, C., Francis, J.J., Hardeman, W.: Behaviour change techniques: the development and evaluation of a taxonomic method for reporting and describing behaviour change interventions (a suite of five studies involving consensus methods, randomised controlled trials and analysis of qualitative da. Health Technol. Assess. **19**(99), 1–187 (2015)
22. Morrissey, E.C., Corbett, T.K., Walsh, J.C., Molloy, G.J.: Behavior change techniques in apps for medication adherence: a content analysis. Am. J. Prev. Med. **50**(5), e143–e146 (2016)
23. OECD: Life expectancy at 65 (2019). https://doi.org/10.1787/0e9a3f00-en. https://data.oecd.org/healthstat/life-expectancy-at-65.htm. Accessed 26 Apr 2019
24. Pal, K., et al.: Computer-based diabetes self-management interventions for adults with type 2 diabetes mellitus. Cochrane Database Syst. Rev. **3** (2013)
25. Smith, C., et al.: Interaction strategies for an affective conversational agent. Presence Teleoperators Virtual Environ. **20**(5), 395–411 (2011)
26. Van Vugt, M., de Wit, M., Cleijne, W.H., Snoek, F.J.: Use of behavioral change techniques in web-based self-management programs for type 2 diabetes patients: systematic review. J. Med. Internet Res. **15**(12), e279 (2013). https://doi.org/10.2196/jmir.2800
27. World Health Organization: Diabetes (2018). https://www.who.int/news-room/fact-sheets/detail/diabetes. Accessed 26 Apr 2019

Towards to Use
Image Mining to Classified Skin Problems
- A Melanoma Case Study

Pamela Coelho, Claudio Goncalves, Filipe Portela[⊠],
and Manuel Filipe Santos

Algoritmi Research Centre, University of Minho,
Azurem Campus, Guimaraes, Portugal
{a71179,a71898}@alunos.uminho.pt, {cfp,mfs}@dsi.uminho.pt

Abstract. Data mining (DM) is the area where are discovery patterns
and the relationship between data. Thus, depending on the type of data,
the process will have different names. In this article is used Image Mining (IM), an area that uses DM techniques to find relationship through
classification or clustering, using image data. Specifically, in this paper
are expressed algorithms that are trying to predict melanomas using skin
lesion and melanoma image's, avoiding the need for a histologic exam.
Furthermore, this avoidance is beneficial in terms of the costs and the
level of intrusion that the patient usually suffers. In relation to the solutions, are presented two trained Convolutional Neural Networks (CNN),
using packages from Keras and TensorFlow. On the other hand, focusing
on the results, the best model was one that only used Keras with an
accuracy value of 91% and a loss value of 36% using the testing data. As
a conclusion, as a last use case for the model, in the long term it could be
used in a preventive way, used to detect if a skin lesion is a melanoma.
These benefits are major improvements in current Healthcare techniques.
Furthermore, the accuracy of the models, considering only that they only
serve as a proof of concept, is considered a "success".

Keywords: Melanoma · Data mining · Classification ·
Artificial intelligence

1 Introduction

With the recent enthusiasm related to big data, there exists the need to create algorithms that will analyse and discover patterns in huge amounts of data.
This way, this phenomenon can be expanded to different areas. In the case of
this article, it will explore, Image Mining (IM), the area witch discovers patterns in images, related to the Healthcare, specifically as a direct application
in melanomas. On the other hand, in this paper it is expected to confirm the
proof of concept that IM can be used in the Healthcare industry, predicting and
detecting melanomas and non-melanonas on images.

Regarding the structure of the document is divided in the background, where
is explained and stated the relevant literature regarding data mining, image mining and material and methods, the section where is explained the methodology

© Springer Nature Switzerland AG 2019
P. Moura Oliveira et al. (Eds.): EPIA 2019, LNAI 11804, pp. 384–395, 2019.
https://doi.org/10.1007/978-3-030-30241-2_33

that is used, CRISP-DM. Additionally, there is the CRISP-DM section, exploring the creation of the Neural Networks (NN) and the results section. As discussion and conclusion, are presented to explicit the comparison of the existing models and to state the future work that will be executed.

2   Background

Nowadays, there is a need to analyse and treat data with the objective of discovering multiple patterns and extract vital knowledge to take the correct and pondered decision. Thus, data mining is a continuous process of discovery, interpretation and investigation of problems related to data [6].

In relation to this section, there will be presented the literature related to Data mining (DM) and Image Mining (IM) in general, specifying some algorithms and ways to solve problems.

2.1   Data Mining

As stated previously, Data Mining (DM) is a process that discovers hidden relations in data, representing them by models that include rules, linear equations, graphs, between others. In a more ample context, DM is defined by the discovery of knowledge based on databases, Knowledge Discovery in Databases (KDD) [6].

This process, the KDD, is defined by the following steps [6]:

- The determination of structure that will be used;
- The decision of how to quantify and compare the adjustment between the different representation of data;
- The choice of the algorithmic process of optimisation regarding the score function;
- The decision of the essential principles of data management for the efficient implementation of the algorithms.

Additionally, the process described previously allows the localisation and interpret patterns that may be key performance indicators (KPI) and furthermore, support decision making [8]. On the other hand,focusing on Healthcare applications, the algorithms can be classified into two categories:

1. Classification, the process of insertion of an object and a concept in a determinate category, based on the properties of the object or concept [5]. This type of algorithms are used with supervise learning techniques.
2. Clustering, an unsupervised learning method that centres in dividing large groups of data into small subgroups or clusters [12].

In the following parts of this article are explored the concepts of classification and clustering, exploring techniques and algorithms that can be applied in the Healthcare sector with Image Mining (IM).

Classification. As stated previously, the concepts of classification is defined by being the process of inserting an object in a specific category [5]. Despite existing multiple techniques that are used when solving classification problems, the following are the most used [10]:

1. Decision Tree Induction (DTI), are trees that classify instances by sorting them based on feature values. Each branch represents a feature to be classified and a value that a node can assume;
2. Bayesian Network (BN), is a graphical model for probability relationships among a set of variable features. This network, illustrated in following Fig. 1, is a directed acyclic graph (DAC) and each node in S is a one-to-one correspondence with multiple features.
3. K-Nearest Neighbor Classifiers, based on the learning analogy and are described by n dimensional numeric attributes. In relation to the implementation of the algorithm, when given an input, a k-nearest neighbor classifier search the pattern space for the k training samples that are closest to the input sample. The "closeness" is defined by the following formula 1 in terms of Euclidean distance:

$$d(X,Y) = \sqrt{\sum_{i=1}^{n}(X_i - Y_i)^2} \tag{1}$$

The previous formula 1 have the variable X, meaning the $xaxis$ coordinate and Y, being the $yaxis$ coordinate in a referential.
4. Support Vector Machine (SVM), a classifier that creates an hyper-plane or multiple hyper-planes in high dimensional space. It works on data points that are classified in that hyper-plane using a maximisation function [12].
5. Neural Networks (NN), an algorithm for classification that uses a gradient descent method and is adaptive in nature. This techniques usually changes its structure and adjusts its weights in order to minimise the error [12].

Clustering. Clustering is used to identify similarities between data points and compare data-points in different groups or clusters [12]. In relation to the algorithmic approach, there are multiple ways to execute clustering, being the following the main ones [12]:

1. Partitioned Clustering (PC), a method where the dataset has 'n' data points partitioned into 'k' groups or clusters. In this particular approach there is a need to define the number of clusters as an input for the algorithm;
2. Hierarchical Clustering (HC), decomposes the data points in a hierarchical way. This process can be executed in multiple ways, being the most common ones the bottom up (aglomerate) or the top down (division) approach.
3. Density Based Clustering (DBC), a technique that handles constraints of the Hierarchical Clusters (HC). Contrary to HC, density clustering method remove the drawback of only discovering spherical clusters and generate arbitrary shapes.

2.2   Image Mining

According to Burger and Burge, despite the capacity to developing a system that allows the manipulation of an image and their elements being attractive, processing an image is still somewhat difficult [3]. Thus, to smooth this difficulty, there is a need to prepare images and study how images can be obtained. Thus, there are multiple ways to obtain an image but, according to the author Burger and Burge, the six following ones are the principal [3]:

1. The camera pinhole, obtaining an image through a camera that has no lenses;
2. Slim lenses, a model that allows an inverse image with better quality;
3. The digital form, the acquisition of a bi-dimensional image (2d) that will be converted to a digital image through a computer;
4. Size and image resolution, components applied to rectangular images. The image resolution will propose the calculus of the distance between objects of the image. In health-care this can be applied when trying to check for a tumour;
5. Coordination systems, that allow obtaining the localisation of an object;
6. The pixel value considered binary words with size k. The exact value of the pixel will change with the size of the image.

Additionally, an image is treated differently in comparison with traditional data. Thus, to a machine compute an image, it must be considered a matrix of pixels mxn, where m and n are the dimensions [11]. On the other hand, one of the most common difficulties presented in images is that they usually carry a lot of noise [4]. Due to this noise and other types of difficulties presented when processing an image, was born the Image Mining (IM) area.

Image Mining (IM) is an extension of Data Mining (DM) in the domain of images [1]. Specifically, it can be seen as an area that combines knowledge from techniques and tools that were created to solve DM problems regarding databases, computer vision, image processing and recovering, statistics, between other [15]. In conclusion, imagine mining, is an area that converges from DM in a way that most of the tools used are known for its work in Data Mining.

3   Materials and Methods

In this section will be explored the methodology used and the a presentation of a method used in Image Mining. This method, Otsu method, is usually used to obtain better results when using classification algorithm.

3.1   Design Science Research Methodology

To build a rigorous and precise model, there is a need to use a methodology. In this case, regarding the main project, it uses Design Science Research (DSR) as principal methodology [9]. Additionally, this article was produced regarding the third phase of the DSR, Design Evaluation, characterised by being a phase where are executed the exploration and prototyping of solutions. Specifically, produce the best accurate results in terms of Data Mining (DM), there is a need to choose a specific methodology according to the area of work that is executed. The one that is selected is the CRoss Industry Standard Process for Data Mining (CRISP-DM), providing a framework for carrying out DM activities [12].

Thus, is divided in six different phases [14]:

- Business understanding focused on the understanding of the project objec-tives and requirements from the business perspective. This step was executed previously, in the project definition;
- Data Understanding, a phase that centres in the initial data acquisition and proceeds with activities in order to get familiar with the data;
- Data preparation, where is covered all the activities regarding the construction of the final data-set;
- Modelling, where various AI models are created and calibrated;
- Evaluation of the multiple models, and scoring regarding the metrics defined;
- Deployment, where the final project will be sent to the client. As the project is a research type, this phase will not be executed.

3.2   The Otsu Method

The Otsu method is used almost every-time when using Image mining and segmentation techniques. Image segmentation is the process of partitioning an image into multiple regions [13]. This method, illustrated by the Fig. 1, is a type of global thresholding in which transform the image in gray values. It requires computing a grey histogram before running an it is characterise to perform satisfactory results when applied to noisy images [13].

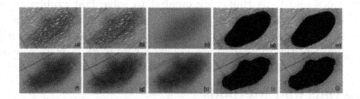

Fig. 1. Visual application of the Otsu method

4   CRISP-DM

To presented the work that was executed regarding the production of this paper, will be used the previously described methodology, CRoss Industry Standard Process for Data Mining (CRISP-DM). To contextualised, are used imaged related to melanomas to train the algorithm. The main objective is to predict if a melanoma is benign or not.

4.1   Business Understanding

In this context, to understand the business is to understand the characteristics of the images that are going to be used. Examples of this like the colour and the texture. In relation to the melanoma images, illustrated in Fig. 2, they can be classified in a clinical point of view by two big groups, the melanocytic and non-melanocityc.

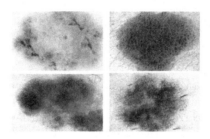

Fig. 2. Melanocytic and non-melanocity lesions. Retired from a Barata [2]

According to Barata, the melanocytic lesions, illustrated in the previous Fig. 2, are formed from melanoma cells that are responsible for the production of melanin pigment [2]. On the other hand, it is important to differentiate melanoma lesions and non-melanoma lesion, so it is important to reinforce the use of for example, birthmark lesions.

4.2   Data Understanding

As the source of the data, is important to state that all the images used in this project, from the type images are from skin lesions of the Instituto Português de Oncologia (IPO) from Oporto city. In relation to the main characteristic of the dataset are presented in the following Table 1:

Table 1. Image data acquisition characteristics

Characteristic	Data
Number of sessions	6
Number of patients	36
Percentage of men	44.4%
Percentage of women	55.6%
Median age	46 years-old
Maximum patient age	76
Minimum patient age	6

Furthermore, in relation to the images, they were taken by two mobile devices (Samsung S4 and HTC One) and a mobile dermoscope with the auxiliary of a Samsung S4. In the following Table 2 is shows the relation between each device and the percentage of images used.

Table 2. Image data devices characteristic

Type of device	Percentage of picture taken
HTC One Smartphone	40%
Samsung S4 Smartphone	30%
Samsung S4 Smartphone + Dermoscope	30%

In one hand the data harvesting process was executed between 2009 and 2013. In relation to the number of images was used 186, with a percentage of approximately 58% corresponding to images of melanomas. Thus, it can be stated that the data used in the following models, was well rounded, having images of skin lesions and/or birthmarks too.

On the other hand, to auxiliary the analysis of and detection of the melanomas, there are a rule called Asymmetry, Border, Color and Diameter (ABCD), focusing on the characteristics presented in their name [7]. To facilitate the understanding of the images was created the following Table 3, with the images and the auxiliary dataset.

Table 3. Information regarding the images and the complementary dataset

Attribute	Description	Possible values
Image ID	Correspond to the image of the lesion	[1, 106]
HTC One Smartphone	If the image was captured with an HTC One	{0, 1}
Samsung S4 Smartphone	If the image was captured with a Samsung S4	{0, 1}
Samsung S4 Smartphone + Dermoscope	If the image was capture with a Dermoscope + Samsung S4	{0, 1}
Asymmetry	Related to the axis of the lesions	{0, 1}
Border	Correspond to level of irregularity around the lesion	[0, 8]
Color	Corresponds to the tonality of a skin lesion	{0, 1}
Melanoma risk	Correspond to the risk associated with a lesion	[1, 3]

In relation to the Table 3, the identification allows the understanding of what image is being used, from 1 to 106. The other rows give information regarding which method was used to capture the image and the ABCD analysis. As an additional transformation was used the Otsu segmentation method and applied the value 0 to pixels with lower value then the result of the function.

4.3   Data Preparation

In this section, were made the following steps ordinarily, with the objective of being used correctly in the data mining process:

1. The images obtained were sliced individually, using an automatic process, with the objective of focusing in a lesion. Each image was obtained based on the location of each two pixels, the superior left edge and the inferior right edge;
2. Recurring the health professional was created an extra attribute and added to the dataset, the result. This attribute can have the value 1 or 0, depending on the image correspondence to a melanoma or not;
3. As it was not applied cross-validation, the dataset was not divided using the 70/30 rule.

The previous steps are executed with the objective of improving the quality of the images, and the accuracy of the data mining models that are stated in the following section Modelling.

4.4   Modelling

Regarding the data mining algorithms, in this modelling process were trained two Convolutional Neural Networks (CNN) models, with the help of the packages TensorFlow and/or Keras. Before understanding how are applied the CNN in Image Mining, is important to understand how a Neural Net (NN) are constituted and which layers should they contain. Thus, a Convolutional Neural Network (CNN) most of the time, have the following types of layers to be chosen from:

- An input layer, the one that receives the shape of the input that will be used in the model;
- Convolutional layer, that can be used as the input layers. It is constituted by a convolutional kernel known as filter, with the objective of extracting the map of the characteristics of the images;
- Max-pooling layer, that has the purpose of reducing the quantity of parameter that will be trained by the network, allowing redundancy control;
- Dropout layer, used to prevent over-fitting;
- Flatten layer, that enables the transformation of the input;
- Dense layer, that describes the dimension of the output layer;
- Output layer, being the final layer of the model.

In the following parts of this section are explored the two models trained, being defined by a tuple in the following Eq. 2, using the structure $T = (<InputVariables>, <OutputVariable>)$

$$T_1 = (< Image\{Height, Width\}, ColorInteger >, < Melanoma? >) \qquad (2)$$

In the previous tuple 2, the first input is an *Image* with two parameters being the *Height* and *Width*. Additionally, the *ColorInteger* is a variable between $[1, 3] \in R$. In contrast as the output, the variable *Melanoma?* represented by $\{1, 0\}$ gives information if an image is or not a melanoma.

First CNN Model. This first Convolutional Neural Network (CNN) Model was trained using 1 input, 4 convolutional, 2 maxpooling, 3 dropout, 1 flatten, 1 dense and 1 output layer. Thus, the scheme, the arrangement of the layers is illustrated in the following Fig. 3.

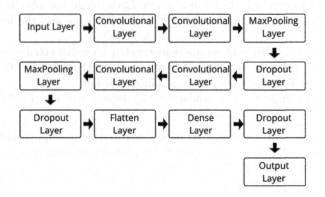

Fig. 3. First CNN Model architecture

As illustrated in the previous Fig. 3, the CNN will receive the $100 \times 100 \times 3$ input, corresponding the dimension of the image and the colour parameter. The convolutional layers are the core layers, used for computation, using a set of filters. Each filter runs on the input and produces an activation. With this, the network will learn which filters are activated in specific characteristics like the borders of the object. In contrast, the pooling and the dropout layer guarantee the elimination of the spacial size and the parameters and the parameters. Regarding the flatten layer, it attenuates the input, controlling the order. As the final layer is used the denser layer, outputting the result.

Second CNN Model. In the section model of CNN is only use two types of layers, the dense and the dropout. In the following Fig. 4 is illustrate the architecture of the second CNN, using 4 dense layers and 3 dropout layers.

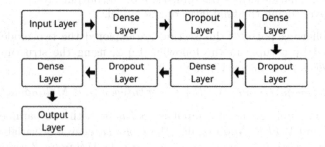

Fig. 4. Second CNN Model architecture

As is illustrated in the previous Fig. 4, the dense layer has neurons that process information about the images while the dropouts are going to eliminate some parameters in a way of controlling the processing time of the network. In relation to the first model, there are no convolutional layers, that are characterised for being the core of the CNN's.

5 Results

The metric that is used to evaluate the models is the accuracy and the variable loss. Additionally, should be stated that a model is more sensible if the biggest is the capacity of hitting a non-melanoma skin lesion. In contrast, a model is specific if the biggest is the capacity of hitting the melanoma lesion. In relation to both of the models, it should be stated that the first model uses the Keras and the Tensorflow packages while the second model only uses the Keras package. In the following Table 4, is shown the results regarding the accuracy and the loss of the two models:

Table 4. Results regarding the two models trained

Model's name	Packages used	Accuracy	Loss
First model	Keras/TensorFlow	≈0.91	≈0.36
Second model	Keras	≈0.58	≈0.69

As final calculus, were executed the following two metrics using the values of True positive (TP), False Positive (FP), True Negative (TN), False Negative (FN). These equations, illustrated in the Eqs. 3 to 6, are calculated to understand the specificity and sensibility of the first (FM) and the second (SM) model.

$$SensibilityFM : TP/(TP + FN) \Leftrightarrow 34/(34 + 6) = 0.85(85\%) \qquad (3)$$

$$SensibilitySM : TP/(TP + FN) \Leftrightarrow 28/(28 + 14) = 0.67(67\%) \qquad (4)$$

$$SpecificityFM : TN/(TN + FP) \Leftrightarrow 15/(15 + 7) = 0.68(68\%) \qquad (5)$$

$$SpecificitySM : TN/(TN + FP) \Leftrightarrow 33/(33 + 1) = 0.97(97\%) \qquad (6)$$

6 Discussion

As a discussion of the results of the models, stated in the following Table 5, it can be stated that both models present low accuracy in the testing phase. The first model presents 91% accuracy and loss of 36% while on the other hand, the second model presents a 58% accuracy, while 69% of loss.

Table 5. Global results regarding the models

Id	Packages used	Accuracy	Loss
1	TensorFlow + Keras	≈0.91	≈0.36
2	Keras	≈0.58	≈0.69

The low accuracy of the second model, stated in the previous Table 4, can be explained by numerous phenomenons like the lack or the specificity of the data. As it was expected, the first model uses more diversity of layers, so it is expected that it presents better results, 91% in comparison with 58%. In conclusion, should be stated that this is only the beginning and is intended as a proof of concept regarding the application of CNN and Image Mining (IM) in detection and analysis of melanomas. Additionally, other tests using cross-validation will be applied in future work and the models will be tunned with the concept of multiple data validation in mind.

7   Conclusion and Future Work

As a conclusion, the use of Convolution Neural Networks for image processing and prediction is a valid approach, having the first model with accuracy around 91% in the testing phase. This result is a valid approach when detecting the images the model was trained with. In a real-world situation, if the images are too different from the ones used in the training phase, this will accuracy will not hold. Although this is only a proof of concept, it is considered a success, as the models are not tuned using cross-validation.

Furthermore, in the next phase and future work, the data will be stratified, will be harvested more images and data in general and will be executed cross-validation and model tuning. In the other hand, will be executed other approaches regarding CNN and will be applied deep learning techniques, focusing on the use of more convolutional layers. The objective is that in future work, the model could reach the accuracy of 90%, meaning that the model could be used instead of a histologist exam, being a non-intrusive alternative to it.

In conclusion, in relation to the techniques stated in this paper, it is important to understand that, the images can be worked with more elaborated computer vision techniques, with the objective of increasing accuracy. Although, regarding this article, should be reinforced that it is only a proof of concept and the objectives were altering the properties of the images to the minimal. Thus, only the Otsu technique is used.

Acknowledgements. This work has been supported by FCT – Fundação para a Ciência e Tecnologia within the Project Scope: UID/CEC/00319/2019 and Deus ex Machina (DEM): Symbiotic technology for societal efficiency gains - NORTE-01-0145-FEDER-000026.

References

1. Balu, R., Devi, T.: Design and development of automatic appendicitis detection system using sonographic image mining. Int. J. Eng. Innov. Technol. (IJEIT) **1**(3), 67–74 (2012)
2. Barata, F.: Automatic detection of melanomas using dermoscopy images. Technical report, Instituto Superior Tecnico Lisboa (2017)
3. Burger, W., Burge, M.J.: Digital Image Processing. Springer, London (2008). https://doi.org/10.1007/3-540-27563-0. www.imagingbook.com
4. Domingos, P.: The master algorithm: how the quest for the ultimate learning machine will remake our world. Am. Libr. Assoc. (2016). https://doi.org/10.5860/choice.194685
5. Gorunescu, F.: Data Mining, Concepts Models and Playlist. Springer, Heidelberg (2011). https://doi.org/10.1007/978-3-642-19721-5
6. Hand, D.J.D.J., Mannila, H., Smyth, P.: Principles of Data Mining. MIT Press, Cambridge (2001)
7. Messadi, M., Cherifi, H., Bessaid, A.: Segmentation and ABCD rule extraction for skin tumors classification. J. Convergence Inf. Technol. **9**(2), 21–34 (2014). https://pdfs.semanticscholar.org/2a7a/bba5a737cde74ebab95e50051cf9488b8987.pdf
8. North, M.: Data Mining for the Masses. A Global Text Project Book (2012). https://docs.rapidminer.com/downloads/DataMiningForTheMasses.pdf
9. Peffers, K., Tuunanen, T., Rothenberger, M.A., Chatterjee, S.: A design science research methodology for information systems research. J. Manage. Inf. Syst. **24**(8), 45–78 (2007). https://doi.org/10.2753/MIS0742-1222240302
10. Phyu, T.N.: Survey of classification techniques in data mining. In: Proceedings of the International MultiConference of Engineers and Computer Scientists (2009)
11. Teixeira, J.W., Annibal, L.P., Felipe, J.C., Ciferri, R.R., Ciferri, C.D.D.A.: A similarity-based data warehousing environment for medical images. Comput. Biol. Med. **66**, 190–208 (2015). https://doi.org/10.1016/J.COMPBIOMED.2015.08.019
12. Tomar, D., Agarwal, S.: A survey on data mining approaches for healthcare. Int. J. Bio-Sci. Bio-Technol. **5**(5), 241–266 (2013). https://doi.org/10.14257/ijbsbt.2013.5.5.25
13. Vala, H., Baxi, A.: A review on Otsu image segmentation algorithm. Int. J. Adv. Res. Comput. Eng. Technol. **2**(2), 387–389 (2013). https://pdfs.semanticscholar.org/ee8b/aed71d46b4d8747c8f2c73ba73f7c4a06130.pdf
14. Wirth, R., Hipp, J.: CRISP-DM: towards a standard process model for data mining. In: Proceedings of the 4th International Conference on the Practical Applications of Knowledge Discovery and Data Mining (2000)
15. Zahradnikova, B., Duchovicova, S., Schreiber, P.: Image mining: review and new challenges. Int. J. Adv. Comput. Sci. Appl. **6**(7), 242–246 (2015)

Artificial Intelligence in Cyber-Physical and Distributed Embedded Systems

Regulating Blockchain Smart Contracts with Agent-Based Markets

Thiago R. P. M. Rúbio$^{(\boxtimes)}$, Zafeiris Kokkinogenis, Henrique Lopes Cardoso, Rosaldo J. F. Rossetti, and Eugénio Oliveira

LIACC/DEI, Faculdade de Engenharia, Universidade do Porto, Rua Dr. Roberto Frias, 4200-465 Porto, Portugal
{reis.thiago,kokkinogenis,hlc,rossetti,eco}@fe.up.pt

Abstract. The fast pace in blockchain development introduced the concept of Smart Contract as a way to deploy digital contracts as pieces of code on the blockchain network. Smart contracts differ from the traditional ones in many aspects related to their automated execution. Still, there are many open issues, such as legal frameworks and regulatory aspects. The study of agreement technologies and agent-based market systems have already dealt with some of these issues and can help us discuss solutions for the future. In this paper, we present an overview of the agreement pipeline, considering regulation-enabled systems and compare the implementation of auction agreements purely on the blockchain with a hybrid approach where markets are active agents that can ensure regulation outside the contractual phase and contract execution runs on blockchain. We have compared the cost of failing negotiations, that is always charged in the blockchain case.

Keywords: Market-based systems · Regulation ·
Multi-agent systems · Blockchain · Smart contracts

1 Introduction

In the last few years, growing efforts in blockchain (BCT) development have made this technology a good approach for solving many distributed problems that usually involved digital property recognition (for either real-world resources or virtual assets). Since its invention, blockchain has always been connected to the Market-Based domain, allowing the creation of virtual currencies to the execution of complex agreements, enabling somehow the traceability of the resources and transactions, as well as the development of Smart Contracts. Smart Contracts are pieces of code deployed to a blockchain network and executed by its nodes. Both deployment and execution operations, whether or not successful, come to at a cost. It is relevant, thus to consider if the agreement logic should be included in the smart contract.

This paper addresses the discussion about the place of the smart contracts in agent-based agreements. Agreement technologies (AT) in Multiagent Systems

© Springer Nature Switzerland AG 2019
P. Moura Oliveira et al. (Eds.): EPIA 2019, LNAI 11804, pp. 399–411, 2019.
https://doi.org/10.1007/978-3-030-30241-2_34

(MASs) have been studied from different perspectives and can be of help in impact's assessment of having "heavier" or "lightweight" contracts in the context of future autonomous negotiations. Our research questions include (a) What is the cost of placing agreement phases inside contracts? and (b) how can smart contracts be used in traditional agreement workflows leveraging on agent-based regulation? We propose a review of the agreement pipeline by considering: (a) Regulation requirements: local regulation (inside the contract) and global (governance over the agreement); (b) Comparing an approach with a whole negotiation protocol inside a smart contract with a hybrid model where a market agent coordinates negotiation and global regulation effects on the contract. We propose the contract cost as a metric to evaluate the value of the negotiation and to run some experiments to observe it in both approaches. We have developed a blockchain middleware REST API and used the Agent Process Modelling (APM) framework to deploy a multi-agent simulation based in business process modelling and a cloud-native environment.

The rest of this paper is as follows: in Sect. 2 we present a literature review about the related concepts, highlighting the main gaps between the related areas; Sect. 3 discusses the use of BCT in agent-based agreements. A simple experiment to compare the use of BCT smart contracts and its results are described in Sect. 4. Finally, the conclusions are discussed in Sect. 6.

2 Background

2.1 Smart Contracts and BCT

Blockchain is a peer-to-peer distributed ledger network that provides a shared, immutable, and transparent append-only register of all the actions that have occurred on it [8]. Nodes are called *miners*, and each one maintains a consistent copy of the ledger. Transactions are grouped into blocks, each hash-chained with the previous block. Such a data structure is the so-called *blockchain*.

The term *smart contract* was proposed by Szabo [14] as a mean of automated transfer of ownership of a property. The contract specifies pre-programmed contractual rules so that its execution takes place when input data meets the stated conditions. In the BTC context, a smart contract is a self-executing program, digitally signed by its creator, running in the distributed environment. Thus, smart contracts implement automated transactions agreed by multiple parties and given their public nature can enable open market-based interactions.

In [13], the benefits of using BCT in cyber-physical systems are reported. However, as mentioned in [11], there are still issues with smart contracts that limit the adoption of the BCT in such organisations. In [6], authors address the legal issues of smart contracts in terms of validity factors, interpretation and contract lifecycle. They state that "fundamental problems can appear concerning the modification and termination of smart contracts". Another major shortcoming of the smart contracts is the lack of control as is reported in [11] since the automated initialisation and execution of the contract cannot be overridden [6]. Non-technical people would find it hard to design and deploy new contracts, even for simple tasks. Because the meaning of the smart contract is hidden into a program code, a participant must understand the requirements and have the capacity to decide to enter into a smart contract. This drawback is very much related to exploitability issues. Finally, another smart contract concern regards operation costs. Transactions on the blockchain are not cost-free due to the economic consensus system. Costs can be due to failure, contract complexity and monitoring, nodes interactions, and network pollution.

2.2 Multiagent Systems and Agreement Technologies

In AT, autonomous software agents enacting human roles establish a settlement, where the adhesion to the contract's terms or not is on the agent's prerogative, and it is regulated by a normative framework. The process of agreement-based coordination can be designed based on two main elements [7]:

- a normative context that determines the rules of the game, i.e. interaction patterns and additional restrictions on agent behaviour
- a call-by-agreement interaction method, where an agreement for action between the agents that respects the normative context is established first; then the actual enactment of the action is requested.

A typical agreement pipeline (Fig. 1) includes the following phases [2]: *Pre-contractual*, *Contractual*, and *Post-contractual*. In the pre-contractual phase, we have the partner selection and proposal creation, and eventually, an agreement will be reached. The contract will be issued during the contractual phase, triggering its execution. Each stage of the contract execution is monitored with the defined obligation framework. Last, in the post-contractual phase, all transactions are performed, and the contract's lifecycle is validated in terms of legal and regulatory measures. All phases are subject to monitoring and validation within the context of a governance regulation framework. There are few uses of blockchain for autonomous and agent-based agreement simulations, but the distributed nature of this technology makes it a good candidate for such a role. [1] present a systematic literature review on the synergy between MAS and BCT. Literature about contracts and normative agreements used to define contracts as a set of rule-based documents [3], but smart contracts can also be considered Finite State Machines, requiring a more complex design process.

3   Agent-Based Agreements and Blockchain

Our analysis points towards two main aspects that must be discussed: (1) the definition of a contract and the associated costs (inside and outside of a blockchain) and (2) the current state of smart contracts integration in the agreement pipeline. Thus, we propose a hybrid approach that combines the traditional view of an agreement with the capabilities of smart contracts, enabling the regulation steps.

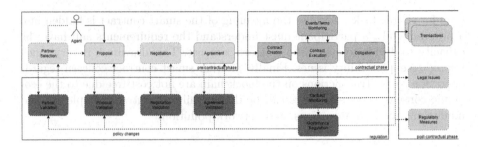

Fig. 1. A typical agreement pipeline

3.1 Agreement and Contract Costs

Every deal has an intrinsically associated cost. The cost of a real-life agreement depends on the complexity of the agreement and its effects. Running computational contracts, such as smart contracts also include the cost of computing operations, it means, each part of the contract process may have its own cost. For example, the reference Ethereum Yellow Paper [15] define the cost of each contract operation regarding the computational operation in the compiled bytecode. The cost value is defined in terms of *gas*, the internal currency of the network that is given for the worker machines in exchange for computation time. The basic unit of gas is called *wei*. Table 1 shows an excerpt of contract operations and their cost, accordingly to [12].

Table 1. Gas cost of some Smart Contract operations in Ethereum

Operation	Gas	Description
ADD/SUB	3	Arithmetic operation
MUL/DIV	5	
POP	2	Stack operation
PUSH	3	
BALANCE	400	Get balance of an account
CREATE	32,000	Create a new account using CREATE

Although the designing of cost-efficient smart contracts are already analysed in some works [4,12] the definition of the total cost of a smart contract could help us investigate the impact of the contract on the other agreement phases. Thus, we propose a semi-formal definition for a contract and its costs.

A Semi-formal Definition of a Contract. A contract represents the binding agreement between two parties that want to exchange goods or services. So, we can define a contract in terms of the *Parties* that want to be involved so that they can exchange some *Items*, their actions are identified by some *Events* expected to occur and the *Obligations* that bind them. The discussion about the legality and validity of a contract is outside of the scope of work.

Definition 1. $Contract = \langle Parties, Items, Events, Obligations \rangle$

The *Parties*, or agents, are the entities responsible for the events. The *Items* regard the set of $resource \in Resources = \{Goods, Services\}$, mapping to some resource *state* which can have an attributed $value \in \mathbb{R}_0^+$ so the parties can exchange resources directly or attribute a value to use as currency in the exchange. Thus,

$$Items \supseteq \{item = \langle resource, state, value \rangle\}$$

Events correspond to the facts that will trigger contract state to change. An $event \in Events$ refers to a *statement* or fact made by a party over some resource, such as a transaction that stores the new state of the resource or place a new value for the item. Also, the *Events* set can be seen as a composition of the *input events* $Events_{in}$ (triggering) and the *output events* $Events_{out}$, $Events_{in}$ result of the contract rules.

$$Event \supseteq \{event = \langle party, statement(item) \rangle\}$$
$$Events = Events_{in} \cup Events_{out}$$

Input events are listened and trigger the evaluation of one or more obligations $obligation \in Obligations$ and its consequences. So an *obligation* is an association of an input event $e \in Events_{in}$, a $condition \in Conditions$ (rule) of the contract regarding that event and the consequences of the condition evaluation.

$$Obligations \supseteq \{obligation_e := condition_e \longrightarrow consequence_{eval}\}$$

The condition evaluation of the event can result true or false. In the affirmative case, we say that the event e **fulfils** the condition and a fulfilment function $Fulf_e$ can give us the fulfilment output events $fuls$. In the same way, when the evaluation function resolves to false, the event **violates** the condition and the consequence might be a set of $viols$ events given by a violation function $Viol_e$.

$$eval(condition, e) = \begin{cases} true, & iff\ condition_e \\ false, & iff\ \neg condition_e \end{cases}$$

$$Fulf(condition, e) = fuls \subseteq Events_{out} \iff eval(condition, e)$$
$$Viol(condition, e) = viols \subseteq Events_{out} \iff \neg eval(condition, e)$$

Therefore, the whole set of consequences of an event is given by the union of the events for those the conditions where fulfiled and the violated conditions.

$$consequences_e = \bigcup \{Fulf(cond, e) \cup Viol(cond, e)\}, \forall cond \in Conditions$$

Calculation of Contract Costs. With the definition of a contract and the functions that allow the evaluation of the conditions and consequences of a contract event, we can then calculate the contract costs.

Definition 2. *Cost function of element x: $\gamma(x) = \gamma_x \in \mathbb{R}_0^+$*

We define a cost function γ that gives the cost of a contract element x. For simplification purposes, the result of $\gamma(x)$ is denoted as γ_x. Assuming that the cost function can be calculated over some contract elements, $\gamma(event) \propto O(event)$ would represent the cost of an event, which is only affected by the complexity of the event. In the same way, the cost of evaluating the conditions when receiving an event does only depend on the conditions complexity $\gamma(eval_e) \propto O(Conditions)$ and finally, the cost of processing the consequences of an event does only regard the complexity of triggering the output events $\gamma(consequence_e) \propto O(events_{out})$. Thus we define the contract cost function:

Definition 3. *Cost function of contract C: $\Gamma(C) = \gamma_{creation}^C + \gamma_{execution}^C$*

The total cost of a contract can be defined by the cost of creating the contract $\gamma_{creation}^C$, which involves the design of the contract and the deployment, and the related costs respectively γ_{design}^C and γ_{deploy}^C. Designing and deploying a contract depends, besides multiple factors, on the document type, complexity of the rules and its bureaucratic-social impacts, as well as the technology and process necessary to execute it. Since we are dealing with smart contracts, we can consider the cost of writing the code, testing and validating, plus the deployment cost in a real blockchain. These costs depends on the contract complexity: $\gamma_{creation}^C \propto O(C)$. Then,

$$\gamma_{creation}^C = \gamma_{design}^C + \gamma_{deploy}^C$$

Finally, the execution cost $\gamma_{execution}^C$ can be written in terms of the events and elements on the contract execution lifecycle.

$$\gamma_{execution}^C = \sum_{i=1}^{n} (\gamma_i^C + \gamma_{eval_i}^C + \gamma_{consequence_i}^C)$$

We have disregarded the value of the items of the contract to analyse only the costs associated with a generic contract. The item values stated in the events should be considered to calculate the total amount paid by some party and summed to the contract cost.

3.2 Hybrid Agent-Based Smart Contracts Agreements

The previous discussion about the contract costs is generic. It means any contract's cost can be calculated regardless of its characteristics. Sometimes getting such costs is a very complex and subjective task. The inherent costs might be shadowed by the contract and events nature. On the other hand, since smart Contracts allow the execution of a contract as code, more agreement tasks tend to execute inside this technological framework and so, are easier to compute.

Smart Contract possibilities also introduce the problem of the *fat contract*[1], it means the contract scope, including more tasks of the agreement pipeline. In such contracts, steps as partner selection or proposal negotiation are considered as parts of the contract, merging pre-contractual and contractual phases, sometimes in an erroneous interpretation of what a contract is. Some papers also highlight the possibility of running auctions or other negotiation protocols in smart contracts [5]. Both from the agreement and legal perspectives, this would not make sense in terms of the traditional definition of a contract [11]. Also, fat contracts would see increased costs since each operation made inside a smart contract is paid (in terms of gas), successful or not.

Figure 2 shows an example of a fat contract, where the agreement pipeline is not fully respected. An agent must first create the contract, which includes negotiation and agreement characteristics in its code. Then, in an off-chain (outside of the smart contract) operation, send the contract reference for a (possible) partner. Just then, this partner can interact with the contract (not the agent) to achieve the agreement and execute the obligations. Running pre-contractual steps as negotiation inside the contract might not even result in a contract at all, since the partners may not achieve an agreement. So why should we do that? For sure, the technological possibilities exist and might be interesting in some specific cases. On the more current scenarios, we believe that agreement technologies should also continue relying on a multi-agent approach. We propose to consider a hybrid approach: from one side it is evident that multi-agent systems can allow richer specifications of agreement pipelines while enabling regulation mechanisms; in the other, we should take advantage of the blockchain and smart contracts as an interesting contract-engine. Mixing both could lead to a truly distributed system where agents could run into its owner's computational nodes with reduced cost, while some regulator agents could put the regulation tasks into action and finally, the smart contract would execute the contractual phase.

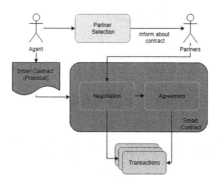

Fig. 2. *Fat contracts* might include negotiation and agreement tasks

---

[1] Similar to the fat client and fat jar concepts used in software engineering.

We consider the existence of a market agent, with an intermediary role: it could facilitate pre-contractual phase tasks by playing as a service hub (help finding partners, contract templates, etc.) but also a regulatory role. The market agent could inherit regulation policies from lawmakers and other regulators to filter invalid proposals or agent's participation, tax or trigger other legal issues and measures to keep the market under regulation boundaries. Contracts made thought the market could be monitored, helping to fill the regulation gap when dealing only with smart contracts. It is worth to mention that negotiation and contracts could also happen aside from the market, and those would not be regulated. Indeed, in such environments, their impact over the market could be monitored by the market agent to trigger also some regulatory measures.

We characterise this scenario in Fig. 3, where all four agreement phases are seen. An agent sends a new proposal to the market agent that could approve or reject it. Here, a proposal is considered as similar to the ones in the ResMAS framework [10]. Thus, the pre-contractual phase can run between the interested parties, eventually communicating with the market agent (to ask for services, etc.). When an agreement is reached, the agents must communicate it with the market agent so a contract template can be applied and a new smart contract deployed to the blockchain. All the involved parties can keep the contract reference for monitoring purposes. In this situation, the smart contract execution is delegated to the contractual phase.

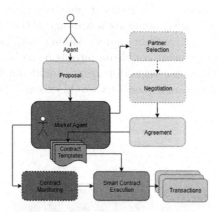

Fig. 3. Hybrid agreements with agent-based markets and smart contracts

4   Agent-Processes and Blockchain API

The development of the microservices as the *de-facto* architecture for distributed web services has to lead the growth of multiple kinds of applications and integration possibilities between them. In this sense, an interesting way to design and deploy cloud-native agents is the Agent Process Modelling [9], where agents are designed as process models. The agents' capabilities include calling web services, for example, interacting with the blockchain. The only things needed is to design and run the agents and to have a callable REST API. A simple agent-process representing the agent role in our approach can be seen in Fig. 4.

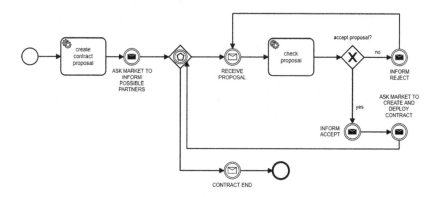

Fig. 4. APM agent for the hybrid approach

4.1 Blockchain Operations and API

Blockchain frameworks can be public, meaning anyone could interact with, paying real money in the exchange, or private. Although many tools can be used to get the blockchain running, few provide a useful REST interface for automatic integration. For this purpose, we have developed our API considering the smart contract capabilities and market-based domain requirements. We have identified three main areas: accounts, transactions, and contracts. Accounts refer to the owners of the resources, transactions to the messages of sending resources or information to other accounts and contracts the logic for automatic transactions.

In our experiments, we have used the Ethereum[2] network, the most accessible custom open source blockchain, by the time of writing, that enables easily running a local blockchain. It was designed towards smart contracts from the beginning and did also support the possibility of running the local network as a web service. Thus, we have built a REST API on top of it to enable automatic agent's interactions. Table 2 shows the API details, accordingly to each of the blockchain domains.

5   Preliminary Assessment of Contract Costs Comparison

In this section, we will present the experimental setup we used for the contract cost comparison in the traditional BCT and the hybrid one.

---

[2] https://www.ethereum.org/.

Table 2. Detailed API for each of the blockchain domains

Domain	Operations	REST Method	URL	Params	Description
Accounts	Create	POST	api/accounts		Creates a new account
	Retrieve	GET	api/accounts api/accounts/:accountId		Retrieves all accounts or an account with specific accountId
	Lock	PUT	api/accounts/:accountId/lock		Locks an account (disable transactions)
	Unlock	PUT	api/accounts/:accountId/lock		Unlocks the account for new transactions
Contracts	Create	Post	api/contracts	code	Compiles and Deploys a new smart contract
	Retrieve	GET	api/contracts api/contracts/:contractId		Retrieves all contracts or a contract with specific contractId
	Execute	POST	api/contracts/:contractId/execute	abi, contractMethod, params, fromAccount, transactionValue	Executes a specific contract method using its public interface (abi)
	Subscribe	POST	api/contracts/:contractId/subscribe	abi, event, filter, subscriptionType	Subscribes to (once, all or past) events emited by a specific contract with using its public interface (abi)
Transactions	Retrieve	GET	api/transactions api/transactions/:transactionId		Finds the details of an specific
	Estimate	POST	api/transactions/estimate	toAccount, value	Estimates the cost of a transaction to another account by the value (data to be sent)
	Execute	POST	api/transactions/execute	toAccount, fromAccount, value	Executes a transaction to another account

5.1   Simulation Settings

We developed a smart contract[3] in Solidity language and deployed it on a local container-based Ethereum blockchain to perform our experiments. The deployment of the contract in the blockchain has a fixed deployment cost according to its complexity $\gamma^C_{deployment} = 415653wei$. Since the design cost of the contract is the same for both cases, we have disregarded it.

The experiment consists of a ten-round negotiation agreement where there is a reservation contract between two agents, a *seller* A and a *buyer* B. We assume that agent B must reserve the item first, paying more than the minimum price (100). Also, we assume that agent B must pay the double of the reservation price for being able to acquire the item completing thus the contract execution. We consider an increasing rejection factor to be applied to each negotiation round. Finally, we assume a probability of failing on paying for the item (50%) to simulate contract violations and a random fluctuation of the *gas* price is drawn from a normal distribution. The same contract runs in both approaches. In the fat contract way, these probabilities of success and failures occur by calling the contract methods. On the other side, in the hybrid approach, the proposals run on agent services.

5.2   Results

Figure 5 shows the results of 100 runs with each configuration. The number of negotiation rounds is increased to evaluate the impact of the negotiation phase in the contract cost. We have calculated the total cost of the contract using the final cost formula defined in Sect. 3.1. The results show the cost of the contract increasing with the number of negotiations for the fat contract, but not for the hybrid, which maintains a nearly linear cost throughout the experiment. Surprisingly, the cost of the hybrid approach is similar to not having negotiation rounds in the fat contract, which corroborates the idea presented in Table 3 summarises the relationship between the cost of failing events depending on the approach and the agreement phase. Of the cost of the pre-contractual phase being processed outside the blockchain.

Table 3. Event cost depending on the agreement phase and type

Agreement Phase	Events	Condition	Cost - Fat Contract	Cost - Hybrid
Negotiation	Send Proposal	Accepted	✓	-
	Send Proposal	Rejected	✓	-
Contract execution	Send Proposal Value	Fulfilled	✓	✓
	Send Proposal Value	Violated	✓	✓

---

[3] https://gist.github.com/MunhozThiago/579102a19b6503b81c3167c19785e469.

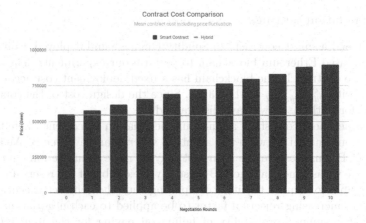

Fig. 5. Comparison of smart contract costs

6   Conclusions

The proliferation of BCT as a platform for decentralised applications, shed light into some inherent limitation of the technology regarding the contractual relationships. In this preliminary work, we address the place of smart contracts within a traditional blockchain and agreement pipeline. We have argued that such a contract should be an integral part of the agreement and not incorporating agreement aspects. Indeed as it has been stated in the literature from a legal point of view and agreement perspective, Smart Contracts might not be real contracts. To that extent, we have reviewed an agreement pipeline from a smart contract perspective and provide a semi-formal definition of contracting elements and associated costs. Following we have proposed a hybrid approach combining multi-agent systems and smart contracts could allow placing regulation mechanisms and discussed how a blockchain REST API could help to experiment with this kind of network. Our experiment has corroborated the hypothesis of the negotiation cost reduction outside the smart contract. For future work, we will consider explicit regulation mechanisms along with the use of more complex contract templates. Finally, we intend to experiment with our proposal considering various domains such as smart grids, logistics, transportation, etc.

References

1. Calvaresi, D., Dubovitskaya, A., Calbimonte, J.P., Taveter, K., Schumacher, M.: Multi-agent systems and blockchain: results from a systematic literature review. In: Demazeau, Y., An, B., Bajo, J., Fernández-Caballero, A. (eds.) PAAMS 2018. LNCS (LNAI), vol. 10978, pp. 110–126. Springer, Cham (2018). https://doi.org/10.1007/978-3-319-94580-4_9
2. Cardoso, H.L.: Virtual organization support through electronic institutions and normative multi-agent systems. In: Handbook of Research on Nature-Inspired Computing for Economics and Management, pp. 786–805. IGI Global (2007)

3. Lopes Cardoso, H., Oliveira, E.: A contract model for electronic institutions. In: Sichman, J.S., Padget, J., Ossowski, S., Noriega, P. (eds.) COIN -2007. LNCS (LNAI), vol. 4870, pp. 27–40. Springer, Heidelberg (2008). https://doi.org/10.1007/978-3-540-79003-7_3

4. Chen, T., Li, X., Luo, X., Zhang, X.: Under-optimized smart contracts devour your money. In: 2017 IEEE 24th International Conference on Software Analysis, Evolution and Reengineering (SANER), pp. 442–446. IEEE (2017)

5. Galal, H.S., Youssef, A.M.: Verifiable sealed-bid auction on the ethereum blockchain. In: Zohar, A., et al. (eds.) FC 2018. LNCS, vol. 10958, pp. 265–278. Springer, Heidelberg (2019). https://doi.org/10.1007/978-3-662-58820-8_18

6. Governatori, G., Idelberger, F., Milosevic, Z., Riveret, R., Sartor, G., Xu, X.: On legal contracts, imperative and declarative smart contracts, and blockchain systems. Artif. Intell. Law **26**(4), 377–409 (2018)

7. Ossowski, S.: Coordination in multi-agent systems: Towards a technology of agreement. In: Bergmann, R., Lindemann, G., Kirn, S., Pěchouček, M. (eds.) MATES 2008. LNCS (LNAI), vol. 5244, pp. 2–12. Springer, Heidelberg (2008). https://doi.org/10.1007/978-3-540-87805-6_2

8. Porru, S., Pinna, A., Marchesi, M., Tonelli, R.: Blockchain-oriented software engineering: Challenges and new directions. In: 2017 IEEE/ACM 39th International Conference on Software Engineering Companion (ICSE-C), pp. 169–171. IEEE (2017)

9. Rúbio, T.R.P.M., Lopes Cardoso, H., Oliveira, E.: Agent process modelling. In: Demazeau, Y., Matson, E., Corchado, J.M., De la Prieta, F. (eds.) PAAMS 2019. LNCS (LNAI), vol. 11523, pp. 277–280. Springer, Cham (2019). https://doi.org/10.1007/978-3-030-24209-1_30

10. Rúbio, T.R., Kokkinogenis, Z., Cardoso, H.L., Oliveira, E., Rossetti, R.J.: ResMAS-a conceptual MAS model for resource-based integrated markets. In: Bajo J. et al. (eds.) Highlights of Practical Applications of Cyber-Physical Multi-Agent Systems. PAAMS 2017. CCIS, vol. 722, pp. 117-129. Springer, Cham (2017). https://doi.org/10.1007/978-3-319-60285-1_10

11. Singh, M.P., Chopra, A.K.: Violable contracts and governance for blockchain applications. arXiv preprint arXiv:1801.02672 (2018)

12. Sklaroff, J.M.: Smart contracts and the cost of inflexibility. U. Pa. L. Rev. **166**, 263 (2017)

13. Skowroński, R.: The open blockchain-aided multi-agent symbiotic cyber-physical systems. Future Gener. Comput. Syst. **94**, 430–443 (2019)

14. Szabo, N.: Formalizing and securing relationships on public networks. First Monday **2**(9) (1997)

15. Wood, G., et al.: Ethereum: A secure decentralised generalised transaction ledger. Ethereum project yellow paper **151**, 1–32 (2014)

Machine Learning Methods
for Radar-Based People Detection
and Tracking

José Castanheira[(✉)], Francisco Curado[iD], Ana Tomé[iD], and Edgar Gonçalves

Department of Electronics and Informatics Engineering, University of Aveiro,
3810-193 Aveiro, Portugal
{jp.castanheira,fcurado,ana,easg}@ua.pt

Abstract. This paper describes the work developed towards the implementation of a radar-based system for people detection and tracking in indoor environments using machine learning techniques. For such, a series of experiments were carried out in an indoor scenario involving walking people and dummies representative of other moving objects. The applied machine learning methods included a neural network and a random forest classifier. The success rates (accuracies) obtained with both methods using the experimental data sets evidence the high potential of the proposed approach.

Keywords: RADAR · Locomotion pattern · RCS · Machine learning

1 Introduction

1.1 Motivation

The number and diversity of applications of radar sensors have been increasing dramatically in recent years, motivated by the emergence of inexpensive, self-contained development kits that permit rapid prototyping and testing of radar-based solutions. The reduced cost and dimension of these systems make them affordable for academic research and permit their integration in small, inexpensive robots.

The immunity of radar signals to some of the main sources of noise (such as dust, fog, rain, strong heat and fire) that disrupt measurements taken with other sensors (such as cameras, laser or infrared) is one of the most important arguments for the adoption of radar as sensory devices in autonomous systems in general and in mobile robotics in particular. Robotic applications currently operational or under development include: obstacle detection and mapping of indoor environments, ground and pavement classification, terrain-referenced navigation,

Funded by Research Project RETIOT PT2020-03/SAICT/2015 - Fundação para a Ciência e Tecnologia.

P. Moura Oliveira et al. (Eds.): EPIA 2019, LNAI 11804, pp. 412–423, 2019.
https://doi.org/10.1007/978-3-030-30241-2_35

Simultaneous Localization and Mapping (SLAM), and detection and tracking of people and objects in motion.

Despite the aforementioned advantages, feature extraction from radar data poses significant challenges to conventional signal processing techniques due to the diversity of artifacts that typically affect unprocessed radar signals. This problem is especially dramatic in indoor environments due to the ubiquity of obstacles (clutter) normally present in these scenarios.

This paper addresses the problem of radar-based detection of walking people in an indoor scenario using machine learning techniques. The method proposed is envisaged as a building block of a more general robust classifier and tracker of people in indoor environments that is currently under development in our laboratory. The aim of the this work is to develop a highly reconfigurable real-time location system (RTLS) that integrates static radars with radars installed on mobile platforms and Internet-of-Things (IoT) devices. The envisioned applications include elderly monitoring and rescue operations in vision-denied environments. The paper does not discuss other sensor alternatives (e.g. vision) because the radar is intended to work as a complementary instrument or as a replacement sensor in scenarios where the alternative sensors are prone to fail.

1.2   Summary of Prior Work

In order to establish a clear context for the methods described in the present paper, we present below a summary of the state of the art in terms of radar-based approaches for people detection and tracking together with an overview of related applications for indoor environments.

According to the main data types and the signal processing techniques applied, the approaches proposed in the literature to detect and track moving persons can be divided into the following categories:

Doppler-Based Detection and Range/Doppler/Azimuth Based Tracking. This approach separates moving people from clutter based essentially on Doppler data (representative of the velocity of the target relatively to the radar); static objects can be easily classified as clutter due to their zero-Doppler attribute while non-zero Doppler measurements associated to people motion are used to initiate and propagate target tracks in time; data association performed for each target relies on additional information regarding the target position in 2D, including its range and bearing provided by a phased array radar. This approach has demonstrated its efficacy to track multiple people with a single, low-cost multiple-input multiple-output (MIMO) radar but it fails in two relevant aspects: (i) it cannot distinguish moving people from other moving targets of approximately the same dimensions (or radar cross section) and (ii) it cannot detect or track a non-walking person even if he/she is performing some task (seated or standing). This approach is illustrated by the demonstrations provided by the Texas Instruments manufacturer of the xWR1642 and xWR1443 families of frequency modulated continuous wave (FMCW) radars; see, e.g., [8] and [6]. It is also adopted in the works of [9] and [5].

Range/Doppler-Based Detection and Range/Doppler/Azimuth Based Tracking. This approach exploits the extended velocity profile (or velocity dispersion) characteristic of human motion that stems from the fact that humans do not move as rigid objects but rather present typical oscillating movements of their members and body; for example, there is a typical spreading and contraction pattern of the velocity profile, with a sinusoidal character, in the case of movement of arms and legs of a walking pedestrian. This approach is obviously more robust and holds a larger application potential in most scenarios where humans are required to interact with other mobile agents (including mobile robots, small vehicles, and other machines with moving parts in general). Typically, during a short time interval (for example, a radar frame of a few tens of milliseconds), walking pedestrians present Doppler profiles with multiple, distinct velocity components centered on a single point in the range domain (due to his small velocity, a walking human practically does not change its position during such a short interval). This is in contrast with the compact, point-shaped profile presented by a rigid moving body (a mobile robot or a car) in the Doppler domain due to its constant velocity during an equivalent period of time. An interesting implementation of the Range-Doppler detection approach is described in [4]. The authors apply a Support Vector Machine to classify pedestrians, vehicles, and other objects in an urban area, using an automotive 24 GHz radar sensor with a bandwidth of 150 MHz as the measuring device. For such, they propose three feature extraction schemes with increasing computational complexity and latency corresponding to increasing classification success rates. The features used in the simplest implementation are the range-velocity profiles and associated dispersion metrics extracted from the set of reflections obtained in a single radar measurement; a more elaborate solution exploits data from multiple buffered radar measurements; the most advanced implementation complements the radar returns with additional feedback information provided by a Kalman-based tracker. In the three solutions, the true positive rates for pedestrians are, 45%, 54%, and 61%, respectively. Another potential application of the Range-Doppler detection approach consists of exploiting the patterns of hands movements of a person in order to detect her presence and even to interpret his gestures (for example as remote commands for a robot). This method is illustrated by the work of [2] that implements a hand gesture recognition system using a machine learning algorithm fed with data from a radar to permit steering small mobile robots without direct human operation. The machine learning implementation of gesture recognition relies on decision trees providing a mean success rate (true positives) of 96%.

Returned Signal Strength-Based Detection. This approach exploits measurements of signal intensity returned from the target that may be used directly, as in the case of classification schemes based on the computed absolute radar cross section (RCS) of targets, or indirectly by exploiting the relative intensity of the echos corresponding to distinct scatterers of the same target. RCS is a property of the target's reflectivity, commonly used to detect and classify airplanes in a wide variation of ranges. In principle, the technique can be applied to distinguish terrestrial targets, because cars, motorcycles, bicycles, and pedestrians have distinct RCS values. In practice, the method may be difficult to apply due to the large dependence of RCS measurements on the orientation of the target relatively to the radar; see, e.g., [7]. To the best of our knowledge RCS has not been applied before to detection and tracking of people. The indirect method is illustrated by the collection of methods proposed in [1] that exploits the 2D radar intensity image of a small object in order to derive a model of its bi-dimensional shape. This is combined with measures of its Doppler spectrum distribution to build a feature vector used by a fuzzy membership function that maps the acquired features onto the corresponding target class. As such, the solution integrates techniques pertaining to the above-mentioned approaches (1) and (2) in order to implement a robust classification system. The success rate (true positives) achieved with this system varies between 40% and 95% depending on the orientation of the pedestrian trajectory (from radial to lateral) relatively to the radar axis.

1.3 Novelty and Main Contributions of the Paper

In this paper we propose a new, robust approach for classification of moving objects based on radar measurements in indoor scenarios. The main novelty of the method is the exploitation of the velocity pattern associated to the collection of points (point cloud) representative of the multiple radar scatterers of a given object that permits a robust distinction between moving rigid bodies and people. Another relevant and novel contribution consists in the utilization of the radar cross section of the observed objects as a classification feature, which is shown to significantly increase the performance of the classifier.

2 Problem Formulation and Proposed Solution

2.1 Basic Terminology

- In radar terminology, any object that can be detected by the radar is often designate as *target*.
- The scalar measure representative of the radial velocity of the target, i.e. its velocity projected onto the central axis of the radar transmitter, is normally designated as *Doppler* since it is computed based on the frequency shift (Doopler effect) incurred by the radar wave due to the target velocity.
- A *frame* constitutes an elementary structure of reflectivity data that characterizes the state of the target in terms of its distance (range) and radial velocity (Doppler), relatively to the radar system.
- The MIMO radar technology considered in this work permits the discrimination of simultaneous reflections from different points in the plane of the radar wave by exploiting the beam-formimg capability of the MIMO system.
- In the present context, a *point cloud* is a collection of points corresponding to individual reflections from a scene acquired at a given instant of time and represented in different positions of the radar sensor grid; these points may correspond to different reflections from a single or multiple targets.

2.2 Problem Formulation

The problem can be formulated as follows: *Given an indoor scenario charac-terized by the presence of a diversity of static and mobile objects, implement a method to unambiguously detect the presence of a walking person and estimate its kinematic properties using range and Doppler data acquired with a low-cost radar.*

2.3 Proposed Solution

The proposed approach relies on the following principles.

The motion of people is characterized by the pendular motion of arms, as well as legs. Other objects, such as robots, usually move as a block. The pattern of motion of people is, therefore, different from the pattern of motion of other mobile agents, and thus, capturing this pattern over time and feeding it to a learning model can provide a mean to dynamically detect people and distinguish them from other objects.

Using a radar to capture the pattern of motion of an object actually implies measuring the velocity of the points that constitute the point cloud of that object and its variation along time. The velocity of a point is given by its associated Doppler value. When some object moves in front of the radar, a series of frames are recorded, and the values of Doppler are stored. In this way, the evolution of the kinematic properties of a target can be stored and indexed to time.

In addition to the utilization of the velocity pattern of the objects observed in a given scenario, we propose to acquire their RCS and use it in order to make the classification more robust.

The RADAR device used was the AWR1642-BOOST EVM from Texas Instruments. In Table 1 details of the chirp can be found.

Table 1. Chirp parameters and respective value.

Chirp Parameter (Units)	Value	Chirp Parameter (Units)	Value
Start Frequency (GHz)	77	Maximum unambiguous range (m)	5
Slope (MHz/us)	60	Maximum radial velocity (m/s)	5.2936
Samples per chirp	128	Azimuth resolution (degrees)	14.5
Chirps per frame	256	Velocity resolution (m/s)	0.0827
Frame duration (ms)	50	Number of transmission antennas	2
Sampling rate (Msps)	2.5000	Range resolution (m)	0.0488
Bandwidth (GHz)	3.0720	Number of reception antennas	4

In this work, the RCS, represented by the Greek letter σ, was calculated using the following equation

$$\sigma = \frac{4\pi^3 d^4 P_r}{\lambda G P_t} \ , \tag{1}$$

where d denotes the distance to the object, P_t and P_r represent the power emitted by the radar and reflected by the target, respectively, λ is the wave length of the radar signal, and G is the ratio between the transmission and reception gain.

The value for P_t is 12.5 dBm, and is later converted to Watts. The transmission and reception gains have the same value of 9 dB, thus $G = 1$. Because the radar chirp used has a bandwidth of 4 GHz (from 77 GHz to 81 GHz), in order to calculate RCS, the wave length used is based on the central frequency, 79 GHz, which corresponds to a wave length of 0.0038 m. Since the received signal is attenuated by a series of filtration steps in the digital signal processor (DSP) pipeline of the radar, the power of the digitized signal after fast Fourier transform (FFT) processing needs to be compensated in order to obtain the total power reflected by the target. This compensation is implemented according to Eq. (2) as explained below; see also [7].

$$P_r = P_{FFT} - [20log_{10}(2^{(nbits-1)}) + 20log_{10}(\sum_{i=0}^{N-1} \omega_i)$$
$$- 20log_{10}(\sqrt{2})] + 10 \tag{2}$$

Where P_{FFT} stands for the power of the signal after analog-to-digital converter (ADC) and FFT processing, *nbits* is the number of ADC bits used (12 in this case), the ω_i summation represented compensates the attenuation effect of windowing prior to the application of the FFT, and the additive term 10 is used to convert from dBFS (dB full-scale) to dBm. Equation (2) is used as a correction factor [7]. The resulting value for power received is later converted from dBm to Watts.

The velocity of the points belonging to the point cloud of a frame are represented by a histogram. The histogram is calculated between -6 and 6 m/s with 150 bins. Therefore the bin size (resolution) is 0,08 m/s. The kinematic of the object can be viewed as an image by the concatenation of the histograms of the object point cloud in all frames. Naturally the values of the bins are color coded.

Based on this configuration, the data acquired in each test is transformed into a single dataset constituted by 151 elements (150 velocity bins plus one value RCS) and with a number of data samples equal to the number of frames. The total dataset is constituted by the collection of all the datasets obtained in all the tests. Hence, in the current experiment, the complete dataset consists of a total of 24455 frames. Out of these 24455 frames, 11285 correspond to people moving, and the remaining 13170 correspond to other moving objects.

When performing measurements using the RADAR, clutter may coexist with the point cloud of an object of interest. It is then important not only to detect this clutter, but to eliminate it, ensuring that these points will not be included in the creation of the dataset. The obvious way to segment the point cloud corresponding to a target is by using an appropriate clustering method. The method chosen in the current implementation was DBSCAN (Density-based spatial clustering of applications with noise); [3]. DBSCAN is a clustering method that relies solely on two base parameters: minimum number of points and minimum distance between them for a set of points to be considered a cluster. Henceforth, minimum number of points will be designated as *MinPts* and the minimum distance will be designated by *Eps*. In the current application, clustering is performed not only in spacial dimension, but also in the velocity dimension. The justification of this strategy is the fact that two closely spaced objects will not be distinguished by the algorithm if we only consider spatial distance between points. However, if we consider clustering in the velocity dimension, then two objects, even if closely spaced, will be distinguished if they have different velocities. This clustering approach is applied in a hierarchical fashion. First, only spacial-based clustering is applied, resulting in an initial set of clusters. Then, to every cluster, velocity based sub-clustering is applied inside each cluster, permitting to discriminate sub-clusters of points whose velocity difference exceeds a predefined threshold. The parameter values of $MinPts = 4$ and $Eps = 0.6$, both in the spatial and velocity dimension, were chosen based on practical experiments.

It is important to remark that with the present configuration of clustering parameters, the method does not decompose the cloud of points of a single person into different clusters; it allows for the coexistence of significant velocity differences in the same cluster in order to contemplate the representation of the pendular motions of the arms and legs of the same person.

3 Experiments

3.1 Scenario Configuration

The tests with the radar were performed in an indoor wide open area, free of obstacles. This simplified scenario is proposed, similarly to other works described in the literature, in order to permit a proof of concept involving the type of classification methods proposed here. The host computer communicates with the sensor via a Raspberry Pi connected directly to the sensor. The device is placed at a height of 1.9 m (in order to stand taller than most people) with an inclination (facing downwards) of about 10°. This placement of the device aims at minimizing the number of people that can be occluded by other people present in the area.

The whole test field contains blue marks that can be found on the ground. They identify the bottom and top left and right corners, as well as the centre of the field and the centre of each one of the sides. There are also blue marks to identify the 30° and 60° mark on the bottom and middle of the field, and the 30° mark at the top of the field (which is coincident with the top left and right corner). The blue marks at the bottom of the two front legs of the tripod serve the purpose of marking the position of the sensor, to ensure the tests are done with the device placed always in the same position. Figure 1 shows a schematic of the test field.

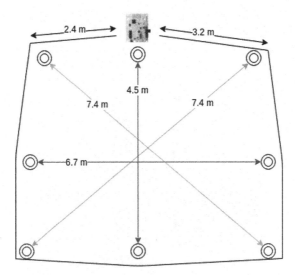

Fig. 1. Schematic of the test field with the trajectories considered represented by bidirectional non-black arrows, and the corners by circumferences. The length of each trajectory is represented in meters.

3.2   Types of Tests Carried Out

To enable a learning model to distinguish people from other objects, representative data sets of both classes of targets had to be provided. Therefore, tests were made with people, but also with objects, such as dummies with a dimension close to that of an adult. Furthermore, with the intent of making this application as inclusive as possible, people with limited mobility were also taken into account by performing tests with a person driving an automated wheelchair.

Each elementary test in this experiment consisted of an object moving in a specific direction. In the test field, 4 types of directions were considered: from one corner to the opposite one (left to right and right to left); from the top centre of the field to the bottom centre; from the centre side of the field to the other centre side. For each direction, the two ways were considered, yielding therefore a total of 8 different trajectories (see Fig. 1). For each trajectory, 10 different tests were performed, for a total of 80 tests for each specific object. Three different types of objects were considered: person walking, person in a wheelchair, and two different dummies. A picture of one of the dummies is shown in Fig. 2, as well as the radar device.

The typical velocity pattern of a person walking in front and to the device is depicted in Fig. 3; the plot clearly shows the dispersion of velocity values associated to the walking person. For other directions, such as diagonal or transversely, the pattern is similar. Figure 4 shows the velocity pattern of the mannequin and of a person in a wheelchair. As can be seen, the velocity pattern of the locomotion of the dummy is clearly different from that of a person. Most of the points of

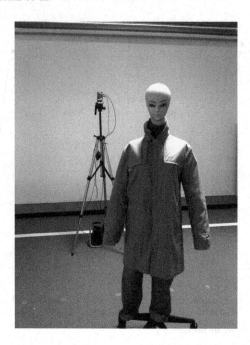

Fig. 2. One of the dummies used in the tests.

a person-related point cloud are located within a defined region of the Doppler, and this can be explained by the fact that most of the points are correspondent to the torso and thus move with the same velocity. However, as a result of the motion of the arms and legs, we can see there is a spread of points along the Doppler dimension. This spread is symmetrical (both in the positive and negative side) and approximately periodic. This is accordance with the movement of the limbs, which have a velocity superior to the rest of the body and travel in opposite directions. On the other hand, the motion pattern of the dummy is rather different. As the dummy moves as a block, the great majority of the points will have the same Doppler value.

4   Learning Models Applied

The learning models used in this paper are implemented in the well-known Python machine learning library named **scikit-learn**. Each model is dependent on a set of parameters. The parameters for which the respective value is omitted are considered to have the default value defined in the aforementioned library. 25% of the dataset (equivalent to 6114 frames) were used for test, while the remaining were applied in the training stage. The dataset was previously shuffled to ensure an equal representation of both classes in both the training and testing set.

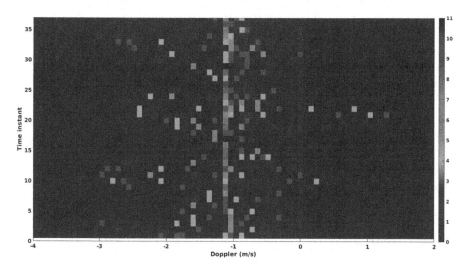

Fig. 3. Velocity pattern of a person walking in front and to the device.

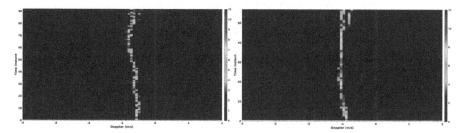

Fig. 4. Velocity pattern of a mannequin (left) and of a person in a wheelchair (right) moving in front and to the device. The Doppler scale is the same as the one in Fig. 3.

4.1 Artificial Neural Network

The first model applied was an artificial neural network. Several values for the hyperparameters were tested. The optimal performance was 85.9%. The values used for the artificial neural network parameters are shown in Table 2. Using the same hyperparameters but ignoring the RCS as a feature, the accuracy is 81.5%. In Table 3 is shown the confusion matrix both in the case the RCS is used and in the case the RCS is not used.

4.2 Random Forests

The second model applied was a Random Forest, with a number of estimators of 500 and a maximum depth of 600, and the random state is set to 0. The accuracy attained was 86%, which is better than the one achieved by the neural network. As in the case for the neural network, when the RCS is not used the accuracy

Table 2. Artificial Neural Network Hyperparameters. *hl* stands for hidden layers.

Activation function	Relu	Num. of hl	4
Num. of neurons (1st to last layer)	100, 70, 50, 20	**Learning rate**	0.001
Maximum iterations	10000	**Random state**	42

Table 3. Artificial Neural Network confusion matrix.

	Predicted Not Person (with RCS)	Predicted Person (with RCS)
Not Person	2890	413
Person	448	2363
	Predicted Not Person (without RCS)	Predicted Person (without RCS)
Not Person	2732	571
Person	559	2252

Table 4. Random Forest confusion matrix.

	Predicted Not Person (with RCS)	Predicted Person (with RCS)
Not Person	2916	387
Person	470	2341
	Predicted Not Person (without RCS)	Predicted Person (without RCS)
Not Person	2821	482
Person	563	2248

decreases, in this case for a value of 82.9%. Table 4 shows the confusion matrix of the Random Forest model.

5   Discussion of Results and Conclusions

As can be seen from the results presented in the previous section, the inclusion of the RCS of each detected target as a classification feature was shown to improve significantly the performance of the target recognition methods in the two studied approaches. Actually, even without using an absolute values of the RCS, whose calibration was beyond the scope of the present study, it is possible to show that the relative values of this parameter, when acquired by the same radar with fixed parameters, is sufficient to discriminate some classes of objects in a given scenario. In our opinions, this constitutes an interesting contribution of the present work.

The overall performance of the classification models tested in this study evidence clearly the high potential of the methods to detect people in indoor environments, even if moving in a wheelchair, and to support the application envisaged in our work.

The work currently in progress at our laboratory includes additional tests with other types of targets and the detection of non-walking people based on movements of the arms and hand gestures.

In future work we intend to test the same methods in more problematic scenarios (e.g. with furniture and other obstacles) in order to assess their performance and the potential adequacy of different models to the different environments. Moreover, different parameters of the classification models will be also tested, and their results evaluated.

References

1. Bartsch, A., Fitzek, F., Rasshofer, R.H.: Pedestrian recognition using automotive radar sensors. Adv. Radio Sci. **10**, 45–55 (2012)
2. Berkius, C., Buck, M., Gustafsson, J., Kauppinen, M.: Human Control of Mobile Robots Using Hand Gestures. Bachelor thesis in Electrical Engineering, Chalmers University of Technology. Gothenburg, Sweden. (2018)
3. Ester, M., Kriegel, H.P., Sander, J., Xu, X.: A density-based algorithm for discovering clusters in large spatial databases with noise. In: Proceedings of the Second International Conference on Knowledge Discovery and Data Mining, KDD 1996, pp. 226–231. AAAI Press (1996)
4. Heuel, S., Rohling, H.: Pedestrian Recognition Based on 24 GHz Radar Sensors, vol. Ultra-Wideband Radio Technologies for Communications, Localization and Sensor Applications, chap. 10, pp. 241–256. InTech (2013)
5. Knudde, N., et al.: Indoor Tracking of Multiple Persons With a 77 GHz MIMO FMCW Radar. In: 2017 European Radar Conference (EURAD), pp. 61–64 (2017)
6. Livshitz, M.: Tracking radar targets with multiple reflection points. https://e2e.ti.com/cfs-file/_key/communityserver-discussions-components-files/1023/Tracking-radar-targets-with-multiple-reflection-points.pdf (2018). Accessed 20 April 2019
7. Machado, S., Mancheno, S.: Automotive FMCW Radar Development and Verification Methods. Master's thesis, Department of Computer Science and Engineering. Chalmers University of Technology. University of Gothenburg, Sweden (2018)
8. Texas-Instruments: People tracking and counting reference design using mmWave radar sensor. ti designs: Tidep-01000 (March 2018)
9. Yamada, H., Wakamatsu, Y., Sato, K., Yamaguchi, Y.: Indoor Human Detection by Using Quasi-MIMO Doppler Radar. In: 2015 International Workshop on Antenna Technology (iWAT), pp. 35–38 (2015)

Artificial Intelligence in Power and Energy Systems

Explorative Spatial Data Mining for Energy Technology Adoption and Policy Design Analysis

Fabian Heymann[1,2(✉)], Filipe Joel Soares[2(✉)], Pablo Duenas[3(✉)], and Vladimiro Miranda[1,2(✉)]

[1] Faculty of Engineering, University of Porto, Porto, Portugal
fabian.heymann@fe.up.pt
[2] INESC TEC, Porto, Portugal
[3] Massachusetts Institute of Technology, 40 Ames Street, Cambridge, MA 02142, USA

Abstract. Spatial data mining aims at the discovery of unknown, useful patterns from large spatial datasets. This article presents a thorough analysis of the Portuguese adopters of distributed energy resources using explorative spatial data mining techniques. These resources are currently passing the early adoption stage in the study area. Results show adopter clustering during the current stage. Furthermore, spatial adoption patterns are simulated over a 20-year horizon, analyzing technology concentration changes over time while comparing three different energy policy designs. Outcomes provide useful indication for both electrical network planning and energy policy design.

Keywords: Diffusion of innovation · Renewable energy · Spatial data mining

1 Introduction

Recently, Portuguese residential consumers have been adopting new distributed energy resources (DER), energy technologies like solar photovoltaics (PV), electric vehicles (EV) and electric heating, ventilation and air conditioning devices (HVAC) [1–3]. With the constant growth in utilization of these technologies experienced in recent years, studies started to focus on the likely impact of such DER, as they are expected to substantially reshape the European energy system [4]. With its Clean Energy For All Europeans package, the European Union (EU) aims at further strengthening the role of consumers and local energy communities within an increasingly decentralized European energy system [5].

Installation and subsequent adequate operation of DER offers several potential benefits, including self-consumption, arbitrage trade, shifted consumption and flexibility provision [5]. The Portuguese government has recently committed to a renewable energy transition as outlined in its National Energy Plan towards 2020 [6]. This strategy includes two main goals: (i) to increase the share of renewable energy on final energy consumption by 40% until 2030; and (ii) to promote microgeneration, mostly by PV, with a target of 300 MW in microgeneration by 2020. Furthermore, ambitious

© Springer Nature Switzerland AG 2019
P. Moura Oliveira et al. (Eds.): EPIA 2019, LNAI 11804, pp. 427–437, 2019.
https://doi.org/10.1007/978-3-030-30241-2_36

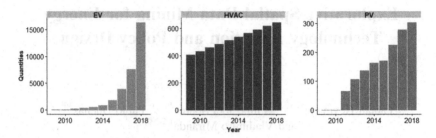

Fig. 1. EV, HVAC (both adopters) and PV (in MW) stock in Portugal 2009–2018

targets to stimulate the uptake of electric mobility technologies is contained. Given the political backing, a strong uptake of DER could be observed in Portugal (Fig. 1).

This motivates a thorough and combined assessment of the spatial patterns of PV, EV, and HVAC adoption. These patterns are especially interesting to electricity network planners, whose job is to connect consumers to generation sources, thus satisfying the rising electricity needs at a constant, balanced and cost-optimized pace. With regard to energy technologies such as DER, network planners are especially interested in understanding timing and magnitude of the appearance of such new appliances [7]. Therefore, the assessment of spatial DER adoption patterns can contribute with important insights both to policy analysis and electricity network planning [8]. Having the analysis of DER adoption patterns as main topic of this paper, the addressed research questions can be differentiated into the following:

- Does the adoption process of EV, HV and HVAC exhibit spatially clustered or homogeneous patterns?
- Can a decomposition of spatial autocorrelation patterns identify EV, PV or HVAC adoption hotspots (or coldspots) that are statistically significant?
- If we simulate technology adoption over time, how are spatial autocorrelation measures (e.g. Moran's I) evolving?

The article is structured the following way: While Sect. 2 is dedicated to a short introduction to the emerging field of spatial data mining, Sect. 3 includes a description of the dataset analysed. Then, Sect. 4 introduces the mathematical framework of spatial autocorrelation and the detection of localized clusters used throughout this work. Section 5 builds on previous explanations and investigates the temporal variability of Moran's I along a 20-year timespan, with a simulated full technology adoption. Section 6 contains conclusions and an outlook on the further applications of the developed application of the previous section.

2 Spatial Data Mining

Data mining or knowledge discovery in data-bases is a growing field that is closely interlinked to Artificial Intelligence (AI) [9]. Spatial data mining is an emerging, very recent research area that has developed on top of data mining research which itself exists since the 1980s [10]. Spatial data mining has been defined as the "the process of discovering interesting and previously unknown, but potentially useful patterns from large spatial datasets" [11]. The main difference to traditional data mining thus lies in the very nature of spatial data. Spatial data intrinsically relate to space, therefore carrying information on location, distance and topology/form of spatial objects [10]. Thus, spatial data is also always assessed with tools that aim to analyze these specific spatial characteristics, such as spatial join, spatial overlay and spatial intersection among others. An extensive overview of the computation of spatial pattern analysis can be found in [12]. In contrast to non-spatial data mining, spatial data mining was said to possess increased complexity [11]. Its main challenges are [10]:

(1) Spatial autocorrelation phenomena
(2) Spatial relationships between observations and their description
(3) The inherent complexity of spatial data

Consequently, the increased complexity and a high computational costs of spatial data processing require the use of efficient spatial data structures and operations [10]. There have been developed several methods that are able to explore and handle the above-mentioned complexities. These can be divided into Exploratory Spatial Data Mining and other advanced techniques. In [13], the authors merge the common spatial clustering tools such as Global Autocorrelation (Moran's I), Hot Spot (Getis-Ord) Analysis, Local Autocorrelation (e.g. Anselins Local Moran I) and Density kernel estimation as Exploratory Spatial Data Mining analyses. On the other hand, more advanced tasks of spatial data mining are the analysis of spatial association rules, spatial trend detection, and spatial outlier analysis [13].

This work will proceed with a thorough Exploratory Spatial Data Mining of DER adopters in Portugal, followed by the application of an advanced tool that allows tracking the variation of spatial autocorrelation structures along a full DER adoption lifetime using a spatiotemporal DER adoption forecasting model.

3   Input Data

In the scope of this work, two datasets have been combined. A set of geo-referenced EV, PV and HVAC adopters (counting 2,632/474/2,111) as point information, obtained by the Portuguese e-mobility charging platform operator and the Portuguese energy agency, together with a highly granular census dataset for Continental Portugal. The EV dataset has been cleaned from commercial users beforehand and sums both Battery EV (BEV) and Plug-In Hybrid EV (PHEV). Likewise, residential PV installation records have been obtained by removing small-scale business. No technology or installation size differentiation have been considered. On the other hand, the HVAC dataset comprises mostly electrical systems of different technical peculiarities. The per-capita distribution of selected energy technologies across Portuguese continental municipalities is shown below (Fig. 2).

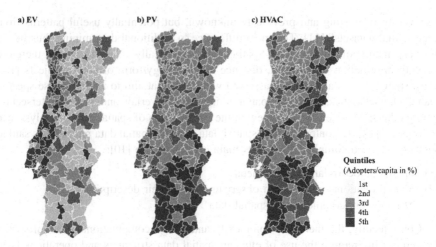

Fig. 2. Spatial distribution of EV, PV and HVAC adopters in municipalities of Continental Portugal. Values are divided into quintiles, (for each technology separately).

While this study differentiates the adoption tendencies between this larger EV, PV and HVAC groups, in-group analysis (e.g. BEV versus PHEV) has been constrained by the shape of datasets available and lies outside the scope of this work.

4 Applying Spatial Data Mining to DER Adopter Patterns

4.1 Global Autocorrelation

This part of this work is dedicated to what has been called "Exploratory Spatial Data Mining" [13]. A widely-applied metric for spatial auto-correlation is Moran's I [12]. Similar to Geary's C or the global Getis-Ord G, it is an autocorrelation test like that is applied on a global scale. Thus, it results in one index. Moran's I provides insight in the observations' tendency having similar (or, linearly correlated) values when compared to their neighbors. Input data can be spatial point, raster or polygon type.

It is a dimensionless, appealing metric, as it produces outputs within $[-1,1]$, where a value of 0 indicates spatial randomness equivalent to show no distinct pattern, 1 represents absolute spatial autocorrelation, and -1 complete dissimilarity similar to a checkerboard pattern [14]. A Moran's I value of -1 implies that all spatial objects are neighbored by the most dissimilar values of the population. An important input represents the weight matrix w_{ij} that contains the neighboring structures of the spatial points or polygons under analysis.

Considering spatial polygons, the neighborhood structure incorporates the degree of adjacency, taking values of 0 (is not neighbor) or 1 (is neighbor). As shown below (Eq. 1), the formula sums up all differences between polygons (i) values y_i and respective neighborhood polygons' (j) values y_j compared to the global mean $\hat{y}$ (also *lagged mean* or *spatial lag*). The resulting value is divided by the variance of each value y_i with respect to the global average $\hat{y}$ and consecutively multiplied with the number of observations n by the spatial weights' matrix w_{ij}. Moran's I is typically computed as stated below:

$$I = \frac{n}{\sum_{i-1}^{n} \sum_{j=1}^{n} W_{ij}} \frac{\sum_{i=1}^{n} \sum_{j=1}^{n} (y_i - \hat{y})(y_j - \hat{y})}{\sum_{i=1}^{n} (y_i - \hat{y})^2} \qquad (1)$$

The output gives a first indication of the spatial autocorrelative structures. However, respective significance levels (p-values) can be either obtained through simulation approaches or by comparing the variances to predefined distributions. Former approach has been explained in [15].

It is important to note that Moran's I values can be computed on the base of spatial point data only. However, in our research question such analysis is limited given the adopter's location dependency from population variables, that is, the spatial distribution of population groups that represent the overall adopter potential. Therefore, spatial point information previously introduced has been superimposed with municipality polygons. This approach allows for the retrieval of a DER adopters/1000 inhabitants ratio, which is better suited to compare the presence of EV, PV or HVAC adopters in differently populated areas to each other.

Moran's I values and p-values obtained for the polygon-based analysis are shown below (Table 1). As shown, results suggest that all three technologies exhibit spatial autocorrelation (Moran's I between 0–1). That means that values are similar to neighboring values, or in other words, are spatially clustered.

Table 1. Spatial autocorrelation for EV, PV and HVAC adopters in Continental Portugal

Value/Technology	EV	PV	HVAC
Moran's I	0.42346	0.37526	0.39532
p-value	<0.01	<0.01	<0.01
Polyg. with values	185	130	161

The p-value has been computed to quantify the probability that the calculated Moran's I values are different from pure chance. As mentioned above, the p-value is approximated using a simulation-based approach firstly presented in [16]. Here, the probability of obtaining Moran's I values above the observed one is calculated using the following formula:

$$p = \frac{m+1}{M+1} \qquad (2)$$

In this equation, m quantifies the number of simulated Moran's I values above the retrieved value. Furthermore, M represents the total number of simulations. As shown in Fig. 3, one-sided exceedance probability distributions for obtaining values larger than the retrieved Moran's I have been generated. In other words, the approach simulates a predefined number of Moran's I values relying on observed values in a permutated way. Thus, it can be observed if such value distributions follow a spatial randomization that is equivalent to accepting the Null hypothesis.

The distribution of the exceedance probability was generated using 600 permutations with equal probability and no repetition. It should be noted that the number of permutations needs to be smaller than the possibilities of rearranging the polygon values to avoid double counting effects that could affect negatively results. This is true for this work.

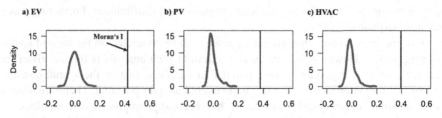

Fig. 3. Exceedance probabilities for 600 permutations

As seen above, outcomes suggest strong evidence for the rejection of the Null hypothesis of spatial randomization with p-values smaller than 0.1% across all technologies. The black vertical bar in the figure indicates the realized Moran's value and the estimated Moran's I value for each technology on Municipal aggregation level. It should be noted that Moran's Is dependency on a predefined neighborhood structure as well as its boundary polygon configuration in an incomplete neighborhood matrix have been criticized in [12]. However, as authors likewise admitted, no optimal treatment of these cases has been found so far.

4.2   Local Autocorrelation

While the previously introduced analysis of spatial autocorrelation (Moran's I) provides insight in the global dispersion/concentration of spatial patterns, attempts have been made to break geographical variation down to study local situations.

In this light, Anselin suggested a new type of model, namely the so called "local indicators of spatial association (LISAs)" [17]. These should comply with two requirements:

- The LISA value of each observation should provide insights to the spatial clustering around that value
- The sum of all LISA observations should be proportional to a global metric of spatial autocorrelation (e.g. all LISA values should sum to a global autocorrelation value).

Latter requirement can be met using index decomposition techniques. In the same work [17], Anselin suggested a LISA based on the decomposition of Moran's I, to retrieve a Local Moran's I. Here, the autocorrelation value associated to each observation is I_i, whereas q_i are the mean-centered values and q_j are the means for all neighbor values of polygon i. Thus, I_i can be retrieved following:

$$I_i = q_i \sum_j w_{ij} q_j \tag{3}$$

Using a permutation Monte-Carlo sampling approach as in the test-statistic approach of Eq. 2, a significance test may be conducted using [17]:

$$z(I_i) = \frac{I_i - E[I_i]}{\sqrt{Var[I_i]}} \tag{4}$$

Here, values of $I_i > 0$ indicate that a cluster of similar values (higher or lower than average) is present. Likewise, values of $I_i < 0$ indicate a combination of dissimilar values (e.g. high values surrounded by low values). In R programing language, this can be computed using the "localmoran" command of the *spdep* package. This command returns the local Moran's I statistic for each polygon, the expected value $E(I_i)$ and variance $Var(I_i)$ under the randomization hypothesis, the test statistic (Eq. 4) as well as the p-value of the above statistic assuming approximate normal distribution [15].

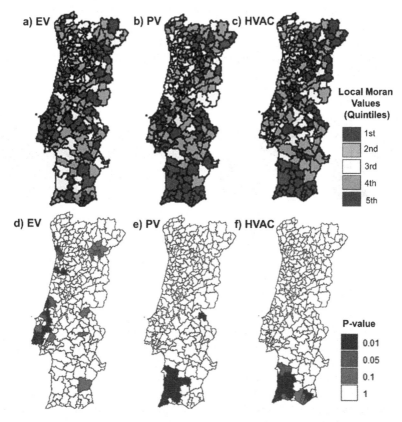

Fig. 4. Spatial distribution of Local Moran I (a, b, c) and respective p-values (d, e, f). Please note that a, b and c are shown in quintiles that are equidistant to 0.

Figure 4 displays outcomes of the local Moran analysis. Results suggest spatial hotspots along the southern cost (PV, HVAC) and Western costs (EV) as well as in some isolated areas in northern-central Portugal (EV, PV, HVAC). Furthermore, all technologies adopter distributions suggest cold spots in the Northern or central areas of Continental Portugal (EV, PV, HVAC). Taking the test statistics analysis into account, the hotspots along the urban centers at Portugal's western coastline (EV) and the southern costal hotspots (PV; HVAC) suggest being significant at levels <1%.

Several techniques to extend the local autocorrelation analysis, taking into account common critiques on the necessary normality assumption (of I_is) and multiple hypothesis testing have been proposed. The interested reader might find a broad overview of such extensions together with case study applications in [15].

5   Spatial Autocorrelation Describing Technology Diffusion

An interesting further application of Moran's I to study large-scale DER diffusion patterns geographically, lies in its potential to describe the stage of maturity of the innovation diffusion process based on analysis of spatial autocorrelation of the adoption patterns. In a thought experiment (Fig. 5), we would expect to see isolated adoption clusters at early adoption. Such patterns would possess low spatial autocorrelation. However, autocorrelation would rise (towards higher spatial autocorrelation) during mid-time of the diffusion process, while a mature technology diffusion would likely see equally distributed DER per capita shares.

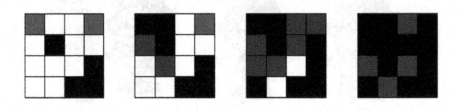

Innovation diffusion process

Fig. 5. Hypothetical technology diffusion process with spatial patterns of adoption stages. Here, white represents "No adoption", light grey "Intermediate adoption" (33%), dark grey "Strong adoption" (66%), and black "Full adoption" (100%).

Hence, spatial autocorrelation, and, especially its change over time, can be used to study and compare technology diffusion processes across countries or case studies. Furthermore, the strength of autocorrelation (maximum value of Moran's I) and its development over time are interesting inputs to benchmark energy policy designs, in case decision makers are concerned about adoption asymmetries across populations.

Therefore, we establish a temporalization of Moran's I model, which compares 20 annual snapshot DER distributions along the technology diffusion process. While the spatiotemporal DER adoption forecasting model has been presented in [8], we further analyze three policy designs that result in different spatial DER distributions. The modelling rationale behind all three policy designs lies in the different ranking of census cells in the queue of DER adoption.

Table 2. Modeling of DER distribution under policy change

DER adopter distributions	High weights on the following census variables
High-performance high income (HP)	Census cells with above average higher education share, large residencies, high shares of housing owners
Low-medium income (LMI)	Census cells with below average higher education share, small and old residencies, high shares of renters
Randomized distribution (RN)	-

While the model uses a global technology forecast for each year as well as spatially granular (neighborhood level) census data, it produces DER shares per municipality for each of the 20 analyzed years. The policy designs are: "high-performance high income (HP)", "Low-medium income (LMI)" and "randomized distribution (RN)". They can be discriminated considering different rankings of census cells that are due next in the adoption process (Table 2). According to the logic presented in this table, subsets of census variables have been used to construct the different census cell rankings (through attributing different weights to each household-count normalized census cell).

Results are shown below (Fig. 6). One can observe spatial autocorrelation growing along the EV adoption process (left side). Interestingly, patterns on the left side (along adoption years) are not linear or follow the expected bell curve outcome (from low adoption – low autocorrelation to medium adoption – high autocorrelation to complete adoption – low autocorrelation). Instead, under a HP policy design, Moran's I increase until year 10 and then fades out to a higher autocorrelation level (0.6). On the other hand, LMI and RN policies see different Moran's I evolutions that stepwise proceed towards a 0.4 or 0.5 autocorrelation value respectively. Moran's I variations on time are very different if compared to EV adoption shares; as DER adoption is not constant over time, such analysis shows remarkable differences. While under a HP policy design, Moran's I would rapidly increase after around 5–10% of adoption, it quickly reaches a plateau, too. Towards the end of the adoption process, autocorrelation reduces slightly again. On the other hand, for LMI and RN policies, spatial autocorrelation remains initially on lower levels (around 0.4) and only reach higher levels (such as the HP plateau) after 90% of EV adoption. That is an interesting outcome as it suggests that LMI and HP trigger less autocorrelated (i.e. more dispersed) DER adoption behavior that might eventually reduce system integration costs of DER.

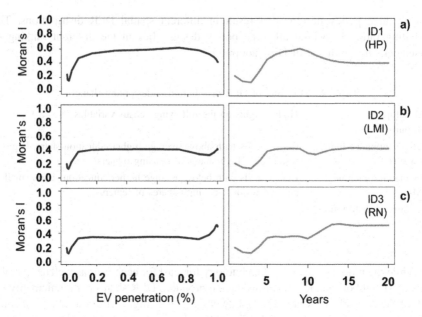

Fig. 6. Global Moran's I values for EV adoption patterns along the years (left side) and relative to EV adoption shares (right side). Results show temporal variations for HP, LMI and RN policy designs (a, b, c respectively).

6 Conclusions and Outlook

This paper presented a thorough analysis of Portuguese DER adopters using explorative spatial data mining techniques. While adoption patterns on municipal level have been characterized using Moran's I and Local Moran's I, the temporal evolution of spatial autocorrelation behavior using EV as a case study has been analyzed, too. Results show similar degree of autocorrelation for all three technologies under analysis (EV, PV, HVAC). Likewise, local clusters (<1% significance level) have been detected, with EV hotspots along the western, densely populated coastline and PV and HVAC mostly along the southern fringe along the Algarve coastline.

On the other hand, this paper provided insights in the effects of policy choice on spatial autocorrelation structures. Using a spatiotemporal technology adoption forecasting model, outcomes suggested that the choice of energy policy measures has strong effects on spatial autocorrelation structures (and thus inequality and network impact) of DER adopters. For example, policy schemes LMI and RN achieve only higher autocorrelation levels after 10 years of adoption. Thus, such incentive schemes might allow deferring electricity network investments given adoption patterns with a higher degree of dispersion. In contrast, one would expect to associate HP adoption patterns with a more pronounced investment to integrate EV charging. This is, as such incentive scheme would produce highly concentrated adoption patterns from early adoption phases onwards.

Concluding, this study serves as promising starting point to further investigate the dependency among spatial autocorrelation behavior of DER adoption patterns, network expansion costs and adoption inequality.

Acknowledgement. The authors gratefully acknowledge the provision of data-sets by the Portuguese Energy Agency (ADENE) and CEiiA. F. Heymann acknowledges the financial support granted under FCT-MIT Portugal Scholarship PD/BD/114262/2016. This work has been co-financed by National Funds through the Portuguese funding agency (Fundação para a Ciência e a Tecnologia) within project: UID/EEA/50014/2019.

References

1. European Alternative Fuels Observatory, Electric vehicle statistics (2017). http://www.eafo. eu/vehicle-statistics/m1. Accessed 1 Jan 2017
2. Portuguese General Direction of Energy and Geology (DGEG), Rapid Statistics - Renewables No. 168 (2018)
3. PORDATA, Households with principal electrical appliances (%) (2018). https://www. pordata.pt/Municipios/Agregados+privados+com+os+principais+equipamentos+domésticos +(percentagem)-824
4. Bell, K.: Methods and tools for planning the future power system: issues and priorities. Modelling Requirements of the GB Power System Resilience during the transition to Low Carbon Energy, no. Paper 5, pp. 1–35 (2015)
5. European Commission, Clean Energy For All Europeans, Brussels (2016)
6. Portuguese Republic, National Renewable Energy Plan (Implementation of the European DIrective 2009/28/CE) (2010)
7. Heymann, F., Melo, J., Martínez, P.D., Soares, F., Miranda, V.: On the emerging role of spatial load forecasting in transmission/distribution grid planning. In: 11th Mediterranean Conference on Power Generation, Transmission, Distribution and Energy Conversion (MEDPOWER 2018) (2018)
8. Heymann, F., Silva, J., Miranda, V., Melo, J., Soares, F.J., Padilha-Feltrin, A.: Distribution network planning considering technology diffusion dynamics and spatial net-load behavior. Int. J. Electr. Power Energy Syst. **106**, 254–265 (2019)
9. Wu, X.: Data mining: an AI perspective. IEEE Comput. Intell. Bull. **4**(2), 5–8 (2004)
10. Koperski, K., Adhikary, J., Hau, J.: Spatial Data Mining: Progress and Challenges Survey paper (1997)
11. Shekhar, S., Zhang, P., Huang, Y.: Spatial data mining. In: Maimon, O., Rokach, L. (eds.) Data Mining and Knowledge Discovery Handbook, pp. 833–850. Springer, Boston (2005). https://doi.org/10.1007/0-387-25465-X_39
12. Gómez-Rubio, V., Bivand, R.S., Pebesma, E.: Applied Spatial Data Analysis with R, 2nd edn. Springer, New York (2013). https://doi.org/10.1007/978-1-4614-7618-4
13. Bhardwaj, A.: Spatial data mining. In: Data Mining Techniques and Tools for Knowledge Discovery in Agricultural Datasets, pp. 153–166. IASRI (2012)
14. Gimond, M.: Intro to GIS and Spatial Analysis [ebook] (2019). https://mgimond.github.io/ Spatial/index.html
15. Comber, L., Brunsdon, C.: R for Spatial Analysis and Mapping. SAGE Publications Ltd., London (2015)
16. Hope, A.C.A.: A simplified Monte Carlo significance test procedure. J. R. Stat. Soc. Ser. B **30**(3), 582–598 (1968)
17. Anselin, L.: Local indicators of spatial association - LISA. Geogr. Anal. **27**, 93–115 (1995)

Distributed Constrained Optimization Towards Effective Agent-Based Microgrid Energy Resource Management

Fernando Lezama[1]([⊠]) [iD], Enrique Munoz de Cote[2,3] [iD], Alessandro Farinelli[4] [iD], João Soares[1] [iD], Tiago Pinto[1] [iD], and Zita Vale[5] [iD]

[1] GECAD-ISEP, Polytechnic of Porto, Porto, Portugal
{flzcl,jan,tcp}@isep.ipp.pt
[2] PROWLER.io, Cambridge, UK
enrique@prowler.io
[3] Department of Computer Science, INAOE, Puebla, Mexico
[4] Computer Science Department, University of Verona, Verona, Italy
alessandro.farinelli@univr.it
[5] Polytechnic of Porto, Porto, Portugal
zav@isep.ipp.pt

Abstract. The current energy scenario requires actions towards the reduction of energy consumption and the use of renewable resources. In this context, a microgrid is a self-sustained network that can operate connected to the smart grid or in isolation. The long-term scheduling of on/off cycles of devices is a critical problem that has been commonly addressed by centralized approaches. In this work, we propose a novel agent-based method to solve the long-term scheduling problem as a distributed constraint optimization problem (DCOP) by modelling future system configurations rather than reacting to changes. Moreover, with respect to approaches based on decentralised reinforcement learning, we can directly encode system-wide hard constraints (such as for example the Kirchhoff law) which are not easy to represent in a factored representation of the problem. We compare different multi-agent DCOP algorithms showing that the proposed method can find optimal/near-optimal solutions for a specific case study.

Keywords: Decentralized · Distributed optimization · Microgrid · Multi-agent systems · Smart grid · Energy resource management

This work has been developed under the MAS-SOCIETY project - PTDC/EEI-EEE/28954/2017 and has received funding from UID/EEA/00760/2019, funded by FEDER Funds through COMPETE and by National Funds through FCT. This work has been also partially supported by the project "GHOTEM" Global HOuse Thermal & Electrical energy Management for Efficiency, Lower emission and Renewables, founded by the Veneto Region through the POR FESR 2014–2020 founding scheme (Action 1.1.4), DGR n. 1139 19 July 2017.

© Springer Nature Switzerland AG 2019
P. Moura Oliveira et al. (Eds.): EPIA 2019, LNAI 11804, pp. 438–449, 2019.
https://doi.org/10.1007/978-3-030-30241-2_37

1   Introduction

A microgrid is a small self-sustained power network, with local distribution and local generators, that uses renewable energy. Moreover, a *smart* microgrid uses a combination of the electric network, local generators, information and communication technologies (ICT), and intelligent systems to provide control in an effective and efficient way [22].

One of the main problems to tackle in a microgrid is the control and management of resources through the scheduling of on/off cycles of devices. An optimal scheduling of devices is traditionally achieved by centralized approaches [12,19]. However, such approaches lack flexibility, since adding new devices to the system implies the recalculation of the entire scheduling, and robustness, because losing the central unit might result in a shut down for the whole system [3,20]. On the other hand, a decentralized approach is more flexible, allowing the addition of new devices and performing the optimization in a distributed way, hence following the trend of intelligent distribution networks (i.e., the SG). Commonly, the decentralized approach has been applied to the scheduling problem without considering long-term optimization [13,14].

Recently, significant effort has been devoted to decentralised solutions that can take into account the dynamics and sequential nature of the environment. A relevant approach in this domain is modeling the problem as a distributed constraint optimization problem (DCOP); see e.g. [9], which provides a review on the current status and future perspectives on DCOP in multiple domains. [4] presents a survey on DCOP to support multi-agent systems (MAS) in complex, real-time, and uncertain environments. The paper proposes a classification of DCOP multiple extensions, focused both on solving methods and applications. The classification identifies future evolutions for DCOP, and identifies challenges in the design of efficient algorithms by adapting approaches from diverse fields. [6] proposes an integrated approach to solve the economic dispatch and demand response problems that simultaneously maximizes the benefits of customers and minimizes the generation costs, and introduces a multi-agent-based algorithm, based on DCOPs, [5] that formalizes a smart home scheduling problem, describes a mapping of this problem to a distributed constraint optimization problem, proposes a distributed algorithm for solving the problem, and presents results from a physically distributed system capable of controlling smart devices through hardware interfacess. Additionally, [2] introduces an algorithm that adopts the optimal asynchronous partial overlay (OPTAPO) technique, which uses distributed constraint agent search to solve distributed DCOP sub-problems in a multi-agent environment. The use of the Dynamic DCOP framework has also been proposed, where the system evolution is modelled as a sequence of canonical DCOPs providing a new solution each time the system changes its configuration [17].

On the other hand, a series of works aims at considering the system dynamics by modelling the transition function for system configurations by using reinforcement learning techniques that can perform computation in a decentralised fashion [1,8,16,21], including cooperative [7] and non-cooperative distributed reinforcement learning approaches [18]. A core component of these approaches is to exploit the structure of the domain, so to have a factored representation of the problem that can be conveniently solved in a decentralized fashion by message passing techniques.

In this paper, we propose a mathematical model for the long-term microgrid control. This is a modification of a former model presented in [10,11], which is optimised for distributed settings. After that, we characterize the mathematical formulation as a DCOP. In the agent-based optimization, to keep the model tractable for long-time horizons, we split the problem into time windows and solve it using different off-the-shelf approaches.

In contrast to approaches based on Dynamic DCOPs, our method explicitly performs long-term optimization by modelling future system configurations rather than reacting to changes. Moreover, with respect to approaches based on decentralised reinforcement learning, we can directly encode system-wide hard constraints (such as for example the Kirchhoff law) which are not easy to represent in a factored representation of the problem[1].

The results show that, even when the agent-based distributed approach provides optimal and near-optimal solutions for small window sizes, it pays a large computational cost associated with the interaction of agents for large window sizes.

2   Problem Formulation for Distributed Settings

Let $G = \{1, \ldots, n\}$ be the set of all generators and $type_i$ be the type of energy produced by each generator $i \in G$. Furthermore, let $E_{G_i}(t)$ be the instantaneous (at timestep t) energy produced by each generator $i \in G$ and $E_{B_j}(t)$ be the instantaneous energy being stored ($E_{B_j}(t) > 0$) or used ($E_{B_j}(t) < 0$) by each battery $j \in B = \{1, 2, \ldots, m\}$ at time t. Because a microgrid is never completely balanced, let $E_{dis}(t)$ be the amount of undelivered ($E_{dis} > 0$) or exceeded ($E_{dis} < 0$) energy at each time. Finally, we use C to refer to costs, where C_{G_i} is associated with the cost of energy production through $type_i$ generator, $C_{B_j^+}/C_{B_j^-}$ with the cost of charging/discharging battery j, and $C_{E_{dis}^-}/C_{E_{dis}^+}$ with the cost of undelivered/exceeded energy. Now that energy generation and storage is defined, let $Load(t)$ captures an aggregated quantity of energy consumption.

The objective is to minimize the cost of generated energy (first term of Eq. (1)) and storage/used battery energy (second term of Eq. (1)), while minimizing the unbalance between production and consumption (third term of Eq. (1)) in the microgrid. This can be formulated as follows:

$$Min \quad f = \sum_{t=1}^{T} \left(\begin{array}{l} \sum_{i \in G} E_{G_i}(t) C_{G_i}(t) - \\ \sum_{j \in B} E_{B_j}(t) \mathbf{C_B}(E_{B_j}(t)) + \\ E_{dis}(t) \mathbf{C_{dis}}(E_{dis}(t)) \end{array} \right) \tag{1}$$

---

[1] Nonetheless, we believe that using decentralised learning approaches for scheduling on/off cycles of devices in the microgrid deserves further investigation, and is definitely an interesting direction for future work.

where $\mathbf{C_B}(.)$ and $\mathbf{C_{E_{dist}}}(.)$ are functions returning the battery and disbalance cost depending on the conditions (i.e., battery charge/discharge status and undelivered/exceeded energy) defined as:

$$\mathbf{C_B}(E_{B_j}(t)) = \begin{cases} C_{B_j^+} & \text{if } E_{B_j}(t) > 0 \quad \text{(battery charging)} \\ C_{B_j^-} & \text{otherwise} \end{cases} \tag{2}$$

$$\mathbf{C_{dis}}(E_{dis}(t)) = \begin{cases} C_{E_{dis}^-} & \text{if } E_{dis}^- > 0 \quad \text{(demand > generation)} \\ C_{E_{dis}^+} & \text{otherwise} \end{cases} \tag{3}$$

Subject to the following constraints:

- Kirchhoff law or power balance:

$$\sum_{i \in G} E_{G_i}(t) - \sum_{j \in B} E_{B_j}(t) + E_{dis}(t) = Load(t) \quad \forall t \tag{4}$$

where $Load(t)$ is the sum of energy required by all consumers at time t. $E_{dis}(t)$ is a variable that balances above equation when $demand \neq generation$, meaning that:

$$E_{dis}(t) = Load(t) - \left(\sum_{i \in G} E_{G_i}(t) - \sum_{j \in B} E_{B_j}(t) \right) \tag{5}$$

$E_{dis}(t)$ takes positive values when $demand > generation$ and negative values otherwise.
- Energy type production limits at time t:

$$0 \leq E_{G_i}(t) \leq cap_G(type_i) \quad \forall i \in G, t \tag{6}$$

where $cap_G(type_i)$ is the limit capacity if generator $type_i$.
- Storage, charge and discharge battery limits at each time t:

$$CH_j(t) \leq cap_B \quad \forall j \in B, t \tag{7}$$
$$\Delta cap_{B-} \leq E_{B_j}(t) \leq \Delta cap_{B+} \quad \forall j \in B, t \tag{8}$$

where CH_j is the current battery $j \in B$ charge level, cap_B is the maximum energy storage capacity of any battery, and $\Delta cap_{B+}/\Delta cap_{B-}$ are the maximum instantaneous (per timestep) charge/discharge rate of any battery.
- State balance of the battery:

$$CH_j(t) = E_{B_j}(t) + CH_j(t-1) \quad \forall j \in B, t \tag{9}$$

- Charge and discharge limits at time t considering period $t-1$:

$$0 \leq E_{B_j}(t) + CH_j(t-1) \leq cap_B \quad j \in B \tag{10}$$

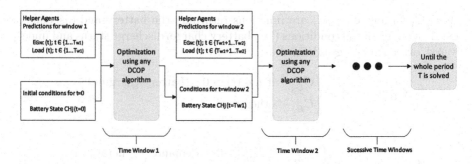

Fig. 1. Optimization using time windows.

The new formulation can also be optimally solved using Mixed-integer Linear Programming (MILP) in a centralized fashion as in [15]. In the next section, we present a long-term decentralized approach using this new formulation that allows solving the problem using agent-based theory and DCOP algorithms.

3   Agent-Based Long-Term Optimization

We consider a microgrid with four types of elements: (i) consumers (i.e., *Load*), (ii) non-controllable generators ($G_{NC} \subseteq G$), (iii) controllable generators ($G_C \subseteq G$) and (iv) storage devices (B).

To model the dispatch problem from Sect. 2 as a DCOP, we need to define agents, variables, domains, and functions according to the mathematical formulation.

First, we assign each type of element to a specific type of Agent. So, in our model we have four types of agents: (i) $\mathcal{A}_{Load}$, (ii) $\mathcal{A}_{G_{NC_k}}$, (iii) $\mathcal{A}_{G_{C_i}}$ and, (iv) $\mathcal{A}_{B_j}$ corresponding to each type of element.

These agents are in charge of variables related to energy production or consumption, i.e., (i) $Load(t)$, (ii) $E_{G_{NC_k}}(t)$, (iii) $E_{G_{C_i}}(t)$, and $E_{B_j}(t)$.

The domains of each variable are defined as: (i) $[0, cap_{Load}]$, (ii) $[0, cap_{G_{NC_k}}]$, (iii) $[0, cap_{G_{C_i}}]$, and (iv) $[\Delta cap_{B-}, \Delta cap_{B+}]$.

Finally, the agents must coordinate their actions to minimize the cost function from Eq. (1), subject to the constraints defined through Sect. 2.

In this model, agents assigned to non-controllable elements (i.e., $\mathcal{A}_{Load}$ and $\mathcal{A}_{G_{NC}}$) are considered helper agents, and their functions are simply to provide the forecast of energy production and consumption in a determined period. That information is taken as an input for agents assigned to controllable elements (i.e., $\mathcal{A}_{G_C}$ and $\mathcal{A}_B$) to perform optimization in a distributed way.

The distributed agent-based model enables to treat the problem as a DCOP, allowing the use of distributed agent algorithms. However, optimally solving a DCOP is known to be an NP-complete problem, hence solving the long-term optimization problem directly will be impractical even for short optimization horizons.

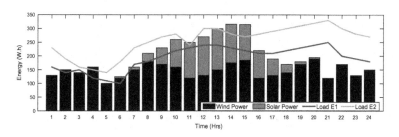

Fig. 2. Forecast of distributed energy sources (DES) and Load for scenarios E1 and E2.

We proposed in our previous work to split the problem in time windows [10]. In this way, for a period T, we can solve the problem by dividing such period T in $N_{windows} = T/n$, where n is the size of the window. This means that for a size $n = 1$ we will solve T windows, for $n = 2$ we will solve T/2 windows and so on. Figure 1 shows the scheme of optimization in time windows. The input for the fist window corresponds to initial conditions of the microgrid (e.g., the battery could start with an initial charge of 100 W, and a fuel-cell generator in off state ready for being activated).

Then, optimization for that window is done by using any of the algorithms to solve the DCOP. The result obtained in that window is used as input for the next window. The process is repeated sequentially until a solution for the long-term period T is obtained.

One disadvantage of this approach is that the optimal solution cannot be guaranteed and depends directly on the size of the window chosen. Small time windows (e.g., size 1) are solved fast since the optimization is done without considering the available knowledge on the future, keeping the information and variable relations low. However, the quality of the solution may not be good enough because of the lack of global vision for the conditions of the successive periods (e.g., wasting all the resources at the current time without considering the demand for the successive time).

In general in this model for an arbitrary window size (WS) and considering only 2 variables (i.e., variable FC owned by agent $\mathcal{A}_{FC}$ and variable B owned by agent $\mathcal{A}_B$), the number of variables grows as a function of (i) $2 * WS$; the number of relations between variables is given by (ii) $WS + WS * (WS - 1)/2$; finally, the domain size grows according to (iii) $|D_{FC}|^{WS} * |D_B|^{WS}$, where $|D_i|$ is the cardinality of the domain of variable i.

It is expected that the quality of the solution improves by increasing the size of the windows. However, as shown in Fig. 3, the number of variables to handle for each agent grows significantly with the size of the windows, hence resulting into an exponential grow of the number of possible configuration to explore.

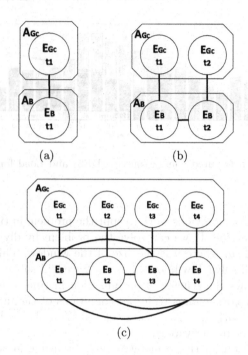

Fig. 3. Agents and variable relations with window sizes of: (a) 1, (b) 2 and (c) 4.

4   Results and Discussion

The reported results consider the Budapest Tech case study presented in [15]. This case study considers a microgrid with one wind generator (G_W), one solar generator (G_S), one fuel cell generator (G_{FC}), and one battery (B). Energy costs are considered constants for simplicity. Such costs and power limits are presented in Table 1.

Table 1. Costs and limits of energy generation [15].

Costs (W/h)	Production limits (W)
$C_{G_W} = 0.4$	$cap_{G_W} = 400$
$C_{G_S} = 0.4$	$cap_{G_S} = 150$
$C_{G_{FC}} = 0.9$	$cap_{G_{FC}} = 80$
$C_{BC} = 0.4$	$\Delta cap_{B+} = [0 - 200]$
$C_{BD} = 0.6$	$\Delta cap_{B-} = [0 - 50]$
$C_{E-} = 1.5$	$cap_B = 200$
$C_{E+} = 1.5$	$CH_{t_0} = 100$

The optimization of on/off cycles was done considering a period of 24 h (i.e., $T = 24$) in intervals of 1 h. Figure 2 presents the forecast of wind energy (E_W), solar power (E_S), and the joint *Load* for two different scenarios (Scenario 2 presents a very high load compared to Scenario 1) at each time t used as an input of the optimization task (all values given in Wh). Also, we consider that the battery starts charged with $CH_{t_0} = 100$ W.

We present the results using DCOP algorithms for the case study with the new proposed model. The optimization procedure was done for different window sizes as explained in Sect. 3. We present results for each DCOP algorithm (i.e., DPOP, MB-DPOP, AFB, and SBB) in terms of percent error (regarding the optimal solution) and number of exchanged messages[2] respectively. The execution times were in the order of 70 mS with a standard deviation of 10 mS. We used a PC with Processor Intel(R) Core(TM) i7-4770 @ 3.40 GHz and 64 GB of RAM.

The first thing to point out is the dependency of the search space and the window size considering variables and domains of the case study. Figure 4 presents a comparison against the model used in [10, 11]. It can be noticed that the number of variables (Fig. 4a) grows linearly, while the number of relations and the domain size present an exponential behavior (Figs. 4b and c). The new model reduces the impact of such exponential growth, making it more suitable for agent-based optimization and allowing the exploration of large window sizes for optimization.

Table 2. Percentage error and number of exchanged messages for scenario 1.

Percentage error				
Window	DPOP	MB-DPOP	AFB	SBB
size 1	0.42	0.42	0.42	0.42
size 2	0.42	0.42	0.42	0.42
size 3	0	0	-	-
size 4	0.42		-	-
Messages				
Window	DPOP	MB-DPOP	AFB	SBB
size 1	192	216	9999	8282
size 2	168	192	8534589	23468014
size 3	160	184	-	-
size 4	156	180	-	-

Tables 2 and 3 show the percent error (i.e., the percent error between the DCOP approach and the optimal solution found with a centralized approach as in [11]) for both scenarios. The experiments confirm that all the algorithms present an exponential growth in the time required to find a solution when the window

---

[2] We used the available implementations of DCOP algorithms by FRODO2 and JaCoP. Both from http://frodo2.sourceforge.net and http://www.jacop.eu.

size increases. For that reason, we limited our analysis to window sizes of 4 since above that window sizes all the algorithms required more than 24 h to find a solution (in fact, AFB and SBB were not able to find a solution with window sizes greater than 2 for both scenarios shown with a "−" mark in Tables 2 and 3).

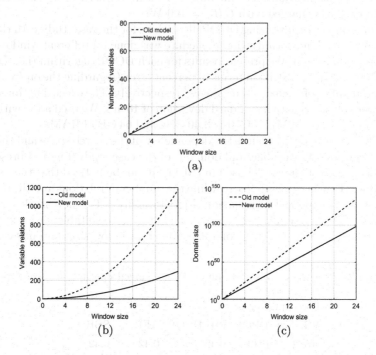

(a)

(b)   (c)

Fig. 4. Comparison of models. Window size and increase of: (a) Variables, (b) Relations, and (c) Domains.

Notice that in both scenarios the percent error improves along with the window size to the point of reaching the optimal value in scenario 1 with a window size of 3. However, a window size of 4 does not present an improvement of the percent error. In fact, the percent error increases for both scenarios. This behavior is explained in Fig. 5, in which we present the configurations found with window sizes of 3 and 4 for specific time slots (i.e., from time slot 17 to 24 for scenario E1 (Figs. 5a and b) and time slot 13 to 20 for scenario E2 (Figs. 5c and d)). For scenario 1, the battery status at time slot 17 is 200 W for both window sizes (i.e., 3 and 4). This means that in both horizons the battery can be discharged 200 W. Both horizons makes the same use of the battery in time slots 17 to 19 (using 120 W of the battery, letting the battery status in 80 W). However, since the horizon of window size 4 does not care about the next four time slots, it decides to use the battery in time slot 20 minimizing its cost for that time slot (a cost of 105 compared to 109.5 using window size 3) but leaving a battery status of 35 W for the next horizon of optimization. As consequence, the battery status is not sufficient to satisfy the demand of time slot 21 (which is the higher demand due to a high load in that specific time slot), given as a result a higher cost due to undelivered energy (remember that nondelivery energy has the greatest cost). That situation does not happen for a window size of 3, in which the battery status for time slots 20–21 is 80 W, and most of that energy can be used in time slot 21 leading to a complete satisfaction of the demand (time slot 21 of Fig. 5a). The same situation is presented in scenario 2 for window size 4, in which the use of the battery in time slot 16 (and the saves for that time slot) leads to a higher use of the fuel cell unit in time slot 17 and insufficient energy in time slot 18 giving as a result a higher cost overall.

Table 3. Percentage error and number of exchanged messages for scenario 2.

Percentage error				
Window	DPOP	MB-DPOP	AFB	SBB
size 1	3.1	3.1	3.1	3.1
size 2	2.9	2.9	3.1	2.9
size 3	2.2	2.2	-	-
size 4	2.9	2.9	-	-
Messages				
Window	DPOP	MB-DPOP	AFB	SBB
size 1	192	216	13269	10550
size 2	168	192	31647420	65315732
size 3	160	184	-	-
size 4	156	180	-	-

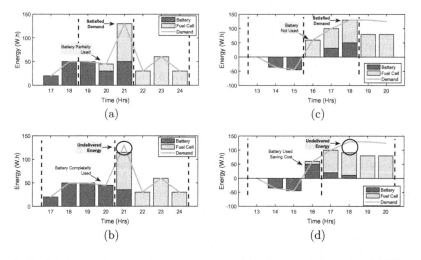

Fig. 5. Explaining the increase in percent error with a larger window size. (a) Dispatch with window size 3 for E1. (b) Dispatch with window size 3 for E2. (c) Dispatch with window size 4 for E1. (d) Dispatch with window size 4 for E2.

5 Conclusions

In this paper, we proposed an agent-based method for decentralized microgrid control. By doing that, the problem of scheduling on/off cycles can be treated as a DCOP, and different multi-agent algorithms can be used to find the solution. The results open research directions for the use of multi-agent systems in the long-term optimization of microgrids. For instance, it is clear the necessity of faster procedures of search, allowing agents to handle large window sizes and improving the quality of the solutions. Also, it has been shown that the quality of the solution when time horizons are used for the optimization procedure does not depend completely on the size, but in an adequate size depending on the scenario. Our method, with respect to approaches based on decentralised reinforcement learning, directly encode system-wide hard constraints (such as for example the Kirchhoff law) which are not easy to represent in a factored representation of the problem. Nonetheless, we believe that using decentralised learning approaches for scheduling on/off cycles of devices in the microgrid deserves further investigation, and is definitely an interesting direction for future work. On the other hand, heuristics and pre-processing strategies can be applied to reduce the configuration search space significantly, thus reducing the run time of the approach in the average case and open another interesting venue for future work.

References

1. Amato, C., Oliehoek, F.A., et al.: Scalable planning and learning for multiagent pomdps. In: AAAI, pp. 1995–2002 (2015)
2. Awasthi, S.K., Vij, S.R., Mukhopadhyay, D., Agrawal, A.J.: Multi-strategy based automated negotiation: BGP based architecture. In: International Conference on Computing, Communication and Automation (ICCCA), pp. 588–593. IEEE (2016)
3. Chaouachi, A., Kamel, R.M., Andoulsi, R., Nagasaka, K.: Multiobjective intelligent energy management for a microgrid. IEEE Trans. Industr. Electron. **60**(4), 1688–1699 (2013)
4. Fioretto, F., Pontelli, E., Yeoh, W.: Distributed constraint optimization problems and applications: a survey. J. Artif. Intell. Res. **61**, 623–698 (2018)
5. Fioretto, F., Yeoh, W., Pontelli, E.: A multiagent system approach to scheduling devices in smart homes. In: Conference on Autonomous Agents and MultiAgent Systems, pp. 981–989 (2017)
6. Fioretto, F., Yeoh, W., Pontelli, E., Ma, Y., Ranade, S.J.: A distributed constraint optimization (DCOP) approach to the economic dispatch with demand response. In: Conference on Autonomous Agents and MultiAgent Systems, pp. 999–1007 (2017)
7. Kofinas, P., Dounis, A., Vouros, G.: Fuzzy Q-learning for multi-agent decentralized energy management in microgrids. Appl. Energy **219**, 53–67 (2018)
8. Kok, J.R., Vlassis, N.: Collaborative multiagent reinforcement learning by payoff propagation. J. Mach. Learn. Res. **7**(Sep), 1789–1828 (2006)
9. Leite, A.R., Enembreck, F., Barthes, J.P.A.: Distributed constraint optimization problems: review and perspectives. Expert Syst. Appl. **41**(11), 5139–5157 (2014)

10. Lezama, F., Palominos, J., Rodríguez-González, A.Y., Farinelli, A., Munoz de Cote, E.: Agent-based microgrid scheduling: an ICT perspective. Mob. Netw. Appl. (2017). https://doi.org/10.1007/s11036-017-0894-x

11. Lezama, F., Palominos, J., Rodríguez-González, A.Y., Farinelli, A., de Cote, E.M.: Optimal scheduling of on/off cycles: a decentralized IoT-microgrid approach. In: Sucar, E., Mayora, O., Muñoz de Cote, E. (eds.) Applications for Future Internet. LNICST, vol. 179, pp. 79–90. Springer, Cham (2017). https://doi.org/10.1007/978-3-319-49622-1_10

12. Lezama, F., Soares, J., Hernandez-Leal, P., Kaisers, M., Pinto, T., Vale, Z.: Local energy markets: Paving the path towards fully transactive energy systems. IEEE Trans. Power Syst, **PP**, 1 (2018)

13. Logenthiran, T., Srinivasan, D., Khambadkone, A.M.: Multi-agent system for energy resource scheduling of integrated microgrids in a distributed system. Electr. Power Syst. Res. **81**(1), 138–148 (2011)

14. Miller, S., Ramchurn, S.D., Rogers, A.: Optimal decentralised dispatch of embedded generation in the smart grid. In: International Conference on Autonomous Agents and Multiagent Systems, vol. 1, pp. 281–288 (2012)

15. Morais, H., Kádár, P., Faria, P., Vale, Z.A., Khodr, H.: Optimal scheduling of a renewable micro-grid in an isolated load area using mixed-integer linear programming. Renewable Energy **35**(1), 151–156 (2010)

16. Nguyen, D.T., Yeoh, W., Lau, H.C., Zilberstein, S., Zhang, C.: Decentralized multi-agent reinforcement learning in average-reward dynamic DCOPs. In: AAAI Conference on Artificial Intelligence, pp. 1341–1342 (2014)

17. Petcu, A., Faltings, B.: Superstabilizing, fault-containing distributed combinatorial optimization. In: Proceedings of the National Conference on Artificial Intelligence, p. 449 (2005)

18. Pourpeighambar, B., Dehghan, M., Sabaei, M.: Non-cooperative reinforcement learning based routing in cognitive radio networks. Comput. Commun. **106**, 11–23 (2017)

19. Soares, J., Pinto, T., Lezama, F., Morais, H.: Survey on complex optimization and simulation for the new power systems paradigm. Complexity **2018**, 1–32 (2018)

20. Su, W., Wang, J., Roh, J.: Stochastic energy scheduling in microgrids with intermittent renewable energy resources. IEEE Trans. Smart Grid **5**(4), 1876–1883 (2014)

21. Teacy, W.L.,et al.: centralized Bayesian reinforcement learning for online agent collaboration. In: International Conference on Autonomous Agents and Multiagent Systems, vol. 1, pp. 417–424 (2012)

22. Vega, A., Santamaria, F., Rivas, E.: Modeling for home electric energy management: a review. Renew. Sustain. Energy Rev. **52**, 948–959 (2015)

A Fuzzy System Applied to Photovoltaic Generator Management Aimed to Reduce Electricity Bill

Marcos Sousa and Filipe Saraiva[✉]

Institute of Exacts and Natural Sciences, Federal University of Pará,
Belém, Pará, Brazil
marksoft@outlook.com, saraiva@ufpa.br

Abstract. Distributed energy production is a trend nowadays in order to reduce the dependence of fossil-based energy sources and the impact of projects like thermoelectrical and hydroelectrical power plants. In addition, distributed energy generators in the side of consumers can reduce the energy fee paid by them to power distribution companies. However, different approaches of decision-making to use (or not) the energy produced by distributed generators can reduce more or less the energy fee. This paper presents a fuzzy system to make decision about when and how much energy will be used by consumers from a photovoltaic generator in a scenario where the generator has a coupled storage energy system and the price of energy sold by distribution company has different values along the day. The proposal uses real datasets for production and energy consumption. The approach is also compared to a non-fuzzy system representing the common way as this technology is currently deployed in real world scenarios. The comparison shows the proposed approach reduces in general 10% the amount of energy fee for the consumer when compared with the common deployed way.

Keywords: Distributed generation · Fuzzy system · Reduction electricity bill

1 Introduction

Distributed generation (DG) is a methodology for energy generation different from the currently most utilized power plants. In power plants scenario, there are big plants localized in far geographic regions producing large amounts of energy and injecting it in the transmission systems. The main energy sources utilized are the hydroelectric, thermoelectric, nuclear, and big farms of photovoltaic and eolic energy [17].

In DG scenario, the generators are small units plugged directly in the consumers load and/or the distribution systems. For this case it is most common the use of renewable sources like photovoltaic energy [6,7].

© Springer Nature Switzerland AG 2019
P. Moura Oliveira et al. (Eds.): EPIA 2019, LNAI 11804, pp. 450–461, 2019.
https://doi.org/10.1007/978-3-030-30241-2_38

DG reduces the need for high-impact projects like new power plants, reduces the use of fossil-based energy sources for electric energy production, improves some characteristics of distribution systems like voltage regulation, and more. Currently, DG is the main technology for the deployment of a more "clean" future for energy distribution in the cities [9].

In addition, the use of DG by consumers reduces the energy bill paid to power distribution companies. When part of the energy demand from the consumer is supplied by a DG device, the energy consumption from the distribution company is reduced, implying in the reduction of the energy bill.

Despite this direct consequence, it is not clear which strategies could be used in order to maximize the reduction of the energy consumed from the distribution companies – or, in other words, how to maximize the use of the DG in order to minimize the energy bill.

There are some studies related to this set of applications available in the literature utilizing several techniques. In [12], machine learning algorithms are applied to forecast the future demand and make decision about the energy use; [11] uses a mixed integer linear programming approach while [10] utilizes a multi-objective version of the technique. [8] utilizes a neural network to design an energy storage system controller for residential photovoltaic generators, and [2] applied fuzzy-system to this same problem. A survey about fuzzy logic applications to renewable energy systems can be find in [18].

This paper proposes a fuzzy system to a specific scenario of DG. For the case, the simulation is applied in a scenario where there are 3 different values for the energy sold by the company, varying throughout the day. It simulates the time intervals where the energy price is high or low, according to the peak of power. This scenery is called in Brazil the "white tariff" [1].

This way, the system must to make decision about when it is more interesting to use or not the energy produced by the distributed generator. In order to allow the decision to postpone the use of the energy produced, the generator has a battery storage coupled.

The simulations were performed using 2 real-world and publicly available datasets, one with power consumption and the other containing photovoltaic energy production. Because the data of energy production is a photovoltaic energy source, the generator simulated is therefore a photovoltaic generator. The measurements utilized for both correspond to one whole year.

The approach was compared to a way as the DG is commonly deployed these days. It is common to generators store the energy in the battery and start to use only in the time-intervals when the price is more expensive. The proposed approach improves the use of the battery storage, reducing the energy consumption from the distribution company and, consequently, the energy bill paid.

The paper is structured as follow. Section 2 describes in more details the simulated scenario. Section 3 describes the proposed fuzzy system, the fuzzy rules, the inputs and outputs. Section 4 discusses the datasets utilized, presents the simulations performed and the results obtained. Finally, Sect. 5 points the conclusions and some future works to extend the studies presented.

2   Application Scenario

Power distribution companies must to manage a characteristic of the energy distribution called peak demand. Peak demand is a specific time interval when the demand for energy from the consumers is higher [17].

In general, it is mandatory for the companies supply consumers with all the electricity requested. Therefore, energy distribution industries must to provide some additional infrastructure in order to supply that high demand just for that small time interval.

There are some ways to reduce the peak demand from the consumers, among that it is possible to charge different values for the electricity along the day, increasing the value when the hours of peak demand is close. It benefits consumers using energy in hours different of the peak, because the electricity is cheaper [13].

That is the background context for the study presented in this paper. The authors are using real electricity consumption fees values provided by a power distribution company called CELPA, from Belém do Pará – a Brazilian city.

CELPA has 3 different fees for electricity distributed in 5 different time intervals. From 0:00 h to 17:29 h and from 22:30 to 23:59 the price by kWh is 0.48 BRL – the most cheap value. From 17:30 to 18:29 and from 21:30 to 22:29, the cost is 0.79 BRL by kWh – it is an intermediary cost. Finally, from 18:30 to 21:29, the price is the most expensive one, 1.23 BRL. This last interval is the peak demand time interval. Figure 1 presents graphically these different prices for the energy bill consumed.

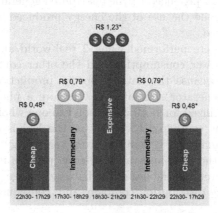

Fig. 1. Prices for each time interval

This scenario brings some problems to consumers because the peak demand time interval is the time interval when the demand is higher – it happens because the consumers need to use electricity in that time. A way to reduce the dependency of energy during the peak demand time interval is combining distributed generators with energy storage devices.

A distributed generator can produce energy to supply the consumer load. However, in a scenario where the cost of electricity in peak demand is more expensive, it is interesting if the consumer could use the energy produced when the energy price from the distribution company is higher.

For some kinds of consumers in some countries, mainly the residential ones, the peak demand time interval is like that utilized by CELPA, in the end of afternoon and in the beginning of the night. Commonly, that time is related to people coming back to home after a work day. This time is also when the photovoltaic energy production is low, because the Sun is going away.

In order to use photovoltaic energy produced during the mornings in the peak demand time interval, the generator must be connected to an energy storage device – a battery. This way, the energy can be utilized when the price from the companies is more expensive, reducing the bill for consumers.

This system architecture described here – a distributed photovoltaic generator plugged to consumer load and to a battery – is a common way how DG companies deploy this kind of system to their customers. For instance, the company EDP sells a system [5] like the presented here.

However, that way how to use energy produced by the DG is not necessarily the best way. This paper proposes an alternative make decision technology based in fuzzy systems to make a better use of the battery, reducing the electricity bill. Next section will describe the proposed approach.

3   Fuzzy System Proposal

The fuzzy system proposal is, in fact, 3 different fuzzy systems, one for each electricity price. The idea behind this approach is allow the system to behave according to the different configurations of the scenario.

Based on this architecture, there is an "input" related to the time to select which fuzzy system will be used.

About the fuzzy systems itself, there are 2 inputs, one named *liquid energy* (E_l) and the other called *State-of-Charge* (SoC).

E_l is the difference between the energy produced by the distributed generator (E_g) and the energy consumed by the consumer load (E_c). If E_l is positive, there is more production than consumption, so that energy can be sent to the battery or to the grid. Case E_l is negative, the production is not enough to supply the electricity demand, so the consumer must to use this energy difference from the battery or from the grid.

SoC is the level of electricity charge stored in the battery. When E_l is positive, it is possible to recharge the battery using that excess of electricity produced. Case E_l is negative, the battery can be used to supply the energy demand.

The output of the fuzzy systems is a decision about if the battery will be charged or discharged. Called E_b, if this variable is positive so the energy will be inserted in the storage device and, case negative, the battery will be used by the consumer load.

Each input has 5 linguistics variables. In the system proposed, those variables has the same label for both inputs. The numeric interval values for each one was created based on the data sets utilized for the simulations.

Figure 2 presents the photovoltaic residential installation architecture utilized in this paper and some of the variables described above.

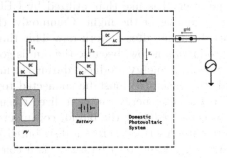

Fig. 2. Residential photovoltaic installation architecture

The linguistic variables for E_l input is as presented in Table 1. Figure 3 presents the pertinence functions to this same variable.

Table 1. Linguistic variables for E_l

Linguistic variable	Acronym	Explanation
Positive big	PB	E_g is very high than E_c
Positive small	PS	E_g is small high than E_c
Zero	ZE	E_g and E_c are equivalents
Negative small	NS	E_g is a bit low than E_c
Negative big	NB	E_g is very low than E_c

For SoC input, the linguistic variables are described in Table 2 and the pertinence functions are presented in Fig. 4:

Finally, for the output E_b related to the energy exchanged with the energy storage device, the linguistics variables are described in Table 3 and the pertinence functions are presented in Fig. 5.

The fuzzy decision is made based on the hour of day, the E_l, and the SoC. If the hour of day is inside the time interval of less expensive electricity cost, the system is more prone to store energy in the battery, depending the SoC. For the intermediate electricity cost, the related fuzzy system uses battery moderately.

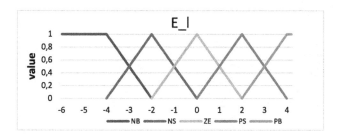

Fig. 3. Pertinence rules for E_l

Table 2. Linguistic variables for SoC

Linguistic variable	Acronym	Explanation
Positive big	PB	Battery is fully charged
Positive small	PS	Around 75% of full charge
Zero	ZE	Close to 50% of the full charge
Negative small	NS	Close to 25% of full charge
Negative big	NB	Battery is almost discharged

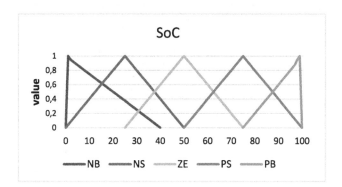

Fig. 4. Pertinence rules for SoC

Table 3. Linguistic variables for E_b

Linguistic variable	Acronym	Explanation
Positive big	PB	Big recharging
Positive small	PS	Small recharging
Zero	ZE	Battery without changes
Negative small	NS	Small discharging
Negative big	NB	Big discharging

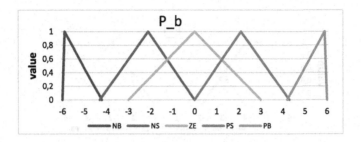

Fig. 5. Pertinence rules for E_b

When the electricity cost is expensive, the system try to use as much as possible the battery charge.

The inference method utilized was Mandami, while the defuzzyfication was calculated by gravity center. The fuzzy rules are presented in tables below: Table 4 presents the rules for the fuzzy system utilized during the most cheap time interval; Table 5 show the rules for the time interval when the price is intermediate; and Table 6 contains the rules for the time interval with the most expensive price.

Table 4. Fuzzy system for the most cheap time interval

E_b		SoC				
		PB	PS	ZE	NS	NB
E_l	PB	ZE	PS	PS	PB	PB
	PS	ZE	PS	PB	PS	PS
	ZE	ZE	ZE	ZE	ZE	ZE
	NS	NB	NS	ZE	ZE	ZE
	NB	NB	NS	ZE	ZE	ZE

Next section will describe the simulations performed, the comparisons with the common approach, and the results obtained.

Table 5. Fuzzy system for the intermediate time interval

E_b		SoC				
		PB	PS	ZE	NS	NB
E_l	PB	ZE	PS	PS	PB	PB
	PS	ZE	PS	PB	PS	PS
	ZE	ZE	ZE	ZE	ZE	ZE
	NS	NB	NB	NS	ZE	ZE
	NB	NB	NB	NS	ZE	ZE

Table 6. Fuzzy system for the most expensive time interval

E_b		SoC				
		PB	PS	ZE	NS	NB
E_l	PB	ZE	PS	PS	PB	PB
	PS	ZE	PS	PS	PS	PS
	ZE	ZE	ZE	ZE	ZE	ZE
	NS	NB	NB	NB	ZE	ZE
	NB	NB	NB	NB	ZE	ZE

4 Computational Simulations and Results

4.1 Simulations Details

For the simulations were used real world datasets of photovoltaic production and residential consumption available by IEEE PES Intelligent System Applications Subcommittee – Task Force on Open Data Sets [14].

The dataset of residential consumption contains measurements from December 2011 to March 2013, in intervals of 15 min. The photovoltaic production data set consists of measurements from January 2013 to December 2013 in intervals of 5 min [15,16]. All these data were measured in locations from Porto, Portugal.

In order to synchronize the data, the simulation utilized the period from January 2013 to December 2013, grouping those in intervals of 15 min.

The photovoltaic panel measured has 0.2 kW of power installed. Because it is very low to the consumption data in analysis, the photovoltaic energy production was multiplied by 13, resulting in a 2.6 kW power installed. It is like if the consumer had 13 photovoltaic panels installed in his residence.

The battery storage has capacity for 70 kWh and the maximum energy flow for charging or discharging allowed is 6 kWh.

To ensure a long life for the battery, power discharging is limited to 25% of the full capacity. In other words, the battery charge can not be less than 17.5 kWh.

In order to do comparisons, two additional simulations of different approaches were performed against the same datasets. These approaches are one without photovoltaic generation – just to verify how much will be the electricity bill for the time in analysis – and other where the battery is utilized only during the intermediate and the most expensive time intervals – like the current commercial products do.

The calculus of electricity bill is made by the sum of the energy consumed in some time interval multiplied by the electricity cost in that time. Let E_t be the energy consumed in the time t and C_t the cost of energy in the time t, the electricity bill B is calculated by Eq. 1:

$$B = \sum_{t}^{T} E_t C_t \tag{1}$$

Where T is the time interval in analysis – for this simulation, the whole year of 2013.

As pointed before, the related energy cost to different time intervals is utilized according to Table 7.

Table 7. Energy costs

Time interval	Costs (BRL)
00:00–17:29	0.48
17:30–18:29	0.79
18:30–21:29	1.23
21:30–22:29	0.79
22:30–23:59	0.48

From 0:00 h to 17:29 h and from 22:30 to 23:59 the price by kWh is 0.48 BRL – the most cheap value. From 17:30 to 18:29 and from 21:30 to 22:29, the cost is 0.79 BRL by kWh – it is an intermediary cost. Finally, from 18:30 to 21:29, the price is the most expensive one, 1.23 BRL. This last interval is the peak demand time interval.

The programming language utilized for the simulations was Java, using the jFuzzyLogic [3,4] library to develop the fuzzy systems. The simulations were performed in a Intel i5 computer running Linux.

4.2   Simulations Results and Discussion

Firstly, the simulation without photovoltaic generation consumed 6767.72 kW from the power distribution company. In terms of costs, it was 4390.00 BRL.

For the system using distributed generator but without fuzzy decision, the energy consumed from the company was 3652.98 kW, costing 2079.88 BRL for the whole year. This value is 53.98% of the house consumption without DG.

For the fuzzy system, the energy consumed from the grid was 2937.09 kW, and the related cost was 1805.91 BRL. This approach reduced the consumption from the grid to just 43.4% of the total consumed energy, and when compared to the system with DG but without fuzzy decision making deployed, it improved in 13.17% in terms of cost.

Table 8 summarizes the numeric difference between the compared approaches.

The fuzzy system proposed reduces the energy bill because it uses the battery in a more smart way. The battery is used more when the energy price is high,

Table 8. Comparison and results for the approaches simulated

	Without DG	DG without Fuzzy	DG with Fuzzy
Grid consumption	6767.72	3652.98	2937.09
Grid consumption (%)	100%	53.98%	43.4%
Energy bill (BRL)	4390.00	2079.88	1805.91

but it is also used when the battery is full (or close to full) and the energy price is low. The not-fuzzy approach starts the use of the battery only when the time interval for intermediate price starts.

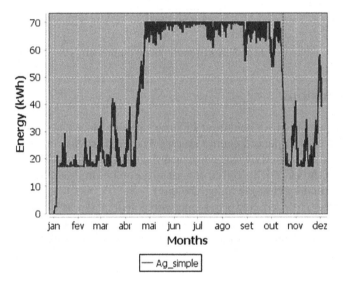

Fig. 6. SoC for the approach without fuzzy

The paper presents some figures with these evaluations in a graphical way. Figure 6 presents the SoC for the approach without fuzzy along the year simulated. It is possible to see the battery is charged in May and after that the consumption from it is small until November. It shows the battery could be used more frequently in the months from May to October in order to reduce the electricity bill.

Figure 7 presents the SoC for the fuzzy approach. Now, the battery is utilized more frequently during all the year. This use impacts positively in the electricity bill, reducing the total amount of money spent for the year.

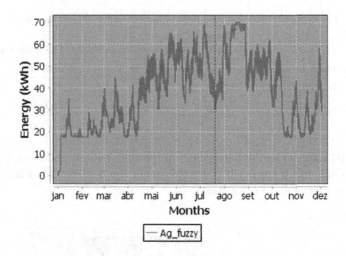

Fig. 7. SoC for the fuzzy approach

5 Conclusions

This paper presented a simulation of fuzzy making decision system embedded in a set of photovoltaic and energy storage system, installed in a residence. The main question addressed by this paper was if a more smart way to use the battery could reduce the electricity bill in the scenario of "white tariff" (when the price of electricity energy changes along the day).

The dataset utilized comprises one whole year and was obtained from real measurements, available in the literature. In order to compare the proposal, were simulated a common photovoltaic+energy storage system without intelligent algorithm (like utilized currently in real world scenario) and a system without DG. The fuzzy proposal reduced the electricity bill more than the proposal without intelligent algorithm, obtaining 13.7% of reduction compared to that proposal.

The results are interesting and open new directions for research in this topic. It is possible to analyze if there is other fuzzy variable configuration to improve the result obtained, maybe optimizing that through a metaheuristic method. Comparisons with other methods can be interesting too, like neural networks.

References

1. ANEEL: Resolução normativa n. 414 (2010)
2. Arcos-Aviles, D., Pascual, J., Marroyo, L., Sanchis, P., Guinjoan, F.: Fuzzy logic-based energy management system design for residential grid-connected microgrids. IEEE Trans. Smart Grid **9**(2), 530–543 (2018)
3. Cingolani, P., Alcala-Fdez, J.: jFuzzyLogic: a robust and flexible fuzzy-logic inference system language implementation. In: 2012 IEEE International Conference on Fuzzy Systems, pp. 1–8. IEEE (2012)

 4. Cingolani, P., Alcalá-Fdez, J.: jFuzzyLogic: a java library to design fuzzy logic controllers according to the standard for fuzzy control programming. Int. J. Comput. Intell. Syst. **6**(sup1), 61–75 (2013)
 5. EDP: Produza e rentabilize energia solar com as baterias solares (2019). https://www.edp.pt/particulares/servicos/baterias/
 6. El-Khattam, W., Salama, M.M.: Distributed generation technologies, definitions and benefits. Electr. Power Syst. Res. **71**(2), 119–128 (2004)
 7. Guerrero, J.M., et al.: Distributed generation: toward a new energy paradigm. IEEE Industr. Electron. Mag. **4**(1), 52–64 (2010)
 8. Henri, G., Lu, N., Carrejo, C.: Design of a novel mode-based energy storage controller for residential PV systems. In: 2017 IEEE PES Innovative Smart Grid Technologies Conference Europe (ISGT-Europe), pp. 1–6. IEEE (2017)
 9. Ipakchi, A., Albuyeh, F.: Grid of the future. IEEE Power Energy Mag. **7**(2), 52–62 (2009)
10. Lokeshgupta, B., Sivasubramani, S.: Multi-objective home energy management with battery energy storage systems. Sustain. Cities Soc. **47**, 101458 (2019)
11. Lopez-Salamanca, H.L., Arruda, L.R., Magatão, L., Rico, J.E.N.: Using a MILP model for battery bank operation in the "white tariff" Brazilian context. In: 2014 5th International Renewable Energy Congress (IREC), pp. 1–6. IEEE (2014)
12. Mishra, A., Irwin, D., Shenoy, P., Kurose, J., Zhu, T.: Smartcharge: cutting the electricity bill in smart homes with energy storage. In: Proceedings of the 3rd International Conference on Future Energy Systems: Where Energy, Computing and Communication Meet, e-Energy 2012, pp. 29:1–29:10. ACM, New York, NY, USA (2012). https://doi.org/10.1145/2208828.2208857, http://doi.acm.org/10.1145/2208828.2208857
13. Newsham, G.R., Bowker, B.G.: The effect of utility time-varying pricing and load control strategies on residential summer peak electricity use: a review. Energy policy **38**(7), 3289–3296 (2010)
14. I.P.I.S.C.T.F on Open Data Sets: Open data sets (2019). http://sites.ieee.org/pes-iss/data-sets/
15. Ramos, S., Pinto, S., Santana, J.A.: Development of a solar cell model using PSCAD. In: 2nd International of Solar Power into Power Systems (2012)
16. Ramos, S., Silva, M., Fernandes, F., Vale, Z.: Modelling real solar cell using PSCAD/MATLAB. In: 2nd International of Solar Power into Power Systems (SIW 2012) (2012)
17. Schlabbach, J., Rofalski, K.H.: Power System Engineering: Planning, Design, and Operation of Power Systems and Equipment. Wiley, Chichester (2014)
18. Suganthi, L., Iniyan, S., Samuel, A.A.: Applications of fuzzy logic in renewable energy systems - a review. Renew. Sustain. Energy Rev. **48**, 585–607 (2015)

Demonstration of an Energy Consumption Forecasting System for Energy Management in Buildings

Aria Jozi[1,2], Daniel Ramos[2], Luis Gomes[1,2], Pedro Faria[1,2(✉)], Tiago Pinto[1,2], and Zita Vale[2]

[1] GECAD – Research Group on Intelligent Engineering and Computing for Advanced Innovation and Development, Porto, Portugal
[2] Institute of Engineering, Polytechnic of Porto (ISEP/IPP), Porto, Portugal
{arjoz, 1150463, log, pnf, tcp, zav}@isep.ipp.pt

Abstract. Due to the increment of the energy consumption and dependency of the nowadays lifestyle to the electrical appliances, the essential role of an energy management system in the buildings is realized more than ever. With this motivation, predicting energy consumption is very relevant to support the energy management in buildings. In this paper, the use of an energy management system supported by forecasting models applied to energy consumption prediction is demonstrated. The real-time automatic forecasting system is running separately but integrated with the existing SCADA system. Nine different forecasting approaches to obtain the most reliable estimated energy consumption of the building during the following hours are implemented.

Keywords: Energy consumption · Energy management system · Forecast

1 Introduction

In the past decades, the dominant lifestyle leads to be more dependent on the energy consuming appliances, and this amount of energy consumption requires more complex and attentive management. Industry, transportation, and buildings are the three main economic sectors with the highest amount of energy [1]. Meanwhile, the highest share belongs to the buildings by 40% of the total energy consumption is consumed in European Union countries and 44% in the USA [2]. This way the energy management in the building becomes one of the most critical roles for the energy systems.

This paper presents the real implementation of a SCADA system in the GECAD facilities. The main functionality of this system is to monitor and manage the energy consumption and generation of the building and control the electrical appliances of the building to have better management of the consumption. A Real-time automatic energy consumption forecasting model is proposed in this work to be added to the SCADA system to take advantage of the influence of a trustable forecasted consumption value on the energy management of the building. This model uses two programming languages namely as R and Python, to implement Five forecasting methods, which are,

© Springer Nature Switzerland AG 2019
P. Moura Oliveira et al. (Eds.): EPIA 2019, LNAI 11804, pp. 462–468, 2019.
https://doi.org/10.1007/978-3-030-30241-2_39

Artificial Neural Network (ANN) [3], Support Vector Regression (SVR) [4], Random Forest (RF) [5], Hybrid Neural Fuzzy Inference System (HyFIS) [6] and Wang and Mendel model (WM) [6]. The forecasting process uses these five methods and based on different available variables, and input data generates nine different hour-ahead forecasted energy consumption values for every hour. The SCADA system, building structure, the implementation of the forecasting model and the Real-time monitored results of the system can be found in the following sections.

2 SCADA Model Implementation

The SCADA system has been implemented in the building N of the GECAD research center facilities, located in Porto, Portugal (see Fig. 1).

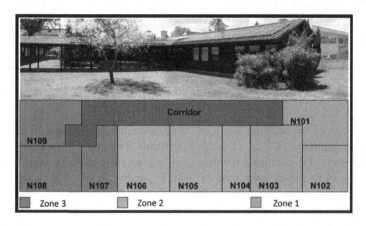

Fig. 1. Office building plane and associated zones

This building includes nine office rooms, namely as N101, N102, ..., N109, plus a corridor. Each one of these rooms contains the typical office equipment, such as computers, Air-condition systems, and lights systems. Also, one of these rooms (N104) is a server room where all the servers of the building are located. This way, since it contains several critical types of equipment, the SCADA system considers a specific consideration for this room. This building is equipped with Programmable Logic Controllers (PLCs), several energy meters, different types of sensors, and one central web-based touch screen console to monitor data and control the loads. As can be seen in Fig. 1, the nine office rooms of this building are divided into three zones [7].

The SCADA system has a set of PLCs, energy meters, sensors, and a central PLC that the other distributed PLCs are connected to this one as the main component. A TCP/IP protocol makes the information exchange between the components of this system. The primary function of this system is to present the real-time information of the building (energy consumption, temperature, humidity, CO_2, generation, etc.) through a monitoring panel and control these variables. A touch screen console is available in building to monitor and control the data. As can be seen in Fig. 2 all of the devices of the building are connected to the SCADA system by a different type of communication protocols and Digital/Analog inputs.

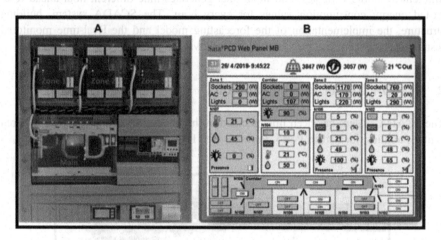

Fig. 2. A: SCADA control panel, B: Real-time data monitoring of SCADA

Every zone of the building has a set of sensors that are mounted to measure the temperature, humidity, CO2, air quality (Volatile Organic Compounds – VOC), presence sensor, and illumination intensity of the rooms. All these sensors are connected to the PLC in their own zone by 0–10 V Analog Input.

The electricity network of the building is based on three phases. Phase 1 feeds sockets of the building, Phase 2 supplies the ACs, and Phase 3 feeds the lighting system. The building has six energy meters that are responsible for measures the consumption and generation of the building. All of these energy meters follow serial communication with MODBUS RS485 protocol. Energy meter #1 to #3 measures the consumption of 3 zones and transmit the data to the distributed PLC of each zone, energy meter #4 measures corridor consumption, meter #5 measures the total consumption of the building, and energy meter #6 measures total generation of the PV system.

3 Forecasting System

According to the importance of having a trustable forecasting result in the energy management systems and its essential influence on the performance of this system, this section presents a forecasting model which has been added to this SCADA system in order to improve the performance and functionalities of this system. This model includes the implementation of 5 different forecasting methods based on two programming languages. The forecasting methods are ANN, SVM, RF, HyFIS, and WM.

The ANNs are based on a model with neurons and weights linked together. More specifically, these methods work with a multilayer model that starts on an input layer, generating the hidden layers based on the inputs, until the obtaining of the output layer [3]. SVM's are a field of supervised machine learning methods and are one of the most known methods in the area of forecasting. The first running kernel of SVM was created by Vapnik in 1963, and the statistical learning theory was implemented further in 1979. Finally, the current form of the SVM approach was presented in 1992, with a paper at the COLT conference [4]. The Random Forest is supported by the creation of a forest containing decision trees supported with rules designed to train the model. The set of decisions will provide the most accurate outcome possible [5]. The HyFIS model is a combination of neuronal networks and fuzzy rule-based systems [8]. WM is also one of the Fuzzy rule-based methods which are known as a simple structured method with the excellent performance [6].

The implementation of this model takes advantage of using two programming languages to implement these forecasting methods. In this model, ANN, SVM, and RF are developed in Python with the TensorFlow library support. Also, this implementation uses R programing language to develop SVM, HyFIS and WM methods. The SVM is implemented in both languages in order to have a better comparison between the performances.

The main objective of this forecasting model is to predict the hour-ahead energy consumption of the building using different methods and different input data. This way, the implemented methods in Python will be executed in every hour and 15 min to predict the energy consumption during the next hour by the time interval of 20 min. As an example, these methods at 12:15 will be executed to predict the energy consumption value of 13:00 to 14:20, 13:20 to 13:40 and 13:40 to 14:00. The combination of the input data for these methods can be seen in Table 1.

Table 1. Details of the forecasting methods

	Language	Input data	Running time	Target time
ANN	Python	Day of week, Consumption of past hour, internal temperature, external temperature	(N−1):15	N:00–N:20
SVM1				N:20–N:40
RF				N:40–(N + 1):00
SVM2	R	Type of the day (Week or Weekend), Peak hour, Consumption of 3 past hours	(N−1):55	N:00–(N + 1):00
HyFIS1				
WM1				
SVM3		Type of the day (Week of weekend), Peak hours, Consumption of past 3 h, external temperature		
HyFIS2				
WM2				

The implemented methods in R are trained at every hour and 55 min to predict the average energy consumption of the next hour. For example, at 12:55 these methods are trained and used to predict the average consumption value from 13:00 to 14:00. Moreover, for every hour these methods are trained twice, with different input train data which means that every implemented method in R for every hour present two different results. The input data and the difference between these data sets are in Table 1.

At every expectation time the system extracts the required data from the main SQL data server of the building and creates the forecasting input data tables to run the algorithms. The recorded data in this database have different time intervals. However, in each case of forecasting the system needs to aggregate the revised data into intended time intervals. This time interval is related to the purpose of the prediction. In case of hour ahead forecasting, the time interval is 60 min and in the cases of 20 min ahead forecasting the data will be aggregated to time interval of 20 min to be used in training process of the methods.

As has been described in Table 1, in this forecasting system, nine values are predicted for the hour-ahead total energy consumption of the building. These different values based on their accuracy, running time and the target time interval, can be used in different purposes. The external temperature has been used in the train data sets to take advantage of the effect of this variable on the usage of the air conditioning system which results as a direct influence on the total consumption value of the building. However, in different situations and different times of the year, the performance of these methods with these input data can be altered, and that is the main reason why this model uses these nine strategies and records all the results.

A Java-based application has been developed in order to calculate the Mean Absolute Percentage Error (MAPE) of the forecasted results. This application at the end of every hour, when the real consumption value of the past hour is available, receives the areal data as well as the forecasted value and calculates the MAPE error of each method.

Figure 3 presents the forecasting errors of these strategies during the April of 2019.

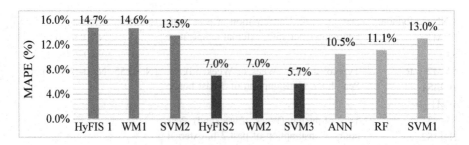

Fig. 3. Average MAPE errors during April of 2019

As one can see in Fig. 3, the implemented methods in R presents the most trustable performance while the value of the external temperature has been used in the input data. The best average MAPE during this month belongs to SVM3 by the average error of 5.67%. To store the results of this forecasting system, a database has been designed using PostgreSQL. This database includes a separated table for the results of every one of these nine forecasting strategies as well as a separated table for the errors of each one. The forecasted values and the errors of each method can be monitored in the real-time energy management system of the building (see Fig. 4). This system is accessible for all of the users of the building.

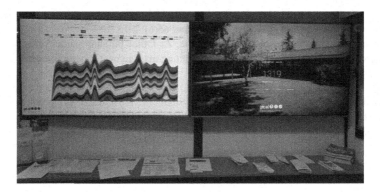

Fig. 4. Realtime energy management system of the building

4 Conclusions

This paper proposes an automatic energy consumption forecasting model for the SCADA system of building N of GECAD facilities located in Porto, Portugal. The model includes the implementation of 5 forecasting algorithms using two programming languages and generates nine hour-ahead different forecasted consumption values for every hour. The results present acceptable errors and are trustable enough to be used for future works such as optimization. The system stores all the results in a database as well as the MAPE error of each forecasted value. These results are accessible for the user through the real-time energy management system of the building.

Acknowledgments. The present work was done and funded in the scope of the following projects: European Union's Horizon 2020 project DOMINOES (grant agreement No 771066), COLORS Project PTDC/EEI-EEE/28967/2017 and UID/EEA/00760/2019 funded by FEDER Funds through COMPETE program and by National Funds through FCT.

References

1. Khosravani, H., Castilla, M., Berenguel, M., Ruano, A., Ferreira, P.: A comparison of energy consumption prediction models based on neural networks of a bioclimatic building. Energies **9**(1), 57 (2016)
2. Jozi, A., Pinto, T., Praça, I., Vale, Z.: Decision support application for energy consumption forecasting. Appl. Sci. **9**(4), 699 (2019)

3. Schaefer, A.M., Udluft, S., Zimmermann, H.-G.: A recurrent control neural network for data efficient reinforcement learning. In: 2007 IEEE International Symposium on Approximate Dynamic Programming and Reinforcement Learning, pp. 151–157 (2007)
4. Boser, B.E., Guyon, I.M., Vapnik, V.N.: A training algorithm for optimal margin classifiers. In: Proceedings of the fifth Annual Workshop on Computational Learning theory - COLT 1992, pp. 144–152 (1992)
5. Biau, G.: Analysis of a Random Forests Model (2010)
6. Riza, L.S., Bergmeir, C., Herrera, F., Benítez, J.M.: frbs: fuzzy rule-based systems for classification and regression in R. J. Stat. Softw. **65**(6) 2015
7. Khorram, M., Abrishambaf, O., Faria, P., Vale, Z.: Office building participation in demand response programs supported by intelligent lighting management. Energy Informatics **1**(1), 9 (2018)
8. Jozi, A., Pinto, T., Praca, I., Silva, F., Teixeira, B., Vale, Z.: Energy consumption forecasting based on Hybrid Neural Fuzzy Inference System. In: 2016 IEEE Symposium Series on Computational Intelligence (SSCI), pp. 1–5 (2016)

Smart Home Appliances Usage Recommendation Using Multi-objective Optimization

Allan Feitosa[✉], Henrique Lacerda, and Abel Silva-Filho

Universidade Federal de Penambuco, Recife, PE, Brazil
{arsf,hfl,agsf}@cin.ufpe.br
http://www.ufpe.br

Abstract. The household appliances are becoming each time more connected to the others and to the internet. Beyond the necessity of improving and increasing the clean and renewable power sources, there is the urge for using the available power sources in more efficient manners. When the concepts of Internet of Things and Computational Intelligence converge, it is enabled a whole field of technologies aiming Smart Home functionality as dweller's comfort, tasks automation and energy saving. This work proposes a Smart Home appliances usage recommendation concept, based on multi-objective optimization to generate balanced recommendations regarding energy usage reduction and dweller's comfort. Those recommendations are also segmented according to the comfort priority of the dwellers in the room. In order to evaluate the priorities, it was implemented a Markov Chain to generate new dweller's presence data from the data set. It was also studied the potential of power saving of the Binary Multi Objective Particle Swarm Optimization over contexts extracted from the data. Results showed that the recommendations have an average power saving potential of 9,76% as well as the possibility of deliver recommendations with different comfort levels according to the priority of the dwellers present in the room.

Keywords: Binary Particle Swarm Optimization ·
Energy usage profiles · Energy saving · Multi objective optimization ·
Recommendation · Smart Home · Smart Home dweller comfort

1 Introduction

The household appliances are becoming each time more connected to the others and to the internet. Among several advantages of that, there are the capacity of obtaining information about how the dweller interacts with the appliances, as weel as the possibility of managing them using computational techniques on behalf of power saving and comfort experience. There is an increasing concern about the emissions of greenhouse gases. In 2017, 56.1% of the whole worlds electricity production was made by the usage of fossil fuel [1].

© Springer Nature Switzerland AG 2019
P. Moura Oliveira et al. (Eds.): EPIA 2019, LNAI 11804, pp. 469–481, 2019.
https://doi.org/10.1007/978-3-030-30241-2_40

Beyond the necessity of improving and increasing clean and renewable power sources, there is the urge for using the available power sources in more efficient manners. The Smart Homes are ubiquitous systems based on Internet of Things. They are able to manage household appliances by using digital smart meters connected to their loads. Hence, those systems make the connection necessary for the information exchanging among the household appliances and computational systems.

When the concepts of Internet of Things and Computational Intelligence converge, it is enabled a whole field of technologies aiming Smart Home functionality, as dweller's comfort, tasks automation and energy saving. Lying the subject of this work at the later one.

Over the last two decades, several works have addressed the field of Smart Home energy saving. Some have performed computationally onerous techniques like brute force data mining and others approaches for recommending actions to the dwellers; others have only intended to predict the dweller's action to automate the future actions; and others have not been addressing the dilemma between power consumption reduction and dweller comfort.

Therefore, this work proposes a Smart Home appliances usage recommendation concept, based on multi-objective optimization to generate recommendations balanced regarding energy usage reduction and dweller's comfort. Those recommendations are also segmented according to the comfort priority of the dwellers in the room.

2   Related Works

In order to generate power saving recommendations for smart home dwellers, [2] described a pattern mining solution named Window Sliding with De-Duplication (WSDD). Their proposal worked in two basic steps, mining patterns of usage for less power consumption from the dweller's past iterations with the appliances, and recommending those mined patterns when convenient. According to their experiments, the WSDD has reached 10% of accepted recommendations. However, the pattern mining process was computationally onerous due to the brute force approach performed at the first step.

Lacerda et al. [3], have developed a multi objective optimization based recommendation system. Their proposal worked based on the dweller's past interaction with the system and the modeling of the dweller's comfort versus energy saving dilemma as a multi-objective optimization problem. The solution group (Pareto Front) returned from the algorithm was a set of recommendations for appliances weekly usage times. Their modeling of solution candidates was high dimensional, once each solution candidate has 86400 dimensions, representing the seconds of a day.

In [4], it was proposed a system based on machine learning to automate actions. The proposal was composed of a Case Based Reasoning and an Artificial Neural Network. When a new context representing the status of the appliances was inputted to the system, the Neural Network, based on the previous accepted suggestions and the dweller's past iteration with the appliances, suggested a set of actions (i.e. turn on/off appliances). However, their system focused more on the dweller's comfort than power saving properly.

The author of [5] have proposed an appliances coordination system based on rescheduling of usage. According to their approach, when a dweller tried to turn an appliance on, if the energy prices were elevated and there was no alternative cheaper power sources, the system rescheduled the usage of the appliance to a more efficient time, out of the peak hours. Although the potential of energy saving, the system does not provide means to address the dweller's comfort.

Thus, the proposed concept of residential appliances usage recommendation approaches the status of the appliances in real time, by implementing a fast and low dimensional multi-objective technique to find balanced solutions between dweller's comfort and energy saving.

3   Binary Multi Objective Optimization

The recommender system proposed is based on a binary version of multi objective particle swarm optimization (BMOPSO) algorithm.

A binary version of Particle Swarm Optimization (PSO) was used in [6]. In their approach, the velocities of the particles were modeled in the same way of the continuous version, but the weights could only be 0 or 1. Therefore they were given by a logistic function given the velocities and a velocity threshold. The updating process of the velocities was given by the following equation.

$$v_i = \omega_i c_1 rand()(p_i - x_i) + c_2 rand()(p_g - x_i) \tag{1}$$

where v_i is velocity of the i-th particle, ω is the inertia weight, $c1$ and $c2$ are constants that ponderate the influence of the local and global influences, respectively and p_i and p_g are the local and global best, respectively.

Besides the binary representation, it were used features of a multi objective version of particle swarm optimization, based on the Pareto Dominance concept as in [7]. According to the Pareto Dominance concept, a solution A dominates a solution B, only if A is not worse than B in any of the objectives and A is better than B in at least one of objective functions. The MOPSO also implements an external archive, where the non dominated particles discovered along the iterative process are stored. At the end of each iteration, each one of the particles is analyzed. If the particle meets at least one of the following rules, it is included to the archive.

- If the archive is empty;
- If the particle domains any other particle from the archive, the dominant replaces the non dominant;
- If the particle is not dominated by any other from the archive and it does not domain any other from the archive.

The particles from the archive are clustered according to their values of the objective functions. Those divisions are denominated hyper cubes. This segmentation is used to define the social influence of the particle. In the MOPSO, the particle suffers influence from the N_{best}, which is obtained by two draws. In the first one, by using the roulette technique with probabilities inversely proportional to the quantity of particles in the hyper cubes, one hyper cube is drawn. If there is more than one particle inside that hyper cube a second drawn is performed to select one of them. Finally, the selected particle is chosen as global influence to the particle whose weights are being updated.

4   Proposed Recommendation System

The main proposal is to perform the BMOPSO over the current status of the appliances and get a set of recommendations. Afterwards, they are segmented accordingly to the comfort priority of the dwellers present in the room. Those steps will be described as follows.

4.1   BMOPSO Recommendation System

The implemented BMOPSO optimizes two concurrent objective functions. The first one is related to the power consumption and the other regards the discomfort level of the solution candidate.

The power consumption of a solution candidate is measured as the quantity of turned on appliances in the solution. As each dimension of a particle represents the status of one appliance in a binary format, thus, zero means turned off and one means turned on. The representation of the power consumption of a solution candidate is given by the sum of its binary dimension values. On the other hand, the discomfort level is given by the euclidean distance between the current state of the appliances inputted to the algorithm and the particle distribution. This distance is inversely proportional to the comfort of the dweller, once it regards how many appliances are suggested to be turned off. The calculation process of the objective functions are described in the Eqs. 2 and 3.

$$C(q) = \sum_{i=1}^{n} q_i \tag{2}$$

$$D(q,p) = \sqrt{\sum_{i=1}^{n}(q_i - p_i)^2} \tag{3}$$

The Eqs. 2 and 3 represent the power consumption and the discomfort level of the solution candidates, respectively. In the Eq. 2, $C(q)$ is the sum of the weights of the q-th particle. And in the Eq. 3, p is the inputted state of the appliances and q is the solution candidate.

The performed technique also implements concepts of the multi-objective and the binary versions aforementioned. Due to the binary representation of the particles, their velocities are represented by two probability values for each weight of the particle. Furthermore, due to the necessity of optimize two distinct objective functions, it is implemented an external archive to receive the non dominated particles.

The BMOPSO operation steps are represented in the Algorithm 1.

Result: Pareto Front with the non-dominated particles
read Parameters;
Initialize Velocities;
Initialize Particles;
Initialize Archive;
Objective Functions;
Archive Search;
Generate Hyper Cubes;
while *iterations Number* $<=$ *maxIter* **do**
    Select N_{best};
    Update P_{Best};
    Calculate Weights and Velocities;
    Mutation;
    Objective Functions;
    Archive Search;
    Generate Hyper Cubes;
end
return Archive;

      Algorithm 1: The proposed recommender BMOPSO.

The steps of the BMOSPO implemented for appliances usage recommendation are described as follows.

- **Read Parameters:** The parameters of the BMOPSO are described in Table 2.
- **Initialize Particles and Initialize Velocities:** The particles are initialized with random binary values in their dimensions. Also, the velocities are initialized, like two probabilities variables for each particle's dimension.
- **Initialize Archive:** Initialization of the archive of non-dominated particles, which is initially empty.
- **Objective Functions:** Calculate the power consumption and the discomfort level as showed in Eqs. 2 and 3, of each particle in the system.
- **Archive Search:** Among the particles, find out the non-dominated ones according to the three rules aforementioned to be stored in the Archive.
- **Generate Hyper Cubes:** According to the hyper cube division factor defined by parameter, each particle in the archive is placed into a hyper cube.
- **Select N_{best}:** Based on hyper cube values, assign a N_{Best} for each particle. Each N_{Best} is a particle from the archive, selected according to the already explained drawn procedure.

- **Update** P_{Bests}**:** For each particle, it is analyzed if its current configuration domains its best version found so far. If positive, the current configuration replaces the previous as the P_{Best} of that specific particle.
- **Calculate Weights and Velocities:** The velocities and weights for each particle are calculated as in the Binary Particle Swarm Optimization described in [6].
- **Mutation:** In the mutation operation, each particle has a probability of receive a noise over its weights. This probability is defined by the mutation parameter.
- **Objective Functions, Archive Search and Generate Hyper Cubes:** Those steps are performed exactly as explained in previous appearances. With exception of the Archive Search that is not empty anymore.

The BMOPSO returns a Pareto Front containing a set of appliance turn on/off recommendations.

4.2   Dweller's Priority Recommendation

After the generation of the recommendations, they are segregated according to their level of energy saving and dweller comfort. The generated Pareto Front solutions are grouped into three clusters. The Fig. 1 show an example of a divided Pareto Front. The solutions are separated in three groups of priorities. The less comfortable solutions group (left side circle) represents the lower priority recommendations. The central group is the medium priority and in the right side circle are the more comfortable solutions, denominated of maximum priority recommendations.

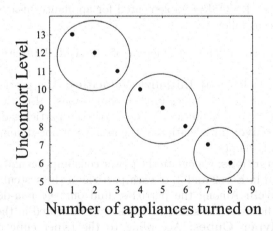

Fig. 1. Pareto front with the generated recommendations.

The delivery of the recommendations works by the following way. A dweller who has more comfort priority receives smoother recommendations (i.e. less power saving, more concerned with comfort). On the other hand, a dweller with lower comfort priority receives the more hard recommendations (i.e. more invasive to its comfort).

The priority level of the recommendations delivered to the dweller is selected according to the dweller with maximum priority which is present in the environment at the moment of the algorithm operation. Also, the experiments realized in this work hypothesize that the dwellers are identified in the environment and their priority levels are already defined.

4.3 Proposed Technique

The Fig. 2 shows a representation of the hole proposed recommendation concept in this work.

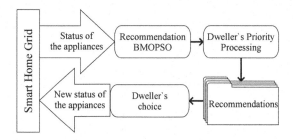

Fig. 2. Proposal scheme.

The stages of the proposed technique are explained as follows.

- The status of the appliances is obtained as a vector in which each component is a binary value representing the ON or OFF state of one appliance as 1 and 0, respectively. Therefore, each dimension of this vector regards to one of the appliances connected to the grid.
- The BMOPSO recommender algorithm receives the current state of the appliances in the format explained in the previous item, and generates a group of optimal recommendations balanced between power saving and dweller's comfort.
- The recommended solutions are divided into three priority groups with equal number of solutions each. In case of the division does not be exact (i.e. same number of solutions assigned to the groups) it is acceptable for the more priority group (Right side circle in the Fig. 1) to have less recommendations.
- According to the higher priority found among the dwellers present at that moment in the environment, the respective group of recommendations is returned as suggestions of appliances turning off actions to reduce the power consumption.
- If one of the recommendations be chosen by a dweller, this recommendation is returned to the grid as the new state of the appliances to be implemented.

The recommendation chosen to the dweller is intended to be used as an action to turn off the appliances which were recommended to do so.

5   Results and Discussion

The experiments were performed by simulations in MATLAB® and R-CRAN platforms. The data were obtained by the Dutch Residential Energy Dataset (DRED) [8], available online. The data available is the instantly power value of 12 appliances in a sampling rate of measure per second, during 152 days.

As the data set only had one column informing the presence of the dweller in the rooms, in order to generate more dweller presence data and to make feasible the dwellers priority tests, it was performed a statistical replication of this data in the following way. From the presence data of the five rooms (Kitchen, LivingRoom, Room1, Room2 and StoreRoom) it were calculated the probabilities of

Table 1. Room changing probabilities

Room	Kitchen	Living	Store	Room1	Room2
Kitchen	0.9985	0.0012	0.0002	0.00003	0
Living	0.0001	0.9999	0.00012	0.0001	0.0001
Store	0.00017	0.00095	0.9986	0.0001	0
Room1	0.0024	0.00078	0.0004	0.9986	0
Room2	0.0001	0.0013	0.0001	0	0.9984

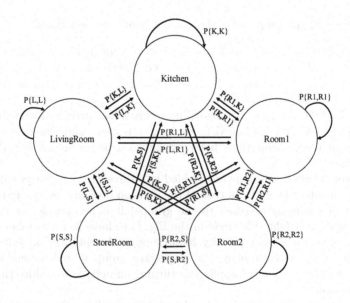

Fig. 3. Room changing possible probabilities.

the dweller commute from one room to each one of the other in the next second. The Table 1 shows those probabilities.

After obtaining the probabilities, a Markov chain was implemented to generate new information about dwellers presence with equal changing probabilities of the original data. The Fig. 3 illustrates the possible probabilities calculated from the original room presence data.

After obtaining the room changing probabilities, the production of new presence data based on the probabilities of the original data was performed in the following way. In the first second, it is drawn a room to the dweller begin. After that, to decide the next movement (change to any other room or stay) the Markov chain is initialized by changing states according to their probabilities. Therefore, each action in the Markov chain will generate a new second of presence data, which is not necessarily equal to the original data, but with equal probabilities distribution.

It were generated two additional presence columns by the Markov process. Those were used as two simulated dwellers presence information beyond the original one, and each one was assigned to one of the three priority levels. Therefore, when the current status of the appliances was captured, also it was taken the highest level of priority among the dwellers present in the environment.

Table 2. BMOPSO Parameters utilized

Parameter	Description	Value
Max_It	Iterations quantity	20
c_1	Local influence factor	1
c_2	Social influence factor	1
P_n	Quantity of particles	50
P_d	Dimensions of the particles	12
P_m	Mutation probability	0.01
Div	Hyper cubes division factor	3

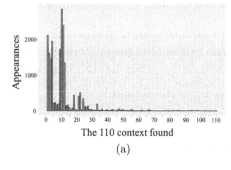
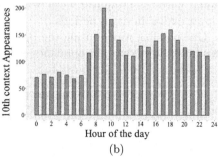

Fig. 4. a: 110 found contexts. b: 10th Context hourly appearances.

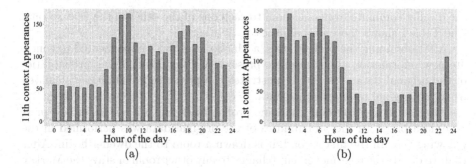

Fig. 5. a: 11th Context hourly appearances. b: 1st Context hourly appearances.

The BMOPSO parameter configuration was defined by performing grid search, varying the parameters and verifying the hyper value behavior. The best performed and used parameters are detailed in the Table 2.

In order to simplifies the nomenclature in the results, the current state of the appliances will be treated as a context. A transformation of the data from data set in contexts revealed 110 independent contexts in all the period analyzed. The Fig. 4a shows the frequency of the contexts appearances in the database.

The Fig. 4a shows the frequencies of the contexts in the data. The right side contexts, from the 30th until the 110 appears in an average of 10 times during all the 152 days analyzed. On the other hand, the 10th appears 2,845 times. In order to verify if the most frequent contexts tend to appear in specific periods of the day, and to evaluate the efficiency of the recommendation over such contexts, an analysis of their hourly appearances was performed. Besides, their recommendations were generated from the BMOPSO. The Figs. 4b, 5a and b shows the hourly appearances of the three most frequent contexts (i.e. 10th, 1st and 11th, respectively).

In the Fig. 4b it is possible to notice that the 10th context has a higher frequency of appearance between 9 AM and 11 AM and at the end of the afternoon, around 18 h. In the same way the Fig. 5a shows the 11th context as having similar patterns of appearances, while the first context, in the Fig. 5b, tend to appear earlier in dawn periods.

One possible way of using the BMOPSO recommender is to generate recommendations to reduce the appliances usage over those most frequent contexts and

Table 3. Estimated power saving of three contexts

Context	Power saving
10th	4.27%
11th	11.58%
1st	2.89%

reuse those recommendations during their most frequent periods. The Table 3 shows estimated average power saving values of the generated recommendations for each of the three analyzed contexts. Those calculation were performed by using the energy values of the appliances from the data set.

The values shown in the Table 3 were obtained by generating the recommendations Pareto Front for each context and calculating the average relative reduction of power of its recommendations in the original data. For instance, if a dweller accepts one of the recommendations for the 10th context, what would be the power consumption reduction when: every time that this context was found, it was replaced by its recommendation.

The mean of energy saving of all the recommendations generated to all the 110 context was 9,76%. Also, the average energy saving by dweller's comfort priority in shown in the Table 4.

Table 4. Estimated power saving of three priorities

Priority level	Average power saving
Low	15.36%
Middle	8.13%
High	4.12%

The Table 4 show that according to the comfort priority of the dwellers, the recommendations can reduce more or less the power consumption of the appliances.

The standard deviation of the hyper value of 30 executions of BMOPSO for the same input context is zero. That means that the same recommendations are being generated for each inputted context. It can be explained by the low complexity of the search. The data set has 12 appliances and in the particles they can be only 0 or 1, resulting in a search space of $2^{12} = 4,096$ possibilities. Those possibilities could be calculated in an exhaustive search with no effort and there was no need of an heuristic search approach. However, an exhaustive search would not be able to determine which of the possibilities composes the Pareto Front for the intersection of the two objective functions (Fig. 1). Furthermore, by using optimization search algorithm the search becomes scalable to any amount of appliances demanded.

6 Conclusion

The work have proposed a concept of residential appliances recommendation with dweller's comfort priority based on multi-objective search. The study performed in the data set showed the potential of power saving of the recommendations when performed over high frequent contexts.

Also, the division of the recommendations according to the dweller's comfort priority can accomplish different levels of comfort and power saving of the solutions according to the priority of the users present in the room.

7   Limitations and Future Works

One of the biggest problem from the simulation works in Smart Home field is to find available data sets. There are few data sets online and most of them do not have good sampling rates or periodicity in the measures. Besides, due to the small amount of appliances, the optimization problem described in this work could be solved by using a deterministic method based on weighted Pareto front. However, as the amount of appliances grows, the possible combinations increase as well as the computational effort to use a deterministic approach.

The experiments have shown the potential of energy saving of the recommendation, however, it is still necessary to give reasonability and usability to them recommendations. The technique described in this work is intended to be the recommendation part of a bigger system evolving the storage of the accepted recommendations per user, which will be able to reuse the accepted recommendations when convenient and generate new recommendation when necessary.

Beyond priority of comfort for the dweller, it could be also interesting to address the usage priority of the appliances in the form of constraints inside the algorithm.

Acknowledgment. The authors are grateful to the Brazilian institutions: FACEPE - Fundacao de Amparo a Ciencia e Tecnologia do Estado de Pernambuco, CIn - Centro de Informatica da UFPE, LIVE - Laboratorio de Inovacao Veicular da UFPE/FCA and UFPE - Universidade Federal de Pernambuco, for the support of this research.

References

1. International Energy Agency: https://www.iea.org/
2. Schweizer, D., Zehnder, M., Wache, H., Witschel, H.F., Zanatta, D., Rodriguez, M.: Using consumer behavior data to reduce energy consumption in smart homes. In: Proceedings of the IEEE 14th International Conference on Machine Learning and Applications (2015)
3. Lacerda, H.F., Feitosa, A.R.S., Silva-Filho, A.G., Santos, W.P., Cordeiro, F.R.: SmartHome energy saving using a multi-objective approach based on appliances usage profiles. In: Mouhoub, M., Langlais, P. (eds.) AI 2017. LNCS (LNAI), vol. 10233, pp. 142–147. Springer, Cham (2017). https://doi.org/10.1007/978-3-319-57351-9_18
4. Nesrine, G., Naouar, G., Ahlame, B., Arslane, Z.: Improving the proactive recommendation in smart home environments: an approach based on case based reasoning and BP-neural network. Int. J. Intell. Syst. Appl. **7**, 29–35 (2015)
5. Mahmood, A., et al.: Home appliances coordination scheme for energy management (HACS4EM) using wireless sensor networks in smart grids. Procedia Comput. Sci. **32**, 469–476 (2014)

6. Zhanga, Y., Wanga, S., Phillips, P., Ji, G.: Binary PSO with mutation operator for feature selection using decision tree applied to spam detection. Knowl.-Based Syst. **64**, 22–31 (2014)
7. Borhanazad, H., Mekhilef, S., Ganapathy, V.G., Mostafa, M.D., Mirtaherid, A.: Optimization of micro-grid system using MOPSO. Renewable Energy **71**, 295–306 (2014)
8. Akshay, S.N., Nambi, U., Lua, A.R., Prasad, V.R.: BuildSys 15. In: Proceedings of the 2nd ACM International Conference on Embedded Systems for Energy-Efficient Built Environments, LocED (2015)

Hyper-parameter Optimization of Multi-attention Recurrent Neural Network for Battery State-of-Charge Forecasting

Aleksei Mashlakov$^{(\boxtimes)}$ ⓘ, Ville Tikka ⓘ, Lasse Lensu ⓘ, Aleksei Romanenko ⓘ,
and Samuli Honkapuro ⓘ

LUT University, Yliopistonkatu 34, 53850 Lappeenranta, Finland
{aleksei.mashlakov,ville.tikka,lasse.lensu,aleksei.romanenko,
samuli.honkapuro}@lut.fi

Abstract. In the past years, a rapid deployment of battery energy storage systems for diverse smart grid services has been seen in electric power systems. However, a cost-effective and multi-objective application of these services necessitates a utilization of forecasting methods for a development of efficient capacity allocation and risk management strategies over the uncertainty of battery state-of-charge. The aim of this paper is to assess the tuning efficiency of multi-attention recurrent neural network for multi-step forecasting of battery state-of-charge under provision of primary frequency control. In particular, this paper describes hyper-parameter optimization of the network with a tree-structured parzen estimator and compares such optimization performance with random and manual search on a simulated battery state-of-charge dataset. The experimental results demonstrate that the tree-structured parzen estimator enables 0.6% and 1.5% score improvement for the dataset compared with the random and manual search, respectively.

Keywords: Battery state-of-charge · Hyper-parameter optimization ·
Multi-attention neural network · Random search ·
Tree parzen estimator

1 Introduction

Battery energy storage systems (BESSs) are expected to be one of the key smart grid technologies residing in all electric grid levels and providing variety of system- or grid-oriented services [11,15]. Primary frequency control (PFC) with a fast dynamic response is one of the lucrative and highest-value application of BESSs from a power system stability and economic perspectives [3,16]. However, many studies conclude that in order to realize the full potential of costly

---

Supported by the DIGI-USER research platform of LUT University, Finland.

P. Moura Oliveira et al. (Eds.): EPIA 2019, LNAI 11804, pp. 482–494, 2019.
https://doi.org/10.1007/978-3-030-30241-2_41

batteries, it requires a multi-objective operation and hence estimation of how its state-of-charge (SOC) capacity will change in different time intervals [10]. Consequently, forecasting methods are of extraordinate importance for the optimal utilization of BESSs in the multi-objective smart grid environment.

Time-series forecasting with deep learning has proven to be efficient tool for a time-dependent decision making in electric power systems. Most of the applications found in the literature can be related to forecasting of wind power generation [9], load consumption [13], market price [24], and solar photo-voltaic (PV) generation [14], respectively. There is, however, a deficit of expertise in forecasting of BESS SOC under the PFC, and the existing research in related domains is limited by rare attempts of frequency deviation forecasting [8].

This paper aims to assess the efficiency of multi-attention recurrent neural network (MARNN) to forecast hourly BESS SOC delta under the PFC on multi-step time intervals. However, the performance of such deep learning models is highly dependent on the selection of model hyper-parameters and, hence, requires comprehensive hyper-parameter tuning prior to an evaluation of the model efficiency. In order to solve this hyper-parameter optimization problem, a tree-structured parzen estimator (TPE) introduced in [5,6] is deployed for the MARNN and described in this paper. Moreover, the results of the paper provide a comparison of the performance of the TPE optimization with a random and manual search. The validation of the optimization approaches is carried out on a simulated BESS SOC dataset generated based on the historical frequency data measured in continental Europe synchronous area.

This paper is structured as follows. Section 2 provides a general overview of the hyper-parameter optimization and the TPE. The description of an applied automatic hyper-parameter tuning methodology including testing dataset, neural network model, hyper-parameter search spaces, and scenarios are given in Sect. 3. The performance evaluation of the results is presented in Sect. 4. Finally, discussion of the results and conclusions are given in Sects. 5 and 6, respectively.

2   Background

2.1   Hyper-parameter Optimization

Hyper-parameter optimization in machine learning assesses the problem of finding a set of optimal hyper-parameters x^* in the domain χ that return the best performance as evaluated on a validation set x:

$$x^* = \arg\min_{x \in \chi} f(x), \tag{1}$$

where the best score is defined as minimum of objective function $f(x)$ that usually corresponds to an error rate or a loss function.

Most of the hyper-parameter optimization techniques can be categorized to manual, grid search, random search, and Bayesian model-based optimization in the increasing order of their efficiency [4]. The highest efficiency of the Bayesian approaches can be explained by taking into account the results of previous evaluations in contrast to the grid and the random search. The efficiency of Bayesian optimization is estimated with a probability model of the objective function based on observed hyper-parameter values:

$$P(f(x)|x). \tag{2}$$

This probability model is called a "surrogate" and represents a high-dimensional response surface of hyper-parameters mapped to the probability of a score on the objective function. Hence, the hyper-parameters in Bayesian optimization are chosen based on greater probability of surrogate model and then evaluated on the actual objective function.

2.2   Tree Parzen Estimator

The Tree-structured Parzen Estimator is a variant of sequential Bayesian model-based optimization. Similar to the other model-based optimizations, in TPE every hyper-parameter has a domain (search space) that is expressed via the probability distributions such as uniform, log-normal, and normal distributions, or categorical variables. However, dissimilar to other algorithms, for each hyper-parameter, the TPE creates two different distributions, where $l(x)$ is a distribution for the hyper-parameters where the value of the objective function is less than the threshold y^*, and $g(x)$ is the distribution that is greater than the threshold. Then, the TPE uses a Bayes rule to build a surrogate model with the probability of the hyper-parameters given the score on the objective function:

$$P(x|f(x)) = \begin{cases} l(x), & \text{if } y < y^* \\ g(x), & \text{if } y \geq y^* \end{cases}. \tag{3}$$

Finally, the next set of hyper-parameters is selected from the surrogate model with aim to maximize Expected Improvement (EI) criteria that is proportional to $l(x)/g(x)$ ratio and promotes a choice of hyper-parameters from $l(x)$ distribution:

$$EI_{y^*}(x) = \frac{\gamma y^* l(x) - l(x) \int_{y^*}^{-\infty} p(y)dy}{\gamma y^* l(x) + (1-\gamma)g(x)} \propto (\gamma + \frac{g(x)}{l(x)}(1-\gamma))^{-1}, \tag{4}$$

where γ is a quantile of the observed y values, so that $\gamma = P(y < y^*)$.

3   Methods

3.1   Automatic Hyper-parameter Tuning

The process of automatic hyper-parameter tuning applied in this paper for the TPE optimization is described in Fig. 1 as sequential Bayesian model-based optimization. This automatic process can be explained as closed loop simulation between the model of a neural network and Bayesian optimizer. The part of the neural network simulation starts with building the neural network model on a set of hyper-parameters from search space, continues with the network training and the evaluation of the network performance on a validation set. A history of such evaluations serves as an input for the optimizer that is using this history to form a surrogate model and obtain new hyper-parameters maximizing EI criteria. This iterative process is repeated until the maximum number of estimations is reached. In the case of random search, such process does not assume any evaluation of the previous results and generates the hyper-parameter set randomly.

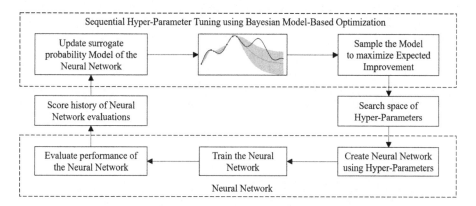

Fig. 1. A sequential automatic hyper-parameter optimization modified from [17].

3.2   Testing Data

The BESS SOC dataset for the automatic hyper-parameter tuning was modelled according to the rules for provision of the PFC that are based on the deviation of locally measured frequency $f(t)$ from the nominal system frequency f_N:

$$\Delta f(t) = f(t) - f_N. \tag{5}$$

A power output at every moment $P_{FCR}(t)$ required for the PFC is defined by a reference droop curve that is shaped by two main parameters, which are an allowed dead-band Δf_{db} and a full activation frequency deviation Δf_{max}:

$$P_{FCR}(t) = \begin{cases} 0, & |\Delta f(t)| \leq |\Delta f_{db}| \\ P_{FCR}^{max}\left(\frac{\Delta f(t)}{|\Delta f_{max}|}\right), & |\Delta f_{db}| < |\Delta f(t)| < |\Delta f_{max}|. \\ P_{FCR}^{max}\left(\frac{\Delta f(t)}{|\Delta f(t)|}\right), & |\Delta f(t)| \geq |\Delta f_{max}| \end{cases} \tag{6}$$

A negative frequency deviation over the dead-band corresponds to a positive reference power output, which in the case of BESS leads to discharging, while BESS charging is provoked by the positive deviation under the same condition.

A BESS is in idle state when the frequency deviation is within the dead-band. When the frequency deviations are larger that the dead-band, BESS regulation power is proportionally increased until the full activation frequency limit is reached. Finally, the deviations that are equal or exceeding $\Delta f_{\max}$ require a maximum reference power. Besides these parameters there is a full activation time for the resources, but BESS can provide continuous support with a small activation time.

Historical grid frequency measurements with 10-s resolution retrieved from the Réseau de Transport d'Électricité (RTE - transmission system operator of France) [21] were utilized as an input parameter for the dataset modelling. The measurements correspond to a continental Europe synchronous area during the time period from October 2014 to April 2019. The droop curve $\Delta f_{\max}$ was set to ±200 mHz with no-activation deadband Δf_{db} of ±10 mHz. A chosen BESS power to energy ratio was equal to 1 as it is one of the most common ratios for PFC according to [11]. The resulted 10-s BESS SOC dataset has been re-sampled to a hourly SOC resolution and is depicted in Fig. 2. The data is stationary with a vivid correlation at 24-h lagged data points that is illustrated in Fig. 3.

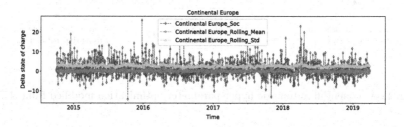

Fig. 2. Raw, standard deviation, and rolling mean values of BESS SOC dataset.

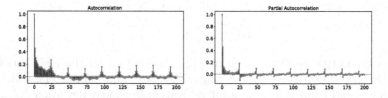

Fig. 3. Autocorrelation and partial autocorrelation plots of BESS SOC dataset with 200-h lag values.

3.3 Model Description

Recurrent Neural Networks (RNNs) that were initially developed for language modelling [23] are one of the state-of-art architecture designs applied for solving sequential forecasting problems in an energy sector [18,22]. A structure of RNN models usually consists of encoder and decoder RNNs represented by a set of long short term memory (LSTM) units or gated recurrent unit (GRU). In this architecture, the former is trying to compress an input sequence into a context vector and the latter attempts to decode this vector in an output sequence.

Attention mechanism is one of the latest advances in neural machine translation [2] that led to significant performance improvements of deep learning models. The main difference with the encoder-decoder RNN is that the attention model develops an aggregate context vector that is filtered specifically for each output time step and memorized in the decoder layer. In this work, MARNN is deployed to assess its effectiveness on the above introduced dataset. A MARNN was implemented based on the model in [20] using Keras 2.0.2 high-level neural networks API [7] with Tensorflow 1.0.1 [1] as backend in the Python 3.6 environment, and an example functional model of this network with two attention heads is visualized in Fig. 4. This functional model can be separated into Input, Encoder, Attention, and Decoder layers.

Fig. 4. An example of a functional model of the MARNN with two attention heads and four decoder units.

3.4   Hyper-parameters

Attention length corresponds to a number of multi-attention heads used in the attention layer and defines possible capability of the attention mechanism. *Number of hidden units* in the decoder layer specifies the number of states kept in the decoder layer and is tightly linked with the attention length. For instance, setting the number to 4 units in case of 24-h input sequence will provide only 4 days saved for the attention at maximum. *Activation function* defines the relevance of the attention by leveling the output of aggregated context vector in a concatenated part of the attention layer. *Dropout* addresses an over-fitting problem by randomly dropping units from the neural network during training. In the model, the dropout was applied to a densely-connected attention and decoder layers, respectively. *Learning rate* is one of the crucial parameters for training. Usually it varies from less than 1 to 10^{-6} with 10^{-2} as default value. In the model, the learning rate was adjusted for Adam optimizer.

3.5   Testing Scenario

A testing scenario applied in this study for the automatic hyper-parameter tuning is presented in Table 1. The parameters of the testing scenario are defined by search spaces and distributions of the above-described hyper-parameters. The search spaces for the number of hidden units and attention heads were set in range from 2 to 14 with randint distribution. Categorical variable choice was used for the activation function to select among None, ReLu, and Sigmoid functions. Finally, an uniform distribution was used for the dropout and the learning rate with corresponding ranges from 0 to 1 and from 10^{-3} to 10^{-2}, respectively.

Table 1. Scenarios for a hyper-parameter optimization of the model.

Hyper-parameter	Search space	Distribution
Attention length	2–14	Randint
Hidden units	2–14	Randint
Activation function	None, Sigmoid, ReLu	Categorical
Dropout 1	0.0–1.0	Uniform
Dropout 2	0.0–1.0	Uniform
Learning rate	10^{-3}–10^{-2}	Uniform

In this work, the automatic hyper-parameter optimization was implemented with Hyperas package [19] that is a wrapper over Hyperopt library [12]. The objective function for the performance evaluation of the MARNN model was Root Mean Square Error (RMSE). Prior to the testing, a difference was applied to the dataset to prevent persistence model properties. Moreover, a MinMax scaling with range from 0 to 1 was utilized for the dataset. A number of maximum iterations was limited to 100 for both algorithms, and a number of epochs was limited to 10 for each trial. A batch size was set equal to 128 data points. Two optimization approaches were used from the Hyperas, which are the TPE and random search.

4   Results

A visualization of the automatic hyper-parameter optimization with the TPE and the random search is presented in Figs. 5, 6 with PairGrid plot and the best optimization parameters are summarized in Table 2 including the optimal

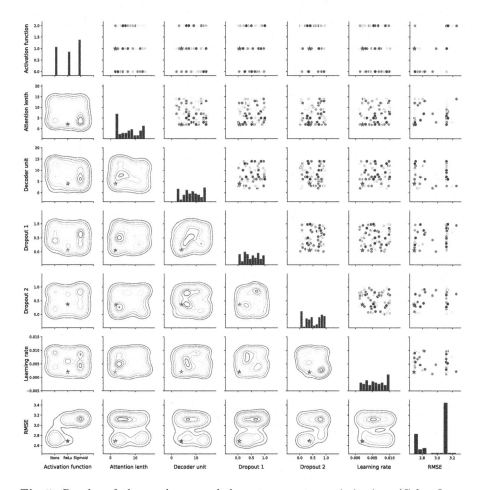

Fig. 5. Results of the random search hyper-parameter optimization. (Color figure online)

manual search parameters. The color of the points in a scatter plot above a diagonal is mapped to a sequential order of the testing trials, where dark blue points correspond to the first trials and dark red to the last trials. A density plots below the diagonal demonstrate the highest concentration of the trials with dark red color and the lowest with dark blue color. The best trial is marked with a red star, and diagonal plots show the distribution of the trials along the search spaces. In both of the methods, some of the testing estimations were removed from the visualization because of the extremely high values of their RMSE scores. In Table 2, the best RMSE score among the methods is marked in bold.

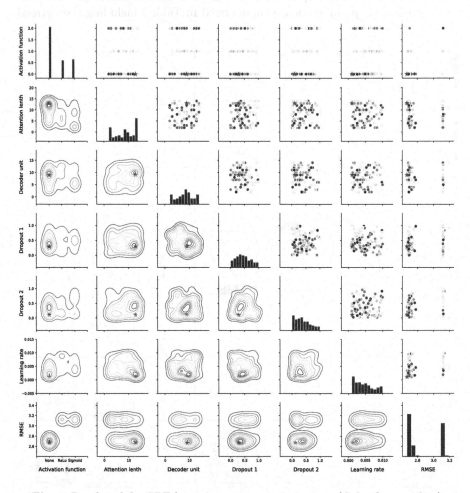

Fig. 6. Results of the TPE hyper-parameter optimization. (Color figure online)

According to the results, the best score was achieved by the TPE method with a difference from random and manual search approaches in 0.6% and 1.5%, respectively. However the scores of all methods are comparable, the hyper-parameters used for their best trials have major dissimilarities. For example, the TPE optimization achieved its best result with None activation function, while ReLU was the best choice for the random search. The TPE was searching for the attention length and the number of decoder units near the highest values of the given search space, while just 2 multi-attention heads and 4 decoder units were used in the random search. This dissimilarity can be also seen from the dropout values where a midpoint area of the interval was used for the dropout 1 and the beginning - for the dropout 2 by the TPE, but the opposite combination was utilized in the random search. However, a partial convergence can be seen in low values for the learning rate in both cases.

Table 2. Results of the model hyper-parameter optimization.

Hyper-parameter	TPE optimization	Random search	Manual search
Attention length	13	2	7
Hidden units	9	4	8
Activation function	None	ReLu	None
Dropout 1	0.295	0.054	0.2
Dropout 2	0.108	0.364	0.2
Learning rate	0.001	0.002	0.01
RMSE	**2.671**	2.688	2.710

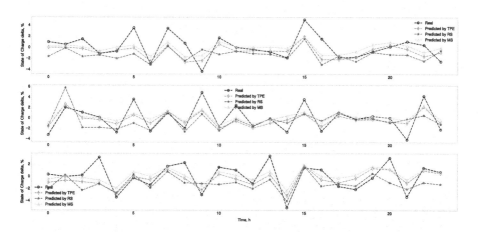

Fig. 7. A performance of the TPE, random search, and manual search optimization methods on unobserved testing data.

A performance of the tested methods is demonstrated in Fig. 7 on 24-h forecasting intervals that were chosen randomly from the testing set. For each of the method, the MARNN was built based on the best trial hyper-parameters, trained during 50 epochs, and tested against BESS SOC testing data.

5 Discussion

The outcomes of the automatic hyper-parameter tuning are inline with the results shown by these optimization algorithms in other studies. The advantages of TPE are in lower number of iterations required for a score improvement compared with the random search and generally higher score performance. However, in this case, the TPE optimization has not improved the neural network accuracy notably, it gave much more understanding about areas with the highest expected improvement. It is also possible that the best results were not achieved because of the low number of testing trials that might not have been sufficient for TPE to select the best hyper-parameters. However, a higher number of trials was not possible due to hardware memory limits. In this situation, a possible approach would be an iterative simulations with several testing search spaces that would be chosen from the most promising areas of each previous optimization test. Moreover, taking into account the similarity of the models results and the different hyper-parameters values used for the different methods, it is possible to conclude that the obtained performance scores are close to the optimal value, and further performance improvement is restricted by the effects of the chosen hyper-parameters on the model score. Moreover, an additional limitation of the utilized approach is that the methods were delivering the best score of each trial based on the last epoch but it is also possible that the lowest score could have been achieved at early epochs. Moreover, a better approach would be to substitute the restriction of fixed number of epochs with early-stopping criteria and to save the best score among the epochs.

6 Conclusions

This paper describes a deployment of the automatic hyper-parameter tuning on top of the MARNN model for forecasting of BESS SOC under the PFC. The TPE optimization was applied for hyper-parameter tuning and compared with the random and manual search. The best score was achieved by the TPE but the close performances were demonstrated by the random and manual search. Taking into consideration the similarity of the results with different hyper-parameters, it is possible to assume the near-optimal values of the chosen hyper-parameters for BESS SOC forecasting.

The future work should resolve the limitations of the current work and investigate the results of TPE optimization for a larger number of trials with different stopping criteria for the trials. Moreover, an assessment of the TPE optimization efficiency for BESS SOC datasets from grid synchronous areas with different provision curve parameters is a matter of interest.

References

1. Abadi, M., et al.: Tensorflow: a system for large-scale machine learning. In: 12th USENIX Symposium on Operating Systems Design and Implementation (OSDI 2016), pp. 265–283 (2016)
2. Bahdanau, D., Cho, K., Bengio, Y.: Neural machine translation by jointly learning to align and translate. arXiv preprint arXiv:1409.0473 (2014)
3. Belonogova, N., et al.: Methodology to define a BESS operating strategy for the end-customer in the changing business environment. In: 2018 15th International Conference on the European Energy Market (EEM), pp. 1–6. IEEE (2018)
4. Bergstra, J., Bengio, Y.: Random search for hyper-parameter optimization. J. Mach. Learn. Res. **13**(Feb), 281–305 (2012)
5. Bergstra, J., Yamins, D., Cox, D.D.: Making a science of model search: hyperparameter optimization in hundreds of dimensions for vision architectures (2013)
6. Bergstra, J.S., Bardenet, R., Bengio, Y., Kégl, B.: Algorithms for hyper-parameter optimization. In: Advances in Neural Information Processing Systems, pp. 2546–2554 (2011)
7. Chollet, F., et al.: Keras (2015). https://keras.io
8. Chourey, D.R., Gupta, H., Kumar, A., Kumar, J., Kumar, A., Mishra, A.: Analyzing effect of system inertia on grid frequency forecasting using two stage neurofuzzy system. J. Inst. Eng. (India): Series B **99**(2), 125–136 (2018)
9. Dong, D., Sheng, Z., Yang, T.: Wind power prediction based on recurrent neural network with long short-term memory units. In: 2018 International Conference on Renewable Energy and Power Engineering (REPE), pp. 34–38. IEEE (2018)
10. Fitzgerald, G., Mandel, J., Morris, J., Touati, H.: The economics of battery energy storage: How multi-use, customer-sited batteries deliver the most services and value to customers and the grid. Rocky Mountain Institute, p. 6 (2015)
11. Hesse, H., Schimpe, M., Kucevic, D., Jossen, A.: Lithium-ion battery storage for the grid a review of stationary battery storage system design tailored for applications in modern power grids. Energies **10**(12), 2107 (2017)
12. Hyperopt: Distributed asynchronous hyperparameter optimization in Python. (2012). https://hyperopt.github.io/hyperopt/. Accessed 30 Apr 2019
13. Kong, W., Dong, Z.Y., Jia, Y., Hill, D.J., Xu, Y., Zhang, Y.: Short-term residential load forecasting based on LSTM recurrent neural network. IEEE Trans. Smart Grid **10**, 841–851 (2017)
14. Muhammad, A., Lee, J.M., Hong, S.W., Lee, S.J., Lee, E.H.: Deep learning application in power system with a case study on solar irradiation forecasting. In: 2019 International Conference on Artificial Intelligence in Information and Communication (ICAIIC), pp. 275–279. IEEE (2019)
15. Müller, M., et al.: Evaluation of grid-level adaptability for stationary battery energy storage system applications in Europe. J. Energy Storage **9**, 1–11 (2017)
16. Obaid, Z.A., Cipcigan, L.M., Abrahim, L., Muhssin, M.T.: Frequency control of future power systems: reviewing and evaluating challenges and new control methods. J. Modern Power Syst. Clean Energy **7**(1), 9–25 (2019)
17. Pedersen, M.E.H.: Hyper-parameter optimization (2018). https://github.com/Hvass-Labs/TensorFlow-Tutorials
18. Petnehází, G.: Recurrent neural networks for time series forecasting. arXiv preprint arXiv:1901.00069 (2019)
19. Pumperla, M.: Hyperas: a very simple convenience wrapper around hyperopt for fast prototyping with keras models (2017). https://maxpumperla.com/hyperas/. Accessed 30 Apr 2019

20. Ratsimbazafy, M.: McKinsey SmartCities traffic prediction (2018). https://github. com/mratsim/McKinsey-SmartCities-Traffic-Prediction
21. RTE: Continental Europe synchronous area frequency data metered by RTE (2019). https://clients.rte-france.com. Accessed 30 Apr 2019
22. Shi, H., Xu, M., Li, R.: Deep learning for household load forecasting–a novel pooling deep RNN. IEEE Trans. Smart Grid 9(5), 5271–5280 (2018)
23. Sutskever, I., Vinyals, O., Le, Q.V.: Sequence to sequence learning with neural networks. In: Advances in Neural Information Processing Systems, pp. 3104–3112 (2014)
24. Toubeau, J.F., Bottieau, J., Vallée, F., De Grève, Z.: Deep learning-based multi-variate probabilistic forecasting for short-term scheduling in power markets. IEEE Trans. Power Syst. 34(2), 1203–1215 (2019)

Gradient Boosting Ensembles
for Predicting Heating and Cooling Loads
in Building Design

Leonardo Goliatt$^{(\boxtimes)}$ (iD), Priscila V. Z. Capriles$^{(\boxtimes)}$ (iD),
and Gisele Goulart Tavares$^{(\boxtimes)}$ (iD)

Federal University of Juiz de Fora, Juiz de Fora, Brazil
{leonardo.goliatt,priscila.capriles}@ufjf.edu.br,
giselegoulart@ice.ufjf.br

Abstract. Project costs, environmental damage and, constructive characteristics such as geometry, thermal properties of materials and weather conditions are required to measure energy efficiency in a building. One way to solve this problem is the application of Machine Learning Methods that estimate a response from a set of data inputs. This paper evaluates the performance of Gradient Boosting machines for predicting cooling and heating loads of residential buildings. With the use of building designs, 768 samples were derived, with eight geometric input variables and two thermal output variables. An exhaustive search with cross-validation was performed to the parameters selection. The performance assessment of the method was checked with the use of four statistical measures and one synthesis index. The results show that Gradient Boosting machines consistently reach a better performance than other machine learning methods like Support Vector Machines and Random Forests. The use of GB resulted in truthful prediction models, contributing to a test of several designs that can bring savings in the initial phase of the project.

Keywords: Energy efficiency · Heating and cooling loads ·
Gradient Boosting · Load forecast

1 Introduction

Energy efficiency's ability to meet world energy demand and change has rapidly improved over the last decade. In many developed and developing countries, energy efficiency has become the first fuel to meet rising energy demand [1]. Energy consumption of buildings, both residential and commercial, has increased reaching figures between 20% and 40% in developed countries and has exceeded the other major sectors: industrial and transportation [2]. Energy performance of buildings is a crucial element to achieve climate and energy objectives, namely a 20% reduction of the greenhouse gases emissions and 20% of primary energy

© Springer Nature Switzerland AG 2019
P. Moura Oliveira et al. (Eds.): EPIA 2019, LNAI 11804, pp. 495–506, 2019.
https://doi.org/10.1007/978-3-030-30241-2_42

savings. Improving the energy performance of buildings is a cost-effective way of fighting against climate change and enhancing energy security [3].

In this context, building energy simulation plays an increasingly significant role in building design, construction operation analyses, diagnostics, commissioning and evaluation of buildings. Simulation tools can help designers to compare various scenarios and identify energy saving potentials and evaluate the energy performance of buildings [4]. However, building energy simulation tools require calibration of simulation models involved in the energy simulation. The calibration process compares the results of the simulation with measured data and adjusts the simulation until its results closely match the observed data. This task can require advanced knowledge of the user and may become time-consuming depending on the simulation settings.

Simulation models for heating and cooling loads can be categorized into three broad groups [5]: (i) calibrated building performance simulation models that embed expert's knowledge of building systems and the historical data; (ii) grey box models that blend a generic simplified representation of a building's physical characteristics and load data [6], and (iii) black box models that attempt to find useful input-output relationships between weather/categorical data and metered load patterns.

In the last years, the interest in the literature for black box models has increasingly growing [7]. Black box models for predicting heating cooling loads have been built by using different methods such as linear regression [8], artificial neural networks [9], support vector machines [10], autoregressive integrated moving average [11], regression splines [12], ensemble models [9], random forests [13], gaussian processes [14], genetic programming [15], extreme learning machines [16], and deep learning approaches [17].

Recently, Gradient Boosting Machines (GB) have been successfully used to perform prediction tasks. Although the efforts that can be found in the literature, there are few examples of Gradient Boosting regression for energy prediction [18]. The objective of this paper comprises using GB that implements a model selection procedure that automatically searches for the best model in a set of user-defined parameters. The resulting model can provide a useful context for the assessment and evaluation of the performance of alternative building designs in the early stages of the design process. In addition, such a model can assists architects to analyze the relative impact of significant parameters of interest while maintaining energy performance standard requirements.

2   Methods

2.1   Dataset

The dataset used in this paper can be found in [19]. The dataset is composed by eight input variables and two output variables. The input variables are: relative compactness (RC), surface area, wall area, roof area, overall height, orientation, glazing area and glazing area distribution. The output variables are the heating loadings (HL) and cooling loadings (CL). To generate different building shapes,

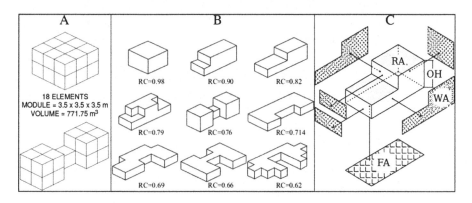

Fig. 1. A: Generation of shapes based on eighteen cubical elements [20]. B: Examples of building shapes [21]. C: Generic definition of building areas, where OH is the Overall Height, RA is the Roof Area, WA is the Wall Area and FA is the Floor Area. Adapted from [13].

eighteen such elements were used according to Fig. 1(A). A subset of twelve shapes with distinct RC values was selected for the simulations as can be seen in Fig. 1(B). Additional details of the simulation experiments are provided by [19] and [20].

2.2   Gradient Boosting Machines

In several problems the goal is, using a training set $\{(x_i, y_i)\}_{i=1}^{N}$ with N samples, to find an approximation $\hat{f}(x)$ to a function $f(x)$ that minimizes the expected value of the loss function

$$L(y, \hat{f}(x)) = \sum_{i}^{N} [y_i - \hat{f}(x_i)]^2. \tag{1}$$

GB approximates f by an additive expansion of the form

$$\hat{f} = \sum_{m=1}^{M} \beta_m h(x, a_m) \tag{2}$$

where the functions $h(x, a)$ are $h(x, a_m)$ is an K-node regression tree and the parameters $\{\beta, a\}$ are jointly fit to the training data in a forward stage wise manner [22]. At each iteration m, a regression tree partitions the variable space into disjoint regions $\{R_{km}\}_{k=1}^{K}$ at the mth iteration. A constant γ_{jm} is assigned to each such region and the predictive rule is $x \in R_{jm} \Rightarrow f(x) = \gamma_{jm}$. Using the indicator notation, the output of h for input x can be written as

$$h(x, \{R_{km}\}_{k=1}^{K}) = \sum_{k=1}^{K} \gamma_{km} I(x \in R_{km}), \quad I(\cdot) = 1 \text{ if } x \in R_{km} \text{ else } 0 \tag{3}$$

with parameters $\{R_{km}, \gamma_{km}\}$, $k = 1, 2, \ldots, J$, $m = 1, \ldots, M$, where γ_{km} is the value predicted in the region R_{km}.

As the model (3) predicts a constant value in each region R_{km}, the solution reduces to

$$\gamma_{km} = \gamma arg\ min \sum_{x_i \in R_{km}} L(y_i, f_{m-1}(x_i) + \gamma), \quad \gamma \text{ constant.} \tag{4}$$

The current approximation $f_{m-1}(x)$ is then updated following the rule

$$\hat{f}_m(x) = \hat{f}_{m-1}(x) + \lambda \sum_{k=1}^{K} \gamma_{km} I(x \in R_{km}) \tag{5}$$

where parameter $0 < \lambda \leq 1$ is called the learning rate.

A substantial improvement in Gradient Boosting's accuracy can be achieved when at each iteration of the algorithm the base learner is fitted on a subsample of the training set drawn at random without replacement. Subsample size is some constant fraction η of the size of the training set. Smaller values of η introduce randomness into the algorithm and help prevent overfitting [23]. The algorithm also becomes faster, because regression trees have to be fit to smaller datasets at each iteration.

Algorithm 1 presents the generic gradient tree-boosting algorithm for regression. The parameter $0 < \lambda \leq 1$ controls the learning rate of the boosting procedure and acts as a regularization parameter, while $0 < \eta \leq 1$ is the fraction of the training observations (without replacement) used to compute the optimal parameters of the model at iteration m. Specific algorithms are obtained by inserting different loss criteria $L(y, f(x))$.

2.3   Model Selection Using Grid Search and Cross-validation

There are a set of parameters that are not learned direct of the training model, called hyperparameters. Those settings are set by an exhaustive search on the hyperparameter space, to find the parameters that provide the best performance of cross-validation. For each possible combination of parameters, the predictive model is evaluated using k-fold cross-validation [24].

Table 1 shows the set the hyperparameters used for each model. The second column describes the parameter names, while the third column displays the list of parameters. The grid size is shown in the last column. For example, the grid size for GB is equal to 350: there are five configurations for learning rate, 10 for subsample and seven configurations for maximum depth (see Table 1). Therefore, the grid size has $5 \times 10 \times 7 = 350$ possible arrangements of parameters.

Algorithm 1: Gradient Boosting algorithm.

Input: Training set $\{(x_i, y_i)\}_{i=1}^{N}$ with N samples where $y_i = f(x_i)$, a differentiable loss function $L(y, f(x))$, the depth of each tree K, the subsampling rate η, learning rate λ and the number of iterations M

Output: Aproximation $\hat{f}(x)$ to $f(x)$

1 Initialize $\hat{f}_0(x) = \gamma arg\ min \sum_{i=1}^{N} L(y_i, \gamma),$ with γ constant

2 **for** $m = 1, \ldots, M$ **do**

3   1. Compute the pseudo-residuals as the negative gradient of the working response

$$r_{im} = - \left[\frac{\partial L(y_i, f(x_i))}{\partial f(x_i)} \right]_{f(x) = \hat{f}_{m-1}(x)}, \text{ for } i = 1, 2, \ldots, N$$

   2. Ramdomly select $\eta \times N$ samples from the dataset (subsampling step)

4   3. Fit a regression tree with K nodes to the pseudo-residuals r_{im} using the $\eta \times N$ samples. This tree is fitted using only those ramdomly selected samples

5   4. Compute the optimal parameters $\gamma_{1m}, \ldots, \gamma_{Km}$ as

$$\gamma_{km} = \gamma arg\ min \sum_{x_i \in R_{km}} L(y_i, \hat{f}_{m-1}(x_i) + \gamma), \text{ for } k = 1, 2, \ldots, K$$

   where R_{km} is the set of x that define the node k

6   5. Update $\hat{f}_m(x) = \hat{f}_{m-1}(x) + \lambda \sum_{k=1}^{K} \gamma_{km} I(x \in R_{km})$.

7 **end**

8 **return** $\hat{f}(x) = \hat{f}_M(x)$

Table 1. Hyperparameters used in model selection step.

Model	Parameters	Hyper-parameter sets	Grid size
GB	Learning rate (λ)	0.05, 0.1, 0.2, 0.3, 0.5	350
	Subsample (η)	0.1, 0.2, 0.3, $\ldots$, 0.9, 1.0	
	Max. depth (K)	Unconstrained, 1, 2, 4, 8, 16, 32	
	No. iterations (M)	200	
	Loss function	Least squares	

3 Computational Experiments

In this section, we present the results obtained for the regressions models described in Sect. 2. We ran each experiment 50 times using 10-fold cross-validation with shuffled data generated by different random seeds. The experiments were conducted based in scikit-learn framework [24] and implementations adapted from [25].

To assess the GB performance we compare the GB results with four machine learning methods from [13]: Decision Trees (DT), Multi-Layer Perceptron Neural Network (MLP), Random Forests (RF) and Support Vector Regression (SVR) and Gaussian Processes (GP). The computational experiments were conducted in the same computational framework described in [13]. In order to evaluate the predictive performance of each model we have used the evaluation metrics shown in Table 2.

Table 2. Performance metrics: $\hat{y}_i$ is the estimated target output, y_i is the corresponding target output, N is the number of samples, p is the number of model parameters, and $\bar{y}$ is the mean of the vector $[y_1, ..., y_N]$. The Synthesis Index (SI) combines RMSE, MAE, MAPE, and $1-R^2$, where M is the number of performance measures and P_i is performance measure, $P_i \in \{\text{RMSE}, \text{MAE}, \text{MAPE}, 1 - R^2\}$. The SI ranges from 0 to 1 and a SI value close to 0 indicates a highly accurate prediction model.

Metric	Expression
R^2	$1 - \frac{\sum_{i=0}^{N-1}(y_i-\hat{y}_i)^2}{\sum_{i=0}^{N-1}(y_i-\bar{y})^2}$
RMSE	$\sqrt{\frac{1}{N}\sum_{i=0}^{N-1}(y_i - \hat{y}_i)^2}$
MAPE	$100 \times \frac{1}{N}\sum_{i=0}^{N-1}\frac{|y_i-\hat{y}_i|}{|y_i|}$
MAE	$\frac{1}{N}\sum_{i=0}^{N-1}|y_i - \hat{y}_i|$
SI	$\frac{1}{M}\sum_{i=1}^{M}\frac{P_i-P_{i,min}}{P_i-P_{i,max}}$

Table 3 displays the summary of averaged statistical measures for cooling load and heating load for each model. Synthesis Index (SI) values close to one indicate a highly accurate prediction model. Observing the statistical measures provided running the computational experiments, we observe that GB has superior performance for heating and cooling loads, as can be seen when comparing the SI values produced by GB and the remaining predictors.

Figure 2 illustrates the values of the four statistical measures averaged in 50 runs for the predicted heating loads and cooling loads. In each bar, the vertical black line indicates the standard deviation. For all machine learning methods implemented here, we can observe that heating loads can be estimated more accurately than cooling loads. This conclusion is in agreement with other studies in the literature [14]. GB achieved better performance when compared with the remaining models for heating loads, as it was able to better capture a nonlinear relationship. Heating loads are estimated with considerably higher accuracy

Table 3. Statistical measures for cooling loads (CL) and heating loads (HL) averaged over 50 runs. The best ones are shown in boldface.

Output	Model	MAE (kW)	R^2	RMSE (kW)	MAPE (%)	SI
HL	GB	**0.224 (0.008)**	**0.999 (8.175e−05)**	**0.341 (0.012)**	**1.114 (0.041)**	**0.0000**
	GP	0.262 (0.010)	0.998 (0.0001507)	0.404 (0.019)	1.395 (0.054)	0.1825
	MLP	0.345 (0.033)	0.994 (0.007)	0.658 (0.357)	1.670 (0.181)	0.7616
	RF	0.327 (0.008)	0.998 (0.0002169)	0.491 (0.022)	1.411 (0.037)	0.3731
	SVR	0.438 (0.015)	0.996 (0.000263)	0.617 (0.021)	2.264 (0.088)	0.8669
CL	GB	0.491 (0.032)	**0.994 (0.001)**	**0.722 (0.081)**	1.973 (0.102)	**0.0085**
	GP	**0.486 (0.023)**	**0.994 (0.001)**	0.763 (0.066)	**1.924 (0.081)**	0.0214
	MLP	0.724 (0.079)	0.979 (0.013)	1.337 (0.357)	2.917 (0.277)	0.6257
	RF	1.008 (0.018)	0.975 (0.001)	1.502 (0.032)	3.760 (0.064)	0.9651
	SVR	1.010 (0.024)	0.975 (0.002)	1.517 (0.046)	3.946 (0.112)	1.0000

than cooling loads because some variables interact more efficiently to provide an estimate of heating loads.

Figure 3 displays the distribution of the parameter learning rate (λ), maximum depth of trees (K), and data subsample (η) according to the model selection procedure. For cooling loads, $\lambda = 0.5$ was selected in 45 out of 50 runs, while GB adopted the subsample equals to 1.0 in 30 out of 50 executions and the others appear distributed in a crescent way from between 0.7, 0.8 and 0.9. The maximum depth $K = 4$ was chosen in all independent runs. For heating loads, the learning rate is distributed between 0.2, 0.3 and 0.5 values, reaching the more significant frequency (31 runs) in $\lambda = 0.5$. For the subsample parameter, the amount with most periodicity was $\eta = 1.0$, in 42 out of 50 executions while K was set to 4 in all runs.

The ANOVA test performs a comparison between the metrics' means in order to verify if tested methods are statistically significantly different from each other. Table 4 presents the results of the ANOVA test, where can be observed that p-value $<10^{-5}$ for MAE, MAPE, R^2 and RMSE metrics. In this way, the ANOVA test indicates the machine learning methods have different means.

Table 4. Anova test for the metrics used to evaluate the method.

Output	Metric	F-value	p-value
HL	MAE (kW)	1060.6569	$<10^{-5}$
	MAPE (%)	1001.1908	$<10^{-5}$
	R^2	15.6564	$<10^{-5}$
	RMSE (kW)	34.8039	$<10^{-5}$
CL	MAE (kW)	1921.5546	$<10^{-5}$
	MAPE (%)	2019.1993	$<10^{-5}$
	R^2	137.4623	$<10^{-5}$
	RMSE (kW)	270.3402	$<10^{-5}$

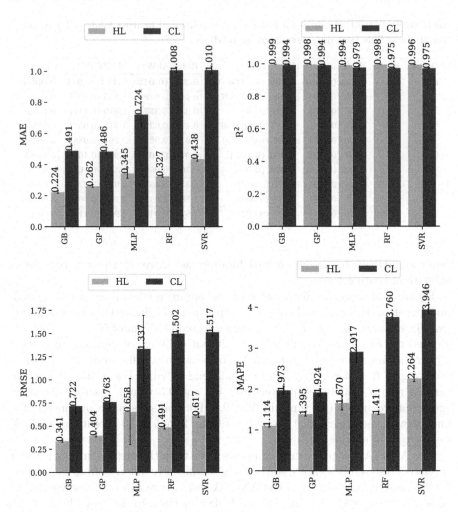

Fig. 2. Barplots for the statistical measures (averaged over 50 runs) for HL and CL. The performance metrics are Mean Absolute Error (MAE), Coefficient of Determination (R^2), Root Mean Square Error (RMSE) and Mean Absolute Percentage Error (MAPE).

Tukey's test, utilized after an ANOVA test, determines the individual means which are significantly different from a set of means. In addition, it shows that a significant difference exists and determines where the gap exists. Table 5 shows the Tukey's test for HL and CL. Only the results for MAPE metric is shown. Columns G_0 and G_1 present the groups which have been compared, while the difference between means appears in the third column. The lower and upper differences between means appear in the fifth and sixth columns, respectively. The last columns display whether the null hypothesis is rejected (or not). From this Table, one can notice that GB and GP produced similar results for heating

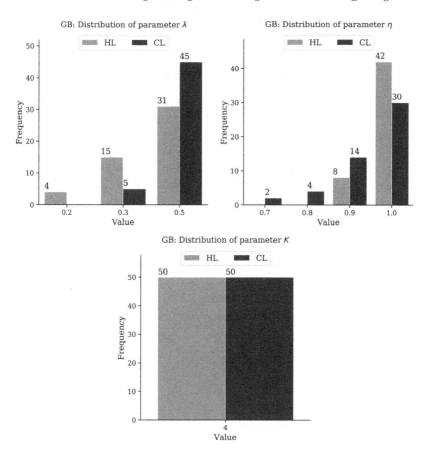

Fig. 3. Distribution of the GB parameters in the final models along 50 runs.

loads, while GB, GP, and RF present equivalent performance for cooling loads according to Tukey's test for MAPE metric.

Tables 6 and 7 present the statistical measures for the best models (along 50 runs) found in this paper. To provide a comparison with other models in the literature, we also show the results collected from other studies. Reference [19] implemented random forests, while [26] developed multivariate adaptive regression splines and gaussian processes were used in [14]. Reference [21] implemented a linear combination of two or more machine learning models. The results presented [15] were obtained by genetic programming, an automated learning of computer programs using a process inspired by biological evolution. The results in [13] were obtained using Random Forests and Multilayer Perceptron Neural Networks. As can be seen in Table 6 for the cooling loads, GB obtained competitive results. For heating loads, GB model reaches the best average performance for all statistical measures reflecting its ability to learn highly nonlinear relationships from data.

Table 5. Tukey test for MAPE.

Output	G_0	G_1	$\mu_{G_0} - \mu_{G_1}$	Lower	Upper	Reject
HL	GB	GP	0.0635	−0.0256	0.1525	False
	GB	MLP	0.3170	0.2279	0.4061	True
	GB	RF	0.1502	0.0611	0.2393	True
	GB	SVR	0.2761	0.1870	0.3652	True
CL	GB	GP	−0.0005	−0.0022	0.0013	False
	GB	MLP	−0.0044	−0.0061	−0.0026	True
	GB	RF	−0.0012	−0.0030	0.0005	False
	GB	SVR	−0.0026	−0.0043	−0.0009	True

Table 6. Heating load – Comparison between the results obtained from the best model of this study.

Reference	MAE (kW)	RMSE (kW)	MAPE (%)	R^2
[19]	0.510	–	2.180	–
[26]	0.340	0.460	–	1.000
[21]	0.236	0.346	–	**0.999**
[15]	0.380	–	**0.430**	–
[13]	0.315	**0.223**	1.350	0.998
[14]	0.262	0.404	1.395	0.998
GB	**0.224**	0.341	1.114	**0.999**

Table 7. Cooling load – Comparison between the results obtained from the best model of this study.

Reference	MAE (kW)	RMSE (kW)	MAPE (%)	R^2
[19]	1.420	–	4.620	–
[26]	0.680	0.970	–	0.990
[21]	0.890	1.566	–	0.986
[15]	0.970	–	3.40	–
[13]	0.565	0.837	2.342	0.991
[14]	**0.486**	0.763	**1.924**	**0.994**
GB	0.491	**0.722**	1.973	**0.994**

This paper focused on the energy consumption of buildings with a limited range of shapes in a specific climate zone. However, the implemented model can be generalized and replicated to other types of buildings in different climate zones. In real world situations, uncertainties in thermal and physical properties of materials can influence thermal performance. In these scenarios [18], data collected from sensor networks such as atmospheric pressure, exterior air temperature and wind speed are important parameters in the prediction of energy loads.

4   Conclusion

This paper evaluated the application of Gradient Boosting machines for the prediction of energy efficiency in residential buildings. The parameters were adjusted through the grid search and trained with cross-validation. The dataset comprises 768 simulated buildings. From the results, GB reaches a good performance for heating loads considering the tested metrics, and an equivalent behavior to the literature for cooling loads. Gradient Boosting arises as an alternative for early prediction of building cooling and heating loads that can potentially avoid the modeling and testing of several prototypes, contributing to savings in the initial phase of the project.

References

1. Friess, W.A., Rakhshan, K.: A review of passive envelope measures for improved building energy efficiency in the UAE. Renew. Sustain. Energy Rev. **72**, 485–496 (2017). https://doi.org/10.1016/j.rser.2017.01.026. http://www.sciencedirect.com/science/article/pii/S136403211730045X
2. Pérez-Lombard, L., Ortiz, J., Pout, C.: A review on buildings energy consumption information. Energy Build. **40**(3), 394–398 (2008)
3. Boermans, T., Grözinger, J.G.: Economic effects of investing in EE in buildings - the beam2 model. In: Background paper for EC Workshop on Cohesion policy (2011)
4. Pan, Y., Huang, Z., Wu, G.: Calibrated building energy simulation and its application in a high-rise commercial building in shanghai. Energy Build. **39**(6), 651–657 (2007)
5. Gunay, B., Shen, W., Newsham, G.: Inverse blackbox modeling of the heating and cooling load in office buildings. Energy Build. **142**, 200–210 (2017). https://doi.org/10.1016/j.enbuild.2017.02.064. https://www.sciencedirect.com/science/article/pii/S0378778816317066
6. Hu, M., Xiao, F., Wang, L.: Investigation of demand response potentials of residential air conditioners in smart grids using grey-box room thermal model. Appl. Energy (2017). https://doi.org/10.1016/j.apenergy.2017.05.099, https://www.sciencedirect.com/science/article/pii/S0306261917306098
7. Azar, E., Nikolopoulou, C., Papadopoulos, S.: Integrating and optimizing metrics of sustainable building performance using human-focused agent-based modeling. Appl. Energy **183**, 926–937 (2016)
8. Chokor, A., El Asmar, M.: Data-driven approach to investigate the energy consumption of LEED-certified research buildings in climate zone 2B. J. Energy Eng. **2**, 05016006 (2016)
9. Jovanović, R., Sretenović, A.A., Živković, B.D.: Ensemble of various neural networks for prediction of heating energy consumption. Energy Build. **94**, 189–199 (2015). https://doi.org/10.1016/j.enbuild.2015.02.052. https://www.sciencedirect.com/science/article/pii/S0378778815001577
10. Al-Shammari, E.T., Keivani, A., Shamshirband, S., Mostafaeipour, A., Yee, P.L., Petković, D., Ch, S.: Prediction of heat load in district heating systems by support vector machine with firefly searching algorithm. Energy **95**, 266–273 (2016). https://doi.org/10.1016/j.energy.2015.11.079. https://www.sciencedirect.com/science/article/pii/S0360544215016424

11. Newsham, G.R., Birt, B.J.: Building-level occupancy data to improve ARIMA-based electricity use forecasts. In: Proceedings of the 2nd ACM workshop on embedded sensing systems for energy-efficiency in building, pp. 13–18. ACM (2010)

12. Roy, S.S., Roy, R., Balas, V.E.: Estimating heating load in buildings using multivariate adaptive regression splines, extreme learning machine, a hybrid model of MARS and ELM. Renew. Sustain. Energy Rev. (2017). https://doi.org/10.1016/j.rser.2017.05.249, https://www.sciencedirect.com/science/article/pii/S1364032117308961

13. Duarte, G.R., Goliatt, L., Capriles, P.V.Z., Lemonge, A.: Comparison of machine learning techniques for predicting energy loads in buildings. Ambiente Construido **17**, 103–115 (2017)

14. Goliatt, L., Capriles, P.V.S.Z., Duarte, G.R.: Modeling heating and cooling loads in buildings using Gaussian processes. In: 2018 IEEE Congress on Evolutionary Computation, CEC 2018, Rio de Janeiro, Brazil, 8–13 July 2018, pp. 1–6 (2018)

15. Castelli, M., Trujillo, L., Vanneschi, L., Popovic, A.: Prediction of energy performance of residential buildings: a genetic programming approach. Energy Build. **102**, 67–74 (2015)

16. Naji, S., et al.: Estimating building energy consumption using extreme learning machine method. Energy **97**, 506–516 (2016). https://doi.org/10.1016/j.energy.2015.11.037. https://www.sciencedirect.com/science/article/pii/S036054421501587X

17. Fan, C., Xiao, F., Zhao, Y.: A short-term building cooling load prediction method using deep learning algorithms. Appl. Energy **195**, 222–233 (2017). https://doi.org/10.1016/j.apenergy.2017.03.064. https://www.sciencedirect.com/science/article/pii/S0306261917302921

18. Candanedo, L.M., Feldheim, V., Deramaix, D.: Data driven prediction models of energy use of appliances in a low-energy house. Energy Build. **140**, 81–97 (2017)

19. Tsanas, A., Xifara, A.: Accurate quantitative estimation of energy performance of residential buildings using statistical machine learning tools. Energy Build. **49**, 560–567 (2012)

20. Pessenlehner, W., Mahdavi, A.: Building morphology, transparence, and energy performance. In: Eighth International IBPSA Conference, Eindhoven, Netherlands, pp. 1025–1032, August 2003

21. Chou, J.S., Bui, D.K.: Modeling heating and cooling loads by artificial intelligence for energy-efficient building design. Energy Build. **82**, 437–446 (2014)

22. Hastie, T., Tibshirani, R., Friedman, J.: The Elements of Statistical Learning - Data Mining, Inference, and Prediction, 2nd edn. Springer, New York (2009). https://doi.org/10.1007/BF02985802

23. Friedman, J.H.: Stochastic gradient boosting. Comput. Stat. Data Anal. **38**(4), 367–378 (2002). https://doi.org/10.1016/S0167-9473(01)00065-2

24. Pedregosa, F., et al.: Scikit-learn: machine learning in python. J. Mach. Learn. Res. **12**, 2825–2830 (2011)

25. Friedman, J.H.: Multivariate adaptive regression splines. Annal. Stat. **19**, 1–67 (1991)

26. Cheng, M.Y., Cao, M.T.: Accurately predicting building energy performance using evolutionary multivariate adaptive regression splines. Appl. Soft Comput. **22**, 178–188 (2014). https://doi.org/10.1016/j.asoc.2014.05.015

Short-Term Streamflow Forecasting for Paraíba do Sul River Using Deep Learning

Luciana Conceição Dias Campos, Leonardo Goliatt da Fonseca[(✉)] ,
Tales Lima Fonseca, Gabriel Dias de Abreu, Letícia Florentino Pires,
and Yulia Gorodetskaya

Federal University of Juiz de Fora, Juiz de Fora, MG, Brazil
lcdcampos@gmail.com, goliatt@gmail.com, taleslimaf@gmail.com,
GABRIEL199716@gmail.com, lepirescomp@gmail.com, yu.gorodetskaya@gmail.com

Abstract. Water resources are essential for sustainable economic and social development, as well as be a vital element for the conservation of ecosystems and the life of all beings on our planet. On the other hand, natural and anthropic disasters from floods and droughts may occur. The modeling of hydrological historical series has extensively been studied in the literature for important applications involving the water resources' planning and management. There are several temporal series prediction's techniques in the literature. Some of them are characterized as classical linear methods whose adjusts for multivariate or multi-input prediction problems can be difficult. On the other hand, artificial neural networks can learn complex nonlinear relationships from time series, and the deep learning model LSTM is considered the most successful type of recurrent neural network capable of directly supporting multivariate prediction problems. This work presents a comparison between two forecasting's models of time series: ARIMA, a classical linear model, and an LSTM neural network, a nonlinear model. As a case study, we used the time series of four measurings' substations of one of the very important Brazilian rivers - the Paraíba do Sul river. These time series are difficult to predict since their history series has flaws and high oscillation in the data. The LSTM, which is a robust model, performs better in analyzing the behavior of this type of time series.

Keywords: Deep learning · Long short-term memory · Time series

1 Introduction

The effective management of available water resources in a river basin requires several aspects, including proper models to be as accurate as possible in predicting future outflows. The economic development and life of the vast majority of people rely on these water resources, which increases the need for improvement in their administration tools. The modeling of hydrological historical series

P. Moura Oliveira et al. (Eds.): EPIA 2019, LNAI 11804, pp. 507–518, 2019.
https://doi.org/10.1007/978-3-030-30241-2_43

has been extensively studied in the literature for important applications such as drought management, water quality policies, flood forecasting, electric generation, environmental management, water services, and more efficient land use in human, industrial and agricultural supply [3,6,12,17].

In recent decades, artificial neural networks have been a valuable tool in many areas of research. The uses of these techniques have also gained ground in the area of water resources, where, in most times, its use in flow prediction presented results compatible or superior to traditional techniques [4,15,21,26,29,33].

Artificial neural networks (RNA) contain adaptive weights along paths between neurons, which can be adapted by a learning algorithm, whose learning occurs through data that are observed until the prediction of the model has a satisfactory result [35].

These techniques are capable of representing complex and non-linear relationships, as well as investigating phenomena from multiple data sources and transform forecast simulations for a data-based practice.

A breakthrough in the artificial neural network field is Deep Learning. Deep-learning networks are distinguished from the more commonplace single-hidden-layer neural networks by their depth; that is, the number of node layers through which data must pass in a multistep process of data's learning. A special kind of recurrent neural network (RNN) architecture used in the field of Deep Learning is Long Short Term Memory networks – called "LSTMs". They are capable of learning long-term dependencies and they work tremendously well on a large variety of problems, like as Natural language processing [24], speech recognition [11] and extreme events requesting [22].

LSTM networks are well-suited to classifying, processing and making predictions based on time series data since there can be lags of unknown duration between important events in a time series. LSTMs were developed to deal with the exploding and vanishing gradient problems that can be encountered when training traditional RNNs, which motivated this work [20,30,36].

This paper aims to assess the viability of using LSTM in forecasting short-term streamflows for time series. To assess the performance of LSTM, we have used historical data from the Paraíba do Sul River (PSR), Brazil. The PSR basin has as main economic activities the industrial and agricultural sectors, and it is characterized by conflicts of multiple uses of its water resources [28,34]. In the last few years, the research on the PSR has been gained increasing attention in several areas. Some efforts include the research on degradation of the aquatic system due to human activities [16], dynamics of sediment transportation [23,32], geological studies [5] and drought identification and characterisation [31]. The prediction of the natural flow of PSR is one of the most important factors for analyses involving the management of this basin. In this way, accurate forecasting tools are essential for a robust and reliable decision-making process.

Historical data from PSR basin have high oscillating and missing data. The success of LSTM in dealing with these data comes from its capacity to capture long-range dependencies over time, which is acquired by the structure of its cell.

The cell is composed of an update gate, output gate and forget gate. These three gates regulate the flow of information into and out of the cell [14].

The secondary aim of the study accomplishes a comparison between ARIMA model [27], a well established statistical approach to streamflow forecasting and the LSTM model, a data-driven non-linear model.

The results of this work show the robust performance of the LSTM model compared to a classic ARIMA model, ensuring that LSTM adheres well to the prediction of the PSR river flow problem.

The rest of this paper is organized as follows: Sect. 2 presents the fundamental concepts around the subject which give context to other sections. Section 3 presents the executed experiment and the results. Section 4 shows the final results and supplies the reader with our contributions to the literature, promoting discussion around the research method with future suggestions.

2 Material and Methods

2.1 Dataset

The dataset used in this paper was provided by the Brazilian National Water Agency (ANA) and compounded by four daily measurement stations located on Paraíba do Sul's river basin. These stations are referenced as 58218000 (UHE FUNIL MONTANTE 2), 58235100 (QUELUZ), 58880001 (SÃO FIDELIS), 58974000 (CAMPOS - PONTE MUNICIPAL) and keeps observations from 1920 until 2016 [2].

Figure 1 shows the location of the Paraíba do Sul river basin and the four cited fluviometric/rainfall stations.

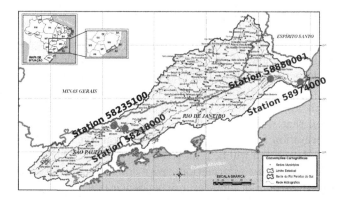

Fig. 1. Location of the Paraíba do Sul river basin and the four fluviometric/rainfall stations. Adapted from [1].

Figure 2 presents time series of the four cited measure stations. It's possible to see, at the raw data, that these series have inconsistencies in their values, containing missing values with long time gaps without registration. In this work, the missing values are treated with the imputation of median values to keep every observation of the series and them improving LSTM performance, once it fits the data.

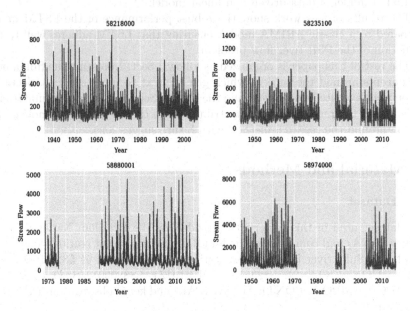

Fig. 2. Streamflow raw data of each measure station, supplied from the Brazilian Agency ANA [2]

2.2 Long Short Term Memory (LSTM)

LSTM is a special type of RNN which are networks with structures of the internal self-looped cell, that allows them to capture data's dynamic temporal behavior. In cases of architectures such as LSTMs, they can capture long time sequences, hence they have been used for time series with success.

LSTM as in Fig. 3 address this problem with an input gate, that specifies the information that will be stored to the cell state, an output gate that specifies which information from cell state will flow as output and a forget gate that decides which information will be removed from cell state. Therefore, these mechanisms from LSTM allows information easily flow through the cells unchanged, providing better learning of long-term dependencies [9].

2.3 Autoregressive Integrated Moving Average (ARIMA)

The autoregressive integrated moving average (ARIMA) models are the most general class of models for forecasting a time series that can to become "stationary" by differencing (when necessary), perhaps in conjunction with nonlinear

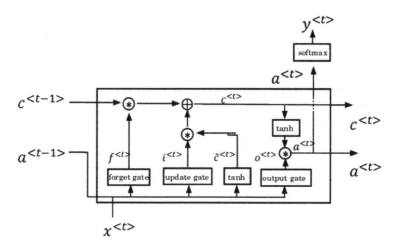

Fig. 3. LSTM cell [25].

transformations such as logging or deflating (when necessary). The process of fitting an ARIMA model is sometimes referred to as the Box-Jenkins method [8].

Lags of the differenced series appearing in the forecasting equation are called "auto-regressive" terms (AR), lags of the forecast errors are called "moving average" terms (MA), and a time series which needs to be differenced to be made stationary is said to be an "integrated" version of a stationary series (I). Each of these components is explicitly specified in the model as a parameter, characterized by 3 terms: p is the order of the AR term, q is the order of the MA term and d is the number of differences required to make the time series stationary.

Given a time series of data X_t where t is an integer index and the X_t are real numbers, the notation ARIMA (p, d, q) model:

1. First, let x denote the d_{th} difference of X, which means:
   - If $d = 0$: $x_t = X_t$.
   - If $d = 1$: $x_t = X_t - X_{t-1}$
   - If $d = 2$: $x_t = (X_t - X_{t-1}) - (X_{t-1} - X_{t-2}) = X_t - 2X_{t-1} + X_{t-2}$
2. In terms of x, the general forecasting equation is present at the Eq. 1:

$$\hat{x}_t = \mu + \phi_1 x_{t-1} + \ldots + \phi_p x_{t-p} - \theta_1 \epsilon_{t-1} - \ldots - \theta_q \epsilon_{t-q} \tag{1}$$

where $\hat{x}_t$ is the forecast of the time series at time t, $\phi_1 \ldots \phi_p$ and $\theta_1 \ldots \theta_q$ are the parameters of the model, and $\epsilon_{t-1} \ldots \epsilon_{t-q}$ is the residual error series and they are white noises, that is, the residuals themselves are independent and identically distributed (i.i.d.).

2.4 Time Series Cross-validation (TSCV)

Cross-validation is a statistical sampling technique to evaluate the generalization of a model from a data set [19]. K-Fold [13] is one of the most used methods among the cross-validation techniques, it eliminates dependency on subsets of validation that compromises most general model selection preventing overfitting.

In a Time series scope, a variation of K-Fold technique that is called Time Series Split (TSS) permits this same generalization gains without shuffling observations.

TSCV as illustrated by Fig. 4 splits all train data in n consecutive samples with train followed by validation, on each split, it maintains already trained and validation subsets as new train data and aggregates another split dividing in train and validation subsets. Validation subsets are the same sized and train keeps growing at each step, in the end, it selects the best model measured by validation set.

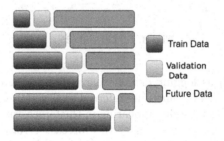

Fig. 4. Time series split example with $k = 6$.

3   Streamflow Estimation Model with LSTM

To carry out the predictions, we selected periods with 14 days in the historical flow series. At every step in the moving window predicting the seventh day ahead.

The predicted flow was considered as a function of finite sets of antecedent flow observations at the stations. The predictive model has the following form:

$$Q_{t+7} = F(Q_t, Q_{t-1}, \cdots, Q_{t-13}) \tag{2}$$

where Q_{t+j} is the streamflow at day $t + j$ and F is an estimation function.

Figure 5 depicts the framework of the proposed approach. The missing data are imputed by the median of the time series, 14-sized rolling windows are generated from data, the last 30% of data is reserved to test set and rest is to train and validate models. The TSCV is the cross-validation method to select the best model and prevent overfitting, this process culminates in the final MAPE evaluation in the test set. This process is performed 30 times resulting in averaged MAPE.

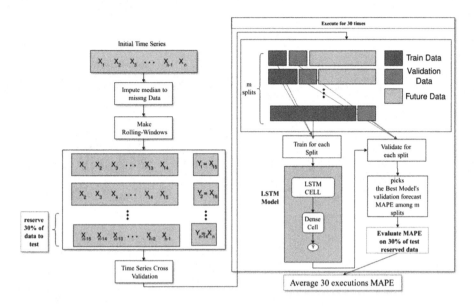

Fig. 5. Streamflow estimation model

3.1   Description of Experiments

ARIMA hyper-parameters as shown in Table 1 was chosen by a grid search with the best in-sample result determining the predictor models configuration as in [27].

Table 1. Hyper-parameters for the ARIMA model at each station.

Station	P	D	Q
58880001	3	0	1
58974000	2	1	0
58218000	2	0	3
58235100	1	0	0

LSTM hyperparameters were set as follows: kernel was initialized in the hidden layer using Xavier algorithm in order to achieve fast convergence [10], mini-batch size equals to 256 as suggested in the literature, and 200 neurons in hidden-layer.

LSTM layer needs two non-linear activation functions that were set to $hard-sigmoid$ and hyperbolic tangent $(tanh)$ as defined in [14] to avoid gradient vanishing problem. The last Layer with one neuron to forecast was composed of a linear activation.

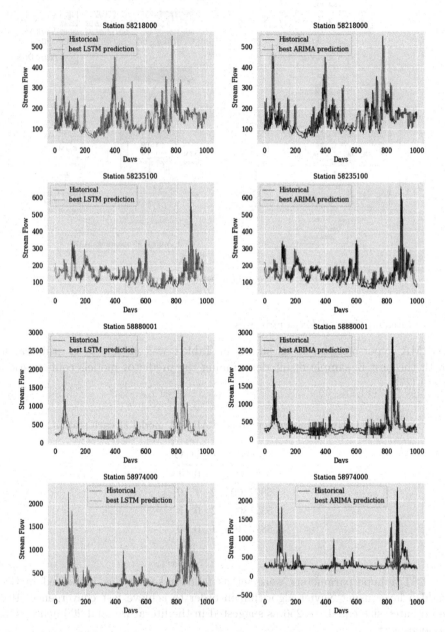

Fig. 6. Last 1000 days of the test set with the best LSTM forecast and historical values at left, and the best ARIMA forecast and historical values at right.

This model was optimized by Adam algorithm [18], time series cross-validation and early-stopping were applied to prevent overfitting [7].

Table 2. Comparison of models MAPEs.

Station	ARIMA	LSTM	Best LSTM
58880001	32.78	27.73 ± 1.01	**25.83**
58974000	26.43	21.29 ± 0.76	**19.74**
58218000	18.53	18.20 ± 0.24	**17.60**
58235100	17.61	15.26 ± 0.32	**14.77**

The main objective of this study was to evaluate the performance of the LSTM in the forecast of the flow of the time series of four stations of measurement of the Paraíba do Sul river. These series, represented in Fig. 2, record strong oscillations, besides present long periods with missing data.

Forecasting in these conditions is a tough mission but we found evidence that LSTM effectively was capable to learn the adversity in this series and predict reasonably well as indicated by Table 2 and Fig. 6.

Figure 6 shows an important problem that this study confronted, the LSTM forecast has some delay when compared to the historical time series. This problem occurs because LSTM is limited by past days, in this sense, we suggest increasing information supply with exogenous variables for future researches.

A limitation of the machine learning approach employed here is that the estimated river flows are reliable only under conditions similar to those that such models have historically experienced. The use of these models to generate predictions in conditions that exceed historical variability may introduce considerable uncertainty into their flow forecasts.

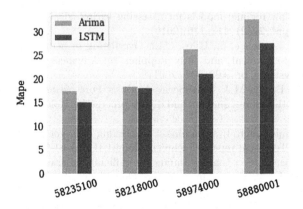

Fig. 7. Comparison of models *MAPE* for each station

In sum of that, Arima as a well-known statistical model to forecast flow performed considerably poor in comparison to LSTM in three of the four stations as saw in Fig. 7 with LSTM out-performing in every Station which corroborates the statement that artificial intelligence algorithms can capture the noise complexity, non-stationarity, dynamism and non-linearity in the data as reported in [35].

4   Conclusions

This work proposes to make the short-term forecast for the time series of the Paraíba River the South through deep learning, more precisely, a model using LSTM. The results of the experiments show that LSTM is a viable approach to prediction time series with high oscillation in data and long periods of missing data. Thus, the prediction results of the model using LSTM surpassed the ARIMA model, a statistical model widely used in forecasting time series of flow.

References

1. Governo do Brasil. https://www.brasil.gov.br/noticias/meio-ambiente. Accessed 27 Mar 2019
2. National water agency. https://www.ana.gov.br/. Accessed 21 Jun 2019
3. Abudu, S., Cui, C.I., King, J.P., Abudukadeer, K.: Comparison of performance of statistical models in forecasting monthly streamflow of Kizil river, China. Water Sci. Eng. **3**(3), 269–281 (2010)
4. Asadi, S., Shahrabi, J., Abbaszadeh, P., Tabanmehr, S.: A new hybrid artificial neural networks for rainfall-runoff process modeling. Neurocomputing **121**, 470–480 (2013)
5. Carelli, T.G., Plantz, J.B., Borghi, L.: Facies and paleoenvironments in paraíba do sul deltaic complex area, north of Rio de Janeiro state. Brazil. J. South American Earth Sci. **86**, 431–446 (2018)
6. Carlisle, D.M., Falcone, J., Wolock, D.M., Meador, M.R., Norris, R.H.: Predicting the natural flow regime: models for assessing hydrological alteration in streams. River Res. Appl. **26**(2), 118–136 (2010)
7. Caruana, R., Lawrence, S., Giles, C.L.: Overfitting in neural nets: backpropagation, conjugate gradient, and early stopping. In: Advances in Neural Information Processing Systems, pp. 402–408 (2001)
8. George, E.P., Box, G.M.J.: Time Series Analysis: Forecasting and Control. Holden-Day Series in time series analysis and digital processing. Holden-Day, San Francisco (1976)
9. Gers, F., Schmidhuber, J., Cummins, F.: Learning to forget: continuous prediction with LSTM. Technical report, Technical Report IDSIA-01-99 (2000)
10. Glorot, X., Bengio, Y.: Understanding the difficulty of training deep feedforward neural networks. In: Proceedings of the Thirteenth International Conference on Artificial Intelligence and Statistics, pp. 249–256 (2010)
11. Graves, A., Jaitly, N., Mohamed, A.R.: Hybrid speech recognition with deep bidirectional LSTM. In: 2013 IEEE Workshop on Automatic Speech Recognition and Understanding, pp. 273–278. IEEE (2013)

12. Guimarãlise da previsibilidade de cheias na bacia do rio uruguai através do modelo mgb-iph (2018)
13. Hastie, T., Tibshirani, R., Friedman, J.: The Elements of Statistical Learning - Data Mining, Inference, and Prediction, 2nd edn. Springer, New York (2009). https://doi.org/10.1007/BF02985802
14. Hochreiter, S., Schmidhuber, J.: Long short-term memory. Neural Comput. 9(8), 1735–1780 (1997). https://doi.org/10.1162/neco.1997.9.8.1735
15. Jain, A., Sudheer, K., Srinivasulu, S.: Identification of physical processes inherent in artificial neural network rainfall runoff models. Hydrol. Process. 18(3), 571–581 (2004)
16. Kahn, J.R., Vásquez, W.F., de Rezende, C.E.: Choice modeling of system-wide or large scale environmental change in a developing country context: lessons from the Paraíba do Sul river. Sci. Total Environ. 598, 488–496 (2017)
17. Khair, A.F., Awang, M.K., Zakaraia, Z.A., Mazlan, M.: Daily streamflow prediction on time series forecasting. J. Theoret. Appl. Inf. Technol. 95(4), 804 (2017)
18. Kingma, D.P., Ba, J.: Adam: a method for stochastic optimization. arXiv preprint arXiv:1412.6980 (2014)
19. Kohavi, R., et al.: A study of cross-validation and bootstrap for accuracy estimation and model selection. IJCAI 14, 1137–1145 (1995)
20. Kratzert, F., Klotz, D., Brenner, C., Schulz, K., et al.: Rainfall-runoff modelling using long short-term memory (LSTM) networks (2018)
21. Krishna, B., Rao, Y.S., Nayak, P.: Time series modeling of river flow using wavelet neural networks. J. Water Resour. Prot. 3(01), 50 (2011)
22. Laptev, N., Yosinski, J., Li, L.E., Smyl, S.: Time-series extreme event forecasting with neural networks at uber. In: International Conference on Machine Learning, pp. 1–5, no. 34 (2017)
23. Miguens, F.C., de Oliveira, M.L., de Oliveira Ferreira, A., Barbosa, L.R., de Melo, E.J.T., de Carvalho, C.E.V.: Structural and elemental analysis of bottom sediments from the Paraíba do Sul River (SE, Brazil) by analytical microscopy. J. South American Earth Sci. 66, 82–96 (2016)
24. Mikolov, T., Karafiát, M., Burget, L., Černocký, J., Khudanpur, S.: Recurrent neural network based language model. In: Eleventh Annual Conference of the International Speech Communication Association (2010)
25. Ng, A., Katanforoosh, K., Mourri, Y.: Sequence models. Deeplearning. AI on Coursera (2018)
26. Patel, S.S., Ramachandran, P.: A comparison of machine learning techniques for modeling river flow time series: the case of upper cauvery river basin. Water Resour. Manag. 29(2), 589–602 (2015)
27. Pena, E.H.M., de Assis, M.V.O., Proença, M.L.: Anomaly detection using forecasting methods ARIMA and HWDS. In: 2013 32nd International Conference of the Chilean Computer Science Society (SCCC), pp. 63–66 (2013). https://doi.org/10.1109/SCCC.2013.18
28. Salomão, M., Molisani, M., Ovalle, A., Rezende, C., Lacerda, L., Carvalho, C.: Particulate heavy metal transport in the lower Paraíba do Sul river basin, Southeastern, Brazil. Hydrol. Process. 15(4), 587–593 (2001)
29. Shafaei, M., Kisi, O.: Predicting river daily flow using wavelet-artificial neural networks based on regression analyses in comparison with artificial neural networks and support vector machine models. Neural Comput. Appl. 28(1), 15–28 (2017)
30. da Silva, I.N., Cagnon, J.Â., Saggioro, N.J.: Recurrent neural network based approach for solving groundwater hydrology problems. In: Artificial Neural Networks-Architectures and Applications. IntechOpen (2013)

31. Sobral, B.S., et al.: Drought characterization for the state of Rio de Janeiro based on the annual SPI index: trends, statistical tests and its relation with ENSO. Atmos. Res. **220**, 141–154 (2019)
32. Trento, A., Vinzón, S.: Experimental modelling of flocculation processes-the case of Paraiba do Sul Estuary. Int. J. Sedim. Res. **29**(3), 378–390 (2014)
33. Valipour, M., Banihabib, M.E., Behbahani, S.M.R.: Comparison of the ARMA, ARIMA, and the autoregressive artificial neural network models in forecasting the monthly inflow of Dez dam reservoir. J. Hydrol. **476**, 433–441 (2013)
34. Vásquez, W.F., de Rezende, C.E.: Willingness to pay for the restoration of the Paraíba do Sul River: a contingent valuation study from Brazil. Ecohydrol. Hydrobiol. (2018)
35. Yaseen, Z.M., El-Shafie, A., Jaafar, O., Afan, H.A., Sayl, K.N.: Artificial intelligence based models for stream-flow forecasting: 2000–2015. J. Hydrol. **530**, 829–844 (2015)
36. Zhang, J., Zhu, Y., Zhang, X., Ye, M., Yang, J.: Developing a long short-term memory (LSTM) based model for predicting water table depth in agricultural areas. J. Hydrol. **561**, 918–929 (2018)

Contextual Simulated Annealing Q-Learning for Pre-negotiation of Agent-Based Bilateral Negotiations

Tiago Pinto[1,2(✉)] and Zita Vale[2]

[1] GECAD – Research Group on Intelligent Engineering and Computing
for Advanced Innovation and Development, Porto, Portugal
[2] Institute of Engineering, Polytechnic of Porto (ISEP/IPP), Porto, Portugal
{tcp, zav}@isep.ipp.pt

Abstract. Electricity markets are complex environments, which have been suffering continuous transformations due to the increase of renewable based generation and the introduction of new players in the system. In this context, players are forced to re-think their behavior and learn how to act in this dynamic environment in order to get as much benefit as possible from market negotiations. This paper introduces a new learning model to enable players identifying the expected prices of future bilateral agreements, as a way to improve the decision-making process in deciding the opponent players to approach for actual negotiations. The proposed model introduces a con-textual dimension in the well-known Q-Learning algorithm, and includes a simulated annealing process to accelerate the convergence process. The proposed model is integrated in a multi-agent decision support system for electricity market players negotiations, enabling the experimentation of results using real data from the Iberian electricity market.

Keywords: Bilateral contracts · Context awareness · Electricity markets · Reinforcement learning

1 Introduction

The Electricity Markets (EM) restructuring placed several challenges to governments and to the companies that are involved in generation, transmission, and distribution of electrical energy [1]. Due to fuel fossil related concerns, the penetration of renewable energy sources has grown. The considerable increase of distributed generation of intermittent nature, makes EM more competitive, and consequently encourage a decrease in electricity prices [2]. However, some recurrent problems must be considered, e.g. the dispatch ability, limitations in the power system network, and the integration of small producers in EM, among others [3]. In order to overcome these problems, some global solutions are being adopted, deeply changing the traditional market models. Nowadays there are several market models, some with clearing mechanisms based on offers optimization, such as most US EM [4]; and other based on symmetric auctions, as in most European countries [5]. However, electricity trade worldwide is also supported by means of bilateral contracts negotiation.

© Springer Nature Switzerland AG 2019
P. Moura Oliveira et al. (Eds.): EPIA 2019, LNAI 11804, pp. 519–531, 2019.
https://doi.org/10.1007/978-3-030-30241-2_44

With the increase of the complexity and unpredictability in EM, increases the need to understand markets' mechanism and how the interaction between the players affects markets outcomes. Simulation and decision support tools have been increasingly used, including several modeling tools based on multi-agent software. Some relevant examples are the simulators EMCAS AMES, GAPEX and MASCEM [6].

Current tools are directed to the study of market mechanisms and interactions among participants, but are not suitable for supporting the decisions of negotiating players in obtaining higher profits in energy transactions. The common behavior of market players in bilateral contracts negotiation is mainly based on the definition of prices and quantities in energy transactions with each competitor. Hence, relevant information, concerning competitors' previous negotiations, can be used to improve the decision process, considering the characteristics of the negotiation. It is essential to consider the concept of context awareness, since it influences the prices and volumes to be negotiated. A review of context analysis mechanism of EM players is presented in [7], which proposes a methodology to define and analyze different negotiation contexts in EM.

This paper presents a learning method to support decisions of players in the pre-negotiation of bilateral contracts, allowing to identify the ideal negotiators to trade with, enhancing the outcomes of the negotiation process. This method is based on the application of reinforcement learning algorithm (RLA), namely the Q-Learning algorithm, to learn the contract price forecasting method that is the closest to reality. This algorithm also determines the best method for each context. The forecast scenarios are determined using different methods to identify the expected price for each amount of energy. However, no method presents a better performance than all others in every situation, only in particular cases and contexts [8]. Thus, these contract prices forecasting are subject to some error degree. Because of that, the quality of definition of the best forecast method is essential for supporting the decision process. Besides the contextual dimension introduced in the learning process, a Simulated Annealing (SA) process [9] is also included to enable accelerating the convergence of the learning process, especially when the number of observations is low.

2   Proposed Methodology

The proposed method uses a learning process based on the assessment of likelihood of occurrence of each alternative scenario of negotiation. Thus, this approach allows the supported player to be prepared for the negotiation scenario that is the most likely to occur and perform the action that generates the best results. Besides, the contextualization of the learning process is enabled, obtaining the expected negotiation scenarios that most reflect the current context.

2.1 Contextual Q-Learning

The bilateral contract price estimation approach is based on the application of the Q-Learning reinforcement learning algorithm, where an agent learns through trial and error. An agent operates in an environment conceptualized by a set of possible states, in which the agent can choose actions from a set of possible actions. Each time that the player performs an action, a reinforcement value is received, indicating the immediate value of the resulting state transition. Thus, the only learning source is the agents' own experience, whose goal is to acquire an actions policy that maximizes its overall performance [10].

The proposed methodology proposes an adaptation of the Q-Learning algorithm [11] to undertake the learning process. Q-Learning is a very popular reinforcement learning method. It is an algorithm that allows the autonomous establishment of an interactive action policy. It is demonstrated that the Q-Learning algorithm converges to the optimal proceeding when the learning Q state-action pairs is represented in a table containing the full information of each pair value [12]. The basic concept behind the proposed Q-Learning adaption is that the learning algorithm can learn a function of optimal evaluation over the whole space of context-scenario pairs $(c \times s)$. This evaluation defines the Q confidence value that each scenario can represent the actual encountered negotiation scenario s in context c. The Q function performs the mapping as in (1):

$$Q : c \times s \rightarrow U \tag{1}$$

where U is the expected utility value when selecting a scenario s in context c. The expected future reward, when choosing the scenario s in context c, is learned through trial and error according to (2):

$$Q_{t+1}(c_t, s_t) = Q_t(c_t, s_t) + \alpha(c_t, s_t)\left[r_{s,c,t} + \gamma \cdot U_t(c_{t+1}) - Q_t(c_t, s_t)\right] \tag{2}$$

where c_t is the kind of context when performing under scenario s_t at time t:

- $Q_t(c_t, s_t)$ represents the value of the previous iteration (each iteration represents each new contract established in the given scenario and context). Generally, the Q value is initialized to 0.
- $\alpha(c_t, s_t)(0 < \alpha \leq 1)$ is the learning rate which determines the extent to which the newly acquired information will replace the old information (e.g. assuming a value of 0 learns nothing; on the other hand, a value of 1 represents a fully deterministic environment).
- $r_{s,c,t}$ is the reward, which represent the quality of the pair context-scenario $(c \times s)$. It appreciates the positive actions with high values and negative with low values, all of them are normalized on a scale from 0 to 1. The reward r is defined in (3):

$$r_{s,c,t} = 1 - \left|RP_{c,t,a,p} - EP_{s,c,t,a,p}\right| \tag{3}$$

where $RP_{c,t,a,p}$ represents the real price that has been established in a contract with an opponent p, in context c, in time t, referring to an amount of power a; and $EP_{s,c,t,a,p}$ is the estimation price of scenario that corresponds to the same player, amount of power and context in time t. All r values are normalized in a scale from 0 to 1.

- $\gamma (0 \leq \gamma \leq 1)$ is the discount factor which determines the importance of future rewards. A value of 0 only evaluates current rewards, and higher values than 0 takes into account future rewards.
- $U_t(c_{t+1})$ is the estimation of the optimal future value which determines the utility of scenario s, resultant in context c. U_t is calculated as in (4):

$$U_t(c_{t+1}) = \max_s Q(c_{t+1}, s) \qquad (4)$$

The Q-Learning algorithm is executed as follows:

- For each c and s, initialize $Q(c, s) = 0$;
- Observe new event (new established contract);
- Repeat until the stopping criterion is satisfied:
  - Select new scenario for current context;
  - Receive immediate reward $r_{s,c,t}$;
  - Update $Q(c, s)$ according to (2);
  - Observe new context c';
  - $c \rightarrow c'$.

After each update, all Q values are normalized according to the Eq. (5), to facilitate the interpretation of values of each scenario in a range from 0 to 1.

$$Q'(c, s) = \frac{Q(c, s)}{max[Q(c, s)]} \qquad (5)$$

The proposed learning model assumes the confidence of Q values as the probability of a scenario in a given context. $Q(c, s)$ learns by treating a forecast error, updating each time a new observation (new established contract) is available again. Once all pairs context-scenario have been visited, the scenario that presents the highest Q value, in the last update, is chosen by the learning algorithm, to identify the most likely scenario to occur in actual negotiation.

2.2 Simulated Annealing Process

SA is an optimization method that imitates the annealing process used in metallurgy. The final properties of this substance depend strongly on the cooling schedule applied, i.e. if it cools down quickly the resulting substance will be easily broken due to an imperfect structure, if it cools down slowly the resulting structure will be well organized and strong. When solving an optimization problem using SA the structure of the substance represents a codified solution of the problem, and the temperature is used to determine how and when new solutions are perturbed and accepted. The algorithm is basically a three steps process: perturb the solution, evaluate the quality of the solution, and accept the solution if it is better than the previous one [13].

The two main factors of SA are the decrease of the temperature and the probability of acceptance. The temperature only decreases when the acceptance value is greater than a stipulated maximum. This acceptance number is only incremented when the probability of acceptance is higher than a random number, which allows some solutions to be accepted even if their quality is lower than the previous. When the condition of acceptance is not satisfied, the solution is compared to the previous one, and if it is better, the best solution is updated. At high temperatures, the simulated annealing method searches for the global optimum in a wide region; on the contrary, when the temperature decreases the method reduces the search area. This is done to try to refine the solution found in high temperatures. This is a good quality that makes the simulated annealing a good approach for problems with multiple local optima. SA, thereby, does not easily converge to solutions near the global optimum; instead this algorithm seeks a wide area always trying to optimize the solution. Thus, it is important to note that the temperature should decrease slowly to enable exploring a large part of the search space. The considered stopping criteria are: the current temperature and the maximum number of iterations. In each iteration is necessary to seek a new solution, this solution is calculated according to (6).

$$newsolution = solution + S \times N(0, 1) \tag{6}$$

solution in (1) refers to the previous solution, because this may not be the best found so far. $N(0, 1)$ is a random number with a normal distribution, the variable S is obtained through (7).

$$S = 0.01 \times (upbound - lwbound) \tag{7}$$

upbound and *lwbound* are the limits of each variable, which prevent from getting out of the limits of the search problem.

The decisive parameters in SA's research are the decrease of temperature and the likelihood of acceptance. 4 variations of the SA algorithm have been implemented, combining different approaches for calculating these two components. It is expected that this will bring different results for different groups, as these components introduce a strong randomness in SA, which makes them reflect in the final results (Table 1).

Table 1. Temperature and probability of acceptance calculation methods

Group	Temperature decreasing	Probability of acceptance	Ref.
1	$T_i = T_{i-1} \times \alpha$	$P = (2\pi T)^{-\frac{D}{2}} e^{\left(\frac{-\Delta x}{K \times T}\right)}$	[14]
2	$T_i = \frac{T_0}{i}$	$P = \dfrac{T_0}{(\Delta x^2 + T^2)^{\frac{(D+1)}{2}}}$	[14]
3	$T_i = T_0 e^{-ci\frac{1}{D}}$	$P = \prod_{d=1}^{D} \dfrac{1}{2(|y_d| + Ti) \ln\left(1 + \frac{1}{T_i}\right)}$	[14]
4	$T_i = T_0 \times \alpha^i$	$T_i = \dfrac{1}{1 + e^{\frac{\Delta x}{Tmax}}}$	[15]

where:

- $\alpha = 0.95$;
- i is the current iteration;
- $\Delta x = y(x^{max} - x^i)$ is the difference between best solution and current solution;
- $K = 1$ is the Boltzmann constant;
- $T_0 = 1$ is the initial temperature;
- D is the number of variables;
- $c = 0.1$;
- $|y_d|$ is the abs of solution current;
- $T_{min} = 1 \times 10^{-10}$;
- $acceptance_{max} = 15$.

3 Results and Discussion

3.1 Case Study Characterization

This section presents a case study to demonstrate the performance of the proposed methodology. A historical database, concerning the past log of established contracts of different EM players, is used to apply the proposed methodology and assess its performance. The used data is based on real data extracted from MIBEL - the Iberian Electricity Market. The dataset can be consulted [16] and is composed by the executed physical bilateral contracts declared in the Spanish System Operator, in the period between 1 July 2007 and 31 October 2008 (16 months/488 days). Each negotiation day is composed by 24 negotiation periods, in a total of 11712 periods. The negotiations were performed by 132 different players (88 Buyers and 44 Sellers) which established 1,797,996 contracts. Table 2 presents a detailed overview of the dataset.

Table 2. Dataset overview

	MIN	AVG	STDEV	MAX
Contracts/Period	128	157	17,78	180
Contracts/Day	147	3 753	485,78	4 287
Contracts/Player	2	27 244	58 653,22	288 160
Contracts/Player/Period	1	5	6,83	29
Power/Period/Contract	1	69,04	6,25	3 575
Power/Player/Contract	1	89,05	223,17	3 575
Power/Period	7 718	10 813	1 346,38	14 128
Power/Day	8 210	258 405,89	34 317,46	316 801
Power/Player	30	1 875 400,33	4 503 101,94	26 081 833

The distinct scenarios, which are the actions that the model may choose, refer to 5 contract price forecast methods, where there is an expected price for each amount of energy (from 1 until 10 MWh). The expected prices for the power amounts are calculated by several forecasting algorithms detailed in [17]. The context awareness is tested through 4 different contexts. The context analysis is carried out by a context analysis mechanism [7], which separates the historic data into different groups or contexts. 47% of the established contracts refer to Context 1, 8% refer to Context 2, 18% to Context 3 and 27% to Context 4.

The overall goal is to update the Q value of each forecast method (scenario) and context whenever there are new contracts. It is also important to test different combinations of input parameters, such as discount factor, learning rate and initial temperature; to analyze the evolution of Q values; and to have a suitable learning mechanism, which chooses the most likely forecast method to occur (i.e. the scenario with a lower forecast error in the current context).

Table 3 shows the comparison of the average error between the predicted price by each scenario and the actual verified price for each of the 4 considered scenarios. The error evaluation is measured using the Mean Absolute Error (MAE), Mean Absolute Percentage Error (MAPE) and Standard Deviation (STD). Using these prediction errors as basis it is possible to assess the quality of each scenario vs context pair, thus enabling to evaluate the quality of the learning process.

Table 3. Prediction error of the five considered scenarios in each of the four considered contexts

Context	Scenario	MAE	MAPE (%)	STD
1	1	13.94	18.43	16.34
	2	8.75	12.48	6.36
	3	3.26	4.12	2.36
	4	19.74	27.39	17.47
	5	12.89	17.62	9.20
2	1	3.67	5.26	4.62
	2	19.84	28.53	15.62
	3	3.82	5.48	4.89
	4	26.84	39.98	18.74
	5	10.31	14.53	8.38
3	1	3.91	7.52	4.93
	2	9.93	14.45	8.22
	3	3.74	7.16	4.53
	4	14.42	19.36	12.60
	5	6.22	9.36	6.83
4	1	5.46	8.63	7.31
	2	20.31	33.16	16.82
	3	24.17	38.28	18.45
	4	8.02	12.21	8.24
	5	15.16	21.75	13.82

From Table 3 it is visible that scenarios with lowest prediction error are: Scenario 1 for Contexts 2 and 4, and Scenario 3 for Contexts 1 and 3. These are the best scenarios (actions) to which the learning model should converge.

3.2 Results

Figure 1 presents the heat maps showing the results quality (overall prediction errors) achieved by the proposed method when applied to each of the contexts independently. The heat maps include the combinations between the values of α and T_0. The dark green zones represent the combinations of α and T_0 that present the best performance in each test, and the red zones represent the worst combinations.

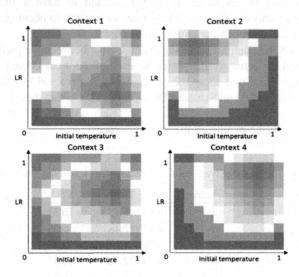

Fig. 1. Sensitivity analysis results for the combination between α and T_0 in the different performed tests.

From Fig. 1 it is seen that the best combination of parameters depends greatly on the number of observations that refer to each of the contexts. In Context 1, being that with the greatest number of observations, the best results arrive when a large T_0 is set, together with a low α. This enables the learning process to learn more slowly, providing enough room for exploration before starting to exploit the best action. On the contrary, in Context 2, which is the context with the smaller number of observations a large α and small T_0 is required, so that the learning process converges more quickly. In Contexts 3 and 4, having a moderate number of observations, the tendency goes to an intermediate level of α associated to a rather large T_0, enabling a moderate learning process, with enough exploration before the final convergence. For illustrative purposes, Fig. 2 shows the convergence process of the proposed model for Context 2, with and without SA.

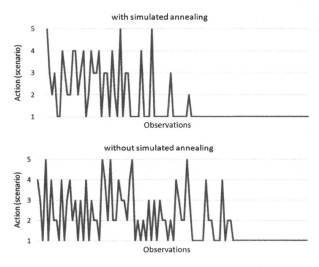

Fig. 2. Convergence process with and without the SA process

Figure 2 shows that, using the SA, the convergence to scenario 1 – the best action for context 2, is faster. There is less exploration, but the exploitation begins much sooner, which is important in contexts such as this one, in which the total number of observations is low.

Using the identified best parametrization, the results of the proposed methodology are compared to several benchmark reinforcement learning algorithms under the same simulation settings, namely the standard Q-Learning, Roth-Erev [18], UCB1 [19] and EXP3 [20]. Table 4 shows the global results, i.e. normalized confidence values (or Q values) in each of the 5 considered scenarios, in each of the 4 considered contexts. Table 5 shows the comparison of the average prediction errors resulting from the scenarios chosen in each iteration by the different algorithms in each context. This enables assessing the overall quality of the learning methods in each context. Note that it is not expected that the achieved error values match those achieved by the best scenarios themselves, as presented in Table 3, because due to the required exploration phase of the reinforcement learning algorithms several different scenarios, even if bad, must be tried, which results in an overall trial and error procedure. However, these average errors enable assessing the algorithms quality in terms of exploration vs exploitation balance, and their capability of converging to the best scenario, as shown by the confidence values in each scenario, as shown by Table 4.

Table 4 shows that the proposed model is able to learn and identify the best scenario for each of the four considered contexts, namely scenario 3 for contexts 1 and 3, and scenario 1 in contexts 2 and 4. On the other hand, all the other state of the art algorithms are able to effectively learn the best global scenario (scenario 1), but, by not including a contextual dimension, they are not able to identify the best scenario for the specific contexts. In summary, the current algorithms are able to learn the best overall approaches, but lack the adaptation capabilities to be able to identify different performances under different contexts.

Table 4. Comparative results between the proposed model and benchmark reinforcement learning algorithms

Algorithm	Context	Scenario				
		1	2	3	4	5
Proposed model	1	0.38	0.75	**1.00**	0.21	0.50
	2	**1.00**	0.30	0.97	0.19	0.69
	3	0.98	0.68	**1.00**	0.42	0.82
	4	**1.00**	0.34	0.29	0.88	0.42
Standard Q-Learning	1	**1.00**	0.41	0.88	0.52	0.65
	2	**1.00**	0.41	0.88	0.52	0.65
	3	**1.00**	0.41	0.88	0.52	0.65
	4	**1.00**	0.41	0.88	0.52	0.65
Roth-Erev	1	1.00	0.28	0.92	0.41	0.56
	2	**1.00**	0.28	0.92	0.41	0.56
	3	**1.00**	0.28	0.92	0.11	0.56
	4	**1.00**	0.28	0.92	0.41	0.56
UCB1	1	1.00	0.23	0.76	0.53	0.72
	2	**1.00**	0.23	0.76	0.53	0.72
	3	**1.00**	0.23	0.76	0.53	0.72
	4	**1.00**	0.23	0.76	0.53	0.72
EXP3	1	1.00	0.32	0.63	0.45	0.42
	2	**1.00**	0.32	0.63	0.45	0.42
	3	**1.00**	0.32	0.03	0.45	0.42
	4	**1.00**	0.32	0.63	0.45	0.42

Table 5 shows that the proposed method is the algorithm that achieves the lowest prediction errors in all four contexts, as result from this method's context aware learning capability. However, some other methods reach very close results in the contexts in which the prediction is from Scenario 1 (identified by all methods as the best one, as seen from Table 4), namely in contexts 2 and 4. Nevertheless, the results from the proposed method are still better in these contexts because it is able to converge faster to the best scenario, by considering the different contexts as independent, while the other methods need for exploration (and more trial and error) to reach the best overall scenario.

The Kruscal-Wallis test is a nonparametric test used to compare three or more independent samples. It indicates if there is a difference between at least two of them. This is used to test the null hypothesis that all populations have equal distribution functions against the alternative hypothesis that at least two of the populations have different distribution functions. In this way it is assumed that equality of averages when equality of equal distributions exists [21]. By the Kruscal-Wallis test it is possible to obtain the value of $p = 0$ that indicates the rejection of the null hypothesis that all data samples have the same distribution at 1% significance level. The comparison between the pairs of groups is made to verify which of the samples differ from each other.

Table 5. Comparison of average prediction errors of the different algorithms in each context

Context	Algorithm	MAE	MAPE (%)	STD
1	Proposed Model	7.45	9.89	8.98
	Std. Q-Learning	11.24	16.28	14.04
	Roth-Erev	10.49	14.87	13.41
	UCB1	15.36	21.04	18.93
	EXP3	18.56	24.90	21.39
2	Proposed Model	4.28	6.46	5.89
	Std.Q-Learning	4.88	7.23	6.68
	Roth-Erev	4.46	6.83	6.03
	UCB1	5.89	9.31	8.72
	EXP3	6.53	10.85	9.38
3	Proposed Model	5.37	8.21	6.98
	Std.Q-Learning	9.16	13.28	9.37
	Roth-Erev	8.43	12.73	9.14
	UCB1	12.54	18.02	12.71
	EXP3	15.11	22.02	17.37
4	Proposed Model	6.22	9.35	8.31
	Std.Q-Learning	6.81	9.97	9.02
	Roth-Erev	7.47	10.28	11.07
	UCB1	6.74	9.63	8.86
	EXP3	7.26	10.15	10.62

The Bonferroni procedure is performed to make the comparison in pairs. Figure 3 represents the 95% confidence interval for all sample groups (5 methods, in which group 1 is the proposed method), in the total of all executions using the three data sets. In this way, it is possible to see which groups differ in the value of the average, using the Bonferroni procedure.

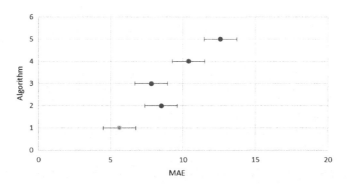

Fig. 3. Bonferroni confidence interval by 95%

Figure 3 shows that all methods have significantly different mean values. Since p = 1 in all these group tests, the null hypothesis where the groups are considered to have similar means with an error of 5% is accepted. Considering this analysis, it is concluded that the applied benchmark methods achieve significantly different results, thus supporting the relevance of the proposed approach.

4   Conclusions

Electricity markets are complex and dynamic environments, involving many entities and a constantly changing negotiation setting. Players acting in this domain need strong decision support solutions in order to be able to take as much benefit from market negotiations as possible.

The model presented in this paper aims at providing decision support to market players by helping them understanding which the best negotiation opponents to negotiate with are. In this way, a learning model for the pre-negotiation stage of bilateral contracts negotiations is presented. This model improved the standard Q-Learning algorithm by including a contextual dimension, thus providing a contextual aware learning model. A simulated annealing process is also included in order to enable accelerating the convergence process when needed, especially when the number of observations is low. Results show that the proposed model is able to undertake context-aware learning, surpassing the results of several benchmark learning algorithms when it comes to contextual learning.

Acknowledgements. This work has received funding from the European Union's Horizon 2020 research and innovation programme under project DOMINOES (grant agreement No 771066) and from FEDER Funds through COMPETE program and from National Funds through FCT under the project UID/EEA/00760/2019.

References

1. Lago, J., De Ridder, F., Vrancx, P., De Schutter, B.: Forecasting day-ahead electricity prices in Europe: the importance of considering market integration. Appl. Energy **211**, 890–903 (2018)
2. Nowotarski, J., Weron, R.: Recent advances in electricity price forecasting: A review of probabilistic forecasting. Renew. Sustain. Energy Rev. **81**, 1548–1568 (2018)
3. Klessmann, C., Held, A., Rathmann, M., Ragwitz, M.: Status and perspectives of renewable energy policy and deployment in the European Union what is needed to reach the 2020 targets? Energy Policy **39**(12), 7637–7657 (2011)
4. MISO Energy. http://www.misoenergy.org. Accessed on August 2018
5. NordPool. http://www.nordpoolspot.com. Accessed on August 2018
6. Soares, J., Pinto, T., Lezama, F., Morais, H.: Survey on complex optimization and simulation for the new power systems paradigm. Complexity **2018**, 32 (2018)
7. Pinto, T., Vale, Z., Sousa, T.M., Praça, I.: Negotiation context analysis in electricity markets. Energy **85**, 78–93 (2015)

8. Pinto, T., Vale, Z., Sousa, T., Praça, I., Santos, G., Morais, H.: Adaptive learning in agents behaviour: a framework for electricity markets simulation. Integr. Comput.-Aided Eng. IOS Press **21**(4), 399–415 (2014)
9. Gerber, M., Bornn, L.: Convergence results for a class of time-varying simulated annealing algorithms. Stoch. Process. Appl. **128**(4), 1073–1094 (2018)
10. Sutton, R.S., Barto, A.G.: Reinforcement Learning: An Introduction. Reinforcement Learning (1998)
11. Rahimi-Kian, A., Sadeghi, B., Thomas, R.J.: Q learning based supplier-agents for electricity markets. IEEE Power Eng. Soc. Gen. Meet. **1**, 420–427 (2005)
12. Watkins, C.J., Dayan, P.: Q-learning. Machine Learning. Machine Learning (1992)
13. Haznedar, B., Kalinli, A.: Training ANFIS structure using simulated annealing algorithm for dynamic systems identification. Neurocomputing **302**, 66–74 (2018)
14. Huang, K.Y., Hsieh, Y.-H.: Very fast simulated annealing for pattern detection and seismic applications. In: 2011 IEEE International Geoscience and Remote Sensing Symposium (IGARSS), pp. 499–502 (2011)
15. Chen, S., Xudiera, C., Montgomery, J.: Simulated annealing with thresheld convergence. In: 2012 IEEE Congress on Evolutionary Computation (CEC), pp. 1–7 (2012)
16. OMIE. ejecucioncbfom (2018). http://www.omie.es/files/flash/ResultadosMercado.html/. Accessed March 2019
17. Pinto, T., Vale, Z., Praça, I., Solteiro, E.J., Lopes, F.: Decision Support for Energy Contracts Negotiation with Game Theory and Adaptive Learning. Energies (2015)
18. Erev, I., Roth, A.E.: Multi-agent learning and the descriptive value of simple models. Artif. Intell. **171**, 423–428 (2007)
19. Burtini, G., Loeppky, J., Lawrence, R.: A Survey of Online Experiment Design with the Stochastic Multi-Armed Bandit. arXiv1510.00757 [cs, stat] (2015)
20. Bouneffouf, D., Féraud, R.: Multi-armed bandit problem with known trend. Neurocomputing **205**, 16–21 (2016)
21. Theodorsson-Norheim, E.: Kruskal-Wallis test: BASIC computer program to perform nonparametric one-way analysis of variance and multiple comparisons on ranks of several independent samples. Comput. Methods Programs Biomed. **23**(1), 57–62 (1986)

Fair Remuneration of Energy Consumption Flexibility Using Shapley Value

Ricardo Faia[1,2], Tiago Pinto[1,2(✉)], and Zita Vale[2]

[1] GECAD – Research Group on Intelligent Engineering and Computing
for Advanced Innovation and Development, Porto, Portugal
{rfmfa, tcp}@isep.ipp.pt
[2] Institute of Engineering, Polytechnic of Porto (ISEP/IPP), Porto, Portugal
zav@isep.ipp.pt

Abstract. This paper proposes a new methodology for fair remuneration of consumers participation in demand response events. With the increasing penetration of renewable energy sources with a high variability; the flexibility from the consumers' side becomes a crucial asset in power and energy systems. However, determining how to effectively remunerate consumers flexibility in a fair way is a challenging task. Current models tend to apply over-simplistic and non-realistic approaches which do not incentivize the participation of the required players. This paper proposes a novel methodology to remunerate consumers flexibility, in a fair way. The proposed model considers different aggregators, which manage the demand response requests within their coalition. After player provide their flexibility, the remuneration is calculated based on the flexibility amount provided by the players, the previous participation in demand response programs, the localization of the players, the type of consumer, the effort put in the provided flexibility amount, and the contribution to the stability of the coalition structure using the Shapley value. Results show that by assigning different weights to the distinct factors that compose the calculation formulation, players remuneration can be adapted to the needs and goals of both the players and the aggregators.

Keywords: Demand response · Fairness · Payoff allocation · Remuneration · Shapley value

1 Introduction

The increasing penetration of renewable energy sources is leading to major changes in power and energy systems all around the world [1]. The importance of consumers is increasing in this context, as they provide the potential to balance the variation of renewable-based generation through consumption flexibility.

This work has received funding from the European Union's Horizon 2020 research and innovation programme under project DOMINOES (grant agreement No 771066) and from FEDER Funds through COMPETE program and from National Funds through FCT under the project UID/EEA/00760/2019 and Ricardo Faia is supported by FCT Funds through and SFRH/BD/133086/2017 PhD scholarship.

© Springer Nature Switzerland AG 2019
P. Moura Oliveira et al. (Eds.): EPIA 2019, LNAI 11804, pp. 532–544, 2019.
https://doi.org/10.1007/978-3-030-30241-2_45

Consumption flexibility may come from multiple sources, such as industry consumers, residential buildings, storage units, or electrical vehicles [2]. The different types of consumers or prosumers enable the system to reach consumption flexibility with different characteristics, e.g. in amount, location, duration and activation time; which makes the flexibility worth differently depending on the needs.

The consumption flexibility may be activated by different means, usually associated to demand response programs or events [3]. Although some changes in current electricity market models are already taking place, market models are still not able to accommodate small-sized energy resources, and therefore, small consumers can only participate in flexibility transactions through aggregators, which guarantee the minimum volume to enable the market participation.

While these aggregators are able to negotiate energy and/or flexibility, how they should distribute their incomes in order to effectively and fairly remunerate the consumers that are providing the flexibility is a challenging task. Although some studies are being made (e.g. [4]), the definition of remuneration models for the participation in demand response is not sufficiently explored, and solutions are not yet adequate.

Lessons in this field can be learnt from artificial intelligence applications which have solved similar problems. An example is in [5] with the application of the Shapley value to divide the profit of a marketers group among them in the scope of a cooperation model among agents in the electricity market. The Shapley value defines how important is each player to the overall cooperation, and what payoff can the player reasonably expect. the optimal cost-sharing rule that optimizes the price of anarchy, followed by the price of stability, is precisely the Shapley value cost-sharing rule. See [6] for a survey of the subject.

The Shapley value determines a payoff for each player based on the player's contribution to the stability of the coalition structure; e.g. in what amount is the player responsible for determining the coalition structure. This, however, does not directly represent the payoff in terms of utility that each player should get as outcome of the game. Considering the specific setup of the problem considered in this work, players payoff is received in the form of a remuneratory monetary compensation for the sale of their consumption flexibility. This is a direct result of players available amount of flexibility, among other considered parameters. Hence, the Shapley value cannot be used as a direct representation of the players payoff, but it can be considered as an influential factor in the payoff calculation, as means of rewarding players for their contribution to the stability of the coalitions structure. In this way, this paper proposes a remuneration definition methodology that distributes the total amount of revenue that the players are entitled to as a whole, among the involved players. This remuneration calculation formulation considers the monetary component that each player should receive from the sale of the flexibility amount, but also several other components that contribute to the quality of the provided service. In specific, the remuneration calculation considers: the flexibility amount, the previous participation in demand response programs, the localization of the player, the type of consumer (residential, industrial, etc.), the effort put in the provided flexibility amount, and the contribution to the stability of the coalition structure (Shapley value). Using the proposed remuneration calculation methodology, it is possible to remunerate the players involved in demand response events in a fair way, enabling the payment for their amount of provided flexibility, but also incentivizing important aspects for the system, such as the relevant type of consumer, the location in the network of the provided flexibility and the effort of the players, as well as their intrinsic contribution for the stability of the coalitions, which is essential for aggregators and operators to be able to define adequate programs directed to the specific groups.

After this introductory section, Sect. 2 presents a discussion on the relevant work related to the present paper. Section 3 provides the formulation and description of the proposed methodology and Sect. 4 presents the results achieved from the application of the proposed model. Finally, Sect. 5 wraps up the paper with the main conclusions from the presented work.

2 Related Work

Developments in game theoretic models have potentiated their application to several research fields, including power and energy systems, see e.g. [7] for an overview on game theoretic methods in this domain. Worth highlighting is the work presented in [8], in which a game-theoretical model for energy scheduling of demand side resources is proposed. [9] presents an energy management model based on game theoretic assumptions, in [10] the optimization of the distribution system planning is performed using game theory, and in [11] a game theory-based strategy for electricity market participation is proposed. Several electricity market-driven simulation systems based on game theory concepts have also been introduced; e.g. [12] introduces a simulation system for energy storage devices management and operation. This problem is defined as a multi-player game, and Nash equilibrium is used to minimize the energy cost by reducing the peak demand. The Short–medium Run Electricity Market Simulator (SREMS) [13] is game theory-based and is able to support scenario analysis in the short-medium term and to evaluate market power.

One relevant, and often disregarded, aspect in this domain is the formation of coalitions between agents, so that they may improve their negotiation power and even for small players to gain access to market opportunities that are only accessible to large players. A recent and relevant review in coalition structure formation is provided in [14]. Consumer and demand response aggregation models in power and energy systems are typically based on clustering approaches. E.g. in [15] consumers are aggregated using an optimization-based clustering approach, as facilitator to their participation in electricity markets. The model proposed in [4] aggregates consumers demand response participation using hierarchical clustering and fuzzy C-means. Several remuneration schemes are also experimented by combining different groups of players and their minimum, average and maximum prices.

Remuneration models are also addressed in [16], which studies current remuneration models in electricity markets and demonstrated the need to extend the current electricity market design by additional remuneration mechanisms to reach imposed quotas of renewable generation and provide investment incentives for new firm capacity. The work presented in [17] considers the sensitivity of users to electricity prices to establish real-time pricing models considering price-based demand response measures by formulating a real-time pricing sale scheme. On the other hand, [18] proposes two formulations of a game-theoretic market equilibrium models for capacity markets with distinctive features. Moreover, the equilibrium models explicitly combine the capacity markets with markets for flexibility and indirect with remuneration for renewable energy sources.

A game-theoretical model is also applied in [5] to define a cooperation model among agents in the electricity market. The Shapley value is used to divide the profit of the marketers group among them. The Shapley value is also used in [19] to support the decision-making process of a peer-to-peer trading mechanism. The proposed game theoretic approach delivers distributed energy management solutions for individuals in the trading process considering both optimality and fairness among prosumers when trading energy among each other. In [20] the Shapley value helps to quantify the marginal contribution of each aggregator when dealing with incentives to electricity users to reduce demand in contingency situations.

The existing applications of the Shapley value in power and energy related problems suggest that this value may be suitable to address the problem discussed in this work. The calculation of the individual remuneration of consumers when participating in demand response events, through the distribution of the total revenue of the corresponding aggregator is presented in the following section.

3 Proposed Methodology

This section presents the proposed methodology for fair remuneration of flexibility provision, including the formulation used in this work. Figure 1 presents the overview of the set up considered by the proposed work.

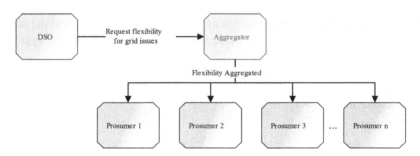

Fig. 1. Flexibility procurement scheme by DSO

As presented by Fig. 1, in cases of need from the system standpoint (e.g. contingency situations), the Distributed System Operator (DSO) requests consumption flexibility to one or several flexibility aggregators. The DSO will use this flexibility to solve issues in the distribution network, such as congestion management. This type of arrangement is proposed in a business model of Dominoes project[1]. Each flexibility

---

[1] http://dominoesproject.eu/about/ - DOMINOES is a project of European Union's Horizon 2020.

aggregator has a number of customers, which may be consumers or prosumers, and uses the flexibility from these customers in order to meet the requests from the DSO. After the costumers provide their flexibility, the DSO remunerates the aggregators for the provided flexibility, and the aggregators must share this income with the customers, in order to remunerate them for their services. Hence, Let N be a finite, non-empty set of customers $\{1, \ldots, n\}$. Any subset C of N is called a coalition and is managed by an aggregator. The *grand coalition* is the set N of all players. A *coalition structure* over N is a collection of non-empty subsets $CS = \{C^1, \ldots, C^k\}$ such that

$$\cup_{j=1}^{k} C^j = N \text{ and}$$

$$C^i \cap C^j = \emptyset \text{ for any } i, j \in \{1, \ldots, k\} \text{ such that } i \neq j.$$

The proposed remuneration definition methodology distributes the total amount of revenue among the involved players. This remuneration calculation formulation considers the monetary component that each player should receive from the sale of the flexibility amount, but also several other components that contribute to the quality of the provided service, namely: the flexibility amount, the previous participation in demand response programs, the localization of the player, the type of consumer (residential, industrial, etc.), the effort put in the provided flexibility amount, and the contribution to the stability of the coalition structure (Shapley value).

In Eq. (1), the aggregator remuneration is presented. In this case, it is considered that the DSO makes a request for flexibility to the aggregator. This request includes the price and amount of flexibility required by the DSO.

$$R_{agg} = Price_{agg} \times A_{agg} \tag{1}$$

where R_{agg} represents the aggregator renumeration in €, $Price_{agg}$ represent the price in €/kW that DSO will pay and A_{agg} is the flexibility amount provided by the aggregator agg.

As shown by Eq. (2), for each aggregator, the sum of the amount of flexibility A_i, in kW, provided by each customer i is equal to the total amount of flexibility provided by the aggregator to the DSO.

$$A_{agg} = \sum_{i=1}^{N} A_i \tag{2}$$

Equation (3) represents the price $Price_i$ that the aggregator will pay to each of its aggregates. The price represents 90% of the price the aggregator receives from the DSO, this represents the profit of 10% to the aggregator.

$$Price_i = 0,9 \times Price_{agg} \tag{3}$$

Equation (4) represents R_i^1, which is in the basis remuneration of player i, and is calculated by multiplying the amount of flexibility provided by customer i by the price payed by the aggregator to player i.

$$R_i^1 = Price_i \times A_i \qquad (4)$$

In (5) is defined the proposed remuneration model R_i^2.

$$R_i^2 = Price_i \times \left(A_i \times \frac{v_i^1}{\sum v^1} \right) \qquad (5)$$

The term R_i^2 represent the renumeration in € for player i and v_i^1 represents a factor which influences the remuneration of each player. This factor is calculated from the attributes of each player, as explained as follows. The term $\sum v$ correspond to the sum of all characteristic function values of all players.

$$v_i^1 = \sum_{j=1}^{NA} w_{j,i}^1 \times At_{i,j}^1 \qquad (6)$$

where $w_{j,i}^1$ is the weight of attribute j considering player i, $At_{j,i}^1$ correspond to the value for attribute j considering player i and NA correspond to the total number of attributes.

$$At^1 = \{participation, location, facility\ type, confort\ affect, Shapley\ value\} \qquad (7)$$

The v_i^1 factor is calculated considering the attributes of each player that should influence the remuneration of the players, either by incentivizing certain characteristics or penalizing them. The considered attributes are (i) the previous participation in demand response programs, in order to benefit the players that contribute regularly to this type of programs, and thus incentivize players participation; (ii) the relevance of the location of each player, *i.e.* if the location of the customer is more or less beneficial to the system (if the reduction of consumption in the specific location contributes to effective power flow); (iii) the relevance of the type of facility, e.g. residential, commercial, industrial; (iv) the effort placed by the customer in the flexibility provision, measures by the relative amount of flexibility provides in relation to the total amount of consumption of the player, in order to reward players that make bigger efforts (provide a larger percentage of relative flexibility); and (v) the contrition of the players to the stability of the coalitions, measured by the Shapley value.

Equation (8) represents the preliminary characteristic function of player i, used to calculate the Shapley value, the term $w_{j,i}^2$ represent the weight for attributes considering all attributes in At^2 set.

$$v_i^2 = \sum_{j=1}^{NA} w_{j,i}^2 \times At_{i,j}^2 \qquad (8)$$

The v_i^2 factor is obtained considering the attributes of each player, except from the Shapley value. I.e. are considered the participation ratio, the location of each player, the type of facility and the comfort affect.

$$At^2 = \{participation, location, facility\ type, confort\ affect\} \tag{9}$$

where, $At_{j,i}^2$ correspond to the value for attribute j considering player i.

Equation (10) specifies the range of the attributes. All attributes are ranged in the interval $[0, 1]$. The calculation of the relevance of the type of facility is performed according to Eq. (11)

$$At_{j,i} = \left\{ \begin{array}{ll} [0, 1], & if\ j = 1, 2, 4 \\ D_c, & else\ if\ j = 3 \end{array} \right\} \tag{10}$$

The relevance of the type of facility is calculated through the diversity D_C among the players included in the same coalition C, considering their intrinsic characteristics. D_C is calculated as in Eq. (11).

$$D_C = \frac{1}{G} \sum_{g=1}^{G} s\sigma_g^C \tag{11}$$

$$s\sigma_g^C = \frac{\sigma_g^C}{\left(\frac{g_{max} - g_{min}}{2} \right)} \tag{12}$$

$$\sigma_g^C = \sqrt{\frac{1}{T_C} \sum_{t=1}^{T_C} \left(g_t - \mu_g^C \right)^2} \tag{13}$$

$$\mu_g^C = \frac{1}{T_C} \sum_{t=1}^{T_C} g_t \tag{14}$$

where G is the number of components that define the diversity of players in each coalition (e.g. volume of flexibility, type of consumer, price). Hence, D_C calculates the average scaled standard deviation $s\sigma_g^C$ in coalition C for all characteristics g in a way that $s\sigma_g^C \in [0, 1]$. For each characteristic g, σ_g^C considers the values associated to each member t of the coalition C. Firstly, the mean value μ_g^C for each characteristic g in the coalition C is calculated as in (14); then we reach the mean deviation σ_g^C of each value of characteristic g (from each player in coalition C) to the mean, as in (13). The standard deviation σ_g^C is scaled according to the maximum and minimum values of g, in order to get $s\sigma_g^C$, as showed in (12). Finally, the average between the $s\sigma_g^C$ of all characteristics is calculated, giving us the value of D_C, as in (11).

The Shapley value is calculated according to Eq. (15). It is one way to distribute the total gains to the players, assuming that they all collaborate. It is a "fair" distribution it is the only distribution with certain desirable properties listed below.

$$\varphi_i(v^2) = \sum_{S \subseteq N \setminus \{i\}} \frac{|S|!(N - |S| - 1)!}{N!} \left(v^2(S \cup \{i\}) - v^2(S) \right) \tag{15}$$

where N is the number of players and the sum extends over all subsets S of N not containing player i. The formula can be interpreted as follows: imagine the coalition being formed one actor at a time, with each actor demanding their contribution $v^2(S \cup \{i\}) - v^2(S)$ as a fair compensation, and then for each actor take the average of this contribution over the possible different permutations in which the coalition can be formed.

4 Numerical Results

4.1 Specifications

The setup of this case study is a set of 3 players, which are part of the same coalition. The aggregator in charge of managing this coalition receives a request from the DSO to provide an amount of flexibility in a certain period in time. Each of the players provides a specific volume of flexibility, and the aggregator uses the proposed approach to calculate the remuneration for each of the players.

Table 1 shows the attributes characterization for all players. The amount is the flexibility value that the player reports. The participation attribute is obtained from an analysis in the historical participation. Location value is obtained by the location of each player in the distribution network. In the facility type value are included the characteristic of each facility. The comfort affect value is related with quantity of load that each player is predisposed to cut, taking into account the total load that is consuming.

Table 1. Attributes characterization for the three considered players

Players	Amount	Participation	Location	Facility type	Comfort affect
A	0	0,5	0,5	0,5	0
B	5	0,9	0,9	0,9	0,9
C	10	0,3	0,3	0,3	0,3

From Table 1 one can see that player A does not provide any flexibility. Player B and player C provide 5 and 10 kW respectively. Player C has a larger amount to sell, but player B has better attributes values. It is expected that the renumeration has into account all attributes and thus fairly remunerate player C, but also compensate player B for the good attributes.

Table 2 presents the values of input for Eq. (6) in term $w_{j,i}^1$. The table considers four different scenarios. In each scenario for each player the sum of all attribute weight must be equal to 1. With the creation of scenarios, we try to study the influence of attributes weight in the final renumeration for each player. In specific, Scenario 1 provides a large weight to the amount, thus expecting to benefit players that provide larger volumes of flexibility regardless of their characteristics; Scenario 2 represents the opposite situation, by rewarding the other characteristics over the amount of flexibility; Scenario 3 considers a more balanced case; and Scenario 4 defines a higher weight for the stability of the coalitions over the remaining attributed.

Table 2. Weight specification for all attributes

Scenario	Players	Amount	Participation	Location	Facility type	Comfort affect	Shapley
1	A	0,75	0,05	0,05	0,05	0,05	0,05
	B	0,75	0,05	0,05	0,05	0,05	0,05
	C	0,75	0,05	0,05	0,05	0,05	0,05
2	A	0,06	0,188	0,188	0,188	0,188	0,188
	B	0,06	0,188	0,188	0,188	0,188	0,188
	C	0,06	0,188	0,188	0,188	0,188	0,188
3	A	0,3	0,14	0,14	0,14	0,14	0,14
	B	0,3	0,14	0,14	0,14	0,14	0,14
	C	0,3	0,14	0,14	0,14	0,14	0,14
4	A	0,1	0,1	0,1	0,1	0,1	0,5
	B	0,1	0,1	0,1	0,1	0,1	0,5
	C	0,1	0,1	0,1	0,1	0,1	0,5

For this case study, the price that the DSO pays to the aggregator for the flexibility is fixed in 0.04 €/kWh. With the application of Eq. (3) the price for each player is 0.036 €/kWh. The flexibility request from the DSO to the aggregator is 15 kW.

4.2   Results

Table 3 presents the value of the characteristic function for all possible coalitions. This function is needed for inputs in the calculation of Shapley value.

Table 3. Values of characteristic function

Scenario	$v^1(A)$	$v^1(B)$	$v^1(C)$	$v^1(AB)$	$v^1(AC)$	$v^1(BC)$	$v^1(ABC)$
1	0	4,18	8,06	4,18	8,06	12,24	12,24
2	0	1,146	0,882	1,146	0,882	2,028	2,028
3	0	2,13	3,21	2,13	3,21	5,34	5,34
4	0	2,13	3,21	2,13	3,21	5,34	5,34

The values of characteristics function are obtained from application of Eq. (8). The $w_{j,i}^2$ are based on values of Table 2 but the weight of Shapley value is removed, and the other weight is normalized in a scale of 0 to 1. In Table 4 are present the values of Shapley values obtained from the application of Eq. (15).

Table 4. Shapley values

Scenario	Players	Shapley value	Relative Shapley value
1	A	1,293	0,106
	B	5,473	0,447
	C	5,473	0,447
2	A	−0,088	0
	B	1,058	0,500
	C	1,058	0,500
3	A	0,360	0,067
	B	2,490	0,466
	C	2,490	0,466
4	A	0,360	0,067
	B	2,490	0,466
	C	2,490	0,466

In Table 4 are present the results of Shapley value and relative Shapley value. The relative Shapley value is a normalization of Shapley value in [0, 1]. Analyzing Table 4, players B and C have, in all scenarios the same Shapley value; meaning that these players' contribution to the stability of the coalition process is the same.

Table 5. Results for the different renumerations approaches

Scenario	Players	Basis	Proposed approach without Shapley value	Shapley value	Proposed approach with Shapley value
1	A	0	0	0,057	0
	B	0,180	0,184	0,241	0,185
	C	0,360	0,356	0,241	0,355
2	A	0	0	0	0
	B	0,180	0,305	0,270	0,291
	C	0,360	0,235	0,270	0,249
3	A	0	0	0,036	0
	B	0,180	0,215	0,252	0,211
	C	0,360	0,325	0,252	0,329
4	A	0	0	0,036	0
	B	0,180	0,215	0,252	0,241
	C	0,360	0,325	0,252	0,299

R. Faia et al.

Table 5 presents the values for the different remunerations approach, namely the basis remuneration, as in Eq. (4), in which the amount of flexibility is multiplied by the price; the proposed approach without considering the Shapley value, which is obtained using Eq. (5) but the term v_i^1 come from Eq. (8). The Shapley value renumeration is obtained using the relative Shapley value present in Table 4 multiplied by the price for flexibility from (3). The proposed approach with Shapley value renumeration is obtained using Eq. (5) and the values for v_i^1 are obtained in (6).

Figure 2 presents the values of Table 5 in order to facilitate the interpretation of the different forms of renumeration.

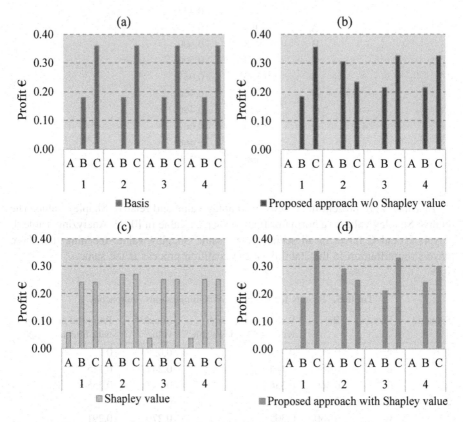

Fig. 2. Different remuneration approaches, (a) Basis renumeration, (b) Proposed approach without Shapley value, (c) Shapley value renumeration and (d) Proposed approach with Shapley value

In Fig. 2 are present the four different types of renumeration. The four plots have in vertical axes the values of profit and in horizontal axes the different scenarios (1, 2, 3 and 4), and for each scenario the respective three players. From Fig. 2(a) it is visible that the basis remuneration is the same regardless of the scenario, with player C receiving twice the payoff of player B, since it provides twice the flexibility amount; and player A receiving nothing. Figure 2(b) shows that in Scenario 1, which defines a very large weight to the amount of flexibility, results are similar to the basis remuneration, similarly to Fig. 2(d). In Scenario 2, which defines a smaller weight for the flexibility amount against the other characteristics, player C is benefited, and has even a larger remuneration than player B even though it provides a smaller amount of flexibility.

In Scenario 3, which considers a more balanced weight distribution, the remuneration distribution is more balanced as well between players B and C, with C being attributed a higher remuneration for its larger amount of flexibility, but player B being rewarded by its good characteristics. Finally, in Scenario 4, considering the Shapley value with larger weight; the remuneration values of both players are more balanced, since their Shapley value is the same, hence, since both contribute the same to the stability of the coalitions, they end up being more balanced.

5   Conclusions

This paper has proposed a methodology to enable a fair renumeration model. The proposed renumeration model considers different player attributes, the participation ratio, the location of each player, the type of facility, the comfort affect and the value of Shapley. Results show that the remuneration can be defined taking into account the attributes of the players and their actual contribution in terms of flexibility amount and stability. It is seen that considering only the Shapley values is not adequate to define a fair remuneration model but considering the Shapley values as part of the remuneration model benefits the remuneration process. For future work it is suggested to explore this proposed methodology with the interaction between a greater number of players, considering also the physical limitations that the distribution network may present.

References

1. Hossain, M.S., Madlool, N.A., Rahim, N.A.: Role of smart grid in renewable energy: an overview. Renew. Sustain. Energy Rev. **60**, 1168–1184 (2016)
2. Tan, K.M., Ramachandaramurthy, V.K., Yong, J.Y.: Integration of electric vehicles in smart grid: a review on vehicle to grid technologies and optimization techniques. Renew. Sustain. Energy Rev. **53**, 720–732 (2016)
3. Müller, T., Möst, D.: Demand response potential: available when needed? Energy Policy **115**, 181–198 (2018)
4. Faria, P., Spinola, J., Vale, Z.: Aggregation and remuneration of electricity consumers and producers for the definition of demand response programs. IEEE Trans. Ind. Inf. **12**, 952–961 (2016)
5. Acuña, L.G., Ríos, D.R., Arboleda, C.P., Ponzón, E.G.: Cooperation model in the electricity energy market using bi-level optimization and Shapley value. Oper. Res. Perspect. **5**, 161–168 (2018)
6. Hart, S.: Shapley value BT - game theory. In: Eatwell, J., Milgate, M., Newman, P. (eds.), pp. 210–216. Palgrave Macmillan UK, London (1989)

7. Saad, W., Han, Z., Poor, H.V., Basar, T.: Game-theoretic methods for the smart grid: an overview of microgrid systems, demand-side management, and smart grid communications. IEEE Signal Process. Mag. **29**, 86–105 (2012)
8. Mohsenian-Rad, A.H., Wong, V.W.S., Jatskevich, J., et al.: Autonomous demand-side management based on game-theoretic energy consumption scheduling for the future smart grid. IEEE Trans. Smart Grid **1**, 320–331 (2010)
9. Gao, B., Zhang, W., Tang, Y., et al.: Game-theoretic energy management for residential users with dischargeable plug-in electric vehicles. Energies **7**, 7499–7518 (2014). https://doi.org/10.3390/en7117499
10. Li, R., Ma, H., Wang, F., et al.: Game optimization theory and application in distribution system expansion planning, including distributed generation. Energies **6**, 1101–1124 (2013)
11. Pinto, T., Praca, I., Morais, H., Sousa, T.M.: Strategic bidding in electricity markets: An agent-based simulator with game theory for scenario analysis. Integr. Comput. Aided Eng. **20**, 335–346 (2013)
12. Vytelingum, P., Voice, T.D., Ramchurn, S.D., et al.: Agent-based micro-storage management for the smart grid. In: Proceedings of the International Joint Conference Autonomous Agents Multiagent Systems, AAMAS, pp. 39–46 (2010)
13. Migliavacca, G.: SREMS: a short-medium run electricity market simulator based on game theory and incorporating network constraints. In: 2007 IEEE Lausanne POWERTECH, Proceedings, pp. 813–818 (2007)
14. Rahwan, T., Michalak, T.P., Wooldridge, M., Jennings, N.R.: Coalition structure generation: a survey. Artif. Intell. **229**, 139–174 (2015)
15. Parvania, M., Fotuhi-Firuzabad, M., Shahidehpour, M.: Optimal demand response aggregation in wholesale electricity markets. IEEE Trans. Smart Grid **4**, 1957–1965 (2013)
16. Gerres, T., Chaves Ávila, J.P., Martín Martínez, F.: Rethinking the electricity market design: remuneration mechanisms to reach high RES shares. Results from a Spanish case study. Energy Policy **129**, 1320–1330 (2019)
17. Zhang, P., Dou, X., Zhao, W., et al.: Analysis of power sales strategies considering price-based demand response. Energy Procedia **158**, 6701–6706 (2019)
18. Höschle, H., De Jonghe, C., Le Cadre, H., Belmans, R.: Electricity markets for energy, flexibility and availability—Impact of capacity mechanisms on the remuneration of generation technologies. Energy Econ **66**, 372–383 (2017)
19. Long, C., Zhou, Y., Wu, J.: A game theoretic approach for peer to peer energy trading. Energy Procedia **159**, 454–459 (2019)
20. Wang, J., Huang, Q., Hu, W., et al.: Ensuring profitability of retailers via Shapley Value based demand response. Int. J. Electr. Power Energy Syst. **108**, 72–85 (2019)

Artificial Intelligence in Transportation Systems

VDS Data-Based Deep Learning Approach for Traffic Forecasting Using LSTM Network

Hongsuk Yi$^{(\boxtimes)}$ and Khac-Hoai Nam Bui🆔

Korea Institue of Science and Technology Information, Daejeon 34141, Korea
hsyi@kisti.re.kr, hoainam.bk2012@gmail.com

Abstract. Traffic forecasting is an important component of the Intelligent Transportation System (ITS). Recently, deep learning has been introduced as a promising method for traffic forecasting to deal with the exponential growth of data in ITS. In this regard, this paper focuses on applying a deep neural network model using LSTM for traffic forecasting based on analyzing data from the Vehicle Detection System (VDS). In particular, we first try to understand the traffic condition by applying visualization techniques. Then, based on the traffic condition, we apply an appropriate deep learning model for predicting traffic flow. Experiments in a certain urban area present promising results by applying the proposed model.

Keywords: Intelligent Transportation System · Traffic forecasting · Deep learning · Long-short term memory · Vehicle Detection System

1 Introduction

ITS is defined as an advanced application which provides innovative services for achieving traffic efficiency by minimizing traffic problems. Recently, with the development of advanced technologies (e.g., IoT, 5G, Fog/Edge computing, and Connected vehicles), many studies have been introduced for improving transportation systems [1,2]. Among approaches, traffic prediction is the main component of ITS to provide the traffic flow guidance system [7]. Particularly, with the development of traffic surveillance systems such as loop detectors and roadside sensors in ITS [10], a large amount of data can be generated and collected every day. In this regard, traffic data analysis and forecasting are able to provide accurate information to drivers and be used for signal optimization [13]. Specifically, Fig. 1 depicts the general process for traffic forecasting. However, with the rapidly increasing traffic demand makes the process difficult to predict. Recently, deep learning models have been introduced for big data-based traffic forecasting to deal with characteristic problems in traffic data such as highly nonlinear, time-varying, and randomness in which the objective is to improve the accuracy for predicting traffic flow [4]. Specifically, some well-known deep learning architectures such as Deep Belief Networks (DBN), Stacked Autoencoder (SAE), Convolution Neural Networks (CNN), Recurrent Neural Network (RNN) have demonstrated capabilities to predict traffic flow with big data.

© Springer Nature Switzerland AG 2019
P. Moura Oliveira et al. (Eds.): EPIA 2019, LNAI 11804, pp. 547–558, 2019.
https://doi.org/10.1007/978-3-030-30241-2_46

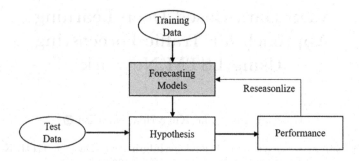

Fig. 1. The workflow for predictive analytics.

In [5], Huang et al. applied DBN architecture for multitask learning to predict traffic flow with promising results. On the other hand, the authors in [8] used SAE to learn generic traffic flow features in terms of nonlinear spatial and temporal correlations from traffic data. Furthermore, RNN, based on the structure, has been introduced as a potential solution for time series data prediction problem [9]. Specifically, the structure of RNN enables cells to memorize the temporal information from previous time intervals [3]. Consequently, Long Short-Term Memory (LSTM) model, a variation of RNN, has been introduced which is able to capture the long temporal features of the input data [12]. Nevertheless, it is difficult to determine which model is clearly better than others in any situation. Furthermore, configuring neural networks is still a challenging problem in which we have to explore different configurations to provide an appropriate model for adapting urban traffic development in terms of improving the efficient use of traffic data.

In this study, we take into account implementing a deep learning model using LSTM-RNN model for traffic prediction VDS data. Specifically, the traffic data collection from VDS has identified as a time series data. Although, there are several time-series forecasting models such as autoregression (AR) or ARIMA [15], however, as we mentioned above, deep learning approach using LSTM network has been proposed in this study since several reasons as follows:

- The model is able to manipulate its memory state which is suitable for the long sequences of the input data.
- The model is able to deal with multiple input variables problem comparing with conventional methods which are difficult to adapt with the multiple input forecasting problems.
- The model is flexible with the predictions in terms of customizing the window sizes (look-back and look-forward) to dynamically predict the traffic flow.

Generally, the contributions of this paper are described as follows:

- Data have collected and analyzed from VDS which are developed in the main roads of an urban area. Furthermore, for analyzing traffic data efficiently, we implement some data analysis techniques to understand the insight of

VDS data. In this regard, the traffic condition in considered areas can be represented.

- We develop a Deep LSTM-RNN model for providing traffic predictions. Specifically, hyper-parameters such as LSTM layers, dropout values, and batch size are defined to train the input data.
- Results in our implementation indicate promising values for VDS data-based traffic forecasting in urban areas.

The rest of this paper is organized as follows: In Sect. 2, the description of the VDS data that we have collected is presented. In Sect. 3, we propose a deep learning model using the LSTM network for traffic flow prediction based on VDS data. Section 4 demonstrates the results of our implementation. Discussions and future works are concluded in Sect. 5.

2 Data Description

The VDS is a type of fixed-point detectors that widely used in traffic surveillance systems for collecting information of traffic flow at a certain point in the road [11]. Specifically, the fixed point traffic information is collected by forming one or more detecting areas at specific points on the road. In this paper, we generated and collected data from VDS in the city of Daejeon, Korea. Figure 2 depicts locations of VDS that have deployed in the considering area. Specifically, there are total 21 fixed-points which have developed in the main roads of the area. Moreover, data was collected during one month for the implementation (from April 1st to April 30th, 2017) and been recorded in every five minutes. Furthermore, Table 1

Fig. 2. The locations of VDSID.

Table 1. Format of VDS traffic data.

Variable	Type	Notation
VDS-ID	String(ID)	VDSID
Time	YYYYMMDDhhmm	REG-HM
Traffic Volume	Integer	TR-VOL
Type-Small	Integer	SM-TR-VOL
Type-Middle	Integer	MD-TR-VOL
Type-Large	Integer	LG-TR-VOL
Speed	Real number	TRVL-SPD
Occupancy Rate	Real number	OCCUPY-RATE

demonstrates the data format that has collected from VDS. Particularly, the data collecting from VDS includes *speed, traffic volume, occupancy rate* and *type*. Particularly, *speed* refers to the average instantaneous velocity of vehicles. In order to collect speed values, multiple loop detectors have been installed on the detecting area. Therefore, multiple loop detectors determine the average speeds of vehicles that have passed between two close points by arranging two or more loop detectors in a row. On the other hand, *traffic volume* indicates the number of vehicles passing the detector. *occupancy rate* data indicates the traditional density (percentage) of the time that vehicle was on the detector during an hour. In particular, the value of *occupancy rate* is used since it is difficult to measure the number of presently vehicles at a specific time on a unit distance. Moreover, the *type* of vehicles also have been determined based on the shape of vehicles which include *Small, Middle,* and *Large* vehicles.

3   Deep LSTM-RNN Model for Traffic Forecasting Based on VDS Data

Recent works have been proved efficient of LSTM-RNN models for traffic data prediction. In [16], authors have proposed a novel deep learning approach for traffic forecast using LSTM. The comparisons with other models such as ARIMA, SVM (Support Vector Machine), and SAE indicate that LSTM can archive a better performance. Furthermore, Yi et al. [14] have been used LSTM model for short-term traffic prediction in highway systems. The experiments have shown promising results. Technically, LSTM network is the variation of RNN which is able to overcome the problems that occur in RNN models (e.g., vanishing gradient problem). Figure 3 illustrates the difference of structure between LSTM and vanilla RNN. Specifically, in a vanilla RNN, it only has hidden states which serve as the memory. Meanwhile, LSTM has both cell and hidden states which includes a cell A, an input gate x, an output gate o, and a forget gate f. The cell state has the ability to remove or add information to the cell. In this regard,

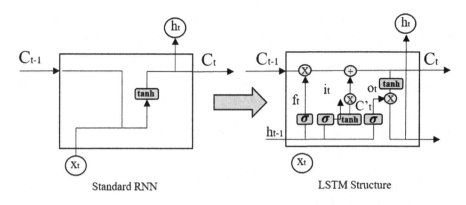

Fig. 3. Structure of a LSTM layer.

LSTM is able to handle the long-term dependency which is also the problem in other conventional RNN models. More detail about the structure of the LSTM model is presented in the following section.

3.1 LSTM-RNN Model

Supporting X denotes the input time series as follows:

$$X = \{x_1, x_2, ..., x_n\} \tag{1}$$

The hidden state of memory cells H and predict output time series Y are respectively determined as follows:

$$\begin{aligned} H &= \{h_1, h_2, ..., h_n\} \\ Y &= \{y_1, y_2, ..., y_n\} \end{aligned} \tag{2}$$

where each $h_t \in H$ and $y_t \in Y$ can be calculated as follow:

$$h_t = H(W_{xh}x_t + W_{hh}h_{t-1} + b_h) \tag{3}$$

$$y_t = W_{hy}h_t + b_y \tag{4}$$

where W and b denotes weight matrices and bias vectors, respectively. Specifically, in deep learning frameworks, weight metrics are stored in separate variables. For instance, W_{xh} is the weight matrix for the input of the hidden layer. Furthermore, the hidden state of memory cells H is computed based on the formulations of each gate in the cell:

$$\begin{aligned} i_t &= \sigma(W_i \cdot [h_{t-1}, x_t, C_{t-1}] + b_i) \\ f_t &= \sigma(W_f \cdot [h_{t-1}, x_t, C_{t-1}] + b_f) \\ o_t &= \sigma(W_o \cdot [h_{t-1}, x_t, C_t] + b_o) \\ h_t &= o_t * tanh(C_t) \end{aligned} \tag{5}$$

where σ and C denote the standard logistic sigmoid function and cell activation vectors, respectively, which can be sequentially calculated as follows:

$$\sigma(x) = \frac{1}{1 + e^{-x}}$$
$$C_t = f_t * C_{t-1} + i_t * \widehat{C}_t \tag{6}$$

where $\widehat{C}$ refers to the candidate value in each computed process of the cell which can be calculated as follows:

$$\widehat{C}_t = tanh(W_C \cdot [h_{t-1}, x_t] + b_C) \tag{7}$$

Consequently, the loss function of the model is computed based on the activation of the hidden layer which depends on the output layer and the hidden layer at the next time step. In this regard, the objective function of the proposed model is to minimize the square error which can be formulated as follows:

$$e = \sum_{t=1}^{n} (y_t - p_t)^2 \tag{8}$$

where p represents the predicted value.

3.2   Model Configuration

Regarding the objective function, in order to minimize the square error, we use Adam optimizer, an adaptive learning rate optimization algorithm for each parameter [6]. In particular, supporting v_t and s_t denote the decaying averages of past and past squared gradients, respectively, which are sequentially calculated as follows:

$$v_t = \beta_1 * v_{t-1} - (1 - \beta_1) * g_t$$
$$s_t = \beta_2 * s_{t-1} - (1 - \beta_2) * g_t^2 \tag{9}$$

where β_1, β_1 are decay rates and g_t denotes the gradient at time t. Consequently, in Adam optimization, bias corrections are implemented as follows:

$$\widehat{v}_t = \frac{v_t}{1 - \beta_1^t}$$
$$\widehat{s}_t = \frac{s_t}{1 - \beta_2^t} \tag{10}$$

In this regard, the Adam update rule of the parameter ω can be formulated as follow:

$$\omega_{t+1} = \omega_t - \eta \frac{\widehat{v}_t}{\sqrt{\widehat{s}_t} + \epsilon} \tag{11}$$

where η denotes the initial learning rate, the epsilon ϵ is a small number to avoid the division by zero ($\epsilon = 10^{-8}$).

Furthermore, Table 2 depicts the configuration of the proposed model. Technically, if we train a model with more layers, the learning is better. However,

Table 2. Hyper-parameters of the proposed model.

Layer (Type)	Output shape	Params #
lstm_1 (LSTM)	(None, 144, 36)	6192
lstm_2 (LSTM)	(None, 36)	10512
dropout_1 (Dropout)	(None, 36)	0
dense_1 (Dense)	(None, 144)	5328
Total params: 22032		
Trainable params: 22032		
Non-trainable params: 0		

the model may run into overfitting problem if we use many layers. Therefore, regarding the dataset that has been collected from VDS, we implement the model including two LSTM layers and one dense layer.

Particularly, one of the potential solutions for reducing the overfitting problem is that we reduce the number of hidden units (neurons) in each LSTM layer. In this study, based on the observation during training the VDS data, the number of neurons in each LSTM layer is around 30 to 40 which can avoid the overfitting problem. More detail of the implemented results is described in the following section.

4 Implementation

For the implementation, we first analyze VDS data to understand the traffic condition. Then, an appropriate Deep LSTM-RNN model is implemented for traffic forecasting in considering areas.

4.1 VDS-based Traffic Data Analysis

Figure 4 depicts traffic volumes from all VDS locations. As results of the figure, we can classify the considering area into three regions based on traffic volumes which are high (e.g, *VDS0022*, *VDS0023*), normal (e.g., *VDS0015*, *VDS0016*), and low traffic (e.g., *VDS0018*) densities. Hence, in this study, we take one VDSID of each region which include *VDS0022* (high density), *VDS0034* (normal density), and *VDS0018* (low density) into account for analyzing traffic condition and predicting traffic flow. Moreover, we also consider data from *VDS0035* since the VDSID is located in the same road but in the opposite direction with *VDS0034*. Figure 5(a) and (b) show traffic volumes and speed of aforementioned VDSIDs locations, respectively. As results, Although, the traffic flows are different, however, the average speeds in the considering areas are quite similar. Specifically, based on this result, we are able to detect abnormal events (e.g., traffic congestion) at a certain time. Furthermore, Fig. 6 depicts the compassion of traffic flows and average speeds between *VDS0034* and *VDS0035* which are

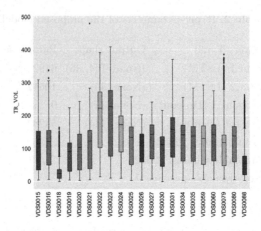

Fig. 4. The traffic volume of all VDS.

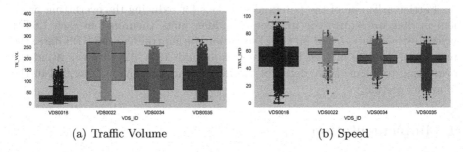

(a) Traffic Volume   (b) Speed

Fig. 5. Traffic conditions in the locations of VDS0018, VDS0022, VDS0034, and VDS0035.

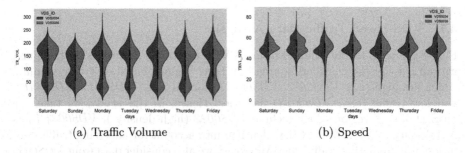

(a) Traffic Volume   (b) Speed

Fig. 6. Traffic condition in a same road with directions.

located on the same road but different direction. As shown in figures, traffic volumes in the directions are similar, however, average speeds of vehicles are different. Generally, the results are useful for the signal optimization problem, in which we take into consideration for our future work regarding this study.

4.2   Experimental Set-Up

In this study, we use *Keras*[1], a python deep learning library to develop our model. The experiments work well by a PC with Core i7 16-GB CPU and 32 GB GPU memories in which the GPU is used for the acceleration. More detail of the experimental settings are described as follows:

- *Input and Output:* The input includes some features such as the traffic volume, speed and occupancy rate of vehicles that have observed in previous time intervals. The output is the traffic prediction of aforementioned features in the next time interval of a certain *VDSID*.
- *Training and Testing Data:* Data have been collected during one month which has been recorded in every five minutes. Therefore, we use the data of the first 23 days as the training set and the last 7 days as the testing set.
- *Architecture:* In order to build the model, several hyper-parameters have to be determined such as the number of LSTM layers, neurons, dropout, and batch size. Moreover, accuracy metrics have been considered for the overall performance evaluation to imply the accuracy of the proposed model.

4.3   Results and Discussions

Traffic Forecasting: regarding the predictions, we compute the traffic flow of considering VDSIDs with twelve hours look-back and two hours look-forward. Figure 7(a) and (b) depict the prediction of traffic flow of *VDS0022* and *VDS0034* locations, respectively. Particularly, the results indicate that in case of high traffic density, the model can predict with better accuracy than low traffic density, especially on weekdays. For more detail, Fig. 8(a) and (b) shows the prediction of the occupancy at the *VDS0022* location on Wednesday and Saturday, respectively. In particular, in Fig. 8(b), at 19:00, the prediction is not accurate cause

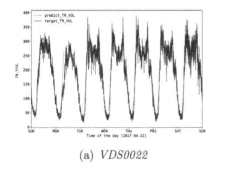
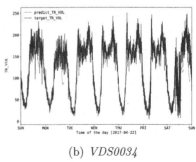

(a) *VDS0022*   (b) *VDS0034*

Fig. 7. Traffic forecasting of *VDS0022* and *VDS0034* locations.

---

[1] https://keras.io/.

there was a problem (e.g., accident or traffic congestion) that had occurred in that time. To deal with this problem, a solution is to reduce the size of look-back (e.g., 1 h or 2 h) to predict the near future (e.g., 1 h). Specifically, we will take the dynamic changing of window sizes (look-back and look-forward) problem in order to improve the accuracy in case of abnormal events as the future works regarding this study.

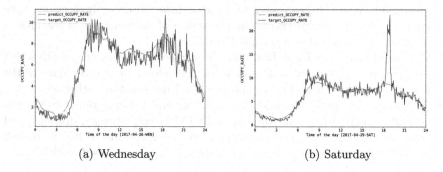

(a) Wednesday   (b) Saturday

Fig. 8. Occupancy rate of *VDS0022* location on Wednesday and Saturday

Accuracy Metrics: regarding the accuracy performance, we take Mean Squared Error (MSE) and Mean Absolute Error (MAE) into account which are sequentially calculated as follows:

$$
\begin{aligned}
MSE &= \frac{1}{n}\sum_{i=1}^{n}\left(f_i - \widehat{f_i}\right)^2 \\
MAE &= \frac{1}{n}\sum_{i=1}^{n}\left| f_i - \widehat{f_i} \right|
\end{aligned}
\tag{12}
$$

where f and $\widehat{f}$ are observation and prediction values, respectively. Figure 9(a) and (b) depict the accuracy metrics of *VDS0018* and *VDS0022* data, respectively. Specifically, the model provides promising results which have converged after 100 epoch. Moreover, we also implement some other common metrics such as Mean Absolute Percentage Error (MAPE), Root Mean Square Error (RMSE), and R Square (R^2) for evaluating the accuracy. The calculations of different accuracy metrics indicate promising results (Table 3) by applying the proposed model for VDS data.

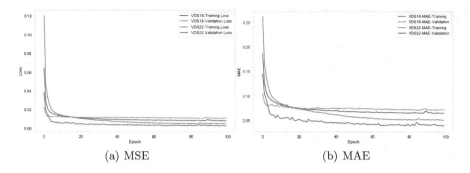

(a) MSE   (b) MAE

Fig. 9. Accuracy metrics of *VDS0018* and *VDS0022*

Table 3. Different accuracy performance indexes of *VDS0022* data

Date	Look-back	Look-forward	MSE	MAE	MAPE	RMSE	R2
Sun	144	24	0.00319	0.03981	18.67132	0.05647	0.63578
Mon	144	24	0.0048	0.04649	28.57718	0.0693	0.51126
Tue	144	24	0.01173	0.05991	35.88783	0.10829	0.55472
Wen	144	24	0.00343	0.04172	26.17659	0.05853	0.75176
Thu	144	24	0.00318	0.0408	24.49447	0.05637	0.71047
Fri	144	24	0.00478	0.04708	27.00742	0.06916	0.7016
Sat	144	24	0.00485	0.04734	23.38833	0.06961	0.69639

5   Conclusion and Future Work

Traffic forecasts are used for several key purposes in ITS to calculate the capacity
of infrastructure. Recently, deep learning models become an emergent issue for
predicting traffic flow. However, defining an appropriate model for forecasting
traffic flow is still a challenge which depends on data generation and collection.
In this study, we take VDS data into account by applying a deep learning approach using LSTM-RNN model to predict traffic flow. The results indicate the
effectiveness of the proposed model. However, the limitation of this study is that
the configuration of the proposed model can not minimize the square error for
all VDS datasets. In this regard, an automated hyper-parameter search for optimizing the accuracy is required which is an interesting issue for our future work
of this study.

Acknowledgment. This work was partly supported by Institute for Information &
communications Technology Promotion (IITP) grant funded by the Korea government
(MSIT) (No. 2018-0-00494, Development of deep learning-based urban traffic congestion prediction and signal control solution system) and Korea Institute of Science and
Technology Information (KISTI) grant funded by the Korea government (MSIT) (K-
19-L02-C07-S01).

References

1. Bui, K.H.N., Jung, J.J.: Internet of agents framework for connected vehicles: a case study on distributed traffic control system. J. Parallel Distrib. Comput. **116**, 89–95 (2018)
2. Bui, K.H.N., Jung, J.J.: Computational negotiation-based edge analytics for smart objects. Inf. Sci. **480**, 222–236 (2019)
3. Che, Z., Purushotham, S., Cho, K., Sontag, D., Liu, Y.: Recurrent neural networks for multivariate time series with missing values. Sci. Rep. **8**(1), 6085 (2018)
4. Chen, D.: Research on traffic flow prediction in the big data environment based on the improved RBF neural network. IEEE Trans. Ind. Inf. **13**(4), 2000–2008 (2017)
5. Huang, W., Song, G., Hong, H., Xie, K.: Deep architecture for traffic flow prediction: deep belief networks with multitask learning. IEEE Trans. Intell. Transp. Syst. **15**(5), 2191–2201 (2014)
6. Kingma, D.P., Ba, J.: Adam: a method for stochastic optimization. In: Proceedings of the 3rd International Conference on Learning Representations (ICLR 2015), San Diego, USA (2015). https://arxiv.org/abs/1412.6980
7. Lana, I., Ser, J.D., Vélez, M., Vlahogianni, E.I.: Road traffic forecasting: recent advances and new challenges. IEEE Intell. Transp. Syst. Mag. **10**(2), 93–109 (2018)
8. Lv, Y., Duan, Y., Kang, W., Li, Z., Wang, F.: Traffic flow prediction with big data: a deep learning approach. IEEE Trans. Intell. Transp. Syst. **16**(2), 865–873 (2015)
9. Ma, X., Tao, Z., Wang, Y., Yu, H., Wang, Y.: Long short-term memory neural network for traffic speed prediction using remote microwave sensor data. Transp. Res. Part C: Emerg. Technol. **54**, 187–197 (2015)
10. Nellore, K., Hancke, G.P.: A survey on urban traffic management system using wireless sensor networks. Sensors **16**(2), 157 (2016)
11. Park, S.H., Kim, S.M., Ha, Y.G.: Highway traffic accident prediction using VDS big data analysis. J. Supercomput. **72**(7), 2815–2831 (2016)
12. Sak, H., Senior, A.W., Beaufays, F.: Long short-term memory recurrent neural network architectures for large scale acoustic modeling. In: 15th Annual Conference of the International Speech Communication Association (INTERSPEECH 2014), pp. 338–342. ISCA (2014)
13. Vlahogianni, E.I., Karlaftis, M.G., Golias, J.C.: Short-term traffic forecasting: where we are and where we're going. Transp. Res. Part C: Emerg. Technol. **43**, 3–19 (2014)
14. Yi, H., Bui, K.N., Jung, H.: Implementing a deep learning framework for short term traffic flow prediction. In: Proceedings of the 9th International Conference on Web Intelligence, Mining and Semantics (WIMS 2019), pp. 7:1–7:8. ACM (2019)
15. Zhang, G.P.: Time series forecasting using a hybrid ARIMA and neural network model. Neurocomputing **50**, 159–175 (2003)
16. Zhao, Z., Chen, W., Wu, X., Chen, P.C., Liu, J.: LSTM network: a deep learning approach for short-term traffic forecast. IET Intell. Transp. Syst. **11**(2), 68–75 (2017)

A Reinforcement Learning Approach to Smart Lane Changes of Self-driving Cars

Fangmin Ye[1], Long Wang[1], Yibing Wang[1(✉)], Jingqiu Guo[2], Ioannis Papamichail[3], and Markos Papageorgiou[3]

[1] Institute of Intelligent Transportation Systems, Zhejiang University, 310058 Hangzhou, China
wangyibing@zju.edu.cn
[2] Key Laboratory of Road and Traffic Engineering of the Ministry of Education (China), Tongji University, Shanghai, China
guojingqiu@hotmail.com
[3] Dynamic Systems and Simulation Laboratory, School of Production Engineering and Management, Technical University of Crete, Chania, Greece
markos@dssl.tuc.gr

Abstract. Lane changes are a vital part of vehicle motions on roads, affecting surrounding vehicles locally and traffic flow collectively. In the context of connected and automated vehicles (CAVs), this paper is concerned with the impacts of smart lane changes of CAVs on their own travel performance as well as on the entire traffic flow with the increase of the market penetration rate (MPR). On the basis of intensive microscopic traffic simulation and reinforcement learning technique, a selfish lane-changing strategy was first developed in this work to enable foresighted lane changing decisions for CAVs to improve their travel efficiency. The overall impacts of such smart lane changes on traffic flow of both CAVs and human-driven vehicles were then examined on the same simulation platform. It was found that smart lane changes were beneficial for both CAVs and the entire traffic flow, if MPR was not more than 60%.

Keywords: Connected and automated vehicles · Smart lane changes · Traffic flow impacts · Microscopic simulation · Q-learning

1 Introduction

In the next decades, road transport and infrastructure are expected to undergo a profound transformation with the rapid development of connected and automated vehicles (CAVs). CAVs hold significant potential in the reduction of road accidents, traffic congestion, travel delay, vehicle emissions, fuel consumption, promising to increase traffic productivity and driver comfort [1, 2].

Vehicles in motion take actions in two dimensions. The longitudinal one aims to maintain desired speeds or keep a safe distance from a preceding vehicle, while the lateral one includes lane keeping or lane changing (for overtaking, merging, exiting, etc.). Owing to V2V and V2I assistance, CAVs may accept shorter inter-vehicle headways for car following, allow for coordinated lane changes, and hence may behave

© Springer Nature Switzerland AG 2019
P. Moura Oliveira et al. (Eds.): EPIA 2019, LNAI 11804, pp. 559–571, 2019.
https://doi.org/10.1007/978-3-030-30241-2_47

more cooperatively than human drivers to achieve greater system-wide benefits in efficiency, safety and environment [3, 4].

A large number of works have been conducted on the longitudinal maneuvers of CAVs, with cooperative adaptive cruise control (CACC) as one of the most promising CAV technologies so far [5–10]. On the other hand, there have been much fewer works on cooperative lane changing for CAVs. So far, most relevant research focuses on the optimal trajectory design for the CAV that is going to do a lane change [11–13]. Unlike the CACC research, the lane-changing works were not meant to determine lane-changing strategies of general applicability; instead, the focus has been on some typical but small scenarios involving a few vehicles on multiple lanes, for both analytical studies and simulation evaluations. Until now, little is known about the impacts of cooperative lane changes of CAVs on traffic flow [14–16]. This paper intends to shed light on this aspect.

Besides efforts from academia, most super automobile companies and internet giants have been engaged in developing their CAVs. Nevertheless, technical paths towards the development and evolution of CAVs are still uncertain. In particular, there is limited publicly available empirical data on how CAVs will behave in traffic flow. It could be argued that a CAV should provide rides of higher efficiency, as long as safety requirements are not violated. For instance, given an origin and a destination as well as a route connecting them, a CAV is supposed to travel in a cleverer way within traffic flow so as to reach the destination earlier than her counterparts of regular vehicles (RVs), i.e. human-driven vehicles. In dense traffic during peak periods, naturally, there is little room for CAVs to get higher speeds by only exploiting their CACC and other longitudinal capabilities, while they could indeed speed up via lane changes to overtake slower vehicles. Therefore, appropriate lane changes are expected to play a significant role in improving CAVs' travel efficiency during peak periods.

To the best of our knowledge, few studies were conducted to develop lane-changing strategies from this perspective (with an aim at travel efficiency). To start with, just imagine what would happen if a number of e.g. Google CAVs were introduced to traffic flow. We believe that it is logical to presume that those CAVs would perform lane changes in a selfish manner so as to maximize their own benefits in terms of travel efficiency without triggering neighboring vehicles' safety concerns. With these in mind, three major questions arise:

(1) Consider a scenario with dense/congested traffic where the entire traffic flow includes only one CAV. What kind of optimal lane-changing strategy should this CAV take so as to adapt herself to various circumstances encountered and hence maximize her own travel efficiency?
(2) With the increasing number of CAVs introduced to traffic flow, each adopting the same selfish lane-changing strategy, could all these CAVs still benefit from their smart lane changes, and what is the overall impact on traffic flow?

No consensus has so far been reached across the related parties (academia, industries, authorities) regarding functional specifications and intelligence standards for CAVs, especially on the lane-changing respect. It is therefore of little significance to explore (1) and (2) through analytical studies. For this reason, a simulation-based optimization approach was applied for this work on an AIMSUN simulation platform that reflects a real freeway infrastructure with real demands. CAVs were then introduced into the platform using SDK and API, and the Q-learning algorithm was applied to develop the aimed CAV lane changing strategy from the scratch. The obtained CAV lane-changing strategy was evaluated on the same simulation platform to determine its impacts on traffic flow.

The paper is organized as follows. Section 2 introduces some key state variables considered. Section 3 formulates the problem from the perspective of reinforcement learning. Section 4 describes the simulation platform setup. Section 5 reports on the obtained results. Section 6 concludes the paper.

2 Environmental State Variables

Figure 1 illustrates a typical situation of lane changing, involving *Vehicle 1*, three following vehicles, *Vehicle 2, 3, 4*, and a number of preceding vehicles. Vehicle 1 is the subject vehicle that may choose to do a lane change. In this work, only CAVs are considered as the subject vehicles, and they intend to gain higher acceleration rates via agile and flexible lane changes. Thus, the difference in each subject vehicle's accelerations before and after a lane change is of a special interest. For clarity, let's first define some state variables that are necessary for the subsequent discussion. First, we have for Vehicle 1:

$$\tilde{a}_{1L} = a_{1L} - a_1 \tag{1}$$

$$\tilde{a}_{1R} = a_{1R} - a_1 \tag{2}$$

where a_1 refers to the acceleration of Vehicle 1 in the current lane (the middle lane); a_{1L} or a_{1R} is the acceleration of Vehicle 1 if she moves to the left or right lane; accordingly, $\tilde{a}_{1L}$ and $\tilde{a}_{1R}$ stand for the respective lane-changing benefits in terms of acceleration gain. Clearly, the benefit due to a lane change can be positive or negative. Based on this nomenclature, we have the following definitions:

$\tilde{a}_{1L}$: Vehicle 1's benefit due to her left lane-change.
$\tilde{a}_{1R}$: Vehicle 1's benefit due to her right lane-change.
$\tilde{a}_{2L}$: Vehicle 2's benefit due to vehicle 1's left lane change.
$\tilde{a}_{4R}$: Vehicle 4's benefit due to vehicle 1's right lane change.
$\tilde{a}_3$: Vehicle 3's benefit due to Vehicle 1's left or right lane change.

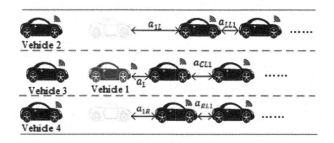

Fig. 1. Vehicles and key variables concerning lane changes.

To take into account also the impacts of downstream traffic conditions on Vehicle 1's lane-changing decisions, more state variables are considered as well:

$\tilde{\mu}_L$: the mean acceleration difference between the middle lane and the left lane for a number N of vehicles in either lane right downstream of Vehicle 1.

$\tilde{\mu}_R$: the mean acceleration difference between the middle lane and the right lane for a number N of vehicles in either lane right downstream of Vehicle 1.

$\tilde{\sigma}_L$: the difference of the standard deviation of accelerations between the middle lane and the left lane for a number N of vehicles in either lane right downstream of Vehicle 1.

$\tilde{\sigma}_R$: the difference of the standard deviation of accelerations between the middle lane and the right lane for a number N of vehicles in either lane right downstream of Vehicle 1.

With respect to Fig. 1, Vehicle 1 has at most three possible lane-changing actions to take at any time, i.e. left lane changing, right lane changing, and staying in the current lane. Without loss of generality, any decision is supposed to be made on the basis of the environmental information that is reflected by the nine state variables defined above.

Without a unified definition, CAVs may refer to connected vehicles, automated vehicles, connected & automated vehicles. Thanks to the rapid development of V2V technologies and the advent of the 5 G era, it is quite possible that ubiquitous vehicle connections may come into practice earlier than mass vehicle automation. The current work is conducted in the context of ubiquitous vehicle connections. More specifically, all vehicles in Fig. 1 are assumed connected vehicles (CVs). Thus, the information of all aforementioned state variables is instantaneously available for Vehicle 1, which is also a self-driving vehicle that can improve her own travel efficient by performing smart lane changes. To avoid confusion, hereafter all subject vehicles like Vehicle 1 are called smart vehicles (SVs) and all other vehicles CVs.

3   The Problem and Reinforcement Learning Solution

3.1   Problem Statement

The problem under discussion is what kind of intelligent lane-changing strategy should be applied by an SV to achieve and maintain on average a higher speed than all counterpart CVs (with the same origin, destination and route as the SV). Due to a large variety of circumstances encountered, it is probably too complicated to address this problem via analytical approaches, hence we have chosen to attack it from a perspective of machine learning and microscopic simulation.

We assume that an SV does not have the capability in performing the desired lane changes when first introduced to traffic flow, but is able to gradually develop such capability by self-learning from the dynamic traffic environment she faces. The SV is not told by any external advisor when to take a lane-changing action. Instead, she has to discover if a lane change is beneficial or not and when to take it or not via trial and error. Most challengingly and interestingly, besides the immediate benefit incurred with a lane-changing action, the SV must learn to evaluate its long-term benefit and become farsighted in conducting lane changes in order to reach her ultimate goal in travel efficiency.

3.2 Problem Formulation and Q-Learning Solution

Reinforcement learning (RL) [17] is well suited to the formulation and handling of the above problem. RL is a computational approach to understanding and automating goal-directed learning from direct interaction with the uncertain environment, without requiring exemplary supervision or complete knowledge of the environment. RL is built upon the framework of Markov decision processes (MDP) [17] to define, in the context of this work, the interaction between an SV and its environment in terms of state, lane-changing actions, and action rewards.

Limited formulation is presented below. The whole journey of a SV is temporally discretized with time steps $t = 0, 1, 2, 3, \ldots$ Let $S_t \in \mathscr{S}$ stand for the environmental state at t, and by Sect. 2, $S_t = \{\tilde{a}_{1L}, \tilde{a}_{1R}, \tilde{a}_{2L}, \tilde{a}_{4R}, \tilde{a}_3, \tilde{\mu}_L, \tilde{\mu}_R, \tilde{\sigma}_L, \tilde{\sigma}_R\}(t)$. The MDP model requires the state space be discrete. The range of each of the 9 state variables is discretized into 6 connected intervals (see Sect. 4.2). Accordingly, any state variable takes values from among 6 possible values, each referring to one specific interval. Let $A_t \in \mathscr{A}$ be the actions at t, and the action set $\mathscr{A}$ includes three elements, left lane changing, right lane changing, and staying in the current lane.

In each time step t, SV senses the environment to get S_t, and on that basis selects an action A_t. One time step later, in part as a consequence of A_t, SV receives a numerical reward R_{t+1}, the acceleration gain of SV, and finds itself in a new state S_{t+1}. The policy $\pi(s, a)$ maps from state $S_t = s$ to probabilities of selecting each possible action $A_t = a$. The objective is to find the optimal policy π^* to maximize the action-value function $q_\pi(s, a)$ for each state-action pair $S_t = s$ and $A_t = a$.

$$q_\pi(s, a) \triangleq \mathbb{E}_\pi \left[\sum_{k=0}^{\infty} \gamma^k R_{t+k+1} | S_t = s, A_t = a \right] \tag{3}$$

where γ denotes the discount factor.

The Q-learning algorithm [17] was applied to approximate $q_{\pi^*}(s, a)$ that drives the smart lane-changing process.

4 Setup for Simulation Study

4.1 The Simulation Environment

A stretch of Freeway A20 (Fig. 2) in the Netherlands was considered to set up the simulation platform. The stretch includes two pairs of on/off-ramps and one lane drop. It starts with three lanes until the lane drop and continues with two lanes. Figure 2 presents real traffic flows collected at the freeway main entry and on-ramps.

Figure 4a displays a heat map with all speed measurements from the site. Congestion was initiated at the merging area of the first on-ramp around 6:30 AM, and spilled back to the upstream of the lane drop. The congestion remained until 8:00 AM. Our simulation platform was built up using enhanced AIMSUN with respect to this freeway example. The simulation platform was calibrated and validated using real measurement data [18]. As shown in Fig. 4, the simulator can well emulate what happened in reality.

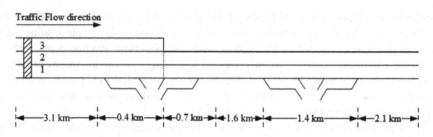

Fig. 2. A stretch of Freeway A20 in the Netherlands.

The simulation environment illustrated in Fig. 4(b) was used as the basis for developing our intelligent lane changing strategy. According to Fig. 3, a simulation run has 4 h. As previously mentioned, two types of vehicles were considered for this study: human-driven connected vehicles (CVs) and self-driving smart vehicles (SVs). No distinction was made between SVs and SVs on their longitudinal behaviors, and the IDM model [19] was used for this aspect.

There are generally two kinds of lane changes, mandatory (unavoidable) ones taking place for the purpose of merging, exiting, etc. While discretionary (opportunistic) ones for improved travel performance. For the current simulation example, throughout the whole journey of each vehicle, SV or CV, mandatory lane changes only happened around the on/off-ramps and lane drop, while it is the discretionary lane changes that make sense during the major part of the journey. Therefore, we presume that the difference between CVs and SVs in the mandatory lane changes is less significant, though SVs would probably be more efficient in performing the lane changes. Also, we presume that any SV is much more capable of increasing her own travel efficiency via discretionary lane changes. All these considerations are summarized in Table 1.

At the start of the simulation study, we let only one SV enter the freeway stretch along with all other CVs. Whenever the SV traverses to exit the stretch, another vehicle right at an origin of the stretch is specified as SV (according to the origin demands) and this new SV enters the stretch immediately.

During one simulation run of 4 h, whenever SV changed the lane, the Q-learning algorithm was applied to update the table for Q(s, a), and the lane-changing strategy in an attempt to get accumulatively a positive acceleration gain for SV. Totally 2200 simulation runs were conducted continuously (with 40 seeds involved), by which the

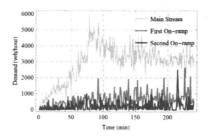

Fig. 3. Traffic demand.

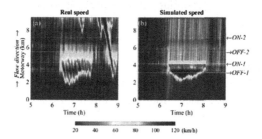

Fig. 4. Spatiotemporal diagrams of (a) real speeds; (b) simulated speeds

Table 1. Comparison of regular vehicle and smart vehicle.

Behavior	Driving mode	
	Connected vehicles (human-driven)	Smart vehicles (self-driving)
Longitudinal maneuvers	IDM	
Discretionary lane changes	Gipps (AIMSUN-default)	Q-Learning
Mandatory lane changes	Heuristic lane changing model	

lane-changing strategy resulting at the end of each run is succeeded by the SV created at the start of the next run for further improvement.

The above settings were used at an early phase of our work, and the learning efficiency for updating SV's lane-changing strategy was found too low. To speed up, we then specified 20% vehicles that enter the freeway stretch over each simulation run of 4 h as SVs, which share the same lane-changing strategy at any time. Whenever an SV changed the lane, the Q-learning algorithm was applied to update the common lane-changing strategy.

4.2 Settings for the Q-Learning Algorithm

The nine environmental state variables considered were empirically discretized such that each variable took values from among 6 possible values, addressing 6 intervals

$(-\infty, -1)$, $[-1, -0.5)$, $[-0.5, 0)$, $[0, 0.5)$, $[0.5, 1)$, $[1, \infty)$. The parameters α and γ for Q-learning were set to be 0.8 and 0.01, respectively, and the ε-greedy policy was applied with $\varepsilon = 0.95$. Ten preceding vehicles of SV in two related lanes were considered for determining state variables $\tilde{\mu}_L$, $\tilde{\mu}_R$, $\tilde{\sigma}_L$ and $\tilde{\sigma}_R$.

5   The Results

5.1   The Journeys of One Single SV

Figure 5 presents the evolution of the total lane-changing benefit by iteration, i.e. the sum of all values in $Q(s, a)$ resulting at the end of each iteration of 4 h. To demonstrate the performance of the lane-changing strategy in improving the travel efficiency of the SV that adopts the strategy, the strategy was first applied to the simulation platform, where only one vehicle entering the freeway stretch was an SV while all other vehicles are CVs each employing the default lane-changing model of AIMSUN for lane changes (Table 1). For this test, only one simulation horizon of 4 h was considered and SV entered the stretch only once, from the mainstream origin right before the peak period.

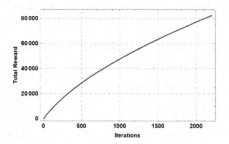

Fig. 5. The total reward in the Q-Table.

The testing results are presented in Fig. 6, where X axis refers to time, and Y axis to the instantaneous speeds of SV. Three curves are plotted in the figure; particularly, the green, red, and blue curves address the speed of SV, the speed of SV's counterpart, and the speed difference of the two. The tiny Y axis on the right-hand side in Fig. 6 refers to the blue curve. The SV's counterpart is an CV that entered the freeway stretch at the same time and same location as SV did. Forty seeds were considered, which affect SV and CV's trip environments. In fact, the curves in Fig. 6 are all seed-mean curves.

It is shown in Fig. 6 that the speed improvement during the heavy congestion is limited, and considerable improvement is obtained during the speed-up processes. Further information is presented in Table 2. As SVs and CVs differ only in their respective lane-changing strategies, the improved travel efficiency for SV is definitely attributed to her adoption of the lane-changing strategy developed via Q-learning. Thus, we have answered Question (1) proposed in Sect. 1. It should be pointed out that the obtained lane-changing strategy is a sort of selfish strategy, which improves the travel performance of the SV adopting the strategy, without considering the interest of any CV. It is also noted that, during heavy congestion, even SV could hardly benefit from her opportunistic lane-changing maneuvers as there is little room on roads for such maneuvers.

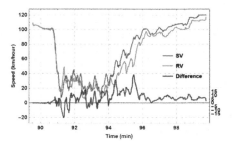

Fig. 6. The speed-time relation. (Color figure online)

Table 2. The improvement in different period.

Average speed improvement (and its relative ratio)		
Before congestion	During congestion	After congestion
0.46 km/h (0.48%)	2.51 km/h (10.58%)	9.82 km/h (12.49%)

5.2   Impacts of SV's Selfish Lane Changes on Traffic Flow

Next, we intend to answer another question: If the selfish lane-changing strategy obtained would be employed by an increasing number of SVs, collectively what impacts would yield for the entire traffic?

Figure 7 presents the histogram of mean journey speeds versus the market penetration rate. For any vehicle, SV or CV, that completes her trip from the origin to destination, her journey speed is calculated as the quotient of her trip length and trip travel time. During each minute, some vehicles exit the stretch and finish their journeys, then the average journey speed of those vehicles is defined as the mean journey speed for that 1-min time interval. As such, over a simulation run of 4 h, we obtained 240 mean journey speeds. Plotting the histograms for those 240 mean journey speeds with respect to each given market penetration rates, we got Fig. 7.

It is noticed from Fig. 7 that, before the market penetration rate of SVs reaches 60%, the more SVs are involved, the higher positive impacts on traffic flow. When the penetration rate rises above 60%, the impacts turn increasingly negative. Since the lane-changing strategy obtained is a selfish one, it is reasonable to postulate that, if this strategy would be employed by too many SVs, interest conflict may take place and eventually deteriorate traffic flow. Figure 7 confirms this postulation and indicates the turning point is 60% in the penetration rate. Of course, this specific value may very likely be simulation-platform dependent, but what really matters is the tendency identified.

To explore what happens when introducing increasingly more SVs into traffic flow, the lane-wise spatiotemporal heat maps of speeds are presented in Figs. 8, 9, 10 and 11. The most striking discovery from these figures is that, as more SVs joined traffic flow, the original congestion right upstream of the lane-drop and first on-ramp (Figs. 2 and 3) in the case of 100% human-driven vehicles was gradually alleviated and eventually removed. This is a remarkable result, indicating that the collective usage of the smart lane-changing strategy could be used as a potential solution to the mitigation of bottleneck congestion. To associate with this finding, Fig. 11 shows that the number of lane changes does increase substantially with the market penetration rate, especially at the upstream of the bottleneck.

Though the histograms in Fig. 7 looks symmetric roughly, it by no means suggests that the situations at the penetration rates of say 30% and 70% are similar; rather they are quite different. It is seen from Figs. 8, 9, and 10 that the increase of the penetration rate removed the congestion on one hand, but it also renders the mean speed across the whole stretch compromised, with the sub-figures getting whiter in colour. This may be because, when the penetration rate becomes sufficiently high, congestion is removed while the adoption of the selfish lane-changing strategy by too many SVs may create interest conflicts, resulting in negative impacts on the entire traffic flow. Thus, we have partly answered Question (2) proposed in the introduction section.

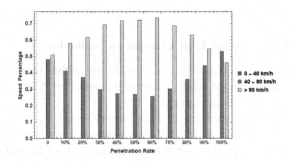

Fig. 7. The statistics of the average journey speed for each minute.

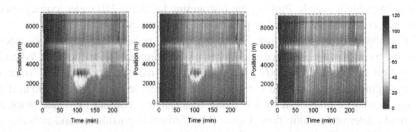

Fig. 8. Lane 1 speed heat maps, 10%, 30%, 70% penetration rate, respectively.

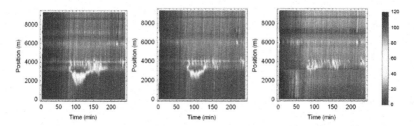

Fig. 9. Lane 2 speed heat maps, 10%, 30%, 70% penetration rate, respectively.

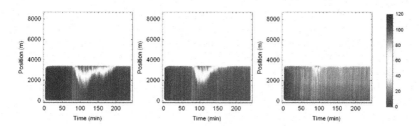

Fig. 10. Lane 3 speed heat maps, 10%, 30%, 70% penetration rate, respectively.

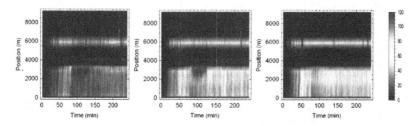

Fig. 11. Lane-changing times heat maps, 10%, 30%, 70% penetration rate, respectively.

6   Conclusion

Based on intensive microscopic simulations associated with reinforcement learning, a selfish lane-changing strategy was determined using the Q-learning algorithm for self-driving smart vehicles (SV). The strategy was found beneficial for the entire traffic as long as the penetration rate of SVs was not more than 60%. When the penetration rate was above 60%, negative impacts on traffic flow arose, possibly because some interest conflict was created due to the adoption of the selfish lane-changing strategy by many SVs. In addition, it was found that the collective use of the obtained lane-changing strategy may be a solution to mitigating bottleneck congestion.

Acknowledgements. This work is supported in part by the National Natural Science Foundation of China (project number: 71771200) and the National Key Research and Development Program of China (project number: 2018YFB1600504; 2017YFE9134700) as well as by the European

Research Council in the frame of the project TRAMAN21/ERC Advanced Grant Agreement n. 321132 under the European Union's Seventh Framework Programme (FP/2007-2013). The authors would like to thank Prof. Bart van Arem and his group for their support in providing information related to the freeway network considered in this work.

References

1. Diakaki, C., Papageorgiou, M., Papamichail, I., Nikolos, I.: Overview and analysis of vehicle automation and communication systems from a motorway traffic management perspective. Transp. Res. Part A Policy Pract. **75**, 147–165 (2015)
2. Muratori, M., Holden, J., Lammert, M., Duran, A., Young, S., Gonder, J.: Potentials for platooning in U.S. highway freight transport. SAE Int. J. Commer. Veh. **10**(1), 45–49 (2017)
3. Dey, K.C., et al.: A review of communication, driver characteristics, and controls aspects of cooperative adaptive cruise control (CACC). IEEE Trans. Intell. Transp. Syst. **17**(2), 491–509 (2016)
4. Bevly, D., et al.: Lane change and merge maneuvers for connected and automated vehicles: a survey. IEEE Trans. Intell. Veh. **1**(1), 105–120 (2016)
5. Desjardins, C., Chaib-draa, B.: Cooperative adaptive cruise control: a reinforcement learning approach. IEEE Trans. Intell. Transp. Syst. **12**(4), 1248–1260 (2011)
6. Milanes, V., Shladover, S.E., Spring, J., Nowakowski, C., Kawazoe, H., Nakamura, M.: Cooperative adaptive cruise control in real traffic situations. IEEE Trans. Intell. Transp. Syst. **15**(1), 296–305 (2014)
7. Amoozadeh, M., Deng, H., Chuah, C.N., Zhang, H.M., Ghosal, D.: Platoon management with cooperative adaptive cruise control enabled by VANET. Veh. Commun. **2**(2), 110–123 (2015)
8. Ge, J.I., Orosz, G.: Dynamics of connected vehicle systems with delayed acceleration feedback. Transp. Res. Part C Emerg. Technol. **46**, 46–64 (2014)
9. Xiao, L., Wang, M., Schakel, W., Arem, B.V.: Unravelling effects of cooperative adaptive cruise control deactivation on traffic flow characteristics at merging bottlenecks. Transp. Res. Part C Emerg. Technol. **96**, 380–397 (2018)
10. Liu, H., Kan, X., Shladover, S.E., Lu, X.-Y., Ferlis, R.E.: Modeling impacts of cooperative adaptive cruise control on mixed traffic flow in multi-lane freeway facilities. Transp. Res. Part C Emerg. Technol. **95**, 261–279 (2018)
11. Nilsson, J., Sjoberg, J.: Strategic decision making for automated driving on two-lane, one way roads using model predictive control. In: 2013 IEEE Intelligent Vehicles Symposium (IV), Gold Coast City, Australia, pp. 1253–1258 (2013)
12. You, F., Zhang, R., Lie, G., Wang, H., Wen, H., Xu, J.: Trajectory planning and tracking control for autonomous lane change maneuver based on the cooperative vehicle infrastructure system. Expert Syst. Appl. **42**(14), 5932–5946 (2015)
13. Tehrani, H., Do, Q.H., Egawa, M., Muto, K., Yoneda, K., Mita, S.: General behavior and motion model for automated lane change. In: 2015 IEEE Intelligent Vehicles Symposium (IV) 2015, COEX, Seoul, South Korea, pp. 1154–1159 (2015)
14. Younes, M.B., Boukerche, A.: A vehicular network based intelligent lane change assistance protocol for highways. In: 2017 IEEE International Conference on Communications (ICC), 2017, Paris, France, pp. 1–6 (2017)
15. Du, Y., Wang, Y., Chan, C.Y.: Autonomous lane-change controller via mixed logical dynamical. In: IEEE 17th International Conference on Intelligent Transportation Systems (ITSC) 2014, Qingdao, China, pp. 1154–1159 (2014)

16. Zheng, Z.: Recent developments and research needs in modeling lane changing. Transp. Res. Part B Methodological **60**, 16–32 (2014)
17. Sutton, R.S., Barto, A.G.: Reinforcement Learning: An Introduction. The MIT Press, Cambridge (2018)
18. Spiliopoulou, A., Perraki, G., Papageorgiou, M., Roncoli, C.: Exploitation of ACC systems towards improved traffic flow efficiency on motorways. In 5th IEEE International Conference on Models and Technologies for Intelligent Transportation Systems: Proceedings, Naples, Italy, pp. 37–43 (2017)
19. Treiber, M., Hennecke, A., Helbing, D.: Congested traffic states in empirical observations and microscopic simulations. Phys. Rev. E **62**(2), 1805–1824 (2000)

LSTM-Based Anomaly Detection: Detection Rules from Extreme Value Theory

Neema Davis[✉], Gaurav Raina, and Krishna Jagannathan

Department of Electrical Engineering, Indian Institute of Technology Madras, Chennai 600 036, India
{ee14d212,gaurav,krishnaj}@ee.iitm.ac.in

Abstract. In this paper, we explore various statistical techniques for anomaly detection in conjunction with the popular Long Short-Term Memory (LSTM) deep learning model for transportation networks. We obtain the prediction errors from an LSTM model, and then apply three statistical models based on (i) the Gaussian distribution, (ii) Extreme Value Theory (EVT), and (iii) the Tukey's method. Using statistical tests and numerical studies, we find strong evidence against the widely employed Gaussian distribution based detection rule on the prediction errors. Next, motivated by fundamental results from Extreme Value Theory, we propose a detection technique that does not assume any parent distribution on the prediction errors. Through numerical experiments conducted on several real-world traffic data sets, we show that the EVT-based detection rule is superior to other detection rules, and is supported by statistical evidence.

Keywords: Anomaly detection · LSTM · Threshold · Extreme Value Theory

1 Introduction

Mobility modeling can aid the design of sustainable transportation systems, making it a crucial part of Intelligent Transportation Systems (ITS). A popular example can be the Mobility-On-Demand service providers such as e-hailing taxis that rely on efficient passenger mobility modeling for rerouting their drivers. The demand for taxis changes dynamically with daily human mobility patterns, along with other non-periodic events. While short-term taxi demand forecasting models may learn periodic patterns in demand [7,12], they are normally unable to accurately capture non-periodic mobility events. It is necessary to detect these unusual events as they often indicate useful, and critical information that can yield instructive insights, and help to develop more accurate prediction models and strategies. This task of finding patterns in data that do not conform to a certain expected behavior is called *anomaly detection*. Transportation networks present several situations where one may find anomalous behavior and patterns.

© Springer Nature Switzerland AG 2019
P. Moura Oliveira et al. (Eds.): EPIA 2019, LNAI 11804, pp. 572–583, 2019.
https://doi.org/10.1007/978-3-030-30241-2_48

For example, sudden spikes in taxi demand might indicate the ending of a concert, drops in traffic speed might be the effect of an unprecedented event such as a road accident, and so on.

The identification of anomalies has been traditionally tackled using statistical and machine learning techniques; for a survey, see [4]. The substantial advances made by deep learning methods in recent years, in various machine learning problems, have encouraged researchers to explore them for anomaly detection as well [3]. The suitability of deep learning models for anomaly detection stems from their unsupervised learning nature and the ability to learn highly complex non-linear sequences. Popular deep learning models such as the Long Short-Term Memory (LSTM) [14] and related Recurrent Neural Networks (RNNs) [13] have shown superior anomaly detection performance compared to traditional anomaly detection models [6]. When presented with normal non-anomalous data, the LSTM can learn and capture the normal behavior of the system. Later, when the LSTM encounters a data instance that deviates significantly from the rest of the set, it generates a high prediction error, suggesting anomalous behavior. This form of prediction-based anomaly detection has found applications in cardiology [5], automobiles [22], radio communications [17], Cyber-Physical Systems (CPS) [10], and telemetry [9], among others.

Prediction-based anomaly detection requires the application of a set of detection rules on the prediction errors. Usually, this is performed by employing a traditional anomaly detection algorithm on top of the prediction errors. Often, the detection rule involves assuming an underlying parametric distribution on the prediction errors, which is mostly Gaussian [14]. In addition to being computationally efficient and mathematically tractable, a distribution based detection rule does not require large memory storage (unlike clustering-based approaches) or suitable kernel functions (unlike Support Vector Machines). If the assumptions regarding the underlying data distribution hold, this technique provides a statistically justifiable solution for anomaly detection. However, its disadvantage is also rooted in this assumption; faithful detection is possible only if the data conforms to a particular distribution.

Given the rise in prediction-based anomaly detection methods and related research [3], it is essential to place increased emphasis on post-prediction error evaluation methods that have received comparatively less focus yet are instrumental for accurate anomaly detection. Since the prediction errors are often assumed to be Gaussian [14], we investigate this assumption by conducting statistical tests on seven diverse real-world data sets. In particular, we compare this Gaussian-based decision rule against decision rules based on Extreme Value Theory (EVT) [1]. An important result from EVT suggests that the extreme values of any distribution follow a Generalized Pareto Distribution (GPD), regardless of the parent distribution. This result allows us to develop a parametric distribution based detection rule on the prediction errors, without making critical assumptions about the input data distribution. Currently, EVT-based detection rules have not been explored for LSTM-based anomaly detection, setting our work apart from the existing literature. Further, we compare these two distribution-based detection rules against a detection rule based on Tukey's method [23] that makes no explicit assumptions on the distribution.

1.1 Our Contributions

We compare three detection rules for LSTM-based anomaly detection: (i) the Gaussian-based detection rule that makes assumptions about the parent distribution, (ii) the EVT-based detection rule that does not assume a parent distribution but makes assumptions about the distribution of the tail, and (iii) the Tukey's method based detection rule that does not make any assumptions on the distribution. The major findings of this paper are as follows:

1. Using the Shapiro-Wilk test for Normality, we reject the null hypothesis that the prediction errors follow the Normal distribution with high confidence.
2. We find that the EVT-based detection rule has superior anomaly detection performance compared to the Gaussian-based detection rule and Tukey's method based detection rule.
3. The false-positive regulator of the EVT-based detection rule has a lower variance than that of the Gaussian-based detection rule, resulting in faster parameter tuning.

The rest of the paper is organized as follows. Section 2 provides a brief description of the data sets. Our anomaly detection methodology, along with the three detection rules and evaluation metrics are explained in Sect. 3. This is followed by a discussion on the statistical tests in Sect. 4. The experimental settings and results are elaborated in Sect. 5. We summarize our contributions in Sect. 6.

2 Data Sets

We consider seven real-world data sets for our comparison study: two taxi demand data sets, three traffic-based data sets, and two data sets from other application domains. The travel time, occupancy and speed data sets are real-time data, obtained from a traffic detector and collected by the Minnesota Department of Transportation. Discussions on the traffic data sets and the temperature sensor data set are available at the Numenta Anomaly Benchmark GitHub repository[1]. Brief descriptions of all data sets used are given below.

1. Vehicular Travel Time (see Footnote 1): The data set is obtained from a traffic sensor and has 2500 readings from July 10, 2015, to September 17, 2015, with eight marked anomalies.
2. Vehicular Speed (see Footnote 1): The data set contains the average speed of all vehicles passing through the traffic detector. A total of 1128 readings for the period September 8, 2015 - September 17, 2015, is available. There are three marked unusual sub sequences in the data set.
3. Vehicular Occupancy (see Footnote 1): There are a total of 2382 readings indicating the percentage of the time, during a 30 s period, that the detector sensed a vehicle. The data is available for a period of 17 days, from September 1, 2015, to September 17, 2015, and has two marked anomalies.

---

[1] https://github.com/numenta/NAB/tree/master/data.

4. New York City Taxi Demand [16]: The publicly available data set contains the pick-up locations and time stamps of street hailing yellow taxi services from the period of January 1, 2016, to February 29, 2016. We pick three time-sequences with clearly evident anomalies from data aggregated over 15 min time periods in $1\,\text{km}^2$ grids.

5. Bengaluru Taxi Demand: This data set is obtained from a private taxi service provider in Bengaluru, India and has GPS traces of passengers booking a taxi by logging into the service provider's mobile application. Similar to the New York City data set, this data is also available for January and February 2016. We aggregate the data over 15 min periods in $1\,\text{km}^2$ grids and pick three sequences with clearly visible anomalies.

6. Electrocardiogram (ECG) [11]: There are a total of 18000 readings, with three unusual sub sequences labeled as anomalies. The data set has a repeating pattern, with some variability in the period length.

7. Machine Temperature (see Footnote 1): This data set contains temperature sensor readings from an internal component of a large industrial machine. The readings are for the period between December 2, 2013, to February 19, 2014. There are a total of 22695 readings taken every 5 min, consisting of four anomalies with known causes.

3   Anomaly Detection

This section outlines our prediction-based anomaly detection, along with the detection strategies.

3.1   Prediction Model

We use the Long Short-Term Memory (LSTM) network [8] as the time-series prediction model. The most recent l_b values of every data set are fed into the model to output l_a future values. We refer to parameters l_b, l_a as look-back and look-ahead respectively. Dropout and early stopping are employed to avoid over-fitting. Before training any neural network model, it is necessary to set suitable values for various hyper-parameters. These parameters define the high-level features of the model, such as its complexity, or capacity to learn. For example, in a neural network model, the important hyper-parameters are the number of hidden recurrent layers, the dropout values, the learning rate, and the number of units in each layer. We use the Tree-structured Parzen Estimator (TPE) Bayesian Optimization [2] to select these hyper-parameters. The output layer is a fully connected dense layer with linear activation. The Adam optimizer is used to minimize the Mean Squared Error.

Each data set is divided into a training set, a hold-out validation set, and a test set. The training set is assumed to be free of anomalies. This is a reasonable assumption in real-world anomaly detection scenarios where the occurrence of anomalous behavior is rare compared to the occurrence of instances of normal behavior. The validation and test set are mixtures of anomalous and non-anomalous data instances. The prediction model is trained on normal data without any anomalies, i.e., on the training data, so that it learns the normal behavior of the time-series. Once the model is trained, anomaly detection is performed by using the prediction errors as anomaly indicators. In this study, the prediction error is defined as the absolute difference between the input received at time t and its corresponding prediction from the model. Next, we discuss three techniques (detection rules) by which the prediction errors can be used to set an anomaly threshold. If any prediction error value lies outside of the threshold, then the corresponding input value can be considered as a possible anomaly.

3.2   Gaussian-Based Detection

The prediction errors from the training data are assumed to follow a Gaussian distribution. The mean, μ, and variance, σ^2, of the Gaussian distribution are computed using the Maximum Likelihood Estimation (MLE). The Log Probability Densities (Log PDs) of errors are calculated based on these estimated parameters and used as anomaly scores [20]. A low value of Log PD indicates that the likelihood of an observation being an anomaly is high. A validation set containing both normal data and anomalies is used to set a threshold τ_g on the Log PD values. The threshold is chosen such that it can separate all the anomalies from normal observations while incurring as few false positives as possible. The threshold is then evaluated on a separate test set.

3.3   EVT-Based Detection

Let X be a random variable and $F(x) = P(X \leq x)$ be its Cumulative Distribution Function (CDF). The tail of the distribution is given by $\bar{F}(x) = P(X > x)$. A key result from the Extreme Value Theory (EVT) [1] shows that the distribution of the extreme values is not highly sensitive to the parent data distribution. This enables us to accurately compute probabilities without first estimating the underlying distribution. Under a weak condition, the extreme events have the same kind of distribution, regardless of the original one, known as the Extreme Value Distribution (EVD):

$$G_\gamma : y \to \exp\left(- \left(1 + \gamma y\right)^{-\frac{1}{\gamma}} \right), \ \gamma \in \mathbb{R}, \ 1 + \gamma y > 0, \tag{1}$$

where γ is the extreme value index of the distribution. By fitting an EVD to the unknown input distribution tail, it is then possible to evaluate the probability of potential extreme events. In some recent work [19], the authors use results from EVT to detect anomalies in a uni-variate data stream, following the Peaks-Over-Threshold (POTs) approach. Based on an initial threshold t, the POTs approach attempts to fit a Generalized Pareto Distribution (GPD) to the excesses, $X - t$. Once the parameters of the GPD are obtained using MLE, the threshold can be computed as:

$$\tau_e = t + \frac{\hat{\sigma}}{\hat{\gamma}}\left(\left(\frac{qn}{N_t}\right)^{-\hat{\gamma}} - 1\right), \tag{2}$$

where $\hat{\gamma}$ and $\hat{\sigma}$ are the estimated parameters of the GPD, q is some desired probability, n is the total number of observations, N_t is the number of peaks, i.e., the number of X_i s.t. $X_i > t$. We calculate $P(X > \tau_e)$ for all the observations and those data instances with $P(X > \tau_e) < q$ can be considered as plausible anomalies. We apply this methodology to the prediction errors obtained from the LSTM. The authors in [19] recommend choosing q in the range $[10^{-3}, 10^{-5}]$ and initial t as the 98% quantile, which we follow in our study.

3.4 Tukey's Method Based Detection

Tukey's method [23] uses quartiles to define an anomaly threshold. It makes no distributional assumptions and does not depend on a mean or a standard deviation. In Tukey's method, a possible outlier lies outside the threshold $\tau_t = Q_3 + 3 \times (Q_3 - Q_1)$, where Q_1 is the lower quartile or the 25th percentile, and Q_3 is the upper quartile or the 75th percentile. The prediction errors from the training, validation and test sets are concatenated, and the lower and upper quartiles are calculated. The values lying outside τ_t are identified as possible outliers.

3.5 Evaluation Metrics

We consider three evaluation metrics for comparing the detection rules: (i) Precision, P, which is the ratio of true positives to the sum of true positives and false positives, (ii) Recall, R, which is the ratio of true positives to the sum of true positives and false negatives, and (iii) F1-score, $F1$, which is the harmonic mean of Precision and Recall. Since F1-score summarizes both Precision and Recall, we consider the detection rule with the highest $F1$ as the superior anomaly detection technique. True positives refer to the correctly predicted anomalies. False positives are the non-anomalies that we incorrectly identify as being anomalies. False negatives refer to the anomalies incorrectly identified as non-anomalous instances.

4   Statistical Tests

We conduct two sets of statistical tests: (i) the Shapiro-Wilk test [18] for testing the Normality of the prediction errors, and (ii) the Anderson-Darling test [21] for checking the compliance of the tail distribution to a Generalized Pareto Distribution (GPD).

The Shapiro-Wilk test [18] calculates a W statistic that tests whether a sample comes from a Normal distribution. The W statistic measures the correlation between the given data and ideal normal scores. If the p-value is less than the chosen significance level (typically less than 0.05), then the null hypothesis can be rejected and there is evidence that the data tested are not Normally distributed. The Anderson-Darling test [21] is used to assess whether a sample of the data comes from a specific probability distribution. The test statistic A^2

measures the distance between the hypothesized distribution and the empirical CDF of the data. Based on the test static and the p-values obtained, the null hypothesis that the data follow a specified distribution can (cannot) be rejected. The Anderson-Darling is a modification of the Kolmogorov-Smirnov (K-S) test [15] and gives more weight to the tails than does the K-S test.

The p-values obtained by conducting the Shapiro-Wilk test on the prediction errors and the Anderson-Darling test on the excesses $X - t$ are given in Table 1. The null hypothesis is rejected for p-values less than 0.001. For all the data sets under study, based on the p-values of the Shapiro-Wilk test, we rejected the null hypothesis that the prediction errors follow a Gaussian distribution. At the same time, statistical evidence from the Anderson-Darling test suggests that the tail distributions of the various prediction errors tend to follow GPD. Hence, while assuming a Normal distribution on the prediction errors may not be suitable for LSTM-based hybrid anomaly detection, a GPD seems to be a more reasonable fit.

Table 1. P-values obtained from the statistical tests. The decision to reject the null hypothesis is taken when the p-values lie below 0.001. The null hypothesis that the prediction errors follow a Gaussian distribution is rejected, and that the tails of the prediction errors follow a Generalized Pareto Distribution is accepted.

Data sets	P-values	
	Shapiro-Wilk test	Anderson-Darling test
Vehicular Travel Time	0.000	0.005
Vehicular Speed	2.38e-22	0.005
Vehicular Occupancy	6.64e-23	0.37
NYC Taxi Demand	2.62e-42	0.14
Bengaluru Taxi Demand	4.45e-43	0.57
Electrocardiogram	0.000	0.002
Machine Temperature	0.000	0.002

5   Experiments

As mentioned in Sect. 3, hyper-parameter optimization is performed prior to the model training process. The chosen set of parameters for each data set is given in Table 2. We follow the same model settings as [20] for the ECG and Machine Temperature data sets. For the traffic speed, travel time and vehicular occupancy data sets, the limited availability of readings suggested look-back and look-ahead times of 1 each. We have over 10 million points for the New York and Bengaluru cities, allowing for a large look-back time. The considerable amount of data in these two cases allows the LSTM to learn better representations of the input data, aiding the anomaly detection process. The models ran for 100 epochs with a batch size of 64, minimizing the Mean Squared Error.

Table 2. The experimental settings for the data sets considered. The optimal set of hyper-parameters for each data set is chosen after running the Tree-structured Parzen Estimator (TPE) Bayesian Optimization.

Data sets	LSTM architecture	l_b, l_a
Vehicular Travel Time	1 Recurrent layer: {20}, Dropout: 0.2, 1 Dense layer: {1}, Learning rate: 0.01	1, 1
Vehicular Speed	1 Recurrent layer: {60}, Dropout: 0.19, 1 Dense layer: {1}, Learning rate: 0.0001	1, 1
Vehicular Occupancy	1 Recurrent layer: {50}, Dropout: 0.23, 1 Dense layer: {1}, Learning rate: 0.0001	1, 1
NYC Taxi Demand	2 Recurrent layers: {50, 20}, Dropout: 0.4, 1 Dense layer: {24}, Learning rate: 0.0001	5760, 24
Bengaluru Taxi Demand	2 Recurrent layers: {20, 10}, Dropout: 0.25, 1 Dense layer: {24}, Learning rate: 0.0001	5760, 24
Electrocardiogram	2 Recurrent layers: {60, 30}, Dropout: 0.1, 1 Dense layer: {5}, Learning rate: 0.05	8, 5
Machine Temperature	2 Recurrent layers: {80, 20}, Dropout: 0.1, 1 Dense layer: {12}, Learning rate: 0.1	24, 12

5.1 Results

Once the predictions are obtained from the models, we applied the three detection rules based on different assumptions. The detection performance obtained on one of the time-sequences from the New York City data set is given in Figs. 1, 2 and 3. The numerical results obtained on evaluating the detection rules using Precision, Recall and F1-score are available in Table 3, along with the values of the false-positive regulators, τ_g and q.

The false-positive regulators are the parameters that impact the performance of the detection algorithms. The false-positive regulator for the Gaussian-based detection rule, τ_g, is chosen for each time-sequence such that the F1-score on the validation errors is maximized. The false-positive regulator for the EVT-based anomaly detection, q, is set from an initialization data stream. An initial threshold t has to be chosen for the EVT-based detection, typically 98% quantile. We set q using the same initialization stream that is used for setting t. The initialization stream contains the prediction errors from the training and validation sets. The probability q is chosen so that the EVT-based anomaly detection picks up all the anomalies from the initialization stream. We observe that the threshold τ_g has a higher variability compared to that of the probability q. While q remains in the range $[10^{-3}, 10^{-5}]$, τ_g varies between -15 and -25. Further, while a single q value is sufficient for different time-sequences from the same data set (e.g., New York City Taxi Demand), different τ_g values are required for different streams of data from the same set. This translates into a relatively slower parameter tuning for the Gaussian-based detection on comparison with that of the EVT-based detection.

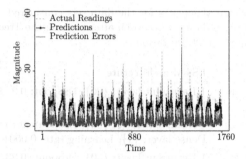

Fig. 1. Performance of the LSTM model. The actual taxi demand values for one of the time-sequences from the New York City is plotted, along with the predictions and prediction errors. True anomaly is at $t = 1366$.

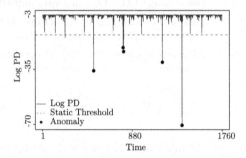

Fig. 2. Performance of the Gaussian-based detection rule on prediction errors obtained from Fig. 1. The threshold is chosen from the validation errors and is seen to result in many false-positives along with the true anomaly at $t = 1366$.

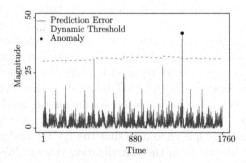

Fig. 3. Performance of the EVT-based detection rule on prediction errors obtained from Fig. 1. The detection rule chooses a threshold, without manual tuning, based on a desired probability. True anomaly detected at $t = 1366$, without incurring any false-positives.

Tukey's method is able to detect most of the anomalies but results in a large number of false-positives, which is not desirable. In other words, Tukey's method has a high Recall, but poor Precision. Only in the ECG data set, the Tukey's method achieves better prediction performance than the others. The fraction of anomalies is higher in the ECG data set, and hence, the anomalies cover a large spectrum above the upper quartile. Since the Tukey's method thresholds the raw prediction errors based on the upper quartile, it results in good anomaly detection for the ECG data set.

Regardless of the application domain, we see that EVT-based detection rules provide consistently better performance that Gaussian-based and Tukey's method based detection rules. These findings suggest that presuming a Gaussian distribution on the prediction errors is a very strong assumption and might not hold for several scenarios. A more sensible assumption would be to assume that the tails follow GPD, which appears to be valid across diverse settings. On the other hand, assuming no distribution can result in multiple false alarms.

Table 3. Evaluation of the detection rules on the data sets considered. The best technique for each data set is shown in bold and shows the superior performance of the EVT-based detection rule.

Data sets		Normality assumption				Tail assumption from EVT				Tukey's method		
		P	R	F1	τ	P	R	F1	q	P	R	F1
Vehicular Travel Time		0.14	0.40	0.21	-20	0.33	0.40	**0.36**	10^{-4}	0.04	0.60	0.07
Vehicular Speed		0.58	1.0	0.73	-18	0.75	0.85	**0.79**	10^{-3}	0.75	0.85	**0.79**
Vehicular Occupancy		1.0	1.0	1.0	-23	1.0	1.0	**1.0**	10^{-5}	0.33	1.0	0.5
NYC Taxi Demand	T1	1.0	1.0	**1.0**	-19	1.0	1.0	**1.0**	10^{-5}	1.0	0.14	0.25
	T2	0.2	1.0	0.33	-17	1.0	1.0	**1.0**	10^{-5}	0.07	1.0	0.14
	T3	0.75	1.0	**0.85**	-15	0.75	1.0	**0.85**	10^{-5}	0.5	1.0	0.66
Bengaluru Taxi Demand	T1	1.0	0.4	0.57	-25	1.0	1.0	**1.0**	10^{-4}	0.31	1.0	0.47
	T2	0.33	1.0	**0.5**	-18	0.33	1.0	**0.5**	10^{-4}	0.04	1.0	0.07
	T3	0.6	0.5	0.54	-25	0.57	0.66	**0.61**	10^{-4}	0.15	0.83	0.26
Electrocardiogram		0.50	0.23	0.32	-23	0.50	0.28	0.36	10^{-4}	0.42	0.57	**0.49**
Machine Temperature		0.004	0.50	0.009	-19	0.10	0.50	**0.16**	10^{-4}	0.002	0.50	0.005

6   Contributions

Across application domains, accurate detection of abnormal patterns plays a vital role in the construction of reliable prediction algorithms. In this paper, we compared three detection rules that can be used with deep learning based anomaly detection, in the context of transportation networks. Each detection rule makes specific assumptions about the distribution of the prediction errors obtained from the Long Short-Term Memory (LSTM) network. Using statistical tests and numerical analysis, we showed that the widely used Gaussian distribution assumption on the prediction errors need not always hold. However, the tails distributions of the prediction errors are seen to follow a Generalized

Pareto Distribution (GPD). This statistical evidence prompted us to devise a set of detection rules based on Extreme Value Theory (EVT).

The EVT-based detection rule consistently achieved more accurate anomaly detection compared to the Gaussian-based detection rule and Tukey's method. More variability was observed in the false-positive regulator values of the Gaussian-based detection rule compared to that of the EVT-based detection rule. The Gaussian-based detection required fixing of different false-positive regulator values for different sequences from the same data set, which in turn necessitated extensive parameter tuning. On the other hand, the EVT-based rule needed only a single value of false-positive regulator to achieve good performance across multiple streams from the same data set.

This paper follows an LSTM-based hybrid approach for anomaly detection. To get a comprehensive overview of various anomaly detection techniques, one should conduct an extensive comparison study of statistical, machine learning, and deep learning based models. Such a study is the next natural avenue for future research. Further, we aim to develop an end-to-end deep anomaly detection model by directly modifying the objective function of the LSTM to detect the anomalies.

References

1. Beirlant, J., Goegebeur, Y., Segers, J., Teugels, J.L.: Statistics of Extremes: Theory and Applications. Wiley, Chichester (2006)
2. Bergstra, J.S., Bardenet, R., Bengio, Y., Kégl, B.: Algorithms for hyper-parameter optimization. In: Advances in Neural Information Processing Systems, pp. 2546–2554 (2011)
3. Chalapathy, R., Chawla, S.: Deep learning for anomaly detection: a survey. arXiv preprint. arXiv:1901.03407 (2019)
4. Chandola, V., Banerjee, A., Kumar, V.: Anomaly detection: a survey. ACM Comput. Surv. **41**, 15 (2009)
5. Chauhan, S., Vig, L.: Anomaly detection in ECG time signals via deep long short-term memory networks. In: Proceedings of the International Conference on Data Science and Advanced Analytics, pp. 1–7. IEEE (2015)
6. Cheng, M., Li, Q., Lv, J., Liu, W., Wang, J.: Multi-scale LSTM model for BGP anomaly classification. IEEE Trans. Serv. Comput. (2018). https://doi.org/10.1109/TSC.2018.2824809
7. Davis, N., Raina, G., Jagannathan, K.: Taxi demand forecasting: a hedge-based tessellation strategy for improved accuracy. IEEE Trans. Intell. Transp. Syst. **19**, 3686–3697 (2018)
8. Gers, F.A., Schmidhuber, J., Cummins, F.: Learning to forget: continual prediction with LSTM. Neural Comput. **12**, 2451–2471 (2000)
9. Hundman, K., Constantinou, V., Laporte, C., Colwell, I., Soderstrom, T.: Detecting spacecraft anomalies using LSTMs and nonparametric dynamic thresholding. In: Proceedings of the International Conference on Knowledge Discovery and Data Mining, pp. 387–395. ACM (2018)
10. Inoue, J., Yamagata, Y., Chen, Y., Poskitt, C.M., Sun, J.: Anomaly detection for a water treatment system using unsupervised machine learning. In: Proceedings of the International Conference on Data Mining Workshops, pp. 1058–1065. IEEE (2017)

11. Keogh, E., Lin, J., Fu, A.: Hot sax: efficiently finding the most unusual time series subsequence. In: Proceedings of the International Conference on Data Mining, pp. 1–8. IEEE (2005)
12. Liao, S., Zhou, L., Di, X., Yuan, B., Xiong, J.: Large-scale short-term urban taxi demand forecasting using deep learning. In: Proceedings of the Asia and South Pacific Design Automation Conference, pp. 428–433. IEEE Press (2018)
13. Lu, C.A.: Traffic scene anomaly detection. Master's thesis, UniversitiTunku Abdul Rahman (2017)
14. Malhotra, P., Vig, L., Shroff, G., Agarwal, P.: Long short term memory networks for anomaly detection in time series. In: Proceedings of the European Symposium on Artifical Neural Networks, Computational Intelligence and Machine Learning, pp. 89–94. Presses universitaires de Louvain (2015)
15. Massey Jr., F.J.: The Kolmogorov-Smirnov test for goodness of fit. J. Am. Stat. Assoc. **46**, 68–78 (1951)
16. New York City Taxi and Limousine Commission: TLC trip record data. https://www.nyc.gov/html/tlc/html/about/trip_record_data.shtml. Accessed 05 Oct 2017
17. O'Shea, T.J., Clancy, T.C., McGwier, R.W.: Recurrent neural radio anomaly detection. arXiv preprint. arXiv:1611.00301 (2016)
18. Shapiro, S.S., Wilk, M.B.: An analysis of variance test for normality (complete samples). Biometrika **52**, 591–611 (1965)
19. Siffer, A., Fouque, P.A., Termier, A., Largouet, C.: Anomaly detection in streams with extreme value theory. In: Proceedings of the International Conference on Knowledge Discovery and Data Mining, pp. 1067–1075. ACM (2017)
20. Singh, A.: Anomaly detection for temporal data using long short-term memory. Master's thesis, KTH Royal Institute of Technology (2017)
21. Stephens, M.A.: EDF statistics for goodness of fit and some comparisons. J. Am. Stat. Assoc. **69**, 730–737 (1974)
22. Taylor, A., Leblanc, S., Japkowicz, N.: Anomaly detection in automobile control network data with long short-term memory networks. In: Proceedings of the International Conference on Data Science and Advanced Analytics, pp. 130–139. IEEE (2016)
23. Tukey, J.: Exploratory Data Analysis. Addison-Wesley, Reading (1977)

Neural Network Based Large Neighborhood Search Algorithm for Ride Hailing Services

Arslan Ali Syed[1]([⊠]), Karim Akhnoukh[2], Bernd Kaltenhaeuser[3],
and Klaus Bogenberger[4]

[1] Mobility Services, Bavairan Motor Works, Munich, Germany
arslan-ali.syed@bmw.de
[2] Technical University of Munich, Munich, Germany
karim.akhnoukh@tum.de
[3] Baden-Wuerttemberg Cooperative State University,
Villingen-Schwenningen, Germany
bernd.kaltenhaeuser@dhbw-vs.de
[4] University of Federal Armed Forces Munich, Munich, Germany
klaus.bogenberger@unibw.de

Abstract. Ride Hailing (RH) services have become common in many cities. An important aspect of such services is the optimal matching between vehicles and customer requests, which is very close to the classical Vehicle Routing Problem with Time Windows (VRPTW).

With the emergence of new Machine Learning (ML) techniques, many researches have tried to use them for discreet optimization problems. Recently, Pointer Networks (Ptr-Net) have been applied to simpler Vehicle Routing Problem (VRP) with limited applicability [14]. We add fixed slots to their approach to make it applicable to RH scenario. The number of slots can vary without retraining the network. Furthermore, contrary to reinforcement learning in [14], we use supervise learning for training.

We show that the presented architecture has the potential to build good vehicle routes for RH services. Furthermore, looking at the effectiveness of Large Neighbourhood Search(LNS) for VRPTW, we combine the approach with LNS by using the trained network as an insertion operator. We generate examples from New York Taxi data and use the solutions generated from LNS for training. The approach consistently produces good solutions for problems of sizes similar to the ones used during training, and scales well to unseen problems of relatively bigger sizes.

Keywords: Long short term memory networks ·
Large Neighborhood Search · Machine Learning ·
Discrete optimization · Ride Hailing

1 Introduction

The large scale availability of high speed wireless internet and the widespread usage of smartphones has marked the beginning of many new and innovative

P. Moura Oliveira et al. (Eds.): EPIA 2019, LNAI 11804, pp. 584–595, 2019.
https://doi.org/10.1007/978-3-030-30241-2_49

transportation services. A lot of focus is now put on viewing people's mobility as a service. Among such services, Ride Hailing (RH) has gained a lot of attention, where a user can order a ride on short notice via a mobile app.

An important aspect in RH is how to match the vehicles to customer requests such that various user and business oriented goals are optimized. Traditionally, this optimization problem comes under the window of Vehicle Routing Problem with Time Windows (VRPTW) or more specifically Dial a Ride Problem (DARP), for which currently Large Neighborhood Search (LNS) based algorithms provide state of the art solutions [9,10]. The dynamic addition of new requests and the limited calculation time provide the biggest challenge for an efficient real time matching algorithm in RH. We suggest that we can benefit from past runs of similar RH problems using Machine Learning (ML) techniques, and get better quick assignment solutions.

Recently, a similar approach has been applied to Vehicle Routing Problem (VRP) with limited applicability using Pointer Networks (Ptr-Net) [14]. We extend their approach to suit for small static RH scenarios or more generally to VRPTW, where all the vehicle positions and customer requests are known in advance. We also present an innovative approach of combining LNS algorithm with NN, by using the trained network as an insertion operator inside LNS. The training and validation problems are taken from the open source New York City (NYC) Taxi data [1].

1.1   Literature Review

The growing market of RH has caused a resurgence of research interests into the VRPTW and DARP [10]. DARP is a special case of pickup and delivery problem with time windows, where both customer convenience and business goals are considered. It is very similar to matching vehicles to customer requests in RH and Ride Sharing (RS) services. However, in DARP vehicles start and end at fixed depots while in RH and RS each vehicle start and end at its own specific location. Therefore, to adopt DARP for RH scenario, each vehicle can be thought of having its own unique start depot, which drastically increases the problem complexity.

DARP has been applied to a wide range of applications. Various exact methods and metaheuristics exist in literature for solving multiple variants of DARP. Usually, the exact methods can solve only small size problems. Therefore, the major focus in literature has been on finding good solutions in a reasonable computation time using various metaheuristics [5,10]. Multiple approaches based on Adaptive Large Neighborhood Search (ALNS) [9,16], Variable Neighborhood Search (VNS) [8,15], Genetic Algorithm (GA) [6] and their Hybrids [12] are generally utilized for this purpose. Among these, the reported current and previous state of the art approaches for static DARP are presented in [9,12], that are based on ALNS and Hybrid Genetic Algorithm (HGA), respectively [10].

Beside the DARP literature, there have been some researches in transportation that simulated the RH scenarios, but many of them did not benefit from the available DARP procedures. The main focus has been to study the impacts and potential of ODM services or an autonomous fleet. Some used commercial microsimulators like Aimsun or MATSim [7,11] for this purpose while others simulated only ODM vehicles inside self built simulation environment [3]. They either used simple heuristics for vehicle dispatching or developed their own procedures for continuous optimization of the problem. However, they did not target the real operation of actual ODM services, where the services get very little time for optimization.

Both VRPTW and DARP have not been directly approached before in literature using Deep Neural Networks (DNN). However, there has been some attempts to solve combinatorial optimization problems with the help of DNN. The first of which is Ptr-Net introduced by [18]. They used it to solve optimization problems like Convex Hull, Delaunay Triangulation and Traveling Salesman Problem (TSP). It is based on supervised learning to generate semi optimal solutions for small sized problems which can not be solved by optimal solvers. They used beam search to consider only valid solutions during the test time.

A modification to the loss function of Ptr-Net was proposed in [13]. Since it depended on supervised learning technique and the solutions used for training were sub optimum, the predicted solutions might outperform the training solutions. Therefore, they added another layer to the loss function that could choose between the current prediction and the approximated supervised solution. During training, it checked if the difference between the predicted solution and the ground truth is less than zero or not; and it treats the loss to be equivalent to zero if it is less than zero. This is a very simple yet effective approach since it makes sure that we do not over train the network with bad solutions.

A Reinforcement Learning (RL) approach based on Ptr-Net was introduced in [4]. They showed the effectiveness of their model by solving combinatorial optimization problems such as TSP and the knapsack problem. A further attempt was made by [14]. They used RL and a simplified version of the Ptr-Net to solve TSP and Capacitated Vehicle Routing Problem (CVRP). They tested their model with one vehicle and up to 100 requests and used beam search in the decoder to obtain their best solutions. They used static and dynamic features for the requests and a mask function to eliminate the set of infeasible solutions on every time step. Additionally, they replaced the Long Short Term Memory (LSTM) network at the encoder with an embedding layer that maps the input to a higher dimensional vector space since the input data is not sequentially dependant. Therefore, the updated embeddings at every time step can be efficiently updated, which decreases the training time significantly. Our implementation is based on this model which is further extended to allow for more vehicles and time constraints.

1.2   Problem Formulation

Consider a fleet V of size m and a set R of l requests. For an RH scenario, we assume that each vehicle can serve only one request at a time. For each request $r \in R$, we have a pickup location r_p, a drop-off location r_d and the time t_r when the request wants to be picked up. The time it takes to travel from r_p to r_d is given as T_r. For each vehicle $v \in V$, let $P_v \subseteq R$ be a set of requests assigned to v, and T_v be the total duration that v will take to serve the requests in P_v. We assume that after serving all requests in P_v the vehicle stays at the drop-off location of the last request. Let d_{max} be a constant indicating the maximum delay allowed for picking up a request. Then, for each request r, the allowed pickup time window is given as $[t_r, t_r + d_{max}]$. For each vehicle $v \in V$, let A_{rv} be the vehicle arrival time at the pickup location of the request r. The delay for the customer pickup can be calculated as $delay_{rv} = \max(0, A_{rv} - t_r)$. Lastly, let c_r be 1 if request r is not covered by any vehicle, otherwise 0. With the above notations, the multi-objective function for the matching problem is given by:

$$\min \alpha \sum_{v \in V} T_v + \beta \sum_{v \in V} \sum_{r \in P_v} delay_{rv} + \delta \sum_{r \in R} c_r \tag{1}$$

where the three terms represent the amount of time traveled by vehicles, the pickup delay of the served customers and the number of unserved customers, respectively. α and β are constant weights for the relative importance of the total travel time of all the vehicles and the total delay to the customers, respectively. δ is a relatively heavy weight for serving the maximum number of customer requests.

2 Methodology

In this section, we present the overall methodology used. We start with the preprocessing step of RV graph, then a brief description of LNS then finally detailed description of our NN.

2.1 Pairwise Request-Vehicle (RV) Graph

We first preprocess an RV graph to reduce the complexity of the RH matching problem and help in the implementation of the algorithms. It is motivated by the ideas of forward time slack in [17] and the RV graph in [3]. We compute a pairwise directed graph for vehicles and requests, with negative edges representing pairwise time slack and positive edges representing the pairwise delay for the pickup. Consider a directed RV graph $G(N, E)$ with set $N = V \cup R$ as nodes and edges E defined as follows:

For a vehicle $v \in V$ and a request $r \in R$, the edge $(v, r) \in E$ if $T_{vr} + t_s - t_r \leq d_{max}$, with a weight $e = T_{vr} + t_s - t_r$; where T_{vr} is the traveling time from the vehicle location to the pickup point of r and t_s is the start time of the vehicle. This implies that starting from the current location, the vehicle can pick up the request with a delay less than d_{max}.

Similarly for two requests r_1 and r_2, the edge $(r_1, r_2) \in E$, with weight $e = T_{r1r2} + T_{r1} + t_{r1} - t_{r2}$, if $T_{r1r2} + T_{r1} + t_{r1} - t_{r2} \leq d_{max}$; where T_{r1} is the travel time from pickup to drop-off location of r_1 and T_{r1r2} is the distance from drop-off of r_1 to pickup of r_2 (And vice versa for edge $(r_2, r_1) \in E$). This means that an imaginary vehicle starting at the pickup point of r_1, drops off r_1 first, and then goes and picks up r_2 such that the delay for picking up r_2 is less than d_{max}.

Algorithm 1. Large Neighbourhood Search (LNS)

---

function SOLVE($sol \in solutions$)

$s_{best} \leftarrow sol$

while stop-criterion not fulfilled **do**

$\hat{s} \leftarrow sol$

remove q requests from $\hat{s}$

reinsert removed requests into $\hat{s}$

if $f(\hat{s}) < f(s_{best})$ **then**

$s_{best} \leftarrow \hat{s}$

if accept($\hat{s}, sol$) **then**

$sol \leftarrow \hat{s}$

return s_{best}

2.2   Large Neighborhood Search (LNS)

LNS is based on the idea of exploring such a large neighborhood of the solution that it's almost impossible to explore it explicitly. In terms of VRPTW, this corresponds to removing q percent requests and inserting them back using a variety of removal and insertion operators respectively, as shown in Algorithm 1. The initial solution is first built using an insertion operator. Ropke and Pisinger [16] first showed LNS effectiveness for VRPTW with pickup and drop off. They introduced a roulette wheel based adaptive scheme for dynamically selecting greedy and (2-, 3-, 4- and k-) regret insertions, and random, shaw and worst removals, and thus termed it as ALNS.

We use the same LNS operators as suggested by Ropke and Pisinger [16], and its solution is used for training NN. However, to adapt the algorithm to RH scenario, we consider that every vehicle has its own station or start location, as mentioned in Sect. 1.1. Furthermore, we introduce a trained NN based insertion operator for final testing as follows:

- **LSTM based Insertion:** The basic aim of using LSTM based insertion inside LNS is to benefit from the past runs on similar problems. We expect that assigning a request to a vehicle path, one at a time, is like a sequence. The traditional insertion operators inside LNS look at various details of the request vehicle combinations and assign a suitable request to a vehicle's path. We expect that an LSTM based network can learn to make such a decision by looking at various features. The details of the used LSTM network architecture will be discussed later.

2.3   Neural Network Architecture

The proposed NN architecture is based on the model mentioned in [14] using dynamic features that are updated before every decoder time step. We also follow the same approach of replacing the Recurrent Neural Network (RNN) encoder presented in the Ptr-Net with an embedding layer for mapping the input to a D-dimensional vector space since the input is not sequentially dependant.

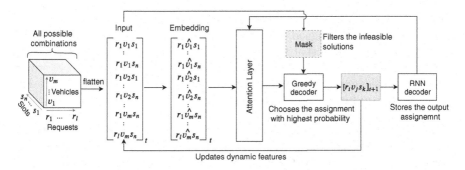

Fig. 1. The network architecture used for the assignment.

The architecture is generalized to cater for multiple vehicles and the pickup time windows of each customer request. For this purpose, every vehicle $v_j \in V$ is assigned a fixed number of slots n, representing the path of the vehicle. n can be adjusted for different problem sizes without the need of retraining. Our model also improves the vehicle path at every decoding time step in order to minimize the overall objective cost. However, in this path correction it guarantees that the request r_i would still be served by v_j (to which it was first assigned) but it can be assigned to a later slot $s_k \in S$ of v_j.

Model Overview. Our input consists mainly of three distinct sets which are: requests, vehicles and slots. These sets are permuted together to generate every possible combination using RV graph. Each cell of the permuted sets has its own dynamic features that change at every decoding step. Then the input cells are mapped to a higher dimensional space using an embedding layer as shown in Fig. 1. At the output, a greedy decoder chooses one specific input (of highest probability) which represents an assignment of a request at a slot within a vehicle's path. The output at every time step is dependant on all the input permutations X_t at the current time step and the outputs of the previous time steps $y_1....y_{t-1}$. Probabilities over different inputs are calculated with the same attention mechanism presented in [14].

Input Features. Each input cell is composed of four features, all of which are dynamic i.e. change every time step depending on the assignment at $t - 1$. Contrary to [14], we did not use any static feature. The dynamic features are:

1. **The cost of assignment:** This feature is similar to the incremental cost Δf_{rv} used in the basic greedy insertion operator for LNS. However, unlike basic greedy, the cost of insertion for r at all the possible insertion positions within v is used. Since all the vehicles are assumed to be empty at the beginning, initially only the cost of assigning requests in the first slot to vehicles is calculated. When a request r_i is assigned to vehicle v_j, the cost of assignment to v_j is recalculated for all requests, that would include the first slot before r_i

and the second slot after it. These possible insertion slots keep increasing as more requests are assigned to v_j. While inserting r_i in v_j at an intermediate slot s_k it is made sure that the requests previously assigned to v_j at s_a where $a \geq k$ would be served in their predefined time window. Otherwise, s_k would not be considered as an insertion option for r_i in v_j and would be masked out. Costs are further normalized by dividing them by the penalty term of neglecting a request (see Sect. 1.2).

2. **Number of outgoing edges in RV Graph:** This feature takes a look one step further in time. For a cell of $r_i v_j s_k$, it considers the number of requests from the set of unmatched requests U that can still be added to the path of v_j at s_b where $b \in [1, n]$, while satisfying the time constraints for the set of requests P_{v_j} already in v_j path. The number of outgoing edges for each input cell is divided by the total number of requests in the problem to be in the range $[0, 1]$.

3. **Number of available vehicles:** It considers the total number of vehicles that are able to serve r_i considering the current path of the vehicles and the time window of the r_i. This feature is request specific such that $r_i v_j s_k$ is the same $\forall j \in [1, m]$ & $k \in [1, n]$. In other words, this feature does not change for same request and different vehicle. The value of this feature is divided by the total number of vehicles in the problem for normalization.

4. **Regret value:** This is also a request specific feature. It's based on the 2-regret insertion concept as used in [16]. Intuitively, it keeps track of the difference between the best and second best insertion cost for a given request. For a request that has just one insertion option available, its regret value is calculated by subtracting its insertion cost from the penalty weight δ of neglecting a request.

Mask Function. The Mask function keeps track of the assignments that are infeasible according to the time window constraints. These infeasible assignments are guaranteed to have a probability of zero and thus they would never be selected by the decoder. If all the inputs have zero probability, then the decoding stops. This also makes sure that there could be no more valid assignments, and thus, the remaining requests (if any) will remain unassigned.

Loss Function. We want to train our neural network to generate solutions whose total cost is minimized. Therefore, the total objective cost of the solutions from the network should be as close as possible to the training solutions. Since these training solutions are not solved up to optimality, we add the *argmax* block from [13] to make sure that the network will not be over trained with bad solutions. The number of unassigned requests per solution are multiplied by the penalty term δ. Then, the loss is further divided by the ground truth solution to account for different magnitudes when the problem size is different. We base our loss function on the one used in [4] by applying the modifications mentioned above.

$$L(\theta) = \frac{1}{B} \sum_{b=0}^{B} \frac{1}{C_{GT}^b} \max \left(\left(\left(\sum_{t=0}^{T^b} c_t^b \right) + \left((l^b - T^b) \times \delta \right) - C_{GT}^b \right), [0] \times B \right) \cdot \sum_{t=0}^{T^b} \log p_\theta(y_t^b) \quad (2)$$

where θ represents the learnable network parameters. B is the batch size, C_{GT}^b is the ground truth objective cost (approximated here) for the whole problem b, l^b is the total number of requests for the problem and T^b is the number of output time steps from the decoder. c_t is the cost of the assignment chosen at decoding time step t and y_t is the probability of the output at this time.

3 Computational Experiments

We used NYC Taxi data for generating requests and vehicles [1]. Vehicles were generated by choosing the trip start positions randomly from the NYC data. Requests were generated from January 2016 for different working days in the morning. Only the trip start time, start location and end location were used for generating the requests. Then Open Source Routing Machine (OSRM) was used for calculating the travel time between different locations [2]. We generated multiple problem instances for the training with the number of vehicles fixed to 10 and varying only the number of requests between $\{10, 20, 30, 40\}$. We denote each problem size by $m^a l^b$, where a and b represent the number of used vehicles and requests in the problem instance, respectively. For each problem size, 1000 samples were generated for training and 300 for testing. Since it was difficult to solve the problem instances upto optimality for the mentioned problem sizes and time windows, LNS with 2-regret insertion and shaw removal operator was used for finding the solutions. LNS was run for 2000 iterations for each of the problem instance and the solutions were used as ground truth for our training process. We trained three different models, which are:

1. **Specific model with $n > 1$:** This model was trained separately on each problem instance until convergence using transfer learning. It was first trained on $m^{10} l^{10}$, then starting from the same weights on $m^{10} l^{20}$, then $m^{10} l^{30}$ and finally on $m^{10} l^{40}$. We use number of slots $n = 6$.
2. **General model:** This model was trained on all the problem instances at once. Each batch contains problems of different sizes. The number of slots $n = 6$ here as well.
3. **General model with $n = 1$:** In this model, the requests are always appended at end of a vehicle's path, i.e. $n = 1$. This eases the model as the features have to be calculated for just one position. This model is specifically important when we want to build vehicle paths incrementally without rescheduling the already assigned requests. Ideally, when we have *perfect* features for the insertion of unassigned request, such a model should be able to build vehicle path optimally by just looking at the dynamic features in the current decoder time step with much less computation time. Therefore, we include such a model in our analysis to test how much close our features are to such an ideal scenario.

The encoder hidden size is set to 128 and the number of layers in the LSTM decoder network to 2. We use a batch size of 64 samples and train for 500 epochs which are enough for convergence. The GPU device used for training is Nvidia quadro M4000 with 8 GB memory. Each epoch containing instances of all the problem sizes for the general model with $n > 1$ takes around 10.4 min while it takes around 7.2 min for the model with $n = 1$.

4   Results and Discussion

In this section we discuss the results of the computational experiments.

4.1   Initial Solution Comparison

In this section we compare the performance of the three models against the 2-regret and basic greedy insertion heuristics of [16] for building the initial solution. Furthermore, since we are also testing a model that only inserts the new requests at the last position, i.e. Generic Model with $n = 1$, we found it reasonable to also test the approaches against modified versions of 2-regret and basic greedy insertions that only inserts the unassigned requests at the last position of vehicle's path. We represent these modified 2-regret and basic greedy by putting $n = 1$.

Figure 2 compares the initial solutions' mean relative objective cost difference to 2000 iteration of LNS and the number of unassigned requests for various insertion strategies. In the simple problem of $m^{10}l^{20}$, all the methods provide very similar solutions. However, when the problem becomes more complicated our general model with $n > 1$ provides better solutions. Additionally, for m^{10} and l^i where $i \in \{20, 30, 40\}$ the general model's performance almost same as the specific model which is trained on every problem size individually. This is very important to ensure that the loss function used is invariant to the magnitude of the problem size. Furthermore, this shows that the general model has already learned what to do in each time step regardless of the size of the problem.

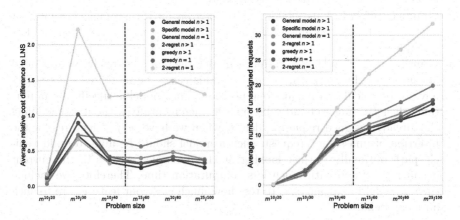

Fig. 2. Comparison of initial solution building using NN models and other LNS insertion heuristics. The problem sizes on the right side of the dashed line correspond to bigger problem sizes on which the NN was never trained.

This is also confirmed when the model is tested on instances of more than double the sizes it was trained on (right side of the dashed line) where the overall cost for the general model is better than the other heuristics. This verifies the fact that the model can generalize and scale well to larger problem instances without retraining.

Besides inside actual LNS, the initial solution approach can be used in a real-time dynamic environment to provide the user with a quick reply when there is no time available for batch optimization.

4.2 Trained Neural Network as Insertion Operator Inside LNS

As introduced in Sect. 2.2, we analyze the performance of the trained NN when used inside LNS as an insertion operator. For this analysis we use only the general model with $n > 1$, as they gave best solution quality for initial solution. We compare it against the ALNS scheme of [16], as multiple LNS operators are almost always better with the adaptive scheme. Additionally, we also test the trained NN along with other operators in ALNS.

We run each problem instance multiple times with each of the used procedures. For this experiment, we select 10 problems for each problem size. Each problem is solved 5 times for each of the procedure with 2000 iterations. We take mean of the 5 solutions and compare it against the best found solution for each of the problems. Hence, the formula used to calculate the solution quality for a problem i using procedure j is given by:

$$(solution\ quality)_i^j = \frac{\frac{1}{5}\sum_{k=1}^{5} cost_k^j}{cost_{best}^i} \tag{3}$$

where $cost_{best}^i$ is the objective cost of the best solution found for problem i regardless of the procedure used and $cost_k^j$ is the objective cost of the solution obtained using j procedure and kth run.

Figure 3 compares the mean solution quality of the NN based LNS, ALNS with NN and traditional ALNS. All procedures are run for 2000 iterations. For small sized problems $m^{10}l^{20}$ all the procedures provide similar quality as the problem is already simple to solve. However, for increasing problem complexity, the NN based approaches are continuously seen to be performing better than the traditional ALNS. For finding good solutions with limited number of iterations and increasing complexity, it is crucial that good requests insertion decisions are taken earlier. Our trained network is interestingly able to take such decisions even for the problem sizes for which the network has never been trained, i.e. ($m^{15}l^{60}$, $m^{20}l^{80}$ and $m^{25}l^{100}$). This shows that, as mentioned in Sect. 2.2, trained model learned how to pick better insertion requests based on seen solutions. Ideally, if we had *perfect* set of features and trained model, then we would expect the LNS to converge in a single iteration. However, in the absence of that, we expect the solution to converge earlier to best solution if we use better features.

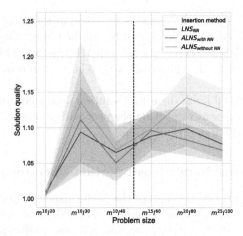

Fig. 3. Comparison of solution quality of trained NN as sole insertion operator inside LNS, trained NN inside ALNS along with other operators and ALNS with only traditional insertion operators. The problem sizes on the right side of the dashed line correspond to bigger problem sizes on which the NN was never trained. The shaded region mark the minimum and the maximum solution quality for each problem size.

5 Conclusion

In this paper, we introduced the concept of fixed number of slots n for generalizing the NN model of [14] for RH scenario. The modification can be used with any VRPTW with minor changes. The experiments show that the network learned how to make good request insertion decisions. The general model with $n > 1$ provided the best solution quality, even for the problem sizes on which it was never trained. Ideally a perfect NN with perfect features set would build solution with just $n = 1$, which can be further looked into in the future.

We also used the trained NN inside LNS and ALNS as an insertion operator which showed an improvement over the traditional ALNS. Such a NN based insertion has great potential inside LNS, as various information that is generally used by individual insertion operators separately for making insertion decisions, can be combined together inside a single NN.

In the future, we propose to try other strategies in the decoder rather than using the greedy decoder directly. This can lead the model to reach a better solution faster inside LNS. We also suggest to use the suggested NN inside an actual dynamic RH simulation environment for quick assignment of vehicles.

References

1. https://www1.nyc.gov/site/tlc/about/tlc-trip-record-data.page
2. http://project-osrm.org/
3. Alonso-Mora, J., Samaranayake, S., Wallar, A., Frazzoli, E., Rus, D.: On-demand high-capacity ride-sharing via dynamic trip-vehicle assignment. Proc. Nat. Acad. Sci. **114**(3), 462–467 (2017)

4. Bello, I., Pham, H., Le, Q.V., Norouzi, M., Bengio, S.: Neural combinatorial optimization with reinforcement learning. arXiv preprint. arXiv:1611.09940 (2016)
5. Cordeau, J.F., Laporte, G.: The dial-a-ride problem: models and algorithms. Ann. Oper. Res. **153**(1), 29–46 (2007)
6. Cubillos, C., Urra, E., Rodríguez, N.: Application of genetic algorithms for the DARPTW problem. Int. J. Comput. Commun. Control **4**(2), 127–136 (2009)
7. Dandl, F., Bracher, B., Bogenberger, K.: Microsimulation of an autonomous taxi-system in Munich. In: 2017 5th IEEE International Conference on Models and Technologies for Intelligent Transportation Systems (MT-ITS), pp. 833–838. IEEE (2017)
8. Detti, P., de Lara, G.Z.M.: Variable neighborhood search algorithms for the multi-depot dial-a-ride problem with heterogeneous vehicles and users. arXiv preprint. arXiv:1611.05187 (2016)
9. Gschwind, T., Drexl, M.: Adaptive large neighborhood search with a constant-time feasibility test for the dial-a-ride problem. Transp. Sci. **53**, 319–622 (2019)
10. Ho, S.C., Szeto, W., Kuo, Y.H., Leung, J.M., Petering, M., Tou, T.W.: A survey of dial-a-ride problems literature review and recent developments. Transp. Res. Part B Methodological **111**, 395–421 (2018)
11. Hörl, S., Ruch, C., Becker, F., Frazzoli, E., Axhausen, K.W.: Fleet control algorithms for automated mobility: a simulation assessment for Zurich. Transp. Res. Part C Emerg. Technol. **102**, 20–31 (2018)
12. Masmoudi, M.A., Braekers, K., Masmoudi, M., Dammak, A.: A hybrid genetic algorithm for the heterogeneous dial-a-ride problem. Comput. Oper. Res. **81**, 1–13 (2017)
13. Milan, A., Rezatofighi, S.H., Garg, R., Dick, A., Reid, I.: Data-driven approximations to NP-hard problems. In: Thirty-First AAAI Conference on Artificial Intelligence (2017)
14. Nazari, M., Oroojlooy, A., Snyder, L., Takác, M.: Reinforcement learning for solving the vehicle routing problem. In: Advances in Neural Information Processing Systems, pp. 9839–9849 (2018)
15. Parragh, S.N., Doerner, K.F., Hartl, R.F.: Variable neighborhood search for the dial-a-ride problem. Comput. Oper. Res. **37**(6), 1129–1138 (2010)
16. Ropke, S., Pisinger, D.: An adaptive large neighborhood search heuristic for the pickup and delivery problem with time windows. Transp. Sci. **40**(4), 455–472 (2006)
17. Savelsbergh, M.W.: The vehicle routing problem with time windows: minimizing route duration. ORSA J. Comput. **4**(2), 146–154 (1992)
18. Vinyals, O., Fortunato, M., Jaitly, N.: Pointer networks. In: Advances in Neural Information Processing Systems, pp. 2692–2700 (2015)

Predicting Air Compressor Failures Using Long Short Term Memory Networks

Kunru Chen[⊠], Sepideh Pashami, Yuantao Fan, and Slawomir Nowaczyk

Center for Applied Intelligent Systems Research,
Halmstad University, Halmstad, Sweden
{kunru.chen,sepideh.pashami,yuantao.fan,slawomir.nowaczyk}@hh.se
http://caisr.hh.se/

Abstract. We introduce an LSTM-based method for predicting compressor failures using aggregated sensory data, and evaluate it using historical information from over 1000 heavy duty vehicles during 2015 and 2016. The goal is to proactively identify trucks that will require maintenance in the near future, so that component replacement can be scheduled before the failure happens, translating into improved uptime. The problem is formulated as a classification task of whether a compressor failure will happen within the specified prediction horizon. A recurrent neural network using Long Short-Term Memory (LSTM) architecture is employed as the prediction model, and compared against Random Forest (RF), the solution used in industrial deployment at the moment. Experimental results show that while Random Forest slightly outperforms LSTM in terms of AUC score, the predictions of LSTM stay significantly more stable over time, showing a consistent trend from healthy to faulty class. Additionally, LSTM is also better at detecting the switch from faulty class to the healthy one after a repair. We demonstrate that this stability is important for making repair decisions, especially in questionable cases, and therefore LSTM model is likely to lead to better results in practice.

Keywords: Fault detection · Predictive maintenance ·
Recurrent neural networks · Long-short term memory

1 Introduction

The current paradigm for transportation vehicle maintenance in industries is a combination of corrective maintenance and preventive maintenance, i.e. to send them to the workshop after a failure occurs in the system, and to maintain based on the pre-planned calendar time. However, this has the following drawbacks: (i) it does not perform maintenance pro-actively before the failure happens; (ii) the fixed maintenance period does not flexibly adapt to the status of the equipment, (iii) it leads to a waste of resources in repairs or replacements of components that still function properly. Therefore, to overcome the drawbacks above, predictive maintenance is being adapted as a new maintenance strategy.

This kind of maintenance pays close attention to the status of the machine, and only suggests repairs and components replacements when they are needed.

P. Moura Oliveira et al. (Eds.): EPIA 2019, LNAI 11804, pp. 596–609, 2019.
https://doi.org/10.1007/978-3-030-30241-2_50

It fixes the drawbacks of the mentioned maintenance planning; however, it takes significantly more effort to implement and to bring it on in the real world. The difficulties of it can be the high cost of sensors for monitoring different components, the unstable or unreliable connectivity, and the lack of well-designed prediction models for a specific type of equipment in a specific usage.

Predictive maintenance depends on data being continuously collected onboard vehicles, and on analyzing this data to understand usage patterns and symptoms of wear. This type of data itself is also a big challenge for data mining methods due to two reasons: (i) there are often several hundred sensors in a vehicle, which results in high dimensionality of the data, with only a small subset being relevant for a particular component; (ii) while there is a lot of data concerning "normal" operation of the vehicles, there are usually very few samples of the failures, which results in high imbalance of different classes in the data.

Many researchers have worked on this topic in the last decade, and some of their works are nowadays implemented in practical settings. Random Forest is one of the successful methods due to its ability to handle highly dimensional and highly imbalanced data. It is also overall one of the easier methods to use, since it does not require a lot of data science expertise to set the parameters. However, Random Forest assumes that each data sample is independent, which is generally not true in equipment monitoring applications. An air compressor failure usually develops gradually and is caused by many different factors, therefore the current state of the vehicle is influenced by the prior usage. The original available data is collected as a time sequence, and different periods in this sequence are highly correlated. Therefore, it is desirable to investigate models that can describe the dynamic behaviours of the system and capture temporal relationship between samples. One example of such methods is Recurrent Neural Network (RNN), and in particular Long Short-Term Memory (LSTM).

In this paper we introduce a prediction model based on LSTM to detect whether an air compressor failure will occur within the next 90 days. Moreover, we conduct an analysis of the stability of prediction results over time, and the effect it has on making maintenance decisions. To this end, we have developed an LSTM model that, while slightly inferior to RF in terms of Area Under the receiver operating characteristic Curve (AUC), provides a significantly better stability of the results, leading to improved vehicle uptime.

2   Related Works

Two common approaches are implemented for diagnosis and prognosis: the model-based paradigm and the data-driven paradigm [16]. The model-based method focuses on building a mathematical or statistical model of expected relations among the signals from the equipment to discover information about the fault [17,18]. In many works [19–21] researchers process the signals using multivariate calculus to learn the status of the equipment. However, it is complex and also challenging to use systems of differential equations to describe the dynamic physical system. On the other hand, data-driven approaches are closely related to machine learning. Through automatic processing of sensor data collected during operations, condition of the equipment can be assessed, and maintenance decisions can be made [22–24].

As for prognosis, Zheng et al. [12] presented a LSTM approach for remaining useful life estimation on three different data set, and the result is compared to that from Support Vector Regression, Relevance Vector Regression, Multi-Layer Perceptron and Convolutional Neural Network (CNN) [25]. The best model that they reported contains three feed forward neural network layers after 2 LSTM layers. There are also researchers who have been using CNN on prognosis. Saxena et al. [26] adopted CNN for RUL estimation on the C-MAPSS dataset by NASA. They divided the sensor data into sliding windows, which means that CNN considers these sliding windows as independent of each other.

This paper builds upon the work of Prytz et al. [1], since it considers the same problem formulation and a very similar dataset, collected from the same truck model. That study has demonstrated that machine learning is a suitable approach to predictive maintenance tasks in the heavy duty vehicles domain, and that the classification setup can lead to significant cost savings while delivering higher uptime. Another study implemented an unsupervised learning [2] to find the interesting relations between measured signals in a truck, whose results later were evaluated by supervised learning classification models [3]. Early results [4] of predicting air compressor failures compared three different classification models (KNN, C4.5 decision trees and Random Forest), and found out that RF achieves the highest AUC score. This work was later continued to find symptoms of wear [5], where a random forest is trained to detect the air compressor failure in a truck before a pre-scheduled workshop visit, and the paper demonstrates economic benefit potential in industrial deployment.

Many researchers have applied RNNs in prognostics because the status of the equipment is time-correlated [6,7]. For predicting system failures, information that is hidden in the past system state can be considered by implementing RNNs. RNNs can also describe the dynamic behaviours of a system and capture the temporal relationship between records; however, the standard RNNs architectures usually suffer from the vanishing and the exploding gradient problem [8]. LSTM is developed by Hochreiter and Schmidhuber [9] to solve this problem. LSTM has been successfully implemented into the applications in different fields, such as Natural Language Processing (NLP), acoustic modelling [10] and handwriting recognition [11]. However, apart from Zheng et al. [12] and Zhao et al. [13], there are not many studies on applying LSTM for diagnosis and prognosis. This is the place where we see the opportunity to further investigate the use of LSTM in the related area of equipment maintenance and industrial transportation applications.

3   Data and Pre-processing

In this paper, we used two datasets from Volvo authorized workshops, *Logged Vehicles Data* (LVD) and *Volvo Service Records* (VSR). The LVD dataset contains aggregated information from various sensors on-board a truck, continuously collected during normal operation. It is downloaded when the truck is in the workshop. However, this poses an interesting challenge, since the length of the interval between two visits (to the workshop) is irregular. Records in VSR dataset are also collected when a truck goes to the workshop. They contain detailed information about the replaced parts and maintenance operations that were performed during the visit.

Subsets of both LVD and VSR are separately used in this paper, we called them *reading table* and *repair table*, respectively. In the reading table, there are more than 160,000 records from about 1,000 Volvo heavy duty trucks collected over 2 years. The records in this table contain information about vehicle configurations and sensor readings. Attributes which reflect the amount of wear, such as mileage, battery mode and hydraulic oil level, are available. Additionally, this data contains information on the working environment of each vehicle.

On the other hand, since we are focusing on the air compressor, a component that does not fail very often, there are less than 200 entries in the repair table. Each of these entries describes when and which truck has been repaired. Clearly, the vast majority of trucks from the reading table never had compressor issues.

There are many missing values in the data. To fill up the missing values, we built a linear interpolation model for each attribute in each truck, with the existing values in that attribute of that truck accordingly. However, in some trucks, there are attributes which are totally absent, or have only a single value, which makes it impossible to do the interpolation. We also use the earliest date in the reading table as the reference date to calculate a new feature called *Age*. To this end, each record has a value of *Age* which is the time distance from the reference date. After unifying the time, for each attribute, all the original values are used to build the interpolation model. As a result, based on the model and the reference date, we filled up all the remaining blanks in the data.

As mentioned before, trucks are not sent to the workshop at fixed time intervals and thus the gap between two LVD records is uneven. This is causing the uneven time-steps in the data, which can be a serious disadvantage when training a model designed for learning sequential data, such as RNN. To solve this problem, we built the global interpolation model to generate synthetic data for each missing day for each of the trucks; so that the data can be represented daily.

If a truck does not have any record in the repair table, we consider it to be a *healthy* truck, and all its record in the reading table will be categorized as negative class (i.e., not requiring a maintenance intervention). On the other hand, any truck that has a repair record is categorized as *faulty* truck. For a faulty truck, a select part of its readout records is categorized as positive class. Clearly, for the classifier to be useful in predictive maintenance setting, it should recommend maintenance intervention only in close vicinity to the failure time. Therefore, we defined a specific condition for positive class, namely, if the record is collected less than 90 days before air compressor repair. In this way, each faulty vehicle has a maximum of 90 faulty records, and all the other records from the same truck are labelled as negative class. This prediction horizon of 90 days is determined by both domain experts and background study [1]. It is based on the fact that air compressor issues require time to develop and it is a gradual process rather than a sudden incident.

4   Methodology

In general, the failure occurs in vehicles over their lifetimes, however, it does not necessarily emerge in the given period of our data collection. Only a small fraction of the LVD records contain information about imminent air compressor failures – the vast majority of the vehicles never develop this problem, and even those that do, are only affected by it through a very short portion of their lifetime. Therefore, these factors contribute to the imbalances in the records on two different levels, truck level and record level, respectively.

After the imbalance problem is handled, the data is fed into prediction models. Random Forest is chosen to be one of the models because it is widely applied in industry, and LSTM is used in our experiments due to its outstanding performance in learning patterns from time-correlated data. Finally, except for the traditional measurements, such as AUC score, a new metric is introduced, focusing on the stability of the model.

4.1   Balancing the Two Classes

On truck level, the imbalance shows that there is too much information about the healthy categories while too little about the faulty one. It is hard for prediction models to learn sufficient knowledge to recognize the minority class, therefore down-sampling of the majority class is necessary. We have selected 200 healthy trucks (preferring those that have the largest number of original reading records) to feed into the experiments. At the same time, it is also desirable to increase the amount of data of the minority class, and we did that through up-sampling using different time windows, as described below.

On record level, for each faulty truck, there are reading records over 2 years (approximately 650 records), but only the 90 records collected just before the failure are labelled as the faulty class. Based on the results from the previous work [1], the closer a record is collected to the failure, the more information concerning that failure is "hidden" in the data. Therefore, it is preferred to mainly use the records collected close to the time when the failure happens. In the experiments, we designed a window with a fixed size to select the preferred records all the records from a (faulty) truck. In this paper, we have decided on a window of size 200 records (days). Therefore, we only selected batches of 200 continuous records from each faulty truck, with a guarantee that the failure happens within these 200 days. In this manner, approximately 45% (90 days out of 200 days) of the data from faulty trucks is labelled as the positive class.

Fig. 1. Window-based up-sampling (the X symbol marks the time of the repair).

Furthermore, as mentioned above, we used the window to up-sample the amount of data from faulty trucks, as shown in Fig. 1. From each of the faulty trucks we selected two subsets of records within the window. We ensured that the repair happens in each of the selected data subsets, however, we consider each subset as a different faulty batch – there is only a limited overlap of the non-faulty data, and the time of failure is different. Although parts of the records from two subsets are exactly the same, since they come from the same actual vehicle, for LSTM or any other sequential learning model the differences in time and the order also matter.

4.2   Prediction Models

Random Forest. Random Forest (RF) [15] is an ensemble of multiple decision trees with a predefined number of trees. In general, bootstrap aggregating repeatedly randomly selects samples in the training set and fits decision trees to those random subsets of the data:

$$\hat{y} = \frac{1}{T} * \sum_{t=1}^{T} f_t(x) \tag{1}$$

RF additionally selects a random subset of the features at each split in training, which makes this algorithm robust in avoiding overfitting problem. When RF makes predictions, it uses the majority voting across all the decision trees in the forest, i.e. it takes the average of predictions from all its decision trees.

Long Short-Term Memory. Artificial Neural Networks (ANNs) are one type of learning models of which operation and architecture are similar to biological neurons in human brain. For the last few decades, ANNs has shown its incredible capacity in machine learning tasks. Though it is powerful, ANNs usually offer individual predictions.

As a particular type of ANNs, the RNN considers that the connections between units form directed cycles. By those cycles, the previous (or sometimes even the future) status of the system can be recurrent in the network, which gives the networks the ability to "remember" the information. With this unique structure, instead of merely patterning feature pairs across attributes, RNNs are also capable to capture dynamic information. Generally, each unit in RNNs makes decisions based on the previous outputs and current input in this way:

$$h^t = g\left(h^{t-1}, x^t\right) \tag{2}$$

where x^t the current input which is a vector-based structure, h^{t-1} is the previous state of this neuron, h^t is the current state, and g is the activation function. Sigmoid (σ), Hyperbolic Tangent (*tanh*), and softmax are the most common choices for the activation function.

LSTM (Hochreiter and Schmidhuber [9]) has been conceptually developed to solve the vanishing and the exploding gradient problem that occurs when training simple RNNs. It is a type of network which has a special structure,

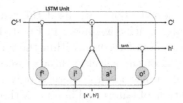

Fig. 2. Structure of LSTM unit

and, thus, it is able to have a better control on information flow in the network. LSTM unit structure at time t is illustrated in Fig. 2.

Assuming that there are m nodes in the unit, x^t, h^t and c^t, respectively, denote input of LSTM, output of LSTM and the cell state, where $h^t \in R^{m \times 1}$ and $C^t \in R^{m \times 1}$. The sensor data collected from each truck is represented in a matrix form $X^n = \left[x^1, x^2, \ldots, x^t, \ldots x^d\right] \in R^{p \times d}$ where d is the duration of the data from a truck, and $x^t = [x_1^t, \ldots, x^t p] \in R^{p \times 1}, t = 1, 2, \ldots d$ is a p-dimensional vector of the reading records at time t.

There are three gates in a LSTM unit: the forget gate, the input gate, and the output gate. Each of them controls the amount of information used in the unit. Generally, based on x^t and h^{t-1}, input gate $i^t \in R^{m \times 1}$ decides which values to use in calculating C^t. Next, forget gate $f^t \in R^{m \times 1}$ determines which information from C^{t-1} should be removed, and which can be used to update C^t. Finally, output gate $O^t \in R^{m \times 1}$ controls what information in C^t to become h^t. In this work, all the LSTM units that are used in the models are implemented as follows:

$$i^t = \sigma(W_i x^t + U_i h^{t-1} + b_i) \tag{3}$$

$$o^t = \sigma(W_o x^t + U_o h^{t-1} + b_o) \tag{4}$$

$$f^t = \sigma(W_f x^t + U_f h^{t-1} + b_f) \tag{5}$$

$$a^t = tanh(W_c x^t + U_c h^{t-1} + b_c) \tag{6}$$

$$C^t = f^t \circ C^{t-1} + i^t \circ a^t \tag{7}$$

$$h^t = o^t \circ tanh(C^{t-1}) \tag{8}$$

where variable weights and bias to be calculated during training process are $W_i, W_o, W_f, W_c \in R^{m \times p}$, $u_i, U_o, U_{f_f}, U_c \in R^{m \times m}$, and $b_i, b_{o\prime}, b_f, b_c \in R^{m \times 1}$. In addition, the $\circ$ is the element-wise multiplication of two vectors, σ is the element-wise logistic sigmoid function, and $tanh$ is the element-wise hyperbolic tangent function.

4.3 Prediction Horizon

Typically in Condition Based Maintenance (CBM) the target variable to predict is Remaining Useful Life (RUL). It provides operators with the most information to base their decision on. However, in our setting, for an OEM with hundreds of thousands of trucks in operation, such a wealth of information is not needed. In fact, it can often confuse unskilled personnel, both at a workshop and at fleet operators. In our case, a binary answer on whether the truck will have any failure before the next visit to the workshop (here estimated as the next 90 days) is perfectly sufficient.

Based on the limited information contained in the data, it is more reasonable to simplify the problem as a binary classification task instead of as a regression. Since the binary output is not as informative as RUL, we define a new metric to measure the stability of the model as compensation. In that sense, the more stable our model is, the more confident the operators can be in the outputs.

4.4   New Metric on Stability

In reality, operators collect new reading record when a truck visits a workshop, and the recurrent neural networks should take both the new record and all the historical records from the truck into account. In our case, the model gives suggested answer on the question: whether this truck needs repair in the next 90 days or not. It is desirable to have stable and confident results rather than the ones that fluctuate often, as the latter might confuse the operator who is supposed to be making maintenance decisions.

For example, when a truck visits the workshop and the model says that it needs to be fixed in the next 90 days, the operators tend to check the results of the recent predictions from the same truck. If the operators get the same predictions on maintenance decision for a few times in a row, they will be much more confident that failures are developing. However, by contrast, if the operators get inconsistent predictions over a period of time, it is difficult for them to understand the condition of the equipment.

We define the point where the prediction switches from one to another as a *jump*, i.e. where the model changes its decision. We count the total amount of jumps as the initial measure of the stability of models. However, not all jumps are equally misleading. Therefore, another measure is designed based on the position of the jump. The intuition is that jumps are expected far away from the time of the failure, close to the 90 days boundary. Such jumps deserve a lower penalty. On the other hand, it is not acceptable, in real world applications, for the jumps to happen close to the failure; thus, such situations receive a higher penalty.

5   Model Creation and Experimental Setup

Our model follows the structure proposed in [12], which implements LSTM for a similar application. Notation L(64,32)D(10,2) refers to a network that has 4 hidden layers with 64 nodes in the first LSTM layer, 32 nodes in the second LSTM layer, followed by 10 and then 2 nodes in the first and the second dense layers. For the model selection, we are using a dropout layer at 0.5 between two LSTM layers; the optimizer is Stochastic Gradient Descent with a learning rate of 0.006, and the activation function is softmax. On the other hand, the random forest is the default version from *scikit-learn* library, and it contains 10 decision trees created using C4.5 algorithm. Gini impurity is used to measure the quality of a split, all notes are expanded until all leaves are pure or until all leaves contain less than 2 samples. We present results evaluated from 4-folds cross-validation.

We have evaluated the results on a setup with 45% faulty records which belongs to 156 trucks (78% of total number of trucks in this setup) and the window size of 200 samples. The 200-days window is randomly located in time, i.e. 200 continuous records out of total approximate 660 reading records in each truck. For the faulty truck, it is guaranteed that all faulty records are included in the selected period. However, for the healthy trucks, in order to avoid the bias to the vehicles which is new or with reduced use, a sufficiently random location of the windows with respect to age is necessary. Figure 3 shows the distribution of the window location from two classes of trucks, they have different distributions in shape; however, on the other hand, different periods of the lifetime are well-covered by the selected windows.

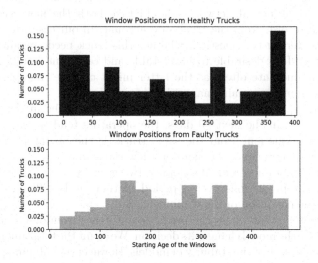

Fig. 3. Distribution of the window locations over vehicle age

6   Results

The results from both Random Forest and LSTM predictions are shown in Table 1. Clearly, Random Forest achieves higher accuracy and AUC score than LSTM models. If that were the only criterion, the preference for this model would be very natural, given also benefits in terms of simplicity and much shorter training time. However, the stability of the results has not been considered.

In particular, one of the challenges with making independent predictions for different reading records in a monitoring scenario is that many methods produce results which are highly unstable – a vehicle would be considered at risk today, but healthy tomorrow. This kind of output is confusing for many end users, such as workshop personnel or fleet operators. It is, of course, possible to use various post-processing methods to smoothen out those results, however, a method that inherently produces results stable over time is preferred and can lead to better decision making by the experts in the field.

Table 1. Results from RF and LSTM in different measurements

	Random Forest	L(64, 32)D(10, 2)
TN	0.92 ± 0.15	0.80 ± 0.13
FP	0.08 ± 0.15	0.20 ± 0.13
FN	0.27 ± 0.34	0.37 ± 0.19
TP	0.73 ± 0.34	0.63 ± 0.19
Accuracy	0.86 ± 0.22	0.74 ± 0.06
Precision	0.83 ± 0.31	0.62 ± 0.07
Recall	0.73 ± 0.34	0.64 ± 0.17
F1-Score	0.78 ± 0.32	0.62 ± 0.09
AUC-Score	0.91 ± 0.17	0.82 ± 0.09

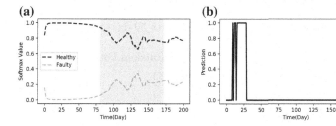

Fig. 4. Example result visualization. Left hand side (a) shows LSTM result from a faulty truck, while right hand side (b) shows Random Forest result from a healthy truck.

In this context, we realize that it is interesting to see how our LSTM model gives prediction over time, to complement the numbers in Table 1. Therefore, we visualize the sequence of predictions for a single truck in a form shown in Fig. 4a. The X-axis corresponds to time and demonstrates the window size of that learning setup. The Y-axis is the outcome of the softmax function: red curve means the probability that the LSTM predicts the data record as a faulty record, while the black curve means the same kind of probability for the healthy one. The blue area corresponds to the ground truth and shows the portion and the position of the faulty period. The repair always happens at the end (right-hand side) of the blue area. The records in the white belong to the healthy (negative) class.

The corresponding example for Random Forest is shown in Fig. 4b. As can be seen, the results are significantly less stable, and can easily be confusing to domain experts – making them reluctant to trust the machine learning models. A comparison of the two models, on different example trucks, is shown in Fig. 5, and more examples are presented in Figs. 7 and 8. These anecdotal examples are, of course, not enough to draw any conclusions, so we propose a method to evaluate this aspect in a rigorous way: *jump*, the new metric mentioned in the Sect. 4.

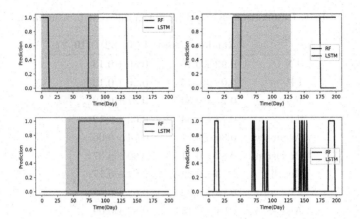

Fig. 5. Comparison of stability between Random Forest and LSTM.

Table 2. Statistic on stability with 30 days threshold

Measurements	Random Forest	LSTM
Number of trucks that has jumps	33	27
Total number of jumps	65	43
Total Penalty	83	74

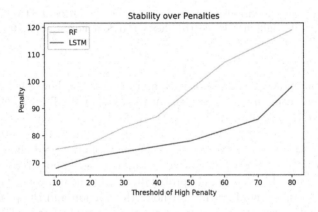

Fig. 6. Penalties from LSTM and Random Forest under high penalty thresholds

We vary a time threshold in the metric, which means the time difference between a jump and the failure. The results shown in Table 2 demonstrate this effect using a 30 days threshold. If the jump happens within 30 days from the failure, it is considered three times as serious as a jump that happens between 30 and 90 days from the failure. In this setting we ignore all jumps that happen earlier, or that happen after the failure. In addition, we adjust the threshold and calculate how the penalty change in response to that, as shown in Fig. 6.

From this perspective it is easy to see that LSTM model outperforms RF in terms of stability of the results.

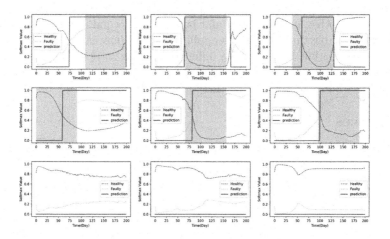

Fig. 7. Example results from LSTM.

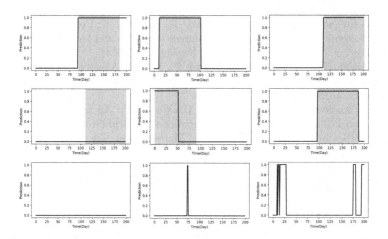

Fig. 8. Example results from Random Forest.

7   Conclusions and Future Works

We have proposed a LSTM model which is able to give stable, consistent prediction overtime. Experiment shows that random forest slightly outperforms LSTM in terms of accuracy and AUC score. Additionally, we also pay attention to the stability of the model. By analysing the predictions given at different time, we demonstrated that this stability is essential for making repair decisions, and for significant improvement on vehicle uptime.

In the future, we would like to investigate three things. First is the reason of the intersections from LSTM, i.e. why does LSTM change its prediction from one class to another at those particular points. The second is which factors make LSTM more stable than RF in this application, and how can we improve it even further. Last the but not the least, different learning setups should be carefully designed and compared with the one used in this paper, i.e. to have different window sizes and also different prediction horizons for improving LSTM models.

References

1. Prytz, R.: Machine learning methods for vehicle predictive maintenance using off-board and on-board data. Licentiate Thesis (2014)
2. Prytz, R., Nowaczyk, S., Byttner, S.: Towards relation discovery for diagnostics. In: Proceedings of the First International Workshop on Data Mining for Service and Maintenance, KDD4Service 2011, San Diego, California (2011)
3. Rognvaldsson, T., Byttner, S., Prytz, R., Nowaczyk, S.: Wisdom of crowds for self-organized intelligent monitoring of vehicle fleets. IEEE Trans. Knowl. Data Eng. (TKDE) (2014)
4. Prytz, R., Nowaczyk, S., Rognvaldsson, T., Byttner, S.: Analysis of truck compressor failures based on logged vehicle data. In: Proceedings of the 9th International Conference on Data Mining (DMIN 2013), Las Vegas, NV, USA, July 2013
5. Prytz, R., Nowaczyk, S., Rognvaldsson, T., Byttner, S.: Predicting the need for vehicle compressor repairs using maintenance records and logged vehicle data. In: Engineering Applications of Artificial Intelligence (2014)
6. Gugulothu, N., Vishnu, T.V., Malhotra, P., Vig, L., Agarwal, P., Shroff, G.: Predicting remaining useful life using time series embeddings based on recurrent neural networks. arXiv:1709.01073 (2017)
7. Liu, J., Saxena, A., Goebel, K., Saha, B., Wang, W.: An adaptive recurrent neural network for remaining useful life prediction of lithium-ion batteries. National Aeronautics and Space Administration, Moffett Field, CA, AMES Research Center, Technical report (2010)
8. Bengio, Y., Simard, P., Frasconi, P.: Learning long-term dependencies with gradient descent is difficult. IEEE Trans. Neural Netw. $5(2)$, 157–166 (1994)
9. Hochreiter, S., Schmidhuber, J.: Long short-term memory. Neural Comput. $9(8)$, 1735–1780 (1997)
10. Sak, H., Senior, A., Beaufays, F..: Long short-term memory recurrent neural network architectures for large scale acoustic modeling. In: Fifteenth Annual Conference of the International Speech Communication Association (2014)
11. Graves, A., Schmidhuber, J.: Offline handwriting recognition with multidimensional recurrent neural networks. In: Advances in Neural Information Processing Systems, pp. 545–552 (2009)
12. Zheng, S., Ristovski, K., Farahat, A., Gupta, C.: Long short-term memory network for remaining useful life estimation. In: 2017 IEEE International Conference on Prognostics and Health Management (ICPHM), pp. 88–95 (2017)
13. Zhao, G., Zhang, G., Liu, Y., Zhang, B., Hu, C.: Lithiumion battery remaining useful life prediction with deep belief network and relevance vector machine. In: 2017 IEEE International Conference on Prognostics and Health Management (ICPHM), pp. 7–13. IEEE (2017)

14. Chen, K., Fan, Y., Pashami, S., Nowaczyk, S.: Recurrent neural networks for fault detection. Master Thesis, Halmstad (2018)
15. Ho, T.: Random decision forests. In: Proceedings of the 3rd International Conference on Document Analysis and Recognition, Montreal, QC, 14–16 August 1995
16. Schwabacher, M., Goebel, K.: A survey of artificial intelligence for prognostics. In: AAAI Fall Symposium, pp. 107–114 (2007)
17. Ahmadimanesh, A., Shahrtash, S.: Transient-based fault-location method for multiterminal lines employing s-transform. IEEE Trans. Power Delivery 28(3), 1373–1380 (2013)
18. Liu, J.: Shannon wavelet spectrum analysis on truncated vibration signals for machine incipient fault detection. Measur. Sci. Technol. 23(5) (2012). https://doi.org/10.1088/0957-0233/23/5/055604
19. Chibani, A., Chadli, M., Shi, P., Braiek, N.: Fuzzy fault detection filter design for t-s fuzzy systems in the finite-frequency domain. IEEE Trans. Fuzzy Syst. 25(5), 1051–1061 (2017)
20. Rai, V.K., Mohanty, A.R.: Bearing fault diagnosis using FFT of intrinsic mode functions in Hilbert-Huang transform. Mech. Syst. Signal Process. 21(6), 2607–2615 (2007)
21. Zhong, G., Yang, G.: Fault detection for discrete-time switched systems in finite-frequency domain. Circuits Syst. Signal Process. 34(4), 1305–1324 (2015)
22. Heimes, F.: Recurrent neural networks for remaining useful life estimation. In: International Conference on Prognostics and Health Management, pp. 1–6. IEEE (2008)
23. Malhi, A., Yan, R., Gao, R.: Prognosis of defect propagation based on recurrent neural networks. IEEE Trans. Instrum. Meas. 60(3), 703–711 (2011)
24. Rigamonti, M., Baraldi, P., Zio, E.: Echo state network for the remaining useful life prediction of a turbofan engine. In: Third European Conference of the Prognostics and Health Management Society (2016)
25. Sateesh Babu, G., Zhao, P., Li, X.-L.: Deep convolutional neural network based regression approach for estimation of remaining useful life. In: Navathe, S.B., Wu, W., Shekhar, S., Du, X., Wang, X.S., Xiong, H. (eds.) DASFAA 2016. LNCS, vol. 9642, pp. 214–228. Springer, Cham (2016). https://doi.org/10.1007/978-3-319-32025-0_14
26. Saxena, A., Goebel, K., Simon, D., Eklund, N.: Damage propagation modeling for aircraft engine run-to-failure simulation. In: International Conference on the Prognostics and Health Management, pp. 1–9. IEEE (2008)

Travel Demand Forecasting: An Evolutionary Learning Approach

Chaima Ahlem Karima Djellab[(✉)], Walid Chaker,
and Henda Hajjami Ben Ghezala

RIADI Laboratory, ENSI, Manouba University, Manouba, Tunisia
{chaima.djellab,walid.chaker,henda.benghezala}@ensi-uma.tn

Abstract. In disaggregate travel demand modeling, we often create an artificial population from a sample of surveyed households and individuals. This synthetic population encompasses the same mobility behaviors as the real one and allows dealing with confidentiality. In this process, Crowdsourcing and Volunteered Geographic Information (VGI) represent very useful data sources. The classical approaches of population synthesis, like synthetic reconstruction and combinatorial optimization, cannot be adapted to manage this huge data. A learning approach is then more suited for the synthesizer to improve the goodness-of-fit of its artificial population as Crowdsourcing data becomes richer. To satisfy such learning requirement, we introduce an evolutionary algorithm for population synthesis. Our results confirm that we can gain incrementality without losing goodness-of-fit.

Keywords: Transport demand modeling ·
Volunteered Geographic Information · Evolutionary algorithms ·
Population synthesis · Goodness-of-fit

1 Introduction

The development of efficient travel urban policies and the introduction of regulating traffic projects (e.g. road reconstruction, rail rehabilitation) cannot be done without adequately modeling the transport demand. Thus, it is necessary to have detailed information about individuals in a given study area, such as household characteristics, home and work locations, to obtain a good forecasting. Census surveys generally do not cover details about the persons habits (e.g. travelling time and mode, visited places, etc) which are essential in such modeling. We can find more dedicated surveys for transportation analysis in which only a population sample is interviewed and data access is restricted to protect people's privacy. However, such micro-data at household and person levels may be efficiently provided by a synthetic population [4] which is a crucial stage for an efficient modeling of the transport demand. This process consists in creating virtual individuals through the expansion of disaggregate public information to reflect recognized aggregate sample data. This virtual population has the same

© Springer Nature Switzerland AG 2019
P. Moura Oliveira et al. (Eds.): EPIA 2019, LNAI 11804, pp. 610–622, 2019.
https://doi.org/10.1007/978-3-030-30241-2_51

demographic characteristics as the real one. However, data provided by the existing surveys are costly, not exhaustive and restricted. In addition, they could not be updated continuously with the newly-collected information about the real population. With the ubiquity of advanced web 2.0 technologies and the location of the sensing hand-held data presented by devices, Volunteered Geographic Information (VGI) is considered as an interesting new data source. VGI is a collaborative application where individuals can produce geographic data, emanating from their own knowledge of a geographic reality, or edit information provided by other contributors who are not necessarily experts in the geographical domain. Indeed, VGI has been successfully applied in several domains including species monitoring [3], soil mapping [18] and cover mapping [3]. In this research work, we aim to use VGI to generate synthetic populations. It is worth-noting that due to the huge mass of the provided information progressing in real time, classical populations synthesizers cannot effectively manage VGI input data because they are not incremental. Indeed, incrementality is a key issue here since it saves time and guarantees output stability. A s a solution, Evolutionary computation is a suited approach that has been applied to deal with various optimization problems [1,2,10,20]. This technique is employed in our work to iteratively enhance the quality of synthetic population. In each generation loop, a subset of synthetic households and the individuals of the previous population are replaced by new ones from the VGI data streaming flow with the consideration of certain criteria: strong similarity between attribute values of the old and the new individual. However, processes related to data acquisition, conflicts detection and elimination are not the scope of this research work. Thus, our goal, in this study, is not to introduce a new technique for the generation of synthetic populations, but to add new functionality in order to improve the resulting population in case where there is a new entry that enriches our source without re-performing the whole process of synthetic population generation. After a brief overview of the existing population synthesis methods in Sect. 2, we introduce in Sect. 3 our requirements for an evolutionary approach. Details about the algorithm adaptation are presented in Sect. 4. Finally, our results are illustrated and discussed in Sect. 5.

2   State of Population Synthesis Advances

Population synthesis techniques are algorithms that take, as inputs, sample population data. They are used to produce a complete list of the studied population's members; each of which has, as output, associated attribute data. In fact, synthetic populations should be statistically representative of the actual populations and show the best estimates of goodness-of-fit. There exists different algorithms for generating synthetic populations:

- **Iterative Proportional Fitting (IPF):** it allows adjusting or fitting contingency table cells to some constraints [5]. It contains two steps: fitting and allocation. In the former, some k-way cross-tabulations of k attributes of households taken from a study area (known as reference or seed table) are available. In the second stage, individual household records are represented (with replacement) from these datasets through Monte Carlo simulation so that the joint multi-way distribution will be satisfied. To cope with this limit, authors in [19], proposed the Iterative Proportional Updating method.

- **Iterative Proportional Updating (IPU):** it is based on iteratively computing weights in the seed data for each household, so that the weighted population will relate the household and individuals' joint distributions [19].
- **Combinatorial optimization (CO):** it begins by considering an initial set of households chosen randomly, and then iteratively replaces an assigned household with another one. If the replacement improves the fit, the households are swapped. If not, the swap is not made. This process is repeated many times until reaching a given termination criterion to find a best-fit synthetic population [6].
- **Fitness-based synthesis (FBS):** it involves choosing a set of households (with replacement) from the seed data so that the tract-level controls will be satisfied [13]. According to this procedure, the synthesis of census tract (i.e. adjusting the initial list) will be iterative. There is a strong resemblance between this algorithm and the previous one; each iteration is based on adding or removing one household (representing all its household members) from the current list. However, in FBS process, two fitness values (type I and type II) are computed for each household. Such algorithm ends if there is no household in seed data with positive values for both type I or type II fitness.

The score card, presented in Table 1, allows evaluating population synthesis algorithms relying on several comparison criteria. Authors, in [16], proved that IPF and IPU are the most applicable methods. They also affirmed that all techniques of population synthesis can reach the convergence criterion. Except IPF, all other methods respect the structural relationship between individuals and households. In addition and based on the fact that even if the provided populations fit to the real one, the already-cited population synthesizers remain static and cannot allow self-improving of the resulting population. Self-improvement means here that the population should be closer to the estimated one following the new added input.

Table 1. Score card of population synthesis methods

Methods/Criteria	IPF	IPU	FBS	CO
Applicability	+	+	−	−
Convergence	+	+	+	+
Relational schema	−	+	−	−
Incrementality	−	−	−	−

3   Evolutionary Algorithm: Why and What?

Evolutionary algorithms (EAs) are heuristically inspired from the mechanism of biological evolution according to which a population of solutions is refreshed iteratively through a number of steps. This evolutive feature is highly required in our application because it leads to an incremental algorithm of generating synthetic populations. Instead of restarting the whole process when entries are added to the input sample, we try to refresh the last generated population by substituting only a limited number of households. The time complexity of the process is drastically reduced. This also allows client applications, such as multi-agent transport simulators, to continue working without reloading the entire travel demand input data. The process of EA starts with the encoding (representation) phase. The latter consists in setting a bridge between the real world and the EA world (the solving space) [7]. The most important and widely-used representations of EAs are: Binary Representations, Integer Representations, Real-valued Representations, Messy Representations, Direct Representations and Parse tree Representation [15]. The second step of an EA is the selection of candidates to be reproduced. It consists in associating to each individual a fitness value. Then, we choose appropriate individuals which are more likely to be treated in the next step according to this value. The selection concept was first inspired by Darwin's survival of the fit test evolutionary principle [12]. In fact, recombining and mixing these solutions for information exchange require the existence of a pair of individuals. Children are thus obtained by combining information from this pair. The cycle of evolutionary process ends if termination criteria are satisfied. Otherwise, it continues. This process improves solutions over generations by promoting survival fitter solutions and eliminating less promising ones [12]. The success of EA applications depends on the parameters setting, such as the choice of its basic ingredients (representation, selection, recombination and replacement) [7]. In our research work, the suited EA approach is GP because it is the youngest GA variant of EAs that uses a particular representation of individuals (Parse trees) [7]. The latter will allows a better support for real data. It is mostly employed to optimize computer programs or mathematical expressions as well as to deal with problems requiring tree-structured solutions. It is also intensively employed to solve classification problems [8,11] and could instead be positioned in machine learning [7].

4   Genetic Programing Adaptation

As previously mentioned, our main objective is to generate a synthetic population faithful to the real population by taking advantage of crowdsourcing data to improve transport demand modeling. Our approach can be summarized as follows: It starts with the *encoding* our approach can be summarized as follows: It starts with the encoding phase which consists in generating a synthetic population using a classical population synthesizer from a sample of the real population. Once we have a new input, our *genetic programming module* triggers automatically to enhance the goodness of fit of the population by following the different GP operators adapted to our solution.

4.1 Preliminary Initialization

This phase consists in generating a synthetic population to initialize our genetic programming module by applying Algorithm 1 based on the IPF method presented in Sect. 2. First, we have $List_{attr}$ containing the list of all the attributes of the population. Dependency graph allows obtaining the most important attribute $attr_{dis}$ attrdis (with the highest information gaining value) and then selecting the attributes strongly correlated to it. Subsequently, we generate a crosstab for each attribute pair. At the end, we remove the attribute $attr_{dis}$ from the $List_{attr}$. The crosstab is adjusted using the IPF method. Attributes values are obtained by respecting the following relation: $(val_{attr_\gamma} \setminus attr_{dis})$. We repeat the same steps until $List_{attr}$ is empty.

Algorithm 1. Pseudo-code of our population synthesizer.

---

1. $List_{attr}$ is the initial list of attributes of the population.
2. Select the most important attributes (discriminant) $attr_{dis}$ by calculating the information gain of each one.
3. Remove $attr_{dis}$ of $List_{attr}$
4. Calculate the correlation value between $attr_{dis}$ and other attributes to determine a dependency priority list.
5. Generate the values of $attr_{dis}$ in the new population following its distribution in each geographical area.
6. Select the attribute that strongly depends on $attr_{dis}$ either $attr_\gamma$, and remove $attr_\gamma$ from the initial attribute list.
7. Draw a table that crosses the values of $attr_{dis}$ with $attr_\gamma$ which will be an IPF entry.
8. Generate the values of $attr_\gamma$ in the new population by respecting $attr_{dis};(val_{attr_\gamma} \setminus attr_{dis})$.
9. Repeat until the processing of all attributes becomes dependent on $attr_{dis}$.
10. Repeat until the processing of all remaining attributes in $List_{attr}$.

4.2 Evolutionary Synthetic Module Operators

Before describing the different components of the applied algorithm, some status concept should be defined. The status is an attribute representing the states of each household and individual of the population; i.e. if the household is added from VGI data stream, its status will be *Real*. However, if it is generated by the classical population synthesizer and directly affixed to the platform VGI, its status will be *Virtual*. Finally, if it is generated by our algorithm, its status will be *Virtual Improved*. These status concepts should be defined to distinguish between the various sources of each household and to match them with the most appropriate treatment. The different GP operators are adapted to our solution as follows (Fig. 1):

- **Representation:** GP is based on using parse trees. It captures expressions in a given syntactic format depending on the problem on hand. In our case, expression is represented as a logical formula (with predicate logic). The following figure shows an example of a parse tree: if the size, the weight and the nombre of persons are less than 2, 0.4 and 4 respectively and the income(month) is more than 2500€, so the household belongs to group 1.

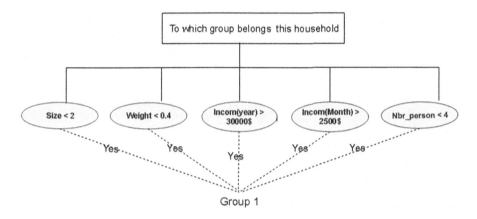

Fig. 1. Parse tree example.

- **Initialization:** this step generates an initial population of households with *Virtual* status obtained from the VGI database. These households must have almost the same characteristics (the same group).
- **Evaluation and Selection:** This step consists in identifying the households or individuals which are the most suited to the problem. In this stage, various selection methods, such as Uniform selection and Proportional selection (by roulette), can be employed. We use the uniform selection that associates, to each household of the initial population, a random value because these households have the same chances of being chosen.
- **Recombination:** In the crossover phase of classic GP algorithms, the subtrees chosen randomly are usually swapped. We revisited this method to improve the quality of our population by initializing an interval for each attribute characterizing the household (or individual) each time a new household (participating households) is added. Each attribute will then be updated, unless the new values is included in the previous range.
- **Replacement:** We define two types of replacement:
  1. Replacing households having *virtual status* with those with *improved virtual status*. These households must belong to the same group; i.e. the

replacement process was carried out randomly as the selection was also random.

2. The step of replacement finished by adding the newly-added households. To do this, we deleted an *improved virtual* household and replaced it with a *real* one, provided that the following elements had to be preserved:

   - Resemblance of characteristics: both households must have almost the same values of attributes; i.e. they must belong to the same group.
   - Neighborhood: after having checked the criterion of resemblance, the two households had to verify the neighborhood criterion. We divided our space into hexadecimal cells. Each cell contained a number of household sharing the same space. We also computed a distance matrix between the different cells. During the nearest household search, if there was an *improved virtual* household in the same cell as the *real* household to be added, we replaced it directly; Otherwise, we used the matrix distance to look for the household belonging to the nearest cell.

The following pseudo-code summarizes the operating mechanism:

Algorithm 2. Pseudo-code of the operating mechanism.

---

1. At (t_0) a synthetic population is generated from the sample of the actual population using Algorithm 1.
2. Add the resulting synthetic population to VGI.
3. At (t_1) a stream of data, containing a number of requests for additions arrives.
4. The Synthetic Evolutionary Process runs automatically.
5. The result of the process are returned to VGI platform.

---

5   Experimental Results

5.1   Data Source and Sampling Methodology

The data set is a subset of survey data collected in 2011 within the Social Diagnosis project which aimed at investigating objective and subjective qualities of life in Poland [9]. The subset data contains sample of 9,322 individuals on 5,628 individuals aged 16 and over. The data subset was obtained using the simple random sampling method. Then we check coverage by verifying that all possible attribute combinations were included in the considered sample. Figure 2 illustrates the used sampling methodology. For the phase of initialization, we took a sample of 2000 households and applied a synthetic population generation method to obtain population (Pop1). On the other hand, for the evolutionary synthetic method, we considered a sample of only 1000 households. The remaining 1000 households are considered in this step as VGI input. The resulting population would play the role of input for the genetic programming module which improved each time the population (Pop2) by adding the new data received from VGI. Among the attributes available in [9], we used in our experiment: (i) for individual level: Place of residence, income, Gender, Age, year of birth, relationship with the head of household; and (ii) for household level: income, size, type, address. We plan to improve this selection in the future by applying data mining techniques.

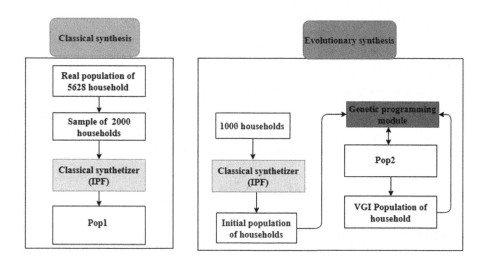

Fig. 2. Sampling method

5.2 Implementation and Evaluation

Our synthetic population generation algorithm and the synthetic evolutionary generator were implemented using the R and java language, respectively. The evaluation phase consists in comparing the goodness-of-fit between a synthetic population generated completely with a classical synthesizer (Pop1) and a synthetic population generated by our algorithm (Pop2). Two parameters are employed in this section to calculate measure of effectiveness (MOE), or goodness-of-fit.

- SRMSE (Standardized root mean squared error): defined to measure the divergence between estimated populations (distribution) frohetic population [21]. SRMSE can be computed as follows:

$$SRMSE = \frac{\sqrt{\sum_{i=0}^{m} \sum_{j=1}^{n} \frac{\left(\bar{\Theta}_{i...j} - \Theta_{i...j}\right)^2}{N}}}{\sum_{i=0}^{m} \sum_{j=1}^{n} \frac{\Theta_{i...j}}{N}} \tag{1}$$

where: N: total number of attributes.
$(\bar{\Theta}_{i...j})$: Estimated frequency of cell (i... j).
$(\Theta_{i...j})$: Corresponding frequency from the real population.
m, n = number of categories for attributes (i... j).

To compute the final RMSE value, we calculated the average sum of SRMSE of each combination of attributes according to the following formula:

$$SRMSE_{final} = \sum_{i=1}^{N} \frac{SRMSE_i}{N_a} \tag{2}$$

where:
N_a: is the number of the made combination.

– MAE (Mean Absolute Error): It is the average over the test sample of the absolute differences between prediction and actual observations where all individual differences had the same weight. It can be calculated as follows:

$$MAE = \frac{1}{n} \sum_{i=1}^{n} \left| \Theta_{i...j} - \bar{\Theta}_{i...j} \right| \tag{3}$$

A Synthetic population was generated to initialize our process (Sect. 4.1). We found an RMSE of 1.1325 and an MAE of 1.0258. Each time a new input was added, the fit of the population improved automatically (Sect. 4.2). The obtained results presented in Fig. 3 show that the SRMSE value of Pop2 (0.975) is very close to Pop1 results (0.968). In addition, the value of MAE (Fig. 4, MAE = 0.893) obtained for Pop2 is nearly equal to the MAE value of Pop1 (MAE = 0.867). Therefore, we notice that our algorithm allowed improving the goodness-of-fit without re-performing the entire process of Algorithm 1.

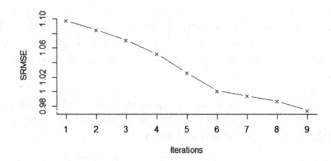

Fig. 3. Value of SRMSE based on the number of iterations for the EVO-SYN approach.

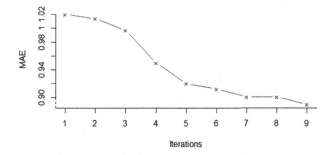

Fig. 4. Value of MAE based on the number of iterations for the EVO-SYN approach.

Correlation analysis the correlation analysis permits checking if our approach preserved the correlations between attributes. Figures 5 and 6 show the correlograms of the real population and the obtained synthetic population. Positive correlations and negative ones are displayed in blue and red, respectively. Obviously, the intensity of the color and the size of the circles are proportional to the correlation coefficients. On the right of the correlogram, the color legend shows the correlation coefficients and the corresponding colors. We note that the correlation coefficients are almost preserved for all attributes (comparing the generated population with the real one).

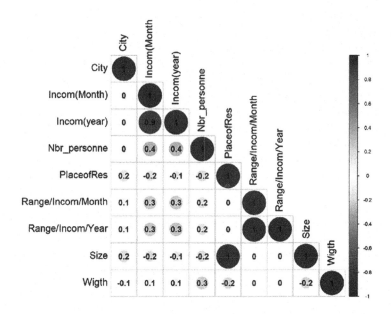

Fig. 5. Correlation matrix of population attributes in real population.

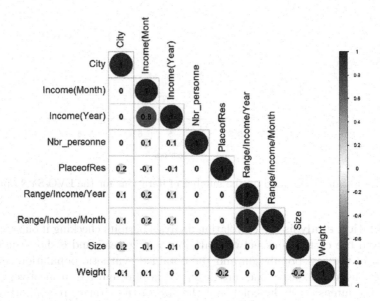

Fig. 6. Correlation matrix of population attributes in synthetic population.

6   Conclusion

There is much to learn with transportation projects which mainly failed due to a bad demand evaluation [14,17]. The interest in developing disaggregated transport demand models has increased over the past decade with the availability of new tools for population Synthesis like in the TransCAD software. However, population synthesis methods are still demanding in term of input survey data. Crowdsourcing and Volunteered Geographic Information (VGI) are then very useful data sources for this process. In fact, such a source provides data stream and the classical approaches (iterative proportional fitting, synthetic reconstruction, etc.) could not be not adapted because their algorithms are not incremental. A learning approach is then more suited for the synthesizer to improve the goodness-of-fit of its artificial population as crowdsourcing data grow. In this work, we adapted an evolutionary algorithm for population Synthesis. Our first results confirm that incrementality can be gained without losing goodness-of-fit. Future works will involve a better consideration of the spatial character of our population by considering not only home locations but others locations like work locations, activity locations (shopping, leisure, etc.). Indeed, it would be interesting to compete several learning approaches, especially for the learning of mobility behavior.

References

1. Aleti, A., Moser, I.: A systematic literature review of adaptive parameter control methods for evolutionary algorithms. ACM Comput. Surv. (CSUR) **49**(3), 56 (2016)
2. Askarzadeh, A.: A memory-based genetic algorithm for optimization of power generation in a microgrid. IEEE Trans. Sustain. Energy **9**(3), 1081–1089 (2018)
3. Auer, M.: Towards using the potential of OpenStreetMap history for disaster activation monitoring. In: ISCRAM (2018)
4. Barthelemy, M., Cornelis, M.: Synthetic populations: review of the different approaches (2012)
5. Beckman, R.J., Baggerly, K.A., McKay, M.D.: Creating synthetic baseline populations. Transp. Res. Part A Policy Pract. **30**(6), 415–429 (1996)
6. Cho, S., Bellemans, T., Creemers, L., Knapen, L., Janssens, D., Wets, G.: Synthetic population techniques in activity-based research. In: Data Science and Simulation in Transportation Research, pp. 48–70. IGI Global (2014)
7. Eiben, A.E., Smith, J.E.: Introduction to Evolutionary Computing, vol. 53. Springer, Heidelberg (2003). https://doi.org/10.1007/978-3-662-05094-1
8. Espejo, P.G., Ventura, S., Herrera, F.: A survey on the application of genetic programming to classification. IEEE Trans. Syst. Man Cybernet. Part C (Appl. Rev.) **40**(2), 121–144 (2010)
9. The council for Social Monitoring (2011). http://www.diagnoza.com/index-en.html
10. Gong, D., Sun, J., Miao, Z.: A set-based genetic algorithm for interval many-objective optimization problems. IEEE Trans. Evol. Comput. **22**(1), 47–60 (2018)
11. La Cava, W., Silva, S., Danai, K., Spector, L., Vanneschi, L., Moore, J.H.: Multidimensional genetic programming for multiclass classification. Swarm Evol. Comput. **44**, 260–272 (2019)
12. Liu, J., Abbass, H.A., Tan, K.C.: Evolutionary Computation and Complex Networks. Springer, Cham (2019). https://doi.org/10.1007/978-3-319-60000-0
13. Ma, L., Srinivasan, S.: Synthetic population generation with multilevel controls: a fitness-based synthesis approach and validations. Comput. Aided Civil Infrastruct. Eng. **30**(2), 135–150 (2014)
14. Pierce, G., Shoup, D.: Getting the prices right: an evaluation of pricing parking by demand in San Francisco. J. Am. Planning Assoc. **79**(1), 67–81 (2013)
15. Rothlauf, F.: Representations for genetic and evolutionary algorithms. Representations for Genetic and Evolutionary Algorithms, pp. 9–32. Springer, Heidelberg (2006). https://doi.org/10.1007/3-540-32444-5_2
16. Ryan, J., Maoh, H., Kanaroglou, P.: Population synthesis: comparing the major techniques using a small, complete population of firms. Geog. Anal. **41**(2), 181–203 (2009)
17. Taylor, M.A.: Critical transport infrastructure in urban areas: impacts of traffic incidents assessed using accessibility-based network vulnerability analysis. Growth Change **39**(4), 593–616 (2008)
18. Yang, D., Fu, C.-S., Smith, A.C., Yu, Q.: Open land-use map: a regional land-use mapping strategy for incorporating openstreetmap with earth observations. Geo-spatial Inform. Sci. **20**(3), 269–281 (2017)
19. Ye, X., Konduri, K., Pendyala, R.M., Waddell, P.: A methodology to match distributions of both household and person attributes in the generation of synthetic populations (2009)

20. Zhang, X., Tian, Y., Cheng, R., Jin, Y.: A decision variable clustering-based evolutionary algorithm for large-scale many-objective optimization. IEEE Trans. Evol. Comput. **22**(1), 97–112 (2018)
21. Zhu, Y., Ferreira, J.: Synthetic population generation at disaggregated spatial scales for land use and transportation microsimulation. Transp. Res. Rec. J. Transp. Res. Board **2429**(1), 168–177 (2014)

Camera Calibration for CNN Based Generic Obstacle Detection

Radu Danescu$^{(\boxtimes)}$ and Razvan Itu

Technical University of Cluj-Napoca,
Memorandumului 28, Cluj-Napoca, Romania
radu.danescu@cs.utcluj.ro

Abstract. The Convolutional Neural Networks (CNNs) have made monocular image processing a powerful obstacle detector, but in order to transform these results into 3D data robust automatic calibration is needed. This paper proposes an unassisted camera calibration algorithm, based on analyzing image sequences acquired from naturalistic driving. The focal distance is computed based on the mean lateral displacement of similar features in consecutive frames, compared with the yaw rate of the vehicle. The height and pitch angle are computed based on the distribution of the lane width values on the image lines, assuming an average lane width is known. The lane markings are detected using the edges on the road, already segmented using the CNN. The yaw angle is computed using the vanishing point (VP) detection, which is performed using the direction of the road gradients. The pitch angle value is dynamically corrected using the VP, and using comparisons between the past frame and the current frame, under multiple correction hypotheses.

Keywords: Camera calibration · Obstacle detection · Deep learning

1 Introduction

Convolutional neuronal networks (CNNs) have become powerful tools for image analysis and segmentation, and for object detection and classification. Due to this technology, road and obstacle areas can be accurately identified, even in difficult and complex scenarios (Fig. 1). However, in order for the segmentation results to become useful as sensorial data, the camera needs to be calibrated with respect to a world reference frame, so that the pixels in the image space can be related to 3D points in the real world.

Camera calibration techniques have been presented since the early 1990s [1], where authors use a stereo camera system and compute the vanishing point (VP) to determine the orientations of the cameras. Similar work with a two camera setup has been presented in [2], whereas in [3] the authors present a monocular based calibration technique that also uses the VP to determine the camera parameters. For the detection of the

This work was supported by a grant of Ministry of Research and Innovation, CNCS - UEFISCDI, project number PN-III-P1-1.1-TE-2016-0440, within PNCDI III.

© Springer Nature Switzerland AG 2019
P. Moura Oliveira et al. (Eds.): EPIA 2019, LNAI 11804, pp. 623–636, 2019.
https://doi.org/10.1007/978-3-030-30241-2_52

VP the technique uses a known pattern that is placed on the road surface. Paper [4] presents another approach that uses the lane lines, but it relies on a prori information such as the lane width and either the camera height or the length of a lane line marking in the scene. Both [3] and [4] use a single camera, rely on flat road assumptions, and the camera is mounted in a fixed position in the scene where only the objects are moving. In [5] the authors stabilize the Inverse Perspective Mapping (IPM) image using the detected vanishing point. Stabilization of the IPM image is done by detecting the VP in each frame and computing the orientation angles, and adjusting the projection matrix accordingly. Other approaches use the optical flow to finds relevant features and determine their correspondences in successive frames. If the vehicle is travelling on a flat road surface and straight, then the line segments defined by the same features in multiple frames will actually define multiple lines that generally intersect in the VP. Such a method based on optical flow is presented in [6].

Fig. 1. Road and obstacle areas segmentation using CNNs.

This paper propose an unassisted complete camera calibration algorithm, based on analyzing image sequences acquired from naturalistic driving. The purpose of our work is to provide a solution that requires no user input and no calibrated intrinsic parameters, is able to work with data acquired from normal traffic, without need for calibration sites, and will continuously refine the parameters as more data becomes available.

2 Solution Overview

The calibration process is based on a sequence of images acquired from a moving vehicle. The camera is assumed to be facing forward, but without careful alignment with the road or with the host vehicle. The camera parameters to be calibrated are the camera focal length, the camera height above the road plane, and the pitch and yaw angles. These parameters will be used to form a projection matrix that can transform the perspective image into a bird-eye view (or Inverse Perspective Mapping, IPM) image [7], where each pixel coordinate will be linearly proportional to the longitudinal and lateral distances in the road plane.

The calibration process is depicted in Fig. 2. The focal distance is computed based on the mean lateral displacement of similar features in consecutive frames, compared with the yaw rate of the vehicle. The height and pitch angle are computed based on the distribution of the lane width values on the image lines, assuming an average lane width is known. The lane markings are detected using the edges on the road, already segmented using the CNN. The yaw angle is computed using the vanishing point (VP) detection, which is performed using the direction of the road gradients. The pitch angle value is dynamically corrected using the VP, and using comparisons between the past frame IPM and the current frame, under multiple correction hypotheses.

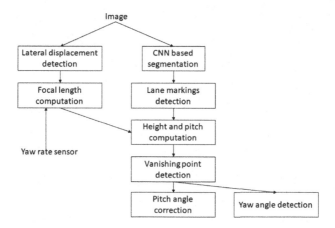

Fig. 2. Overview of the automatic camera calibration process.

For the purpose of identifying the drivable road surface we have employed a convolutional neural network. The solution is based on the popular U-Net [8] architecture and uses pairs of images as input while training the network. The image pairs are composed of the normal image captured in the traffic scenario (color image) and the labeled road image, a binary image where the mask is labeled with 1 and non-road/background is labeled with 0. The training and validation images were gathered from 3 main segmentation databases: KITTI [9], Berkeley Deep Drive (BDD) [10] and CityScapes [11]. We have used a total of 11500 images from these 3 sources from which we have extracted labeled masks with only the road surface.

The network is structured as an encoder-decoder, where the encoder layers have the role of extracting the relevant features from the source image, whereas decoder layers will "build" the prediction mask. U-Net features an equal number of encoder and decoder layers and it also has direct ("skip") connections between them.

The network is able to successfully segment images acquired using different camera setups and with different characteristics. This is especially valuable, as the results are not dependent on calibration, and the segmentation results can be used in the calibration process.

3 Calibration of the Focal Length

The focal length of the camera is the most important intrinsic parameter, as it controls the scaling of the 3D scene when projected to the image space. While the focal length of a lens is usually expressed in millimeters, for image processing related tasks the focal length is expressed in pixels, thus making abstraction of the physical parameters of the lens and of the image sensor. As we'll assume that the principal point of the camera is in the middle of the image (V/2 and H/2, V – image height, H – image width), the focal length will be the only intrinsic parameter needing calibration.

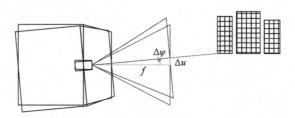

Fig. 3. The principle behind the automatic calibration of the focal length: the angular motion of the camera equipped vehicle translates in a lateral motion of the observed scene in the image space.

The vehicle's rotation due to traffic maneuvers such as turning left or right at intersections will have the effect of translating the points of the observed scene along the lateral coordinate in the image space (the u axis), as seen in Fig. 3. The relation between the image space displacement Δu and the angular rotation $\Delta \psi$ depends on the focal distance (expressed in pixel units):

$$f = \frac{\Delta u}{\Delta \psi} \tag{1}$$

The rotation is computed as the product between the yaw rate of the vehicle and the elapsed time between frames:

$$\Delta \psi = \dot{\psi} \Delta t \tag{2}$$

Ideally, if the lateral displacement of the same feature between two consecutive frames can be determined accurately, the focal distance can be computed instantly. However, there are multiple factors that prevent a quick focal length calibration:

- Noise in the yaw rate measurement. The noise can be caused either by an inaccurate yaw rate sensor, or by vibrations of the vehicle/sensor assembly. For example, in our experiment the camera and the sensor are housed inside a smartphone mounted on the windshield with a suction cup, and the non-rigid mount allows the system to vibrate.

– Noise in the lateral displacement measurement. This can be due to imperfect image processing matching algorithms, or to independently moving targets.
– A very small amplitude of the yaw rate will cause numerical instability when applying Eq. (1).

For the reasons stated above, the method for determining the focal distance will perform the following steps:

1. For each frame, compute the lateral displacement and the yaw displacement, and insert them into lists.
2. Filter the lists using a 15 neighbor median filter, to remove the noise (as shown in Fig. 4).
3. For the yaw displacements higher than 0.3° (to prevent numerical instabilities and noise based values when driving in a straight line), compute the candidate focal value using Eq. (1). Insert this value in a list.
4. When enough candidate values are in the focal length list (at least 50 in our implementation), compute the final focal value as the median value of them (Fig. 5).

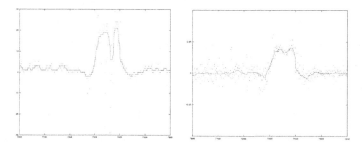

Fig. 4. Left: the average lateral displacement in the image space (in pixels, vs. frame number). Right: The average yaw displacement between frames (radians vs. frame number). Orange dots: the unfiltered signal; blue continuous line: signal after applying the median filter. (Color figure online)

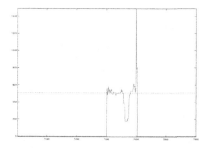

Fig. 5. The focal length candidates list (blue), and the median value (dotted orange line) (Color figure online).

4 Calibration of the Camera Height and of the Pitch Angle

The principle of height and pitch calibration is based on the relation between the projected width of a known world structure in the image plane and the actual 3D width of the structure.

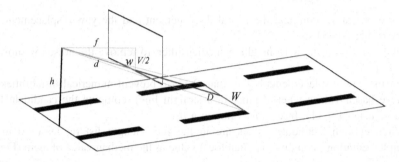

Fig. 6. The projected width of a known 3D structure in the image plane, at the bottom of the image.

As we can see from Fig. 6, the relation between the projected lane width w and the 3D lane width W is:

$$\frac{w}{W} = \frac{d}{D} \tag{3}$$

The distance inside the camera (in pixels) depends on the focal distance and vertical position (v) in the image. Assuming that the position is at the bottom of the image, and that the image height is V, d can be computed as:

$$d = \sqrt{f^2 + (V/2)^2} \tag{4}$$

Using Eqs. (3) and (4) we can compute the distance D between the optical center and the 3D structure of known width. If this structure is the lane on the road, this distance depends on the camera vertical half field of view θ, the pitch angle α, the camera height above the road plane, h, and the row position of the vanishing point, v_0, as shown in Fig. 7.

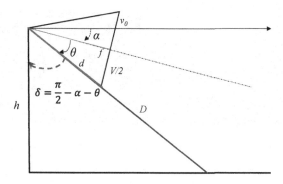

Fig. 7. The relation between the distance to the known structure, D, and the camera parameters.

The pitch angle α and the camera height h can be found using Eqs. (5), (6) and (7).

$$\tan \alpha = \frac{\frac{V}{2} - v_0}{f} \tag{5}$$

$$h = D \cos \delta \tag{6}$$

$$\delta = \frac{\pi}{2} - \alpha - \theta \tag{7}$$

Therefore, if we know the projected width of a lane on the bottom line of the image, w_B, and the row coordinate of the vanishing point, v_0, we can find the camera height above the road plane and the pitch angle. The algorithm for extracting the required information from an image sequence must perform the following steps for each frame:

1. Perform Canny edge detection on the road area pixels, to extract road edges.
2. For each image line, select pairs of edges having gradients of similar magnitude and opposing direction, to identify lane markings.
3. Select pairs of lane markings, left and right of the image central axis, to identify a candidate lane width (as shown in Fig. 8).
4. Use the pair (v, w) found at step 4 to increase the value of a 2D voting array, as shown in Fig. 9.

When enough frames are processed, the voting array will look like the one in Fig. 9. There will be an obvious linear distribution of the high values. If we fit a line to these values, using the Hough transform, the intersection of this line width the $w = 0$ column will give us the row coordinate of the vanishing point, v_0 (the place where the lane will have no width), and the intersection of the line with the $v = V$ line will give us w_B, the width of the lane at the bottom of the image. Due to the fact that the vote accumulation process is performed on multiple frames, there is no need for a perfect lane detector to extract the markings, nor for a perfectly stable camera, or for a perfectly known lane width.

Fig. 8. Extracting road edges, and lane marking widths for multiple image lines.

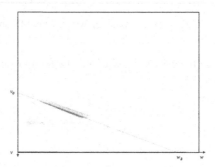

Fig. 9. Relation between the image row coordinate and the detected lane width - the voting array.

5 Calibration of the Yaw Angle

After performing the calibration steps previously described, we know the focal distance, the camera height above the road plane, the pitch angle, and the image row coordinate of the vanishing point. In order to estimate the yaw angle (the camera's rotation angle around the vertical axis), we also need the column position of the vanishing point. This point is the intersection of the parallel features on the road (such as lane markings, curbs, other road edges) in the image space.

The principle behind vanishing point computation is based on the computation of intersections of various lines. Usually, an edge detector is employed as the first detection step, followed by a line extractor such as the Hough transform. However, using these steps implies deciding, sometimes arbitrary, which pixels are edges, and how many pixels should be aligned for a line to be considered valid. Our approach is based on the magnitude and direction of the gradient, without thresholding or line fitting.

For each pixel below the vanishing point search region (defined by v_0 and a margin of error), we compute the magnitude and direction of the gradient. The direction of the possible line that passes through the pixel is given by the perpendicular to the gradient's direction, as shown in Fig. 10. We will follow this line, and when the line crosses the search region, a vote will be added to an accumulation 2D array. The vote will have the amount proportional to the pixel's gradient magnitude, so that the transition pixels (edge pixels) will have a greater influence. For the pixels left of the image central axis,

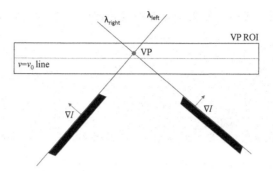

Fig. 10. The vanishing point (VP) is the intersection of the lines that pass through road edges. The direction of these theoretical lines is perpendicular to the gradient direction.

the votes will be recorded in a left array, $A_L(v, u)$, and for the pixels right to the image central axis, the pixels will be recorded in a right array, $A_R(v, u)$.

As the vanishing point is the intersection of the lines from all directions, the final vote array A is computed as the product between the left and right arrays. For increased stability, we will smooth the voting array both in space, by using a Gaussian filter G, and in the time, by using a fading memory averaging. The fading memory coefficient ρ is 0.95, but it can be adjusted to be higher for a higher frame rate.

$$A = \rho A_{past} + (1 - \rho) A_{current} * G \tag{8}$$

The vanishing point will be the point that maximizes the sum of its neighbors in a local window of the smoothed voting array (Fig. 11). The width (and also height) of the window is one third of the height of the VP search window.

The vanishing point detection algorithm will be applied to each captured frame, and will serve two purposes. First, it will be used to determine the camera yaw angle with respect to the vehicle's longitudinal axis. Due to the fact that the vehicle will maneuver during the calibration process, multiple positions of the vanishing point must be collected in a list, and the median u coordinate of these points (we'll denote it u_0) will be used to extract the yaw angle φ, using Eq. (9). By H we denote the image width.

$$\tan \varphi = \frac{\frac{H}{2} - u_0}{f} \tag{9}$$

After enough frames have been processed, the camera parameters are calibrated. The calibration can be either stopped, and the camera parameters assumed to be fixed, or it can run continuously, refining the parameters as more data becomes available.

Fig. 11. VP detection steps: a,b – left and right voting arrays; c-product array superimposed on the original image; d-detected VP.

6 Continuous Correction of the Pitch Angle

The real pitch angle of the camera with respect to the road surface will not be stable, and will vary around the static value determined in the calibration phase. We have identified two types of changes of the pitch angle:

- Slow changes, which can be of quite a significant amplitude, and will remain stable for multiple frames. These changes usually appear due to a slope of the road, either uphill or downhill.
- Fast changes, due to vibrations of the camera with respect to the car body, or of the car due to imperfections of the road surface. These changes are fast, but usually of low amplitude, and tend to go back to zero quickly.

For the first type of change, we will use the vanishing point algorithm. The time filtering of the voting array will make the vanishing point stable enough not to produce noisy corrections, but also fast enough to cope with gradual change such as the change of the road's slope. If we denote by v_0 the vanishing point line detected in Sect. 4 (which is a statistical value computed from multiple frames, based on lane markings), and by v_i the vanishing line determined using the VP algorithm described in Sect. 5, for the current frame i, the correction to the pitch angle can be determined as:

$$\Delta\alpha = \frac{v_0 - v_i}{f} \tag{10}$$

For coping with the second type of pitch variation, we cannot rely on the vanishing point, as the temporal filtering will prevent it from reacting to quick changes. The solution for detecting the small variations is to generate multiple hypotheses around the pitch value already corrected by the vanishing point. The hypotheses will cover a small angular amplitude (0.5°, with a 0.05° step), and will be used to generate inverse perspective mapping (IPM) transforms (Fig. 12). Each such transform will be compared to the previous frames' transform, and the angle that causes the minimum distance between corresponding pixels will be selected as the instantaneous correction.

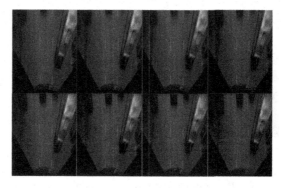

Fig. 12. Correction of the small and fast pitch angle variations by generating multiple IPM images.

7   Results

The system was tested on a sequence of 13000 frames, acquired at 14 fps using a smartphone mounted in the windshield of a passenger car. The yaw rate was provided by the phone's own sensor. The phone was mounted using a suction cup, at a height of approximately 120 cm above the road plane.

The calibration algorithm was run in two modes: with focal length calibration, and without. In the first operation mode the system was able to find the focal length value of 507 pixels after 3000 frames (most of them being straight line driving, therefore useless). A calibration using the Caltech camera calibration toolkit estimated the focal length value for the same camera at 504 pixels, and the computation of the focal length using the phone's API gave us the value 502. Therefore, the yaw rate based focal length estimation is in agreement with the correct value.

The second mode was with the focal length assumed to be known (already calibrated). This time, the calibration process was much quicker: the estimated height of the camera converged to 121.7 cm after 150 frames, and while there was no ground truth for the pitch and yaw angles, the Inverse Perspective Image created using the projection matrix formed by the height and the two angles was correctly generated (the road markings are parallel, and the direction of the road when driving in straight line is aligned with the columns of the IPM image).

For assessing the effect of pitch angle correction, we have analyzed the evolution in time of the distance to the closest obstacle structure ahead of our vehicle, as determined by the CNN based segmentation mapped in the IPM image. The slow pitch angle changes are shown in Figs. 13 and 14. When driving uphill, the incorrect pitch angle makes the obstacles appear further away, and when driving downhill the obstacles appear closer. The correction of the pitch angle will correct the distance to the obstacle, and will also make the road delimiters parallel again (non-parallel markings are an important visual clue that the pitch angle is not correct).

634   R. Danescu and R. Itu

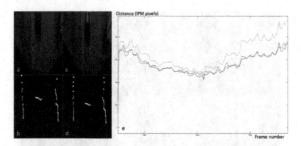

Fig. 13. Pitch angle continuous calibration – uphill road: a- IPM image using static pitch angle, b-obstacle borders on the static pitch IPM, c- IPM image using dynamic pitch angle, d-obstacle borders for dynamic pitch IPM, e-distance comparison (yellow – original IPM, blue-vanishing point corrected pitch, orange – both pitch corrections) (Color figure online).

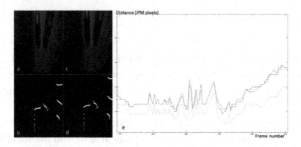

Fig. 14. Pitch angle continuous calibration – downhill road: a- IPM image using static pitch angle, b-obstacle borders on the static pitch IPM, c- IPM image using dynamic pitch angle, d-obstacle borders for dynamic pitch IPM, e-distance comparison (yellow – original IPM, blue-vanishing point corrected pitch, orange – both pitch corrections) (Color figure online).

The difference between VP based pitch correction, and fast pitch correction based on IPM hypotheses is visible especially when detecting obstacles that are near the far edge of the IPM image. In Fig. 15 we can see such a case, and the fast oscillations make the obstacle appear and disappear, a behavior that can seriously affect the performance of an obstacle tracker. The fully corrected pitch angle proved to be more stable.

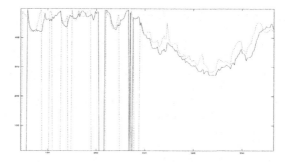

Fig. 15. Comparison between the VP based pitch correction (blue line) and the fast correction (orange) (Color figure online).

8   Conclusions and Future Work

This work presented a solution for unassisted automatic calibration designed to work alongside a CNN based obstacle detector. The segmentation provided by the CNN helps the calibration process by identifying the road features, and, in turn, the calibration process provides the means for assigning longitudinal and lateral distance to the obstacle structures identified by segmentation. The focal length, camera height above the road surface, and the pitch and yaw angles are all calibrated as the vehicle drives normally through traffic, without constraints of scenario. The parameter that changes frequently, the pitch angle, is constantly corrected, taking into account both the slow change causes such as driving uphill/downhill, and the fast change causes such as road surface imperfections or other vibration sources.

In the future, this calibration system will be integrated in a complete road and obstacle tracking system, able to provide 3D data from a single monocular camera.

References

1. Caprile, B., Torre, V.: Using vanishing points for camera calibration. Int. J. Comput. Vis. **4**, 127–139 (1990)
2. Wildenauer, H., Hanbury, A.: Robust camera self-calibration from monocular images of Manhattan worlds. In: CVPR, pp. 2831–2838 (2012)
3. Masoud, O., Papanikolopoulos, N.: Using geometric primitives to calibrate traffic scenes. In: Proceedings IEEE/RSJ International Conference Intelligent Robots and Systems, vol. 2, pp. 1878–1883 (2004)
4. Wang, K., Huang, H., Li, Y., Wang, F.Y.: Research on lane-marking line based camera calibration. In: International Conference on Vehicular Electronics and Safety, ICVES (2007)
5. Zhang, D., Fang, B., Yang, W., Luo, X., Tang, Y.: Robust inverse perspective mapping based on vanishing point. In: Security, Pattern Analysis, and Cybernetics (SPAC), pp. 458–463 (2014)
6. Tan, S., Dale, J., Anderson, A., Johnston, A.: Inverse perspective mapping and optic flow: a calibration method and a quantitative analysis. Image Vis. Comput. **24**(2), 153–165 (2006)

7. Bertozzi, M., Broggi, A.: GOLD: a parallel real-time stereo vision system for generic obstacle and lane detection. IEEE Trans. Image Process. 7(1), 62–81 (1998)
8. Ronneberger, O., Fischer, P., Brox, T.: U-Net: convolutional networks for biomedical image segmentation. In: Navab, N., Hornegger, J., Wells, W.M., Frangi, A.F. (eds.) MICCAI 2015. LNCS, vol. 9351, pp. 234–241. Springer, Cham (2015). https://doi.org/10.1007/978-3-319-24574-4_28
9. Geiger, A., Lenz, P., Urtasun, R.: Are we ready for autonomous driving? The KITTI vision benchmark suite. In: Computer Vision and Pattern Recognition, pp. 3354–3361 (2012)
10. Yu, F., et al.: BDD100 K: A Diverse Driving Video Database with Scalable Annotation Tooling (2018). arXiv preprint: 1805.04687
11. Cordts, M., et al.: The cityscapes dataset for semantic urban scene understanding. In: Computer Vision and Pattern Recognition, pp. 3213–3223 (2016)

Counting Cars from Aerial Videos Using Deep Learning

Caio H. S. Polidoro, Wellington V. M. de Castro, José Marcato,
Geison Salgado Filho, and Edson T. Matsubara[⊠]

Federal University of Mato Grosso do Sul, Campo Grande, Brazil
cpolidoro@gmail.com, wellingtonvcastro@gmail.com, jrmarcato@gmail.com,
geisonfilho.gr@gmail.com, edsontm@facom.ufms.br

Abstract. Counting vehicles in heavy traffic areas is not an easy task, even for a trained human. Recent advances in real-time object detection using convolutional neural network can jointly detect and identify objects. We propose a straightforward application of using real-time object detection algorithm to count the number of vehicles in high traffic areas. The user defines marks on the road where the proposal counts the number of vehicles crossing the marks. The proposal achieves 87.24% average correct counting in a video sequence with real-time performance.

Keywords: Deep learning · Counting cars · Traffic flow

1 Introduction

Aerial video streams are generated by almost omnipresent traffic video cameras in major cities and more recently by drones with integrated video cameras. Considering the massive amount of video streams, the extraction of useful information that should make cities smarter and safer is a challenging task. Humans are limited by the number of simultaneous videos that a person can watch, which bottlenecks the process. This paper proposes the use of machine learning algorithms to count the number of cars in real-time automatically. Counting the number of cars in real time is essential information for intelligent and real-time traffic management and control of streets and roads of big cities.

To fulfill the motivations above, we used an object detection model that localizes and identifies a known set of objects in an image. We defined vehicles as objects and used the current state-of-the-art real-time object detection algorithm known as YOLOv2 [10] as the proposal's object detector. However, the object detection alone cannot estimate traffic flow. To face this challenge, we combined YOLOv2 with two algorithms: non-maximum bounding box suppression and a centroid tracker. The former drops redundant detection and the latter detects the same object in different frames of the video. Thus, our system uses reliable information to count the actual number of vehicles in a video sequence, not just in a static image.

© Springer Nature Switzerland AG 2019
P. Moura Oliveira et al. (Eds.): EPIA 2019, LNAI 11804, pp. 637–649, 2019.
https://doi.org/10.1007/978-3-030-30241-2_53

The proposed solution receives a video sequence and a set of pre-annotated control flow lines by the user as input and outputs an estimation of the total amount of vehicles that passed through these control flow lines. The control flow lines are segments drawn by the user that indicate regions of interest where the vehicles should be counted, Fig. 1 shows examples. The goal of the proposal is to count the number of vehicles crossing the green lines.

Fig. 1. Operation of the system with the control flow lines (green lines) defined by the user. (Color figure online)

Our application required training on a dataset with images of cars in a bird's-eye view, even though there are plenty of vehicle datasets available, we couldn't find one that suited our needs. For that reason, we used a smartphone and a drone to collect and then annotate video sequences of traffic, resulting in a vehicle dataset composed of four classes: car, truck, motorcycle, and bus with both a bird's-eye view and a horizontal-like view. This dataset was a fundamental element of our work and the results achieved. Our main contributions are as follows:

- real-time traffic flow rate estimator from aerial video. We propose a methodology to count the number of cars using object detector algorithms. In this work we adopted YOLOv2, but the proposal can work with the user's preferred object detection algorithm. The proposal differs from others on the literature due to its robustness to work with videos captured from drones.
- a labelled dataset for traffic flow estimation. The dataset is composed of high-resolution videos and over 2800 annotated frames with bounding boxes of car, truck, motorcycle, and bus classes. During the execution of this study, we could not find any labelled drone dataset public available that fit our needs.

This work is organized as follows: in Sect. 2 we briefly explain related works that inspired our efforts to fill gaps in the current models. In Sect. 3 we present our proposal and auxiliary algorithms used to accomplish the task of counting vehicles in a video sequence. We bring forward our approach on how we conducted the experiments, presenting our results on three video sequences and discoursing about the proposal's struggle on specific situations in Sect. 4, besides that, we introduce our novel dataset that was developed due to unavailability of a suited one for our task at the time. Finally, in Sect. 5 we conclude and expose future work ideas.

2 Related Work

The counting vehicles problem is closely related to Multiple Object Tracking (MOT). Luo et al. [6] presents a literature review on MOT algorithms and indicates that deep learning models have great potential to solve MOT problems but more research effort is needed. Jo et al. [5] shows a MOT study using YOLOv2 and Kalman filter. Their results show a precision of 90.8% and 75.8% using TUD-Crossing and ETH-Crossing datasets where the majority of the objects are people crossing streets.

Madellos et al. [7] developed a system that implements Background Subtraction and applies it to supervise traffic. The study contribution is the reconstruction of the background that does not require input for identification. Moreover, they present robust results in images with different scenarios of lighting and angle. Nonetheless, their system is dependent on images that were generated by devices mounted on static structures, which is not viable for this work.

The Horn-Schunk algorithm is used by [2] to estimate Optical Flow, which enables object detection through the intensity of displacement between frames. Also, their proposal applies a Median Filter to remove noise from the images. The main advantages of the system are its low computational cost and its ability to discard objects that frequently are mistaken for vehicles in other methods.

Harsha and Anne [4] developed a vehicle detection, tracking and speed measurement model. They implemented a background subtraction model based on multi-directional filtering, which allowed better performances during object detection and tracking experiments. The speed measurement identifies objects with identical IDs across frames, maps the real distance of the input image, and compares it to the prediction. Their approach could not be applied for our work because the system cannot be used on images with several lanes on the road, which makes it unfeasible for us to use it on images with unconventional angles (i.e. provided by drones).

The 2018 NVIDIA AI City Challenge [8] Task 1 identify the speed of vehicles on the main thruways in all frames of all given videos. The videos streams were recorded from fix position cameras (not from drones). They have provided the participants with 27 videos, each 1 min in length, recorded in 4 locations.

The challenge's organizers labelled the dataset, using a control group that drove vehicles according to a planned route and the GPS information defined the ground truth data. The winning solution also used YOLOv2 as their detector, combined with clustering-based method. In contrast to their work, our strategy uses the output of the YOLOv2 detector and filters it through two algorithms that adjust the data, so the system is capable of recognizing bounding boxes belonging to the same vehicle, avoiding counting errors while maintaining a low computational cost.

3   Proposal

Our proposal uses the CNN architecture of YOLOv2 combined with auxiliary algorithms such as Non-maximum Bounding Box Suppression and Centroid Tracker to detect the position and count the vehicles in images. Figure 2 shows the system overview. The vehicle detection is explained in Sect. 3.1, the filtering in Sect. 3.3 and in Sect. 3.4 we explain our tracking strategy.

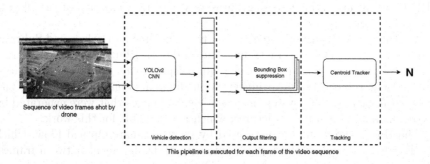

Fig. 2. System flowchart. N is the number of vehicles counted during the video sequence.

3.1   YOLOv2: You Only Look Once

Most object detection algorithms consist of an image classifier applied to multiple crops of the input image obtained through a sliding window. Applying Convolutional Neural Networks to every crop is intrinsically expensive by means of computational cost. YOLOv2's approach solves this issue by designing the network that evaluates the image in a single pass, instead of modelling it as multiple classification problems. This feature enables real-time object detection which reflects the desired performance to our problem. Besides predicting the object's class, the network also predicts the position of the bounding box that contains the object.

Unified Detection with Anchor Boxes. Anchor boxes are a set of pre-selected bounding boxes that the model will use to predict the real boxes. In YOLOv2, they are inferred directly from the training set using K-Means clustering algorithm with Eq. 1 as metric distance, with IOU standing for Intersection Over Union, that is, the ratio between the area of intersection with the area of the union of two bounding boxes.

$$d(box, centroid) = 1 - IOU(box, centroid) \tag{1}$$

Architecture. The YOLOv2 architecture, presented in Fig. 3, remains with the premise of real-time object detection, like the prior YOLO, but it implements recent advances in the deep learning field. In the new architecture, batch normalization was added after every single layer of the network leading to an improvement of 2% in mean Average Precision (mAP). Mean Average Precision is a common metric in tasks like object detection and information retrieval. It is calculated in different ways, depending on the task. In object detection, it is the average between the average precision of all classes within the dataset, as shown in Eq. 2.

$$MAP = \frac{\sum_q^Q AveP(q)}{Q} \tag{2}$$

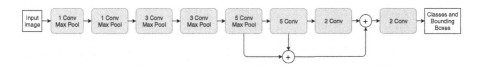

Fig. 3. YOLOv2's architecture diagram.

The image is split into a $S \times S$ grid and for every cell of the grid, B bounding boxes are predicted. The network predicts 5 coordinates for every bounding box: t_x, t_y, t_w, t_h and t_o. Also note that besides the 5 coordinates, the output has to take into account the amount of object classes (C) that we wish to detect. Finally, the output is composed of the $S \times S$ grid with every grid cell containing $D = B \times (5 + C)$ values.

For a complete understanding of the improvements in the YOLO framework, the original article [10] is a must-read.

YOLOv2 Loss Function. The YOLOv2 loss function, in Eq. 3, is composed of three specialized parts, each one responsible for one feature. The features are: localization, classification and objectness. Localization is the centroid and bounding box size, classification is assigning an object class to a bounding box and objectness is how confident the model is that there actually is an object inside the bounding box.

The first two lines are related to the localization loss, one thing to note is the square root at the width and height. This is a mathematical trick to penalize more the network's wrong predictions on small bounding boxes, since a small absolute error in a small bounding box is worse than the same absolute error on a big bounding box. The third line is concerned with the objectness loss, it is responsible of correcting the network when it makes false positives and false negatives mistakes in objectness score confidence. The fourth line is the classification loss, it is the squared difference of the predicted class probabilities and real ones for the j_{th} bounding box in the i_{th} cell. The λs are used to weight the loss function, making it more sensible to a specific feature.

$$Loss = \lambda_{coord} \sum_{i=0}^{S^2} \sum_{j=0}^{B} 1_{ij}^{obj} [(x_i - \hat{x}_i)^2 + (y_i - \hat{y}_i)^2]$$

$$+ \lambda_{coord} \sum_{i=0}^{S^2} \sum_{j=0}^{B} 1_{ij}^{obj} [(\sqrt{w_i} - \sqrt{\hat{w}_i})^2 + (\sqrt{h_i} - \sqrt{\hat{h}_i})^2]$$

$$+ \sum_{i=0}^{S^2} \sum_{j=0}^{B} 1_{ij}^{obj} (C_i - \hat{C}_i)^2 + \lambda_{noobj} \sum_{i=0}^{S^2} \sum_{j=0}^{B} 1_{ij}^{noobj} (C_i - \hat{C}_i)^2$$

$$+ \sum_{i=0}^{S^2} \sum_{j=0}^{B} 1_{ij}^{obj} \sum_{c \in classes} (p_i(c) - \hat{p}_i(c))^2 \tag{3}$$

Where:

- $x, y, \hat{x}, \hat{y}$ are the predicted and ground truth bounding box's centroid coordinates
- $w, h, \hat{w}, \hat{h}$ are the predicted and ground truth width and height of the bounding box
- $C, \hat{C}$ are the predicted and ground truth bounding box objectness score, i.e. how strongly it thinks there is an object inside
- $p(c), \hat{p}(c)$ are the predicted and ground truth conditional class probability for class c given a detected object
- 1_{ij}^{obj} is 1 when there really is a real object, and 0 otherwise
- 1_{ij}^{noobj} is the complement of 1_{ij}^{obj}
- λ are scalars

Model's Restrictions. Just as YOLOv1, YOLOv2 predicts a maximum number of objects per grid cell and consequently for all image, so in a scenario where there are more vehicles than the maximum number of output predictions some objects would not be counted. To soften this restriction we proposed the use of regions of interest (ROI) to count the vehicles as explained in Sect. 4. Since the size of the ROI is very small compared to the whole image, it is likely to have a limited number of objects inside it, leading to less errors of this nature.

3.2   Network Training

Originally, YOLOv2 was written in C language, but due to its popularity and researchers' interest, several versions written in Python have been made, we chose to work with a Tensorflow [1] implementation [11]. We used the available pre-trained weights on the VOC dataset and fine-tuned the model by training the net on our dataset, in order to suit it to our purpose. Our model is avaiable at http://lia.facom.ufms.br/wp/obtaining-real-time-traffic-flow-from-aerial-images-using-deep-learning/.

3.3   Output Filtering (Non-maximum Bounding Box Suppression)

The output of an object detector is a set of bounding boxes, and it is common for this kind of algorithm to predict more than one bounding box with similar positions for the same object, as can be seen in Fig. 4.

To solve this issue, a bounding box suppression algorithm was applied. The algorithm was based on Tomasz Malisiewicz's algorithm available on MATLAB, the implementation can be found in Algorithm 1. Figure 4 illustrates the result of the process, in the left is a common output from an object detector, and in the right is the output after the bounding box suppression algorithm was applied. This is a fundamental technique to avoid counting more vehicles than there really are in the scene. The algorithm works as follows: sort all the generated bounding boxes by their confidence score and iterate through all of them, starting from the one with the highest confidence score, put the current box in a list of selected boxes, for every sorted box, check if the intersection area surpasses a threshold, if it does, delete the box from the sorted boxes list. At the end, all the boxes in the selected boxes list should be the actual objects, avoiding duplicates.

Given that the algorithm iterates through all the bounding boxes (n boxes) and for each one of them it also calculates the intersection area with the remaining boxes, the algorithm's complexity is $O(n^2)$. However, this is not a problem when the time to calculate the intersection area between the boxes is compared to the inference time of the network's forward pass.

Fig. 4. In this example the yellow bounding box is the box with the higher confidence score and overlapping area ratio. (Color figure online)

Algorithm 1. Bounding box suppression

---

  selected boxes ← empty
  sorted boxes ← bounding boxes sorted in descending order by the confidence scores
  while sorted boxes **is not** empty **do**
    current box ← first bounding box of sorted boxes
    append current box to selected boxes
    for all bounding boxes **in** sorted boxes **do**
      calculate intersection area ratio with the current box
      if intersection area ratio is greater than threshold t **then**
        delete the bounding box from sorted boxes
      end if
    end for
  end while
  return selected boxes

3.4   Tracking

An object detector is sufficient to estimate the amount of objects in a single image, however, it is not suitable for videos. This happens because the video is a sequence of frames, and if we blindly count the amount of bounding boxes, as the sequence goes on, the same object would be counted several times instead of just one.

Thus, it is necessary to define when a detected object on frame $n + 1$ corresponds to the same object detected on frame n. To overcome this challenge, a tracker was incorporated in our solution to identify the correspondence between vehicles in the sequence of frames.

The algorithm works as follows: in the first iteration all the centroids of the detected bounding boxes are listed, and for each centroid a counter variable named "missing" is initialized as zero. This variable is incremented every time it's correspondent centroid is missing in the current frame. After the first frame, the iterations follow the steps in Algorithm 2: for every centroid in frame n, we find it's correspondent one in frame $n + 1$ by using the Nearest Neighbor Algorithm, which is a very simple algorithm that provided fairly good results, if there are centroids that were detected and not used to update an old centroid, then a new object is in the frame, if there are more old centroids than new ones, it means that an object left the frame.

Since the algorithm iterates through all n centroids calculating their euclidean distances to the m new centroids, the algorithm's complexity is $O(n.m)$. For the same reason as Algorithm 1, the computational cost of this algorithm is not a problem.

Algorithm 2. Centroid tracker

---

new centroids ← centroids of given bounding boxes
for all centroids **do**
    for all new centroids **do**
        calculate the euclidean distance between the centroid and the new centroid
    end for
    centroid ← closest new centroid
    for every centroid that was updated **do**
        set the centroid's missing variable to 0
    end for
end for
if number of new centroids is greater than the number of centroids **then**
    append centroid list with new centroids that weren't used to update the list of centroids
else if number of new centroids is lower than the amount of centroids **then**
    for every centroid that was not updated **do**
        increment the centroid's missing variable
        if value of missing variable is greater than threshold t **then**
            delete the centroid from the list
        end if
    end for
end if

---

4 Experiments

To evaluate our proposal, we used human performance as baseline. Therefore, the experiments were designed to compare the quantity of vehicles counted by the model with the quantity counted by humans.

4.1 Dataset

We have produced a dataset composed of two different points of view of streets in the city. On the first one, the camera was placed on a bridge above a two-way street, which allowed us to have both front and back view of the vehicles. On the second one, a drone was used to make a video in a bird's-eye view of a busy roundabout. In total, the dataset is composed of 2866 frames that contain 38599 cars, 9275 motorcycles, 2175 trucks and 1111 buses. The labels follow the well-known format of the PASCAL Visual Object Classes (VOC) Challenge Dataset [3]. We used the DarkLabel tool [9] to annotate the frames. The dataset is available at http://weblia.facom.ufms.br/~datasets/carspybara-vehicle-dataset/.

Bridge Set. Two video sequences of length 1 min 30 s and 2 min 30 s were captured using a Samsung Galaxy S6 smartphone, using its 16 MP camera with 1920×1080 resolution. The sequences were captured from a bridge, pointing the camera at a two-way street that was right below the viaduct, generating a horizontal-like view of the vehicles passing by.

Roudabout Set. We have collected five video sequences with duration between three and four minutes in an urban area, with a DJI Phantom 4 Pro drone using a 60 fps 20 MP camera with 5472 × 3078 resolution, at 60 m height and 1.77 cm/px GSD. Out of the five sequences, two were annotated with four classes: truck, car, motorcycle and bus. These two videos were used as train set.

4.2   Experiments

The model does not identify the vehicles's path automatically, so we defined ROIs where there is traffic flow in order to perform the counting. These ROIs are defined by the bounding box of the lines drawn by the user, as is shown in green in Fig. 1. Even when the lines are perfectly aligned with the image axes the intersection algorithm implementation still works to evaluate the intersection between the vehicles' bounding boxes and the lines. Note that since the ROIs are drawn and attributed to specific coordinates of the video, the drone must be stationary.

Absolute Counting. In this experiment the total amount of vehicles was counted by a human in each scene and compared with the estimated value by the model. We used video sequences 0162 and 0166 to fine tune the model and 163, 164 and 167 as the test set. Figure 5 shows the comparison. The total amount of vehicles are 1023 and 910 for humans and model respectively. The difference of 113 vehicles represents 88.9% of average correct counting.

Counting at Each Second. We proceed our experimental evaluation investigating when the model count differs from the human count at each second. Using video sequence 0164, we computed the absolute value of the difference between the two counts, calculated overtime. Figure 6 shows the graph of the accumulated error over time. It is interesting to see a sudden rise between 80 s and 110 s. In the next section we further investigate this intriguing result.

Investigation of Increasing Error Between 80 s and 110 s on 0164 Video Sequence. The experiment of counting the amount of vehicles at each second shows that the error rate increases dramatically between 80 s and 110 s of the 0164 video sequence. Looking at the video sequence, we verified a small traffic jam at the scene, as shown in Fig. 7 highlighted by the green rectangle.

To assess the hypothesis that the model is more error-prone on traffic jam, we evaluate the result again, but now looking only at the right road of Fig. 7. The right road has no close obstacle (intersection or traffic light). Therefore during the video sequence 0164, no congestion was observed in that region. We denoted this region as *no traffic jam area*. The human count for this sequence was 69 vehicles, and the model counted 66 vehicles. That is, the system achieved a correct count rate of 95.6% at *no traffic jam area*.

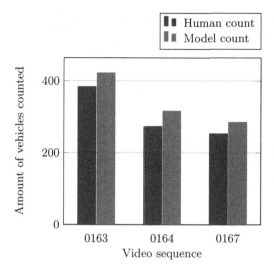

Fig. 5. Comparison between the amount of vehicles counted by a human and the amount counted by the model.

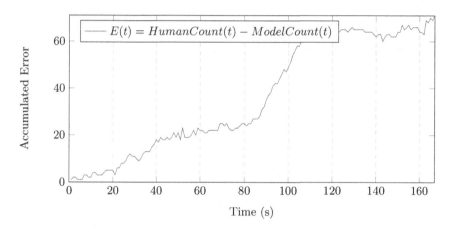

Fig. 6. Counting error overtime for the 0164 video sequence.

Fig. 7. Scenario where the model makes more counting errors. (Color figure online)

To further investigate this result, Fig. 8 shows the accumulated error at *no traffic jam area*. We can observe that the model still makes a few mistakes but the accumulated error reaches a plateau after 50 s and stays consistent between 2 and 5 errors.

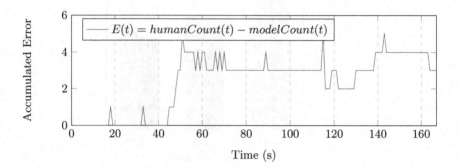

Fig. 8. Counting error overtime for *no traffic jam area*.

To assess the performance of the proposal, we measured the average frame per second processed by the system. Using Nvidia Titan X GPU the system process 32.7 fps on the roundabout dataset.

5   Conclusion and Future Work

Our work developed a real-time vehicle counting system using a state-of-the-art CNN architecture combined with simple yet powerful algorithms that turned a solution for the task of object detection in single images into a robust system that can be used on real-time video sequences. We also created a labelled dataset with four vehicle classes (car, motorcycle, bus and truck) consisting of bird's-eye and front view scenes. This dataset is publicly available, so other researchers can train their own models on it and make further improvements on the approaches to this challenging task. We also made the CNN's weights available so anyone can fine tune it, or just run the model without the need of training it.

For further work we intend to enhance the model's counting precision by trying different strategies for tracking such as data association algorithms (Joint Probabilistic Data Association, Hungarian Algorithm, Multiple Hypothesis Testing Algorithm), we also expect that these algorithms solve our proposal's issue with traffic jam areas. In the future, adding speed prediction can be of great value for this work, so we could measure vehicles average speed, supplying richer and more complete data about traffic. We also want to embed the counting system at the Remotely Piloted Aircraft (RPA) using mobile CNN architectures, in order to accomplish that, we must provide an interface so the user can remotely draw the input lines for the ROIs on an actual stream of the drone's footage.

References

1. Abadi, M., et al.: Tensorflow: a system for large-scale machine learning. In: OSDI, vol. 16, pp. 265–283 (2016)
2. Aslani, S., Mahdavi-Nasab, H.: Optical flow based moving object detection and tracking for traffic surveillance. Int. J. Electr. Comput. Energ. Electron. Commun. Eng. **7**(9), 1252–1256 (2013)
3. Everingham, M., Van Gool, L., Williams, C.K., Winn, J., Zisserman, A.: The pascal visual object classes (VOC) challenge. Int. J. Comput. Vis. **88**(2), 303–338 (2010)
4. Harsha, S.S., Anne, K.: A highly robust vehicle detection, tracking and speed measurement model for intelligent transport systems. Int. J. Appl. Eng. Res. **11**(5), 3733–3742 (2016)
5. Jo, K., Im, J., Kim, J., Kim, D.S.: A real-time multi-class multi-object tracker using YOLOv2. In: 2017 IEEE International Conference on Signal and Image Processing Applications (ICSIPA), pp. 507–511. IEEE (2017)
6. Luo, W., et al.: Multiple object tracking: a literature review (2014). arXiv preprint arXiv:1409.7618
7. Mandellos, N.A., Keramitsoglou, I., Kiranoudis, C.T.: A background subtraction algorithm for detecting and tracking vehicles. Expert Syst. Appl. **38**(3), 1619–1631 (2011)
8. Naphade, M., et al.: The 2018 NVIDIA AI city challenge. In: Proceedings of the IEEE Conference on Computer Vision and Pattern Recognition Workshops, pp. 53–60 (2018)
9. Programmer, D.: DarkLabel1.3 - Image Labeling and Annotation Tool (2017). http://darkpgmr.tistory.com/16
10. Redmon, J., Farhadi, A.: YOLO9000: better, faster, stronger. In: Proceedings of the IEEE Conference on Computer Vision and Pattern Recognition, pp. 7263–7271 (2017)
11. Trieu, T.: Darkflow (2018). https://github.com/thtrieu/darkflow

How the Quality of Call Detail Records Influences the Detection of Commuting Trips

Joel Pires[1], Aldina Piedade[1], Marco Veloso[1],
Santi Phithakkitnukoon[2(✉)], Zbigniew Smoreda[3],
and Carlos Bento[1(✉)]

[1] Center for Informatics and Systems of the University of Coimbra (CISUC),
Coimbra, Portugal
bento@dei.uc.pt
[2] Department of Computer Engineering, Faculty of Engineering,
Chiang Mai University, Chiang Mai, Thailand
santi@eng.cmu.ac.th
[3] Sociology and Economics of Networks and Services Department,
Orange Labs, Issy-les-Moulineaux, France

Abstract. Call Detail Records provide information on the origin and destination of voice calls at the level of the base stations in a cellular network. The low spatial resolution and sparsity of these data constitutes challenges in using them for mobility characterization. In this paper we analyze the impact on the detection of commuting patterns of four parameters: density of base stations per square kilometer, average number of calls made and received per day per user, regularity of these calls, and the number of active days per user. In this study, we use CDRs collected from Portugal over a period of fourteen months. Based on the result of our study, we are able to infer the commuting patterns of 10.42% of the users in our data set by considering users with at least 7.5 calls per day. Accounting users with over 7.5 calls per day, on average, does not result in a significant improvement on the result. Concerning the inference of routes in the home-to-work direction and vice versa, we examined users who connect to the cellular network, on average, every 17 days to everyday, which results in a 0.27% to 11.1% of trips detected, respectively. Finally, we found that with 208 days of data we are able to infer 5.67% of commuting trips and this percentage does not improve significantly by considering more data.

Keywords: Call Detail Records · Commuting trip ·
Origin-Destination matrices

1 Introduction

The use of opportunistic data for generation of mobility patterns (generated for other uses, but opportunistically used for mobility studies) instead of more traditional methods like surveys, has various advantages, namely lower cost, larger comprehensiveness and shorter periodicity when compared to the use of surveys. By using data from mobile operators, we can access a greater variety of data, much longer observations and much detailed information about the user. The main sources of data are:

© Springer Nature Switzerland AG 2019
P. Moura Oliveira et al. (Eds.): EPIA 2019, LNAI 11804, pp. 650–662, 2019.
https://doi.org/10.1007/978-3-030-30241-2_54

cellular network-based data and data from the smartphone sensors [1]. One of the types of network-based data mostly used to infer mobility patterns are Call Detail Records (CDRs). CDRs are fundamentally metadata on the voice calls. In general, they have the following fields [2]: timestamp, caller's ID, ID of the person that receives the call, call duration, ID of the originating cellular tower of the call and ID of the terminating cellular tower. As these data were not specifically gathered for this task, they need careful preparation, namely eliminating those that do not contribute or degrade the analysis process.

The use of CDRs for analysis of mobility comprises various challenges: oscillation phenomenon, spatial resolution, and data sparsity. Oscillation ("Ping-Pong effect") [3] comprises swapping the association of the user's terminal between neighbor cell towers even when the user is not moving. That happens because of load balances between different cells within a certain user's range [4]. A common criteria to detect this swapping is the detection of highly unrealistic speeds (above 1000 km/h), being it an evidence that we are in a presence of an oscillation [4]. Another challenge is the spatial resolution resultant from the distribution of base stations that is very different between dense urban areas, sparse urban areas, and rural areas. The precision of location estimation depends on the cellular towers' density and it is reported to vary between several hundred meters to several kilometers in rural areas [5]. The temporal sparsity is another problem of CDRs. It is affected by the number of calls the user performs or receives (a CDR is only issued when a call takes place). For an average user, the number of calls per day is small and irregularly distributed along the time window, so CDRs are coarse-grained which means that they have low spatial resolution concerning users' location estimation. Various approaches are used to work on these problems. We can use data from various days for the same user (for pendular trips), we can consider only users evolving on dense urban areas, or users with high number of calls. These are examples of the challenges on using CDRs to infer user's activities and locations traveled during the day, which results into lower quality of the Origin-Destination (OD) matrices generated by CDRs.

Current literature does not provide enough solutions on how to overcome these difficulties, especially on how good a dataset needs to be to infer mobility patterns. In general the focus is on developing OD matrices from the fusion of CDRs with data coming from traffic sensors [2] to develop OD matrices. For instance, traffic counters in different locations are used to validate the origin-destination predictions. Using non-supervised learning algorithms, Augusto et al. [6] tries to infer users' trips from their CDRs and then, from the travel behavior, characterize the mobility of the population. The work by Zhao et al. [7] is particularly interesting because, by using a fusion of CDRs and mobile internet accesses, they propose a supervised learning technique to detect if there are hidden visited places between those that can be seen by looking through CDRs. This study tells us if there are hidden visited places or not, but it does not provide the location of the hidden places. Another noteworthy study is the one by Bento et al. [8]. This study pretends to estimate the origins and destinations of the users' trips in Senegal using CDRs as well. Commuting and other irregular trips are inferred. This study is very interesting but has some limitations. They used CDRs at the granularity of a district level, so no actual location of the cellular towers was provided. The work by Jundee et al. [9] constitutes an step forward on the sense that it proposes two different techniques to infer the exact routes in commuting trips (home to workplace and workplace to home) using only CDRs. In order to detect home and workplace locations, it was done a subsampling so that "each user must have at least 100 total connections during the morning commuting hours (7AM–11AM) and 100 connections during the evening commuting hours (3PM–7PM)." To infer the exact commuting routes, they used the Google Maps API. With the workplace and home locations previously inferred, Google Maps Platform generate the routes that it considers being the most probable between the given workplace and home locations for each user. After that, they apply a method that enables to choose the right route among the options that the API suggests. To do that, two techniques are considered: the first one is the method of "Minimum Distance" and the second one is the "Method of Maximum Overlap" [9]. The principal limitation observed with this approach is that the different frequencies of call activity in the different cellular towers were not considered in any of these two techniques, which can lead to misleading results. Besides having some limitations, this work is helpful in finding a viable way of detecting commuting routes and the respective modes of transport.

Phithakkitnukoon et al. [10] proposed to follow the same methodology and fixing precisely the limitation above-mentioned. Nonetheless, the study comprises other limitations: (1) it should have been supported on a higher volume of data; (2) it is assumed that the users move using just one of the following transport modes - car or bus – where in fact the user can walk, bike, use by subway, train or tram; (3) it is not taken into consideration that the user can change the transport mode in the middle of the trip; (4) the calculation of the exact commuting routes can be highly optimized by estimating travel times and intermediate activated cell towers (cell towers activated during a commuting trip that do not correspond to the home or workplace location); (5) taking into the account the challenges that we have to face relatively to the oscillation phenomenon and others, the pre-process and treatment of the data should be more elaborated; (6) not forgetting the challenges of temporal sparsity and spatial resolution of the CDRs, a more detailed series of filters on the users' data in the dataset is necessary in order to end up with a subsample of users greatly apt to be used in the following stages of the learning process. Besides these limitations, the main methodology followed in this work is promising, so we will apply our efforts to develop an optimized version of that methodology that will answer to those limitations. In this paper we will take into consideration to overcome limitations (5) and (6) that have a significant impact on the effectiveness of the next steps of the methodology.

This paper is structured in five sections. Section 2 describes the dataset that we used in this study. In Sect. 3 the research approach is explored, detailing all the processing of the data, the methodology used in selecting the right users to infer commuting routes and the experiments performed to assess the quality requirements needed in a CDR dataset. Section 4 presents the results of the experiments as well as a discussion of them. Section 5 closes the study with the main conclusions obtained and possible opportunities for new research challenges.

2   Dataset Characterization

The dataset that we used consists of CDRs from citizens of the entire Portugal (including Madeira and Azores islands) provided by one of the largest telecom operators. It corresponds to a period of a year and two months of records, from 2nd of April 2006 to 30th of June 2007. These records were registered for billing purposes. The dataset contains incoming and outgoing calls from a total of almost 2 million mobile phone users (1.899.216 users in total and 1.890.018 on Continental Portugal). Nothing was registered about SMS's sent/received or internet accesses or other type of network-based data. This constitutes a total of 435.701.911 records from approximately 18% of the Portuguese population in 2007 and covers all the 308 Portuguese municipalities. The total number of different cellular towers presented in the dataset is 2243. On average, the coverage is 90 km^2 per cellular tower, however, in dense urban areas like Porto, this coverage drops to 0.125 km^2 per cellular tower. In order to have a notion of the different coverage area of each cell tower, a Voronoi Diagram was developed (see Fig. 1a. As already emphasized, it is notorious by the figure that the regions of Porto and Lisbon are the municipalities with higher density of antennas. It is also perceived

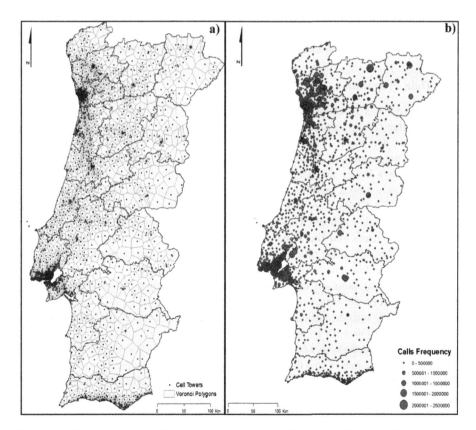

Fig. 1. (a) Voronoi diagram of all the cell towers across Continental Portugal (b) Proportional circles map of the calls frequency across Continental Portugal (Color figure online)

the high variability of cellular tower densities in our dataset. To perceive how the call activity is distributed geographically across the country, a proportional circles map was created based on the call's density (see Fig. 1b). The bigger the green balls, the more intense is the call activity. As we can see, Porto and Lisbon (as well as its surroundings) constitute the districts that have the highest call activity. So, as expected, the geographic distribution of tower density is a mirror of the geographic distribution of call activity. We can also conclude that there is a tendency to coastal regions to have higher call activity than inland regions. The anonymity, privacy, and security of the users had to be guaranteed and, consequently, cellular numbers were anonymized and a unique hash code (code ID) was generated for each user before we received the data. Aside from oscillation phenomenon, the ID's of the antennas are the ones that were closer to the user in the moment of the call. The fields included in each CDR are: timestamp, caller's ID, ID of the person to whom the user is calling, call duration, ID of the originating cellular tower and ID of the terminating cellular tower of the call.

3 Research Approach

First, an elaborated process of data cleaning of the entire 435.701.911 records was carried out. From the remaining CDRs, a meticulous process of users' selection was done. With all the eligible users collected, multiple experiments were performed.

3.1 Data Preparation

The first step was to clean every record with "NULL" values or any field with a negative value (every value of the CDR must be positive). A total of 16 CDRs were deleted. Next step was to delete duplicated records as well as records that reference cell towers that are unknown. A total of 12.810.045 CDRs were eliminated (2.9% of the original dataset). It was also needed to check if the minimum and maximum values for all fields were within a credible range (e.g. check if a duration of a call is absurdly long). Also, 254 CDRs were deleted because they had every field equal except the duration of the call. 4 pair of CDRs were erased as well because they had the same pair of intervenient users and the same timestamp, but the duration and the cell towers involved in the call were different. Finally, we focused on cases in which a call comprises more than one record. This can happen because the user is moving or because of the ping-pong effect. We know that we are facing a case like this when the difference between the timestamps of two consecutive calls is equal to zero. In these cases, if the cell towers participating in the call remained the same, we merged the CDRs into one CDR with its final duration being the sum of durations of the pair of calls. Another situation is when the originating cell tower or the terminating one change, that means one of two things: or the user legitimately moved from one place to another during a call, or the call suffered from the ping-pong effect. With that in mind, distances between the base stations involved in the calls and the travelling speeds of the users were estimated having in mind to delete CDRs which represent a travelling speed higher than 400 km/h. All these cases resulted in merging 1524 contiguous CDRs and deleting 333 CDRs that are oscillation cases. After the pre-processing we ended up with a total of 422.889.747 CDRs (97% of the original dataset).

3.2 Selection of Data for Prediction

As we are using CDRs. we have to deal with challenges like low spatial resolution and temporal sparsity of the call activity. In practice, that means that we need not only to have a higher quantity of data but also a more refined methodology to select relevant data. So, a random selection of the CDRs for generation of the prediction model can lead to data that is not appropriate to infer commuting patterns. Actually, there are various criteria that we have to fulfill in order to obtain the right set of users for further analysis. Figure 2 gives us an overview of the selection process and how the various steps are related to each other. Therefore, the first criteria that needs to be met is to filter CDRs in order to obtain only users that have call activity on weekdays. As we are talking about commuting trips, it does not make sense to consider the contrary. After that, we need to identify the workplace and home of the users. In order to do that we followed the technique used by Santi et al. in [10]. The home of the user is assumed to be the cellular tower in which most activity was registered during the hours that the user is supposed to be at home, namely, from 10PM to 7AM. Conversely, the work-place of the user is assumed to be the cellular tower in which was registered most call activity during the working hours (9AM to 12PM and from 2PM to 5PM). With this approach we are ignoring users in the dataset that have more than one home and/or more than one workplace, as well as users that work during the night. Only users that have a well-defined and distinct home and workplace locations were considered in the following steps of the commuting trips inference. A strong assumption that is made is that the user will not change home or workplace during the period of study. The next step is to select users that have call activity during the morning and/or the evening. The morning corresponds to the period between 5AM and 12PM. The evening corresponds to the period between 3PM and 12AM. The next task is find the users with call activity at home and in the workplace during morning hours. This is essential to determine if it is possible to infer home to workplace trips (entering the workplace). Analogously, we want to know if it is possible to determine the inverse trip, in other words, workplace to home trips (exiting the workplace), by selecting the users that have call activity at home and in the workplace during evening hours. Once it is done, it is time to observe how many users have call activity along the trip home to workplace or vice-versa, as it is explained in Fig. 3. To do that, we observe the transitions home to workplace and vice-versa in consecutive calls along the different user's active days. For home to workplace routes, we select the following pair of calls in each user's day of activity: last call associated to the home cell tower and first call associated to the workplace cell tower. For workplace to home routes, the process is the reverse: last call associated to the workplace cell tower and first call associated to the home cell tower. Then we compute the difference between the calls' timestamps and select the pair of calls that registered the minimum difference for each user. That difference will be our estimated travel time, the timestamp of the first call will be stored as the starting timestamp and the timestamp of the second call will be stored as the end timestamp. Finally, to obtain the intermediate activated towers, we look for the calls that happen between the stored starting timestamp and end timestamp in the user's set of active days.

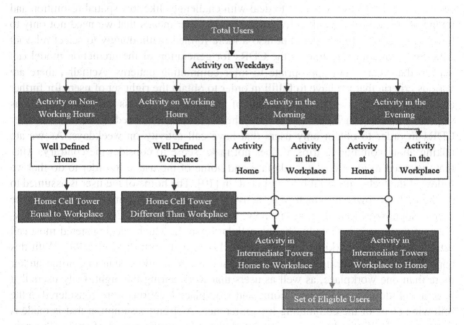

Fig. 2. The methodology to select the users for which we can infer commuting patterns

3.3   Designing the Experiment

The two main requirements to guarantee the success of our approach to infer commuting routes are: (a) users must have a distinct home and workplace location; (b) users must have call activity in intermediate towers between home to workplace and/or vice-versa. We consider four quality parameters under analysis: (1) Tower Density for each municipality (TD); (2) Average Number of Calls made/received per Day (ANCD); (3) Regularity of the Call Activity (call activity every x days) (RCA); (4) Number of Different Active Days (temporal window) (NDAD). Intuitively the last three variables affect the ability to identify workplaces, homes and intermediate towers, and the first variable (TD) mainly affects the ability to distinguish the home from the workplace and to distinguish possible intermediate towers from the home and workplace (origin and destination of the trip). To demonstrate this, multiple experiments were made and are presented in this paper.

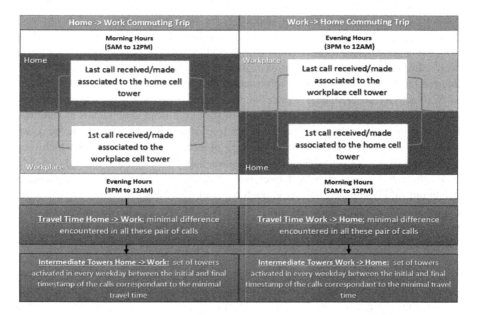

Fig. 3. Reasoning behind the calculation of travel times and intermediate towers

First, we will vary the values of the last three variables and we'll develop a chart for each one of them that encapsulates the percentage of users that have: (1) call activity on weekdays; (2) an well-identified home and workplace; (3) call activity at home and in the workplace in the morning; (4) call activity at home and in the workplace in the evening; (5) call activity during their routes home to work and/or work to home.

Secondly, we need to consider areas with different tower densities across the multiple municipalities to answer to the question: considering the universe of users who have enough call activity to have a well-identified home and workplace in each municipality, what is the percentage of users that still have the home location distinct from the workplace location in that municipality? To answer to this question, we developed an experiment that relates the different values of cell towers densities and the percentage of users that have distinct home from workplace. We are assuming that a user does not work in the same building where he/she lives.

4   Results and Discussion

The methodology described above was applied to our dataset. Table 1 presents some insights collected during the selection of the 1.890.018 users from the dataset. From the whole dataset, we can only infer the routes home to workplace or vice-versa of 10.2% of the total number of users and the routes home to workplace and vice-versa of 1.2% of the total number of users. The criteria that makes us lose more users from the initial dataset is, in descending order of impact: (1) a well-defined home and workplace; (2) call activity at home and in the workplace in the evening. In the work of Santi et al. [11], the approach used to infer home and workplace locations of the users has already been validated as being a good approximation of the actual locations by comparing the inferred results with actual census information. According to Fig. 4, except for the line of "Call activity on Weekdays", each line has a similar behavior – high growth in low values of ANCD until it reaches the elbow of the curve from which tends to stabilize. Having in consideration statistical measures (e.g. standard deviation, mean, etc.), we concluded that the values of ANCD for each plotted line (in the order in which they appear in the Fig. 4) from which this stabilization happen are 0.1, 6.3, 6.3, 7.1, 7.5, 8.5. In practice, this means that a dataset with users that, on average, receive/make a maximum of 7.5 calls per day is enough to avail 10.42% of the total users to infer routes home/workplace or vice-versa. Moreover, if we extend the threshold to a maximum of 8.5 calls per day, we can avail 3.31% of the total users to infer routes home/workplace and vice-versa. Adding users to our dataset with higher thresholds does not result into significant percentage gains. In Fig. 5, the behavior of the plotted lines is the reverse - coming from high values of RCA the lines remain stable in values close to 0% until they reach the elbows of the curves from which the peak is achieved. Considering again the same previously mentioned statistical measures, we concluded that the values of RCA for each plotted line (in the order in which they appear in the Fig. 5) from which this stabilization happen are 1.4, 33.5, 30.7, 24.4, 16.8, 9.4 days. So, if we include in our dataset users with a RCA of 16.8 or higher, we can only avail a maximum of 0.27% of them to infer routes home/workplace or vice-versa and, if RCA = 9.4 or higher, we can only avail a maximum of 0.035% users to infer routes home/workplace and vice-versa. Conversely, if we have users with a RCA less than 16.8 in our dataset, we can notice a significant higher growth (that can go up to 11.1%) in the percentage of users from which we can infer routes home to workplace or vice versa. Looking to Fig. 6, we see that the elbow of the curve of each line is becoming more and more attenuated until becoming practically linear. Hereupon, we conclude that the higher the value of NDAD of the users, the bigger the percentage of them from which we can infer commuting patterns. For example, if we have in our dataset users with a maximum amount of 208 days (average for the green plotted data) of call activity, we can obtain 5.67% of them to compute routes home/workplace or vice-versa. Yet, to reach only 1.427% of users from which we can compute routes home/workplace and vice-versa, the threshold needs to be 228 days (average for the cyan plotted data). From the Fig. 7 we understand that as long we are increasing the average coverage area per cell, the percentage of users that have a distinct cell for home and for workplace (considering the universe of users that have a well-identified home and workplace) will decrease (not linearly) until it reaches 0% for TD > 370 Km^2/cell. On average, the percentage of users obtained is 13% with a standard deviation of 10.7%. So, if we choose users from our dataset that are from a municipality with a tower density less than 7 Km^2/cell, then we will obtain more than 13% of them with a well identified home and workplace.

Table 1. Statistical results of filtering our dataset

Parameter of filtering the users	Number of users left	Percentage of remaining users relatively to the initial dataset	Percentage of eliminated users
Call Activity on **Weekdays**	1857772	98.3%	–1.7%
Well-defined **Home and Workplace**	932671	49.3%	–49%
Call Activity at **Home and in the Workplace in the Morning**	872356	46.2%	–1.9%
Call Activity at **Home and in the Workplace in the Evening**	329715	17.5%	–28,7%
Call Activity **During the trip Home-Workplace or Workplace-Home** (with home, workplace and intermediate towers distinct)	209659 192150	11.1% 10.2%	–6,4% –0,9%
Call Activity **During the trip Home to Workplace and Workplace to Home** (with home, workplace and intermediate towers distinct)	69154 53163	3.7% 1.2%	–6,5% –2,5%

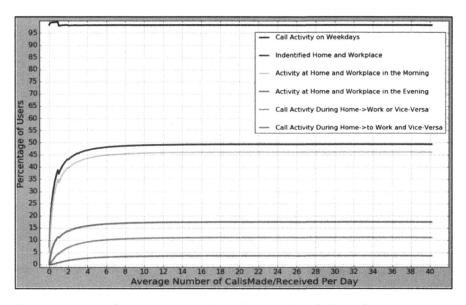

Fig. 4. Percentage of remaining users that satisfy certain criterion. The percentages are cumulative - e.g. the percentage for 6 calls per day is a sum of percentages of 0 to 6 calls per day.

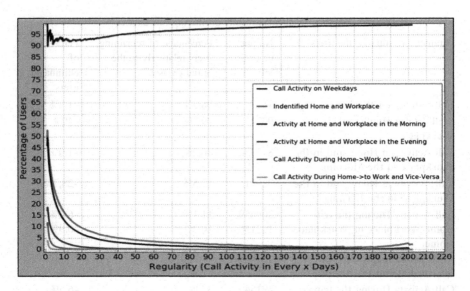

Fig. 5. Percentage of remaining users that satisfy certain criterion. The percentages are cumulative - e.g. the percentage for a regularity of 10 days is a sum of percentages of 10 to 205 days.

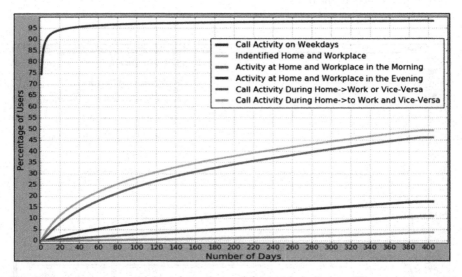

Fig. 6. Percentage of remaining users that satisfy certain criterion. The percentages are cumulative - e.g. the percentage for 120 active days is a sum of percentages of 0 to 120 active days.

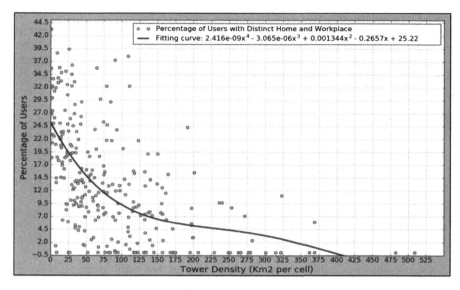

Fig. 7. Variation of the percentage of the users with distinct home and workplace

5 Conclusion

Following a methodology that selects the proper users through multiple criteria, we studied how the variation in four quality parameters of a CDR dataset can potentiate or constrain the percentage of users from which we are able to infer commuting routes. After the experiments, we concluded that a dataset with users that, on average, receive/make a maximum of 7.5 calls per day is adequate to infer commuting routes of 10.42% of them. Adding users with more than 7.5 calls per day into the dataset does not result in a significant increase in that percentage value. Only if we have in our dataset users with a regularity of less than 16.8 days, we can see a significant growth (that can go from 0.27% to 11.1%) in the percentage of users from which we can infer routes in home-to-workplace direction or vice versa. A dataset constituted by users with a maximum amount of 208 days of call activity allows us to infer commuting patterns of 5.67% of the users. So, this study is important for those who want to infer mobility patterns using CDRs and need to know what the optimal threshold for multiple quality parameters are to process and subsample the data. It gives also an overview of what the quality of the results is going to be, knowing in advance the characteristics of the dataset. For a given set of characteristic variables of the dataset or subset, it is shown to be possible to estimate the percentage of data or users that we could ignore or carry on adequately for detecting commuting patterns. This work can serve as a basis for future research in detecting exact commuting routes and respective transport modes using a CDR dataset. Detecting other activity locations besides home or workplace and other routes besides the commutes can be among others to be further explored in the future. In addition, these conclusion and insights are contextualized to the Portuguese reality. So, it would be interesting to see similar experiments in other countries for comparative study and different mobility profiles.

Acknowledgements. This work had the financial support of the program Centro 2020 and Portugal 2020 of project SUSpENsE - Sustainable built environment under natural hazards and extreme events (CENTRO-45-2015-1) and MITPortugal Exploratory Project UMove - Understanding User's Needs, Preferences and Social Interactions for the Design of Future Mobility Services. We thank the anonymous referees for their valuable suggestions.

References

1. Wang, Z., He, S.Y., Leung, Y.: Applying mobile phone data to travel behaviour research: a literature review. Travel Behav. Soc. **11**, 141–155 (2018)
2. Charisma, F., González, M.C.: Development of Origin–Destination Matrices Using Mobile Phone Call Data (2018)
3. Nikolic, M., Bierlaire, M.: Review of transportation mode detection approaches based on smartphone data. In: 17th Swiss Transport Research Conference, May 2017
4. Wang, F., Chen, C.: On data processing required to derive mobility patterns from passively-generated mobile phone data. Transp. Res. Part C **87**, 58–74 (2018)
5. Chen, C., Bian, L., Ma, J.: From traces to trajectories: how well can we guess activity locations from mobile phone traces? Transp. Res. Part C **46**, 326–337 (2014)
6. Augusto, G., et al.: A trip to work: estimation of origin and destination of commuting patterns in the main metropolitan regions of Haiti using CDR. Dev. Eng. **3**, 133–166 (2018)
7. Zhao, Z., Zhao, J., Koutsopoulos, H.N.: Individual-Level Trip Detection Using Sparse Call Detail Record Data Based on Supervised Statistical Learning (2016)
8. Demissie, M.G., Antunes, F., Bento, C.: Inferring Origin-Destination Flows Using Mobile Phone Data : A Case Study of Senegal (2016)
9. Jundee, T.: Inferring Commuting Flows using CDR Data : A Case Study of Lisbon, Portugal (2018)
10. Phithakkitnukoon, S., Sukhvibul, T., Demissie, M., Smoreda, Z., Natwichai, J., Bento, C.: Inferring social influence in transport mode choice using mobile phone data. EPJ Data Sci. **6**(1), 11 (2017)
11. Phithakkitnukoon, S., Smoreda, Z., Olivier, P.: Socio-geography of human mobility: a study using longitudinal mobile phone data. PLoS ONE **7**(6), 1–9 (2012)

Warranty Claim Rate Prediction Using Logged Vehicle Data

Reza Khoshkangini[(✉)], Sepideh Pashami, and Slawomir Nowaczyk

Center for Applied Intelligent Systems Research (CAISR), Halmstad University,
Halmstad, Sweden
{reza.khoshkangini,sepideh.pashami,slawomir.nowaczyk}@hh.se

Abstract. Early detection of anomalies, trends and emerging patterns can be exploited to reduce the number and severity of quality problems in vehicles. This is crucially important since having a good understanding of the quality of the product leads to better designs in the future, and better maintenance to solve the current issues. To this end, the integration of large amounts of data that are logged during the vehicle operation can be used to build the model of usage patterns for early prediction. In this study, we have developed a machine learning system for warranty claims by integrating available information sources: Logged Vehicle Data (LVD) and Warranty Claims (WCs). The experimental results obtained from a large data set of heavy duty trucks are used to demonstrate the effectiveness of the proposed system to predict the warranty claims.

Keywords: Warranty claim predictive · Machine learning · Fault detection

1 Introduction

Vehicle manufacturers aim to increase customer satisfaction by ensuring high product quality. As customers expect continued improvement in the quality of products together with increased functionality, vehicles are becoming more personalized and specialized. Such product diversity is desired by manufacturers' sale divisions as means of attracting customers' attention. However, the diversity in products becomes more challenging when trying to understand weak spots and flawed designs. A novel AI system is needed to deal with the huge amount of historical data for immediate recognition of emerging quality issues.

Warranty claims (WCs) refer to problems reported by customers, related to maintenance, repair or replacement of vehicle's components during the warranty period. Growth in the number of claims for certain components is often an indicator of a quality issue. This will also translate into an increase in costs that a manufacturer has to pay on warranty claims and a decrease in customer's trust and satisfaction. Therefore, it is important to detect the imminent increase of the claim rate as quickly as possible, or even to predict it before it happens.

© Springer Nature Switzerland AG 2019
P. Moura Oliveira et al. (Eds.): EPIA 2019, LNAI 11804, pp. 663–674, 2019.
https://doi.org/10.1007/978-3-030-30241-2_55

Analyzing WCs [12,14] with the aim of deriving useful knowledge from products during their operations enables the manufacturers to increase awareness of the quality problems. It also supports OEMs in making decisions to initiate corrective actions as soon as possible. Predicting warranty claims, however, is a challenging task. A failure can be caused by different factors, across different components and due to different usage patterns. In complex systems such as modern heavy-duty trucks there are thousands of potential components to monitor, with complex inter-dependencies.

Over the past decades, significant efforts have been undertaken among researchers and manufactures to develop various algorithms for detecting quality problems in the vehicles [8,12,15]. In this context, and from the state of the art, we can categorize the studies into three approaches, namely Lifetime Distributions, Stochastic Process and Artificial Neural Networks [28]. For example, under the umbrella of lifetime distribution approach, a warranty claim prediction model is introduced in [13] based on a piecewise application of Weibull and exponential distributions in order for intrinsic failure period and early failure period. In [21] a probabilistic model is developed on the bases of time and a time-dependent quantity including the amount of usage. Similarly, Chukova et al. in [7] exploited two variables such as age and mileage of the vehicle to estimate the mean cumulative number of claims. In the frame of Stochastic process, Kalbfleisch et al. in [12] developed a prediction approach that works based on the date of warranty claims (rather than the failure date), in which a log-linear Poisson model is used to predict the claims. Another interesting forecasting method has been done in [10], where mixed non-homogeneous Poisson process (NHPP) used to predict the warranty claims. In artificial neural network context, multi-layer perceptron (MLP) [25,26], and radial basis [19] algorithms have been used. Within these algorithms, Kalman filter [27], time series and linear regression models are used in order for building the models to predict the number of warranty claims [6,24].

Despite the significant progress in this area, most works on predicting warranty claims are age-based approaches (both in terms of time and mileage) without taking the vehicles' usage into account, despite the fact that only such multidimensional data contains complete information. However, there are several recent investigations in the automotive domain on using Machine Learning approaches for predictive maintenance where vehicle's usage are considered [17,18]. We believe that warranty claim prediction could be formulated in a similar fashion so that it can benefit from logged sensory data collected on-board of vehicles.

Sensors, wireless communications, and instrumentation such as a telematic equipment support Original Equipment Manufacturers (OEMs) to continuously monitor the vehicles during their operation [16]. The Logged Vehicle Data (LVD) data consists aggregated information about vehicle usage patterns during their life time. The huge amount of LVD and warranty claims data allows for building a machine learning system to effectively model the vehicles past behavior to predict which and when the specific component is going to fail [23]. Although this strategy can be bridge a gap in traditional claim's predictions that are mostly constructed based on two parameters, dealing with a multi-dimensional data itself creates new concerns for choosing relevant parameters.

In this study we aim to detect the quality issues ahead of time (early detection) by monitoring the increases in the warranty claim rate predictions. Thus, we have developed machine learning approaches for predicting individual warranty claims, which can then be aggregated to give OEMs indications of the claim rate within overall vehicle population. In particular, the proposed early detection approach consists of four main modules: *Data Integration*, where LVD and WCs data are integrated into a combined time series to be used as an input of the system; *Feature Selection* for identifying the most relevant subset of parameters, taking advantage of two algorithms implemented in a parallel way; *Feature Extraction* to derive additional, hidden information from the selected features in a format suitable for the prediction algorithms; and *Learning and Prediction* module to train the model based on the data collected from thousands of heavy duty trucks during three years of operation. We focus on two failures connected to the power train and the fuel system. In essence, we formulate this warranty claim prediction as a supervised classification problem of whether or not a vehicle is going to have a warranty claim during the next month.

The rest of the paper is organized as follows; In Sect. 2 the information about both data sets, LVD and WC, are described. Section 3 presents the proposed methods and detailed descriptions of the modules. Section 4 describes the experimental evaluation and the results, which is followed by discussion and summary of the work in Sect. 5.

2   Data Presentation

Large amount of data is a necessity for the success of the systems that operate on the basis of learning and predicting the future event. In this study, we utilize two data sets: Logged Vehicle Data (LVD), that mainly contains usage and specification of the vehicles, and Warranty Claim (WC) data, consisting of vehicles' claims information during their life time.

2.1   Logged Vehicle Data (LVD)

The logged vehicle data (LVD) used in this study were collected over the three years from commercial trucks. Over this time more than 300.000 data points from 6.000 unique vehicles were collected in a structured entry. The LVD consists of the aggregated information about vehicles' usage. The values of most parameters are collected each time a vehicle visits an authorized workshop for repair or service. A subset of parameters is also collected through telematics. In general, two types of parameters were logged in this data set. The first type describes the configuration of the vehicles, for instance, the type of the engine, gearbox, etc., expressed as categorical features; the second type denotes to the usage of the vehicle during its operation, for instance, aggregated parameters such as total fuel consumption, usage of compressors, etc. Out of the 375 parameters contained in the LVD data, we have focused on 296 parameters numerical parameters that capture actual vehicle usage over time, and excluded the categorical features.

2.2 Claim Data

Claim data captures the history of failures in vehicles during the warranty period, collected by the OEM authorized workshops around the world. In particular, the claim dataset shows which component of which vehicle has been replaced at which date. The parts and components are defined by the normalized identification codes in four different levels of detail. This claim data set contains parameters such as *Vehicle Id*, as well as the name and code of the components that have been replaced, and claim date.

3 Proposed Method

Borrowing from the taxonomy introduced in [28], our proposed early warranty claim prediction system can be characterized as a *multi-dimensional* approach, since it considers multiple parameters at once to build the prediction model. Figure 1 illustrates the conceptual overview of the system and its modules, consisting of *Data Integration*, *Feature Selection*, *Feature Extraction*, and *Learning and Prediction*, described below.

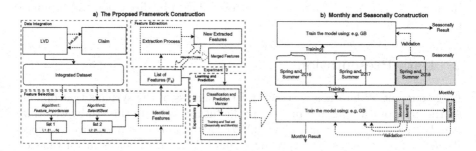

Fig. 1. The conceptual view of the framework with its' four main modules (a), and the formulation of training and test sets; monthly and seasonally (b).

3.1 Data Integration

The purpose of this module is to merge the LVD and claim datasets, creating an integrated dossier with both the usage and failure information for all the vehicles. We merge the two datasets based on vehicles "Chassis id", "Date of readout" and "Date of claim report". To this end, we select a time-window of one month preceding each warranty claim, and consider this to be the interval in which the symptoms of imminent failure are most likely to be visible, and when the vehicle usage has the highest effect on a failure. The integrated data set contains a new feature named "Failure" (as the target feature f_t) so that it has a value of 1 for a given row if and only if a claim for the specific component of interest has been reported within a month from the readout date.

3.2   Feature Selection

Within hundreds of parameters logged in the LVD, collected from multiple sensors installed in different places throughout the vehicle, we expect only a small subset to be informative for predictive lifetime of a particular component of interest. Thus, given a set of features $F = \{f_1, f_2, \ldots, f_t\}$, without the loss of generality we assume that f_t is the variable corresponding to the component failure. In this context, the target feature indicates whether the component has failed within a month of the data readout. In this module we aim to identify a subset $F_s \subset F$ of the features that are highly relevant for predicting the target.

It is expected that every feature selection algorithm takes into account different aspects of the data to select the most valuable features. Several studies have demonstrated the usefulness of *ensemble* methods in machine learning. Hence, in this module, we combine two different algorithms, namely *SelectKBest* [29] and *Feature Importance* [2] algorithms[1], in a parallel fashion to pick the most informative subset of features. In the first algorithm, we used ANOVA F-value [9] between features/label for this selection problem, which is a time efficient algorithm with high performance. In the second method, a type of random decision tree class (**Extra Tree classifier**) is exploited in order to select the most informative features. In fact, this classifier runs a meta estimator, which fits a set of randomized decision trees on multiple sub-samples of the data set [4]. Feature importance is selected since it enables the module to take advantage of deeply compressed and global inside the behaviors, by taking into consideration both the main feature impact and the interaction impact [1]. Eventually, to achieve the desired list of features $F_s = \{f_1, f_2, \ldots, f_m, f_t\}$ in this selection manner (as it is illustrated in Fig. 1), the common subset of features from the output of each algorithm is selected to build the model.

3.3   Feature Extraction

This third module aims to generate new features. Unlike the previous one, where the goal is to reduce the dimensionality of the data [11], in this case we want to find the hidden information that can not be directly recognized by classification algorithms. It has been shown before, in a related study [20], that different ways to represent data collected on-board vehicles lead to different classification performance.

As mentioned above, we excluded the categorical data to evaluate our approach on the parameters which are logged using on-board sensors. These parameters express the cumulative data, in which the value of each parameter is incremented over time. Therefore we calculate the difference between subsequent data points, to capture the rate of change of these parameters. This allows us to characterize the resulting changes as significant, moderate, low and no deviations. An example is shown in Fig. 2, where significant and moderate changes are highlighted by red and blue colors, respectively. The subplots show the changes in

---

[1] We have used *sklearn.feature_selection* [5] library (Python) implementations of these feature selection algorithms.

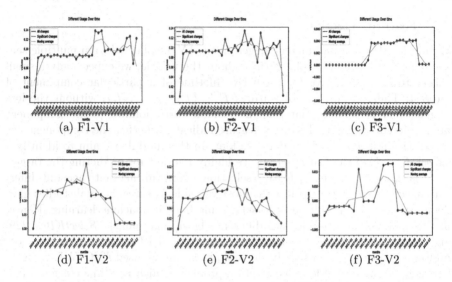

Fig. 2. Usage changes between different features (Color figure online)

three different features (F1, F2 and F3) from two distinct vehicles (V1 and V2). As it can be seen in the plots, these movements (up and downs) form distinctive patterns. As an example, in Fig. 2a, there are two significant changes that happened in 2017, and similar pattern occurs in 2018. Another clear pattern can be seen in Fig. 2b. This hidden information indicate a particular usage of the vehicle, is likely to be very useful for building the model in *Learning and Prediction* module. The green line in all subplots also shows the moving average of the changes during the vehicles operation.

We conduct this extraction on the list of the features (F_s), which are obtained and selected from the *Feature Selection* module described in Sect. 3.2. Thus, to construct the data set to be trained by the classifier, we have merged these extracted changes as extra parameters to the list F_s, to get $F_{se} = \{f_{0s}, f_{1s}, f_{2s}, \ldots, f_{ms}, f_{0ex}, f_{1ex}, \ldots, f_{mex}\}$. The work-flow of this process is illustrated in Fig. 1a.

3.4 Learning and Prediction

This module concerns the learning and prediction of the warranty claim given the vehicles usage. The action flow is detailed in Fig. 1a, where the module receives two types of data sets to train and build the model for conducting different experiments. The first data is injected from *Feature Selection* module in order to answer Experiments 1 and 2, while the second data is received from *Feature Extraction* module to tackle Experiment 3. Partitioning the incoming data into training and validation sets is distinct and it is constructed based on the objective of different experiments.

4   Experimental Evaluation and Results

The main task of the prediction service is to provide reliable support for workshops to decrease the warranty cost, which is beneficial for both company and the customers. In this experimental evaluation, we illustrate how machine learning algorithms can be leveraged for failure detection taking into account not only age and mileage, but multiple parameters which express vehicle past behaviors during their operation. In the following sections we report the results of three different experiments.

4.1   Experiment 1

In this experiment we focus on the issue of predicting warranty claims within fuel system, taking into account the usage of vehicles in the past. In particular we evaluate the effect of seasonality in the predictions. The detailed information of how we construct the training and test sets the *monthly* and *seasonal* cases are described below. In both cases we have used two years (2016–2017) of data to train the model, and one year (2018) to evaluate it. Due to highly unbalanced data (healthy vs unhealthy vehicles), we select only the vehicles that have at least one claim during their three years of operation.

Monthly: In this monthly setup, 42.000 samples with 19 features are selected. To train the model, we employed GradientBoostingClassifier (GB)[2], which works based on a type of decision tree (CART) [22]. Once the model is trained using 30.000 data samples, the test set is used with 12.000 data points to validate the classification method. This is done through 12 partitions, one per month, as shown in Fig. 1b. The result from each partition is depicted in the plot in Fig. 3a.

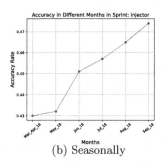

(a) Monthly   (b) Seasonally

Fig. 3. Monthly and seasonally accuracy in 2018.

Figure 3a shows the monthly accuracy performance over the year. Within the twelve months validation, the maximum performance that we could obtain is ∼50% correctly classification in the last month. The unbalanced data in the

---

[2] We took the advantage of *sklearn* library in Python to employ this classifier to build the model.

training and test sets might be the reason of this low accuracy performance throughout the year. Although the accuracy value indicates low performance, this figure with regard to the very low baseline shows an admissible result. In addition, the GB classifier provides the area under the curve (AUC) [3] with 0.66 (average over all partitions in the test set) showing that the model works better than random classification.

To have an in-depth look at the performance of the prediction over time, a distinguishable pattern can be seen between the first and the second six-month of the year. It basically reveals that over the months the data is getting more meaningful which has a contribution to the model. This explains the consistent growth of the accuracy through months.

Seasonally: To evaluate this experiment we have trained the model based on data logged during the Spring and Summer (March–September) over two years, and validated it over the same period the following year. For this experiment, in total 20.000 data points are considered for training set and 3720 for validation set. The conceptual view of training and test sets in monthly and seasonally experiments are illustrated in Fig. 3. Similar to the monthly evaluation, we observed that accuracy over the first six-months is increasing starting from 43% to ~48%, however we did not obtain a high accuracy value. Taking into consideration both monthly and seasonally plots, we can observe quite similar results in accuracy metrics. In contrast with monthly, though, a much worse AUC value of 56% was achieved in this experiment. To have an in-depth look at both monthly and seasonally evaluation results, we can observe a very similar pattern for the common months with respect to accuracy rate. Thus, we can conclude that prediction of fuel system claims is not dependent on the seasonality.

4.2   Experiment 2

In this experiment we distinguish two types of vehicles: healthy and non-healthy ones. Healthy vehicles are those that do not have any failure claim during their lifetime, while non-healthy ones have at least one failure. At this stage we do not, however, distinguish *when* the failure happened. To differentiate from the previous experiment, here we consider a component which is part of power train. We have also selected a balanced dataset consisting of 7.000 data samples. Then, 100 times iteration have been executed to randomly select 20% of the data as the test set and the rest of the data is considered as the training set to build the model. Receiver Operating Characteristic curve is depicted in Fig. 4a. It shows that the BG classifier performs very well in predicting the healthy and un-healthy vehicles, with $AUC = 0.86$. True negative and true positive ratios depicted in the confusion matrix (see Fig. 4b), demonstrate a high performance of the classifier (0.84 and 0.73, respectively).

Based on these results we can conclude that although the model cannot express *when* a vehicle is going to fail, it performs very well by identifying vehicles which will have a failure during their lifetime.

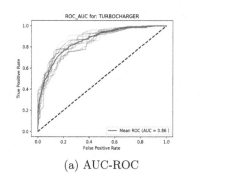
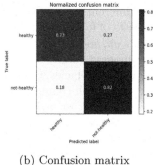

(a) AUC-ROC   (b) Confusion matrix

Fig. 4. Performance evaluation for Experiment 2.

4.3 Experiment 3

In this final experiment we intend to exploit the value of hidden information, which is described in Sect. 3.3, to optimize the performance of the classifier. Therefore we use 38 features, including the original (19 parameters) and the extracted ones (19 parameters). Otherwise the configuration and implementation is analogous to that which was used in Experiment 2.

Table 1. The comparison results in Experiments 2 and 3.

	True Positive	True Negative	AUC	# of Features	Significant Changes		Function Group
					Decreasing	Increasing	
Feature Selection	0.73	0.84	0.86	19	x	x	Turbo Charger
Feature Extraction	0.84	0.77	0.89	34	yes	yes	Turbo Charger

Table 1 illustrates the comparison between Experiments 2 and 3. Concerning AUC and true positive rates, which are particularly important for the warranty claim prediction, we can clearly observe that patterns collected from the *Extraction* module have increases the predictive performance. They lead to more than 10% improvement in predicting the failure. Although, in AUC we slightly could improve the performance, taking into account these high numbers of samples, 3% indicates an admissible improvement for this early warranty claim prediction.

5   Discussion and Conclusion

In this study, we have presented a system for early prediction of warranty claims by exploiting the information about usage of vehicles. This is a significant improvement over current industry standard, since learning from such rich data allows capturing different aspects of the component wear. The proposed prediction approach consists of four separate modules: *Data Integration, Feature Selection, Feature Extraction,* and *Learning and Prediction*. The proposed system is able to predict the number of failures over time given the vehicles usage. In addition, capable of predicting the vehicles which are going to fail in a specific time interval. This is beneficial for both commercial vehicles manufactures and for their customers, since it will lead to cost savings during warranty, and increase satisfaction of customers with the company and quality of the product.

Experimental evaluation has been done on the data collected from thousands of Volvo vehicles operating all over the world. The aim of the evaluation was to assess whether our machine learning approach is able to reliably predict the warranty claims for individual vehicles. This way the prediction can be used to improve maintenance, as well as to allow early interventions in case of quality problems. We have evaluated our proposed solution through three different experiments. In the first experiment we have demonstrated that the proposed machine learning system can reliably predict the warranty claims over time, in particular when we train the model and validate it monthly. From the results obtained by comparing monthly and seasonal predictions one can conclude that prediction of fuel system component is not dependent on seasons. The evaluation results in the second experiment show that the system is able to predict which vehicles are at risk of failure much more accurately then when this failure will occur. One limitation of this evaluation that should be remarked is that we can not predict the date of failures. This gives us a strong motivation to investigate more on this evaluation as the future work to take time interval–e.g., monthly and seasonally– into consideration to predict the risk of failures. We have learned from Experiment 3 that additional hidden information can be extracted from the logged features, and that pre-processing the data before presenting it to classifiers can lead to significant increase in the performance. In this case we have observed 10% improvement at predicting the warranty claims.

As future work, one promising extension of the proposed framework would be to extend the *Feature Extraction* module, in order to derive more information from the extracted changes in different parameters. In particular, more structured descriptions of the number and relations of subsequent changes (e.g., number of increases and decreases, or the relative trends in them) promise to be even more informative.

References

1. Altmann, A., Toloşi, L., Sander, O., Lengauer, T.: Permutation importance: a corrected feature importance measure. Bioinformatics **26**(10), 1340–1347 (2010)
2. Behrens, T., Zhu, A.X., Schmidt, K., Scholten, T.: Multi-scale digital terrain analysis and feature selection for digital soil mapping. Geoderma (2010)
3. Bradley, A.P.: The use of the area under the ROC curve in the evaluation of machine learning algorithms. Pattern Recogn. **30**(7), 1145–1159 (1997)
4. Breiman, L.: Classification and Regression Trees. Routledge, New York (2017)

5. Buitinck, L., Louppe, G.: API design for machine learning software: Experiences from the scikit-learn project (2013)
6. Chen, J., Lynn, N., Singpurwalla, N.: Forecasting warranty claims (1996)
7. Chukova, S., Robinson, J.: Estimating mean cumulative functions from truncated automotive warranty data. Modern Stat. Math. Methods Reliab. **10**, 121 (2005)
8. Corbu, D., Chukova, S., O'Sullivan, J.: Product warranty: Modelling with 2D-renewal process. Int. J. Reliab. Saf. (2008)
9. Faul, F., Erdfelder, E., Lang, A.G., Buchner, A.: G* power 3: A flexible statistical power analysis program for the social, behavioral, and biomedical sciences. Behavior Res. Methods **39**(2), 175–191 (2007)
10. Fredette, M., Lawless, J.F.: Finite-horizon prediction of recurrent events, with application to forecasts of warranty claims. Technometrics **49**(1), 66–80 (2007)
11. Hira, Z.M., Gillies, D.F.: A review of feature selection and feature extraction methods applied on microarray data. Adv. Bioinform. **2015** (2015)
12. Kalbfleisch, J., Lawless, J., Robinson, J.: Methods for the analysis and prediction of warranty claims. Technometrics **33**(3), 273–285 (1991)
13. Kaminskiy, M.P., Krivtsov, V.V.: G-renewal process as a model for statistical warranty claim prediction. In: 2000 Proceedings Annual Reliability and Maintainability Symposium, International Symposium on Product Quality and Integrity (Cat. No. 00CH37055), pp. 276–280. IEEE (2000)
14. Karim, R., Suzuki, K.: Analysis of warranty claim data: A literature review. Int. J. Qual. Reliab. Manage. **22**(7), 667–686 (2005)
15. Kleyner, A., Sanborn, K.: Modelling automotive warranty claims with build-to-sale data uncertainty. Int. J. Reliab. Saf. (2008)
16. Lawless, J.: Statistical analysis of product warranty data. Int. Stat. Rev. **66**(1), 41–60 (1998)
17. Nowaczyk, S., Prytz, R., Rögnvaldsson, T., Byttner, S.: Towards a machine learning algorithm for predicting truck compressor failures using logged vehicle data. In: 12th Scandinavian Conference on Artificial Intelligence, Aalborg, Denmark, November 20–22, 2013, pp. 205–214. IOS Press (2013)
18. Prytz, R., Nowaczyk, S., Rögnvaldsson, T., Byttner, S.: Predicting the need for vehicle compressor repairs using maintenance records and logged vehicle data. Eng. Appl. Artif. Intell. **41**, 139–150 (2015)
19. Rai, B., Singh, N.: Forecasting warranty performance in the presence of the 'maturing data' phenomenon. Int. J. Syst. Sci. **36**(7) (2005)
20. Rögnvaldsson, T., Nowaczyk, S., Byttner, S., Prytz, R., Svensson, M.: Self-monitoring for maintenance of vehicle fleets. Data Min. Knowl. Disc. **32**(2), 344–384 (2018)
21. Singpurwalla, N.D., Wilson, S.P.: Failure models indexed by two scales. Adv. Appl. Prob. **30**(4), 1058–1072 (1998)
22. Steinberg, D., Colla, P.: Cart: Classification and regression trees. Top Ten Algorithms Data Min. **9**, 179 (2009)
23. Vaiciukynas, E., Ulicny, M., Pashami, S., Nowaczyk, S.: Learning low-dimensional representation of bivariate histogram data. IEEE Trans. Intell. Transp. Syst. **19**(11), 3723–3735 (2018)
24. Wasserman, G.S.: An application of dynamic linear models for predicting warranty claims. Comput. Ind. Eng. **22**(1), 37–47 (1992)
25. Wasserman, G.S., Sudjianto, A.: A comparison of three strategies for forecasting warranty claims. IIE Trans., 967–977 (1996)
26. Wasserman, G., Sudjianto, A.: Neural networks for forecasting warranty claims. Intell. Eng. Syst. Through Artif. Neural Netw. (2001)

27. Welch, G., Bishop, G., et al.: An Introduction to the Kalman Filter (1995)
28. Wu, S.: Warranty data analysis: A review. Qual. Reliab. Eng. Int. **28**(8), 795–805 (2012)
29. Yang, Y., Pedersen, J.O.: A comparative study on feature selection in text categorization. In: ICML, vol. 97, p. 35 (1997)

Anomaly Detection in Vehicle Traffic Data Using Batch and Stream Supervised Learning

David Faial[1]([✉]) [ID], Flavia Bernardini[2] [ID], Leandro Miranda[2] [ID],
and José Viterbo[2] [ID]

[1] Instituto de Ciência e Tecnologia, Universidade Federal Fluminense,
Rio das Ostras, RJ, Brazil
dfaial@id.uff.br
[2] Instituto de Computação, Universidade Federal Fluminense, Niterói, RJ, Brazil
{fcbernardini,viterbo}@ic.uff.br,
leandromiranda@id.uff.br

Abstract. Anomaly detection in the execution time of vehicular traffic routes is important in smart cities context. This is due to identified anomaly situations allow replanning traffic in large cities. However, this is a problem of difficult treatment, since it is difficult to label such data. This fact leads to some works in literature tackle the problem using unsupervised or semi-supervised learning algorithms. Techniques for labeling data allow using supervised learning. On the other hand, data streams raises questioning the performance of batch and stream learning algorithms. The purpose of this work is to present a process of anomaly detection in the execution time of vehicle traffic routes. Part of the proposed process was evaluated, using data collected in real scenarios. The results were promising for two of the evaluated routes.

Keywords: Vehicle traffic data · Anomaly detection ·
Stream supervised learning

1 Introduction

The number of people living in cities is increasing. Thus, several services need to be offered with quality to their citizens. In an overview, the concept of Intelligent Cities encompasses different terms organized in three dimensions [12]: (i) Technological Dimension, based on the use of infrastructures, especially ICT, to improve and transform life and work within a city in a relevant way; (ii) Human Dimension, based on people, education, learning and knowledge (key factors for a so-called intelligent city); and (iii) Institutional Dimension, based on governance and policy, as cooperation between stakeholders and institutional governments is very important in designing and implementing smart initiatives. Several initiatives have taken place in several cities, in Brazil and in the world, to address at least one of these dimensions, or at the intersections, since a city be a living environment in which people are inserted and at the same time transform this environment. In a more specific view, linked to the technological dimension, the concept of Smart Cities originated from the term Information City, where Information and Communication Technologies (ICTs) become relevant in

© Springer Nature Switzerland AG 2019
P. Moura Oliveira et al. (Eds.): EPIA 2019, LNAI 11804, pp. 675–684, 2019.
https://doi.org/10.1007/978-3-030-30241-2_56

city services. According to [7], a city is defined as smart when its investments feed sustainable economic development by a better quality of life, be they in human and social capital, or in urban transport and ICT infrastructure, highlighting the wise management of natural resources through participatory government. Thus, urban mobility is seen, in this more specific view, as an axis that needs attention in the cities, which indicates priority in this theme.

In many large cities, such as Rio de Janeiro and cities that surround it often present traffic problems such as accidents, repairs, among others, which may increase the time of delay in routes realized in these cities. One difficulty with this scenario is to identify events related to traffic anomalies. In addition, another difficulty is to label the data as anomalous. An alternative is to use the human being in the process. However, when a huge amount of data is available, techniques to make an initial estimate of what is considered an anomaly can be used.

The purpose of this work is to present a process for labeling and detection of anomalies in the execution time of routes by vehicles in urban traffic. Batch machine learning and stream learning algorithms can be used in our presented process. To evaluate the performance of the process, data collected from real scenarios are used. The results were considered promising.

This work is divided as follows: Sect. 2 presents the theoretical reference for anomaly detection and batch learning and data stream, as well as related work. Section 3 presents the proposed process. Section 4 presents the performed experiments and the obtained results. Section 5 presents a literature review, which shows some possible new ways to future work and improvements of our process. Section 6 concludes this work and presents future work.

2 Background

Anomaly detection is related to problems of finding patterns in data that do not agree with the expected behavior. These nonconformities are better known as anomalies, but can also be called discrepancies, outliers, discordant observations, exceptions, aberrations, surprises, peculiarities or contaminants. It is an important topic because data anomalies can translate real, often critical anomalies in a wide variety of domains [10].

A simple approach to anomaly detection is to define a region that represents the normal behavior of the domain under analysis and to consider any observations outside this region as an anomaly. It seems like a simple approach, but several factors make it a challenge, such as: (i) It is often difficult to define a region that represents normal behavior with comprehensiveness for all possible cases. In addition, the definition of the boundary between normal and anomalous behavior is not precise, making it possible for an anomalous observation close to the border to be classified as normal, and vice versa. (ii) When anomalies are the result of malicious actions, in many cases, those responsible for actions will adapt to make their actions look normal, making it more difficult to define what is normal. (iii) In many domains, normal behavior evolves over time, and thus a representation of normal behavior at a given moment may not be representative in the future. (iv) The accuracy needed to identify an anomaly may be different in the various application domains. For example, in the medical field a small deviation in a patient's body temperature may characterize an anomaly, while a similar variation in the stock of a market may be considered as normal. The application of a technique developed for a domain is not from simple transference to another. (v) It is difficult to find labeled data for the training and validation of anomaly detection models, and when they are found they are generally unbalanced. (vi) The data may contain noises similar to real anomalies, which makes it difficult to distinguish between one and the other. Most existing anomaly detection techniques solve only one set of problems. This is due to the applicability of the techniques is induced by the nature and availability of the data, types of anomalies and the domain of the application.

Based on the existing labels, anomaly detection can use one of the following three approaches [10]: Supervised, Semi-Supervised and Unsupervised Anomaly Detection. Supervised Anomaly Detection typically constructs a prediction model for normal vs. anomaly based on a training dataset. The new occurrences are compared with the model to determine which class it fits into. There are two important issues: (i) The number of anomalous instances is much smaller than the number of normal instances in the training set. Different works tackle unbalanced classes for anomaly detection [4]; (ii) The difficulty of obtaining a representative dataset, mainly for the class of anomaly. Techniques for injecting artificial anomalies into the data for the training set are presented in some works [1, 14]. One technique that has been widely used to overcome the two previous issues is One Class Classification - OCC, which consists of using only instances of a class in training [16]. For Semi-supervised Anomaly Detection, the training dataset has labels only for a portion of the instances, usually small and with the normal class. A limited set of anomaly detection studies only assume the anomalous class in the training set and is not commonly used. The difference of OCC and semi-supervised anomaly detection is that in the first all training instances are labeled with the normal class; in the second, only one part of this set is labeled with the normal class and the other part is unlabeled. Unsupervised Anomaly Detection uses unlabeled training data. It usually assumes that normal instances are more frequent than anomalies [10].

The nature of the data is one of the key factors in anomaly detection. Input data is usually collections of instances, also called objects, registers, points, vectors, patterns, events, cases, observations, or entities. Each instance is described by a set of features, also called attributes, variables, characteristics, fields or dimensions [15]. Examples may be related to other instances, such as in sequential, spatial, temporal, and graphical data. This relationship between the instances can be an important feature for the domain. Labels typically associated with data in detecting anomalies are "normal" or "anomalous". Obtaining accurate labeled data as well as a set representing all types of domain behavior is expensive. It is more difficult to obtain labels for anomalous behavior than for normal behavior, and in some cases the occurrence of anomalous event is rare.

Although supervised learning for anomaly detection presents many issues, in this work we propose and investigate the effectiveness of using supervised anomaly detection. Historically, research and application of machine learning has focused on batch learning where typically a stationary database is available, and it is expected that the data do not change over time. In this case, all training set data is available in memory, and an algorithm learns a decision model after iteratively processes all data.

The logic behind this practice is that the instances are generated randomly according to some stationary distribution [6]. However, the use of supervised learning techniques for stream learning can be promising, since the data are presented as data streams, also referred to as a continuous data stream. This characteristic in the data led to new needs for machine learning, *i.e.*, the need for (i) new sampling techniques, (ii) new learning algorithms, (iii) ways of processing data at the speed at which they are available, and (iv) ability to forget outdated data [2, 6]. Batch learning algorithms can learn concepts in data stream. For this, a period of data to perform the models training is necessary [6]. On the other hand, several learning algorithms are available in the literature to process data stream [2], including decision tree induction algorithms [5] for predictive learning, among others.

3   A Process for Labeling and Anomaly Detection in Vehicle Traffic Data

For the construction of the process, we initially carried out a study on real data to identify the characteristics and a better understanding of the issues inherent to the problem explored. Afterwards, we build the process and validate part of the process using the data available. At the end of this paper, we present the limitations of the work, and how the process can be adapted to scenarios where the user is available to improve the detection of anomaly.

3.1   Data Source and Characteristics

To model the problem of anomaly detection in vehicle routes, real data were collected through a partnership with a company that offers navigation products, which provided access to an API for collection of route instances. To simplify our experimentation process, we explore three route sizes, which we call long, medium, and short. The first is performed on average at 39 km, the second on average at 6 km, and the third on average at 3 km. Data were collected from the routes in the city of Rio de Janeiro. The journeys were selected because they were carried out frequently in the daily life of people in Rio, so they were considered good candidates for the analyzes of this work.

Data Characteristics: We collected 52,000 instances of routes in six months, with a five-minute interval between collections. The instances were collected in an intercalated way, that is, every five minutes an instance of each route was collected (short, medium and long). Each route instance contains the following features: Distance in meters; Total travel time in seconds; Departure date; Departure time; Day of the week; and Post-Holiday or not. These data were also used by Pinto [13]. An example of an instance of a long route is shown in Table 1.

Table 1. A long route instance.

Distance (meters)	Total time	Departure date	Departure time	Day
27069	2905	01-04-2018	16	Sunday

We analyzed the data to extract interesting information from the collected data. Thus, we construct a scatter plot for each type of route (short, medium or long), in which the horizontal axis represents the day of the week, the vertical represents the route duration time of the route. Figures 1 and 2 shows the graph constructed for short and medium route data. We can check some rather non-standard course times for Saturday, Sunday and a few more for Monday. Particularly on Saturday, we can see that most routes are grouped in a range of 3200 to 3800 s. From this analysis, we built our process, presented in what follows.

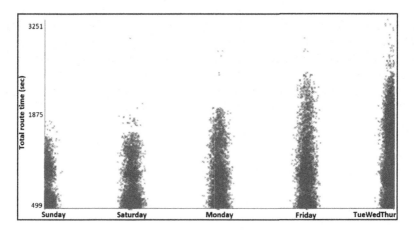

Fig. 1. Short route data dispersion graph

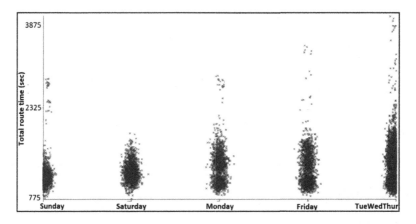

Fig. 2. Medium route data dispersion graph

3.2 Process Definition

Figure 3 shows the proposed process for detection of vehicle traffic anomalies. Step 1 is responsible for collecting data, as presented in the previous section. After, the data must be pre-processed (Step 2). In this step, features referring to the anomalous data context, such as days of the week, for example, can be constructed. This was inspired by what was observed in the analysis of the data collected. Step 3 is responsible for labeling the data. In a first collection, when there is no machine learning model built and there is no interaction with the user, as is the case of the experiments performed in this work, data can be automatically labeled using statistical techniques. After the first iteration of the cycle, there is a built model, which is used to predict anomalies. In this way, the model is used to diagnose anomalous execution times. In addition, the data can also be labeled either by the automatic technique or by the user, when available. After labeling, data goes to Step 4, so that an update of the model is performed, if a learning algorithm is used for stream learning, or for a new model to be constructed (batch learning). The process repeats itself constantly. A parameter of the execution of this process is related to the time of collection of data for construction of the models when using batch algorithm. Similarly, if using stream learning algorithms, another parameter is the time that must be considered for concept drift, parameter of several stream learning algorithms, including VFDT, used in the experiments of this work.

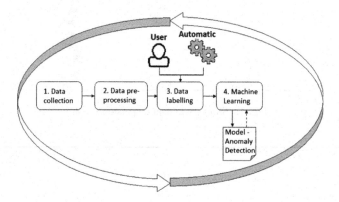

Fig. 3. A process for detection of vehicle traffic data anomalies

In this work, we evaluated only the first cycle of the presented process, considering only the automatic labeling through statistical techniques, and the use of batch learning and stream learning algorithms. The results obtained are presented in the next section.

4   Case Study

4.1   Dataset

Before inputting the collected instance to the algorithm, day of the week columns need to be unpivoted, to avoid being considered different features by the algorithm. Table 2 shows the same route before pre-processing.

After pre-processing, the instance format has the following features: Distance, Route execution time, Departure date, Departure time, Monday, Tuesday, Wednesday,

Table 2. A collected long route instance.

Dist. (m)	Route time (s)	Departure date	Departure time	Day of the week	Post-holiday
27069	2905	04/01/2018	4 pm	Tuesday	0

Thursday, Friday, Saturday and Sunday. The day of the week is indicated by a "1" in its respective feature name, and "0" for all the other feature days. Table 3 shows an instance of a long route instance, executed on a Tuesday, at 4 pm, and it is not a day after any holiday (Post-Holiday feature equals zero).

Table 3. A post-processed long route instance.

Dist. (m)	Route Time (s)	Dep. Date	Dep. Time	Mon.	Tue.	Wed.	Thur.	Fri.	Sat.	Sun.	Post-Holiday
27069	2905	04/01/2018	4 pm	0	1	0	0	0	0	0	0

To label each instance as anomalous or not anomalous, the total route time (in seconds) was considered. Considering Saturday's route times, we note that most routes are grouped in a range of 3200 to 3800 s. Within this group of routes on Saturday, the journey time between them differs from a maximum of 10.5%. The first route that runs away from this pattern differs by 25.7% from the route duration time of the previous route. For Saturday, this is a limiting value if the route execution time of a route is anomalous or not, that is: a route duration time that is equal to or above the limiting value is considered anomalous for the Saturday. We repeat the same technique for every day of the week.

The limiting value defines the separation of the two route classes: anomalous and normal (non-anomalous). To calculate the limiting value, it is necessary to verify the variation of each travel time of an instance I in relation to the travel time of an earlier instance I-1. If the variation between I and I-1 travel time is less than or equal to twice the variation between instances I-1 and I-2, instance I is considered normal, otherwise it is considered anomalous. It should be noted that twice the variation between instances is a parameter of the technique. Table 4 shows the numbers of anomalous instances for each route. 10,000 instances were used per route type collected. It is observed that, as in most cases of anomaly detection, the imbalance of the data is quite large.

Table 4. Number of anomalous instances per route.

Route type	#Normal	#Anomalies
Long	9893	107
Medium	9781	219
Short	9942	58

4.2   Model Construction

Using the technique presented for data labeling, Weka tools [9] were used to construct the models using batch algorithms, and MOA [2] were used to construct the models using data stream. We used the SVM (Support Vector Machine) and M5 (Model Decision Tree) algorithms as batch algorithms, and the Very Fast Decision Tree (VFDT) algorithm as a stream learning algorithm. To generate the stream from the original data file, MOA uses the *ArffFileStream* function. Since the data is temporal, we construct the models in the first 2/3 of the collected data (66%) and evaluate the performance in the remaining data (34% of the data). Table 5 shows the percentage of correctly classified anomalies. We can observe that the VFDT is the one that presents the best performance, among all the algorithms used. In addition, the choice of data stream learning algorithms (stream learning algorithms) facilitates the execution of the proposed process by us.

Table 5.   Number of anomalous instances per route.

Route type	SVM	M5	VFDT
Long	60,68%	59.26%	81.90%
Medium	46.32%	52.02%	74.01%
Short	26.27%	29.72%	38.8%

5   Literature Review

Ruiz-Blázquez, Muñoz-Organero and Sánchez Fernández [3] explore the use of unsupervised and supervised learning algorithms, including logit and SVM, for finding outliers traffic congestion in smart city traffic data from vehicle sensors. A small part of the data was manually labeled for the supervised task. Related to unsupervised algorithms, their results show that even if the data are not normally distributed all the techniques present similar outcomes. In general, clustering methods work worse than density-based methods. Regarding to supervised algorithms, SVM showed a slightly better behavior. This work strengthen our presented process. However, the authors did not explore stream learning algorithms.

Markou, Rodrigues and Pereira [11] present a methodology for identifying anomalies on traffic networks and correlates them with special events using internet data. They justify their work due to, in some occasions, unexpected and unwanted demand patterns are noticed in the traffic network that lead to system failures and cost implications. Their main subject of interest is the investigation of why traffic congestion is happening as well why there are demand fluctuations in days were there are no apparent reasons for the occurrence of such phenomena. The authors used kernel density analysis, considered as an Unsupervised Anomaly Detection approach. Their methodology allowed to detect the affected areas as well as the significance of the observed differences compared to the average day. In our work, we used a simple technique to label the data in the first interaction of our process, that we consider an unsupervised approach, to allow using supervised learning algorithms. So, improving our labeling approach with more robust techniques could be useful in future work.

A different approach is proposed by Gu, Zhen and Chen [8]. They propose to mine tweet texts to extract incident information on both highways and arterials as an efficient and cost-effective alternative to existing data sources. The process of adaptive data acquisition establishes a dictionary of important keywords and their combinations that can imply traffic incidents (TI). Mining tweets holds great potentials to complement existing traffic incident data in a very cheap way. This is an interesting approach to increment our proposed approach in the future.

6 Conclusions and Future Work

The main goal of this work was to present a process for the diagnosis of anomalies during execution of vehicle routes. One hypothesis confirmed by the analyzed and collected data is that there are events in the traffic that lead to much longer execution times than are usually executed. A problem in the process of detecting anomalies is in the labeling of the data. For this reason, we use techniques inspired by descriptive statistics for data labeling. However, in the proposed process, it is also possible to use user-labeled data for data labeling, and to combine both labeling for updating the models.

As a first experiment of process evaluation, we needed to know if the constructed features allow the detection of anomalies. In addition, another question is related to the performance of the algorithms. Our question was whether batch algorithms outperform stream learning algorithms. In the results obtained in our experiments, we observed that the algorithm of stream learning used obtained the best performance. In addition, it is possible to detect, with high accuracy, medium and long route anomalies. However, the results of the short route are not very promising. Further analysis and studies on the data set of this route need to be made. These results may have been influenced by the constructed features, or the exploited algorithms are not the most adequate. It is important to observe that the use of data visualization facilitated the experimentation phase, since the success of experiment attempts could be guided by the visual structure of the data when displayed in graphs and other types of visualization, such as scatter plots presented in this paper.

In future work, besides we presented in Sect. 5, we intend to collect more data to (i) evaluate the composition of the labeling, and how the performance of the algorithms used; and (ii) extending the experiments using other batch and data stream algorithms.

References

1. Abe, N., Zadrozny, B., Langford, J.: Outlier detection by active learning. In: Proceedings of 12th ACM SIGKDD International Conference on Knowledge Discovery and Data Mining, Philadelphia, PA, USA, pp. 504–509. ACM (2006)
2. Bifet, A., Gavaldà, R., Holmes, G., Pfahringer, B.: Machine Learning for Data Streams: with Practical Examples in MOA. MIT Press, Cambridge (2018)

3. Ruiz-Blázquez, R., Muñoz-Organero, M., Sánchez Fernández, L.: Evaluation of outliers detection algorithms for traffic congestion assessment in smart city traffic data from vehicle sensors. Int. J. Heavy Veh. Syst. **25**(3/4), 308–321 (2018)
4. Chawla, N.V., Japkowicz, N., Kotcz, A.: Editorial: special issue on learning from imbalanced data sets. SIGKDD Explor. Newsl. **6**(1), 1–6 (2004)
5. Domingos, P., Hulten, L.: Mining high-speed data streams. In: Proceedings of 6th ACM SIGKDD International Conference on Knowledge Discovery and Data Mining, pp. 71–80 (2000)
6. Faceli, K., Lorena, A.C., Gama, J., Carvalho, A.C.P.L.F.: Artificial Intelligence: A Machine Learning Approach (*in Portuguese*). Rio de Janeiro (2011)
7. Giffinger, R., Gudrun, H., Haindlmaier, G.: Smart cities ranking: an effective instrument for the positioning of the cities. ACE Archit. City Environ. **4**(12), 7–25 (2010)
8. Gu, Y., Zhen, Q., Chen, F.: From twitter to detector: real-time traffic incident detection using social media data. Transp. Res. Part C Emerg. Technol. **67**, 321–342 (2016)
9. Hall, M., Frank, E., Holmes, G., Pfahringer, B., Reutemann, P., Witten, I.H.: The WEKA data mining software: an update. SIGKDD Explor. Newsl. **11**(1), 10–18 (2009)
10. Lima, H.T., Bernardini, F.: Spatiotemporal anomaly detection applied to flow measurement points in natural gas production plants. J. Inf. Data Management **8**(2), 163 (2017)
11. Markou, I., Rodrigues, F., Pereira, F.C.: Demand pattern analysis of taxi trip data for anomalies detection and explanation. In: Proceedings of 96th Annual Meeting of the Transportation Research Board (2017)
12. Nam, T., Pardo, T.A.: Conceptualizing smart city with dimensions of technology, people, and institutions. In: Proceedings of 12th Annual International Digital Government Research Conference–DGO 2011, pp. 282–291 (2011)
13. Pinto, A.: Proposal of a Method for Predicting Vehicle Traffic Conditions (*in Portuguese*). Master in Computing Systems Master Thesis, Universidade Federal Fluminense (2016)
14. Steinwart, I., Hush, D., Scovel, C.: A classification framework for anomaly detection. J. Mach. Learn. Res. **6**, 211–232 (2005)
15. Tan, P.-N., Steinbach, M., Kumar, V.: Introduction to Data Mining. Addison-Wesley Longman Publishing Co. Inc, Boston (2005)
16. Tax, D.: One-Class Classification: Concept-Learning in the Absence of Counter-Examples. Ph.D Thesis – Technische Universiteit Delft (2001)

Predicting the Impact of Text-Reading Using Decision Trees

Eftihia G. Nathanail[1]($\boxtimes$), Panos D. Prevedouros[2], Md. Mintu Miah[2],
and Rafaela De Melo Barros[2]

[1] University of Thessaly, 38334 Volos, Greece
enath@uth.gr
[2] University of Hawaii at Manoa, 2540 Dole Street, Honolulu, HI 96822, USA

Abstract. Various road safety analyses prove that cell phone usage cause driver distraction which, in turn, has become a leading cause for crashes. Various studies have focused on different cell phone operations such as hand-held or hand-free conversation, number dialing and text writing and reading and examined how they affect driving performance. Research efforts have been also placed on investigating the effects of sociodemographic characteristics on distraction and related them to the reaction of the drivers under distraction and the resulting speed, lane changes, lateral placement, deceleration, incidents and many other variables. The primary aim of this paper is to implement a decision trees approach in predicting the degree of influence of text reading on driving performance and associate it with self-reported behavioral and sociodemographic attributes. Data were based on a sample of 203 taxi drivers in Honolulu, who drove on a realistic driving simulator. Driving performance measures were collected under non-distraction and text-reading conditions. Among them, line encroachment incident and maximum driving blind time changes were used in combination with sociodemographic characteristics (gender, age, experience, educational level, race) and behavioral constructs (past behavior, behavior, behavioral beliefs, control beliefs, risk appreciation and descriptive norms) and decision trees were built.

The analysis revealed that important predictors for maximum driving blind time changes are sociodemographic and past behavior attributes. The accuracy of the prediction increases in the case of line encroachment incident changes, with the addition of behavioral beliefs, control beliefs, risk appreciation, descriptive norms and past behavior.

Keywords: Distraction · Text reading · Road safety

1 Introduction

Driver distraction is the status under which drivers refrain from focusing on driving, as they get engaged in other side tasks not related to driving. When such a condition occurs, driver awareness, decision making and driving performance diminish and the probability of road incidents or crashes increase [1].

© Springer Nature Switzerland AG 2019
P. Moura Oliveira et al. (Eds.): EPIA 2019, LNAI 11804, pp. 685–696, 2019.
https://doi.org/10.1007/978-3-030-30241-2_57

The National Highway Traffic Safety Administration (NHTSA) reported that 3,477 people were killed and 391,000 were injured in 2015 in accidents involving distracted driving; and 14% of the total traffic crashes are identified as distracted accidents [1]. Other studies estimate 25-30% of accidents are attributed to distracted drivers [2]. Two main sources of distraction have been identified in literature, inside and outside the vehicle. Inside the vehicle distraction is caused by usage of on-board mobile devices, mainly cell phones, conversation with passengers, eating, drinking, smoking and other. These tasks seem to mainly affect driving performance and safety. In particular to on board devices, hand-held or hand-free conversation, number dialing, and text writing and reading have been proven to affect significantly driving behavior and performance [3].

Texting affects variability in speed, following distance, line encroachments and missed lane changes, and increase the time that the driver does not have eyes on the road [4]. Most studies have considered sociodemographic characteristics, mainly age and gender as the main influencers for the impact of distracted driving, owing to texting. Young drivers seem to be the age group being most vulnerable to driving inattention [5], caused by visual, auditory, biomechanical and cognitive distraction [6]. Older drivers have a larger lateral control variation than younger age groups, when they are occupied in visual and manual tasks [7]. Both age and gender affect speed adjustment [8] and lane excursions [9] under distraction. Professional drivers have attracted the attention of researchers and found that they are less prone to distraction than non-professional [10, 11].

Self-reported behavioral data in combination with sociodemographic characteristics and parameters, such as past behavior and beliefs has not been attempted yet. The primary aim of this paper is to implement decision trees approach in predicting the degree of influence of text reading on driving performance and associate it with self-reported behavioral and sociodemographic attributes. Data were based on a sample of 203 taxi drivers in Honolulu, who drove on a driving simulator. Driving performance measures were collected under non-distraction and text-reading conditions. Among them, line encroachment incident and maximum driving blind time changes were used in combination with sociodemographic characteristics (gender, age, experience, educational level, race) and behavioral constructs (past behavior, behavior, behavioral beliefs, control beliefs, risk appreciation and descriptive norms) and decision trees were built.

2   Method

2.1   Data Collection

The study was conducted on the driving simulator of the University of Hawaii's Traffic and Transportation Laboratory (TTL) in the Department of Civil and Environmental Engineering. The simulator was provided by the company Charley's Taxi and Limousine which operates a fleet of approximately 250 vehicles in Honolulu. The 203 participants in the experiment were drivers who work for the same company, and they were recruited as part of the requirements for their continuing education insurance credits. Before the experiment, drivers had to complete a questionnaire addressing two sets of attributes. The first set included demographic questions on gender, age, education level and driving experience; the second, investigated behavioral aspects related to driving and following the principles of behavioral modeling [12], it included (Table 1) the components, below:

- Behavior: "While driving, how often do you make or take phone calls, read emails or text messages, send emails or text messages, surf the net or social media, use GPS or map service" (Attributes B1.1–B1.5)
- Behavior: "What is your typical speed when you drive on a freeway with 55 mph speed limit and light traffic, on a major urban street with speed limit 25 mph and moderate traffic, on a rural highway with speed limit 45 mph" (Attributes B2.1–2.6)
- Control Beliefs: "What are the chances of getting arrested after drinking and driving in Hawaii", "If all drivers are trained in safe driving, how safe would be the roads?", "What are the chances of getting a speeding ticket?" (Attributes CB1–3)
- Descriptive Norms: "What are the chances of a driver in your area to get a speeding ticket?" (Attribute DN1)
- Risk Appreciation: "How many trips did you drive at night, in the last two weeks?" and "Do you drive less when it rains?" (Attributes R1–2)
- Behavioral Beliefs: "Do you think that enforcement is too strict in Hawaii?" (Attribute BB1)
- Past Behavior: "Have you been stopped by the police", "issued a ticket", "been involved in an accident", been involved in an accident owing to using your cell phone" (Attributes PB1–PB6)

Then, the subjects drove the simulator for 10–15 min, to familiarize themselves with the reaction of the various controls, such as steering wheel, accelerator and brakes. After given some explanations about the driving scenario of the experiment, all drivers drove along a rural highway with two lanes per direction and frequent merging and diverging sections with moderate traffic, for approximately 9 min. During their drive, subjects had to read the messages every time they were displayed on the mobile device installed on the dashboard. Three texts were displayed from low to moderate complexity, similar to the messages they receive on their business-as-usual. Their reactions were recorded, including maximum blind driving time and line encroachment incidents. These two were selected to be further analysed here, as the first is the direct measurement of the distraction owing to text reading and the latter its impact.

2.2 Data Analysis

The database was formulated containing the demographic, self-reported behavioural attributes and driving performance measurements with and without text reading. Some further analysis was done to the driving performance, to calculate their difference between the two conditions.

The analysis was based on Structure-Activity Relationships and it used decision trees. Decision tree models can be used to select the number and kind of variables required for the conduct of a research, assess the relative importance of these variables and create non-linear decision boundaries that fit data very well. They handle any missing values in a dataset, predict outcomes based on past data and improve the handling of variables by allowing merging values when their number is too high [13]. Decision Trees are among the popular approaches to represent classifiers with extended applicability in many disciplines, such as statistics, data mining, machine learning etc. [14].

The most commonly used decision trees are the CART and the C4.5 based model. However, C4.5. proves to be more flexible than CART, as it allows for more that binary decisions. For ranking test, C4.5 uses information-based criteria, while CART the Gini diversity index. CART prunes trees using a cost-complexity model (the parameters of this model are estimated by cross-validation) while C4.5 uses a single-pass algorithm derived from binomial confidence limits. Still, the greatest advantage of C4.5 is linked with its attitude when some case values are unknown, as it apportions the case probabilistically among the outcomes, while CART looks for surrogate tests that approximate the outcomes.

The J48 classifier is a decision tree implementation of the C4.5 algorithm in the open source software WEKA (Waikato Environment for Knowledge Analysis) [15–20]. It has proved that it produces more correctly classified objects than the Naive Bayes classifier [16]. J48 is also shown to produce better results Support Vector Machines (SMVs), a supervised learning model, while having the same classification accuracy (100%) with Multilayer Perceptron (MLP), which is an artificial neural network model [20]. The C4.5 algorithm and its J48 WEKA version have been used in a wide range of cases across many disciplines [15, 18, 19, 21, 22].

Changes of the two dependent variables, maximum blind driving time (mean values) and line encroachment incidents were calculated between the no texting and texting conditions. They were further transformed into nominal variables, following the specification of the classifier. Three values were considered, reflecting the decision tree class labels "more", "null" and "less", corresponding to higher, equal and less driving blind time or encroachment incidents, respectively, while texting as compared to the no texting. The list of the dependent variables and influencing attributes is depicted in Table 1.

3 Data Analysis and Results

3.1 Participants and Driving Performance

The sample was composed of 203 participants, 175 male (86.2%) and 28 female (13.8%). All of them are professional taxi drivers. The mean age is 53.3 years with standard deviation 11.58 and the mean driving experience is 32.71 years with standard deviation 12.44. Most of them are between 46–55 (31.5%) and 56–65 (36.5%) years old. The majority are high school graduates (39.4%) followed by some college education (23.2%) and bachelor's degree (20.2%). Most of them are Korean (38.9%), followed by Japanese (13.3%), Chinese (11.8%), Filipino (9.9%) and Vietnamese (9.4%).

Table 1. Decision tree attributes.

Code	Maximum blind drive time changes	Line encroachment incident changes	Attribute
DE1		node	gender
DE2	Root node	node	age
DE3			race
DE4	node	node	education
DE5	node	node	driving.experience
B1.1		node	phone.calls
B1.2	node		read.messages
B1.3			send.messages
B1.4			surf.the.net
B1.5	node	node	use.maps
B2.1		node	speed.on.freeway.with.speed.limit.of.55.mph.in.light.traffic
B2.2			more.than.speed.on.freeway.with.speed.limit.of.55.mph.in.light.traffic
B2.3			speed.on.a.major.city.street.with.speed.limit.of.25.mph.moderate.traffic.and.green.light
B2.4			more.than.speed.on.a.major.city.street.with.speed.limit.of.25.mph.moderate.traffic.and.green.light
B2.5	node		speed.on.a.rural.highway.with.a.speed.limit.of.45.mph
B2.6			more.than.speed.on.a.rural.highway.with.a.speed.limit.of.45.mph
CB1		node	What.do.you.think.are.the.chances.of.arrest.after.drinking.and.driving.in.Hawaii
CB2		Root node	If.all.drivers.are.trained.in.safe.driving.the.roads.would.be.safer
CB3		node	chance.of.you.receiving.a.speeding.ticket.in.Hawaii
DN1			chance.for.the.typical.driver.in.your.area.of.receiving.a.speeding.ticket
R1			In.the.last.two.weeks.how.many.trips.did.you.drive.at.night
R2		node	Do.you.drive.less.when.it.rains
BB1		node	Do.you.think.that.blood.alcohol.level.is.too.strict.in.Hawaii
PB1			Have.you.taken.your.vehicle.for.inspection.and.maintenance

(continued)

Table 1. (*continued*)

Code	Maximum blind drive time changes	Line encroachment incident changes	Attribute
PB2			Have.you.been.stopped.by.the.Police
PB3		node	Were.you.issued.a.citation
PB4			Have.you.had.a.DUI
PB5			Have.you.been.involved.in.a.traffic. accident
PB6			did.any.of.these.accidents.involve. your.cell.phone.use
Total number of attributes	6	13	

Table 2 indicates the mean values of the driving performance indicators, along with their statistical significance. As the data are not normally distributed and belong to two dependent groups (same subjects under the two conditions), the non-parametric Wilcoxon Z test was performed. It is observed that both indicators have shown to be affected by the texting, and the have been both increased significantly.

Table 2. Driving performance while no texting and texting (Source: 3)

Driving performance indicator	Mean (Std. Dev.)		Diff.	N	Wilcoxon Z	Sig.
	No texting	Texting				
Maximum blind driving time (s)	1.2 (1.56)	2.25 (1.96)	1.05	203	−8.364	0.000
Line encroachment incidents	0.9 (1.42)	4.07 (3.92)	3.17	203	−9.857	0.000

4 Building the Classification Tree Models

Each decision tree is formulated by the main classifier (root node), which depicts the basic attribute for the classification, followed by other attributes, called interior nodes, and ending at the class labels (leaf or end nodes). Every class label is described by the correctly and the incorrectly classified instances (observations used by the tree) when following the specific path from the root to the leaf node. Paths starting at the same node are mutually exclusive, and the classification is such that it maximizes the Information Gain [22]. As a decision tree development may lead to a very large number of leaf nodes, the selected J48 classifier was set-up with a post-pruning method. Post-pruning is the process of evaluating the decision error (estimated % of misclassifications) at each decision junction and propagating this error up the tree. At each junction, the algorithm compared the weighted error of each child node versus the misclassification error if the child nodes were deleted and the decision node were assigned the class label of the majority class.

Maximum Blind Driving Time Change. The tree developed for the maximum blind driving time change has 15 leaves and its size is 29 (total number of nodes). The main classifier (root node) is the age (DE2) and the branches formulated for subjects more years old and less or equal than 40 years old.

The tree has classified correctly 85.7868% of the instances with a high statistical significance indicated in the value of the Kappa statistic 0.5289. Table 3 depicts the summary of the tree statistics and Table 4 shows the performance of the tree for each of the three examined classes. Expected accuracy by class is high for more and less time, but there are no correctly classified instances for no change (null), as all 8 observed instances were classified in the other two classes. This is not considered as a problem, owing to the small proportion of null instances over the total (0.6%). For the other two classes, true positive rates range from 0.56 to 0.97 and class recall is high calculated to a weighted average of 0.858. The Receiver Operator Characteristic (ROC) under the curve is 0.806 on the average, indicating a high statistical dependence. The confusion matrix in Table 5 indicates the classification of the instances by actual observation class. The exact number of the correctly/not correctly classified instances is represented in the tree graph inside each parenthesis at the end nodes (Fig. 1).

Table 3. Statistics for the classification of maximum blind driving time changes.

Correctly Classified Instances	88.3249%
Incorrectly Classified Instances	11.6751%
Kappa statistic	0.7051
Mean absolute error	0.1251
Root mean squared error	0.2488
Relative absolute error	42.9391%
Root relative squared error	65.4402%
Total Number of Instances	197

Table 4. Decision tree accuracy by class of maximum blind driving time changes.

Class	TP Rate[a]	FP Rate[b]	Precision[c]	Recall[d]	F-Measure[e]	MCC[f]	ROC Area[g]	PRC Area[h]
1 (null)	0.000	0.000	?	0.000	?	?	0.806	0.145
2 (more)	0.974	0.500	0.871	0.974	0.920	0.583	0.801	0.908
3 (less)	0.556	0.037	0.769	0.556	0.645	0.592	0.827	0.636
Weighted Avg.	0.858	0.395	?	0.858	?	?	0.806	0.827

[a]True Positive Rate (correctly identified)
[b]False Positive Rate (incorrectly identified)
[c]Precision is the probability that a (randomly selected) retrieved instance is relevant
[d]Recall is the probability that a (randomly selected) relevant instance is retrieved in a search
[e]F-Measure is the harmonic mean of precision and recall (F-Measure = 2* (Precision* Recall)/ (Precision+Recall))
[f]Matthews Correlation Coefficient
[g]The area under the ROC curve as the Wilcoxon-Mann-Whitney statistic
[h]The area under the precision-recall curve

There are 7 paths that lead to an anticipated increase in the number of maximum blind time while text reading, as compared to no text reading. The attributes which affect the increase are depicted in Table 1, whereas the combination of their values is indicated in Fig. 1.

Table 5. Confusion matrix of maximum blind driving time changes.

Observations	Classified as		
	Null	More	Less
Null	0	6	2
More	0	149	4
Less	0	16	20

Line Encroachment Incident Change. The tree developed for the line encroachment incident change has 27 leaves and its size is 52 (total number of nodes). The main classifier (root node) is the control belief parameter (CB2) which examines the perception of the subjects on how to enhance road safety.

The tree has classified correctly 88.32% of the instances with a high statistical significance indicated in the value of the Kappa statistic 0.7051. Table 6 depicts the summary of the tree statistics and Table 7 shows the performance of the tree for each of the three examined classes. Expected accuracy by class is also high. True positive rates range from 0.64 to 0.97 and class precision and recall are high in all classes with an weighted average of 0.883. Their harmonic mean (F-measure) is equal to 0.877 and the Receiver Operator Characteristic (ROC) under the curve is 0.916, indicating a high statistical dependence. The confusion matrix in Table 8 indicates the classification of the instances by actual observation class. The exact number of the correctly/not correctly classified instances is represented in the tree graph inside each parenthesis at the end nodes (Fig. 2).

Table 6. Statistics for the classification of line encroachment incident changes.

Correctly Classified Instances	88.3249%
Incorrectly Classified Instances	11.6751%
Kappa statistic	0.7051
Mean absolute error	0.1251
Root mean squared error	0.2488
Relative absolute error	42.9391%
Root relative squared error	65.4402%
Total Number of Instances	197

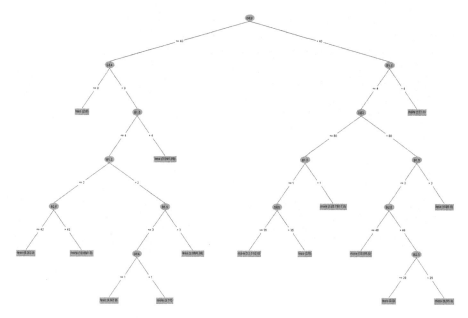

Fig. 1. Decision tree of maximum blind driving time changes.

Table 7. Decision tree accuracy by class of line encroachment incident changes.

Class	TP Rate[a]	FP Rate[b]	Precision[c]	Recall[d]	F-Measure[e]	MCC[f]	ROC Area[g]	PRC Area[h]
1 (less)	0.667	0.023	0.778	0.667	0.718	0.690	0.963	0.781
2 (more)	0.972	0.315	0.891	0.972	0.930	0.722	0.906	0.947
3 (null)	0.636	0.012	0.913	0.636	0.750	0.726	0.932	0.781
Weighted Avg.	0.883	0.233	0.883	0.883	0.877	0.719	0.916	0.901

[a]True Positive Rate (correctly identified)
[b]False Positive Rate (incorrectly identified)
[c]Precision is the probability that a (randomly selected) retrieved instance is relevant
[d]Recall is the probability that a (randomly selected) relevant instance is retrieved in a search
[e]F-Measure is the harmonic mean of precision and recall (F-Measure = 2* (Preci-sion*Recall)/ (Precision + Recall))
[f]Matthews Correlation Coefficient
[g]The area under the ROC curve as the Wilcoxon-Mann-Whitney statistic
The area under the precision-recall curve

There are 14 paths that lead to an anticipated increase in the number of line encroachment incidents while text reading, as compared to no text reading. The attributes which affect the increase are depicted in Table 1, whereas the combination of their values is shown in Fig. 2.

Table 8. Confusion matrix of line encroachment incident changes.

	Classified as		
Observations	Less	More	Null
Less	14	7	0
More	2	139	2
null	2	10	21

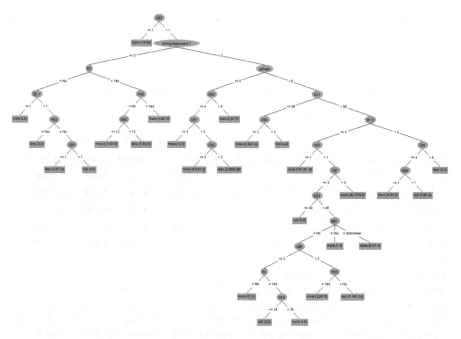

Fig. 2. Decision tree of line encroachment incident changes.

5   Conclusions

Decision trees have been developed to estimate the impact of text reading while driving. Two main distraction variables have been examined, maximum blind driving time, which is the direct effect of text reading and line encroachment incidents, which are the further consequences of distraction. A set of attributes was considered including demographic characteristics, and self-reported behavioral constructs; behavior, control beliefs, behavioral beliefs, descriptive norms, risk appreciation and past behavior.

From the analysis of the data it is observed that 78% of the drivers increased the maximum time driving blind and the rest either reduced it or were not affected, while text reading. Similarly, 73% of the drivers increased the line encroachment incidents while text reading than in the case of no reading, while 17% were not affected. Decision trees predicted these changes with an accuracy of 85.7868% for the maximum blind driving time and 88.32% for the line encroachment incidents.

The associations built between these two variables and the attributes affecting them showed a strong impact of age on maximum blind driving time changes, supported by education and driving experience, and behaviour. Line encroachment incident changes are mainly affected by the perception of the drivers about the measures to increase road safety, and also by most of the demographic characteristics and a combination of constructs related to behaviour, control beliefs, behavioral beliefs, risk appreciation and past behaviour. Associations of the attributes with the dependent variables indicated high statistical dependence with a high accuracy.

The study outcomes suggest that the driving performance is not solely affected by the typical demographic attributes, met widely in literature, but the behavioral profile should be also considered and incorporated in the estimation of the impact of distractive tasks while driving.

References

1. NHTSA, Research Note Distracted Driving 2013. Dot Hs 812 132, 2013, vol. 2015: p. 1–5. doi.org/DOT HS 811 379
2. National Highway Traffic Safety Administration. Traffic Safety Facts Research Notes 2016: Distracted Driving.S. Department of Transportation, Washington, DC: NHTSA (2015). https://crashstats.nhtsa.dot.gov/Api/Public/ViewPublication/812517External. Accessed 25 March 2019
3. Miah, M. MD. Prevedouros, P.D.: Effects of Reading Text While Driving: Analysis of 200 Honolulu Taxi Drivers on a Simulator. Paper 19–00455 presented at the 98th Annual Meeting of the Transportation Research Board (2019)
4. Hosking, S., Young, K., Regan, M.: The effects of text messaging on young drivers. Hum. Factors Ergon. Soc. **51**(4), 582–592 (2009). https://doi.org/10.1177/0018720809341575
5. Buckley, L., Chapman, R., Sheehan, M.: Young driver distraction: State of the evidence and directions for behavior change programs. J. Adolesc. Health **54**(5 Suppl), S16–S21 (2014)
6. Ranney, T. Mazzae,, E., Garrott, R., Goodman, M.M.: NHTSA driver distraction research: past, present, and future. NHTSA report. 2000, 10 May 2006. http://www-nrd.nhtsa.dot.gov/departments/nrd-13/driverdistraction/PDF/233.PDF
7. Bao, S., Guo, Z., Flannagan, C., Sullivan, J., Sayer, J.R., DeBlanc, D.: distracted driving performance measures. Transp. Res. Rec. J. Transp. Res. Board **2518**, 68–72 (2015)
8. Ayalon, A., Barkai, R., Frumkin, A., Karkanas, P.: Geochronology, Speed variation for different drivers, situation and road geometry; simulator and survey analysis, p. 1–40. Taylor & Francis, Milton Park (2010). https://doi.org/10.1016/j.quagei.2010.03.003
9. Choudhary, P., Velaga, N.R.: Analysis of vehicle-based lateral performance measures during distracted driving due to phone use. Transp. Res. Part F: Traffic Phychology Behav. **44**, 120–133 (2017). https://doi.org/10.1016/j.trf.2016.11.002

10. Adamos, G., Nathanail, E.: Do road safety communication campaigns work? How to assess the impact of a national fatigue campaign on driving behavior. Transp. Res. Rec. J. Transp. Res. Board **2364**, 62–70 (2013)
11. Hankins, M., Frenc, D., Horne, R.: Statistical guidelines for studies on the theory of reasoned action and the theory of planned behaviour. Phychology Health **15**, 151–161 (2000)
12. Song, Y., Lu, Y.: Decision tree methods: applications for classification and prediction. Shanghai Arch. Psychiatry **27**(2), 130–135 (2015)
13. Breiman, L., Friedman, J.H., Olshen, R.A., Stone, C.J.: Classification and Regression Trees. Wadsworth Publishing Group, Belmont (1984)
14. Gao, W., Tang, W., Wang, X.: Application of an improved C4.5 algorithm in performance analysis. Appl. Mech. Mater. **380–384**, 1681–1684 (2013)
15. Patil, T., Sherekar, S.: Performance analysis of Naive Bayes and J48 classification algorithm for data classification. Int. J. Comput. Sci. Appl. **6**(2), 256–261 (2013)
16. Kapoor, P., Rani, R.: Efficient decision tree algorithm using J48 and reduced error pruning. Int. J. Eng. Res. Gen. Sci. **3**(3), 1613–1621 (2015)
17. Kaur, G., Chhabra, A.: Improved J48 classification algorithm for the prediction of diabetes. Int. J. Comput. Appl. **98**(22), 13–17 (2014)
18. Acharia, T., Yang, I., Lee, D.: Application of J48 decision tree for the identification of water bodies using landsat 8 OLI imagery. In: 2nd International Electronic Conference on Sensors and Applications (2015)
19. Ahishakiye, E., Omulo, E., Taremwa, D., Niyonzima, I.: Crime prediction using decision tree (J48) classification algorithm. Int. J. Comput. Inf. Technol. **6**(3), 188–195 (2017)
20. Dota, M., Cugnasca, C., Barbosa, D.: Comparative analysis of decision tree algorithms on quality of water contaminated with soil. Ciencia Rural **45**(2), 267–273 (2015)
21. Yan, N., Ju, W., Fang, H., Sato, R.: Application of J48 decision tree classifier in emotion recognition based on chaos characteristics. In: International Conference on Automation, Mechanical Control and Computational Engineering, Changsha, China (2015)
22. Kumar, A.: Design and Applications of Decision Trees. Int. J. Comput. Sci. Trends Technol. **2**(4), 94–98 (2014)

Artificial Life and Evolutionary Algorithms

Benchmarking Collective Perception: New Task Difficulty Metrics for Collective Decision-Making

Palina Bartashevich[(✉)] and Sanaz Mostaghim

Faculty of Computer Science, Otto von Guericke University, Magdeburg, Germany
{palina.bartashevich,sanaz.mostaghim}@ovgu.de
http://www.ci.ovgu.de

Abstract. This paper presents nine different visual patterns for a Collective Perception scenario as new benchmark problems, which can be used for the future development of more efficient collective decision-making strategies. The experiments using isomorphism and three of the well-studied collective decision-making mechanisms are conducted to validate the performance of the new scenarios. The results on a diverse set of problems show that the real task difficulty lies not only in the quantity ratio of the features in the environment but also in their distributions and the clustering levels. Given this, two new metrics for the difficulty of the task are additionally proposed and evaluated on the provided set of benchmarks.

Keywords: Collective decision making · Collective perception · Benchmarking · Multi-agent systems · Isomorphism

1 Introduction

In the past decade, researchers have shown an increased interest in the study of self-organizing collective decision-making (further denoted as CDM) using multi-agent and swarm robotics systems. There are two typical scenarios to test the performance of such systems, Site Selection and Collective Perception [9,13]. However, unlike in optimization, there are no standard benchmark functions (artificial landscapes) for these scenarios. In this paper, we intend to propose a new set of benchmarks, particularly for Collective Perception, along with two new metrics to quantify the *difficulty of the task* for more comprehensive validation and comparison of new CDM methodologies.

We focus on the Collective Perception [14], where the individuals move in an environment with a certain pattern and make a collective decision about the specific features derived from this pattern. In particular, in this paper, the final collective decision has to be taken on which color is prevalent in the scene.

The Site Selection mechanisms [9] are slightly different. There, the individuals start their movements from a certain region in the environment, the "nest", explore alternative sites for other opinions and go back to the "nest" to exchange the new explored opinions with other individuals. Although the latter is mostly observed in nature, i.e. the behaviour of honeybees and ants, multiple returns

© Springer Nature Switzerland AG 2019
P. Moura Oliveira et al. (Eds.): EPIA 2019, LNAI 11804, pp. 699–711, 2019.
https://doi.org/10.1007/978-3-030-30241-2_58

to the "nest" cost extra time and energy, which are ones of the most critical limitations in the robotic systems. While in the collective perception s cenario the agents are able to act and decide directly "on the fly" during the exploration without going back to the starting point. Among possible applications are the monitoring of the air and water quality, the concentration estimate of $CO2$ and oxygen in the burning buildings, or the frequency evaluation of the scattered natural resources in the hard-to-reach areas.

The most common benchmark scenario for collective perception is a randomly generated 2D square grid, mostly equiprobably painted with two colors, black and white [12,14]. In this paper, we aim to develop new benchmark problems representing various features which can be used as a baseline for further validation of the CDM strategies. Our benchmark contains a set of nine different patterns, taken from the matrix visualization literature [2–4]. Unlike the existing Collective Perception scenario with random distribution of the features [8,14], these visual patterns contain certain structural information, i.e. clustering, which can cover a diverse representation of various real-world scenarios. In order to validate the proposed benchmarks, we investigate the influence of different feature distributions on the performance of the existing CDM methods, which are primarily used in the current state-of-the-art [13], the *majority rule* (DMMD), the *voter model* (DMVD) and the *direct comparison* (DC).

In order to verify how general is the proposed benchmarking approach, we refer to the recent study [1], which has shown a positive impact of a special kind transformation in the environment, namely isomorphism, on the CDM performance. Different from [1], here, we use isomorphism to prove that the color-ratio difficulty, mostly examined in the previous research, is an intrinsic property of a certain CDM strategy, while the clustering level of the features is the actual *difficulty of the task*. To support this claim, we introduce two new metrics to specify the task difficulty for the CDM and perform the analysis of the proposed benchmarks based on them.

The paper is organized as follows. In Sect. 2, we provide the related work on collective perception. Afterwards, we describe new task difficulty metrics along with the multi-agent simulation in Sect. 3. Section 4 presents the evaluation of the obtained results and the paper is concluded in Sect. 5 including some discussion.

2 Related Work

The Collective Perception scenario was originally introduced in 2010 by Morlino et al. [8], who studied how a swarm of robots can collectively encode the density of black spots on the ground using flashing signals. In [14], Valentini et al. compared the performance of several CDM strategies in the context of Collective Perception, considering two black-and-white static grid setups: the easiest one with the proportion of the prevailing color closely twice of another, and the most difficult one, characterized by almost equal color ratio. Later, Strobel et al. in [12] tested the same CDM approaches on more percentage variations. In [6], Ebert et al. investigated for the first time a 3-feature case and demonstrated a new decentralized decision-making algorithm with a dynamic task allocation strategy to classify a 3-colored grid. Prasetyo et al. in [10] has considered an application of a CDM to the dynamic Site Selection problem, where the quality of two sites is changing over time. Recently, Valentini has also published a book [13] about the design and analysis of CDM strategies for the best-of-n problems. However, in the application part, attention mainly for $n = 2$ is paid. So far, all the research in this area has studied either the quality or the total amount of the features in the environment (i.e. global information), as a measure for the *task difficulty*, ignoring their actual distributions.

3 Methodology

For the generation of benchmark environments, we refer to the matrix visualization literature [2–4] and consider nine of the most important visual patterns, which can be observed in visual matrices (see the top of Fig. 2). In order to prevent the attachment of the further simulation results to the concrete configuration, for each type of the pattern and the color-ratio, a random environment with the same visual structure as the whole class corresponding to this pattern is generated. For some color ratios (e.g. 48% black and 52% white, see top Fig. 2), the patterns may contain some artifacts, due to the insufficient amount of available cells to shape the pattern. That is, random black cells placed out of the pattern or, vice a verse, white cells disrupting the pattern can be observed.

3.1 Pattern Metrics

In order to classify the considered patterns, we propose the following metrics:

– *Entropy* (E_c): It measures the density of the clusters in pattern P.

To calculate E_c, we need to detect clusters C_i in P. Without loss of generality, we assume that black color determines the pattern and, hence, clustering. Therefore, let $|C_i|$ denotes the number of black cells that belong to the cluster C_i and N_{bl} is the total number of black cells in P. Then, the metric E_c is defined as follows:

$$E_c = \frac{H_c^{max} - H_c}{H_c^{max}} \tag{1}$$

$$H_c = -\sum_{i=1}^{M} \frac{|C_i|}{N_{bl}} \log_2 \frac{|C_i|}{N_{bl}} \tag{2}$$

$$H_c^{max} = -\sum_{N_{bl}} \frac{1}{N_{bl}} \log_2 \frac{1}{N_{bl}}, \tag{3}$$

where M is the number of clusters, H_c^{max} is the maximum entropy. The value of E_c increases with decreasing number of clusters ($E_c \to 1$ is ordered, $E_c \to 0$ is random). However, the value of E_c does not characterize how this cluster (or clusters) looks like, i.e. is it compact (e.g. as a "block") or more sparse (e.g. as a "chain"). To address this issue, we also consider the following metric:

- *Moran Index* (MI): It estimates the level of connectivity between clusters (if any) in pattern P.

In our case, MI is calculated as the correlation of the colors between adjacent cells c_i and c_j in P, where N is the total number of cells:

$$MI = \frac{N}{\sum_{ij}^{N} w_{ij}} \cdot \frac{\sum_{ij}^{N} w_{ij}(c_i - \bar{c})(c_j - \bar{c})}{\sum_{i}^{N} (c_i - \bar{c})^2}. \tag{4}$$

The value of c_i is equal to 1 if it is black, and 0 if it is white; $\bar{c}$ is the mean of all cell values in P and $\bar{c} = N_{bl}/N$. The values of w_{ij}, $w_{ij} = w_{ji}$, define the the degree of spatial closeness of the cells c_i and c_j, i.e. $w_{ij} = 1$ if the cells c_i and c_j have a common side, i.e. placed as ⊹ (where ⊹ shows which cells neighbour a central one), otherwise $w_{ij} = 0$. The more ⊹-connected black cells are in a pattern, the closer the value of MI is to 1. When colors tend to be more randomly distributed, then $MI \to 0$ (i.e. random pattern gives $MI = 0$). Alternation of white and black (like in a chessboard) brings $MI \to -1$.

- *Color Ratio*: It describes the *"task difficulty"* from [12,13].

It is calculated as $\rho_b^* = \frac{N_{bl}}{N_{wh}}, \rho_b^* \in [0,1]$, taking into account that $N_{wh} > N_{bl}$. The more visible is the difference between the amount of colors, the lower is the value of ρ_b^* (e.g. $34\% - 66\%$, $\rho_b^* \approx 0.52$). As soon as the proportions of the colors are coming closer to each other, $\rho_b^* \to 1$ (e.g. $48\% - 52\%$, $\rho_b^* \approx 0.92$).

3.2 Multi-agent Simulation

To conduct the experiments, we implement a multi-agent simulation along with nine pattern generators in MatlabR2017a. The environment is defined by a square grid of 20×20 cells, 1×1 unit each, painted over in black and white. Without loss of generality, we consider that in all the considered environments the white color is prevailing. As in the previous research [12], we consider 100 iterations in simulation as 1 s, and we plot the simulation environment each 10 iterations (i.e. 0.1 s). We use a swarm of 20 agents, initially assigned with half for opinion white and half for black, keeping the other agents parameters similar to Valentini et al.'s work [15]. Each agent can be in one of the two alternating states: (1) *exploration*, where it moves and only estimates the quality of its current opinion, or (2) *dissemination*, when it moves and only exchanges its own opinion with the others. At the end of the state (2), it makes a decision on either to keep or to switch its current opinion. The communication between agents is set only pairwise for each 0.1 s in a random order within the distance of 5 units and only if both of them are in states (2). Each agent logs the opinions of its neighbors during the last 0.3 s of its (2) state and takes the last 2 opinions to decide based on one of the mentioned in Sect. 1 decision-making strategies (further denoted as DMs). Two metrics, *Exit probability* (E_N) and *Consensus time* ($T_N^{correct}$), are used to evaluate the performance of DMs. E_N measures the ratio of successful runs among all simulations. The simulation is considered successful, if the collective reached consensus on the correct option. $T_N^{correct}$ defines the number of iterations until all the individuals come up with the same opinion.

4   Experimental Study

4.1   Pattern Characteristics

In order to determine how the patterns quantitatively differ from each other, we evaluate the mean values and the standard deviations of *Entropy* and *Moran Index* over 100 generations of each pattern (see Fig. 1-left). According to the preliminary calculations, the metrics' values mainly differ only within a pattern type and are not affected by the change of the color ratio (as intended). The Kruskal-Wallis ANOVA analysis of MI values reveals that there is a significant difference ($p < 0.01$) between all the grid-patterns, except for *"Off-diagonal"* and *"Block"*. Referring to the same analysis of the E_c values, we group the patterns correspondingly to their non-significant differences with the others (see Fig. 1): (1) *"Off-diagonal"* and *"Block"* (in blue); (2) *"Stripe"* and *"Band-Random-Width"* (in green); (3) *"Band-Stripe"*, *"Bandwidth"* and *"Star"* (in red). Therefore, patterns belonging to the same group have a non-significant difference ($p > 0.01$) in distributions of their E_c values. However, all of them are significantly different ($p < 0.01$) according to their Moran indexes, except of the first group. *"Band"* and *"Random"* do not belong to any of the formed groups and are significantly different ($p < 0.01$) from all the others in both parameters. We expect similar results in the CDMs performance on the patterns within the same group.

4.2   Experiment I - Influence of the Patterns

The goal of the first experiment is to show the influence of different pattern configurations and their respective color ratios on the performance trend of CDMs. We perform 40 simulation runs with maximum 400 s each. That is, if the swarm was not able to reach the consensus during these 400 s or came to the wrong decision before the time expired, the simulation is stopped and the run is considered as unsuccessful.

Figure 2 shows the mean consensus time calculated only among successful runs and the exit probability obtained on nine different patterns for the three tested CDMs within eight variants of color ratio. The curves are created by local regression over boxplots (not reported here) with shading areas of 95% confidence interval. The DMVD strategy shows rather stable results for all "difficulties" (ρ_b^*) in both $T_N^{correct}$ and E_N on all the patterns (except for *P5-Stripe*), while the performance of DMMD and DC differs among the patterns. However, the exit probability of DMVD for the most of the patterns (i.e. P3-P9) is mainly observed by the chance level. *P1-Random* does not have any structure and was primarily the focus of the previous studies. We also obtained here the similar trend for the CDMs as in [12].

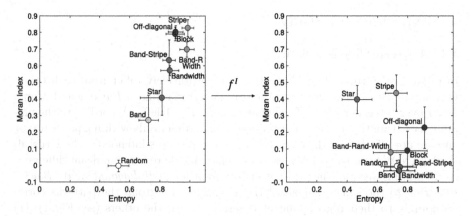

Fig. 1. Scatter diagram of the statistics for patterns characteristics (means (points) and standard deviations (bars)) "before" (left) and "after" applying isomorphism (right). Colors indicate the belonging to one and the same group. (Color figure online)

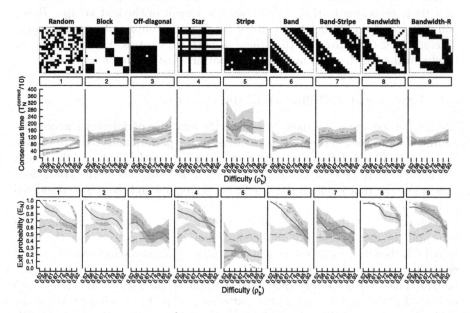

Fig. 2. Consensus time ($T_N^{correct}$) and exit probability (E_N) over eight types of the task difficulty ρ_b^* for each of nine patterns (top row). Dashed (red), solid (green) and dot-dashed (blue) lines correspond to the DMVD, DMMD and DC strategies respectively. (Color figure online)

Patterns *P4-Star* (performed by horizontal and vertical lines) and *P6-Band* (by diagonals of the upper and lower triangles) show similar results to *P1-Random* in $T_N^{correct}$ for all three CDM strategies. In addition, we obtain here the lowest value of consensus time for DMMD among all the other considered patterns and DMs (of around 40 s), which is slightly increasing for higher ρ_b^*. Nevertheless, the $T_N^{correct}$ performance of DC strategy on P4 and P6 is worse than on P1, increasing in $T_N^{correct}$ and rapidly decreasing in E_N after $\rho_b^* \approx 0.72$. The E_N result for DMMD is similar and reaches the chance level by $\rho_b^* \approx 0.92$. The considered patterns, i.e. P1, P4 and P6, are characterized by $MI < 0.5$ and different values of E_c.

P8-Bandwidth (visual rhombus-like enclosure with fixed width around the main diagonal, $MI = 0.572 \pm 0.029$, $E_c = 0.866 \pm 0.06$) is "the second best" pattern after P1, P4 and P6, where DMMD is still one of the fastest strategies among the others with "ups and downs" in the performance between $\rho_b^* = [0.61, 0.79]$ and $\rho_b^* = (0.79, 0.92]$ respectively. DC, here, is characterized by the linear growth in $T_N^{correct}$ with increasing ρ_b^*. For $\rho_b^* \approx 0.92$ the DMs strategies perform actually the same (even with equal exit probabilities), while for other ρ_b^* the E_N resembles the similar trend as in P1 for all DMs.

In patterns *P9-Bandwidth-Rand* (the same as P8 but with random width, $MI = 0.698 \pm 0.046$, $E_c = 0.98 \pm 0.048$) and *P7-Band-Stripe* (the same as P6 but lines are clustered, $MI = 0.633 \pm 0.122$, $E_c = 0.861 \pm 0.041$), there is no single DM strategy which is better than the other one in terms of consensus time (DC even shows the highest $T_N^{correct}$ in P7 with the linearly decreasing E_N, getting lower than the chance level for $\rho_b^* > 0.79$). On P9, the E_N trend of DMMD and DC is similar.

P2-Block and *P3-Off-diagonal* (for both $MI \approx 0.8$, $E_c \approx 0.9$) are characterized by similar visual structures with the difference that in P3 there are only two rectangular coherent areas in the corners of off-diagonal, while in P2 the blocks must cover the whole main diagonal and only for higher ρ_b^* some possible blocks are added in the off-corners. The performance of DMMD strategy here is worse than DMVD and is not significantly better than DC for all ρ_b^*. In P3, DMMD and DC have higher $T_N^{correct}$ than in P2 along with non significantly different exit probabilities, which are lower than in P2, and both are characterized by the rapid decline to the chance level, which does not significantly change after $\rho_b^* > 0.72$.

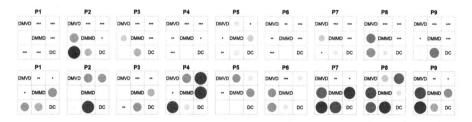

Fig. 3. The heatmaps of p-values (i.e. $^*p < .05$, $^{**}p < .01$, $^{***}p < .001$) according to the Mann-Whitney U-test indicating a statistically significant difference in the performance between DMs on each pattern. The lower triangular (LT) part of the matrix corresponds to the results "before" a nd the upper to the "after" applying isomorphism (top row: $\rho_b^* \approx 0.52$; bottom row: $\rho_b^* \approx 0.92$).

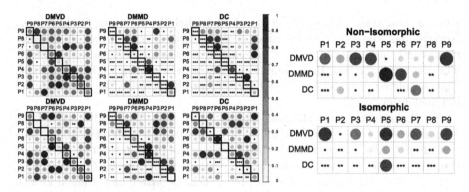

Fig. 4. The heatmaps of significance levels according to the Mann-Whitney U-test for the difference in the performance of the DMs within the patterns (on the left) and on one DM strategy with itself between the highest and the lowest values of ρ_b^* on each pattern (on the right). Left: The lower (LT) and the upper triangular (UT) parts of the matrix correspond to the results "before" and "after" isomorphic changes (top row: $\rho_b^* \approx 0.52$; bottom row: $\rho_b^* \approx 0.92$). The diagonal elements show how the performance of a certain DM strategy on one pattern changes after applying isomorphism. The size of the circles reflects the same value as the color intensity.

P5-Stripe (clustered vertical/horizontal lines, $MI = 0.827 \pm 0.051$, $E_c \rightarrow 1$) is a notable exception among the other patterns. The performance of DMVD strategy here is the best one among the others in both $T_N^{correct}$ and E_N with a slight decreasing of consensus time for higher ρ_b^*, followed by DMMD, while DC shows its the worst performance. The DC strategy completely fails for $\rho_b^* > 0.79$ (with $E_N \rightarrow 0$) and is characterized by the high variability for lower ρ_b^* with the lowest E_N than the other DMs. However, the exit probability for both DMMD and DC strategies here is less than by the chance.

Discussion. The obtained results confirm our initial claim that the real **task difficulty** lies not in the amount of prevailing feature (i.e. ρ_b^*) but in the distribution of the features. Our analysis shows that in the patterns with low density of clustering ($MI \leqslant 0.6$ and $E_c < 0.8$: P1, P4, P6, P8) the DMMD performs the best, while for the patterns with higher clusterization ($0.6 < MI \leqslant 0.8$ and $E_c \rightarrow 1$: P2, P3, P5, P7, P9) the DMMD performance significantly drops. P5 is the hardest pattern among all of the others ($MI > 0.8$, $E_c \rightarrow 1$), where the DMMD has the highest time with the lowest probability of reaching the consensus. The DC strategy shows mostly similar consensus time as DMMD within the patterns and the color-ratios but with higher variability and more rapidly decrease in the exit probability at higher ρ_b^* than the DMMD (in P4, P5, P7 and P9). It also completely fails in P5 (after $\rho_b^* > 0.79$). The results obtained by the DMVD in all of the considered patterns are mostly due to the chance. Figures 5 and 6 (both left) support the above conclusions.

4.3   Experiment II - Isomorphic Patterns

In order to evaluate the generalizability of the proposed benchmarks, in the second experiment, we use isomorphic transformations, firstly considered in [1]. Such transformations allow us easily to construct a large variety of structurally identical objects at the global level (i.e. environments with similar connectivity interactions and sharing the same amount of features). There, the grid of black-and-white cells is identified with a certain undirected graph via its incidence matrix [1], resembling the corresponding pattern with '0's and '1's instead of white and black colors. To construct an isomorphic environment to the given, we multiply an incidence matrix of the current environment, $M \in \mathbb{Z}_2^{k \times k}$, on two random permutation matrices, $P, Q \in \mathbb{Z}_2^{k \times k}$, as follows: $M' = PMQ$. Doing by this, we aim to investigate the performance of CDM even on a more diverse set of benchmark problems. In the following, we fix two extreme color ratios (the easiest and the hardest ones), namely $\rho_b^* \approx 0.52$ and $\rho_b^* \approx 0.92$, and study the influence of isomorphism on the consensus time and the exit probability within various patterns using different CDMs. Additionally, we also investigate how the isomorphic changes differ between the patterns.

The results show a clear difference in the performance of the CDM strategies in both metrics, $T_N^{correct}$ and E_N, before (Figs. 5 and 6-left) and after applying the isomorphism on the patterns (Figs. 5 and 6-right). The comparison is supported by Figs. 3 and 4 showing the levels of significant difference in the consensus time between the DMs, patterns and color-ratios, according to the Mann-Whitney U-test. From the data in Fig. 4, we can see that the DMVD strategy has no significant difference on its performance either within the patterns "before" or "after" the isomorphic changes nor within the "difficulties". Along with Figs. 5 and 6, one can claim that it completely relies on a random chance. For the DMMD and DC strategies the picture is different. The DMMD and DC performances are significantly improved on isomorphic patterns with respect to the initial ones (see the diagonal elements in Fig. 4-left), and are characterized by a decrease in the consensus time and increase in the exit probability for both considered "difficulties" (Figs. 5 and 6). While the $T_N^{correct}$ values, obtained on the patterns before the transformation, mostly significantly differ between each other (see the LT-parts in Fig. 4), after transformations the differences in $T_N^{correct}$ within the patterns disappear (especially for $\rho_b^* \approx 0.92$, see the UT-parts in Fig. 4). However, for $\rho_b^* \approx 0.52$, P4-Star and P5-Stripe indicate a statistically significant increment in $T_N^{correct}$ among the other "after"-patterns but both are not statistically different between each other for both DMMD and DC (see P4-P5 columns and rows of the UT-parts in Fig. 4-left). Interestingly, the DMs strategies indicate a significantly different performance in the consensus time with each other on all "after"-patterns (except P5, where only DMVD and DC differ with $p < 0.05$) for $\rho_b^* \approx 0.52$ (see the UT-parts in the top row of Fig. 3). But this is not true for the "before" case (see the top row, the LT-parts in Fig. 3): there is even no significant differences between the DMMD and the DC on all the patterns (except P1). For $\rho_b^* \approx 0.92$ (see the bottom row, UT-parts in Fig. 3), the differences within all the DMs strategies on "after"- P2, P4-Star,

P. Bartashevich and S. Mostaghim

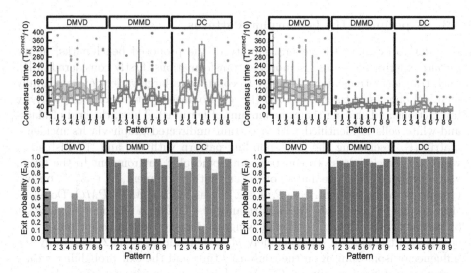

Fig. 5. Comparison of consensus time ($T_N^{correct}$) and exit probability (E_N) within patterns "before" (left) and "after" applying isomorphism (right) for the "task difficulty" of $\rho_b^* \approx 0.52$. The curves are fitted via local regression with shading areas representing 95% confidence interval.

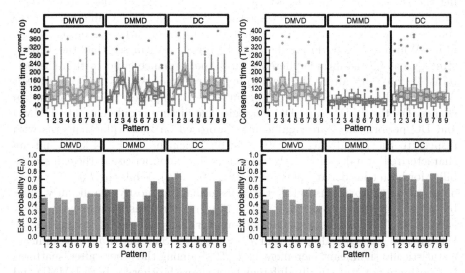

Fig. 6. The same comparison as in Fig. 5 but for the "task difficulty" of $\rho_b^* \approx 0.92$.

P5-Stripe and P8 are non-significant, and even on the other patterns there is no significant difference in the DMMD and the DC performance. However, the consensus time of the strategies itself has significantly decreased after isomorphism. In summary, the DC strategy yields the best performance on isomorphic patterns, followed by the DMMD and then the DMVD, regardless of the color ratios. The analysis in Fig. 4-right shows that the isomorphic transformations do not considerably change the influence of the ρ_b^*-"difficulty" on the DMs. That is, the DMMD is significantly worsening on one and the same "before"- and "after"-patterns (i.e. P1-P3 and P8), while for DC this holds for all "before"- (except P2, P6 and P7) and "after"-patterns (except P5 and P9).

Discussion. Although an isomorphism preserves the global structure of the environment, the characteristics of the patterns with high density of clustering after applying isomorphic mappings have changed. From the data in Fig. 1, we can see that almost all "after"-patterns are characterized by $E_c \in [0.7, 0.8]$ and significantly decreased MI values (i.e. $MI \approx 0$), except for *P3-Off-diagonal*, *P4-Star* and *P5-Stripe*, where $MI \in [0.2, 0.5]$. Interestingly, exactly on these exceptions for both ρ_b^* (the easiest and the hardest) the analysis illustrates a significant increase in $T_N^{correct}$ w.r.t. other patterns. These findings support the results of our first experiment, indicating that the higher density of clustering significantly degrades the performance of CDM. To sum up, the difference in the performance of a certain CDM approach vanishes on isomorphic patterns and narrows to its intrinsic properties, thereby underlining the generalization and necessity of the proposed benchmarks.

5   Discussion and Conclusion

In this paper, we extended a Collective Perception scenario, used in the swarm robotics research, with nine different patterns to test the generalizability of the existing collective decision-making strategies and to promote the future development of the new ones. Previous research examined only a single and the easiest example of the environment, considering the proportion of the features as a "task difficulty" for decision makers. However, our benchmark study reveals that the "difficulty" connected with the ratio of the colors (i.e. global information) is mainly related to the intrinsic property of a certain CDM method, while the distribution of the features in the environment (i.e. local information) is the actual *difficulty of the task*. In this scope, we also proposed and examined two new metrics that have shown to be a good choice to define the difficulty and to predict the behavior of the CDM. Experiments on isomorphic test problems were also conducted to support the study. Isomorphism has been already proven to be an effective tool to design a diverse set of digital cognitive games [11]. Similar, in this work, we used isomorphism to diversify the set of the benchmarks. At the same time, our results fully support the previous research [1] on a bigger set of problems, where isomorphic changes in the environment result in the speed up of CDM. From this side, a collective perception is considered as a cognitive activity mediated in human brains. There, isomorphism is described as the brain moving objects in order to facilitate a decision-making process. While for humans it is more relevant to mentally re-order the objects to enhance the problem solving [5] (e.g. to figure out the prevailing color), to make direct changes in the real environment with acting swarm of robots seems to be problematic. However, if the agents will be able to build individually or collectively a cognitive map of the environment during the exploration process (i.e. latent learning [7]), isomorphic transformations can be used inside their "inner world" [16] to assist a CDM, without the need to be adapted to the specific scenario.

References

1. Bartashevich, P., Mostaghim, S.: Positive impact of isomorphic changes in the environment on collective decision-making. In: Proceedings of the ACM Genetic and Evolutionary Computation Conference Companion (2019)
2. Behrisch, M., Bach, B., Hund, M., Delz, M., et al.: Magnostics: Image-based search of interesting matrix views for guided network exploration. IEEE Trans. Vis. Comput. Graph. **23**(1), 31–40 (2017)
3. Behrisch, M., Blumenschein, M., Kim, et al.: Quality metrics for information visualization. EuroVis STAR (2018)
4. Behrisch, M., Bach, B., Henry Riche, N., Schreck, T., Fekete, J.D.: Matrix reordering methods for table and network visualization. Comput. Graph. Forum **35**(3), 693–716 (2016)
5. Bilge, A.R., Taylor, H.A.: Framing the figure: Mental rotation revisited in light of cognitive strategies. Mem. Cognit. **45**(1), 63–80 (2017)
6. Ebert, J.T., Gauci, M., Nagpal, R.: Multi-feature collective decision making in robot swarms. In: Proceedings of the 17th International Conference on Autonomous Agents and Multi-Agent Systems (2018)
7. Jensen, R.: Behaviorism, latent learning, and cognitive maps: Needed revisions in introductory psychology textbooks. Behav. Anal. **29**(2), 187–209 (2006)
8. Morlino, G., Trianni, V., Tuci, E.: Collective perception in a swarm of autonomous robots. In: Proceedings of the International Joint Conference on Computational Intelligence, vol. 1, pp. 51–59. SciTePress (2010)
9. Passino, K.M., Seeley, T.D.: Modeling and analysis of nest-site selection by honeybee swarms: the speed and accuracy trade-off. Behav. Ecol. Sociobiol. **59**, 427–442 (2005)
10. Prasetyo, J., De Masi, G., Ranjan, P., Ferrante, E.: The best-of-n problem with dynamic site qualities: achieving adaptability with stubborn individuals. In: Dorigo, M., Birattari, M., Blum, C., Christensen, A.L., Reina, A., Trianni, V. (eds.) ANTS 2018. LNCS, vol. 11172, pp. 239–251. Springer, Cham (2018). https://doi.org/10.1007/978-3-030-00533-7_19
11. Sedig, K., Haworth, R.: Creative design of digital cognitive games: Application of cognitive toys and isomorphism. Bull. Sci. Technol. Soc. **32**(5), 413–426 (2012)
12. Strobel, V., Castelló Ferrer, E., Dorigo, M.: Managing byzantine robots via blockchain technology in a swarm robotics collective decision making scenario. In: Proceedings of the 17th International Conference on Autonomous Agents and Multi-Agent Systems, pp. 541–549 (2018)
13. Valentini, G.: Achieving Consensus in Robot Swarms: Design and Analysis of Strategies for the best-of-n Problem. SCI, vol. 706. Springer, Cham (2017). https://doi.org/10.1007/978-3-319-53609-5

14. Valentini, G., Brambilla, D., Hamann, H., Dorigo, M.: Collective perception of environmental features in a robot swarm. In: Dorigo, M., et al. (eds.) ANTS 2016. LNCS, vol. 9882, pp. 65–76. Springer, Cham (2016). https://doi.org/10.1007/978-3-319-44427-7_6
15. Valentini, G., Ferrante, E., Dorigo, M.: The best-of-n problem in robot swarms: Formalization, state of the art, and novel perspectives. Front. Robot. AI **4**, 9 (2017)
16. Ziemke, T., Jirenhed, D.A., Hesslow, G.: Internal simulation of perception: A minimal neuro-robotic model. Neurocomputing **68**, 85–104 (2005)

Maximum Search Limitations: Boosting Evolutionary Particle Swarm Optimization Exploration

Mário Serra Neto[1]($\boxtimes$) (iD), Marco Mollinetti[2], Vladimiro Miranda[3] (iD),
and Leonel Carvalho[3] (iD)

[1] INESC TEC and University of Porto (FCUP), Porto, Portugal
mario.t.ribeiro@inesctec.pt
[2] Systems Optimization Laboratory, University of Tsukuba, Tsukuba, Japan
marco.mollinetti@gmail.com
[3] INESC TEC and University of Porto (FEUP), Porto, Portugal
{vmiranda,lcarvalho}@inesctec.pt

Abstract. The following paper presents a novel strategy named Maximum Search Limitations (MS) for the Evolutionary Particle Swarm Optimization (EPSO). The approach combines EPSO standard search mechanism with a set of rules and position-wise statistics, allowing candidate solutions to carry a more thorough search around the neighborhood of the best particle found in the swarm. The union of both techniques results in an EPSO variant named MS-EPSO. MS-EPSO crucial premise is to enhance the exploration phase while maintaining the exploitation potential of EPSO. Algorithm performance is measured on eight unconstrained and two constrained engineering design optimization problems. Simulations are made and its results are compared against other techniques including the classic Particle Swarm Optimization (PSO). Lastly, results suggest that MS-EPSO can be a rival to other optimization methods.

Keywords: Swarm Intelligence · Particle Swarm Optimization ·
Position-wise statistics · Engineering design problems

1 Introduction

Particle Swarm Optimization (PSO) is a prominent Swarm Intelligence (SI) algorithm proposed by Kennedy and Eberhart [3] based on the social behavior of groups of animals found in nature, e.g., bird flocks and fish schools. By simulating the collective intelligence that these animals features when in motion as a whole group, PSO carries optimization tasks in the search space by constantly changing the velocity of a set of candidate solution (particles).

Despite its relative success in solving continuous optimization problems, PSO displays several documented performance issues [4]. To address these issues and at the same improve the robustness of the algorithm, a hybrid approach that combines Evolutionary Strategies (ES) with the classic PSO was proposed by

© Springer Nature Switzerland AG 2019
P. Moura Oliveira et al. (Eds.): EPIA 2019, LNAI 11804, pp. 712–723, 2019.
https://doi.org/10.1007/978-3-030-30241-2_59

Miranda and Fonseca [10]. The algorithm - Evolutionary Particle Swarm Optimization (EPSO) - adapts the original particle update rule by inserting self-adaptive properties for the control parameters and replicas of the particle for an enhanced exploitation phase. This adaptation in particular has had many successful cases, reported to be used by researchers to win several optimization competitions where the versions of EPSO were either standalone or combined approaches [16].

Previous results obtained by the authors suggests that EPSO can indeed find promising solutions at the cost of a higher frequency of premature convergence to local optima if the exploration phase does not generate particles with higher quality. With that in mind, we introduce a new strategy named Maximum Search Limitations (MS) to the exploration phase in EPSO (MS-EPSO). The premise of MS-EPSO is to cover EPSO exploration deficiencies without introducing major changes to the latter. To validate the proposed algorithm, MS-EPSO is evaluated in six unconstrained benchmarks and four engineering design problems in order to assess its performance and robustness. Results are compared to the original versions of PSO, EPSO and other established optimization methods.

The paper is organized as follows: Sect. 2 describes the features of PSO and EPSO, while Sect. 3 explains the MS-EPSO. Section 4 describes the experiments and its results are discussed in Sect. 5. Lastly, Sect. 6 outlines the conclusion of the paper.

2   PSO and EPSO

In this section both algorithms are outlined. Moreover, the update processes as well as relevant variables are explained.

2.1   PSO

The set of candidate solutions is called particles, where each has a position and velocity. Position is updated at each generation using the following movement rule:

$$x_i^{new} = x_i + v_i^{new}, \tag{1}$$

where i represents the i-th particle. v_i^{new} is computed as:

$$v_i^{new} = w_1 * v_i + \phi_1 * w_2 * (\hat{x} - x) + \phi_2 * w_3 * (x_g - x), \tag{2}$$

where ϕ_1 and ϕ_2 are uniformly random numbers sampled along the $[0, 1]$ interval. Each weight (w) is defined before running the algorithm. If the new position is better than the local best position in its trajectory, the local best position $(\hat{x})$ is updated and, in case this new local best is also the best of the entire population, x_g is modified. Components of (1) and (2) are described in Table 1.

The position update rule (2) can be divided by the addition operator into three distinct terms, each regulated by weights w_1, w_2 and w_3, respectively [15].

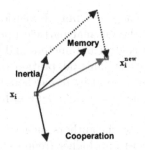

Fig. 1. Depiction of the PSO particle movement [10]

First term is the inertia which represents the capability of the particle to keep moving in same direction. The second term is related to the memory, attracting the particle to the best point ever visited in its trajectory. Lastly, the third term, cooperation, guides the particle towards the current best point in the swarm. Figure 1 illustrates the influence of each component in the position update.

Table 1. PSO components [3]

Attribute	Symbol	Description
Particle position	x	Solution for a specific problem
Local best position	$\hat{x}$	Best solution found by the particle
Global best position	x_g	Best solution found by the swarm
Particle fitness	-	Value of the solution
Local best fitness	-	Value of the best solution found by the particle
Global best fitness	-	Value of the best solution found by the swarm
Particle velocity	v	Values to update the position (Movement Rule)
Static weights	w_1 w_2 w_3	Control parameters for the movement rule

2.2 EPSO

Inspired by the PSO and Evolutionary Strategies (ES) [1], EPSO introduces a self-adapting recombination mechanism and stochastic (or elitist) tournament to PSO. Table 2 describes the new components added by EPSO.

Table 2. EPSO new components [9]

Attribute	Symbol	Description
Mutation rate	τ	Control parameter for weight mutation
Communication factor	P	Control parameter for information trading
Replicas	r	Replicas for the each particle
Strategic weights	w_1^* w_2^* w_3^* w_4^*	Control parameters for movement rules

EPSO performs five steps per iteration in its original form. Foremost, particles are replicated R times. Then, replicas have its weights mutated according to (3) while the original particle retains their previous set of weights:

$$w^*_{rk} = w_{ik} + \tau N(0,1). \tag{3}$$

where $N(0,1)$ is a random number sampled from a normal distribution with mean 0 and standard deviation 1. The process that follows, called reproduction phase, updates the replicas position using (1). However, the $v^{new}_i - i$th term is calculated using the new movement formula:

$$v^{new}_i = w^*_{i1} * v_i + w^*_{i2} * (\hat{x} - x) + w^*_{i3} * P[(x^*_g - x)]. \tag{4}$$

Besides the strategic weights, the (4) adds a communication factor: a binary mask containing components of value 1 with probability p, where p stands for the communication probability [8]. Furthermore, (4) introduces a perturbation in the global best as x^*_g:

$$x^*_g = x_g * (1 + w_{i4} * N(0,1)). \tag{5}$$

Next, replicas and the original particle are evaluated and a tournament selection between the best replica and the particle is performed. The winner of the tournament is assigned as the new particle and its weights are maintained. Lastly, the new particle is compared against the local and global best solution in the same fashion as the PSO.

3   MS-EPSO

EPSO was able to overcome a crucial issue found in the PSO by introducing genetic operators of the ES: if the particle local best is the same as the global best, the cooperation term would be zero, resulting in a movement provided only by the inertia and memory. However, at the same time, it failed to address another problem: if a particle moves to a new local best position at generation t, its memory term in consecutive iterations will be zero. When a term is zero, the update rule (4) does not perform proper local search.

Obviously, a desirable outcome would be to intensify the local search in the region of said particle instead of halting it by having the memory term set to zero. Taking that into account, we propose a strategy, called maximum search limitation (MSL) that regulates the behavior of the EPSO movement rule by detecting convergence of solutions to accumulation points.

3.1   Maximum Search Limitations

The MSL is composed by several components: particle update rules, position-wise statistics (x_μ, $x_g\mu$, x_σ and $x_g\sigma$) and a new local and global parameters named Particle Local Limit (PLL) and Maximum Local Limit (MLL), respectively. Table 3 describes the MSL components added to EPSO algorithm.

Table 3. MS-EPSO new components

Attribute	Symbol	Description
Position mean	x_{i_μ}	Position-wise mean
Best position mean	x_{g_μ}	Best position-wise mean
Position standard deviation	x_{i_σ}	Position-wise standard deviation
Best position standard deviation	x_{g_σ}	Best position-wise standard deviation
Particle local limit	PLL	Local limit for limitation strategy
Maximum local limit	MLL	Upper bound for the local limit
Particle strategy	EXP	1 for exploration; 0 for EPSO movement

In MS-EPSO, after standard solution initialization, position-wise statistics are calculated for each particle. Instead of replicating each particle after initialization, a decision process is carried by MS-ESPO taking three rules into consideration. These rules decide which will be updated first, replicas or the original solution. Their definitions is as follows:

1. **If** PPL_i has not surpassed MLL and EXP_i is 1, generate a new particle x_{new} sampled from a multivariate normal distribution, where $x_{new} \sim x_{g_\mu} + \mathcal{N}x_{g_\sigma}(0, I)$. Evaluate x_{new}, generate R replicas and update each replica with (4).
2. **If** PPL_i has not surpassed MLL and EXP_i is 0, apply the standard EPSO search for this particle giving priority to replicas.
3. **If** PPL_i surpassed MLL, generate a new particle x_{new} sampled from a normal distribution, where $x_{new} \sim x_{i_\mu} + \mathcal{N}x_{i_\sigma}(0, I)$ and a new set of weights sampled from a uniform distribution ranging between $[0, 1]$. PLL_i is set to zero and also EXP_i if it is the first time that the particle has adopted this rule. Evaluate x_{new}, generate R replicas and update each replica with (4).

After applying the rules, the algorithm conducts the same selection process of EPSO, searching for the best position between best replica and particle and comparing it to the local and global best. If the particle was capable of moving to a better local best position, the new position statistics are calculated, then compared against the global best. In case of failure, the PLL value of the respective particle is increased by one. The main rationale of this approach is to search for the best mean and standard deviation possible in order to generate a new particle during the exploration phase, as opposed to searching for the best D components of the solution.

When particle exploration mode is turned off (EXP_i is 0), it will never come back into this strategy, thus changing the search mechanism to the classic EPSO until the stopping criteria is reached. This is due that, if MS strategy is maintained until termination, an issue similar to another version of the EPSO, the Cross Entropy EPSO (CEEPSO) [13] is likely to arise: lack of a thorough local search, requiring yet again the inclusion of another technique to complement the search.

The last rule regulates the search mechanism. If the particle does not locate better regions *MLL* times, the search strategy will be modified for the next iteration. The most important step in this rule is to displace particles out of bad local optima and place them in the neighborhood of its best position found.

To illustrate the benefits from the inclusion of the third term when the local best was the same as the current particle, Fig. 2 shows a single particle movement based on normal distribution search for the *Rosenbrock* 2D function, where the global optimum is inside the red circle.

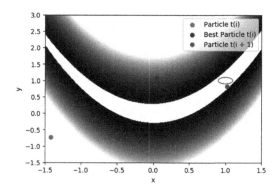

Fig. 2. Movement performed by a single particle using $x_g \mu$ and $x_g \sigma$ in MS-EPSO

4 Experiment

To analyze whether the proposed approach exert any influence to the performance of EPSO, 6 instances of well-known landscape functions designed to validate the capability of metaheuristics to handle various challenging aspects when optimizing a continuous function, such as ruggedness, multimodality and deceptive global optima. In addition to that 4 constrained engineering design optimization problems featuring linear and nonlinear constraints, and have been previously solved using a variety of other techniques [5,12,18,20] which is useful to determine the quality of the solutions produced by the proposed approach.

Following the guidelines of [11] and [6], selected unconstrained functions for this experiment are shown in Table 4. They are grouped by their characteristics: Differentiable or Non-differentiable (D or Nd); Separable or Non-separable (S or Ns); Unimodal or Multimodal (U or M). Table 5 describes the standards for the engineering design problems.

Parameters shared between the algorithms are: population size as 50. Algorithms with replicas uses 1 single replica, leading to a population with size 25; the total number of function evaluations (FE's) are $2 * 10^5$ for unconstrained problems and $1 * 10^5$ for design problems. Algorithm-specific parameters are: for PSO, values are chosen from [19], 0.6 for inertia factor (w_1) and 1.8 to cognitive and social

Table 4. Landscape functions

Name	No	Dim	Range	Definition	Opt.
Damavandi	F1	2	[0, 14]	DNsM	0.0
DeVilliersGlasser02	F2	5	[1, 60]	DNsM	0.0
Griewank	F3	30	[−100, 100]	DNsM	0.0
Rastrigin	F4	30	[−5.12, 5.12]	DNsM	0.0
Rosenbrock	F5	30	[−30, 30]	DNsM	0.0
Schwefel06	F6	30	[−500, 500]	NdNsM	0.0

Table 5. Engineering design functions

Name	Dim	Constraints	Version [5]
Design of pressure vessel (DPV)	4	4	1
Speed Reducer Design (SRD-11)	7	11	-
Three-bar truss (TBT)	2	3	-
Weight tension/compression (MWTCS)	3	4	-

parameters (w_2, w_3); Regarding EPSO parameters the authors do not suggest values in the paper, but the code available in [7] points that τ is 0.2 and the communication probability is 0.9; in MS-EPSO the unique parameter is MLL is defined by Particles * Problem Dimension, but if this value surpass an upper bound of 100, MLL will be 100 in order to circumvent the normal distribution issue; lastly, the algorithm is compared with Differential Evolution (DE) [17] with *best1bin* strategy, F value is 0.5 and CR is 0.9. It is worth mentioning that the algorithms use Deb Rules [2] to handle constraints during the selection process.

5   Results

The following section presents the results obtained by the method in both constrained and unconstrained experiments. For comparative purposes, the statistical metrics used are: mean, standard deviation, median, Mann-Whitney U (MWU) test and best-worst results obtained by 30 distinct runs with different seeds.

5.1   Unconstrained Function Experiment

For the unconstrained problems, Figs. 3, 4, 5, 6, 7 and 8 reports the mean convergence achieved during the process, while Table 6 in next page shows the statistical results, where values less than 10^{-10} are represented as zero.

In Table 6, it is possible to verify that MS-EPSO achieved the best results, including the best *worst* value, for all landscape functions. Individually, EPSO is the second best in F1, F3 and F5, while DE in F2 and F4. The results obtained

Table 6. Experiment with unconstrained functions

No.	Algorithm	Mean	Median	Std. Dev	Best	Worst
F1	PSO	2.0	2.0	0.0	2.0	2.0
	EPSO	1.8	2.0	0.6	0.0	2.0
	MS-EPSO	**1.46**	**2.0**	**0.8844**	**0.0**	**2.0**
	DE	2.0	2.0	0.0	2.0	2.0
F2	PSO	5620.4012	6344.275	4456.1999	0.3382	10674.7455
	EPSO	354.6191	0.3382	1889.2850	0.0	10528.5451
	MS-EPSO	**12.4013**	**0.3382**	**29.4839**	**0.0**	**111.8927**
	DE	25.8360	0.3991	71.3312	0.0250	315.3606
F3	PSO	1.2281	1.2227	0.0963	1.0516	1.4674
	EPSO	0.0022	0.0	0.0063	0.0	0.0295
	MS-EPSO	**0.0**	**0.0**	**0.0**	**0.0**	**0.0**
	DE	0.0207	0.0135	0.0201	0.0	0.0682
F4	PSO	133.6427	133.1711	27.6952	78.8659	206.3065
	EPSO	54.5236	57.2100	28.7096	1.9899	134.3190
	MS-EPSO	**13.4982**	**12.9344**	**12.0239**	**0.0**	**42.7831**
	DE	47.1278	44.7730	12.5944	29.8487	94.5208
F5	PSO	169050.5709	140931.5580	113945.1897	18083.5788	411478.4490
	EPSO	0.9616	0.0035	2.1833	0.0	10.1682
	MS-EPSO	**2.543E−05**	**0.0**	**0.0**	**0.0**	**0.0004**
	DE	1.4617	0.0	1.9211	0.0	1.9211
F6	PSO	0.0	0.0	0.0	0.0	0.0
	EPSO	0.0	0.0	0.0	0.0	0.0
	MS-EPSO	0.0	0.0	0.0	0.0	0.0
	DE	0.0	0.0	0.0	0.0	0.0

by MWU test when comparing MS-EPSO with the second bests suggests that for F1, F3, F4, F5, the samples found in MS-EPSO are sampled by a different distribution ($p < 0.05$), indicating that MS-EPSO has statistical significance. For F2, MS-EPSO is better than DE, but both are samples by the same distribution, resulting in no statistical significance ($p > 0.05$), likewise in F6 but it happens with all algorithms. The convergence plots illustrate this significance while the number of FE's increases. However, it is possible to notice that in Fig. 8 EPSO reached the bottom level faster than other algorithms.

5.2 Constrained Experiment: Engineering Design

For constrained problems, if the algorithm was not capable of finding a solution without violations, the run is considered invalid. The sum of each invalid run is represented by SIR, grouped with all metrics from the previous experiment presented in Table 7.

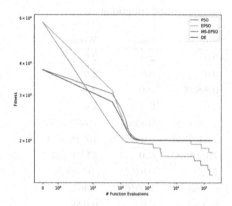

Fig. 3. *Damavandi* function convergence

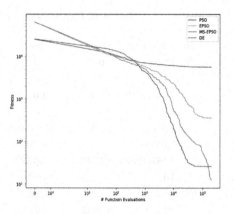

Fig. 4. *DeVG02* function convergence

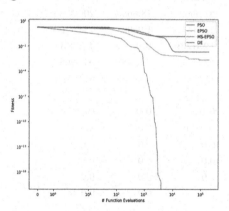

Fig. 5. *Grienwank* function convergence

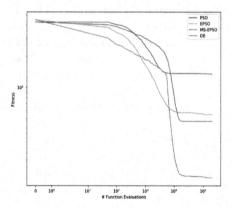

Fig. 6. *Rastrigin* function convergence

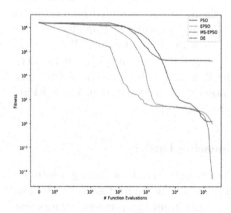

Fig. 7. *Rosenbrock* function convergence

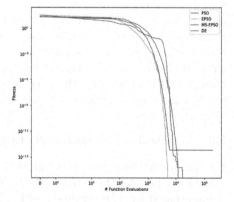

Fig. 8. *Schwefel06* function convergence

Table 7. Experiment with engineering design functions

Design	Algorithm	Mean	Median	Std. Dev	Best	Worst	SIR
DPV	PSO	6091.6634	5924.7044	377.6837	5885.3327	7319.0007	0
	EPSO	6399.8912	6268.0292	480.8715	5885.3649	7319.0007	0
	MS-EPSO	6217.2251	6030.0320	363.0227	5885.3345	7176.1426	0
	ADX [20]	**5885.3331**	-	**0.0001**	**5885.3329**	-	0
	TLBO [12]	6059.7143	-	-	6059.7143	-	0
SRD11	PSO	-	-	-	-	-	8
	EPSO	2894.3825	2894.3821	0.0013	2894.3821	2894.3879	0
	MS-EPSO	2894.3882	2894.3821	0.0307	2894.3821	2894.5534	0
	EQABC [18]	**2894.3821**	-	**7.86E−6**	**2894.3821**	-	0
	ADX [20]	2894.3827	-	0.0012	2894.3823	-	0
TBT	**PSO**	**263.8958**	**263.8958**	**1.031E−14**	**263.8958**	**263.8958**	**0**
	EPSO	263.8963	263.8959	0.0008	263.8958	263.8988	0
	MS-EPSO	263.8960	263.8958	0.0005	263.8958	263.8991	0
	ADX [20]	263.8958	-	3.77E−07	263.8958	-	0
MWTCS	PSO	-	-	-	-	-	21
	EPSO	-	-	-	-	-	19
	MS-EPSO	0.0127	0.0001	0.0127	0.0126	0.0134	0
	EQABC [18]	0.0126	-	2.18E−5	0.0126	-	0
	ADX [20]	**0.0126**	-	**2.06E−07**	**0.0126**	-	**0**

The results points that MS-EPSO achieved better overall performance regarding the experiment. Individually, in DPV and TBT where all algorithms found feasible solutions, PSO performed better than the EPSO and MS-EPSO, but MS-EPSO achieved better results when compared to EPSO, highlighting the capabilities of the enhanced exploration phase. The best result for these problems were found by ADX, a genetic algorithm combined with diversity control which shares the first position with PSO. For SRD11, the best result was found by EQABC, which is an algorithm that combines the evolutionary strategies found in EPSO with the mechanisms from Artificial Bee Colony (ABC) and Quick ABC (QABC) algorithms. In this particular set, MS-EPSO failed to have a better mean when compared to EPSO. Lastly, in MWTCS, between PSO versions, MS-EPSO was the only capable of finding a feasible solution, but did not achieve the best result possible.

In general, the results suggest that as long as the initial population has constraints, MS strategy can assist the EPSO to move its particles to positions without violations, but does not help when the initial set is feasible. For all problems, the strategy trade between MS and EPSO was, in average, performed after its maximum limit plus 25 generations, indicating that the parameter must be further analyzed.

6 Conclusion

Results indicate that MS strategy may enhance the exploration phase in EPSO algorithm, increasing the quality of the solutions and leading to a better outcome. Overall, performance of MS-EPSO for unconstrained problems was shown to be better than constrained problems, indicating that additional constraint handling rules has to be introduced when solving problems with constraints. On the other hand, results of the unconstrained problems point that the algorithm may produce interesting results on more complex domains, for example the parameter tuning of deep neural networks and large scale problems.

In any case, and as expected and demonstrated in many benchmark competitions, EPSO and its variants is a very competitive approach as far as a meta-heuristic can be. Further tests on neural networks, large scale problems, mechanical design and power systems is to be done to further investigate the performance of MS strategy in EPSO. Besides applications, a parameter analysis to search the best strategy trade-off will be applied to enhance the proposed method.

Finally, this paper was focusing on strategies enhancing the performance of an algorithm guided by the EPSO logic, and all the tests were done with random initialization of the first population. But another initialization process has been successfully attempted, in the CE-EPSO variant: to use a Cross Entropy to produce a suitable population (a first order exploration phase), followed by an EPSO development. This variant has won consecutive IEEE PES Modern Meta-Heuristic Optimization competitions in power systems [14], since 2014, and it will be interesting to investigate if the MS-EPSO strategy can further enhance the EPSO phase of the CE-EPSO approach.

Acknowledgments. This paper was produced under conditions provided by funding by the ERDF – European Regional Development Fund through the Operational Programme for Competitiveness and Internationalization - COMPETE 2020 within project POCI-01-0145-FEDER-006961, and by national funds through the FCT – Portuguese Foundation for Science and Technology, as part of project UID/EEA/ 50014/2013

References

1. Beyer, H.G.: Toward a theory of evolution strategies: self-adaptation. Evol. Comput. **3**(3), 311–347 (1995)
2. Deb, K.: An efficient constraint handling method for genetic algorithms. Comput. Methods Appl. Mech. Eng. **186**(2–4), 311–338 (2000)
3. Eberhart, R., Kennedy, J.: A new optimizer using particle swarm theory. In: Proceedings of the Sixth International Symposium on Micro Machine and Human Science, MHS 1995, pp. 39–43. IEEE (1995)
4. Engelbrecht, A.P.: Computational Intelligence: An Introduction. Wiley, London (2007)
5. Garg, H.: Solving structural engineering design optimization problems using an artificial bee colony algorithm. J. Ind. Manag. Optimization **10**(3), 777–794 (2014)

6. Jamil, M., Yang, X.S.: A literature survey of benchmark functions for global optimization problems. Int. J. Math. Model. Numer. Optimisation **4**(2), 150–194 (2013)
7. Miranda, V.: EPSO code. http://epso.inesctec.pt/epso-code-c. Accessed 27 Mar 2019
8. Miranda, V., Alves, R.: Differential evolutionary particle swarm optimization (DEEPSO): a successful hybrid. In: 2013 BRICS Congress on Computational Intelligence and 11th Brazilian Congress on Computational Intelligence, pp. 368–374. IEEE (2013)
9. Miranda, V., Fonseca, N.: EPSO-best-of-two-worlds meta-heuristic applied to power system problems. In: Proceedings of the 2002 Congress on Evolutionary Computation, CEC 2002 (Cat. No. 02TH8600), vol. 2, pp. 1080–1085. IEEE (2002)
10. Miranda, V., Fonseca, N.: EPSO-evolutionary particle swarm optimization, a new algorithm with applications in power systems. In: IEEE/PES Transmission and Distribution Conference and Exhibition, vol. 2, pp. 745–750. IEEE (2002)
11. Molga, M., Smutnicki, C.: Test functions for optimization needs. In: Test Functions for Optimization Needs, p. 101 (2005)
12. Rao, R.V., Savsani, V.J., Vakharia, D.: Teaching-learning-based optimization: a novel method for constrained mechanical design optimization problems. Comput. Aided Des. **43**(3), 303–315 (2011)
13. Rueda, J., Erlich, I., Lee, K.: 2017 smart grid operation problems. http://sites.ieee.org/psace-mho/2017-smart-grid-operation-problems-competition-panel/. Accessed 27 Mar 2019
14. Rueda, J., Erlich, I., Lee, K.: Modern heuristic optimization. http://sites.ieee.org/psace-mho/. Accessed 27 Mar 2019
15. Shi, Y., Eberhart, R.C.: Parameter selection in particle swarm optimization. In: Porto, V.W., Saravanan, N., Waagen, D., Eiben, A.E. (eds.) EP 1998. LNCS, vol. 1447, pp. 591–600. Springer, Heidelberg (1998). https://doi.org/10.1007/BFb0040810
16. Soares, J., Lezama, F., Vale, Z., Rueda, J.: Evolutionary computation in uncertain environments: a smart grid application. http://www.gecad.isep.ipp.pt/WCCI2018-SG-COMPETITION/. Accessed 27 Mar 2019
17. Storn, R., Price, K.: Differential evolution-a simple and efficient heuristic for global optimization over continuous spaces. J. Glob. Optimization **11**(4), 341–359 (1997)
18. Teixeira, O.N., et al.: Evolutionary quick artificial bee colony for constrained engineering design problems. In: Rutkowski, L., Scherer, R., Korytkowski, M., Pedrycz, W., Tadeusiewicz, R., Zurada, J.M. (eds.) ICAISC 2018. LNCS (LNAI), vol. 10842, pp. 603–615. Springer, Cham (2018). https://doi.org/10.1007/978-3-319-91262-2_53
19. Vesterstrom, J., Thomsen, R.: A comparative study of differential evolution, particle swarm optimization, and evolutionary algorithms on numerical benchmark problems. In: Proceedings of the 2004 Congress on Evolutionary Computation (IEEE Cat. No. 04TH8753), vol. 2, pp. 1980–1987. IEEE (2004)
20. Yasojima, E.K.K., de Oliveira, R.C.L., Teixeira, O.N., Pereira, R.L.: CAM-ADX: a new genetic algorithm with increased intensification and diversification for design optimization problems with real variables. Robotica **37**(9), 1595–1640 (2019). https://doi.org/10.1017/S026357471900016X

Interval Differential Evolution Using Structural Information of Global Optimization Problems

Mariane R. Sponchiado Cassenote$^{(\boxtimes)}$ ⓘ, Guilherme A. Derenievicz ⓘ, and Fabiano Silva ⓘ

Informatics Department, Federal University of Paraná, Curitiba, Brazil
{mrscassenote,gaderenievicz,fabiano}@inf.ufpr.br

Abstract. Differential Evolution (DE) algorithms are a promising strategy to Numerical Constrained Global Optimization Problems (NCOP). Most DE recent variants are applied to black-box optimization problems, where the analytical structure of the NCOP instance is unknown. In this paper we present an Interval Differential Evolution (InDE) algorithm that explores the structural information of the problem. The instance structure is represented by a hypergraph Epiphytic decomposition, where the variables are intervals. InDE algorithm is based on several strategies used in state-of-the-art DE implementations. Based on structural information, our approach extracts a subset of variables of the instance that are critical to the search process. The DE population individuals encode only this subset of variables. The other variables of the instance are valuated by a linear cost constraint propagation over the hypergraph structure. Our experiments show that the use of structural information associated with interval local consistency techniques significantly improves the performance of DE algorithm.

Keywords: Structural decomposition · Differential Evolution · Global optimization

1 Introduction

A *Numerical Constrained Global Optimization Problem* (NCOP) consists of finding an assignment of values to a set of variables $\mathcal{V} = \{x_1, \ldots, x_D\}$ that minimizes an objective function $f : \mathbb{R}^D \mapsto \mathbb{R}$ subject to a set of m constraints of the form $g_i(x_{i_1}, \ldots, x_{i_k}) \leq 0$ called *constraint network*, where $\{x_{i_1}, \ldots, x_{i_k}\} \subseteq \mathcal{V}$ is the *scope* of the i-th constraint, $1 \leq i \leq m$, and D is the *dimension* of the instance.

Differential Evolution (DE) [12] has become one of the most used evolutionary algorithms to tackle NCOPs due to its performance in recent competitions of the IEEE Congress of Evolutionary Computing (CEC), winning the last editions

This work was supported by CAPES – Brazilian Federal Agency for Support and Evaluation of Graduate Education within the Ministry of Education of Brazil.

of the constrained real-parameter optimization track. In CEC competitions, the state-of-the-art algorithms are evaluated in the context of black-box optimization, where the analytical structure of the NCOP instance is unknown.

On the other hand, interval branch and pruning algorithms have been widely used in the last few decades to rigorously solve NCOPs [1,6,7]. These algorithms combine local consistency techniques with a complete investigation of the search space. In many approaches, the local consistency is based on the analytical structure of the NCOP instance [5]. In this context, the *Relaxed Global Optimization* (OGRe) solver, proposed in [3], is an interval method that explores the structural information represented by a hypergraph. The algorithm uses the constraint hypergraph to determine the amount of local consistency that guarantees a solution to be found efficiently. This is ensured by the existence of a particular decomposition of the hypergraph, called Epiphytic decomposition, that extracts a subset of variables of the instance that are critical to the search method. The main issue of the solver is that the search is performed over a relaxed version of the instance, where a tolerance $\varepsilon > 0$ is considered to satisfy some constraints of the problem (with ε set empirically). Another issue is the high computational cost of the branch and pruning approach.

In this paper, we propose an *Interval DE* (InDE) algorithm that uses the Epiphytic decomposition as a source of structural information of the NCOP instance. Such decomposition allows the DE to perform its operations only on a subset of the instance variables, whilst others are valuated by constraint propagation. At each fitness evaluation, a local consistency procedure allows the pruning of unfeasible values from the intervals assigned to that subset of variables. Differently from OGRe, the proposed algorithm solves the original instance by dynamically defining the ε tolerance during the search. The processing time is limited by the maximum number of fitness evaluations, given as input.

The proposed InDE algorithm is based on several strategies used in state-of-the-art algorithms of the CEC competitions, like IUDE [15] and LSHADE44 [10]. We evaluate our approach in an experimental set of 80 instances from the COCONUT Benchmark [11]. Experiments show that the use of structural information associated with interval consistency techniques significantly improves the performance of the DE algorithm. In addition, we find solutions with better approximations than the OGRe solver.

The remainder of this paper is organized as follows: Sect. 2 contains the main concepts about interval algorithms for global optimization, and the approach used in OGRe [3]. Section 3 presents the classical DE algorithm. Section 4 introduces our InDE approach. Experiments and discussions are presented in Sect. 5, and Sect. 6 concludes the paper.

2   Interval Algorithms for Global Optimization

Interval arithmetic was proposed in the 60's as a formal approach to analyze rounding errors on computational systems [9]. A *closed interval* $X = [\underline{x}, \overline{x}]$ is the set of real numbers $X = \{x \in \mathbb{R} \mid \underline{x} \leq x \leq \overline{x}\}$, where $\underline{x}, \overline{x} \in \mathbb{R}$ are the *endpoints* of X. The *width* of an interval X is $\omega(X) = \overline{x} - \underline{x}$ and its *midpoint* is $\mu(X) = (\underline{x} + \overline{x})/2$. An interval can be defined by its width and midpoint as follows: $X = [\mu(X) - \omega(X)/2, \ \mu(X) + \omega(X)/2]$. A *box* is a tuple of intervals $(X_1, X_2, \ldots, X_n)$. Given two intervals X and Y the *interval extension* of any binary operator $\circ$ well defined in $\mathbb{R}$ is defined by:

$$X \circ Y = \{x \circ y \mid x \in X, \ y \in Y \text{ and } x \circ y \text{ is defined in } \mathbb{R}\}.$$

The set $X \circ Y$ can be an interval, the empty set or a disconnected set of real numbers (a *multi-interval*). It is possible to compute $X \circ Y$ for all algebraic and the most common transcendental functions only by analyzing the endpoints of X and Y [6,9], e.g., $[\underline{x}, \overline{x}] + [\underline{y}, \overline{y}] = [\underline{x} + \underline{y}, \overline{x} + \overline{y}]$, $[\underline{x}, \overline{x}] \cdot [\underline{y}, \overline{y}] = [\min\{\underline{xy}, \underline{x}\overline{y}, \overline{x}\underline{y}, \overline{xy}\}, \max\{\underline{xy}, \underline{x}\overline{y}, \overline{x}\underline{y}, \overline{xy}\}]$ etc.

Since the late eighties, interval arithmetic has been used to deal with numerical constrained problems in a rigorous way by combining consistency techniques from the constraint programming community with *Branch and Bound* (B&B) algorithms [1,6,7]. A central work in this context is the Numerica modeling language [16], whose core algorithm forms the basis of most current interval solvers. Interval methods compute a set of atomic boxes that contains an optimum solution of the NCOP instance. Generally, such methods are composed by three main phases that are repeatedly applied until a solution is found:

- **Pruning phase:** contractors that guarantee some level of local consistency are applied, removing from variables' domain values that surely do not constitute a feasible solution of the problem. On numeric context, these contractors are generally implemented using interval arithmetic;
- **Local search:** cheap search methods are used to detect if the current box contains a feasible solution of the instance that can be used as an upper bound for the optimum solution. The Newton method is an example of a local search method that can be applied in this phase;
- **Branching phase:** a variable is chosen and its domain is bisected to continue the search in a recursive fashion. Good heuristics for choosing the variable and the side of its domain to be searched first are essential for the performance of the method.

In the pruning phase, contractors of Generalized Arc-Consistency (GAC) and its relaxed forms Hull Consistency and Box Consistency are generally used. GAC [8] guarantees that any valuation of a single variable can be extended to others variables whilst satisfying a constraint. On ternary numerical constraints of the form $x_1 = x_2 \circ_1 x_3$ this property is ensured by (1), where X_i is the domain of x_i, and $\circ_2$ and $\circ_3$ are the inverse operations of $\circ_1$ that hold the condition $(x_1 = x_2 \circ_1 x_3) \Leftrightarrow (x_2 = x_1 \circ_2 x_3) \Leftrightarrow (x_3 = x_1 \circ_3 x_2)$:

$$(X_1 \subseteq X_2 \circ_1 X_3) \wedge (X_2 \subseteq X_1 \circ_2 X_3) \wedge (X_3 \subseteq X_1 \circ_3 X_2). \tag{1}$$

If a ternary constraint is not GAC, this propriety can be easily achieved by computing the intersection of each relevant domain with the respective *projection function*:

$$\texttt{GAC\_contractor}(x_1 = x_2 \circ_1 x_3) := \begin{cases} X_1 \leftarrow X_1 \cap (X_2 \circ_1 X_3) \\ X_2 \leftarrow X_2 \cap (X_1 \circ_2 X_3) \\ X_3 \leftarrow X_3 \cap (X_1 \circ_3 X_2). \end{cases} \tag{2}$$

Strictly, the box (X_1, X_2, X_3) generated by (2) is not complete due to the finite precision of machine numbers. Furthermore, domains may be disconnected sets of real numbers (multi-intervals). Generally, in order to apply the GAC contractor on k-ary constraints a procedure of decomposition that transforms the constraint into an equivalent set of ternary constraints is used [4]. For example, with an auxiliary variable z_1 the constraint $x_1(x_2 - x_1) = 0$ is decomposed into a network of two new constraints: $x_2 - x_1 = z_1$ and $x_1 z_1 = 0$. Contractor (2) is then repeatedly applied to both constraints until a fixed box is obtained or a maximum number of steps is reached.

In the constraint programming context, a *constraint hypergraph* $\mathcal{H} = (\mathcal{V}, E)$ is a structural representation of a constraint network where $\mathcal{V}$ is a set of vertices representing variables and E is a set of edges representing scopes of constraints. In [3] this structural representation is extended to NCOP instances by encoding the objective function $f(x_1, \ldots, x_D)$ as a new constraint $z = f(x_1, \ldots, x_D)$ on the network, where z is called the *root* variable of the network and its domain Z equals the image of f under the box $(X_1, \ldots, X_D)$. The authors found a relationship between the constraint hypergraph and the amount of consistency that guarantees a backtrack-free solution, i.e., a search that solves the NCOP instance without encountering any conflict. This relationship is ensured by the existence of a particular decomposition of the constraint hypergraph called Epiphytic decomposition.

An *Epiphytic decomposition* [3] of the constraint hypergraph $\mathcal{H} = (\mathcal{V}, E)$ according to $z \in \mathcal{V}$ is a triple $(\mathcal{A}, \Omega, t)$, where $\mathcal{A} = (\mathcal{A}_1, \ldots, \mathcal{A}_n)$ is an ordered set of disjointed hypergraphs $\mathcal{A}_i = (V_i, E_i)$ obtained by removing from $\mathcal{H}$ a set of edges Ω, and $t : \Omega \mapsto V_\Omega$ is a function that associates each edge $e_i \in \Omega$ with one vertex $t(e_i) \in e_i$ such that: (i) $\mathcal{A}_1$ is a rooted tree in z (i.e., connected and Berge-acyclic); (ii) $\forall \mathcal{A}_{i>1} \in \mathcal{A}$ there is at most one $e_i \in \Omega$ such that $t(e_i) \in V_i$ and $\mathcal{A}_i$ is a rooted tree in $t(e_i)$ (or in any other vertex if such edge e_i does not exist); and (iii) if $t(e_i) \in V_i$, then $e_i \setminus \{t(e_i)\} \subseteq \bigcup_{j=1}^{i-1} V_j$.

Figure 1 shows an Epiphytic decomposition $(\mathcal{A}, \Omega, t)$ according to v_1 of the Rosenbrock function $f(x, y) = 100(x - y^2)^2 + (1 - y)^2$ encoded as a ternary network, where $\mathcal{A} = \{\mathcal{A}_1, \mathcal{A}_2\}$, $\mathcal{A}_1 = (\{v_1, \ldots v_{13}\}, \{e_1, \ldots, e_6\})$, $\mathcal{A}_2 = (\{v_{14}\}, \emptyset)$, $\Omega = \{e_7\}$ and $t(e_7) = v_{14}$.

It was showed that an Epiphytic decomposed NCOP instance can be solved in a backtrack-free manner if the network satisfies a combination of GAC and Relational Arc Consistent (RAC) [3]. Such consistencies enable a complete instantiation of the network from the initial assignment $\langle z = \min Z \rangle$ that minimizes the objective function. RAC is a local consistency proposed in [2] that guarantees any consistent assignment to all variables except one x_j, in the scope of a

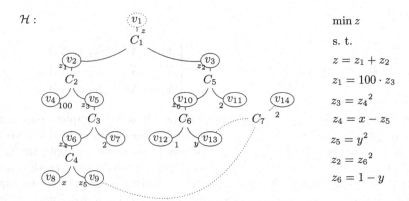

Fig. 1. An Epiphytic decomposition according to v_1 of the ternary encoded Rosenbrock function. Labels below vertices indicate the variables they represent.

constraint, to be extended to x_j whilst satisfying the constraint. A constraint of the form $x_1 = x_2 \circ_1 x_3$ is RAC w.r.t. x_1 if $X_1 \supseteq X_2 \circ_1 X_3$.

More specifically, [3] showed it suffices that only the constraints represented by edges $e_i \in \Omega$ are RAC w.r.t. the variable represented by $t(e_i)$, while the other constraints are GAC. An Epiphytic decomposition can be found in linear time w.r.t. the number of instance's operators, however, not all instances have such decomposition. Besides that, it was showed that all instances from an experimental set of COCONUT Benchmark [11] have Epiphytic decompositions.

While the GAC contractor shrinks the domain of variables, an RAC contractor must tighten the constraint on $e_i \setminus \{x_j\}$. If such constraint does not exist it must be added to the network, changing the structure of the hypergraph and its Epiphytic decomposition. To avoid that, [3] proposed a domain filtering algorithm that achieves a relaxed form of RAC. The proposed algorithm forms the basis of a global optimization solver called OGRe (Relaxed Global Optimization)[1] that is a variation of the usual interval B&B for global optimization.

OGRe considers a tolerance ε on constraints represented by the Ω set; therefore, it considers a relaxed version of the original instance. On the pruning phase, the GAC contractor (2) is applied to shrink variables' domain. As a local search strategy, OGRe attempt the entire instantiation of the network in a backtrack-free manner, starting by the initial valuation $\langle z = \min Z \rangle$. If some constraint in Ω is not satisfied with tolerance ε its variables must be narrowed to achieve a better approximation of RAC. Thus, on the branching phase, a variable from the non ε-feasible constraint in Ω is chosen and its domain is bisected to continue the search in a recursive fashion.

---

[1] https://gitlab.c3sl.ufpr.br/gaderenievicz/OGRe.

3 Differential Evolution

Differential Evolution (DE) was introduced by Storn and Price [12] using a floating-point encoding evolutionary algorithm for global optimization over continuous spaces. The classical DE consists of an evolutionary loop over generations of a population $\mathbf{p}$ of individuals. An individual is an assignment of values to all variables of the instance, represented by a vector $\mathbf{x} = (a_1, a_2, \ldots, a_D)$ where $a_i \in X_i$ is a value from the domain of the variable x_i, $1 \leq i \leq D$. A population $\mathbf{p}$ is a set of NP individuals. We denote by $\mathbf{p}_g$ the population on the g-th generation, $0 \leq g \leq G$.

DE follows the general procedure of an evolutionary algorithm. During each generation, the operators of mutation, crossover and selection are performed on the population until a termination condition is satisfied, like a fixed maximum number of fitness evaluations ($MaxFEs$). The initial population ($\mathbf{p}_0$) is randomly generated according to a uniform distribution over $X_1 \times \cdots \times X_D$. In the mutation phase of each generation, a mutation operator is applied to generate a *mutant vector* $\mathbf{v}_i$ for each individual $\mathbf{x}_i$ (called *target vector*) of the population. In the classical DE, several mutation operators have been proposed; for example, DE/rand/1 is described as follows:

$$\mathbf{v}_i = \mathbf{r}_1 + F \cdot (\mathbf{r}_2 - \mathbf{r}_3), \tag{3}$$

where $\mathbf{r}_1$, $\mathbf{r}_2$ and $\mathbf{r}_3$ are three mutually distinct individuals randomly selected from the population $\mathbf{p}_g$, and F is the scaling factor. Other popular mutation operators are the DE/current-to-pbest/1 (4) and the DE/current-to-rand/1 (5):

$$\mathbf{v}_i = \mathbf{x}_i + F \cdot (\mathbf{r}_{\text{pbest}} - \mathbf{x}_i) + F \cdot (\mathbf{r}_1 - \mathbf{r}_2), \tag{4}$$
$$\mathbf{v}_i = \mathbf{x}_i + s \cdot (\mathbf{r}_1 - \mathbf{x}_i) + F \cdot (\mathbf{r}_2 - \mathbf{r}_3), \tag{5}$$

where s is a uniformly distributed random number between 0 and 1, p is a value in $[1, NP]$, and $\mathbf{r}_{\text{pbest}}$ is an individual randomly chosen from the p best individuals of the current population.

In the classical DE, after the mutation step a crossover operation is applied to each pair of the target vector $\mathbf{x}_i$ and its corresponding mutant vector $\mathbf{v}_i$ to generate a new individual $\mathbf{u}_i$, called *trial vector*. The basic version of binomial crossover is defined as follows:

$$\mathbf{u}_{ij} = \begin{cases} \mathbf{v}_{ij}, & \text{if } rand_{ij} \leq CR \text{ or } j = j_{rand} \\ \mathbf{x}_{ij}, & \text{otherwise,} \end{cases}$$

where $\mathbf{u}_{ij}$, $\mathbf{v}_{ij}$ and $\mathbf{x}_{ij}$ are the j-th element of the vectors $\mathbf{u}_i$, $\mathbf{v}_i$ and $\mathbf{x}_i$, respectively. The value $rand_{ij}$ is a uniformly distributed random number between 0 and 1, CR is the crossover rate and $j_{rand} \in \{1, \ldots, D\}$ is a randomly chosen index which ensures that the trial individual gets at least one component from the mutant vector. Finally, a selection operator is performed on $\mathbf{x}_i$ and $\mathbf{u}_i$ and the best one according to a fitness evaluation function is selected as a target vector of the next generation.

4   The Proposed Approach

In this section we describe the proposed InDE algorithm. Our approach uses a new representation for the individuals: instead of each individual be an assignment of real values to all variables of the NCOP instance, only the variables present in constraints of the Ω set of an Epiphytic decomposition are considered. Moreover, the representation is based on intervals, i.e., an individual is an assignment of intervals to variables (a box). The population is a set of boxes that covers parts of the search space, instead of just points in this space as the classical DE. This allows to use the GAC contractor (2) to prune unfeasible solutions. OGRe's local search is used to compute the fitness of each individual. The proposed approach uses interval adaptations of the main features of DE algorithms presented in the last CEC competitions on constrained real-parameter optimization, especially IUDE [15] and LSHADE44 [10], first places on CEC 2018 and CEC 2017, respectively. The components of InDE are discussed below.

4.1   Interval Population

An interval individual is a vector of intervals $\mathbf{X} = (A_1, A_2, \ldots, A_D)$, where $A_i \subseteq X_i$ is an interval. A population $\mathbf{p}$ is a set of NP interval individuals and $\mathbf{p}_g$ denotes the interval population on the g-th generation.

OGRe uses a multi-interval representation of variables' domain for a better use of the GAC contractor. A multi-interval can be represented by an union of intervals and a multi-interval box is a short way of describing a combinatorial of intervals. For example, the multi-interval box $([-2, -1] \cup [1, 2], [0, 2])$ represents both the boxes $([-2, -1], [0, 2])$ and $([1, 2], [0, 2])$. In our approach we split multi-intervals in a combinatorial representation.

The initial population is generated by the top level branching tree of OGRe's B&B. Each node of the search tree contains a consistent multi-interval box. Each multi-interval box is splitted into a set of interval boxes (individuals) that are added to the initial population. The nodes are iteratively processed until the number of individuals is NP. This strategy guarantees that the initial population covers all search space. Then, the individuals' fitness are evaluated using OGRe's backtrack-free local search (Sect. 4.3). As this procedure is subject to numerical rounding errors, it is possible that some individuals are considered inconsistent. In this case, substitute individuals are randomly generated from the initial consistent box by varying the endpoints of an interval.

Inspired by IUDE, the current population is divided into two sub-populations A and B of size $NP/2$. The current population of NP size is sorted at the beginning of each generation w.r.t. their individuals' fitness. This ensures that the sub-population A will be composed by the best $NP/2$ individuals according to the ε constrained method described in Sect. 4.3. We use these sub-populations to control the application of the mutation operations. In sub-population A we apply a pool of three mutation strategies, promoting the exploitation of the fitter solutions that can speed up the convergence. In order to better allocate the computational resources, in sub-population B an adaptive selection scheme is used to apply only one mutation operator.

DE traditionally employs the one-to-one comparison between target vectors and trial vectors to select the individuals for the next generation. In order to explore promising directions of the search, we maintain an additional memory with the trial vectors that were not selected for the next generation. When a multi-interval box is splitted into interval individuals, only the one with best fitness value is compared to the target vector, others are added to the additional memory. Periodically, the current population (comprising the two sub-populations) and the additional memory are merged and sorted. Then, the new population is composed by the NP best individuals, and the additional memory is emptied.

We use the Linear Population Size Reduction scheme proposed in LSHADE [14] to linearly reduce the population. In this scheme, NP^{max} is the population size at the beginning of the search and NP^{min} is the population size at the end. At each generation the new population size is calculated and if it is different from the current size, the worst individuals are deleted from the population until it has the appropriate size.

4.2   Interval Operations

Like in IUDE, a pool of three mutation operators consisting of DE/rand/1, DE/current-to-$p$best/1 and DE/current-to-rand/1 is used. In the top sub-population A, each one of the three strategies is used to generate new trial vectors, employing three fitness evaluations for each target vector. Since the sub-population A contains the $NP/2$ best members of the current population, we adopted the same modified ranking-based parent selection used in IUDE. Thus, in the mutation operation the base vector and the terminal vector are selected from the sub-population A.

Since an interval is defined by its width (ω) and midpoint (μ), mutant operators can be applied over midpoints as on real values representation. However, they must be extended to deal with interval widths. Equations 6, 7 and 8 are the result of applying interval arithmetic to the classical mutation operators.

The interval version of DE/rand/1 operator (3) combines $\mathbf{r}_1$, $\mathbf{r}_2$ and $\mathbf{r}_3$ to generate a mutant vector $\mathbf{v}_i$. The j-th element of $\mathbf{v}_i$ is defined by:

$$\mu(\mathbf{v}_{ij}) = \mu(\mathbf{r}_{1j}) + F \cdot (\mu(\mathbf{r}_{2j}) - \mu(\mathbf{r}_{3j})), \tag{6}$$

$$\omega(\mathbf{v}_{ij}) = \omega(\mathbf{r}_{1j}) + F \cdot (\omega(\mathbf{r}_{1j}) \cdot (\omega(\mathbf{r}_{2j})/\omega(\mathbf{r}_{3j})) - \omega(\mathbf{r}_{1j})).$$

The other two mutation operators are defined in the same manner. The interval version of DE/current-to-$p$best/1 (4) combines the target vector $\mathbf{x}_i$ with two randomly selected individuals $\mathbf{r}_1$ and $\mathbf{r}_2$, and with $\mathbf{r}_{\text{pbest}}$, one of the p best individuals of the population. The resulting mutant vector is defined by:

$$\mu(\mathbf{v}_{ij}) = \mu(\mathbf{x}_{ij}) + F \cdot (\mu(\mathbf{r}_{\text{pbest}j}) - \mu(\mathbf{x}_{ij})) + F \cdot (\mu(\mathbf{r}_{1j}) - \mu(\mathbf{r}_{2j})), \tag{7}$$

$$\omega(v_{ij}) = \omega(x_{ij}) + F \cdot (\omega(r_{\text{pbest}j}) - \omega(x_{ij})) + F \cdot (\omega(x_{ij}) \cdot (\omega(r_{1j})/\omega(r_{2j})) - \omega(x_{ij})).$$

The interval version of DE/current-to-rand/1 (5) combines the target vector x_i with three randomly selected individuals r_1, r_2 and r_3. The resulting mutant vector is defined by:

$$\mu(v_{ij}) = \mu(x_{ij}) + s \cdot (\mu(r_{1j}) - \mu(x_{ij})) + F \cdot (\mu(r_{2j}) - \mu(r_{3j})), \tag{8}$$

$$\omega(v_{ij}) = \omega(x_{ij}) + s \cdot (\omega(r_{1j}) - \omega(x_{ij})) + F \cdot (\omega(x_{ij}) \cdot (\omega(r_{2j})/\omega(r_{3j})) - \omega(x_{ij})),$$

where s is a random number between 0 and 1. This strategy does not use crossover operator, i.e., trial vector u_i is a copy of mutant vector v_i.

As in IUDE, in the top sub-population A, the three trial vectors generated corresponding to each target vector are compared among themselves, and the trial vector generation strategy with the best trial vector scores a win. At every generation, the success rate of each strategy is evaluated over the period of previous L generations, where L is the learning period. For example, the success rate (SR) of strategy 1 on the learning period $L = 25$ is given by $SR_1 = NW_1/(NW_1 + NW_2 + NW_3)$, where NW_i is the number of wins of the strategy i in the previous 25 generations. In the bottom sub-population B, the probability of employing a trial vector generation strategy is equal to its recent success rate on the top sub-population A over the previous L generations.

The setting of values for the F and CR parameters is problem dependent and may change according to the region of the search space being visited. For this reason, we use the parameter adaptation scheme applied in LSHADE44. Thus, it is employed a pair of memories M_F and M_{CR} for the strategies DE/rand/1 and DE/current-to-pbest/1. As DE/current-to-rand/1 does not use crossover, we only use one memory M_F. It is important to note that only successful trial vectors in the sub-population A are used in the adaptation of parameters, since only in this sub-population the three strategies are used for each individual.

4.3   Fitness Evaluations

To compute the fitness value of an individual we use OGRe's pruning and local search strategies. First, the GAC contractor (2) shrinks the intervals by removing inconsistent values. Then, we try the instantiation of the entire network in a backtrack-free fashion starting by the initial valuation $\langle z = \min Z \rangle$. Unlike OGRe, we allow the constraints in the Ω set of the Epiphytic decomposition to be instantiated regardless of the tolerance required to satisfy them. The sum of all these tolerances makes the constraint violation value $\phi(x)$ of the individual (if the contractor entails an empty interval we define $\phi(x) = \infty$), while the $f(x)$ value is simply defined by $\min Z$. The consistent individual obtained from the GAC contractor may contain multi-intervals. Thus, we split this multi-interval box into a set of interval individuals, adding to the population the one with the best fitness value (if it is better than the target vector) and putting in the additional memory all the other generated interval individuals. It is worth noting that unlike usual DE methods, a new individual is not defined only by the mutation and crossover operations, but also by the GAC contractor that shrinks its interval values.

We use the ε constrained method [13] to compare two individuals, similarly to IUDE and LSHADE44. In this method, the fitness value of an individual $\mathbf{x}$ is composed by two values: the objective function value $f(\mathbf{x})$ and the constraint violation value $\phi(\mathbf{x})$. The ε comparisons are defined basically as a lexicographic order in which $\phi(\mathbf{x})$ precedes $f(\mathbf{x})$, i.e., the feasibility is more important than the minimization of the objective function. This precedence is adjusted by the parameter ε. Given two individuals $\mathbf{x}_1$ and $\mathbf{x}_2$ with fitness $(f(\mathbf{x}_1), \phi(\mathbf{x}_1))$ and $(f(\mathbf{x}_2), \phi(\mathbf{x}_2))$, respectively, $\mathbf{x}_1$ is better than $\mathbf{x}_2$ iff the following conditions are satisfied:

$$(f(\mathbf{x}_1), \phi(\mathbf{x}_1)) <_\varepsilon (f(\mathbf{x}_2), \phi(\mathbf{x}_2)) \Leftrightarrow \begin{cases} f(\mathbf{x}_1) < f(\mathbf{x}_2), & \text{if } \phi(\mathbf{x}_1) \leq \varepsilon, \phi(\mathbf{x}_2) \leq \varepsilon \\ f(\mathbf{x}_1) < f(\mathbf{x}_2), & \text{if } \phi(\mathbf{x}_1) = \phi(\mathbf{x}_2) \\ \phi(\mathbf{x}_1) < \phi(\mathbf{x}_2), & \text{otherwise.} \end{cases}$$

The ε level declines as the generation increases:

$$\varepsilon = \begin{cases} \varepsilon_0 \cdot (1 - \frac{g}{T})^{cp}, & \text{if } 0 < g < T \\ 0, & \text{if } g \geq T \end{cases} \text{, with } cp = \frac{-\log\varepsilon_0 + \lambda}{\log(1 - T)},$$

where ε_0 is the constraint violation of the top θ-th individual in the initial population. The ε level is updated at each generation g until the number of generations exceeds T, from this point the ε level is set to 0 to prefer solutions with minimum constraint violation.

5   Experimental Results

In order to verify the performance of our approach, 80 functions were chosen from the COCONUT Benchmark [11] and tested in 25 independent runs. These functions were selected according to an increasing number of variables and constraints. The maximal number of fitness evaluations was set to $MaxFEs = 20000 \times |V_\Omega|$, where $|V_\Omega|$ is the number of variables on the Ω set. Initial population size was defined as $NP^{max} = 12 \times |V_\Omega|$ and the minimal size was $NP^{min} = 6$. The DE/current-to-pbest/1 operator used $p = 20\%$ of the population. The length of historic memory was $H = 5$. The additional memory and the current population $\mathbf{p}_g$ were merged and sorted every 50 generations and the learning period L was set to 25 generations. Parameters of ε level were $\theta = 0.5$ and $T = 0.75 \times G$, where G is the maximum number of generations. GAC contractor was applied a maximum of 1000 iterations. We chose the exponential version of the classical crossover operator because it outperformed the binomial one in most cases. The timeout was set to 7200 s.

Our experiments considered the OGRe solver, the proposed InDE and a DE variant that uses the same strategies, but does not use interval representation neither structural decomposition. In this case, the variables are represented as real values and the NCOP instance is handled as black-box optimization. As the optimal solution of all instances are known, we used the absolute distance from these values as a performance measure (absolute error). Only solutions that respect all constraints of the instance (feasible) were considered. The maximum tolerance used in OGRe was $\varepsilon = 10^{-1}$.

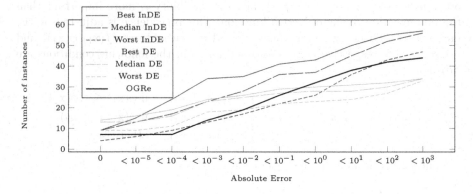

Fig. 2. Accumulated absolute error of the solutions found.

Figure 2 shows the number of instances solved with a given maximum absolute error. The lines show the best, the median and the worst solutions of 25 runs of InDE and the real parameter DE. For OGRe we only show the best solution of each instance among several parameter settings [3]. Instances with absolute error greater than 10^3 were disregarded.

Our InDE approach found feasible solutions for 71.25% of the 80 instances, with 11.25% of optimal solutions and 42.5% with an better approximation than 10^{-3}. Although the real-parameter DE found more optimal solutions than the other approaches, it found feasible solutions for only 42.5% of instances. In general, given a maximum absolute error ($maxAE$), in our experiments the InDE found a solution far from the optimal by at most $maxAE$ for a greater number of instances than OGRe and real-parameter DE. It is worth noting that the InDE's search outperformed OGRe's B&B using the same local consistence procedure. The average time of the 25 executions of the 80 instances, including the timeouts, was 1891.23 s for the InDE, 0.19 s for the DE and 2258.31 s for the OGRe. The processing times of InDE and OGRe are significantly higher due to the local consistency process.

6   Conclusion

In this work, an Interval Differential Evolution (InDE) algorithm was proposed to solve constrained optimization problems. InDE combines the main strategies of state-of-the-art algorithms of the CEC competitions on real-parameter optimization [10,15] with the Epiphytic decomposition approach [3], that allows the structural exploration of the NCOP instances. With this decomposition InDE executes its operators only on a subset of variables, while the others are valuated by a linear propagation through the network of constraints.

The performance of the proposed InDE on the functions of COCONUT Benchmark [11] reveals that the algorithm is capable of finding feasible solutions to more problems. In addition, the comparative analysis with real-parameter black-box DE showed that the exploration of structural information of the instances considerably improves the performance of the search method. Thus, this paper shows that the use of structural decomposition in optimization meta-heuristics is a promising investigation direction.

Some future works include extending the InDE to optimize unconstrained problems by removing the ε constrained component. Another aspect to be analyzed is the possibility of reducing the amount of InDE parameters, making them self-adaptive. In addition, our experimental evaluation can be extended by the use of other contractors and different structural decompositions of instances.

References

1. Araya, I., Reyes, V.: Interval branch-and-bound algorithms for optimization and constraint satisfaction: a survey and prospects. J. Glob. Optim. **65**(4), 837–866 (2016)
2. Dechter, R., van Beek, P.: Local and global relational consistency. Theor. Comput. Sci. **173**(1), 283–308 (1997)
3. Derenievicz, G.A., Silva, F.: Epiphytic trees: relational consistency applied to global optimization problems. In: van Hoeve, W.-J. (ed.) CPAIOR 2018. LNCS, vol. 10848, pp. 153–169. Springer, Cham (2018). https://doi.org/10.1007/978-3-319-93031-2_11
4. Faltings, B., Gelle, E.M.: Local consistency for ternary numeric constraints. In: 15th International Joint Conference on Artificial Intelligence, pp. 392–397 (1997)
5. Freuder, E.C.: A sufficient condition for backtrack-free search. J. ACM **29**(1), 24–32 (1982)
6. Hansen, E., Walster, G.W.: Global Optimization Using Interval Analysis. Monographs and Textbooks in Pure and Applied Mathematics. Marcel Dekker, New York (2004)
7. Kearfott, R.B.: An interval branch and bound algorithm for bound constrained optimization problems. J. Glob. Optim. **2**(3), 259–280 (1992)
8. Mackworth, A.K.: On reading sketch maps. In: 5th International Joint Conference on Artificial Intelligence, pp. 598–606. Morgan Kaufmann, San Francisco (1977)
9. Moore, R.E.: Interval Analysis. Prentice-Hall, Englewood Cliffs (1966)
10. Poláková, R.: L-shade with competing strategies applied to constrained optimization. In: 2017 IEEE Congress on Evolutionary Computation (CEC), pp. 1683–1689. IEEE (2017)
11. Shcherbina, O., Neumaier, A., Sam-Haroud, D., Vu, X.-H., Nguyen, T.-V.: Benchmarking global optimization and constraint satisfaction codes. In: Bliek, C., Jermann, C., Neumaier, A. (eds.) COCOS 2002. LNCS, vol. 2861, pp. 211–222. Springer, Heidelberg (2003). https://doi.org/10.1007/978-3-540-39901-8_16
12. Storn, R., Price, K.: Differential evolution - a simple and efficient heuristic for global optimization over continuous spaces. J. Glob. Optim. **11**(4), 341–359 (1997)

13. Takahama, T., Sakai, S.: Constrained optimization by the ε constrained differential evolution with an archive and gradient-based mutation. In: IEEE Congress on Evolutionary Computation, pp. 1–9. IEEE (2010)
14. Tanabe, R., Fukunaga, A.S.: Improving the search performance of shade using linear population size reduction. In: 2014 IEEE Congress on Evolutionary Computation (CEC), pp. 1658–1665. IEEE (2014)
15. Trivedi, A., Sanyal, K., Verma, P., Srinivasan, D.: A unified differential evolution algorithm for constrained optimization problems. In: 2017 IEEE Congress on Evolutionary Computation (CEC), pp. 1231–1238. IEEE (2017)
16. Van Hentenryck, P.: Numerica: a modeling language for global optimization. In: 15th International Joint Conference on Artificial Intelligence, pp. 1642–1647. Morgan Kaufmann, San Francisco (1997)

Hierarchical Classification of Transposable Elements with a Weighted Genetic Algorithm

Gean Trindade Pereira[1]([✉]), Paulo H. R. Gabriel[2]([✉]) [iD],
and Ricardo Cerri[1]([✉]) [iD]

[1] Federal University of São Carlos, São Carlos 43017-6221, Brazil
{gean.pereira,cerri}@ufscar.br
[2] Federal University of Uberlândia, Uberlândia 38400-902, Brazil
phrg@ufu.br

Abstract. Most of the related works in Machine Learning (ML) are concerned with Flat Classification, in which an instance is often associated with one class within a small set of classes. However, in some cases, instances have to be assigned to many classes simultaneously, and these classes are arranged in a hierarchical structure. This problem, called Hierarchical Classification (HC), has received special attention in some fields, such as Bioinformatics. In this context, a topic that has gained attention is the classification of Transposable Elements (TEs), which are DNA fragments capable of moving inside the genome of their hosts. In this paper, we propose a novel hierarchical method based on Genetic Algorithms (GAs) that generates HC rules and classifies TEs in many hierarchical levels of its taxonomy. The proposed method is called Hierarchical Classification with a Weighted Genetic Algorithm (HC-WGA), and is based on a Weighted Sum approach to deal with the accuracy-interpretability trade-off, which is a common and still relevant problem in both ML and Bioinformatics. To the best of our knowledge, this is the first HC method to use such an approach. Experiments with two popular TEs datasets showed that our method achieves competitive results with most of the state-of-the-art HC methods, with the advantage of presenting an interpretable model.

Keywords: Weighted Sum approach · Genetic Algorithms ·
Hierarchical Classification · Rule induction · Transposable Elements

1 Introduction

In Machine Learning (ML), the Classification problem usually consists of assigning instances to one class within a set of classes. In Hierarchical Classification (HC) [17], classes are organized in a hierarchical structure and each instance may be simultaneously associated with multiple classes in a hierarchical path. Considering a path $1/1/2$ from a tree-structured hierarchy, where "/" separates

© Springer Nature Switzerland AG 2019
P. Moura Oliveira et al. (Eds.): EPIA 2019, LNAI 11804, pp. 737–749, 2019.
https://doi.org/10.1007/978-3-030-30241-2_61

levels, $1/1/2$ would be a subclass of $1/1$, which in turn, is a subclass of 1, forming a complete path through the hierarchy. Thus, the set of class labels in a HC problem can be represented by a matrix $\mathbf{V} = \{\mathbf{v}_{\mathbf{x}_1}, \mathbf{v}_{\mathbf{x}_2}, ..., \mathbf{v}_{\mathbf{x}_N}\}$, in which $\mathbf{v}_{\mathbf{x}_i}$ is the c-dimensional binary class array associated with an instance $\mathbf{x}_i$ in a hierarchical structure with c classes. Each position j of the class array $\mathbf{v}_{\mathbf{x}_i}$ corresponds to a class that is set to 1 if $\mathbf{x}_i$ is assigned to class j, or 0 otherwise.

Many peculiarities compose a HC problem, such as: (i) the hierarchical structure used, which is basically a Tree or a Directed Acyclic Graph, (ii) the depths in which a classification is performed, being Mandatory Leaf-Node Prediction (MLNP) or Non-Mandatory Leaf-Node Prediction (NMLNP), and (iii) the exploration approaches applied to a hierarchy, which are called *Local* and *Global* [17].

In the Local approach, multiple classifiers are trained using local information about the classes and predictions often follow a top-down strategy, exploring the hierarchy towards the leaves [2]. Moreover, there are three types of Local methods, known as LCN (Local Classifier per Node), LCPN (Local Classifier per Parent Node) and LCL (Local Classifier per Level) [17]. In contrast, the Global approach uses a single classifier to deal with an entire hierarchy of classes and predictions occur in a single step [18]. Another difference between these strategies is the type of algorithms used. Whereas the Local approach uses well-established algorithms such as Decision Trees and Naive Bayes to produce a hierarchy of classifiers, the Global approach usually does not use conventional algorithms, unless they are heavily adapted to deal with a hierarchy of classes at once.

One of the major areas for applying HC is Bioinformatics, in which ML methods usually lead to better predictions in comparison to standard methods that often uses homology [10]. In this context, a topic that has gained attention is the study of Transposable Elements (TEs), which are fragments of DNA capable of moving within the genome of their hosts [9]. Due to the large number of TEs discovered in the mid-80s, a system for its classification became necessary. It was then that Finnegan [3] proposed the first classification system reported in the literature, which was, in fact, a hierarchical taxonomy. For that reason, the HC approach can be seen as a natural way of treating the classification of these elements. According to recent research, TEs can be related to mutations in a variety of organisms, being responsible for the genetic variability of many species [9]. Consequently, the correct classification of TEs can bring benefits such as understanding the evolution of several species, including biological pathogens [11].

Despite the importance of designing methods that can automatically classify TEs at multiple levels of their hierarchy, as well as generate interpretable models, just a few works seem to pay attention to these concerns. One of the reasons is that building interpretable classifiers without loss of predictive performance is a challenging task, since these two objectives are naturally conflicting. Therefore, an interesting solution is to consider Multi-Objective approaches to deal with multiple and conflicting objectives [4]. Given this lack in the literature, this paper proposes a novel Global hierarchical method called Hierarchical Classification with a Weighted Genetic Algorithm (HC-WGA). Our proposal is based on Genetic Algorithms to generate HC rules and classify TEs in many hierarchical levels. The method follows a Multi-Objective Weighted Sum approach in order to better deal with the trade-off between accuracy and interpretability, which represents a common and still relevant problem for both ML and Bioinformatics.

Although the definition of interpretability is broad and sometimes vague, it is a common consensus that a model is said to be interpretable if it is understandable to a human being [8,15]. Thus, we consider that our method generates an interpretable model, since it generates a set of HC rules. Besides, in this work we evaluate interpretability in relation to the complexities of the rules models generated by HC-WGA (number of rules and number of tests in the rules). We consider two TE datasets structured according to the hierarchical taxonomy proposed by Wicker *et al.* [19], and compare our proposal with other state-of-the-art HC methods. As results, HC-WGA achieve competitive prediction performance in addition to present an interpretable list of HC rules.

2   Related Works

Vens *et al.* [18] proposed a global method called Clus-HMC which generates a single Decision Tree (DT) considering an entire class hierarchy. Clus-HMC treats DTs as a hierarchy of clusters, in which the root node contains all the training instances and the remaining are recursively divided into smaller groups, as the hierarchy is explored toward the leaves. Therefore, predictions are made using a distance-based metric which calculates how similar an instance is to some DT.

Nakano *et al.* [11] proposed two LCPN methods called nlLCPN (non-leaf Local Classifier per Parent Node) and LCPNB (Local Classifier per Parent Node and Branch) along with two LCL methods, called LCL+SWV (Sum of Weighted Votes) and LCL+SP (Simple Prune), all of them based on Neural Networks. While nlLCPN tries to avoid the error propagation through the hierarchy by modifying the hierarchy and enabling NMLNP, the LCPNB besides modifying the hierarchy considers the prediction probabilities in all the hierarchical paths when classifying an instance, hoping that predictions in deeper levels could correct the errors in higher levels. On the other hand, the LCL methods use two different inconsistency correction procedures known as SWV and SP. LCL+SWV performs a sum of the predictions' probabilities to decide which predictions should be replaced, whilst LCL+SP just eliminates all the predicted classes whose super-classes were not predicted. Later, Nakano *et al.* [10] extended these methods using Stacked Denoising Auto-Encoders, reporting better results.

Santos *et al.* [16] applied several traditional classifiers such as Decision Trees, Naive Bayes and Support Vector Machines following the LCN strategy to classify TEs. The authors investigated strategies for selecting positive and negative instances during the induction of local hierarchical models, analyzing how these strategies affected the local information about classes during the training. As result, they recommended the best strategy based on empirical analysis.

Pereira, Santos and Cerri [14] proposed a global method based on Genetic Algorithms to induce and evolve HC rules, called Hierarchical Classification with a Genetic Algorithm (HC-GA). This method was able to classify TEs with good predictive performance and generate interpretable lists of rules. Later, Pereira and Cerri [13] improved HC-GA with the implementation of more fitness functions, which were evaluated in the prediction of all levels of the TEs hierarchy.

Although these methods being capable of making predictions at the four levels of the TEs' hierarchy with good predictive performances, the majority are not interpretable, except for Clus-HMC. However, Clus-HMC does not present such a good performance in comparison with others. Thus, we propose a method that is, at the same time, able to classify TEs in all levels of its hierarchy with good performance and that generates an interpretable model.

3   Hierarchical Classification with Weighted Sum

This section presents a novel Global-based Multi-Objective method for HC problems called **H**ierarchical **C**lassification with a **W**eighted **G**enetic **A**lgorithm (HC-WGA)[1], which can handle multiple objectives such as interpretability and predictive performance in order to generate a set of HC rules.

HC-WGA explore the simplicity of the Weighted Sum approach [4], that consists of transforming a Multi-Objective Optimization Problem (MOOP) into a simple one by using a weighted formula. In that formula, objectives are expressed together as one function and weights are associated with them, representing their importance to the problem [1]. An example of that weighted formula is: $Fitness = w_1 \cdot obj_1 + w_2 \cdot obj_2 + w_3 \cdot obj_3$, in which w_1, w_2 and w_3 are the weights assigned to each objective, which are combined in a linear way into a single value that represents the commitment of all objectives in solving a MOOP. These weights guide the search for solutions, thus changing the set of weights modifies the space to be explored within the space of possible solutions, directing the search to certain regions of interest.

The Weighted Sum approach has a relatively simple implementation as an advantage since it only requires to change the objective function into a weighted formula, allowing a rapid adaptation of simple optimization methods to multi-objective. As consequence, HC-WGA is a natural extension of its previous single-objective method HC-GA [13,14]. Despite simplifying a MOOP, HC-WGA is still able to handle multiple objectives at a low cost using a set of different weights.

3.1   Population Initialization and Individual Encoding

In HC-WGA, a population is created by a seeding process where training instances are randomly selected and their features are used to create individuals (rules' antecedents). Thus, each instance's feature has a pt probability of being activated (used as a test) in an antecedent. Usually, a low value of pt is chosen since a high value would result in rules with many active tests, which in turn, it would cover a few instances or only the seed instance. This seeding process ensures that each individual will cover at least one training instance (its own seed instance), and an instance is considered covered if all the rule's active

---

[1] Available at https://github.com/geantrindade/HC-WGA (20 June 2019).

tests are satisfied by the instance's features. This process is repeated until a population with the desired number of rules is generated.

An individual in HC-WGA is an array of fixed-length with real values representing the antecedent of a rule. Each set of four positions in this array represents one test related to a feature from the training set, where tests are encoded by a 4-tuple{FLAG, OP, Δ_1, Δ_2}. The possible components of this tuple are: (i) a FLAG, that receives 0 or 1 indicating if the corresponding test is been used or not (activated or deactivated); (ii) an operator (OP), that defines one of the possible operators used in a test of a given feature (numerical or categorical), and; (iii) the Δ genes, that receives real number values or indexes (in the case for categorical features), used as test conditions.

HC-WGA is capable of working with categorical and numerical features. However, since the adopted datasets contain just numerical values, only operators $\leq$ and $\geq$ were used. When creating a new population, these operators are chosen at random. So in case of choosing $\leq$ in the test, Δ_1 is set to 0 (not used) while Δ_2 receives the value of the feature being tested. Otherwise, using $\geq$ as operator, the opposite occurs. Also, it is possible to check whether a feature belongs to a certain range, such as $\Delta_1 \leq A_k \leq \Delta_2$, where Δ values are the lower and upper bounds for the numeric feature in the test. In that case, Δ values are randomly chosen in a way that the value for the test condition would satisfy the instance's feature, which also happens in the creation of a new population.

3.2 Rule's Consequent Construction

A rule's consequent in HC-WGA is a mean class array $\overline{\mathbf{v}}$ of real values representing probabilities of class assignment. Once an antecedent of a rule r is built, it is possible to calculate its consequent by using the equation $\overline{\mathbf{v}}_{r\,i} = \frac{|S_{r\,i}|}{|S_r|}$, which is obtained dividing the set of instances covered by rule r that are classified in class i ($S_{r\,i}$), by the set of instances covered by r (S_r). Thus, each of its i_{th} positions is a real value between $[0, 1]$ representing the probability of a given instance to belong to a class i in the hierarchy. For instances that satisfy the antecedent of r, this array can be used to classify those instances. Moreover, a threshold is always applied to the consequent arrays to obtain the final predictions. Here, we use a threshold of 0.5 (often used in literature), so if the i_{th} value in the array is greater than or equals to 0.5, it receives 1. Otherwise, the position is set to 0.

3.3 Fitness Functions

A variety of functions implemented in HC-GA [13,14] were combined with sets of weights and used in HC-WGA, where each one addresses the objective of predictive performance (Hierarchical Measures and $AU(\overline{PRC})$) or interpretability (Percentage Coverage and Variance Gain), being presented in the following:

1. Hierarchical Measures: hierarchical versions of F1 Score, Precision and Recall, proposed to consider the hierarchical relationships among classes [7];

2. Area Under the Precision Recall Curve $(AU(\overline{PRC}))$: HC-WGA outputs values in $[0, 1]$ for each class, which can be interpreted as the likelihood of assignment. This allows to calculate the Precision-Recall curves (PR-curves), obtained applying multiple thresholds in the outputs, what results in different Precision and Recall values or points within the PR space. Thus, the union of these points forms a PR-curve, making possible to calculate the area under the curve. A PR-point is obtained using the micro-average of Precision and Recall through equations $\overline{P} = \frac{\sum_i TP_i}{\sum_i TP_i + \sum_i FP_i}$ and $\overline{R} = \frac{\sum_i TP_i}{\sum_i TP_i + \sum_i FN_i}$, where i ranges from 1 to number of classes $|C|$, whereas True Positives, False Positives, and False Negatives are represented by TP, FP, and FN. With the PR-points, it is possible to calculate the $AU(\overline{PRC})$, where its value ranges between $[0, 1]$ and which the higher, the better;

3. Percentage Coverage (PC): measures the percentage of instances covered by a given rule. It is obtained by equation $PC(r) = \frac{|S_r|}{|S|}$, where S_r is the set of instances covered by a rule r and S is the total set of instances;

4. Variance Gain (VG): measures the decrease of variance among instances covered by a rule and instances not covered. In other words, VG partitions the set of instances in sets of similar instances [18]. Its formal definition is $VG(r, S) = var(S) - \frac{|S_r|}{|S|} \cdot var(S_r) - \frac{|S_{\neg r}|}{|S|} \cdot var(S_{\neg r})$, where the training set S is divided into the set of instances covered by rule r (S_r) and the set of instances not covered by rule r $(S_{\neg r})$. The VG of a rule r is then calculated with respect to set S. The calculation of VG also involves the Variance (var) of the sets of instances being considered (S, S_r or $S_{\neg r}$). So, considering one set, Variance is obtained by the mean square distance between each of the training instances' consequent and the mean consequent array of the set.

3.4 Sequential Covering Strategy

Along with the evolutionary process, a *sequential covering strategy* (also known as "separate-and-conquer") is applied to induce HC rules that classify instances from a hierarchical dataset. During this procedure, rules are induced and used to cover instances, which are immediately removed from the training set. This allows the generation of new rules that will cover the remaining instances when the evolutionary process is restarted.

Always after a population is generated, a local search is performed. This local search aims to ensure that generated rules will cover between a minimum and a maximum number of instances, thus preventing rules of being too general or too specific, which could compromise the model accuracy and interpretability. Then, after calculating the population fitness and the beginning of the evolutionary process, an *Elitism* operator is applied to the best e rules from the current population. Therefore, a set of $p - e$ parent rules (where p is the population size) is selected using *Tournament Selection*, which enables the *Uniform Crossover* to be applied between these rules, generating the offsprings. That crossover is a specialized crossover created to combine similar rules, and once is finished, the new population can be submitted to a *Bit-flip Mutation*. This mutation operator changes the binary FLAG genes according to a rate mr, determining which instances will have their genes values changed from 0 to 1 and vice-versa.

At the end of the first generation, the best rule from the current population is saved only based on its *fitness*. From the second generation onwards, all rules are ordered by their fitness and compared to the best rule from the previous generation. If a new rule has its fitness higher than the current best rule, it becomes the new best rule. The evolutionary process is executed until a maximum number of generations is reached or until the population convergence, which occurs when the same rule remains as the best rule after a specific number of generations.

After the end of the evolutionary process, the best rule is saved in a final set of rules and the instances covered by this rule are removed from the training set. This process is then restarted by the creation of a new set of rules considering only the remaining instances. This sequential covering strategy is repeated until all or almost all (a stop criteria defined) training instances are covered. Moreover, at the end of this whole procedure, HC-WGA checks if there are instances left uncovered. If so, they are classified using a default rule, which simply classifies instances using the mean class array of all classes in the training set.

3.5 Classification Phase

Given a set of rules, instead of using the first rule that covers a test instance $\mathbf{x}_i$, we adopted a selection strategy that showed better results [14]. This strategy works as follows: (i) from a set of rules, select rules that covers $\mathbf{x}_i$; (ii) search in the training set for similar instances to $\mathbf{x}_i$ by comparing features and considering a *range* (defined incrementally until similar instances are found), as well as a *tolerance* value of 90% (a minimum percentage of similarity), i.e., $feature_{train} \geq feature_{test} - range$ **AND** $feature_{train} \leq feature_{test} + range$; ($iii$) calculate the hierarchical F-measure (hF) [7] of the selected rules considering only the similar training instances; and (iv) choose the best rule according to its hF.

4 Methodology

4.1 Hierarchical Transposable Elements Datasets

The hierarchical datasets adopted are composed by TEs sequences collected from two public repositories, called PGSB[2] and REPBASE[3]. In fact, PGSB [12] is composed only by plant repeat sequences while REPBASE [6] contains sequences of repetitive DNA from different eukaryotic species. Both datasets are public available[4] and have been used in several related works [10,13,14,16].

Table 1 shows some statistics about these datasets organized according to a tree-based hierarchical taxonomy proposed by Wicker *et al.* [19], which is

---

[2] Available at http://pgsb.helmholtz-muenchen.de/plant/ (20 June 2019).

[3] Available at http://girinst.org/repbase/ (20 June 2019).

[4] Available at https://github.com/geantrindade/TEsHierarchicalDatasets (20 June 2019).

continuously adopted by the scientific community [11]. The features consist of
k-mers quantified in the DNA sequences with sizes of 2, 3 and 4. The number
of instances refers to the total number of instances without the division in train
and test subsets. The remaining statistics are the number of levels, the number
of classes in each level of the hierarchy and the number of leaf node classes.

Table 1. Datasets statistics.

	PGSB	REPBASE
Features	336	336
Instances	18678	34559
Hierarchical levels	4	4
Classes per level	2/4/3/5	2/5/12/9
Leaves	11	24

Table 2. HC-WGA hyperparameters.

Parameter	Value
Number of Generations	25/50/**100**
Population Size	25/50/**100**
Min of Covered Instances per Rule	**10**
Max of Covered Instances per Rule	**9000**
Max of Uncovered Instances	**10**
Crossover Rate	10%/30%/**90%**
Mutation Rate	10%/**30%**/90%
Tournament Size	**3**
Individuals Selected by Elitism	**2**/3/4
Probability of Using a Test (pt)	1%/**3%**/9%

4.2 Baselines, Hyperparameters and Evaluation Measures

In our experiments we included both Global and Local methods applied to the
same datasets. From Global, results of HC-GA [13] and Clus-HMC [14] were
compared. Results from LCN reported in [16] using traditional classifiers were
also included. The recent work of [10] improving the results introduced in [11]
using LCL and LCPN were also reported. Regarding HC-WGA, it was built from
scratch using only Java without any evolutionary framework. Table 2 shows its
final hyperparameters (in bold) which were obtained by grid search considering
only the training folds of a 10-fold cross-validation strategy.

As evaluation measures we applied hierarchical Precision (hP), hierarchical
Recall (hR) and hierarchical F-measure (hF) [7]. Furthermore, to verify the exis-
tence of statistically significant differences among results, the paired Wilcoxon
Rank Sum Test [5] with a significance level $\alpha = 0.05$ was used.

5   Experiments and Discussion

Considering the fitness functions implemented and tested individually in HC-
GA, each one addressing the objective of predictive performance or interpretability, they are combined in HC-WGA using a set of different weights aiming to
find solutions that optimize both objectives. Therefore, from the predictive performance group, we adopted hF and $AU(\overline{PRC})$ whilst for the interpretability
group, PC and VG were used. Only hF was chosen because it is the harmonic
mean of hP and hR. Therefore, five variations of weights were used for each combination of functions: (i) 0.2+0.8, (ii) 0.4+0.6, (iii) 0.5+0.5, (iv) 0.6+0.4 and (v)

Table 3. Predictive performance and interpretability analysis of the HC-WGA.

Fitness	Weights	Level 1	Overall	Leaves	Rules	Tests	perRule
PGSB							
$hF+PC$	20-80%	0.50 ± 0.17	0.40 ± 0.12	0.61 ± 0.10	4	20	5
	40-60%	0.61 ± 0.14	0.50 ± 0.12	0.61 ± 0.08	4	19	5
	50-50%	0.58 ± 0.17	0.47 ± 0.13	0.64 ± 0.08	5	30	5
	60-40%	0.62 ± 0.17	0.50 ± 0.14	0.58 ± 0.15	10	66	6
	80-20%	**0.94 ± 0.01**	**0.87 ± 0.01**	**0.83 ± 0.01**	1011	7198	7
$hF+VG$	20-80%	**0.94 ± 0.01**	**0.87 ± 0.01**	**0.83 ± 0.01**	958	6758	7
	40-60%	**0.94 ± 0.01**	**0.87 ± 0.01**	**0.83 ± 0.01**	1025	7376	7
	50-50%	**0.94 ± 0.01**	**0.87 ± 0.01**	**0.83 ± 0.01**	1037	7438	7
	60-40%	**0.94 ± 0.01**	**0.87 ± 0.01**	**0.83 ± 0.01**	1043	7527	7
	80-20%	**0.94 ± 0.01**	**0.87 ± 0.01**	**0.83 ± 0.01**	1047	7561	7
$AU(\overline{PRC})+PC$	20-80%	0.64 ± 0.19	0.53 ± 0.19	0.60 ± 0.05	4	**18**	4
	40-60%	0.55 ± 0.20	0.45 ± 0.15	0.75 ± 0.03	17	106	6
	50-50%	0.69 ± 0.14	0.61 ± 0.12	0.70 ± 0.05	55	360	6
	60-40%	0.84 ± 0.05	0.77 ± 0.05	0.75 ± 0.03	263	1716	6
	80-20%	0.93 ± 0.01	0.85 ± 0.01	0.80 ± 0.01	368	2224	6
$AU(\overline{PRC})+VG$	20-80%	**0.94 ± 0.01**	0.86 ± 0.01	0.81 ± 0.01	461	2978	6
	40-60%	0.93 ± 0.01	0.86 ± 0.01	0.81 ± 0.01	446	2868	6
	50-50%	**0.94 ± 0.01**	0.86 ± 0.01	0.80 ± 0.01	434	2763	6
	60-40%	0.93 ± 0.01	0.86 ± 0.01	0.81 ± 0.01	429	2739	6
	80-20%	0.93 ± 0.01	0.85 ± 0.01	0.80 ± 0.01	423	2664	6
REPBASE							
$hF+PC$	20-80%	0.28 ± 0.23	0.19 ± 0.16	0.19 ± 0.05	4	28	6
	40-60%	0.38 ± 0.21	0.25 ± 0.12	0.25 ± 0.07	14	105	7
	50-50%	0.60 ± 0.09	0.49 ± 0.06	0.47 ± 0.08	509	4220	8
	60-40%	0.75 ± 0.02	0.62 ± 0.01	0.58 ± 0.02	1240	10211	8
	80-20%	**0.89 ± 0.01**	**0.78 ± 0.01**	0.69 ± 0.01	2415	18823	8
$hF+VG$	20-80%	0.88 ± 0.01	0.77 ± 0.01	0.68 ± 0.01	1902	14608	8
	40-60%	**0.89 ± 0.01**	**0.78 ± 0.01**	0.69 ± 0.01	2396	18538	8
	50-50%	**0.89 ± 0.01**	**0.78 ± 0.01**	**0.70 ± 0.01**	2397	18640	8
	60-40%	**0.89 ± 0.01**	**0.78 ± 0.01**	0.69 ± 0.01	2405	18675	8
	80-20%	**0.89 ± 0.01**	**0.78 ± 0.01**	**0.70 ± 0.01**	2404	18654	8
$AU(\overline{PRC})+PC$	20-80%	0.34 ± 0.19	0.20 ± 0.12	0.17 ± 0.05	4	22	5
	40-60%	0.35 ± 0.12	0.20 ± 0.08	0.17 ± 0.05	4	**20**	4
	50-50%	0.35 ± 0.13	0.18 ± 0.09	0.14 ± 0.03	5	23	5
	60-40%	0.84 ± 0.03	0.66 ± 0.03	0.42 ± 0.04	152	902	5
	80-20%	0.86 ± 0.02	0.68 ± 0.03	0.42 ± 0.05	188	1133	6
$AU(\overline{PRC})+VG$	20-80%	0.87 ± 0.01	0.72 ± 0.02	0.55 ± 0.04	412	2648	6
	40-60%	0.86 ± 0.02	0.70 ± 0.02	0.52 ± 0.05	402	2561	6
	50-50%	0.88 ± 0.01	0.71 ± 0.01	0.53 ± 0.05	404	2579	6
	60-40%	0.87 ± 0.02	0.70 ± 0.03	0.49 ± 0.05	392	2481	6
	80-20%	0.87 ± 0.01	0.69 ± 0.02	0.47 ± 0.05	385	2431	6

0.8+0.2. These values represent percentages, thus, in the case of $0.8 \cdot hF + 0.2 \cdot PC$, the final value of the weighted sum will consist of hF value representing 80% of the sum, plus the PC value corresponding to 20%.

Table 3 shows some results from HC-WGA according to hF values and corresponding standard deviations. In addition to the overall performance (*Overall*) achieved by each weighted formula, these results include predictions for the first level (*Level 1*) and for the leaf classes of the TEs hierarchy (*Leaves*), since these two levels hold the most general and specific knowledge about the classes. Moreover, Table 3 also shows some statistics regarding the interpretability of the sets of rules generated by each weighted formula. This analysis includes the number of rules (*Rules*), the number of active tests in a whole set of rules (*Active Tests*), and the average number of tests per rule (*perRule*).

As seen in Table 3, experiments with $hF + VG$ showed the best results in both datasets, followed by $hF(80\%) + PC(20\%)$ with comparable values. Also, is seen that the best configurations in *Overall*, also presented higher values for *Level 1*. This correlation makes sense and has a theoretical justification, since in HC errors made by classifiers at levels closer to the root are usually propagated through the hierarchy, degrading the predictions' quality. Consequently, showing high predictive performance at the highest levels contribute to fewer errors being propagated as predictions become more specific, reflecting in the overall performance and in specific cases such as leaf class prediction.

Other configurations considered as good solutions were $AU(\overline{PRC})$ (80%) + $PC(20\%)$ and $AU(\overline{PRC}) + VG$ (with any weight variation), since comparable results were achieved in PGSB. However, these configurations did not maintain the good performance in REPBASE, differing from the others with statistical significance. Although, regarding the results in both datasets as tie-breaking criterion, $hF + VG$ with 50-50% and 80-20% achieved the best performance.

Concerning the interpretability comparisons in Table 3, it is possible to notice that changing the weights significantly affects the models' interpretability. Since functions related to predictive performance were combined with functions related to interpretability, when weights favor one side, the results are guided to optimize that function. This scenario is more clearly seen in formulas containing PC, which when favored, ends up generating simpler and smaller models. Unlike the weighted formulas in which PC is included and received more weight, configurations composed of VG did not present the same behavior or, at least, not with the same strength. In $hF + VG$, discrete changes in the models' complexity were noticed, whilst in $AU(\overline{PRC}) + VG$, an inversion of the expected behavior happened, since more weight to VG increased the model's complexity.

Configurations where PC received more weight obtained the best results, being the combinations $hF + PC$ and $AU(\overline{PRC}) + PC$ using the weights 20–80%, and thus, considerably favoring the function oriented to interpretability. In general, considering all the evaluated criteria and both datasets, $AU(\overline{PRC})(20\%) + PC(80\%)$ showed the best and most stable results. The worst results were obtained by configurations that prioritized the performance functions, being $hF(80\%) + PC(20\%)$ and all combinations of weights for $hF + VG$.

Table 4. Hierarchical F-measures achieved by HC methods.

	PGSB	REPBASE
HC-GA	0.87 ± 0.007	0.78 ± 0.007
HC-WGA	0.87 ± 0.006	0.77 ± 0.005
Clus-HMC	0.85 ± 0.004	0.71 ± 0.006
LCN-C4.5	0.83 ± 0.023	0.65 ± 0.035
LCN-RF	0.87 ± 0.028	0.64 ± 0.039
LCN-NB	0.55 ± 0.136	0.51 ± 0.070
LCN-KNN	0.86 ± 0.025	0.63 ± 0.055
LCN-MLP	0.85 ± 0.015	0.66 ± 0.040
LCN-SVM	0.76 ± 0.014	0.64 ± 0.036
LCL-SWV	0.89 ± 0.020	0.86 ± 0.010
LCL-SP	0.89 ± 0.020	0.86 ± 0.020
LCPN	0.89 ± 0.020	0.85 ± 0.010
nlLCPN	0.90 ± 0.020	**0.87 ± 0.010**
LCPNB	**0.91 ± 0.020**	**0.87 ± 0.010**

Table 5. Models induced by global methods.

		PGSB	REPBASE
HC-GA	Rules	1180	2507
	Tests	8749	19889
	perRule	7	8
HC-WGA	Rules	**1037**	**2397**
	Tests	**7438**	**18640**
	perRule	7	8
Clus-HMC	Rules	1375	2433
	Tests	18103	29941
	perRule	13	11

Table 4 compares the performances of the previously mentioned HC methods according to hierarchical F-measure. Most methods showed competitive and comparable results in PGSB, except for LCN-C4.5, LCN-NB and LCN-SVM, which did not achieve similar values. HC-WGA achieved the same result as HC-GA and was competitive with LCL-SWV and LCL-SP. Also, HC-WGA was superior to the state-of-the-art Global method Clus-HMC and all the LCN methods. However, the best and statistically superior results for PGSB were obtained by nLLCPN and LCPNB, with hF of 0.90 and 0.91, respectively. In REPBASE, HC-WGA did not outperform HC-GA but still proved to be competitive with it and superior to Clus-HMC and the LCN methods. Still, the best results were again achieved by nlLCPN and LCPNB, both with a hF of 0.87 and followed closely by LCL-SWV and LCL-SP, with a hF of 0.86.

Table 5 compares the rules generated by HC-WGA and the other Global methods. As shown, HC-GA and HC-WGA achieved similar results, obtaining even the same number of tests per rule (*perRule*). Comparing the results of Clus-HMC against HC-GA and HC-WGA, the latter generated more interpretable rules in all criteria and for both datasets. In short, HC-WGA overcomes HC-GA and Clus-HMC in PGSB and REPBASE with statistical significance.

6   Conclusions and Future Works

This work presented a novel Global method based on Genetic Algorithms that generates HC rules, called Hierarchical Classification with a Weighted Genetic Algorithm (HC-WGA). This method follows a Weighted Sum approach in order to better deal with the accuracy-interpretability trade-off. Experiments with PGSB and REPBASE, two datasets for TEs classification, showed that HC-WGA achieves competitive results with the state-of-the-art HC methods, and with the advantage of generating an interpretable model. Besides, it was verified that HC-WGA can generate smaller sets of rules containing simpler rules than HC-GA with comparable predictive performance.

As future works, we intend to apply HC-WGA in more complex hierarchical datasets related to other problems such as protein function prediction. Also, we plain to better analyze some functions such as VG that showed an unexpected behavior. Moreover, other Multi-Objective approaches can be explored, such as the Lexicographic method as well as methods based on Pareto front [1,4].

Acknowledgment. This study was financed by the Coordenação de Aperfeiçoamento de Pessoal de Nível Superior - Brazil (CAPES) - Finance Code 001, as well as by the Sao Paulo Research Foundation (FAPESP), grants 2015/14300-1 and 2016/50457-5.

References

1. Bandaru, S., Ng, A.H., Deb, K.: Data mining methods for knowledge discovery in multi-objective optimization: part a-survey. Expert Syst. Appl. **70**, 139–159 (2017)
2. Costa, E.P., Lorena, A.C., Carvalho, A.C.P.L.F., Freitas, A.A., Holden, N.: Comparing several approaches for hierarchical classification of proteins with decision trees. In: Sagot, M.-F., Walter, M.E.M.T. (eds.) BSB 2007. LNCS, vol. 4643, pp. 126–137. Springer, Heidelberg (2007). https://doi.org/10.1007/978-3-540-73731-5_12
3. Finnegan, D.J.: Eukaryotic transposable elements and genome evolution. Trends Genet. **5**, 103–107 (1989)
4. Freitas, A.A.: A critical review of multi-objective optimization in data mining: a position paper. SIGKDD Explor. Newsl. **6**(2), 77–86 (2004)
5. Hollander, M., Wolfe, D.A., Chicken, E.: Nonparametric Statistical Methods. Wiley, New York (2013)
6. Jurka, J., Kapitonov, V.V., Pavlicek, A., Klonowski, P., Kohany, O., Walichiewicz, J.: Repbase update, a database of eukaryotic repetitive elements. Cytogenet. Genome Res. **110**(1–4), 462–467 (2005)
7. Kiritchenko, S., Matwin, S., Nock, R., Famili, A.F.: Learning and evaluation in the presence of class hierarchies: application to text categorization. In: Lamontagne, L., Marchand, M. (eds.) AI 2006. LNCS (LNAI), vol. 4013, pp. 395–406. Springer, Heidelberg (2006). https://doi.org/10.1007/11766247_34
8. Lipton, Z.C.: The mythos of model interpretability. arXiv preprint arXiv:1606.03490 (2016)
9. McClintock, B.: The Significance of Responses of the Genome to Challenge. World Scientific Pub. Co., Singapore (1993)
10. Nakano, F.K., Mastelini, S.M., Barbon, S., Cerri, R.: Improving hierarchical classification of transposable elements using deep neural networks. In: 2018 International Joint Conference on Neural Networks (IJCNN), pp. 1–8. IEEE (2018)
11. Nakano, F.K., Pinto, W.J., Pappa, G.L., Cerri, R.: Top-down strategies for hierarchical classification of transposable elements with neural networks. In: 2017 International Joint Conference on Neural Networks (IJCNN), pp. 2539–2546. IEEE (2017)
12. Nussbaumer, T., et al.: MIPS PlantsDB: a database framework for comparative plant genome research. Nucleic Acids Res. **41**(D1), D1144–D1151 (2012)
13. Pereira, G.T., Cerri, R.: Hierarchical and non-hierarchical classification of transposable elements with a genetic algorithm. J. Inf. Data Manage. **9**(1), 163–178 (2018)

14. Pereira, G.T., Santos, B.Z., Cerri, R.: A genetic algorithm for transposable elements hierarchical classification rule induction. In: 2018 IEEE Congress on Evolutionary Computation (CEC), pp. 1–8. IEEE (2018)
15. Poursabzi-Sangdeh, F., Goldstein, D.G., Hofman, J.M., Vaughan, J.W., Wallach, H.: Manipulating and measuring model interpretability. arXiv preprint arXiv:1802.07810 (2018)
16. Santos, B.Z., Pereira, G.T., Nakano, F.K., Cerri, R.: Strategies for selection of positive and negative instances in the hierarchical classification of transposable elements. In: 2018 7th Brazilian Conference on Intelligent Systems (BRACIS), pp. 420–425. IEEE (2018)
17. Silla, C.N., Freitas, A.A.: A survey of hierarchical classification across different application domains. Data Min. Knowl. Disc. **22**(1–2), 31–72 (2011)
18. Vens, C., Struyf, J., Schietgat, L., Džeroski, S., Blockeel, H.: Decision trees for hierarchical multilabel classification. Mach. Learn. **73**(2), 185–214 (2008)
19. Wicker, T., et al.: A unified classification system for eukaryotic transposable elements. Nat. Rev. Genet. **8**(12), 973–982 (2007)

A Comparison of Genetic Algorithms and Particle Swarm Optimization to Estimate Cluster-Based Kriging Parameters

Carlos Yasojima[✉], Tiago Araújo, Bianchi Meiguins, Nelson Neto, and Jefferson Morais

Faculty of Computer Science, Federal University of Pará, Belém, Pará, Brazil
takeshiyasojima@gmail.com,
{tiagoaraujo,bianchi,nelsonneto,jmorais}@ufpa.br

Abstract. Kriging is one of the most used spatial estimation methods in real-world applications. Some kriging parameters must be estimated in order to reach a good accuracy in the interpolation process, however, this task remains a challenge. Various optimization methods have been tested to find good parameters of the kriging process. In recent years, many authors are using bio-inspired techniques and achieving good results in estimating these parameters in comparison with traditional techniques. This paper presents a comparison between well known bio-inspired techniques such as Genetic Algorithms and Particle Swarm Optimization in the estimation of the essential kriging parameters: nugget, sill, range, angle, and factor. In order to perform the tests, we proposed a methodology based on the cluster-based kriging method. Considering the Friedman test, the results showed no statistical difference between the evaluated algorithms in optimizing kriging parameters. On the other hand, the Particle Swarm Optimization approach presented a faster convergence, which is important in this high-cost computational problem.

Keywords: Bio-inspired algorithms · Artificial Intelligence · Geostatistic · Kriging

1 Introduction

Kriging is a geostatistical interpolation technique that predicts the value of observations in unknown locations, based on previously collected data. The kriging error or interpolation error is minimized by studying and modeling the spatial distribution of points already obtained. This spatial distribution or spatial variation is expressed in the form of an experimental variogram [9].

The variogram is the basis for the application of the kriging method. Thus, the kriging process is defined in three main steps. First, the experimental variogram is calculated. Then, the theoretical variogram is modeled to represent the experimental variogram. Finally, the value of a given point is predicted using the built theoretical model.

© Springer Nature Switzerland AG 2019
P. Moura Oliveira et al. (Eds.): EPIA 2019, LNAI 11804, pp. 750–761, 2019.
https://doi.org/10.1007/978-3-030-30241-2_62

Artificial Intelligence techniques have been used to improve the kriging process as shown in [2, 8, 10, 13, 15], however, it is still a challenge to determine what method is better suited for a given database. As stated in [8] and applied in [10], bio-inspired algorithms, in general, are suitable to help define the theoretical variogram parameters. Furthermore, these types of algorithms do not require a single initial seed value as input, but rather an interval.

Several researchers have implemented bio-inspired algorithms to optimize theoretical variogram parameters, such as Genetic Algorithms (GA) [2, 10, 15], and more recently Particle Swarm Optimization (PSO) [12]. However, which to the best of the authors knowledge, there is no systematic comparison in relation to accuracy and convergence of the kriging parameters estimation as well computational processing effort of these algorithms considering the same scenario of study.

This paper applies the cluster-based kriging method designed by [1]. In this method, the spatial data are divided into different subgroups by the K-means clustering method [14], where each data point is interpolated using only data from the same group. A limitation of the cluster-based method proposed by [1] is the task of defining a single theoretical variogram model for all groups, without considering that distinct regions of the analyzed database may present specific behaviors during the kriging process. Therefore, we propose the estimation and optimization of different parameters to each group. Some problems encountered in this kind of improvement, such as cluster overlapping and unknown point classification, are solved using the K-Nearest Neighbour (KNN) algorithm [14] and data preprocessing.

In this context, the purpose of this paper is to evaluate well known bio-inspired techniques such as Genetic Algorithms and Particle Swarm Optimization when applied in the estimation of the essential kriging parameters. As said, in order to perform tests, the cluster-based kriging method was applied and a GA and PSO model was built for each cluster. The results showed that both algorithms were statistically equal in optimizing the variogram parameters. However, PSO converged faster than GA. This conclusion is important because the adopted methodology (cluster-based kriging, interpolation cost function, and so forth) presents a high computational cost. Therefore, it is essential to reduce the number of iterations of optimization algorithms.

This paper is organized as follows. Section 2 consists of the theoretical background involving important concepts for the understanding of this paper. In Sect. 3, the steps of the proposed methodology are detailed. Section 4 presents the database used in this work besides the results of the experiments performed. Finally, Sect. 5 presents the final considerations.

2 Background

2.1 Kriging

Kriging is an interpolation technique widely used in geostatistics to predict spatial data. This method takes into account the characteristics of regional variables autocorrelation. These variables have some spatial continuity, which allows the data obtained by the sampling of specific points to be used to parameterize the prediction of points where the value of the variable is unknown [9].

Let Z be a set of observations of a target variable (response variable) denoted as $\{z(s_1), z(s_2), \ldots, z(s_N)\}$, where $s_i = (x_i, y_i)$ is a point in a geographical space; x_i and y_i are its coordinates (primary locations); and N is the number of observations.

Values of the target variable at some new location s_0 can be derived using a spatial prediction model. The standard version of kriging is called ordinary kriging (OK), where the predictions are based on the model:

$$\hat{z}_{OK}(s_0) = \sum_{i=1}^{n} w_i(s_0).z(s_i) = \lambda_0^T.\mathbf{z} \tag{1}$$

where λ_0 is a vector of kriging weights (w_i), and $\mathbf{z}$ is the vector of N observations at primary locations.

So, in order to estimate the weights, we calculate the semivariances $\gamma(h)$ based on the differences between the neighboring values:

$$\gamma(h) = \frac{1}{2}E[(z(s_i) - z(s_i + h))^2] \tag{2}$$

where $z(s_i)$ is the observation of the target variable at some point location, and $z(s_i + h)$ is the observation of the neighbour at a distance $s_i + h$.

Suppose that there are N point observations, this yields $N \times (N - 1)/2$ pairs for which a semivariance can be calculated. If we plot all semivariances versus their separation distances a variogram cloud is produced. For an easier visualization of this variogram cloud, the values are commonly averaged for a standard distance called "lag". If we display such averaged data, then we get the standard experimental variogram, which can be seen in Fig. 1.

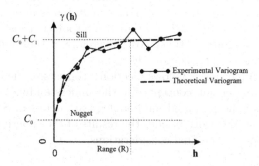

Fig. 1. Example of a final variogram model.

Once we calculate the experimental variogram, we can fit it using a theoretical model, such as linear, spherical, exponential, Gaussian, among others.

The variograms are commonly fitted using a cost function (e.g. weighted least squares [3]). Hence, the main objective is to minimize this cost function. In this work, in order to simplify the experiments, we only use the exponential theoretical model, which is given by

$$\gamma(h) = C_0 + C_1 \left(1 - EXP \left(-3 \left(\frac{h}{R} \right)^2 \right) \right) \tag{3}$$

where R is the range of influence or simply range, which is the coordinate where the model starts to flatten out; C_0 is the nugget effect, which can be attributed to measurements errors or spatial sources of variation at distances smaller than the sampling interval; and $C_O + C_1$ is the sill, which is the value that the model attains at the range R. These parameters, also called coefficients, determine the theoretical variogram as illustrated in Fig. 1.

Once we have estimated the theoretical model, we can use it to derive semi-variances at all locations and solve the kriging weights. The ordinary kriging (OK) weights are solved multiplying the covariances:

$$\lambda_0 = \mathbf{C}^{-1}.\mathbf{c_0}; \qquad C(|h| = 0) = C_0 + C_1 \tag{4}$$

where $\mathbf{C}$ is the covariance matrix derived for $N \times N$ observations and $\mathbf{c_0}$ is the vector of covariances at a new location. Note that the $\mathbf{C}$ is in fact a $(N + 1) \times (N + 1)$ matrix if it is used to derive kriging weights, since one extra row and column are used to ensure that the sum of weights is equal to one:

$$\begin{bmatrix} C_{(s_1,s_1)} & \cdots & C_{(s_1,s_N)} & 1 \\ \vdots & \ddots & \vdots & \vdots \\ C_{(s_N,s_1)} & \cdots & C_{(s_N,s_N)} & 1 \\ 1 & \cdots & 1 & 0 \end{bmatrix}^{-1} \cdot \begin{bmatrix} C_{(s_0,s_1)} \\ \vdots \\ C_{(s_0,s_N)} \\ 1 \end{bmatrix} = \begin{bmatrix} w_1(s_0) \\ \vdots \\ w_N(s_0) \\ \varphi \end{bmatrix} \tag{5}$$

where φ is the *Lagrange multiplier*. After calculating the weights, the prediction is then given by Eq. 1.

When the experimental variogram is distinct for two or more directions, we have an anisotropic phenomenon [9]. The anisotropy is calculated considering a certain angle from 0 to 180°, and a factor given by

$$Anisotropy factor = \frac{a_2}{a_1} \tag{6}$$

where a_1 and a_2 are the biggest and smallest radius of the ellipse (area of effect in the kriging process), respectively. This factor varies between 0 and 1, with 1 being an isotropic model. Therefore, in case of anisotropy, five parameters are used to estimate the theoretical variogram model: nugget, sill, range, angle, and the anisotropy factor.

2.2 Population Diversity Index

The standard population diversity (SPD) describes the level of variation in a certain population. Greater diversity implies greater variability of the population [16]. Considering a population with P individuals $(G_1, G_2,...,G_p)$, given that each individual (or particle) has T parameters (or genes), we can denote $G_i = (G_{i,1}, G_{i,2},...,G_{i,T})$. So, the general mean for each gene T is given by

$$G_T^{ave} = \frac{1}{P} \sum_{i=1}^{P} G_{i,T} \qquad (7)$$

In the normalization step, the standard deviation for each gene T in relation to the population P is calculated by

$$\sigma(G_T^{ave}) = \sqrt{\frac{1}{P} \sum_{i=1}^{P} (G_{i,T} - G_T^{ave})^2} \qquad (8)$$

Finally, the variability of the population P in each generation of the bio-inspired algorithm is given by

$$SPD = \frac{1}{T} \sum_{j=1}^{T} (\frac{\sigma(G_j^{ave})}{G_j^{ave}}) \qquad (9)$$

3 Methodology

The cluster-based kriging method [1] was adopted to evaluate GA and PSO algorithms. In this scenario, we first applied a preprocessing step using standardization algorithms and a statistical measure to remove outliers. After that, the K-means algorithm was used to find U groups of data. In this clustering step, the KNN algorithm was used to minimize the cluster overlapping problem, improving the clustering groups. For each group, the bio-inspired algorithms were used to find the kriging parameters, in other words, a model was built for each cluster u. Then, the unknown points (test data) were allocated via KNN to one of the previously built clusters and interpolated by the respective model.

The flow chart that describes the proposed methodology can be seen in Fig. 2. For each number of cluster (1 to 5), this process was repeated 10 times in the 10-fold cross-validation. Each iteration was performed using different training and test data sets.

3.1 Cost Function and Evaluation Metric

The fitness function used in GA and PSO algorithms was obtained by applying the kriging process at each data point (leave-one-out cross-validation) of the training data (90% of the database). Regarding the evaluation metric, the 10-fold cross-validation was applied. For both cases, fitness and evaluation, the

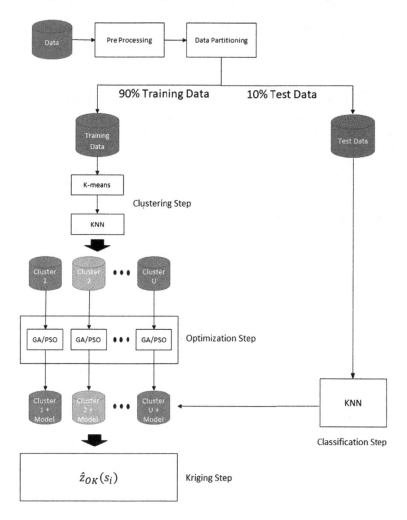

Fig. 2. Flowchart of the proposed methodology.

interpolation cost function (Eq. 10) was employed [10]. More specifically, the normalized mean squared error (NMSE) index was used as figure of merit and calculated by

$$NMSE_u = \frac{1}{\sigma^2 .n} \sum_{i=1}^{n} [\hat{z}(s_i) - z(s_i)]^2 \tag{10}$$

where $\hat{z}(s_i)$ is the predicted value of the target variable obtained by the kriging method at the hidden point s_i; $z(s_i)$ is the real value of the target variable at the hidden point s_i; n is the total number of points in the cluster u; and σ^2 is the variance of the target variable considering the cluster u data. A lower NMSE indicates a better prediction value. The NMSE index of the database is given by

$$NMSE = \sum_{u=1}^{U} NMSE_u \tag{11}$$

It is important to point out that the leave-one-out cross-validation was used only to calculate the fitness function of each solution (GA and PSO). In order to measure the accuracy, we applied the 10-fold cross-validation. So, the studied database was randomly partitioned in 90% for training and 10% for test in each iteration. In all, 10 iterations with different partitions were performed for each number of clusters. The average of these 10 tests was calculated in the end.

3.2 Data Preprocessing

In the data preprocessing step, the spatial information x and y, and the target variable, piezometric wells in this work, were normalized between 0 and 1. This procedure is important to ensure that every variable has the same weight in the clustering process and to avoid cluster overlapping. In the sequel, we used the Z-score measure with 99% confidence level to remove outliers.

3.3 Data Clustering

K-means [14] is one of the simplest unsupervised learning algorithms that solve the clustering problem. This clustering algorithm partitions the database into U clusters, where the user provides the value of U. In this work, the K-means method was chosen based on the solution proposed by [1], however, it is important to observe that any other clustering method can be used in the proposed methodology. Remembering that the main objective is to evaluate the performance and behavior of GA and PSO bio-inspired optimization methods.

After the preprocess and partition tasks, the training data was split into U clusters using the spatial information x and y, and the target variable. As shown in [1], the clustering process often results into overlapped clusters. This problem impairs the correct allocation of unknown (new) data into the clusters. So, in order to minimize the overlapping, all data were previously normalized between 0 and 1, and the KNN algorithm was applied in order to enhance the data grouping by allocating the current point based on the k neighbors. For example, the black circle highlighted in Fig. 3(a) demonstrates data overlapping, which was reduced with the application of the proposed methodology, as can be seen in Fig. 3(b).

3.4 Optimization Phase

For each cluster obtained by the K-means technique, we applied an optimization algorithm (GA and PSO) to find optimal kriging parameters: nugget, sill, range, factor, and angle. The accuracy of the interpolation are directly correlated to how good these parameters are. Each bio-inspired algorithm was evaluated based on the best set of parameters.

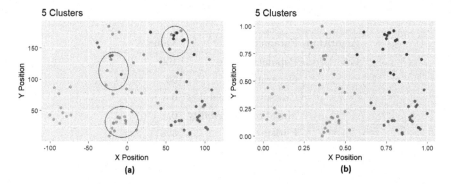

Fig. 3. Example of data clustering: (a) Original data clustering with overlapping and (b) Normalization + KNN data clustering.

3.5 Classification

The KNN algorithm was applied in order to classify the test data points into one of the previously built clusters based only on the spatial coordinates. Then, the kriging process was carried out and the error was calculated.

4 Experiments and Results

4.1 Database

The studied database represents the mountainous region of Wolfcamp Aquifer in West Texas/New Mexico [1]. This study area was already employed in other works [1,3] and classified as irregularly spaced with anisotropic data. This database contains 85 data points, including the spatial coordinates (x and y) and piezometric wells information (target variable).

4.2 Experiments

In order to evaluate and compare the results for the two studied bio-inspired algorithms, a manual tuning process was performed. The population size and the number of iterations were the same for both algorithms, and other specific parameters were manually tested. The final values are shown in Table 1. The GA code was designed on the R package GA [11] and the PSO code was also implemented using the R language programming.

For convenience, some parameters of the experimental variogram were fixed, such as the number of lags (= 1), the model type (= exponential), and the nugget effect (= 0). So, the chromosome (GA) and the particle (PSO) had the following variables: sill, range, angle, and factor. Their lower and upper bounds were defined, after the normalization step, as: range (= 0 to d); sill (= 0 to σ^2); angle (= 0 to 180°); and factor (= 0 to 1); where d is the maximum distance between two points and σ^2 is the target variable variance.

Table 1. GA and PSO parameters.

Algorithm	Parameter	Value
GA	Population Size	100
	Generations	50
	Crossover Probability	0.8
	Mutation Probability	0.1
	Elitism	5%
	Selection Method	Roulette
	Crossover Method	Real Coded [4]
	Mutation Method	Real Coded [5]
PSO	Particles	100
	Iterations	50
	Social Constant	2
	Cognitive Constant	2
	Inertia Range	0.4 to 0.8

GA and PSO fitness from one to five clusters in the optimization phase are described in Table 2. For more than one cluster settings, the results were obtained by summing the NMSE errors (Eq. 11). Because of the computational cost, 10 executions for each number of clusters were performed, each one using 90% of the database and the leave-one-out process. Note that the best results (or lowest errors) were obtained with five clusters for both algorithms and the average and standard deviation tend to decrease as the number of clusters increases. PSO always achieved better fitness than GA, but we can infer that GA is more stable, since PSO presented a higher standard deviation.

Table 2. Best fitness/NMSE, fitness average and fitness standard deviation.

		Number of clusters				
		1	2	3	4	5
GA	Best fitness	0.357	0.341	0.353	0.310	**0.287**
	Average	0.458	0.457	0.441	0.407	**0.381**
	Std. Dev.	0.098	0.051	0.036	0.038	0.044
PSO	Best fitness	0.354	0.299	0.314	0.269	**0.222**
	Average	0.739	0.625	0.537	0.513	**0.498**
	Std. Dev.	0.712	0.300	0.114	0.111	0.110

Figure 4 presents GA and PSO convergence curves from one to five clusters in the optimization phase. The results showed that PSO converges faster than

GA, in other words, PSO reached the best result found by GA before the tenth generation in most cases. Since it is a high computational cost process, this kind of information is relevant considering future works. This better convergence is probably explained by the fact that PSO presented populations with higher diversity level, as will be discussed in the sequel.

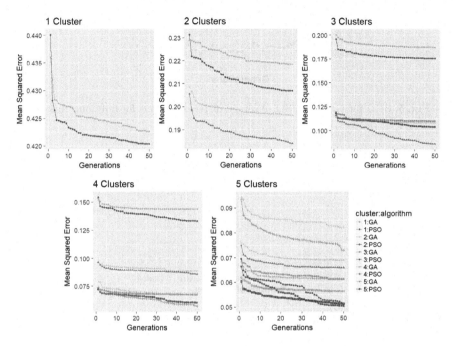

Fig. 4. Convergence charts for one to five clusters. Each line represents the average of 10 executions of GA or PSO.

In Fig. 5, we can see the standard population diversity (SPD) calculated for both algorithms. PSO had a much higher variation in the population than its counterpart GA. Obviously, a high diversity does not guarantee a better result, but it is a good indicator that the population is well spread out in the search space. Figure 5 shows the SPD values for the configuration with one cluster, just as an example, since the behavior was similar in the other settings.

Figure 6 presents the results of the classification step that were calculated using the 10-fold cross-validation process. More specifically, each iteration (= 10 for each number of clusters) used 10% of the database to test the kriging parameters previously estimated with the remaining 90%. The p-value obtained by the Friedman test [7] was 0.17, indicating that the error difference between GA and PSO was not statistically significant.

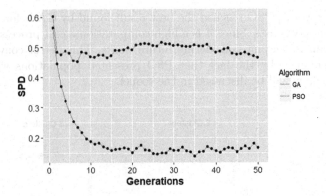

Fig. 5. SPD for GA and PSO. Average of 10 executions for only one cluster.

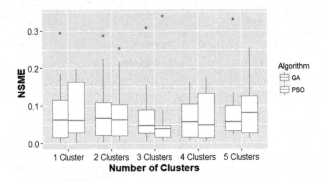

Fig. 6. Boxplot of NMSE considering the classification step for GA and PSO from one to five clusters. Average of 10 executions for each number of clusters.

5   Conclusions

The results obtained with the proposed methodology demonstrated that, based on the Friedman test, the evaluated algorithms (GA and PSO) are statistically equivalents when estimating the kriging parameters on the studied database. However, in the optimization phase, PSO converged faster than GA in all scenarios (1 to 5 clusters), which is an important conclusion.

Furthermore, exploring different parameters and customizing other operators could be interesting tasks to thoroughly assess the strengths of each method. Other topics that would add value to this research are: (i) reduce the computational processing time; (ii) test other techniques and databases in the proposed methodology; and (iii) discuss the impact of the clustering-based method on the stationary hypothesis. Stationary data is one whose statistical properties such as mean, variance, among others, are all constant over the spatial domain, which is suitable for the kriging process [9]. In [6], the author states that including the spatial coordinates in the clustering step, like the proposed methodology, does not guarantee the stationary hypothesis.

References

1. Abedini, M., Nasseri, M., Ansari, A.: Cluster-based ordinary kriging of piezometric head in west texas/new mexico-testing of hypothesis. J. Hydrol. **351**(3–4), 360–367 (2008)
2. Abedini, M., Nasseri, M., Burn, D.: The use of a genetic algorithm-based search strategy in geostatistics: application to a set of anisotropic piezometric head data. Comput. Geosci. **41**, 136–146 (2012)
3. Cressie, N.: Fitting variogram models by weighted least squares. J. Int. Assoc. Math. Geol. **17**(5), 563–586 (1985)
4. Deep, K., Thakur, M.: A new crossover operator for real coded genetic algorithms. Appl. Math. Comput. **188**(1), 895–911 (2007)
5. Deep, K., Thakur, M.: A new mutation operator for real coded genetic algorithms. Appl. Math. Comput. **193**(1), 211–230 (2007)
6. Fouedjio, F.: A spectral clustering approach for multivariate geostatistical data. Int. J. Data Sci. Anal. **4**(4), 301–312 (2017)
7. Gibbons, J.D., Fielden, J.D.G.: Nonparametric Statistics: An Introduction, vol. 90. Sage, Newbury Park (1993)
8. Gonçalves, Í.G., Kumaira, S., Guadagnin, F.: A machine learning approach to the potential-field method for implicit modeling of geological structures. Comput. Geosci. **103**, 173–182 (2017)
9. Hengl, T.: A Practical Guide to Geostatistical Mapping, vol. 52. Hengl, Amsterdam (2009)
10. Li, Z., Zhang, X., Clarke, K.C., Liu, G., Zhu, R.: An automatic variogram modeling method with high reliability fitness and estimates. Comput. Geosci. **120**, 48–59 (2018)
11. Scrucca, L., et al.: GA: a package for genetic algorithms in R. J. Stat. Softw. **53**(4), 1–37 (2013)
12. Wang, Z., Chang, Z., Luo, Q., Hua, S., Zhao, H., Kang, Y.: Optimization of riveting parameters using kriging and particle swarm optimization to improve deformation homogeneity in aircraft assembly. Adv. Mech. Eng. **9**(8) (2017). https://doi.org/10.1177/1687814017719003
13. Wei, Z., Liu, Z., Chen, Q.: GA-based kriging for isoline drawing. In: 2010 International Conference on Environmental Science and Information Application Technology (ESIAT), vol. 2, pp. 170–173. IEEE (2010)
14. Witten, I.H., Frank, E., Hall, M.A., Pal, C.J.: Data Mining: Practical Machine Learning Tools and Techniques. Morgan Kaufmann, Cambridge (2016)
15. Xialin, Z., Zhengping, W., Zhanglin, L., Chonglong, W.: An intelligent improvement on the reliability of ordinary kriging estimates by a GA. In: 2010 Second WRI Global Congress on Intelligent Systems (GCIS), vol. 2, pp. 61–64. IEEE (2010)
16. Yasojima, E.K.K., de Oliveira, R.C.L., Teixeira, O.N., Pereira, R.L.: CAM-ADX: a new genetic algorithm with increased intensification and diversification for design optimization problems with real variables. Robotica **37**, 1–46 (2019)

A 3-Step Cartesian Genetic Programming for Designing Combinational Logic Circuits with Multiplexers

José Eduardo Henriques da Silva and Heder Soares Bernardino[✉]

Universidade Federal de Juiz de Fora, Juiz de Fora, MG, Brazil
{jehenriques,heder}@ice.ufjf.br

Abstract. The design of digital circuits has been widely investigated in the literature but the evolution of complex combinational logic circuits is not an easy task for Cartesian Genetic Programming (CGP). We propose here a new approach in order to increase the capacity of CGP in finding feasible circuits (those with the same response of the truth table). The proposed procedure uses a 3-step evolution by coupling a 2-input multiplexer in each circuit's output. These multiplexers divide the truth table and the similarity between its inputs is maximized. Thus, don't-care situations are generated for the controls of the multiplexers, making the evolution of CGP easier. Also, a variant of the standard evolutionary strategy commonly adopted in CGP is proposed, where the following procedures are considered: (i) the Single Active Mutation (SAM), (ii) the Guided Active Mutation (GAM), and (iii) a crossover. The proposed methods are applied to combinational logic circuits with multiple outputs and the results obtained are compared to those found by a standard CGP with SAM. Benchmark problems with inputs from 9 to 12 are used in the computational experiments, and the objective is to find circuits that match the truth tables. The results show that (i) the combination of crossover, SAM, and GAM increases the performance of CGP, and (ii) the proposed 3-step method is the only technique tested here able to obtain feasible solutions in all independent runs.

1 Introduction

The design of digital electronic circuits is a task that requires time and knowledge of specific rules. The complexity of this task increases with the number of inputs and outputs. The evolutionary computation has shown to be a powerful tool for designing circuits and rose the so-called Evolvable Hardware (EH), which consists in the use of evolutionary computation techniques in the design and implementation of hardware in general [21].

Several methods can be found in the literature for designing combinational logic circuits, such as those developed by Coello and collaborators [1–5], and Miller and collaborators [12–15]. Miller proposed the Cartesian Genetic Programming (CGP), in which programs are represented as directed acyclic graphs (DAGs) composed by an array of nodes. These nodes have genes that encode

© Springer Nature Switzerland AG 2019
P. Moura Oliveira et al. (Eds.): EPIA 2019, LNAI 11804, pp. 762–774, 2019.
https://doi.org/10.1007/978-3-030-30241-2_63

their functions and their connections from the other nodes. In addition, CGP is pointed out as the most efficient technique for the evolution of digital circuits [20]. Most of these circuits are combinational logic circuits (CLCs), that is, digital circuits whose outputs are represented only by a combination of its inputs. There are no memory elements.

Despite the success of the application of CGP to this type of task when compared to other evolutionary computation techniques, some recently published papers still work with the same problems of 15 years ago and are walking through a very challenging scenario for balancing the real needs of the industry with the capacity of designing circuits via CGP [19]. The most complex circuit already evolved using CGP is presented in [22], which consists of a 28 input benchmark circuit. The evolution of more complex circuits using CGP can be found only minimizing the number of gates of known models [20].

CGP presents difficulties in evolving complex circuits. However, CGP is still used for solving this type of problem as it is efficient in obtaining circuits that escape the traditionalism of human design. This advantage especially occurs when the goal is to find more compact circuits in terms of reducing the number of logic gates. Thus, several works aim to increase the CGP's capability of exploring the search space. For instance, mutation operators are proposed for CGP in [7] (Single Active Mutation, SAM) and [17] (Guided Active Mutation, GAM), while crossover operators are presented in [9,10,16,23]. Also, an approach that uses multiplexers in CGP can be found in [11].

Initially, we propose here an approach using the crossover operator presented in [16], and combining two mutation strategies (SAM and GAM) aiming to reduce the number of evaluations needed to find feasible solutions. The crossover adopted found good results when designing of CLCs in [16], and the combination of SAM and GAM increased the success rate and reduced the number of objective functions evaluations required to obtain a feasible solution in [18].

Another method is also proposed here for evolving combinational logic circuits where a 2-input (and a controller) multiplexer is coupled in each circuit's output and evolving the candidate solutions using 3 steps. In the first and second steps, the inputs of the multiplexers are improved: the inputs must match the outputs of the truth table and the similarity between the values in the pair of inputs of each multiplexer is maximized. The controllers of the multiplexers are evolved in the third step. We intend with this procedure to decrease the computational budget required for CGP to find a feasible solution, that is, a circuit with the same outputs presented in the truth table.

As the number of evaluations required to find a feasible solution decreases, more computational resources are available for the circuit optimization phase in terms of reducing the number of logic elements. In addition, as a large set of logic gates are used in the CGP function set, the optimized circuits found tends to have fewer logic elements. Thus, we intend here to reduce the number of evaluations needed to find a feasible solution. The results of the proposed methods are compared to those obtained by CGP, all these approaches include a 2-input multiplexer as a logic element in the function set.

2   Cartesian Genetic Programming

Cartesian Genetic Programming (CGP) was proposed by Miller [12] and, despite his initial intention of evolving digital circuits, CGP is nowadays applied in several areas, such as robot controllers [6], neural networks [7], and image classifiers [8]. In CGP, the programs are DAGs represented by a matrix of processing nodes and each node contains genes that describe its function and connections to the other nodes. Each node connects to other ones on its left columns in the matrix, as shown in Fig. 1, where a CGP individual with a 4×3 matrix and which represents a model with 3 inputs and 2 outputs is presented. CGP's representation has three user-defined parameters: number of columns (n_c) and rows (n_r) of the matrix that encodes the graph, and levels-back (lb). Levels-back is the number of columns (on the left side) in which each node can be connected.

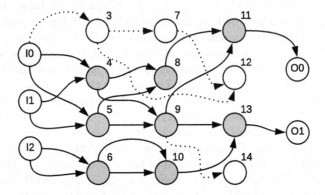

Fig. 1. Example of a CGP individual with *levels-back=number of columns*. Inactive nodes (those ones which do not interfere in the output) are in white. The circuit (phenotype) is formed by the active nodes and their connections.

The most common search technique used in CGP is an Evolution Strategy (ES) [12] $(1 + \lambda)$-ES, where λ is the number of new solutions generated at each iteration. In this case, the best individual considering the parent and the λ new generated candidate solutions is selected to the next generation.

In CGP, the most used mutation operator is the point mutation [12]. However, when using the point mutation, the changes may occur only in inactive nodes leading to a lack of modifications in the phenotype. The Single Active Mutation (SAM) [7,8] is another common mutation operator and was proposed for reducing the wasted objective functions evaluations. In SAM, the modifications caused by the mutation occur up to an active node is modified. Thus, SAM ensures that one active node is changed. The Guided Active Mutation (GAM) [18] consists of modifying active(s) node(s) on the subgraph from the inputs to the output with the smallest number of correct values when compared to the truth table. Thus, GAM does not mutate subgraphs which already matches their corresponding values in the truth table. Similarly to GAM, SAM also reduces the waste of computational budget.

Miller [12] highlights that crossover operators have received little attention in CGP. Walker [23] proposed a crossover for multi-chromosome structures where the circuits are represented by a set of arrays of equal length and each array represents a subcircuit for a given output. Thus, each node can connect to another node into the same chromosome or directly to a primary program input, and the crossover combines the chromosomes which generate the best outputs.

A recent approach uses an idea similar to that presented in [23] and was proposed in [16], where a good performance was obtained in the designing of combinational logic circuits. However, a single chromosome is adopted in [16]. The proposed crossover creates the new individuals using the subgraphs that encode the best outputs present in the individuals of the current population and it is applied during the selection step of the evolution strategy. The individuals generated by the crossover share the active nodes which are common in different outputs (keeping the graph structure of the whole circuit). When the problem contains only a single output, the crossover approach will select the individual with the best fitness, such as the standard CGP. Thus, this approach is mainly suitable for problems with multiple outputs. In addition, inactive nodes are present throughout the genotype, so that the neutral genetic drift can occur.

3   The Proposed Approaches

Here, two techniques are proposed: (i) a CGP method combining a crossover [16] with SAM [7,8] and GAM [18], and (ii) a 3-step optimization process using a multiplexer in each output of the circuit and the search method in (i).

The crossover adopted found good results when designing of CLCs in [16], and the combination of SAM and GAM increased the success rate and reduced the number of objective functions evaluations required to obtain a feasible solution in [18]. The use of crossover and GAM showed an improvement in reducing the number of evaluations needed for finding a feasible solution, as related in [16,18]. These approaches are detailed in the following sections.

3.1   CGP with Crossover, SAM and GAM

In previous experiments involving CLCs, GAM reduced the number of evaluations needed to find feasible solutions. However, GAM achieved low success rates (number of independent runs in which a feasible solution is obtained) when compared to SAM. Aiming an approach that increases success rates and requires few objective function evaluations in order to find a feasible solution, it is proposed here the combination of SAM, GAM, and a recombination operator.

This approach, labeled here as X-SG-MUX, modifies the $(1 + \lambda)$-ES commonly used in CGP by an $(1 + \lambda_{SAM} + \lambda_{GAM})$-ES, where the new individuals are generated using both SAM and GAM [18]. Also, the crossover proposed in [16] is incorporated in the search process in order to generate circuits in each generation using the best parts of all the offspring. Here, $\lambda_{SAM} = \lambda_{GAM} = 2$ and a pseudocode is presented in Algorithm 1.

Algorithm 1. ES 1+λ modification (X-SG-MUX procedure)

1: $\mu = 1$
2: $\lambda_{SAM} = 2$
3: $\lambda_{GAM} = 2$
4: Stopping Criteria $\leftarrow$ reach the maximum number of allowed objective function evaluations or find a feasible solution
5: **for** individuals $\mu + \lambda_{SAM} + \lambda_{GAM}$ **do**
6:     Create a Random Individual(i)
7:     Evaluate Individual(i)
8: **end for**
9: $\mu \leftarrow$ best individual of the initial population
10: **while** Stopping Criteria is not reached **do**
11:     **for** i in λ **do**
12:         **if** i = 0 or i = 1 **then**
13:             Mutate the parent (μ) with (SAM) and create a new offspring k_i
14:         **end if**
15:         **if** i = 2 or i = 3 **then**
16:             Mutate the parent (μ) with (GAM) and create a new offspring k_i
17:         **end if**
18:         Evaluate Individual(k_i)
19:     **end for**
20:     $\mu \leftarrow$ Apply Crossover($\mu + \lambda_{SAM} + \lambda_{GAM}$)
21: **end while**

3.2   3-Step CGP with Multiplexers

Preliminary experiments were performed in order to analyze the behavior of CGP in several situations in fictitious problems. Circuits with 4 inputs and a single output, and some Boolean expressions were considered in these tests. The results of these experiments indicated that CGP performed better in problems where the Boolean function is simplifiable. Considering this observed feature, the proposed method consists in the use of multiplexers coupled to the circuit outputs as the multiplexer is an element capable of dividing the truth table with respect to its inputs. Given this division of the truth table, the final Boolean expression of the circuit is obtained partly from the inputs and the control. In this way, the desired expression is obtained through three logic expressions: I0, I1, and control. We propose here a 3-step approach for finding feasible combinational circuits with a 2-input multiplexer (and a control) coupled to each output of the circuit. With this architecture, we aim to reduce the number of objective function evaluations needed for finding a feasible solution. Given a fixed computational budget for the designing procedure, reducing the number of evaluations needed for finding a feasible solution implies a greater amount of computational resources for a later optimization step. As a consequence, one expects an improvement in the quality of the circuits evolved.

Considering a multiplexer in each output of the circuit, the 3 steps of the proposal are: (i) to maximize the number of correct values used as inputs of the multiplexers (at least one input of each multiplexer must be equals to its corresponding output of the truth table); (ii) to maximize the similarities between the pair of inputs of each multiplexer; and (iii) to maximize the number of correct outputs of the evolved circuit (given by the multiplexers) when compared to the truth table. As a result, the circuit created by the proposed method contains an additional 2-input multiplexer for each output. In the cases where the set of gates does not include multiplexers, this gate can be replaced by its equivalent with basic gates (NOT, AND, and OR).

In the first step, the circuit is improved in order to generate at least one input for each multiplexer with the same value in the corresponding output of the truth table. Thus, for each multiplexer, at least one of its input is the correct output of the truth table. As a consequence, the desired truth table can be divided between the inputs of the multiplexer. Also, both inputs can be equal and a "don't-care" case occurs.

In order to increase the number of don't-care situations, the second step modifies the circuit in order to maximize the number of similarities between the pair of inputs of the multiplexers. One can notice that these values must correspond to the outputs of the truth table. The greater the number of similarities the easier it is to obtain the control (third step), as the control can give any value in don't-care situations.

In the third step, the control is evolved. The objective is to determine a controller which correctly selects the outputs of the multiplexes based on their inputs (I0 or I1). The outputs of the circuit (given by the outputs of the multiplexes) are compared with the output of the truth table. This step concludes the designing of a (hopefully) feasible solution.

A particular case occurs when we obtain 100% similarity between the inputs I0 and I1 of the multiplexer. In this case, there are only don't-cares situations in the multiplexes and, therefore, the constraints imposed by the truth table are met. On the other cases (those with not only don't-cares), the CGP effort is focused only on those outputs in which the control of the multiplexes must select the correct output based on their inputs.

The computational budget allowed to the search technique is divided into the three steps and these amounts are expressed as a percentage. Here, 30% of the number of evaluations are used in both the first and second steps, and the remaining of the computational budget (70%) is used in the third step. This number was chosen empirically in such a way that the similarities obtained after the second step are greater than 50%. An illustration of the evolution in 3 steps is presented in Fig. 2 and an example of individual is shown in Fig. 3.

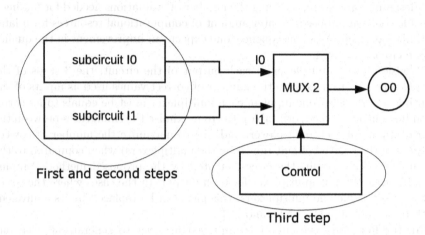

Fig. 2. Illustration indicating where the 3 steps of the proposed method are applied. First, the goal is to find the correct outputs of the truth table but considering the inputs I0 and I1 of the multiplexer. The second step consists of the maximization of the number of equal values of the inputs I0 and I1. Finally, the objective of the third step is to evolve the multiplexer's control. Each similarity obtained in the second step represents a don't care situation, and the optimization of the third step does not use the lines of the truth table with these don't care cases. Thus, the second step aims to reduce the number of lines of the truth table which must be evaluated and aims to decrease the complexity of the controller.

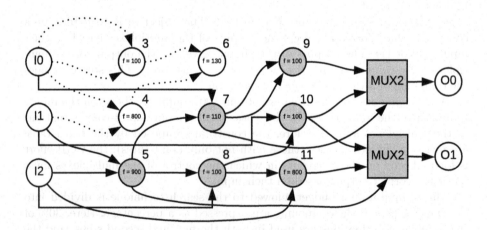

Fig. 3. Illustrative example of a candidate solution when the 3-step evolution is adopted. This individual encodes a circuit with 3 inputs and 2 outputs. Consequently, there are 2 multiplexes. The active and inactive nodes are, respectively, in gray and white. Continuous lines defines the edges between the active nodes and they form the phenotype.

Besides the 3 steps for evolving the candidate solutions and the representation with multiplexers, the proposed method modifies the standard $(1+\lambda)$-ES commonly used in CGP. The crossover procedure proposed in [16] and the $(1+\lambda_{SAM}+\lambda_{GAM})$-ES presented in [18], with $\lambda_{SAM} = \lambda_{GAM} = 2$ are also used. Thus, the proposed method takes advantage of both mutation operators, namely, SAM and GAM.

Considering an illustrative example where a 4 input and 1 output circuit is evolved by the 3-step evolution method, Table 1 shows the result of evaluating an initial individual where I0 and I1 are the multiplexer's inputs, D is the desired logic level in the truth table, and the match column is marked with an "X" when at least of the multiplexer's inputs corresponds to the value in D (I0 equals D, or I1 equals D). These inputs with the same value of D are shown in parentheses. The first step ends when I0 or I1 equals D for all lines of the truth table as shown in Table 2. Then, the second step begins using this obtained candidate solution and the objective is to maximize the similarities between the multiplexer's inputs. An example of the evaluation of a candidate solution at the end of the second step is shown in Table 3. When the 30% computational resources allowed for the first and second steps is reached, the third step starts the evolution of the multiplexer's control. The evaluation of a final circuit (generated using the remaining 70% of the computational budget) is presented in Table 4 where the column Control presents the desired logic levels where 0, 1, and "X" means that the result of the circuit is given, respectively, by I0, I1, and that there is a don't care situation. The program is ended when a feasible solution is found, or when the maximum number of circuit evaluations is reached.

Table 1. Truth table – initial individual.

I0	I1	D	Match
0	1	0	X (I0)
0	1	0	X (I0)
1	1	0	-
1	1	1	X (I0, I1)
1	1	1	X (I0, I1)
1	1	0	-
0	0	1	-
1	1	0	-

Table 2. Truth table – first step.

I0	I1	D	Match
0	1	0	X (I0)
0	1	0	X (I0)
1	0	0	X (I1)
1	1	1	X (I0, I1)
0	1	1	X (I1)
0	1	0	X (I0)
1	1	1	X (I0, I1)
1	0	0	X (I1)

4   Computational Experiments

Computational experiments were performed in order to comparatively analyze the performance of the proposed methods. Three techniques are used: CGP with SAM (labeled as CGP) [12], the proposed CGP with an $(1+\lambda_{SAM}+\lambda_{GAM})$-ES and crossover (X-SG-MUX), and the proposed 3-step technique (X-CGP-3E).

Table 3. Truth table – second step.   **Table 4.** Truth table – final solution.

I0	I1	D	Match
0	0	0	X (I0, I1)
0	0	0	X (I0, I1)
1	0	0	X (I1)
1	1	1	X (I0, I1)
1	1	1	X (I0, I1)
0	0	0	X (I0, I1)
1	1	1	X (I0, I1)
0	1	0	X (I0)

I0	I1	D	Match	Control
0	0	0	X (I0, I1)	X
0	0	0	X (I0, I1)	X
1	0	0	X (I1)	1
1	1	1	X (I0, I1)	X
1	1	1	X (I0, I1)	X
0	0	0	X (I0, I1)	X
1	1	1	X (I0, I1)	X
0	1	0	X (I0)	0

We adopted $n_r = 1$ and lb $= n_c$. CGP was applied with $\lambda = 4$, and $\lambda_{SAM} = \lambda_{GAM} = 2$ are adopted when X-SG-MUX or X-CGP-3E is used.

The function set is $\Gamma = \{\text{AND, OR, NOT, XOR, WIRE, MUX}\}$, except for the standard CGP where the MUX was not used. MUX represents a 2-input multiplexer. In this way, each CGP's node is represented here by 4 genes, such as, {I0, I1, F, C}, where I0 and I1 are the two inputs, F is the function, and C is the control of the node (only used by MUX nodes).

The functions NOT and WIRE are unary. Thus, a mutation is considered active only when the modification occurs in I0 or F. Furthermore, the functions AND, OR and XOR are binary, and modifications in C are not considered a mutation of an active node. Modifications in C are considered active mutations only when the function MUX is used. As a consequence, we guarantee that all mutations will generate offspring phenotypically different from their parents.

The problems used in the experiments are presented in Table 5, and they are benchmarks problems from LGSynth 91'[1]. The source code of the proposal is available[2]. The number of columns (n_c) and the maximum number of objective function evaluations were defined considering the complexity of the problems. Thus, larger values are used for the most complex problems. These values are also presented in Table 5. The number of independent runs is 10 for all the tested problems, except for problem br1 where 3 independent runs were performed as it has the largest truth table. Minimum (Best), median, mean, standard deviation (Std), maximum (Worst) number of objective functions required to find a feasible circuit are presented. Also, median absolute deviation (MAD), interquartile range (IQR), and success rate (SR), the percentage of independent runs in which a feasible solution is found, are shown.

[1] https://ddd.fit.cvut.cz/prj/Benchmarks/LGSynth91.pdf.
[2] https://github.com/ciml/ciml-lib.

4.1   Results

The results obtained by CGP, X-SG-MUX, and X-CGP-3E are shown in Table 6. According to these results, CGP did not perform well. The only problem in which CGP obtained a feasible solution was clpl, and this solution was found in 1 of the 10 independent runs. X-SG-MUX solved 2 of the 5 problems and obtained the best results in clpl. However, X-SG-MUX (i) was able to solve 2 of the 5 problems, (ii) reached 80% of success rate in clpl problem, and (iii) obtained results worse than those found by X-CGP-3E in newtpla2. Finally, X-CGP-3E (i) obtained the best overall results in all metrics for all problems tested here, except clpl; and (ii) was able to reach 100% of success rate in all problems.

Table 5. Problems used in the experiments where ni is the number of inputs, no is the number of outputs, nc is the number of columns of the candidate solutions, and Max. Eval. is the maximum number of objective function evaluations.

Problem	ni	no	nc	Max. Eval.
dk27	9	9	200	400,000
clpl	11	5	300	400,000
br1	12	8	500	1,000,000
newtpla1	10	2	200	200,000
newtpla2	10	4	400	500,000

Table 6. Summary of the results obtained by CGP, X-SG-MUX and X-CGP-3E approaches. The best values obtained for each problem are in boldface.

Problem	Best	Median	Mean	Std	Worst	MAD	IQR	SR
CGP								
dk27	-	-	-	-	-	-	-	0%
clpl	211350	**211350**	**211350**	-	**211350**	-	211350	10%
br1	-	-	-	-	-	-	-	0%
newtpla1	-	-	-	-	-	-	-	0%
newtpla2	-	-	-	-	-	-	-	0%
X-SG-MUX								
dk27	-	-	-	-	-	-	-	0%
clpl	**100466**	216526	218983,5	1.08E5	342416	84189	138964,5	80%
br1	-	-	-	-	-	-	-	0%
newtpla1	-	-	-	-	-	-	-	0%
newtpla2	189299	278260	273980	6,08E4	341269	40848	77144	50%
X-CGP-3E								
dk27	**123745**	**156512.5**	**158624.5**	**2.76E4**	**198965**	**24492.5**	**43632.5**	100%
clpl	180001	228051.5	268011.3	**8.13E4**	388787	42535.5	134845.75	100%
br1	**403575**	**569877.5**	**569877.5**	**2.35E5**	**736180**	**166302.5**	**166302.5**	100%
newtpla1	**60001**	**62552.5**	**65262.8**	**6.25E3**	**76163**	**2525.5**	**6613.25**	100%
newtpla2	**156588**	**209780**	**212944.1**	**4.82E4**	**298121**	**37462.5**	**68653.75**	100%

772 J. E. Henriques da Silva and H. Soares Bernardino

A statistical analysis was performed on the problems in which the feasible results were obtained by at least two of the search techniques considered here: clpl and newtpla2. The Kruskal-Wallis test indicates that there is no statistical difference between the methods for clpl (p-value=0.46), and there is a difference for the results when newtpla2 is considered (p-value= 0.05). In the last case, the results obtained by X-CGP-3E are better than those found by X-SG-MUX; CGP found no feasible circuit. As a result, the proposed X-CGP-3E obtained the best results (or they are statistically equivalent to the best ones) in all the tested cases and it is the only method able to achieve 100% of success rate.

5 Concluding Remarks and Future Work

A new method for evolving combinational logic circuits (CLC) via Cartesian Genetic Programming (CGP) was introduced, where solutions are evolved in 3 steps: (i) optimizing the inputs of the multiplexers placed in each circuit's output, (ii) optimizing the similarity between the pairs of inputs of each multiplexer, and (iii) optimizing the controls of the multiplexers with respect to the expected output values for the circuit. Also, Single Active Mutation (SAM), Guided Active Mutation (GAM) and a crossover are used by the proposed X-CGP-3E.

The proposed method was compared to a baseline CGP with SAM, and to a CGP approach with a single (standard) evolution, and with the same crossover and mutation operators used by X-CGP-3E (X-SG-MUX). We can conclude that the proposed 3-step evolution method: (i) obtained the best results with respect to all metrics considered here, except for clpl, where X-SG-MUX (with respect to best) and CGP (with respect to the median and mean) performed better; (ii) found the best results (or statistically equivalent to the best) in all the problems considered here; and (iii) was the only technique considered here which reached 100% of success rate for all the problems tested.

We also intend to apply the proposed method to more complex problems in order (i) to evaluate its computational limits, and (ii) to address needs from the industry. Finally, another future work is a sensitivity analysis with respect to the number of active nodes modified by GAM.

Acknowledgments. We thanks the support provided by CNPq (grant 312682/2018-2), FAPEMIG (grant APQ-00337-18), Capes, PPGCC/UFJF, PPGMC/UFJF.

References

1. Coello, C., Aguirre, A., Buckles, B.: Evolutionary multiobjective design of combinational logic circuits. In: Proceedings of the 2nd NASA/DoD Workshop on Evolvable Hardware, pp. 161–170. IEEE (2000)
2. Coello, C.A.C., Aguirre, A.H.: Design of combinational logic circuits through an evolutionary multiobjective optimization approach. AI EDAM **16**(1), 39–53 (2002)
3. Coello, C.A.C., Alba, E., Luque, G.: Comparing different serial and parallel heuristics to design combinational logic circuits. In: Proceedings of the NASA/DoD Conference on Evolvable Hardware, pp. 3–12 (2003)

4. Coello Coello, C.A., Luna, E.H., Aguirre, A.H.: Use of particle swarm optimization to design combinational logic circuits. In: Tyrrell, A.A.M., Haddow, P.C., Torresen, J. (eds.) ICES 2003. LNCS, vol. 2606, pp. 398–409. Springer, Heidelberg (2003). https://doi.org/10.1007/3-540-36553-2_36
5. Coello Coello, C.A., Zavala, R.L.G., García, B.M., Aguirre, A.H.: Ant colony system for the design of combinational logic circuits. In: Miller, J., Thompson, A., Thomson, P., Fogarty, T.C. (eds.) ICES 2000. LNCS, vol. 1801, pp. 21–30. Springer, Heidelberg (2000). https://doi.org/10.1007/3-540-46406-9_3
6. García, B.M., Coello, C.A.C.: An approach based on the use of the ant system to design combinational logic circuits. Mathware Soft Comput. 9(2–3), 235–250 (2002)
7. Goldman, B.W., Punch, W.F.: Reducing wasted evaluations in cartesian genetic programming. In: Krawiec, K., Moraglio, A., Hu, T., Etaner-Uyar, A.Ş., Hu, B. (eds.) EuroGP 2013. LNCS, vol. 7831, pp. 61–72. Springer, Heidelberg (2013). https://doi.org/10.1007/978-3-642-37207-0_6
8. Goldman, B.W., Punch, W.F.: Analysis of cartesian genetic programming's evolutionary mechanisms. IEEE Trans. Evol. Comput. 19(3), 359–373 (2015)
9. Husa, J., Kalkreuth, R.: A comparative study on crossover in cartesian genetic programming. In: Castelli, M., Sekanina, L., Zhang, M., Cagnoni, S., García-Sánchez, P. (eds.) EuroGP 2018. LNCS, vol. 10781, pp. 203–219. Springer, Cham (2018). https://doi.org/10.1007/978-3-319-77553-1_13
10. Kalkreuth, R., Rudolph, G., Droschinsky, A.: A new subgraph crossover for cartesian genetic programming. In: McDermott, J., Castelli, M., Sekanina, L., Haasdijk, E., García-Sánchez, P. (eds.) EuroGP 2017. LNCS, vol. 10196, pp. 294–310. Springer, Cham (2017). https://doi.org/10.1007/978-3-319-55696-3_19
11. Manfrini, F., Barbosa, H.J., Bernardino, H.S.: Optimization of combinational logic circuits through decomposition of truth table and evolution of sub-circuits. In: 2014 IEEE Congress on Evolutionary Computation (CEC), pp. 945–950. IEEE (2014)
12. Miller, J.F.: Cartesian genetic programming. In: Miller, J. (ed.) Cartesian Genetic Programming. NCS, pp. 17–34. Springer, Heidelberg (2011)
13. Miller, J.F.: An empirical study of the efficiency of learning boolean functions using a cartesian genetic programming approach. In: Proceedings of the Conference on Genetic and Evolutionary Computation, pp. 1135–1142. Morgan Kaufmann, Burlington (1999)
14. Miller, J.F., Job, D., Vassilev, V.K.: Principles in the evolutionary design of digital circuits - part i. Genet. Program. Evolvable Mach. 1(1–2), 7–35 (2000)
15. Miller, J.F., Smith, S.L.: Redundancy and computational efficiency in cartesian genetic programming. IEEE Trans. Evol. Comput. 10(2), 167–174 (2006)
16. da Silva, J.E.H., Bernardino, H.S.: Cartesian genetic programming with crossover for designing combinational logic circuits. In: Proceedings of the Brazilian Conference on Intelligent Systems (BRACIS), pp. 145–150. IEEE (2018)
17. da Silva, J.E.H., Manfrini, F.A.L., Bernardino, H.S., Barbosa, H.J.C.: Biased mutation and tournament selection approaches for designing combinational logic circuits via cartesian genetic programming. Anais do Encontro Nacional de Inteligência Artificial e Computacional (ENIAC), pp. 835–846 (2018)
18. da Silva, J.E.H., de Souza, L.A.M., Bernardino, H.S.: A guided active mutation for designing combinational logic circuits via cartesian genetic programming. In: Proceedings of the International Conference on Machine Learning, Optimization, and Data Science (LOD), pp. 1–12. Springer (2019)
19. Stepney, S., Adamatzky, A. (eds.): Inspired by Nature. ECC, vol. 28. Springer, Cham (2018). https://doi.org/10.1007/978-3-319-67997-6

20. Vasicek, Z.: Cartesian GP in optimization of combinational circuits with hundreds of inputs and thousands of gates. In: Machado, P., et al. (eds.) EuroGP 2015. LNCS, vol. 9025, pp. 139–150. Springer, Cham (2015). https://doi.org/10.1007/978-3-319-16501-1_12

21. Vasicek, Z.: Bridging the gap between evolvable hardware and industry using cartesian genetic programming. In: Stepney, S., Adamatzky, A. (eds.) Inspired by Nature. ECC, vol. 28, pp. 39–55. Springer, Cham (2018). https://doi.org/10.1007/978-3-319-67997-6_2

22. Vasicek, Z., Sekanina, L.: How to evolve complex combinational circuits from scratch? In: International Conference on Evolvable Systems (ICES), pp. 133–140. IEEE (2014)

23. Walker, J.A., Miller, J.F., Cavill, R.: A multi-chromosome approach to standard and embedded cartesian genetic programming. In: Proceedings of the 8th Annual Conference on Genetic and Evolutionary Computation, pp. 903–910. ACM (2006)

Extending Local Search in Geometric Semantic Genetic Programming

Mauro Castelli[1], Luca Manzoni[2], Luca Mariot[2(✉)], and Martina Saletta[1]

[1] NOVA Information Management School (NOVA IMS), Universidade Nova de Lisboa, Campus de Campolide, 1070-312 Lisbon, Portugal
{mcastelli,msaletta}@novaims.unl.pt
[2] Dipartimento di Informatica Sistemistica e Comunicazione (DISCo), Università degli Studi di Milano Bicocca, Viale Sarca 336, 20126 Milan, Italy
{luca.manzoni,luca.mariot}@unimib.it

Abstract. In this paper we continue the investigation of the effect of local search in *geometric semantic genetic programming* (GSGP), with the introduction of a new general local search operator that can be easily customized. We show that it is able to obtain results on par with the current best-performing GSGP with local search and, in most cases, better than standard GSGP.

1 Introduction

Genetic programming (GP) [12], in particular in the standard tree-based representation, has proved to be a powerful method to automatically build symbolic expressions and programs for solving problems in a wide variety of domains. Recently, the introduction of Geometric Semantic Genetic Programming (GSGP) and the new ideas related to the definition of Geometric Semantic Operators (GSO) [15] allowed to solve problems more efficiently and to produce better solutions [3,5,10]. Recently, GSGP has been improved by replacing the mutation GSO with a local search operator: the application of this local search operators allows the search to rapidly improve in the first few generations, thus increasing the speed of convergence [6]. However, the effect of local search and the best way to employ it in conjunction with GSGP are still not well understood. In fact, among the several possible ways of combining GSGP with local search, only one, called GSGP-LS, has been investigated in [6]. Here, we introduce a new method to perform this local search operation, namely by defining a generic set of functions to locally modify a candidate GP individual. In particular, the possibility of modifying the set of functions allows one to easily customize the local search operator, by making it suited for the problem at hand.

We compare our newly proposed method, which we call GSGP-reg, with GSGP and GSGP-LS, showing that in most cases GSGP-reg outperforms GSGP and achieves results similar to those of GSGP-LS, although with a different "fitness profile". That is, the problems in which GSGP-LS and GSGP-reg produce

© Springer Nature Switzerland AG 2019
P. Moura Oliveira et al. (Eds.): EPIA 2019, LNAI 11804, pp. 775–787, 2019.
https://doi.org/10.1007/978-3-030-30241-2_64

overfitting solutions are not the same, showing that the selection of the best local search operators for GSGP is still an open (and interesting) problem.

The paper is organized as follows: Sect. 2 recalls the basic concepts of GSGP, while Sect. 3 provides a short survey of the existing works linking local search with GP. Then, Sect. 4 defines our proposed integration of local search in GSGP, namely GSGP-reg. In Sect. 5 the settings of the experiments performed are then introduced and the datasets used are described in Sect. 6. The results of the experiments and their discussion are the topics of Sect. 7. Finally, some directions for future research are highlighted in Sect. 8.

2   Geometric Semantic Genetic Programming

GSGP was originally defined by Moraglio and coworkers in 2012 [15]. The main idea is that mutation and crossover operators can be defined in such a way that the effects on the semantics of the individuals are predictable, differently from the usual syntactic crossover and mutation. They were successful in defining those operators, and proved that GSO induce a unimodal fitness landscape, in which the unique global optimum is known and the fitness is derived from the distance from this global optimum.

In particular, the geometric semantic crossover between two trees T_1 and T_2 is defined as

$$R \cdot T_1 + (1 - R) \cdot T_2$$

where R is a randomly generated tree with outputs in $[0, 1]$. The geometric semantic mutation of a tree T is defined as:

$$T + ms \cdot (R_1 - R_2)$$

where ms is a positive constant (called the *mutation step*) and both R_1 and R_2 are randomly generated trees with outputs in $[0, 1]$.

While GSGP produces a "nice" fitness landscape, in its original formulation the crossover operator induces an exponential increase in the size of the individuals with respect to the number of generations, as already remarked when GSGP was introduced [15]. A different representation of the individual was introduced shortly after in [18], where the individuals are still trees at the logical level, but they are represented in memory as directed graphs. This new way of implementing GSGP allowed to obtain better performances than classical tree-based GP with shorter execution times.

3   Related Work

This section reports some of the most important works related to the method described in the rest of this paper. Most of the existing methods were specifically designed for standard syntax-based GP and taking into account symbolic regression problems. Thus, it is fundamental to frame the context in which the existing techniques were developed.

The main objective in addressing a symbolic regression problem is to search for the symbolic expression $K^O : \mathbb{R}^p \to \mathbb{R}$ that best fits a particular training set $\mathbb{T} = \{(x_1, y_1), \ldots, (x_n, y_n)\}$ of n input/output pairs with $x_i \in \mathbb{R}^p$ and $y_i \in \mathbb{R}$.

Then, following the same formulation proposed by Castelli and coauthors [6], a symbolic regression problem can be formally defined as

$$(K^O, \boldsymbol{\theta}^O) \leftarrow \underset{K \in \mathbb{G}; \theta \in \mathbb{R}^m}{arg\ min}\ f(K(x_i, \theta), y_i) \text{ with } i = 1, \ldots, p\ ,$$

where $\mathbb{G}$ is the solution or syntactic space defined by the primitive set $\mathbb{P}$ (functions and terminals), while f is the fitness function based on the distance between a program's output $K(x_i, \theta)$ and the expected output y_i (such as the root mean square error–RMSE), and $\theta \in \mathbb{R}^m$ is a particular parametrization of the symbolic expression K.

Standard GP operators work at the syntax level, without taking into account the effects on the semantics. Nonetheless, GP was able to successfully solve problems in different domains [13]. Despite that, the impossibility to optimize the parameters of the model translates into significant limitations, such as search stagnation, bloat [19] and solutions that are poorly understandable [6,14]. This is mostly due to the fact that GP performs a highly-exploratory search, characterized by large fitness changes when a modest syntactic modification occurs and vice-versa [6].

Different works were proposed to include a local search strategy into evolutionary algorithms [9,16]. The common idea shared by these methods consists of defining an operator that, given a candidate solution, is able to exploit the local region around that solution to search for the best neighbor.

Considering the particular case of GP, it is possible to distinguish two main methods for applying a local search (LS) strategy: apply LS either on the syntax or on the numerical parameters of the program [6,14].

With respect to the first approach, Azad and Ryan [2] proposed the use of local search to change the fitness of individuals during their lifetime. While the proposed system was not the first attempt to include LS in GP, it was easy to understand and cheap to implement [2]. Their results show that GP with LS outperforms standard GP over different symbolic regression problems. Moreover, they show that the system uses the available genetic material more efficiently than standard GP, and that the training process produces smaller individuals.

With respect to the second approach, several works are worth to be mentioned. In [17], authors studied the effectiveness of gradient search optimization of numeric leaf values in GP individuals. The results reported by the authors showed that local learning yielded an improved approximation accuracy, even if they optimized only the value of the terminal nodes of the trees.

A similar approach was proposed in the work of Zhang and Smart [22], where a LS algorithm was integrated into the GP search process to optimize the value of the terminal nodes.

In [21] the authors investigated a Lamarckian memetic GP, incorporating a LS strategy to refine GP individuals expressed as syntax trees. The authors tested different heuristic methods to determine which individuals should be subject to LS, showing that better results can be obtained by applying LS to all individuals in the population or to a subset of the best individuals. All in all, the results demonstrated that including a LS strategy in GP is beneficial both in terms of convergence and performance, as well as limiting code growth.

The use of LS in GP for symbolic regression was also proposed in [14], where the authors integrated a LS optimizer as an additional search operator. The results showed that the use of the LS operator helps improving the convergence and performance of tree-based GP, while reducing the size (i.e., the number of nodes) of the trees.

With respect to GSGP, to the best of our knowledge, the only work published in this line of research is the one proposed in [6], where the authors modified the original geometric semantic mutation (GSM) operator to integrate a greedy LS optimizer. Given an individual T, the resulting operator (called GSM-LS) was defined as follows:

$$T' = \alpha_0 + \alpha_1 \cdot T + \alpha_2 \cdot (R_1 - R_2)$$

where R_1 and R_2 are random trees with output in $[0, 1]$, while $\alpha_i \in \mathbb{R}$. In particular, α_2 replaces the mutation step parameter ms that characterizes the geometric semantic mutation operator.

As reported in [6], the GSM-LS operator tries to determine the best linear combination of the parent tree and the random trees used to perturb it, and it is local in the sense of the linear problem defined by the GSM operator. When compared against the original GSM operator, GSM-LS was able to improve the convergence speed of the search process, and reduced the size of the resulting solution [4,6,8,11].

4   A New Way to Perform Local Search

In this paper we build on top of the GSGP-LS idea, whereby differently from the work described in [6], we apply LS to all the individuals during a separate step after mutation and crossover.

Let $T : \mathbb{R}^p \to \mathbb{R}$ be a GP individual encoded by a tree which is defined over a set of primitives $\mathbb{P}$, and let $s(T) = (T(x_1), T(x_2), \ldots, T(x_n))$ be its semantic vector computed on the inputs $X = (x_1, \ldots, x_n)$, where $x_i \in \mathbb{R}^p$ and $T(x_i) \in \mathbb{R}$ for all $i \in \{1, \cdots, p\}$. Further, let $Y = (y_1, \ldots, y_n) \in \mathbb{R}^n$ be the vector of target values associated to X. In particular, the *training set* $\mathbb{T} = \{(x_1, y_1), \cdots, (x_n, y_n)\}$ is the diagonal of the Cartesian product $X \times Y$. In what follows, we assume that the fitness f of the individual T is the *mean squared error* (MSE) of T in predicting Y from X, i.e.

$$f(T) = \frac{1}{n} \sum_{i=1}^{n} (T(x_i) - y_i)^2 \ .$$

Remark that, however, our local search method can be defined with any order-preserving transformation of the MSE as the underlying fitness function, such as the *RMSE*.

A first idea to introduce a local search step in GSGP is to define a regression problem that aims at minimizing the error between the values in the vector $s(T)$ and Y as follows: find two coefficients $\alpha^*, \beta^* \in \mathbb{R}$ that minimize the sum of the squares of the differences between $\alpha T(x_i) + \beta$ and y_i. Formally, for all $i \in \{1, \cdots, n\}$ we have

$$T'(x_i) = \alpha^* T(x_i) + \beta^* \ , \ \text{where} \ (\alpha^*, \beta^*) = \underset{\alpha, \beta \in \mathbb{R}}{arg \ min} \left\{ f(\alpha T(x_i) + \beta) \right\} \ .$$

In other words, the original tree T is replaced by an affine transformation T', which is then encoded as a new GP individual. Since $\alpha = 1$ and $\beta = 0$ is a valid solution, the resulting individual T' will not have a worse fitness than that of the original individual T over the training set.

The idea of replacing a tree with an affine transformation of it can be generalized to allow more complex transformations of a GP tree. In particular, let $\mathcal{F} = \{f_1, \ldots, f_k : \mathbb{R} \to \mathbb{R}\}$ be a collection of k real functions. We can thus define the semantic vectors for all $1 \leq i \leq k$ as

$$s(f_i \circ T) = (f_i(T(x_1)), f_i(T(x_2)), \cdots, f_i(T(x_n))) \ .$$

Similarly to the affine transformation case, one can define a regression problem using the components of the vectors $s(f_i \circ T)$ in the following way: find k coefficients $\alpha_1^*, \cdots, \alpha_k^* \in \mathbb{R}$ that minimize the sum of the squares of the differences between y_i and $T'(x_i)$, where

$$T'(x_i) = \sum_{j=1}^{k} \alpha_j f_j(T(x_i)) = \alpha_1^* f_1(T(x_i)) + \alpha_2^* f_2(T(x_i)) + \cdots + \alpha_k^* f_k(T(x_i)) \quad (1)$$

for all $1 \leq i \leq n$. Therefore, the formulation of the regression problem becomes

$$(\alpha_1^*, \cdots, \alpha_k^*) = \underset{\alpha_1, \cdots \alpha_k \in \mathbb{R}}{arg \ min} \left\{ f \left(\sum_{j=1}^{k} \alpha_j f_j(T(x_i)) \right) \right\} \ . \quad (2)$$

Clearly, one obtains a direct generalization of the previous regression problem if set $\mathcal{F}$ includes both a non-zero constant function and the identity function. The goodness of the solutions obtained by solving this linear regression problem depends on the particular set $\mathcal{F}$, which can include non-linear functions as well.

Our modified version of GSGP uses the linear regression problem defined by Eq. (1), with coefficient given by Eq. (2), as an additional local search step that tries to exploit the structure of the candidate solutions. In particular, this step is applied at each generation over all individuals in the current population after having applied semantic crossover and mutation, and before the insertion in the new population.

5   Experimental Settings

In the following, GSGP denotes standard Geometric Semantic GP, GSGP-LS the variant of GSGP with the local search mutation operator introduced in [6], and GSGP-reg the regression-based method described in Sect. 4.

The set of functional symbols employed in the experiments was $\{+, -, \times, \div\}$, where $\div$ is division, protected by returning 1 when the denominator is sufficiently close to 0. The set of terminal symbols was the set of all input variables over which the symbolic expression encoded by a GP individual is defined. In particular, no fixed constant was used in the terminal set. All GSGP variants investigated in our experiments adopted a generational evolutionary strategy, using tournament selection with tournament size $t = 4$. Each offspring individual was created by applying either semantic crossover or mutation, with a probability respectively of 0.6 and 0.4. The population size was set at 250 individuals, generated through a ramped half-and-half method with a maximum initial depth of 6. Survival of the best candidate solution in the population was assured by employing elitism with replacement of a random individual. The trees used in the semantic mutation and crossover operators were randomly generated with a maximum depth of 6, and their values constrained between 0 and 1 by using a logistic function.

Both GSGP-LS and GSGP-reg performed the local search step only for the first 10 generations; then, the algorithm switched to GSGP. As shown in [6], this limits the overfitting introduced by the local search procedure. Further possibilities, like the application every k generations, will be the aim of future investigations. As for GSGP-reg, we performed some preliminary explorations with different sets of functions for the regression step. This showed that a good trade-off between performances on the training set and the avoidance of overfitting was given by the four functions $f_1(x) = 1$ (constant), $f_2(x) = x$ (identity), $f_3(x) = \max(0, x)$ (positive part), and $f_4(x) = \min(0, x)$ (negative part).

In all considered problems, a 70/30 random split between train and test sets was used. To ensure the statistical validity of the results, we performed 100 runs of 500 generations on each test problem, using a different random split of training and test sets in each run. We used the RMSE as the fitness function to minimize in all problems.

For all test problems we recorded the median and the median absolute deviation (MAD) of the fitness obtained by the best individual of the population, since they are more resistant to outliers than the average and the standard deviation. The results obtained by the three methods on the test sets were also compared among themselves using the Mann-Whitney U-test, adopting the alternative hypothesis that the fitness achieved by the first method (either GSGP or GSGP-LS) was greater, and thus worse, than the fitness achieved by the second method (either GSGP-LS or GSGP-reg). The significance level adopted for the tests was $\alpha = 0.05$. The Mann-Whitney U-test was used since it makes no assumption on the distribution underlying the samples.

6 Regression Problems Used for Testing

We performed our experiments over five regression problems. In particular, the first three come from the domain of pharmacokinetics, and concern the prediction of three different parameters featured by a set of chemical compounds that are considered for potential drug development, and which are represented by their molecular structure. On the other hand, the last two problems pertain civil engineering, and specifically consist in predicting two parameters of concrete based on the mix of ingredients used to produce it. We briefly describe each of the considered problems, and summarize in a table the dimensions of the respective datasets at the end of this section. For further information, the reader may refer to [1,6] for the pharmacokinetics problems and to [7,20] for the concrete problems. In our experiments we adopted the same datasets used in those works. Table 1 summarizes the sizes of the five considered datasets. The "#Features" row includes both the input features and the output value of the parameter.

Table 1. Sizes of the considered datasets.

	%F	%PPB	TOX	COMP	SLUMP
#Instances	260	131	234	1030	102
#Features	242	627	627	8	9

Human Oral Bioavailability (%F). Human Oral Bioavailability (shortened as %F) is a pharmacokinetic parameter which measures the quantity of an orally-administered drug that actually reaches blood circulation after being processed by the liver. The dataset adopted in our experiments is composed of 260 molecules instances, each of them represented by 241 molecular descriptors and the corresponding value of %F.

Plasma Protein Binding (%PPB). Plasma Protein Binding (indicated as %PPB in what follows) is a parameter more specific than %F, since it measures the quantity of drug that reaches circulation and further attaches to plasma proteins in the blood. The dataset is composed of 131 molecules instances, where each instance is described by 626 features and the associated value of %PPB.

Median Lethal Dose (TOX). Median Lethal Dose (informally referred to as *toxicity*, and abbreviated as TOX) measures the quantity of drug which is necessary to kill half of the test organisms. As noted in [1], one can have different toxicity parameters depending on the specific test organism and administration route. The parameter considered in our experiments is the one used in [1,6], which concerns mice as test organisms and oral supplying as an administration route. The dataset is composed of 234 molecules instances which, as in the %PPB dataset, are described by 626 features and the corresponding value of TOX.

Concrete Compressive Strength (COMP). Concrete Compressive Strength (abbreviated as COMP in the following) is a parameter that measures how much a particular mix of concrete can resist compression forces. The dataset of our experiments is composed of 1030 instances of concrete mix, each described by 7 features (i.e. the ingredients composing the mix) and the corresponding value of COMP.

Concrete Slump (SLUMP). Concrete Slump (indicated as SLUMP) is a parameter that measures the consistency of fresh concrete. The dataset employed for our tests is composed of 102 instances described by 8 input features, plus the corresponding SLUMP value.

7   Experimental Results

Figures 1, 2, 3, 4 and 5 report the plots of the median fitness for the three compared methods (GSGP, GSGP-LS and GSGP-reg) over the five considered datasets. In particular, the left part (respectively, right part) of each figure refers to the median fitness achieved by each method in 500 generations over 100 experimental runs on the training set (respectively, test set) of the relevant problem. The median fitness is also reported in Table 2 for each problem, along with the associated median absolute deviation (MAD). In general, one can see from the plots of the training sets that both GSGP-LS and GSGP-reg perform better than pure GSGP over all considered datasets. This is an expected outcome, since as observed in [6] local search tends to overfit the datasets when applied to each generation of the GSGP algorithm. As discussed in Sect. 5, this is the reason why we investigated a hybrid version of both GSGP-LS and GSGP-reg, where the local search step is not applied after 10 generations. On the other hand, one can still observe on the test sets that GSGP-LS and GSGP-reg generally fare better than pure GSGP, except over the %PPB and TOX datasets. In the former case, our generalization of local search is the worse performer among the three algorithms, the median fitness values of GSGP and GSGP-LS being lower than GSGP-reg and close to each other. In the latter, GSGP-reg actually scores the best performance, while GSGP-LS achieves the highest median fitness after 500 generations. Regarding the comparison of the two versions of GSGP with local search, one cannot rely on the plots alone, except for the %PPB and TOX datasets. In fact, as it can be seen in the right parts of Figs. 1, 4 and 5, the plots of the median fitness values of GSGP-LS and GSGP-reg are almost superimposed. For this reason, we performed a more thorough comparison using the Mann-Whitney U-test. Table 3 reports the p-values of all three comparisons (GSGP vs. GSGP-LS, GSGP vs. GSGP-reg and GSGP-LS vs. GSGP-reg) over the test sets of the five considered problems. However, by looking at the fourth column of Table 3, it can be seen that under the considered significance level ($\alpha = 0.05$) one cannot reject the null hypothesis, i.e. that the performance of GSGP-LS is not worse than that of GSGP-reg over %F, COMP and SLUMP. The p-value corresponding to the %PPB dataset actually shows that GSGP-LS

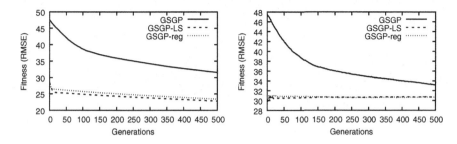

Fig. 1. Median fitness on the training (left) and test (right) sets for the %F dataset.

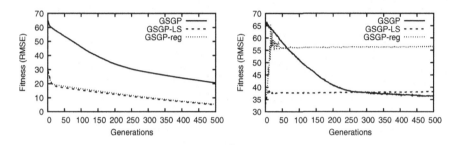

Fig. 2. Median fitness on the training (left) and test (right) sets for the %PPB dataset.

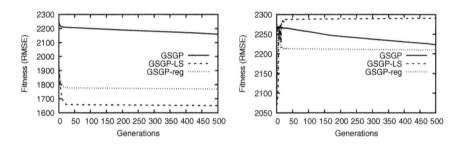

Fig. 3. Median fitness on the training (left) and test (right) sets for the TOX dataset.

is not worse than GSGP-reg as well. On the other hand, the null hypothesis is rejected for the TOX dataset ($p = 0.0316$), thereby confirming our observation above regarding the median fitness plot on the test set of Fig. 3. As a final note, for both GSGP-LS and GSGP-reg, the additional computational resources needed did not increase significantly the time required to perform the evolution.

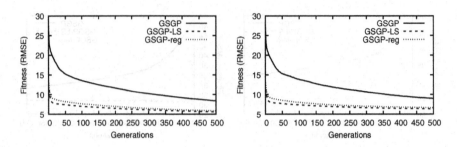

Fig. 4. Median fitness on the training (left) and test (right) sets for the COMP dataset.

Table 2. Median and MAD of the fitness obtained by the best individual.

Dataset			GSGP	GSGP-LS	GSGP-reg
%F	Training set	Median	31.5945	**22.8211**	23.4196
		MAD	0.7531	0.3585	0.3733
	Test set	Median	33.2053	**30.7070**	30.7311
		MAD	1.2162	2.0702	3.2942
%PPB	Training set	Median	20.5467	**4.8129**	5.2265
		MAD	0.7768	0.7783	1.0574
	Test set	Median	**36.5051**	38.2085	56.3562
		MAD	5.0257	4.0538	25.0935
TOX	Training set	Median	2159.6356	**1650.8873**	1768.6019
		MAD	68.2308	48.0973	52.6530
	Test set	Median	2223.4332	2290.4879	**2209.9571**
		MAD	157.9263	328.4134	210.1360
COMP	Training set	Median	8.3835	**5.5940**	5.8519
		MAD	0.4053	0.1002	0.1618
	Test set	Median	8.9826	**6.3625**	6.6204
		MAD	0.6422	0.2255	0.2179
SLUMP	Training set	Median	1.6911	**0.8124**	0.8956
		MAD	0.2336	0.0757	0.0746
	Test set	Median	4.4309	**2.8535**	2.9441
		MAD	0.8338	0.4305	0.4482

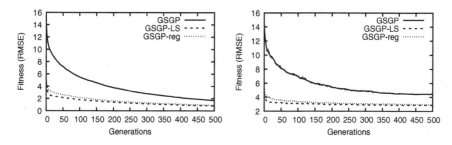

Fig. 5. Median fitness on the training (left) and test (right) sets for the SLUMP dataset.

Table 3. p-values obtained with the Mann-Whitney U test.

Dataset	GSGP vs GSGP-LS	GSGP vs GSGP-reg	GSGP-LS vs GSGP-reg
%F	3.0863E−7	0.0933	0.7386
%PPB	0.7159	0.9999	0.9999
TOX	0.9952	0.8231	0.0316
COMP	2.5092E−33	2.0975E−28	0.9999
SLUMP	1.1896E−16	2.4460E−20	0.7425

8 Conclusion

In this paper we have defined a new local search operator for GSGP called GSGP-reg, and compared it with both the classical version of GSGP and the current best performing combination of GSGP with local search, called GSGP-LS, as defined in [6]. We were able to outperform classical GSGP in most cases, and our proposed method is on par with the performances of GSGP-LS. However, the problems in which GSGP-reg and GSGP-LS show overfitting are different. Therefore, it would be interesting to understand what causes similar performances in certain datasets and remarkably different generalization behavior in others.

There are multiple interesting research directions still open. First of all, an in-depth study of the best functions families $\mathcal{F}$ to be employed for regression should be performed, thereby expanding the preliminary exploration presented here, and analyzing how each of these families influences the learning process and the ability to generalize. The regression method can also be tuned in multiple ways. For example, one could generate multiple regression models on different subsets of the training data and select one with the best generalization on the part of the training set that was not used for the generation of the linear regression model. Finally, for classification problems a similar method can be employed by using logistic regression instead of the traditional linear regression.

Acknowledgments. This work was partially supported by national funds through FCT (Fundação para a Ciência e a Tecnologia) under project DSAIPA/DS/0022/2018 (GADgET).

References

1. Archetti, F., Lanzeni, S., Messina, E., Vanneschi, L.: Genetic programming for computational pharmacokinetics in drug discovery and development. Genet. Program. Evolvable Mach. **8**(4), 413–432 (2007)
2. Azad, R.M.A., Ryan, C.: A simple approach to lifetime learning in genetic programming-based symbolic regression. Evol. Comput. **22**(2), 287–317 (2014)
3. Castelli, M., Manzoni, L., Vanneschi, L., Silva, S., Popovič, A.: Self-tuning geometric semantic genetic programming. Genet. Program. Evolvable Mach. **17**(1), 55–74 (2016)
4. Castelli, M., Trujillo, L., Vanneschi, L.: Energy consumption forecasting using semantic-based genetic programming with local search optimizer. Comput. Intell. Neurosci. **2015**, 57 (2015)
5. Castelli, M., Trujillo, L., Vanneschi, L., Popovič, A.: Prediction of relative position of ct slices using a computational intelligence system. Appl. Soft Comput. **46**, 537–542 (2016)
6. Castelli, M., Trujillo, L., Vanneschi, L., Silva, S., et al.: Geometric semantic genetic programming with local search. In: Proceedings of the 2015 Annual Conference on Genetic and Evolutionary Computation, pp. 999–1006. ACM (2015)
7. Castelli, M., Vanneschi, L., Silva, S.: Prediction of high performance concrete strength using genetic programming with geometric semantic genetic operators. Expert Syst. Appl. **40**(17), 6856–6862 (2013)
8. Castelli, M., Vanneschi, L., Trujillo, L., Popovič, A.: Stock index return forecasting: semantics-based genetic programming with local search optimiser. Int. J. Bio-Inspired Comput. **10**(3), 159–171 (2017)
9. Chen, X., Ong, Y.S., Lim, M.H., Tan, K.C.: A multi-facet survey on memetic computation. Trans. Evol. Computat. **15**(5), 591–607 (2011)
10. Enríquez-Zárate, J., et al.: Automatic modeling of a gas turbine using genetic programming: an experimental study. Appl. Soft Comput. **50**, 212–222 (2017)
11. Hajek, P., Henriques, R., Castelli, M., Vanneschi, L.: Forecasting performance of regional innovation systems using semantic-based genetic programming with local search optimizer. Comput. Oper. Res. **106**, 179–190 (2019)
12. Koza, J.R.: Genetic Programming: On the Programming of Computers by Means of Natural Selection. MIT press, Cambridge (1992)
13. Koza, J.R.: Human-competitive results produced by genetic programming. Genet. Program. Evolvable Mach. **11**(3–4), 251–284 (2010)
14. Trujillo, L., et al.: Local search is underused in genetic programming. In: Riolo, R., Worzel, B., Goldman, B., Tozier, B. (eds.) Genetic Programming Theory and Practice XIV. GEC, pp. 119–137. Springer, Cham (2018). https://doi.org/10.1007/978-3-319-97088-2_8
15. Moraglio, A., Krawiec, K., Johnson, C.G.: Geometric semantic genetic programming. In: Coello, C.A.C., Cutello, V., Deb, K., Forrest, S., Nicosia, G., Pavone, M. (eds.) PPSN 2012. LNCS, vol. 7491, pp. 21–31. Springer, Heidelberg (2012). https://doi.org/10.1007/978-3-642-32937-1_3
16. Neri, F., Cotta, C., Moscato, P.: Handbook of Memetic Algorithms, vol. 379. Springer, Heidelberg (2012)

17. Topchy, A., Punch, W.F.: Faster genetic programming based on local gradient search of numeric leaf values. In: Proceedings of the 3rd Annual Conference on Genetic and Evolutionary Computation, GECCO2001, pp. 155–162, Morgan Kaufmann Publishers Inc., San Francisco (2001)
18. Vanneschi, L., Castelli, M., Manzoni, L., Silva, S.: A new implementation of geometric semantic GP and its application to problems in pharmacokinetics. In: Krawiec, K., Moraglio, A., Hu, T., Etaner-Uyar, A.Ş., Hu, B. (eds.) EuroGP 2013. LNCS, vol. 7831, pp. 205–216. Springer, Heidelberg (2013). https://doi.org/10.1007/978-3-642-37207-0_18
19. Vanneschi, L., Castelli, M., Silva, S.: Measuring bloat, overfitting and functional complexity in genetic programming. In: Proceedings of the 12th Annual Conference on Genetic and Evolutionary Computation, pp. 877–884. ACM (2010)
20. Yeh, I.C.: Modeling of strength of high-performance concrete using artificial neural networks. Cem. Concr. Res. **28**(12), 1797–1808 (1998)
21. Z-Flores, E., Trujillo, L., Schütze, O., Legrand, P.: Evaluating the effects of local search in genetic programming. In: Tantar, A.-A., Tantar, E., Sun, J.-Q., Zhang, W., Ding, Q., Schütze, O., Emmerich, M., Legrand, P., Del Moral, P., Coello Coello, C.A. (eds.) EVOLVE - A Bridge between Probability, Set Oriented Numerics, and Evolutionary Computation V. AISC, vol. 288, pp. 213–228. Springer, Cham (2014). https://doi.org/10.1007/978-3-319-07494-8_15
22. Zhang, M., Smart, W.: Genetic programming with gradient descent search for multiclass object classification. In: Keijzer, M., O'Reilly, U.-M., Lucas, S., Costa, E., Soule, T. (eds.) EuroGP 2004. LNCS, vol. 3003, pp. 399–408. Springer, Heidelberg (2004). https://doi.org/10.1007/978-3-540-24650-3_38

Author Index

Printed in the United States
By Bookmasters